DICCIONARIO DE BOLSILLO

INGLÉS-ESPAÑOL Y ESPAÑOL-INGLÉS

POR

WESSELY, GIRONÉS, TOLHAUSEN, Y PAYN

ENMENDADO, CON INCLUSIÓN DE LOS TÉRMINOS MÁS MODERNOS

———————

HANDY DICTIONARY

OF THE

ENGLISH AND SPANISH LANGUAGES

BY

WESSELY, GIRONÉS, TOLHAUSEN, AND PAYN

THOROUGHLY REVISED AND EXTENDED BY THE INCLUSION OF
WORDS IN MODERN USE

BY

F. A. KIRKPATRICK, M.A.

PHILADELPHIA

DAVID McKAY COMPANY

WASHINGTON SQUARE

1947

PRONUNCIACIÓN APRÓXIMATIVA
DEL INGLÉS

Las vocales inglesas expresan varias graduaciones de sonidos; los principales son los siguientes:—

ā (v.g. *fate, hate*) se pronuncia como *e* en *dedo*.

ă (v.g. *fat, hat*)   "   "   *a* en *papa*, pero breve y de golpe.

ē (v.g. *mete*)   "   "   *i*.

ĕ (v.g. *met*)   "   "   *e* en *guerra*.

e final (v.g. *fate, mete, note*) es muda, teniendo el efecto de alargar la silaba antecedente.

ī (v.g. *bite*) se pronuncia como *ai* en *baile*.

ĭ (v.g. *bit*)   "   "   *i* en *igual*, pero breve y de golpe.

ō (v.g. *note*)   "   "   *o* en *solo*.

ŏ (v.g. *not*)   "   "   *o* en *sol*.

ū (v.g. *acute*)   "   "   *iu* en *viuda*.

ŭ (v.g. *cut*)   "   "   entre *a* y *u*, pero breve y de golpe.

w   "   "   como *hu* en *hueco*.

y final (v.g. *happy*) se pronuncia como *e* en *monte*.

g se pronuncia como *g* en el idioma italiano.

h se aspira.

j se pronuncia como la *g* suave Italiana (v.g. *Giorgionc*).

qu (v.g. *question*) se pronuncia como *cu* en *cuestión*.

sh se pronuncia como *ch* en el idioma francés.

th   "   "   *z* en castellano.

APPROXIMATE PRONUNCIATION OF SPANISH.

a is pronounced as in *father*.

e is commonly pronounced as *a* in *hate*.

e before two consonants (e.g. *puente, guerra*) is pronounced as *e* in *get*.

e final (e.g. *puente, monte*) is pronounced as *y* in *happy*.

i is pronounced as *i* in *routine*.

o " " *o* in *sole;* but before two consonants (e.g. *consta*) and also in some monosyllables (e.g. *sol.*) it has a shorter sound, resembling *o* in *off*.

u is pronounced as in *rule*.

c before *e* and *i* is pronounced as *th* in *thank*.

d and *t* are pronounced with a very sharp dental sound, almost as if aspirated, much as the Irish peasantry pronounce these letters.

d final (e.g. *usted, Madrid*) is a soft aspirate, sometimes almost mute.

g before *e* and *i* is a strong guttural aspirate.

h is practically mute.

j is a strong guttural aspirate.

ll is pronounced almost as *k* in *valiant*.

ñ is pronounced as *gn* in *Bologna*, almost as *ni* in *onion*.

qu " " *k*, the *u* being mute.

y before a vowel is pronounced as in English.

y final (e.g. *rey, hay*) has the sound of the Spanish *i*.

z is pronounced as *th* in *thank*.

GENDERS OF SPANISH SUBSTANTIVES

1. Substantives ending in *-a, -d, -z, -ión* are usually feminine. Other terminations are usually masculine.

2. Substantives signifying males are masculine, regardless of termination. Substantives signifying females are feminine Thus *poeta* is masculine; *guía* and *centinela* may be either masculine or feminine.

3. All names of rivers are masculine, as *el Guadiana*.

Names of countries, provinces, and towns are masculine, unless ending in *-a*. Thus *Cádiz, Valladolid* are masculine; *Granada, Sevilla* are feminine.

ABBREVIATIONS
ABREVIATURAS

a. = adjective, *adjetivo*.
ad. = adverb, *adverbio*.
am. = Americanism, *Americanismo*.
ar. = arithmetic, *arithmética*.
arch. = architecture, *arquitectura*.
art. = article, *articulo*.
art = art, *arte, artístico*.
bot. = botany, *botánica*.
c. = conjunction, *conjunción*.
chem. = chemistry, *química*.
col. = colloquial, *familiar, vulgar*.
com. = commerce, *comercio*.
eccl. = ecclesiastical, *eclesiástico*.
fig. = figurative, *figurativo, metafórico*.
gr. = grammar, *gramática*.
in comp. = in compounds, *usado en palabras compuestas*.
interj. = interjection, *interjección*.
law, leg. = law term, *jurisprudencia*.
mar. = maritime, *marina*.
med. = medicine, *arte médica*.
mil. = military, *milicia, guerra*.
mus. = music, *música*.
obs. = obsolete, *anticuado, desusado*.

orn. = ornithology, birds, *ornitología, aves*.
p. = participle, *participio*.
pl. = plural, *plural*.
poet. = poetical, *poético*.
pn. = pronoun, *pronombre*.
pr. = preposition, *preposición*.
rail. = railway, *ferrocarril*.
rel. pn. = relative pronoun, *pronombre relativo*.
Scot. = Scotch, *Escocés*.
sf. = feminine substantive, *sustantivo femenino*.
sm. = masculine substantive, *sustantivo masculino*.
theatr. = theatre, *teatro*.
v.a. = verb active, *verbo activo*.
v. aux. = auxiliary verb, *verbo auxiliar*.
v. def. = verb defective, *verbo defectivo*.
v. imp. = verb impersonal, *verbo impersonal*.
v. n. = verb neuter, *verbo neutro*.
v. r. = verb reflexive, *verbo reflexivo*.
zool. = zoology, *zoología, animales*.

A

á, pr. to, in, at, according to, on, by, for, of.

ababa, sf. red poppy, corn-rose.

abacería, sf. grocery.

abacero, sm. grocer.

abacial, a. abbatial.

ábaco, sm. abacus (of a column); multiplication-table.

abad, sm. abbot.

abada, sf. female rhinoceros.

abadejo, sm. codfish; yellow wren; Spanish fly.

abadengo, ga, a. abbatial.

abadesa, sf. abbess.

abadía, sf. abbey; abbacy.

abajo, ad. under, underneath; below.

abalanzar, v.a. to balance, to counterpoise; to dart, to impel; —, v.n. to rush on with impetuosity; to venture.

abalear, v.a. to fan or winnow (corn).

abalorio, sm. glass-bead.

aballestar, v.a. (mar.) to haul a cable.

abanderado, sm. (mil.) ensign; standard-bearer.

abanderizador, ra, sm. ringleader, agitator.

abanderizar, v.a. to band together.

abandonamiento, sm. abandonment.

abandonar, v.a. to abandon; -se, to despond, to despair; to give one's self up.   [debauchery.

abandono, sm. abandonment, forlornness,

abanicar, v.a. to fan.

abanico, sm. fan.

abaniquero, sm. fan-maker.

abanto, sm. dwarf vulture.

abaratar, v.a. to cheapen.

abarca, sf. shoe of coarse leather, worn by Spanish peasants.

abarcadura, sf. abarcamiento, sm. embrace.   [contain.

abarcar, v.a. to clasp, to embrace, to

abarcón, sm. iron ring, hoop.

abarquillar, v.a. to shape like a boat; -se, to curl up; to be cocked.

abarracarse, v.r. to take shelter in a hut.

abarraganamiento, sm. concubinage.

abarraganarse, v.r. to live in concubinage.

abarrancadero, sm. boggy place; precipice; difficult business.

abarrancamiento, sm. fall into a pit or trap; embarrassment.

abarrancar, v.a. to dig holes; -se, to become embarrassed.

abarrotar, v.a. to tie down; (mar.) to stow (cargo).

abarrote, sm. (mar.) small stowage.

abastecedor, ra, sm. purveyor, caterer.

abastecer, v.a. to purvey.

abastecimiento, sm. provision; provisions.

abastionar, v.a. to fortify with bastions.

abasto, sm. supply of provisions.

abatanar, v.a. to full cloth.

abate, sm. abbé.

ábate! take care!

abatido, da, a. dejected, low-spirited, faint; abject, mean.

abatimiento, sm. low spirits, depression.

abatir, v.a. to throw down; to humble; -se, to descend, to stoop.

abdicación, sf. abdication.

abdicar, v.a. to abdicate.

abdomen, sm. abdomen.

abecé, sm. alphabet.

abecedario, sm. spelling-book, primer.

abedul, sm. birch-tree.

abeja, sf. bee; — maestra o madre, queen-bee.

abejar, sm. bee-hive.

abejarrón, sm. horse-fly.

abejero, sm. bee-keeper.

abejón, sm. drone; hornet.

abellacarse, v.r. to degrade one's self.

aberración, sf. aberration.

abertal, a. (geol.) easy to cleave.

abertura, sf. aperture, chink, cleft; (fig.) plain dealing; (mus.) overture.

abestiar, v.a. to stupefy.

abeto, sm. fir-tree.

abetunado, da, a. bituminous.

abierto, ta, a. open; sincere; frank.

abigarrar, v.a. to variegate, to dapple, to chequer; to diversify.

abigeato, sm. (leg.) cattle-theft.

abigeo, sm. cattle-thief.

abigotado, da, a. wearing long whiskers.

abintestato, a. intestate.

abismal, a. abysmal; -es, s.pl. clasp nails.

abismar, v.a. to hurl down, to humble.

abismo, sm. abyss; gulf; hell.

abitaque, sm. rafter.

abjuracion; sf. abjuration.

abjurar, v.a. to abjure, to recant upon oath.   [gation.

ablandamiento, sm. mollification, miti-

ablandar, v.a. & n. to mollify, to soften.

ablativo, sm. (gr.) ablative.

ablucion, sf. ablution, lotion.

abnegación, sf. abnegation.

abnegar, v.a. to renounce.

abobado, da, a. silly, idiotic.

abobamiento, sm. stupefaction.

abobar, v.a. to stupefy.

abocamiento, sm. meeting, interview.

abocar, v.a. to seize with the mouth; -se, to meet by agreement.

abocardado, da, a. wide-mouthed.

abocinar, v.n. to fall upon one's face.

abochornar, v.a. to swelter; to provoke; -se, to be angry with; to blush.

abofetear, v.a. to slap.

abogacia, sf. advocacy.

abogada, sf. mediatrix; advocate's wife.

abogado, sm. advocate; mediator.

abogar, v.n. to advocate; to intercede.

abolengo, sm. ancestry; inheritance from ancestors.

abolición, sf. abolition, abrogation.

abolir, v.a. to abolish.

abolorio, sm. ancestry.

abolsado, da, a. puckered.

abolladura, sf. lump; inequality.

abollar, v.a. to emboss; to dent; to confound; to tire, to bore.

abollonar, v.a. to emboss.

abominable, a. abominable, cursed.

abominación, sf. abomination, cursed-

abominar, v.a. to detest.   [ness.

abonado, da, a. creditable, rich; fit for; subscriber.   [another.

abonador, sm. & f. person who is bail for

abonamiento, sm. surety, bail.

abonanzar, v.n. to clear up (the weather).

abonar, v.a. to bail; to insure; to improve; to make good an assertion; to manure; to give one credit; -se, to subscribe to; —, v.n. to clear up.

abonaré, sm. (com.) cheque.

abono, sm. subscription; surety, bail; dung, manure.

abordador, sm. boarder; intruder.

abordaje, sm. act of boarding a ship.

abordar, v.a. (mar.) to board.

abordo, sm. act of boarding a ship.

aborrachado, da, a. high coloured.

aborrascarse, v.r. to grow stormy; to get tipsy,

aborrecer, v.a. to hate, to abhor; to desert (of birds).

aborrecible, a. hateful, detestable.

aborrecimiento, sm. abhorrence, hatred.

abortamiento, sm. abortion.   [abortion.

abortar, v.n. to miscarry, to have an

abortivo, va, a. abortive.

aborto, sm. abortion; monster.

abortón, sm. abortion of a quadruped.

aborujarse, v.r. to be muffled up.

abotagarse, v.r. to be swollen.

abotinado, da, a. in the form of a boot.

abotonar, v.a. to button; -se, to bud.

abovedar, v.a. to arch, to vault.

aboyar, v.a. (mar.) to lay down buoys.

abra, sf. bay; mountain-gorge, mountain-canyon.

abracijo, sm. embrace, hug.

abrasador, ra, sm. & f. burner; —, a. burning.

abrasamiento, sm. burning.

abrasar, v.a. to burn; to parch the ground; to squander; -se, to be agitated by a violent passion.   [wood.

abrasilado, da, a. of the colour of Brazil-

abrazadera, sf. clamp, clasp.

abrazador, ra, sm. & f. embracer.

abrazamiento, sm. embracing.

abrazar, v.a. to embrace; to surround; to contain; to admit.

abrazo, sm. embrace.

ábrego, sm. south-west wind.   [cattle.

abrevadero, sm. watering-place for

abrevar, v.a. to water cattle.

abreviación, sf. abbreviation, abridgment; shortening.

abreviador, ra, sm. & f. abridger; —, a. shortening.   [accelerate.

abreviar, v.a. to abridge, to cut short; to

abreviatura, sf. abbreviation.

abribonarse, v.r. to act the scoundrel.

abridero, sm. nectarine.

abridor, sm. nectarine-tree; opener; — de láminas, engraver.

abrigar, v.a. to shelter; to protect; -se, to take shelter.   [mantle.

abrigo, sm. shelter; protection; aid;

abril, sm. April.

abrillantador, sm. diamond cutter.

abrillantar, v.a. to cut (a diamond) into facets.

abrimiento, sm. opening.   [close.

abrir, v.a. to open; to unlock; to dis-

abrochador, sm. button-hook.   [on.

abrochar, v.a. to button on, to clasp

abrogación, sf. abrogation.

abrogar, v.a. to abrogate.

abrojo, sm. (bot.) caltrop; -s, pl. sunken

abromado, da, a. hazy, foggy.   [rocks.

abroquelarse, v.r. to shield oneself; to defend oneself,

abrótano, sm. (bot.) southern-wood.
abrumador, ra, a. troublesome, annoying.
abrumar, v.a. to overwhelm ; to molest.
abrutado, da, a. brutish.
absceso, sm. abscess.
absolución, sf. forgiveness ; absolution.
absoluto, ta, a. absolute, independent ; unconditional ; imperious.
absolutorio, a. absolutory.
absolver, v.a. to absolve.
absorbencia, sf. absorption. [ent.
absorbente, sm. & a. (med.) absorb-
absorber, v.a. to absorb (also fig.) ; -se, v.r. to be astonished.
absorto, a. amazed.
abstenerse, v.r. to abstain.
abstinencia, sf. abstinence.
abstinente, a. abstinent, abstemious.
abstracción, sf. abstraction ; retirement.
abstracto, ta, a. abstract.
abstraer, v.a. to abstract ; — de, to pass over in silence ; -se, to become lost in thought.
abstraído, a. retired.
abstruso, sa, a. abstruse.
absurdidad, sf., absurdo, sm. absurdity.
absurdo, da, a. absurd.
abubilla, sf. hoopoe.
abuela, sf. grandmother.
abuelo, sm. grandfather ; ancestor.
abultado, da, a. bulky, large, massive.
abultar, v.a. to increase, to enlarge ; —, v.n. to be bulky.
abundancia, sf. abundance.
abundante, a. abundant, copious.
abundar, v.n. to abound.
aburrido, da, a. weary ; bored.
aburrimiento, sm. tediousness. [hazard
aburrir, v.a. to vex, to weary ; (col.) to
aburujar, v.a. to press or heap together.
abusar, v.a. to abuse.
abusivo, va, a. abusive.
abuso, sm. ill-usage, misuse.
abyección, sf. abjectness.
acá, ad. here, hither.
acabado, da, a. perfect, accomplished.
acabalar, v.a. to complete.
acaballerado, da, a. gentleman-like.
acaballerar, v.a. to render genteel.
acabar, v.a. & n. to finish, to complete ; to achieve ; to terminate in any-thing ; to die, to expire ; -se, to grow feeble.
acabildar, v.a. to unite, to assemble.
acacia, sf. acacia.
academia, sf. academy ; literary society.
académico, sm. academician ; —, a. academical.
acaecedero, ra, a. incidental.
acaecer, v.n. to happen.
acaecimiento, sm. event, incident.

acal, sm. canoe.
acalenturarse, v.r. to be feverish.
acalia, sf. (bot.) marsh-mallows.
acallar, v.a. to quiet, to hush, to silence ; to soften, to assuage, to appease.
acamar, v.a. to lay flat (corn).
acampamento, sm. (mil.) encampment.
acampar, v.a. (mil.) to encamp.
acampo, sm. common pasture.
acanalar, v.a. to flute, to groove.
acandilado, da, a. peaked, pointed.
acanelado, da, a. of a cinnamon colour.
acanillado, da, a. ribbed.
acanto, sm. (bot.) acanthus.
acantonamiento, sm. cantonment.
acantonar, v.a. (mil.) to quarter, to billet.
acañonear, v.a. to cannonade.
acaponado, da, a. effeminate.
acardenalar, v.a. to beat black and blue ; -se, to be covered with livid spots.
acariciar, v.a. to fondle, to caress.
acarreador, sm. carrier.
acarrear, v.a. to convey in a cart ; to carry ; to occasion.
acarreo, sm. carriage, portage. [by chance.
acaso, sm. chance, hap, hazard ; —, ad.
acatarrarse, v.r. to catch cold.
acaudalado, da, a. rich, wealthy.
acaudalar, v.a. to hoard up riches.
acaudillador, sm. commander of troops.
acaudillar, v.a. to command troops.
acceder, v.n. to accede.
accesible, a. attainable ; of easy access.
acceso, sm. access.
accesorias, sf. pl. out-buildings.
accesorio, ria, a. accessory, additional.
accidental, a. accidental, casual.
accidentarse, v.r. to have a fit.
accidente, sm. accident ; haphazard.
acción, sf. action, operation ; battle ; position, posture ; (com.) share.
accionar, v.n. to gesticulate.
accionista, sm. shareholder.
acebo, sm. holly-tree.
acebuche, sm. wild olive-tree.
acebuchina, sf. wild olive.
acecinar, v.a. to salt meat and smoke it ; -se, to wither.
acechador, sm. listener. [upon.
acechar, v.a. to lie in ambush for, to spy
acecho, sm. lying in ambush, waylaying.
acedar, v.a. to sour ; to displease, to disquiet.
acedera, sf. (bot.) sorrel.
acedia, sf. acidity ; squeamishness ; roughness ; asperity of address.
acedo, da, a. acid, acetous.
aceitar, v.a. to oil.
aceite, sm. oil.
aceitera, sf. oil-cruet.
aceitería, sf. oilshop ; oil-mill.

aceitero, sm. oil-seller ; oil-cruet.

aceitoso, sa, a. oily.

aceituna, sf. olive.

aceitunado, da, a. olive-green.

aceitunero, sm. olive-seller.

aceituno, sm. olive-tree.

aceleracion, s. acceleration.

aceleradamente, ad. swiftly, hastily.

acelerar, v.a. to accelerate ; to hurry.

acelga, sf. (bot.) beet.

acemila, sf. beast of burden. [muleteers.

acemilar, a. belonging to mules and

acemilería, sf. mule-stable.

acemilero, sm. muleteer.

acemite, sm. fine bran ; grits.

acendrar, v.a. to refine (metals) ; to free from blemish.

acensar, acensuar, va. to assess (for taxa-

acento, sm. accent. [tion.

acentuación, sf. accentuation.

acentuar, v.a. to accentuate.

aceña, sf. water-mill.

aceñero, sm. keeper of a water-mill.

acepar, v.n. to take root.

acepción, sf. meaning, acceptation ; favouritism. [chips, pl.

acepilladura, sf. smoothing with a plane ;

acepillar, v.a. to plane ; to brush.

aceptable, a. acceptable ; worthy of acceptance.

aceptación, sf. acceptation ; approbation ; acceptance (of a bill).

aceptador, ra, s. acceptor.

aceptar, v.a. to accept, to admit.

acepto, to, a. agreeable. [mill-trench.

acequia, sf. canal, channel, drain ;

acequiar, v.a. to drain with water-cuts.

acequiero, sm. inspector of canals. [walk.

acera, sf. flag-way, pavement ; side-

acerar, v.a. to steel.

acerbidad, sf. acerbity, rigour.

acerbo, ba, a. rigorous, harsh, rude ; cruel.

acerca, pr. about, relating to.

acercar, v.a. to bring near.

acerico, acerillo, sm. pin-cushion ; small bed-pillow.

acerino, na, a. made of steel.

acero, sm. steel ; (fig.) courage.

acérrimo, ma, a. most strenuous, very vigorous.

acertado, da, a. fit, proper ; prudent.

acertador, ra, sm. & f. dead-shot, true

acertajo, sm. riddle. [prophet.

acertar, v.a. & n. to hit (the mark) ; to conjecture right ; to turn out true ; —, v.n. to happen unexpectedly ; to take root.

acertijo, sm. riddle.

acervar, v.a. to accumulate.

acervo, sm. heap, pile ; (leg.) totality of tithes.

acetato, sm. (chem.) acetate.

acetosa, sf. (bot.) sorrel. [fount.

acetre, sm. small bucket ; holy-water-

aciago, ga, a. unlucky, ominous.

acial, sm. twitch (for holding a horse).

aciano, sm. corn-flower.

acíbar, sm. aloes-tree ; (fig.) bitterness, displeasure.

acibarar, v.a. to add juice of aloes ; to gall ; to imbitter.

acicalador, sm. polisher ; burnisher, burnishing-stick. [nishing.

acicaladura, sf., acicalamiento, sm. bur-

acicalar, v.n. to polish, to furbish ; -se, to dress in style ; to paint one's face.

acidez, sf. acidity.

ácido, sm. acid ; —, da, a. acid, sour.

acidular, v.a. to acidulate.

acídulo, a, a. acidulous.

acierto, sm. act and effect of hitting dexterity, right judgment, chance.

acijado, da, a. copperas coloured.

acije, sm. copperas.

acimboga, sf. citron-tree.

ación, sf. stirrup-leather.

acipado, da, a. well milled (of broadcloth).

acirate, sm. landmark (to show boundaries). [wall.

acitara, s. rails of a bridge ; partition-

acitrón, sm. candied lemon.

aclamación, sf. acclamation. [cry up.

aclamar, v.a. to applaud, to huzza ; to

aclarar, v.a. to clear ; to brighten ; to explain ; to clarify ; -se, to clear up (the weather).

aclimatar, v.a. to acclimatize.

aclocarse, v.r. to brood.

acobardar, v.a. to intimidate.

acoceador, ra, sm. & f. kicking horse.

acocear, v.a. to kick.

acocharse, v.n. to squat, to stoop down.

acochinar, v.a. (col.) to assassinate ; to injure.

acodar, v.a. to lean the elbow upon ; to lay layers of vines.

acodillar, v.a. to bend at an angle.

acodo, sm. (bot.) layer, scion, shoot.

acogedizo, za, a. gathered promiscuously.

acogedor, ra, sm. & f. harbourer.

acoger, v.a. to receive ; to protect ; to harbour ; -se, to take refuge. [ence.

acogida, sf. reception ; asylum ; conflu-

acogimiento, sm. gathering.

acogollar, v.a. to cover delicate plants with straw.

acogombrar, v.a. to earth up (plants).

acogotar, v.a. to kill by a blow on the

acolchar, v.a. to quilt. [neck.

acólito, sm. acolyte ; assistant.

acollarar, v.a. to yoke horses, &c. ; to couple hounds.

acometedor, ra, sm. & f. aggressor.

acometer, v.a. to attack ; to undertake.

acometida, sf., acometimiento, sm. attack, assault.

acomodado, da, a. commodious ; suitable, convenient, fit ; wealthy.

acomodamiento, sm. accommodation.

acomodar, v.a. to accommodate, to arrange ; —, v.n. to fit, to suit ; -se, to condescend, to comply. [phorical.

acomodaticio, cia, a. figurative, meta-

acomodo, sm. accommodation ; employment.

acompañador, ra, sm. & f. companion ; (mus.) accompanist.

acompañamiento, sm. attendance ; (mus.) accompaniment.

acompañar, v.a. to accompany ; to join ; (mus.) to accompany ; -se, to consult with others.

acompañante, sm. & f. accompanist.

acompasado, da, a. accurate, even ; composed ; well-proportioned.

aconchar, v.a. to arrange ; (mar.) to strand.

acondicionado, da, a. conditioned, of a (good or bad) disposition.

acondicionar, v.a. to dispose ; -se, to acquire a certain position.

acongojar, v.a. to oppress, to afflict.

acónito, sm. (bot.) aconite, monk's hood.

aconsejable, a. advisable. [sellor.

aconsejador, ra, sm. adviser, coun-

aconsejar, v.a. to advise ; -se, to take advice.

aconsonantar, v.a. & n. to rhyme.

acontecedero, ra, a. possible to happen.

acontecer, v.imp. to happen.

acontecimiento, sm. event, incident.

acopado, da, a. cup-shaped, bell-shaped.

acopar, v.n. (mar.) to bend or arch boards.

acopiamiento, acopio, sm. gathering, storing.

acopiar, v.a. to gather, to store up.

acoplar, v.a. to couple ; to adjust or fit (timber-work).

acoquinar, v.a. to intimidate.

acorazonado, a. heart-shaped.

acorcharse, v.r. to dry up and shrivel (of acordado, da, a. deliberate. [fruits).

acordar, v.a. to concert ; to tune musical instruments ; —, v.n. to agree ; -se, to come to an agreement ; to remember.

acorde, a. conformable, accordant ; —, s. accord.

acordeón, sm. (mus.) accordion.

acordonar, v.a. to lace ; (mil.) to surround with a cordon.

acornear, v.a. to gore with the horns.

ácoro, sm. (bot.) sweet cane, sweet grass.

acorralar, v.a. to shut up cattle or sheep in pens ; to intimidate.

acorrucarse. See acurrucarse.

acortar, v.a. to abridge, to shorten ; -se, to be bashful.

acorullar, v.a. to ship oars.

acosar, v.a. to pursue close ; to molest.

acostar, v.a. to put to bed, to lay flat ; -se, to incline to one side (of buildings) ; (mar.) to lie along.

acostumbradamente, ad. customarily.

acostumbrar, v.a. to accustom ; —, v.n. to be accustomed.

acotación, sf. setting bounds ; quotation in the margin.

acotar, v.a. to set bounds ; to quote ; -se, (obs.) to escape from justice.

acotillo, sm. large sledge-hammer.

acoyundar, v.a. to yoke oxen.

acre, a. acid, sharp.

acrecencia, sf., acrecentamiento, sm. increase, augmentation.

acrecentar, acrecer, v.a. to increase, to augment.

acreditar, v.a. to assure, to affirm ; to accredit ; -se, to gain credit.

acreedor, sm. creditor.

acribadura, sf. sifting.

acribar, v.a. to sift ; to pierce like a sieve.

acribillar, v.a. to pierce like a sieve ; to molest, to torment.

acriminación, sf. accusation.

acriminador, ra, sm. & f. accuser.

acriminar, v.a. to exaggerate a fault ; to accuse.

acrimonia, sf. acrimony ; asperity.

acrisolar, v.a. to refine, to purify.

acristianar, v.a. (col.) to christen, to baptize. [tize.

aceitud, sf. acrimony.

acróbata, sm. acrobat.

acromático, ca, a. achromatic.

acta, sf. (leg.) act, record.

acritud, sf. attitude, posture.

actividad, sf. activity ; liveliness. [sets.

activo, va, a. active, diligent ; s. as-

acto, sm. act, action ; act of a play ; thesis.

actor, sm. player, comedian ; plaintiff.

Actos, s.pl. Acts of the Apostles.

actriz, sf. actress.

actuación, sf. actuation, operation.

actuado, da, a. experienced.

actual, a. actual, present.

actualidad, sf. actuality.

actuar, v.a. to practice ; to support (a thesis) ; to instruct.

actuario, sm. actuary.

Acuario, —, sm. Aquarius (sign of the zodiac).

acuartelamiento, sm. quartering of troops.

acuartelar, v.a. (mil.) to quarter troops.

acuático, ca, a. aquatic.
acuátil, a. aquatic.   [bucket.
acubado, da, a. resembling a pail or
acucharado, da, a. spoon-like.
acuchillado, da, a. slashed ; experienced,
  skilful.   [bully.
acuchillador, ra, s. quarrelsome person,
acuchillar, v.a. to cut ; -se, to fight with
  knives.
acudimiento, sm. aid, assistance.
acudir, v.n. to come up, to have recourse
  to, to assist, to succour.
acueducto, sm. aqueduct.
ácueo, ea, a. watery.
acuerdo, sm. deliberation ; resolution ;
  agreement.
acullá, ad. on the other side, yonder.
acumular, v.a. to accumulate, to heap
  together.   [precaution ; jointly.
acumulativamente, ad. (law) by way of
acuñación, sf. coining.
acuñador, sm. coiner.
acuñar, v.a. to coin, to mint ; to wedge
  in, to fasten with wedges.
acuosidad, sf. wateriness.
acuoso, sa, a. watery.
acurrucarse, v.r. to muffle one's self up ;
acusación, sf. accusation.   [to squat.
acusador, ra, sm. & f. accuser.
acusar, v.a. to accuse ; to reproach.
acusativo, sm. (gr.) accusative.
acusatorio, ria, a. accusatory.
acuse, sm. acknowledgment, declaring
  (at cards).
acústica, sf. acoustics, pl.
acústico, ca, a. acoustic.
achacar, v.a. to impute.
achacoso, sa, a. sickly, unhealthy.
achaparrado, da, a. stunted.
achaque, sm. habitual indisposition ; excuse ; vice ; subject, matter.
achaquiento, ta, a. sickly.
acharolar, v.a. to japan, to varnish.
achicado, da, a. childish.   [boats.
achicador, sm. (mar.) scoop for baling
achicadura, sf. diminution, reduction.
achicar, v.a. to diminish ; to bale a boat.
achicharrar, v.a. to fry meat too much ;
  to over-heat.
achicoria, sf. (bot.) chicory.
achinar, v.a. (col.) to intimidate.
achisparse, v.r. to get tipsy.
achocar, v.a. to knock, to dash against;
  (col.) to hoard (money).
achuchar, v.a. to crush with a blow.
achulado, da, a. waggish, frolicsome.
adagio, sm. adage ; proverb ; (mus.)
  adagio.
adalid, sm. chief, commander.
adamado, da, a. girl-like ; effeminate.
adamantino, na, a. adamantine.

adamascado, da, a. damask-like.
adaptable, a. adaptable.
adaptar, v.a. to adapt.
adaraja, sf. projecting stones left to continue a wall.
adarga, sf. oval shield.
adargar, v.a. to shield.
adarme, sm. half a drachm ; a trifle.
adarve, sm. flat top of a wall.
adatar, v.a. to book (an expense).
adecenar, v.a. to divide troops into com-
  panies of ten.
adecuación, sf. fitness.
adecuado, da, a. adequate, fit.
adecuar, v.a. to fit, to accommodate, to
  proportion.
adefesio, sm. folly, nonsense.
adefueras, sf. pl. suburbs.
adehala, sf. gratuity.   [ture.
adehesar, v.a. to convert land into pas-
adelantado, da, a. anticipated ; (ant.)
  governor of a province.
adelantamiento, sm. progress, improvement, advancement.
adelantar, v.a. & n. to advance, to accelerate ; to pay beforehand ; to ameliorate, to improve.
adelante, ad. opposite, farther off ; on
  ward ; henceforth.
adelfa, sf. (bot.) rose-bay.
adelgazar, v.a. to make thin or slender ;
  to discuss with subtlety.
ademán, sm. gesture ; attitude.
ademar, v.a. to prop (mines).
además, ad. moreover, besides.
adentellar, v.a. to bite ; to indent ;
  — una pared, to leave bricks to continue a wall.
adentro, ad. within ; inwardly.
aderezar, v.a. to dress, to adorn ; to prepare ; to clean, to repair.
aderezo, sm. adorning ; finery ; arrangement.
ad(i)estrador, sm. & f. instructor, teacher.
ad(i)estrar, v.a. to guide ; to teach, to
  instruct ; -se, to practise.
adeudado, da, a. indebted.   [indebted.
adeudar, v.a. to pay duty ; -se, to be
adeudo, s. import-duty.
adherencia, sf. adhesion, cohesion ; alliance, kindred.
adherente, a. adherent, cohesive.
adherir, v.n. to adhere.
adhesión, sf. adhesion ; cohesion.
adiamantado, da, a. adamantine.
adición, sf. addition ; (law) entry into an
  inheritance.
adicionar, v.a. to make additions.
adicto, ta, a. addicted, devoted to.
adietar, v.a. to put on a diet.
adinerado, da, a. moneyed, rich.

adiós, á dios, interj. good-bye ; —, sm. farewell. [heritance].

adir, v.a. (leg.) to enter upon (an in-

aditamento, sm. addition.

adiva, sf., **adive,** sm. jackal.

adivinación, sf. divination. [sayer.

adivinador, ra, sm. & f. diviner, sooth-

adivinanza, sf. enigma ; divination.

adivinar, v.a. to foretell ; to conjecture.

adivino, na, sm. & f. diviner, sooth-sayer ; fortune-teller.

adjetivar, v.a. to make the adjective agree with the substantive.

adjetivo, sm. adjective.

adjudicación, sf. adjudication.

adjudicar, v.a. to adjudge ; -se, to appropriate to one's self.

adjunto, ta, a. adjoining ; sm. partner.

adminicular, v.a. to support with legal proof.

adminículo, sm. support ; legal proof or evidence.

administración, sf. administration.

administrador, ra, sm. & f. administrator.

administrar, v.a. to administer.

administrativo, va, a. administrative.

admirable, a. admirable, marvellous.

admiración, sf. admiration ; wonder ; (gr.) note of exclamation.

admirar, v.a. to surprise ; to admire.

admisible, a. admissible.

admisión, sf. admission, acceptance.

admitir, v.a. to receive, to let in ; to concede ; to permit.

adobado, sm. pickled pork.

adobar, v.a. to dress ; to pickle ; to stew ; to tan hides.

adobe, sm. adobe, sun-dried brick.

adobería, sf. brick-field ; tanyard.

adobo, sm. repairing, mending ; pickle-sauce ; rouge ; ingredients for dressing leather or cloth. [nary.

adocenado, da, a. very common, ordi-

adocenar, v.a. to count, sell or make by dozens ; to despise.

adolecer, v.n. to be seized with illness.

adolescencia, sf. adolescence.

adolescente, a. adolescent, young.

¿ adónde ? ad. whither ?, where ?

adopción, sf. adoption.

adoptador, ra, sm. & f. adopter.

adoptar, v.a. to adopt.

adoptivo, va, a. adoptive.

adoración, sf. adoration, worship.

adorador, ra, sm. & f. adorer.

adorar, v.a. to adore ; to love exceedingly. [America).

adoratorio, sm. temple of idols (in

adormecer, v.a. to put to sleep ; to calm.

adormecimiento, sm. drowsiness, sleepi-

adormidera, sf. (bot.) poppy. [ness.

adornar, v.a. to embellish, to ornament.

adornista, sm. painter of ornaments.

adorno, sm. adornment ; ornament, dec-

adquirir, v.a. to acquire. [oration.

adquisición, sf. acquisition.

adra, sf. turn, successive order.

adragante, sm. gum tragacanth.

adrales, sm. pl. rails or hurdles of carts.

adrede, ad. purposely. [post.

adscribir, v.a. to appoint a person to a

aduana, sf. custom-house.

aduanar, v.a. to enter goods at the custom-house ; to pay duty.

aduanero, sm. custom-house officer.

aduar, sm. nomadic village of Arabs ; gipsy encampment.

aduendado, da, a. ghostly.

adufe, sm. tambourine.

adufero, sm. tambourine-player.

aduja, sf. (mar.) coiled cable.

adujar, v.a. (mar.) to coil a cable.

adulación, sf. adulation.

adulador, ra, s. flatterer ; fawner.

adular, v.a. to flatter ; to fawn.

adulear, v.n. to bawl, to cry out.

adulero, sm. driver of horses (or mules).

adulterar, v.a. & n. to adulterate ; to commit adultery.

adulterino, na, a. begotten in adultery ; misborn ; falsified.

adulterio, sm. adultery. [teress.

adúltero, ra, sm. & f. adulterer, adul-

adulto, ta, a. adult, grown-up.

adunar, v.a. to unite, to join.

adunia, ad. abundantly.

adusto, ta, a. gloomy, intractable.

advenedizo, za, a. exotic, foreign.

advenimiento, sm. arrival ; Advent.

adventicio, cia, a. adventitious ; acci-

adverbio, sm. adverb. [dental.

adversario, sm. adversary ; antagonist.

adversidad, sf. adversity, calamity.

adverso, sa, a. adverse, calamitous.

advertencia, sf. advertence ; attention to ; advice.

advertido, da, a. skilful, intelligent.

advertir, v.a. to advert, to take notice of ; to give heed ; to mark.

Adviento, sm. Advent.

adyacente, a. adjacent.

aechar, v.a. to winnow, to sift.

aecho, sm. winnowing.

aéreo, rea, aerial ; airy, fantastic.

aerolito, sm. aerolite.

aeronauta, sm. aeronaut ; airman.

aeroplano, sm. aeroplane.

aerostática, sf. aerostatics.

afabilidad, sf. affability.

afable, a. affable, complacent.

afaca, sf. yellow vetch.

afán, sm. anxiety, solicitude.

afanar, v.n. & r. to toil ; to be over-solicitous.

afanoso, sa, a. solicitous ; painstaking.

afear, v.a. to deform, to misshape ; —, (fig.) to blacken, to calumniate.

afección, sf. affection ; fondness, attachment.

afectación, sf. affectation. [ment.

afectadamente, ad. affectedly ; for appearance's sake.

afectar, v.a. to affect ; to feign.

afecto, sm. affection ; passion ; —, ta, a. affectionate ; disposed ; reserved.

afectuoso, sa, a. affectionate ; moving ; tender.

afeitar, v.a. to shave ; to paint the face.

afeite, sm. paint, rouge.

afelpado, da, a. shaggy.

afeminado, da, a. effeminate.

afeminar, v.a. to enervate.

aferrar, v.a. to grapple, to grasp, to seize ; (mar.) to furl ; to anchor.

afestonado, a. worked in a wavy pattern.

afianzar, v.a. to bail, to guarantee ; to prop.

afición, sf. affection ; fancy, liking.

aficionado, da, sm. & f. amateur, connoisseur.

aficionar, v.a. to inspire affection ; -se, to give one's mind to, to take a taste

afijo, ja, a. (gr.) affix. [for.

afiladera, sf. whetstone.

afilado, a. sharp.

afilar, v.a. to whet, to sharpen, to grind.

afiligranado, da, a. filigree-like.

afilón, sm. whetstone.

afilosofado, sm. person who plays the philosopher. [affinity.

afín, a. adjoining ; —, sm. relation by

afinación, sf. completion ; refining ; tuning of instruments.

afinar, v.a. to complete ; to tune musical instruments ; to refine.

afinidad, sf. affinity ; analogy.

afirmación, sf. affirmation.

afirmar, v.a. to secure, to fasten ; to affirm, to assure.

afirmativa, sf. affirmation.

afirmativo, va, a. affirmative.

aflicción, sf. affliction, grief, heart-ache, painfulness.

aflictivo, va, a. afflicting. [ment.

afligir, v.a. to afflict, to grieve, to torment.

aflogisticar, v.a. to render incombustible.

aflojar, v.a. to loosen, to slacken, to relax ; —, v.n. to grow weak ; to abate ; to grow cool in fervour.

afluente, a. abundant ; loquacious ; — sm. affluent, tributary stream.

afollar, v.a. to blow with bellows.

afondar, v.a. to put under water ; (mar.) to sink ; —, v.n. to go to the bottom.

aforar, v.a. to gauge ; to measure ; to calculate the duty on goods.

aforismo, sm. aphorism.

aforístico, ca, a. aphoristical.

aforo, sm. gauging ; custom-house examination of goods or luggage.

aforrar, v.a. to line (clothes) ; to stuff.

aforro, sm. lining ; sheathing.

afortunado, da, a. fortunate, happy.

afosarse, v.r. (mil.) to entrench one's self.

afrancesar, v.a. to frenchify.

afrenta, sf. outrage ; insult ; infamy.

afrentar, v.a. to affront ; to insult.

afrentoso, sa, a. ignominious ; insulting.

afretar, v.a. (mar.) to scour.

afrontar, v.a. to confront ; to reproach one to one's face with a crime.

afuera, ad. abroad ; outward ; | — | stand out of the way !

afueras, sm. pl. environs of a place.

afufar(se), v.n. & r. (col.) to run away, to escape.

afuste, sm. gun-carriage.

agabachado, da, a. (col.) frenchified.

agachadiza, sf. snipe.

agacharse, v.r. to stoop, to squat.

agalla, sf. gall-nut ; -s, pl. glands of the throat ; wind-galls of horses ; gills of fishes. [galls.

agallado, da, a. steeped in an infusion of

agallón, sm. large gall-nut ; -es, pl. strings of large silver beads ; wooden beads used for rosaries.

agamuzado, da, a. chamois coloured.

agarbarse, v.r. to cower, to squat.

agarradero, sm. anchoring-ground ; hold, haft ; (fig.) refuge.

agarrado, da, a. miserable, stingy.

agarrafar, v.a. to grapple hard in a scuffle.

agarrar, v.a. to grasp, to seize, to gripe.

agarro, sm. grasp.

agarrotar, v.a. to tie down.

agasajador, ra, a. officious, complacent.

agasajar, v.a. to receive and treat kindly ; to regale.

agasajo, sm. graceful reception ; kindness ; friendly present.

ágata, sf. agate.

agavillar, v.a. to tie up corn in sheaves ; -se, to associate with a gang of sharpers.

agazapar, v.a. (col.) to catch a person ; -se, to hide one's self.

agencia, sf. agency.

agenciar, v.a. to solicit, to obtain.

agencioso, sa, a. diligent, active ; officious.

agente, sm. agent, actor ; attorney.

agestado, da, (bien ó mal-) good- or bad looking.

agibilibus, sm. (col.) application, industry.

agilidad, sf. agility, nimbleness. [active.

agilitar, v.a. to render nimble, to make agio, sm. agio.

agio, sm. agio.

agiotador, agiotista, sm. money-changer, bill-broker, stock-broker.

agiotaje, sm. stock-jobbing.

agitación, sf. agitation.

agitanado, da, a. gipsy-like.

agitar, v.a. to agitate, to move.

aglomerar, v.a. to agglomerate, to conglomerate.

agnación, sf. consanguinity.

agnado, da, agnaticio cia, (leg.) a. consanguineous.

agnición, sf. (dramatic) recognition.

Agnus déi, sm. Agnus Dei, wax medal blessed by the Pope.

agobiar, v.a. to bend down to the ground; to oppress.

agolparse, v.a. to assemble in crowds.

agonía, sf. agony.

agonizar, v.a. to assist dying persons; —, v.n. to be in the agony of death, to agonise.

agorar, v.a. to divine; to augur.

agorero, sm. augurer; diviner. [(corn).

agorgojarse, v.r. to be destroyed by grubs

agostar, v.a. to scorch, to wither; —, v.n. to pasture cattle on stubbles in summer.

agostero, sm. harvesters' boy; religious mendicant (who begs corn in August).

agostizo, za, a. born in August.

agosto, sm. August (month); harvest-time. [drain off.

agotar, v.a. to exhaust; to consume; to

agraciado, da, a. graceful, genteel.

agraciar, v.a. to embellish; to grace; to grant, to concede.

agradable, a. agreeable; lovely.

agradar, v.a. to please, to gratify.

agradecer, v.a. to acknowledge a favour; to thank.

agradecido, da, a. thankful.

agradecimiento, sm. gratitude, gratefulness, thankfulness.

agrado, sm. agreeableness, courteousness; will, pleasure; liking.

agramadera, sf. brake (for dressing flax or hemp). [a brake.

agramar, v.a. to dress flax or hemp with

agramiza, sf. stalk of hemp; refuse of hemp. [aggrandize.

agrandar, v.a. to enlarge, to extend; to

agranujado, da, a. grained.

agrario, ria, a. agrarian.

agravación, sf. aggravation.

agravar, v.a. to make heavier, to oppress; to exaggerate.

agravatorio, ria, a aggravating; (leg.) compulsory.

agraviador, ra, s. injurer, offender.

agraviar, v.a. to wrong, to injure; -se, to be aggrieved; to be piqued.

agravio, sm. offence, injury.

agraz, sm. verjuice; unripe grape; en —, unseasonably. [bush.

agrazón, sm. wild grape; gooseberry

agregación, sf. aggregation.

agregado, sm. aggregate; attaché.

agregar, v.a. to aggregate, to heap together; to collate; to muster.

agresión, sf. aggression, attack.

agresor, sm. aggressor, assaulter.

agreste, a. rustic; uncultivated.

agrete, a. bitter-sweet. [asperate.

agriar, v.a. to sour, to acidify; to ex-

agricultura, sf. agriculture.

agridulce, a. half sweet and half sour.

agrietar, v.a. to split.

agrillo, lla, a. sourish, sharp to the taste.

agrimensor, sm. land-surveyor, surveyor.

agrimensura, sf. land-surveying.

agrimonia, sf. (bot.) agrimony.

agrio, a. sour, acrid; rough, craggy; sharp, rude, unpleasant; —, sm. acidity of the juice of certain fruits.

agrónomo, sm. surveyor.

agrumarse, v.r. to clog.

agrupar, v.a. to group, to cluster, to agrura, sf. acidity. [crowd.

agrura, sf. acidity.

agua, sf. water; lustre of diamonds; — llovediza, rain-water; — fuerte, aqua fortis. [rain.

aguacero, sm. short heavy shower of

aguachirle, sf. sour wine.

aguada, sf. fresh-water hold or supply on board ship; water-colour; painting in water-colours.

aguaderas, sf. pl. wooden framework for the carriage of jars of water by mules.

aguadero, sm. watering-place for cattle, horse-pond.

aguador, sm. water-carrier.

aguaje, sm. rapid current of sea-water; (mar.) spring-tide.

aguamanil, sm. water-jug for the wash-hand stand; wash-hand stand.

aguamanos, sm. water for washing the hands. [stone).

aguamarina, sf. aqua marina (precious

aguamiel, sf. hydromel.

aguanieve, sf. sleet; lap-wing.

aguanoso, sa, a. aqueous.

aguantar, v.a. to sustain, to suffer.

aguante, sm. firmness; patience.

aguapié, sm. inferior wine.

aguar, v.a. to mix water with wine; -se, to be submerged. [grant time.

aguardar, v.a. to expect, to wait for; to

aguardentería, sf. brandy-shop.

aguardentero, sm. keeper of a liquor-shop.

aguardiente, sm. brandy.

aguardo, sm. place where a sportsman waits to fire at the game, stand.

aguarrás, sf. spirit of turpentine.

aguatocha, sf. fire-engine.

aguaza, sf. juice extracted from trees by incision.

aguazal, sm. marsh.   [marshy.

aguazarse, v.r. to become boggy or

aguazo, sm. painting in gouache.

agudeza, sf. keenness, sharpness; acuteness; acidity; smartness.

agudo, da, a. sharp-pointed; keen-edged; smart; fine; acute, witty;

aguijada, sf. spur, goad.   [brisk.

aguijar, v.a. to prick, to spur, to goad; to stimulate.   [stimulation.

aguijón, sm. sting of a bee, wasp, &c.:

aguijonear, v.a. to prick, to spur; to stimulate.

águila, sf. eagle; a gold coin.

aguileño, ña, a. aquiline; hawk-nosed.

aguilucho, sm. eaglet.

aguinaldo, sm. Christmas-box.

aguja, sf. needle; bodkin; magnetic needle; (rail.) switch, siding; — de media, knitting-needle.

agujar, v.a. to prick with a needle: to sew, to stitch; to knit.

agujazo, sm. prick with a needle.

agujerear, v.a. to pierce, to bore.

agujero, sm. hole; needle-maker; needle-seller.

agujeta, sf. leather-strap; lace; -s, pl. pour-boire given to post-boys; pains from fatigue.

agujetería, sf. haberdasher's shop.

aguosidad, sf. lymph.

aguoso, sa, a. aqueous.

agusanarse, v.r. to be worm-eaten.

agustiniano, agustino, sm. monk of the order of St. Augustin.

aguzadera, sf. whetstone.

aguzanieve, sf. wagtail.   [late.

aguzar, v.a. to whet, to sharpen; to stimu-

aherrojar, v.a. to put in chains or irons.

ahí, ad. there.

ahidalgado, da, a. gentleman-like, noble.

ahijada, sf. goddaughter.

ahijado, sm. godson.

ahijar, v.a. to adopt as one's child; —, to bring forth young; to bud.

ahilarse, v.r. to grow faint for want of nourishment; to grow ropy (of wine).

ahilo, sm. faintness for want of food. inanition.

ahinco, sm. earnestness, eagerness.

ahitar, v.a. to surfeit; to cloy.

ahogar, v.a. to throttle, to smother; to drown, to suffocate; to oppress; to quench.

ahogo, sm. suffocation, anguish, pain.

ahojar, v.n. to eat the leaves of trees.

ahondar, v.a. to sink, to deepen; —, v.n. to penetrate far into a thing.

ahora, ad. now, at present; — —, just now; —, c. whether, or.

ahorcajarse, v.r. to sit astride.

ahorcar, v.a. to hang.

ahormar, v.a. to set on a form; to fit.

ahorquillado, da, a. forked.

ahorquillar, v.a. to prop up with forks.

ahorrar, v.a. to enfranchise, to emancipate; to save; to economize; to shun (labour).

ahorrativo, va, a. frugal, thrifty, saving; niggardly, stingy.

ahorro, sm. saving; thrift.

ahoyar, v.a. to dig holes for trees.

ahuchar, v.a. to hoard up.

ahuecar, v.a. to hollow, to scoop out; -se, to grow haughty.

ahumar, v.a. to smoke, to cure in smoke.

ahuyentar, v.a. to put to flight.

aijada, sf. See aguijada.

airarse, v.r. to grow angry.

airazo, sm. violent gust of wind.

aire, sm. air; wind; gracefulness of manners; aspect, countenance; musical composition; buen —, good-humour.

airearse, v.a. to take the air.

airón, sm. violent gale.

airoso, sa, a. airy; windy; graceful, genteel; successful.

aislado, da, a. insulated, isolated.

aislar, v.a. to isolate.

ajar, sm. garlic-field; —, v.a. to spoil, to tarnish; to abuse.

aje, sm. chronic ailment.

ajedrez, sm. chess (game); grating.

ajedrezado, da, a. chequered.

ajenabe, sm. wild mustard.

ajenjo, sm. wormwood, absinthium.

ajeno, na, a. belonging to another; foreign, strange; insane; contrary to; ignorant; unsuitable.

ajenuz, sm. fennel-flower.

ajetrearse, v.a. to bustle; to toil.   [tion.

ajetreo, sm. activity; bustling disposi-

ají, sm. red Indian dwarf-pepper.

ajicola, sf. glue made of scraps of leather boiled with garlic.

ajimez, sm. arched window with a pillar in the centre to support it.

ajipuerro, sm. (bot.) leek.

ajo, sm. garlic; garlic-sauce; paint for ladies; (col.) discreditable transaction taken part in by several persons.

ajobar, v.a. to carry heavy loads upon one's back.

ajolio, sm. sauce made of oil and garlic.

ajonje, sm. bird-lime.   [cheese.

ajoqueso, sm. dish made of garlic and

ajorca, sf. anklets ; bracelets.

ajordar, v.a. to bawl, to cry out.

ajornalar, v.a. to hire by the day.

ajuar, sm. household furniture.

ajudiado, da, a. Jewish.

ajuiciado, da, a. judicious, prudent, sensible.

ajustar, v.a. to regulate, to adjust ; to concert ; to settle a balance.

ajuste, sm. agreement, pact ; accommodation.

ajusticiar, v.a. to execute a malefactor.

al, art. for **á el.**

ala, sf. wing ; aisle ; row, file ; brim of the hat ; auricle ; -s, pl. (mar.) upper-studding sails ; protection.

alabandina, sf. manganese.

alabanza, sf. praise, applause.

alabar, v.a. to praise, to applaud.

alabarda, sf. halberd.

alabardero, sm. halberdier.

alabastrado, da, a. resembling alabaster.

alabastrino, na, a. of alabaster.

alabastro, sm. alabaster ; gypsum.

álabe, sm. drooping branch of an olive-tree ; flier of a water-mill ; fan-wheel.

alabearse, v.r. to warp.

alabeo, sm. warp, warping.

alacena, sf. cupboard, small cupboard in the wall ; wainscot-chest.

alacrán, sm. scorpion ; ring of the mouth-piece of a bridle ; stop, hook.

alacranado, da, a. bitten by a scorpion ; vicious.

alada, sf. fluttering of the wings.

aladares, sm. pl. love-curls.

alado, da, a. winged.

álaga, sf. (bot.) spelt.

alama, sf. gold or silver cloth.

alambicado, da, a. given sparingly, grudgingly.

alambicar, v.a. to distil ; to investigate closely.

alambique, sm. alambic ; still.

alambre, sm. copper ; copper-wire ; sheep-bells.

alambrera, sf. wire-netting.

alameda, sf. poplar-avenue ; public garden.

álamo, sm. poplar, poplar-tree ; — temblón, aspen-tree.

alampar(se), v.a. & r. to long, to wish earnestly.

alamud, sm. door-bolt ; bar of a gate.

alancear, v.a. to dart, to spear ; to wound with a lance.

alano, sm. boar-hound.

alar, sm. birdsnare, noose.

alarbe, sm. Arabian ; unmannerly person.

alarde, sm. military review ; ostentation ; hacer —, to boast.

alargar, v.a. to lengthen ; to extend.

alarida, sf. hue and cry.

alarido, sm. outcry, shout.

alarife, sm. architect.

alarma, sf. alarm.

alarmar, v.a. to alarm, to call to arms.

alarmista, sm. alarmist.

alatón, sm. latten, brass.

alazán, ana, a. sorrel-coloured (of horses).

alazo, sm. blow with the wings.

alba, sf. dawn of day, dayspring ; alb, surplice.

albacea, sm. testamentary executor.

albaceazgo, sm. office of a testamentary executor.

albada, sf. morning-serenade.

albahaca, sf. (bot.) sweet basil. [passport.

albalá, sm. & f. quittance, certificate ;

albanega, sf. hair-net.

albañal, albañar, sm. common sewer ; gully-hole.

albañil, sm. mason, bricklayer.

albañilería, sf. masonry.

albar, a. white, whitish.   [house.

albarán, sm. bill or placard for letting a

albarazado, da, a. affected with the white leprosy ; pallid, pale.

albarazo, sm. white leprosy.

albarcoquero, sm. apricot-tree.

albarda, sf. pack-saddle for beasts of burden ; slice of bacon.

albardar, v.a. to saddle with a pack-saddle.

albardilla, sf. small pack-saddle ; coping ; ridge ; mother-wool.

albaricoque, sm. apricot.

albaricoquero, sm. apricot-tree.

albarillo, sm. country-dance tune for the guitar ; small kind of apricot.

albarrada, sf. dry wall ; trench.

albayalde, sm. white-lead, ceruse.

albazano, na, a. of a dark chestnut colour.

albear, v.a. to whiten.   [arbitrament.

albedrío, sm. free-will, freedom of will ·

albéitar, sm. farrier, veterinary surgeon.

albeitería, sf. farriery.

albengala, sf. muslin.

albentola, sf. fine bag-net.

alberca, sf. reservoir, cistern.

albérchiga, sf. peach.

albergar, v.a. to lodge, to harbour ; -se to take a lodging.

albergue, sm. lodging-house, harbour ; charity-school for orphans.

albina, sf. marshy ground inundated with sea-water.

albo, ba, a. white.
albogue, sm. bagpipe ; cymbal.
albohol, sm. bind-weed.
albóndiga, sf. forcemeat-ball.
albor, sm. (poet.) dawn.
alborada, sf. first dawn of day ; (mil.) action fought at the dawn of day ; morning-watch.
alborear, v.n. to dawn.
alborga, sf. mat-weed sandal.
albornía, sf. large glazed jug.
albornoz, sm. coarse woollen stuff ; moorish cloak. [a bargain.
alboroque, sm. treat at the conclusion of
alborotadizo, za, alborotado, da, a. restless, turbulent.
alborotapueblos, s. disturber.
alborotar, v.a. to disturb, to agitate.
alboroto, sm. noise, disturbance, tumult, riot.
alborozar, v.a. to exhilarate. [riot.
alborozo, sm. joy, gaiety.
albricias, sf. pl. reward given for good news ; ¡ — ! joy ! joy !
albufera, sf. lagoon.
albugíneo, nea, a. albuminous.
albugo, sm. albugo (eye-disease).
albur, sm. dace (pez).
albura, sf. whiteness.
alcabala, sf. tax on sales.
alcacel, alcacer, sm. young corn.
alcachofa, sf. artichoke.
alcahaz, sm. large bird-cage.
alcahazar, v.a. to cage birds.
alcahuete, ta, sm. & f. pimp, bawd.
alcahuetear, v.a. to pander.
alcahuetería, sf. bawdry.
alcaide, sm. governor of a castle ; jailor, warden.
alcaidesa, sf. wife of a governor *or* jailor.
alcaidía, sf. governorship ; governor's district.
alcalde, sm. mayor ; justice of the peace.
alcaldía, sf. office and jurisdiction of an alcalde.
alcalino, na, a. alkaline. [alcalde.
alcamonías, sf. pl. various kinds of aromatic seeds.
alcance, sm. reach, extent ; arm's length ; range of fire-arms ; capacity, ability ; hit ; deficit.
alcancía, sf. money-box ; (mil.) handgrenade.
alcanfor, sm. camphor. [grenade.
alcanforado, da, a. camphorated.
alcantarilla, sm. small bridge ; drain ; conduit under ground.
alcanzado, da, a. necessitous, wanting.
alcanzar, v.a. to overtake, to come up with, to reach ; to get, to obtain ; to outlive ; to be a creditor ; —, v.n. to suffice ; to reach.
alcaparra, sf., **alcaparro,** sm. caper-bush ; caper.

alcaraván, sm. bittern.
alcaravea, sf. caraway-seed.
alcartaz, sm. paper-bag.
alcatifa, sf. fine carpet.
alcatraz, sm. pelican.
alcayata, sf. hook ; clothes-hook ; staple.
alcázar, sm. castle, palace.
alcazuz, sm. liquorice.
alce, sm. the cut (at cards).
alcista, sm. bull (Stock Exchange).
alción, sm. halcyon.
alcoba, sf. alcove ; bedroom.
alcohol, sm. antimony ; alcohol.
alcoholar, v.a. to paint with antimony ; to rectify spirits.
alcorán, sm. Alcoran, Koran.
alcoranista, sm. expounder of the Koran.
alcornoque, sm. cork-tree ; person of uncouth manners.
alcrebite, sm. sulphur, brimstone.
alcuza, sf. oil-bottle.
aldaba, sf. knocker ; clapper ; cross-bar.
aldabada, sf. rap with a knocker ; sudden fear. [knocker.
aldabazo, sm. violent rap with the
aldabear, v.n. to knock at the door with
aldea, sf. hamlet. [the knocker.
aldeana, sf. countrywoman ; lass.
aldeano, sm. villager ; —, a. rustic.
aleación, sf. art of alloying metals.
alear, v.n. to flutter ; —, v.a. to alloy.
aleccionar, v.a. to teach.
alegación, sf. allegation.
alegar, v.a. to allege, to quote.
alegato, sm. allegation ; (law) plaintiff's
alegoría, sf. allegory. [deposition.
alegórico, ca, a. allegorical.
alegorizar, v.a. to allegorise.
alegrar, v.a. to gladden ; to lighten ; to exhilarate ; to enliven ; to beautify ; -se, to rejoice ; to grow merry with drinking.
alegre, a. merry, joyful, content.
alegría, sf. mirth, gaiety ; (bot.) oilygrain.
alegro, sm. (mus.) allegro.
alegrón, sm. sudden joy ; sudden flicker.
alejamiento, sm. removal.
alejar, v.a. to remove to a greater distance.
alelar, v.a. to stupefy. [tance.
alelí, sm. (bot.) winter gilliflower.
aleluya, sf. alleluiah ; Easter-time.
alemán, sm. German.
alemana, sf. (old) Spanish dance.
alentar, v.n. to respire, to breathe ; —, v.a. to animate.
alepín, sm. a kind of bombasine.
alerce, sm. larch-tree.
alero, sm. gable-end ; eaves.
alerta, ad. attentively ; interj. hullo ! (sentinel's cry).

alertamente. ad. vigilantly, attentively, on the watch.

alertar, v.a. to render vigilant.

alesna, sf. awl.

alesnado, da, a. awl-shaped.

aleta, sf. fin.

aletargarse, v.r. to fall into a lethargic state, to sink to sleep.

aletazo, sm. blow from a wing.

aletear, v.n. to flutter, to flit, to flicker.

aleteo, sm. flapping of wings; fluttering.

aleve, a. treacherous, perfidious.

alevosía, sf. treachery, perfidy.

alevoso, sa, a. treacherous, perfidious.

alfabéticamente, ad. alphabetically.

alfabético, ca, a. alphabetical.

alfabeto, sm. alphabet.

alfajor, sm. gingerbread.

alfalfa, sf. (bot.) lucern.

alfanjazo, sm. cutlass-wound.

alfanje, sm. hanger, cutlass.

alfaquí, sm. Mussulman jurisconsult.

alfar, sm. pottery; potter's clay.

alfarería, sf. potter's art.

alfarero, sm. potter.

alfeñicado, a. sugared; delicate.

alfeñique, sm. sugar-paste; weakling.

alferecía, sf. epilepsy.

alférez, sm. ensign.

alfil, sm. bishop (at chess).

alfiler, sm. pin (to fasten clothes); -es, pl. pin-money.

alfilerazo, sm. prick of a pin.

alfolí, sm. granary; salt warehouse.

alfoli(n)ero, sm. keeper of a granary or magazine.

alfombra, sf. carpet.

alfombrar, v.a. to carpet.

alfombrero, sm. carpet-maker.

alfombrilla, sf. (med.) scarlatina.

alfóncigo, sm. pistachio (tree or nut).

alforja, sf. saddle-bag, knapsack.

alforjero, sm. maker or seller of saddle-bags. [bags.

alga, sf. (bot.) sea-weed.

algaida, sf. sand-dune.

algalia, sf. civet; civet-cat. [berish.

algarabía, sf. Arabic tongue; gabble, gib-

algarada, sf. loud cry.

algarroba, sf. (bot.) carob.

algarrobera, sf., algarrobo, sm. (bot.) carob-tree.

algazara, sf. huzza (cry of Moors); hub-bub of a multitude.

álgebra, sf. algebra.

algebrista, sm. algebraist.

álgido, a. (med.) icy-cold.

algo, pn. somewhat, something, ought; —, ad. somewhat. [ton-wool.

algodón, sm. cotton; cotton-plant; cot-

algodonado, da, a. filled with cotton.

algodonal, sm. cotton-plantation.

algodonero, sm. cotton-plant; dealer in cotton, cotton-broker.

algoso, sa, a. full of sea-weed.

alguacil, sm. constable; watchman.

alguien, pn. somebody.

algún, alguno, na, a. any; — tanto, ad. a little, rather.

alhaja, sf. furniture; jewel.

alhajar, v.a. furnish.

alharaca, sf. clamour, vociferation.

alheña, sf. (bot.) common privet, dog-wood; corn-blight.

alhoja, sf. lark.

alhóndiga, sf. public granary.

alhondiguero, sm. keeper of a public granary. [granary.

alhucema, sf. lavender.

aliacán, sm. jaundice.

aliacanado, da, a. jaundiced.

aliado, da, a. allied.

alianza, sf. alliance, league.

aliarse, v.r. to be allied.

alias, ad. otherwise.

alible, a. nourishing.

alicaído, da, a. lame-winged; weak, de-pressed. [ning.

alicantina, sf. artifice, stratagem, cun-

alicates, sm. pl. pincers, nippers.

aliciente, sm. attraction, incitement.

alicionar, v.a. to teach.

alicuanta, a.f. aliquant (number).

alicuota, a.f. aliquot (quantity).

aliento, sm. breath, respiration; cou-rageousness.

alifafe, sm. tumour (on a horse's hock); (col.) habitual ailment.

aligacion, sf. incorporation, coalition; (arith.) alligation.

aligar, v.a. to tie, to unite.

aligeramiento, sm. alleviation.

aligerar, v.a. to lighten; to alleviate; to hasten.

alijador, sm. (mar.) lighter.

alijar, v.a. (mar.) to lighten, to lighter; sm. uncultivated ground. [viation.

alijo, sm. lightening of a ship; alle-

alimentación, sf. alimentation, mainten-ance, nourishment.

alimentar, v.a. to feed, to nourish.

alimenticio, cia, a. nutritious, nutritive.

alimento, sm. aliment, food; -s, s.pl. alimony.

alindar, v.a. to fix limits; to delimitate.

alineación, sm. delimitation.

alinear, v.a. to measure by line, to arrange in line.

aliñar, v.a. to adorn; to season.

aliño, sm. dress, ornament, decoration; apparatus. [footed.

alípede, a. (poet.) with winged feet; swift-

aliquebrado, da, a. broken-winged; de-jected, low-spirited.

alisadura, sf. planing, smoothing, polishing ; -s, s.pl. shavings, cuttings.

alisar, v.a. to plane, to polish ; to smoothe ; to mangle.

aliseda, sf. plantation of alder-trees.

aliso, sm. alder-tree.

alistado, da, a. striped.

alistador, sm. accountant ; one who enlists.   [levy.

alistamiento, sm. enrolment, conscription,

alistar, v.a. to enlist, to enrol.

aliviador, ra, sm. assistant.

aliviar, v.a. to lighten ; to ease, to relieve, to mollify.

alivio, sm. alleviation, mitigation ; com-

aljaba, sf. quiver.   [fort.

aljez, crude gypsum.

aljibe, sm. cistern.   [basin.

aljofaina, sf. earthen jug ; wash-hand

aljofar, sm. misshapen pearl ; dew-drop.

aljofarar, v.a. to adorn with pearls.

aljor, sm. crude gypsum.

aljuba, sf. a Moorish garment.

alma, sf. soul ; human being ; principal part of a thing ; conscience ; energy ; mould for casting statues.   [zine.

almacén, sm. warehouse, store, maga-

almacenaje, sm. warehouse rent , housage.

almacenar, v.a. to store, to lay up.

almacenero, sm. warehouse-keeper.

almáciga, sf. mastich ; (bot.) nursery.

almaden, sm. mine.

almadía, sf. Indian canoe ; raft.

almadraba, sf. tunny-fishery ; tunny-net.

almadreña, sf. wooden shoe.

almaganeta, sf. sledge-hammer.

almagrar, v.a. to tinge with red ochre, to ruddle.

almagre, sm. red ochre, ruddle.

almanaque, sm. almanac.

almanaquero, almanaquista, sm. maker or vendor of almanacs.

almargo, sm. (bot.) glass-wort.

almarjal, sm. plantation of glass-wort ; low marshy ground.

almártaga, sf. litharge ; a sort of halter.

almástiga, sf. mastich.

almastigado, da, a. containing mastich.

almazara, sf. oil-mill.

almazarero, sm. oil-miller.

almazarrón, sm. ochre ; raddle.

almena, sf. battlement.

almenado, da, a. embattled.

almenaje, sm. series of turrets around a rampart.   [battlements.

almenar, v.a. to crown a rampart with

almendra, sf. almond.

almendrada, sf. almond-milk.

almendrado, da, a. almond-like ; —, sm. macaroon.

almendrera, sf., almendrero, almendro, sm. almond-tree.

almez(o), sm. nettle-tree, lotus-tree.

almeza, sf. lotus-berry.

almiar, sm. stack of hay.

almíbar, sm. syrup ; treacle ; -es, pl. preserved fruit.

almibarar, v.a. to preserve fruit in sugar ; to conciliate with soft and endearing words.

almidón, sm. starch.   [spruce.

almidonado, da, a. starched ; affected

almidonar, v.a. to starch.

almilla, sf. under waistcoat ; short military jacket ; pork-chop.

alminar, sm. minaret.   [wife.

almiranta, sf. flag-ship ; the admiral's

almirantazgo, sm. admiralty, admiral's

almirante, sm. admiral.   [dues.

almirez, sm. brass mortar.

almizclar, v.a. to musk.

almizcle, sm. musk.

almizcleña, sf. grape-hyacinth.

almizcleño, ña, a. musky.

almizclera, sf. musk-rat.

almo, ma, a. supporting ; nourishing ; (poet.) venerable, holy.

almocafre, sm. gardener's hoe.

almodrote, sm. hodge-podge.

almofía, sf. wash-hand basin.

almofrej, sm. bag for bedding.

almohada, sf. pillow, bolster ; cushion.

almohadilla, sf. small pillow ; working-

almohadón, sm. large cushion.   [case.

almohaza, sf. curry-comb.   [ostler.

almohazador, sm. groom, stable-boy,

almohazar, v.a. to curry.

almojábana, sf. cheese-cake.

almoneda, sf. auction.

almonedear, v.a. to sell by auction.

almoraduj, sm. sweet marjoram.

almorí, sm. sweetmeat-cake.

almorranas, sf.pl. hemorrhoids.

almorrefa, sf. mosaic-tile floor.

almorta, sf. chickling vetch.

almorzada, sf. double-handful of grain. &c.

almorzado, da, a. one who has breakfasted.

almorzar, v.a. to breakfast.

almotacén, sm. inspector of weights and measures.

almotacenazgo, sm. office of an inspector of weights and measures.

almozárabe, sm. Christian who lived under the Moors.

almud, sm. a measure of grain.

almudada, sf. piece of ground which it takes half a fanega of grain to sow.

almuerza, sf. double-handful (of grain, fruits, &c.).

almuerzo, sm. breakfast ; the midday meal. [sore (of animals).
alobadado, da, a. bitten by a wolf ; plague-
alobunado, da, a. wolf-coloured.
alocado, da, a. crack-brained ; foolish, inconsiderate.
alocución, sf. allocution.
alodio, sm. allodium.
áloe, sm. (bot.) aloes.
aloja, sf. metheglin, mead. [age.
alojamiento, sm. lodging ; (mar.) steer-
alojar, v.a. to lodge.
alojería, sf. place where mead is pre-pared and sold.
alojero, sm. eller of mead ; box near the pit in some theatres of Spain.
alomado, da, a. crook-backed (of horses).
alomar, v.a. to distribute equally the strength of a horse ; —, v.n. to grow strong and vigorous. [feathers.
alón, sm. wing of a bird stripped of its
alondra, sf. lark.
alopiado, da, a. composed of opium.
aloque, a. light-red (wine).
alosa, sf. shad (fish). [ing pottery.
alpañata, sf. piece of leather for smooth-
alpargata, sf. hempen shoe.
alpargatar, v.a. to make hempen shoes.
alpargatero, sm. manufacturer of hempen shoes. [wheedler.
alpargatilla, sm. crafty fellow ; (col.)
alpiste, sm. canary-seed.
alpistela, alpistera, sf. cake made of flour, eggs, sesamum, and honey . [seed.
alpistero, sm. sieve for sifting canary-
alquería, sf. grange, farm-house.
alquifol, alquifou, sm. potter's ore.
alquiladizo, za, a. for hire.
alquilador, ra, sm. (& f.) one who hires out (carriages).
alquilar, v.a. to let, to hire.
alquiler, sm. wages, hire ; house-rent.
alquimia, sf. alchemy.
alquímico, ca, a. alchemical.
alquimista, sm. alchemist.
alquitara, sf. alembic.
alquitarar, v.a. to distil.
alquitrán, sm. tar, liquid pitch.
alquitranado, sm. (mar.) tarpaulin.
alquitranar, v.a. to tar.
alrededor, ad. around.
alrededores, sm.pl. environs.
alta, sf. discharge from hospital.
altanería, sf. haughtiness. [proud.
altanero, ra, a. haughty, arrogant, vain,
altar, sm. altar ; — de ánima, altar of indulgence ; — mayor, high-altar.
altarero, sm. decorator of altars for festi-
altea, sf. (bot.) marsh-mallow. [vals.
alterabilidad, sf. alterableness ; muta-bility.

alterable, a. alterable, mutable.
alteración, sf. alteration, mutation ; strong emotion ; disturbance, tumult.
alterar, v.a. to alter, to change ; to dis-turb.
altercación, sf., altercado, sm. alterca-tion, controversy ; quarrel, contest, strife.
altercador, ra, sm. (& f.) wrangler.
altercar, v.a. to dispute, to altercate, to quarrel.
alternación, sf. alternation.
alternar, v.a. & n. to alternate.
alternativa, sf. alternative.
alternativo, va, a. alternate.
alteza, sf. height, elevation.
Alteza, sf. Highness (title).
altibajo, sm. downright blow in fencing ; uneven ground ; -s, pl. (col.) vicissi-tudes of human affairs, ups and downs.
altillo, sm. hillock.
altísimo, ma, a. extremely high, high-most ; —, sm. the Most High, God.
altisonante, altísono, na, a. high-sound-ing, pompous, fustian.
altitonante, a. (poet.) thundering, high-sounding.
altivez, sf. haughtiness, huff.
altivo, va, a. haughty, proud, high-flown.
alto, ta, a. high, elevated ; arduous, difficult ; eminent ; enormous, atro-cious ; —, sm. height ; storey ; high-land ; (mil.) halt ; (mus.) alto ; pasar por —, to omit, ignore.
altozano, sm. hillock.
altramuz, sm. (bot.) lupine.
altura, sf. height ; highness ; moun-tain summit ; altitude ; -s, pl. the alubia, sf. kidney-bean. [heavens.
alucinación, sf., alucinamiento, sm. hal-lucination.
alucinar, v.a. to blind, to deceive ; -se, to deceive oneself, to labour under a delusion.
aludir, v.n. to allude.
alumbrado, da, a. aluminous ; —, sm. illumination. [birth.
alumbramiento, sm. illumination ; child-
alumbrar, v.a. to light ; to enlighten, to instruct ; to soak in alum-water ; -se (col.) to be intoxicated.
alumbre, sm. alum.
alumbrera, sf. alum-mine.
aluminado, da, a. impregnated with alum.
aluminio, sm. aluminium.
aluminoso, sa, a. aluminous.
alumno, na, sm. foster-child ; disciple, pupil. [tusked.
alunado, da, a. lunatic ; spasmodic ; long-
alusión, sf. allusion, hint.
alusivo, va, a. allusive.

alustrar, v.a. tó give lustre, to polish.
alutación, sf. grains of gold, brought to light by washing.
aluvión, sf. alluvion.
álveo, sm. bed of a river.
alvéolo, sm. socket of a tooth; cell of a honey-comb.
alza, sf. advance in price.
alzacuello, sm. stock (for the neck).
alzadamente, ad. wholesale.
alzado, sm. plan of a building showing front elevation; -s, pl. spare stores; —, da, a. fraudulent (of a bankrupt); wholesale.
alzadura, sf. elevation.   [bid.
alzamiento, sm. rise; elevation; higher
alzaprima, sf. lever.
alzaprimar, v.a. to lever; (fig.) to excite.
alzapuertas, sm. (drama) rôle of a mute servant.
alzar, v.a. to raise, to lift up, to heave; to construct, to build; to hide; to lock up; to cut cards; to plough for the first time; -se, to rise in rebellion; -se con algo, to carry away.
allá, ad. there; thither; in other times.
allanar, v.a. to level, to flatten; to overcome difficulties; to pacify; to subdue; -se, to submit; to tumble down.
allegadizo, za, a. swept or scraped together.
allegado, da, a. near, proximate; —, sm. relative, follower.   [approach.
allegar, v.a. to collect, to gather; to
allende, ad. on the other side.
allí, ad. there, in that place.
alloza, sf. green almond.
allozo, sm. wild almond-tree.
ama, sf. mistress, house-wife; — de llaves, house-keeper; — de leche, nurse.
amabilidad, sf. amiability, loveliness.
amable, a. amiable, lovely.
amador, ra, sm. & f. lover, sweetheart.
amadroñado, da, a. strawberry-like.
amaestrado, da, a. taught; artfully contrived.
amaestrar, v.a. to teach, to instruct.
amagar, v.a. to threaten.
amago, sm. threat; indication; symptom.   [n. to yield, to lessen.
amainar, v.a. (mar.) to lower a sail; —,
amajadar, v.n. to pen sheep.
amalgama, sf. amalgam.
amalgamación, sf. amalgamation.
amalgamar, v.a. to amalgamate.
amamantar, v.a. to suckle.
amancebamiento, sm. concubinage.
amancebarse, v.r. to live in concubinage.
amancillar, v.a. to stain, to defile; to injure; to tarnish.

amanecer, v.n. to dawn.
amanerado, da, a. affected.
amanerarse, v.r. to be affected.
amanojar, v.a. to gather by handfuls.
amansador, ra, sm. & f. tamer, subduer; soother.
amansamiento, sm. taming.
amansar, v.a. to tame, to domesticate; to soften, to meeken.
amantar, v.a. to cloak.
amante, sm. lover.   [copyist.
amanuense, sm. amanuensis, clerk,
amañar, v.a. to do a thing cleverly; -se, to accustom one's self to do things cleverly.
amaño, sm. skill, dexterity; -s, s.pl. tools; implements; intrigue.
amapola, sf. (bot.) poppy.
amar, v.a. to love.
amaranto, sm. (bot.) amaranth.
amargar, v.a. to embitter; to exasperate; —, v.n. to be bitter.
amargo, ga, a. bitter, acrid; painful; —, sm. bitterness; bitters (liquor).
amargón, sm. (bot.) dandelion.
amargor, sm. bitterness; sorrow, vexation, distress.
amargoso, sa, a. bitter.
amargura, sf. bitterness; sorrow.
amaricado, da, a. effeminate.
amarillazo, za, a. pale yellow.
amarillear, v.n. to turn yellow.
amarillejo, ja, amarillento, ta, a. yellowish.
amarillez, sf. yellowness of the skin.
amarillo, lla, a. yellow; —, sm. jaundice.
amarinar, v.a. (mar.) to man, to equip.
amarra, sf. cable; martingale.
amarradero, sm. a post to make fast to; (mar.) mooring-berth.
amarrar, v.a. to tie, to fasten.   [tackle.
amarrazones, sm. pl. (mar.) ground-
amartelar, v.a. to court, to make love; -se, to fall in love with.
amartillar, v.a. to hammer; to cock (a gun or pistol).
amasadera, sf. kneading-trough.
amasadijo, sm. bread-dough.
amasadura, sf. kneading.
amasar, v.a. to knead; (fig.) to arrange, to prepare, to settle.
amasijo, sm. dough; mixed mortar; bread-dough; medley.
amatista, sf. amethyst.
amatorio, ria, a. relating to love.
amazona, sf. amazon; masculine woman.
ámbar, sm. amber.
ambarino, na, a. amber.
ambición, sf. ambition.
ambicionar, v.a. to crave, to covet.
ambicioso, sa, a. ambitious.

ambiente, sm. surrounding atmosphere.

ambigú, sm. supper.

ambigüedad, sf. ambiguity.

ambiguo, gua, a. ambiguous, doubtful, equivocal.

ámbito, sm. circuit, circumference.

ambos, bas, pn. both.

ambrosia, sf. ambrosia ; any delicious liquor ; (bot.) buck-thorn.

ambulancia, sf. ambulance.

ambulante, a. ambulatory ; movable.

ambulativo, va, a. of a roving disposition.

amedrentar, v.a. to frighten, to terrify, to intimidate.

amelga, sf. ridge between two furrows.

amelgar, v.a. to open furrows with the plough.

amelonado, da, a. melon-shaped.

amen, sm. amen, so be it ; — de, besides.

amenaza, sf. threat, menace.

amenazar, v.a. to threaten, to menace.

amenizar, v.a. to render pleasant ; to adorn a speech. [(of language).

ameno, na, a. pleasant, delicious; flowery

amerengado, a. (fig.) fair-spoken.

ametalado, da, a. brass-coloured.

amicísimo, a. most friendly.

amiento, sm. chin-strap.

amiga, sf. female friend ; concubine ; school-mistress. [able.

amigable, a. amicable, friendly ; suit-

amigo, sm. friend ; comrade ; lover ; —, ga, a. friendly.

amilanar, v.a. to frighten, to terrify.

amillaramiento, sm. tax-assessment.

amillarar, v.a. to assess.

amillonado, da, a. liable to pay a certain tax, called millones ; very rich.

amistad, sf. friendship ; juncture ; gallantry ; civility, favour ; desire.

amistar, v.a. & r. to reconcile.

amistoso, sa, a. friendly, cordial.

amito, sm. amice.

amnistía, sf. amnesty.

amo, sm. master of a house ; proprietor, owner ; foster-father ; overseer.

amoblar, v.a. to furnish.

amodorrarse, v.r. to grow sleepy.

amohecerse, v.r. to grow mouldy.

amohinar, v.a. to put out of humour.

amojamado, da, a. dry, meagre.

amojonar, v.a. to set landmarks.

amoladera, sf. whetstone, grindstone.

amolador, sm. grinder ; bungler, bore.

amoladura, sf. whetting, grinding, sharpening.

amolar, v.a. to whet, to grind, to sharpen.

amoldar, v.a. to mould ; to bring one to his duty.

amolletado, da, a. loaf-shaped.

amomo, sm. (bot.) Guinea-grains.

amonedar, v.a. to coin.

amonestación, sf. advice, admonition ; publication of marriage-bans.

amonestar, v.a. to advise, to admonish to publish banns of marriage.

amoniaco, sm. ammonia.

amontillado, vino —, pale sherry.

amontarse, v.r. to take to the woods.

amontonar, v.a. to heap together, to accumulate.

amor, sm. love ; fancy ; the object of love ; — mío, mis -es, my love ; — propio, self-love ; -es, pl. gallantry ; amours.

amoratado, da, a. livid.

amorcillo, sm. flirtation. [lovely

amoroso, sa, a. affectionate, loving,

amorrar, v.n. to hang one's head.

amorronar, v.a. to signal with a flag.

amortajar, v.a. to shroud (a corpse).

amortecer, v.a. to deaden ; -se, to faint.

amortiguar, v.a. to mortify, to deaden ; to temper.

amortización, sf. entail ; redemption (of a tax or debt).

amortizar, v.a. to entail (an estate) ; to redeem (a tax or debt).

amoscar, v.a. to whisk flies ; -se, to drive off flies with the tail (of animals) ; to fly into a passion at nothing.

amostachado, a. moustachioed.

amotinador, a. mutineer.

amotinamiento, sm. mutiny.

amotinar, v.a. to excite rebellion ; -se, to mutiny.

amovible, a. removable.

ampara, sf. (law) distraint.

amparar, v.a. to shelter, to favour, to protect ; to sequestrate ; -se, to claim protection. [refuge, asylum.

amparo, sm. protection, help, support ;

ampelita, sf. cannel-coal. [ment.

ampliación, sf. amplification, enlarge-

ampliar, v.a. to amplify, to enlarge, to extend, to expand.

ampliativo, va, a. amplifying.

amplificar, v.a. to amplify.

amplio, lia, a. ample, extensive.

amplitud, sf. amplitude, extension, largeness.

ampo (de la nieve), sm. whiteness.

ampolla, sf. blister (on the cuticle) ; phial, cruet.

ampollar, v.a. to raise blisters ; -se, to rise in bubbles ; —, a. bubble-shaped.

ampolleta, sf. small phial ; hour-glass ; — de arena, powder-box.

amputación, sf. amputation.

amputar, v.n. to amputate.

amuchachado, da, a. boyish, childish.

amueblar, v.a. to furnish.

amugronar, v.a. to lay (vine-shoots).
amujerado, da, a. effeminate.
amuleto, sm. amulet.   [nition.
amunicionar, v.a. to supply with ammu-
amurada, sf. (mar.) bulwark.
amurallar, v.a. to surround with walls.
amurcar, v.a. to gore.
amurco, sm. blow with the horns.
amusco, a. dark-brown.
amusgar, v.a. to lay back the ears; to
    half-close one's eyes to see better.
ana, sf. ell (-measure).
anabaptista, sm. anabaptist.
anacoreta, sm. anchorite, hermit.
anacorético, ca, a. relating to a hermit.
anacronismo, sm. anachronism.
ánade, sm. & f. duck.
anadear, v.n. to waddle.
anadeja, sf. duckling.
anadino, na, sm. & f. young duck.
anadón, sm. duck.
anafalla, sf. thick-corded silk stuff.
anafe, sm. portable stove.
anagálida, sf. (bot.) pimpernel.
anagrama, sг. anagram.
anales, sf.pl. annals.
análisis, sf. analysis.
analista, sm. writer of annals.
analítico, ca, a. analytical.
analizar, v.a. to analyse.
analogía, sf. analogy.
analógico, ca, análogo, ga, a. analagous.
anana, sm. pine-apple.
anaquel, sm. shelf in a book-case.
anaranjado, da, a. orange-coloured.
anarquía, sf. anarchy.
anárquico, ca, a. anarchical, confused.
anarquista, sm. anarchist.
anascote, sm. serge.
anata, sf. annates.
anatema, sf. anathema.
anatematizar, v.a. to anathematize.
anatomía, sf. anatomy.
anatómico, ca, a. anatomical.
anatomista, sm. anatomist.   [sect.
anatomizar, v.a. to anatomize, to dis-
anca, sf. buttocks of a horse.
ancianar, v.n. (poet.) to grow old.
ancianidad, sf. old age; antiquity.
anciano, na, a. old, stricken in years.
ancla, sf. anchor; — de esperanza, sheet-
    anchor.   [ground; anchorage.
anclaje, sm. act of anchoring; anchor
anclar, v.n. to anchor.
anclote, sm. grapnel.
ancón, sm. anconada, sf. small bay.
ancoraje, sm. anchorage.
ancorar, v.a. See anclar.
ancorero, sm. anchor-smith.
ancho, cha, a. broad, wide, large; —
    sm. breadth, width.

anchoa, sf. anchovy.
anchura, sf. width, breadth.
andadero, ra, a. accessible, passable.
andado, sm. (col.) step-son; —, da, a.
    beaten, much frequented; threadbare.
andador, sm. stroller; leading string;
    alley or small walk in a garden; —, ra,
    a. fast-going.
andadura, sf. walk; pace; amble.
andana, sf. row, rank, line; tier of guns.
andanada, sf. (mar.) broadside.
andaniño, sm. go-cart in which children
    learn to walk
andar, v.n. to go, to walk; to fare; to
    act, to proceed, to behave; to elapse;
    to move (machines).
andaraje, sm. wheel of a well.
andarín, sm. fast walker.
andas, sf.pl. hand-barrow, bier.
andén, sm. shelf; pavement; (am.)
    side-walk; (rail.) platform; horse-
    path round the draw-well.
ándito, sm. gallery around a building.
andorrear, v.a. to stroll.
andorrera, sf. street-walker.
andrajo, sm. rag (of worn clothes).
andrajoso, sa, a. ragged.
andrógino, sm. hermaphrodite.
andrómina, sf. trick, fraud, artifice.
andullo, sm. roll of tobacco; (mar.)
    fender.
andurriales, sm. pl. by-ways.
aneaje, sm. alnage, ell-measure.
anear, v.a. to measure by the ell.
aneblar, v.a. to cloud, to darken.
anécdota, sf. anecdote.
anegadizo, za, a. easily inundated.
anegar, v.a. to inundate, to submerge.
anejo, ja, a. joined, connected, dependent.
anexar, v.a. to annex, to join.
anexidades, sf.pl. appertinent rights.
anexión, sf. annexation.
anéxo. See anejo.
anfibio, bia, a. amphibious; —, sm.
    amphibium.
anfibología, sf. words of double meaning.
anfion, sm. opium.
anfiteatro, sm. amphitheatre.
angarillas, sf.pl. hand-barrow; cruet-
ángaro, sm. signal-smoke.   [stand.
ángel, sm. angel.
angelical, a. angelical, heaven-born.
angelote, sm. large figure of an angel (on
    altars); fat, good-natured child.
angina, sf. quinsy.
angla, sf. cape.
anglicismo, sm. anglicism.
angostar, v.a. to narrow, to contract.
angosto, ta, a. narrow, close, strait. [sage.
angostura, sf. narrowness; narrow pas-
angra, sf. small bay.

anguarina, sf. loose coat hanging down to the knees.

anguila, sf. eel. [ner-stone.

angular, a. angular; piedra —, sf. corangulema, sf. tow; -s, pl. fulsome flatángulo, sm. angle, corner. [tery.

anguloso, sa, a. angled, cornered.

angustia, sf. anguish; heart-ache.

angustiar, v.a. to vex, to torment.

anhelar, v.n. to breathe with difficulty; —, v.a. to wish eagerly.

anhelo, sm. vehement desire, longing.

anheloso, sa, a. very desirous.

anidar, v.n. to nestle, to make a nest; to dwell, to inhabit.

anillo, sm. ring.

ánima, sf. soul; bore of a gun; -s, pl. bell-ringing at sunset; á las -s, at sunset.

animal, sm. & a. animal.

animalazo, sm. big animal. [cule.

animalejo, sm. small animal, animalanimalucho, sm.ugly, hideous animal.

animar, v.a. to animate, to enliven, to abet, to comfort, to revive.

ánimo, sm. soul; courage; mind, intention, meaning, will; thought; ¡—! come on!

animosidad, sf. valour, courage, boldness; animosity, dislike.

animoso, sa, a. courageous, spirited.

aniñarse, v.r. to act in a childish manner.

aniquilar, v.a. to annihilate, to destroy; -se, to decline, to decay; to humble; to consume.

anís, sm. (bot.) anise.

anisar, v.a. to tincture with anise.

anisete, sm. anisette. [versary.

aniversario, ria, a. annual; —, sm. anniano, sm. anus.

anoche, ad. last night.

anochecer, v.n. to grow dark.

anodinar, v.a. to treat with an anodyne.

anodino, na, a. (med.) anodyne.

anomalía, sf. anomaly.

anómalo, la, a. anomalous.

anonadar, v.a. to annihilate; to lessen; -se, to humble one's self.

anónimo, ma, a. anonymous.

anotación, sf. annotation, note.

anotar, v.a. to annotate, to note.

ánsar, sm. goose.

ansarería, sf. place where geese are reared.

ansarero, sm. goose-herd.

ansia, sf. anxiety, eagerness, hankering.

ansiar, v.a. to desire exceedingly.

ansioso, sa, a. anxious, eager.

anta, sf. tapir; (arch.) antes (pillar).

antagonista, sm. antagonist.

antaño, ad. last year.

antártico, ca, a. antarctic.

ante, sm. dressed buffalo skin; first course of dishes; —, pr. before; in the presence of.

anteado, da, a. buff-coloured.

anteanteanoche, ad. three nights ago.

anteanteayer, ad. three days ago.

antebrazo, sm. fore-arm.

antecama, sf. bed-carpet.

antecámara, sf. antechamber.

antecamarilla, sf. room leading to the king's antechamber.

antecedente, sm. & a. antecedent.

anteceder, v.a. to precede.

antecesor, ra, sm. & f. predecessor; forefather.

antecoger, v.a. to drive before one; to gather in fruit before the due time.

antecristo, sm. antichrist.

antedata, sf. antedate.

antedatar, v.a. to antedate.

antediluviano, na, a. antediluvian.

antelación, sf. priority.

antemano, ad. de —, beforehand.

antemeridiano, na, a. antemeridional.

antemural, sm. (mil.) outworks, fortresswall.

antemuralla, sf. antemuro, sm. (mil.) rampart, parapet.

antena, sf. feeler, antenna.

antenallas, sf.pl. pincers.

antenombre, sm. title prefixed to a proper name (as Don, San, &c.).

anteojo, sm. spy-glass; eye-glass; — de larga vista, telescope; — de puño, opera-glass; -s, pl. spectacles.

antepagar, v.a. to pay in advance.

antepasado, da, a. passed, elapsed; -s, sm.pl. ancestors.

antepecho, sm. (mil.) breastwork, parapet; footstep of a coach; harness.

antepenúltimo, ma, a. antepenultimate.

anteponer, v.a. to prefer.

antepuerta, sf. door-hangings.

antera, sf. (bot.) anther.

anterior, a. anterior, fore, former.

anterioridad, sf. anteriority, priority; preference.

antes, pr. before; —, ad. first, rather, better.

antesala, sf. antechamber; hacer —, to wait in an antechamber.

antestatura, sf. light, hasty entrenchment of palisadoes and sand-bags.

antevíspera, sf. day before; the eve of a feast.

anticipación, sf. anticipation.

anticipar, v.a. to anticipate; to forestall.

anticuado, da, a. antiquated.

anticuar, v.a. to make obsolete.

anticuario, sm. antiquary, antiquarian.

antídoto, sm. antidote.

antífona, sf. antiphony, anthem.

antigualla, sf. monument of antiquity; antique.

antiguamente, ad. anciently, of old.

antigüedad, sf. antiquity, oldness; the times of yore; the ancients.

antiguo, gua, a. antique, old, ancient; —, sm. senior.

antimonárquico, ca, a. antimonarchic.

antimonio, sm. antimony.

antinacional, a. antinational.

antipapa, sm. anti-pope.

antipara, sf. screen; gaiter.

antipatía, sf. antipathy.

antipático, ca, a. antipathetical.

antipodas, sm.pl. antipodes.

antítesis, sf. (gr.) antithesis.

antojadizo, za, a. capricious, fanciful.

antojarse, v.r. to long, to desire earnestly; to itch.   [horses).

antojera, sf. spectacle-case; blinker (of

antojo, sm. whim; longing, fancy.

antorcha, sf. torch, taper.

antro, sm. (poet.) cavern, den, grotto.

antropófago, sm. man-eater, cannibal.

antropología, sf. anthropology.

antruejar, v.a. to wet with water, or play some joke at a carnival.   [nival.

antruejo, sm. the three days of the car-

antuvión, sm. sudden stroke or attack.

anual, a. annual.

anualidad, sf. yearly recurrence.

anubarrado, da, a. clouded (of linens and silks).   [to become clouded.

anublar, v.a. to cloud, to obscure; -se, to

anudar, v.a. to knot, to join; -se, to waste away.

anuencia, sf. condescension, compliance.

anuente, a. condescending, courteous.

anulación, sf. abrogation.

anular, v.a. to annul; —, a. annular.

anulativo, va, a. making void.

anunciar, v.a. to announce.

anuncio, sm. advertisement.

anverso, sm. obverse (in coins).

anzuelo, sm. fish-hook; allurement;

aña, sf. hyæna.   [kind of fritters.

añadidura, sf. addition.

añadir, v.a. to add.

añafea, sf. brown paper.

añafil, sm. Moorish trumpet.

añagaza, sf. bird-call.

añal, a. & sm. yearling.

añalejo, sm. ecclesiastical almanac.

añascar, v.a. to collect lumber or odds and ends.

añejar, v.a. to make old; -se, to grow old; to become stale.

añejo, ja, a. old, stale, musty.

añicos, sm.pl. bits, small pieces; hacerse —, to overheat one's self.

añil, sm. indigo plant; indigo.

añinos, sm.pl. fleeces of yearling lambs.

año, sm. year; -s, pl. birth-day.

añojal, sm. fallow land.

añojo, sm. a yearling calf.

añudar, v.a. to make fast; to unite.

aojar, v.a. to charm, to bewitch, to fascinate.

aojo, sm. witchery, fascination.

aorta, sf. aorta (the great artery).

aovar, v.a. to lay eggs.

apabilar, v.a. to prepare the wick of a wax-candle; -se, to expire.

apacentadero, sm. pasture, grazing-ground.

apacentar, v.a. to tend grazing cattle.

apacible, a. affable, gentle, placid, quiet.

apaciguar, v.a. to appease, to pacify, to calm.

apacheta, sf. cairn, heap of stones.

apadrinar, v.a. to support, to favour, to patronise.

apagador, sm. extinguisher.

apagar, v.a. to quench, to extinguish; to damp; to destroy; to soften.

apalabrar, v.a. to appoint a meeting; to bespeak.

apalancar, v.a. to lift with a lever.

apalear, v.a. to cane, to drub, to shovel grain (to prevent its being spoilt).

apancora, sf. crab.   [water.

apantanar, v.a. to make a pool of stagnant

apantuflado, da, a. slipper-like.

apañado, da, a. cloth-like.

apañar, v.a. to grasp; to pilfer; to patch; -se, to get ready.

apaño, sm. (col.) patch.

apañuscar, v.a. to rumple; to crush.

apapagayado, da, a. parrot-like.

aparador, sm. buffet, sideboard; work-shop of an artisan; estar de —, to be dressed for receiving visitors.

aparar, v.a. to dig and heap the earth round plants; to prepare, to arrange.

aparato, sm. apparatus; preparation; ostentation, show, circumstance.

aparcería, sf. partnership in a farm.

aparcero, sm. partner; associate.

aparear, v.a. to match; to couple; -se, to be paired off by twos.

aparecer, v.n. to appear.

aparecido, sm. ghost.

aparejar, v.a. to prepare; to harness horses; to rig a ship.

aparejo, sm. preparation; harness, gear; sizing of a piece of linen on which something is to be painted; (mar.) tackle, rigging; -s, pl. tools, implements.   [to pretend.

aparentar, v.a. to make a false show;

aparente, a. apparent; convenient.

aparición, sf. apparition.

apariencia, sf. appearance, outside.

aparrado, da, a. crooked (applied to trees and plants). [a shop.

aparroquiar, v.a. to bring customers to

apartadero, sm. siding, road-side.

apartadijo, sm. small part.

apartadizo, za, a. shy, retiring. [ment.

apartado, sm. detached or private apart-

apartar, v.a. to separate, to divide, to dissuade ; to remove ; to sort ; **-se,** to withdraw ; to be divorced ; to desist. [the stage.

aparte, ad. apart, separately ; aside on

aparvar, v.a. to arrange the corn for being threshed.

apasionado, da, a. passionate ; suffering, devoted to ; fond.

apasionar, v.a. to excite a passion.

apatía, sf. apathy.

apático, ca, a. apathetic, indifferent.

apea, sf. tether. [accommodation.

apeadero, sm. horse-block ; house of

apeador, sm. land-surveyor.

apear, v.a. to dismount ; to measure lands ; to take a thing ; (col.) to dissuade.

apechugar, v.a. to push with the breast ; to undertake a thing with spirit and boldness.

apedreado, da, a. pitted with small-pox ; parti-coloured.

apedrear, v.a. to pelt with stones, to stone ; **—,** v.n. to hail.

apego, sm. attachment, fondness.

apelación, sf. appeal.

apelado, da, a. of the same colour.

apelambrar, v.a. to steep hides in pits of lime-water.

apelante, sm. appellant.

apelar, v.n. to appeal ; to have recourse to ; to be of the same colour.

apelativo, a. (gr.) nombre **—,** sm. generic name.

apelmazar, v.a. to compress.

apellar, v.a. to dress leather.

apellidar, v.a. to call by name ; to proclaim. [epithet.

apellido, sm. surname ; family-name ;

apenas, ad. scarcely, hardly.

apéndice, sm. appendix, supplement.

apeñuscar, v.a. to rumple, to crush.

apeo, sm. survey, mensuration of land ; props and stays for underpinning a building.

apeonar, v.a. to run swiftly.

aperador, sm. wheelwright.

aperar, v.a. to carry on the trade of a cartwright.

apercibimiento, apercibo, sm. readiness, provision.

apercibir, v.a. to prepare ; to provide ; to warn, to advise.

apercollar, v.a. to seize by the collar.

aperdigar, v.a. to broil.

aper.tivo, a. & s. appetiser, cock-tail.

apernar, v.a. to seize by the hough or

apero, sm. sheep-fold. [ham.

aperreado, da, a. harassed, dog-weary.

aperrear, v.a. to throw to the dogs to be torn to pieces ; to molest ; **-se,** to worry one's self to death. [cleft.

apertura, sf. aperture, opening, chink,

apesadumbrar, v.a. to cause trouble and affliction.

apesgar, v.a. to overload, to press down.

apestar, v.a. to infect with the pestilence ; to produce an offensive smell.

apetecer, v.a. to long, to hanker.

apetecible, a. desirable.

apetitivo, va, a. appetising. [desire.

apetito, sm. appetite ; that which excites

apetitoso, sa, a. pleasing to the taste, appetising. [horses.

apezuñar, v.n. to tread heavily (of

apicarado, da, a. roguish, knavish.

apiadarse, v.r. to feel pity.

apice, sm. summit, point ; smallest part of a thing.

apilar, v.a. to pile up.

apimpollarse, v.r. to shoot, to germinate.

apiñado, da, a. pyramidal ; pine-shaped.

apiñar, v.a. to press things close together ; **-se,** to clog, to crowd.

apio, sm. (bot.) celery. [kill.

apiolar, v.a. to gyve a hawk ; (col.) to

apisonar, v.a. to ram down earth.

apitonar, v.n. to put forth shoots ; to bud ; **—,** v.a. to pick (as hens do their eggs) ; **-se** (col.), to rail at each other.

aplacable, a. appeasable.

aplacar, v.a. to appease, to pacify.

aplanadera, sf. roller for levelling the ground.

aplanar, v.a. to level, to flatten ; to astonish ; **-se,** to fall to the ground.

aplanchado, da, a. ironed, smoothed ; **—,** sm. parcel of linen to be ironed ; ironing linen.

aplanchadora, sf. ironer.

aplanchar, v.a. to iron linen.

aplantillar, v.a. to adjust or fit a stone, a piece of timber or a board, according to model. [confound

aplastar, v.a. to flatten, to crush ; to

aplaudir, v.a. to applaud ; to extol.

aplauso, sm. applause, approbation, praise. [to postpone.

aplazar, v.a. to cite for a given date ;

aplicable, a. applicable.

aplicación, sf. application, attention.

aplicado, da, a. studious, industrious.

aplicar, v.a. to apply ; to clasp ; to attribute ; -se, to devote one's self to anything ; to earn a living.

aplomado, da, a. lead-coloured ; leaden ; heavy, dull.

aplomar, v.n. to plumb ; -se, to tumble, to fall to the ground.

aplomo, sm. self-possession.

apocado, da, a. pusillanimous.

Apocalipsis, sm. Apocalypse. [contract.

apocar, v.a. to lessen, to diminish ; to

apócrifo, fa, a. apocryphal ; fabulous.

apodar, v.a. to give nick-names.

apoderado, da, a. representing a person ; —, sm. proxy, attorney. [thing.

apoderarse, v.r. to take possession of a

apodíctico, ca, a. apodeictic.

apodo, sm. nick-name, sobriquet.

apolillar, v.a. to gnaw or eat clothes ; -se, to be moth-eaten.

apología, sf. apology.

apoltronarse, v.r. to grow lazy, to loiter.

apomazar, v.a. to glaze printed linens with pumice-stone.

apoplejía, sf. apoplexy.

apoplético, ca, a. apoplectic.

aporcar, v.a. to cover plants with earth.

aporrar, v.n. to stand mute, to remain silent ; -se, to become importunate.

aporrear, v.a. to cudgel, to knock ; -se, to have a fight ; to drudge.

aportadera, sf. provision-chest for portage by mules.

aportadero, sm. landing-place.

aportar, v.n. to arrive at a port.

aportillar, v.n. to make a breach in a wall ; to break down, to break open.

aposentar, v.a. to harbour ; to house.

aposento, sm. room, apartment ; inn ; a temporary habitation ; opera-box.

aposesionar, v.a. to put in possession, to endow ; -se, to take possession.

aposición, sf. (gr.) apposition. [cation.

apósito, sm. external medicinal aplposta, ad. on purpose.

apostadero, sm. stand, station ; (mar.) station ; dock-yard.

apostar, v.a. to bet, to lay a wager ; to post soldiers.

apostasía, sf. apostasy.

apóstata, sm. apostate.

apostatar, v.n. to apostatize.

apostema, sf. abscess, tumour.

apostilla, sf. marginal note ; postscript.

apóstol, sm. apostle.

apostolado, sm. apostleship.

apostólico, ca, a. apostolical.

apostrofar, v.a. to apostrophise.

apóstrofe, sf. apostrophe.

apóstrofo, sm. (gr.) apostrophe.

apoteosis, sf. apotheosis.

apoyar, v.a. to prop, to support, to favour, to patronise ; —, v.n. to rest on ; to lie ; -se, to lean upon.

apoyo, sm. prop, stay, support ; protection. [spectable.

apreciable, a. appreciable, valuable, reapreciar, v.a. to appreciate, to estimate, to value.

aprecio, sm. appreciation ; esteem.

aprehender, v.a. to apprehend, to seize ; to conceive. [perception.

aprehensión, sf. apprehension, seizure :

aprehensivo, va, a. apprehensive, quick to understand ; fearful.

apremiar, v.a. to press ; to compel.

apremio, sm. pressure, constriction ; judicial compulsion.

aprender, v.a. to learn ; — de memoria, to learn by heart.

aprendiz, sm apprentice.

aprendizaje, sm. apprenticeship.

aprensar, v.a. to press, to calender.

apresar, v.a. to seize, to grasp ; to capture an enemy's ship.

aprestar, v.a. to prepare, to make ready.

apresto, sm. preparation.

apresurar, v.a. to accelerate, to hasten, to expedite.

apretadillo, lla, a. somewhat constrained, rather hard put to it.

apretado, da, a. mean, miserable, closehanded, hard, difficult.

apretadura, sf. compression.

apretar, v.a. to compress, to tighten ; to constrain ; to distress ; to urge earnapretón, sm. pressure. [estly

apretura, sf. pressure of crowd.

apriesa, ad. in a hurry.

aprieto, sm. crowd ; conflict ; exigence.

aprisa, ad. swiftly, promptly.

aprisco, sm. sheep-fold, sheep-cot.

aprisionar, v.a. to imprison.

aproar, v.n. (mar.) to turn a ship's head to any part.

aprobación, sf. approbation.

aprobar, v.a. to approve.

aproches, sm.pl. (mil.) approaches.

aprontar, v.a. to prepare, to get ready.

apropiación, sf. appropriation, assumpapropiar, v.a. to appropriate. [tion.

aprovechable, a. profitable. [gress.

aprovechamiento, sm. profit, utility ; proaprovechar, v.n. to profit, to make progress ; —, v.a. to use profitably.

aproximar, v.a. to approach.

aptitud, sf. aptitude, fitness, ability.

apto, ta, a. apt, fit, able ; clever.

apuesta, sf. bet, wager.

apulgarar, v.a. to press with the thumb.

apuntación, sf. annotation ; musical note ; aim.

puntado, da, a. pointed. [marker.
puntador, sm. prompter; billiard-
puntalar, v.a. to prop ; (mar.) to shore
a vessel.
puntar, v.a. to aim ; to level, to point
out ; to mark, to fix ; to prompt
(theatre) ; —, n. to begin to appear ;
-se, to begin to turn, to be pricked
(of wine). [ing.
punte, sm. annotation ; stage-prompt-
puñetear, v.a. to strike with the fist.
purado, da, a. poor, destitute of means ;
difficult.
purar, v.a. to purify, to clear up, to
verify ; to exhaust ; to tease and
perplex ; to press hard, to constrain.
puro, sm. want, indigence ; pain, affliction ; difficulty, dilemma.
quejar, v.a. to fatigue, to afflict.
quel, -la, -lo, pn. that ; he, she ; -los,
-las, pl. those.
querenciarse, v.r. to become fond of a
place (applied to cattle).
quese, sa, so, pn. (obs.) that.
queste, ta, to, pn. (obs.) this, that.
quí, ad. here, in this place.
quiescencia, sf. consent. [lull.
quietar, v.a. to quiet, to appease, to
quilatar, v.a. to assay gold and silver.
quilea, sf. (bot.) milfoil.
quilino, na, a. aquiline.
quilón, sm. north wind.
ra, sf. altar.
rabesco, sm. arabesque.
rado, sm. plough.
rador, sm. plough-man. [tariff.
rancel, sm. fixed price of provisions ;
rándano, sm. bilberry, cranberry.
randela, sf. pan of the socket of a
candlestick ; ruffles of shirts.
ranzada, sf. a measure of land. [lustre.
raña, sf. spider ; sea-spider ; chandelier,
rañar, v.a. to scratch ; to scrape ; to
corrode.
raño, sm. scratch, slight wound.
rar, v.a. to plough.
rabellón, sm. gutter.
rbitrar, v.a. to arbitrate.
rbitrariedad, sf. arbitrariness. [trary.
rbitrario, ria, arbitrativo, va, a. arbi-
rbitrio, sm. free-will ; means, expedient,
way ; arbitration, arbitrament ; compromise. [triver.
rbitrista, sm. schemer, projector, con-
rbitro, sm. arbiter, arbitrator.
rbol, sm. tree ; (mar.) mast.
rbolado, da, a. forested ; wooded ; —,
sm. wood-land.
rboladura, sf. masting, masts.
rbolar, v.a. to hoist, to set upright.
rboleda, sf. copse.

arbolete, sm. branch of a tree for fasten-
ing lime-twigs.
arbolista, sm. arborist.
arbollón, sm. gutter.
arbóreo, rea, a. arboreous.
arbusto, sm. shrub.
arca, sf. chest, wooden box ; sepulchral
urn ; — del Testamento, — féderis,
ark of the Covenant.
arcabucería, sf. number of cross-bows ;
manufactory of arquebuses.
arcabucero, sm. arquebusier, gunsmith.
arcabuz, sm. arquebuse.
arcada, sf. rising of the stomach before
vomiting ; arcade.
arcaduz, sm. conduit or pipe for conveying water ; draw-well bucket.
arcáico, ca, a. archaic.
arcaísmo, sm. archaism.
arcángel, sm. archangel.
arcano, sm. secret, mystery.
arce, sm. maple-tree.
arcilla, sf. argil, clay.
arcilloso, sa, a. clayey, argillaceous.
arcipreste, sm. archpriest.
arco, sm. arc, arch ; fiddle-bow ; hoop ;
— del cielo, — iris, rainbow.
archiducado, sm. archdukedom.
archiducal, a. archducal.
archiduque, sm. archduke.
archiduquesa, sf. archduchess.
archipiélago, sm. archipelago.
archivar, v.a. to deposit among archives.
archivero, archivista, sm. keeper of the
archivo, sm. archives. [records.
arder, v.n. to burn, to blaze.
ardid, sm. stratagem, artifice, cunning.
ardido, da, a. heated (of grain, tobacco,
&c.) ; in a state of fermentation.
ardiente, a. ardent, flagrant, burning,
passionate ; active, fervid, fiery.
ardilla, sf. squirrel.
ardor, sm. great heat ; valour, vivacity.
fieriness, fervour.
ardoroso, sa, a. fiery, restless.
arduo, dua, a. arduous, difficult.
área, sf. area ; measure of 100 sq. metres.
arena, sf. sand ; grit ; arena.
arenal, sm. sandy ground.
arenga, sf. harangue, speech.
arengar, v.n. to harangue.
arenisco, ca, arenoso, sa, a. sandy ; arenaceous. [herring.
arenque, sm. herring ; — ahumado, red-
areómetro, sm. aerometer.
argadijo, argadillo, sm. reel, bobbin ;
restless person.
argado, sm. prank, trick, artifice.
argamandijo, sm. small implements.
argamasa, sf. mortar, cement for build-
argamasar, v.a. to make mortar. [ing.

árgana, sf. crane (machine); -s, pl. horse-baskets, paniers.

argentado, da, a. silver-like.

argentar, v.a. to silverplate; to colour with silver.

argentería, sf. gold or silver embroidery.

argentino, na, a. silvery.

argolla, sf. large iron ring; pillory.

argucia, sf. subtlety.

argüe, sm. windlass.   [pose.

argüir, v.n. to argue, to dispute, to op-

argumentación, sf. argumentation.

argumentar, v.n. to argue, to dispute; to conclude.

argumento, sm. argument.

aria, sf. (mus.) aria, tune, air.   [rain.

aridez, sf. dryness, drought, want of

árido, da, a. dry; barren.   [zodiac].

Aries, sm. Aries, the Ram (sign of the

ariete, sm. battering-ram.   [soil].

arijo, ja, a. light, easily tilled (applied to

arillo, sm. a small hoop; ear-ring.

arimez, sf. projecting part of a building.

arisco, ca, a. fierce, rude, untractable.

aristarco, sm. severe critic.

aristocracia, sf. aristocracy.

aristócrata, sm. aristocrat.

aristocrático, ca, a. aristocratical.

aritmética, sf. arithmetic.

aritmético, ca, a. arithmetical.

arlequín, sm. harlequin, buffoon.

arma, sf. weapon, arms; — falsa, false alarm.

armada, sf. navy, war-fleet, armada.

armadía, sf. raft.

armador, sm. ship-owner; privateer, cruiser; jacket, jerkin.

armadura, sf. armour; frame-work.

armamento, sm. warlike preparation, armament.

armar, v.a. to furnish with arms; to man; to arm; to fit up, to contrive, to set on foot; — la, (col.) to cheat at cards.

armario, sm. clothes-press; cupboard.

armatoste, sm. hulk; lumber; frame.

armazón, sf. wooden frame; hulk of a ship; fishing-tackle.

armelina, sf. ermine-skin.

armería, sf. armoury; heraldry; art of armour-making.

armero, sm. armourer; keeper of arms.

armilla, sf. bracelet.

armiño, sm. ermine.

armipotente, a. (poet.) mighty in war.

armisticio, sm. armistice.

armonía, sf. harmony.

armónico, ca, a. harmonical.

armonioso, sa, a. harmonious.

arna, sf. bee-hive.

arnés, sm. harness; gear, trapping.

arnilla, sf. small bee-hive.

aro, sm. hoop of wood; iron staple.

aroca, sf. Portuguese linen.

aroma, sm. & f. aroma; fragrance.

aromaticidad, sf. aromatic quality.

aromático, ca, a. aromatic.

aromatizar, v.a. to perfume.

arpa, sf. harp.

arpado, da, a. serrated, toothed.

arpar, v.a. to tear to pieces, to rend.

arpegio, sm. (mus.) arpeggio.

arpeo, sm. grappling-iron.

arpía, sf. (poet.) harpy.

arpillera, sf. sack-cloth.

arpista, sm. harper.

arpón, sm. harpoon.

arponado, da, a. like a harpoon.

arponar, v.a. to harpoon.

arponero, sm. harpooner.

arqueada, sf. (mus.) stroke or movement of the violin-bow.

arqueado, da, a. arched, vaulted.

arquear, v.a. to arch; to gauge the dimensions of ships.   [ship

arqueo, sm. arcuation; gauging of a

arqueología, sf. archæology.

arquería, sf. arcade.

arquero, sm. hoop-maker; cashier.

arqueta, sf. small trunk.

arquitecto, sm. architect.

arquitectónico, ca, a. architectonic.

arquitectura, sf. architecture.

arquitrabe, sm. architrave.

arrabalero, ra, a. suburban; —, sm. & f. common person, churl.

arrabio, sm. cast-iron.

arracada, sf. ear-ring.

arracimarse, v.r. to cluster.

arráez, sm. Arab or Moorish captain.

arraigar, v.n. to take root; (leg.) to give security.

arraigo, sm. landed property.

arramblar, v.a. to cover with sand (of torrents); to sweep away.

arrancadera, sf. bell of the bell-wether.

arrancar, v.a. to pull up by the roots; to force out; to wrest; to draw out (a tooth).

arrancasiega, sf. mowing of stunted corn; altercation, dispute.

arranque, sm. extirpation; fit of passion; sudden impulse.

arrapiezo, arrapo, sm. tatter, rag.

arras, sf.pl. dowry; earnest-money.

arrasar, v.a. to demolish, to destroy; —, v.n. to clear up (weather).

arrastrado, da, a. miserable, afflicted; (fig.) rascally.

arrastrar, v.a. & n. to creep, to crawl; to drag along the ground; to lead at cards.

arrastre, sm. dragging, haulage ; knocking-mill.

arrayán, sm. myrtle.

¡ arre ! gee !, geho !, go on !

arrear, v.a. to urge on horses, mules, &c.

arrebañar, v.a. to scrape together, to pick up.

arrebatado, da, a. rapid, violent, impetuous ; rash, inconsiderate.

rebatar, v.a. to carry off, to snatch with hurry ; to enrapture.

arrebaniia, sf. carrying off a thing precipitately out of a crowd.

arrebato, arrebatamiento, sm. seizure ; fury, ecstasy, passion. [rouge.

arrebol, sm. red appearance of the sky ;

arrebolar, v.a. to paint red ; to rouge.

arrebozarse, v.r. to swarm (of bees, &c.).

arrebujar, v.a. to crumple ; to wrap up.

arrecafe, sm. (bot.) cardoon ; sharewort.

arrecife, sm. causeway ; reef.

arrecirse, v.r. to grow stiff with cold.

arredrar, v.a. to remove to a greater distance ; to terrify.

arredro, ad. backwards.

arregazado, da, a. turned up ; cocked.

arregazar, v.a. to truss, to tuck up the skirts of clothes.

arreglado, a. regular, moderate.

arreglar, v.a. to regulate ; to adjust.

arreglo, sm. rule, order ; **con — á,** according to.

arregostarse, v.r. to relish.

arrejacar, v.a. to hoe.

arrejaco, sm. fish-spear ; (orn.) swift martlet. [dent.

arrejaque, sm. three-pronged fork, tri-

arrellanarse, v.r. to sit at ease ; to make one's self comfortable.

arremangar, v.a. to tuck up one's sleeves or petticoats.

arremango, sm. tucking up of clothes.

arremeter, v.a. to assail, to attack ; to seize suddenly.

arremetida, sf. attack, assault.

arremolinarse, v.r. to eddy.

arrendadero, sm. stable-ring.

arrendado, da, a. manageable, tractable (of horses).

arrendador, sm. lessor, hirer ; landlord.

arrendajo, sm. mocking-bird ; mimic, buffoon.

arrendamiento, sm. lease ; letting.

arrendar, v.a. to rent, to let out, to lease ; to tie a horse by the reins ; to imitate. [farmer.

arrendatario, ria, sm. & f. tenant ; lessee ;

arreo, sm. dress, ornament ; **-s,** pl. dependencies ; **—,** ad. successively, uninterruptedly.

arrepápalo, sm. sort of fritter or bun.

arrepentido, da, a. repentant. [tence.

arrepentimiento, sm. repentance, peni-

arrepentirse, v.r. to repent.

arrepistar, v.a. to grind or pound rags into a fine pulp (in paper-mills).

arrequives, sm.pl. ornaments ; circumstances of a case ; requisites.

arrestado, da, a. intrepid, bold.

arrestar, v.a. to arrest, to imprison ; **-se,** to undertake a bold enterprise.

arresto, sm. boldness in undertaking an enterprise ; prison, arrest.

arrezafe, sm. place full of thistles, brush-wood, and brambles.

arriada, sf. flood, overflowing.

arriano, na, a. Arian.

arriar, v.a. (mar.) to lower, to strike.

arriata, sf., arriate, sm. hot-bed, shelving-bed ; causeway.

arriba, ad. above, over, up, high, on high, overhead ; aloft.

arribada, sf. arrival of a vessel in port.

arribar, v.n. (mar.) to put into a harbour ; to fall off to leeward ; to arrive.

arribo, sm. arrival.

arriendo, sm. lease, farm rent.

arriería, sf. mule-driver's trade.

arriero, sm. muleteer.

arriesgado, da, a. dangerous ; daring.

arriesgar, v.a. to risk, to hazard, to expose to danger.

arrimadero, sm. scaffold ; stick or support to lean upon.

arrimadillo, sm. wainscot, pannelling.

arrimadizo, a. sustaining, sustainable ; **—,** sm. parasite, sponger.

arrimador, sm. back-log in a fire-place.

arrimar, v.a. to approach, to put near ; to lay aside ; **-se,** to lean on, to rest against ; to displace.

arrinconar, v.a. to put a thing in corner ; to lay aside ; to drive from office ; **-se,** to retire, to withdraw.

arriscado, da, a. forward, bold, audacious, impudent ; brisk.

arriscador, sm. olive gleaner.

arrizar, v.a. (mar.) to reef ; to tie or lash.

arroba, sf. weight of twenty-five pounds ; measure (thirty-two pints) ; **por -s,** by wholesale.

arrobadizo, za, a. feigning ecstasy.

arrobamiento, sm. rapture ; amazement, rapturous admiration.

arrobarse, v.r. to be intensely amazed, to be in ecstasy.

arrocero, sm. rice-grower ; rice-merchant.

arrocinado, da, a. stupid, asinine ; ass-like (applied to horses). [stupid.

arrocinarse, v.r. to become dull and

arrodillar, v.a. to make to kneel ; **—,** n. to bend the knee ; **-se,** to kneel.

arrodrigar, arrodrigonar, v.a.to prop vines.
arrogación, sf. arrogation ; adoption.
arrogancia, sf. arrogance, haughtiness ; high spirit.
arrogante, a. haughty, proud, assuming ; valiant, spirited, gallant ; **caballo —,** mettlesome, spirited horse.
arrogar, v.a. to arrogate ; to appropriate to one's self.
arrojadizo, za, a. easily cast or thrown.
arrojado, da, a. rash, inconsiderate ; bold, fearless.
arrojar, v.a. to dart, to fling, to jet ; to dash ; to shed (a fragrance) ; to emit (light) ; to shoot, to sprout.   [ness.
arrojo, sm. boldness, intrepidity, fearless-
arrollar, v.a. to roll up, to revolve, to enwrap ; to sweep away ; to confound (an opponent).
arromadizarse, v.r. to catch cold.
arromar, v.a. to blunt.
arrompido, sm. broken ground.
arropar, v.a. to clothe, to dress.
arrope, sm. must (new wine boiled until it is as dense as a syrup).
arropea, sf. irons, fetters, pl.
arrostrar, v.a. to perform in a cheerful manner ; to encounter dangers.
arroyada, sf. gorge, torrent.
arroyar, v.a. to overflow sown ground.
arroyo, sm. rivulet.
arroz, sm. rice.
arrozal, sm. rice-field.
arruar, v.n. to grunt like a wild boar.
arrufar, v.a. to curve.
arrufianado, da, a. impudent ; ruffianly.
arruga, sf. wrinkle ; rumple.
arrugar, v.a. to wrinkle ; to rumple, to fold ; **-se,** to shrivel ; to die.
arruinar, v.a. to demolish ; to ruin.
arrullador, ra, a. flattering, cajoling.
arrullar, v.a. to lull to rest ; to court, to bill and coo.
arrullo, sm. cooing of pigeons ; lullaby.
arrumaco, sm. caress ; curl of the lips.
arrumaje, sm. cargo-stowage.
arrumar, v.a. to stow cargo.   [horizon.
arrumazón, sm. (mar.) stowing ; cloudy
arrumbar, v.a. to set aside as useless lumber ; to refute or silence in conversation ; to decant wine ; **-se,** (mar.) to steer the proper course.   [cards.
arrunflarse, v.r. to have a " flush " at
arsenal, sm. arsenal ; dock-yard.
arsénico, sm. arsenic.
arte, sm. & f. art ; skill ; artfulness ; rudiments of grammar.
artefacto, sm. manufacture.
artejo, sm. finger-point.
arteria, sf. artery.   [ful.
artero, ra, a. dexterous, cunning, art-

artesa, sf. kneading-trough ; wooden bowl.
artesano, sm. artisan, workman.
artético, ca, a. arthritical, gouty.
ártico, ca, a. arctic, northern.
articulación, sf. articulation, clear and distinct pronunciation.
articular, v.a. to articulate, to pronounce distinctly.   [article ; condition.
artículo, sm. article ; clause ; point ; (gr.)
artífice, sm. artisan ; artist.
artificial, a. artificial.
artificio, sm. workmanship, craft ; artifice, cunning, trick.
artificioso, sa, a. skilful, ingenious ; art ful, cunning.
artillar, v.a. to mount cannon.
artillería, sf. gunnery ; artillery.
artillero, sm. artillery-man.
artimaña, sf. trick.
artista, sm. artist ; craftsman.
arúspice, sm. augurer, soothsayer.
arveja, sf. (bot.) vetch.
arvejo, sm. (bot.) bastard chick-pea.
arzobispado, sm. archbishopric.
arzobispal, a. archiepiscopal.
arzobispo, sm. archbishop.
arzón, sm. bow of a saddle.
as, sm. ace ; Roman copper coin.
asa, sf. handle, haft, hold.
asado, sm. roast-meat.
asador, sm. turn-spit.   [cattle.
asadura, sf. chitterlings ; toll paid for
asaetinado, da, a. silky, satiny.
asalariar, v.a. to give a fixed salary.
asaltar, v.a. to storm a position ; to assail, to fall upon.
asalto, sm. assault, storm against a place.
asamblea, sf. assembly, meeting.
asar, v.a. to roast.
asargado, da, a. serge-like.
asativo, va, a. boiled in its own juice.
asbestino, na, a. asbestine.
asbesto, sm. asbestos.
ascalonia, sf. (bot.) shallot.
ascendencia, sf. ascending line ; line of descent.   [s. up-train.
ascendente, a. ascending ; (rail.) **tren —,**
ascender, v.n. to ascend ; to be promoted to a higher dignity.
ascendiente, sm. forefather ; influence
Ascensión, sf. feast of Ascension.
ascenso, sm. promotion to a higher dig-
ascensor, sm. lift.   [nity or station.
asceta, sm. ascetic.
ascético, ca, a. ascetic.
asco, sm. nausea, loathing.
ascua, sf. red hot coal.
¡ ascuas ! how it hurts ! good heavens !
aseado, da, a. clean, elegant, neat.
asear, v.a. to set off, to adorn.

asedado, da, a. silky.
asediar, v.a. to besiege.
asedio, sm. siege.
aseglararse, v.r. to secularize one's self.
asegundar, v.a. to repeat.
aseguración, sf. insurance.
asegurador, sm. insurer.
asegurar, v.a. to secure; to insure; to affirm; to bail. [alike.
asemejar, v.a. to assimilate, to make
asenderear, v.a. to persecute; to force one's way.
asenso, sm. assent, consent.
asentaderas, sf.pl. buttocks.
asentadillas, ad. (á —) sitting on horseback like a woman.
asentar, v.a. to place on a chair or other seat; to suppose; to affirm, to assure; to adjust; to note; —, v.n. to sit down; to settle; to sit (of clothes); -se, to settle (of liquids).
asentir, v.n. to acquiesce, to concede.
asentista, sm. purveyor, contractor.
aseo, sm. cleanliness, neatness.
asequible, a. attainable, obtainable.
aserción, sf. assertion, affirmation.
aserradero, sm. saw-mill.
aserraduras, sf.pl. saw-dust.
aserrar, v.a. to saw; to scrape (upon a fiddle).
asertivo, va, a. affirmative.
asesar, v.n. to become prudent.
asesinar, v.a. to assassinate.
asesinato, sm. assassination.
asesino, sm. assassin; impostor, cheat.
asesor, sm. assessor.
asesorarse, v.r. to employ counsel.
asestar, v.a. to aim, to point.
aseverar, v.a. to asseverate, to affirm
asfalto, sm. asphaltum. [solemnly.
así, ad. so, thus, in this manner; therefore, so that; also; — bien, as well; — que, so that, therefore; así, así, so, so; middling; — que —, whether this or that way; como —, even so, just so. [pretext.
asidero, sm. handle, hold; occasion,
asido, da, a. fastened, tied, attached.
asiduo, dua, a. assiduous.
asiento, sm. chair, bench, stool; seat; contract; entry; residence.
asignación, sf. assignation; destination.
asignar, v.a. to assign; to attribute.
asignatura, sf. catalogue of university lectures for one year. [clavicle.
asilla, sf. small handle; slight pretext.
asilo, sm. asylum, refuge.
asimilar, v.a. to assimilate; —, v.n. to resemble. [manner.
asimismo, ad. similarly, in the same
asimplado, da, a. silly-looking.

asir, v.a. & n. to grasp, to seize; to hold, to grip, to take root.
asistencia, sf. actual presence; assistance; help; — de Sevilla, magistracy of Seville. [at court.
asistenta, sf. hand-maid; servant-maid
asistente, sm. assistant, helper; chief officer of justice at Seville; officer's servant, orderly.
asistir, v.n. to be present, to assist; —, v.a. to help, to minister, to further; to attend a sick person.
asma, sf. asthma.
asmático, ca, a. asthmatic.
asna, sf. she-ass, jenny-ass.
asnada, sf. foolish action.
asnal, a. asinine.
asnallo, sm. worm-seed.
asnazo, sm. a large jack-ass. [der.
asnería, sf. stud of asses; egregious blun-
asnico, ca, sm. & f. little ass; andiron.
asnillo, lla, sm. & f. little ass; grasshopper; field-cricket.
asno, sm. ass; stupid fellow.
asobarcar, v.a. to pick up and put under one's arm.
asocarronado, a. waggish; crafty.
asociación, sf. association; co-partner-
asociado, sm. associate. [ship.
asociar, v.a. to associate.
asolanar, v.a. to parch, to dry up (of easterly winds).
asolar, v.a. to destroy, to devastate; -se, to settle, to clear (of liquids).
asolear, v.a. to expose to the sun; -se, to be sunburnt. [canals).
asolvarse, v.r. to be stopped (of pipes,
asomada, sf. sudden appearance, apparition.
asomar, v.n. to begin to appear; to peep; -se, (col.) to be flustered with wine. [easily frightened.
asombradizo, za, a. fearful, timid,
asombrar, v.a. to frighten, to amaze; to astonish; (poet.) to obscure, to overshadow. [ment.
asombro, sm. dread, terror; astonish-
asombroso, sa, a. astonishing, marvellous.
asomo, sm. mark, token, indication; conjecture.
asonancia, sf. assonance; harmony.
asordar, v.a. to deafen.
asortir, v.a. to assort.
asotanar, v.a. to build arched cellars.
aspa, sf. reel, bobbin.
aspar, v.a. to reel; to crucify; to vex, to mortify; -se á gritos, to cry out loudly, to yell. [mation.
aspaviento, sm. astonishment; excla-
aspecto, sm. appearance, aspect.
aspereza, sf. asperity, acerbity.

asperges, sm. sprinkling with holy-water ; **quedarse —,** (col.) to be disappointed.

asperillo, sm. bitterness of unripe fruit.

áspero, ra, a. rough, rugged ; craggy, hirsute, knotty ; horrid ; harsh, hard ; crabbed ; severe, austere, gruff.

asperón, sm. grindstone.

aspersión, sf. aspersion, sprinkling.

aspersorio, sm. water-sprinkler.

áspid, sm. asp ; adder.

aspiración, sf. aspiration.

aspirante, sm. aspirant, aspirer.

aspirar, v.a. to inspire the air ; to aspire ; (gr.) to aspirate.

asqueroso, sa, a. loathsome, squeamish.

asta, sf. lance ; horn ; handle of a pencil, [brush.

ástaco, sm. cray-fish.

asterisco, sm. asterisk.

asterismo, sm. constellation.

astil, sm. handle, shaft. [ber.

astilla, sf. chip of wood, splinter of tim-

astillar, v.a. to chip.

astillazo, sm. crack, blow from a splinter ; damage which results from an enterprise to those who have not been its principal authors.

astillero, sm. holdfast for soldiers' arms ; dockyard, shipwright's yard.

astral, a. astral.

astricción, sf. astriction.

astrictivo, va, a. astrictive, styptic.

astricto, ta, a. contracted, compressed.

astringente, a. astringent.

astringir, a. to astringe, to contract.

astro, sm. star.

astrología, sf. astrology.

astrológico, ca, a. astrological.

astrólogo, sm. astrologer.

astronomía, sf. astronomy.

astronómico, ca, a. astronomical.

astrónomo, sm. astronomer.

astroso, sa, a. unlucky ; sordid.

astucia, sf. cunning, slyness.

asturión, sm. pony.

astuto, ta, a. cunning, sly, astute.

asueto, sm. holidays ; vacation.

Asunción, sf. Assumption.

asunto, sm. subject, matter treated upon ; affair, business.

asurarse, v.r. to be burnt in cooking (applied to meat).

asurcar, v.a. to furrow sown land for the purpose of rooting out the weeds.

asustar, v.a. to frighten ; **-se,** to be frightened.

atabacado, da, a. tobacco-coloured.

atabal, sm. kettle-drum. [kettle-drums.

atabalear, v.n. to make a noise like

atabalero, sm. kettle-drummer.

atabe, sm. small vent left in water-pipes.

atabernado, da, a. retailed in taverns.

atabladera, sf. roller for corn-land.

atablar, v.a. to roll land sown with corn.

atacado, da, a. irresolute ; narrow-minded. [poniard.

atacador, sm. aggressor ; ramrod ; (col.)

atacar, v.a. to fit clothes tight to the body ; to force the charge into fire-arms with a ramrod ; to attack, to onset.

atado, sm. bundle, parcel ; **—, da,** a. pusillanimous, easily embarrassed ; attached.

atador, sm. sheaves-binder.

atafagar, v.a. to stupefy ; to take away one's breath ; to tease.

atafetanado, da, a. resembling tiffany.

ataharre, sm. broad crupper of a pack-

ataborma, sf. (orn.) osprey. [saddle.

ataire, sm. moulding in the panels and frames of doors and windows.

atajadizo, sm. partition-wall.

atajar, v.a. to cut off ; to intercept, to stop, to obstruct ; **-se,** to be confounded with dread.

atajasolaces, sm. kill-joy.

atajea, atajía, sf. sewer.

atajo, sm. cross-path, by-path, short cut.

atalaya, sf. watch-tower ; **—,** sm. guard in a watch-tower.

atalayar, v.a. to overlook the country and sea-coast from a watch-tower ; to spy into the action of others.

atanquía, sf. depilatory ; refuse of silk.

ataque, sm. attack ; trenches ; fit of the palsy, &c. ; verbal dispute.

ataquizar, v.a. to lay vine-shoots.

atar, v.a. to tie, to bind, to fasten ; to stop ; **-se,** to be embarrassed or perplexed,

ataracea, sf. marquetry, checker-work.

ataracear, v.a. to checker, to inlay.

atarantado, da, a. bitten by a tarantula ; surprised, amazed. [walks.

atarazana, sf. arsenal ; shed in rope-

atarazar, v.a. to bite.

atarear, v.a. to impose a task ; **-se,** to overdo one's self.

atarjea, sf. protecting vault over the pipes of an aqueduct ; small drain.

atarquinar, v.a. to bemire.

atarugar, v.a. to wedge ; to silence ; **-se,** to be perplexed.

atasajar, v.a. to cut meat into small pieces and dry it in the sun.

atascar, v.a. to stop a leak ; to throw an obstacle in the way ; **-se,** to be-

ataúd, sm. coffin. [come bogged.

ataujía, sf. damaskeen.

ataujiado, da, a. damaskeened. [adorn.

ataviar, v.a. to dress out, to trim, to

atavío, sm. dress, ornament, finery.

atediar, v.a. to disgust ; -se, to be tired.

ateísmo, sm. atheism.

ateísta, sm. atheist. [to daunt.

atemorizar, v.a. to strike with terror,

atemperación, sf. moderation.

atemperar, v.a. to temper, to soften, to assuage ; to accommodate.

atenaz(e)ar, v.a. to tear off the flesh with pincers.

atención, sf. attention, heedfulness ; civility, complaisance ; observance, consideration ; en —, attending ; in consideration of ; as regards.

atender, v.n. to be attentive ; —, v.a. to heed, to hearken ; to look at.

atentado, da, a. discreet, prudent, moderate ; noiseless ; —, sm. attempt, transgression, offence.

atentar, v.a. to attempt (crime) ; to go about a thing deliberately.

atento, ta, a. attentive ; heedful ; observing ; mindful ; polite, courteous, mannerly ; compliant ; notable ; —, pr. in consideration. [tion.

atenuación, sf. attenuation ; maceraatenuar, v.a. to diminish, to macerate, to mince.

ateo, ea, a. atheistic ; —, sm. & f. atheist.

atercianado, da, a. afflicted with the tertian fever.

aterciopelado, da, a. velvet-like.

aterirse, v.r. to grow stiff with cold.

aterrar, v.a. to prostrate ; to terrify ; -se, to be terrified.

aterronar, v.a. to clod, to coagulate.

aterrorizar, v.a. to frighten, to terrify.

atesorar, v.a. to treasure or hoard up riches.

atestación, sf. testimony, evidence.

atestado, da, a. stubborn ; —, sm. certificate.

atestar, v.a. to cram, to stuff ; to overstock ; to attest, to witness.

atestiguar, v.a. to witness, to attest.

atetado, da, a. mammiform.

atetar, v.a. to suckle. [trees.

atetillar, v.a. to lay bare the roots of

atezado, da, a. black. [black.

atezar, v.a. to blacken ; -se, to grow

atiborrar, v.a. to stuff with wool, &c. ; to cram with food.

aticismo, sm. atticism.

atigrado, da, a. tiger-coloured.

atildar, v.a. to mark with the tilde (ñ) ; to censure ; to deck, to adorn.

atinar, v.n. to touch the mark, to reach the point ; to hit ; to guess.

atiriciarse, v.r. to grow jaundiced, to get the jaundice.

atisbadero, sm. peep-hole.

atisbador, sm. pryer.

atisbar, v.a. to pry, to examine closely.

atisuado, da, a. tissue-like.

atizador, sm. poker. [to stir up.

atizar, v.a. to stir the fire with a poker ;

atizonar, v.a. to fill up the chinks in a wall ; -se, to be smutted.

atlántico, ca, adj. atlantic.

atlas, sm. atlas (collection of maps) ; kind of rich silk.

atleta, sm. wrestler.

atlético, ca, a. athletic.

atmósfera, sf. atmosphere.

atmosférico, ca, a. atmospherical.

atoar, v.a. to tow a vessel. [ing.

atocinar, v.a. to cut up a pig for salt-

atocha, sf. (bot.) esparto grass.

atolondramiento, sm. stupefaction, consternation. [to be stupefied.

atolondrar, v.a. to stun, to stupefy ; -se,

atolladero, sm. bog ; obstacle ; impediment.

atollar, v.n. to stick in the mire.

atomismo, sm. atomical philosophy.

átomo, sm. atom ; mote. [knees.

atondar, v.a. to urge a horse with the

atonía, sf. (med.) weakness, debility.

atónito, ta, a. astonished, amazed.

atontar, v.a. to stun, to stupefy ; -se, to grow stupid.

atorarse, v.r. to stick in the mire.

atormentadamente, ad. anxiously.

atormentar, v.a. to torment, to give pain.

atorozonarse, v.r. to suffer from gripes or colic (of horses).

atorrante, sm. (col. am.) vagabond, idler.

atortolar, v.a. to intimidate ; to confuse.

atosigar, v.a. to poison ; to harass, to oppress.

atrabancar, v.a. to hurry.

atracadero, sm. landing-place.

atracar, v.a. to bring a ship to shore ; (col.) to glut, to pamper.

atracción, sf. attraction.

atractivo, va, a. attractive ; magnetic ; —, sm. charm, grace.

atraer, v.a. to attract, to allure.

atrafagado, da, a. over-busy, overworked.

atrafagar, v.n. to exhaust one's self.

atragantarse, v.r. to have someth ng stick in the throat, to choke ; to stick fast in conversation.

atraidorado, da, a. treacherous.

atraillar, v.a. to leash.

atramparse, v.r. to be caught in a snare ; to be stopped or blocked up ; to be involved in difficulties.

atrancar, v.a. to bar a door ; to take long steps ; to skip (in reading).

atrapar, v.a. to overtake, to nab ; to deceive.

atrás, ad. backwards ; past ; **hacia —**, (col.) quite the contrary.

atrasado, da, a. in arrear.

atrasar, v.a. to outstrip, to leave behind ; to hinder another's fortune ; to postpone ; — **el reloj**, to put back a watch.

atraso, sm. backwardness ; loss of fortune ; arrears of money.

atravesado, da, a. squint-eyed ; oblique ; cross-grained, perverse ; mongrel, degenerate.

atravesaño, sm. cross-timber.

atravesar, v.a. to lay across ; to traverse, to cross ; to pass over ; to trump a trick ; **-se**, to get in the way ; to thwart one's purpose.

atreguado, a. rash, precipitate.

atresnalar, v.a. to collect sheaves of corn into heaps.

atreverse, v.r. to dare, to venture.

atrevido, da, a. bold, audacious, daring.

atrevimiento, sm. boldness, audacity.

atribución, sf. attribution, imputation.

atribuir, v.a. to attribute, to ascribe ; to impute.

atribular, v.a. to vex, to afflict.

atributivo, va, a. attributive.

atributo, sm. attribute.

atrición, sf. attrition.

atril, sm. mass-book desk.   [ment.

atrincheramiento, sm. (mil.) intrench-

atrincherar, v.a. to intrench.

atrio, sm. porch ; portico.

atrito, ta, a. contrite, penitent.

atro, ra, a. (poet.) black.

atrocidad, sf. atrocity.

atrochar, v.n. to take by-paths.

atrochemoche, ad. criss-cross.

atrofia, sf. atrophy.

atrófico, ca, a. affected with atrophy.

atrompetado, da, a. trumpet-like.

atronado, da, a. unadvised, thoughtless, rash.

atronarse, v.r. to be thunderstruck.

atronerar, v.a. to make embrasures in a wall.

atropado, da, a. grouped, clumped. [wall.

atropar, v.a. to assemble in groups.

atropellado, da, a. hasty, precipitate.

atropellar, v.a. to trample ; to run down ; to hurry, to flurry ; **-se**, to hurry one's self too much.

atroz, a. atrocious, heinous, cruel.

atrozar, v.a. (mar.) to truss a yard to the mast.

atufar, v.a. to vex, to plague ; **-se**, to be on the fret (applied to wine) ; to be angry.

atún, sm. tunny-fish.   [angry.

atunara, sf. tunny-fishery.   [careless.

aturdido, da, a. hare-brained ; stupid,

aturdimiento, sm. stupefaction ; astonishment ; dullness.

aturdir, v.a. to perturbate, to confuse ; to stupefy.

atusar, v.a. to cut the hair ; to shear.

auca, sf. goose.

audacia, sf. audacity, boldness.

audaz, a. audacious, bold.

audiencia, sf. audience ; audience-chamber ; a court of oyer and terminer.

auditivo, va, a. auditory.

auditorio, sm. auditory.

auge, sm. the pinnacle of power ; apogee

augur, sm. augurer.   [of a planet.

augusto, ta, a. august, majestic.

aula, sf. auditory, lecture-room.

aullar, v.n. to howl.

aullido, aullo, sm. howling.

aumentar, v.a. to augment, to increase ; —, v.n. to grow larger.   [ing.

aumentativo, va, a. increasing, enlarg-

aumento, sm. augmentation, increase ; promotion, advancement.

aun, ad. yet, as yet, nevertheless ; still, farther, even, further.

aunar, v.a. to unite, to assemble.

aunque, ad. though, although.

¡aupa! up, up !   [larity.

aura, sf. gentle breeze ; — **popular**, popu-

áureo, rea, a. golden, gilt.

auréola, sf. glory ; nimbus.

aurícula, sf. (bot.) bear's-ear.

auricular, a. auricular.

aurífero, ra, a. (poet.) containing gold.

aurora, sf. first dawn of the day ; (poet.) origin *or* first appearance of a thing ; — **boreal**, north light.

aurragado, da, a. badly tilled.

auscultar, v.a. (med.) to sound.

ausencia, sf. absence.

ausentarse, v.r. to absent one's self.

ausente, a. absent.   [tection.

auspicio, sm. auspice ; prediction ; pro-

austero, ra, a. austere, severe ; crabbed.

austral, austrino, na, a. austral, southern.

austro, sm. south wind.

auténtica, sf. certificate.

autenticar, v.a. to authenticate.

autenticidad, sf. authenticity.

auténtico, ca, a. authentic.   [da-fe.

autillo, sm. horned owl ; secret auto

auto, sm. judicial sentence ; warrant, edict, ordinance ; — **de fe**, auto-da-fe, sentence given by the Inquisition.

autocracia, sf. autocracy.

autócrata, sm. autocrat.

autógrafo, sm. autograph.   [ton.

autómato, ta., automatic ; — sm. automa-

automóvil, sm. motor-car.

autonomía, sf. autonomy.

autopsia, sf. autopsy.

autor, sm. author ; maker ; **writer** ; (drama) manager, impressario.

autora, sf. authoress.
autorcillo, sm. bad writer.
autoría, sf. managership of a theatre.
autoridad, sf. authority.
autoritativo, va, a. authoritative.
autorización, sf. authorisation.
autorizar, v.a. to authorise.
autorzuelo, sm. scribbler.
auxiliar, v.a. to aid, to help, to assist; to attend a dying person; —, a. auxiliary.
auxilio, sm. aid, help, assistance.
avadarse, v.r. to become fordable.
avalentado, da, a. bragging, vainly boasting.
avalorar, v.a. to estimate, to value; to heighten the value of a thing; to inspirit, to animate.
avalúo, sm. estimate, valuation.
avambrazo, sm. fore-arm.
avance, sm. (mil.) advance, attack.
avantrén, sm. (mil.) limbers of a gun-carriage.
avanzada, sf. (mil.) vanguard.
avanzar, v.a. & n. to advance.
avanzo, sm. (com.) account, balance.
avaricia, sf. avarice.
avariento, ta, a. avaricious, covetous.
avaro, ra, a. avaricious, miserly.
avasallar, v.a. to subdue, to enslave.
ave, sf. bird; fowl. [muffin.
avechucho, sm. sparrow-hawk; ragamuffin.
avecindar, v.a. to admit to the privileges of a citizen; -se, to approach, to join.
avejentar, v.n. to look more than one's age.
avejigar, v.a. to blister. [age.
avellana, sf. filbert, hazel-nut.
avellanar, sm. plantation of hazels.
avellanarse, v.r. to shrivel, to grow as dry as a nut.
avellano, sm. hazel-nut tree.
Ave María, sf. Ave, the angel's salutation of the Holy Virgin.
avena, sf. oats.
avenamiento, sm. drainage.
avenar, v.a. to drain or draw off water.
avenate, sm. water-gruel.
avenencia, sf. agreement, bargain; union, concord.
aveníceo, cea, a. oaten.
avenida, sf. flood, inundation; avenue, approach; concurrence of several things.
avenido, da, a. agreed. [things.
avenir, v.a. to reconcile; to accommodate; to get reconciled; to join, to consent. [fan.
aventador, sm. winnower; fan; fire-fan.
aventadura, sf. wind-gall.
aventajado, da, a. advantageous, profitable; beautiful, excellent.
aventajar, v.a. to surpass, to excel.

aventar, v.a. to fan; to expel; -se, to be puffed up. [chance.
aventura, sf. adventure, event, incident;
aventurar, v.a. to venture, to risk.
aventurero, ra, a. adventurous.
avergonzar, v.a. to shame, to abash; -se, to be ashamed. [sea; aviary.
avería, sf. (mar.) average, damage by
averiado, da, a. damaged by sea-water.
averiarse, v.r. to suffer damage at sea.
averiguación, sf. investigation.
averiguar, v.a. to inquire, to investigate, to explore. [birds.
averío, sm. beast of burden; flight of
averno, sm. (poet.) hell. [rence.
aversión, sf. aversion, dislike; abhor
avestruz, sm. ostrich.
aviación, sf. aviation.
aviador, ra, sm. & f. airman, aviator.
aviar, v.a. to provision, to provide for a journey; to accoutre; to hasten the execution of a thing; -se, to get ready.
avidez, sf. covetousness.
ávido, da, a. (poet.) greedy, covetous.
aviejarse, v.r. to grow old.
aviento, sm. winnowing-fork.
avieso, sa, a. irregular, out of the way; mischievous, perverse. [and spirit.
avigorar, v.a. to inspire with vigour
avilantez, sf. forwardness, boldness.
avillanado, da, a. clownish, mean, vile,
avillanar, v.a. to debase. [base.
avinado, da, a. tasting or smelling of wine.
avinagrado, da, a. crabbed, peevish, bad-
avinagrar, v.a. to acidify. [tempered.
avío, sm. preparation, provision.
avión, sm. (orn.) martin.
avisado, da, a. prudent, cautious; sagacious, skilful; **mal —**, ill advised, injudicious. [to admonish.
avisar, v.a. to inform, to give notice;
aviso, sm. information, intelligence, notice; warning, hint; prudence; care; counsel.
avispa, sf. wasp. [counsel.
avispado, da, a. lively, brisk, vivacious.
avispar, v.a. to spur; -se, to be peevish.
avispero, sm. wasps' nest.
avispón, sm. hornet.
avistar, v.a. to descry at a distance; to have an interview, to transact business. [ness.
avituallar, v.a. (mil.) to victual.
avivar, v.a., to enliven, to encourage.
avizorar, v.a. to spy, to search narrowly.
avocar, v.a. to carry a law-suit into a superior court.
avucasta, sf. (orn.) widgeon.
avutarda, sf. bustard, wild turkey.
axioma, sm. axiom, maxim.
¡ay! alas! **¡—de mí!** alas! poor me!
aya, sf. governess, instructress.
ayer, ad. yesterday; lately.

ayo, sm. tutor, governor.

ayuda, sf. help, aid ; support ; syringe ; —, sm. deputy, assistant.

ayudante, sm. (mil.) adjutant, aid-de-camp.

ayudar, v.a. to aid, to help, to assist, to further.

ayunar, v.a. to rast, to abstain from food.

ayunas, (en) ad. fastingly ; without knowledge.

ayuno, sm. fast, abstinence from food ; —, na, a. fasting.

ayunque, sm. anvil.

ayuntamiento, sm. town-council.

azabachado, da, a. jet-black.

azabache, sm. jet.

azacán, sm. water-carrier.

azada, sf. spade, hoe.

azadón, sm. pick-axe, grub-axe.

azafata, sf. queen's waiting-woman.

azafrán, sm. saffron.

azafranar, v.a. to dye with saffron.

azagador, sm. cattle-path.

azahar, sm. orange or lemon flower,

azainadamente, ad. perfidiously ; viciously.

azar, sm. hazard, unforeseen disaster, unexpected accident ; unfortunate card or throw at dice ; disappointment ; impediment.

azarbe, sm. irrigation-trench.

azarja, sf. silk-reel.   [ous.

azaroso, sa, a. hazardous, unlucky, ominous.

aznallo, sm. Scotch fir.

azoe, sm. (chem.) nitrogen.

azófar, sm. latten-brass.

azogadamente, ad. in a quick and restless manner.

azogar, v.a. to overlay with quicksilver ; — la cal, to slake lime ; -se, to suffer from quicksilver poisoning ; to be in a state of agitation.

azogue, sm. quicksilver, mercury ; -s, pl. ships which carry quicksilver.

azoguería, sf. amalgamating-works.

azolar, v.a. to cut timber with a hatchet.

azor, sm. goshawk.   [agitated.

azorar, v.a. to frighten, to terrify ; to be

azorrarse, v.r. to feel a heaviness in the head.   [bummer.

azotacalles, sm. lounger, loafer ; (am.)

azotaina, sf. drubbing, sound flogging.

azotar, v.a. to whip, to lash ; to horsewhip.   [calamity.

azote, sm. whip, lash given with a whip ;

azotea, sf. platform, flat roof of a house.

azúcar, sm. sugar ; — de pilón, loaf-sugar ; — piedra ó cande, sugar-candy; — terciado ó moreno, brown sugar.

azucarado, da, a. sugared ; sugary.

azucarar, v.a. to sugar, to sweeten.

azucarero, sm. sugar-basin ; confectioner.

azucena, sf. white lily.   [tioner.

azud, sf. dam with a sluice or flood-gate.

azuda, sf. water-works for irrigation.

azuela, sf. chip-axe.

azufaifa, sf. jujube.

azufaifo, sm. jujube-tree.   [sulphurous.

azufrado, da, a. whitened with sulphur ;

azufrar, v.a. to fumigate with sulphur.

azufre, sm. sulphur, brimstone.

azufroso, sa, a. sulphureous.

azul, a. blue ; — celeste, sky blue ; — turquí, Turkish or deep blue.

azulado, da, a. azure, bluish.

azular, v.a. to dye blue.

azulear, v.n. to have a bluish tint.

azulejo, sm. glazed coloured tile.

azulenco, a. bluish.   [gallon).

azumbre, sf. liquid measure (half a

azutero, sm. sluice-master.

azuzador, ra, sm. & f. instigator.

azuzar, v.a. to set on dogs ; to irritate, to stir up.

B

baba, sf. drivel, slaver.

babada, sf. thigh-bone.

babadero, babador, sm. bib, chin-cloth.

babaza, sf. slime ; foam or froth from the mouth.

babear, v.n. to drivel, to slaver.

babera, sf. chin-piece of a helmet ; foolish, silly fellow.

babero, sm. chin-cloth.   [or dreaming.

babia, sf. estar en —, to be absent-minded

babieca, sm. (col.) ignorant, stupid fellow.

babilonia, sf. es una —, it is all uproar and confusion.

babor, sm. (mar.) larboard, port side.

babosa, sf. slug.

babosear, v.a. to beslaver.

baboso, sa, a. drivelling, slavering.

babucha, sf. oriental slipper.

bacalao, bacallao, sm. cod-fish.

bacanales, st.pl. bacchanals.

bacante, sf. bacchant.

bacía, sf. basin ; barber's basin.

bacinica, sf. small basin.

báculo, sm. walking-stick ; support ; — pastoral, bishop's crosier.

bachiller, sm. bachelor ; —, a. (col.) garrulous, loquacious.

bachillerear, v.n. to babble, to prattle.

badajo, sm. clapper of a bell.

badana, sf. dressed sheep-skin.

badil, badila, sf. fire-shovel, poker.
badulaque, sm. (col.) stupid fellow.
bagaje, sm. beast of burden; army-baggage.
bagajero, sm. driver of beasts of burden.
bagatela, sf. bagatelle, trifle.
bahía, sf. bay.
bailador, ra, sm. & f. dancer.
bailar, v.n. to dance.
bailarín, ina, sm. & f. dancer.
baile, sm. dance, ball; bailiff.
bajá, sm. bashaw, pacha.
baja, sf. fall, diminution; (mil.) casualty.
bajada, sf. descent; inclination.
bajamar, sf. low water.
bajar, v.a. to lower, to let down; to
   abate (the price); to lessen; to
   humble; to bend downwards; —,
   v.n. to descend; to grow less; -se,
   to crouch; to lessen.
bajel, sm. vessel, ship.
bajelero, sm. ship-owner, ship-master.
bajete, sm. (mus.) baritone.
bajeza, sf. meanness, abjectness; little-ness; lowliness, fawningness.
bajío, sm. shoal, sand-bank; decline.
bajo, ja, a. low; abject, despicable;
   faint; common; dull (of colours);
   bent; —, pr. under, underneath, be-low; —, ad. low (of the voice); —,
   sm. (mus.) base; low place; -s, pl.
   under-petticoats of women.
bajón, sm. bassoon.
bajonero, sm. player on the bassoon.
bala, sf. ball, bullet, shot; bale of paper;
   printer's inking-ball.
baladí, a. mean, despicable, worthless.
baladre, sm. rose-bay.
baladrón, sm. boaster, bully.
baladronada, sf. boast, brag, bravado.
baladronear, v.n. to boast, to brag.
bálago, sm. hay-rick; soap-suds.
balance, sm. fluctuation; equipoise;
   balance of accounts; rolling of a ship.
balancear, v.a. & n. to balance; to roll;
   to hold in equipoise; to waver.
balancín, sm. swing-bar of a cart; mint-ing-mill; rope-dancer's pole.
balandra, sf. (mar.) sloop.
balanza, sf. scale; pair of scales; com-parative estimate. [mint).
balanzario, sm. balancer, weigher (in the
balar, v.n. to bleat as a sheep.
balaustrada, sf. balustrade.
balaustre, sm. baluster.
balazo, sm. blow of a bullet or cannon-ball, shot.
balbuciente, a. stammering, stuttering.
balcón, sm. balcony.
balconaje, sm. range of balconies.
baldar, v.a. to cripple.

balde, sm. bucket; de —, ad. gratis, for
   nothing; en —, in vain.
baldés, sm. piece of dressed skin.
baldío, día, a. untilled, uncultivated.
baldón, sm. reproach, insult.
baldosa, sf. fine square tile.
balduque, sm. red tape.
balería, sf. pile of balls or bullets.
balido, sm. bleating, bleat.
balija. See **valija.**
balijero. See **valijero.**
balín, sm. buck-shot.
balón, sm. large football; bale of goods.
balota, sf. ballot.
balsa, sf. pool; raft, float; ferr
balsámico, ca, a. balmy.
bálsamo, sm. balsam, balm. [floats.
balsear, v.a. to cross rivers on ferries or
balsero, sm. ferry-man.
balsopeto, sm. large pouch carried near
   the breast; bosom.
baluarte, sm. bastion; bulwark.
balumbo, sm. bulk of things heaped to-gether.
ballena, sf. whale; whale-bone.
ballenato, sm. cub of a whale.
ballenero, sm. (mar.) whaler.
ballesta, sf. crossbow.
ballestada, sf. shot from a crossbow.
ballestear, v.a. to shoot with a crossbow.
ballestera, sf. (mil.) loop-hole. [bow-men.
ballestería, sf. archery; crossbows; cross-
ballestero, sm. archer; crossbow-maker;
   king's armourer.
ballestilla, sf. small crossbow.
bamba, sf. (col.) fluke (at billiards).
bambalina, sf. hanging scenery of a
   theatre representing sky or ceiling.
bambolear, v.n. to reel.
bamboleo, sm. reeling, staggering.
bambolla, sf. ostentation, vain show.
bambú, bambuc, sm. bamboo.
banana, sf. banana, plantain.
banano, sm. plantain-tree.
banasta, sf. large basket.
banastero, sm. basket maker.
banasto, sm. large round basket.
banca, sf. bench; washing-box.
bancal, sm. garden-bed, parterre; carpet.
bancarrota, sf. bankruptcy.
banco, sm. bench; carpenter's bench;
   bench of rowers; bank.
banda, sf. sash; ribbon; band of
   troops; party; gang; crew; covey;
   bank, border.
bandada, sf. covey.
bandearse, v.r. to shift for one's self.
bandeja, sf. salver.
bandera, sf. banner, standard; flag.
banderilla, sf. small decorated dart used
   at a bull-fight.

C

banderillear, v.a. to plant banderillas in a bull's neck or shoulder.
banderillero, sm. thrower of banderillas.
banderín, sm. cockade.
banderizo, za, a. factious.
banderola, sf. bannerol.
bandido, sm. bandit, highwayman.
bando, sm. faction, party.
bandolera, sf. bandoleer.
bandolero, sm. highwayman.
bandolín, sm. (mus.) mandolin.
bandullo, sm. belly.
bandurria, sf. bandore (musical instrument resembling a fiddle).
banquero, sm. banker.
banqueta, sf. three-legged stool.
banquete, sm. banquet.
baña, sf., bañadero, sm. pool, puddle (in which wild boars wallow).
bañar, v.a. to bathe ; to tub ; to water, to irrigate ; to candy ; to wash over a painting with a second coat of transparent colours.
bañero, sm. bath-keeper.
bañista, sm. bather.
baño, sm. bath ; bathing-place ; bathing-tub ; varnish ; crust of sugar ; coat of paint put over another.
baqueta, sf. ramrod, gun-stick ; drumstick ; (mil.) gantlet.
baquetazo, sm. blow of a ramrod.
baqueteado, da, a. inured, habituated.
báquico, ca, a. bacchanal.
baraja, sf. pack of cards.
barajadura, sf. shuffling of cards.
barajar, v.a. to shuffle cards ; to entangle.   [railing.
barandilla, sf. small balustrade, small
baratero, sm. card-sharper, black-leg.
baratijas, sf.pl. trifles, toys.
baratillero, sm. fripperer.
baratillo, sm. frippery.
barato, ta, a. cheap ; de —, gratis ; —, sm. cheapness, low price ; money given by the winners at a gaming-table to the by-standers as part of the
baratura, sf. cheapness.   [gain.
baraúnda, sf. noise, hurly-burly.
barba, sf. chin ; beard ; — á —, face to face ; —, sm. actor who personates old
barbacana, sf. (mil.) barbican.   [men.
barbada, sf. lower jaw of a horse ; dab (fish).   [keep bees ; to take root.
barbar, v.n. to grow a beard ; to rear or
barbaridad, sf. barbarity, barbarism ; rashness ; rudeness.
barbarie, sf. barbarism ; rusticity.
barbarismo, sm. barbarism (form of speech) ; (poet.) crowd of barbarians.
bárbaro, ra, a. barbarous ; rash, bold, daring ; rude, unpolished.

barbechar, v.a. to plough.   [ploughings.
barbechera, sf. series of successive
barbecho, sm. first ploughing, fallow.
barbería, sf. barber's shop.
barbero, sm. barber.
barbeta, sf. (mar.) rackline.
barbiblanco, ca, a. white-bearded.
barbicano, na, a. grey-beard.
barbihecho, a. fresh shaved.
barbilampiño, ña, a. thin-bearded.
barbilucio, cia, a. pretty, genteel.
barbilla, sf. chin-point.
barbinegro, gra, a. black-bearded.
barbirrubio, bia, a. red-bearded.
barbo, sm. barbel (fish).   [beard.
barbón, sm. man with a thick, strong
barbosa, sf. layer, provine.
barbote, sm. chin-cloth.
barbudo, da, a. long-bearded.
barbulla, sf. confused noise.
barbullar, v.a. to talk loudly and confusedly.   [of tongues.
barbullón, ona, a. loud talking ; babel
barca, sf. boat, barge.
barcada, sf. passage in a ferry-boat ; boat full of persons or goods.
barcaje, sm. fare.
barco, sm. boat, barge ; bark.
barda, sf. bard.
bardal, sm. mud-wall, covered at the top with straw, brush or fence-wood.
bardana, sf. common burdock.
bardar, v.a. to cover the top of walls with straw or brushwood.
baritono, sm. (mus.) baritone.
barloar, v.a. (mar.) to lay alongside.
barloventear, v.n. (mar.) to tack, to tack about.
barlovento, sm. (mar.) weather-gauge.
barniz, sm. varnish ; Japan paint ; printer's ink.
barnizar, v.a. to varnish.
barómetro, sm. barometer.
barón, sm. baron.
baronesa, sf. baroness.
baronía, sf. barony ; baronage.
barquear, v.n. to cross in a boat.
barquero, sm. bargeman.
barquilla, sf. (mar.) log ; thin boat-formed pastry-cake.
barquillero, sm. wafer-baker.
barquillo, sm. wafer.
barquín, sm. large bellows for furnaces.
barquinazo, sm. thud of a falling body.
barquino, sm. wine-bag.
barra, sm. crowbar, lever ; ingot, or bar of gold, silver, &c. ; rock, sandbank ; de — á —, from place to place.
barrabasada, sf. trick, plot, intrigue.
barraca, sf. hut (for soldiers or for fisher-
barraganete, sm. top-timber.   [men,

barranca, sf., barranco, sm. deep break made by mountain-floods ; cleft, glen, fissure ; embarrassment, difficulty.

barrancoso, sa, a. full of breaks and holes.

barrar, barrear, v.a. to barricade, to forbar.

barreda, barrera, sf. turn-pike. [tify.

barredero, sm. mop. [residue.

barreduras, s.pl. sweepings ; remains,

barrena, sf. borer, gimlet, auger.

barrenar, v.a. to bore ; (fig.) to frustrate one's designs.

barrendero, sm. sweeper, dust-man.

barreno, sm. large borer ; hole made with a borer or auger ; blasting-hole.

barreño, sm. earthen pan ; tub.

barrer, v.a. to sweep ; to carry off the whole.

barrera, sf. clay-pit, barrier ; turn-pike.

barrero, sm. potter ; clay-pit.

barretear, v.a. to strengthen with bars.

barretero, sm. one who works with a crowbar, wedge or pick (in mines).

barriada, sf. suburb, ward of a city.

barrica, sf. keg, small barrel.

barricada, sf. barricade.

barrido, sm. sweeping.

barriga, sf. abdomen, belly ; pregnancy ; (mar.) middle part of a vessel.

barrigudo, da, a. big-bellied.

barril, sm. barrel ; jug.

barrilame, sm., barrilería, sf. number of barrels collected in one place.

barrilero, sm. cooper.

barrilete, sm. keg ; holdfast ; (mar.) mouse.

barrilla, sf. (bot.) salt-wort, barrilla.

barrillar, sm. barrilla-pits.

barrio. sm. district or quarter of a town.

barrizal, sm. clay-pit.

barro. sm. clay, mud.

barroso, sa, a. muddy ; mud-coloured, brown (of horses).

barrote, sm. iron-work of doors, windows, tables ; ledge of timber.

barrueco, sm. pearl of irregular shape.

barruntador, sm. conjecturer.

barruntamiento, sm. conjecture, guess.

barruntar, v.a. to foresee, to conjecture.

barrunto, sm. conjecture.

bártulos, sm.pl. affairs, business.

barzón, sm. idle walk.

barzonear, v.n. to loiter.

basa, sf. (arch.) base (of a column) ; basis ; base.

basada, sf. crane, derrick.

basalto, sm. basalt, basaltes.

basca, sf. squeamishness, nausea.

bascosidad, sf. nastiness, filth.

base, sf. base, basis.

basílica, sf. basilica (cathedral).

basilisco, sm. basilisk, cockatrice.

basquear, v.n. to be squeamish.

basquiña, sf. upper petticoat worn by

basta, sf. basting. [Spanish women.

bastante, a. sufficient, enough.

bastar, v.n. to suffice, to be proportioned to something, to be enough.

bastarda, sf. bastard-file ; italic (type).

bastardear, v.n. to degenerate ; to bastardize.

bastardía, sf. bastardy ; meanness.

bastardo, da, a. bastard, spurious ; —, sm. bastard. [slightly.

bastear, v.a. to stitch loosely, to sew

bastero, sm. maker and seller of pack-saddles.

bastidor, sm. embroidery-frame ; side-scene ; -es, pl. scenery (on the stage).

bastilla, sf. hem, seam. [visions.

bastimentar, v.a. to supply with pro-

bastimentero, sm. purveyor.

bastimento, sm. supply of provisions ; (mar.) vessel.

bastión, sm. (mil.) bastion.

basto, sm. pack-saddle for beasts of burden ; —, ta, a. coarse, rude, unpolished.

bastón, sm. cane, stick ; truncheon ; staff of command ; military command.

bastonazo, sm. blow of a stick.

bastoncillo, sm. narrow lace.

bastonear, v.a. to stir must with a stick to prevent its becoming ropy.

bastonero, sm. marshal or manager of a ball, steward of a feast ; assistant jail-keeper. [at cards.

bastos, sm.pl. clubs (one of the four suits

basura, sf. sweepings ; dung, ordure.

basurero, sm. dustman ; dung-hill.

bata, sf. morning-gown ; refuse of silk.

batacazo, sm. thud of a fall.

batahola, bataola, sf. hurly-burly, bustle.

batalla, sf. battle, combat, fight ; agitation of the mind.

batallador, sm. combatant, warrior.

batallar, v.n. to battle, to fight ; to fence with foils ; to dispute.

batallón, sm. (mil.) battalion.

batán, sm. fulling-mill.

batanar, v.a. to full cloth. [roughly.

batanear, v.a. (col.) to beat, to handle

batanero, sm. fuller.

batata, sf. sweet potato.

batea, sf. painted tray or hamper of japanned wood ; washing-trough.

batel, sm. boat.

batería, sm battery ; impression made on the mind or body.

batera, sf. mantua-maker.

batida, sf. battue, game-drive.

batidera, sf. beater (instrument for beating and mixing mortar).

batidero, sm. clashing of one thing against another; collision; uneven ground.

batido, da, a. shot (applied to silks): beaten (as roads); —, sm. batter of flour and water for making the host; wafers, biscuits.

batidor, sm. scout; ranger; outrider; one of the life-guards, who rides before a royal coach; — **de oro,** gold-beater.

batiente, sm. jamb or post of a door.

batihoja, sm. gold-beater; artisan who works iron and other metal into sheets; warp of cloth.

batir, v.a. to beat, to dash; to clash, to clap; to demolish; to move in a violent manner; to strike (of the sun).

batista, sf. batiste, cambric.

baturrillo, sm. hotch-potch, salmagundi.

baúl, sm. trunk; (col.) belly.

bauprés, sm. (mar.) bow-sprit.

bausán, ana, sm. & f. guy; fool; idiot.

bautismal, a. baptismal.

bautismo, sm. baptism.

bautisterio, sm. baptistery.

bautizar, v.a. to baptise, to christen.

bautizo, sm. baptism.

baya, sf. berry; husk, cod.

bayeta, sf. baize (kind of cloth).

bayetón, sm. coating.

bayo, ya, a. cream-coloured (of a horse).

bayoneta, sf. bayonet.

bayonetazo, sm. thrust with a bayonet.

baza, sf. trick (at cards).

bazar, sm. bazaar.

bazo, sm. spleen, milt; —, **za,** a. yellowish brown.

bazofia, sf. offal; refuse; hog-wash.

bazucar, v.a. to stir liquids by shaking.

bazuqueo, sm. stirring of liquids by shaking.

be, baa (cry of sheep).

beata, sf. sister of charity; devotee.

beatería, sf. bigotry.

beaterio, sm. house of sisters of charity.

beatificación, sf. beatification.

beatificar, v.a. to beatify; to exalt; to make happy.

beatífico, ca, a. beatific.

beatilla, sf. French lawn.

beatísimo, ma, a. most holy; — **padre,** sm. most holy father (the pope).

beatitud, sf. beatitude, blessedness.

beato, ta, a. happy, blessed; devout; —, sm. devotee; bigot.

bebedera, sm. drinking-trough; place where birds resort to drink.

bebedizo, za, a. drinkable.

bebedizo, sm. love-potion.

bebedor, ra, sm. & f. tippler, drunkard.

beber, v.a. to drink.

bebida, sf. drink, beverage.

bebido, da, a. half tipsy.

bebistrajo, sm. bad drink, washy stuff.

beborretear, v.a. to sip.

beca, sf. part of a collegian's dress worn over the gown; fellowship; allowance, scholarship; **-s,** pl. strips of velvet, &c., with which the forepart of cloaks is lined by way of ornament.

becabunga, sf. (bot.) brook-lime.

becada, sf. (orn.) wood-cock.

becafigo, sm. fig-pecker.   [dragon.

becerra, sf. she-calf; —, sm. (bot.) snap-

becerrillo, sm. dressed calf-skin.

becerro, sm. calf; calf-skin; register in which are entered the privileges and appurtenances of cathedral churches and convents; — **marino,** sea-calf.

bedel, sm. beadle.

bedelía, sf. beadleship.

bedija, sf. See **vedija.**

befa, sf. jeer, scoff, mock; garland.

befar, v.a. to mock, to ridicule.

befo, fa, a. blubber-lipped.

bejucal, sm. reed-plot, reed-bank.

bejuco, sm. pliant cane or reed; liana.

bejuquillo, sm. small gold chain.

beldad, sf. beauty.

beleño, sm. (bot.) hen-bane.

bélico, ca, a. warlike, martial.

belicoso, sa, a. martial, pugnacious.

beligerante, a. belligerent.

bellacamente, ad. knavishly, roguishly.

bellaco, ca, a. artful, sly; cunning, roguish.   [night-shade.

belladama, belladona, sf. (bot.) deadly-

bellaquear, v.a. to cheat, to play roguish

bellaquería, sf. knavery, roguery. [tricks.

belleza, sf. beauty.

bello, lla, a. beautiful, handsome, fair, fine; perfect.

bellota, sf. acorn; smelling-bottle (in the shape of an acorn).

bellote, sm. large round-headed nail.

bellotear, v.n. to feed on acorns (applied

bellotera, sf. acorn season.   [to swine).

bemol, sm. (mus.) b-flat.

bendecir, v.a. to consecrate; to bless; to praise, to exalt.

bendición, sf. benediction.

bendito, ta, a. saint, blessed; simple, silly.

bendícite, sm. grace at meals; clergyman's leave of absence.

benedictino, benito, sm. Benedictine.

beneficencia, sf. beneficence.

beneficiado, sm. incumbent of a benefice.

beneficiador, sm. benefactor; improver; careful administrator.

beneficiar, v.a. to benefit; to work and improve (mines or land).

beneficiario, sm. beneficiary.

beneficio, sm. benefit, favour, kindness; labour, culture; profit; benefit-night; benefice.

benéfico, ca, a. beneficent, kind.

benemérito, ta, a. meritorious.

beneplácito, sm. good-will, approbation.

benevolencia, sf. benevolence, well-wishing. [kind-hearted.

benévolo, la, a. benevolent, favourable,

benignidad, sf. benignity; mildness of the weather.

benigno, na, a. benign; kind; mild,

beodo, da, a. drunk; drunken.

berberis, sm. barberry, berberry.

Bercebú, sm. (fam.) the devil.

bergamota, sf. bergamot (sort of pear).

bergamote, bergamoto, sm. bergamot-tree. [ruffian.

bergante, sm. brazen-faced villain,

bergantín, sm. (mar.) brig.

beril, sm. beryl, a precious stone.

berlina, sf. landau, berlin.

bermejear, v.n. to incline to vermilion.

bermejizo, za, a. reddish.

bermejo, ja, a. vermilion.

bermejura, sf. vermilion.

bermellón, sm. vermilion. [boasts.

bernardinas, sf.pl. fanfaronade, false

bernardo, sm. Bernardine monk.

berra, sf. coarse water-cress plant.

berrear, v.n. to low, to bellow.

berrenchín, sm. grunting of a boar; crying of angry children. [colours.

berrendo, da, a. tinged with two different

berrido, sm. bellowing of a calf.

berrín, sm. child in a violent passion.

berrinche, sm. anger, passion, sulkiness (applied to children).

berrizal, sm. place full of water-cress.

berro, sm. water-cress.

berroqueño, ña, a. granite-like; piedra — a, granite.

berruga, sf. wart.

berza, sf. cabbage.

besalamano, sm. formal note.

besamanos, sm. kissing of hands; lévee; court-day.

besar, v.a. to kiss; (col.) to knock up against one another; -se, (col.) to knock one's head against another's.

beso, sm. kiss; collision of persons or things.

bestia, sf. beast; animal; dunce, idiot.

bestiaje, sm. herd of beasts of burden.

bestial, a. bestial, brutal.

bestialidad, sf. bestiality.

besugo, sm. sea-bream (fish).

besuqueo, sm. repeated kisses.

betún, sm. bitumen.

bezar, sf. bezoar (stone). [wound.

bezo, sm. blubber-lip; proud flesh in a

biazas, sf.pl. leather-saddlebags.

Biblia, sf. Bible.

bíblico, ca, a. biblical.

bibliófilo, sm. book-lover, book-worm.

bibliografía, sf. bibliography.

bibliográfico, ca, a. bibliographical.

bibliógrafo, sm. bibliographer.

bibliómano, na, a. bibliomaniac.

biblioteca, sf. library.

bibliotecario, sm. librarian.

bicicleta, sf. bicycle.

biciclista, sm. & f. bicyclist.

bicho, sm. vermin; hop o' my thumb; mal —, (col.) rascal.

bicoca, sf. (obs.) small fort; (col.) trifle.

bielda, sf. pitchfork with six or seven prongs.

bieldar, v.a. to winnow corn.

bieldo, bielgo, sm. winnowing-fork.

bien, sm. good, utility, benefit; welfare; -es, pl. property, riches, land; —, ad. well, right; very; willingly; heart ily; — que, although.

bienal, a. biennial.

bienandanza, sf. prosperity, success.

bienaventurado, da, a. blessed, happy, fortunate; simple, silly.

bienaventuranza, sf. beatitude; prosperity; -s, pl. the eight beatitudes of

bienestar, sm. well-being. [the gospel.

bienhablado, da, a. well-spoken; civil, courteous.

bienhadado, da, a. lucky, happy.

bienhechor, ra, sm. & f. benefactor.

bienio, sm. space of two years.

bienquisto, ta, a. generally esteemed and

bienvenida, sf. welcome. [beloved.

bigamia, sf. bigamy.

bígamo, sm. bigamist.

bigardear, v.n. (col.) to live licentiously.

bigardía, sf. dissoluteness; trick, turn, jest.

bigardo, sm. friar of loose morals; lubber.

bigornia, sf. anvil.

bigote, sm. whisker, moustache; tener -s, to be firm and undaunted.

bilioso, sa, a. bilious.

bilis, sf. bile.

bilorta, sm. See vilorta.

billar, sm. billiards, pl.

billear, v.a. to make cannons (at billiards).

billero, sm. billiard-player.

billete, sm. billet, label; (rail.) ticket, railway-ticket; — directo, through-ticket; — de ida y vuelta, return-ticket.

bimestre, a. of two months' duration; —, sm. space of two months; two months' pay. [the second time.

binar, v.a. to plough a piece of ground for

binario, sm. binary.

binazón, sf. second ploughing.
binóculo, sm. opera-glass.
biografía, sf. biography.
biógrafo, sm. biographer.
biombo, sm. screen.
bípedo, sm. biped.
biplano, sm. biplane.
biricú, sm. sword-belt.
birla, sf. bowl for playing.
birlar, v.a. to knock down at one blow
(at nine-pins) ; to dispossess.
birlocha, sf. paper-kite.
birlocho, sm. barouche.
birreta, sf. cardinal's red cap.
birretina, sf. grenadier's cap.
bisabuela, sf. great-grandmother.
bisabuelo, sm. great-grandfather.
bisagra, sf. hinge ; shoemaker's polisher.
bisiesto, a. bissextile ; año —, leap-year.
bisnieto, sm. great-grandson.
bisnieta, sf. great-granddaughter.
bisojo, ja, a. squint-eyed.
bisoñada, bisoñería, sf. inconsiderate
speech or action.
bisoño, ña, a. raw, undisciplined ; novice.
bisonte, sm. bison.
bitor, sm. (orn.) rail, king of the quails.
bituminoso, sa, a. bituminous.
bivac, sm. See vivac.   [lantly.
bizarramente, ad. courageously, gal-
bizarrear, v.n. to act in a spirited and
gallant manner.   [ality, generosity.
bizarría, sf. gallantry, valour ; liber-
bizarro, rra, a. brave, gallant ; high-
spirited ; generous.
bizco, ca, a. squint-eyed.
bizcochero, sm. maker or seller of biscuits ; confectioner.
bizcocho, sm. sea-biscuit ; cake.
bizma, sf. cataplásm, poultice.
bizmar, v.a. to apply a poultice ; —, sf.
great-granddaughter.
biznieto, ta. See bisnieto, ta.
bizquear, v.n. to squint.   [(orn.) magpie.
blanca, sf. half a maravedí ; mite ;
blanco, ca, a. white, blank ; —, sm.
first form, prime (printing) ; blank,
mark (to shoot at) ; — a ropa, linen,
linen-cloth ; en —, in vain.
blancura, sf. whiteness ; hoariness.
blandear, v.n. to soften ; to make one
change his opinion ; —, v.n. to yield,
to give way.   [&c. ; -se, to quiver.
blandir, v.a. to brandish a sword, lance,
blando, da, soft, smooth ; cotton-like ;
mellowy ; lithe ; mild, gentle.   [stick.
blandón, sm. wax-taper ; church-candle-
blanducho, cha, a. flabby, loose, insecure.
blandura, sf. softness ; daintiness, delicacy ; gentleness of temper ; mild
temperature.

blanqueador, ra, sm. & f. bleacher.
blanqueadura, sf. bleaching ; whitening.
blanquear, v.a. to bleach ; to whitewash ;
to give coarse wax to bees in winter ;
—, v.n. to show whiteness.
blanquecer, v.a. to blanch metal.
blanquecino, na, a. whitish.
blanqueo, sm. whitening ; whitewash.
blanquete, sm. white rouge.
blanquición, sf. blanching (of metals).
blanquimiento, sm. bleaching liquid.
blanquizco, ca, a. whitish.
blasfemable, a. blamable.
blasfemador, ra, sm. & f. blasphemer.
blasfemamente, ad. blasphemously.
blasfemar, v.n. to blaspheme.
blasfematorio, ria, a. blasphemous.
blasfemia, sf. blasphemy ; gross verbal
insult.   [blasphemer.
blasfemo, ma, a. blasphemous ; —, sm.
blasón, sm. heraldry, blazonry ; honour,
glory.
blasonador, ra, sm. & f. boaster, braggart.
blasonar, v.a. to blazon ; —, n. to blow
one's own trumpet.
bledo, sm. (bot.) wild amaranth ; no me
importa un —, I don't care a straw.
blondo, da, a. light-haired ; fair ; blonde.
bloquear, v.a. to blockade.
bloqueo, sm. blockade.
blusa, sf. blouse.
boato, sm. ostentation, pompous show.
bobada, sf. folly, foolishness.
bobático, ca, a. (col.) silly, stupid.
bobear, v.a. to act or talk in a stupid
manner ; to dally ; to loiter about.
bobería, sf. folly, foolishness.
bóbilis, ad. de —, (col.) without more ado.
bobinas, sf.pl. bobbins.
bobo, ba, sm. & f. dunce ; stage-buffoon ;
—, ba, a. stupid, silly.
boca, sf. mouth ; entrance, opening ;
mouth of a river ; — á —, ad. by
word of mouth ; á pedir de —, to one's
heart's content.
bocací, bocacín, sm. buckram.
bocadillo, sm. luncheon given to labourers
in the field.
bocado, sm. morsel, mouthful.
bocal, sm. pitcher ; mouth-piece of a
trumpet.
bocamanga, sf. sleeve-wrist.
bocanada, sf. mouthful of liquor.
bocateja, sf. end of ridge-tile.
bocel, sm. fluting ; fluting-plane.
bocina, sf. bugle-horn ; speaking-trum-
bocinero, sm. horn-blower.   [pet.
bocón, sm. wide-mouthed person ; braggart.   [heat ; blush.
bochorno, sm. sultry weather, scorching
bochornoso, sa, a. shameful, reproachful.

boda, sf. nuptials, pl. [warehouse.
bodega, sf. wine-cellar ; harvest of wine ;
bodegón, sm. chop-house, eating-house ;
tippling-house.
bodegonero, sm. eating-house keeper.
bodigo, sm. small loaf of finest flour.
bodijo, sm. unequal marriage ; hedge-marriage.
bodoque, sm. pellet ; dunce, idiot.
bodorrio, sm. *See* bodijo.
bodrio, sm. poor soup made of leavings ;
hodge-podge.
bofes, sm.pl. lungs, lights.
bofetada, sf. slap, box on the ear.
bofetón, sm. box on the ear ; folding-doors on the stage.
boga, sf. rowing ; cackerel (fish) ; estar en —, to be fashionable.
bogada, sf. stroke at rowing.
bogador, sm. rower.
bogar, v.n. to row, to paddle.
bohemio, sm. short cloak formerly worn by the guard of archers ; gipsy.
boj, sm. box, box-tree.
boja, sf. mug-wood, southern-wood.
bojar, bojear, v.a. to sail round an island *or* cape, and measure the coast-line thereof ; to scrape off the rough integuments of leather ; —, v.n. to measure around.
bojedal, sf. plantation of box-trees.
bojeo, sm. circumnavigation ; doubling of a cape.
bola, sf. ball ; globe ; bolus ; game of bowls ; (fam.) lie, fib ; escurrir la —, to take French leave, to run away.
bolazo, sm. blow of a bowl.
bolear, v.n. to knock the balls about (billiards) ; to bowl for a wager.
boleo, sm. Spanish dance ; bowling-green.
bolero, sm. a Spanish dance ; dancer ; runaway child. [let.
boleta, sf. entrance-ticket ; soldier's bill.
boletero, sm. ticket-collector.
boletín, sm. warrant given for the payment of money ; ticket for the quartering of soldiers ; bulletin.
boliche, sm. king-ball at skittles ; small fish caught in a drag-net near the shore ; drag-net.
bolichero, sm. keeper of a skittle alley.
bolillo, sm. small bowl ; bobbin ; starching-frame ; -s, pl. starched cuffs worn by counsellors of state ; paste-nuts.
bolina, sf. (mar.) bowline ; noise, scuffle ; ir á la —, to sail on a wind.
bolo, sm. nine-pin ; notch-board of a winding-staircase.
bolsa, sf. purse ; purse-net ; money ; Exchange.

bolsería, sf. purse-manufactory.
bolsillo, sm. pocket ; money ; fortune.
bolsista, sm. speculator on change.
bolso, sm. purse of money.
bolsor, sm. key-stone.
bollero, sm. pastry-cook.
bollo, sm. small Spanish cake.
bollón, sm. brass-headed nail.
bollonado, da, a. adorned with brass-headed nails.
bomba, sf. pump ; bomb ; dar á la —, to pump ; de fuego ó de vaho, steam engine ; — de apagar incendios, fire-engine.
bombarda, sf. bomb-ketch.
bombardear, v.a. to bombard.
bombardeo, sm. bombardment.
bombardero, sm. bombardier.
bombasí, sm. bombasine, dimity.
bombazo, sm. report of a bursting bomb.
bombo, sm. large drum.
bonachón, sm. good-natured person.
bonancible. a. calm, fair, serene (applied to the weather at sea). [perity.
bonanza, sf. fair weather at sea ; pros-
bonazo, za, a. good-natured, kind.
bondad, sf. goodness ; suavity ; kindness, courtesy ; exellence, healthfulness.
bondadoso, sa, a. bountiful. [ness.
bonetada, sf. salutation made by raising the hat. [secular clergyman.
bonete, sm. clerical hat ; college-cap ;
bonetero, sm. cap-maker.
bonico, ca, a. pretty good, passable.
bonitamente, ad. carefully, cunningly, quietly.
bonito, ta, a. pretty good, passable ; pretty ; pleasing, graceful.
boñiga, sf. cow-dung.
boqueada, sf. act of opening the mouth ; la última —, the last gasp.
boquear, v.n. to gape, to gasp ; to breathe one's last ; —, v.a. to pronounce, to utter a word.
boquera, sf. sluice in an irrigating canal.
boquerón, sm. anchovy ; large hole.
boquete, sm. gap, narrow entrance.
boquiabierto, ta, a. with the mouth open ; gaping.
boquiancho, cha, a. wide-mouthed.
boquiangosto, ta, a. narrow-mouthed.
boquiduro, ra, a. hard-mouthed (of horses): [plied to horses).
boquifresco, ca, a. fresh-mouthed (ap-
boquifruncido, da, a. having the mouth contracted.
boquihundido, da, a. having the mouth sunk in from age or want of teeth.
boquilla, sf. little mouth ; mouth-piece.
boquimuelle, a. soft-mouthed ; easily led.

boquirroto, ta. a. loquacious, garrulous.
boquirrubio, bia, a. (fig.) simple, easily imposed upon.
boquiseco, ca, a. dry-mouthed.
boquituerto, ta, a. wry-mouthed.
borbollar, v.n. to bubble out.
borbollón, borbotón, sm. bubbling; á borbollones, in hurry and confusion.
borceguí, sm. buskin, half-boot.
borda, sf. (mar.) board; hut.
bordado, sm. embroidery.
bordadora, sf. embroiderer.
bordadura, sf. embroidery.
bordaje, sm. side-planks of a ship.
bordar, v.a. to embroider; to do anything artistically.
borde, sm. border; margin; (mar.) board.   [ward.
bordear, v.n. (mar.) to ply to wind-
bordo, sm. board of a ship.
bordón, sm. pilgrim's staff; base of a stringed musical instrument.
bordura, sf. embroidery.
boreal, a. boreal, northern.
Bóreas, sm. Boreas, north-wind.
borla, sf. tassel; tuft; doctor's cap.
bornear, v.a. to bend, to turn or twist.
borní, sm. merlin, dwarf-falcon.
borona, sf. millet; maize.
borra, sf. yearling ewe; goat's hair; nap raised on cloth by shearers; hairy wool.
borracha, sf. leather-bag for wine.
borrachear, v.n. to get drunk habitually.
borrachera, sf. drunkenness; hard-drinking; revelry; madness.
borrachez, sf. intoxication.
borracho, cha, a. drunk, intoxicated; inflamed by passion.
borrachón, sm. great drinker, tippler.
borrachuela, sf. (bot.) ray-grass.
borrador, sm. foul copy; waste-book; blotting-book.
borraja, sf. (bot.) borage.
borrajear, v.a. to scribble.
borrar, v.a. to blot or efface; to blur; to cloud, to obscure.
borrasca, sf. storm, violent squall of wind; hazard, danger.
borrascoso, sa, a. stormy.
borrasquero, sm. reveller.
borregada, sf. large flock of sheep or lambs.
borrego, ga, sm. hogget; yearling lamb; simpleton; blockhead.
borreguero, sm. shepherd who tends lambs.
borrén, sm. panel of a saddle.
borrica, sf. she-ass, jenny-ass.
borricada, sf. drove of asses; cavalcade on asses; foolish action.

borrico, sm. ass, jack-ass; blockhead.
borrilla, sf. down or bloom on fruit.
borriqueño, ña, a. asinine.
borriquero, sm. ass-driver.   [dolt.
borro, sm. wether under two years old;
borrón, sm. ink-blot, blur; rough draft of a writing; first sketch of a painting; stain, tarnish; unworthy action.
borronear, v.a. to sketch; to scribble.
boscaje, sm. boscage; landscape (in painting).
bosque, sm. forest, grove.
bosquejar, v.a. to make a sketch of a painting; to explain a thought rather obscurely; to make a rough model of a figure.
bosquejo, sm. sketch; unfinished work.
bostezar, v.n. to yawn; to gape.
bostezo, sm. yawn, yawning.
bota, sf. wine-bag; boat.
botador, sm. thrower, driver; punch (tool); crow's bill.
botafuego, sm. linstock.
botalón, sm. (mar.) boom.
botana, sf. plug, stopple.
botánica, sf. botany.
botánico, ca, a. botanic.
botánico, botanista, sm. botanist.
botar, v.a. to cast, to fling, to launch.
botarate, sm. mad-cap, blustering person.
botarga, sf. gaskins; harlequin's costume: harlequin; motley dress of a harlequin; buffoon.
botasilla, sf. (mil.) signal given with a trumpet for the cavalry to saddle.
botavante, sm. (mar.) pike.   [boat.
bote, sm. thrust with a pike or lance;
botella, sf. bottle, flask.
botequin, sm. small boat.
botica, sf. apothecary's shop.
boticario, sm. apothecary.
botija, sf. earthen jar with a short and narrow neck.
botijo, botijón, sm. plump little child.
botillería, sf. shop for ices and cool drinks.   [liquids.
botillero, sm. preparer or seller of iced
botín, sm. buskin, half-boot; spatter-dash; gaiter; booty.
botinero, sm. (mil.) booty guard; one who makes or sells gaiters.
botiquín, sm. travelling medicine-chest.
botivoleo, sm. catching of a ball at the rebound.
botón, sm. button; (bot.) bud.
botonadura, sf. set of buttons for a suit of clothes.
botonazo, sm. thrust given with a foil.
botonero, ra, sm. & f. button-maker; button-seller.
bóveda, sf. arch, vault; crypt.

boya, sf. (mar.) buoy; float, piece of cork fastened to a fishing-net.

bóyada, sf. drove of oxen.

boyante, p. & a. buoyant, floating; sailing well; fortunate, successful.

boyar, v.n. (mar.) to take the water.

boyardo, sm. boyar.

boyera, boyériza, sf. ox-stall, cow-house.

boyero, sm. ox-herd.

boyezuelo, sm. young ox.

boyuno, na, a. belonging to cattle.

bozal, sm. muzzle; —, a. novice, inexperienced in business.

bozo, sm. down which precedes the beard; headstall of a horse.

brabante, sm. Brabant linen.

braceada, sf. violent movement of the arms.

braceaje, sm. coinage; coining of money.

bracear, v.n. to swing the arms; —, v.n. (mar.) to brace.

bracero, sm. day-labourer; strong-armed [man.

bracmán, sm. Brahmin. [(dog).

braco, ca, a. flat-nosed; —, s. pointer

braga, sf. breeches, pl.

bragadura, sf. fork of the body; fork of a pair of breeches. [persuaded.

bragazas, sm. (col.) one who is easily

braguero, sm. truss, braces.

bragueta, sf. front of breeches.

braguillas, sm. child breeched for the first time; dwarfish person.

brama, sf. rut.

bramadera, sf. rattle.

bramadero, sm. rutting-place. [linen.

bramante, sm. pack-thread; bramant

bramar, v.n. to roar, to bellow; to storm, to bluster; to be in a passion.

bramido, sm. cry uttered by wild beasts; clamour of persons enraged; roaring of the elements.

brancada, sf. drag-net, sweep-net.

brandal, sm. (mar.) back-stay.

branquia, sf. gill (of a fish).

brasa, sf. live coal; estar hecho unas -s. to be all in a blaze.

braserillo, sm. foot-warmer.

brasero, sm. brazier.

brasil, sm. Brazil-wood; rouge.

brasilado, da, a. ruddy. [etto.

brasilete, sm. Jamaica-wood, brazil-

bravamente, ad. bravely, gallantly, cruelly; finely, extremely well.

bravata, sf. bravado, boast, braggadocio.

braveador, ra, sm. & f. bully.

bravear, v.n. to bully, to hector.

braveza, sf. fury of the elements.

bravío, vía, a. ferocious, savage, wild; coarse; —, sm. fierceness, savageness.

bravo, va, a. brave, valiant; bullying; savage, fierce; rude, unpolished;

sumptuous; excellent, fine; ¡—! bravo! [boast.

bravura, sf. ferocity; courage; bravado,

braza, sf. fathom. [full.

brazada, sf. extension of the arms; arm-

brazado, sm. arm-full.

brazaje, sm. (mar.) number of fathoms, depth of water.

brazal, sm. bracer (piece of armour); biceps; arm pad of wood or leather (at ball-play).

brazalete, sm. bracelet.

brazo, sm. arm; branch of a tree; valour, strength, power; á —, man to man; á — partido, in unarmed conflict.

brazuelo, sm. small arm; fore-leg of beasts; branch of the mouth-bit of a bridle. [wrapping up wares.

brea, sf. pitch; tar; coarse canvas for

brear, v.a. to pitch; to tar; to vex, to plague; to play a joke upon.

brebaje, sm. beverage.

brecha, sf. (mil.) breach; impression made upon the mind; batir en —, (mil.) to make a breach; to persecute.

brega, sf. strife, contest; pun, jest, trick.

bregar, v.n. to contend, to struggle; to struggle with difficulties; —, v.a. to work up dough on a board with a rolling-pin.

breña, sf. craggy, broken ground full of brakes and brambles.

breñal, breñar, sm. briars, underwood.

breñoso, sa, a. craggy and brambled.

brete, sm. fetters, shackles; (fig.) perplexity; difficulties, pl. [acorn.

breva, sf. early black fig; early large

breval, sm. early fig-tree.

breve, sf. apostolic brief; (mus.) brief; —, a. brief, short; en —, shortly.

brevedad, sf. brevity, shortness, conciseness. [letter used in printing).

breviario, sm. breviary; brevier (small

brezal, sm. heath.

brezo, sm. (bot.) heath, heather, ling.

briaga, sf. rope made of bass-weed.

briba, sf. truancy, idleness. [cally.

bribón, ona, a. vagrant; knavish, ras-

bribonada, sf. knavery, mischievous trick.

bribonear, v.n. to rove; to lead a vagabond's life. [gar's trade.

bribonería, sf. life of a vagabond; beg-

bricho, sm. spangle.

brida, sf. bridle; horsemanship; (fig.) restraint, check, curb.

bridar, v.a. to bridle; to curb.

brigada, sf. brigade.

brigadier, sm. brigadier.

brillador, ra, a. brilliant, radiant.

brillante, a. brilliant; bright, shining; —, sm. diamond; brilliant.

brillar, v.n. to shine; to sparkle, to glisten; to shine in talents *or* merits.

brillo, sm. brilliancy, brightness.

brincador, ra, sm. & f. jumper, leaper.

brincar, v.n. to leap, to jump, to gambol; to omit something, to skip; to fly into a passion.

brinco, sm. leap, jump, bounce; gambol.

brindar, v.n. to drink one's health, to toast; —, v.a. to invite; to allure.

brindis, sf. health, toast.

brío, sm. strength, vigour; spirit, courage.

briosamente, ad. spiritedly, courageously.

brioso, sa, a. vigorous, full of spirit; courageous, lively.

brisa, sf. breeze.

brisca, sf. a card game.

briscar, v.a. to embroider with gold *or* silver twist mixed with silk.

broca, sf. reel for twist; drill; shoemaker's tack.

brocado, sm. gold or silver brocade; —, **da**, a. embroidered, like brocade.

brocal, sm. kerb-stone of a well; metal rim of the scabbard of a sword.

brocatel, sm. stuff made of hemp and silk.

bróculi, sm. broccoli.

brocha, sf. painter's brush, pencil.

brochada, sf. stroke with a pencil.

brochado, da, a. figured (of stuffs).

brochadura, sf. set of hooks and eyes.

broche, sm. clasp; brooch.

brochón, sm. plasterers' brush.

broma, sf. clatter, noise; joke, jest.

bromear, v.n. to jest; to bore with dull talking. [panion.

bromista, sm. merry fellow; jolly companion.

bronce, sm. bronze, brass; (poet.) trumpet.

bronceado, sm. bronzing. [pet.

broncear, v.a. to bronze.

broncería, sf. brass-works; brass-ware.

broncista, sm. worker in bronze.

bronco, ca, a. rough, coarse; hard, nonelastic; crusty; crabbed; rude, hoarse; harsh (to the ear).

bronquedad, sf. rudeness of manners; unmalleability.

broquel, sm. shield, buckler; (fig.) support, protection; **rajar -es**, to bully, to swagger.

brotadura, sf. budding.

brotar, v.n. to bud, to germinate; to gush, to rush out; to break out, to appear (applied to the small-pox, &c.).

broza, sf. bark; vegetable rubbish; brush-wood; farrago; printer's brush.

brozar, v.a. to brush type.

brucero, sm. brush-maker.

bruces, ad., á —, de —, face downwards.

bruja, sf. witch, hag.

brujear, v.n. to practise witchcraft.

brujería, sf. witchcraft.

brujidor, sm. glaziers' nippers.

brujir, v.a. to pare glass.

brujo, sm. sorcerer.

brújula, sf. sea-compass.

brujulear, v.a. to turn up one card after another; to discover by deduction; to conjecture.

brujuleo, sm. exposure of cards (at card games); close examination; conjecture. [ture.

brulote, sm. fire-ship.

bruma, sf. (mar.) haziness.

brumal, a. foggy.

brunela, sf. (bot.) prunella.

bruno, sm. prune.

bruñido, sm. polish, burnish.

bruñidor, sm. burnisher (person and instrument). [on rouge.

bruñir, v.a. to burnish; to polish; to put

bruñola, sf. prunello.

brusco, ca, a. rude, peevish, forward.

brutal, a. brutal, brutish; —, sm. brute, rude person. [tion.

brutalidad, sf. brutality; 'brutal action.

bruto, sm. brute; rude, immoral person; —, **ta**, a. coarse, unpolished, in a rough state.

bu, sm. bogey, word used by nurses to frighten children into silence.

buba, sf. pustule; -s, pl. venereal disease

bubático, ca, a. infected with the venereal disease. [of matter.

bubón, sm. large morbid tumour, full

buboso, sa, a. afflicted with pustules.

bucear, v.n. to dive.

buceo, sm. diving. [hound).

bucero, a. black-nosed (applied to a

bucle, sm. curl.

bucólica, sf. pastoral poetry; (fam.) food.

buchada, sf. draught *or* mouthful of liquor.

buche, sm. craw, crop, stomach of quadrupeds; mouthful; sucking ass; pucker *or* crease in clothes; (fig.) bosom.

buchete, sm. blown-out cheek.

buen, a. good.

buenamente, ad. easily, commodiously.

buenaventura, sf. fortune, good luck.

bueno, na, a. good; fair; fit, proper; sociable, agreeable; sound, healthy; useful; **de buenas á buenas**, freely, willingly; — **está**, enough, no more.

buenpasar, sm. comfortable subsistence.

buey, sm. ox, bullock.

¡buf! pooh, pooh!

bufa, sf. jeer, scoff, taunt, mock.

búfala, sf. female buffalo.

bufalino, na, a. belonging to buffaloes.

búfalo, sm. buffalo.
bufanda, sf. scarf.
bufar, v.n. to choke with anger; **to huff;** to snort.
bufete, sm. desk, writing-table; office of a lawyer.
bufido, sm. blowing of an animal; snorting of a horse; huff.
bufo, sm. buffoon on the stage; —, **fa,** a. comic; **ópera -a,** sf. comic opera.
bufón, sm. buffoon; jester; —, **ona,** a. funny, comical. [castic taunt.
bufonada, sf. buffoonery; raillery, sarbufonearse, v.r. to jest, to make fun of.
bufonería, sf. buffoonery.
buhedera, sf. embrasure, loop-hole.
buhero, sm. owl-keeper.
buho, sm. owl; an unsocial man.
buhonería, sf. pedlar's box.
buhonero, sm. pedlar, hawker.
buitre, sm. vulture. [a. vulturine.
buitrero, sm. vulture-fowler; —, **ra,**
bujería, sf. gewgaw, bauble, knick-knack.
bujeta, sf. box made of box-wood; perfume-box.
bujía, sf. wax-candle.
bula, sf. papal bull.
bulbo, sm. (bot.) bulb.
bulboso, sa, a. bulbous. [Santa Cruzada.
bulero, sm. distributor of bulls of the
buleto, sm. apostolic letter.
bulla, sf. confused noise, clatter; crowd; **meter —,** to make a noise.
bullaje, sm. crowd.
bullanguero, sm. rioter.
bullebulle, sm. busy-body.
bullicio, sm. bustle; tumult, uproar.
bullicioso, sa, a. lively, restless, noisy, clamorous, busy; turbulent; boister-
bullidor, ra, a. noisy, turbulent. [ous.
bullir, v.n. to boil; (fig.) to bustle, to fluster; —, v.a. to manage a business.
bullón, sm. boiling dye; metal boss on binding of a book.
bulto, sm. bulk; tumour, swelling; bust; luggage; (am.) baggage; **-s á la mano,** pl. (rail.) small luggage; **á —,** vaguely, without exactitude; **en —,** by the lump. [of buns.
buñolero, ra, sm. & f. maker or seller
buñuelo, sm. bun; pan-cake, fritter.

buque, sm. bulk, capacity of a ship; hull of a ship; vessel, ship.
burdel, sm. brothel.
burdo, da, a. coarse (of stuffs).
bureo, sm. amusement, diversion.
bureocracia, sf. bureaucracy.
bureocrático, a. bureaucratic.
burga, sf. thermal waters, pl.
burgomaestre, sm. burgomaster.
buril, sm. burine, graver.
burilada, sf. stroke of a burine.
buriladura, sf. engraving.
burilar, v.a. to engrave.
burla, sf. scoff, mockery, sneer; trick, slight deceit; hoax; **de -s,** in jest.
burlar, v.a. to mock, to scoff; to hoax, to abuse, to play tricks, to deceive; to frustrate; **-se,** to jest, to laugh at.
burlesco, ca, a. burlesque, comical, funny.
burlón, ona, sm. & f. wag.
burra, sf. she-ass.
burrada, sf. drove of asses; stupid action.
burrajo, sm. dry stable-dung for fuel.
burrero, sm. ass-keeper who sells asses' milk. [jack, saw-horse.
burro, sm. ass, donkey; stupid fellow;
burujo, sm. dregs of pressed olives.
busca, sf. search, examination.
buscada, sf. research, inquiry.
buscador, ra, sm. & f. searcher, investi-
buscapié, sm. (fig.) feeler. [gator.
buscapiés, sm. crackers (fireworks).
buscar, v.a. to seek, to search; to look for or after; to hunt after.
buscarruidos, sm. quarrelsome fellow.
buscavidas, sm. prying person, spy, busybody. [sharper,
buscón, sm. searcher; cheat, pilferer,
busilis, sm. point in question; main point of an argument.
busola, sf. sea-compass.
busto, sm. bust.
butaca, sf. arm-chair; fauteuil (in theatre). [gaskins.
butifarra, sf. sausage made in Catalonia;
buz, sm. **hacer el —,** to do homage or pay respect to.
buzo, sm. diver.
buzón, sm. conduit, canal; letter-box; post-box; cover of a cistern, pond, jar, &c.

C

cabal, a. just, exact; perfect, complete, accomplished. [artifice.
cábala, sf. rabbinical learning; intrigue,
cabalgada, sf. horseback excursion; cavalcade; (mil.) foray.
cabalgador, sm. rider; horseman.

cabalgadura, sf. sumpter-mule, sumpter-horse, beast of burden.
cabalgar, v.n. to parade on horseback; to take part in a cavalcade; to spring
cabalista, sm. cabalist. [to horse.
cabalístico, ca, a. cabalistic.

caballa, sf. horse-mackerel (fish).

caballaje, sm. stud of stallions. [horses.

caballar, a. belonging to *or* resembling

caballejo, sm. trave, wooden frame for shoeing unruly horses.   [man.

caballerear, v.n. to set up for a gentle-

caballeresco, ca, a. knightly; chivalrous.

caballerete, sm. spruce young gentleman.

caballería, sf. cavalry; cavalry-horse; chivalry; knighthood; knight-errantry.

caballeriza, sf. stable; number of horses, mules, &c., standing in a stable.

caballerizo, sm. head-groom of a stable.

caballero, sm. knight; cavalier; gentleman; rider; horseman; horse-soldier; **— andante,** knight-errant.

caballeroso, sa, a. noble, gentlemanlike.

caballerote, sm. graceless, unpolished gentleman.

caballete, sm. ridge of a roof; ridge of a ploughed field; horse (instrument of torture); painter's easel; hemp-brake; trestle.   [horse.

caballico, sm. hobby-horse, rocking-

caballo, sm. horse; (at chess) knight; á **—,** on horseback.

caballuno, na, a. belonging to a horse.

cabaña, sf. shepherd's hut, cottage; hovel; flock of ewes; drove of asses for carrying corn; line drawn on a billiard-table, within which the players must play.

cabañal, sm. mule *or* sheep track (of travelling *or* migratory herds).

cabañero, ra, a. belonging to the droves of travelling mules and asses.

cabañil, sm. keeper of asses for carrying corn.

cabecear, v.n. to nod with sleep; to shake one's head; (mar.) to pitch.

cabeceo, sm. nod, shaking of the head.

cabecera, sf. upper end of a hall; bed-pillow; vignette.

cabecilla, sm. ringleader.

cabecita, sf. wrong-headed person.

cabellera, sf. long hair spread over the shoulders; wig; tail of a comet.

cabello, sm. hair of the head.

cabelludo, da, a. hairy, overgrown with hair.

caber, v.n. to fit (as into a box), to find room; **—,** v.a. to contain, to hold.

cabestraje, sm. bridle-money; money paid to a driver for conducting cattle to market.

cabestrar, v.a. to halter; **—,** v.n. to fowl with a stalking-ox.   [halter.

cabestrear, v.n. to be led easily by the

cabestrillo, sm. sling, splint; necklace; gold chain.

cabestro, sm. halter; bell-ox.

cabeza, sf. head; top; end; **chief;** leader; beginning of a thing.

cabezada, sf. head-shake; pitching of a ship; head-stall of a bridle; head-band of a book; upper-leather of a boot.

cabezal, sm. pillow; compress.

cabezo, sm. summit of a hill.

cabezón, sm. collar of a shirt; opening in a garment for the passage of the head; nose-band.   [head.

cabezorro, sm. large disproportioned

cabezudo, da, a. large-headed; thick-headed; head-strong, obstinate.

cabezuela, sf. small head; simpleton; coarse flour; rose-bud.

cabida, sf. content, capacity; **tener — con una persona,** to be in high favour with one.

cabildo, sm. chapter (of a cathedral *or* collegiate church); meeting of a chapter; corporation of a town.

cabizbajo, ja, cabizcaído, da, a. crest-fallen; pensive; thoughtful.

cabiztuerto, ta, sm. wry-headed; hypo-**cable,** sm. (mar.) cable.   [critical.

cabo, sm. extremity; cape, head-land.

cabotaje, sm. coasting-trade; pilotage.

cabra, sf. goat.

cabrahigo, sm. wild fig-tree.   [sold.

cabrería, sf. place where goats' milk is

cabrero, sm. goat-herd.

cabrestante, sm. (mar.) capstan.

cabrilla, sf. prawn; **-s,** pl. Pleiades (constellation); heat-marks on the legs.

cabrio, sm. (arch.) rafter, roof-spar;

cabrío, sm. flock of goats.   [chevron.

cabriola, sf. caper; gambol.

cabriol(e)ar, v.n. to cut capers; to curvet.

cabriolé, sm. cabriolet, gig.

cabrita, sf. small female kid; kid-skin.

cabritero, sm. dealer in kids; seller of kid-skins.

cabritilla, sf. dressed kid-skin.

cabrito, sm. kid.

cabrón, sm. buck, he-goat; one who consents to the adultery of his wife.

cabronada, sf. infamous action which a man permits against his own honour.

cabruno, na, a. goatish.

cacahual, cacaotal, sm. plantation of chocolate-trees.

cacao, sm. (bot.) smooth-leaved chocolate nut-tree; cocoa.

cacareador, ra, sm. & f. crowing cock; cackling hen; cackler; braggart.

cacarear, v.n. to crow, to cackle; to brag, to boast.

cacareo, sm. crowing of a cock, cackling of a hen; boast, brag.

cacera, sf. canal, channel, conduit.
cacería, sf. hunting-party.
cacerina, sf. cartridge-box.
cacerola, sf. stewing-pan.   [caries.
caceta, sf. small pan used by apothe-
cacique, sm. Cazique (tribal chief of
   American Indians).
caco, sm. pickpocket, coward.
cacofonía, sf. harsh unharmonious sound.
cacha, sf. handle of a knife.
cachalote, sm. sperm-whale.
cachamarín, sm. (mar.) lugger.
cachar, v.a. to break in pieces.
cacharro, sm. coarse earthen pot; sherd.
cachaza, sf. inactivity, tardiness.
cachemira, sf. cashmere.
cachera, sf. coarse, shaggy cloth.
cachete, sm. cheek; blow with the fist.
cachetero, sm. short, broad, sharp-
   pointed knife; bull-fighter who kills
   the bulls with the cachetero.
cachetudo, da, a. chubby-cheeked.
cachicán, sm. farm-overseer.
cachidiablo, sm. hobgoblin.
cachigordete, a. thick and short.
cachiporra, sf. cudgel.
cachivache, sm. broken crockery-ware,
   old trumpery; despicable fellow.
cacho, sm. slice, piece (applied to lemons,
   oranges, &c.); game of chance at
   cards.   [beasts.
cachonda, a. ruttish, proud (of female
cachorrillo, sm. pocket-pistol.
cachorro, rra, sm. & f. whelp or puppy;
   cub (of any animal).
cachucha, sf. Spanish dance and its tune.
cachuela, sf. fricassee made of the livers
   and lights of rabbits.
cachupín, sm. Spanish settler in Mexico.
cada, pn. every; every one; each.
cadalso, sm. scaffold.
cadarzo, sm. floss-silk.
cadáver, sm. corpse, cadaver.
cadavérico, cá, a. cadaverous.
cadena, sf. chain; series, link.
cadencia, sf. cadence.
cadente, a. declining; harmonious, mellifluous (of declamation).
cadera, sf. hip.
caderillas, sf.pl. crinoline, hoop.
cadete, sm. (mil.) cadet.
caducar, v.n. to dote, to be senile; to
   lapse (of a legacy, etc.).
caduceo, sm. caduceus; herald's staff.
caducidad, sf. decrepitude; fragility.
caduco, ca, a. worn out; enfeebled by
   age, decrepit; perishable; mal —,
   sm. epilepsy.
caedizo, za, a. tottering, frail.
caedura, sf. loose threads dropping from
   the loom in weaving.

caer, v.n. to fall; to tumble down; to
   lapse; to befall, to happen, to come to
   pass; to die.
café, sm. coffee-tree; coffee; coffee-
   house.
cafetera, sf. coffee-pot.
cafetero, sm. coffee-house keeper.
cafeto, sm. coffee-tree.
cáfila, sm. multitude of people, animals
   or other things; caravan.
cafre, a. savage, inhuman; rude, uncivil.
cagafierro, sm. scoria, dross of iron.
cagajón, sm. horse-dung.
cagalar, sm. rectum.   [and mice.
cagarruta, sf. dung of sheep, goats,
cagatinta, sm. term of contempt for
   attorney's clerks.
cagón, ona, sm. & f. person afflicted with
   diarrhœa; cowardly person.
cahiz, sm. measure of corn (about 12
   English bushels).
cahizada, sf. tract of land which requires
   about one cahiz of grain to be properly
   sown.
caída, sf. fall, falling; declivity, descent.
caídos, sm.pl. arrears of rent or taxes.
caimán, sm. caiman, alligator; cunning
   man.   [fall.
caimiento, sm. low spirits; languidness;
caja, sf. box, case, coffin; chest in
   which money is kept; exchange-
   office; libro de —, cash-book.
cajero, sm. cashier, cash-keeper.
cajeta, sf. snuff-box; poor-box.
cajetín, sm. very small box.
cajista, sm. compositor.
cajón, sm. chest of drawers; locker;
   book-shelf.
cal, sf. lime; — viva, quicklime.
cala, sf. creek, small bay; small piece
   of melon, &c.; hole made in a wall to
   judge of its thickness; (mar.) hold.
calabacera, sf. pumpkin-plant; pumpkin seller.
calabacero, sm. retailer of pumpkins.
calabacín, sm. small, young, tender
   pumpkin.
calabacino, sm. wine-gourd.
calabaza, sf. gourd, calabash, pumpkin;
   — vinatera, bottle-calabash.
calabazada, sf. blow with the head.
calabazate, sm. preserved pumpkin.
calabozo, sm. dungeon.
calada, sf. rapid flight of birds of prey.
calado, sm. open work in metal, wood or
   linen.   [ment
calador, sm. probe (surgeon's instru-
calafate, sm. (mar.) calker.
calafatear, v.a. (mar.) to calk.
calafateo, sm. (mar.) calking.
calafatería, sf. (mar.) calking.

calambre, sm. spasm, cramp.
calamidad, sf. misfortune, calamity, misery.   [tunate.
calamitoso, **sa**, a. calamitous, unfor-
cálamo, sm. (bot.) sweet flag; pen; shepherd's flute; **currente** —, off-hand.   [what fuddled.
calamocano, a. estar ó ir —, to be some-
calandrajo, sm. rag hanging down from a garment; ragamuffin.
calandria, sf. calender.
calaña, sf. specimen; character, quality.
calar, v.a. to penetrate, to pierce; to discover a design; — **las cubas**, to gage a barrel; **-se**, to introduce one's self; to insinuate one's self into; to stoop (of a hawk).   [rake.
calavera, sf. skull; hot-brained fellow.
calaverada, sf. ridiculous, foolish action.
calaverear, v.n. to act foolishly.
calcañar, sm. heel-bone.
calcar, v.a. to copy a drawing by pressing, to trace; to trample on.
calcáreo, **rea**, a. calcareous.
calce, sm. tire of a wheel.
calceta, sf. stocking.
calcetería, sf. trade of a hosier.
calcetero, **ra**, sm. one who makes, mends or sells thread-stockings; knitter.
calcina, sf. mortar.
calcinar, v.a. to calcine.
calco, sm. counter-drawing, tracing.
calcografía, sf. art of copper-engraving.
calculable, a. calculable.   [tion.
calculación, sf. calculation, computa-
calculador, sm. calculator, computer.
calcular, v.a. to calculate, to reckon, to compute.
cálculo, sm. calcule, calculation, computation; (med.) gravel.
calda, sf. warmth, heat; warming or heating; **-s**, pl. hot baths.
caldear, v.a. to weld iron; to warm, to heat.
caldera, sf. caldron, kettle, boiler; **las -s de Pero Botero**, (col.) hell.
calderada, sf. a caldron-full.
caldereria, sf. brazier's shop.
calderero, sm. brazier, copper-smith.
caldereta, sf. small caldron; — **de agua bendita**, holy-water fount.
calderilla, sf. holy-water fount; copper-
caldero, sm. caldron.   [coin.
calderón, sm. copper, large caldron; (mus.) fermata-sign.
calderuela, sf. dark lantern (used by sportsmen to drive partridges into the
caldo, sm. broth.   [net).
caldoso, **sa**, a. having much broth or gravy.   [month.
calendas, sf.pl. calends, first day of every

calendario, sm. almanac, calendar.
calentador, sm. warming-pan.
calentar, v.a. to warm; to heat; **-se**, to grow hot, to dispute warmly; to be ruttish or proud (of beasts).
calentura, sf. fever.
calenturiento, **ta**, a. feverish; fever-sick.
calera, sf. lime-kiln.
calería, sf. lime-kiln.
calero, sm. lime-burner.
calesa, sf. calash, cab.   [man.
calesero, sm. driver of a calash, cab-
calesín, sm. single horse-chaise.
caletre, sm. understanding, judgment, discernment.
calibre, sm. calibre; (fig.) sort, kind.
calidad, sf. quality, condition, character: kind.
cálido, **da**, a. warming, heat-giving.
caliente, a. hot; fiery, vehemently; **en** —, on the spot, immediately.
califa, sm. caliph.
califato, sm. caliphate.
calificación, sf. qualification; judgment, censure; proof.
calificar, v.a. to qualify; to authorise; to attest; to ennoble; **-se**, to prove one's noble birth.
caligrafía, sf. calligraphy.
calígrafo, sm. one who writes a beautiful hand.
cáliz, sm. chalice; flower-cup.
calizo, **za**, a. calcareous.
calma, sf. calm; calmness, smooth sea.
calmante, sm. (med.) anodyne.
calmar, v.a. to calm, to quiet, to pacify; —, v.n. to be becalmed.
calmoso, **sa**, a. calm; tranquil.
calofriarse, v.r. to shiver with fever.
calofrío, sm. shivering with fever.
calor, sm. heat, hotness, ardour, fieriness
calórico, sm. caloric.
calorífero, sm. heating apparatus.
calumnia, sf. calumny.   [slanderer.
calumniador, **ra**, sm. & f. calumniator
calumniar, v.a. to calumniate, to slander
calumnioso, **sa**, a. calumnious, slanderous.
caluroso, **sa**, a. warm, hot; lively.
calva, sf. bald pate.
calvario, sm. Calvary; (fig.) debts.
calvicie, sf. baldness.
calvinismo, sm. Calvinism.
calvinista, sm. Calvinist.
calvo, **va**, a. bald; barren.
calza, sf. trousers, pl.; stockings, pl.
calzada, sf. causeway, highway.
calzado, sm. any kind of shoe or foot-covering.
calzador, sm. shoeing-horn.
calzadura, sf. putting on of shoes; felloe of a cart-wheel.

calzar, v.a. to shoe ; to strengthen with iron *or* wood ; to stop a wheel ; to carry a ball of a certain size (of fire-arms).

calzón, sm. breeches, pl.

calzonazo, sm. (col.) weak fellow.

calzoncillos, sm.pl. drawers.

callada, sf. dish of tripe ; **de —, á las -s,** ad. without noise, privately.   [less.

callado, da, a. silent, reserved, noise-

callandico, ad. in a low voice ; silently.

callar, v.n. to keep silence, to be silent, to hold one's tongue ; to conceal, to

calle, sf. street ; lane ; alley.   [hush.

callear. v.a. to clear the walks in a vineyard of loose branches.

calleja, sf. lane, narrow passage.

callejear, v.a. to loiter about the streets.

callejero, ra, a. loitering, rambling.

callejón, sm. narrow path.

callejuela, sf. lane, narrow passage ; subterfuge, shift.   [tripe.

callo, sm. corn ; wen ; callus ; **-s,** pl.

callosidad, sf. callosity.

calloso, sa, a. callous ; horny.

cama, sf. bed, couch ; litter.

camachuelo, sm. linnet.

camada, sf. brood of young animals ; **— de ladrones,** nest of rogues.

camafeo, sm. cameo.

camal, am. halter.

camaleón, sm. chameleon.

camaleopardo, sm. cameleopard.

camamila, sf. camomile.   [decades.

camándula, sf. rosary of one or three

camandulería, sf. hypocrisy, insincerity, dissimulation.

camandulero, a. full of tricks, hypocritical.

cámara, sf. hall ; chamber ; king's court.

camarada, sm. comrade, companion.

camaranchón, sm. garret.   [houses.

camarera, sf. head waiting-maid in great

camarero, sm. valet de chambre.

camarilla, sf. coterie of private advisers of the king.

camarín, sm. shrine behind an altar.

camarista, sm. a member of the supreme council of **la Cámara ; —,** sf. maid of honour of the queen of Spain.

camarón, sm. shrimp.

camarote, sm. cabin.

camasquince, sm. (col.) meddler.

camastrón, sm. cunning fellow.   [ter.

cambalache, sm. traffic by exchange, bar-

cambalachear, v.a. to barter.

cambalachero, sm. barterer.

cambiable, a. fit to be exchanged.

cambiar, v.a. to barter, to exchange ; to change ; to alter ; to give or take money on bills.

cambija, sf. basin of water.

cambio, sm. barter, exchange ; **course** of exchange ; bank ; alteration, change.

cambista, sm. money-changer.

cambray, sm. cambric, fine linen.

cambrón, sm. common buck-horn.

cambronal, sm. thicket of briers, brambles, and thorns.

camella, sf. she-camel ; trough.

camellero, sm. driver of camels.

camello, sm. camel.   [plough.

camellón, sm. ridge turned up by the

camilla, sf. pallet ; couch ; clothes-horse.

caminador, sm. good walker.

caminante, sm. traveller, walker.

caminar, v.n. to travel ; to walk, to

caminata, sf. long walk.   [march.

camino, sm. highroad ; way ; **— real,** highway ; **de —,** in one's way, going along.

camisa, sf. shirt ; shift, chemise.

camisola, sf. ruffled shirt.

camisolín, sm. shirt-front.

camisote, sm. coat of mail.

camorra, sf. quarrel, dispute.

camorrista, sm. & f. quarrelsome person.

campamento, sm. (mil.) encampment, camp, lager.

campana, sf. bell.

campanada, sf. sound of a bell ; (fig.) scandal.

campanario, sm. belfry.

campanear, v.a. to peal ; to divulge.

campanela, sf. rapid rotation upon one foot in a Spanish dance.

campaneo, sm. bell-ringing, chime ; affected manner of walking.

campanero, sm. bell-founder ; bell-man.

campanilla, sf. hand-bell ; uvula.

campanillazo, sm. signal given with a bell.

campanillear, v.a. to ring a small bell often.

campante, p. & a. excelling, surpassing.

campanudo, da, a. wide, puffed up ; pompous, high-sounding.

campánula, sf. bell-flower.   [paign.

campaña, sf. level country ; (mil.) cam-

campar, v.n. to encamp ; to excel.

campeador, sm. warrior ; surname of the Cid.

campear, v.n. to be in the field ; to frisk about in the fields ; to excel.   [wood.

campeche, sm. Campeachy-wood, cam-

campeón, sm. champion.

campesino, na, campestre, a. rural.

campiña, sf. flat tract of arable land.

campo, sm. country ; field ; camp ;

camposanto, sm. cemetery.   [ground.

camuesa, sf. pippin.

camueso, sm. pippin-tree ; simpleton.

can, sm. dog; (poet.) dog-star.
cana, sf. measure (=two ells).
canal, sm. channel, canal.
canas, sf.pl. grey hair.
canalizar, v.a. to canalise.
canalizo, sm. narrow channel, strait.
canalón, sm. large gutter.
canalla, sf. mob, rabble, populace.
canana, sf. cartridge-box.
canapé, sf. canopy, sofa.
canario, sm. canary-bird.
canasta, sf. basket, hamper.
canastilla, sf. small basket.
canasto, sm. large basket.
cancamusa, sf. trick, fraud.
cancel, sm. screen (at church-doors).
cancelación, canceladura, sf. cancellation, erasion.
cancelar, v.a. to cancel, to expunge; to efface from the memory.
cancelaría, sf. papal chancery, place where grants and licences are expe-
caucelario, sm. chancellor.   [dited.
cáncer, sm. cancer (ulcer).   [zodiac.
Cáncer, sm. Cancer, Crab (sign of the
cancerarse, v.r. to be afflicted with a cancer.
canceroso, sa, a. cancerous.
canciller, sm. chancellor.
canción, sf. song, ballad.
cancionero, sm. song-book.
candado, sm. padlock.
candela, sf. candle, lamp.
candelabro, sm. candlestick.
Candelaria, sf. Candlemas.
candelero, sm. candlestick; chandelier.
candente, a. red-hot.
candidato, sm. candidate.   [simple.
cándido, da, a. white, snowy; candid;
candil, sm. kitchen- or stable-lamp.
candilada, sf. oil or grease spot.
candilejas, sf.pl. footlights.
candonga, sf. servile civility (intended to deceive); old mule no longer fit for service.
candongo, ga, a. cajoling, fawning.
candonguear, v.a. to jeer.
candor, sm. candour, ingenuousness.
canela, sf. cinnamon.
canelo, sm. cinnamon-tree.
canelón, sm. icicle (hanging from the eaves); sugar-stick with a slice of cinnamon.
canevás, sm. canvas.
cangreja, sf. brig-sail, gaff-sail.
cangrejo, sm. craw-fish, crab.
cangrena, sf. gangrene.   [grene.
cangrenarse, v.r. to be affected with gan-
cangrenoso, sa, a. gangrenous.
canguro, sm. kangaroo.
caníbal, sm. cannibal, man-eater.

canícula, sf. dog-days.
canijo, ja, a. weak, sickly.   [spool.
canilla, sf. shin-bone; tap of a cask;
caninez, sf. canine appetite.
canino, na, a. canine; hambre -a, sf. canine appetite.   [Indies.
caniquí, sf. fine muslin (from the East
canje, sm. interchange, exchange.
canjear, v.a. to exchange.
cano, na, a. hoary, grey-headed.
canoa, sf. canoe.
canoero, sm. one who steers a canoe.
canon, sm. canon (law); catalogue; (mus.) canon.
canonesa, sf. canoness.
canongía, sf., canonicato, sm. canonry; canonicate.
canónico, ca, a. canonical.
canónigo, sm. canon, prebendary.
canonista, sm. canonist.
canonización, sf. canonisation.
canonizar, v.a. to canonise.
canoro, ra, a. canorous, tuneful.
canoso, sa, a. hoary, grey-headed.
cansado, da, a. weary, wearied, tired; tedious, tiresome.
cansancio, sm. lassitude, fatigue.
cansar, v.a. to weary, to fatigue; to harass, to molest; -se, to grow weary.
cantable, a. tunable.
cantada, sf. (mus.) cantata.
cantaleta, sf. pun, jest, joke.
cantar, sm. song; -es, pl. Solomon's Song; —, v.a. to sing; to creak; (at cards) to call out the score.
cántara, sf. pitcher; wine-measure (containing about 32 pints).
cantárida, sf. Spanish fly, cantharis.
cantarín, sm. opera-singer; fellow who is always singing.
cantarina, sf. opera-singer.
cántaro, sm. pitcher; ballot-box; llover á -s, to rain heavily, to pour.
cantatriz, sf. songstress.
cantera, sf. quarry.
cantería, sf. trade of a stone-cutter.
cantero, sm. stone-cutter.
cántico, sm. canticle; — de los -s, the song of Solomon.
cantidad, sf. quantity; number.
cantimplora, sf. syphon; vessel for cooling liquors.
cantina, sf. canteen.
cantinela, sf. short song; irksome repetition of a subject.
cantinero, sm. butler.
cantizal, sm. stony ground.
canto, sm. stone; edge; singing, song; canto (poet.).
cantón, sm. corner; canton.
cantonearse. See contonearse.

cantonera, sf. corner-clips.

cantor, ra, sm. & f. singer ; songstress.

cantorral, sm. place full of stones.

canturía, sf. vocal music.

canutillo, sm. stalk of a straw.

caña, sf. cane, reed ; stalk ; — dulce, sugar-cane.

cañada, sf. dale, glen, cleft.

cañal, sm. pond-grate ; fish-garth.

cañamar, sm. hemp-field.

cañamiel, sm. sugar-cane.

cáñamo, sm. hemp ; hempen cloth.

cañamón, sm. hemp-seed.

cañavera, sf. common reed-grass.

cañaveral, sm. reed-plot, reed-bank.

cañazo, sm. blow with a cane.

cañería, sf. conduit of water, water-pipe.

cañiza, sf. kind of coarse linen.

cañizo, sm. hurdle.

caño, sm. tube, pipe ; sewer.

cañón, sm. tube, pipe ; cannon.

cañonazo, sm. cannon-shot.

cañonear, v.a. to cannonade.

cañoneo, sm. cannonade.

cañonera, sf. embrasure.

cañonería, sf. pipes of an organ.

cañutillo, sm. bugle (glass ornaments).

cañuto, sm. internode of a cane, phalange ; pipe, tube.

caoba, sf. mahogany.

caos, sm. chaos ; confusion.

capa, sf. cloak ; mantle ; layer, stratum ; cover ; pretext ; de — y gorra, in a plain manner.

capacidad, sf. capacity ; extent ; talent.

capachero, sm. basket-maker.

capacho, sm. hamper ; frail.

capada, sf. quantity portable in a person's cloak.

capador, sm. sow-gelder ; gelder's whistle.

capadura, sf. castration, gelding.

capar, v.a. to geld ; (fig.) to castrate, to curtail.

caparazón, sm. caparison.

caparra, sf. earnest-money.

caparrosa, s. copperas.   [of the mint.

capataz, sm. overseer, foreman ; warden

capaz, a. capacious, capable, spacious, roomy ; fit, apt ; ingenious, clever.

capazo, sm. rush-basket, frail.

capcionar, v.a. to seize, to arrest.

capcioso, sa, a. captious.

capear, v.a. to rob a passenger of his cloak ; to flourish one's cloak before a bull ; —, v.n. (mar.) to lay to.

capelo, sm. dues received in ancient times by bishops from their clergy ; red hat (of a cardinal).

capellada, sf. toe-piece of a shoe.

capellán, sm. chaplain ; almoner.

capellanía, sf. chaplainship.

capellar, sm. Moorish cloak.

capellina, sf. (mil.) spike-helmet ; hood worn by country-people.

capeo, sm. challenging of a bull with a cloak.

capero, sm. priest who wears the cope or pluvial in churches.

caperuza, sf. hood.   [parasite.

capigorrista, capigorrón, sm. vagabond ;

capilar, a. capillary.

capilla, sf. hood ; cowl ; chapel.

capilleja, sf. small chapel.   [for sewing.

capillejo, sm. small hood ; skein of silk

capiller(o), sm. sexton, churchwarden.

capillo, sm. child's cap ; hood of a hawk.

capilludo, da, a. resembling a monk's cowl.   [finger.

capirotazo, sm. fillip, blow with the

capirote, sm. hood.

capisayo, sm. short cloak.

capiscol, sm. precentor.

capitación, sf. poll-tax.

capital, sm. capital, stock ; sum of money put out at interest ; —, sf. capital, metropolis ; —, a. capital, principal.

capitalista, sm. capitalist.

capitalizar, v.a. to capitalize.

capitán, sm. captain.

capitana, sf. flag-ship.

capitanear, v.a. to be in command ; to lead.

capitanía, sf. captainship, captaincy.

capitel, sm. capital (of a column).

capitolio, sm. capitol.

capítula, sf. (eccl.) lesson, part of the Scriptures read at divine service.

capitulación, sf. capitulation ; agreement ; -ones, pl. matrimonial contract.

capitular, v.a. to conclude an agreement ; (mil.) to capitulate ; to. accuse by public authority ; —, v.n. to sing prayers at divine service ; —, sm. capitular ; —, a. capitulary.

capitulario, sm. antiphonal, antiphoner.

capítulo, sm. chapter of a cathedral ; assembly of religious orders ; chapter (section of a book).

capolar, v.a. to mince.

capón, sm. eunuch ; gelding ; capon ; anchor-stopper.

caponar, v.a. to geld ; to curtail ; to tie up vine-branches.

caponera, sf. coop (for capons).

caporal, sm. chief, ringleader ; (mil.) corporal.

capotear, v.a. to hoodwink.

capote, sm. cloak.

capotón, sm. large wide coat.

capotudo, da, a. frowning.

Capricornio, sm. Capricorn (sign of the zodiac).

capricho, sm. caprice, whim, fancy; (mus.) irregular but pleasing composition. [obstinate.

caprichoso, sa, a. capricious, whimsical;

caprichudo, da, a. stubborn, capricious.

caprino, na, a. goatish.

cápsula, sf. (bot.) capsule.

captar, v.a. to captivate.

captura, sf. capture, seizure.

capucha, sf. circumflex; cap, fur-cap, cowl, hood of a woman's cloak; monk's hood.

capuchina, sf. (bot.) great Indian cress.

capuchino, sm. Capuchin monk; —, **na,** a. appertaining to Capuchin friars.

capucho, sm. cowl or hood forming part of a monk's dress.

capullo, sm. cocoon; bud.

cara, sf. face, visage; — **á** —, face to face.

carabina, sf. carbine, carabine.

carabinero, sm. carabinier. [chub.

cárabo, sm. horned owl; earth-beetle;

caracol, sm. snail; winding staircase.

caracolear, v.n. to caracole.

carácter, sm. character; quality; condition; hand-writing.

característico, ca, a. characteristic.

caracterizar, v.a. to characterize.

caramanchón, sm. garret.

carámbano, sm. icicle; flake of ice.

carambola, sf. cannon (at billiards); trick. [liards).

carambolear, v.n. to cannon (at billiards).

caramelo, sm. caramel.

caramente, ad. dearly. [ing.

caramillo, sm. small flute; tale-carrying.

carantamaula, sf. hideous mask.

carantoña, sf. hideous mask; painted old woman.

carantoñero, sm. wheedler, cajoler.

carátula, sf. pasteboard-mask; histrionic [art.

caravana, sf. caravan.

caravanera, sf. caravansary.

caray, sm. tortoise-shell.

carbón, sm. charcoal; — **de piedra,** coal.

carbonada, sf. grilled meat; kind of pancake.

carboncillo, sm. charcoal-pencil.

carbonear, v.n. to burn charcoal.

carbonera, sf. coal-pit, coal-mine.

carbonería, sf. coal-yard; coal-shed.

carbonero, sm. charcoal-burner; coal-merchant.

carbónico, ca, a. carbonic.

carbonilla, sf. coal-dust.

carbonizar, v.a. to carbonise.

carbono, sm. (chem.) carbon. [pustule.

carbunclo, carbunco, sm. carbuncle; red

carcaj, sm. quiver, socket.

carcajada, sf. horse-laugh.

carcamal, sm. nick-name for old people.

carcaño, sm. heel-bone.

cárcel, sf. prison, gaol, jail.

carcelaje, sm. prison-fees.

carcelería, sf. imprisonment.

carcelero, sm. jailor.

cárcola, sf. treadle.

carcoma, sf. wood-worm; dust made by the wood-louse; grief; anxious concern.

carcomer, v.a. to gnaw, to corrode; **-se,** to grow worm-eaten.

carcomido, da, a. worm-eaten. [wool).

carda, sf. teazel, teasel; card (for

cardador, sm. carder, comber.

cardadura, sf. carding.

cardar, v.a. to card (wool); to raise the wool on cloth with a teasel.

cardenal, sm. cardinal; cardinal bird; weal, bruise.

cardenalato, sm. cardinalate. [dinal.

cardenalicio, cia, a. belonging to a cardenencha, sf. teasel; card, comb.

cardenillo, sm. rust of copper; verdigris.

cárdeno, na, a. livid.

cardero, sm. card-maker.

cardillo, sm. golden thistle.

cardinal, a. cardinal, principal.

cardo, sm. thistle.

cardón, sm. (bot.) teasel. [ing wool.

carducha, sf. large iron comb for comb-

carduzador, sm. carder.

carduzar, v.a. to card or comb wool.

carear, v.a. to confront criminals; to compare; to tend a drove of cattle; **-se,** to assemble for business.

carecer, v.n. to want.

carena, sf. careening; careen; ship.

carenar, v.a. to careen a ship.

careo, sm. (law) confrontation.

carero, ra, a. in the habit of selling things dear.

carestía, sf. scarcity, want; famine; dearness.

careta, sf. pasteboard-mask.

careto, ta, a. blazed (applied to horses).

carey, sm. tortoise-shell.

carga, sf. load, freight, pack; cargo; charge (of a fire-arm); impost, tax; (fig.) burden of the mind, heaviness.

cargadas, sf.pl. a game at cards.

cargadero, sm. loading-place.

cargadilla, sf. increase of a debt newly contracted. [mer.

cargador, sm. freighter; loader; ram-

cargamento, sm. (mar.) cargo.

cargar, v.a. to load, to burden, to freight; to attack the enemy; to charge a gun; to clog; to impose taxes; to impeach.

cargazón, sf. cargo (of a ship) ; heaviness of the head.

cargo, sm. burden, loading ; employment, dignity ; office ; charge, care ; obligation ; accusation.

carguío, sm. cargo of merchandize.

cariaguileño, ña, a. long-faced and crook-nosed.

cariampollado, a. round-faced.

cariancho, cha, a. broad-faced, chubby.

cariarse, v.r. to decay (a tooth or bone).

caribe, sm. savage.

caricatura, sf. caricature.

caricia, sf. caress.

caricioso, sa, a. a fondling, caressing. [pl.

caridad, sf. charity ; benevolence ; alms,

caridoliente, a. sad-faced.

caries, sf. caries, cariosity. [face.

carifruncido, da, a. having a wrinkled

carigordo, da, a. full-faced.

carilargo, ga, a. long-visaged.

carilucio, cia, a. smooth-faced.

carilla, sf. mask used by bee-keepers.

carilleno, na, a. full-faced. [ioned.

carinegro, gra, a. swarthy-complex-

cariño, sm. fondness, tenderness ; endearing expression. [loving.

cariñoso, sa, a. affectionate, endearing ;

cariota, sf. wild carrot.

carirraído, da, a. brazen-faced, impudent.

carirredondo, da, a. round-faced.

caritativo, va, a. charitable.

cariz, sm. aspect of the weather.

carlán, sm. justice of the peace in Arragon.

carlanca, sf. spiked dog-collar.

carlancón, sm. sly-boots, dodger.

carmelita, sf. Carmelite.

carmen, sm. Carmelite order.

carmenador, sm. wool-carder.

carmenar, v.a. to card wool ; to pull out the hair of the head ; to cheat.

carmes, sm. kermes.

carmesí, sm. crimson ; purple.

carmín, sm. & a. carmine.

carnada, sf. bait, lure.

carnaje, sm. salt beef.

carnal, a. carnal, fleshy ; sensual ; —, sm. time of the year in which meat may be eaten.

carnalidad, sf. lustfulness, fleshliness.

carnaval, sm. carnival.

carnaza, sf. fleshy part of a hide ; abundance of meat.

carne, sf. flesh ; meat ; pulp (of fruit).

carnecilla, sf. carnosity, caruncle.

carnerada, sf. flock of sheep.

carneraje, sm. tax laid on sheep.

carnerear, v.a. to fine the proprietor of sheep which have done damage.

carnerero, sm. shepherd.

carneril, sm. sheep-walk. [vault.

carnero, sm. sheep, mutton ; family-

carneruno, na, a. belonging to sheep.

carnestolendas, sf.pl. Shrovetide, Shrove-Tuesday.

carnicería, sf. shambles, slaughter-house ; carnage, slaughter.

carnicero, sm. butcher ; —, ra, a. carnivorous. [mals.

carnicol, sm. hoof of cloven-footed ani-

carnívoro, ra, a. carnivorous.

carniza, sf. refuse of meat, offal.

carnosidad, sf. proud flesh ; fatness ; fleshiness. [rowy ; pulpous.

carnoso, sa, carnudo, a. fleshy ; mar-

caro, ra, a. dear, costly ; beloved, affectionate ; —, ad. dearly.

caroca, sm. caress.

carocha, sf. eggs of the queen-bee.

carochar, v.a. to lay and hatch eggs (applied to the queen-bee).

caromomia, sf. dry flesh of a mummy.

carona, sf. saddle-cloth ; part of the animal's back on which the saddle lies.

caroquero, sm. wheedler, flatterer.

carótida, sf. the carotid artery.

carozo, sm. core of a pomegranate.

carpa, sf. carp (fish) ; part torn off a bunch of grapes.

carpeta, sf. portfolio.

carpintear, v.a. to carpenter. [shop.

carpintería, sf. carpentry ; carpenter's

carpintero, sm. carpenter ; — de blanco, joiner ; — de carretas, cartwright ; — de obras de afuera, carpenter who timbers or roofs houses ; — de ribera, shipwright.

carpo, sm. wrist, carpus.

carraca, sf. carack (ship) ; rattle.

carral, sm. barrel, butt, vat.

carraleja, sf. a kind of beetle.

carralero, sm. cooper.

carrasca, sf. carrasco, sm. evergreen oak.

carraspada, sf. negus, mulled wine.

carraspera, sf. hoarseness.

carrasqueño, ña, a. harsh, sharp ; belonging to the evergreen oak.

carrera, sf. career, course, race ; race-ground ; high-road ; alley ; row, line ; course of life ; á — abierta, at full speed.

carreta, sf. long narrow cart.

carretada, sf. cart-load ; great quantity ; á -s, in abundance.

carretaje, sm. cartage.

carrete, sm. small reel for winding off silk, &c. ; fishing-pulley.

carretear, v.a. to cart ; to drive a cart ; -se, to draw unevenly.

carretela, sf. light coach.

carretera, sf. high-road.

carretería, sf. number of carts ; trade of a carman ; cartwright's yard.

carretero, sm. cartwright ; carman.

carretilla, sf. go-cart ; squib, cracker ; wheelbarrow.

carretón, sm. go-cart (for children).

carriego, sm. osier fish-basket.

carril, sm. cart-way ; cart-rut ; furrow.

carrillada, sf. hog's cheek ; box on the

carrillo, sm. cheek ; tackle.   [ears.

carrilludo, da, a. chub-cheeked.

carriola, sf. truckle-bed ; small chariot ; curricle.

carrizo, sm. common reed grass.

carro, sm. cart.

Carro, sm. Charles' Wain.

carrocín, sm. chaise, curricle.

carromatero, sm. waggoner.

carromato, sm. two-wheeled cart.

carroña, sf. carrion.   [scab.

carroñar, v.a. to infect sheep with the

carroño, ña, a. putrid, rotten.

carroza, sf. state-coach.

carruaje, sm. carriage.

carta, sf. letter ; map ; — blanca, carte-blanche ; — credencial ó de creencia, credentials, pl. ; — certificada, registered letter.

cartabón, sm. rule (drawing-tool).

cartapacio, sm. memorandum-book ; scholar's portfolio.

cartazo, sm. (col.) insulting letter.

cartearse, v.r. to keep up a correspondence by letter.

cartel, sm. placard ; hand-bill ; — de comedia, play-bill.

cartela, sf. slip of paper ; cornice.   [case.

cartera, sf. portfolio, pocket-book ; letter-

cartero, sm. letter-carrier, postman.

cartilaginoso, sa, a. cartilaginous.

cartílago, sm. cartilage.

cartilla, sf. primer.   [ment ; cartoon.

cartón, sm. pasteboard ; metal orna-

cartonero, sm. pasteboard-maker.

cartuchera, sf. (mil.) cartridge-box ; cartridge-pouch.

cartucho, sm. cartridge.

cartuja, sm. Carthusian order.

cartujo, sm. Carthusian monk.

cartulario, sm. cartulary.

cartulina, sf. card, visiting-card.

carvi, sm. caraway-seed.

casa, sf. house ; home ; — de campo, country-house ; — de locos, mad-house ; — de moneda, mint ; — de posada, lodging-house.

casaca, sf. coat.

casación, sf. abrogation.

casadero, ra, a. marriageable.

casamata, sf. (mil.) casemate.   [maker.

casamentero, ra. sm. & f. marriage-

casamiento, sm. marriage.

casapuerta, sf. porch.

casaquilla, sf. short jacket.

casar, v.a. to marry ; (fig.) to unite ; -se, to marry.

casar, v.a. to abrogate.

casatienda, sf. shop and house combined.

casca, sf. husks of grapes ; bark.

cascabel, sm. rattle, little round bell ; rattle-snake.

cascabelada, sf. jingling of small bells ; inconsiderate speech or action.

cascabelear, v.a. to feed one with vain hopes ; —, v.n. to act with levity.

cascaciruelas, sm. (col.) mean, despicable fellow.

cascada, sf. cascade, water-fall.

cascajal, sm. place full of pebbles.

cascajo, sm. gravel ; fragments of broken vessels ; rubbish ; copper coin.

cascajoso, sa, a. gravelly.   [bits.

cascamajar, v.a. to pound a thing to

cascanueces, sm. nut-cracker.

cascar, v.a. to crack, to break into pieces ; to lick, to beat ; -se, to be broken open.

cáscara, sf. rind, peel, husk ; bark.

¡ cáscaras ! exclamation of surprise.

cascarilla, sf. Peruvian bark, quinine.

cascarón, sm. egg-shell ; niche for the sacrament.

cascarrón, na, a. rough, harsh, rude.

cascarudo, da, a. thick-skinned, thick-peeled.

casco, sm. skull, cranium ; fragments of a pot ; helmet ; hulk of a ship ; crown of a hat ; hoof of a horse.

cascote, sm. rubbish, fragments of material used in building.

cascudo, da, a. large-hoofed.

caseoso, sa, a. caseous, cheesy.

casera, sf. bachelor's housekeeper.

casería, sf. messuage ; economical management of a house.

caserío, sm. series of houses ; village.

caserna, sf. (mil.) bomb-proof shelter.

casero, sm. landlord ; —, ra, a. domestic ; familiar ; house-keeping.

caseta, sf. cottage.

casi, ad. almost, nearly ; — que, — —, very nearly.

casia, sf. (bot.) quassia.   [board.

casillas, sf.pl. backgammon ; draught-

casillero, sm. set of pigeon-holes.

casimiro, sm. kerseymere.

casino, sm. club, club-house.

caso, sm. case, occurrence, event ; hap, casualty ; occasion ; (gr.) case ; en — de eso, in that case ; en todo — at all events ; — que, in case.   [riage.

casorio, sm. (col.) inconsiderate mar-

caspa, sf. dandriff ; scurf.
¡ cáspita ! wonderful !
casquetazo, sm. blow with the head.
casquete, sm. helmet, casque ; cataplasm.
casquiblando, da, a. soft-hoofed.
casquiderramado, da, a. wide-hoofed.
casquijo, sm. gravel.
casquilucio, cia, a. gay, frolicsome.
casquilla, sf. cell of the queen-bee.
casquillo, sm. iron socket with which a spear is shod ; point of an arrow.
casquimuleño, ña, a. narrow-hoofed (like mules). [quality.
casta, sf. cast, race, lineage ; breed ; kind,
castaña, sf. chestnut ; jug in the shape of a chestnut ; — pilonga, dried chestnut.
castañal, castañar, sm. chestnut-grove.
castañeta, sf. castanet.
castañetear, v.n. to rattle the castanets in dancing. [burn, chestnut.
castaño, sm. chestnut-tree ; —, ña, a. aucastañuela, sf. castanet.
castañuelo, la, a. chestnut-coloured.
castellán, sm. governor of a castle.
castellanía, sf. castellany, district belonging to a castle. [ish.
castellano, sm. Castilian language, Spancastidad, sf. chastity.
castigar, v.a. to chastise, to punish , to afflict. [correction.
castigo, sm. chastisement, punishment ;
castillejo, sm. castlet ; go-cart (for little children).
castillete, sm. small castle. [bee.
castillo, sm. castle ; cell of the queen-
castizo, za, a. of a noble descent ; pure, uncorrupt.
casto, ta, a. pure, chaste.
castor, sm. beaver.
castoreo, sm. (med.) castoreum.
castra, sf. pruning of plants and trees.
castrar, v.a. to geld, to castrate ; to prune ; to cut the honey-combs out of bee-hives. [of hives.
castrazón, sf. cutting honey-combs out
casual, a. casual, accidental.
casualidad, sf. casualty, accident.
casucha, sf. miserable hut.
casuísta, sm. casuist.
casulla, sf. chasuble.
cata, sf. tasting.
catábulo, sm. stable.
catacumbas, sf.pl. catacombs.
catadura, sf. face, countenance.
catafalco, sm. funeral canopy over a bier.
catalejo, sm. telescope.
catálogo, sm. catalogue.
cataplasma, sf. cataplasm, poultice.
catapulta, sf. catapult.

catar, v.a. to taste ; to inspect, to examine ; to judge ; to esteem.
catarata, sf. cataract (disease of the eye) ; water-fall, cascade.
catarral, a. catarrhal.
catarriento, ta, a. catarrhal.
catarro, sm. catarrh.
catarroso, sa, a. catarrhal, catarrhous.
catártico, ca, a. cathartic, purging.
catastro, sm. general tax on land.
catástrofe, sf. catastrophe.
catavino, sm. small cup for tasting wine ; -s, sm. wine-taster ; tippler.
catecismo, sm. catechism.
cátedra, sf. professor's chair.
catedral, a. & sf. cathedral.
catedrático, sm. professor of a university.
categoría, sf. category ; rank.
categorico, ca, a. categorical, decisive.
catequismo, sm. catechism.
catequista, sm. catechist.
catequizar, v.a. to catechise.
caterva, sf. mob.
cato, sm. Japan earth.
catolicismo, sm. catholicism.
católico, ca, a. & sm. catholic.
catorcena, sf. set of fourteen.
catorceno, na, a. fourteenth.
catre, sm. small bedstead ; trestle-bed.
catricofre, sm. bed-closet.
cauce, sm. drain.
caución, sf. caution, security, guaranty.
caucionar, v.a. to guarantee. [rubber.
caucho, sm. (am.) caoutchouc, india-
cauda, sf. train of a bishop's robe.
caudal, sm. property, fortune, wealth ; fund, stock ; plenty.
caudaloso, sa, a. carrying much water (speaking of rivers).
caudillo, sm. commander, chief, leader.
causa, sf. cause ; occasion ; motive, reason ; law-suit ; á — de, considering, because of.
causal, a. causal. [occasion.
causar, v.a. to cause, to produce ; tc
causídico, ca, a. belonging to law-suits.
causón, sm. burning fever which lasts only some hours. [a. caustic.
cáustico, sm. (med.) caustic ; —, ca,
cautela, sf. caution, prudence ; heedfulness. [tions.
cautelar, v.a. to take necessary precau-
cauteloso, sa, a. cautious, heedful.
cauterio, sm. cautery.
cauterizar, v.a. to cauterize ; to reproach with severity.
cautivar, v.a. to take prisoner in war ; to captivate, to charm.
cautiverio, sm. captivity ; confinement.
cautivo, va, sm. & f. captive.
cauto, ta, a. cautious, wary.

cava, sf. digging and earthing of vines ; wine-cellar.

cavar, v.a. to dig up, to excavate ; —, v.n. to penetrate far into a thing ; to think profoundly ; to paw (of horses).

caverna, sf. cavern, cave.

cavernoso, sa, a. cavernous.

cavidad, sf. cavity, hollow.

cavilación, sf. over-subtlety ; captious hesitation. [ties.

cavilar, v.a. to cavil, to raise difficul-

caviloso, sa, a. captious, cavillous.

cayada, sf., **cayado,** sm. shepherd's hook.

cayo, sm. rock, shoal.

caz, sm. canal, trench.

caza, sf. chase ; game.

cazadero, sm. hunting-ground. [man.

cazador, sm. hunter, huntsman, sports-

cazamoscas, sm. fly-catcher, gnat-snapper (bird).

cazar, v.a. to chase, to hunt.

cazcalear, v.n. to fidget.

cazcarria, sf. splashings of dirt, pl.

cazo, sm. copper saucepan with an iron handle ; ladle.

cazolero, ra, a. over-officious, officious.

cazuela, sf. stewing-pan.

cazumbrón, sm. cooper.

cazurro, rra, a. silent, taciturn.

¡ce! hark ! come hither !

cea, sf. thigh-bone.

ceática, sf. (med.) sciatica.

ceba, sf. fattening (of animals).

cebada, sf. barley.

cebadazo, za, a. of barley. [horses.

cebadera, sf. fodder-bag ; nose-bag (for

cebadura, sf. feeding of animals.

cebar, v.a. & n. to feed animals, to fatten; to keep up a fire ; to prime ; to let off (a rocket) ; (fig.) to bite, to take hold.

cebellina, sf. sable ; sable-skin.

cebo, sm. food ; bait, lure ; priming.

cebolla, sf. onion.

cebolleta, sf. shallot.

cebollino, sm. onion-seed.

cebolludo, da, a. bulbous.

cebón, -na, a. fatted.

cebra, sf. zebra.

cebruno, a. reddish brown. [ce.''

cecear, v.a. to lisp ; to call one by ,, ce-

cecial, sm. cod (fish).

cecina, sf. hung beef, salt beef.

cedazo, sm. hair-sieve, strainer.

ceder, v.a. to grant, to resign, to yield, to give up ; —, v.n. to submit, to comply, to give in ; to abate, to grow

cedrino, na, a. made of cedar. [less.

cedro, sm. cedar.

cédula, sf. slip of paper ; bill ; decree ; schedule ; — **de cambio,** bill of exchange.

céfalo, sm. mullet.

céfiro, sm. zephyr.

cegar, v.n. to grow blind ; —; v.a., to deprive of sight ; to darken.

cegarrita, sm. (col.) short-sighted person ; **á -s,** with shut eyes.

cegato, ta, a. short-sighted.

ceguedad, sf. blindness.

ceja, sf. eye-brow ; edging of clothes ; (mus.) bridge of a stringed instrument ; brow of a mountain.

cejar, v.n. to go backward ; to slacken, to give in.

cejijunto, ta, a. with meeting eye-brows.

cejo, sm. thick mist or fog which usually arises from rivers. [artful trick.

celada, sf. Burgundy helmet ; ambush ;

celaje, sm. light clouds.

celar, v.n. & a. to fulfil with care ; to watch over ; to conceal ; to engrave.

celda, sf. cell.

celdilla, sf. cellule.

celebérrimo, ma, a. most celebrated.

celebración, sf. celebration ; praise.

celebrar, v.a. to celebrate ; to praise ; — **misa,** to say mass.

célebre, a. famous, renowned ; gay ; agreeable in conversation.

celebridad, sf. celebrity, fame.

celebro, sm. skull ; brain ; fancy.

celemín, sm. dry measure (the 12th part of a fanega).

celeridad, sf. celerity, velocity.

celeste, a. heavenly ; sky-blue.

celestial, a. heavenly ; perfect ; excellent.

celibato, sm. celibacy. [lent.

célibe, sm. bachelor.

celo, sm. zeal ; rut (in animals).

celosía, sf. lattice of a window.

celoso, sa, a. zealous ; jealous.

célula, sf. cellule.

celular, a. cellular.

cementar, v.a. to cement.

cena, sf. supper.

cenacho, sm. market-basket.

cenador, sm. one who sups ; arbour.

cenagal, sm. quagmire.

cenagoso, sa, a. miry, marshy.

cenar, v.a. to sup.

cenceño, ña, a. lean, thin, slender.

cencerrada, sf. rough music, hubbub clatter, Dutch concert.

cencerrear, v.n. to jingle continually ; to play badly ; to make a dreadful noise.

cencerro, sm. cow-bell ; **á -s tapados,** privately, by stealth.

cencerrón, sm. grape which remains after the vintage.

cendal, sm. crape ; fine linen.

cenefa, sf. fringe.

cenicero, sm. ash-pit.
ceniciento, ta, a. ash-coloured.
cenit, sm. zenith.
ceniza, sf. ashes, pl.; miérco - les de —, Ash-Wednesday.
cenojil, sm. garter.
censatario, sm. land-owner paying a head-rent or quit-rent.
censo, sm. census; poll-tax.
censor, sm. censor, reviewer, critic; censorious person.
censual, a. belonging to a quit-rent.
censualista, sm. owner of a head-rent.
censura, sf. critical review; censure, blame. [censure, to blame.
censurar, v.a. to review, to criticise; to
centauro, sm. Centaur.
centavo, sm. (am.) cent.
centella, sf. lightning; spark.
centellar, centellear, v.n. to sparkle.
centena, sf. hundred.
centenadas, ad. á —, by hundreds.
centenal, sm. rye-field.
centenario, ia, a. centenary, secular; —, sm. centennial.
centeno, sm. rye; na, a. hundredth.
centésimo, ma, a. centesimal, hundredth.
centílitro, sm. centilitre.
céntimo, sm. cent, centime (100th part of a peseta or franc).
centinela, sm. & f. sentry, sentinel; — avanzada, advanced guard; — per- dida, forlorn hope; — á caballo, vedette.
centón, sm. cento (literary composition of scraps from other authors).
central, centrical, a. central, centric.
centralizar, v.a. to centralize.
céntrico, ca, a. focal.
centrífugo, ga, a. centrifugal.
centrípeto, ta, a. centripetal.
centro, sm. centre; principal object.
centuplicar, v.a. to centuplicate.
céntuplo, pla, a. centuple, hundredfold.
centuria, sf. century.
cénzalo, sm. gnat.
ceñido, da, a. moderate, economical; en- circled with rings.
ceñidor, sm. belt, girdle.
ceñir, v.n. to gird, to surround, to circle; to environ; to reduce, to abbreviate, to abridge.
ceño, sm. frown; ferrule.
ceñudo, da, a. frowning, grim.
cepa, sf. stock of a vine; origin of a family.
cepilladuras, sf.pl. wood-shavings.
cepillo, sm. plane; brush.
cepo, sm. block; trap, snare; poor- box; stocks (for prisoners); (fig.) entanglement.

cequí, cequín, sm. sequin (coin).
cera, sf. wax; wax-taper, wax-candle; side-walk; -s, pl. the cells of wax and honey formed by bees.
cerafolio, sm. (bot.) common chervil.
cerbatana, sf. pea-shooter; acoustic trumpet.
cerca, sf. inclosure; fence; -s, pl. ob- jects placed in the foreground of a painting; —, ad. near, at hand, close by; — de, close, near.
cercano, na, a. near, close by, adjoining.
cercar, v.a. to inclose, to environ, to circle; to fence.
cercenar, v.a. to pare; to retrench, to clip; to lop off; to reduce, to lessen; to curtail, to cut away; to abridge.
cerceta, sf. widgeon.
cercillo, sm. tendril of the vine.
cerciorar, v.a. to assure, to ascertain, to affirm. [place.
cerco, sm. encirclement; blockade of a
cerda, sf. strong hair growing in a horse's tail or mane; bristle.
cerdear, v.n. to go lame; to be out of tune; to evade a request.
cerdo, sm. hog, pig.
cerdoso, sa, cerdudo, da, a. bristly.
cerebelo, sm. cerebel, the little brain.
ceremonia, sf. ceremony.
ceremonial, a. & sm. ceremonial.
ceremonioso, sa, a. ceremonious.
cerería, sf. wax-chandler's shop.
cerero, sm. wax-chandler; idle vagrant.
cereza, sf. cherry.
cerezo, sm. cherry-tree.
cerilla, sf. taper; match.
cermeña, sf. muscadine pear.
cernada, sf. leached ashes.
cerneja, sf. fetlock.
cerner, v.a. to sift; —, v.n. to bud and blossom; to drizzle; -se, to waddle.
cernido, sm. sifting.
cernidura, sf. siftings, pl.
cero, sm. zero. [into a cake.
cerón, sm. dregs of pressed wax formed
ceroso, a. waxy. [fear.
cerote, sm. cobbler's wax; (fig.) panic.
cerquillo, sm. tonsure.
cerquita, ad. at a small distance. [mal.
cerrada, sf. backbone-hide of an ani-
cerradero, sm. staple of a lock; —, ra, a. serving for locking. [locked.
cerradizo, za, a. that which may be
cerrado, da, a. close, reserved; con- cealed; thick-grown.
cerradura, sf. locking-up; lock; — de golpe, spring-lock.
cerrajear, v.n. to do locksmith's work.
cerrajería, sf. trade of a locksmith; lock- smith's shop.

cerrajero, sm. locksmith.
cerramiento, sm. stopping-up ; inclosure; finishing of the roof of a building.
cerrar, v.a. & n. to close, to shut ; to obstruct a passage ; to lock ; to engage the enemy ; — la cuenta, to close an account ; -se, to be shut up ; to be cicatrized ; to grow dark.
cerrazón, sf. dark and cloudy weather which precedes tempests.
cerrero, ra, a. running wild on the hills ; caballo —, an unbroken horse.
cerril, a. mountainous, rough ; wild, uncerrión, sm. icicle.   [tamed.
cerro, sm. hill ; neck of an animal ; backbone ; en —, nakedly, barely.
cerrojo, sm. bolt of a door.
certamen, sm. literary controversy.
certero, ra, a. aiming with certainty ; sure, unerring.
certeza, certidumbre, sf. certainty.
certificación, sf. certificate.
certificado, sm. certificate.
certificar, v.a. to certify, to affirm.
certificatorio, ria, a. authenticating.
cerúleo, lea, a. ceruleous, sky-blue.
cerval, cervario, ria, a. belonging to a deer or resembling it.
cervatillo, sm. small deer.
cervato, sm. fawn.
cervecería, sf. brew-house, brewery.
cervecero, sm. brewer.
cerveza, sf. beer, ale.
cervicabra, sf. gazelle.
cerviguillo, sm. big nape.
cerviz, sf. nape of neck.
cervuno, na, a. deer-coloured.
cesación, sf. cessation, ceasing, pause, discontinuation.
cesar, v.n. to cease, to desist.
César, sm. Roman emperor.
cesáreo, rea, a. imperial.
cesible, a. that which may be ceded.
cesión, sf. cession, transfer.
cesionario, sm. cessionary.
césped, sm. sod, turf covered with grass ; grass-plot.   [are cut.
cespedera, sf. field where green sods
cesta, sf. basket, pannier.
cestada, sf. basket-full.
cestería, sf. basket-shop ; basket-stand.
cestero, sm. basket-maker.
cesto, sm. large basket.
cetrino, na, a. citrine, lemon-coloured ; jaundiced, melancholic.
cetro, sm. sceptre.
cía, sf. hip-bone.
ciar, v.n. to go back ; (mar.) to backwater ; (fig.) to slacken in the pursuit of an affair.
ciática, sf. sciatica, hip-gout.

ciático, ca, a. sciatical.
cibera, sf. mill-hopper ; grist put at once in the hopper ; all seeds or grains ; husks, grounds.
cicatear, v.n. to be niggardly.
cicatería, sf. niggardliness.
cicatero, ra, a. niggardly, sordid.
cicatriz, sf. cicatrice ; gash.
cicatrizar, v.a. to cicatrise.
ciclo, sm. cycle.
cíclope, ciclope, sm. Cyclops.
cicuta, sf. (bot.) hemlock.
cidra, sf. citron.
cidro, sm. citron-tree.
ciegamente, ad. blindly.
ciego, ga, a. blind.
cielo, sm. heaven ; atmosphere ; climate ; — de la cama, tester of a bed ; — de coche, roof of a coach ; — de la boca, roof of the palate.
ciempiés, sm. centipede.
cien, a. one hundred.
ciencia, sf. science.
cieno, sm. mud, mire.
científico, ca, a. scientific.
ciento, a. one hundred ; —, sm. a hundred ; juego de los -s, piquet (game at cientopiés, sm. centipede.   [cards)
cierna, sf. blossom of vines, corn, &c.
cierne, en —, in blossom ; estar en —, to be in its infancy.
cierre, sm. closing, closure.
cierro, sm. enclosure.   [certainly.
cierto, ta, a. certain, doubtless ; por —,
cierva, sf. hind.   [stag-beetle.
ciervo, sm. deer, hart, stag ; — volante,
cierzo, sm. cold northerly wind.
cifra, sf. cipher ; abbreviation.
cifrar, v.a. to write in ciphers ; to abridge.
cigarra, sf. cicala.   [ette.
cigarro, sm. cigar ; — de papel, cigar-
cigarrero, sm. cigar-seller.
cigarrista, sm. one who smokes many cigars.
cigarrillo, sm. cigarette.
cigoñal, sm. pole of a draw-well.
cigüeña, sf. stork ; crank of a bell.
cigüeño, sm. male stork.
cilicio, sm. hair-shirt.
cilíndrico, ca, a. cylindric.
cilindro, sm. cylinder.
cilla, sf. granary.
cillerero, sm. cellarer (of monastery).
cilleriza, sf. stewardess in a nunnery.
cillero, sm. keeper of a granary ; granary.
cima, sf. summit ; nap ; top of trees.
cimbalillo, sm. small bell.
címbalo, sm. cymbal.
cimbel, sm. decoy-pigeon.
cimborio, cimborrio, sm. cupola.
cimbra, sf. centring of an arch.

cimbrado, sm. quick movement in a Spanish dance.

cimbr(e)ar, v.a. to brandish a rod or wand; — á alguno, to give one a drubbing; —, v.n. to bend, to vibrate.

cimbreño, ña, a. pliant, flexible.

cimbronazo, sm. thrust of a foil.

cimentado, sm. refinement of gold.

cimentar, v.a. to lay the foundation of a building; (fig.) to establish principles; to refine metals.

cimenterio, sm. cemetery, churchyard.

cimento, sm. cement.

cimera, sf. crest of a helmet.

cimero, ra, a. uppermost; at the very top.　　　[work; basis, origin.

cimiento, sm. foundations; ground-

cimitarra, sf. cimeter, falchion.

cimorra, sf. glanders, pl.

cinabrio, sm. cinnabar; vermilion.

cinamomo, sm. bead-tree.

cinc, sm. zinc.

cincel, sm. chisel.

cincelador, sm. engraver, sculptor.

ciucelar, v.a. to chisel, engrave.

cinco, a. & sm. five.

cincuenta, sm. fifty.

cincuenteno, na, a. fiftieth.

cincha, girth.

cinchar, v.a. to girth.

cinchera, sf. girth-place.

cincho, sm. broad belt of labourers.

cingaro, ra, s. gipsy.

cíngulo, sm. girdle; band, wreath.

cínico, ca, a. cynical.

Cinosura, sf. Cynosure, the Lesser Bear.

cinta, sf. ribbon; estar en —, to be with child.　　　　　[tunny-fishery.

cintagorda, sf. coarse hempen net for the

cinteado, da, a. adorned with ribands.

cintero, sm. riband-weaver.

cintillo, sm. hat-band.

cinto, sm. belt, girdle; (poet.) zodiac.

cintura, sf. girdle; waist.

cinturón, sm. broad-sword belt.

ciprés, sm. cypress-tree.

cipresal, sm. grove of cypress-trees.

cipresino, na, a. resembling or belonging to cypress.

circo, sm. circus.

circuir, v.a. to surround, to encircle.

circuito, sm. circuit; circumference.

circulación, sf. circulation; currency.

circular, a. circular, circulatory; —, v.n. to circulate.

círculo, sm. circle; circumference; district; orb; compasses.

circumpolar, a. near the pole.

circuncidar, v.a. to circumcise

circuncisión, sf. circumcision.

circundar, v.a. to surround, to encircle.

circunferencia, sf. circumference.

circunferencial, a. circumferential, surrounding.　　　　　[flex.

circunflejo, ja, a., acento —, sm. circum-

circunloquio, sm. circumlocution.

circunscribir, v.a. to circumscribe.

circunscripción, sf. circumscription.

circunspección, sf. circumspection.

circunspecto, ta, a. circumspect, cautious.

circunstancia, sf. circumstance.

circunstanciado, da, a. circumstantial, detailed.

circunstantes, sm.pl. bystanders.

circunvalar, v.a. to surround; to circumvallate.　　　　　[jacent.

circunvecino, na, a. neighbouring, ad-

cirial, sm. large candlestick.

cirio, sm. church-candle.

cirro, sm. indurated gland; cirrus

ciruela, sf. plum, prune.　　　[(cloud).

ciruelo, sm. plum-tree.

cirugía, sf. surgery.

cirujano, sm. surgeon.　　　　[nature.

ciscar, v.a. to make dirty; -se, to ease

cisco, sm. coal-dust.

cisión, sf. incision.

cisma, sm. & f. schism; disturbance.

cismático, ca, a. schismatic.　　[cian.

cisne, sm. swan; (fig.) an eminent musi-

cisquero, sm. pouncing-bag.

cister, sm. Cistertian order.

cisterna, sf. cistern.

cisura, sf. incisure, incision.

cita, sf. citation, quotation; rendezvous.

citación, sf. quotation; summons.

citano, sm. such a one.

citar, v.a. to make an appointment to meet a person; to convoke; to cite; to quote; to summon; to give judicial notice.

cítara, sf. (mus.) zither.

citara, sf. wall of thickness of one brick.

citarista, s. zither-player.

citatorio, ria, a. (law) citatory.

citerior, ad. hither, nearer.

cítola, sf. mill-clapper.

ciudad, sf. city; civic body.

ciudadano, sm. citizen; —, na, a. civil; citizen-like.

ciudadela, sf. citadel.

cívico, ca, a. civic.　　　　[civil.

civil, a. civil; polite, courteous; (law)

civilización, sf. civilisation.

civilizar, v.a. to civilise.

civismo, sm. patriotism.

cizalla, sf. shears for clipping metal; filings of gold or other metal.

clamar, v.a. to cry out in a mournful tone; to show a want of something.

clamor, sm. clamour, outcry; exclamation; peal of passing-bells.

clamorear, v.a. to clamour; —, v.n. to toll the passing-bell.

clamoreo, sm. continued outcry.

clamoroso, sa, a. clamorous.

clandestino, na, a. clandestine, secret, concealed.

clara, sf. (col.) white of an egg; short interval of fair weather on a rainy day.

claraboya, sf. sky-light.

clarea, sf. mulled wine.

clarear, v.n. to dawn; -se, to be transparent; to clear up.

clarete, a. vino —, sm. claret.

claridad, sf. brightness, clearness.

clarificar, v.a. to brighten; to clarify.

clarificativo, va, a. purificatory, clarifying.

clarín, sm. trumpet; trumpeter. [ing.

clarinero, sm. trumpeter. [clarinet.

clarinete, sm. clarinet; player on the

claro, ra, a. clear, bright; intelligible; evident, manifest; —, sm. open space; sky-light. [ing).

claroscuro, a. light and shade (in painting).

clase, sf. class, rank; order.

clásico, ca, a. classical.

clasificación, sf. classification.

clasificar, v.a. to classify.

claudicar, v.n. to halt, to limp.

claustral, a. claustral.

claustro, sm. cloister; congregation of graduates of a university.

cláusula, sf. period; clause.

clausular, v.a. to close a period.

clausura, sf. monastic enclosure; conclusion of a session.

clava, sf. club, heavy stick.

clavado, da, a. furnished with nails; exact, precise.

clavar, v.a. to nail; to fasten in, to force in; to drive into; to drive a wedge; (fig.) to cheat, to deceive.

clavazón, sf. set of nails.

clave, sf. key-stone; key of a cipher; (mus.) clef; —, sm. harpsichord, pianoforte.

clavel, sm. (bot.) common pink.

clavera, sf. mould for nail-heads; hole in a horse-shoe.

clavero, sm. aromatic clove-tree.

clavetear, v.a. to garnish with nails.

clavicordio, sm. harpsichord.

clavícula, sf. clavicle, collar-bone.

clavija, sf. pin, peg.

clavo, sm. nail; corn (on the feet); clove.

clemencia, sf. clemency.

clemente, a. clement, merciful.

clerecía, sf. clergy.

clerical, a. clerical. [clergyman.

clericato, sm. state and dignity of a

clérigo, sm. clergyman.

clero, sm. clergy.

cliente, sm. client.

clientela, sf. clientship.

clima, sm. climate.

clin, sf. See crin.

clínica, sf. clinical surgery or hospital.

clínico, ca, a. clinical.

clisaje, sm. stereotyping.

clisar, v.a. to stereotype.

clister, sm. clyster.

clivoso, sa, a. (poet.) declivous.

clo-clo, sm. clucking of a hen.

cloaca, sf. sewer.

cloque, sm. grapnel; harpoon.

cloquear, v.a. to cluck.

cloqueo, sm. clucking. [time.

cloquera, sf. hatching of fowls; brooding

cloquero, sm. harpooner in the tunny-fishery.

clorosis, sf. green-sickness. [decrepit.

clueco, ca, a. clucking, hatching; (fig.)

coacción, sf. compulsion.

coactivo, va, a. coercive.

coadjutor, sm. coadjutor, assistant.

coadyuvar, v.a. to help, to assist.

coagular, v.a. to coagulate, to curd.

coágulo, sm. coagulated blood.

coalición, sf. coalition, confederacy.

coarrendador, sm. joint partner in the rent of a property; co-lessor.

coartación, sf. obligation; obligation of an incumbent to receive ordination.

coartada, sf. (law) alibi.

coartar, v.a. to limit, to restrict, to recoba, sf. (col.) practical joke. [strain.

cobalto, sm. cobalt.

cobarde, a. coward, timid.

cobardía, sf. cowardice.

cobertera, sf. pot-lid; procuress.

cobertizo, sm. small shed; hovel.

cobertura, sf. coverlet; covercle; prerogative of the Spanish grandees to appear with covered head before their sovereign.

cobija, sf. gutter-tile.

cobijar, v.a. to cover, to shelter.

cobradero, ra, a. recoverable.

cobrador, sm. collector of rents.

cobranza, sf. recovery or collection of money.

cobrar, v.a. to recover, to collect (money); -se, to come to one's self.

cobre, sm. copper; kitchen-furniture.

cobrizo, za, a. coppery.

cobro, sm. collection of money.

cocar, v.a. to make grimaces; to coax.

coccíneo, nea, a. of a purple colour.

cocción, sf. coction, concoction.

coceador, ra, a. kicker (of horses).

cocear, v.a. to kick, to fling out; (fig.) to repugn, to resist. [bake-house.

cocedero, ra, a. easily cooked; —. sm.

cocedizo, za, a. easily boiled.
cocer, v.a. to boil ; to bake (bricks, &c.) ; to digest ; —, v.n. to boil ; to ferment ; -se, to suffer intense pain.
cocido, da, a. boiled ; (fig.) skilled, experienced ; —, sm. olla, a dish of boiled meat and vegetables.
cocimiento, sm. decoction ; dyer's bath.
cocina, sf. kitchen.
cocinar, v.a. to cook.
cocinera, sf. cook-maid, female cook.
cocinero, sm. cook.
cocinilla, sf. spirit-stove.
cocle, sm. grapnel.
cóclea, sf. endless screw.
coclear, v.a. to catch with a harpoon ; —, v.n. to cluck. [bear.
coco, sm. cocoa-tree ; cocoa-nut ; bugcocodrilo, sm. crocodile ; (fig.) false, faithless person.
cocoso, sa, a. worm-eaten.
cochambre, sm. dirty, stinking object.
cochambrería, sf. heap of nasty and filthy objects. [ing.
cochambroso, sa, a. nasty, filthy, stinkcocharro, sm. wooden cup.
cochastro, sm. little sucking wild boar.
coche, sm. coach, carriage ; (rail.) -cama, sleeping-car.
cochear, v.n. to drive a coach.
cochera, sf. coach-house.
cocheril, a. belonging to coachmen.
cochero, sm. coachman.
cochifrito, sm. fricassee.
cochina, sf. sow.
cochinería, sf. dirtiness, foulness.
cochinilla, sf. cochineal. [sm. pig.
cochino, na, a. dirty, nasty, filthy ; —,
cochiquera, sf. pig-sty.
codaste, sm. (mar.) stern-post.
codazo, sm. blow given with the elbow.
codear, v.a. to elbow.
códice, sm. old manuscript.
codicia, sm. covetousness, cupidity, greediness.
codiciable, a. covetable.
codiciar, v.a. to covet, to desire eagerly.
codicilar, a. pertaining to a codicil.
codicilo, sm. (law) codicil.
codicioso, sa, a. greedy, covetous ; diligent, laborious.
código, sm. code of laws.
codillo, sm. knee of horses and other quadrupeds ; angle ; crotch of a tree ; codille, a term at ombre.
codo, sm. elbow.
codorniz, sf. quail.
coerción, sf. coercion, restraint.
coercitivo, va, a. coercive.
coetáneo, nea, a. contemporary.
coeterno, na, a. coeternal.

coevo, va, a. coeval.
coexistencia, sf. coexistence.
coexistente, a. coexistent.
coexistir, v.n. to coexist.
cofa, sf. (mar.) top.
cofia, sf. coif ; silken hair-net.
cofín, sm. small basket for fruit.
cofrade, sm. colleague.
cofradía, sf. confraternity.
cofre, sm. trunk.
cofrero, sm. trunk-maker.
cogedera, sf. hive used to gather an escaped swarm of bees.
cogedizo, za, a. gatherable. [box.
cogedor, sm. collector, gatherer ; dustcogedura, sf. gathering.
coger, v.a. to catch, to lay hold of, to occupy, to take up ; to surprise.
cogitabundo, da, a. pensive, thoughtful.
cogitar, v.a. to reflect, to meditate.
cognoscitivo, va, a. cognitive.
cogollo, sm. heart of a lettuce, cabbage, &c. ; shoot of a plant.
cogote, sm. occiput.
cogujada, sf. crested lark. [bolster.
coguión, sm. corner of a mattress or
cogulla, sf. cowl, monk's hood. [gether.
cohabitar, v.n. to cohabit, to live tocohechar, v.a. to bribe, to suborn.
cohecho, sm. bribery ; season for ploughing the ground.
coheredera, sf. co-heiress.
coheredero, sm. co-heir, joint-heir.
coherencia, sf. coherence.
coherente, a. coherent, cohesive.
cohete, sm. sky-rocket.
cohetero, sm. rocket-maker.
cohibir, v.a. to prohibit, to restrain.
cohombral, sm. cucumber-bed.
cohombro, sm. cucumber.
cohonestar, v.a. to give an honest appearance to an action.
cohorte, sm. cohort.
coincidencia, sf. coincidence.
coincidente, a. coincident.
coincidir, v.n. to coincide.
coito, sm. coition, cohabitation.
cojear, v.n. to go lame, to halt, to hobble ; to deviate from virtue.
cojera, sf. lameness, halting.
cojijoso, sa, a. peevish, irritable.
cojín, sm. cushion.
cojo, ja, a. lame, cripple, halt.
cojudo, da, a. entire (of animals).
cok, sm. coke.
col, sf. cabbage.
cola, sf. tail ; train (of a gown) ; glue ; de la —, behind, backwards.
colación, sf. collation (luncheon) ; collation of a (benefice).
colacionar, v.a. to collate, to compare.

colada, sf. bleaching of linen ; bleached [linen.
coladera, sf. strainer, colander.
coladero, sm. colander ; narrow passage.
colador, sm. colander.
coladura, sf. straining, filtering.
colanilla, sf. small bolt.
colapez, colapiscis, sf. isinglass.
colar, v.a. & n. to strain, to filter ; to pass through a strait place ; to collate (to a benefice) ; (col.) to drink wine.
colateral, a. collateral.
colcha, sf. coverlet, counterpane.
colchadura, sf. quilting.
colchar, v.a. to quilt.
colchero, sm. quilt-maker.
colchón, sm. mattress.
colchonero, sm. mattress-maker.
coleada, sf. wagging of an animal's tail.
colear, v.n. to wag the tail.
colección, sf. collection. [collect.
colecta, sf. distribution of a tax ; (eccles.)
colectar, v.a. to collect taxes.
colecticio, cia, a. assembled without discipline (of troops).
colectivo, va, a. collective.
colector, sm. collector, gatherer.
colega, sm. colleague. [legatee.
colegatario, ria, sm. & f. co-heir, joint
colegial, a. collegial, collegiate ; —, sm. collegian, school-boy ; iglesia —, sf. collegiate church.
colegiala, sf. female member of a seminary or college.
colegiata, sf. collegiate church.
colegio, sm. college. [infer.
colegir, v.a. to collect, to deduce ; to
cólera, sf. bile ; anger, fury, rage.
cólera-morbo, sm. (med.) cholera.
coléricamente, ad. in a rage.
colérico, ca, a. choleric ; passionate.
coleta, sf. queue, pig-tail ; (fig.) appendix.
coleto, sm. doublet, leather jacket.
colgadero, sm. hook to hang things upon ; —, ra, a. fit to be hung up.
colgadizo, sm. projecting roof ; —, za, a. pendent, suspended.
colgadura, sf. tapestry ; bed-furniture.
colgajo, sm. tatter, rag.
colgar, v.a. to hang ; to suspend ; to adorn with tapestry ; —, v.n. to be suspended.
colibrí, sm. humming-bird, colibri.
cólica, sf. colic. [the tail.
colicano, na, a. having grey hair in
cólico, sm. colic.
colicorto, a. short-tailed (of animals).
colicuar, v.a. to colliquate, to melt, to dissolve ; -se, to become liquid.
coliflor, sm. cauliflower. [ance.
coligación, sf. connexion, union, alli-
colilla, sf. stump of a cigar.

colina, sf. hill, hillock.
colinabo, sm. turnip.
coliseo, sm. opera-house, theatre.
colisión, sf. collision ; friction. [suit.
colitigante, sm. litigant ; party to a law-
colmar, v.a. to heap up.
colmena, sf. hive, bee-hive. [house.
colmenar, sm. bee-hive stand, bee-
colmenero, sm. bee-master.
colmenilla, sf. morel (mushroom).
colmillo, sm. eye-tooth.
colmilludo, da, a. having eye-teeth ; (fig.) sagacious, quick-sighted.
colmo, sm. heap ; completion, crown ; height ; á —, plentifully.
colocación, sf. arrangement ; situation ; employment.
colocar, v.a. to arrange, to place ; to provide with an employment.
colodra, sf. milking-pail ; wooden can with which wine is measured.
colodrillo, sm. back of the head.
colofonia, sm. rosin.
colon, sm. (gr.) two points (:) ; colon, the largest of the intestines.
colonia, sf. colony ; silk ribbon two fingers' wide.
colonial, a. colonial.
colonizar, v.a. to colonise.
colono, sm. colonist ; farmer.
coloquio, sm. colloquy.
color, sm. colour, hue, dye ; rouge, pretext ; so —, on pretence, under pretext.
coloración, sf. colouring, coloration.
colorado, da, a. ruddy.
colorar, v.a. to colour ; to make plausible ; —, v.n. to blush with shame.
colorativo, va, a. colorific.
colorear, v.a. to colour ; to palliate, to excuse ; —, v.n. to grow red.
colorete, sm. rouge (paint). [tence.
colorido, sm. colouring ; pretext, pre-
colorín, sm. linnet ; vivid colour.
colorir, v.a. to colour.
colorista, sm. colourist.
colosal, a. colossal.
coloso, sm. colossus. [to guess.
columbrar, v.a. to discern at a distance ;
columna, sf. column.
columnata, sf. colonnade.
columpiar, v.a. to swing to and fro.
columpio, sm. swing, see-saw.
coluna, sf. column.
colusión, sf. collusion.
colusorio, ria, a. collusive.
colza, sf. (bot.) colza.
collado, sm. hill.
collar, sm. necklace, necklet.
collera, sf. collar ; gang of convicts chained together.
collón, sm. (col.) coward.

collonería, sf. (col.) cowardice.
coma, sf. (gr.) comma ; (med.) coma.
comadre, sf. joint sponsor ; comrade.
comadreja, sf. weasel. [gossip.
comadrero, ra, a. gossiping.
comadrón, sm. man-midwife.
comandancia, sf. command.
comandante, sm. commander.
comandita, sf. sleeping partnership.
comanditario, ria, a. sleeping (partner).
comandar, v.a. to command.
comarca, sf. territory, district ; boundary, limit. [ing upon.
comarcano, na, a. neighbouring, border-
comarcar, v.a. to plant trees in a straight
line ; —, v.n. to border, to confine
upon. [warped] ; convexity.
comba, sf. curvature (of timber when
combar, v.a. to bend ; -se, to warp.
combate, sm. combat, conflict ; fighting.
combatidor, sm. combatant.
combatir, v.a. & n. to combat, to fight ;
to attack ; to contradict.
combinación, sf. combination.
combinar, v.n. to combine.
combo, ba, a. bent, crooked, warped ;
-s, sm.pl. stand for casks ; gawn-tree.
combustible, a. combustible ; —, sm.
combustible ; fuel.
comedero, sm. dining-room.
comedero, ra, a. eatable.
comedia, sf. comedy. [dian.
comediante, sm. player, actor, come-
comediar, v.a. to divide into equal shares.
comedido, da, a. polite, gentle.
comedirse, v.r. to govern one's self.
comedor, ra, sm. & f. eater ; feeder ;
—, sm. dining-room.
comendador, sm. knight commander of a
military order. [nunnery.
comendadora, sf. mother superior of a
comendaticio, cia, a. (eccles.) (letters) of
commendation.
comendatorio, ria, a. recommending, introductory (of letters). [pound.
comentar, v.a. to comment, to ex-
comentario, sm. commentary.
comento, sm. comment.
comenzar, v.n. to commence, to begin.
comer, v.a. to eat, to chew ; to dine ; to
consume ; to take a piece at chess.
comerciable, a. marketable ; sociable.
comercial, a. commercial. [man.
comerciante, sm.trader, merchant,trades-
comerciar, v.a. to trade ; to have intercourse with.
comercio, sm. trade ; commerce ; communication, intercourse ; company of
merchants.
comestible, a. eatable ; -s, s.pl. all sorts
of provisions.

cometa, sm. comet ; —, sf. kite.
cometer, v.a. to commit, to charge ; to
intrust ; to attack ; to attempt.
comezón, sf. itch ; ardent desire.
cómico, ca, a. comic, comical ; theatrical ;
—, sm. & f. actor, actress.
comida, sf. eating, food ; dinner..
comidilla, sf. (col.) hobby.
comilón, ona, a. great eater, glutton.
comino, sm. cumin (plant or seed).
comisaría, sf. comissaryship.
comisario, sm. commissary.
comisión, sf. trust, commission ; mandate ; committee.
comisionado, sm. commissionary ; commissioner. [pute.
comisionar, v.a. to commission, to de-
comisionista, sm. commission-agent.
comiso, sm. confiscation.
comistrajo, sm. hodge-podge.
comitiva, sf. suite, retinue, followers.
cómitre, sm. boatswain on board a galley.
como, ad. how, in what manner ; as ;
why ; in such a manner ; in what
manner ; like ; — quiera, however.
cómoda, sf. chest of drawers. [broker.
comodatario, sm. (law) borrower ; pawn-
comodato, sm. (law) loan.
comodidad, sf. comfort ; convenience ;
profit, interest ; -es, pl. wealth, estate.
cómodo, da, a. convenient, commodious ;
comfortable ; —, sm. utility, profit,
benefit.
compacto, ta, a. compact, close, dense.
compadecer, v.a. to pity ; -se, v.r. to
agree with each other.
compadrar, v.n. to become a godfather.
compadrazgo, sm. godfathership.
compadre, sm. joint godfather ; comrade, friend.
compadrería, sf. intimacy, companionship.
compaginar, v.a. to join, to couple.
compañero, ra, sm & f. companion, friend;
compeer, comrade ; partner.
compañía, sf. company, society ; part
nership.
comparación, sf. comparison.
comparar, v.a. to compare, to confront.
comparativo, va, a. comparative.
comparecer, v.n. to appear before a
judge.
comparendo, sm. (leg.) summons.
comparición, sf. (leg.) appearance.
comparsa, sm. & f. (theat.) super.
comparte, sm. joint party in a law-suit.
compartimiento, sm. compartment.
compartir, v.a. to divide into equal parts.
compás, sm. pair of compasses ; (mus.)
measure ; rule, rule of life. [pass.
compasar, v.a. to measure with a com-

compasión, sf. compassion, commiseration.

compasivo, va, a. compassionate.

compatible, a. compatible, consistent with.

compatriota, sm. & f. countryman; countrywoman; fellow-citizen.

compeler, v.a. to compel, to constrain.

compendiar, v.a. to epitomize, to abridge.

compendio, sm. epitome, abridgment, summary.

compendioso, sa, a. brief, abridged, compendious.

compensación, sf. compensation; recompense.

compensar, v.a. & n. to compensate; to make amends; to recompense.

competencia, sf. competition, rivalry; competence.

competente, a. competent, sufficient.

competer, v.n. to be one's due.

competición, sf. competition.

competidor, sm. competitor, rival.

competir, v.n. to vie; to compete with, to rival.

compilación, sf. compilation.

compilador, sm. compiler.

compilar, v.a. to compile.

compinche, sm. (col.) comrade, crony.

complacencia, sf. pleasure; compliance.

complacer, v.a. to consent, to yield gracefully; -se, to be pleased with.

complaciente, a. obliging, good-natured.

complemento, sm. complement, complement.

completar, v.a. to complete.   [tion.

completo, ta, a. complete, perfect.

complexión, sf. bodily constitution.

complexionado, da, a.; bien ó mal —, of a good or bad constitution.

complexo, sm. complex.

complicar, v.a. to complicate.

cómplice, sm. & f. accomplice.

complicidad, sf. complicity.

complot, sm. (col.) plot, intrigue.

complotar, v.a. to conspire, to plot.

componedor, sm. composer, author; compositor.

componer, v.a. to compose; to compound; to construct; to mend, to repair; to strengthen, to restore; to garnish; to adjust; to reconcile; to compose, to calm.

comportable, a. supportable, tolerable, sufferable.

comportar, v.a. to suffer, to tolerate; -se, to comport, to behave one's self.

composición, sf. composition; composure, making; adjustment; •agreement; musical or literary composition; modest appearance.

compositor, sm. composer compositor.

compostura, sf. composition, composure; mending, repairing; neatness of dress; accommodation, adjustment; modesty, demureness.

compota, sf. stewed fruit.

compotera, sf. fruit-dish.

compra, sf. purchase; daily household marketing.

comprador, ra, sm. & f. buyer; caterer.

comprar, v.a. to buy, to purchase.

comprender, v.a. to include, to contain; to comprehend, to understand.

comprensible, a. comprehensible.

comprensión, s. comprehension.

comprensivo, va, a. comprehensive.

compresible, a. compressible.   [sure.

compresión, s. compression, compressivo, va, a. compressive.

comprimir, v.a. to compress; to repress, to restrain; -se, to subdue one's passion.   [prove.

comprobar, v.a. to verify, to confirm; to compromoter, v.a. to compromise; to render one answerable; to endanger.

compromisario, sm. arbitrator, umpire.

compromiso, sm. compromise.

compuerta, sf. half door; sluice.

compuesto, sm. compound; —, ta, a. composed, compounded; made up.

compulsa, sf. attested copy of an instrument.   [copy.

compulsar, v.a. to make an authentic compulsivo, va, a. compulsive.

compulsorio, ria, a. ordering an authentic copy to be made.

compunción, sf. compunction, contrition.

compungirse, v.r. to feel compunction.

compungivo, va, a. pricking, stimulating.

computación, sf. computation.

computar, v.a. to compute.

cómputo, sm. computation, calculation.

comulgar, v.a. & n. to administer the sacrament; to communicate.

común, a. common, usual, general; —, sm. community, public; en —, jointly.

comunal, a. belonging to the community; common, usual; —, sm. commonalty.

comunero, ra, a. popular; —, sm. joint holder of a tenure of lands.

comunicación, sf. communication.

comunicar, v.a. to communicate; -se, to have intercourse; to correspond.

comunicativo, va, a. communicative.

comunidad, sf. commonalty; community.   [common possession.

comunión, sf. communion; fellowship;

comuña, s. wheat mixed with tares.

con, pr. with; by; — que, then, therefore.

conato, sm. endeavour, effort; •crime attempted but not executed.

cóncava, concavidad, sf. concavity.

cóncavo, va, a. concave.

concebir, v.a. & n. to conceive; to become pregnant.

conceder, v.a. to give; to grant; to concede, to allow.

concejal, sm. member of a council.

concejil, a. relating to public boards.

concejo, sm. civic body of a small town; town-hall.

concentración, sf. concentration.

concentrar, v.a. to concentrate.

concéntrico, ca, a. concentric. [ceit.

concepción, sf. conception; idea, conceptear, v.n. to abound in witty saying.

conceptible, a. conceivable. [ings.

concepto, sm. conceit, thought; judgment, opinion. [to think.

conceptuar, v.a. to conceive, to judge,

conceptuóso, sa, a. sharp, witty; sententious.

concerniente, a. concerning, relating.

concernir, v.imp. to regard, to concern.

concertar, v.a. to concert, to settle; to adjust; to conclude an agreement; to compose differences; —, v.n. to agree, to accord.

concesión, sf. concession.

conciencia, sf. conscience.

concierto, sm. concert; agreement; accommodation; (mus.) concert; de —, according to agreement.

conciliación, sf. conciliation, reconciliation.

conciliar, v.a. to conciliate, to reconcile; —, a. belonging to councils.

conciliativo, va, a. conciliatory.

concilio, sm. council; Council of the Church.

concinidad, sf. harmony.

concino, na, a. harmonious, tasteful.

concisión, sf. conciseness.

conciso, sa, a. concise, brief.

concitar, v.a. to excite; to stir up.

conciudadano, sm. fellow-citizen; fellow-countryman.

cónclave, conclave, sm. conclave.

concluir, v.a. to conclude, to end, to complete; to convince; to infer, to deduce; to disarm an adversary by grasping the hilt of his sword.

conclusión, sf. conclusion, end; consequence.

concluyente, a. conclusive. [quence.

concolega, sm. fellow-collegian.

concomerse, v.r. to shrug the shoulders, to give a shrug. [panying.

concomitante, a. concomitant, accompanying.

concordancia, sf. concordance, concord; harmony.

concordar, v.a. to harmonize; —, v.n. to agree.

concordato, sm. concordate.

concorde, a. concordant, agreeing.

concordia, sf. conformity, union, harmony; de —, by common consent.

concreción, sf. concretion.

concretar, v.a. to combine, to put together; -se, v.r. to confine one's self to one subject.

concreto, ta, a. concrete.

concubina, sf. concubine.

concubinato, sm. concubinage.

concúbito, sm. coition.

conculcar, v.a. to trample under foot.

concupiscencia, sf. concupiscence, lust.

concurrencia, sf. convention of persons assembly; competition.

concurrir, v.n. to meet; to concur; to contribute.

concurso, sm. concourse; crowd.

concusión, sf. concussion, shaking; extortion and embezzlement.

concusionario, ria, a. guilty of extortion and peculation.

concha, sf. shell; oyster; tortoise-shell.

conchabanza, sf. the making one's self comfortable; plotting, conspiracy.

conchabar, v.a. to join, to unite; -se, to plot, to conspire. [shells.

conchado, da, a. scaly, covered with

conchil, sm. rock-shell.

conchudo, da, a. scaly, crustaceous; cunning, crafty.

condado, sm. earldom, county.

condal, a. relating to an earl.

conde, sm. earl, count.

condecente, a. suitable.

condecorar, v.a. to adorn, to embellish.

condenable, a. damnable.

condenación, condena, sf. condemnation.

condenar, v.a. to condemn; to refute; to disapprove.

condenatorio, ria, a. (leg.) damnatory.

condensación, sf. condensation.

condensar, v.a. to condense, to thicken.

condesa, sf. countess.

condesado, sm. earldom.

condescendencia, sf. condescension, compliance.

condescender, v.a. to condescend, to yield, to comply.

condestable, sm. constable.

condestablía, sf. constableship.

condición, sf. condition, quality; state, footing; rank; clause, stipulation.

condicionado, da, a. conditioned.

condicional, a. conditional, not absolute.

condicionar, v.n. to agree.

condigno, a. condign.

condimentar, v.a. to season.

condimento, sm. condiment, seasoning.

condiscípulo, sm. fellow-disciple, fellow-scholar.

condolecerse, condolerse, v.r. to condole.
condonación, sf. pardoning, forgiving.
condonar, v.a. to pardon, to forgive.
conducción, sf. conveyance; carriage (the act); conduct; payment for conducting.
conducente, a. suitable, satisfactory.
conducir, v.a. to convey, to conduct; —, v.n. to be serviceable, to conduce; -se, to conduct one's self. [veyance.
conducta, sf. conduct, behaviour; con-
conductivo, va, a. conducive.
conducto, sm. conduit, drain. [guard.
conductor, sm. conductor, guide; (rail.)
conejal, conejar, sm. rabbit-warren.
conejera, sf. warren, rabbit-burrow.
conejero, ra, a. trained to hunt rabbits.
conejo, ja, sm. & f. rabbit.
conejuna, sf. rabbit fur.
conejuno, na, a. belonging to rabbits; rabbit-like.
conexidades, sf.pl. (law) all matters pertinent to the principal subject.
conexión, sf. connection, conjunction.
conexo, xa, a. connected, united.
confabular, v.a. to confabulate, to discuss.
confalón, sm. gonfalon, banner, standard.
confección, sf. (med.) electuary. [serves.
confeccionar, v.a. to make up into con-
confederación, sf. confederacy.
confederado, a. confederate.
confederar, v.a. -se, to confederate.
conferencia, sf. conference, lecture.
conferenciar, v.a. to hold a conference.
conferir, v.a. to compare; to discuss; to grant, to confer.
confesar, v.a. to confess; to avow.
confesión, sf. confession, avowal.
confesionista, sm. Lutheran.
confeso, sa, a. (law) confessed.
confesonario, sm. confessional.
confesor, sm. confessor. [forward.
confiado, da, a. a confident; arrogant,
confiador, sm. (law) joint surety.
confianza, sf. confidence, boldness; assurance; intimacy; en —, confidentially. [to feed with hope.
confiar, v.a. & n. to confide, to trust in;
confidencia, sf. confidence.
confidencial, a. confidential.
confidente, sm. confidant; —, a. true, faithful, trusty.
configurar, v.a. to configure.
confín, sm. limit, boundary.
confinar, v.a. & n. to exile; to confine; to border upon.
confirmación, sf. confirmation. [borate.
confirmar, v.a. to confirm; to corro-
confiscación, sf. confiscation, forfeiture.
confiscar, v.a. to confiscate. [candy.
confitar, v.a. to preserve (fruits); to

confite, sm. sweet-meat.
confitera, sf. sugar-plum box.
confitería, s. confectioner's shop.
confitero, sm. confectioner. [jam.
confitura, sf. preserved or potted fruit;
conflación, sf. melting metals.
conflagración, sf. conflagration.
conflicto, sm. conflict.
confluencia, sf. confluence.
confluir, v.n. to join (applied to rivers and sea-currents).
conformar, v.a. to conform, to fit; —, v.n. to suit, to fit; -se, to submit, to agree.
conforme, a. conformable, suitable; —, ad. according to.
conformidad, sf. conformity; patience, resignation; de —, by common consent; in company.
confortación, sf. comfort, consolation.
confortar, v.a. to comfort; to strengthen; to console. [dial.
confortativo, va, a. comfortable, cor-
confracción, sf. fracture.
confraternidad, sf. confraternity.
confrontación, sf. confrontation.
confrontar, v.a. to confront.
confundir, v.a. to confound, to jumble; to perplex; to huddle; to throw into confusion.
confusamente, ad. confusedly.
confusión, sf. confusion, disorder; tumultuous medley; perplexity, perturbation; obscurity; humiliation.
confuso, sa, a. confused, confounded; obscure; perplexed.
confutación, sf. confutation, conviction.
confutar, v.a. to confute.
congelación, sf. congelation.
congelar, v.a. to congeal.
congeniar, v.n. to be congenial; to agree in character.
congerie, sf. congeries.
congestión, sf. (med.) congestion.
conglutinar, v.a. to join, to stick together; v.n. to unite, to adhere. [ing.
congoja, sf. anguish, pang, heart-break-
congojoso, sa, a. afflictive, painful.
congraciar, v.a. to ingratiate, to flatter.
congratulación, sf. congratulation.
congratular, v.a. to congratulate.
congregación, sf. congregation, assembly.
congregar, v.a. to assemble, to collect.
congreso, sm. congress. [a priest.
congrua, sf. a competent sustenance for
congruamente, ad. conveniently, becomingly. [tunity.
congruencia, sf. convenience, oppor-
congruente, congruo, ua, a. corresponding; convenient, suitable.
cónico, ca, a. conical.

conjetura, sf. conjecture.
conjetural, a. conjectural.
conjeturar, v.a. to conjecture.
conjugación, sf. (gr.) conjugation.
conjugar, v.a. (gr.) to conjugate.
conjunción, sf. conjunction.
conjuntamente, ad. together.
conjunto, ta, a. united, conjunct ; allied,
kindred ; —, sm. sum, total.
conjuración, sf. conspiracy, plot.
conjurado, sm. conspirator.
conjurador, sm. exorcist ; conspirator.
conjuramentar, v.a. to bind by an oath ;
to administer an oath.   [exorcise.
conjurar, v.n. to conspire, to plot ; to
conjuro, sm. conjuration, exorcism.
conmemoración, sf. remembrance ; commemoration ; requiem.
conmemorar, v.a. to commemorate.
conmensal, sm. commensal, messmate.
conmensuración, sf. comparative measurement.   [gard to a standard.
conmensurar, v.a. to measure with re-
conmigo, pn. with me.
conmilitón, sm. comrade, fellow-soldier.
conminación, sf. commination, threat.
conminar, v.a. to threaten.
conminatorio, ria, a. comminatory,
threatening.   [compassion.
conmiseración, sf. commiseration; pity,
conmoción, sf. commotion ; concussion ;
fretting ; tumult, disturbance.
conmover, v.a. to move ; to disturb.
conmutación, sf. commutation, exchange.
conmutar, v.a. to commute ; to barter,
to exchange.   [nature.
connatural, a. natural ; according to
connaturalizarse, v.r. to accustom one's
self
connivencia, sf. connivance.   [relation.
connotación, sf. connotation ; distant
connotado, sm. relationship.
connotar, v.a. to imply.   [lock.
connubio, sm. (poet.) matrimony, wed-
cono, sm. cone.
conocedor, ra, sm. & f. connoisseur.
conocer, v.a. to know, to understand ;
-se, to know one another.
conocido, da, sm. & f. acquaintance,
acquaintant.
conocimiento, sm. knowledge, understanding ; connoisseurship ; cognition ; acquaintance ; (mar.) bill of
landing.   [condition.
conque, conj. so, accordingly ; sm. (col.)
conquista, sf. conquest ; acquisition.
conquistador, sm. conqueror.
conquistar, v.a. to conquer.
conreinar, v.n. to reign at the same time
with another.   [mentioned.
consabido, da, a. already known ; above-

Consagración, sf. consecration.
consagrar, v.a. to consecrate.
consanguíneo, nea, a. consanguineous.
consanguinidad, sf. consanguinity.
conscripto, a. conscript.
consecución, sf. attainment.
consecuencia, sf. consequence ; conclusion ; por —, therefore.
consecuente, a. consequent ; —, sm.
consequence.   [quential.
consecutivo, va, a. consecutive ; conse-
conseguir, v.a. to attain, to get, to obtain.
conseja, sf. fable, tale.
consejero, sm. counsellor.
consejo, sm. counsel, advice ; council ;
council-house.
consentido, a. hen-pecked.
consentir, v.a. to consent, to agree ; to
comply, to acquiesce.
conserje, sm. porter, door-keeper.
conserva, sf. conserve.
conservación, sf. conservation.
conservador, ra, a. conservative.
conservar, v.a. to preserve ; to guard ;
to candy fruit.
conservatorio, sm. conservatoire ; —,
ria, a. preservative.
considerable, a. considerable.
consideración, sf. consideration, notice,
care ; reflection.
consideradamente, ad. considerately.
considerado, a. prudent, considerate.
considerar, v.a. to consider.
consigna, sf. (mil.) watch-word.
consignación, sf. consignment ; destination.
consignador, sm. one who consigns goods
to a foreign correspondent.
consignar, v.a. to consign ; to deposit.
consignatario, sm. consignee.
consigo, pn. with one's self.
consiguiente, a. consequent, consecutive.
consistencia, sf. consistence, stability ;
solidity.
consistente, a. consistent, firm, solid.
consistir, v.n. to consist ; to be contained ; to be composed.
consistorio, sm. consistory ; town-hall.
consocio, sm. partner, companion.
consolación, sf. consolation.   [able.
consolador, ra, a. consolatory, comfort-
consolar, v.a. to console, to comfort, to
cheer.
consolidar, v.a. to consolidate ; -se, (law)
to tie up interest with principal.
consolidativo, va, a. healing.   [ence.
consonancia, sf. consonance ; congru-
consonante, sm. rhyme ; —, sf. (gr.)
consonant ; —, a. agreeable, conformable.

consorcio, sm. partnership, society.

D

consorte, sm. consort, companion, partner ; accomplice.

conspiración, sf. conspiracy, plot.

conspirador, sm. conspirator, plotter.

conspirar, v.n. to conspire, to plot.

constancia, sf. constancy, steadiness, immutability.   [able.

constante, a. constant, firm, unalterable.

constar, v.imp. to be evident, certain ; to be composed of, to consist of.

constelación, sf. constellation.

consternación, sf. consternation.

consternar, v.a. to strike with amazement, to confound.

constipación, sf. cold ; costiveness.

constipar, v.a. to affect with cold ; to constipate ; -se, to take cold.

constitución, sf. constitution (in all senses).

constitucional, a. constitutional.

constituir, v.a. to constitute ; to establish ; to appoint.   [sential.

constitutivo, va, a. constitutive, essential.

constituyente, sm. constituent.

constreñimiento, sm. constraint.

constreñir, v.a. to constrain, to force ; (med.) to constipate.

constricción, sf. constriction, contraction.

constrictivo, va, a. astringent.

construcción, sf. construction.

construir, v.a. to form, to build, to construct ; to construe.

construpar, v.a. to deflour.

consuegro, gra, sm. & f. parents of two children who marry.

consuelo, sm. consolation, comfort ; joy, merriment.

cónsul, sm. consul ; member of the tribunal of commerce.   [commerce.

consulado, sm. consulate ; tribunal of

consular, a. consular.

consulta, sf. consult, consultation.

consultación, sf. consultation.

consultar, v.a. to consult, to ask advice ; to give advice.

consultivo, va, a. consultative.

consultor, ra, sm. & f. adviser, counsel.

consumación, sf. consummation, perfection, finishing.

consumado, da, a. consummate, complete, perfect, accomplished, exquisite ; —, sm. jelly-broth.

consumar, v.a. to consummate, to finish, to perfect.

consumir, v.a. to consume, to destroy ; to waste, to exhaust ; -se, to waste away, to languish.

consumo, sm. consumption of provisions and merchandise.

consunción, sf. (med.) consumption ; wasting.

consustancial, a. consubstantial.

contabilidad, sf. accounts ; book-keeping.

contacto, sm. contact.

contadero, ra, a. countable.

contado, da, a. scarce, rare ; fixed, settled ; de —, instantly ; in hand ; al —, cash, ready money.

contador, a. computer, reckoner ; accountant ; counter (table) ; counter (for games).   [office.

contaduría, sf. counting-house ; box-

contagiar, v.a. to infect.

contagio, sm. contagion.

contagioso, sa, a. contagious.   [lution.

contaminación, sf. contamination, pollution.

contaminar, v.a. to contaminate ; to infect by contagion ; to corrupt.

contante, sm. ready money.

contar, v.a. to count, to reckon, to compute, to calculate ; — con, to rely upon.

contemplación, sf. contemplation.

contemplar, v.a. to contemplate, to consider, to study ; to meditate ; to flatter, to comply.

contemplativo, va, a. contemplative.

contemporáneo, nea, a. contemporary.

contemporizar, v.n. to temporise.

contencioso, sa, a. contentious ; quarrelsome.   [to contest, to debate.

contender, v.n. to contend, to strive ;

contendiente, sm. competitor.

contener, v.a. to contain, to comprehend ; to refrain ; to repress.

contenido, da, a. moderate, temperate, modest ; —, sm. tenour, contents.

contentadizo, za, a. bien —, easily contented ; mal —, hard to please.

contentar, v.a. to content, to satisfy, to please ; -se, to be pleased or satisfied.

contento, ta, a. glad ; pleased ; content ; —, sm. content, satisfaction.

contera, sf. ferule of stick.

contestación, sf. answer, reply ; debate, disputation.

contestar, v.a. to answer, to reply ; to prove, to attest ; —, v.n. to agree ; to accord.

conteste, a. confirming the evidence of another.

contexto, sm. context, intermixture.

contienda, sf. contest, dispute debate.

contigo, pn. with thee.

contigüidad, sf. contiguity.

contiguo, gua, a. contiguous, close.

continencia, sf. continence, abstinence, moderation.

continental, a. continental.

continente, sm. abstinence ; countenance ; continent, mainland ; —, a. abstinent, moderate.

contingencia, sf. accidental possibility, contingency.

contingente, a. fortuitous, accidental; —, sm. contingency.

continuación, sf. continuation, lengthening; continuity.

continuar, v.a. & n. to continue. [less.

continuo, nua, a. continuous, ceaseless.

contonearse, v.r. to walk in an affected manner. [ing.

contoneo, sm. affected manner of walking.

contorno, sm. environs, pl.; contour, outline; **en —,** round about.

contorsión, sf. contortion, wry motion.

contra, pr. against, contrary to, opposite to.

contra-almirante, sm. rear-admiral.

contrabajo, sm. counter-bass; bass-viol.

contrabalanzear, v.a. to counterbalance.

contrabandista, sm. smuggler, contrabandist. [gling.

contrabando, sm. contraband trade, smuggling.

contrabatería, sf. (mil.) counter-battery.

contracambio, sm. exchange.

contracción, sf. contraction.

contradanza, sf. country-dance.

contradecir, v.a. to contradict, to gainsay. [opposition.

contradicción, sf. contradiction, verbal opposition.

contradictorio, ria, a. contradictory, opposite to.

contradique, sm. buttress of a dyke.

contraer, v.a. & n. to contract, to shrink; to make a bargain; **-se,** to shrink up.

contraescarpa, sf. (mil.) counter-scarp.

contraescritura, sf. deed annulling another. [ress.

contrafoso, sm. outer ditch of a fortress.

contrafuero, sm. violation of a privilege.

contrafuerte, sm. buttress.

contraguardia, sf. counterguard.

contrahacer, v.a. to counterfeit, to falsify; to pirate the works of an author.

contrahaz, sm. wrong side of cloth.

contrahecho, cha, a. deformed, miscreated; counterfeited.

contralor, sm. steward of royal palace.

contralto, sm. (mus.) contralto.

contramaestre, sm. (mar.) boatswain.

contramalla, sf. double net for catching fish. [double meshes.

contramallar, v.a. to make nets with double meshes.

contramandar, v.a. to countermand.

contramarca, sf. countermark; customs stamp duty. [glass window.

contramarco, sm. counter-frame of a glass window.

contramarcha, sf. counter-march.

contramarchar, v.a. to counter-march.

contramarea, sf. (mar.) tide meeting another.

contramesana, sf. mizen-mast.

contramina, sf. countermine.

contraminar, v.a. to counter-mine; to counter-work.

contra-natural, a. unnatural.

contraorden, sm. countermand. [party.

contrapasar, v.n. to join the opposite party.

contrapaso, sm. back step.

contrapelo, ad. against the grain.

contrapesar, v.n. to counterpoise.

contrapeso, sm. counterpoise; ropedancer's pole.

contraponer, v.a. to compare, to oppose.

contraposición, sf. comparison, contrast.

contraprueba, sf. (printing) second proof, revise. [house.

contrapuerta, sf. inner hall-door of a house.

contrapuntearse, v.r. to quarrel with abusive language.

contrapunto, sm. (mus.) counterpoint.

contrapunzón, sm. carpenter's punch.

contraquilla, sf. (mar.) false keel.

contrariar, v.a. to contradict, to oppose, to counteract. [tion.

contrariedad, sf. contrariety, opposition.

contrario, sm. opponent, antagonist; contrary; —, **ria,** a. contrary, opposite; adverse, abhorrent; **por el —,** on the contrary; **en —,** against.

contrarrestar, v.a. to resist, to oppose; to strike back a ball.

contrarresto, sm. player who is to strike back the ball; opposition, contradiction.

contrarrevolución, sf. counter-revolution.

contrarronda, sf. (mil.) counter-round.

contrasellar, v.a. to counterseal. [word.

contraseña, sf. countersign; (mil.) watchword.

contrastar, v.a. to contrast, to oppose; to resist, to contradict; to assay metals; to examine measures and weights.

contraste, sm. assayer of the mint; assayer's office; assayer of weights and measures; contrast; opposition, strife; (mar.) sudden change of the wind.

contrata, sf. contract.

contratación, sf. trade, commerce.

contratante, sm. contractor; trader.

contratar, v.a. to trade, to traffic; to contract, to stipulate. [fortune.

contratiempo, sm. disappointment, mis fortune.

contratista, sm. contractor.

contrato, sm. contract, pact.

contratreta, s. counterplot.

contratrinchera, s. counter-trench.

contravalar, v.a. to form a line of contravallation.

contravención, sf. contravention.

contraveneno, sm. antidote.

contravenir, v.n. to contravene, **to** transgress; to oppose.

contraventana, sf. window-shutter.
contraventor, ra, sm. & f. offender, transgressor.
contribución, sf. contribution ; tax.
contribuir, v.a. to contribute.
contributario, sm. contributor, payer of taxes.   [tributory.
contribuyente, v.a. contributing ; contribution.
contrición, sf. contrition, penitence.
contrincante, sm. competitor.
contristar, v.a. to afflict, to sadden.
contrito, ta, a. contrite, penitent.
controversia, sf. controversy, dispute.
controversista, sm. controversialist.
controvertir, v.a. to controvert, to dispute.
contumacia, sf. obstinacy, stubbornness ; (law) contumacy.
contumaz, a. obstinate, stubborn ; (law) contumacious.
contumelia, sf. contumely, abuse.
contumelioso, sa, a. contumelious.
contundente, a. striking, decisive.
contundir, v.a. to beat together ; to bruise ; to cause a contusion.
conturbación, sf. perturbation.
conturbar, v.a. to perturbate, to disquiet.
contusión, sf. contusion.
convalecencia, sf. convalescence, recovery from disease.
convalecer, v.n. to recover from sickness ; to recover lost prosperity or power.
convecino, na, a. neighbouring.
convencer, v.a. to convince.
convencimiento, sm. conviction.
convención, sf. convention, pact.
convencional, a. conventional, agreed upon by compact.
conveniencia, sf. utility, profit ; convenience ; ease, commodity.
conveniente, a. useful, convenable, conformable.   [cordance.
convenio, sm. convention, contract, accordance.
convenir, v.n. to agree, to coincide ; to compromise ; to fit, to suit, to correspond ; to assemble.
conventículo, sm. conventicle.   [nery.
convento, sm. convent, monastery, nunnery.
conventual, a. monastic.
convergencia, sf. convergence.
conversable, a. conversable, sociable.
conversación, sf. conversation, easy talk ; commnication.   [gether.
conversar, v.n. to converse ; to live together.
conversión, sf. conversion, change.
converso, sm. convert.
convertir, v.a. to convert.
convexidad, sf. convexity.
convexo, xa, a. convex.
convicción, sf. conviction.

convicto, ta, a. convicted (found guilty).
convidar, v.a. to invite, to bid ; to allure, to persuade ; **-se**, to offer one's service.
convincente, a. convincing.   [service.
convite, sm. invitation ; banquet.
convocar, v.a. to convoke, to assemble.
convocatorio, ria, a. that which convokes.
convólvulo, sm. (bot.) convolvulus.
convoy, sm. convoy, conduct, escort, retinue, suit.
convoyar, v.a. to convoy, to escort.
convulsión, sf. convulsion.
convulsivo, va, a. convulsive.
conyugal, a. conjugal, connubial.
cónyuges, sm.pl. married couple, husband and wife.
coñac, sm. brandy.
cooperación, sf. co-operation.
cooperador, ra, sm. & f. co-operator.
cooperar, v.a. to co-operate.
cooperativo, va, a. co-operative.
coopositor, sm. competitor.
coordinar, v.a. to arrange, to classify.
copa, sf. wine-glass ; top of a tree ; brazier ; **sombrero de —**, top-hat ; **-s**, pl. hearts (at cards).
copado, da, a. tufted.
copera, sf. cupboard.
copero, sm. cup-bearer.
copete, sm. toupee ; tuft ; top, summit.
copetudo, da, a. tufted ; supercilious on account of one's noble descent.
copia, sf. plenty, abundance ; copy, transcript ; copy of a picture.
copiador, sm. copyist ; copier ; **libro —**, copy-book.
copiar, v.a. to copy ; to imitate, to draw from life ; (poet.) to describe, to depict.   [ful.
copioso, sa, a. copious, abundant, plentiful.
copista, sm. copyist.
copita, sf. dram ; small glass.
copla, sf. couplet ; sarcastic remark.
coplear, v.n. to make couplets.
coplero, sm. poetaster ; ballad-seller.
copo, sm. small bundle of cotton, flax, &c., put on the distaff to be spun ; flake of snow.
copón, sm. cibary (cup used in Catholic churches).
copudo, a. tufted, tufty, bushy.
cópula, sf. joining of two things together ; cupola ; (gr.) copula.
copulativo, va, a. copulative.
coqueta, sf. coquette, flirt.
coquetear, v.n. to coquet.
coquetería, sf. coquetry, flirtation.
coquillo, sm. cocoa-nut (of the Indian palm-tree).   [children.
coquito, sm. grimace made to amuse children.
coracero, sm. cuirassier.

coracha, sf. leather sack, used for the transport of cocoa, tobacco, &c., from America.

coraje, sm. courage ; anger, passion.

corajudo, da, a. angry, passionate.

coral, sm. coral ; -es, pl. strings of corals ; —, a. choral.

coralero, sm. worker or dealer in corals.

coralina, sf. sea-coralline.

corambre, sf. hides and skins, dressed or undressed.

corambrero, sm. dealer in hides.

coranvobis, sm. pomposity.

coraza, sf. cuirass.

corazón, sm. heart ; core ; benevolence ; courage ; centre ; pith of a tree ; de —, heartily.

corazonada, sf. inspiration ; quick decision ; presentiment. [ing-crop.

corbachada, sf. lash given with a hunt-

corbacho, sm. hunting-crop.

corbata, sf. cravat, neckerchief.

corbatín, sm. cravat with a clasp.

corbato, sm. cooler.

corbeta, sf. corvet (light vessel with three masts and square sails).

corcel, sm. steed, charger.

corcino, sm. small deer.

corcova, sf. hump ; protuberance.

corcovado, da, a. hump-backed, crooked.

corcovear, v.n. to curvet, to cut capers.

corcovo, sm. curvet ; caper.

corchea, sf. (mùs.) crotchet.

corchera, sf. cork wine-cooler.

corcheta, sf. eye of a hoor or clasp.

corchete, sm. clasp ; locket ; tipstaff, constable ; bench-hook of a carpenter's bench. [stopple.

corcho, sm. cork ; bee-hive ; cork-

cordaje, sm. (mar.) cordage.

cordel, sm. cord, rope ; (mar.) line.

cordelazo, sm. lash given with a rope.

cordelería, sf. rope-walk.

cordelero, sm. rope-maker.

corderillo, sm. dressed lamb-skin.

cordero, sm. lamb ; dressed lamb-skin ; meek, gentle man. [cordial.

cordial, a. cordial, affectionate ; —, sm.

cordialidad, sf. cordiality.

cordillera, sf. range of mountains.

cordobán, sm. cordovan leather.

cordón, sm. cord, string ; twisted lace ; military cordon. [coins.

cordoncillo, sm. braid ; milled edge of

cordonería, sf. lace-making.

cordonero, sm. lace-maker ; rope-maker.

cordura, sf. prudence, practical wisdom, judgment. [leather hide.

corezuelo, sm. sucking-pig ; smal

corifeo, sm. coryphoeus.

corista, sm. chorister.

coriza, sf. dry catarrh.

corladura, sf. gold-varnish.

cornada, sf. thrust with a bull's horn.

cornadura, sf. horns, pl. [pl.

cornamenta, sf. horns of an animal,

cornamusa, sf. cornemuse ; sort of rustic flute. [of the eye).

córnea, sf. cornea (second integument

cornear, v.n. to butt with the horns.

corneja, sf. crow.

cornejo, sm. cornel-tree.

córneo, ea, a. horny.

cornerina, sf. onyx.

corneta, sf. cornet ; hunting-horn ; cornet (ensign). [horses.

cornezuelo, sm. instrument for bleeding

cornijal, sm. corner of a building.

cornisa, sf. cornice.

corno. See **cornejo.**

cornucopia, sf. cornucopia, horn of plenty ; branched candlestick.

cornudo, da, a. horned.

coro, sm. choir, quire ; chorus.

corolario, sm. corollary.

corona, sf. crown ; coronet ; top of the head ; clerical tonsure ; crown (silver coin) ; regal power ; monarchy ; honour, splendour, decoration ; halo.

coronación, sf. coronation.

coronar, v.a. to crown ; to complete, to perfect ; to ornament the top of a building.

coronario, ria, a. relating to a crown.

coronel, sm. (mil.) colonel.

coronela, sf. colonel's wife.

coronilla, sf. crown of the head.

coroza, sf. coronet of pasteboard, worn as a mark of infamy.

corozo, sm. a species of palm.

corpanchón, sm. huge carcass.

corpiño, sm. bodice.

corporación, sf. corporation, guild.

corporal, a. corporal ; —, sm. altar linen.

corporalidad, sf. corporality.

corpóreo, rea, a. corporeal.

corporificar, v.a. to embody.

corpudo, da, a. corpulent, bulky.

corpulencia, sf. corpulence.

corpulento, ta, a. corpulent, bulky.

Corpus, sm. Corpus-Christi day.

corpúsculo, sm. corpuscle.

corral, sm. fenced enclosure ; yard ; (fig.) blank space in notebooks of students who have neglected a lecture.

corralero, sm. keeper of a yard.

corraliza, sf. yard.

correa, sf. leather strap, thong ; flexibility.

correaje, sm. equipment of straps.

correar, v.a. to draw out wool and prepare it for use.

corrección, sf. correction; reprehension; amendment.

correctivo, va, a. corrective.

correcto, ta, a. exact, correct.

corrector, sm. corrector; proof-reader.

corredera, sf. race-ground; movable shutter; leaf (of table); upper grinding-stone.

corredizo, za, a. easy to be untied.

corredor, sm. runner; race-horse; corridor; broker.

corredura, sf. liquor which flows over the brim.

correduría, sf. trade of a broker; brokerage.

correero, sm. strap-maker.

corregencia, sf. co-regency.

corregente, sm. co-regent.

corregidor, sm. corregidor (Spanish magistrate).

corregidora, sf. wife of a corregidor.

corregir, v.a. to correct, to amend; to reprehend; to mitigate.

correjel, sm. English sole-leather.

correlación, sf. correlation.

correlativo, va, a. correlative.

correncia, sf. (col.) looseness of the belly.

correo, sm. express, courier; post-boy; post-office; bag of letters; **á vuelta de —,** by return of post.

correo, sm. (leg.) accomplice.

correoso, sa, a. flexible.

correr, v.a. & n. to run; to flow; to blow (applied to the wind); to pass away; to go easily; to act heedlessly; **-se,** to be ashamed; to fly into a passion.

correría, sf. incursion; leather strap.

correspondencia, sf. correspondence; relation; intercourse, reciprocal intelligence; proportion.

corresponder, v.n. to make a suitable return; to correspond, to answer; to agree, to be congruent; **-se,** to correspond; to esteem one another.

correspondiente, a. correspondent, conformable, suitable.

corresponsal, sm. correspondent.

corretaje, sm. brokerage.

corretear, v.a. to rove, to ramble.

correvedile, sm. (col.) tale-bearer.

corrida, sf. course, race; **de —,** at full speed.

corrido, da, a. of over weight or measure; expert; artful; ashamed.

corriente, sf. course of rivers; current; course, progression; **—,** a. current; easy; generally received; common, general; fluent; running; marketable.

corrillero, sm. idler, vagabond.

corrillo, sm. circle of persons; **-s,** pl. town-talk.

corro, sm. circle for conversation; group of people; **-s,** pl. gossip.

corroborar, v.a. to corroborate, to strengthen.

corroer, v.a. to corrode.

corromper, v.a. to corrupt; to alter the form of a thing; to seduce; to bribe, to suborn; **—,** v.n. to stink; **-se,** to rot, to putrify.

corrosión, sf. corrosion.

corrosivo, va, a. corrosive.

corrupción, sf. corruption, putrefaction; spurious alteration in a book or writing; depravity.

corruptela, sf. corruption; (law) abuse.

corruptible, a. susceptible of corruption.

corruptivo, va, a. corruptive.

corrupto, ta, a. corrupted, corrupt.

corruptor, sm. corruptor, misleader.

corrusco, sm. offal, broken bread.

corsario, sm. corsair, privateer; **—, ria,** a. cruising.

corsé, sf. corset, stays.

corta, sf. felling of wood.

cortabolsas, sm. pick-pocket.

cortadera, sf. chisel for cutting hot iron; knife for extracting honeycombs.

cortadillo, sm. small drinking-glass; **echar -s,** to speak in an affected manner; to drink wine.

cortador, sm. butcher; **-es,** pl. incisors; **—, ra,** a. cutting.

cortadura, sf. cut; cutting; incision; fissure; **-s,** pl. shreds, cuttings, parings.

cortafrío, sm. cold chisel.

cortafuego, sm. fire-proof wall.

cortapapel, sm. paper-knife.

cortapicos y callares, hold your tongue !

cortapiés, sm. thrust made at the legs in fencing.

cortaplumas, sm. pen-knife.

cortar, v.a. to cut, to cut off, to curtail; to separate, to hew, to chop; (mil.) to cut off part of the enemy's army; to cut (at cards); to interrupt; to abridge; **-se,** to be ashamed or confounded; to coagulate.

corte, sm. edge of knife, &c.; abscission, cutting; out; felling of trees; **—,** sf. court, capital town; retinue, suite; yard; courtship, flattery; tribunal; **-s,** sf.pl. cortes, Spanish Parliament.

cortedad, sf. smallness, littleness; stupidity; shyness; pusillanimity.

cortejante, a. courtier, gallant.

cortejar, v.a. to make love; to court; to attend.

cortejo, sm. homage; courtship; gift, present; gallant; wooer.

cortés, a. courteous, genteel, polite.

cortesanazo, za, a. awkwardly civil.

cortesanía, sf. courtesy, politeness.

cortesano, na, a. connected with the court; courteous, gentle; —, sm. & f. courtier; -na, sf. courtesan.

cortesía, sf. courtesy, good manners, pl. ; formal conclusion of a letter.

corteza, sf. bark; peel; crust; outward appearance; rusticity.

cortezudo, da, a. barky; rustic, un- [mannerly.

cortina, sf. curtain.

cortinaje, sm. set of curtains for a house.

corto, ta, a. short; scanty, narrow, small, little; stupid; pusillanimous, fearful; concise; defective; á la -a ó á la larga, sooner or later.

cortón, sm. a kind of beetle.

coruscar, v.n. (poet.) to glitter. [ing.

corusco, ca, a. (poet.) brilliant, glitter-

corva, sf. ham; curb (disease in horses' knees).

corvadura, sf. curvature; bend of an arch.

corvaza, sf. curb (disease).

corvejón, sm. hough, hock; spur of a cock. [(nar.) corvet, sloop of war.

corveta, sf. curvet, bound of a horse;

corvetear, v.n. to curvet.

corvo, va, a. bent, crooked. [deer.

corzo, za, sm. & f. roe-deer, fallow-

corzuelo, sm. wheat which has been left in the husks by the thrashers.

cosa, sf. thing; — de entidad, important thing; no hay tal —, no such thing; —, ad. about, little more or less.

cosaco, sm. cossack.

coscarse, v.r. to shrug the shoulders.

coscoja, sf. scarlet-oak; dry leaves of the kermes-oak; knob on the cross-bit of a bridle.

cosecha, sf. harvest; harvest-time; de su —, of one's own invention.

cosechar, v.a. to crop, to reap.

cosechero, sm. husbandman; vintager.

cosedera, sf. seamstress, needle-woman.

coser, v.a. to sew; to join.

cosicosa, sf. riddle.

cosido, sm. stitching, sewing; — de cama, quilts and blankets of a bed.

cosmético, sm. cosmetic.

cosmopolita, a. & sm. & f. cosmopolite, cosmopolitan. [inquietude.

cosquillas, sf.pl. tickling; (fig.) agitation;

cosquilloso, sa, a. ticklish; easily offended.

costa, sf. cost, price; charge, expense; fatigue, labour; coast, shore; á toda —, at all costs. [a ship.

costado, sm. side; (mil.) flank; side of

costal, sm. sack, large bag; rammer, paviour's beetle.

costalada, sf. fall flat on the ground.

costaneras, sf.pl. rafters, timbers, pl.

costanero, ra, a. sloping; coasting.

costar, v.n. to cost; to cause detriment or loss. [at first cost.

coste, sm. cost, expense; á — y costas,

costear, v.a. to pay the cost; —, v.n. to sail along the coast.

costera, sf. side of a bale of goods; fisherman's basket; outside quire of a ream of paper.

costero, ra, a. outward; (mar.) coasting.

costilla, sf. rib; (fig.) wife; stave; wealth.

costillaje, costillar, sm. human ribs.

costo, sm. cost, price, expense.

costoso, sa, a. costly, dear, expensive.

costra, sf. crust; broken biscuit given to the galley-slaves.

costrada, sf. Spanish seed-cake.

costroso, sa, a. crusty.

costumbre, sf. custom, habit. [of a rope.

costura, sf. seam; needle-work; splicing

costurera, sf. seamstress.

cota, sf. coat of mail.

cotarrera, sf. a gadding woman.

cotarro, sm. refuge for beggars.

cotejar, v.a. to compare, to confront.

cotejo, sm. comparison, collation.

cotí, sm. ticking used for mattresses.

cotidiano, na, a. daily.

cotilla, sf. stays, pl.

cotillero, sm. stay-maker.

cotillón, sm. cotillon (dance).

coto, sm. enclosure of pasture-grounds: district; land-mark.

cotón, sm. printed cotton.

cotonada, sf. printed calico.

cotonía, sf. dimity.

cotorra, sf. small parrot; (col.) loquacious woman. [woman.

cotorrera, sf. hen-parrot; prattling

cotorrería, sf. loquacity.

coturno, sm. cothurnus; buskin.

covacha, sf. small cave, grotto.

covachuela, sf. office of secretary of state.

covanillo, sm. basket for gathering grapes.

coyunda, sf. strap with which oxen are tied to the yoke. [juncture.

coyuntura, sf. joint articulation; con-

coz, sf. kick; recoil of a gun; flowing back of a flood; á coces, by dint of kicking.

cráneo, sm. skull, head-pan.

crápula, sf. intoxication.

crasitud, sf. grease, fat; corpulency.

craso, sa, a. fat, greasy, thick.

cráter, sm. crater of a volcano.

creación, sf. creation. [author.

creador, sm. the Creator, God; creato.

crear, v.a. to create, to make ; to establish.   [rise (of prices).

crecer, v.n. to grow, to increase ; to

creces, sf.pl. augmentation, increase ; additional quantity of corn paid by a farmer to a public granary, besides what he borrowed from it.

crecida, sf. freshet, flood (of rivers).

crecido, da, a. grown, increased ; grave, important.

creciente, sf. freshet ; leaven ; crescent (moon) ; (mar.) rising tide.

crecimiento, sm. increase ; rise of price.

credencia, sf. (eccles.) credence.

credencial, a. giving assurance or guarantee.

credibilidad, sf. credibility.   [tation.

crédito, sm. credit ; belief, faith ; repu-

credo, sm. creed.

credulidad, sf. credulity.

crédulo, la, a. credulous.   [sion.

creencia, sf. credence, belief ; persua-

creer, v.a. to believe ; to think ; to credit.

creíble, a. credible, believable.   [resis.

crema, sf. cream ; custard ; (gr.) diæ-

crencha, sf. parting of the hair.

crepúsculo, sm. twilight.

cresa, sf. maggot, larva.

crespo, pa, a. crisp, curled ; angry, displeased ; affected (style).

crespón, sm. crape.   [birds.

cresta, sf. cock's-comb ; crest of some

crestado, da, a. crested.

crestón, sm. crest of a helmet.

creta, sf. chalk.

cría, sf. breed or brood of animals ; hatch ; suckling ; infant ; young animal.

criada, sf. maid-servant, hand-maid.

criadero, sm. nursery for trees ; breeding-place ; —, ra, a. fruitful, prolific.

criadilla, sf. testicle ; small loaf in the form of a testicle ; truffle.

criado, sm. servant ; —, da, a. educated, instructed, bred.

criador, sm. Creator ; breeder ; —, ra, a. fruitful, fecund.

crianza, sf. breeding, education.

criar, v.a. to create, to produce ; to breed, to procreate ; to nurse ; to suckle ; to foster.

criatura, sf. creature ; babe.

criba, sf. sieve ; riddle.

cribar, v.a. to sift.

cribo, sm. sieve.

crimen, sm. crime, guilt.

criminal, a. criminal.

criminalidad, sf. criminality.

criminalista, sm. criminal lawyer

crin, sf. mane, horse-hair.

criollo, lla, a. & sm. & f. Creole.

cripta, sf. crypt.   [a mature deliberation.

crisis, sf. crisis ; judgment passed after

crisma, sm. & f. (eccles.) chrism.

crismera, sf. chrismatory.

crisol, sm. crucible.

crisolada, sf. crucible full of metal.

cristal, sm. crystal ; crystal-glass ; looking-glass ; (poet.) water.

cristalino, na, a. crystalline.

cristalización, sf. crystallisation.

cristalizar, v.a. to crystallise.

cristiandad, sf. Christendom.

cristianismo, sm. Christianity.

cristianizar, v.a. to christianize.

cristiano, na, a. & sm. & f. Christian.

Cristo, sm. Christ.

cristus, sm. alphabet.

criterio, sm. criterion.

crítica, sf. critic.

criticador, sm. critic, censurer.

criticar, v.a. to criticise.

crítico, ca, a. & sm. & f. critical ; critic, censurer ; affected refiner of style and language.

crónica, sf. chronicle.

crónico, ca, a. chronic.

cronista, sm. chronicler.

cronología, sf. chronology.

cronológico, ca, a. chronological.

cronómetro, sm. chronometer.

cruce, sm. crossing, crossroads ; railway junction.

crucera, sf. withers of a horse.

crucero, sm. crossing of nave and transepts ; cross-bearer ; (mar.) cruising-station ; cruiser ; cruising-squadron ; Cross (southern constellation).

crucificar, v.a. to crucify ; to molest, to

crucifijo, sm. crucifix.   [torment.

crudeza, sf. unripeness ; rudeness ; cruelty ; vain boasting ; indigestion.

crudo, da, a. raw, crude ; green, unripe ; rude, cruel ; unfinished, immature ; hard of digestion ; blustering, boasting ; immature (of tumours).

cruel, a. cruel ; (fig.) insufferable ; severe, hard ; bloody, violent.   [ageness.

crueldad, sf. cruelty, inhumanity, sav-

cruento, ta, a. bloody, cruel.   [ling.

crujido, sm. crack, creak, clash, crack-

crujir, v.n. to crackle, to rustle.

crustáceo, cea, a. crustaceous ; —, sm. crustacean.

cruz, sf. cross (as instrument, order, ensign of the Christian religion, line) ; (fig.) trial of patience, &c.

cruzada, sf. crusade ; indulgences granted to those who support the crusade.

cruzado, sm. cruzado (old Spanish coin) ; crusader.

cruzamiento, sm. crossing.

cruzar, v.a. to cross; to cross a road; (mar.) to cruise; -se, to be knighted; to take the cross; to cross the legs (of horses).

cuaderna, sf. (mar.) timber-work forming the ribs of a ship.

cuadernillo, sm. small parcel of paper.

cuaderno, sm. parcel of paper stitched together; note-book; punishment of students.

cuadra, sf. hall; large room; stable.

cuadrado, da, a. square, quadrate; perfect; —, sm. square, quadrate; clock (in stockings); gusset of a shirt sleeve; de —, in front, face to face; squared.

cuadragenario, ria, a. forty years old.

cuadragesimal, a. quadragesimal, lenten.

cuadragésimo, ma, a. fortieth. [cornered.

cuadrangular, a. quadrangular, four-

cuadrángulo, sm. quadrangle.

cuadrante, sm. quadrant; dial-plate of a sun-dial; square board put up in churches, pointing out the order of masses to be celebrated.

cuadrar, v.a. & n. to square; to square timbers; to multiply a number by itself; to fit, to suit, to correspond.

cuadratura, sf. quadrature.

cuadriforme, a. four-faced.

cuadrilátero, ra, a. quadrilateral.

cuadrilongo, ga, a. quadrangular, oblong.

cuadrilla, sf. gang, crew, troop, band; one of the four divisions of sheepmasters forming the board of Mesta.

cuadrillero, sm. chief of a gang.

cuádriple, a. quadruple, four-fold.

cuadriplicado, da, a. quadrupled.

cuadrisílabo, ba, a. quadri-syllabic.

cuadriyugo, sm. cart with four horses.

cuadro, sm. square; picture; picture-frame; window-frame; parterre in a garden; (mil.) square body of troops.

cuadrúpedo, da, a. quadruped.

cuadruplicar, v.a. to quadruplicate.

cuádruplo, pla, a. quadruple, fourfold.

cuajada, sf. butter, curd, coagulated fat.

cuajaleche, sf. (bot.) yellow goose-grass.

cuajamiento, sm. coagulation.

cuajar, sm. runnet-bag (of ruminants).

cuajar, v.a. to coagulate; to curdle; to ornament too much; —, v.n. to succeed; to please; -se, to coagulate, to curdle.

cuajarón, sm. grume, clot, gore.

cuajo, sm. rennet; coagulation.

cual, rel. pr. which; he who; like, such; one, other; —, ad. as; how.

cuál, inter. pr. what? which?

cualidad, sf. quality.

cualquier, cualquiera, a. anyone, some-one, anybody, somebody.

cuan, ad. how, as.

cuando, ad. when; in case that; if; although; de — en —, from time to time; — más, — mucho, at most, at best; — menos, at least.

cuándo, inter. ad. when?

cuantía, sf. quantity; rank, distinction.

cuantidad, sf. quantity.

cuantioso, sa, a. numerous, copious.

cuanto, ta, rel. pr. as many as, as much as, all, that, whatever; —, ad. respecting, whilst; — más, the more as; en — á, with regard to; por —, inasmuch as.

cuánto, inter. pr. how much? how many?

cuarenta, a. forty.

cuarentena, sf. space of forty days; Lent; (mar.) quarantine. [sermons.

cuaresma, sf. Lent; collection of Lent

cuaresmal, a. lenten.

cuarta, sf. quarter; quart at piquet; quadrant (of a circle); (mar.) quarter (point of the compass).

cuartal, sm. quartern loaf; quarter (dry measure).

cuartana, sf. (med.) quartan fever.

cuartanal, a. quartan.

cuartanario, ria, a. abouring under a quartan.

cuartear, v.a. to quarter, to divide into four parts; -se, to split into pieces.

cuartel, sm. quarter, fourth part; quarter of a city; barrack billeting of soldiers; dwelling, home.

cuartelero, sm. soldier in each company who keeps their apartment clean.

cuarterón, sm. quadroon, quarter; panel.

cuarteta, sf. (poet.) quatrain.

cuartilla, sf. fourth part of an arroba, or sixteenth part of a quintal; fourth part of a sheet of paper; pastern of horses.

cuartillo, sf. pint; fourth part of a peck in grain; fourth part of a real.

cuarto, sm. fourth part; quarter; dwelling, room, apartment; copper coin worth four maravedís; quartering (in heraldry); -s, pl. cash, money; —, ta, a. fourth.

cuartón, sm. large joist.

cuarzo, sm. quartz.

cuasi, ad. almost, nearly.

Cuasimodo, sm. first Sunday after Easter.

cuatralbo, ba, a. having four white feet

cuatrero, sm. horse-thief. [(horses).

cuatrinca, sf. union of four persons or things; four cards of the same value.

cuatro, a. four; —, sm. figure four; (mus.) quartet.

cuatrocientos, tas, a. four hundred.

cuatropea, sf. horse-tax.

cuatropeado, sm. step in dancing.

cuatrotanto, sm. quadruple amount.

cuba, sf. task; (fig.) toper, drunkard.

cubero, sm. cooper.   [tub.

cubertura, sf. cover, covering.

cubeta, sf. small barrel; bucket.

cubeto, sm. small barrel.

cubicar, v.a. to cube a number.

cúbico, ca, a. cubic.   [of a ship.

cubierta, sf. cover, covert; pretext; deck

cubierto, sm. dish-cover; shelter; cover, place at table; course of dishes.

cubil, sm. lair of wild beasts.

cubilete, sm. copper pan for baking pies, &c.; tumbler; dice-box; small pie stuffed with mince-meat.

cúbito, sm. ulna.

cubo, sm. cube; pail; mill-pool. [herds

cubrepán, sm. fire-shovel, used by shep-

cubrir, v.a. to cover; to palliate; to disguise; to roof (a building); -se, to put on one's hat.

cuca, sf. edible cyperus.

cucaña, sf. greased pole; any thing acquired with little trouble and at other people's expense.

cucañero, sm. (col.) parasite.

cucaracha, sf. cockroach.

cucarda, sf. cockade.   [posture.

cuclillas, (en —,) ad. in a squatting

cuclillo, sm. cuckoo; (fig.) cuckold.

cucurucho, sm. paper bag.

cuchara, sf. spoon.

cucharada, sf. spoonful, ladleful.

cucharón, sm. ladle; large spoon.

cuchichear, v.n. to whisper.

cuchicheo, sm. whispering.

cuchichero, ra, sm. & f. whisperer.

cuchilla, sf. large kitchen-knife; chopping-knife; ancient poniard; (poet.) sword; bookbinder's knife.

cuchillada, sf. cut with a knife; gash; -s, pl. wrangles, quarrels.

cuchillería, sf. cutler's shop; street or quarter of cutlers' shops.

cuchillero, sm. cutler.

cuchillo, sm. knife; triangular gore, gusset of a garment.

cuchufleta, sf. joke, jest, fun.

cuelga, sf. cluster of grapes hung up for use; birthday present.

cuello, sm. neck; neck of a bottle; collar of a priest's garment; shirt-collar.

cuenca, sm. pilgrim's bowl; eye-socket.

cuenco, sm. earthen bowl.

cuenta, sf. computation, calculation; account; narrative; bead of a rosary; reason, satisfaction.   [skinflint.

cuentagarbanzos, sm. niggardly person,

cuentista, sm. tale-bearer.

cuento, sm. a million; butt-end of a spear, &c.; prop, support; fable; tale, story.

cuerda, sf. cord; string for musical instruments; match for firing a gun; spring of a watch or clock; Spanish measure of about 8 yards; dar —, to wind (a watch).   [his senses.

cuerdo, da, a. prudent, judicious; in

cuerna, sf. horn vessel into which cows, &c., are milked; stag's horn; hunt-

cuerno, sm. horn.   [ing-horn.

cuero, sm. hide, skin, leather; (fig.) great drinker.

cuerpo, sm. body; corpse.

cuervo, sm. raven, crow.

cuesco, sm. kernel; stone (of fruits).

cuesta, sf. hill; slope; ir — abajo, to go down hill; — arriba, up hill; with difficulty; á -s, on the shoulders.

cuestión, sf. question; dispute; quarrel; problem.   [lematical.

cuestionable, a. questionable, prob-

cuestionar, v.a. to question, to dispute.

cuestor, sm. questor; alms-gatherer.

cuestura, sf. questorship.

cueva, sf. cave, grotto, den.

cuévano, sm. great basket for carrying grapes to the wine-press.

cuezo, sm. hod.

cugujada, sf. sky-lark.

cugulla, sf. cowl, monk's hood.

cuidado, sm. care, heed, solicitude; fear; custody, charge.   [lant.

cuidadoso, sa, a. careful, heedful, vigi-

cuidar, v.a. to heed, to care; to mind, to look after.

cuita, sf. grief, affliction, trouble.

cuitado, da, a. anxious, wretched, miserable; timid.

culada, sf. fall on one's backside.

culantrillo, sm. (bot.) maidenhair fern.

culantro, sm. (bot.) coriander.

culata, sf. breech of a gun; screw-pin; back part of any thing.

culcusido, sm. (col.) botch-work.

culebra, sf. snake.

culebrear, v.n. to meander.

culebrina, sf. (mil.) culverin.

culero, sm. clout; disease in birds; —, ra, a. slothful, lazy.   [socket.

culo, sm. breech, buttocks; bottom,

culpa, sf. misdemeanour, culpableness; guilt.

culpable, a. culpable; guilty.

culpado, da, sm. & f. culprit.

culpar, v.a. to accuse, to blame.

cultivación, sf. cultivation, culture.

cultivador, sm. cultivator.

cultivar, v.a. to cultivate.

cultivo, sm. cultivation; improvement; culture.

culto, ta, a. pure, elegant, correct; polished; enlightened, civilised; —, sm. culture; worship.

cultura, sf. culture; elegance of style.

cumbre, sf. top, summit; greatest height of favour, fortune, &c.

cumpleaños, sm. birthday.

cumplido, da, a. large, plentiful; faultless; polished, polite, courteous; —, sm. compliment.

cumplimentar, v.a. to compliment.

cumplimentero, ra, a. full of compliments; complaisant.

cumplimiento, sm. compliment; accomplishment; perfection; abundance.

cumplir, v.a. to execute; to provide; to fulfil; —, v.n. to be convenient; to suffice; -se, to be realized.

cumquibus, sm. (col.) money.

cúmulo, sm. heap, pile; (fig.) press of business.

cuna, sf. cradle; (fig.) native country; family, lineage; origin.

cundir, v.n. to spread (of stains); to grow, to increase; to propagate.

cuña, sf. wedge. [in-law.

cuñado, da, sm. & f. brother- or sister-

cuño, sm. die for coining money; impression made by the die.

cuociente, sm. (ar.) quotient.

cuota, sm. quota.

cupé, sm. small closed carriage; brougham.

cupón, sm. coupon, interest-ticket.

cúpula, sf. cupola, dome.

cupulino, sm. lantern (small cupola raised upon another).

cuquillo, sm. cuckoo.

cura, sm. parson, parish priest; —, sf. care, healing.

curable, a. curable, healable.

curazao, sm. curaçoa.

curación, sf. cure, healing.

curador, ra, sm. & f. overseer; guardian; curator, administrator.

curaduría, sf. guardianship.

curandero, sm. quack.

curar, v.a. to attend, to treat, to cure, to heal; to prescribe (for a patient).

curatela, sf. guardianship.

curativo, va, a. curative, healing.

curato, sm. cure of souls; parish.

cureña, sf. gun-carriage; á — rasa, (mil.) without a breastwork.

curia, sf. ecclesiastical court where church affairs are examined and decided in Rome; care and skill.

curial, a. belonging to the Roman curia; —, sm. member of the Roman curia; usher of court.

curiosidad, sf. curiosity; neatness; object of curiosity, rarity.

curiosear, v.n. to be inquisitive.

curioso, sa, a. curious; neat, fine, beautiful; careful, attentive, diligent.

curruca, sf. (orn.) babbling warbler.

currutaco, sm. beau, fop; —, a. foppish affected.

cursado, da, a. skilled; versed.

cursante, a. frequenting; assiduous; —, sm. student, scholar.

cursar, v.a. to frequent; to do a thing often; to attend (a course of lectures). [a university].

cursillo, sm. short course of lectures (in a university).

cursi, a. (col.) flashy, pretentious, aping the fashion.

cursivo, va, a. cursive. [lectures, &c.].

curso, sm. course, direction; course (of curtidor, sm. tanner, leather-dresser.

curtidos, sm.pl. tanned leather.

curtiduría, sf. tan-yard.

curtir, v.a. to tan (leather); to sunbrown; to inure to hardships.

curva, sf. curve; (mar.) knee.

curvatura, sf. curvature.

curvilíneo, nea, a. curvilinear.

curvo, va, curved, bent.

cuscurro, sm. little crust of bread.

cúspide, sf. point.

custodia, sf. custody, keeping, hold; guard, escort; monstrance; reliquary in churches.

custodio, sm. guard, keeper, watchman.

cutáneo, nea a. cutaneous.

cúter, sm. (mar.) cutter.

cutí, sm. ticking (for mattress).

cutícula, sf. cuticle. [another.

cutir, v.a. to knock one thing against

cutis, sm. & f. skin.

cuyo, ya, pn. of which, of whom, whose.

Ch

chabacanada, sf. very vulgar word or observation. bungling.

chabacano, na, a. coarse, unpolished;

chacal, sm. jackal. [taste.

chacolí, sm. light red wine of a sourish

chacota, sf. noisy mirth. [mirth.

chacotear, v.n. to indulge in noisy

chacotero, ra, a. waggish.

cháchara, sf. chit-chat, chatter, idle talk.

chacharear, v.n. to chatter, to jabber.

chacharería, sf. garrulity.

chacharero, sm. prater.

chafaldita, sf. teasing, chaff.

chafalditero, sm. teaser.

chafallar, v.a. to botch, to mend.

chafallo, sm. coarse patch.

chafallón, ona, sm. & f. botcher.

chafar, v.a. to flatten, to crush ; to cut one short in his discourse.   [sword.

chafarote, sm. short broad Turkish

chafarrinada, sf. blot or stain in clothes.

chafarrinar, v.a. to blot, to stain. [&c.

chafarrinón, sm. blot, stain.

chaflán, sm. blaze of a horse ; slope.

chal, sm. shawl.

chalán, sm. hawker, huckster ; cunning dealer ; horse-dealer.

chalanear, v.a. to sell things artfully; to deal in horses.

chalanería, sf. sharp dealing.

chaleco, sm. waistcoat.

chalote, sm. shallot-garlic.

chalupa, sf. (mar.) sloop.

chamarra, sf. garment made of sheep-skins or of very coarse frieze.

chamarreta, sf. short loose jacket.

chambelán, sm. chamberlain.

chambra, sf. woman's dressing-gown.

chamelote, sm. camelot.

chamorra, sf. shorn head.

chamorro, sm. (bot.) beardless wheat.

champurrar, v.a. to mix liquors ; to speak gibberish.

chamuscado, da, a. tipsy, flustered with wine ; addicted to some vice.

chamuscar, v.a. to singe, to scorch.

chamusquina, sf. scorching ; (fig.) scolding, wrangling.

chancero, ra, a. jocose, sportive, merry ; —, sm. (col.) young thief.

chanciller, sm. chancellor.

chancillería, sf. chancery.

chancleta, sf. slipper.

chancla, sf. old shoe.

chanclo, sm. patten, clog.

chanfaina, sf. ragout of livers and lights ; worthless thing.

chanflón, ona, a. coarse, badly made ; —, sm. money beaten out to appear larger.

chantre, sm. precentor.   [larger.

chantría, sf. office of a precentor.

chanza, sf. joke, jest, fun.   [sonnette.

chanzoneta, sf. joke, jest ; merry chan-

chapa, sf. thin metal plate which serves to strengthen or adorn the work it covers ; rouge.

chaparro, sm. evergreen oak-tree.

chaparrón, sm. violent shower of rain.

chapear, v.a. to garnish with metal plates.

chapería, sf. ornament consisting of a number of metal plates.

chapetón, sm. (col. am.) new-comer ; European, new chum.

chapín, sm. clog, patten.

chapitel, sm. capital of a column.

chaple, sm. graver, tool used in engraving.

chapodar, v.a. to lop trees.

chapotear, v.a. to wet with a sponge ; —, v.n. to paddle in the water ; to dab.

chapucear, v.a. to botch, to bungle.

chapucería, sf. clumsy performance, bungling work.

chapucero, sm. nail-maker ; bungler ; —, ra, a. clumsy, rude.

chapurrar, v.a. to speak gibberish ; to mix liquors.   [ing.

chapuz, sm. act of ducking or sous-

chapuzar, v.a. & n. to duck ; to dive ; to souse.

chaqueta, sf. jacket.

chaquete, sm. game resembling back-gammon.

charca, sf. pool.

charco, sm. puddle.

charla, sf. idle chit-chat, prattle.

charlador, ra, sm. & f. prater, garrulous person.

charladuría, sf. garrulity, gossip.

charlar, v.n. to prattle, to chatter.

charlatán, sm. prater, idle talker ; quack ; mountebank.

charlatanería, sf. garrulity ; quackery.

charnela, sf. hinge, joint.

charol, sm. varnish.

charolar, v.a. to varnish ; to japan.

charolista, sm. varnisher, japanner.

charpa, sf. holster.

charrada, sf. speech or action of a clown ; a village dance ; tinsel, tawdriness.

charretera, sf. epaulet.

charro, sm. churl ; —, rra, a. gaudy.

chascarillo, sm. good story.

chasco, sm. fun, joke ; sell, droll, dis-illusionment ; lash.

chasquear, v.a. to crack a whip ; —, v.n. to play tricks ; to cheat.   [Peru].

chasquí, sm. foot-messenger, runner (in

chasquido, sm. crack of a whip ; crack.

chasquista, sm. person fond of tricks.

chata, sf. flat-bottomed boat.

chato, ta, a. flat, flattish ; flat-nosed.

chatón, sm. bezel.

chelín, sm. shilling.

chibalete, sm. compositor's table.

chibor, sm. baboon.

chicada, sf. herd of sickly lambs.

chicarrero, sm. slipper-maker.

chico, ca, a. little, small ; —, sm. little boy.   [lantry.

chicolear, v.a. to joke, to jest in gal-

chicoleo, sm. jest in gallantry, joke.

chicorrotín, a. very small (applied to children).

chicote, ta, sm. end of a cable.

chicha, sf. meat (used only in speaking to children) ; (am.) a sort of beer.

chicharra, sf. froth-worm, harvest-fly.

chicharrero, sm. hot place *or* climate.
chicharro, sm. young tunny-fish ; horse-mackerel. [left in the pan.
chicharrón, sm. morsel of fried lard
chichisbeo, sm. attendance paid to a lady ; gallant, attendant on a lady.
chichón, sm. bump on the head. [dren].
chichonera, sf. tumbling-cap (for chil-
chifla, sf. whistle ; paring-knife.
chifladera, sf. whistle. [to tipple.
chiflar, v.n. to whistle ; to mock ; to jest ;
chifle, sm. whistle, call.
chiflete, chiflo, sm. whistle.
chiflido, sm. sound of a whistle.
chilindrina, sf. trifle. [the head.
chilindrón, sm. game at cards ; cut in
chilla, sf. hunter's decoy-whistle ; tablas de—, thin boards.
chillar, v.n. to scream, to shriek ; to crackle, to creak ; to hiss in frying.
chillido, sm. squeak, shriek.
chillón, sm. bawler ; common crier ; nail, tack ; —, a. shrill, loud.
chimenea, sf. chimney. [china silk.
china, sf. pebble ; porcelain ; china-ware ;
chinarro, sm. large pebble.
chinazo, sm. blow with a pebble.
chincharrazo, sm. blow with a sword.
chincharrero, sm. place infested by ver-
chinche, sf. bug. [min.
chinchorrería, sf. impertinence ; mis-chief.
chinchorro, sm. fishing-boat ; drag-net.
chinchoso, sa, a. (col.) peevish, trouble-
chinela, sf. slipper. [some.
chino, na, a. chinese ; (am.) half-caste
chiquero, sm. pig-sty. [native.
chiquichaque, sm. sawyer.
chiquirritín, sm. little boy.
chiribitil, sm. garret.
chirogota, sf. (col.) jest.
chirimía, sf. clarion ; —, sm. clarion-player. [trifle.
chirinola, sf. game played by boys ;
chiripa, sf. fluke, fortunate chance.
chiripear, v.a. to have luck in a game.
chiripero, sm. one who is lucky at games of chance.
chirivía, sf. (bot.) parsnip ; wagtail.
chirla, sf. mussel. [ler.
chirlador, ra, sm. & f. clamorous pratt-
chirlar, v.n. to prattle.
chirlo, sm. large wound in the face.
chirriar, v.n. to hiss ; to creak ; to chirp.
chirrido, sm. chirping of birds.
chirrío, sm. creaking noise made by the wheels of a cart.
chirrión, sm. tumbrel ; scraper (on a violin).
chirrionero, sm. scavenger.
chirumbela, sf. shawm, cornet.

chisgarabís, sm. superficial meddler.
chisguete, sm. small draught of wine.
chisme, sm. scandal.
chismear, v.a. to tattle, to carry tales.
chismoso, sa, a. tattling, tale-bearing.
chispa, sf. spark ; very small diamond ; short gun ; small particle ; slight in-toxication.
chispazo, sm. the flying off of a spark from the fire, and the damage it does ; tale mischievously circulated.
chispear, v.n. to sparkle ; to drizzle.
chispero, ra, a. emitting sparks.
chisporrotear, v.n. to sparkle, to hiss (of liquids).
chisposo, sa, a. sparkling.
chistar, v.a. to mumble, to mutter.
chiste, sm. fine witty saying ; joke, jest.
chistoso, sa, a. gay, cheerful ; funny.
¡ chite ! silence ! hush !
chiticalla, sm. discreet and silent person.
chiticallar, v.a. to keep silence ; not to make a noise.
¡ chito ! ¡ chitón ! hush ! ; mum ! mum !
chocar, v.n. to strike, to knock ; to en-counter, to rush against each other ; to fight, to combat ; —, v.a. to pro-voke.
chocarrear, v.n. to act the buffoon.
chocarrería, sf. buffoonery.
chocarrero, sm. buffoon ; —, ra, a. scur-rilous, buffoon-like.
chocolate, sm. chocolate.
chocolatera, sf. chocolate-pot.
chocolatero, sm. chocolate manufacturer.
chochear, v.n. to dote.
chocho, a. doting.
chofes, sm.pl. lungs, pl.
chofeta, sf. chafing-dish.
chofista, sm. a poor fellow who lives upon livers and lights.
cholla, sf. (col.) skull ; brains.
chopo, sm. black poplar-tree.
choque, sm. shock, collision ; (mil.) skir-mish ; dispute, contest ; jar.
choquezuela, sf. knee-pan, patella, rotula.
choricero, sm. sausage-maker *or* -seller.
chorizo, sm. pork-sausage.
chorlito, sm. curlew, gray plover.
chorrear, v.n. to drop from a spout, to gush, to drip ; to come successively.
chorrera, sf. spout ; rush of water ; mark left by water ; frill of a shirt.
chorretada, sf. water (or other liquid) rushing from a spout.
chorrillo, sm. (col.) the continual coming-in and out-going of money.
chorro, sm. gush ; á -s, abundantly.
chorrón, sm. dressed hemp.
chotacabras, sf. (orn.) goat-sucker.
choto, sm. sucking-kid.

chotuno, na, a. sucking.
chova, sf. jack-daw.
choza, sf. hut, shepherd's cottage.
chozuela, sf. small hut.
chubasco, sm. squall.
chucero, sm. (mil.) pikeman.
chuchear, v.a. to fowl with calls, gins, and nets; to whisper.
chuchería, sf. gewgaw, bauble; toy.
chuchero, sm. bird catcher.
chucho, sm. dog; word used to call a dog.
chuchumeco, sm. a sorry, contemptible little fellow.
chueca, sf. hollow of a joint.
chufeta, sf. jest, joke; coal-pan.
chufleta, sf. taunt, jeer.
chufletear, v.n. to sneer, to taunt.
chufletero, ra, a. taunting, sneering.
chulada, sf. droll speech or action.
chulear, v.a. to jest, to joke.
chuleta, sf. chop, cutlet.
chulo, la, sm. & f. jester, rogue, loafer; bull-fighter's assistant.

chunga, sf. jest, joke; estar de —, to be in good humour.
chunguearse, v.r. to be in good humour.
chupa, sf. waistcoat; jacket.
chupadero, ra, a. sucking.
chupador, sm. teether. [upon.
chupar, v.a. to suck; (fig.) to sponge
chupetear, v.a. to suck gently.
chupetín, sm. doublet.
chupón, sm. sucker (twig); —, ona, sm. & f. swindler, sponger.
churdón, sm. raspberry syrup.
churre, sm. thick dirty grease.
churriento, ta, a. greasy.
churruscarse, v.r. to be scorched.
churrusco, sm. over-toasted bread.
churumbela, sf. shawm.
chuscada, sf. pleasantry, drollery.
chusco, ca, a. pleasant, droll, merry.
chusma, sf. rabble, mob.
chus ni mus, ad. (col.) (no decir —), not to say a word.
chuzo, sm. little spear or pike; llover á -s, to pour heavily.

D

dable, a. easy, possible.
dádiva, sf. gift, present.
dadivoso, sa, a. generous, open-handed.
dado, sm. die (pl. dice).
daga, sf. dagger.
dalmática, sf. dalmatica.
dallador, sm. mower.
dallar, v.a. to mow grass.
dalle, sm. scythe.
dama, sf. lady, gentlewoman; mistress; queen (in the game of draughts); actress who performs the principal parts.
damascado, da, a. damask-like.
damasco, sm. damask (stuff); damson (plum). [bling damask.
damasina, sf. light silk stuff resem-
damasquino, na, a. damaskeened.
damería, sf. prudery; scruples.
damero, sm. draught-board.
damisela, sf. young gentlewoman; girl about town. [to injure.
damnificar, v.a. to hurt, to damage,
danza, sf. dance.
danzador, ra, sm. & f. dancer. [son.
danzante, sm. dancer; fickle, airy per-
danzar, v.n. to dance; to meddle.
danzarín, sm. fine dancer; meddling person. [jure.
dañar, v.a. to hurt, to damage; to in-
dañino, na, a. noxious; mischievous.
daño, sm. damage, prejudice, loss.
dañoso, sa, a. hurtful, noxious.

dar, v.a. to give; to supply, to minister, to afford; to deliver; to bestow; to strike; to communicate; -se priesa, to make haste.
dardo, sm. dart.
data, sf. date; article put down in an account; condition, quality.
datar, v.a. to date.
dataría, sf. Datary (office where the pope's bulls are expedited).
datario, sm. principal officer of the Datary.
dátil, sm. (bot.) date.
datilado, da, a. resembling a date.
dativo, sm. (gr.) dative.
dato, sm. datum; fact.
dauco, sm. carrot.
de, pr. of; from; for; by; to.
deán, sm. dean.
deanato, sm. deanship.
debajo, a. under, underneath, below.
debate, sm. debate, discussion, contest, altercation. [discuss.
debatir, v.a. to debate, to argue, to
debe, sm. (com.) debit; — y haber, debit and credit.
deber, sm. obligation, duty; debt; —, v.a. to owe; to be obliged.
debidamente, ad. justly; duly, exactly, perfectly. [pusillanimous.
débil, a. feeble, weak; sickly; frail;
debilidad, sf. debility, weakness.
debilitar, v.a. to debilitate, to weaken.

débito, sm. debt; liability.
década, sf. decade.
decadencia, sf. decay, decline. [fade.
decaer, v.n. to decay, to decline, to
decágramo, sm. ten grammes.
decaimiento, sm. decay, decline.
decalitro, sm. ten litres.
decálogo, sm. the Decalogue.
decampar, v.n. to decamp.
decanato, sm. seniority.
decano, sm. senior. [cant.
decantar, v.a. to cry up, to puff; to de-
decapitación, sf. decapitation, beheading.
decapitar, v.a. to behead.
decena, sf. denary, lot of ten.
decenal, a. decennial.
decencia, sf. decency.
deceno, na, a. tenth.
decentar, v.a. to begin to use; **-se,** to
injure the skin or body.
decente, a. decent, honest.
decible, a. expressible.
decidir, v.a. to decide, to determine.
décima, sf. tenth; tithe; stanza of ten
lines.
decimal, a. decimal; belonging to tithes.
décimo, ma, a. tenth.
décimoctavo, va, deciocheno, na, a.
eighteenth.
décimocuarto, ta, a. fourteenth.
décimonono, na, a. nineteenth.
décimoquinto, ta, a. fifteenth.
décimoséptimo, ma, a. seventeenth.
décimosexto, ta, a. sixteenth.
décimotercio, cia, a. thirteenth.
decir, v.a. to say, to tell, to speak; to
name; **— de sí,** to affirm anything.
decisión, sf. decision, determination, resolution; sentence.
decisivo, va, a. decisive, final.
declamación, sf. declamation, discourse,
oration; oratorical invective; declamatory style of reading.
declamador, ra, a. & sm. & f. declaimer,
declamatory. [gue.
declamar, v.n. to declaim, to haran-
declaración, sf. declaration; (law) deposition.
declarar, v.a. to declare, to manifest;
to expound; to explain; (law) to depose; **-se,** to declare one's opinion.
declaratorio, ria, a. declaratory, explana-
declinable, a. (gr.) declinable. [tory.
declinación, sf. declination, descent; decline; (gr.) declination.
declinar, v.n. to decline; to decay, to degenerate; **—,** v.a. (gr.) to decline.
declive, sm. declivity.
decocción, sf. decoction.
decomiso, sa, a. confiscated.
decoración, sf. decoration.

decorar, v.a. to decorate; to adorn; to
illustrate.
decoro, sm. honour, respect; circumspection; honesty; decency.
decoroso, sa, a. decorous, decent.
decrecer, v.n. to grow less, to decrease.
decremento, sm. decrease, diminution.
decrepitar, v.n. to decrepitate; to
crackle in the fire.
decrépito, ta, a. decrepit, crazy, worn
out with age.
decrepitud, sf. decrepitude.
decretal, sf. letter of the pope which de-
cides a question of ecclesiastical law;
—, a. decretal.
decretar, v.a. to decree, to determine; to
give a decree in a suit. [decree.
decreto, sm. decree, decision; judicial
décuplo, pla, a. decuple, tenfold.
decuria, sf. group of ten.
decursas, sf.pl. (law) arrears.
decurso, sm. course of time.
dechado, sm. sample, pattern; sampler;
model of virtue and perfection.
dedada, sf. a pinch (of anything), a
finger-full. [ing-glass.
dedal, sm. thimble; very small drink
dedalera, sf. (bot.) fox-glove.
dedicación, sf. dedication; consecration.
dedicar, v.a. to dedicate, to devote, to
consecrate; **-se,** to apply one's self to.
dedicatoria, sf. dedication.
dedo, sm. finger; toe; the forty-eighth
part of a Spanish yard; hand of a
clock; finger's breadth, small bit; **—**
meñique, little finger; **— pulgar,**
thumb; **— del corazón,** middle-
finger; **— anular,** ring-finger.
deducción, sf. deduction, derivation,
consequence.
deducir, v.a. to deduce, to infer; to
allege in pleading; to subtract.
defamación, sf. defamation.
defección, sf. defection, apostasy.
defectible, a. imperfect, deficient.
defectivo, va, a. defective.
defecto, sm. defect, defectiveness;
maimedness. [faulty.
defectuoso, sa, a. defective, imperfect,
defender, v.a. to defend, to protect; to
justify, to assert, to maintain; to prohibit, to forbid; to resist, to oppose.
defensa, sf. defence, justification, apology; guard, shelter, protection, fence;
(mil.) flanking defences.
defensiva, sf. defensive.
defensivo, sm. defence, safeguard; **—,**
va, a. defensive.
defensor, ra, sm. & f. defender, protector;
lawyer, counsel.
deferente, a. pliant, docile.

deferir, v.n. to defer ; to yield to another's opinion ; —, v.a. to delegate.
definición, sf. definition ; decision.
definir, v.a. to define, to describe, to explain ; to decide.
definitivo, **va**, a. definitive.
deforme, a. deformed, ugly.
deformidad, sf. deformity, ugliness ; gross error.
defraudación, s. fraud, usurpation.
defraudador, sm. defrauder, usurper.
defraudar, v.a. to defraud, to cheat ; to usurp ; to disturb.
defuera, a. externally, outwardly.
defunción, sf. death.
degeneración, sf. degeneracy.
degenerar, v.n. to degenerate.
degollación, sf. decollation, beheading.
degolladero, sm. throttle ; abattoir ; seat near the orchestra (in theatres).
degollador, sm. headsman, executioner.
degollar, v.a. to cut the throat ; to destroy, to ruin.
degradación, sf. degradation.
degradar, v.a. to degrade ; -se, to degrade *or* demean one's self.
degüello, sm. throat-cutting ; neck of a bottle.
degustar, v.a. to taste liquors.
dehesa, sf. pasture-ground.
dehesar, v.a. to turn arable land into pasture.
dehesero, sm. keeper of a pasture-ground.
deicidio, sm. deicide, murder of Christ.
deidad, sf. deity, divinity.
deificación, sf. deification.
deificar, v.a. to deify.
deífico, a. divine.
deísmo, sm. deism.
deísta, sm. deist.   [tude.
dejadez, s. slovenliness, neglect, lassi-
dejado, **da**, a. slovenly, idle, indolent ; dejected.
dejar, v.a. to leave, to let, to quit ; to omit ; to permit, to allow ; to leave, to forsake ; to bequeath ; -se, to abandon one's self (to).
dejo, sm. end, termination ; negligence, laziness ; after-taste ; particular accentuation on the last syllable of words.
del, of the (contraction of **de el**).
delación, sf. accusation, denunciation.
delantal, sm. apron.
delante, ad. before, in front ; in the presence of.   [thing ; advantage.
delantera, sf. forefront, forepart *or* some-
delantero, **ra**, a. foremost ; —, sm. one who takes the lead ; postillion.
delatable, a. accusable, blamable.
delatar, v.a. to accuse, to denounce.

delator, sm. accuser, informer, denouncer, delator.
delectación, sf. pleasure, delight ; — **morosa**, deliberate indulgence of some sensual pleasure, contrary to good manners.
delegación, sf. delegation, substitution.
delegado, sm. delegate, deputy.
delegar, v.a. to delegate.
deleitable, a. delightful.
deleitar, v.a. to delight.
deleite, sm. pleasure, delight ; lust.
deleitoso, **sa**, a. pleasing, delightful.
deletrear, v.a. to spell ; to examine ; to conjecture.
delfín, sm. dolphin ; dauphin.
delgadez, sf. thinness.
delgado, **da**, a. thin, delicate, light ; slender, lean ; acute, fine, ingenious ; little, scanty.
deliberación, sf. deliberation ; resolution
deliberadamente, ad. deliberately.
deliberar, v.n. to consider, to deliberate ; —, v.a. to decide.
deliberativo, **va**, a. deliberative.
delicadeza, sf. tenderness, softness ; exquisiteness ; delicacy, daintiness ; subtlety.
delicado, **da**, a. delicate, tender ; faint ; finical ; exquisite ; delicious, dainty ; slender, subtle.
delicia, sf. delight, pleasure.
delicioso, **sa**, a. delicious, delightful.
delincuente, sm. delinquent.
delineación, sf. delineation.   [describe.
delinear, v.a. to delineate, to sketch ; to
delinquir, v.n. to transgress the law.
delirar, v.n. to delirate, to rave ; to talk nonsense.
delirio, sm. delirium ; dotage ; nonsense.
delito, sm. transgression of a law, crime.
delta, sm. delta.
demagogo, sm. demagogue.
demanda, sf. demand, claim ; pretension, complaint ; request ; -s y respuestas, haggling ; altercation.
demandadero, **ra**, sm. & f. messenger of a nunnery *or* a jail.
demandado, **da**, sm. & f. defendant.
demandador, sm. alms-collector ; plaintiff, demandant ; claimant ; suitor.
demandar, v.a. to demand, to ask, to petition ; to claim ; to covet.
demarcación, sf. demarcation ; boundary-line.
demarcar, v.a. to mark out.
demás, a. the rest, the others ; **y así de lo** —, and so on ; **estar** —, to be over and above ; to be useless *or* superfluous ; **por** —, in vain, to no purpose.

demasía, sf. excess ; abundance ; daring ; insolence ; **en —,** excessively.

demasiado, da, a. excessive, too much ; overbold ; **—,** ad. too.

demencia, sf. madness.

demente, a. mad, insane.

demérito, sm. demerit.

demeritorio, ria, a. without merit.

democracia, sf. democracy.

demócrata, sm. democrat.

democrático, ca, a. democratical.

demoler, v.a. to demolish ; to destroy.

demolición, sf. demolition.

demonio, sm. demon.

demora, sf. delay ; (mar.) bearings.

demorar, v.a. to delay ; **—,** v.n. to live, to stay.

demostrable, a. demonstrable.

demostración, sf. demonstration ; manifestation. [to manifest.

demostrar, v.a. to prove, to demonstrate,

demostrativo, va, a. demonstrative.

denegación, sf. denial, refusal.

denegar, v.a. to deny, to refuse.

dengue, sm. prudery ; tippet. [grace.

denigración, sf. defamation, stigma, disgrace.

denigrar, v.a. to blacken ; to calumniate.

denodado, da, a. bold, intrepid, audacious.

denominación, sf. denomination. [cious.

denominar, v.a. to name.

denotar, v.a. to denote, to express.

densidad, sf. density ; obscurity.

denso, sa, a. dense, thick ; compact.

dentado, da, a. dentated, toothed.

dentadura, sf. set of teeth.

dental, a. dental. [to cut teeth.

dentar, v.a. & n. to indent ; to teeth,

dentellada, sf. gnashing of the teeth ; nip ; pinch with the teeth ; **á -s,** snappishly, peevishly.

dentellado, da, a. denticulated.

dentellear, v.a. to bite. [jealousy.

dentera, sf. setting on edge of teeth ; (fig.)

dentición, sf. dentition, teething.

denticular, a. like teeth, toothed.

dentista, sm. dentist.

dentro, ad. within.

dentudo, da, a. uneven-toothed.

denuedo, sm. boldness, intrepidity.

denuesto, sm. affront, insult.

denuncia, sf. denunciation.

denunciable, a. capable of being denounced.

denunciación, sf. denunciation.

denunciador, sm. denunciator, accuser.

denunciar, v.a. to denounce ; to prognosticate ; to promulgate.

denunciatorio, ria, a. denunciatory.

deparar, v.a. to offer, to present.

departamento, sm. department ; (rail.) compartment.

dependencia, sf. dependency, relation, affinity ; business, affair.

depender, v.n. to depend, to be dependent on. [lower ; clerk.

dependiente, sm. dependant, client, fol-

deplorable, a. deplorable, lamentable.

deplorar, v.a. to deplore.

deponer, v.a. to depose, to declare ; **to** remove ; to deposit.

deportación, sf. deportation.

deportar, v.a. to deport.

deposición, sf. deposition.

depositar, v.a. to deposit, to confide.

depositaría, sf. depository.

depositario, sm. depositary, trustee.

depósito, sm. deposit.

depravación, sf. depravity. [corrupt.

depravar, v.a. to deprave, to vitiate, to

deprecación, sf. petition ; earnest entreaty.

depresión, sf. depression, abasement.

deprimir, v.a. to depress, to humble, to deject.

depuración, sf. purification. [filter.

depurar, v.a. to cleanse, to purify, to

derecha, sf. right hand, right side ; **á -s,** right ; well done.

derechamente, ad. directly, straight ; rightly, prudently.

derechera, sf. direct road.

derecho, cha, a. right ; straight ; just ; perfect ; certain ; **—,** sm. right, justice, law ; just claim ; tax, duty ; fee.

derechura, sf. rectitude, right way.

derivación, sf. derivation ; source ; origin.

derivar, v.a. & n. to derive ; (mar.) to deflect from the course.

derivativo, va, a. derivative.

derogación, sf. derogation, abolition ; deterioration ; diminution. [reform.

derogar, v.a. to derogate, to abolish

derogatorio, ria, a. derogatory.

derrama, sf. assessment of a tax. [thrift.

derramador, ra, a. & sm. prodigal, spend-

derramamiento, sm. effusion, waste ; dispersion.

derramar, v.a. to drain off water ; **to** spread ; to spill ; to scatter, to waste, to shed ; **-se,** to be spread, to fly abroad.

derrame, sm. leakage ; waste.

derredor, sm. circumference, circuit ; **al —, en —,** round about.

derrengado, da, a. bent, crooked.

derrengar, v.a. to injure the back ; to twist. [tion, fusion.

derretimiento, sm. melting ; liquefac-

derretir, v.n. to melt ; to consume, to expend ; **-se,** to fall in love very easily ; to be impatient, to fret.

derribar, v.a. to demolish; to throw down; -se, to throw one's self down on the ground.   [molished building.

derribo, sm. demolition; ruins of a de-
derrocar, v.a. to hurl down, to demolish.
derrochador, ra, a. & sm. prodigal.
derrochar, v.a. to dissipate.
derrota, sf. ship's course; road, path; defeat of an army.
derrotar, v.a. (mar.) to cause to fall off; to destroy; to defeat.
derrotero, sm. ship's course; (fig.) course, way.
derruir, v.a. to demolish.
derrumbadero, sm. precipice; thorny or arduous affair; risk.
derrumbar, v.a. to precipitate.
desabarrancar, v.a to extricate, to rescue.   [from.
desabastecer, v.a. to cut off supplies
desabillé, sm. deshabille, undress.
desabonarse, v.r. to withdraw one's sub-scription.   [to blossom.
desabotonar, v.a. to unbutton; -se,
desabrido, da, a. tasteless, insipid; peev-ish.   [less.
desabrigado, da, a. uncovered; shelter-
desabrigar, v.a. to uncover, to deprive of clothes or shelter.   [tution.
desabrigo, sm. exposure, nakedness; desti-
desabrimiento, sm. insipidity; asperity of temper; ill-humour.
desabrir, v.a. to spoil flavour of; to vex, to plague; to harass; -se, to be angry.   [unbosom.
desabrochar, v.a. to unclasp; -se, to
desacalorarse, v.r. to take the fresh air; to cool one's self.
desacatamiento, sm. disrespect.
desacatar, v.a. to treat in a disrespectful manner.
desacato, sm. disrespect, incivility.
desacertado, da, a. blundering.
desacertar, v.a. to err, to commit a mistake.   [blunder.
desacierto, sm. error, gross mistake.
desacobardar, v.a. to encourage.
desacomodado, da, a. destitute of con-veniences; incommodious; unem-ployed.   [trouble.
desacomodamiento, sm. incommodity,
desacomodar, v.a. to incommode, to molest; -se, to lose one's place.
desacompañamiento, sm. want of com-pany.   [pany.
desacompañar, v.a. to leave the com-
desaconsejado, da, a. inconsiderate, ill-advised.   [to colours.]
desacordado, da, a. discordant (applied
desacordar, v.a. to untune; -se, to be forgetful; to be at variance.

desacorde, a. discordant.
desacorrolar, v.a. to let the flock or cattle out of the fold.
desacostumbrado, da, a. unusual.
desacostumbrar, v.a. to disuse.
desacotar, v.a. to lay open a pasture-ground; to withdraw a prohibition.
desacreditar, v.a. to discredit.
desacuerdo, sm. derangement; discord-ance, disagreement, disunion.   [order.
desaderezar, v.a. to undress; to dis-
desadeudar, v.a. to pay one's debts, to get out of debt.
desadormecer, v.a. to wake, to rouse from sleep; to rouse from mental stupor.   [or decorations.
desadornar, v.a. to divest of ornaments
desadorno, sm. want of embellishments or charms.
desafecto, sm. disaffection.
desaferrar, v.a. to weigh anchor; to loosen; -se, to let go one's hold; to give up.
desafiador, sm. challenger.
desafiar, v.a. to challenge, to call out (to fight a duel).
desaficionar, v.a. to destroy one's affec-tion for anything.
desafinar, v.a. to untune.   [combat.
desafío, sm. challenge; struggle, contest,
desaforado, da, a. huge; disorderly, lawless, impudent.
desaforar, v.a. to encroach upon one's rights; (mil.) to deprive of rights; -se, to be outrageous.   [anything.
desaforrar, v.a. to take the lining from
desafortunado, da, a. unfortunate, un-lucky.   [cess.
desafuero, sm. act of injustice; ex-
desagarrar, v.a. to release.   [gant.
desagraciado, da, a. ungraceful, incle-
desagraciar, v.a. to deform, to disfigure.
desagradable, a. disagreeable, unpleasant.
desagradar, v.a. to displease.
desagradecido, da, a. ungrateful.
desagradecimiento, sm. ingratitude.
desagrado, sm. asperity, harshness; dis-pleasure.   [an injury.
desagraviar, v.a. to make amends for
desagravio, sm. relief, satisfaction.
desagregar, v.a. to disjoin, to separate.
desaguadero, sm. channel, drain.
desaguador, sm. irrigating channel.
desaguar, v.a. to draw off water; —, v.n. to empty or to flow into the sea.
desaguazar, v.a. to drain or draw off the water from a thing.
desagüe, sm. channel, drain; extraordi-nary expense.
desahijar, v.a. to wean; -se, to swarm (of bees).

desahitarse, v.r. to relieve indigestion.

desahogado, da, a. petulant, impudent.

desahogar, v.a. to ease pain ; -se, to recover ; to unbosom.

desahogo, sm. ease, alleviation from pain ; freedom of speech.

desahuciar, v.a. to discourage ; to give up (an invalid) ; to dismiss a tenant.

desahucio, sm. dismissal of a tenant.

desahumar, v.a. to free from smoke.

desairado, da, a. graceless ; unsuccessful.

desairar, v.a. to disregard, to slight.

desaire, sm. disdain ; rebuff, slight.

desajustar, v.a. to disproportion ; -se, to withdraw from an agreement.

desajuste, sm. disturbance of proper or regular conditions.

desalar, v.a. to cut off the wings ; to take the salt out of fish or salt meat ; -se, to run with open arms.

desalentar, v.a. to put out of breath ; to discourage.

desalfombrar, v.a. to uncarpet.

desaliento, sm. dismay.

desaliñar, v.a. to discompose.

desaliño, sm. slovenliness ; carelessness.

desalmado, da, a. cruel, inhuman, impious.

desalmarse, v.r. to desire very ardently

desalmenado, da, a. without turrets.

desalojar, v.a. to dislodge ; —, v.n. to move to other lodgings.

desalterar, v.a. to allay, to assuage, to settle. [in the dark.

desalumbrado, da, a. dazzled ; groping

desamarrar, v.a. to unmoor ; to untie.

desamoldar, v.a. to unmould ; to discompose. [mutiny.

desamotinarse, v.r. to withdraw from

desamparar, v.a. to forsake, to abandon, to relinquish. [ness.

desamparo, sm. abandonment ; helpless-

desamueblar, v.a. to unfurnish.

desancorar, v.a. (mar.) to weigh anchor.

desandar, v.a. to retrace one's steps.

desandrajado, da, a. ragged, in tatters.

desangrar, v.a. to bleed one to excess ; to drain ; to exhaust.

desanidar, v.n. to forsake the nest ; —, v.a. to dislodge from a post.

desanimar, v.a. to discourage.

desanudar, v.a. to untie ; to extricate, to disentangle.

desapacibilidad, sf. rudeness, churlishness, peevishness. [harsh.

desapacible, a. disagreeable, unpleasant,

desapadrinar, v.a. to disapprove.

desaparear, v.a. to unmatch.

desaparecer, v.a. to remove out of sight ; —, v.n. -se, to disappear.

desaparejar, v.a. to unharness beasts ; (mar.) to unrig a ship.

desapasionar, v.a. to root out a passion.

desapego, sm. alienation of affection ; coolness ; disinterestedness.

desapercibido, da, a. unprovided.

desapercibimiento, sm. unpreparedness.

desapestar, v.a. to disinfect.

desapiadado, da, a. merciless.

desaplicación, sf. want of application.

desaplicado, da, a. indolent, careless, neglectful.

desapoderar, v.a. to dispossess ; to repeal a power of attorney.

desapolillar, v.a. to free from moths ; -se, to take the air when it is cold and sharp. [out of his lodgings.

desaposentar, v.a. to turn someone

desaposesionar, v.a. to dispossess.

desapoyar, v.a. to cut the ground from beneath one's feet. [value.

desapreciar, v.a. to depreciate, to under-

desaprender, v.a. to unlearn.

desapretar, v.a. to slacken, to loosen.

desaprisionar, v.a. to release from confinement ; -se, to extricate one's self from difficulties.

desaprobación, sf. disapprobation.

desaprobar, v.a. to disapprove, to reprove

desapropiamiento, sm. alienation.

desapropiarse, v.r. to alienate.

desaprovechado, da, a. useless, unprofitable ; backward.

desaprovechamiento, sm. backwardness.

desaprovechar, v.a. to misspend, to turn to a bad use. [props.

desapuntalar, v.a. to take away the

desapuntar, v.a. to unstitch.

desarbolar, v.a. to unmast a ship.

desarbolo, sm. unmasting a ship.

desarenar, v.a. to clear a place of sand.

desarmadura, sf. disarming.

desarmar, v.a. to disarm ; to disband ; to dismount (a cannon) ; to take to pieces ; (fig.) to pacify.

desarme, sm. disarmament of ships ; breaking up of an army. [pate.

desarraigar, v.a. to root out ; to extir-

desarraigo, sm. eradication.

desarrapado, da, a. ragged

desarrebozar, v.a. to unmuffle ; to manifest, to discover. [out.

desarrebujar, v.a. to unfold, to spread

desarregladamente, ad. in a disorderly way.

desarreglado, da, a. immoderate.

desarreglar, v.a. to disorder, to derange.

desarreglo, sm. disorder, derangement ; licentiousness.

desarrimar, v.a. to remove ; to dissuade.

desarrollar, v.a. to unroll, to unfold ; -se, to be unfolded, to open.

desarropar, v.a. to undress.

desarrugar, v.a. to smooth, to take out wrinkles.

desarrumar, v.a. to unload a ship.

desasear, v.a. to make dirty; to discompose.

desaseo, sm. disorder.

desasimiento, sm. letting loose; disinterestedness.

desasir, v.a. to loosen, to disentangle; -se, to extricate one's self.   [ners.

desasnar, v.a. (fig.) to polish one's manners.

desasosegar, v.a. to disquiet, to disturb.

desasosiego, sm. restlessness, feverishness.

desastrado, da, a. wretched, miserable; ragged.

desastre, sm. disaster; misfortune.

desatacar, v.a. to loosen, to untie; — una escopeta, to draw the charge out of a gun.

desatadura, sf. untying.

desatar, v.a. to untie, to loose; to separate; to unriddle; -se, to give rein to one's tongue; to lose all reserve.

desatascar, v.a. to draw out of the mire; to extricate one from difficulties.

desataviar, v.a. to strip off decorations.

desatavío, sm. want of neatness in dress.

desatención, sf. want of attention, absence of mind; want of politeness.

desatender, v.a. to pay no attention; to disregard, to contemn.

desatentado, da, a. inconsiderate; thoughtless; excessive.

desatento, ta, a. inattentive, careless; rude, uncivil.

desatesorar, v.a. to spend a treasure.

desatinado, da, a. extravagant; —, sm. fool, madman.

desatinar, v.a. & n. to derange one's mind; to throw into a violent passion; to talk nonsense; to reel; to stagger.   [nonsense.

desatino, sm. extravagance; staggering;

desatollar, v.a. to pull out of the mire.

desatolondrar, v.a. to bring someone to himself; -se, to recover one's senses, to come to one's self.

desatontarse, v.r. to come to one's self (from a faint, &c.).

desatracar, v.a. (mar.) to sheer off.

desatrancar, v.a. to unbar; to clean a

desatufarse, v.a. to grow calm.   [well.

desaturdir, v.a. to rouse from a state of dizziness or stupor.

desautorizar, v.a. to disauthorise.

desavahar, v.a. to let off steam; to cool

desavecindado, da, a. deserted, unpeopled.

desavecindarse, v.r. to change one's domicile.

desavenencia, sf. discord, disagreement.

desavenido, da, a. discordant, disagreeing.

desavenir, v.a. to discompose, to disconcert.   [unprofitable.

desaventajado, da, a. disadvantageous,

desaviar, v.a. to lead astray from the high road.   [means.

desavío, sm. going astray; want of

desavisado, da, a. ill-advised.

desavisar, v.a. to countermand.

desayunarse, v.r. to breakfast.

desayuno, sm. breakfast.

desazón, sf. insipidity; disgust; uneasiness; unfitness, sterility.   [humoured.

desazonado, da, a. ill-adapted; ill-

desazonar, v.a. to render tasteless; to disgust; -se, to become indisposed.

desbancar, v.a. to clear a room of the benches; to break the bank (in gambling); (fig.) to supplant.

desbandarse, v.r. to disband, to disperse.

desbarajuste, sm. confusion.

desbaratado, da, a. debauched, lewd.

desbaratar, v.a. to destroy; to dissipate; — la paz, to break the peace; —, v.n. to talk nonsense; -se, to be confounded.

desbarate, sm. ruin; dissipation.

desbarbado, a. beardless.   [limits.

desbarrar, v.n. to slip, to go beyond

desbarretar, v.a. to unbar, to unbolt.

desbarrigado, da, a. little-bellied.

desbarrigar, v.a. to rip up, to open the belly.   [extravagance; frenzy.

desbarro, sm. slipping; (fig.) nonsense,

desbastar, v.a. to smooth; to polish; to waste; to purify one's morals and manners.

desbaste, sm. hewing, smoothing.

desbastecido, da, a. without sufficient provisions.

desbautizarse, v.r. (fig.) to be irritated.

desbecerrar, v.a. to wean (animals).

desblanquecido, da, a. whitish.

desbocado, da, a. open-mouthed (applied to a cannon); wild (applied to a horse); foul-mouthed, indecent.

desbocar, v.a. to break the neck of a jar; —, v.n. to disembogue; -se, to take the bit between the teeth; to use abusive language.   [of a vessel.

desboquillar, v.a. to break the mouth

desbordamiento, sm. overflow, flood.

desborrar, v.a. to cut off the loose threads of stuff.

desbragado, da, a. without breeches.

desbrevarse, v.r. to lose strength (of wine).

desbrozar, v.a. to clear away rubbish.

desbrozo, sm. clearing away rubbish.

desbuchar, v.a. to disclose one's secrets; to ease the stomach (applied to birds of prey)

descabal, a. incomplete.
descabalar, v.a. to make incomplete; to impair.
descabalgar, v.n. to alight from a horse; —, v.n. to dismount.
descabellado, da, a. dishevelled; disorderly; wild, unrestrained; disproportional; violent.
descabellar, v.a. to disorder the hair.
descabezado, da, a. light-headed, giddy.
descabezar, v.a. to behead; to lop off; -se, to puzzle one's brains.
descabullirse, v.r. to steal away; to elude difficulties.
descaderar, v.a. to sprain the hip.
descaecer, v.n. to decline, to decay.
descaecimiento, sm. weakness; languor.
descalabazarse, v.r. to puzzle one's brains. [head; imprudent.
descalabrado, da, a. wounded on the
descalabradura, sf. contusion or wound in the head.
descalabrar, v.a. to break or wound the head; to attack one's character.
descalabro, sm. calamitous event, considerable loss.
descalcez, sf. nudity of the feet; barefootedness of monks.
descalificar, v.a. to disqualify.
descalzar, v.a. -se, to pull off the shoes and stockings.
descalzo, za, a. barefooted.
descaminar, v.a. to misguide, to lead astray.
descamisado, da, a. shirtless; very poor.
descampado, da, a. disengaged, free, open.
descampar, v.n. to leave off working.
descansado, da, a. reposing; rested, refreshed; quiet.
descansar, v.n. to rest from labour and fatigue; to pause in the execution of a thing; to repose, to sleep; — las tierras, to lie fallow or at rest.
descanso, sm. rest, repose. [bread.
descanterar, v.a. to cut the crust off
descantillar, v.a. to pare off; to lessen.
descañonar, v.a. to pluck (feathers); (fig.) to trick one out of his money.
descaperuzar, v.a. to uncover the head.
descarado, da, a. impudent, barefaced.
descararse, v.r. to behave insolently.
descarga, sf. disburdening, unloading; volley, discharge.
descargadero, sm. wharf.
descargador, sm. unloader, stevedore.
descargar, v.a. to unload, to discharge; -se, (law) to clear oneself.
descargo, sm. discharge, acquittal, justification. [burden.
descargue, sm. alleviation from any
descariño, sm. coolness, loss of affection.

descarnar, v.a. to strip off the flesh; -se to squander one's wealth.
descaro, sm. impudence.
descarriar, v.a. to lead astray; to separate cattle from one another; -se, to deviate. [off the rails.
descarrilamiento, sm. (rail.) running
descarrilar, v.n. (rail.) to leave or run off the rails. [der.
descarrillar, v.a. to tear the jaws asun-
descarrio, sm. losing of one's way.
descartar, v.a. to discard; to dismiss; -se, to excuse one's self.
descarte, sm. cards discarded; discarding; evasion, subterfuge.
descasar, v.a. to separate a husband and wife. [-se, to fall off.
descascarar, v.a. to decorticate, to husk;
descaspar, v.a. to remove dandriff from
descasque, sm. decortication. [the head.
descastado, a. degenerate; ungrateful.
descebar, v.a. to unprime fire-arms.
descendencia, sf. descent, offspring.
descendente, a. descending; (rail.) tren —, sm. down-train.
descender, v.n. to descend; to flow; to be derived from. [scendant.
descendiente, a. & sm. descending; de
descensión, sf. descent, descending.
descenso, sm. descent; degradation.
desceñir, v.a. to ungird.
descepar, v.a. to uproot, to root up; to clear a wood.
descerar, v.a. to take the empty combs from a bee-hive.
descercado, da, a. open, unfortified.
descercar, v.a. to destroy or pull down a wall.
descerrajar, v.a. to force a lock; to discharge fire-arms.
descifrar, v.a. to decipher; to unravel.
descinchar, v.a. to ungirth a horse.
desclavar, v.a. to draw out nails.
descoagular, v.a. to dissolve.
descobijar, v.a. to uncover, to undress.
descocado, da, a. bold, impudent.
descocar, v.a. to free trees from insects; -se, to be impudent.
descoco, sm. impudence, sauciness.
descoger, v.a. to unfold, to expand.
descogollar, v.n. to prune plants.
descogotado, da, a. bare-necked.
descogotar, v.a. to knock off the horns of a stag at one blow.
descolar, v.a. to dock.
descolchar, v.a. to untwist a cable.
descolgar, v.a. to unhang; -se, to come down gently; to glide; to run (of streams). [teeth.
descolmillar, v.a. to draw out the eye-
descolorar, v.a. to discolour.

descolorido, da, a. pale, colourless.

descollar, v.n. to overtop, to excel, to surpass. [lent; huge.

descomedido, da, a. impudent, inso-
descomedirse, v.r. to be rude or disrespectful. [proportionate.

descompasado, da, a. excessive; dis-
descompasarse, v.r. to exceed all rule and measure.

descomponer, v.a. to discompose, to set at variance, to disconcert; -se, to be out of temper; to be indisposed; to change for the worse (of the weather); (chem.) to decompose.

descomposición, sf. disagreement, dis-composure; decomposition.

descompostura, sf. disagreement; dis-order, confusion; want of modesty.

descompuesto, ta, a. impudent, insolent.

descomunal, a. uncommon; unmea-
desconceptuar, v.a. to discredit. [sured.

desconcertado, da, a. disorderly, slovenly.

desconcertar, v.a. to disturb; to con-found; to disconcert; -se, to disagree; to exceed limits; to be out of joint; to be dislocated.

desconcierto, sm. discomposure; dis-order, confusion; indolence, negli-gence; sprain. [ful.

desconfiado, da, a. diffident, mistrust-
desconfianza, sf. diffidence; jealousy.

desconfiar, v.n. to mistrust, to suspect.

desconforme, a. discordant, contrary; unequal, unlike.

desconformidad, sf. disagreement, oppo-sition; inequality, unlikeness, dis-similitude.

desconocer, v.a. to disown, to disavow; to be totally ignorant of a thing; not to know a person; not to acknow-ledge (a favour received).

desconocido, da, a. ungrateful; dis-guised; unknown. [imprudent.

desconsiderado, da, a. inconsiderate,

desconsolado, da, a. comfortless, painful; sick with indigestion.

desconsolar, v.a. to afflict.

desconsuelo, sm. affliction, trouble; dis-order of the digestive organs.

descontar, v.a. to discount; to abate, to diminish.

descontentadizo, za, a. squeamish, easily disgusted. [displease.

descontentar, v.a. to discontent, to
descontento, sm. dissatisfaction, disgust.

desconvenible, a. discordant, disagreeing, dissimilar.

desconveniencia, sf. incommodity, in-convenience; discord, disunion; dis-similitude. [gruous.

desconveniente, a. inconvenient; incon-

desconvenir, v.n. to disagree; not to suit. [of a tree.

descopar, v.a. to lop off the branches

descorazonar, v.a. to pull out the heart; to dishearten, to discourage.

descorchar, v.a. to strip off the bark; to break a bee-hive; to uncork.

descordar, v.a. to unstring an instrument.

descornar, v.a. to dis-horn.

descorrer, v.n. to run back, to flow away; —, v.a. to draw back.

descortés, a. impolite, uncivil. [ness.

descortesía, sf. incivility, want of polite-

descortezar, v.a. to decorticate; to strip (bark); to flay; (fig.) to polish.

descosedura, sf. unseaming a seam.

descoser, v.a. to unpick; to separate; -se, to give rein to one's tongue.

descosido, sm. idle talker.

descostillar, v.a. to break the ribs; -se, to fall violently on one's back.

descostrarse, v.r. to scale off.

descotar, v.a. to remove the restrictions against the use of a path or road.

descoyuntamiento, sm. dislocation; pain from over-exertion.

descoyuntar, v.a. to disjoint bones; to vex, to molest.

descrédito, sm. discredit.

descreer, v.a. to disbelieve. [describe.

describir, v.a. to draw, to delineate; to
descripción, sf. delineation; description; inventory.

descriptivo, va, a. descriptive.

descruzar, v.a. to uncross. [order.

descuadernar, v.a. to unbind; to dis-
descuajar, v.a. to dissolve, to liquefy; to pluck up weeds; to frighten.

descuajo, sm. eradication.

descuartizar, v.a. to quarter (to divide the body into four parts); to carve.

descubierta, sf. (mil.) reconnaissance; á la —, openly, clearly.

descubierto, sm. solemn exposition of the sacrament; deficit.

descubridor, ra, sm. & f. discoverer; in-vestigator; (mil.) scout.

descubrimiento, sm. discovery.

descubrir, v.a. to discover, to disclose; to uncover; to reveal; mil.) to reconnoitre.

descuello, sm. excessive stature; pre-eminence; haughtiness.

descuento, sm. discount.

descuerno, sm. contempt; affront.

descuidado, da, a. careless, negligent.

descuidar, v.a. & n. to neglect, to relieve from care; to render careless.

descuido, sm. indolence, carelessness, negligence, forgetfulness; want of at-tention, incivility; improper action; al —, affectedly careless.

descular, v.a. to break the bottom *or* end of a thing.

desde, pr., since, after, from; — luego, thereupon.

desdecir, v.n. to degenerate; to differ, to disagree; to tumble down; -se, to gainsay; to retract.

desdén, sm. disdain, scorn, contempt.

desdentado, da, a. toothless.

desdentar, v.a. to draw out teeth.

desdeñable, a. contemptible, despicable.

desdeñar, v.a. to disdain, to scorn; -se, to be disdainful. [tuous.

desdeñoso, sa, a. disdainful; contemp-

desdicha, sf. misfortune, calamity; great poverty. [miserable.

desdichado, da, a. unfortunate, wretched.

desdoblar, v.a. to unfold, to spread open.

desdorar, v.a. to take off the gilding; to tarnish. [reputation.

desdoro, sm. dishonour, blot on one's

deseable, a. desirable.

desear, v.a. to desire, to wish; to require, to demand.

desecación, sf. desiccation.

desecar, v.a. to dry.

desechar, v.a. to depreciate; to reject, to reprove; to refuse: to exclude, to reprobate; to lay aside.

desecho, sm. residue, remainder; refuse, offal; contempt.

desedificar, v.a. to scandalise.

desellar, v.a. to unseal.

desembalar, v.a. to unpack.

desembanastar, v.a. to take out of a basket; to talk at random; -se, to break out (of a person confined).

desembarazar, v.a. to disembarrass; to clear; to disencumber; -se, to be extricated from difficulties.

desembarazo, sm. disembarrassment; liberty to do a thing.

desembarcadero, sm. landing-place.

desembarcar, v.a. to unship, to disembark; —, v.n. to disembark, to land.

desembarco, sm. landing; unshipment; descent, hostile landing.

desembargar, v.a. to raise an embargo.

desembargo, sm. (law) raising an embargo. [bargo.

desembarque, sm. landing.

desembaular, v.a. to unpack; to disclose one's secret thoughts.

desembelesarse, v.r. to recover from amazement. [or canal.

desembocadero, sm. mouth of a river

desembocar, v.n. to disembogue.

desembolsar, v.a. to empty a purse; to disburse. [diture.

desembolso, sm. disbursement, expen-

desemborrachar, v.a. to sober; —, v.n. to grow sober.

desemboscarse, v.r. to get out of the woods; to get clear of an ambuscade.

desembozar, v.a. to unmuffle.

desembozo, sm. uncovering of the face.

desembravecer, v.a. to tame, to domesticate.

desembriagar, v.a. & r. to sober; to recover from drunkenness.

desembrollar, v.a. to disentangle, to disembroil.

desembuchar, v.a. to disgorge; to unbosom.

desemejante, a. dissimilar, different.

desemejanza, sf. dissimilitude, unlikeness.

desemejar, v.n. to be dissimilar.

desempalagar, v.a. to clean one's palate, to restore the appetite. [(glass).

desempañar, v.a. to unswathe; to clean

desempapelar, v.a. to unwrap.

desempaquetar, v.a. to unpack.

desemparejar, v.a. to unmatch.

desempedrar, v.a. to unpave.

desempeñar, v.a. to redeem; to extricate from debt; to fulfil (a promise).

desempeño, sm. redeeming a pledge performance of an obligation.

desemperezar, v.n. to relinquish habits of laziness.

desempolvorar, v.a. to free from dust.

desemponzoñar, v.a. to expel poison.

desenalbardar, v.a. to take off a packsaddle.

desenamorar, v.a. to destroy love.

desencabalgar, v.a. (mil.) to dismount cannon.

desencabestrar, v.a. to disentangle a beast from the halter.

desencadenar, v.a. to unchain; to dissolve all connection *or* obligation.

desencajar, v.a. to take a thing out of its place.

desencajonar, v.a. to take out of a box.

desencalabrinar, v.a. to remove dizziness.

desencallar, v.a. to float a stranded vessel.

desencaminar, v.a. to lead astray.

desencantar, v.a. to disenchant.

desencantarar, v.a. to draw by lot the names of persons for office.

desencanto, sm. disenchantment.

desencapotar, v.a. to strip off one's cloak; to uncover; to make manifest; to raise and keep up the head of a horse; -se, to recover one's temper. [prejudice.

desencaprichar, v.a. to dissuade from

desencerrar, v.a. to free from confinement; to open, to unclose.

desenclavar, v.a. to draw out nails; to tear from its place.

desenclavijar, v.a. to take out the pegs of a musical instrument.

desencoger, v.a. to unfold ; -se, to grow

desencolar, v.a. to unglue.   [bold.

desencolerizarse, v.r. to grow calm or appeased.

desenconar, v.a. to cure an inflammation ; to appease one's passion ; -se, to become milder.   [passion.

desencono, sm. cooling of anger or

desencordar, v.a. to unstring.

desencordelar, v.a. to untie, to unrope.

desencorvar, v.a. to straighten.

desendemoniar, desendiablar, v.a. to exorcise.

desenfadado, da, a. free, unembarrassed ; gay, wide, spacious.   [appease.

desenfadar, v.a. to assuage (anger) ; to

desenfado, sm. ease ; facility ; calmness, relaxation.   [of a gown.

desenfaldar, v.a. to let fall the train

desenfangar, v.a. to clear from mud or filth.

desenfardar, desenfardelar, v.a. to open bales of goods.

desenfrenar, v.a. to unbridle ; -se, to give play to one's passions ; to fly into a passion.

desenfreno, sm. licentiousness.

desenfundar, v.a. to take out of a bag.

desenfurecerse, v.r to grow calm ; to lay aside anger and passion.

desenganchar, v.a. to unhook.

desengañado, da, a. undeceived ; despicable, ill-executed.

desengañar, v.a. to undeceive, to free from error, to disabuse, to free from a mistake, to set right.

desengaño, sm. disillusionment ; naked truth ; reproach, upbraiding.

desengarzar, v.a. to unravel.

desengastar, v.a. unset (a jewel).

desengrasar, v.a. to free from grease.

desengrosar, v.a. to extenuate, to make lean.

desenhebrar, v.a. to unthread.

desenjaezar, v.a. to unharness.

desenjaular, v.a. to uncage.

desenlabonar, v.a. to unlink.

desenlace, sm. climax ; end of an affair.

desenladrillar, v.a. to take up floor-tiles.

desenlazar, v.a. to unlace ; to distinguish.

desenlosar, v.a. to unpave.

desenlutar, v.a. to leave off mourning ; to banish sorrow.

desenmarañar, v.a. to disentangle.

desenmudecer, v.a. to remove an impediment of speech ; to break a long silence.

desenojar, v.a. to appease ; -se, to amuse one's self.

desenojo, sm. abatement of anger.

desenredar, v.a. to disentangle ; -se, to extricate one's self.

desenrizar, v.a. to uncurl.

desenrollar, v.a. to unroll.

desenroscar, v.a. to untwist, to unroll.

desensartar, v.a. to unthread ; to un ravel.

desensillar, v.a. to unsaddle.   [pride.

desensoberbecerse, v.r. to moderate one's

desensortijado, da, a. out of joint.

desentablar, v.a. to rip off planks ; to disturb ; to embroil.

desentenderse, v.r. to turn a deaf ear.

desenterramiento, sm. disinterment.

desenterrar, v.a. to disinter, to unbury ; to recall to memory.

desentoldar, v.a. to take away an awning , to strip a thing of its ornaments.

desentonación, sf dissonance.

desentonar, v.a. & n. to humble ; to be out of tune ; -se, to raise the voice disrespectfully.   [voice.

desentono, sm. discord ; rude tone of

desentornillar, v.a. to unscrew.

desentorpecer, v.a. to free from torpor ; -se, to become lively, smart or pert.

desentrañar, v.a. to gut, to eviscerate ; to probe ; -se, to give away all one's fortune for love.

desentristecer, v.a. to banish sadness and grief.   [prive of authority.

desentronizar, v.a. to dethrone ; to desentumecer, v.a. to restore motion to torpid limbs.   [to light.

desenvainar, v a. to unsheath ; to bring

desenvenenar, v.a. to cure from poison.

desenvergar, v.a. to furl a sail.

desenvoltura, sf sprightliness ; cheerfulness ; impudence, boldness ; lewd posture or gesture ; graceful, easy delivery of one's sentiments and thoughts.

desenvolver, v.a. to unfold, to unroll ; to decipher, to unravel ; -se, to be forward.

desenvuelto, ta, a. forward ; licentious.

deseo, sm. desire, wish.

deseoso, sa, a. desirous.

deserción, sf. desertion.

desertar, v.a. to desert, to forsake one's colours or post.

desertor, sm. deserter, fugitive.

deservicio, sm. disservice.

deservir, v.a. to fail in duty.

deseslabonar, v.a. to unlink.

desesperación, sf. despair, desperation ; anger, fury.

desesperado, da, a. desperate, hopeless.

desesperanzar, v.a. to deprive of hope ; to make desperate.

desesperar, v.a. to make desperate ; v.n. & r. to despair.

desesterar, v.a. to take away the mats from a room.

desestimación, sf. disesteem, crying down.

desestimar, v.a. to disregard, to contemn.

desfajar, v.a. to ungird.

desfalcar, v.a. to cut off ; to embezzle.

desfalco, sm. lopping, embezzlement.

desfallecer, v.n. to pine, to fall away ; to faint ; —, v.a. to weaken.

desfallecimiento, sm. languor, fainting.

desfavorecer, v.a. to neglect ; to contemn ; to injure, to hurt ; to contradict, to oppose.

desfigurar, v.a. to disfigure, to deform ; to disguise ; -se, to be disfigured by passion.

desfijar, v.a. to unsettle, to remove.

desfilar, v.n. (mil.) to defile.

desflemar, v.a. to clear from phlegm.

desfloración, sf. defloration.

desflorar, v.a. to deflower ; to tarnish.

desflorecer, v.n. to wither.

desfogar, v.a. to give vent to ; -se, to give vent to one's passion or anger.

desfogue, sm. venting of one's passion.

desfondar, v.a. to break the bottom of any vessel ; to scuttle.

desfortalecer, v.a. to demolish a fortress, to dismantle. [pieces.

desgajar, v.a. to lop off ; to break in

desgalgadero, sm. rugged, declivitous

desgalgar, v.a. to precipitate. [place.

desgana, sf. disgust, want of appetite ; aversion, reluctance.

desganar, v.a. to deprive of the pleasure of doing something ; -se, to lose all pleasure in doing a thing ; to lose one's appetite.

desganchar, v.a. to lop off.

desgargantarse, v.r. to become hoarse by brawling.

desgargolar, v.a. to shed the seed.

desgaritar, v.n. (mar.) to lose the course.

desgarrado, da, a. licentious, dissolute.

desgarrar, v.a. to rend, to tear ; -se, to withdraw, to retire. [idle boast.

desgarro, sm. rent, breach ; impudence,

desgarrón, sm. large rent ; piece of cloth torn off.

desgastar, v.a. to consume, to waste ; to corrode ; -se, to weaken one's self.

desglosar, v.a. to scratch out MS. notes or remarks. [ment.

desglose, sm. erasure of a note or com-

desgobernar, v.a. to disturb the order of government ; to misgovern ; to dislocate ; to steer an unsteady course ; -se, to make affected movements.

desgobierno, sm. misgovernment, mismanagement. [to disjoint.

desgonzar, v.a. to separate ; to unhinge ;

desgoznar, v.a. to unhinge ; -se, to distort the body. [pleasantness.

desgracia, sf. misfortune, disgrace ; un-

desgraciado, da, a. unfortunate, unhappy, miserable ; out of favour ; disagreeable.

desgraciar, v.a. to displease, to injure ; -se, to fall out with ; to go wrong.

desgranar, v.a. to shake out the grain.

desgreñar, v.a. to dishevel ; to disorder.

desguarnecer, v.a. to strip of ornaments : to disgarnish ; to dismantle.

desguazar, v.a. to trim timber.

deshabitado, da, a. deserted, uninhabited, desolate. [tion ; to unpeople.

deshabitar, v.a. to quit one's habita-

deshabituar, v.a. to disaccustom.

deshacedor, sm. — de agravios, avenger of injuries.

deshacer, v.a. to undo, to destroy ; to cancel, to efface ; to rout an army ; to spend profusely ; to melt ; to cut up, to divide ; to dissolve in a liquid ; to violate a treaty ; to diminish ; to disband troops ; -se, to grieve, to mourn ; to disappear ; to do a thing with vehemence ; to grow feeble or meagre.

desharrapado, da, a. shabby, ragged, in tatters.

deshebillar, v.a. to unbuckle.

deshebrar, v.a. to unthread ; to divide into filaments. [farewell.

deshecha, sf. simulation, fiction ; polite

deshechizar, v.a. to disenchant.

deshechizo, sm. disenchantment.

deshecho, cha, a. undone ; borrasca -a, violent tempest. [to melt.

deshelar, v.a. to thaw ; -se, to thaw.

desherbar, v.a. to weed.

desheredamiento, sm. disinheriting.

desheredar, v.a. to disinherit ; -se, to degenerate.

deshermanar, v.a. to remove the likeness or similarity of things ; -se, to fall out or quarrel with one's brother.

desherrar, v.a. to unchain ; to unshoe

deshielo, sm. thaw. [horses.

deshilachar, v.a. to ravel, to unweave.

deshilado, sm. open-work ; —, da, a. marching in file. [into lint.

deshilar, v.a. to unravel ; to convert

deshincar, v.a. to tear up what is nailed fast.

deshinchar, v.a. to reduce a swelling ; to appease ; -se, to go down (as a swelling) ; to abate presumption.

deshojar, v.a. to strip off the leaves.

deshollejar, v.a. to peel, to pare.

deshollinador, sm. chimney-sweeper, sweep ; scraper for sweeping chimneys.

deshollinar, v.a. to sweep chimneys ; to clean ; to examine attentively.

deshonestidad, sf. immodesty, indecency; lewdness. [unreasonable.

deshonesto, ta, a. immodest; lewd;

deshonor, sm. dishonour; insult.

deshonorar, v.a. to dishonour, to dismiss.

deshonra, sf. dishonour.

deshonrabuenos, sm. calumniator, libeller; he who degenerates from his ancestors.

deshonrar, v.a. to affront, to insult, to defame; to dishonour; to deflower.

deshonroso, sa, a. dishonourable, indecent.

deshora, sf. unseasonable time.

deshuesar, v.a. to rid of bones. [dry.

deshumedecer, v.a. to dry; -se, to grow

desidia, sf. idleness, indolence.

desidioso, sa, a. lazy, idle.

desierto, ta, a. deserted, solitary; —, sm. desert, wilderness.

designación, sf. designation.

designar, v.a. to design, to intend; to appoint; to express, to name.

designio, sm. design, purpose; road, course.

desigual, a. unequal, unlike; uneven.

desigualar, v.a. to make unequal or dissimilar; -se, to excel, to surpass.

desigualdad, sf. inequality, dissimilitude; inconstancy; knottiness, unevenness

desimpresionar, v.a. to undeceive.

desinclinar, v.a. to desincline

desinfección, sf. disinfection.

desinficionar, v.a. to disinfect.

desinflamar, v.a. to cure an inflammation.

desinterés, sm. disinterestedness.

desinteresado, da, a. disinterested.

desistir, v.n. to desist, to cease.

desjarretadera, sf. knife for houghing cattle. [string; to weaken.

desjarretar, v.a. to hough, to ham-

deslamar, v.a. to clear of mud.

deslastrar, v.a. to unballast a ship.

deslavado, da, a. impudent, barefaced.

deslavadura, sf. surface washing.

deslavar, v.a. to wash superficially.

deslazar, v.a. to unlace.

desleal, a. disloyal; perfidious. [faith.

deslealtad, sf. disloyalty, breach of

deslechugar, v.a. to prune vines.

desleir, v.a. to dilute, to dissolve.

deslenguado, da, a. foul-mouthed, free-tongued.

deslenguar, v.a. to cut out the tongue; -se, to be abusive.

desliar, v.a. to untie.

desligar, v.a. to loosen, to unbind; (fig.) to explain.

deslindar, v.a. to mark the limits.

deslinde, sm. demarcation. [weakness.

desliz, sm. slip, sliding; (fig.) slip,

deslizadero, sm. slippery place.

deslizadizo, za, a. slippery, slippy, glib.

deslizar, v.n. to slip, to slide; to speak carelessly.

deslomar, v.a. to break the back, to distort the loins.

deslucimiento, sm. disgrace, dishonour.

deslucir, v.a. to tarnish; to obscure.

deslumbramiento, deslumbre, sm. overpowering lustre; dazzling.

deslumbrar, v.a. to dazzle; to puzzle.

deslustrar, v.a. to tarnish; to obscure; to vilify.

deslustre, sm stain; disgrace, ignominy.

deslustroso, sa, a. unbecoming, ugly.

desmadejamiento, sm. languor.

desmadejar, v.a. to enervate, to produce languor.

desmán, sm. misconduct; misfortune, disaster.

desmandar, v.a. to countermand; to revoke; -se, to stray; to misbehave.

desmangar, v.a. to take off the handle of anything. [ward.

desmanotado, da, a. unhandy, awk-

desmantelado, da, a. ruinous, dilapidated.

desmantelar, v.a. to dismantle; to abandon, to forsake; (mar.) to unmast.

desmarañar, v.a. to disentangle.

desmayado, da, a. pale, wan; dismayed, appalled.

desmayar, v.n. to be dispirited or faint-hearted; —, v.a. to dismay, to dispirit; -se, to faint.

desmayo, sm. swoon; dismay.

desmedido, da, a. disproportioned.

desmedirse, v.r. to exceed measure.

desmedrar, v.n. to decrease, to decay; —, v.a. to impair. [worse.

desmejorar, v.a. to debase, to make

desmelenar, v.a. to dishevel.

desmembración, sf. dismemberment.

desmembrar, v.a. to dismember; to curtail; to separate.

desmentida, sf. giving the lie.

desmentir, v.a. to give the lie.

desmenuzar, v.a. to crumble, to chip; to examine minutely.

desmeollar, v.a. to take out the marrow.

desmerecer, v.a. to be unworthy of.

desmerecimiento, sm. demerit, ill desert.

desmesurado, da, a. excessive; huge; immeasurable.

desmesurar, v.a. to perturbate, to put out; to put out of order; -se, to talk impudently, to forget one's self.

desmigajar, v.a. to crumble, to break into bits.

desmigar, v.a. to crumble bread.

desmochar, v.a. to lop; to mutilate.

desmoche, sm. mutilation.

desmontar, v.a. to cut down wood; to remove a heap; to uncock fire-arms; to dismount (rider); to dismount (cannon); —, v.n. to dismount, to alight, &c.

desmonte, sm. felling; clearing a wood.

desmoralización, sf. demoralisation.

desmoralizar, v.a. to demoralise.

desmoronadizo, za, a. dilapidated, ruinous, rickety. [little.

desmoronar, v.a. to destroy little by

desnarigar, v.a. to cut off the nose.

desnatar, v.a. to skim milk; to take the choicest part.

desnaturalizar, v.a. to denaturalise; -se, to forsake one's country.

desnevar, v.a. to thaw, to dissolve.

desnivel, sm. unevenness of the ground.

desnucar, v.a. to break the neck.

desnudar, v.a. to strip; to discover, to reveal; -se, to undress.

desnudez, sf. nakedness.

desnudo, da, a. naked, bare, uncovered; (fig.) plain, evident.

desobedecer, v.a. to disobey.

desobediencia, sf. disobedience; insubordination.

desobediente, a. disobedient.

desocupación, sf. leisure, want of occupation.

desocupar, v.a. to quit, to empty; -se, to retire from a business.

desoir, v.a. to pretend not to hear.

desojarse, to strain the sight by looking steadfastly at a thing.

desolación, sf. desolation; affliction.

desolado, da, a. desolate, disconsolate.

desolar, v.a. to lay waste; to harass.

desoldar, v.a. to unsolder.

desolladero, sm. slaughter-house.

desollado, da, a. impudent, insolent, saucy. [to fleece.

desollar, v.a. to flay, to skin; (fig.)

desorden, sm. disorder, confusion.

desordenado, da, a. disorderly.

desordenar, v.a. to disorder; -se, to get out of order.

desorejar, v.a. to crop the ears.

desorganización, sf. disorganization.

desorganizar, v.a. to disorganize. [cloth.

desorillar, v.a. to cut off the selvage of

desovar, v.n. to spawn.

desove, sm. spawning; spawn.

desovillar, v.a. to follow a clue.

despabiladeras, sf.pl. snuffers.

despabilado, da, a. watchful, vigilant.

despabiladura, sf. snuff of the candle.

despabilar, v.a. to snuff; (fig.) to despatch briefly; to rob; -se, to rouse.

despacio, ad. slowly, leisurely; little by little.; ¡ — ! softly ! gently !

despacito, ad. gently, leisurely.

despachaderas, sf.pl. surly words in answer.

despachar, v.a. to despatch; to expedite; -se, to make haste.

despacho, sm. despatch, expedition; cabinet; office; counting-house; commission; warrant, patent; expedient.

despachurrar, v.a. to crush. [der.

despaldillar, v.a. to dislocate the shoul-

despalmar, v.a. to clean and calk the bottoms of ships; to pare a horse's hoof.

despampanar, v.a. to prune the shoots of vines; (fig.) to unbosom. [even.

desparejar, v.a. to make unequal or un-

desparpajar, v.a. to undo in a disorderly manner; to prattle at random.

desparpajo, sm. pertness of speech or action.

desparramar, v.a. to disseminate; to squander, to lavish; -se, to be dissipated.

despartir, v.a. to divide. [pated.

despatarrarse, v.r. (col.) to fall on the ground with the legs wide spread.

despavesar, v.a. to snuff the candle.

despavorido, a. frightened.

despearse, v.r. to be footsore.

despechar, v.a. to enrage, to irritate; -se, to despair.

despecho, sm. indignation; vexation; spite; dismay, despair; derision, scorn; á —, in spite of.

despechugar, v.a. to cut off the breast of a fowl; -se, to uncover the breast.

despedazar, v.a. to tear into pieces, to cut asunder; to mangle; -se de risa, to burst into fits of laughter.

despedida, sf. farewell.

despedir, v.a. to discharge, to dart; to dismiss from office; -se, to take leave.

despegado, da, a. rough, sullen, sour of temper.

despegar, v.a. to unglue; -se, to withdraw one's affection. [ness.

despego, sm. asperity; want of love,cool-

despeinar, v.a. to entangle the hair.

despejado, da, a. sprightly, quick, sagacious; clear.

despejar, v.a. to clear away obstructions; -se, to cheer up; to amuse one's self; to clear up (weather).

despejo, sm. removal of obstacles; sprightliness; grace.

despeluzar, v.a. to make the hair stand on end; -se, to stand erect.

despellejar, v.a. to skin. [pl

despensa, sf. pantry, larder; provisions,

despensero, ra, sm & f. butler, caterer; steward on board ship; distributer.

despeñadero, sm. precipice; (fig.) bold and dangerous undertaking.

despeñar, v.a. to precipitate; -se, to throw one's self headlong. [belly.

despeño, sm. precipitate fall; flux of the

despepitarse, v.r. to vociferate; to act imprudently. [squanderer.

despe.diciador, ra, sm. & f. spendthrift,

desperdiciar, v.a. to squander.

desperdicio, sm. prodigality, profusion; residuum, remains.

desperdigar, v.a. to separate, to scatter.

desperezarse, v.r. to stretch oneself.

despernado, da, a. weary, tired.

despernar, v.a. to break the legs.

despertar, v.a. to awaken, to rouse from sleep; to excite; —, v.n. & r. to wake up; to grow lively or sprightly.

despierto, ta, a. awake; vigilant; alert; brisk, sprightly.

despilfarrar, v.a. to waste, to squander.

despilfarro, sm. slovenliness; waste; mismanagement.

despintar, v.a. to paint out; to obscure; to mislead; —, v.n. to degenerate.

despique, sm. vengeance, revenge.

desplantar, v.a. to eradicate; to transplant; -se, to lose one's erect posture (in fencing or dancing). [ing.

desplante, sm. oblique posture in fenc-

desplegadura, sf. explication, unfolding.

desplegar, v.a. to unfold, to display; to explain, to elucidate; (mar.) to unfurl.

desplomar, v.a. to make a wall bulge out; -se, to bulge out; to fall flat.

desplomo, sm. jutting out of a wall.

desplumar, v.a. to deplume, to strip feathers; (fig.) to despoil.

despoblación, sf. depopulation.

despoblado, sm. desert.

despoblar, v.a. to depopulate; to desolate; -se, to become depopulated.

despojar, v.a. to despoil; to deprive of; -se, to undress.

despojo, sm. spoliation; plunder; -s, pl. chitterlings; offal.

despolvar, v.a. to dust.

despolvorear, v.a. to brush, to dust, to beat (carpets, &c.).

desportillar, v.a. to break the neck of a bottle, pot. [cuffed.

desposado, da, a. newly-married; hand-

desposar, v.a. to marry, to betroth; -se, to be betrothed or married.

desposeer, v.a. to dispossess.

desposeimiento, sm. dispossession.

desposorio, sm. betrothal.

déspota, sm. despot.

despotado, sm. despotic government.

despótico, ca, a. despotic, despotical.

despotismo, sm. despotism.

despreciable, a. contemptible, despicable

despreciar, v.a. to depreciate, to despise.

desprecio, sm. scorn, contempt.

desprender, v.a. to unfasten, to loosen, to separate; -se, to give way, to fall down; to extricate oneself.

desprendimiento, sm. alienation, disinterestedness. [dice.

despreocupar, v.a. to free from preju-

desprevenido, da, a. unprovided, unprepared.

desproporción, sf. disproportion.

despropósito, sm. absurdity.

desproveer, v.a. to deprive of provisions; (mil) to deprive of ammunition.

desprovisto, ta, a. unprovided.

después, ad. after, afterwards.

despumar, v.a. to skim.

despuntar, v.a. to blunt; (mar.) to double; —, v.n. to sprout; to dawn; to be lively.

desquiciar, v.a. to unhinge; to discompose, to disorder.

desquijarar, v.a. to break the jaws.

desquitar, v.a. to retrieve; -se, to win one's money back; to take revenge; to get satisfaction. [retaliation.

desquite, sm. recovery of a loss; revenge,

desreglado, da, a. disorderly, irregular.

desreglarse, v.r to be irregular, to be ungovernable.

desrizar, v.a. to uncurl.

destacamento, sm. (mil.) detachment.

destacar, v.a. (mil.) to detach (a body of troops); -se, to stand out, to be prominent.

destajar, v.a. to undertake; to contract.

destajero, sm. piece-worker.

destajo, sm. piece-work; contract.

destapar, v.a. to uncover; -se, to be uncovered.

destapiar, v.a. to pull down mud-walls.

destaponar, v.a. to uncork.

destazar, v.a. to cut to pieces. [less

destejar, v.a. to untile; to leave defence

destejer, v.a. to unweave, to ravel.

destello, sm. sparkle, glimmer.

destemplado, da, a. inharmonious, incongruous; intemperate.

destemplanza, sf. intemperateness; excess; disorder.

destemplar, v.a. to distemper, to alter, to disconcert; to dissolve; to untune: -se, to be ruffled; to be ill with a fever; to grow blunt; to act improperly.

destemple, sm. discordance; disorder.

desteñir, v.a. to discolour.

desterradero, sm. desert, wilderness.

desterrar, v.a. to banish; **to expel, to drive away.**

destetar, v.a. to wean.
destete, sm. weaning.
destierro, sm. exile, banishment.
destilación, sf. distillation.
destiladera, sf. still.
destilador, sm. distiller.
destilar, v.a. & n. to distil.
destilatorio, sm. distillery.
destinar, v.a. to destine, to intend.
destino, sm. destiny; fate, doom; destination; office.
destitución, sf. destitution, abandonment.
destituir, v.a. to deprive.   [head.
destocar, v.a. to uncoif; to uncover the
destorcer, v.a. to untwist; to uncurl; (fig.) to arrange, to put in order.
destornillador, sm. screw-driver.
destornillar, v.a. to unscrew; (fig.) to act or speak rashly.   [separate.
destrabar, v.a. to unfetter; (fig.) to
destramar, v.a. to unweave; to break off an intrigue.
destrenzar, v.a. to unplait (hair).
destreza, sf. dexterity, cleverness, cunning, expertness, skill.
destripar, v.a. to disembowel.
destripaterrones, sm. (col.) day-labourer.
destriunfar, v.a. to draw all the trumps at cards.   [tered.
destrocar, v.a. to return a thing bar-
destrón, sm. blind man's guide.
destronamiento, sm. dethronement.
destronar, v.a. to dethrone.
destroncar, v.a. to lop, to cut short; to maim, to cut to pieces; (fig.) to ruin, to frustrate.
destrozar, v.a. to destroy, to break into pieces; (mil.) to defeat.   [massacre.
destrozo, sm. destruction; (mil.) defeat,
destrucción, sf. destruction, ruin.
destructivo, va, a. destructive.
destrueque, sm. mutual restitution of things bartered or exchanged.
destruir, v.a. to destroy.
desuellacaras, sm. impudent person.
desuello, sm. (fam.) flaying; impudence; exorbitant price.
desuncir, v.a. to unyoke.
desunión, sf. separation, disjunction; discord, dissension.
desunir, v.a. to separate, to disunite.
desurdir, v.a. to unweave cloth.
desusar, v.a. to disuse.
desuso, sm. disuse; obsoleteness.
desvaído, da, a. tall and graceless.
desvalido, da, a. helpless, destitute.
desván, sm. garret.
desvanecer, v.a. to divide into imperceptible parts; to cause to vanish; to undo, to remove; to swell with pride; -se, to grow vapid, to become insipid;

to vanish; to be affected with giddiness.
desvanecido, a. giddy; proud.
desvanecimiento, sm. pride, haughtiness; giddiness; swoon.
desvarío, sm. delirium; giddiness; inconstancy, caprice; extravagance.
desvedar, v.a. to revoke a prohibition against a thing.   [be watchful.
desvelar, v.a. to keep awake; -se, to
desvelo, sm. want of sleep; watchfulness.
desvenar, v.a. to clear the veins of flesh; to extract from the veins of mines.
desvencijar, v.a. to disunite, to weaken, to divide; -se, to be ruptured; to be relaxed.
desvendar, v.a. to take off a bandage.
desventaja, sf. disadvantage, damage.
desventura, sf. misfortune, calamity.
desventurado, da, a. unfortunate, calamitous.   [less.
desvergonzado, da, a. impudent, shame-
desvergonzarse, v.r. to speak in an impudent manner.   [word.
desvergüenza, sf. impudence; shameless
desviar, v.a. to divert from the right way; to dissuade; to parry (at fencing).
desvío, sm. turning away, going astray; aversion; disdain; indifference.
desvirtuar, v.a. to rob of virtue or strength.   [nutely.
detallar, v.a. to detail, to relate mi
detalle, sm. detail.
detención, sf. detention; delay.
detener, v.a. to stop, to detain; to arrest; to keep back; to reserve; to withhold; -se, to tarry, to stay.
detenido, da, a. sparing, niggardly; slow, inactive.
detentar, v.a. to detain.
deterioración, sf. deterioration, damage.
deteriorar, v.a. to deteriorate.
deterioro, sm. deterioration.
determinación, sf. determination, resolution; boldness.   [lute.
determinado, da, a. determinate; reso-
determinar, v.a. to determine.
determinativo va, a. definitive.
detestable, a. detestable, execrable.
detestación, sf. detestation, abomination.
detestar, v.a. to detest, to abhor.
detonación, sf. detonation.   [slander.
detractar, v.a. to detract, to defame, to
detractor, ra, a. & sm. & f. slandering, slanderer.
detrás, ad. behind.
detrimento, sm. detriment, damage, loss.
deuda, sf. debt; fault; offence.
deudo, da, a. parent; kindred.
deudor, ra, sm. & f. debtor.

Deuteronomio, sm. Deuteronomy.

devanadera, sf. reel, spool.

devanador, ra, sm. & f. winder ; core of a ball of thread.

devanar, v.a. to wind.   [to dote.

devanear, v.n. to rave, to talk nonsense ;

devaneo, sm. delirium ; idle pursuit.

devantal, sm. apron.

devastación, sf. devastation, desolation.

devastador, ra, a. devastating.

devastar, v.a. to desolate, to waste.

devengar, v.a. to earn, to deserve.

devoción, sf. devotion, piety ; strong affection.

devocionario, sm. prayer-book.

devolución, sf. (law) devolution.

devolver, v.a. to return ; to restore.

devorar, v.a. to devour, to swallow up.

devoto, ta, a. devout, pious, devotional ; strongly attached.

dezmar, v.a. to tithe.

día, sm. day.

diabla, (á la —,) ad. carelessly ; rudely.

diablillo, sm. acute, clever man.

diablo, sm. devil, Satan ; person of a perverse temper ; ugly, cunning or subtle person.

diablura, sf. devilry.

diabólico, ca, a. diabolical, devilish.

diacitrón, sm. candied peel.

diaconato, sm. deaconship, diaconate.

diaconisa, sm. deaconess.

diácono, sm. deacon.

diadema, sm. & f. diadem ; halo.

diafanidad, sf. transparency, pellucidness.

diáfano, na, a. diaphanous, transparent, pellucid.

diafragma, sm. diaphragm.   [diagnostic.

diagnóstico, sm. diagnosis ; —, ca, a.

diagonal, a. diagonal.

dialéctica, sf. logic, dialectic.

dialéctico, sm. logician ; —, ca, a. dialectical, logical.

dialecto, sm. dialect.

diálogo, sm. dialogue.

diamante, sm. diamond.

diamantino, na, a. adamantine.

diamantista, sm. lapidary.

diametral, a. diametrical.

diámetro, sm. diameter.

diana, sf. (mil.) reveillé.

diantre, sm. deuce, devil.

diapasón, sm. (mus.) diapason.

diario, sm. journal, diary ; daily newspaper ; daily expense ; —, ria, a. daily

diarista, sm. journalist.

diarrea, sf. diarrhœa.

diatónico, a. (mus.) diatonic.

diatriba, sf. diatribe.

dibujador, ra, a. designer.   [scribe.

dibujar, v.a. to draw, to design ; to de-

dibujo, sm. drawing, sketch, draught ; description.

dicción, sf. diction, style, expression.

diccionario, sm. dictionary.

diciembre, sm. December.

dictado, sm. a title of dignity or honour.

dictador, sm. dictator.

dictadura, sf. dictatorship.

dictamen, sm. opinion, notion.

dictar, v.a. to dictate.

dicterio, sm. sarcasm, taunt.

dicha, sf. happiness, good fortune ; por —, á —, by chance.

dicharacho, sm. vulgar expression.

dicho, sm. saying, sentence ; declaration ; witticism.

dichoso, sa, a. happy, prosperous.

diente, sm. tooth ; fang, tusk ; jag.

diestra, sf. right hand ; (fig.) favour, support, protection.

diestro, tra, a. right ; dexterous, skilful, clever ; sagacious, prudent ; sly, cunning ; favourable, propitious ; —, sm. skilful fencer ; halter, bridle.

dieta, sf. diet, regimen ; diet, assembly ; daily salary of judges.

diez, a. & sm. ten.   [take the tenth.

diezmar, v.a. to decimate ; to tithe ; to

diezmero, sm. tithe-payer.

diezmesino, na, a. ten months old.

diezmo, sm. tithe ; —, ma, a. tenth.

difamación, sf. defamation.

difamar, v.a. to defame, to libel.

difamatorio, ria, a. defamatory, calumnious.

diferencia, sf. difference ; á —, with the difference ; -s, pl. controversies, disputes.

diferencial, a. differential, different.

diferenciar, v.a. to differentiate, to distinguish ; -se, to differ, to distinguish oneself.

diferente, a. different, unlike.

diferir, v.a. to defer, to put off ; to differ.

difícil, a. difficult.

dificultad, sf. difficulty.   [obstruct.

dificultar, v.a. to raise difficulties ; to

dificultoso, sa, a. difficult ; painful.

difidencia, sf. distrust.

difidente, a. distrustful.

difundir, v.a. to diffuse, to outspread ; to divulge.

difunto, ta, a. dead, deceased ; late.

difusión, sf. diffusion.   [circumstantial.

difuso, sa, a. copious ; large ; prolix,

digerible, a. digestible.

digerir, v.a. to digest ; to bear with patience ; to adjust, to arrange.

digestible, a. digestible.

digestión, sf. digestion, concoction.

digestivo, va, a. digestive.

dignación, sf. condescension.
dignarse, v.r. to condescend, to deign.
dignidad, sf. dignity, rank ; grandeur of mien ; church dignitary.
digno, na, a. worthy, meritorious ; suitable, correspondent.
digresión, sf. digression.
dij, dije, sm. trinket ; -es, pl. toys.
dilacerar, v.a. to dilacerate.
dilación, sf. delay.
dilapidar, v.a. to dilapidate.
dilatable, a. capable of postponement.
dilatación, sf. dilatation, extension ; greatness of mind ; calmness.
dilatado, da, a. large, numerous ; prolix ; spacious, extensive.
dilatar, v.a. to dilate, to expand ; to spread out ; to defer, to protract ; -se, to expatiate ; to speak largely and copiously.
dilatorio, ria, a. dilatory.
dilección, sf. dilection, love, affection, good will.
dilecto, ta, a. loved, beloved.
dilema, sm. dilemma.
diligencia, sf. diligence ; affair, business ; stage-coach.
diligenciar, v.a. to set in motion.
diligenciero, sm. agent. [swift.
diligente, a. diligent, assiduous, prompt,
dilucidación, sf. explanation, illustration.
dilucidar, v.a. to elucidate, to explain.
dilucidario, sm. commentary.
diluviano, a. diluvian.
diluviar, v.n.imp. to rain like a deluge.
diluvio, sm. deluge, inundation ; vast abundance.
dimanación, sf. emanation.
dimanar, v.n. to spring from ; to originate, to flow from. [city, bulk.
dimensión, sf. dimension ; extent, capa-
dimes, sm.pl., **andar en — y diretes,** to contend, to argue.
diminución, sf. diminution. [retail.
diminutamente, ad. diminutively ; by
diminutivo, va, a. diminutive.
diminuto, ta, a. defective, faulty, small.
dimisión, sf. resignation of post.
dimisorias, sf.pl. (eccl.) dimissory letters.
dimitir, v.a. to give up, to abdicate.
dinámica, sf. dynamics.
dínamo, sm. dynamo (electric engine).
dinastía, sf. dynasty.
dineral, sm. large sum of money.
dinero, sm. coin, money, coinage.
dintel, sm. lintel.
diocesano, na, a. diocesan.
diócesis, sm. diocese.
Dios, sm. God ; **á —,** farewell, adieu.
diosa, sf. goddess.
diploma, sm, diploma, patent.

diplomacia, diplomática, sf. diplomacy.
diplomático, ca, a. diplomatic.
diplomatizar, v.a. to act the diplomatist.
diptongo, sm. diphthong.
diputación, sf. deputation ; object of a deputation.
diputado, sm. deputy.
diputar, v.a. to depute ; to constitute.
dique, sm. dyke, dam, mole. [stration.
dirección, sf. direction ; guidance, admini-
directivo, va, a. directive. [evident.
directo, ta, a. direct, straight ; apparent,
director, sm. director ; conductor ; president ; manager.
directora, sf. directress, governess.
directorio, ria, a. directive, directorial ; —, sm. directory.
dirigir, v.a. to direct ; to conduct ; to dedicate a work ; to regulate, to govern ; -se, to address oneself.
dirimir, v.a. to dissolve, to separate ; to accommodate differences.
discernimiento, sm. discernment ; appointment of a guardian.
discernir, v.a. to discern, to distinguish ; to appoint a guardian.
disciplina, sf. discipline.
disciplinar, v.a. to discipline.
discípulo, sm. disciple, scholar.
disco, sm. disk ; face of the sun or moon ; lens of a telescope.
díscolo, la, a. ungovernable ; peevish.
discordancia, sf. disagreement, discordance.
discordante, a. dissonant, discordant.
discordar, v.n. to discord, to disagree.
discorde, a. discordant ; (mus.) dissonant.
discordia, sf. discord, disagreement ; contrariety of opinion.
discreción, sf. discretion ; acuteness of mind, sharpness of wit ; **á —,** at the will of another.
discrepar, v.n. to differ.
discreto, ta, a. discreet ; ingenious, witty, eloquent.
disculpa, sf. apology, excuse.
disculpar, v.a. to exculpate, to excuse, to acquit, to absolve.
discurrir, v.n. to ramble about, to run to and fro ; to discourse upon a subject ; to discuss ; —, v.a. to invent, to contrive ; to meditate. [plative.
discursivo, va, a. discursive ; contem-
discurso, sm. discourse ; ratiocination ; discourse, conversation ; dissertation ; space of time.
discusión, sf. discussion.
discutir, v.a. to discuss.
disecar, v.a. to dissect.
disección, sf. dissection, anatomy.
disector, sm. dissector, anatomist.

diseminar, v.a. to scatter as seed; to disseminate, to propagate.

disensión, sf. dissension, misunderstanding, contest, strife; cause of dissension. [sion.

disentería, sf. dysentery.

disentimiento, sm. dissent, disagreement.

disentir, v.n. to dissent, to disagree.

diseñador, sm. designer.

diseñar, v.a. to draw, to design.

diseño, sm. design, draught; description; picture.

disertación, sf. dissertation, discussion.

disertar, v.a. to dispute, to debate, to argue.

disfavor, sm. disregard, want of favour.

disforme, a. ugly, monstrous, formless;

disfraz, sm. mask, disguise. [huge.

disfrazar, v.a. to disguise, to conceal; to cloak, to dissemble.

disfrutar, v.a. to enjoy.

disfrute, sm. enjoyment.

disgustar, v.a. to disgust; to offend; -se, to be displeased, to fall out.

disgusto, sm. disgust, aversion; ill-humour; grief, sorrow; á —, in spite of.

disidente, a. & s. dissident, dissenter.

disimulación, sf. dissimulation; hypocrisy.

disimulado, da, a. reserved, dissembled; á lo —, dissemblingly; reservedly.

disimular, v.a. to dissemble; to cloak; to hide; to tolerate.

disimulo, sm. dissimulation.

disipación, sf. dissipation; (chem.) resolution into component parts; resolution into vapour.

disipado, da, a. prodigal, lavish.

disipador, ra, a. & sm. & f. spendthrift.

disipar, v.a. to dissipate, to disperse, to scatter; to lavish.

dislate, sm. nonsense, absurdity.

dislocación, sf. dislocation.

dislocar, v.r. to dislocate.

disminuir, v.a. to diminish.

disoluble, a. dissoluble.

disolución, sf. dissolution; lewdness; licentiousness.

disolutivo, va, a. dissolvent.

disoluto, ta, a. dissolute, licentious, lewd.

disolver, v.a. to loosen, to untie; to dissolve, to disunite; to melt, to liquefy; to interrupt.

disonancia, sf. dissonance; disagreement, discord.

disonante, a. dissonant, inharmonious; (fig.) discordant

disonar, v.n. to disagree in sound; to disagree; to be repugnant.

dísono, na, a. dissonant.

dispar, a. unlike, unequal, different.

disparador, sm. shooter; trigger of a gun.

disparar, v.a. & n. to shoot, to discharge, to fire; to let off; to throw with violence; to talk nonsense; -se, to run headlong; to stoop, to dart down upon a prey. [extravagant.

disparatado, da, a. inconsistent, absurd,

disparatar, v.a. to talk nonsense.

disparate, sm. nonsense, absurdity, extravagance.

disparidad, sf. disparity, inequality.

disparo, sm. discharge, explosion.

dispendio, sm. extravagant expense; voluntary loss of life, honour or fame.

dispendioso, sa, a. costly, expensive.

dispensa, sf. dispensation, exemption.

dispensable, a. dispensable. [tion.

dispensación, sf. dispensation, exemption.

dispensador, sm. dispenser; distributer.

dispensar, v.a. to dispense; to excuse, to dispense with; to distribute.

dispersión, sf. dispersion.

disperso, sa, a. dispersed.

displicencia, sf. displeasure, dislike.

displicente, a. displeasing, offensive; angry, fretful.

disponer, v.a. & n. to arrange; to dispose, to prepare; to dispose of; to resolve.

disponible, a. disposable. [resolve.

disposición, sf. disposition, ordering; resolution; command; power, authority.

dispuesto, ta, a. disposed, fit, ready; bien —, quite well; mal —, indisposed

disputa, sf. dispute, controversy. [ill.

disputable, a. disputable, controvertible.

disputador, sm. disputant, disputer.

disputar, v.a. & n. to dispute, to controvert, to question; to debate, to argue.

distancia, sf. distance, interval; differ-

distante, a. distant, far off. [ence.

distar, v.n. to be distant; to be different.

dístico, sm. distich.

distinción, sf. distinction; difference; prerogative; á —, in contradistinction. [spicuous.

distinguido, da, a. distinguished, conspicuous.

distinguir, v.a. to distinguish; to see clearly and at a distance to discern; to esteem; -se, to distinguish oneself.

distintivo, sm. distinctive mark; particular attribute.

distinto, ta, a. distinct, different; clear.

distracción, sf. distraction, want of attention.

distraer, v.a. to distract; -se, to be absent-minded, to be inattentive.

distraído, da, a. absent, inattentive; dissolute, licentious.

distribución, sf. distribution, division, separation; arrangement.

distribuidor, sm. distributer.
distribuir, v.a. to distribute, to dispose.
distributivo, va, a. distributive.
distrito, sm. district ; territory.
disturbar, v.a. to disturb, to interrupt.
disturbio, sm. disturbance, interruption.
disuadir, v.a. to dissuade.
disuasión, sf. dissuasion.
disyunción, sf. disjunction ; (gr.) disjunctive particle.
disyunta, sf. (mus.) change of key.
disyuntivo, va, a. disjunctive.
diurno, na, a. diurnal ; daily ; —, sm. prayer-book.
diuturnidad, sf. long endurance.
diuturno, na, a. long-lived, lasting.
diva, sf. a celebrated songstress.
divagar, v.n. to wander ; to digress.
diván, sm. Divan (supreme council among the Turks).
divergencia, sf. divergence.
divergente, a. divergent.
diversidad, sf. diversity ; variety of things.
diversificar, v.a. to diversify, to vary.
diversión, sf. diversion ; sport, amusement ; (mil.) diversion. [sundry.
diverso, sa, a. diverse, different ; several.
divertido, da, a. amused ; amusing.
divertimiento, sm. diversion, amusement, pastime, sport.
divertir, v.a. to divert (the attention) ; to amuse, to entertain ; (mil.) to divert the enemy ; -se, to sport, to dally.
dividendo, sm. (ar. & com.) dividend.
dividir, v.a. to divide, to disunite, to separate ; -se, to break up a friendship.
divinidad, sf. divinity ; Supreme Being.
divinizar, v.a. to deify ; to sanctify.
divino, na, a. divine, heavenly ; excel-
divisa, sf. posy, motto, device. [lent.
divisar, v.a. to perceive indistinctly, to descry.
divisible, a. divisible.
división, sf. division ; partition ; separation ; difference ; (gr.) hyphen.
divisor, sm. (ar.) divisor.
divisorio, ria, a. dividing.
divorciar, v.a. to divorce, to separate ; -se, to be divorced. [union.
divorcio, sm. divorce ; separation, disdivulgación, sf. publication.
divulgar, v.a. to publish, to divulge.
dobladillo, sm. hem.
doblado, sm. measure of the fold in cloth ; —, da, a. robust, thick-set ; deceitful, dissembling.
dobladura, sf. fold.
doblar, v.a. & n. to double, to fold ; to bend ; to ring the passing-bell ; -se, to bend, to bow, to submit.

doble, a. double ; thick-set, robust ; artful, deceitful ; al —, doubly ; —, sm. passing-bell.
doblegar, v.a. to bend, to curve.
doblete, a. false jewel. [duplicity.
doblez, sm. crease ; fold ; —, sm. & f.
doblón, sm. doubloon.
doce, a. & sm. twelve.
docena, sf. dozen.
docenal, a. sold by the dozen.
doceno, na, a. twelfth.
dócil, a. docile, tractable. [ness.
docilidad, sf. docility, compliance, gentledocto, ta, a. learned.
doctor, sm. doctor ; physician.
doctora, sf. doctoress ; wife of a physician or doctor.
doctorado, sm. doctorate, doctorship.
doctoral, a. doctoral ; —, sf. canonry called doctoral in the Spanish cathedrals ; —, sm. canon of the doctoral.
doctorando, sm. one who is on the point of taking out his degrees as doctor.
doctorear, v.n. to play the doctor.
doctrina, sf. doctrine, instruction ; science ; Christian preaching. [nal.
doctrinal, sm. catechism ; —, a. doctridoctrinar, v.a. to teach, to instruct.
documento, sm. document ; muniment, record. [asses, mules, &c.
dogal, sm. rope tied round the neck of
dogma, sm. dogma.
dogmático, ca, a. dogmatical.
dogmatista, sm. dogmatist.
dogmatizador, dogmatizante, sm. dogmatizer, dogmatist.
dogmatizar, v.a. to dogmatize.
dogo, sm. terrier.
dolencia, sf. disease, affliction.
doler, v.n. to hurt ; to ache ; to be repugnant ; to be sorry ; -se, to repent ; to regret ; to sympathise.
doliente, a. suffering ; sorrowful.
dolo, sm. fraud, deceit. [tion.
dolor, sm. pain, aching, ache ; afflicdolorido, da, a. afflicted, painful, heartsick ; —, sm. chief mourner, the nearest relation of a person deceased.
doloroso, sa, a. sorrowful, afflicted, dolorous, dismal ; painful.
doloso, sa, a. deceitful, knavish.
domable, a. tameable.
domador, ra, sm. & f. tamer ; subduer ; horse-breaker.
domadura, sf. taming, subduing.
domar, v.a. to tame ; to subdue, to master.
domeñar, v.a. to make tractable, to tame.
domesticable, a. tameable.
domesticar, v.a. to domesticate.
domesticidad, sf. domesticity.

doméstico, ca, a. domestic ; —, sm. domestic, servant.

domiciliado, da, a. domiciled.

domiciliarse, v.r. to establish oneself in a residence.   [abode.

domicilio, sm. habitation, domicile, home.

dominación, sf. dominion, authority.   [power.

dominador, sm. ruler.

dominante, a. dominant, domineering.

dominar, v.a. to dominate ; to moderate.

dómine, sm. dominie, schoolmaster.

domingo, sm. Sunday.   [Sunday.

dominguero, ra, a. done or worn on

dominguillo, sm. straw doll.

dominica, sf. Sunday (in ecclesiastical language).

dominical, a. manorial ; dominical.

dominico, sm. friar of the order of Saint Dominic.

dominio, sm. dominion, domination, power, authority ; domain.   [ment.

dominó, sm. domino (a masquerade gar-

Don, sm. Don (title for a gentleman).

donación, sf. donation, gift.

donado, da, sm. & f. lay-brother ; lay-sister.   [giver.

donador, ra, sm. & f. donor, bestower.

donaire, sm. grace, elegance ; witty saying.   [stow.

donar, v.a. to make free gifts, to bestow.

donatario, sm. recipient.

donativo, sm. free contribution.

doncel, sm. page.   [maid.

doncella, sf. virgin, maiden ; lady's-

doncellez, sf. virginity, maidenhood.

donde, ad. where ; — quiera, anywhere ; ¿ de dónde ? whence ? ¿ por dónde ? by what way ? for what reason ?

donillero, sm. swindler, sharper ; cheat.

donoso, a. gay, witty ; pleasant, comely.

doña, sf. title of lady.

doquier, doquiera, ad. anywhere.

dorada, doradilla, sf. a kind of fish.

doradillo, sm. fine wire ; wagtail.

dorado, da, a. gilt ; —, sm. gilding.

dorador, sm. gilder.

doradura, sf. gilding.

dorar, v.a. to gild ; (fig.) to palliate.

dórico, ca, a. Doric.

dormidero, ra, a. sleepy, soporific ; —, sm place where cattle repose.

dormidor, sm. great sleeper.   [abed.

dormilón, ona, a. & sm. & f. sleepy ; lie-

dormir, v.n. to sleep ; -se, to fall asleep.

dormitar, v.n. to doze, to be half asleep.

dormitorio, sm. dormitory.

dorsal, a. dorsal.

dorso, sm. back.

dos, a. & sm. two.

doscientos, tas, a.pl. two hundred.

dosel, sm. canopy.

doselera, sf. valance.

dosis, sf. dose, dosis.

dospuntos, sm. (gr.) colon.

dotación, sf. dotation, endowment.

dotador, ra, sm. one who endows ; donor ; institutor.

dotal, a. dotal.

dotar, v.a. to endow.

dote, sm. & f. dower, dowry ; -s, pl. gifts of nature ; endowments.

dovelar, v.a. to hew a stone in curves.

dovelas, sf.pl. curved sides of the keystone of an arch.

dozavo, va, sm. twelfth part.

dracma, sf. drachm.

drago, sm. dragon-tree.

dragón, sm. a dragon ; (mil.) dragoon.

dragona, sf. shoulder-knot.

drama, sm. drama.

dramática, sf. dramatic art.

dramático, ca, a. dramatic.

dramatizar, v.a. to dramatize.

dríada, dríade, sf. dryad.

driza, sf. (mar.) halyard.

droga, sf. drug ; stratagem, artifice.

droguería, sf. druggist's shop ; drug-sister.   [trade.

droguero, sm. druggist.

droguista, sm. druggist ; cheat, impostor.

dromedario, sm. dromedary.

dual, a. dual.

dualidad, sf. duality.

dubitativo, va, a. doubtful, dubious.

ducado, sm. duchy, dukedom ; ducat.

ducal, a. ducal.

ducha, sf. douche.

ducho, cha, a. dexterous ; accustomed.

ducientos, tas, a. (obs.) two hundred.

duda, sf. doubt, suspense, hesitation.

dudable, a. dubious, doubtful.

dudar, v.a. to doubt.   [tain.

dudoso, sa, a. doubtful, dubious, uncer-

duela, sf. stave of cask.

duelista, sm. duellist ; quarreller.

duelo, sm. duel ; grief ; affliction ; mourning, funeral ; -s, pl. troubles ; afflictions.

duende, sm. elf, hobgoblin.

dueña, sf. mistress, owner ; duenna.

dueño, sm. owner ; master.

dulce, a. sweet ; pleasing to the taste ; mild, soft, gentle, meek ; —, sm. sweetmeat.

dulcificante, a. sweetening.

dulcificar, v.a. to sweeten.

dulzaina, sf. German flute.

dulzaino, a. excessively sweet.

dulzura, sf. sweetness ; gentleness, graciousness ; pleasant manner.

dúo, sm. (mus.) duo, duet.

duodécimo, ma, a. twelfth.

duplicación, sf. duplication.
duplicado, sm. duplicate.
duplicar, v.a. to double, to duplicate; to repeat.
duplicidad, sf. duplicity; falseness.
duplo, sm. double.
duque, sm. duke.
duquesa, sf. duchess.
dura, sf. duration, continuance.
durable, a. durable, lasting.
duración, sf. duration.
duradero, ra, a. lasting, durable.
durante, p. & a. during.
durar, v.n. to last, to continue.
durazno, sm. peach.

durazno, duraznero, sm. peach-tree.
dureza, sf. hardness, solidity, firmness; acerbity; steadiness; callosity; — de vientre, costiveness; — de oído, hardness of hearing.
durillo, a. rather hard.
durmiente, p. & a. sleeping; —, sm. dormer, dormant; -s, pl. sleepers.
duro, ra, a. hard, solid; unjust; oppressive, rigorous, cruel; stubborn; avaricious; rude, harsh, peevish, rough; —, sm. dollar; five pesetas.
duunvir, sm. one of the duumviri.
duunvirato, sm. duumvirate.
dux, sm. doge (of Venice and Genoa).

E

é, c. and.
ea, interjection used to awaken attention; ¡ — pues! well then! let us see!
ebanista, sm. cabinet-maker.
ébano, sm. ebony.
ebullición, sf. ebullition, boiling over.
Eccehomo, sm. picture of Ecce Homo.
eclesiástico, sm. clergyman, ecclesiastic; —, ca, a. ecclesiastical.
Eclesiástico, sm. Ecclesiasticus.
eclipsable, a. that may be eclipsed.
eclipsar, v.a. to eclipse, to outshine.
eclipse, sm. eclipse.
eclíptica, sf. ecliptic.
eco, sm. echo.
economía, sf. economy.
económico, ca, a. economical; avaricious.
económo, sm. economist.
ecuación, sf. equation.
ecuador, sm. equator.
ecuestre, a. equestrian.
eculeo, sm. wooden horse (for torture).
ecuménico, ca, a. œcumenical, universal.
echadizo, za, a. waste, worthless; sent as a spy; exposed (of children); —, sm. foundling.
echar, v.a. to cast, to throw, to dart, to jet; to cast away; to shoot, to bud; -se, to lie, to rest, to stretch oneself at [full length.
edad, sf. age.
edecán, sm. (mil.) aide-de-camp.
edición, sf. edition; publication.
edicto, sm. edict.
edificación, sf. construction; edification.
edificar, v.a. to build; to fabricate; to construct; to edify. [tive.
edificativo, va, a. exemplary, instruc-
edificio, sm. building, structure.
editor, sm. editor, publisher.
educación, sf. education. [cator.
educador, ra, sm. & f. instructor, edu-

educando, da, sm. & f. pupil, scholar.
educar, v.a. to educate, to instruct.
educción, sf. drawing forth, eduction, extraction. [bring out.
educir, v.a. to educe, to extract, to
efectivamente, ad. effectually, powerfully; certainly.
efectivo, va, a. effective, true, certain.
efecto, sm. effect; consequence; purpose; -s, pl. effects, goods; en —, in fact, in truth.
efectuar, v.a. to effect, to bring about.
efemérides, sf.pl. diary. [lition.
efervescencia, sf. effervescence, ebul-
eficacia, sf. efficacy.
eficaz, a. efficacious, effective.
eficiente, a. efficient, effective.
efigie, sf. effigy, image.
efímero, ra, a. ephemeral.
efluvio, sm. effluvium.
efugio, sm. subterfuge.
efusión, sf. effusion.
égida, sf. shield, protection.
égloga, sf. eclogue.
egoísmo, sm. selfishness.
egoísta, sm. self-seeker. [markable.
egregio, gia, a. egregious, eminent, re-
eje, sm. axle-tree.
ejecución, sf. execution.
ejecutable, a. performable.
ejecutar, v.a. to execute, to perform; to put to death; (law) to distrain, to seize.
ejecutivo, va, a. executive.
ejecutor, ra, sm. & f. executor; executioner.
ejecutoria, sf. (law) writ of execution.
ejecutorial, a. executory.
ejecutoriar, v.a. to obtain a verdict in one's favour; to prove.
ejecutorio, ria, a. (law) executory.

ejemplar, sm. exemplar ; example ; —, a. exemplary.

ejemplificar, v.a. to exemplify.

ejemplo, sm. example ; comparison ; pattern, copy ; por —, for instance.

ejercer, v.a. to exercise.

ejercicio, sm. exercise.

ejercitación, sf. exercise, practice.

ejercitar, v.a. to exercise ; -se, to practise.

ejército, sm. army.

ejido, sm. town pasture.

el, art. m. the.

él, ella, ello, pn. he, she, it.

elaboración, sf. elaboration.

elaborado, da, a. elaborate.

elaborar, v.a. to elaborate.

elación, sf. elation.

elasticidad, sf. elasticity.

elástico, ca, a. elastic.

elección, sf. election, discernment, choice.

electivo, va, a. elective.

electo, sm. elect.

elector, sm. elector.

electorado, sm. electorate.

electoral, a. electoral.

electricidad, sf. electricity.

eléctrico, ca, a. electric, electrical.

electrización, sf. electrification.

electrizar, v.a. to electrify.

electuario, sm. electuary.

elefante, sm. elephant.

elegancia, sf. elegance.

elegante, a. elegant, fine.

elegía, sf. elegy.

elegible, a. eligible.

elegidos, sm.pl. the elect, the blessed.

elegir, v.a. to choose, to elect.

elemental, a. elemental.

elemento, sm. element ; -s, pl. elements, rudiments, first principles.

elevación, sf. elevation ; highness ; exaltation, dignity ; ecstasy, rapture ; haughtiness, pride, height ; altitude.

elevar, v.a. to raise ; to elevate ; to heave ; -se, to be enraptured ; to be puffed up, to be conceited.

elidir, v.a. to weaken, to enervate.

elipse, sf. (geom.) ellipse.

elipsis, sf. (gr.) ellipsis.

Eliseo, Elisio, sm. Elysian fields, pl.

elixir, sm. elixir.

elocución, sf. elocution.

elocuencia, sf. eloquence.

elocuente, a. eloquent.

elogiador, sm. eulogist, praiser.

elogiar, v.a. to praise, to eulogise.

elogio, sm. eulogy, praise.　　[tion.

elucidación, sf. elucidation, explana-

eludir, v.a. to elude, to escape by stratagem.

emanación, sf. emanation.

emanar, v.n. to emanate.

emancipación, sf. emancipation.　[free.

emancipar, v.a. to emancipate, to set

embadurnar, v.a. to besmear, to bedaub.

embajada, sf. embassy.

embajador, sm. ambassador.

embalaje, sm. packing, package.

embalar, v.a. to bale, to pack in bales.

embaldosado, sm. tile-floor.

embaldosar, v.a. to pave with flags.

embalijar, v.a. to pack into a portmanteau.

embalsadero, sm. pool of rain-water.

embalsamador, sm. embalmer.

embalsamar, v.a. to embalm.

embanastar, v.a. to put into a basket.

embarazada, a. pregnant.

embarazar, v.a. to embarrass ; -se, to become intricate.　　[pregnancy.

embarazo, sm. embarrassment ; obstacle ;

embarazoso, sa, a. difficult, intricate, entangled.

embarbecer, v.n. to be getting a beard.

embarcación, sf. embarkation ; any vessel or ship.

embarcadero, sm. quay, wharf.

embarcar, v.a. to embark ; -se, to go on shipboard ; (fig.) to engage in any affair.

embarco, sm. embarkation.

embargar, v.a. to lay under embargo ; to impede, to restrain.

embargo, sm. embargo, sequestration ; sin —, notwithstanding.

embarnizador, sm. varnisher.

embarnizadura, sf. varnishing.

embarnizar, v.a. to varnish ; (fig.) to set off.

embarque, sm. embarkation.　　[bug.

embarrador, sm. plasterer ; cheat, hum-

embarradura, sf. plastering (of walls, etc.), laying on of mortar.

embarrancarse, v.r. to bemire oneself.

embarrar, v.a. to plaster.

embarrilar, v.a. to pack in barrels.

embastar, v.a. to baste, to sew roughly.

embate, sm. breakers, pl., surf, surge ; impetuous attack.

embaucador, sm. sharper, impostor.

embaucamiento, sm. deception, illusion.

embaucar, v.a. to deceive, to impose upon.　　[cram.

embaular, v.a. to pack in a trunk ; to

embazar, v.a. to tinge, to shade ; (fig.) to astonish ; to impede, to stop, to check ; —, v.n. to be amazed ; -se, to become tired ; to be ashamed.

embebecer, v.a. to astonish, to stupefy ; to amuse ; -se, to be struck with amazement.

embebecimiento, sm. amazement, aston-ishment.

embeber, v.a. to imbibe; to soak; to include; to squeeze, to press; —, v.n. to shrink; -se, to be enraptured; to retain firmly in the mind.

embelecar, v.a. to impose upon, to de-ceive. [tion.

embeleco, sm. fraud, delusion, imposi-

embelesamiento, sm. rapture.

embelesar, v.a. to amaze, to astonish.

embeleso, sm. amazement, ravishment.

embellecer, v.a. to embellish, to adorn.

emberrincharse, v.r. to fly into a violent passion (of children).

embestida, sf. assault, violent attack.

embestir, v.a. to assail, to attack.

embetunar, v.a. to cover with gum-resin or bitumen. [grow white.

emblanquecer, va. to whiten; -se, to

emblema, sm. emblem. [faction.

embobamiento, sm. astonishment; stupe-

embobar, v.a. to amuse, to divert from, to distract; -se, to be in suspense, to stand gaping.

embobecer, v.a. to stultify, to stupefy; -se, to become stupefied or stultified.

embobecimiento, sm. stupefaction.

embocadero, sm. mouth of a channel or of a river.

embocadura, sf. mouth-piece.

embocar, v.a. to put into one's mouth; to swallow in haste; to enter by a pass; to deceive.

embodegar, v.a. to warehouse.

embolar, v.a. to put balls on the ends of bull's horns. [reviler.

embolismador, ra, sm. & f. detracter,

embolismar, v.a. to propagate malicious rumours.

embolismo, sm. imbroglio; confusion.

émbolo, sm. sucker of a pump.

embolsar, v.a. to put into a purse; to reimburse.

embolso, sm. putting of money into a purse, repayment. [ebriate.

emborrachar, v.a. to intoxicate, to in-

emborrar, v.a. to stuff with hair; to comb the wool a second time; to cram. [rage.

emborrascar, v.a. to provoke, to en-

emborricarse, v.r. to be stupefied.

emborrizar, v.a. to give the first combing to wool. [bush.

emboscada, sf. ambuscade; (mil.) am-

emboscar, v.a. (mil.) to post in ambush; -se, to retire into the thickest part of a forest; (mil.) to lie in ambush.

embotadura, sf. bluntness.

embotar, v.a. to blunt; (fig.) to enervate, to debilitate.

embotellar, v.a. to bottle wine.

embotijar, v.a. to put in jars; -se, to swell; to be in a passion.

embozado, da, a. covered; involved.

embozar, v.a. to muffle; (fig.) to cloak, to dissemble.

embozo, sm. part of a cloak; muffling the face; muffling of one's face.

embravecer, v.a. to enrage, to irritate; —, v.n. to grow strong and healthy (of plants). [sion.

embravecimiento, sm. fury, rage, pas-

embrazar, v.a. to clasp a shield.

embreadura, sf. pitching or tarring of a ship.

embrear, v.a. to pitch a ship.

embriagar, v.a. to intoxicate, to in-ebriate; to transport, to enrapture.

embriaguez, sf. intoxication, drunken-ness; rapture, transport of mind.

embridar, v.a. to bridle.

embrión, sm. embryo.

embrocar, v.a. to pour out of one vessel into another, to decant. [founder.

embrollador, ra, sm. & f. entangler, con-

embrollar, v.a. to entangle, to embroil.

embrollo, sm. imposture; embroiling.

embrollón, ona, sm. & f. tale-bearer, im-postor; entangler.

embromar, v.a. to cajole, to wheedle, to chaff.

embrujar, v.a. to bewitch.

embrutecer, v.a. to stupefy.

embuchado, sm. pork sausages.

embuchar, v.a. to cram.

embudar, v.a. to put through a funnel; to insnare, to trick.

embudo, sm. funnel; fraud, artifice.

embuste, sm. fraud, imposition; quibble, humbug; -s, pl. gew-gaws, trinkets.

embustero, ra, sm. & f. impostor, cheat.

embutido, sm. inlaid work.

embutir, v.a. to inlay; to cram.

emendar, v.a. to correct, to amend.

emérito, a. retired, pensioned.

emético, ca, a. emetic.

emigración, sf. emigration, migration.

emigrado, da, a. & sm. & f. emigrant,

emigrar, v.n. to emigrate.

eminencia, sf. eminence.

eminente, a. eminent, high; excellent conspicuous.

emisario, sm. emissary.

emitir, v.a. to emit, to send forth; to let go, to let fly.

emoliente, a. emolient, softening.

emolumento, sm. emolument, fee, profit, advantage.

empachar, v.a. to impede, to embarrass; to cram, to surfeit; -se, to be ashamed, to be confounded.

empacho, sm. bashfulness, timidity; embarrassment.   [ful, timid.

empachoso, sa, a. embarrassing; bash-

empadronamiento, sm. register of taxable persons.

empadronar, v.a. to register.

empalagamiento, sm. surfeiting, surfeit.

empalagar, v.a. to loathe; to disgust; to trouble.

empalago, sm. disgust, nausea.

empalagoso, a. loathsome; troublesome.

empalar, v.a. to empale.

empalizada, sf. (mil.) palisade or palisado.

empalizar, v.a. to palisade.

empalmadura, sf. joining of two pieces of wood; welding of metals.

empalmar, v.a. to join the ends of two pieces of timber.

empalme, sm. (rail.) junction.

empanada, sf. meat-pie.

empanar, v.a. to cover with paste.

empantanar, v.a. to submerge; to drag in the mire; to complicate.

empañadura, sf. swaddling of children.

empañar, v.a. to swaddle, to swathe; to tarnish, to obscure, to vilify.

empapar, v.a. to soak; -se, to steep oneself.

empapelar, v.a. to wrap up in paper.

empaquetar, v.a. to pack goods into bales.

emparedamiento, sm. confinement; cloister.

emparedar, v.n. to confine, to immure.

emparejadura, sf. equalisation.

emparejar, v.a. to level; to match, to fit, to equalise.   [by marriage.

emparentar, v.n. to become related

emparrado, sm. vine-arbour.

emparrar, v.a. to embower.

empastar, v.a. to paste; to paint over.

empatadera, sf. check; deadlock.

empatar, v.a. to equal; to check; to cut short.   [lock.

empate, sm. equality of votes; dead-

empavesar, v.a. to deck out with flags; (mar.) to dress a ship.

empecatado, da, a. turbulent, incorrigible.   [inflexible.

empedernir, v.a. to harden; -se, to be

empedrado, sm. pavement.

empedrador, sm. paver, paviour.

empedrar, v.a. to pave.   [pitch.

empega, sf. varnish of pitch; mark of

empegado, sm. (mar.) tarpaulin.

empegadura, sf. varnish of pitch put on vessels.

empegar, v.a. to pitch.

empeine, sm. groin; instep.

empellejar, v.a. to cover with skins.

empellón, sm. push, heavy blow; -ones, rudely.

empenachar, v.a. to adorn with plumes.

empeñar, v.a. to pawn, to pledge; to engage, to oblige; -se, to bind oneself; to persist in a resolution; to interced e

empeño, sm. obligation; engagement; perseverance.

empeorar, v.a. to make worse; —, v.n. & r. to grow worse.

emperador, sm. emperor.

emperatriz, sf. empress.

emperejilar, v.a. to trick out.

emperezar, v.n. & r. to be lazy or indolent; —, v.a. to retard.

empero, c. yet, however.

emperrarse, v.r. to be obstinate.

empezar, v.a. to begin, to commence.

empinadura, sf. elevation, raising.

empinar, v.a. to raise; to exalt; to drink much; -se, to stand on tiptoe; to rise high.

empíreo, sm. empyrean (the highest heaven); —, rea, a. celestial.

empírico, sm. quack, empiric; —, ca, a. empirical.

empirismo, sm. empiricism.

empizarrado, sm. slate-roofing.   [slate.

empizarrar, v.a. to slate, to roof with

emplastadura, sf. plastering.

emplastar, v.a. to plaster; to paint the face; to impede; -se, to bedaub one's hands or feet.

emplasto, sm. plaster.   [paritor.

emplazador, sm. (law) summoner, ap-

emplazamiento, sm. summons, citation.

emplazar, v.a. to summon.

empleado, sm. official.

emplear, v.a. to employ; to occupy; to commission.   [pation.

empleo, sm. employ, employment, occu-

emplomador, sm. plumber.

emplomar, v.a. to solder.

emplumar, v.a. to adorn with feathers; -se, to get feathers.

emplumecer, v.n. to begin to get feathers.

empobrecer, v.a. to reduce to poverty; —, v.n. to become poor.

empobrecimiento, sm. impoverishment.

empodrecer, v.a. to corrupt; —, v.n. to putrify.   [powder.

empolvar, v.a. to powder, to sprinkle

empolladura, sf. swarm (of bees).

empollar, v.a. to hatch.

emponzoñador, ra, sm. & f. poisoner.

emponzoñamiento, sm. poisoning.

emponzoñar, v.a. to poison; to taint, to corrupt.

emporcar, v.a. to soil, to dirty.

emporio, sm. emporium.

empotrar, v.a. to mortise.

emprendedor, sm. undertaker.

emprender, v.a. to undertake.

empreñar, v.a. to impregnate.

empresa, sf. symbol, motto; enterprise, undertaking; design, purpose.

empresario, sm. manager of a theatre.

empréstito, sm. loan.

empringar, v.a. to grease.

empujar, v.a. to push, to shove.

empuje, sm. impulse; pushing.

empujón, sm. impulse, push; á -ones, pushingly, rudely.

empuñadura, sf. hilt of a sword.

empuñar, v.a. to clutch, to grip with the fist.

emulación, sf. emulation.

emular, v.a. to emulate, to rival.

émulo, sm. competitor, rival.

emulsión, sf. emulsion.

en, pr. in; on, upon.

enaguas, sf.pl. petticoat.   [mind.

enajenación, sf. alienation; absence of

enajenamiento, sm. change of affection; rapture; astonishment.

enajenar, v.a. to alienate; to astonish; -se, to fall out.

enalbardar, v.a. to saddle beasts of burden; to cover with batter.

enamoradamente, ad. lovingly.

enamoradizo, za, a. inclined to love.

enamorado, da, a. in love, enamoured, love-sick.

enamoramiento, sm. falling in love.

enamorar, v.a. to inspire love; to captivate, -se, to fall in love.

enamoricarse, v.r. to be slightly in love.

enano, na, a. dwarfish; —, sm. dwarf.

enarbolar, v.a. to hoist, to raise high.

enardecer, v.a. to fire with passion, to inflame.

enarenar, v.a. to fill with sand.

enarrar, v.a. to narrate.   [horse.

encabalgar, v.a. to provide horses, to

encabestrar, v.a. to guide by a halter; -se, to be entangled in the halter.

encabezamiento, sm. register of persons liable to pay a tax; heading.

encabezar, v.a. to make up the tax-roll; -se, to compound for taxes.

encabritarse, v.r. to rear (of horses).

encadenamiento, sm. linking together; connection, sequence.

encadenar, v.a. to chain, to link together; to connect, to unite.

encajadura, sf. encasing.

encajar, v.a. to encase, to drive in, to adjust; to introduce something with craft and cunning; -se, to thrust oneself in.   [inlaid work.

encaje, sm. joining together; lace;

encajera, sf. lace-woman.

encajonado, sm. mud-wall supported by pillars of bricks.

encajonar, v.a. to pack in a box, to lay in a chest.

encalabrinar, v.a. to make confused; -se, to become obstinate.

encaladura, sf. whitening, whitewash.

encalar, v.a. to whitewash.

encallar, v.n. (mar.) to run aground; to be checked.

encallecer, v.n. to get corns.

encamarse, v.r. to lie abed.

encaminar, v.a. to guide, to show the way; -se, to take a road.

encandecer, v.a. to heat to a white heat.

encanecer, v.n. to grow grey; to grow old.   [quill.

encanillar, v.a. to wind thread on a

encantador, ra, a. & sm. & f. enchanting, charming; enchanter; enchantress; sorcerer, sorceress.

encantamiento, sm. enchantment.

encantar, v.a. to enchant, to charm.

encantarar, v.a. to put into a jar or a pitcher.

encanto, sm. enchantment, spell, charm.

encañado, sm. conduit of water; hedge of canes or reeds.

encañar, v.a. to enclose with a hedge of cane; to convey water through conduits.

encañizada, sf. weir made of cane and reeds to enclose fish.

encañonar, v.a. & n. to put into pipes; to begin to grow fledged; to fold.

encañutar, v.a. to flute; to plait.

encapado, da, a. cloaked.

encaperuzarse, v.r. to cover one's head with a hood.

encapillar, v.a. to put over one's head.

encapotar, v.a. to cover with a cloak; -se, to be clouded; to look sullen.

encapricharse, v.r. to become stubborn.

encapuchar, v.a. to cover with a hood.

encaramar, v.a. to raise; to extol.

encarar, v.n. to face, to come face to face.

encarcelación, sf. incarceration.

encarcelar, v.a. to imprison.

encarecer, v.a. to raise the price; (fig.) to enhance, to exaggerate.

encarecimiento, sm. enhancement; exaggeration; con —, ardently.

encargado, sm. agent; *chargé d'affaires*.

encargar, v.a. to charge, to commission.

encargo, sm. charge, commission; office, employ.

encarnación, sf. incarnation; flesh-colour.

encarnado, da, a. incarnate; dyed flesh-colour; —, sm. flesh-colour.

encarnar, v.n. to be incarnate, to heal over; —, v.a. to give flesh-colour; -se, to incorporate one thing with another.

encarnizado, da, a. fleshed; blood-shot, inflamed.

encarnizar, v.a. to satiate with flesh; to provoke, to irritate; -se, to be glutted with flesh; to be cruelly minded. [scription.

encartamiento, sm. outlawry, pro-

encartar, v.a. to proscribe; to summon; to enter in the register; to include.

encasquetar, v.a. to cram a hat on to one's head; (fig.) to induce one to adopt *or* espouse an opinion; -se, to be headstrong.

encastar, v.a. to improve a race of animals; to procreate, to generate.

encastillar, v.a. to fortify with castles; —, v.n. to make the cell of the queen-bee; -se, to shut oneself up for defence in a castle; to be heady.

encenagado, da, a. mixed with mud.

encenagamiento, sm. wallowing in dirt *or* mire.

encenagarse, v.r. to wallow.

encender, v.a. to kindle, to light, to set on fire; to inflame, to incite; to foment; -se, to fire, to take fire; to fly into a passion.

encendido, da, a. inflamed; high-coloured.

encendimiento, sm. inflammation; glow.

encerado, sm. oil-cloth; window-blind; sticking-plaster.

encerar, v.a. to wax; to fill *or* stiffen with wax.

encerotar, v.a. to wax thread.

encerrar, v.a. to shut up, to confine; to contain; -se, to withdraw from the world.

encespedar, v.a. to turf.

encía, sf. gum (of the teeth).

encíclica, sf. encyclical epistle.

enciclopedia, sf. cyclopædia, encyclopedia.

enciclopédico, ca, a. encyclopedian.

encierro, sm. confinement, enclosure; cloister; prison.

encima, ad. above, over; at the top; over and above, besides.

encina, sf. evergreen oak.

encinar, sm. evergreen oak-grove.

encintar, v.a. to garnish with ribbons.

enclaustrado, da, a. shut up in cloisters.

encalvadura, sf. groove.

enclavar, v.a. to nail.

enclavijar, v.a. to join closely; to put pegs in a musical instrument.

enclenque, a. sickly.

encobertado, a. wrapped up.

encoger, v.a. to contract, to shorten; to shrink; -se, to be low-spirited; to humble oneself.

encogidamente ad. meanly, abjectly.

encogido, da, a. pusillanimous, timid, narrow-minded.

encogimiento, sm. contraction; constriction; pusillanimity.

encohetar, v.a. to throw squibs at bulls (at bull-fights).

encojar, v.a. to cripple, to lame; -se, to grow lame; to feign sickness.

encoladura, sf. gluing.

encolar, v.a. to glue. [tate.

encolerizar, v.a. to provoke, to irri-

encomendar, v.a. to recommend; -se, to commit oneself to another's protection.

encomienda, sm. commission, charge; message; patronage, protection; -s, pl. compliments.

encomio, sm. encomium, praise, commendation.

enconar, v.a. to inflame, to irritate.

encono, sm. malevolence, rancour.

enconoso, sa, a. hurtful, prejudicial; malevolent. [be met.

encontradizo, za, a. that which may

encontrado, da, a. opposite, in front.

encontrar, v.a. & n. to meet, to encounter; to assemble, to come together; -se, to encounter in an hostile manner, to clash; to be of contrary opinions. [ful.

encopetado, da, a. presumptuous, boast-

encorajar, v.a. to give courage, to inflame; -se, to be in a rage.

encorchar, v.a. to hive bees. [ments.

encordar, v.a. to chord musical instru-

encordelar, v.a. to tie with cords; to cord a bed. [ness.

encorvadura, sf. act of bending; crooked-

encorvar, v.a. to bend, to crook.

encostrar, v.a. to crust, to incrust; to rough-cast.

encrespar, v.a. to curl, to frizzle; -se, to become boisterous; to be involved in quarrels.

encrestado, da, a. (fig.) haughty, lofty.

encrestarse, v.r. to get the crest (applied to a young cock).

encrucijada, sf. cross-way.

encrudecer, v.a. to make raw; to exasperate, to irritate.

encuadernación, sf. binding books.

encuadernador, sm. bookbinder.

encuadernar, v.a. to bind books; to reconcile.

encubar, v.a. to put liquids into casks.

encubiertamente, ad. secretly; deceitfully.

encubierto, ta, a. hidden, concealed.

encubridor, ra, sm. & f. concealer, harbourer; receiver of stolen goods.

encubrimiento, sm. concealment, hiding.

encubrir, v.a. to hide, to conceal.

encuentro, sm. chock, justle; encounter.

encumbrado, da, a. high, elevated.

encumbramiento, sm. elevating; height.

encumbrar, v.a. to raise, to elevate; to mount, to ascend a height; -se, to be raised. [gar.

encurtir, v.a. to souse in pickle or vine-

encharcarse, v.r. to be inundated.

endeble, a. feeble, weak.

endecasílabo, ba, a. consisting of eleven syllables.

endecha, sf. dirge.

endechar, v.a. to lament with dirges; -se, to grieve, to mourn.

endemoniado, da, a. possessed with the devil; devilish.

endemoniar, v.a. to possess with the devil; to irritate, to provoke.

enderezadamente, ad. justly, rightly; directly. [tion.

enderezamiento, sm. guidance, direc-

enderezar, v.a. to rectify, to set right; to address; -se, to stand upright.

endiablada, sf. mummery. [ugly.

endiablado, da, a. devilish, diabolical;

endilgar, v.a. (col.) to direct.

endiosar, v.a. to deify; -se, to be puffed up with pride.

endosante, sm. endorser. [change.

endosar, v.a. to endorse a bill of ex-

endoso, sm. endorsement.

endrina, sf. sloe.

endrino, sm. sloe-tree.

endulzar, v.a. to sweeten; to soften.

endurecer, v.a. to harden, to indurate; -se, to become cruel, to grow hard.

endurecidamente, ad. pertinaciously.

endurecimiento, sm. hardness; obsti-nacy; hardness of heart.

enebro, sm. (bot.) common juniper.

enemigo, ga, a. inimical, hostile; —. sm. enemy; fiend.

enemistad, sf. enmity, hatred.

enemistar, v.a. to set at enmity.

energía, sf. energy, power, vigour; strength of will.

enérgico, ca, a. energetic; expressive.

energúmeno, na, sm. & f. demoniac, one possessed.

enero, sm. January.

enervar, v.a. to enervate.

enfadadizo, za, a. irritable, irascible.

enfadar, v.a. to vex, to molest, to trouble.

enfado, sm. trouble, vexation.

enfadoso, sa, a. vexatious, troublesome.

enfaldar, v.a. & r. to tuck up (clothes).

enfardar, v.a. to pack, to bale goods.

enfardelar, v.a. to make up into bales.

énfasis, sm. & f. emphasis.

enfático, ca, a. emphatic.

enfermar, v.n. to fall ill; —, v.a. to make sick; to weaken.

enfermedad, sf. indisposition, illness.

enfermería, sf. infirmary, hospital.

enfermero, ra, sm. & f. sick-nurse; hos pital nurse or attendant.

enfermizo, za, a. infirm, sickly.

enfermo, ma, a. sick, ill, indisposed.

enfervorizar, v.a. to heat, to inflame, to incite.

enfeudar, v.a. to enfeoff. [enfilade.

enfilar, v.a. to put in a row; (mil.) to

enfiteusis, sf. copyhold, alienation of the usufruct. [tenant.

enfiteuta, sm. copyholder; perpetual

enflaquecer, v.a. to weaken, to thin; -se, to fall away. [ening.

enflaquecimiento, sm. maceration, weak-

enfoscarse, v.r. to be troubled or per plexed; to be immersed in business; to be cloudy.

enfrascar, v.a. to pour liquid into a flask; -se, to be entangled in bram-bles; to be involved in difficulties.

enfrenar, v.a. to bridle; to curb, to re-strain. [front

enfrente, ad. over against, opposite, in

enfriadera, sf. cooler, refrigerator.

enfriamiento, sm. refrigeration.

enfriar, v.a. to cool, to refrigerate; -se, to cool down.

enfurecer, v.a. to irritate, to enrage; -se, to grow boisterous or furious (of the wind and sea); to become furious or enraged. [frown.

enfurruñarse, v.r. to grow angry, to

engalanar, v.a. to adorn, to deck.

engallado, da, a. erect, upright.

engallarse, v.r. to carry it high, to be haughty.

enganchador, sm. (mil.) recruiter.

enganchar, v.a. to hook; to ensnare; to enlist.

enganche, sm. recruiting.

engañabobos, sm. impostor; fooltrap.

engañadizo, za, a. deceivable, easily de-ceived. [ceiver.

engañador, sm. cheat, impostor, de-

engañar, v.a. to deceive, to cheat; -se, to be deceived; to make a mistake.

engañifa, sf. deceit, trick.

engaño, sm. mistake, misunderstanding, deceit, fraud.

engañoso, sa, a. deceitful, artful, false.

engarabatar, v.a. to hook; -se, to grow crooked.

engarabitarse, v.r. to climb, to mount.

engaritar, v.a. to place sentry-boxes; to deceive in a dexterous manner.

engarzar, v.a. to enchain, to link; to curl.

engastar, v.a. to set (a jewel).

engaste, sm. setting.

engastrimismo, sm. ventriloquism.

engastrimita, sm. ventriloquist.

engatar, v.a. to cheat in a dexterous manner. [coaxing.

engatusamiento, sm. deception, cheat,

engatusar, v.a. to coax.

engazar, v.a. to enchain, to link.

engendrar, v.a. to beget, to engender, to produce.

engendro, sm. fœtus, embryo; mal —, low breed; a perverse youth.

engolfar, v.n. to enter a gulf; -se, to be engaged in arduous undertakings or difficult affairs. [to find delight in.

engolosinar, v.a. to give a taste for; -se,

engomadura, sf. gumming.

engomar, v.a. to gum.

engordar, v.a. to fatten; -se, to grow fat; to grow rich. [stacle.

engorro, sm. (fam.) embarrassment, ob-

engorroso, sa, a. troublesome, cumbrous.

engrandecer, v.a. to augment, to aggrandise; to exaggerate.

engrandecimiento, sm. increase, aggrandisement; exaggeration.

engrasar, v.a. to grease, to oil, to fat.

engreimiento, sm. presumption, vanity.

engreir, v.a. to make proud; -se, to grow proud. [or fighting.

engrescar, v.a. to goad into quarrelling

engrifar, v.a. to irritate; to displease.

engrosar, v.a. to make fat; —, v.n. to increase in bulk.

engrudamiento, sm. pasting; gluing.

engrudar, v.a. to paste.

engrudo, sm. paste.

engualdrapar, v.a. to caparison a horse.

enguijarrar, v.a. to pave with pebbles.

engullidor, ra, sm. & f. devourer; gobbler

engullir, v.a. to swallow, to gobble, to glut. [with flour.

enharinar, v.a. to cover or besprinkle

enhebrar, v.a. to thread a needle.

enhestar, v.a. to erect, to set upright.

enhilar, v.a. to thread.

enhorabuena, sf. congratulation; felicitation; —, ad. well and good.

enhoramala, ad. in an evil hour.

enigma, sm. enigma, riddle. [scure.

enigmático, ca, a. enigmatical, dark, ob-

enjabonadura, sf. soaping.

enjabonar, v.a. to soap; to insult with foul language and blows.

enjaezar, v.a. to caparison a horse.

enjalbegar, v.a. to whitewash the walls of a building.

enjalma, sf. pack-saddle.

enjalmero, sm. pack-saddle maker.

enjambradero, sm. place where bees swarm to form their hives.

enjambrar, v.a. to gather a scattered swarm of bees; —, v.n. to swarm; to multiply.

enjambrazón, sf. swarming of bees.

enjambre, sm. swarm of bees; crowd

enjaretado, sm. grating. [multitude.

enjaular, v.a. to cage; to imprison.

enjebar, v.a. to steep in lye.

enjebe, sm. lye-steeping; bucking.

enjergar, v.a. (col.) to set a business going.

enjertal, sm. nursery of grafted trees.

enjoyar, v.a. to adorn with jewels; to set a ring with precious stones; to heighten the brilliancy of a thing.

enjuagadura, sf. rinsing of the mouth.

enjuagar, v.a. to rinse the mouth and teeth; to rinse clothes.

enjuague, sm. water used to rinse the mouth; intrigue. [clothes-horse.

enjugador, ra, sm. & f. one who dries;

enjugar, v.a. to dry; to wipe off; -se, to dry up; to grow lean.

enjuiciar, v.a. to bring into court; to pass judgment.

enjuncar, v.a. to tie with rush ropes.

enjutar, v.a. to dry.

enjutez, sf. dryness.

enjuto, ta, a. dried.

enlace, sm. connection, coherence; link; kindred, affinity; marriage.

enladrillado, sm. pavement of brick.

enladrillador, sm. bricklayer.

enladrillar, v.a. to pave with bricks.

enlardar, v.a. to rub with grease, to baste.

enlazable, a. which can be fastened together. [to lace.

enlazar, v.a. to join, to unite; to knit,

enlodar, v.a. to bemire. [mad.

enloquecer, v.a. to madden, to make

enloquecimiento, sm. enraging, maddening.

enlosar, v.a. to lay a floor with flags.

enlozanarse, v.r. to boast of one's dexterity or strength.

enlucido, sm. plaster.

enlutar, v.a. to put into mourning; -se to go into mourning. [timber.

enmaderar, v.a. to roof a house with

enmarañar, v.a. to entangle, to involve in difficulties; to puzzle. [yellow.

enmarillecerse, v.r. to become pale or

enmaromar, v.a. to tie with a rope.

enmascarar, v.a. to mask; -se, to go in disguise, to masquerade. [tion.

enmendación, sf. emendation, correc-

enmendar, v.a. to correct, to reform; to repair, to compensate.

enmienda, sf. correction, amendment; emendation; reward; compensation; parliamentary amendment.

enmohecer, v.a. to cover with mould; -se, to grow mouldy or musty; to rust.

enmudecer, v.n. to grow dumb; to be silent; —, v.a. to silence.

ennegrecer, v.a. to blacken; to darken, to obscure.

ennoblecer, v.a. to ennoble.

ennoblecimiento, sm. ennoblement, nobilitation.

enojadizo, za, a. fretful, peevish.

enojar, v.a. to irritate, to make angry; to teaze; to molest; to offend; -se, to be boisterous. [passion.

enojo, sm. peevishness; anger, choler.

enojoso, sa, a. offensive, vexatious.

enorgullecer, v.a. to fill with pride.

enorme, a. enormous, vast, huge; horrible; wicked beyond measure.

enormidad, sf. enormity, monstrosity.

enramada, sf. arbour.

enramar, v.a. to cover with branches.

enranciarse, v.r. to grow rancid.

enrarecer, v.a. to thin, to rarefy.

enredadera, sf. climbing plant; bindweed.

enredador, ra, sm. & f. entangler; tattler, tale-bearer; busybody.

enredar, v.a. to entangle, to ensnare, to confound, to perplex; to puzzle; to set at enmity; -se, to fall in love (of unlawful love).

enredo, sm. entanglement; perplexity, embarrassment; imposition; mischievous lie; plot of a play.

enredoso, sa, a. full of snares and difficulties. [embroidery.

enrejado, sm. trellis-work; open-work

enrejar, v.a. to fix a grating to a window; to grate, to lattice.

enriquecer, v.a. to enrich; to adorn; —, v.n. to grow rich.

enriscado, da, a. mountainous, craggy.

enriscamiento, sm. taking refuge among rocks. [rocks.

enriscarse, v.r. to take refuge among

enristrar, v.a. to couch the lance; to range, to file; (fig.) to meet a difficulty.

enristre, sm. couching a lance.

enrizar, v.a. to curl.

enrobustecer, v.a. to make robust.

enrodar, v.a. to break on the wheel.

enrojecer, v.a. to make red-hot

enronquecer, v.a. to make hoarse; —, v.n. to grow hoarse.

enroscadura, sf. act of twisting. [up.

enrosear, v.a. to twist; -se, to curl or roll

ensalada, sf. salad; medley.

ensaladera, sf. salad-bowl. [by spells.

ensalmar, v.a. to set bones; to heal

ensalmo, sm. enchantment, spell.

ensalobrarse, v.r. to become putrid, as stagnant water.

ensalzar, v.a. to exalt, to aggrandize; to exaggerate; -se, to boast.

ensamblador, sm. joiner.

ensanchar, v.a. to widen, to extend, to enlarge; -se, to assume an air of importance. [widening.

ensanche, sm. dilatation, augmentation;

ensangrentar, v.a. to stain with blood; -se, to be vindictive; to proceed in a cruel and barbarous manner.

ensañado, a. courageous.

ensañar, v.a. to irritate, to enrage.

ensartar, v.a. to string (beads, etc.); (fig.) to go through a long story.

ensayar, v.a. to assay precious metals; to rehearse; to examine, to prove; -se, to exercise oneself.

ensayo, sm. assay, trial, proof; rehearsal of a play.

ensebar, v.a. to grease.

ensenada, sf. creek.

enseña, sf. colours, pl., standard.

enseñanza, sf. teaching, instruction.

enseñar, v.a. to teach, to instruct; -se, to accustom oneself.

enseres, sm.pl. chattels, pl.

ensillado, da, a. hollow-backed.

ensilladura, sf. saddle of a horse's or mule's back.

ensillar, v.a. to saddle.

ensoberbecer, v.a. to make proud; -se, to become proud; to become boisterous.

ensordecer, v.a. to deafen; —, v.n. to grow deaf; to become silent.

ensordecimiento, sm. deafness.

ensortijamiento, sm. curling the hair.

ensortijar, v.a. to form into a ring; to curl.

ensuciar, v.a. to stain, to soil; to pollute; -se, to allow oneself to be bribed by presents.

entablado, sm. floor made of boards.

entablar, v.a. to cover or floor with boards; to introduce, to arrange, to set on foot.

entablillar, v.a. (med.) to put in splints.

entallador, sm. sculptor; engraver.

entalladura, sf. sculpture; engraving.

entallar, v.a. to sculpture, to carve; to engrave; —, v.n. to fit (of clothes).

entalle, sm. groove, notch.

entallecer, v.n. to shoot, to sprout (of plants).

entapizar, v.a. to hang with tapestry.

entarimar, v.a. to cover a floor with boards.

ente, sm. entity, being; ridiculous man.

enteco, ca, a. weak, thin.

entenado, da, sm. & f. step-child.
entendederas, sf.pl. (col.) understanding, judgment.
entender, v.a. & n. to understand, to comprehend; to remark, to take notice of; to reason, to think; á mi —, in my opinion; -se, to understand each other.   [knowing.
entendido, da, a. wise, learned, prudent.
entendimiento, sm. understanding, knowledge, judgment.
enteramente, ad. entirely, completely.
enterar, v.a. to inform thoroughly; to instruct.
entereza, sf. entirety; integrity; uprightness; perfection; firmness of mind.
enterizo, za, a. entire, complete.
enternecer, v.a. to soften; to move to compassion.   [softening.
enternecimiento, sm. compassion, pity, tenderness.
entero, ra, a. entire; perfect, complete; sound; just, right; pure, uncorrupted; strong, robust; uncastrated; por —, entirely, completely.
enterrador, sm. grave-digger.
enterrar, v.a. to inter, to bury.
entibiar, v.a. to cool.
entidad, sf. entity, real being; (fig.) consideration, importance.
entierro, sm. burial; tomb, grave.
entiznar, v.a. to besmirch, to defame.
entoldar, v.a. to cover with an awning; to hang the walls with clothes; -se, to dress pompously.
entonación, sf. modulation; intonation; blowing of the bellows of an organ; (fig.) presumption, pride.
entonador, sm. organ-blower; player of the first verse of a psalm.
entonar, v.a. to tune, to intone; to blow an organ; -se, to be puffed up with pride.
entonces, ad. then, at that time.
entonelar, v.a. to barrel.
entontecer, v.a. to make stupid; —, v.n. & r. to grow stupid.
entontecimiento, sm. growing stupid.
entorchado, sm. twisted cord which serves for embroideries.
entorchar, v.a. to twist a cord; to cover cords for musical instruments with wire.
entornar, v.a. to turn.   [wire.
entornillar, v.a. to make anything in the form of a screw.
entorpecer, v.a. to benumb; to stupefy.
entorpecimiento, sm. torpor, numbness, stupefaction.   [eye.
entortar, v.a. to bend; to pull out an eye.
entrada, sf. entrance, entry; entrance ticket.

entrambos, bas, pn.pl. both.
entrampar, v.a. to entrap, to ensnare; to involve in difficulties; to deceive; to encumber an estate with debts; -se, to become indebted.
entrañable, a. intimate, affectionate.
entrañas, sf.pl. entrails, intestines, pl.
entrapujar, v.a. to bandage with rags.
entrar, v.a. & n. to enter, to go in; to commence.
entre, pr. between; in; — año, in the course of the year; — manos, in hand.
entreacto, sm. (theat.) interval.
entreabrir, v.a. to half open a door, to leave it ajar.
entrecano, na, a. greyish.
entrecejo, sm. the space between the eyebrows; frowning supercilious look.
entrecoger, v.a. to catch, to intercept.
entrecubiertas, sf.pl. (mar.) betweendecks.
entredicho, sm. prohibition; interdict.
entrefino, na, a. between coarse and fine.
entrega, sf. delivery; conveyance.
entregar, v.a. to deliver; to give up.
entrelazar, v.a. to interlace.
entrelistado, da, a. striped, variegated.
entremedias, ad. in the meantime.
entremés, sm. interlude.
entremeter, v.a. to put one thing between others; -se, to meddle; to interfere.   [da, a. meddling.
entremetido, sm. meddler, obtruder; —,
entremetimiento, sm. interposition; meddling.
entreoir, v.a. to hear without perfectly understanding what is said.
entrepaño, sm. panel.   [decks.
entrepuentes, sm.pl. (mar.) betweenentrerrenglonadura, sf. interlineal note.
entrerrenglonar, v.a. to write between lines.
entresaca, sf. cutting down trees, in order to thin a wood.
entresacar, v.a. to sift, to thin (a wood).
entresuelo, sm. entresol.
entretalladura, sf. sculpture in bas-relief.
entretallar, v.a. to sculpture in basrelief; to slash (cloth).
entretejer, v.a. to interweave.
entretela, sf. buckram, stiff or strong linen.
entretener, v.a. to amuse; to entertain, to divert; -se, to amuse oneself.
entretenido, da, a. pleasant, amusing; doing business in an office in hopes of obtaining a place.
entretenimiento, sm. amusement, entertainment.   [see imperfectly.
entrever, v.a. to have a glimpse of, to
entreverado, da, a. variegated, streaky.

entreverar, v.a. to intermix, to mix to-
entrevista, sf. interview.   [gether.
entripado, da, a. contained in the entrails.
entristecer, v.a. to sadden, to afflict.
entrojar, v.a. to put up grain in barns.
entroncar, v.n. to belong to the same
  family.
entronización, sf. elevation to a throne
entronizar, v.a. to enthrone.
entronque, sm. relationship with the
  chief of a family.
entruchada, sf. clandestine operation,
  underhand business.   [a snare.
entruchar, v.a. to decoy, to lure into
entumecer, v.a. to benumb; —, v.n. to
  swell, to surge.
entumecimiento, sm. swelling; torpor.
enturbiar, v.a. to make turbid; to obscure, to confound.   [ture.
entusiasmar, v.a. to transport, to enrap-
entusiasmo, sm. enthusiasm.
entusiasta, sm. enthusiast.   [over.
enumeración, sf. enumeration, counting
enumerar, v.a. to enumerate.
enunciación, sf. enunciation, declaration.
enunciar, v.a. to enunciate, to declare.
envainar, v.a. to sheathe, to sheath.
envalentonar, v.a. to encourage, to inspirit.
envanecer, v.a. to make vain; to swell
  with pride; -se, to become proud.
envaramiento, sm. stiffness, numbness.
envarar, v.a. to benumb.
envasador, sm. funnel.   [to excess.
envasar, v.a. to put in casks; to drink
envejecer, v.a. to make old; —, v.n. to
  grow old.
envejecido, da, a. grown old; looking old.
envenenador, ra, sm. & f. poisoner.
envenenar, v.a. to envenom, to poison.
envenenamiento, sm. poisoning.
envestidura, sf. investiture.
envestir, v.a. to invest.
enviado, sm. envoy, messenger.
enviar, v.a. to send, to transmit, to convey, to despatch.
enviciar, v.a. to vitiate, to corrupt; -se,
  to be excessively fond of.
envidia, sf. envy; emulation.
envidiable, a. enviable.
envidiar, v.n. to envy, to grudge.
envidioso, sa, a. envious; invidious,
  jealous.   [to degrade oneself.
envilecer, v.a. to vilify, to debase; -se,
envinagrar, v.a. to put vinegar into anything.
envío, sm. (com.) remittance of goods.
enviscar, v.a. to smear with bird-lime;
  to irritate.
envite, sm. invitation.   [widow.
enviudar, v.n. to become a widower or

envoltorio, sm. bundle of clothes.
envolturas, sf.pl. swaddling- or swathing-
  clothes, pl.
envolver, v.a. to involve; to wrap up,
  -se, to be implicated in an affair.
enyesadura, sf. plastering with gypsum.
enyesar, v.a. to plaster.
enyugar, v.a. to yoke cattle.
enzainarse, v.r. to squint, to have a cast
  in one's eye.
enzarzado, da, a. matted.
enzarzar, v.a. to throw among brambles
  and briers; to sow discord; -se, to be
  entangled among brambles and briers;
  to be involved in difficulties.
épico, ca, a. epic.
epicúreo, rea, a. epicurean.
epidemia, sf. epidemic disease.
epidémico, ca, a. epidemic.
epidermis, sf. epidermis, cuticle.
Epifanía, sf. Epiphany.
epígrafe, sf. inscription; motto, device.
epigrama, sm. epigram.
epilepsia, sf. epilepsy.   [up.
epilogar, v.a. to recapitulate, to sum
epílogo, sm. epilogue.
epiqueya, sf. (leg.) equity.
episcopado, sm. episcopacy; bishopric.
episcopal, a. episcopal.
episódico, ca, a. episodical.
episodio, sm. episode.
epístola, sf. epistle, letter.
epistolar, a. epistolary.
epistolario, sm. collection of epistles.
epitafio, sm. epitaph.
epitalamio, sm. nuptial song.
epíteto, sm. epithet.
epitomar, v.a. to epitomize.
epítome, sm. epitome, compendium.
época, sf. epoch.
epopeya, sf. epopee.
equidad, sf. equity, honesty; fair price;
  impartiality, justice.
equidistar, v.n. to be equidistant.
equilátero, ra, a. equilateral, having all
  sides equal.
equilibrar, v.a. to balance.
equilibrio, sm. equilibrium.
equinoccial, a. equinoctial.
equinoccio, sm. equinox.
equipaje, sm. luggage; equipment;
  (mar.) crew of a ship.
equipar, v.a. to fit out, to equip, to furnish, to accoutre.
equitación, sf. horsemanship.
equitativo, va, a. equitable; just. [tion
equivalencia, sf. equivalence, compensa-
equivalente, a. equivalent.
equivaler, v.n. to be of equal value.
equivocación, sf. mistake, error, mis
  understanding.

equivocar, v.a. & r. to mistake, to mis-conceive, to misunderstand.

equívoco, ca, a. equivocal, ambiguous; —, sm. equivocation, quibble.

era, sf. era; thrashing-floor; plot in a garden.

eral, sm. two-year-old ox.   [fisc.

erario, sm. Exchequer, public treasury;

erección, sf. foundation, establishment; erection, elevation.

eremítico, ca, a. hermit-like, solitary.

erguir, v.a. to erect, to raise up straight; -se, to be elated with pride.

erial, a. untilled, uncultivated.

erigir, v.a. to erect, to raise, to build; to establish.

erisipela, sf. (med.) erysipelas.

erizamiento, sm. standing on end (of hair, etc.).

erizar, v.a. & r. to bristle.

erizo, sm. hedgehog.

ermita, sf. hermitage.

ermitaño, sm. hermit.

erradizo, za, a. wandering to and fro.

errante, a. errant, erring, roving.

errar, v.a. to do amiss; to mistake; —, v.n. to go astray, to err.

errata, sf. error in printing.   [nately.

erre, — que —, ad. pertinaciously, obsti-

erróneo, nea, a. erroneous.

error, sm. error, mistake, fault.

eructar, v.n. to belch, to eructate.

eructo, sm. belch, eructation.

erudición, sf. erudition, learning.

erudito, ta, a. learned, lettered.

erupción, sf. eruption, outbreak.

erutación, sf. eructation, belching.

esbelto, ta, a. tall, genteel, well-shaped.

esbirro, sm. bailiff, apparitor.

escabechar, v.a. to pickle.

escabeche, sm. pickle; pickled fish.

escabel, sm. foot-stool.

escabrosidad, sf. unevenness, roughness; asperity.

escabroso, sa, a. rough, uneven; craggy, crabbed; rude, unpolished.

escabullirse, v.r. to escape, to evade; to slip through one's fingers.

escala, sf. ladder; (mus.) scale.

escalada, sf. escalade.   [walls.

escalador, sm. climber, he who scales

escaldado, da, a. cautious, suspicious.

escaldar, v.a. to scald.   [wary.

escalera, sf. staircase; ladder.

escalfador, sm. barber's pan for keeping water warm; chafing-dish.

escalfar, v.a. to boil eggs; to heat.

escalón, sm. step of a stair; degree of dignity.

escalpela, sm. scalpel.

escama, sf. scale of fish or reptile.

escamadura, sf. scale-like embroidery.

escamar, v.a. to scale; to alarm; —, v.n. to embroider scale or shell fashion.

escamoso, sa, a. scaly.

escamotar, v.a. to make a thing dis appear from one's hands (in con-juring).   [v.a. to clean a place.

escampar, v.n. to cease raining, —,

escanciar, v.a. to pour out wine.

escandalizador, sm. scandal-monger.

escandalizar, v.a. to scandalise; -se, to be scandalised.

escándalo, sm. scandal.

escandaloso, sa, a. scandalous; turbu-lent.

escaño, sm. bench with a back.

escapada, sf. escape, flight.

escapar, v.n. to escape.

escaparate, sm. shop-front; cupboard (in Havana).

escapatoria, sf. escape, flight; excuse.

escape, sm. escape, flight; escapement (part of a watch); á todo —, with the utmost velocity.

escapulario, sm. scapulary.

escarabajear, v.n. to crawl to and fro like insects; to scribble; to sting, to give pain.

escarabajo, sm. black-beetle; scrawl, scribble; short, ill-shaped person.

escaramujo, sm. dog-rose.

escaramuza, sf. skirmish; dispute, quarrel.   [puter.

escaramuzador, sm. skirmisher; dis-

escaramuzar, v.a. to skirmish.

escarapela, sf. cockade.

escarbadientes, sm. tooth-pick.   [ing.

escarbadura, sf. act and effect of scratch-

escarbaorejas, sm. ear-pick.

escarbar, v.a. to scratch the earth (as fowls do); to inquire minutely into.

escarcha, sf. white frost.

escarchar, v.n. to be frozen.

escarda, sf. hoe.

escardadera, sf. woman employed to clear corn-fields of weeds.

escardador, sm. weeder.

escardar, v.a. to weed.

escarlata, sf. scarlet (colour); scarlet (cloth); kermes.

escarlatín, sm. coarse kind of scarlet.

escarlatina, sf. scarlet-fever, scarlatina.

escarmenar, v.a. to comb, to pick wool.

escarmentar, v.n. to be tutored by ex-perience; to take warning; —, v.a. to punish severely.   [chastisement.

escarmiento, sm. warning, caution;

escarnecer, v.a. to mock, to ridicule.

escarnio, sm. scoff, contemptuous ridicule.

escarola, sf. (bot.) endive.

escarpa, sf. declivity; scarp.

escarpado, da, a. sloped, craggy. [down.

escarpar, v.a. (mil.) to escarp, to slope

escarpia, sf. hook.

escarpidor, sm. wide, large-toothed comb.

escarpín, sm. sock; pump (shoe).

escasear, v.a. to give sparingly and with reluctance; to spare; —, v.n. to grow less, to decrease.

escasez, sf. scantiness, niggardliness.

escaso, sa, a. small, short, little; sparing, niggardly; scanty, defective.

escatimar, v.a. to curtail, to lessen; to haggle; to corrupt the sense and meaning of words.

escena, sf. stage; scene.

escénico, ca, a. scenic.

escepticismo, sm. scepticism.

escéptico, ca, a. sceptic, sceptical.

esclarecer, v.a. to lighten; to illuminate; to illustrate; —, v.n. to dawn.

esclarecido, da, a. illustrious, noble.

esclarecimiento, sm. dawn; splendour, renown.

esclavina, sf. tippet.

esclavitud, sf. slavery, servitude.

esclavo, va, am. & f. slave, captive.

esclusa, sf. sluice, flood-gate.

escoba, sf. broom, besom.

escobada, sf. sweeping slightly.

escobazo, sm. blow given with a broom.

escobilla, sf. brush; small broom.

escobillón, sm. artillery-sponge.

escocer, v.n. & r. to smart.

escofina, sf. rasp.

escofinar, v.a. to rasp.

escoger, v.a. to choose, to select.

escogidamente, ad. choicely, selectly.

escolar, sm. scholar, student; —, a. scholastic.

escolástico, ca, a. scholastic; —, sm. professor of theology.

escolio, sm. scholion, comment.

escollo, sm. sunken rock.

escolta, sf. (mil.) escort, convoy.

escoltar, v.a. to escort. [purify.

escombrar, v.a. to remove obstacles; to

escombro, sm. rubbish; mackerel.

esconce, sm. corner, angle.

escondedero, sm. lurking-place.

esconder, v.a. to hide, to conceal; to dissemble; to contain; -se, to lie hid.

escondidas, escondidillas, (á —) ad. in a secret manner.

escondite, sm. concealment; hiding; juego de —, hide and seek.

escondrijo, sm. hiding-place.

esconzado, da, a. angular.

escopeta, sf. firelock, gun; á tira de —, within gun-shot.

escopetazo, sm. gun-shot; gun-shot wound.

escopetear, v.a. to discharge a gun repeatedly; -se, to discharge fire-locks at each other; to insult each other with foul language.

escopeteo, sm. discharge of fire-arms.

escopetero, sm. musketeer. [timber.

escopleadura, sf. mortise-hole made in

escoplear, v.a. to chisel out.

escoplo, sm. chisel.

escorbútico, ca, a. scorbutic.

escorbuto, sm. scurvy.

escoria, sf. dross; lee; worthless thing.

escorial, sm. dross-heap.

escoriar, v.r. to skin.

Escorpio, sm. Scorpio, Scorpion (sign of the zodiac).

escorpión, sm. scorpion.

escorzonera, sf. viper-grass. [set.

escotadura, sf. curve of a jacket or corescotar, v.a. to cut out a garment about the neck; to slope; to pay one's share.

escote, sm. slope of a garment; one's share of a reckoning at a club.

escotero, ra, a. free, disengaged.

escotilla, sf. (mar.) hatchway.

escotillón, sm. trap-door.

escozor, sm. smart pain.

escriba, sm. scribe (among the Hebrews).

escribanía, sf. office of a notary; escritoire.

escribano, sm. notary, scrivener.

escribiente, sm. amanuensis.

escribir, v.a. to write; to compose literary works. [ment.

escrito, sm. literary composition; docuescritor, sm. writer, author.

escritorio, sm. counting-house, writingdesk; office, study.

escritura, sf. writing; deed; Scripture.

escriturar, v.a. to bind oneself legally.

escrofula, sf. scrofula.

escrupulizar, v.n. to scruple, to doubt.

escrúpulo, sm. doubt, scruple, scrupulousness.

escrupulosidad, sf. scrupulosity.

escrupuloso, sa, a. scrupulous; exact.

escrutinio, sm. scrutiny, enquiry.

escrutiñador, sm. scrutiniser, enquirer.

escuadra, sf. carpenter's square; squadescuadrar, v.a. to square. [ron.

escuadrón, sm. squadron, troop of horse.

escuadronar, v.a. to form troops in squadrons.

escucha, sf. sentinel, sentry; scout.

escuchar, v.a. to listen, to hearken.

escudar, v.a. to shield; to guard from danger. [squire.

escudero, sm. shield-bearer; page;

escudilla, sf. porringer. [porringers.

escudillar, v.a. to pour out broth into

escudo, sm. shield, buckler ; scutcheon of a lock ; Crown (gold coin).

escudriñamiento, sm. investigation, scrutiny.   [to examine into.

escudriñar, v.a. to search, to pry into ;

escuela, sf. school.

esculpir, v.a. to sculpture.

escultor, sm. sculptor, carver.   [tor.

escultura, sf. sculpture ; work of a sculp-

escupidera, sf. spittoon.

escupidura, sf. spittle.

escupir, v.a. to spit.

escurriduras, sf.pl. dregs, lees.

escurrir, v.a. to drain to the dregs ; —, v.n. to drop ; to slip, to slide ; to glide slowly ; -se, to slip away.

esdrújulo, la, a. accented on antepenultimate syllable.

ese, esa, eso, pn. that.

esencia, sf. essence.

esencial, a. essential ; principal.

esfera, sf. sphere ; globe.

esférico, ca, a. spherical.

esferoide, sf. spheroid.

esfinge, sm. sphinx.   [ant.

esforzado, da, a. strong, vigorous, vali-

esforzar, v.a. to strengthen ; -se, to exert oneself, to make an effort ; to be confident.   [effort.

esfuerzo, sm. courage, spirit, vigour ;

esgrima, sf. fencing ; maestro de —, fencing-master.

esgrimador, sm. fencer ; fencing-master.

esgrimir, v.a. to fence.   [striking fire.

eslabón, sm. link of a chain ; steel for

eslabonar, v.a. to link ; to unite.

esmaltador, sm. enameller.

esmaltar, v.a. to enamel.

esmalte, sm. enamel.

esmerado, da, a. high-finished, nice.

esmeralda, sf. emerald.   [pains.

esmerar, v.a. to polish ; -se, to take

esmeril, sm. emery.

esmerilar, v.a. to polish with an emery.

esmero, sm. careful attention ; nicety.

esófago, sm. gullet ; throat.

esotro, tra, a. this or that other.

espabiladeras, sf.pl. snuffers, pl., candle-snuffer.

espabilar, v.a. to snuff a candle.

espaciar, v.a. to extend, to dilate, to spread ; to insert spaces (print.) ; -se, to amuse oneself.   [slowness.

espacio, sm. space, capacity ; distance ;

espaciosidad, sf. spaciousness, capacity.

espacioso, sa, a. spacious, roomy ; slow.

espada, sf. sword ; spades (in cards) ; —, m. swordsman (in bull-ring).

espadachín, sm. bully.

espadería, sf. sword-cutler's shop.

espadero, sm. sword-cutler.

espadilla, sf. scotching-handle.

espadín, sm. small short sword.

espalda, sf. shoulder ; shoulder of a bastion ; back, back-part.

espaldar, sm. back-piece of armour ; back-board ; espalier in gardens.

espaldilla, sf. shoulder-blade.

espalmar, v.a. to pare a horse's hoof for shoeing.

espantable, a. horrid, terrible ; marvellous, wonderful.   [frightened.

espantadizo, za, a. timid, easily

espantajo, sm. scarecrow ; bug-bear.

espantar, v.a. to frighten, to daunt ; to chase or drive away.

espanto, sm. fright ; menace, threat ; wonder, surprise.   [wonderful.

espantoso, sa, a. a frightful, dreadful ;

español, ola, a. Spanish.

españoleta, sf. ancient Spanish dance.

esparaván, sm. sparrow-hawk.

esparavel, sm. casting-net, drag-net.

esparcir, v.a. to scatter ; to divulge ; -se, to amuse oneself.

espartería, sf. place where mats of esparto are made or sold.

espartero, sm. maker and seller of esparto-work.   [grass.

esparto, sm. (bot.) esparto, feather-

espárrago, sm. asparagus.

espasmo, sm. spasm.

espátula, sf. spatula.

especería, sf. grocer's shop, grocery ; spices.

especia, sf. spice.   [specially.

especial, a. special, particular ; en —,

especialidad, sf. speciality.

especie, sf. species, sort, kind ; matter ; motive.

especiero, sm. dealer in spices

especificación, sf. specification

especificar, v.a. to specify.

específico, ca, a. specific.

especioso, sa, a. neat, beautiful, finished with care ; specious.

espectáculo, sm. spectacle.

espectador, sm. spectator.

espectro, sm. spectre, phantom, ghost, apparition.

especulación, sf. speculation, contemplation ; commercial scheme.

especulador, ra, sm. & f. speculator.

especular, v.a. to speculate.

especulativo, va, a. a speculative ; thoughtful.

espejismo, sm. mirage.

espejo, sm. looking-glass, mirror.

espera, sf. stay, waiting ; (law) respite, adjournment.

esperanza, sf. hope ; (mar.) áncora de —, sheet-anchor.

esperanzar, v.a. to give hope.   [for.
esperar, v.a. to hope ; to expect, to wait
esperma, sf. sperm.
espesar, v.a. to thicken, to condense ;
-se, to grow thick, to solidify.
espeso, sa, a. thick, dense.
espesor, sm. thickness.
espesura, sf. thickness, density, solidity.
espetar, v.a. to spit ; to transfix ; -se,
to be stiff and stately.
espetera, sf. kitchen-furniture.
espetón, sm. skewer.
espía, sm. & f. spy.
espiar, v.a. to spy, to lurk.
espichar, v.a. to prick ; —, v.n. to die.
espiga, sf. ear (of corn) ; fusee of a
bomb ; sail of a galley.
espigadora, sf. gleaner.
espigar, v.n. to shoot into ears ; to grow,
to increase ; —, v.a. to glean.
espigón, sm. ear of corn.
espina, sf. thorn ; fish-bone ; — crespa,
gooseberry.
espinaca, sf. (bot.) spinage.
espinar, v.a. to prick with thorns ; —,
sm. thorn-brake, bramble-thicket ;
arduous undertaking.
espinazo, sm. spine, back-bone.
espinilla, sf. shin-bone.
espino, sm. thorn, prickly tree.   [ous.
espinoso, sa, a. thorny, arduous, danger-
espión, sm. spy.
espiral, a. spiral ; —, sf. spiral line.
espirar, v.a. to exhale.
espirenque, sm. leech.
espiritar, v.a. to possess with the devil ;
to wish someone to the devil ; to irritate, to agitate ; -se, to be possessed
with an evil spirit.
espíritu, sm. spirit, soul ; genius ; ardour, courage ; el — Santo, the Holy
Ghost ; -s, pl. demons, hobgoblins,
m.pl.
espiritual, a. spiritual ; ghostly.
espiritualidad, sf. spirituality ; principle
and effect of what is spiritual.
espiritualizar, v.a. to spiritualize, to refine the intellect.   [lively.
espirituoso, sa, a. spirituous ; vivid,
espita, sf. tap of a cask.
espitar, v.a. to tap.   [dent.
esplendente, pa. (poet.) shining, resplen-
esplendidez, sf. splendour, magnificence.
espléndido, da, a. splendid, magnificent ;
brilliant.
esplendor, sm. splendour.
espliego, sm. (bot.) lavender.
esplín, sm. spleen.
espolazo, sm. violent prick with a spur.
espolear, v.a. to spur, to instigate, to
incite.

espoleta, sf. fuse.
espolique, sm. running footman.
espolón, sm. spur of a cock ; terrace ;
chilblain, kibe.
espondeo, sm. spondee.
esponja, sf. sponge.
esponjadura, sf. act of sponging.
esponjar, v.a. to sponge ; -se, to be
puffed up with pride.
esponjoso, sa, a. spongy.
esponsales, sm.pl. espousals, pl.
espontaneidad, sf. spontaneity.
espontáneo, nea, a. spontaneous.
esportillero, sm. porter.
esportillo, sm. pannier, market-basket.
esposas, sf.pl. manacles, handcuffs, pl.
esposo, sm. husband.   [spur.
espuela, sf. spur ; stimulus ; (bot.) lark-
espuerta, sf. pannier, basket.
espulgar, v.a. to clear of vermin ; to
examine closely.
espuma, sf. froth, foam.
espumadera, sf. skimmer.
espumajear, v.n. to froth at the mouth.
espumajoso, sa, a. foamy, frothy, full of
spume.   [scum.
espumar, v.a. to skim, to take off the
espumarajo, sm. foam, froth (from the
mouth).
espumoso, sa, a. frothy, foamy.
espurio, ria, a. spurious ; adulterated ;
corrupted.
esputo, sm. spittle, saliva.
esquela, sf. billet, note, slip of paper.
esqueleto, sm. skeleton.
esquife, sm. skiff, small boat.
esquilador, sm. sheep-shearer.
esquilar, v.a. to shear.
esquileo, sm. sheep-shearing.
esquilmar, v.a. to gather and get in
the harvest ; to harvest.
esquilmo, sm. farm products.   [cattle.
esquilón, sm. small bell, bell worn by
esquina, sf. corner, angle.
esquinado, da, a. cornered, angled.
esquinazo, sm. corner, angle.
esquivar, v.a. to shun, to avoid, to
evade ; -se, to be disdainful.
esquivez, sf. disdain, scorn.
esquivo, va, a. scornful ; shy, reserved.
estabilidad, sf. stability.
estable, a. stable, firm.
establecer, v.a. to establish.
establecimiento, sm. establishment.
establo, sm. stable.
estaca, sf. stake ; stick, cudgel.
estacada, sf. (mil.) palisade ; paling.
estacar, v.a. to enclose with stakes.
estacazo, sm. blow given with a stake.
estación, sf. situation ; season of the
year ; station ; railway-station.

estacional, a. belonging to the seasons.

estacionario, ria, a. stationary.

estadio, sm. race-course; furlong.

estadista, sm. statesman; politician.

estadística, sf. statistics.

estadístico, ca, a. statistical.

estado, sm. state, condition; **hombre de —**, statesman; politician.

estafa, sf. trick, imposition.

estafador, sm. impostor, swindler.

estafar, v.a. to deceive, to defraud.

estafermo, sm. quentia (game).

estafeta, sf. courier, express.

estafetero, sm. postmaster.

estallar, v.n. to crack, to burst; to break out into fury.

estallido, sm. crack, crackling, crash.

estambre, sm. worsted; stamen of flowers.

estamento, sm. formerly each of the three estates composing the Cortes of Aragon.

estameña, sf. serge.

estampa, sf. print, stamp; pattern, model.

estampador, sm. printer.

estampar, v.a. to print. [ing prints.

estampería, sf. office for printing or. sell-

estampido, sm. report of a gun, &c.;

estampilla, sf. signet. [crack.

estancar, v.a. to check (a current); to monopolise; to prohibit, to suspend.

estancia, sf. stay, sojourn; mansion; (am.) cattle-ranch; bedroom; (poet.) stanza.

estanco, sm. forestalling, monopoly; place where monopoly goods are sold, tobacco shop; —, ca, a. stanch, sea-worthy.

estandarte, sm. banner, standard.

estanque, sm. pond, basin.

estanquillero, sm. tobacconist.

estanquillo, sm. tobacconist's shop.

estante, sm. shelf (for books); -s, pl. props of the cross-beams.

estañador, sm. tinman.

estañadura, sf. tinning.

estañar, va. to tin.

estaño, sm. tin. [etc.).

estar, v.n. to be (of position, state,

estática, sf. statics.

estatua, sf. statue.

estatuario, sm. statuary.

estatura, sf. stature.

estatuto, sm. statute, law.

este, sm. east; —, ta, to, pn. this.

estera, sf. mat.

esterar, v.a. to cover with mats.

estercolar, v.a. to dung, to manure; —, v.n. to void the excrements.

estercolero, sm. dung-hill; dung-pit.

estereotipar, v.a. to stereotype.

estereotipia, sf. stereotypography.

esterero, sm. mat-maker.

estéril, a. sterile, barren.

esterilidad, sf. sterility, barrenness.

esterilla, sf. lace of gold or silver.

esterlino, na, a. sterling.

esteva, sf. plough-handle; long stick.

estevado, da, a. bow-legged.

estiércol, sm. dung; excrement.

estigio, gia, a. Stygian.

estilar, v.n. to use, to be accustomed; —, v.a. to arrange, to draw up.

estilo, sm. style; use, custom.

estima, sf. esteem. [teem-

estimable, a. estimable, worthy of es-

estimación, sf. estimation, valuation account.

estimar, v.a. to estimate, to value; to esteem; to judge; to thank, to ac-knowledge.

estimular, v.a. to sting, to stimulate, to excite, to goad.

estímulo, sm. sting, stimulus.

estío, sm. summer.

estipendiario, sm. stipendiary.

estipendio, sm. stipend, salary.

estipulación, sf. stipulation.

estipular, v.a. to stipulate.

estirar, v.a. to dilate, to stretch out; to prolong, to drag out.

estirón, sm. pulling; hauling; rapid growth.

estirpe, sf. race, origin, stock.

estocada, sf. stab.

estofa, sf. quilted stuff; quality.

estofado, da, sm. stew.

estofar, v.a. to quilt; to stew.

estola, sf. stole.

estolidez, sf. stupidity.

estólido, da, a. stupid, stolid.

estomacal, a. stomachic.

estomagar, v.a. to disgust; to enrage.

estómago, sm. stomach.

estopa, sf. tow.

estopilla, sf. fine spinning-flax.

estopín, sm. quick-match.

estopón, sm. coarse tow.

estoque, sm. rapier.

estorbo, sm. hindrance, impediment.

estornudar, v.n. to sneeze.

estornudo, sm. sneeze. [this other.

estotro, tra, pn. contraction for este otro.

estrada, sf. causeway. [court.

estrado, sm. drawing-room; -s, pl. law-

estrafalario, ria, a. slovenly, uncleanly dressed; extravagant.

estragar, v.a. to deprave, to corrupt.

estrago, sm. ravage; havoc. [lar.

estrambótico, ca, a. extravagant, irregu-

estratagema, sf. stratagem; trick.

estrategia, sf. strategy.

estratégico, ca, a. strategical. [paper.

estraza, sf. rag; papel de —, brown

estrechar, v.a. to tighten; to contract, to compress; -se, to bind oneself strictly; to reduce one's expenses; to be intimate.

estrechez, sf. straitness, narrowness; intimate union; poverty.

estrecho, sm. strait; narrow passage between two mountains; —, cha, a. narrow, close; strait, tight; intimate; rigid, austere; exact; poor, indigent.

estregadura, sf. friction, rubbing.

estregar, v.a. to rub one thing against another.

estrella, sf. star. [poached eggs.

estrellado, da, a. starry; huevos -s,

estrellar, v.a. to dash to pieces.

estremecer, v.a. to shake, to make tremble; -se, to shake, to tremble.

estremecimiento, sm. trembling, shaking.

estrena, estrenas, sf. New-Year's gift; handsel.

estrenar, v.a. to handsel; to regale; to use for the first time; to begin, to initiate. [tiveness.

estreñimiento, sm. obstruction, cos-

estreñir, v.a. to restrain; -se, to restrain oneself.

estrépito, sm. noise, clamour, bustle, noisiness, obstreperousness.

estrepitoso, sa, a. noisy.

estribar, v.n. to prop; to be supported.

estribillo, sm. burden of a song.

estribo, sm. buttress; stirrup; step on the side of a coach; perder los -s, to lose courage.

estricto, ta, a. strict, exact; severe.

estrofa, sf. strophe.

estropajo, sm. dish-clout.

estropajoso, sa, a. ragged; despicable; mean; stammering.

estropear, v.a. to maim, to cripple.

estructura, sf. structure.

estruendo, sm. clamour, noise; confusion, bustle; pomp, ostentation.

estrujadura, sf. pressure, compressing.

estrujar, v.a. to press, to squeeze.

estuche, sm. case (for scissors, jewels, &c.); (fig.) a clever fellow.

estuco, sm. stucco.

estudiante, sm. scholar, student.

estudiantina, (á la —,) ad. in the manner of students.

estudiar, v.a. to study.

estudio, sm. study; study (room); — general, university.

estudioso, sa, a. studious.

estufa, sf. stove; hot-house.

estufador, sm. stewing-pan.

estufero, sm. stove-maker.

estufilla, sf. muff; small brasier.

estupefacción, sf. stupefaction.

estupefacto, a. petrified with astonishment; stupefied.

estupendo, da, a. stupendous, marvellous.

estupidez, sf. stupidity.

estúpido, da, a. stupid.

estupor, sm. stupor; astonishment

estuprador, sm. ravisher, deflourer.

estuprar, v.a. to violate, to deflour.

estupro, sm. ravishment, rape.

etapa, sf. (mil.) rations.

etcétera, adv. et cetera, and so on

éter, sm. ether.

etéreo, rea, a. ethereal.

eternidad, sf. eternity, everlasting.

eternizar, v.a. to eternalize, to perpetuate.

eterno, na, a. eternal.

ética, sf. ethics.

ético, ca, a. ethical, moral.

etimología, sf. etymology.

etimológico, ca, a. etymological.

etiqueta, sf. etiquette, formality

Eucaristía, sf. Lord's Supper.

eucarístico, ca, a. eucharistical.

eufonía, sf. euphony.

eufónico, ca, a. euphonious.

Euro, sm. Eurus, the east-wind.

evacuación, sf. evacuation; issue.

evacuar, v.a. to evacuate, to empty.

evadir, v.a. to evade, to escape.

evangélico, ca, a. evangelical.

evangelio, sm. gospel.

evangelista, sm. evangelist; gospeller.

evangelizar, v.a. to evangelize.

evaporar, v.a. & n. to evaporate; to pass away; to grow vapid.

evasión, sf. evasion, escape; subterfuge, poor excuse.

eventual, a. eventual, fortuitous.

evidencia, sf. evidence, manifestation.

evidente, a. evident, clear, manifest.

evitable, a. avoidable.

evitar, v.a. to avoid. [tion.

evocación, sf. evocation; pagan invoca-

evocar, v.a. to evoke.

evolución, sf. evolution.

exacción, sf. exaction; impost. [tate.

exacerbar, v.a. to exasperate, to irri-

exactitud, sf. exactness, exactitude.

exacto, ta, a. exact, punctual, assiduous.

exageración, sf. exaggeration. [ating.

exagerador, ra, a. amplifying; exagger-

exagerar, v.a. to exaggerate, to amplify.

exaltación, sf. exaltation, elevation.

exaltar, v.a. to exalt, to elevate; to praise, to extol; -se, to be excited, to be violent.

examen, sm. examination, trial, inquiry.

exámetro, sm. hexameter (verse).
examinación, sf. examination.
examinador, sm. examiner.
examinando, sm. candidate.
examinar, v.a. to examine.
exánime, a. spiritless, weak, dead.
exasperación, sf. exasperation.
exasperar, v.a. to exasperate, to irritate.
excavación, sf. excavation.
excavar, v.a. to excavate, to dig out.
excedente, a. excessive, exceeding.
exceder, v.a. to exceed, to surpass, to excel, to outdo.
excelencia, sf. excellence.
Excelencia, sf. Excellency (title).
excelente, a. excellent.
excelso, sa, a. elevated, sublime, lofty.
excentricidad, sf. eccentricity.
excéntrico, ca, a. eccentric.
excepción, sf. exception.
excepto, ad. except that, excepting.
exceptuar, v.a. to except, to exempt.
excesivo, va, a. excessive.
exceso, sm. excess.
excitar, v.a. to excite.
exclamación, sf. exclamation.
exclamar, v.a. to exclaim, to cry out.
excluir, v.a. to exclude.
exclusión, sf. exclusion.
exclusivamente, exclusive, ad. exclusively.
exclusivo, va, a. exclusive.
excogitable, a. imaginable; to be thought out.
excogitar, v.a. to excogitate, to strike out by thinking.
excomulgar, v.a. to excommunicate.
excomunión, sf. excommunication.
excoriación, sf. excoriation, flaying.
excoriar, v.a. to excoriate, to flay.
excremento, sm. excrement.
excursión, sf. excursion ; liquidation of a debtor's estate.
excusa, sf. excuse, apology, plea.
excusable, a. excusable.
excusado, da, a. superfluous, useless ; preserved ; exempted, privileged ; —, sm. privy, water-closet.
excusalí, sm. apron, pinafore.
excusar, v.a. to excuse ; to exempt ; to shun, to avoid ; -se, to decline a request.
execrable, a. execrable, accursed.
execración, sf. execration, curse.
execrar, v.a. to execrate, to curse.
exención, sf. exemption, immunity, privilege.
exentar, v.a. to exempt, to privilege.
exento, ta, a. exempt, free ; —, sm. a rank in the Spanish life-guards.
exequias, sf.pl funeral rites, obsequies.
exhalación, sf. exhalation ; velocity.

exhalar, v.a. to exhale ; -se to evaporate.
exhausto, ta, a. exhausted.
exhibición, sf. exhibition.
exhibir, v.a. to exhibit.
exhortación, sf. exhortation.
exhortar, v.a. to exhort.
exhorto, sm. letters requisitorial sent by one judge to another.
exhumación, sf. exhumation.
exhumar, v.a. to disinter, to exhume.
exigencia, sf. exigence, want.
exigible, a. requirable.
exigir, v.a. to demand, to require.
exiguo, gua, a. exiguous, small.
eximio, mia, a. eximious, famous, very eminent.
eximir, v.a. to exempt, to privilege.
existencia, sf. existence, existency, being.
existente, a. existing, existent.
existir, v.n. to exist, to be.
éxito, sm. end, termination, issue.

Éxodo, sm. Exodus.
exoneración, sf. exoneration.
exonerar, v.a. to exonerate, to unburden.
exorbitancia, sf. exorbitance.
exorbitante, a. exorbitant, excessive, immoderate.
exorcismo, sm. exorcism.
exorcista, sm. exorciser, exorcist.
exorcizar, v.a. to exorcise.
exordio, sm. exordium.
exótico, ca, a. exotic.
expansión, sf. expansion, extension.
expansivo, va, a. expansive. [grate.
expatriarse, v.r. to be exiled ; to emi-
expectación, sf. expectation.
expectativa, sf. right or claim respecting some future thing ; hope of obtaining a reward.
expectoración, sf. expectoration.
expectorar, v.a. to expectorate.
expedición, sf. expedition ; speed, activity.
expedicionario, a. expeditionary.
expediente, sm. affair of easy settlement ; collection of documents ; expedient ; pretext ; provision, means.
expedir, v.a. to expedite, to despatch.
expeditivo, va, a. expeditious.
expedito, ta, a. prompt, expeditious, speedy.
expeler, v.a. to expel.
expender, v.a. to spend, to lay out.
expensas, sf.pl. expenses, charges.
experiencia, sf. experience ; trial. [pert.
experimentado, da, a. experienced, ex-
experimental, a. experimental.
experimentar, v.a. to experience ; to experiment.
experimento, sm. experiment, trial.

experto, ta, a. expert, experienced.
expiación, sf. expiation; purification.
expiar, v.a. to atone for; to expiate; to purify.
expiatorio, ria, a. expiatory.   [last.
expirar, v.n. to expire, to breathe the
explanada, sf. esplanade.
explanar, v.a. to explain.
explayar, v.a. to extend, to dilate; -se, to amuse oneself.
explicación, sf. explanation.
explicaderas, sf.pl. (col.) manner in which anything is explained; facility of explaining.
explicar, v.a. to explain, to expound; -se, to speak plainly; to explain oneself.
explícito, ta, a. explicit, clear, distinct.
exploración, sf. exploration.
explorador, ra, sm. & f. explorer.
explorar, v.a. to explore.
explosión, sf. explosion.
exponente, sm. (ar.) exponent.
exponer, v.a. to expose; to explain.
exposición, sf. exposition; exhibition,
expósito, ta, a. exposed.   [show.
expresar, v.a. to express.
expresión, sf. expression.
expresivo, va, a. expressive; energetic.
expreso, sa, a. express, clear, manifest, not dubious; —, sm. express, courier.
exprimir, v.a. to squeeze out; to express.
ex profeso, ad. avowedly, on purpose.
expuesto, ta, a. exposed.
expulsar, v.a. to expel, to drive out.
expulsión, sf. expulsion.
expulso, sa, a. expelled; outcast.
expurgación, sf. expurgation, purification.
expurgar, v.a. to purify, to expurgate.
exquisito, ta, a. exquisite, consummate, excellent.
extasi, éxtasis, sm. ecstasy, enthusiasm.
extático, ca, a. ecstatical.
extender, v.a. to extend, to stretch out; -se, to be extended; to increase in bulk; to swell: to be elated with pride.
extensión, sf. extension; extent.
extensivo, va, a. extensive.
extenso, sa, a. extensive.

extenuación, sf. extenuation, feebleness, debility.   [tate.
extenuar, v.a. to extenuate, to debili-
exterior, a. exterior, external; —, sm. exterior, outward appearance.
exterioridad, sf. outward appearance; outside; superficies; pomp, ostenta
exteriormente, ad. externally.   [tion.
exterminador, sm. exterminator.
exterminar, v.a. to exterminate, to root out.   [tion.
exterminio, sm. extermination, extirpa-
externo, na, a. external, outward; foreign.
extinción, sf. extinction.
extinguible, a. extinguishable.
extinguir, v.a. to quench; to extinguish.
extirpación, sf. extirpation, extermination.
extirpar, v.a. to extirpate, to root out.
extorsión, sf. extortion.
extra de, pr. besides.   [cestry.
extracción, sf. extraction; origin, an
extractar, v.n. to abridge.
extracto, sm. extract.
extraer, v.a. to extract; to export.
extrajudicial, a. extra-judicial.
extramuros, a. without the walls.
extranjero, ra, sm. & f. stranger, foreigner; —, a. foreign, outlandish.
extrañar, v.a. to banish; to remove; to wonder at; to reprimand.
extraño, ña, a. foreign; rare; singular, strange, odd.
extraordinario, ria, a. extraordinary, uncommon, odd.
extravagancia, sf. extravagance.
extravagante, a. & f. extravagant.
extraviar, v.a. to mislead; -se, to lose one's way.
extravío, sm. deviation; irregularity.
extremado, da, a. extreme; accomplished.
extremaunción, sf. extreme unction.
extremidad, sf. extremity.
extremo, ma, a. extreme, last; —, sm. extreme, highest degree; en —, por —, extremely.
extrínseco, ca, a. extrinsic, external.
exuberancia, sf. exuberance, luxuriance.

F

fábrica, sf. manufacture; factory; fabric.
fabricante, sm. manufacturer.
fabricar, v.a. to build, to construct; to fabricate, to manufacture.
fabril, a. belonging to manufacturers or workmen.

fabuco, sm. beech-mast.   [mon talk.
fábula, sf. fable; fiction; rumour, com-
fabulista, sm. fabulist.
fabuloso, sa, a. fabulous, fictitious.
facción, sf. faction; feature; (mil.) duty.
faccioso, sa, a. factious, turbulent.

fácil, a. facile, easy.
facilidad, sf. facility, ease.
facilitar, v.a. to facilitate.
facineroso, a. wicked, detestably bad.
facistol, sm. lectern ; book-rest.
factible, a. feasible, practicable.
facticio, cia, a. factitious.
factor, sm. performer ; (ar.) factor ; (com.) factor, agent.
factoría, sf. factory ; office.
factura, sf. invoice.
facultad, sf. faculty.
facultativo, va, optional ; —, sm. master of a science or art ; doctor.
facha, sf. appearance, aspect, mien, face.
fachada, sf. façade, face, front.
fachenda, sf. vanity ; —, sm. busybody.
fachendear, v.a. to pretend to have important business on hand ; to bustle.
faena, sf. task, labour, fatigue.
faja, sf. belt, waist-band, wrapper, band ; bajo —, by book-post, under open cover.
fajar, v.a. to swathe.
fajina, sf. sheaf, faggot.
falacia, sf. fallacy, fraud.
falange, sf. phalanx.   [cious.
falaz, a. deceitful, fraudulent ; falla-
falda, sf. skirt ; lap ; flap ; train ; brow of a hill ; **perrillo de —,** lap-dog.
faldellín, sm. short under-petticoat.
faldero, ra, a. belonging to the lap ; fond of being constantly among women ; perrillo —, lap-dog.
faldillas, sf.pl. small skirts of a jacket.
faldón, sm. long flowing skirt ; bandelet.
falible, a. fallible.
fallar, v.a. to give sentence, to judge ; to trump (at cards).
fallecer, v.n. to die.
fallecimiento, sm. decease, death.
fallido, da, a. disappointed, frustrated ; bankrupt.
fallo, sm. judgment, sentence.
falsamente, ad. falsely.   [truthful.
falsario, ria, a. falsifying, forging ; un-
falsear, v.a. to falsify, to counterfeit ; —, v.n. to slacken ; not to agree in sound.
falsedad, sf. falsehood ; untruth, fib.
falsete, sm. bung.
falsificación, sf. falsification.
falsificador, sm. falsifier.   [counterfeit.
falsificar, v.a. to falsify, to forge, to
falso, sa, a. false, untrue ; deceitful ; feint.
falta, sf. fault, defect, want ; slight crime, failure, flaw.
faltar, v.n. to be wanting ; to fail ; not to fulfil one's promise ; to die.
falto, ta, a. wanting, defective ; jejune ; miserable, wretched ; mad.

faltriquera, sf. pocket.
falúa, sf. (mar.) officer's boat, launch.
fama, sf. fame ; reputation, name.
familia, sf. family.
familiar, a. familiar, domestic ; frequent ; —, sm. domestic ; college-servant.
familiaridad, sf. familiarity.
familiarizar, v.a. to familiarise ; -se, to become familiar.
famoso, sa, a. famous, renowned ; noted.
fámulo, sm. servant of a college.
fanal, sm. ship's lantern.
fanático, ca, a. fanatical ; enthusiastic.
fandango, sm. fandango (Spanish dance).
fanega, sf. a dry measure of about an English bushel and a half..
fanfarria, sf. empty brag.
fanfarrón, sm. bully, hector.   [brag.
fanfarronada, sf. fanfaronade, boast,
fanfarronear, v.n. to bully, to brag.
fanfarronería, sf. fanfaronade, brag.
fango, sm. mire, mud.
fangoso, sa, a. muddy, miry.
fantasía, sf. fancy ; phantasy ; caprice ; presumption.
fantasma, sf. phantom.
fantasmagoría, sf. phantasmagoria.
fantástico, ca, a. fantastic, whimsical ; presumptuous.
faquín, sm. porter, carrier.
faramalla, sf. imposition, artful trick ; prattling ; —, sm. treacherous man.
faramallón, sm. tattling, deceitful man.
farándula, sf. profession of a low comedian ; artful trick.
farandulero, sm. actor, player ; idle tattler, deceitful talker.
faraute, sm. messenger ; interpreter ; principal manager ; meddling fellow.
fardel, sm. fardel, bag, knapsack.
fardo, sm. bale of goods, parcel.
farfantón, sm. boasting babbler.
farfantonada, sf. idle boast.
farfulla, sm. stammering person.
farfullar, v.a. to talk stammeringly ; to do in a hurry and confusion.
farisaico, ca, a. pharisaical.
farisaísmo, sm. pharisaism.
fariseo, sm. pharisee ; very tall, ugly person.
farmacéutico, ca, a. pharmaceutical.
farmacia, sf. pharmacy.
faro, sm. (mar.) lighthouse.
farol, sm. lantern, street-lamp.
farolear, v.n. to act the busybody.
farolero, sm. lantern-maker ; lamp-lighter.
fárrago, sm. farrago, medley.
farsa, sf. farce ; company of players.
farsante, sm. actor, player ; mountebank.

fascinación, sf. fascination; deceit.
fascinar, v.a. to fascinate; to enchant; to deceive.
fase, sf. phase. [to offend.
fastidiar, v.a. to excite disgust; to grate,
fastidio, sm. squeamishness; disgust.
fastidioso, sa, a. fastidious; nauseous; tedious.
fastoso, sa, a. proud, ostentatious.
fatal, a. fatal; mortal; unfortunate.
fatalidad, sf. fatality, mischance, ill luck.
fatalismo, sm. fatalism.
fatalista, sm. fatalist.
fatiga, sf. toil, fatigue.
fatigar, v.a. to fatigue, to tire, to harass.
fatigoso, sa, a. tiresome, troublesome.
fatuidad, sf. fatuity, foolishness, silliness.
fatuo, tua, a. fatuous, stupid, foolish, silly, trifling.
fausto, ta, a. happy, fortunate; —, sm. splendour, pomp.
faustoso, sa, a. haughty, ostentatious.
fautor, sm. partisan, supporter.
favor, sm. favour, protection, good graces. [propitious.
favorable, a. favourable, advantageous,
favorecer, v.a. to favour, to protect.
favorito, ta, a. favourite, beloved.
faz, sf. face. [my honour.
fe, sf. faith, belief; á — mía, upon
fealdad, sf. ugliness; turpitude, dishonesty.
Febo, sm. (poet.) Phœbus (the sun).
febrero, sm. February.
febril, a. febrile, feverish.
fecundar, v.a. to fertilise.
fecundidad, sf. fecundity, fertility.
fecundo, da, a. fruitful, fertile.
fecha, sf. date (of a letter, &c.).
fechar, v.a. to date.
fechoría, sf. action, exploit.
felicidad, sf. felicity, happiness.
felicitar, v.a. to congratulate, to felicitate
feligrés, esa, sm. & f. parishioner.
feligresía, sf. rural parish.
feliz, a. happy, fortunate.
felonía, sf. treachery, felony.
felpa, sf. plush; drubbing.
felpilla, sf. corded silk for embroidering.
felpudo, da, a. shaggy; —, sm. fur rug.
femenil, a. feminine, womanly.
femenino, na, a. feminine, female.
fementido, da, a. false, unfaithful.
fenecer, v.a. to finish, to conclude; —, v.n. to die.
fenecimiento, sm. termination, end.
fenómeno, sm. phenomenon.
feo, ea, a. ugly, deformed.
feracidad, sf. feracity, fertility.
feraz, a. fertile, fruitful.
féretro, sm. bier, hearse.

feria, sf. feast-day, holiday; fair, market-day.
feriar, v.a. to buy at the fair; to barter; to give fairings; to suspend.
fermentación, sf. fermentation.
fermentar, v.n. to ferment.
fermento, sm. ferment; leaven.
ferocidad, sf. ferocity, wildness; cruelty.
feroz, a. ferocious, cruel, savage.
ferrocarril, sm. railway.
ferruginoso, sa, a. ferruginous.
fértil, a. fertile, fruitful. [ness.
fertilidad, sf. fertility, fecundity, fruitful-
fertilizar, v.a. to fertilise.
férula, sf. cane.
ferviente, a. fervent, ardent.
fervor, sm. fervour, zeal, ardour.
fervoroso, sa, a. fervent, ardent, fervid, passionate.
festejar, v.a. to feast; to court, to woo.
festejo, sm. courtship; feast.
festín, sm. feast.
festividad, sf. festivity; solemnization of some occurrence.
festivo, va, a. festive, gay, merry; día —, holiday.
festón, sm. garland; festoon. [toons.
festonear, v.a. to ornament with fes-
fétido, da, a. fetid, stinking.
feto, sm. fœtus.
feudal, a. feudal.
feudalidad, sf. feudality.
feudatario, sm. & a. feudatory. [lord.
feudo, sm. fief; tribute paid to a feudal
fiado, da, a. confident; al —, upon trust; en —, upon bail.
fiador, sm. surety (person); loop of a cloak; staple.
fiambre, a. & sm. cold (meat).
fianza, sf. caution, security, bail.
fiar, v.a. to bail; to sell on trust; to commit to another, to credit; —, v.n. to confide.
fiat, sm. consent; (law) fiat.
fibra, sf. fibre.
fibroso, sa, a. fibrous.
ficción, sf. fiction.
ficticio, cia, a. fictitious.
ficha, sf. counter (at games).
fidedigno, na, a. worthy of credit.
fideicomisario, sm. trustee.
fideicomiso, sf. bequest in trust. [ity.
fidelidad, sf. fidelity; loyalty; punctual-
fideos, sm.pl. vermicelli.
fiebre, sf. fever.
fiel, a. faithful, loyal; —, sm. clerk of the market; needle of a balance.
fielazgo, sm. office of the town-clerk.
fieltro, sm. felt; rain-cloak.
fiera, sf. wild beast.
fierabrás, sm. bully, braggart.

fiereza, sf. fierceness, cruelty, ferocity.

fiero, ra, a. fierce, cruel, ferocious; rough, rude.

fierro, sm. iron. [days, vacations.

fiesta, sf. feast; festivity; -s, pl. holifigón, sm. eating-house, chop-house.

figonero, sm. eating-house keeper.

figura, sf. figure, shape.

figurable, a. figurable, that which may be figured.

figuración, sf. imagination.

figurado, da, a. figurative.

figurar, v.a. to figure; -se, to fancy, to imagine.

figurativo, va, a. figurative.

figurón, sm. self-important person.

fijacarteles, sm. bill-sticker.

fijar, v.a. to fix, to fasten; -se, to fix or settle itself in a place.

fijo, ja, a. fixed, firm; settled, permanent; attentive.

fila, sf. row, line of soldiers; in a line.

filamento, sm. filament.

filantropía, sf. philanthropy, good-nature.

filántropo, sm. philanthropist; -s, pl. burdock.

filete, sm. fillet; hem; ridge.

filetear, v.a. to adorn with fillets.

filiación, sf. filiation.

filial, a. filial.

filiar, v.n. to prove one's descent, &c.

filibustero, sm. freebooter.

filigrana, sf. filigree.

filisteo, tea, a. tall, gigantic.

filo, sm. edge (of a sword, &c.).

filología, sf. philology.

filológico, ca, a. philological.

filólogo, sm. philologist.

filosofar, v.a. to philosophize.

filosofía, sf. philosophy.

filosófico, ca, a. philosophical.

filosofismo, sm. sophistry.

filósofo, sm. philosopher.

filtración, sf. filtration.

filtrar, v.a. to filter, to strain.

filtro, sm. filter; love-potion.

fin, sm. end, termination, conclusion; al —, at last; en —, por —, finally, lastly.　　　　[tion, conclusion.

final, a. final; —, sm. end, termina-

finalizar, v.a. to finish, to conclude; —, v.n. to be finished.

finalmente, ad. finally, at last.

financiero, sm. financier.

finca, sf. real estate.

fineza, sf. fineness, perfection; delicacy; beauty; friendly zeal; small, friendly gift; courtesy.

fingido, da, a. feigned, dissembled, sham.

fingimiento, sm. simulation, pretence, false appearance.

fingir, v.a. to feign, to pretend.

finiquito, sm. close of an account; final receipt or discharge.

finito, ta, a. finite, limited, bounded.

fino, na, a. fine, perfect, pure; delicate, nice, polite; acute, sagacious.

finura, sf. fineness.

firma, sf. signature, subscription.

firmamento, sm. firmament, sky, heaven.

firmar, v.a. to sign, to subscribe.

firme, a. firm, stable, strong, secure; constant, resolute.

firmeza, sf. firmness, stability, constancy.

fiscal, sm. public prosecutor; fiscal.

fiscalía, sf. office and business of the fiscal.

fiscalizar, v.a. to accuse, to criticize.

fisco, sm. fisc, fiscal, exchequer. [scoff.

fisga, sf. three-pronged harpoon; raillery.

fisgar, v.a. to mock, to scoff, to jeer.

fisgón, sm. punster, buffoon.

física, sf. physics.

físico, ca, a. physical; real; —, sm. physician; physique, bodily constitu-

fisonomía, sf. physiognomy. [tion.

fisonomista, sm. physiognomist.

fístola, sf. fistula.

flaco, ca, a. lean, meagre; feeble, languid.

flacura, sf. meagreness.

flagelación, sf. flagellation.

flagelante, sm. flagellant.

flagrante, a. flagrant; en —, in the act, red-handed.

flagrar, v.n. to glow, to flame.

flamante, a. flaming, bright; quite new.

flan, sm. custard.

flanco, sm. flank.

flanquear, v.a. (mil.) to flank.

flaquear, v.n. to flag; to grow spiritless; to slacken.

flaqueza, sf. leanness, extenuation, meagreness, feebleness, weakness.

flato, sm. flatulency; gust of wind.

flatulento, ta, a. flatulent.

flauta, sf. (mus.) flute.

flautado, da, a. resembling a flute; —, sm. stop of an organ.

flautero, sm. flute-maker.

flautista, sm. flute-player, flutist.

flecha, sf. arrow. [maker.

flechero, sm. archer, bowman; bow-

flema, sf. phlegm.

flemático, ca, a. phlegmatic.

flemón, sm. gumboil.

flemoso, sa, a. pituitous.

flemudo, da, a. dull, sluggish.

fletar, v.a. to freight (a ship).

flete, sm. (mar.) freight.

flexibilidad, sf. flexibility.

flexible, a. flexible, pliant; docile.

flojedad, sf. feebleness, laxity, laziness, negligence.

flojo, ja, a. flexible, lax, slack; insipid, feeble; lazy. [ficial flowers.

flor, sf. flower; -es de mano, artiflorear, v.a. to adorn with flowers; to flourish (of swords); (mus.) to flourish.

florecer, v.n. to blossom.

florero, sm. flower-pot.

floresta, sf. forest, thicket, grove; fine delightful place.

florete, sm. fencing-foil.

floretista, sm. fencer.

florido, da, a. florid; choice, excellent.

florín, sm. florin.

florista, sm. florist.

flota, sf. fleet.

flotación, flotadura, sf. floating, flotation.

flotante, a. floating.

flotar, v.n. to float.

flote, sm. floating; á —, buoyant.

flotilla, sf. small fleet, flotilla.

fluctuación, sf. fluctuation; uncertainty.

fluctuar, v.n. to fluctuate; to be irresolute.

fluidez, sf. fluidity, liquidness.

fluido, da, a. fluid; (fig.) fluent; —, sm. fluid.

fluir, v.n. to flow. [vientre, diarrhœa.

flujo, sm. (med.) flux; flowing; — de

fluvial, a. fluvial.

fluxión, sf. fluxion.

foca, sf. seal.

foco, sm. focus; centre.

fofo, fa, a. spongy, soft, bland.

fogata, sf. blaze.

fogón, sm. hearth; touch-hole of a gun.

fogosidad, sf. excessive vivacity, fieriness.

fogoso, sa, a. fiery, ardent, fervent; impetuous, boisterous.

foguear, v.a. to accustom soldiers or horses to stand fire; to clean firearms by firing off a small quantity of gun-powder in them.

foliación, sf. pagination (of books).

foliar, v.a. to page.

follados, sm.pl. old-fashioned trunk-hose.

follaje, sm. foliage. ·

follero, sm. one who makes or sells belfolletín, sm. serial story.

folletista, sm. pamphleteer.

folleto, sm. pamphlet.

fomentación, sf. fomentation.

fomentar, v.a. to foment; to patronise; to excite. [tronage.

fomento, sm. fermentation; fuel; pafonda, sf. hotel, inn, lodging-house.

fondeadero, sm. anchoring-ground, anchorage.

fondear, v.a. to sound; to search (a ship); —, v.n. to cast anchor

fondista, sm. innkeeper.

fondo, sm. bottom; depth, strength of character; space covered by anything; -s, pl. stocks, funds, capital; dar —, to cast anchor; á —, perfectly, completely; —, da, a. profound.

fontanería, sf. art of making waterworks; conduit-pipes, water-duct.

fontanero, sm. conduit-maker, turncock.

forajido, da, a. & sm. & f. outlaw.

forastero, ra, a. strange, exotic; —, sm. stranger. [oppose.

forcejar, v.n. to struggle, to strive, to

forcejudo, da, a. strong, robust.

forense, a. forensic.

forjador, sm. framer, forger.

forjadura, sf. forging. [vent.

forjar, v.a. to forge; to frame; to informal, sf. form, shape, fashion.

formación, sf. formation; form, figure.

formal, a. formal; prop., genuine; serious, grave. [gravity.

formalidad, sf. formality; punctuality;

formalizar, v.a. to form; to formalize; -se, to grow formal, to affect gravity.

formar, v.a. to form, to shape.

formidable, a. formidable, dreadful, terrific.

formón, sm. paring-chisel; punch.

fórmula, sf. formula.

formulario, sm. formulary.

fornicación, sf. fornication.

fornicador, sm. fornicator.

fornicar, v.n. to commit fornication.

fornitura, sf. accoutrements.

foro, sm. court of justice; bar; background of the stage.

forradora, sf. lining (of clothes).

forraje, sm. forage.

forrajeador, sm. forager.

forrajear, v.a. to forage.

forrar, v.a. to line.

forro, sm. lining.

fortalecer, v.a. to fortify, to strengthen, to encourage.

fortaleza, sf. fortitude, valour, courage; strength, vigour; (mil.) fortress, stronghold.

fortificación, sf. fortification.

fortificar, v.a. to strengthen, to comfort; to fortify a place.

fortín, sm. (mil.) small fort.

fortuito, ta, a. fortuitous.

fortuna, sf. fortune. [galleys.

forzado, sm. criminal sentenced to the

forzar, v.a. to force. [of draughts.

forzosa, sf. decisive move at the game

forzoso, sa, a. indispensable, necessary.

forzudo, da, a. strong, vigorous.

fosfórico, ca, a. phosphoric.

fósforo, sm. phosphorus; match.

fósil, a. & sm. fossil.

foso, sm. pit ; moat, ditch, fosse.

frac, sm. evening-coat, dress-coat.

fracasar, v.n. to crumble, to break into pieces ; to collapse.

fracaso, sm. downfall, ruin, destruction.

fracción, sf. fraction.

fractura, sf. fracture.

fracturar, v.a. to break a bone. [smell.

fragancia, sf. fragrance, sweetness of

fragante, a. fragrant, odoriferous ; en —, in the act itself, red-handed.

fragata, sf. (mar.) frigate.

frágil, a. brittle, frail.   [firmity.

fragilidad, sf. fragility, brittleness ; in-

fragmento, sm. fragment.

fragosidad, sf. roughness of the road ; imperviousness of a forest.

fragoso, sa, a. craggy, rough, uneven.

fragrancia, sf. fragrance ; (fig.) reputation for virtue.

fragrante, a. fragrant, odoriferous.

fragua, sf. forge.

fraguar, v.a. to forge ; to contrive ; —, v.n. to solidify, to harden (of mortar, clay, &c.).

fraile, sm. friar, monk.

frambuesa, sf. raspberry.

frambueso, sm. raspberry-cane.

francés, sa, a. French.

franco, sm. franc (coin) ; —, ca, a. frank ; generous, liberal.

francolín, sm. Indian partridge.

franela, sf. flannel.

franja, sf. fringe.

franquear, v.a. to exempt ; to franchise ; to disengage ; to stamp letters ; -se, to give oneself up to the service of others ; to unbosom oneself.   [rosity.

franqueza, sf. freedom, liberty ; gene-

franquicia, sf. immunity from taxes.

frasco, sm. flask ; powder-horn.

frase, sf. phrase.

frasquera, sf. bottle-case, liquor-case.

fraternal, a. fraternal, brotherly.

fraternidad, sf. fraternity, brotherhood.

fratricida, sm. & f. fratricide.

fratricidio, sm. fratricide (murder of a brother).

fraude, sm. fraud, deceit, cheat.

fraudulento, ta, a. fraudulent, deceitful.

frecuencia, sf. frequency.

frecuentación, sf. frequentation.

frecuentar, v.a. to frequent.

frecuente, a. frequent.

fregadero, sm. scullery.

fregado, sm. scouring of kitchen utensils ; (fig.) intrigue ; underhand work.

fregador, sm. dish-clout.

fregar, v.a. to rub ; to cleanse, to scour.

fregona, sf. kitchen-maid.

freidura, sf. frying.

freír, v.a. to fry.

frenesí, sm. frenzy ; extravagant caprice.

frenético, ca, a. mad, lunatic, insane.

frenillo, sm. impediment of the tongue.

freno, sm. bridle ; (rail.) brake.

frente, sf. front ; face ; — á —, face to face ; en —, opposite ; (mil.) front

fresa, sf. strawberry.   [rank.

fresal, sm. strawberry-bed.

frescachón, ona, a. plump, blooming, healthy-looking.

fresco, ca, a. fresh, cool ; new ; recent ; plump, ruddy ; brisk, gay ; —, sm. fresh air.

frescura, sf. freshness ; frankness ; smart repartee ; carelessness.

fresno, sm. ash-tree.

freza, sf. spawn.   [ence.

frialdad, sf. frigidity, coldness ; indiffer-

fricación, sf. friction.

fricasé, sm. fricassee.

fricción, sf. friction.

friega, sf. friction with flannel.

frígido, da, a. (poet.) cold.

frío, fría, a. cold, frigid ; indifferent ; —, sm. cold ; fresh air ; shivering.

friolento, ta, a. chilly.

friolera, sf. trifle.

frisar, v.a. to rub against the grain ; —, v.n. to resemble ; to approach.

friso, sm. frieze ; wainscot.

frisón, sm. large draught-horse.

fritada, sf. dish of fried meat or fish.

frito, ta, p. & a. fried.

frivolidad, sf. frivolity.

frívolo, la, a. frivolous, trifling.

frondosidad, sf. foliage, tuft of leaves.

frondoso, sa, a. leafy, abounding with leaves.

frontal, sm. front-ornament of an altar.

frontera, sf. frontier.

fronterizo, za, a. concerning frontiers ; opposite, over against.

frontis, sm. façade.

frontispicio, sm. frontispiece.

frontón, sm. wall for playing at fives.

frotación, frotadura, sf. friction, rubbing.

frotar, v.a. to rub.

fructífero, ra, a. fructiferous, fruitful.

fructificar, v.n. to fructify, to bear fruit.

fructuoso, sa, a. fruitful ; useful.

frugal, a. frugal, sparing.

frugalidad, sf. frugality, parsimony.

fruncidor, sm. plaiter, folder.

fruncimiento, sm. wrinkling, corrugation ; imposture.

fruncir, v.a. to plait ; to knit ; to reduce to a smaller size ; to conceal the truth ; — las cejas, to knit the eyebrows ; —los labios, to curl the lips,

fruslería, sf. trifle, futility.

frustrar, v.a. to frustrate; to disappoint; -se, to miscarry.

fruta, sf. fruit.

frutal, sm. fruit-tree.

frutera, sf. fruit-woman.

frutero, sm. fruiterer; fruit-basket.

frutilla, sf. strawberry (in Peru); round shell of which rosaries are made.

fruto, sm. fruit; benefit, profit.

fuego, sm. fire.

fuelle, sm. bellows; tale-bearer.

fuente, sf. fountain; original, first principle; source; issue; dish.

fuera, ad. without; outside; over and above; ¡ — ! out of the way !

fuero, sm. municipal law; jurisdiction; privileges granted to a province, city, or corporation; charter.

fuerte, sm. fortification, fort; —, a. vigorous, stout; strong; —, ad. strongly.

fuerza, sf. force, strength, vigour; valour; courage; violence, coercion; á — de, by dint of; -s, pl. troops.

fuga, sf. flight, escape.

fugarse, v.r. to escape, to fly.

fugaz, a. fugitive; volatile; perishable.

fugitivo, va, a. & sm. & f. fugitive.

fulano, na, sm. & f. such a one.

fulgente, a. (poet.) brilliant.

fulgurar, v.n. to emit flashes of light.

fullería, sf. cheating, card-sharping; cogging, fallacy.

fullero, sm. card-sharper, cheat.

fulminación, sf. flash; report; thundering.

fulminar, v.a. to fulminate.

fumada, sf. whiff.

fumadero, sm. smoking-room.

fumar, v.a. & n. to smoke. [tobacco.

fumarada, sf. puff of smoke, a pipeful of

fumigación, sf. fumigation.

fumigatorio, ria, a. fumigatory.

fumosidad, sf. smokiness.

fumoso, sa, a. smoky.

funámbulo, sm. rope-dancer.

función, sf. function; solemnity, festival; fight, battle.

funda, sf. case, sheath.

fundación, sf. foundation; groundwork.

fundador, sm. founder.

fundamental, a. fundamental.

fundamento, sm. foundation, groundwork; reason, cause.

fundar, v.a. to found; to establish, to ground.

fundible, a. fusible.

fundición, sf. fusion; foundry.

fundidor, sm. founder.

fundir, v.a. to melt metals, to smelt.

fúnebre, a. mournful, sad; funereal.

funeral, a. funeral; á la -a, (mil.) with arms reversed; -es, sm.pl. funeral, obsequies.

funerario, ria, a. funeral, funereal.

funesto, ta, a. funereal, mournful, sad, dismal. [the utmost speed.

furia, sf. fury, rage; á toda —, ad. with

furibundo, da, a. furious.

furioso, sa, a. furious.

furor, sm. fury.

furrier, sm. quarter-master.

furtivamente, ad. by stealth.

furtivo, va, a. furtive.

fusil, sm. fusil, firelock.

fusilazo, sm. musket-shot.

fusilero, sm. fusileer.

fusión, sf. fusion.

fusique, sm. kind of snuff-box.

fuste, sm. staff, shaft; tree and bows of a saddle; shaft of a lance; fust of a column.

fútil, a. futile, trifling.

futilidad, sf. futility.

futuro, ra, a. & sm. future.

G

gabacho, cha, a. (col.) French, Frenchy.

gabán, sm. great-coat; sack.

gabardina, sf. smock.

gabarra, sf. (mar.) lighter (boat).

gabela, sf. tax, duty.

gabinete, sm. cabinet.

gaceta, sf. newspaper.

gacetero, sm. newswriter; newsvendor.

gacetilla, sf. paragraph.

gacetista, sm. newsmonger.

gachas, sf.pl. pap, porridge.

gacho, dha, a. (curved, bent downwards; á gachas, on all fours.

gafa, sf. kind of hook; -s, pl. spectacles.

gaita, sf. bagpipe.

gaitería, sf. gay and gaudy dress.

gaitero, sm. bag-piper, bag-pipe player; —, ra, a. gay, gaudy, showy.

gaje, sm. salary, wages; -s, pl. fees.

gajo, sm. branch of a tree broken off; part torn off a bunch of grapes.

gala, sf. court-dress; día de —, court-day; holiday; graceful, pleasing address; parade; hacer —, to glory in having done a thing.

galafate, sm. artful thief; cunning rogue.

galán, sm. gallant, gentleman in full dress; courtier; lover; —, **ana, a.** gallant, fine, neat, elegant.

galante, a. gallant, courtly; brave, generous, liberal; elegant.

galanteador, sm. wooer, lover.

galantear, v.a. to court, to woo.

galanteo, sm. gallantry, courtship.

galantería, sf. gallantry, elegance; liberality, generosity.

galápago, sm. fresh-water tortoise.

galardón, sm. reward, recompense.

galardonar, v.a. to reward, to recompense.

galbana, sf. laziness, idleness, indolence.

galbanero, ra, a. lazy, indolent.

galenismo, sm. doctrine of Galen.

galeón, sm. (mar.) galleon.

galeota, sf. (mar.) galliot.

galeote, sm. galley-slave.

galera, sf. (mar.) galley; wagon.

galería, sf. gallery.

galgo, sm. greyhound.

gálico, ca, a. venereal.

galicoso, sa, a. syphilitic.

galocha, sf. clog, golosh.

galón, sm. shoulder-knot, decoration.

galope, sm. gallop; haste, hurry.

galopear, v.n. to gallop.

galopín, sm. ragamuffin.

galvánico, ca, a. galvanic.

galvanismo, sm. galvanism.

galladura, sf. tread (in an egg).

gallarda, sf. a Spanish dance.

gallardear, v.n. to do anything gracefully or elegantly.

gallardete, sm. (mar.) pendant, streamer.

gallardía, sf. genteelness, elegance, gracefulness; activity, briskness; liberality.

gallardo, da, a. gay, graceful, elegant, genteel; magnanimous; generous; brave, daring.

gallear, v.a. to tread (as birds); —, v.n. to raise the voice menacingly; to assume an air of importance.

galleta, sf. sea-biscuit.

gallillo, sm. uvula. [blindman's buff.

gallina, sf. hen; (fig.) coward; — ciega;

gallinero, sm. poulterer; cock loft, henroost women's gallery of a Spanish theatre.

gallineta, sf. sand-piper (bird).

gallipavo, sm. turkey.

gallito, sm. beau, coxcomb.

gallo, sm. cock; cock of the walk.

gama, sf. (mus.) gamut; doe, she-deer.

gamella, sf. yoke for oxen and mules; large wooden trough.

gamo, sm. buck of the fallow deer.

gamuza, sf. chamois.

gana, sf. appetite; desire; **de buena —**, with pleasure, voluntarily; **de mala —**, unwillingly, with reluctance.

ganadería, sf. breeding or feeding of cattle. [cattle.

ganadero, sm. cattle-owner; dealer in

ganado, sm. cattle.

ganancia, sf. gain, profit, lucre.

ganancial, a. lucrative.

ganancioso, sa, a. gainful.

ganapán, sm. porter, carrier.

ganar, v.a. to gain, to win.

gancho, sm. hook; crook.

ganga, sf. little pin-tailed grouse; bed of minerals; bargain.

gangoso, sa, a. snuffling.

gangrena, sf. gangrene.

gangrenarse, v.r. to become gangrenous.

gangrenoso, sa, a. gangrenous.

ganguear, v.n. to snuffle, to speak through the nose.

gangueo, sm. snuffling.

gansarón, sm. gosling; tall thin man.

ganso, sa, sm. & f. gander; goose; tall slender person.

gañote, sm. wind-pipe.

garabatear, v.a. to catch with a hook; to scrawl, to scribble.

garabato, sm. hook, pot-hook; -s, pl. scrawling letters or characters; improper gestures or movements of the hands and fingers.

garante, sm. guarantee.

garantía, sf. warranty, guarantee.

garantir, v.a. to guarantee.

garañón, sm. jack-ass.

garapiña, sf. ice, ice-cream; the congealed particles of any liquid; kind of black lace.

garapiñar, v.a. to ice.

garapiñera, sf. ice-safe.

garba, sf. sheaf. [with chick-peas.

garabanzal, sm. piece of ground sown

garbanzo, sm. chick-pea.

garbanzuelo, sm. spavin.

garbear, v.n. to affect elegance or fineness.

garbillo, sm. riddle (coarse sieve).

garbo, sm. gracefulness, elegance of manner; generosity; cleverness.

garboso, sa, a. genteel, graceful; liberal, generous.

garduña, sf. pole-cat, house-marten.

gargajear, v.n. to spit.

gargajo, sm. phlegm, spittle.

garganta, sf. throat, gullet; instep; mountain-flood, torrent; narrow pass between mountains or rivers.

gargantilla, sf. necklace.

gárgara, sf., **gargarismo**, sm. gargling, gargle.

garganizar, v.a. to gargle.
gargüero, sm. gullet; wind-pipe.
garita, sf. (mil.) sentry-box.
garitero, sm. master of a gaming-house; gamester.
garlito, sm. snare.
garnacha, sf. counsellor's robe.
garra, sf. claw, talon, paw; clutch, hand.
garrafa, sf. decanter.
garrafal, a. great, vast, huge.
garrapata, sf. tick (insect).
garrapatear, v.n. to scribble, to scrawl.
garrapato, sm. scrawl.
garrocha, sf. goad.
garrotazo, sm. blow with a cudgel.
garrote, sm. cudgel; capital punishment in Spain, performed by strangling with an iron collar.
garrotillo, sm. diphtheria.
garrucha, sf. pulley.   [ling.
gárrulo, la, a. chirping; chattering, prattgarulla, sf. waste grapes; (fig.) rabble.
garza, sf. heron (bird).
garzo, za, a. blue-eyed.   [of a helmet.
garzota, sf. night-heron; plumage; crest
gas, sm. gas.
gasa, sf. gauze.
gasconada, sf. gasconade.
gaseoso, sa, a. gaseous, aerated.
gasómetro, sm. gasometer.
gastador, ra, a. & sm. & f. spendthrift, prodigal; corrupter; (mil.) pioneer.
gastar, v.a. to expend; to waste; to plunder; to digest; -se, to become rotten.
gasto, sm. expense, cost.
gastronomía, sf. gastronomy.
gata, sf. she-cat; á -s, on all fours.
gatada, sf. clawing; robbery effected in an artful manner; artful action.
gatear, v.n. to climb up; —, v.a. to scratch or claw; to steal.
gatera, sf. cat's hole.
gatesco, ca, a. feline, catlike.
gatillazo, sm. click of the trigger in firing.
gatillo, sm. tooth-pincer; trigger of a gun.
gato, sm. cat; screw-jack.
gatuno, na, a. catlike, feline.
gaucho, sm. Argentine cow-boy.
gaudeamus, sm. feast, entertainment, merry-making.
gaveta, sf. drawer of a desk, locker.
gavia, sf. (mar.) top, crow's nest; pit into which a tree is transplanted with its roots; cell for mad persons; -s, pl. top-sails of the main and fore-mast.
gavilán, sm. (orn.), sparrow-hawk.
gavilla, sf. sheaf of corn; gang of suspicious persons.
gavota, sf. gavotte (French dance).

gazapera, sf. warren.
gazapo, sm. young rabbit; artful knave; great lie.
gazmoñada, gazmoñería, sf. prudery, hypocrisy.   [critical.
gazmoñero, ra, gazmoño, na, a. hypogaznate, sm. throttle, wind-pipe.
gazpacho, sm. vegetable hodge-podge.
gazuza, sf. keenness of stomach.
gemelo, la, sm. & f. twin.
gemido, sm. groan, moan, howl.
Géminis, sm. Gemini, Twins (sign of the zodiac).
gemir, v.n. to groan, to moan.
genciana, sf. (bot.) gentian.
gendarma, sm. gendarme.
gendarmería, sf. gendarmery.
genealogía, sf. genealogy.
genealógico, ca, a. genealogical.   [race.
generación, sf. generation; progeny,
general, a. general; en —, generally, in general; —, sm. general.
generala, sf. (mil.) general (a beat of the drum).
generalato, sm. generalship.
generalidad, sf. generality.
generalísimo, sm. generalissimo.
generalizar, v.a. to generalize.
genérico, ca, a. generic.
género, sm. genus; sex, gender; -s, pl. goods, commodities.
generosidad, sf. generosity.
generoso, sa, a. noble, generous.
genial, a. genial.
genio, sm. genius.
genital, a. genital; -es, pl. genitals.
genitivo, sm. (gr.) genitive case.
genízaro, ra, a. begotten by parents of different nations; composed of different species; —, sm. janizary.
gente, sf. people; nation; family; army, troops.
gentecilla, gentezuela, sf. mob, rabble.
gentil, sm. pagan, heathen; —, a. genteel, elegant, excellent.
gentileza, sf. genteelness, elegance of be haviour; politeness.
gentilhombre, sm. gentleman.
gentílico, ca, a. pagan, heathenish. [ism
gentilidad, sf., gentilismo, sm. heathengentío, sm. crowd, multitude.
gentualla, sf. rabble, mob.
genuflexión, sf. genuflection.
genuino, na, a. genuine, pure.
geografía, sf. geography.
geográfico, ca, a. geographical.
geógrafo, sm. geographer.
geología, sf. geology.
geómetra, sm. geometrician.
geometría, sf. geometry.
geométrico, ca, a. geometrical, geometric.

geranio, sm. (bot.) geranium.
germen, sm. germ, bud; source, original cause.
germinar, v.n. to germinate, to bud.
gerundio, sm. (gr.) gerund.
gesolreut, sm. (mus.) the first sign or clef to music.
gesticular, v.a. to gesticulate.
gesto, sm. face, visage; grimace; aspect, appearance; resemblance.
giganta, sf. giantess.
gigante, sm. giant; —, a. gigantic.
gigantesco, ca, a. gigantic, giant.
gigantilla, sf. pasteboard figure with large head. [academy.
gimnasio, sm. gymnasium; school,
gimnástica, sf. gymnastics.
gimnástico, ca, a. gymnastic.
ginebra, sf. rattle; gin, Geneva.
gineta, sf. civet-cat.
girafa, sf. giraffe.
giraldilla, sf. weathercock.
girándula, sf. catherine-wheel (firework).
girante, sm. drawer of bills of exchange.
girar, v.n. to turn round; to remit by bills of exchange.
girasol, sm. sun-flower.
giro, sm. turning round; circulation of bills; turn; direction, tendency.
girón, sm. facing of a garment; rag.
gitanear, v.a. to flatter, to wheedle.
gitanería, sf. wheedling, flattery.
gitanesco, ca, a. gipsy-like.
gitano, na, sm. & f. gipsy; sly fellow; person of a genteel, pleasing address.
glacial, a. icy.
glacis, sm. sloping bank, glacis.
gladiator, sm. gladiator, prize-fighter.
glándula, sf. gland.
glanduloso, sa, a. glandulous.
globo, sm. globe; sphere; orb; en —, by the lump; — aerostático, balloon.
globoso, sa, a. globular.
glóbulo, sm. globule.
gloria, sf. glory.
gloriarse, v.r. to glory, to take pride; to take delight in anything.
glorieta, sf. bower, arbour.
glorificación, sf. glorification; praise.
glorificador, sm. glorifier.
glorificar, v.a. to glorify; -se, to boast.
glorioso, sa, a. glorious.
glosa, sf. gloss.
glosador, sm. commentator, glosser.
glosar, v.a. to gloss.
glotón, ona, sm. & f. glutton.
glotonería, sf. gluttony.
glutinoso, sa, a. glutinous, viscous.
gobernación, sf. government; administration.
gobernador, sm. governor.

gobernalle, sm. rudder, helm.
gobernar, v.a. to govern; to regulate; to direct.
gobierno, sm. government.
gobio, sm. whiting (fish). [sion.
goce, sm. enjoyment, fruition; posses-
goleta, sf. schooner.
golfo, sm. gulf, bay.
golilla, sf. Spanish collar; magistrate who wears the golilla.
golondrina, sf. swallow. [sire.
golosina, sf. dainty, titbit; cupidity, de-
goloso, sa, a. gluttonous.
golpe, sm. blow, stroke, hit; knock; unfortunate accident; de —, all at once.
gollete, sm. gullet, spout.
golpear, v.a. to beat, to knock; to give blows; to bruise.
goma, sf. gum; india-rubber.
gomosidad, sf. gumminess, viscosity.
gomoso, sa, a. gummy, viscous.
góndola, sf. gondola.
gondolero, sm. gondolier.
gordiflón, ona, a. very corpulent.
gordo, da, a. fat, corpulent, plump.
gordura, sf. grease; fatness, corpulence, obesity.
gorgojo, sm. grub, weevil.
gorgojoso, sa, a. full of grubs or weevils.
gorgorita, sf. bubble.
gorgoritear, v.n. to warble, to trill.
gorgorito, sm. quiver of the voice; trill.
gorigori, sm. (col.) funeral dirge.
gorjear, v.n. to warble; (mus.) to trill, to shake.
gorjeo, sm. trilling; quaver; chirping.
gorra, sf. cap, bonnet.
gorrión, sm. sparrow.
gorro, sm. round cap.
gota, sf. drop; gout; — coral ó caduca, falling-sickness; — serena, amaurosis.
gotear, v.a. to fall drop by drop.
gotera, sf. gutter; fringe of bed-hangings.
gótico, ca, a. Gothic.
gotoso, sa, a. gouty.
gozar, v.a. to enjoy, to have possession or fruition of; -se, to rejoice.
gozne, sm. hinge.
gozo, sm. joy, pleasure.
gozoso, sa, a. joyful, cheerful, content, glad, merry, pleased.
grabado, sm. engraving.
grabador, sm. engraver.
grabar, v.a. to engrave; — al agua fuerte, to etch.
gracejo, sm. joke, jest, mirth; graceful deliverance.
gracia, sf. grace; favour; affability; benevolence; pardon. [perfection.
graciosidad, sf. gracefulness, beauty.

gracioso, sa, a. graceful, beautiful; funny, pleasing; benevolent; gratuitous; —, sm. buffoon, clown.

grada, sf. step of a staircase; harrow; -s, pl. (law) bar; seats of an amphitheatre.

gradería, sf. series of seats or steps.

gradilla, sf. hand-ladder; tile-mould.

grado, sm. step; degree; will, pleasure.

graduación, sf. graduation; (mil.) rank.

gradual, a. gradual.

graduando, sm. candidate for academical degrees.

graduar, v.a. to graduate.

grajo, sm. jack-daw (bird).

grama, sf. dog's grass.

gramática, sf. grammar.

gramatical, a. grammatical.

gramático, sm. grammarian.

gran, a. for grande, great.

grana, sf. grain; cochineal; scarlet grain; fine scarlet cloth.

granada, sf. pomegranate; (mil.) grenade.

granadero, sm. (mil.) grenadier.

granadilla, sf. passion-flower.

granado, da, a. large, remarkable; illustrious; —, sm. pomegranate tree.

granar, v.a. to form seed.

granate, sm. garnet (precious stone).

granazón, sf. seeding.

grande, a. great; —, sm. grandee (Spanish nobleman).

grandeza, sf. greatness; grandeur; grandeeship; body of grandees.

grandiosidad, sf. greatness, grandeur; magnificence.

grandioso, sa, a. grand, magnificent.

grandor, sm. size, bigness, extent, magnitude.

granear, v.a. to sow grain in the earth; to engrave; to grain leather.

granero, sm. granary.

granito, sm. granite.

granizada, sf. copious fall of hail; multitude of things which fall in abundance.

granizar, v.n. to hail. [dance.

granizo, sm. hail.

granja, sf. farm.

grano. sm. grain.

granoso, sa, a. granular.

grasa, sf. suet, fat; grease.

grasiento, ta, a. greasy; rusty, filthy.

gratificación, sf. gratification, recompense.

gratificar, v.a. to gratify, to reward, to recompense.

gratis, a. gratis, for nothing.

gratitud, sf. gratitude, gratefulness.

grato, ta, a. grateful.

gratuito, ta, a. gratuitous.

grava, sf. gravel.

gravamen, sm. charge, obligation; nuisance. [molest.

gravar, v.a. to burden, to oppress, to

grave, a. weighty, heavy; grave, important; haughty; troublesome; grievous.

gravedad, sf. gravity; importance.

gravemente, ad. gravely, seriously.

gravitación, sf. gravitation. [down.

gravitar, v.a. to gravitate; to weigh

gravoso, sa, a. onerous, unbearable.

graznar, v.n. to croak; to cackle; to

graznido, sm. croak, cackle. [gaggle.

greda, sf. fuller's earth.

greguería, sf. outcry, confused clamour.

gremio, sm. lap; society; company, guild, corporation.

greña, sf. entangled, clotted hair.

greñudo, da, a. dishevelled.

gresca, sf. clatter, tumult, outcry, confusion; wrangle, quarrel.

grey, sf. flock (of sheep and goats); congregation of the faithful.

grieta, sf. crevice, crack, chink.

grifo, sm. griffin.

grifón, sm. cock for water.

grilletes, sm.pl. shackles, fetters. [irons.

grillo, sm. cricket (insect); -s, pl. fetters,

grima, sf. fright, horror.

gris, sm. gray colour; meniver (Russian squirrel); (col.) cold, sharp weather.

gritador, ra, sm. & f. clamourer, bawler.

gritar, v.n. to cry out, to clamour, to bawl. [cry of many voices.

gritería, sf. outcry, clamour, confused

grito, sm. cry, scream; á — herido, with a clamorous cry.

grosella, sf. fruit of the red currant.

grosellero, sm. currant-bush.

grosería, sf. coarseness, ill-breeding.

grosero, ra, a. coarse, rude, unpolished.

grosura, sf. suet, tallow.

grotesco, ca, a. grotesque.

grúa, sf. crane (machine).

gruesa, sf. gross (twelve dozen).

grueso, sa, a. bulky, gross; large; coarse; —, sm. corpulence.

grulla, sf. crane (bird). [pith of trees.

grumo, sm. clod; curd; cluster, bunch;

grumoso, sa, a. clotted.

gruñido, sm. grunt, grunting; growl.

gruñidor, ra, sm. & f. grunter, mumbler.

gruñir, v.n. to grunt; to creak (of hinges, &c.).

grupa, sf. hind-quarters, buttock.

grupera, sf. crupper.

grupo, sm. group.

gruta, sf. grotto, grot.

grutesco, sm. grotesque.

guadaña, sf. scythe.

guadañero, sm. mower.

gualderas, sf.pl. side-supports.

gualdrapa, sf. horse-cloth ; tatter, rag.

guantada, sf. slap given with the palm of the hand.

guante, sm. glove ; -s, pl. pourboire.

guantería, sf. glover's shop ; glover's art.

guantero, sm. glover.·

guapear, v.n. to boast of one's courage ; to take a pride in fine dress.

guapeza, sf. courage ; ostentation in dress.

guapo, pa, a. stout, courageous ; valiant, bold ; spruce, neat ; ostentatious ; gay, sprightly.

guarda, sm. & f. guard, keeper ; —, sf. custody, wardship, keeping.

guardaaguja, sm. (rail.) switchman, pointsman.

guardaalmacén, sm. store-keeper.

guardabosque, sm. keeper of a forest.

guardacantón, sf. stone road-post.

guardacostas, sm. guard-ship, cruiser.

guardafuegos, sm. fender. [sword, &c.

guardamonte, sm. guard of a gunlock,

guardapiés, sm. women's black petticoat.

guardapolvo, sm. dust-coat ; dust-guard.

guardar, v.a. to keep, to preserve ; to guard ; -se, to be upon one's guard, to avoid, to abstain from.

guardarropa, sf. wardrobe ; —, sm. keeper of a wardrobe.

guardasellos, sm. Keeper of the Seal.

guardavía, sm. (rail.) line-keeper.

guardia, sf. guard, defence, protection ; (mar.) watch ; —, sm. guardsman (soldier), policeman. [dian.

guardián, ana, sm. & f. keeper ; guar-

guardianía, sf. guardianship.

guardilla, sf. garret ; skylight.

guarecer, v.a. to aid, to succour ; to guard ; to cure ; -se, to take refuge.

guarida, sf. den, couch of a wild beast ; shelter ; lurking-place.

guarismo, sm. cipher.

guarnecer, v.a. to garnish ; to equip ; to garrison ; to set (in gold, &c.) ; to adorn.

guarnición, sf. flounce, furbelow ; gold setting ; sword-guard ; garniture ; (mil.) garrison.

guarnicionero, sm. harness-maker.

guasón, sm. joker, jester.

guedeja, sf. ear-lock ; lion's mane.

guerra, sf. war ; hostility.

guerreador, ra, a. warlike.

guerrear, v.a. to war, to wage war.

guerrero, sm. warrior ; —, ra, a. martial, warlike.

guerrilla, sf. war of partisans ; body of skirmishers ; irregular troop.

guía, sm. & f. guide.

guiar, v.a. to guide.

guija, sf. pebble, pebble-stone. [bles.

guijarral, sm. place abounding in peb-

guijarrazo, sm. blow with a pebble.

guijarro, sm. pebble.

guijarroso, sa, a. pebbly.

guijo, sm. gravel.

guillotina, sf. guillotine.

guillotinar, v.a. to guillotine.

guinda, sf. cherry.

guindal, sm. cherry-tree.

guindilla, sf. capsicum.

guindola, sf. life-buoy.

guinea, sf. guinea (gold coin).

guiñada, sf. wink, hint.

guiñapo, sm. tatter, rag.

guiñar, v.a. to wink, to hint. [writing).

guión, sm. standard ; hyphen (in

guirigay, sm. gibberish, confused language.

guirindola, sf. frill. [guage.

guirnalda, sf. garland, wreath.

guisado, sm. ragout, fricassee.

guisandero, ra, sm. & f. cook.·

guisante, sm. (bot.) pea.

guisar, v.a. to stew, to cook.

guiso, sm. cooked dish.

guisote, sm. rough dish of meat.

guitarra, sf. guitar. [player.

guitarrero, sm. guitar-maker guitar-

guitarrista, sm. guitar-player.

gula, sf. gluttony.

gusano, sm. maggot, worm.

gusarapo, sm. water-worm.

gustar, v.a. to taste, to relish ; to like, to love ; to experience ; —, v.n. to please, to be tasteful.

gusto, sm. taste ; pleasure, delight ; liking, mind ; election, choice.

gustosamente, ad. tastefully ; very desirously.

gustoso, sa, a. dainty ; tasty, pleasant.

gutagamba, sf. gamboge.

gutural, a. guttural.

H

haba, sf. (bot.) bean.

haber, v.aux. to have ; —, v.imp. to happen ; to exist ; to fall out, to befall ; —, sm. property, goods and chattels ; (com.) credit.

habichuela, sf. kidney-bean. [apt.

hábil, a. able, clever, skilful, ·dexterous,

habilidad, sf. ability, cleverness, dexterity, aptitude. [tion.

habilitación, sf. habilitation, qualifica-

habilitado, sm. (mil.) regimental treasurer.

habilitar, v.a. to qualify, to enable.

habitable, a. habitable, lodgeable.

habitación, sf. habitation, abode, lodging, dwelling, residence.

habitante, sm. inhabitant, dweller.

habitar, v.a. to inhabit, to reside.

hábito, sm. dress, habit; habitude, custom.

habitual, a. habitual, customary.

habituar, v.a. to accustom; -se, to accustom oneself.

habitud, sf. habitude.

habla, sf. speech; language; discourse; talk, conversation.

hablador, ra, a. & sm. & f. prattler.

habladuría, sf. impertinent speech.

hablar, v.a. to speak; to talk; to reason, to converse, to harangue.

hablilla, sf. rumour, report; little tale.

hacedero, ra, a. feasible, practicable.

hacedor, ra a. causing; —, sm. creator; steward, farm-bailiff; agent.

hacendado, sm. man of property; —, da, a. landed.

hacer, v.a. & n. to make, to do, to practise; to perform; to effect; to correspond; to matter; to fit, to suit; -se, to become. [hitherward.

hacia, ad. towards; about; — acá, hitherward.

hacienda, sf. landed property; estate, fortune, wealth.

hacina, sf. stack, rick.

hacinar, v.a. to stack *or* pile up sheaves of corn; to hoard.

hacha, sf. large taper; axe, hatchet; — de viento, flambeau, torch.

hachazo, sm. blow with an axe.

hachero, sm. torch-stand; (mil.) pioneer.

hachón, sm. large torch.

hado, sm. fate, destiny.

halagar, v.a. to cajole, to flatter.

halago, sm. cajolery, caress.

halagüeño, ña, a. attractive, flattering.

halcón, sm. falcon.

halconero, sm. falconer.

hálito, sm. breath; gentle breeze.

hallar, v.a. to find; to meet with; to discover; -se, to find oneself, to be in a place.

hallazgo, sm. finding, discovery; reward given for finding.

hambre, sf. hunger; famine; eagerness, desire, greediness.

hambrear, v.n. to be hungry.

hambriento, ta, a. hungry; starved; greedy, eager.

haragán, ana, sm. & f. idler, loiterer.

haraganear, v.n. to lead an idle life, to loiter.

haraganería, sf. idleness, laziness.

harapo, sm. rag, tatter.

haraposo, a. ragged.

harina, sf. flour.

harinero, sm. meal-man; meal-box; —, ra, a. made of flour.

harinoso, sa, a. mealy.

harnero, sm. sieve. [gust.

hartar, v.a. to cloy, to satiate; to disgust.

harto, ta, a. satiated; sufficient; —, ad. enough.

hartura, sf. satiety; plenty, abundance

hasta, ad. until, as far as; even.

hastío, sm. loathing; disgust.

hatajo, sm. small herd of cattle; assemblage, collection.

hato, sm. clothes, wearing-apparel; herd of cattle, flock of sheep; heap, cluster; crowd, multitude.

haya, sf. species of beech.

haz, sm. faggot, bundle of brush-wood; —, sf. right side of cloth; surface of the ground.

hazaña, sf. exploit, achievement.

hazmerreir, sm. laughing-stock, butt.

¡he! (imperative of **haber**), behold, look here.

hebilla, sf. buckle.

hebillaje, sm. collection of buckles.

hebra, sf. needleful; filament, fibre.

hebraico, ca, a. belonging to the Hebrews.

hebraísmo, sm. Hebraism.

hebreo, sm. Hebrew; (fig.) merchant; —, ea, a. Hebraic, Jewish.

hectolitro, sm. a hundred litres.

hechicería, sf. witchcraft; charm.

hechicero, ra, a. charming, bewitching.

hechizar, v.a. to bewitch; to enchant; to charm.

hechizo, sm. bewitchment, enchantment; —, za, a. artificial.

hecho, cha, a. complete, perfect; —, sm. action; act, feat; point contested.

hechura, sf. form, shape, fashion; making; workmanship; creature; client.

heder, v.a. to stink, to smell badly.

hediondez, sf. strong stench.

hediondo, da, a. fetid, stinking.

hedor, sm. stench, stink.

helada, sf. frost.

helado, da, a. frozen; glacial, icy; astonished; astounded; —, sm. ice-cream.

helar, v.a. & n. to congeal; to freeze; to astonish, to amaze; -se, to be frozen; to turn into ice; to congeal.

helecho, sm. fern.

hélice, sf. helix, spiral; (mar.) propeller, screw.

Hélice, sf. Great Bear (constellation).

hembra, sf. female.

hemisferio, sm. hemisphere.

hemorragia, sf. hemorrhage.

henchir, v.a. to fill up; -se, to fill or gorge oneself.

hendedura, sf. fissure, chink, crevice.

hender, v.a. to cleave, to split; to go through; to open a passage.

heno, sm. hay.

heraldo, sm. herald.

herbaje, sm. herbage, pasture.

herbolario, sm. herbalist; ridiculous, extravagant man.

herborizar, v.n. to botanise.

heredad, sf. patrimony, inherited property; fruitful ground.

heredar, v.a. to inherit.

heredera, sf. heiress.

heredero, sm. heir.

hereditario, ria, a. hereditary.

hereje, sm. & f. heretic.

herejía, sf. heresy.

herencia, sf. inheritance, heritage, hereditament; heirship.

herida, sf. wound, hurt.

herido, da, a. wounded, hurt.

herir, v.a. to wound, to hurt; to affect, to touch, to move; to offend.

hermafrodita, sm. hermaphrodite.

hermana, sf. sister; — de la caridad, sister of charity.

hermanar, v.a. to match, to suit, to acknowledge as a brother; —, v.n. to fraternise.

hermanastra, sf. step-sister, half-sister.

hermanastro, sm. step-brother, half-brother.   [brotherhood.

hermandad, sf. fraternity; conformity;

hermano, sm. brother; —, na, a. matched; resembling.

hermético, ca, a. hermetical, chemical.

hermosear, v.a. to beautify, to embellish, to adorn.

hermoso, sa, a. beautiful, handsome.

hermosura, sf. beauty.

hernia, sf. hernia, rupture.

héroe, sm. hero.   [or virtue.

heroicidad, sf. heroism, heroic courage

heroico, ca, a. heroic.

heroína, sf. heroine.

heroísmo, sm. heroism.

herpe, sm. & f. herpes, tetters, pl.

herrada, sf. well-bucket.

herrador, sm. farrier, blacksmith.

herradura, sf. horse-shoe.

herraje, sm. iron-work.

herramienta, sf. set of tools for workmen; iron-work; (fig.) teeth, grinders

herrar, v.a. to shoe horses.

herrería, sf. iron-works; forge; clamour, confused noise.

herrero, sm. smith.   [tity.

hervidero, sm. ebullition; great quan-

hervir, v.n. to boil; to be fervent.

hervor, sm. ebullition.

heterogeneidad, sf. heterogeneousness.

heterogéneo, nea, a. heterogeneous

hética, sf. phthisis.

hético, ca, a. hectic, hectical.

hexámetro, sm. hexameter.

hez, sf. lee, dregs; dross.

hidalgo, ga, sm. & f. hidalgo; hidalga (gentleman or gentlewoman).

hidalguía, sf. nobility.

hidra, sf. hydra.

hidráulica, sf. hydraulics.

hidráulico, ca, a. hydraulic.

hidrofobia, sf. hydrophobia.

hidrógeno, sm. (chem.) hydrogen.

hidropesía, sf. dropsy.

hidrópico, ca, a. hydropical.

hiedra, sf. ivy.

hiel, sf. gall, bile.

hielo, sm. frost, ice.

hiena, sf. hyæna.

hierro, sm. iron; -s, pl. irons, fetters.

hígado, sm. liver; (fig.) courage, valour.

higo, sm. fig.

higuera, sf. fig-tree.

hijastro, tra, sm. & f. step-child.

hijo, ja, sm. & f. son; daughter; child; young of animals.

hijodalgo, sm. hidalgo; gentleman.

hijuela, sf. patch; piece of stuff; by-lane; rural postman.

hila, sf. row, line; lint to lay on sores.

hilacha, sf. filament or threads ravelled out of cloth.

hilado, sm. spun flax, wool, &c.

hilador, ra, sm. & f. spinner.

hilandero, sm. spinner; spinning-room.

hilar, v.a. to spin.

hilera, sf. row, line, file.

hilo, sm. thread; wire.

hilván, sm. basting.

hilvanar, v.a. to tack, to sew slightly; to perform in a hurry.

himeneo, sm. (poet.) marriage.

himno, sm. hymn.

hin, sm. neighing.   [foot.

hincapié, sm. firm planting of one's

hincar, v.a. to thrust in, to drive into.

hinchado, da, a. swollen; vain, arrogant.

hinchar, v.a. to swell; -se, to swell; to be elated with arrogance.

hinchazón, sf. swelling, tumid inflammation; ostentation, vanity.

hinojo, sm. knee; (bot.) fennel.

hipar, v.n. to hiccough.   [cone.

hipérbola, sf. hyperbola, section of a

hipérbole, sf. hyperbole, exaggeration.

hiperbólico, ca, a. hyperbolical.

hipo, sm. hiccough.

hipocondría, sf. hypochondria.

hipocóndrico, ca, a. hypochondriac.

hipocresía, sf. hypocrisy.

hipócrita, a. & sm. hypocritical; hypo-[crite.

hipódromo, sm. hippodrome, circus.

hipopótamo, sm. hippopotamus.

hipoteca, sf mortgage.

hipotecar, v.a. to mortgage.

àipotecario, ria, a. belonging to a mortgage; —, sm. mortgagee.

hipótesis, sf. hypothesis.

hipotético, ca, a. hypothetical.

hisopo, sm. (bot.) hyssop; water-sprinkler.

hispano, na, a. (poet.) Spanish. [terical.

histérico, sm. hysterics; —, ca, a. hys-

historia, sf. history; tale, story.

historiador, ora, sm. & f. historian, historiographer.

historiar, v.a. to narrate; to record in painting.

histórico, ca, a. historical historic; —, sm. historian.

historieta, sf. short story, short novel.

hito, sm. landmark; guide-post; mark to shoot at; á —, fixedly.

hocicar, v.a. to break up the ground with the snout; —, v.n. to fall on the nose.

hocico, sm. snout; (fig.) face; meter el — en todo, to meddle in everything.

hocicudo, da, a. long-snouted; blubber-lipped.

hogar, sm. hearth, fire-place; (fig.) house, residence, home.

hogaza, sf. large loaf.

hoguera, sf. bonfire; blaze.

hoja, sf. leaf; blade of a sword; half of each of the principal parts of a coat, &c.; — de lata, tin.

hojalatero, sm. tin-man.

hojaldre, sf. puff-paste.

hojarasca, sf. fallen leaves; foliage: useless trifles. [book.

hojear, v.a. to turn the leaves of a

hojuela, sf. skins of olives after pressing

¡ hola ! hullo !

holgado, da, a. loose, wide, broad; at leisure; in easy circumstances.

holganza, sf. ease, tranquillity of mind; recreation, amusement.

holgar, v.n. to rest; -se, to sport, to be pleased. [vagabond

holgazán, ana, sm. & f. idler, loiterer,

holgazanear, v.n. to idle, to loiter, to lounge.

holgazanería, sf. idleness, indolence.

holgura, sf. width, breadth; ease, repose; feasting.

hollejo, sm. pellicle, peel.

hollín, sm. soot.

holliniento, ta, a. sooty.

holocausto, sm. holocaust.

hombre, sm. man; human being; ombre (game at cards); — de bien, upright man.

hombría de bien, sf. probity; integrity.

hombro, sm. shoulder.

hombruno, na, a. manlike, virile, manly.

homenaje, sm. homage.

homicida, sm. & f. murderer; —, a. homicidal, murderous.

homicidio, sm. murder.

homilía, sf. homily.

homogeneidad, sf. homogeneity.

homogéneo, nea, a. homogeneous.

homólogo, ga, a. homologous; synonym-honda, sf. sling. [ous.

hondazo, sm. throw with a sling.

hondero, sm. slinger.

hondo, da, a. profound, deep; difficult.

hondonada, sf. dale; glen.

hondura, sf. depth, profundity. [ity.

honestidad, sf. honesty, modesty; urban-honesto, ta, a. honest; modest.

hongo, sm. mushroom; fungus.

honor, sm. honour.

honorable, a. honourable. [salary.

honorario, ria, a. honorary; —, sm.

honorífico, ca, a. creditable, honourable.

honra, sf. honour, reverence; reputation; chastity (in women); -s, pl. funeral honours.

honradez, sf. honesty, probity.

honrado, da, a. honest, honourable, reputable.

honrar, v.a. to honour; to praise.

honrilla, sf. nice point of honour.

honroso, sa, a. honourable; honest.

hopalanda, sf. fur cloak.

hora, sf. hour; -s, pl. canonical hours; devotional book, prayer-book.

horadar, v.a. to bore from side to side.

horario, sm. hour-hand.

horca, sf. gallows; pitchfork.

horcajadas, horcajadillas, (á —) ad. astride. [thighs.

horcajadura, sf. fork formed by the two

horchata, sf. sherbet.

horizontal, a. horizontal.

horizonte, sm. horizon.

horma, sf. mould.

hormero, sm. last-maker.

hormiga, sf. ant.

hormiguear, v.n. to itch.

hormiguero, sm. ant-hill; place where there is a crowd of people moving.

hornacho, sm. shaft of a mine.

hornada, sf. batch of bread.

hornaza, sf. goldsmith's furnace.

hornero, sm. baker.

hornillo, sm. portable stove.

horno, sm. oven ; furnace.

horóscopo, sm. horoscope.

horquilla, sf. forked stick.   [nary.

horrendo, da, a. horrible ; extraordi-hórreo, sm. granary.

horrible, a. horrid, horrible.   [ing.

horrísono, na, a. (poet.) dreadful-sound-

horror, sm. horror, fright.

horrorizar, v.a. to cause horror ; -se, to be terrified.   [ful.

horroroso, sa, a. horrid, hideous, fright-

hortaliza, sf. garden-stuff, pot-herbs.

hortelano, sm. gardener, horticulturist ; ortolan (bird).

hortera, sf. wooden bowl ; —, sm. nick-name of shop-boys in Madrid.

hospedador, ra, sm. & f. one who kindly receives and entertains guests and strangers, entertainer.

hospedaje, sm. kind reception of guests ; board and lodging.

hospedar, v.a. to lodge and entertain strangers and travellers.

hospedería, sf. hospice.

hospedero, sm. hospitaller.

hospicio, sm. hospice ; asylum.

hospital, sm. hospital.

hospitalario, ria, a. applied to the re-ligious communities which keep hos-pitals.   [hospital.

hospitalero, ra, sm. & f. warden of a

hospitalidad, sf. hospitality.

hostería, sf. inn, tavern, hostelry.

hostia, sf. host ; wafer.

hostigar, v.a. to trouble, to molest, to gall, to tire.

hostil, a. hostile, adverse.

hostilidad, sf. hostility.

hostilizar, v.a. to attack.

hoy, ad. to-day, this day ; de — en ade-lante, henceforth, henceforward.

hoya, sf. hole, pit ; sepulture.

hoyo, sm. hole, pit, excavation.

hoyoso, sa, a. full of holes.

hoz, sf. sickle, reaping-hook.

hozar, v.a. to grub.

hucha, sf. large chest in which labouring people keep clothes, money, etc. ; money-box.

huebra, sf. extent of ground which a yoke of oxen can plough in a day ; pair of mules with a ploughman let out for a day's work.

hueca, sf. notch at the end of a spindle.

hueco, ca, a. hollow, concave ; empty, vain, ostentatious ; —, sm. interval ; gap, hole ; office vacant, vacancy.

huelga, sf. rest, repose ; ecreation ; fallow ground ; strike of workmen ; lock-out of employees.

huella, sf. track, footstep.

huérfano, na, a. & sm. & f. orphan.

huero, ra, a. empty, addled.

huerta, sf. orchard, kitchen-garden.

huerto, sm. walled garden, kitchen garden.

huesa, sf. grave, sepulture.

hueso, sm. bone ; stone, core.

huesoso, sa, a. bony.

huésped, da, sm. & f. guest, lodger ; inn-keeper, host ; stranger.

hueste, sf. army in campaign.

huesudo, da, a. bony.

huevar, v.n. to begin to lay eggs.

huevera, sf. egg-cup.

huevero, ra, sm. & f. dealer in eggs.

huevo, sm. egg ; spawn.

huída, sf. flight, escape.

huir, v.n. to fly, to escape.

hule, sm. oil-cloth.

hulla, sf. coal.

humanarse, v.r. to become man (applied to the Son of God); to become hu-mane or meek.

humanidad, sf. humanity ; benevolence ; corpulence ; -es, pl. humanities, pl., human learning.

humano, na, a. human ; humane, kind.

humareda, sf. clouds of smoke.

humeante, a. smoking, steaming (of blood, &c.).

humear, v.n. to smoke.   [ness.

humedad, sf. humidity, moisture, wet-

humedecer, v.a. to moisten, to wet, to soak.   [damp.

húmedo, da, a. humid, wet, moist,

humero, sm. funnel, shaft of a chimney.

humildad, sf. humility, humbleness ; meanness ; submission.

humilde, a. humble.

humillación, sf. humiliation, submission.

humilladero, sm. small chapel outside a village.

humillar, v.a. to humble ; to subdue ; -se, to humble oneself.

humo, sm. smoke ; fume.

humor, sm. humor, humour.

humorada, sf. graceful sprightliness.

humorado, da, a. full of humours ; well-or ill-disposed.

humoroso, sa, a. humorous.

humoso, sa, a. smoky.

hundir, v.n. to submerge ; to sink, to overwhelm ; to confound ; -se, to sink, to go to the bottom ; to hide, to lie hid.

huracán, sm. hurricane.

hurgar, v.a. to stir ; to excite.

hurón, sm. ferret ; busybody.

huronear, v.a. to ferret.

huronera, sf. ferret-hole ; lurking-place.

hurraca, sf. magpie.

hurtadillas (á), ad. by stealth.
hurtar, v.a. to steal, to rob.
hurto, sm. theft, robbery.
husar, sm. (mil.) hussar.
husillo, sm. clamp-screw; -s, pl. drains.

husma, andar á la —, to pry into a thing,
to spy out a secret.
husmear, v.a. to scent; to pry, to peep.
huso, sm. spindle.
huta, sf. hut.

I

ictericia, sf. jaundice.
ida, sf. departure; sally; billete de —
y vuelta, return-ticket.
idea, sf. idea; scheme.
ideal, a. ideal.
idealmente, ad. ideally. [trive.
idear, v.a. to conceive; to think, to con-
idéntico, ca, a. identical.
identidad, sf. identity.
identificar, v.a. to identify.
idilio, sm. idyll.
idioma, sm. idiom.
idiosincrasia, sf. idiosyncrasy.
idiota, sm. idiot. [phrase.
idiotismo, sm. ignorance; idiomatic
idólatra, sm. idolater.
idolatrar, v.a. to idolize; to love with
excessive fondness.
idolatría, sf. idolatry.
ídolo, sm. idol.
idóneo, nea, a. idoneous, fit, suitable.
iglesia, sf. church.
ignominia, sf. ignominy, infamy.
ignominioso, sa, a. ignominious.
ignorancia, sf. ignorance.
ignorante, a. ignorant, stupid. [know.
ignorar, v.a. to be ignorant of, not to
igual, a. equal, similar; al —, equally.
igualar, v.a. to equalize, to equal; to
match; —, v.n. to be equal; -se, to
agree.
igualdad, sf. equality.
igualmente, ad. equally. [pork.
ijada, sf. flank; side of pork or bacon;
ijadear, v.n. to pant, to palpitate.
ijar, sm. flanks, pl.
ilación, sf. inference, deduction.
ilegal, a. illegal, unlawful.
ilegalidad, sf. illegality.
ilegitimar, v.a. to render illegitimate.
ilegitimidad, sf. illegitimacy.
ilegítimo, ma, a. illegal; illegitimate.
ileso, sa, a. unhurt.
ilícito, sa, a. illicit, unlawful.
ilimitado, da, a. unlimited.
iluminación, sf. illumination.
iluminar, v.a. to illumine, to illuminate,
to enlighten.
ilusión, sf. illusion.
ilusivo, va, a. illusive. [ary.
iluso, sa a. deceived; fanatical; vision-

ilusorio, ria, a. illusory.
ilustración, sf. illustration; explanation.
ilustrado, da, a. highly educated, instructed, competent.
ilustrar, v.a. to illustrate; to inspire; to
instruct, to civilise.
ilustre, a. illustrious, celebrated.
imagen, sf. image.
imaginable, a. imaginable.
imaginación, sf. imagination, fancy;
conceit, idea.
imaginar, v.n. to imagine.
imaginaria, sf. (mil.) reserve guard.
imán, sm. loadstone, magnet.
imbécil, a. weak, feeble, imbecile
imbecilidad, sf. imbecility. [mind.
imbuir, v.a. to imbue; to infuse into the
imitable, a. imitable. [tion of.
imitación, sf. imitation; á —, in imita-
imitador, ra, sm. & f. imitator.
imitar, v.a. to imitate, to copy; to
counterfeit.
impaciencia, sf. impatience. [ate.
impacientar, v.a. to irritate, to exasper-
impaciente, a. impatient.
impar, a. unequal, odd; uneven.
imparcial, a. impartial.
imparcialidad, sf. impartiality.
impasibilidad, sf. impassibility.
impasible, a. impassible.
impavidez, sf. intrepidity.
impávido, da, a. dauntless, intrepid.
impedimento, sf. impediment, obstacle.
impedir, v.a. to impede, to hinder.
impeler, v.a. to impel; to incite, to
stimulate.
impenetrable, a. impenetrable, impervious; incomprehensible.
impenitencia, sf. impenitence.
impenitente, a. impenitent.
impensado, da, a. unexpected, unforeseen
imperativo, va, a. & sm. imperative.
imperatorio, ria, a. imperial.
imperceptible, a. imperceptible.
imperdible, sm. safety-pin.
imperfección, sf. imperfection.
imperfecto, ta, a. imperfect. [perial.
imperial, sm. roof of a coach; —, a. im-
impericia, sf. want of experience.
imperio, sm. empire. [haughty.
imperioso, sa. a. imperious; arrogant,

imperito, ta, a. unlearned, unskilled.
impermeable, a. & sm. impermeable; waterproof.
impermutable, a. immutable.
impersonal, a. impersonal.
impertérrito, ta, a. intrepid.
impertinencia, sf. impertinence; want of tact; importunity. [nate.
impertinente, a. impertinent; importu-
imperturbable, a. imperturbable.
impetración, sf. impetration.
impetrar, v.a. to solicit; to obtain by solicitation.
ímpetu, sm. impetus; impetuosity.
impetuoso, sa, a. impetuous.
impiedad, sf. impiety; cruelty.
impío, pia, a. impious.
implacable, a. implacable, inexorable.
implicación, sf. implication.
implicar, v.a. to implicate, to involve; to entangle.
implícito, ta, a. implicit.
implorar, v.a. to implore.
impolítica, sf. incivility.
impolítico, ca, a. impolitic; impolite.
imponderable, a. incalculable.
imponer, v.a. to impose, to inflict; to impute falsely; to advise; -se, to inspire respect.
importación, sf. importation.
importancia, sf. importance, import.
importante, a. important, considerable.
importar, v.imp. to be important, to matter. [value.
importe, sm. amount or gross amount,
importunación, sf. importunity.
importunar, v.a. to importune.
importunidad, sf. importunity.
importuno, na, a. importunate; unreasonable.
imposibilidad, sf. impossibility.
imposibilitar, v.a. to render impossible.
imposible, a. impossible; extremely difficult.
imposición, sf. imposition; impost.
impostor, sm. impostor, cheater.
impostura, sf. false imputation; imposture, deceit, cheat.
impotencia, sf. impotence.
impotente, a. impotent. [sible.
impracticable, a. impracticable, unfea-
imprecación, sf. imprecation, curse.
imprecar, v.a. to imprecate, to curse.
imprecatorio, ria, a. containing curses, damnatory, abusive.
impregnar, v.a. to impregnate.
imprenta, sf. printing; printing-office.
imprescindible, a. not to be put aside; unavoidable.
impresión, sf. impression; stamp; print; impression, edition; influence.

impresionar, v.a. to make an impression on, to impress.
impreso, sm. printed work.
impresor, sm. printer.
imprevisto, ta, a. unforeseen; unprovided against. [stamp.
imprimir, v.a. to print; to imprint; to
improbable, a. improbable, unlikely.
improbo, ba, a. corrupt, wicked; laborious, painful.
improperar, v.a. to upbraid, to taunt, to chide, to abuse.
improperio, sm. contemptuous reproach, taunt.
impropiedad, sf. impropriety.
impropio, pia, a. improper; unfit; misbecoming. [be prorogued.
improrrogable, a. that which cannot
improvisar, v.a. to extemporize, to improvise.
improviso, sa, a. improvised, unforeseen; not provided against; de —, unexpectedly.
imprudencia, sf. imprudence.
imprudente, a. imprudent.
impudencia, sf. impudence.
impudente, a. impudent, shameless.
impúdico, ca, a. unchaste; shameless, brazen-faced.
impuesto, sm. tax, impost, duty.
impugnación, sf. opposition, contradiction.
impugnar, v.a. to impugn, to oppose.
impulsivo, va, a. impulsive.
impulso, sm. impulsion.
impune, a. unpunished.
impunidad, sf. impunity; guiltlessness.
impureza, sf. impurity.
impuro, ra, a. impure, foul.
imputable, a. imputable, chargeable.
imputar, v.a. to impute.
inaccesible, a. inaccessible.
inacción, sf. inaction.
inadmisible, a. inadmissible. [tion.
inadvertencia, sf. carelessness, inatten-
inadvertido, da, a. inadvertent, inconsiderate.
inagotable, a. inexhaustible.
inaguantable, a. insupportable, insufferable, intolerable.
inajenable, a. inalienable.
inalterable, a. unalterable.
inapelable, a. without appeal, final.
inapetencia, sf. want of appetite.
inapreciable, a. invaluable.
inaudito, ta, a. unheard of. [tion.
inauguración, sf. inauguration, consecra-
inaugurar, v.a. to inaugurate.
incansable, a. indefatigable.
incapacidad, sf. incapacity, inability; stupidity.

incapaz, a. incapable, unable. [less.
incauto, ta, a. incautious, unwary, heed-
incendiar, v.a. to kindle, to set on fire.
incendiario, ria, sm. & a. incendiary.
incendio, sm. fire, conflagration; combustion.
incensar, v.a. to perfume, to incense.
incensario, sm. incensory, censer.
incentivo, sm. incitement, spur.
incertidumbre, sf. incertitude, uncertainty.
incesante, a. incessant, continual.
incesto, sm. incest.
incestuoso, sa, a. incestuous.
incidencia, sf. incidence; accident.
incidente, sm. incident, accident.
incidir, v.n. to fall into (an error).
incienso, sm. incense.
incierto, ta, a. uncertain, doubtful.
incisión, sf. incision, cut.
incisivo, va, a. incisive.
inciso, sm. (gr.) comma.
incitación, sf. incitement.
incitar, v.a. to incite, to excite.
incitativo, va, a. inciting, stimulating.
incivil, a. unpolished, uncivil.
inclemencia, sf. inclemency, severity;
á la —, without shelter.
inclinación, sf. inclination.
inclinar, v.a. to incline; —, v.n. to resemble; to incline; to be favourably
disposed to.
ínclito, ta, a. famous, illustrious.
incluir, v.a. to include, to comprise.
inclusa, sf. foundling-hospital.
inclusión, sf. inclusion.
inclusive, ad. inclusively.
incluso, sa, a. included.
incoativo, va, a. initiative.
incobrable, a. irrecoverable. [cognito.
incógnito, ta, a. unknown; de —, in-
incoherencia, sf. incoherence.
incoherente, a. incoherent.
incombustible, a. incombustible.
incomodar, v.a. to incommode.
incomodidad, sf. inconvenience, annoyance. [venient.
incómodo, da, a. incommodious, incon-
incomparable, a. incomparable, matchless.
incompatibilidad, sf. incompatibility.
incompatible, a. incompatible.
incompetencia, sf. incompetence.
incompetente, a. incompetent.
incompleto, ta, a. incomplete.
incomplexo, xa, a. simple.
incomprensible, a. incomprehensible.
incomunicación, sf. want of communication; isolation.
incomunicado, da, a. without communication, isolated; in solitary confinement.

inconcebible, a. inconceivable.
inconexo, xa, a. unconnected, incoherent;
independent.
incongruencia, a. incongruity.
incongruo, grua, a. incongruous, disproportionate.
inconmensurable, a. immeasurable.
inconquistable, a. unconquerable.
inconsecuencia, sf. inconsequence. [less.
inconsiderado, da, a. inconsiderate, heed-
inconsolable, a. inconsolable.
inconstancia, sf. inconstancy, unsteadiness, levity.
inconstante, a. inconstant, variable, fickle.
incontestable, a. indisputable, incontrovertible, incontestable. [tity.
incontinencia, sf. incontinence; unchas-
incontinente, a. incontinent.
incontrastable, a. insurmountable.
inconveniencia, sf. inconvenience, incommodity; unsuitableness.
inconveniente, a. inconvenient, unsuitable. [tion.
incorporación, sf. incorporation, annexa-
incorporar, v.a. to incorporate. [terial.
incorpóreo, rea, a. incorporeal, imma-
incorrecto, ta, a. incorrect.
incorregible, a. incorrigible.
incorruptible, a. incorruptible.
increado, da, a. uncreated.
incredulidad, sf. incredulity.
incrédulo, la, a. incredulous.
increíble, a. incredible.
incremento, sm. increment, increase;
growth; (gr.) augmentation. [ing.
increpación, sf. reprehension; scold-
increpar, v.a. to chide, to reprehend, to
scold.
incruento, ta, a. bloodless.
inculcar, v.a. to inculcate.
inculpabilidad, sf. innocence.
inculpable, a. blameless.
inculpar, v.a. to accuse, to blame.
inculto, ta, a. uncultivated, uneducated;
rude.
incumbencia, sf. incumbency; duty.
incumbir, v.n. to be incumbent upon one.
incurable, a. incurable; irremediable.
incuria, sf. negligence.
incurrir, v.n. to incur.
incursión, sf. incursion, incurring.
indagación, sf. search, inquiry.
indagar, v.a. to search, to inquire. [ful.
indebido, da, a. undue, illegal, unlaw-
indecencia, sf. indecency.
indecente, a. indecent.
indecible, a. inexpressible, unutterable.
indecisión, sf. irresolution, indecision.
indeciso, sa, a. irresolute; undecided.
indeclinable, a. firm, unshaken; (gr.) indeclinable.

indecoroso, sa, a. indecent, unbecoming, indecorous.
indefectible, a. unfailing.
indefenso, sa, a. defenceless.
indefinible, a. indefinable.
indefinido, da, a. indefinite.
indeleble, a. indelible.
indeliberado, da, a. unpremeditated.
indemnización, sf. indemnification; indemnity.
indemnizar, v.a. to indemnify.
independencia, sf. independence.
independiente, a. independent.
indestructible, a. indestructible.
indeterminado, da, a. indeterminate; indetermined, irresolute.
indevoto, ta, a. not devout.
indiana, sf. chintz, printed cotton.
indiano, sm. Nabob; South American.
indicación, sf. indication.
indicar, v.a. to indicate.
indicativo, va, a. & sm. indicative.
indice, sm. mark, sign; hand of a watch or clock; index, table of contents; forefinger, index.
indicio, sm. indication, mark; sign, token.
indiferencia, sf. indifference, unconcern.
indiferente, a. indifferent.
indigena, a. indigenous, native.
indigencia, sf. indigence, poverty, need.
indigente, a. indigent, poor, in want.
indigestión, sf. indigestion.
indigesto, ta, a. undigested; indigestible; not properly thought or worked out.
indignación, sf. indignation, anger.
indignar, v.a. to irritate, to provoke.
indignidad, sf. indignity; meanness.
indigno, na, a. unworthy, disgraceful.
indigo, sm. indigo-plant; indigo.
indirecta, sf. innuendo, hint, cue.
indirecto, ta, a. indirect.
indisciplinado, da, a. undisciplined.
indiscreción, sf. indiscretion, imprudence.
indiscreto, ta, a. indiscreet, inconsiderate.
indisculpable, a. inexcusable.
indisoluble, a. indissoluble.
indispensable, a. indispensable.
indisponer, v.a. to disable; to indispose.
indisposición, sf. indisposition, slight disorder.
indispuesto, ta, a. indisposed.
indisputable, a. indisputable, incontrovertible.
indistinto, ta, a. indistinct.
individual, a. individual.
individualidad, sf. individuality. [ally.
individualizar, v.a. to specify individu-
individuo, sm. individual.
indivisible, a. indivisible.

indócil, a. indocile; headstrong.
indocilidad, sf. indocility.
indole, sf. disposition, temper, peculiar genius.
indolencia, sf. indolence, indifference.
indolente, a. indolent, indifferent.
indómito, ta, a. untamed, ungoverned.
inducción, sf. induction, persuasion.
inducir, v.a. to induce.
inductivo, va, a. inductive.
indulgencia, sf. indulgence, forgiveness.
indulgente, a. indulgent.
indultar, v.a. to pardon; to exempt.
indulto, sm. pardon, amnesty; privilege, exemption.
industria, sf. industry.
industrial, a. industrial.
industriar, v.a. to teach, to instruct.
industrioso, sa, a. industrious; ingenious.
inédito, ta, a. not published, unedited.
inefable, a. ineffable, unspeakable, unutterable.
ineficacia, sf. inefficacy.
ineficaz, a. inefficacious. [tude.
ineptitud, sf. inability, unfitness, inepti-
inepto, ta, a. inept, unfit; incapable.
inercia, sf. inertia; inactivity.
inerme, a. disarmed, without arms.
inerte, a. inert, dull, sluggish; unskilful, awkward.
inescrutable, a. unscrutable. [seen.
inesperado, da, a. unexpected, unfore-
inestimable, a. inestimable.
inevitable, a. unavoidable. [actness.
inexactitud, sf. inaccuracy, want of ex-
inexacto, ta, a. inaccurate.
inexorable, a. inexorable.
infalibilidad, sf. infallibility.
infalible, a. infallible. [disgraceful.
infamante, a. defamatory; opprobrious,
infamar, v.a. to defame.
infame, a. infamous.
infamia, sf. infamy.
infancia, sf. infancy.
infando, da, a. infamous, unspeakably abominable.
infanta, sf. infanta (Princess of the royal blood of Spain); infant (female child under seven years old).
infante, sm. Prince; infant; infantryman, foot-soldier.
infantería, sf. infantry.
infanticida, sm. infanticide (person).
infanticidio, sm. infanticide (murder).
infantil, a. infantile, infantine.
infanzón, sm. nobleman.
infatigable, a. indefatigable.
infausto, ta, a. unlucky, unfortunate, luckless, fatal.
infección, sf. infection.
infectar, v.a. to infect.

infecto, ta, a. infected.
infelicidad, sf. misfortune, infelicity.
infeliz, a. unhappy, unfortunate.
inferior, a. inferior.
inferioridad, sf. inferiority.
inferir, v.a. to infer.
infernal, a. infernal, hellish.
infestar, v.a. to overrun, to harass, to annoy an enemy by incursions; to infect.
nficionar, v.a. to infect; to corrupt.
infidelidad, sf. infidelity; treachery.
infiel, a. infidel; faithless; disloyal godless.
infierno, sm. hell.
infiltración, sf. (med.) infiltration.
infiltrarse, v.r. to infiltrate.
ínfimo, ma, a. lowest, lowermost.
infinidad, sf. infinity, immensity.
infinitivo, sm. (gr.) infinitive.
infinito, ta, a. infinite, immense; —, ad. infinitely, immensely.
inflamable, a. inflammable.
inflamación, sf. inflammation; fervour.
inflamar, v.a. to inflame; to kindle desires.
inflamatorio, ria, a. inflammatory.
inflar, v.a. to inflate, to swell with wind.
inflexibilidad, sf. inflexibility.
inflexible, a. inflexible.
influencia, sf. influence.   [upon.
influir, v.a. to influence, to prevail
influjo, sm. influx, influence.
información, sf. information; intelligence given; instruction, judicial inquiry.   [forms.
informal, a. contrary to established
informalidad, sf. informality.
informar, v.a. to inform.
informe, sm. information, account; —, a. shapeless, formless.
infortunio, sm. misfortune, ill luck.
infracción, sf. infraction; breach, contravention, violation, trespass.
infractor, sm. violator.
infrascripto, infrascrito, a. underwritten, undersigned.   [less.
infructífero, ra, a. unfruitful; use-
infructuoso, sa, a. fruitless, unproductive, unprofitable.
infundado, da, a. groundless.
infundir, v.a. to infuse, to inspire.
infusión, sf. infusion.
infuso, sa, a. infused, introduced.
ingeniar, v.a. to conceive; to contrive; -se, to work in the mind, to endeavour to find out.
ingeniero, sm. engineer.
ingenio, sm. genius; engine; mèans, expedient; — de azúcar, sugar-mill.
ingenioso, sa, a. ingenious.

ingenuidad, sf. ingenuousness; candour, frankness.
ingenuo, nua, a. ingenuous.
ingerir, v.a. to insert; to introduce, to inclose; -se, to interfere officiously.
ingle, sf. groin.
inglés, esa, a. English.
ingratitud, sf. ingratitude, unthankfulness.   [agreeable.
ingrato, ta, a. ungrateful, thankless; dis-
ingrediente, sm. ingredient.
ingreso, sm. entrance; receipts, income.
inhábil, a. unable, incapable; awkward.
inhabilitar, v.a. to disqualify, to disable.
inhabitable, a. uninhabitable.
inherente, a. inherent.
inhibición, sf. inhibition, prohibition.
inhibir, v.a. to inhibit, to prohibit.
inhibitorio, ria, a. prohibitory.
inhumanidad, sf. inhumanity.
inhumano, na, a. inhuman.
inicial, a. initial.
iniciar, v.a. to initiate; -se, (eccl.) to receive the first orders.
iniciativo, va, a. initial, initiatory.
inicuo, cua, a. iniquitous, unjust.
inimaginable, a. unimaginable, incon-
inimitable, a. inimitable.   [ceivable.
ininteligible, a. unintelligible.
iniquidad, sf. iniquity, injustice.
injertar, v.a. to ingraft a tree.
injerto, sm. graft.
injuria, sf. injury.   [doer.
injuriador, ra, sm. & f. injurer, wrong-
injuriar, v.a. to injure.
injurioso, sa, a. injurious; offensive.
injusticia, sf. injustice.
injusto, ta, a. unjust.
inmaculado, da, a. immaculate.
inmarcesible, a. never-fading.
inmediatamente, ad. close by; immediately, forthwith.   [mediate
inmediato, ta, a. closely adjacent; im
inmemorial, a. immemorial.
inmensidad, sf. immensity.
inmenso, sa, a. immense, infinite.
inmensurable, a. inmeasurable.
inminente, a. imminent.
inmoble, a. immovable; constant.
inmoderado, da, a. immoderate.
inmodesto, ta, a. immodest.
inmolar, v.a. to sacrifice.
inmortal, a. immortal.
inmortalidad, sf. immortality.
inmortalizar, v.a. to immortalize.
inmóvil, a. immovable.
inmovilidad, sf. immobility.
inmueble, a. (law) real (estate).
inmundicia, sf. nastiness, filth.
inmundo, da, a. filthy, dirty; obscene.
inmune, a. free, exempt.

inmunidad, sf. immunity, privilege.
inmutabilidad, sf. immutability.
inmutable, a. immutable.
inmutar, v.a. to change, to alter ; -se, to be excited, to be moved.
innato, ta, a. inborn, natural.
innecesario, ria, a. unnecessary.
innegable, a. incontestable, incontrovertible.
innoble, a. ignoble ; mean of birth.
innovación, sf. innovation.
innovador, ra, sm. & f. innovator.
innovar, v.a. to innovate.   [less.
innumerable, a. innumerable, number-
inobediencia, sf. disobedience.
inobediente, a. disobedient.   [ance.
inobservancia, sf. inadvertency ; inobserv-
inocencia, sf. innocence.
inocentada, sf. (col.) simple speech.
inocente, a. innocent.
inoculación, sf. inoculation.
inocular, v.a. to inoculate.
inoficioso, sa, a. inofficious.   [sudden.
inopinado, da, a. unexpected, unforeseen,
inquietar, v.a. to disquiet, to disturb.
inquieto, ta, a. restless, unquiet.
inquietud, sf. inquietude, anxiety.
inquilino, na, sm. & f. tenant ; lodger.
inquirir, v.a. to examine, to trace.
inquisición, sf. inquisition ; judicial inquiry.
inquisidor, sm. inquirer ; inquisitor.
insaciable, a. insatiable.
insalubre, a. insalubrious, unwholesome.
insalubridad, sf. insalubrity.
insano, na, a. insane, mad.
inscribir, v.a. to inscribe.
inscripción, sf. inscription.
insecto, sm. insect.
insensatez, sf. stupidity, folly
insensato, ta, a. insensate, stupid, mad
insensibilidad, sf. insensibility.
insensible, a. insensible ; imperceptible.
insensiblemente, ad. by degrees.
inseparable, a. inseparable.
inserción, sf. insertion.
insertar, v.a. to insert.
inservible, a. unserviceable.
insidioso, sa, a. insidious.
insigne, a. notable.
insignia, sf. badge ; -s, pl. insignia.
insinuación, sf. insinuation.
insinuar, v.a. to insinuate.
insipidez, sf. insipidity.
insípido, da, a. insipid.
insistencia, sf. persistence, steadiness.
insistir, v.n. to insist.
insociable, a. unsociable.
insolencia, sf. insolence, imprudence, effrontery.
insolente, a. insolent, impudent.

insolvencia, sf. insolvency.
insolvente, a. insolvent.
insondable, a. unfathomable ; inscrutable.
insoportable, a. insupportable.
inspección, sf. inspection, survey, control.
inspeccionar, v.a. to inspect, to oversee.
inspector, sm. inspector, superintendent.
inspiración, sf. inspiration.
inspirar, v.a. to inspire.
instabilidad, sf. instability, inconstancy, fickleness, mutability, fugitiveness, fragility ; giddiness.
instable, a. unstable, inconstant, changing, mutable, fickle, fugacious.
instalación, sf. installation.
instalar, v.a. to install.
instancia, sf. insistence ; memorial (document).
instantaneo, nea, a. instantaneous.
instante, a. urgent ; —, sm. instant ; al —, immediately, instantly.
instar, v.a. to press, to urge a request or petition ; to impugn the solution of a question ; —, v.n. to be pressing or urgent ; to be imminent.   [stigation.
instigación, sf. incitement, impulse, in-
instigar, v.a. to instigate.
instinto, sm. instinct.
institución, sf. institution ; -ones, pl. elements of a science.
instituir, v.a. to institute ; to instruct.
instituto, sm. institute, school.
instrucción, sf. instruction.   [knowledge.
instructivo, va, a. instructive, conveying
instructor, sm. instructor, teacher.
instruir, v.a. to instruct, to teach.
instrumental, a. instrumental.
instrumentista, sm. musical player.
instrumento, sm. instrument ; machine, means, expedient.
insubsistente, a. groundless.   [quacy.
insuficiencia, sf. insufficiency, inade-
insuficiente, à. insufficient, inadequate
insufrible, a. insufferable, insupportable.
insulsez, sf. insipidity ; dullness, rudeness.   [flat ; tactless.
insulso, sa, a. insipid ; dull, heavy ;
insultar, v.a. to insult.
insulto, sm. insult ; sudden and violent attack.   [able.
insuperable, a. insuperable, insurmount
insurgente, sm. insurgent.
insurrección, sf. insurrection.
intacto, ta, a. untouched ; entire ; intact.
integral, a. integral, whole.
integridad, sf. integrity.
integro, gra, a. integral, entire ; upright, honourable ; (com.) gross (opposed to net).
intelectual, a. intellectual.   [standing.
inteligencia, sf. intelligence ; under-

inteligente, a. intelligent.
inteligible, a. intelligible.
intemperancia, sf. intemperance.
intemperie, sf. inclemency of weather.
intempestivo, va, a. unseasonable.
intención, sf. intention, design, meaning,
view.
intencionado, da, a. inclined, disposed.
intendencia, sf. administration ; employment of an intendant ; district
ruled by intendant.
intendente, sm. intendant.
intensión, sf. intensity.
intenso, sa, a. intense, ardent.
intentar, v.a. to try ; to intend, to design.
intento, sm. intent, purpose, design.
intentona, sf. extravagant design ;
chimerical attempt. [stancy.
intercadencia, sf. interruption ; incon-
intercadente, a. variable.
intercalación, sf. intercalation, insertion.
intercalar, v.a. to intercalate, to insert.
interceder, v.n. to intercede.
interceptar, v.a. to intercept.
intercesión, sf. intercession, mediation,
entreaty. [mediator.
intercesor, ra, sm. & f. intercessor,
interés, sm. interest ; concern, advantage ; profit.
interesado, da, a. interested. [venient.
interesante, a. interesting, useful, con-
interesar, v.n. & r. to be concerned or
interested in ; —, v.a. to interest ;
to concern, to give a share in.
interin, ad. in the interim, in the meantime. [office.
interinidad, sf. temporary holding of
interino, na, a. provisional (of an employ
or office).
interior, na, a. interior, internal ; —,
sm. interior, inside ; -es, pl. entrails,
intestines.
interioridades, sf.pl. private affairs.
interjección, sf. (gr.) interjection.
interlineal, a. interlineal.
interlocución, sf. dialogue.
intermediar, v.a. to interpose.
intermedio, dia, a. intermediate ; —,
sm. interval, intermedium ; interlude.
interminable, a. interminable, endless.
intermisión, sf. intermission, interruption
intermitente, a. intermittent.
internar, v.a. to remove a person inland ;
—, v.n. to penetrate ; -se, to insinuate ; to wheedle.
interno, a. interior, internal.
interpelación, sf. interpellation.
interpelar, v.a. to appeal to. [tion.
interpolación, sf. interpolation ; interrup-
interpolar, v.a. to interpolate ; to interrupt.

interponer, v.a. to interpose. [tion.
interposición, sf. interposition ; media-
interpretación, sf. interpretation.
interpretar, v.a. to interpret, to explain ;
to translate.
interprete, sm. interpreter.
interregno, sm. interregnum.
interrogación, sf. interrogation.
interrogante, a. interrogative.
interrogar, v.a. to interrogate.
interrogatorio, sm. interrogatory.
interrumpir, v.a. to interrupt. [ance.
interrupción, sf. interruption, discontinu-
intersección, sf. intersection.
intervalo, sm. interval. [tion.
intervención, sf. intervention, media-
intervenir, v.n. to intervene, to mediate.
interventor, ra, sm. & f. intervener.
intestado, da, a. intestate.
intestino, na, a. intestinal, internal, interior ; —, sm. intestine.
intimación, sf. intimation, hint.
intimar, v.a. to intimate.
intimidad, sf. intimacy.
intimidar, v.a. to intimidate.
íntimo, ma, a. internal, innermost ; intimate, familiar.
intitular, v.a. to entitle.
intolerable, a. intolerable, insufferable.
intolerancia, sf. intolerance.
intolerante, a. intolerant.
intramuros, a. within the walls. [trable.
intransitable, a. impassable, impene-
intransitivo, va, a. (gr.) intransitive.
intratable, a. intractable, ungovernable.
intrepidez, sf. intrepidity.
intrépido, da, a. intrepid, daring.
intriga, sf. intrigue.
intrigante, sm. intriguer.
intrigar, v.n. to intrigue.
intrincar, v.a. to entangle, to involve ;
to confound. [essential.
intrínseco, ca, a. intrinsic, internal ;
introducción, sf. introduction. [sinuate.
introducir, v.a. to introduce ; -se, to in-
introductor, sm. introducer.
introito, sm. entrance, entry.
intrusión, sf. intrusion, obtrusion.
intruso, sa, a. intrusive, obtrusive.
intuición, sf. intuition.
intuitivo, va, a. intuitive.
inundación, sf. inundation, deluge.
inundar, v.a. to inundate, to overflow.
inusitado, da, a. unusual.
inútil, a. useless.
inutilidad, sf. uselessness.
inutilizar, v.a. to render useless.
invadir, v.a. to invade.
invalidar, v.a. to invalidate, to nullify.
inválido, da, a. invalid, null ; —, sm.
(mil.) invalid.

invariable, a. invariable.
invasión, sf. invasion.
invasor, ra, sm. & f. invader.
invectiva, sf. invective.
invencible, a. invincible.
invención, sf. invention.
inventar, v.a. to invent.
inventariar, v.a. to make an inventory.
inventario, sm. inventory.
invento, sm. invention.
inventor, sm. inventor.
inverisimil, a. unlike, improbable.
inverisimilitud, sf. unlikelihood, improbability.
invernaculo, sm. green-house, hot-house.
invernadero, sm. (mil.) winter-quarters.
invernar, v.n. to pass the winter ; to be the winter season.
invernizo, za, a. winterly.
inversión, sf. inversion.
inverso, sa, a. inverted, reciprocal.
invertir, v.a. to invert.
investidura, sf. investiture.   [inquest.
investigación, sf. investigation, research ;
investigar, v.a. to investigate, to search out.
investir, v.a. to invest.
inveterarse, v.r. to become antiquated, to grow old.
invicto, ta, a. unconquerable.
invierno, sm. winter.
inviolabilidad, sf. inviolability.
inviolable, a. inviolable.
invisible, a. invisible.
invocación, sf. invocation.
invocar, v.a. to invoke.
involuntario, ria, a. involuntary.
invulnerable, a. invulnerable.
ir, v.n. to go, to walk ; -se, to go away, to depart.
ira, sf. anger, wrath.
iracundo, da, a. passionate, enraged.

íris, sf. rainbow; íris (of the eye); water-lily.
ironía, sf. irony.
irónico, ca, a. ironical.
irracional, a. irrational.
irradiación, sf. irradiation.
irrazonable, a. unreasonable.
irreconciliable, a. irreconcileable. [able.
irrecusable, a. not to be refused ; inevit-
irreflexión, sf. rashness, inconsideration.
irrefragable, a. irrefragable, irrefutable.
irregular, a. irregular, abnormal.
irregularidad, sf. irregularity, anomaly.
irreligioso, sa, a. irreligious, impious.
irremediable, a. irremediable.   [able.
irremisible, a. irremissible, unpardon-
irreparable, a. irreparable, irretrievable.
irresistible, a. irresistible.
irresolución, sf. irresolution.
irresoluto, ta, a. irresolute.
irreverencia, sf. irreverence, want of reverence, respect or veneration.
irreverente, a. irreverent.
irrevocable, a. irrevocable.
irrisible, a. ludicrous.
irrisión, sf. mockery, mocking laughter.
irrisorio, ria, a. laughable.
irritación, sf. irritation ; wrath.
irritar, v.a. to irritate, to exasperate (law) to annul.
irrupción, sf. irruption, inroad.
isla, sf. isle, island.
isleño, ña, sm. & f. islander.
isleta, sf. islet.
islote, sm. small barren island.
israelita, sm. Israelite, Jew.
istmo, sm. isthmus.
italiano, sm. Italian language.
ítem, ad. also, item.
itinerario, a. & sm. itinerary.
izar, v.a. (mar.) to hoist.
izquierdo, da, a. left ; left-handed.

J

jabalí, sm. wild boar.
jabalina, sf. wild sow ; javelin.
jabón, sm. soap.
jabonado, sm. washing with soap . parcel of linen washed with soap
jabonadura, sf. soap-suds ; lather.
jabonar, v.a. to soap.
jabonería, sm. soap-house.
jabonero, sm. soap-boiler.
jaca, sf. nag, pony.
jácara, sf. country song or dance tune.
jacarear, v.n. to sing jácaras.
jacinto, sm. hyacinth.
jaco, sm. wretched nag.

jactancia, sf. boasting.
jactancioso, sa, a. boastful, vain-glorious.
jactarse, v.r. to boast.
jaculatoria, sf. ejaculatory prayer, short and hurried prayer.
jaez, sm. harness.
jalapa, sf. jalap.
jalea, sf. jelly.
jalear, v.a. to urge on hounds.
jaleo, sm. halloo.
jaletina, sf. gelatine.
jamás, ad. never ; para siempre —, for ever.
jamón, sm. ham.

jándalo, la, a (col.) having the gait and dialect of an Andalusian. —

jaque, sm. check (at the game of chess); — y mate, check-mate.

jaquear, v.a. to check.

jaqueca, sf. megrim, head-ache.

jáquima, sf. halter.

jarabe, sm. syrup.

jarana, sf. merry clatter, outcry.

jarcia, sf. bundle, packet; bundle or heap of odds and ends; (mar.) tackle.

jardín, sm. garden.

jardinería, sf. gardening.

jardinero, ra, sm. & f. gardener.

jareta, sf. lace-hole.

jarope, sm. medical draught.

jarra, sf. jug, jar, pitcher; en —, de -s, with arms placed akimbo; with hands to the sides.

jarrete, sm. hock, hough.

jarretera, sf. garter.

jarro, sm. jug.

jarrón, sm. large jug, urn.

jaspe, sm. jasper.

jaspear, v.a. to marble, to speckle.

jaula, sf. cage; cell for mad persons.

jauría, sf. pack of hounds.

jazmín, sm. jessamine.

jefe, sm. chief, head, leader.

jengibre, sm. (bot.) ginger.

jerarquía, sf. hierarchy.

jerárquico, a. hierarchical.

Jerez, vino de-, sm. sherry. [jargon.

jerga, sf. coarse frieze, any coarse cloth;

jergón, sm. coarse mattress. [honour.

jerife, sm. sherif, Moorish title of

jerigonza, sf. jargon, gibberish.

jeringa, sf. syringe.

jeringar, v.a. to syringe, to squirt.

jeringazo, sm. clyster.

jeroglífico, a. hieroglyphical; —, sm. hieroglyph, hieroglyphic.

Jesucristo, sm. Jesus Christ.

jesuíta, sm. Jesuit.

jesuítico, ca, a. jesuitical.

jiba, sf. hump-back.

jibado, a. hump-backed.

jibia, sf. cuttle-fish.

jícara, sf. chocolate-cup.

jigote, sm. minced meat.

jilguero, sm. linnet.

jineta, sf. horsemanship.

jinete, sm. cavalier.

jocoserio, ria, a. jocoserious.

jocosidad, sf. jocosity.

jocoso, sa, a. waggish, good-humoured.

jornada, sf. journey; military expedition; act (of a Spanish play); — rompida, fight, battle.

jornal, sm. day-work; journal; á —, by the day.

jornalero, sm. day-labourer.

joroba, sf. hump.

jorobado, da, a. hump-backed. [dance.

jota, sf. letter J; jot, tittle; Spanish

joven, a. young; —, sm. & f. youth; young woman.

jovial, a. jovial, gay, merry.

jovialidad, sf. joviality, gaiety.

joya, sf. jewel; present, gift.

joyería, sf. jeweller's shop.

joyero, sm. jeweller. [toe.

juanete, sm. knuckle-bone of the great

jubilación, sf. festivity.

jubilar, v.a. to pension off; to superannuate; to lay aside as useless; —, v.n. to become a pensioner; to rejoice.

jubileo, sm. jubilee.

júbilo, sm. joy, merriment, festivity.

jubón, sm. doublet, jacket. ·

judaico, ca, a. Judaical, Jewish.

judaísmo, sm. Judaism, Jewish religion.

judaizar, v.a. to judaize.

Judas, sm. (fig.) traitor.

judía, sf. French bean, kidney-bean.

judicatura, sf. judicature; dignity of a judge.

judicial, a. judicial, juridical.

judío, día, a. Jewish; —, sm. Jew.

juego, sm. play, amusement, diversion, sport; game, gambling; -s, pl. public games of the ancients.

jueves, sm. Thursday.

juez, sm. judge.

jugada, sf. playing of a card.

jugador, ra, sm. & f. player; gamester.

jugar, v.a. & n. to play, to sport, to trifle, to toy; to gamble, to game; to intervene; to mock; to fit, to work smoothly.

jugarreta, sf. bad play, unskilful playing.

jugo, sm. sap, juice.

jugoso, sa, a. juicy, succulent.

juguete, sm. toy, plaything, gew-gaw, trinket.

juguetear, v.n. to trifle, to fool.

juguetón, ona, a. playful.

juicio, sm. judgment.

juicioso, sa, a. judicious, prudent.

julepe, sm. julap.

julio, sm. July (month).

jumento, ta, sm. & f. beast of burden; ass; stupid person. [ship).

junco, sm. (bot.) rush; junk (Chinese

juncoso, sa, a. full of rushes.

junio, sm. June (month). [meeting.

junta, sf. congress, assembly, council,

juntamente, ad. jointly; at the same time.

juntar, v.a. to join, to unite; -se, to meet, to assemble; to be closely united.

junto, ad. near, close to ; (de) por —, by the bulk, in the lump.

juntura, sf. juncture ; joint.

Júpiter, sm. Jupiter (planet) ; (chem.) tin.

jura, sf. oath of allegiance.

jurado, sm. jury ; juror, juryman ; jurat.

jurador, ra, sm. & f. swearer.

juramentar, v.a. to swear ; -se, to bind oneself by an oath.

juramento, sm. oath.

jurar, v.a. to swear, to make oath.

jurídico, ca, legal, juridical.

jurisconsulto, sm. lawyer, jurist.

jurisdicción, sf. jurisdiction, legal authority.   [dence.

jurisperito, sm. master of jurisprudence.

jurisprudencia, sf. jurisprudence.

jurista, sm. jurist, lawyer. [—, certainly.

juro, sm. right of perpetual property ; de

justa, sf. joust, tilt, tournament.

justamente, ad. justly, just.

justicia, sf. justice ; equity.

justiciero, ra, a., sm. & f. observant of justice ; executing justice.

justificación, sf. justification ; adjustment of lines of type.

justificado, da, a. justified ; conformable to justice.

justificar, v.a. to justify ; to prove, to set right ; to adjust lines of type.

justificativo, va, a. justificatory.

justillo, sm. sleeveless vest.

justipreciar, v.a. to estimate anything.

justo, ta, a. just ; lawful ; honourable —, sm. just and pious man ; al — ad. fitly, duly ; punctually.

juvenil, a. juvenile, youthful.

juventud, sf. youthfulness, youth.

juzgado, sm. tribunal ; judicature.

juzgar, v.a. & n. to judge.

K

kaleidoscopio, sm. kaleidoscope.

kan, sm. Khan, oriental prince.

kermes, sm. fair, public festival.

kilogramo, sm. kilogram.

kilómetro, sm. kilometre.

kiosco, sm. kiosk.

L

la, art. f. the.

laberinto, sm. labyrinth.

labia, sf. (fam.) winning eloquence.

labio, sm. lip ; brim, edge of anything.

labor, sf. labour, task ; needlework ; husbandry, tillage.

laboratorio, sm. laboratory.

laboriosidad, sf. laboriousness, assiduity.

laborioso, sa, a. laborious.

labrado, da, a. worked (applied to figured cloth) ; —, sm. cultivated land.

labrador, ra, sm. & f. labourer ; cultivator, farmer ; peasant.

labrantío, tía, a. arable.   [land.

labranza, sf. tillage ; husbandry ; tilled

labrar, v.a. to work ; to labour ; to cultivate the ground ; to build.

labriego, sm. peasant.

lacayo, sm. lackey, footman.

lacerar, v.a. to tear to pieces, to lacerate.

lacería, sf. misery, poverty, wretchedness ; fatigue.

lacio, cia, a. faded, withered ; languid.

lacónico, ca, a. laconic, concise.

laconismo, sm. laconism.   [vice.

lacra, sf. mark left by a wound ; fault,

lacrar, v.a. to injure one's health ; to damage financially.

lacre, sm. sealing-wax.

lactancia, sf. time of giving suck.

ladear, v.a. to move to one side ; to incline ; —, v.n. to incline to one side ; -se, to incline to an opinion or party.

ladera, sf. declivity.

ladilla, sf. louse.

ladino, na, a. sagacious, cunning, crafty.

lado, sm. side ; party ; ¡á un —! clear the way !

ladrar, v.n. to bark.

ladrido, sm. barking ; vociferation.

ladrillal, ladrillar, sm. brick-kiln.

ladrillo, sm. brick.

ladrón, sm. thief, robber, highwayman.

ladronera, sf. den of robbers.

ladronicio, sm. larceny, theft, robbery

lagaña, sf. weakness of eyes.

lagañoso, sa, a. blear-eyed.

lagar, v.a. press-house ; wine-press.

lagarero, sm. wine-presser ; one employed in olive-pressing.

lagartija, sf. small lizard.

lagarto, sm. lizard ; sly, artful person.

lago, sm. lake ; — de leones, den of lions.

lágrima, sf. tear.

lagrimal, sm. lachrymary bag.

lagrimoso, sa, a. weeping, shedding tears.

laguna, sf. lake ; lagoon ; gap, lacuna.

lagunoso, sa, a. marshy, fenny.

laical, a. lay, laical.   [country.
lama, sf. mud, slime, ooze; flat, even
lamedor, ra, sm. & f. licker; entice-
    ment, allurement.
lamedura, sf. act of licking.
lamentable, a. lamentable, deplorable,
    pitiable.
lamentación, sf. lamentation.
lamentar, v.a. to lament, to bewail; —,
    v.n., -se, to lament, to complain, to
lamento, sm. lamentation.   [cry.
lamer, v.a. to lick, to lap.
lámina, sf. plate, sheet of metal; copper-
    plate, engraving, print.
lámpara, sf. lamp.
lamparero, sm. lamp-lighter.
lamparilla, sf. night-light.
lamparón, sm. scrofula.
lampiño, ña, a. beardless.
lampión, sm. large lantern.
lamprea, sf. lamprey (fish).
lana, sf. wool.
lanar, a. woolly.
lance, sm. cast, throw; favourable op-
    portunity; chance, haphazard; sud-
    den quarrel.
lancear, v.a. to wound with a lance.
lancero, sm. pikeman, lancer.
lanceta, sf. lancet.
lancetada, sf. lancing, cut of a lancet.
lancha, sf. barge, lighter; launch.
lanchón, sm. (mar.) lighter.
langosta, sf. locust; lobster; sharper,
    swindler.
langostín, sm. small locust.
languidez, sf. languor.
lánguido, da, a. languid, faint, weak;
    langorous, languishing.
lanudo, da, a. woolly, fleecy.
lanza, sf. lance, spear; pole of a coach;
    -s, pl. duty paid by the nobility (in
    lieu of military services).
lanzada, sf. stroke with a lance.
lanzadera, sf. shuttle.
lanzar, v.a. to throw, to dart, to launch,
    to fling; (law) to eject.
lapicero, sm. metal pencil-case.
lápida, sf. flat stone, on which inscrip-
    tions are engraved.
lapidario, sm. —, ria, a. lapidary.
lápiz, sm. lead-pencil; black chalk used
    in drawing; black lead.
lapizar, v.a. to pencil, to sketch.
lapso, sm. lapse.
lardar, lardear, v.a. to baste.
lardoso, sa, a. greasy, fatty.
lares, sm.pl. household-gods; home.
larga, sf. delay, adjournment.
largamente, ad. fully, at length.
largar, v.a. to loosen, to slacken; to let
    go; -se, to set sail.

largo, ga, a. long; large, generous,
    liberal; copious; á la -a, at length,
    extensively; —, ad. largely, pro-
    fusely.   [generosity.
largueza, sf. length, largeness; liberality
largura, sf. length, longitude.
lascivia, sf. lasciviousness; lewdness.
lascivo, va, a. lascivious; lewd.
lasitud, sf. lassitude, weariness.   [pity.
lástima, sf. compassion, pity; object of
lastimar, v.a. to hurt; to wound; to
    move to compassion; -se, to be
    moved to compassion; to grieve.
lastimero, ra, a. sad, mournful; lament
    able.
lastimoso, sa, a. grievous, mournful.
lastrar, v.a. to ballast a ship.
lastre, sm. ballast; motive.
lateral, a. lateral.
latido, sm. pant, palpitation.
latigazo, sm. lash, crack of a whip.
látigo, sm. thong of a whip.
latín, sm. Latin tongue.
latinajo, sm. dog Latin.
latinidad, sf. Latinity, Latin tongue.
latinizar, v.a. to latinize.
latino, na, a. Latin.
latir, v.n. to palpitate.
latitud, sf. breadth; width; latitude
lato, ta, a. ample, large, diffuse, exten-
latón, sm. brass, latten.   [sive.
latonero, sm. brazier.   [only.
latría, sf. worship, adoration due to God
latrocinio, sm. larceny, theft, robbery.
laud, sf. lute (musical instrument).
laudable, a. laudable, praiseworthy.
láudano, sm. laudanum.
laude, sf. tombstone with an epitaph;
    -s, pl. Lauds.
laurear, v.a. to crown with laurel; to
    honour, to reward.
laurel, sm. (bot.) laurel; laurel-crown
    as a reward.
lauréola, sf. crown of laurel.
lavabo, sm. wash-stand.   [terer.
lavacaras, sm. (fig. & tam.) mean flat-
lavadero, sm. washing-place; laundry.
lavadura, sf. wash, washing.
lavamanos, sm. washhand-stand.
lavandera, sf. laundress.
lavar, v.a. to wash; to whitewash.
lavativa, sf. clyster.
lavatorio, sm. act of washing; medicinal
    lotion; ceremony of washing the feet
    on Holy Thursday.
laxante, a. & sm. (med.) laxative.
laxar, v.a. to loosen, to soften.
laxitud, sf. laxity; laxness; weariness
laxo, xa, a. lax, slack; (fig.) vague.
layar, v.a. to turn up the ground with
    fork.

lazada, sf. running knot.
lazareto, sm. lazaretto, lazaret. [man.
lazarillo, sm. boy who guides a blind
lazo, sm. slip-knot ; snare, trick ; tie ;
le, pn. him, her. [bond.
real, a. loyal ; faithful.
lealtad, sf. loyalty.
lebrel, sm. greyhound.
lebrillo, sm. glazed earthen-ware pan.
lección, sf. reading ; lesson ; lecture ;
lector, sm. reader, lecturer. [lection.
lectoría, sf. lectureship.
lectura, sf. reading, lecture.
leche, sf. milk.
lechera, sf. milkwoman, dairymaid.
lechería, sf. cow-house, dairy.
lechigada, sf. litter (of animals).
lecho, sm. bed ; litter.
lechón, sm. sucking pig ; dirty fellow.
lechuga, sf. lettuce. [lettuce.
lechugado, da, a. having leaves like
lechuguino, sm. bed of small lettuces.
lechuza, sf. owl.
leer, v.a. to read ; to lecture.
lega, sf. lay-sister.
legacía, sf. embassy, legation.
legado, sm. deputy, legate ; legacy.
legajo, sm. bundle of loose papers tied
together.
legal, a. legal ; loyal, faithful.
legalidad, sf. legality, fidelity.
legalización, sf. legalization.
legalizar, v.a. to legalize.
legar, v.a. to depute ; to bequeath.
legatario, sm. legatee.
legible, a. legible.
legión, sf. legion.
legionario, ria, a. legionary.
legislación, sf. legislation.
legislador, sm. legislator, lawgiver.
legislar, v.a. to legislate.
legislativo, va, a. legislative, lawgiving.
legislatura, sf. legislature.
legista, sm. legist. [paternal estate.
legítima, sf. (law) legal portion of
legitimación, sf. legitimation.
legitimar, v.a. to legitimate.
legitimidad, sf. legitimacy.
legítimo, ma, a. legitimate, lawful.
lego, sm. lay-brother.
legua, sf. league.
legumbre, sf. vegetable.
leído, da, a. well-read.
lejano, na, a. distant, remote, far.
lejía, sf. lie, lye.
lejos, ad. at a great distance, far off ;
, sm. perspective, distant prospect.
lelo, la, a. stupid, ignorant.
lema, sm. argument of a poem explained
in the title.; lemma.
lencería, sf. drapery ; linen-draper's shop.

lencero, sm. draper.
lendroso, sa, a. lousy.
lengua, sf. tongue ; language, tongue.
lenguaje, sm. language ; mode of speech.
lenidad, sf. lenity, mildness.
lenitivo, va, a. lenient, mitigant ; —
sm. emollient.
lente, sm. & f. lens.
lenteja, sf. (bot.) lentil.
lentitud, sf. slowness.
lento, ta, a. slow, tardy, lazy.
leña, sf. fire-wood.
leñador, sm. woodman, wood-cutter.
leñera, sf. place for fire-wood
leñero, sm. wood-merchant.
leño, sm. block, log ; trunk of a tree.
leñoso, sa, a. woody.
Leo, Leo (sign of the zodiac).
león, sm. lion ; beau, dandy.
leona, sf. lioness. [fallow.
leonado, da, a. lion-coloured, tawny ;
leonera, sf. lion-cage.
leonero, sm. keeper of lions.
leopardo, sm. leopard.
lepra, sf. leprosy.
leproso, sa, a. leprous. [prehension
lerdo, da, a. slow, heavy ; dull of com-
lesión, sf. hurt, damage, wound ; injury.
lesna, sf. awl.
letal, a. mortal, deadly.
letanía, sf. litany.
letárgico, ca, a. lethargic.
letargo, sm. lethargy.
letra, sf. letter ; handwriting ; printing-
type ; words of a song ; bill of exchange ; -s, pl. letters, learning.
letrado, da, a. learned, lettered ; —, sm.
lawyer ; professor of law.
letrero, sm inscription.
letrilla, sf. short poem, generally written
to be sung to music.
letrina, sf. privy.
leva, sf. act of weighing anchor ; (mil.)
levy ; (mar.) press.
levadizo, za, a. that can be lifted or
raised ; puente —, drawbridge.
levantamiento, sm. elevation ; insurrection.
levantar, v.a. to raise, to lift up, to
heave ; to build up ; to elevate, to
promote ; -se, to rise ; to get up from
bed ; to stand up.
levante, sm. Levant ; east ; east-wind.
leve, a. light ; trifling.
levita, sm. levite ; —, sf. frock-coat.
Levítico, sm. book of Leviticus.
ley, sf. law ; loyalty.
leyenda, sf. reading, legend.
lía, sf. bass-rope.
liar, v.a. to tie, to bind, to faggot.
libación, sf. libation

libelo, sm. petition; written charge against a prisoner; lampoon, libel.
liberal, a. liberal, generous.
liberalidad, sf. liberality, generosity.
libertad, sf. liberty, freedom; independence; freeness. [liberator.
libertador, ra, a. & sm. & f. deliverer,
libertar, v.a. to free, to liberate; to exempt, to clear from an obligation.
libertinaje, sm. libertinism, licentiousness. [tious, lewd.
libertino, na, sm. & f. dissolute, licen-
liberto, sm. freed man.
libra, sf. pound; — **esterlina,** pound sterling. [zodiac).
Libra, —, sf. Libra, scales (sign of the
librar, v.a. to free, to rescue, to deliver; to dispatch, to expedite; — **bien ó mal,** to get over a thing well or ill; **-se,** to escape.
libre, a. free; exempt; innocent.
librea, sf. livery.
librejo, sm. little book, pamphlet.
libremente, ad. freely; boldly; audaciously, impudently.
librería, sf. book-seller's shop; library.
librero, sm. book-seller; — **papelero,** stationer.
libreta, sf. note-book.
libro, sm. book. [ousness.
licencia, sf. permission, license; licenti-
licenciado, sm. licentiate.
licenciamiento, sm. taking of the degree of licentiate. [license.
licenciar, v.a. to permit, to allow; to
licencioso, sa, a. licentious, dissolute.
liceo, sm. lyceum, school.
lícitamente, ad. lawfully, licitly.
lícito, ta, a. lawful.
licor, sm. liquor.
lid, sm. contest, fight; dispute.
lidiador, sm. combatant.
liebre, sf. hare.
liendre, sf. louse.
lienzo, sf. linen; canvas; picture; façade of a building. [tion; alloy
liga, sf. garter; bird-lime; league, coali-
ligadura, sf. ligature, binding.
ligar, v.a. to tie, to bind, to fasten; to alloy (metal); to confederate; **-se,** to league; to be allied; to bind one-
ligazón, sf. union, connection. [self.
ligereza, sf. lightness; levity.
ligero, ra, a. light, swift, easy.
lija, sf. angel-fish; fish-skin.
lijar, v.a. to smooth, to polish.
lila, sf. lilac-tree; lilac-flower; Lisle
lima, sf. file. [thread.
limadura, sf. filing.
limar, v.a. to file; to polish.
limbo, sm. limbo.

limitación, sf. limitation, restriction.
limitado, da, a. limited.
limitar, v.a. to limit; to restrain.
límite, sm. limit, boundary.
limítrofe, a. limiting, bordering.
limo, sm. slime, mud.
limón, sm. lemon.
limonada, sf. lemonade.
limonar, sm. plantation of lime-trees.
limosna, sf. alms, charity. [table
limosnero, sm. almoner; —, **ra,** a. chari-
limpiadientes, sm. tooth-pick.
limpiador, sm. cleanser, scourer.
limpiar, v.a. to scour, to cleanse, to clear, to purify.
limpieza, sf. cleanliness, neatness; chastity; integrity; purity of blood.
limpio, pia, a. clean; limpid, neat; pure
limpión, sm. cleansing, cleaning.
linaje, sm. lineage, race, descent.
linar, sm. flax-field.
linaza, sf. linseed.
lince, sm. lynx.
lindar, v.n. to be contiguous.
linde, sm. landmark, boundary.
lindero, sm. landmark, boundary.
lindeza, sf. neatness, elegance.
lindo, da, a. neat, handsome, pretty.
línea, sf. line; boundary, limit.
lineal, a. lineal.
linear, v.a. to draw lines.
linfa, sf. lymph.
linfático, ca, a. lymphatic.
lino, sm. flax.
linterna, sf. lantern.
lío, sm. bundle, parcel.
liquidación, sf. liquidation.
liquidar, v.a. to liquefy, to melt; to clear accounts.
líquido, da, a. liquid.
lira, sf. lyre.
lirio, sm. (bot.) lily.
lis, sf. fleur-de-lis.
lisiar, v.a. to lame; to hurt a limb.
liso, sa, a. plain, even, flat smooth.
lisonja, sf. adulation, flattery.
lisonjear, v.a. to flatter.
lisonjero, sm. flatterer; —, **ra,** a. fawning; flattering; pleasing.
lista, sf. stripe; list, catalogue.
listo, ta, a. ready, prompt, active.
listón, sm. ribbon; lath. [dour.
lisura, sf. smoothness; sincerity, can-
litera, sf. litter.
literal, a. literal.
literario, ria, a. literary.
literato, ta, a. learned, lettered; —, sm. literary man.
literatura, sf. literature.
litigante, sm. litigant. [cause.
litigar, v.a. to litigate, to carry on a

litigio, sm. law-suit.
litigioso, sa, a. litigious.
litografía, sf. lithography.
litográfico, ca, a. lithographic.
litografiar, v.a. to lithograph.
litógrafo, sm. lithographer.
litoral, a. littoral.
litro, sm. litre (measure).
liturgia, sf. liturgy.
litúrgico, ca, a. liturgical.
liviandad, sf. lightness; levity, imprudence; incontinence.
liviano, na, a. light; imprudent; unchaste; -s, sm.pl. lungs.
lívido, da, a. livid.
lo, pn. it; —, art. neutr. the.
loable, a. laudable.
loar, v.a. to praise; to approve.
loba, sf. she-wolf.
lobanillo, sm. wen, chafe.
lobato, sm. wolf-cub.
lobo, sm. wolf.   [sad.
lóbrego, ga, a. murky, obscure, gloomy;
lobreguez, sf. obscurity darkness.
lobuno, na, a. wolfish.
local, a. local.
localidad, sf. locality.
localizar, v.a. to localize.
loco, ca, a. mad, crack-brained.
locuacidad, sf. loquacity.
locuaz, a. loquacious, garrulous.
locución, sf. mode of speech; phrase.
locura, sf. madness, frenzy, folly; ab-
locutorio, sm. parlour.   [surdity.
lodazal, sm. muddy place.
lodo, sm. mud, mire.
lodoso, sa, a. muddy, miry.
logaritmo, sm. logarithm.
lógica, sf. logic.
lógico, ca, a. logical; —, sm. logician.
lograr, v.a. to gain, to obtain.
logrear, v.n. to lend on interest.
logrero, sm. usurer.   [usury.
logro, sm. gain, benefit; interest;
loma, sf. hillock.
lombarda, sf. red cabbage.
lombriz, sf. worm.   [(needle-work).
lomillo, sm. small loin; cross-stitch
lomo, sm. loin; back of a book; double
of any cloth; ridge between two furrows.
lona, sf. canvas.
lóndiga, sf. granary.   [tience.
longanimidad, sf. long-suffering, pa-
longaniza, sf. sausage.
longitud, sf. length; longitude.
lonja, sf. Exchange; grocer's shop;
warehouse; slice.
lonjista, sm. grocer.
loor, sf. (poet.) praise.   [to revel.
loquear, v.n. to play the fool; to rejoice,

loquero, sm. keeper of a mad-house.
loro, sm. parrot.
lorri, sm. (rail.) lorry.
losa, sf. flag-stone.
lote, sm. lot.
lotería, sf. lottery.
loza, sf. delft, crockery.
lozanear, v.n. to act ostentatiously.
lozanía, sf. verdure, exuberant growth
of plants; vigour; vivacity.
lozano, na, a. luxuriant; sprightly.
lucero, sm. morning-star, day-star.
lúcido, da, a. shining, magnificent,
splendid; clear, lucid.
luciérnaga, sf. glow-worm.
lucimiento, sm. splendour, lustre, applause; brightness.
lucio, cia, a. lucid, bright.
lucir, v.n., -se, to shine, to be brilliant;
to dress to advantage.
lucrativo, va, a. lucrative.
lucro, sm. gain, profit, lucre.
lucha, sf. struggle, strife.
luchador, sm. wrestler.
luchar, v.a. to wrestle, to struggle.
ludibrio, sm. mockery, derision.
luego, ad. presently, immediately; soon
afterwards.
lugar, sm. place, spot; village; employment, office; dignity; cause; motive; en — de, instead of, in lieu of.
lugareño, ña, a. & sm. & f. belonging to a
village; villager.
lugarteniente, sm. lieutenant, deputy.
lúgubre, a. sad, gloomy; dismal.
lujo, sm. luxury, profusion, ostentation.
lujoso, sa, a. showy, profuse, lavish,
sumptuous, luxurious.
lujuria, sf. lewdness; licentiousness.
lujurioso, sa, a. voluptuous, lewd, licentious.
lumbre, sf. fire; spark.
lumbrera, sf. luminary; sky-light.
luminaria, sf. illumination; perpetual
altar-lamp.
luminoso, sa, a. luminous, lucid.
luna, sf. moon; glass plate for mirrors.
lunar, sm. mole; stain of infamy; —, a.
lunar.
lunático, ca, a. lunatic, moon-struck.
lunes, sm. Monday.
luneta, sf. stall (in theatre); eye-glass.
lupanar, sm. brothel.
lustre, sm. gloss, lustre; splendour.
lustro, sm. lustrum (space of five years).
lustroso, sa, a. bright, brilliant.
luteranismo, sm. Lutheranism.
luterano, na, sm. & f. Lutheran.
luto, sm. mourning (dress).
luz, sf. light; candle; day; information, hint; knowledge, science.

Ll

llaga, sf. wound, sore.

llagar, v.a. to wound, to hurt.

llama, sf. flame; llama (animal).

llamada, sf. call; (mil.) drum-beat to summon troops.

llamador, sm. door-knocker. [tion.

llamamiento, sm. calling; convoca-

llamar, v.a. to call; to summon, to cite; to invoke; to knock at the door.

llamarada, sf. sudden blaze of fire; burst of merriment.

llana, sf. trowel; page (of a book, &c.).

llanada, sf. wide tract of level ground; plain.

llano, na, a. plain, even, level, smooth; meek, affable; plain, clear, evident; frank, open; —, sm. level field, plain.

llanta, sf. tyre.

llanto, sm. flood of tears, cry.

llanura, sf. evenness, level; vast tract of level ground.

llares, sm.pl. pot-hook. [key.

llave, sf. key; — maestra, master-

llavero, sm. keeper of the keys of a place, custodian; key-ring.

llegada, sf. arrival, coming.

llegar, v.a. to arrive; to reach; -se, to proceed to some place; to unite.

llena, sf. overflow; flood.

llenar, v.a. to fill, to stuff, to gorge; to overwhelm (with compliments, kindness, &c.); -se, to feed gluttonously; to lose patience.

lleno, na, a. full, replete; complete; de —, entirely, fully.

llevadero, ra, a. tolerable.

llevar, v.a. to carry, to convey, to transport; to bear; to introduce.

llorar, v.a. & n. to weep, to cry; to be wail.

lloriquear, v.n. to whine.

lloro, sm. weeping, crying.

llorón, na, a. & sm. & f. weeper.

lloroso, sa, a. mournful, full of tears.

llovediza (agua —), sf. rain-water.

llover, v.imp. to rain.

lloviznar, v.imp. to drizzle.

lluvia, sf. rain.

lluvioso, sa, a. rainy.

M

macaco, ca, sm. & f. monkey.

macana, sf. club, mace.

macareno, na, a. bragging, boasting.

macarrones, sm.pl. macaroni.

macarse, v.r. to rot (of fruit).

macear, v.a. to pound with a mallet; to knock.

macerar, v.a. to macerate, to soften.

macero, sm. mace-bearer.

maceta, sf. flower-pot. [withered.

macilento, ta, a. lean, extenuated;

macizo, za, a. massive, solid. [bore.

machaca, sm. & f. tiresome person.

machacar, v.a. to pound, to crush; to importune, to molest. [dious.

machacón, ona, a. importunate, te-

machada, sf. flock of he-goats; stupidity.

machete, sm. cutlass.

macho, sm. male animal; mule; goat; hook to catch in an eye; —, a. masculine, male; vigorous.

machón, sm. buttress.

machorra, sf. barren female.

machucadura, sf. pounding, bruising.

machucar, v.a. to pound, to bruise.

machucho, cha, a. mature, ripe; judicious.

madama, sf. madam. [hair.

madeja, sf. skein of thread; lock of

madera, sf. timber, wood.

maderería, sf. timber-yard.

madero, sm. beam of timber.

madrastra, sf. stepmother.

madraza, sf. very fond mother.

madre, sf. mother; womb, matrix; bed of a river.

madreperla, sf. mother of pearl.

madreselva, sf. honey-suckle.

madrigal, sm. madrigal. [place.

madriguera, sf. burrow; den, lurking-

madrina, sf. godmother.

madrona, sf. mother who spoils her children by over-indulgence.

madroño, sm. strawberry-tree, arbutus.

madrugada, sf. dawn; de —, at break of day.

madrugador, ra, a. & sm. & f. early riser

madrugar, v.n. to get up early; to be beforehand.

madurar, v.a. to ripen; —, v.n. to ripen, to grow ripe; to arrive at maturity.

madurez, sf. maturity; prudence, wisdom.

maduro, ra, a. ripe, mature; prudent, judicious.

maestra, sf. mistress; schoolmistress, master's wife.

maestrante, sm. academician.

maestranza, sf. riding-school; dockyard; arsenal. [military order.
maestrazgo, sm. grand-mastership of a
maestre, sm. grand-master of a military order; ship-master.
maestresala, sm. chief waiter at a nobleman's table in Spain.
maestría, sf. mastership.
maestro, sm. master; teacher; —, tra, a. masterly, principal.
magia, sf. magic.
mágico, ca, a. magical; —, sm. magician.
magisterio, sm. mastery; mastership;
magistrado, sm. magistrate; magistracy.
magistral, a. magisterial.
magistratura, sf. magistracy.
magnanimidad, sf. magnanimity.
magnánimo, ma, a. magnanimous.
magnate, sm. magnate.
magnesia, sf. magnesia.
magnético, ca, a. magnetic.
magnetismo, sm. magnetism.
magnetizar, v.a. to magnetize.
magníficat, sf. the Magnificat. [dour.
magnificencia, sf. magnificence, splen-
magnífico, ca, a. magnificent, splendid.
magnitud, sf. magnitude; greatness, grandeur.
maguo, na, a. great.
mago, ga, sm. & f. magician.
magra, sf. rasher, slice of pork.
magro, gra, a. meagre.
magulladura, sf. bruise, contusion.
magullar, v.a. to bruise, to contuse.
mahometano, s. & a. Mohammedan.
mahometanismo, sm. Mohammedanism.
mahón, sm. nankeen.
maitines, sm. pl. matins.
maíz, sm. maize, Indian corn.
maizal, sm. field sown with Indian corn.
majada, sf. sheep-fold.
majadería, sf. absurd speech; insult.
majadero, ra, a. dull, silly; —, sm. gawk, block-head.
majadura, sf. pounding, bruising.
majar, v.a. to pound.
majestad, sf. majesty.
majestuoso, a. majestic(al).
majo, sm. boaster; gallant; low-class dandy.
majuela, sf. hawthorn-hips. [thorn.
majuelo, sm. vine newly planted; haw-
mal, sm. evil, hurt, injury; illness; —, a. (used only before masculine substantives) bad; —, ad. ill, badly.
mala, sf. mail, trunk, travelling-box.
malamente, ad. badly, perversely.
malandrín, sm. a. malign, perverse.
malavenido, da, a. quarrelsome.
malaventura, sf. calamity, misfortune.
malaventurado, da, a. unfortunate.

malbaratador, ra, a. & sm. & f. spendthrift, lavish. [tent.
malcontento, ta, a. discontented, malcon-
maleriado, da, a. ill-bred, ill-behaved, unmannerly; naughty.
maldad, sf. wickedness.
maldición, sf. malediction, cursing.
maldito, ta, a. perverse, wicked; damned, cursed. [destroy.
malear, v.a. to injure, to corrupt; to
maledicencia, sf. slander, calumny.
maleficiar, v.a. to adulterate, to corrupt; to bewitch.
maleficio, sm. witchcraft, enchantment.
maléfico, ca, a. mischievous, maleficent.
maleta, sf. portmanteau.
malevolencia, sf. malevolence.
malévolo, la, a. malevolent.'
maleza, sf. wickedness, malice; bramblebrake; thicket.
malgastar, v.a. to waste, to lavish.
malhablado, da, a. foul-mouthed.
malhecho, sm. flagitious action, wrong
malhechor, ra, sm. & f. malefactor.
malhumorado, da, a. ill-humoured, peevish. [cunning artifice.
malicia, sf. malice, perversity; suspicion;
maliciar, v.a. to corrupt, to adulterate; —, v.n. to suspect maliciously.
malicioso, sa, a. malicious, wicked, malign.
malignidad, sf. malignity, malice.
maligno, na, a. malignant, malicious.
malmandado, da, a. disobedient.
malo, la, a. bad; wicked; sickly, ill.
malograr, v.a. to lose (a chance); to miss; -se, to fail. [riage.
malogro, sm. disappointment, miscar-
malparado, da, a. injured, hurt.
malparida, sf. woman who has had a miscarriage.
malparir, v.n. to miscarry.
malparto, sm. abortion.
malquisiar, v.a. to set at variance.
malquisto, ta, a. hated, detested.
malrotar, v.a. to misspend, to lavish.
malsano, na, a. sickly; unwholesome.
maltratamiento, sm. ill-treatment.
maltratar, v.a. to treat ill, to abuse, to
malva, sf. (bot.) mallow. [maltreat.
malvado, da, a. wicked, perverse.
malvasía, sf. malmsey (wine).
malversación, sf. malversation. [bezzle.
malversar, v.a. to misapply; to em-
malvís, sm. (orn.) red-wing.
malla, sf. mesh, mash; coat of mail.
mallo, sm. mallet; bowls (game).
mama, sf. mamma.
mamar, v.a. to suck; to cram.
mamarrachada, sf. collection of daubs; foolish action or speech.

mamarrachista, sm. dauber. [ment.
mamarracho, sm. daub ; grotesque orna-
mameluco, sm. Mameluke ; dolt.
mamola, sf. chuck under the chin.
mamón, ona, sm. & f. sucking animal ;
child who is suckled for a long time.
mamotreto, sm. memorandum-book.
mampara, sf. screen.
mampostería, sf. rubble-work.
maná, sm. manna. [multitude.
manada, sf. flock, drove of cattle ; crowd,
manantial, sm. source, spring ; origin.
manar, v.n. to spring from ; to distil
from ; to issue ; to abound.
manceba, sf. concubine.
mancebo, sm. youth.
mancilla, sf. spot, blemish.
manco, ca, a. one-handed ; mained, faulty.
mancomún, de —, ad. jointly, by common
consent.
mancomunar, v.a. to associate, to unite ;
to make two or more persons pay
jointly the costs of a law-suit ; -se,
to act together, to join in the execution of a thing.
mancomunidad, sf. union, fellowship.
mancha, sf. stain, spot.
manchado, da, a. spotted.
manchar, v.a. to stain, to soil.
manda, sf. offer, proposal ; legacy
mandado, sm. mandate ; command ;
errand, message. [ment.
mandamiento, sm. mandate ; command-
mandar, v.a. to command, to order ; to
offer ; to bequeath ; to send.
mandarín, sm. mandarin.
mandatario, sm. representative, agent.
mandato, sm. mandate, order ; ecclesiastical ceremony of washing twelve
persons' feet on Maundy Thursday
mandíbula, sf. jaw-bone.
mandil, sm. coarse apron.
mando, sm. command, authority, power.
mandón, ona, a. imperious, domineering ;
—, sm. imperious, haughty person.
manecilla, sf. book-clasp ; hand (of clock).
manejable, a. manageable.
manejar, v.a. to manage ; -se, to recover
movement after an injury.
manejo, sm. management, administration ; horsemanship, manège.
manera, sf. manner, mode ; kind.
manes, sm.pl. manes, pl. (souls of the
dead).
manga, sf. sleeve ; tube ; water-spout ;
straining-bag.
mango, sm. handle, haft.
mangonear, v.n. to loiter.
manguito, sm. muff.
manía, sf. frenzy, madness.
maniatar, v.a. to manacle, to band-cuff.

maniático, ca, a. maniac, mad, frantic.
manicuro, sm. manicure, chiropodist.
manifactura, sf. manufacture.
manifestación, sf. manifestation.
manifestar, v.a. to manifest, to declare.
manifiesto, ta, a. manifest, open, clear ;
—, sm. act of exposing the Holy Sacrament ; manifesto.
manilla, sf. bracelet ; hand-cuff, manacle.
maniobra, sf. handiwork ; handling ;
cleverness in handling ; (mil.) manœuvre.
maniobrar, v.a. to work with the hands ;
to work a ship ; (mil.) to manœuvre
troops ; to intrigue.
maniota, hobble.
manipulación, sf. manipulation.
manipular, v.a. (fam.) to manipulate.
maniqueo, a, a. Manichean.
maniquí, sm. mannikin.
manir, v.a. to hang meat.
manirroto, ta, a. wasteful, too liberal.
manjar, sm. food, victuals.
mano, sf. hand ; hand of a clock or
watch ; first hand at play ; á —, at
hand ; with the hand.
manojo, sm. bundle of herbs, etc.
manopla, sf. gauntlet ; coachman's whip.
manosear, v.a. to handle.
manoseo, sm. handling.
manotada, sf. blow with the hand.
manoteo, sm. manual gesticulation.
mansedumbre, sf. meekness, gentleness
mansión, sf. sojourn, residence ; abode.
manso, sa, a. tame ; gentle, soft ; —,
sm. leading male in a flock of goats,
sheep or cattle.
manta, sf. blanket ; thrashing, drubbing
mantear, v.a. to toss in a blanket.
manteca, sf. fat ; butter.
mantecada, sf. buttered toast.
mantecado, sm. butter-cake.
mantecoso, sa, a. buttery.
mantel, sm. table-cloth.
mantelería, sf. table-linen.
manteleta, sf. mantelet.
mantellina, sf. mantle.
mantener, v.a. to maintain, to support ,
to nourish ; -se, to support oneself.
mantenimiento, sm. maintenance ; subsistence.
manteo, sm. cloak of priests and students.
mantequera, sf. churn.
mantequero, sm. butter-man.
mantequilla, sf. butter-cake.
mantilla, sf. mantilla, head-covering for
women ; cloak ; horsecloth ; swaddling-clothes.
manto, sm. mantle ; cloak, robe.
mantón, sm. large veil ; shawl.
manuable, a. tractable, manageable.

manual, a. manual, handy ; easily performed with the hand ; —, sm. manual.

manubrio, sm. handle.

manufactura, sf. manufacture.

manumitir, v.a. to release from slavery.

manuscrito, sm. manuscript ; —, a. written.   [ance.

manutención, sf. maintaining ; maintenmanzana, sf. apple.

manzanal, manzanar, sm. orchard.

manzanilla, sf. camomile.

manzano, sm. apple-tree.

maña, sf. handiness, dexterity, cleverness, cunning, artifice ; evil habit *or* custom.

mañana, sf. morning, morrow ; —, ad. to-morrow.

mañoso, sa, a. skilful, handy ; cunning.

mapa, sm. map.

mapamundi, sf. map of the world.

maquila, v.a. miller's due for grinding corn.

máquina, sf. machine ; (rail) engine.

maquinación, sf. machination.

maquinador, ra, sm. & f. schemer, machinator.

maquinalmente, ad. mechanically.

maquinar, v.a. to machinate ; to plot.

maquinaria, sf. mechanics.   [chanician.

maquinista, sm. engine-driver, memar, sm. & f. sea.

maraña, sf. shrub, thicket ; perplexity, puzzle ; intrigue.

marasmo, sm. (med.) marasmus.

maravedí, sm. maravedi (smallest Spanish coin, now obsolete).

maravilla, sf. wonder ; marvel ; á —, marvellously.

maravillar, v.a.·to surprise, to astonish ; -se, to wonder, to be astonished.

maravilloso, sa, a. wonderful, marvellous.

marca, sf. province, district ; due measure *or* weight of anything ; mark.

marcar, v.a. to mark ; to observe, to note, to designate.

marcial, a. martial, warlike ; frank. informal.

marco, sm. door-case, window-case ; picture-frame ; mark (weight of eight ounces) ; branding-iron.

márcola, sf. pruning-hook.

marcha, sf. march.

marchamar, v.a. to mark goods at the custom-house.

marchamo, sm. mark put on goods at the custom-house.

marchar, v.n. to go ; to go off ; to march.

marchitable, a. perishable.

marchitar, v.a. to wither ; to fade ; to deprive of vigour.

marchito, ta, a. faded, withered.

marea, sf. tide.

mareaje, sm. art of navigating a ship.

marear, v.a. to work a ship ; to molest ; -se, to be sea-sick.   [ance in a crowd.

marejada, sf. sea-swell, surge ; disturbmareo, sm. sea-sickness.

marfil, sm. ivory.   [winkle.

margarita, sf. pearl ; common daisy ; perimargen, sm. & f. margin ; border.

marginal, a. marginal.   [the margin.

marginar, v.a. to make annotations on

marica, sf. magpie ; milksop.

maricón, sm. coward, poltroon.

maridable, a. matrimonial.

marido, sm. husband.

marimacho, sm. virago.

marimanta, sf. bugbear.

marimorena, sf. dispute, quarrel.

marina, sf. navy.

marinaje, sm. seamanship ; crew.

marinar, v.a. to salt fish.   [men.

marinería, sf. seamanship ; body of seamarinero, ra, a. marine ; —, sm. mariner ; sailor.

marinesco, ca, a. nautical.

marino, na, a. marine ; —, sm. mariner, seaman.

mariposa, sf. butterfly ; night-light.

mariscal, sm. marshal ; farrier ; blacksmith.

marisco, sm. sea-shell.

marital, a. marital.

marítimo, ma, a. maritime, marine.

Maritornes, sf. ill-shaped, awkward woman.

marmita, sf. flesh-pot, porridge-pot.

marmitón, sm. scullion.

mármol, sm. marble.

marmolista, sm. worker in marble.

marmóreo, ea, a. marbled, marble.

marmota, sf. marmot.

maroma, sf. rope.

marqués, sm. marquis.

marquesa, sf. marchioness.

marquesado, sm. marquisate.

marrajo, sm. white shark ; —, ja, a. sly, cunning.

marrano, na, sm. & f. pig.

marras, ad. long ago, long since.

marro, sm. quoits (game) ; disappointment, failure.

marrón, sm. quoit, pitcher.   [trick.

marrullería, sf. knavery, cunning ; prank, marrullero, ra, a. crafty, cunning.

marsellés, sm. shooting-jacket.

marsopa, marsopla, sf.·porpoise.

marta, sf. marten.

martes, sm, Tuesday.

martillada, sf. blow with a hammer.

martillar, v.a. to hammer.

martillo, sm. hammer.

martinete, sm. sand-martin ; hammer in copper-works ; copper-mill.

mártir, sm. & f. martyr.

martirio, sm. martyrdom.

martirizar, v.a. to martyrize.

martirologio, sm. martyrology.

marzo, sm. March.

mas, ad. but, yet.

más, —, ad. more ; besides, moreover ; á — tardar, at latest ; sin — ni —, without more ado.

masa, sf. dough, paste ; mortar ; mass.

mascadura, sf. mastication.

mascar, v.a. to chew.

máscara, sm. & f. mask ; masker, masquerader ; pretext.

mascarada, sf. masquerade.

mascarilla, sf. small mask.

mascarón, sm. figure-head.

mascujar, v.n. to masticate with difficulty ; to mumble.

masculino, a. masculine, male.

mascullar, v.a. to falter in speaking, to mumble.

masera, sf. kneading-trough.

masticación, sf. mastication.

masticar, v.a. to masticate, to chew.

mástil, sm. (mar.) top-mast.

mastín, sm. mastiff.

mata, sf. shrub ; sprig, blade ; coppice ; lock of matted hair.

matachín, sm. merry-Andrew ; dance performed by grotesque figures.

matadero, sm. slaughter-house.

matador, sm. slayer.

matadura, sf. saddle-gall.

matanza, sf. slaughtering ; massacre.

matar, v.a. to kill ; to execute ; to murder ; to quench, to extinguish fire ; to slack lime ; to gall a horse, —se, to kill oneself, to commit suicide.

matasanos, sm. quack, charlatan, empiric.

matasiete, sm. bully, braggadocio.

mate, a. unpolished, dull ; — sm. checkmate.

maté, sm. beverage of *yerla Paraguaya*.

matemática, sf. mathematics.

matemático, ca, a. mathematical ; —, sm. mathematician. [matter (pus).

materia, sm. matter, materials ; subject ;

material, a. material, corporal ; rude ; uncouth ; —, sm. ingredient, materials, pl.

materialismo, sm. materialism.

materialista, sm. materialist.

maternal, a. maternal, motherly. [liness.

maternidad, sf. motherhood, mother-

materno, na, a. maternal, motherly.

matiz, sm. shade of colour ; shading.

matizar, v.a. to mix colours well ; to matón, sm. bully. [beautify.

matorral, sm. shrub, thicket.

matraca, sf. wooden rattle ; jest coxcomb. [mock, to ridicule.

matraquear, v.a. to jest, to scoff, to

matricida, sm. & f. matricide (person).

matricidio, sm. matricide (murder).

matrícula, sf. register, list.

matricular, v.a. to matriculate ; to enrol.

matrimonial, a. matrimonial, connubial.

matrimonio, sm. marriage, matrimony.

matriz, sf. matrix, womb ; mould, form.

matrona, sf. matron.

matute, sm. smuggling.

matutear, v.a. to smuggle.

matutero, ra, sm. & f. smuggler.

matutino, na, a. matutinal.

maula, sf. rubbish ; deceitful tricks, imposition ; —, sm. cheat, bad payer.

maulero, sm. impostor, cheat, swindler.

maullar, v.a. to mew.

maullido, sm. mew, cry of a cat.

mauseolo, mausoleo, sm. mausoleum.

máxima, sf. maxim.

máxime, ad. principally. [great.

máximo, ma, a. chief, principal ; very

mayo, sm. May ; May-pole.

mayor, a. greater, larger ; elder ; —, sm. superior ; major ; —, sf. first proposition in a syllogism ; por —, wholesale ; -es, sm. pl. forefathers.

mayoral, sm. head-shepherd, driver (of carriage), leader.

mayorazgo, sm. entail ; entailed estate ; heir in tail.

mayordomo, sm. steward.

mayoría, sf. advantage, excellence, superiority ; majority.

mayormente, ad. principally, chiefly.

mayúscula, sf. capital letter.

maza, sf. club ; mace ; importunate, troublesome fellow.

mazada, sf. blow with a mallet.

mazapán, sm. marchpane.

mazmorra, sf. dungeon.

mazo, sm. mallet ; bundle of ribands ; importunate, tiresome person.

mazorca, sf. ear of corn.

me, pn. me.

meadero, sm. urinal.

mear, v.n. to make water.

mecánica, sf. mechanics ; mean, despicable thing ; management.

mecánico, ca, a. mechanical ; —, sm. mechanician.

mecanismo, sm. mechanism.

mecer, v.a. to stir, to agitate ; to rock ; to dandle a child to rest.

mecha, sf. wick ; bacon with which fowls and meat are larded.

mechar, v.a. to lard.

mechero, sm. burner of a lamp; socket of a candlestick; —, de gas, burner.

mechinal, sm. square stones left projecting in a wall to be continued.

mechón, sm. large lock of hair; large bundle of threads or fibres.

medalla, sf. medal.

medallón, sm. medallion.

media, sf. stocking.

mediación, sf. mediation, intervention.

mediador, sm. mediator; go-between.

medianero, ra, a. mediating, interceding.

medianía, sf. moderation; mean.

mediano, na, a. moderate, middling; mediocre.

mediante, ad. by means of.

mediar, v.n. to be in the middle; to intercede for another; to mediate.

medicina, sf. physic; medicine.

medicinal, a. medicinal.

medicinar, v.a. to medicine.

médico, sm. physician; —, ca, a. medical.

medida, sf. measure.

medidor, sm. measurer.

mediero, sm. hosier.

medio, dia, a. half; á medias, by halves; —, sm. middle; expedient; way, mean; medium. [ocre.

mediocre, a. middling, moderate, mediocridad, sf. mediocrity.

mediodía, sm. noon, midday.

medir, v.a. to measure; -se, to be moderate.

meditación, sf. meditation.

meditar, v.a. to meditate. [inland.

mediterráneo, nea, a. mediterranean;

medra, sf. progress, improvement.

medrar, v.n. to thrive, to prosper; to improve. [ble.

medroso, sa, a. fearful, timorous; terri-

medula, médula, sf. marrow; principal substance; (fig.) pith. [rowy.

meduloso, sa, a. full of marrow, mar-

mejido, da, a. beaten up (of eggs).

mejilla, sf. check.

mejor, a. & ad. better. [growth.

mejora, sf. improvement, melioration.

mejorar, v.a. to improve, to ameliorate, to heighten; to cultivate; to mend; —, v.n. to recover, to grow well from a disease or calamity; -se, to improve, to grow better.

mejoría, sf. improvement, melioration; mending; repairs; improvement in health; advantage; superiority.

melada, sf. toasted bread steeped in honey.

melancolía, sf. melancholy. [gloomy.

melancólico, ca, a. melancholy, sad,

melena, sf. hair hanging over the eyes; dishevelled hair; mane.

melenudo, da, a. having bushy hair.

melífero, ra, a. productive of honey.

melifluo, flua, a. honey-mouthed; melli-fluous.

melindre, sf. fritters made with honey; prudery; affectation.

melindrear, v.n. to act the prude.

melindroso, sa, a. prudish, finical.

melocotón, sm. peach.

melodía, sf. melody.

melodioso, sa, a. melodious.

melodrama, sf. melodrama.

melón, sm. melon.

melonar, sm. bed of melons.

melosidad, sf. sweetness.

meloso, sa, a. honied; mellow.

melote, sm. molasses, treacle.

mella, sf. notch in edged tools; gap.

mellado, da, a. gap-toothed. [tarnish.

mellar, v.a. to notch; to damage, to

mellizo, za, a. twin.

membrana, sf. membrane.

membranoso, sa, a. membranous, filmy.

membrete, sm. memorandum, note; line of a letter containing the name of the addressee; invitation card.

membrillo, sm. quince-tree; quince.

membrudo, da, a. strong, robust; mem-bered. [the quick and the dead.

mementos, sm.pl. prayers at mass for

memorable, a. memorable.

memoria, sf. memory; memoir; -s, pl. compliments. [morial, brief.

memorial, sm. memorandum-book; me-

memorialista, sm. amanuensis; writer of petitions for others.

mención, sf. mention.

mencionar, v.a. to mention.

mendicante, a. mendicant, begging; —, sm. mendicant.

mendigar, v.a. to ask charity, to beg.

mendigo, sm. beggar.

mendiguez, sf. beggary. [beggars.

mendrugo, sm. broken bread given to

menear, v.a. to move from place to place; to manage; -se, to be brisk and active, to stir about.'

meneo, sm. waddling motion of the body

menester, sm. necessity, need, want; -es, pl. natural necessities, pl.

menesteroso, sa, a. needy, necessitous.

menestra, sf. pottage; soup.

menestral, sm. tradesman, handicrafts-man. [disgrace.

mengua, sf. decay, decline; poverty;

menguado, da, a. cowardly; foolish; avaricious; hora -a, fatal moment.

menguante, sf. ebb-tide, low-water; de-cline.

menguar, v.n. to decay, to fall off ; to ail, to diminisl .

menor, sm. & f. minor (one under age) ; minor (second proposition in the syllogism) ; —, a. less, smaller, minor ; por —, by retail, in small parts ; minutely.

menoría, sf. inferiority ; minority.

menos, ad. & sm. less ; with exception of ; á lo —, por lo — at least.

menoscabar, v.a. to lessen ; to make worse : to reduce. [ration, loss.

menoscabo, sm. diminution, deterioration.

menospreciar, v.a. to undervalue ; to despise, to contemn.

menosprecio, sm. contempt, scorn.

mensaje, sm. message, errand.

mensajero, sm. messenger.

mensual, a. monthly.

mentado, da, a. famous, renowned.

mental, a. mental, intellectual.

mentar, v.a. to mention. [meaning.

mente, sf. mind, understanding ; sense,

mentecato, ta, a. silly, crack-brained.

mentidero, sm. talking-corner.

mentir, v.a. to lie.

mentira, sf. lie, falsehood.

mentiroso, sa, a. lying. [minutely.

menudear, v.a. to repeat, to detail

menudencia, sf. trifle ; minuteness ; -s, pl. small matters.

menudillos, sm.pl. giblets of fowls.

menudo, da, a. small ; minute ; of no moment ; á —, repeatedly, often ; por —, minutely ; by retail ; -s, sm.pl. giblets.

meñique, sm. little finger.

meollo, sm. marrow. [low.

mequetrefe, sm. insignificant, noisy fel-

meramente, ad. merely, solely.

mercader, sm. dealer, trader.

mercadería, sf. commodity, merchandise ; trade.

mercado, sm. market ; market-place.

mercancía, sf. trade, traffic ; saleable goods.

mercantil, a. commercial, mercantile.

merced, sf. wages, favour, grace, mercy ; will, pleasure ; religious military order, whose chief object was to redeem captives ; estar á —, to live at another's expense. [mercenary.

mercenario, sm. day-labourer ; —, a.

mercería, sf. mercery.

mercero, sm. haberdasher.

mercurial, a. mercurial.

mercurio, sm. mercury, quick-silver.

merecedor, ra, a. deserving.

merecer, v.n. to deserve, to merit.

merecido, da, a. meritorious.

merendar, v.n. to take a light collation.

merengue, sm. meringue.

meretricio, cia, a. meretricious.

mergo, sm. (orn.) plungeon. [dional.

meridiano, sm. meridian ; —, a. meri-

meridional, a. southern, meridional.

merienda, sf. luncheon ; light refreshment. [merino (sheep).

merino, sm. shepherd ; —, na, a.

mérito, sm. merit, desert.

meritorio, ria, a. meritorious.

merluza, a. cod.

merma, sf. waste, leakage.

mermar, v.n. to waste, to diminish.

mermelada, sf. marmelade. [pure.

mero, sm. pollack ; —, ra, a. mere,

merodeador, sm. (mil.) marauder. [ing.

merodear, v.n. to pillage, to go maraud-

mes, sm. month.

mesa, sf. table ; committee ; —redonda, table d'hôte, ordinary.

mesada, sf. monthly pay or wages.

mesana, sf. (mar.) mizen-mast.

mesar, v.a. to tear one's hair out.

meseta, sf. landing (of a staircase).

Mesías, sm. Messiah.

mesón, sm. inn, hostelry.

mesonero, sm. inn-keeper.

mestizo, za, a. of mixed breed or race.

mesura, sf. grave deportment ; politeness ; moderation.

mesurado, da, a. moderate ; modest ; gentle ; prudent.

metafísica, sf. metaphysics.

metafísico, ca, a. metaphysical ; —, sm. metaphysician.

metáfora, sf. metaphor.

metafórico, ca, a. metaphorical.

metal, sm. metal ; brass, latten ; compass or strength of the voice.

metálico, ca, a. metallic.

metalurgia, sf. metallurgy.

metamorfósis, sf. metamorphosis, transformation.

metátesis, sf. metathesis, transposition.

metéoro, sm. meteor.

meteorología, sf. meteorology.

meter, v.a. to place, to put ; to occasion ; -se, to intermeddle, to interfere.

metódico, ca, a. methodical.

método, sm. method.

metralla, sf. grape-shot.

métrico, ca, a. a metrical.

metro, sm. metre ; verse.

metrópoli, sf. metropolis ; archiepiscopal church ; mother-country.

metropolitano, sm. metropolitan.

mezcla, sf. mixture, medley.

mezclar, v.a. to mix, to mingle ; -se, to mix ; to be connected by marriage.

mezquindad, sf. penury, poverty ; avarice ; meanness.

mezquino, na, a. poor, indigent ; avaricious, mean.

mezquita, sf. mosque.

mí, pn. acc. & dat. of pronoun yo ; —, a. my.

mico, sm. monkey.

microscópico, ca, a. microscopical.

microscopio, sm. microscope.

miedo, sm. fear, dread.

miel, sf. honey. [fish ; rake.

mielga, sf. (bot.) lucern ; small dog-

miembro, sm. member.

mientras, c., while ; — tanto, meantime.

miércoles, sm. Wednesday.

mierda, sf. excrement, ordure.

mies, sf. harvest. [crumbs.

miga, sf. crumb ; -s, pl. fried bread-

migaja, sf. scrap, crumb, small particle.

migajón, sm. crumb without crust.

migar, v.a. to crumble.

mijo, sm. (bot.) millet.

mil, sm. a thousand.

milagro, sm. miracle, wonder.

milagroso, sa, a. miraculous.

milano, sm. (orn.) kite.

milésimo, ma, a. thousandth.

milicia, sf. militia.

miliciano, sm. militia-man ; —, na, a. military. [the army.

militar, a. military ; —, v.n. to serve in

milla, sf. mile.

millar, sm. thousand.

millón, sm. million.

millonario, sm. millionaire.

mimar, v.a. to coax, to wheedle, to flatter ; to fondle, to caress.

mimbre, sm. twig of an osier.

mímico, ca, a. mimic.

mimo, sm. buffoon ; mime ; endearment, petting.

mimoso, sa, a. delicate, fond.

mina, sf. conduit, subterraneous canal ; mine ; source of water.

minador, sm. miner.

minar, v.a. to undermine, to mine.

mineral, sm. mineral ; spring of water ; —, a. mineral.

mineralogía, sf. mineralogy. [alogy.

mineralógico, ca, a. belonging to miner-

minero, sm. miner.

miniatura, sf. miniature.

mínima, sf. (mus.) minim.

mínimo, ma, a. least, smallest.

minio, sm. red-lead.

ministerio, sm. ministry (office).

ministril, sm. tipstaff ; petty officer of justice ; minstrel.

ministro, sm. minister ; Minister of state ; magistrate.

minorar, v.a. to lessen, to diminish.

minoridad, sf. minority.

minucioso, sa, a. superfluously exact.

minúscula, a. small (applied to letters).

minuta, sf. minute, first draught of an agreement. [or clock.

minutero, sm. minute-hand of a watch

minuto, sm. minute.

mío, mía, a. my, mine.

miope, a. near-sighted.

mira, sf. sight of a gun ; needle or point for directing the sight ; estar á la —, to be on the look-out.

mirada, sf. glance ; gaze.

mirador, ra, sm. & f. spectator, looker-on ; —, sm. watch-tower, gazebo.

miramiento, sm. consideration ; circumspection.

mirar, v.a. to behold, to look ; to observe, to spy ; —, v.imp. to concern ; por lo que mira á, as to, concerning ; -se, to consider one's own interests.

mirlo, sm. blackbird.

mirón, cna, a. & sm. & f. prier ; inquisitive, officious.

mirra, sf. myrrh.

mirto, sm. myrtle.

misa, sf. mass.

misal, sm. missal.

misantropía, sf. misanthropy.

misántropo, sm. misanthropist.

miscelánea, sf. miscellany.

miserable, a. miserable, wretched, unhappy ; exhausted ; avaricious.

miserere, sm. the Miserere.

miseria, sf. misery ; niggardliness ; trifle.

misericordia, sf. mercy ; clemency.

misericordioso, sa, a. merciful, clement.

misión, sf. mission.

misionero, sm. missionary.

mismo, ma, a. same, similar.

misterio, sm. mystery.

misterioso, sa, a. mysterious, mystical.

mística, sf. mystical theology.

místico, ca, a. mystic, mystical.

mitad, sf. moiety, half.

mitigación, sf. mitigation.

mitigar, v.a. to mitigate.

mitología, sf. mythology.

mitológico, ca, a. mythological.

mitones, sm.pl. mittens.

mitra, sf. mitre.

mitrado, a. mitred.

mixtión, sf. mixing, mixture.

mixto, ta, misto, ta, a. mixed, mingled.

mixtura, sf. mixture.

mocadero, sm. pocket-handkerchief.

mocedad, sf. youthfulness.

moción, sf. motion.

moco, sm. mucus ; snuff of a candle.

mocosidad, sf. mucosity.

mocoso, sa, a. snively ; mucous.

mochila, sf. knapsack.

mocho, cha, a. dishorned, polled; cropped, shorn; lopped; maimed, mutilated.

mochuelo, sm red owl.

moda, sf. fashion, mode.

modelar, v.a. to model, to form.

modelo, sm. model, pattern.

moderación, sf. moderation; temperance.

moderado, da, a. moderate, temperate.

moderar, v.a. to moderate.

moderno, na, a. modern.

modestia, sf. modesty, decency.

modesto, ta, a. modest.

modificación, sf. modification; limita- [tion.

modificar, v.a. to modify; to moderate.

modista, sf. milliner, dressmaker.

modo, sm. mode, method, manner moderation; mood.

modorra, sf. drowsiness.

modorrar, v.a. to render heavy with sleep; -se, to become over-ripe.

modorro, rra, a. drowsy, sleepy.

modulación, sf. modulation.

modular, v.a. to modulate.

mofa, sf. mockery.

mofador, ra, sm. & f. scoffer, scorner.

mofar, v.a. & r. to deride; to mock; to scoff.

mofeta, sf. fire-damp.

moflete, sm. chubby cheek. [sponger.

mogollón, sm. hanger-on, parasite,

mohecer, v.a. to cover with mould.

mohina, sf. animosity, desire of revenge, resentment, grudge.

mohino, na, a. fretful, peevish.

moho, sm. moss, mould.

mohoso, sa, a. mouldy, musty; mossy.

mojadura, sf. act of moistening or wetting.

mojar, v.a. to wet, to moisten; —, v.n. (col.) to meddle, to interfere.

moje, sm. broth.

mojicón, sm. cuff, punch.

mojiganga, sf. masquerade; mummery.

mojigato, a. hypocritical.

mojón, sm. land-mark.

moldar, v.a. to mould.

molde, sm. mould; model.

moldura, sf. moulding.

mole, sf. bulk.

molécula, sf. molecule. [bore.

moledor, sm. grinder; tiresome fellow,

moler, v.a. to grind, to pound; to vex, to molest; to waste, to consume by use. [trouble.

molestar, v.a. to vex, to molest, to

molestia, sf. injury, molestation.

molesto, ta, a. vexatious, troublesome.

molicie, sf. tenderness, softness.

molienda, sf. act of grinding or pounding; fatigue, lassitude.

molinero, sm. miller.

molinete, sm. windlass; turnstile.

molinillo, sm. hand-mill.

molino, sm. mill.

mollar, a. soft, pappy; credulous.

molleja, sf. gizzard.

mollera, sf. crown of the head.

mollete, sm. muffin.

momentáneo, nea, a. momentaneous.

momento, sm. moment.

momería, sf. mummery.

momio, mia, a. meagre, lean.

momia, sf. mummy.

momo, sm. buffoonery, grimaces.

mona, sf. female monkey; ludicrous imitator; drunkenness.

monacal, a. monastic, monkish.

monacillo, sm. acolyte. [object.

monada, sf. grimace; treasure; pretty

monago, monaguillo, sm. acolyte.

monarca, sm. monarch.

monarquía, sf. monarchy.

monárquico, ca, a. monarchical.

monasterio, sm. monastery, cloister.

monástico, ca, a. monastic.

monda, sf. pruning of trees.

mondadientes, sm. toothpick.

mondadura, sf. cleaning, cleansing; -s, pl. parings, peelings.

mondar, v.a. to clean, to cleanse; to husk, to peel; to deprive of money

mondo, da, a. neat, clean, pure; — y lirondo, without any admixture.

mondongo, sm. paunch, tripe.

moneda, sf. money, coinage.

moned(e)ar, v.a. to coin.

monedero, sm. coiner.

monería, sf. grimace, mimicry; trifle, gewgaw.

monetario, sm. cabinet of coins.

monición, sf. admonition; publication of the banns (of marriage).

mónita, sf. cunning, craft.

monitor, sm. admonisher; monitor; (mar.) monitor (ship).

monje, sm. monja, sf. monk; nun.

mono, na, a. neat, pretty, nice; —, sm. monkey, ape.

monólogo, sm. monologue.

monopolio, sm. monopoly. [liser.

monopolista, sm. monopolist, monopo-

monosílabo, ba, a. monosyllabical; —, sm. monosyllable.

monotonía, sf. monotony.

monótono, na, v.n. monotonous.

monstruo, sm. monster.

monstruosidad, sf. monstrosity.

monstruoso, sa, a. monstrous.

monta, sf. amount, sum total.

montaña, sf. wooded or hilly country, forest.

montañés, esa, a. pertaining to the mountains; mountainous; —, s. mountaineer, Cantabrian.

montañoso, sa, a. mountainous.

montar, v.n. to mount (on horseback); to amount to.

montaraz, a mountainous; wild, untamed.

monte, sm. mountain; wood, forest; difficulty; a card game.

montera, sf. peasant's cap.

montería, sf. hunting, chase.

montero, sm. huntsman, hunter.

montés, esa, montesino, na, a. bred or found in a forest or mountain.

montón, sm. heap, pile; mass, cluster; á -ones, abundantly, by heaps.

montuoso, sa, a. mountainous, hilly.

montura, sf. mount (horse, etc.); saddle.

monumento, sm. monument; catafalque raised in churches on Holy Thursday.

monzón, sm. monsoon.

moña, sf. doll.

moño, sm. chignon, roll of hair, top-knot; crest or top-knot of birds.

moquear, v.n. to blow the nose.

moquero, sm. pocket-handkerchief.

moquete, sm. blow on the face or nose.

moquillo, sm. pip (disease in fowls).

moquita, sf. snivel.

morada, sf. habitation, abode, residence.

morado, da, a. violet, mulberry-coloured.

morador, sm. inhabitant, lodger.

moral, sm. mulberry-tree; —, sf. morals, ethics; —, a. moral.

moralidad, sf. morality.

moralista, sm. moralist.

moralizar, v.n. to moralise.

moralmente, ad. morally.

morar, v.n. to inhabit, to dwell.

moratoria, sf. delay granted to a debtor.

mórbido, da, a. morbid, diseased; soft, mellow.

morboso, sa, a. diseased, morbid.

morcilla, sf. black-pudding.

mordacidad, sf. sarcasm.

mordaz, a. corrosive, biting; sarcastic.

mordaza, sf. gag.

mordedura, sf. bite.

morder, v.a. to bite.

mordiscar, v.a. to gnaw, to nibble.

mordisco, mordiscón, sm. bite.

morena, sf. sea-eel.

moreno, na, a. brown, swarthy.

morga, sf. dregs of oil.

moribundo, da, a. dying.

morigeración, sf. temperance.

morigerar, v.a. to moderate.

morillo, sm. andiron.

morir, v.n. to die, to expire; -se, to go out, to be extinguished; to be benumbed.

morisco, ca, a. Moorish; —, sm. name given to the Moors who remained in Spain after the Christian re-conquest.

morisma, sf. Mohammedan sect; multitude of Moors.

moriaco, ca, a. affecting ignorance and stupidity.

moro, ra, a. Moorish.

morondanga, sf. hodge-podge.

morondo, da, a. bald; leafless.

morosidad, sf. slowness, delay, tardiness, dilatoriness.

moroso, sa, a. slow, tardy, heavy.

morrada, sf. butting with the heads between two people.

morral, sm. fodder-bag, nose-bag. sportsman's-bag.

morralla, sf. hotch-potch. [of a sheep.

morrillo, sm pebble; fat of the nape

morriña, sf. murrain; sadness, melancholy.

morrión, sm. morion, spike-helmet.

morro, sm. any round skull-like object; overhanging lip; promontory, cape.

morrudo, da, a. blubber-lipped.

mortaja, sf. shroud, winding-sheet; mortise.

mortal, a. mortal; fatal, deadly.

mortalidad, sf. mortality.

mortandad, sf. excessive mortality.

morterete, sm. small mortar for firing at festivities.

mortero, sm. mortar (cannon).

mortífero, ra, a. fatal. [trouble.

mortificación, sf. mortification; vexation,

mortificar, v.a. to mortify; to afflict, to vex. [mortuary.

mortuorio, sm. burial, funeral; —, a.

moruno, na, a. Moorish.

mosaico, ca, a. Mosaic; mosaic.

mosca, sf. fly. [prater.

moscardón, sm. large gad-fly; bore,

moscatel, a. muscatel grape. [fellow.

moscón, sm. large fly; crafty, deceitful

mosquero, sm. fly-trap; fly-flap.

mosquetería, sf. body of musketeers; musketry.

mosquetero, sm. musketeer.

mosquitero, sm. mosquito-net.

mosquito, sm. gnat, mosquito; tippler.

mostachón, sm. marchpane.

mostaza, sf. mustard; mustard-seed.

mostillo, sm. sauce made of must.

mosto, sm. must, new wine.

mostrador, sm. shop-counter.

mostrar, v.a. to show, to exhibit; -se, to appear, to show oneself.

mostrenco, ca, a. ownerless; vagabond, vagrant; stupid, dull.

mota, sf. bit of thread, &c., sticking to cloth; slight defect or fault.

mote, sm. nickname.

motejar, v.a. to censure, to ridicule.

motilar, v.a. to cut off the hair, to crop.

motín, sm. mutiny.   [a motive.

motivar, v.a. to give a reason, to assign

motivo, sm. motive, cause, reason.

motor, sm. mover, motor; motor-car; —, a. movable.

motriz, a. motive, causing.

movedizo, za, a. movable; variable, inconstant.

mover, v.a. to move; to touch pathetically; to stir up; to excite.

movible, a. movable.

móvil, a. movable.

movilidad, sf. mobility; inconstancy.

movimiento, sm. movement, motion; sedition.

moza, sf. girl, lass; maid-servant.

mozo, za, a. young; —, sm. youth, lad; man-servant.

mozuelo, sm. boy, youth.

muceta, sf. bishop's cape.

muchacha, sf. girl; lass.

muchachada, sf. boyish trick.

muchacho, sm. boy; lad; —, cha, a. boyish, girlish.

muchedumbre, sf. multitude, plenty.

mucho, cha, a. much, abundant; —, ad. much.

muda, sf. change, alteration; act of moulting.

mudable, a. changeable, variable, mutable.

mudanza, sf. change; mutation; inconstancy.

mudar, v.a. to change; to mew, to moult; to change one's voice; -se, to change; to change sentiments and manners; to shift; to change house.

mudez, sf. dumbness.

mudo, da, a. dumb; silent, mute.

mueble, sm. piece of furniture.

mueblaje, sm. furniture, set of furniture.

mueca, sf. grimace, wry face.

muela, sf. upper mill-stone; grindstone; mill-dam; hillock; molartooth, back-tooth.

muelle, a. tender, delicate, soft; —, sm. spring (of watch, etc.); quay, wharf, mole.

muérdago, sm. (bot.) mistletoe.

muermo, sm. glanders.

muerte, sf. death.

muerto, sm. corpse; —, ta, a. dead.

muesca, sf. notch, groove.

muestra, sf. pattern, sample; copy written to be imitated by boys; indicative sign; specimen, design, model; (mil.) muster-roll; dial, face of clock; watch.

mugido, sm. lowing of an ox.

mugir, v.n. to low, to bellow.   [&c.

mugre, sm. dirt sticking to clothes,

mugriento, ta, a. greasy, dirty, filthy.

mujer, sf. woman.

mujeril, a. womanish, womanly.

mula, sf. mule.

muladar, sm. manure-heap; anything very dirty.

mular, a. belonging to mules.

mulatero, sm. muleteer.

mulato, a. mulatto.

muleta, sf. crutch.

mulo, sm. mule.

multa, sf. mulct, fine, penalty.

multar, v.a. to fine.

multiplicación, sf. multiplication.

multiplicador, ra, sm. & f. multiplier; (ar.) multiplicator.

multiplicando, sm. (ar.) multiplicand.

multiplicar, v.a. to multiply.

multíplice, a. multiple; multiplicious.

multiplicidad, sf. multiplicity.

multitud, sf. multitude, great number.

mullir, v.a. to beat up, to soften.

mundano, na, a. mundane, worldly.

mundinovi, mundonuevo, sm. rareeshow, magic-lantern.

mundo, sm. world.

munición, sf. ammunition.

municionar, v.a. to munition.

municipal, a. municipal.

munificencia, sf. munificence, liberality.

muñeca, sf. wrist; doll.

muñeco, sm. puppet; effeminate fellow.

muñidor, sm. beadle of a corporation; messenger.   [limb.

muñón, sm. stump of an amputated

muralla, sf. rampart, wall.

murciélago, sm. bat.

murmullo, sm. murmur, mutter.

murmuración, sf. backbiting, privy calumny.   [backbiter.

murmurador, ra, sm. & f. detractor,

murmurar, v.a. to murmur, to purl; to backbite.   [stream.

murmurio, sm. murmuring of a

muro, sm. wall.

murria, sf. heaviness of the head.

musa, sf. Muse.   [vermin.

musaraña, sf. shrew-mouse; hobgoblin;

muscular, a. muscular.

músculo, sm. muscle.

muselina, sf. muslin.

museo, sm. museum.

musgo, sm. moss.

música, sf. music.

musical, a. musical.

músico, ca, s. musician; —, a. musical.

muslo, sm. thigh.

mustiamente, ad. sadly, in a melancholy manner.

mustio, tia, a. parched, withered ; sad, sorrowful ; musty.
mutabilidad, sf. mutability, inconstancy.
mutación, sf. mutation, change.

mutilación, sf. mutilation.
mutilar, v.a. to mutilate, to maim.
mutual, mutuo, tua, a. mutual, reciprocal
muy, ad. very ; greatly.

N

nabal, nabar, sm. turnip-field ; —, a. made of turnips.
nabo, sm. turnip.
nácar, sm. mother of pearl, nacre.
nacarado, da, a. set with mother of pearl ; pearl-coloured.
nacer, v.n. to be born, to bud, to shoot (of plants) ; to rise ; to grow.
nacido, da, a. innate, inborn ; apt, fit : —, sm. tumour, abscess ; -s, pl. all men born.
nacimiento, sm. birth ; Nativity.
nación, sf. nation.
nacional, a. national.
nacionalidad, sf. nationality.
nada, sf. nothing ; una —, a trifle ; —, ad. in no way, by no means.
nadaderas, sf.pl. swimming-bladders (for learning to swim).
nadadero, sm. swimming-place.
nadador, ra, sm. & f. swimmer.
nadar, v.n. to swim.
nadie, pn. nobody, no one.
nado, á —, ad. afloat.
naipe, sm. playing-card.
nalga, sf. buttock, rump.
ñao, sf. ship, vessel.
naranja, sf. orange.   [orange-water.
naranjada, sf. conserve of oranges ;
naranjado, da, a. orange-coloured.
naranjal, sm. orangery.
naranjero, sm. orange-seller.
naranjo, sm. orange-tree.
narciso, sm. (bot.) daffodil ; narcissus flower ; fop, coxcomb.
narcótico, ca, a. narcotic.
nardo, sm. spikenard.   [big-nosed.
narigón, sm. large nose : —, ona. a.
narigudo, da, a. big-nosed.
nariz, sf. nose ; sense of smelling.
narración, sf. narration.
narrar, v.a. to narrate, to tell.
narrativa, sf. narrative, relation ; talent for narration.
nata, sf. cream.
natal, a. natal, native.
natalicio, cia, a. natal.
natillas, sf.pl. custard.
natividad, sf. nativity.
nativo, va, a. native.
natural, sm. temper, natural disposition ; —, a. natural, native ; common, usual ; ingenuous, unaffected.

naturaleza, sf. nature.
naturalidad, sf. birthright ; naturalness ; ingenuity, candour.
naturalista, sm. naturalist.
naturalizar, v.n. to naturalize ; -se, to become accustomed.
naufragar, v.n. to be shipwrecked, to suffer wreck ; to suffer ruin.
naufragio, sm. shipwreck.
náufrago, ga, a. shipwrecked.
náusea, sf. nauseousness, nausea.
náutica, sf. art of navigating.
navaja, sf. clasp-knife ; razor.
navajada, sf. gash given with a knife.
navajero, sm. razor-case.
naval, a. naval.
nave, sf. ship ; nave.
navegable, a. navigable.
navegación, sf. navigation
navegador, navegante, sm. navigator.
navegar, v.n. to navigate.
naveta, sf. censer.
navidad, sf. nativity ; Christmas.
navío, sm. ship.
náyade, sf. naiad, water-nymph.
neblina, sf. mist, fog.
nebuloso, sa, a. misty, cloudy, nebulous, foggy, hazy, drizzling.
necear, v.n. to talk nonsense.
necedad, sf. gross ignorance, stupidity ; imprudence.
necesaria, sf. privy, water-closet.
necesario, ria, a. necessary.
necesidad, sf. necessity, need, want.
necesitado, da, a. necessitous, needy.
necesitar, v.a. to necessitate, to oblige, to compel ; to want, to need.
necio, cia, a. ignorant, stupid, foolish ; imprudent.
necrología, sf. necrology, an account of persons deceased.
necrologia, sm. obituary.
néctar, sm. nectar.   [able.
nefando, da, a. base, nefarious, abomin-
nefario, ria, a. nefarious, abominable.
negación, sf. negation.
negado, a. incapable, unfit.
negar, v.a. to deny ; to refuse ; -se, to decline to do a thing.   [tive.
negativa, sf. negation ; repulse ; nega-
negativo, va, a. negative.
negligencia, sf. negligence.   [less.
negligente, a. negligent, careless, heed-

negociación, sf. negotiation.

negociante, sm. & f. trader, dealer

negociar, v.n. to negotiate (bills of exchange, political affairs). [tion.

negocio, sm. business, affair; negotiation.

negrear, v.n. to grow black, to appear black. [blackamoor.

negro, gra, a. black; —, sm. negro,

negrura, sf. blackness.

negruzco, ca, a. blackish.

nene, sm., nena, sf. baby.

neófito, sm. neophyte.

nervio, sm. nerve.

nervioso, sa, a. nervous.

nervudo, da, a. nervous, vigorous.

nesga, sf. gore (of a gown).

neto, ta, a. neat, pure; (com.) net, nett.

neutral, a. neutral, neuter.

neutralidad, sf. neutrality.

neutralizar, v.a. to neutralize.

neutro, tra, a. neutral, neuter.

nevada, sf. heavy fall of snow.

nevar, v.n. to snow.

nevera, nevería, sf. ice-house.

ni, c. neither, nor.

nicho, sm. niche.

nido, sm. nest; habitation.

niebla, sf. fog, mist.

nieto, ta, sm. & f. grandchild.

nieve, sf. snow.

nigromancia, sf. necromancy.

nigromante, sm. necromancer.

nigromántico, ca, a. necromantic.

nimiamente, ad. excessively. [nicety.

nimiedad, sf. excess; extravagant

nimio, mia, a. excessive, too much.

ninfa, sf. nymph.

ningún, ninguno, na, a. none, not one, neither. [the eye.

niña, sf. little girl; pupil, apple of

niñada, sf. puerility, childishness.

niñear, v.n. to act like a child.

niñera, sf. nursemaid.

niñería, sf. puerility, childish action.

niñero, ra, a. fond of children.

niñez, sf. childhood.

niño, ña, a. childish; —, sm. & f. child, infant; desde —, from infancy, from a child.

níspero, sm. medlar-tree.

níspola, sf. medlar.

nitro, sm. nitre, saltpetre. [level.

nivel, sm. level, plane; á —, perfectly

nivelador, sm. leveller.

nivelar, v.a. to level.

no, ad. no; not.

noble, a. noble, illustrious, generous.

nobleza, sf. nobleness, nobility.

noción, sf. notion, idea.

nocivo, va, a. noxious, hurtful.

nocturno, na, a. nocturnal, nightly.

noche, sf. night; — buena, Christmas Eve; ¡ buenas —s ! good night !

nodriza, sf. nurse.

nogal, sm. walnut-tree.

nómade, a. nomad, nomadic.

nombradía, sf. fame, reputation.

nombramiento, sm. nomination; appointment. [to appoint.

nombrar, v.a. to name; to nominate,

nombre, sm. name; title; reputation.

nomenclatura, sf. nomenclature; cata-nómina, sf. catalogue. [logue.

nominador, sm. nominator.

nominal, a. nominal.

nominativo, sm. (gr.) nominative.

non, a. odd, uneven.

nonada, sf. trifle.

nonagenario, ria, a. ninety years old; —, sm. & f. nonagenarian.

nonagésimo, ma, a. ninetieth.

nono, na, a. ninth. [standing.

no obstante, ad. nevertheless, notwithnordest(e), sm. north-east.

noria, sf. chain-pump; draw-well.

norma, sf. square (tool); rule.

noroeste, sm. north-west.

norte, sm. north; polar star; rule, guide.

nos, pn. we.

nosotros, tras, pn. we, ourselves.

nostalgia, sf. home-sickness.

nota, sf. note, notice, remark.

notable, a. notable, remarkable.

notar, v.a. to note, to mark; to remark.

notaría, sf. notary's office.

notario, sm. notary.

noticia, sf. notice, knowledge, information, note; news.

noticiar, v.a. to give notice.

noticioso, sa, a. informed; learned.

notificación, sf. notification.

notificar, v.a. to notify, to inform.

notoriedad, sf. notoriety.

notorio, ria, a. notorious.

novación, sf. renewal of an obligation formerly contracted.

noval, a. newly broken ground, and the fruits it produces. [anything.

novato, ta, a. new, commencing in

novator, sm. innovator.

novecientos, tas, a. nine hundred.

novedad, sf. novelty, modernness; turn for the worse (in health); admiration excited by novelties.

novela, sf. novel, story, fiction.

novelero, ra, a. fond of novels; fond of hearing and telling news; new-fangled; inconstant; —, sm. news-monger.

novena, sf. term of nine days' worship.

novenario, sm. novenary.

noveno, na, a. ninth.

noventa, sm. ninety.
novia, sf. bride ; woman betrothed.
noviciado, sm. novitiate.
novicio, sm. novice.
noviembre, sm. November.
novilunio, sm. new-moon.
novilla, sf. heifer.
novillada, sf. drove of young bulls ; fight of young bulls.
novillo, sm. young bull or ox.
novio, sm. bridegroom.
novísimo, **ma**, a. newest ; —, sm. either of the four last events of man (death, judgment, heaven and hell).
nubada, sf. shower of rain ; plenty.
nubado, **da**, a. clouded (of stuffs).
nubarrón, sm. heavy shower of rain, large cloud.
nube, sf. cloud ; film.
nublado, sm. clouds announcing a storm.
nublar, v.a. to cloud ; -se, v.r. to cloud over ; to be afflicted, to be clouded.
nuca, sf. nape, scruff of the neck.
núcleo, sm. kernel of a nut.
nudillo, sm. knuckle.
nudo, sm. knot ; knuckle.
nudoso, **sa**, a. knotty.
nuera, sf. daughter-in-law.
nuestro, **tra**, a. our.
nueva, sf. news.
nueve, sm. & a. nine.

nuevo, **va**, a. new, modern, fresh ; ¿ qué hay de — ? is there any news ? what news ?
nuez, sf. walnut ; Adam's apple ; —) moscado ó de especia, nutmeg.
nulidad, sf. nullity.
nulo, **la**, a. null.
numen, sm. divinity ; inspiration poetical genius.
numeración, sf. numeration.
numerador, sm. numerator.
numeral, a. numeral.
numerar, v.a. to number, to count.
numerario, **ria**, sm. hard cash, coin.
numérico, **ca**, a. numerical.
número, sm. number ; cipher.
Números, sm.pl. the book of Numbers.
numeroso, **sa**, a. numerous.
nunca, ad. never.
nuncio, sm. messenger ; Nuncio.
nuncupativo, **va**, a. (law) verbally pronounced.
nupcial, a. nuptial.
nupcias, sf.pl. nuptials, wedding.
nutra, **nutria**, sf. otter.
nutrición, sf. nutrition.
nutrimento, sm. food, aliment, nourishment ; nutrition.
nutrir, v.a. to nourish.
nutritivo, **va**, a. nutritive, nourishing.
nutriz, sf. nurse.

Ñ

ñagaza, sf. bird-call.
ñaque, sm. hodge-podge.
ñoclos, sm.pl. kind of macaroons.

ñoño, **ña**, a. decrepit, impaired by age.
ñoñería, sf. dotage.

O

ó, c. or ; either.
¡ o ! interj. oh !
obcecación, sf. obduracy.
obcecar, v.a. to blind, to darken.
obedecer, v.a. to obey.
obediencia, sf. obedience.
obediente, a. obedient.
obelisco, sm. obelisk.
obenques, sm.pl. (mar.) shrouds, pl.
obertura, sf. (mus.) overture.
obesidad, sf. obesity, fatness.
obeso, **sa**, a. obese, fat.
óbice, sm. obstacle.
obispado, sm. bishopric ; episcopate.
obispillo, sm. boy-bishop ; large black-pudding ; crop of a fowl.
obispo, sm. bishop.   [ception.
objeción, sf. objection, opposition, ex-

objetar, v.a. to object, to oppose.
objetivo, **va**, a. objective.
objeto, sm. object.
oblación, sf. oblation, offering.
oblada, sf. funeral offering.
oblata, sf. money given to defray expense of celebrating mass ; host and chalice offered before being consecrated in the celebration of mass.
oblea, sf. wafer.
oblicuidad, sf. obliquity.
oblicuo, **cua**, a. oblique.
obligación, sf. obligation ; debenture.
obligado, sm. public contractor.
obligar, v.a. to oblige.
obligatorio, **ria**, a. obligatory.
oblongo, **ga**, a. oblong.
oboe, sm. hautboy, oboe.

óbolo, sm. obolus.

obra, sf. work ; means, virtue, power ; toil, work, labour, employment.

obrada, sf. day's work.

obrador, ra, sm. & f. workman, work-woman ; artificer ; workshop.

obrar, v.a. to work ; to operate, to act ; to put into practice. [labourer.

obrero, ra, sm. & f. workman ; day-

obscenidad, sf. obscenity.

obsceno, na, a. obscene.

obscurecer, v.a. to obscure, to darken ; —, v.n. to grow dark ; -se, to disappear.

obscuridad, sf. obscurity ; darkness.

obscuro, ra, a. obscure, dark.

obsequiar, v.a. to court, to entertain.

obsequio, sm. compliance ; civility, courteous attention.

obsequioso, sa, a. obsequious, attentive, civil.

observación, sf. observation ; remark.

observador, sm. observer. [reverence.

observancia, sf. observance ; ceremonial

observar, v.a. to observe.

observatorio, sm. observatory.

obstáculo, sm. obstacle, impediment, hindrance. [hinder.

obstar, v.n. to oppose, to obstruct, to

obstinación, sf. obstinacy, stubbornness.

obstinado, a. obstinate.

obstinarse, v.r. to be obstinate.

obstruir, v.a. to obstruct ; -se, to be blocked up, to be obstructed.

obtener, v.a. to obtain.

obturar, v.a. to stop up.

obtuso, sa, a. obtuse, blunt.

obué, sm. (mus.) hautboy.

obús, sm. (mil.) howitzer ; shell.

obvención, sf. perquisite.

obviar, va, to obviate, to prevent.

obvio, via, a. obvious, evident.

ocasión, sf. occasion, opportunity, danger, risk.

ocasional, a. occasional.

ocasionar, v.a. to cause, to occasion ; to move, to excite.

ocaso, sm. setting (of sun, etc.).

occidental, a. occidental, western.

occidente, sm. occident, west.

océano, sm. ocean.

ocio, sm. leisure ; pastime.

ociosidad, sf. idleness, leisure.

ocioso, sa, a. idle ; vacant ; profitable.

ocre, sm. ochre.

octava, sf. octave.

octavo, va, a. eighth.

octubre, sm. October.

ocular, a. ocular ; —, sm. eye-glass.

oculista, sm. oculist.

ocultación, sf. concealment.

ocultar, v.a. to hide, to conceal.

oculto, ta, a. hidden, concealed, secret.

ocupación, sf. occupation ; business, employment.

ocupar, v.a. to occupy, to hold an office ; -se, to be busy, to follow a business.

ocurrencia, sf. occurrence, accident ; idea occurring to the mind ; witticism.

ocurrir, v.n. to meet ; to occur, to happen.

ochavado, da, a. octagonal, eight-sided.

ochavar, v.a. to form an octagon.

ochavo, sm. small brass coin of two maravedies (now obsolete).

ochenta, a. eighty.

ocho, sm. & a. eight.

ochocientos, a. eight hundred.

oda, sf. ode. [another.

odiar, v.a. to hate ; -se, to hate one

odio, sm. hatred.

odioso, sa, a. odious, hateful.

odorífero, ra, a. odoriferous, fragrant.

odre, sm. wine-bag ; drunkard.

oeste, sm. west.

ofender, v.a. to offend, to injure ; -se, to be vexed ; to take offence.

ofensa, sf. offence, injury.

ofensivo, va, a. offensive, injurious.

ofensor, sm. offender.

oferta, sf. offer ; offering. [clerk.

oficial, sm. workman, artificer ; officer ;

oficiala, sf. work-woman.

oficiar, v.a. to officiate, to minister (of clergymen, &c.).

oficina, sf. workshop ; office, counting-house, business-room.

oficio, sm. office, employ, occupation, ministry ; function ; official letter ; trade, business ; -s, pl. divine service.

oficiosidad, sf. diligence ; officiousness ; importunity. [dling.

oficioso, sa, a. officious, diligent ; med-

ofrecer, v.a. to offer ; to present ; to exhibit ; -se, to occur, to present itself.

ofrecimiento, sm. offer, promise.

ofrenda, sf. offering, oblation.

ofrendar, v.a. to offer to God.

ofuscación, sf. dimness of sight ; obfuscation. [scure.

ofuscar, v.a. to darken, to render ob-

oídas, de ó por —, by hearsay.

oído, sm. hearing ; ear ; touch-hole.

oidor, sm. hearer ; Judge.

oir, v.a. to hear ; to listen ; to understand.

ojal, sm. button-hole.

¡ ojalá ! would to God ! God grant !

ojalar, v.a. to make button-holes.

ojeada, sf. eye-glance, ogle.

ojear, v.a. to rouse or put up game ; to frighten.

g

ojera, sf. dark line under the eye.
ojeriza, sf. spite, grudge, ill-will.
ojete, sm. eyelet-hole in clothes.
ojiva, sf. pointed arch.
ojival, a. ogival, Gothic.
ojo, sm. eye ; sight ; eye of a needle ; arch of a bridge.
ola, sf. wave.
olaje, sm. succession of waves, seaswell.
oleada, sf. surge ; violent emotion.
olear, v.a. to administer extreme unction.
óleo, sm. oil ; extreme unction ; holy oil.
oler, v.a. to smell, to scent ; —, v.n. to smell ; to smack of.
olfato, sm. odour ; scent.
oligarquía, sf. oligarchy.
oligárquico, ca, a. oligarchical.
olímpico, ca, a. olympic.
Olimpo, sm. (poet.) heaven.
oliva, sf. olive ; olive-tree ; owl.
olivar, sm. olive-grove.
olivo, sm. olive-tree.
olmo, sm. elm-tree.
olor, sm. odour, scent.
oloroso, sa, a. fragrant, odorous.
olvidadizo, za, a. forgetful.
olvidar, v.a. to forget.
olvido, sm. forgetfulness.
olla, sf. round pot ; whirl-pool ; — podrida, stew of meat and vegetables.
ollería, sf. pottery.
ollero, sm. potter.
ombligo, sm. navel.
ominoso, sa, a. ominous.
omisión, sf. omission.
omitir, v.a. to omit.
omnibus, sm. omnibus.
omnipotencia, sf. omnipotence.
omnipotente, a. omnipotent, almighty.
omniscio, scia, a. all-knowing.
once, sm. & a. eleven.
onceno, na, a. eleventh.
onda, sf. wave.   [-se, to see-saw.
ondear, v.a. to undulate ; to fluctuate ; to see-saw.
oneroso, sa, a. burdensome.
ontología, sf. ontology.
onza, sf. ounce ; linx.
onzavo, va, a. eleventh ; —, sm. eleventh part
opacidad, sf. opacity, gloom ; darkness.
opaco, ca, a. opaque, dark ; melancholy, gloomy.
opción, sf. option, choice.
ópera, sf. opera.
operación, sf. operation.
operar, v.n. to operate, to act.
operario, sm. operator, labourer.
opiata, sf. opiate.
opilar, v.a. to obstruct.
ópimo, ma a. rich, fruitful.

opinable, a. problematic.
opinión, sf. opinion.
opio, sm. opium.
opíparo, ra, a. sumptuous.
oponer, v.a. to oppose ; -se, to oppose, to be opposite.
oportunidad, sf. opportunity.
oportuno, na, a. seasonable, opportune.
oposición, sf. opposition ; competition of skill.
opositor, sm. opposer, opponent.
opresión, sf. oppression.
opresivo, va, a. oppressive.
opresor, sm, oppressor.
oprimir, v.a. to oppress ; to crush, to press, to squeeze.
oprobio, sm. opprobrium, ignominy.
optar, v.a. to choose, to elect.
optativo, sm. (gr.) optative.
óptica, sf. optics.
óptico, ca, a. optical ; —, sm. optician.
optimista, sm. optimist.
óptimo, ma, a. best.   [verse
opuesto, ta, a. opposite, contrary, adverse
opulencia, sf. wealth, riches.
opulento, ta, a. opulent, wealthy.
opúsculo, sm. opuscule, pamphlet.
oración, sf. oration, speech ; prayer -ones, pl. prayers at sunset.
oráculo, sm. oracle.
orador, sm. orator.
orar, v.n. to harangue ; to pray.
orate, sm. & f. lunatic, madcap.
oratoria, sf. oratory, rhetorical skill.
oratorio, sm. oratory ; oratorio ; —, ria, a. rhetorical.   [tial body.
orbe, sm. orb, sphere, the earth ; celesórbita, sf. orbit.
orden, sm. order, rule, regulation ; —, sf command.
ordenación, sf. arrangement ; ordination ; edict, ordinance.   [orders.
ordenando, sm. candidate for holy
ordenanza, sf. order ; statute, ordinance ; ordination.
ordenar, v.a. to arrange ; to order ; to ordain ; -se, to take holy orders.
ordeñar, v.a. to milk.
ordinal, a. ordinal.
ordinario, ria, a. ordinary, common ; —, sm. ordinary ; established judge of ecclesiastical cases ; carrier, carman ; de —, regularly, commonly, ordinarily.
orear, v.a. to cool, to refresh ; to air ; -se, to take the air.
orégano, sm. wild marjoram.
oreja, sf. ear.
orejón, sm. preserved peach ; nobleman of the ancient nobility of Peru.
oreo, sm breeze, fresh air.
orfandad, sf. orphanage.

organero, sm. organ-builder.
orgánico, ca, a. organic.
organista, sm. organist. [ment.
organización, sf. organization; arrange-
organizar, v.a. to organize.
órgano, sm. organ.
orgullo, sm. pride, haughtiness.
orgulloso, sa, a. proud, haughty.
oriental, a. oriental, eastern.
oriente, sm. orient; east.
orificio, sm. orifice, mouth, aperture.
origen, sm. origin, source; native country; family, extraction. [original.
original, a. original, primitive; —, sm.
originalidad, sf. originality.
originar, v.a. & n. to originate.
orilla, sf. limit, border, margin; edge of
cloth; footpath in a street; shore.
orillar, v.a. to arrange, to order.
orillo, sm. list, selvage.
orín, sm. rust.
orina, sf. urine.
orinal, sm. chamber-pot.
orinar, v.n. to make water.
oriundo, da, a. derived from.
orla, sf. list, selvage, border.
orladura, sf. border, edging, list.
orlar, v.a. to border, to edge. [ment.
ornamento, sm. ornament, embellish-
ornato, sm. apparel, ornament.
oro, sm. gold; -s, pl. diamonds (cards).
oropel, sm. tinsel.
orquesta, sf. orchestra.
ortiga, sf. (bot.) nettle.
ortodoxia, sf. orthodoxy.
ortodoxo, xa, a. orthodox.
ortografía, sf. orthography.
ortográfico, ca, a. orthographical.
o.uga, sf. (bot.) rocket; caterpillar.
orujo, sm. peel of pressed grapes.
orza, sf. gallipot, crock.
os, pn. you.
osa, sf. she-bear.
osadamente, ad. boldly, daringly.
osadía, sf. boldness, intrepidity; zeal,
fervour.
osamenta, sf. skeleton.

osar, v.n. to dare, to venture.
osario, sm. charnel-house.
oscilación, sf. oscillation.
oscilar, v.n. to oscillate.
ósculo, sm. kiss.
oscurecer, v.a. & n. to darken.
oscuridad, sf. darkness.
oscuro, ra, a. dark, obscure.
osificarse, v.r. to ossify.
oso, sm. bear; — blanco, polar bear.
ostensible, a. ostensible, apparent.
ostensión, sf. show, exhibition, manifestation.
ostentación, sf. ostentation, ambitious
display. [boast, to brag.
ostentar, v.a. to show; —, vn. to
ostentoso, sa, a. sumptuous, ostentatious.
ostra, sf. oyster.
ostrera, sf. oyster-bed; oyster-woman.
osudo, da, a. bony, full of bones.
otoñal, a. autumnal.
otoñar, v.n. to spend the autumn-
season; to grow in autumn; -se, to
be seasoned (of earth after rain).
otoño, sm. autumn. [contract.
otorgamiento, sm. grant, licence, license;
otorgar, v.a. to grant, to consent.
otro, tra, a. another, other. [item.
otrosí, ad. besides, moreover; —, sm.
ova, sf. sea-weed.
ovación, sf. ovation.
ovalado, da, a. oval.
óvalo, sm. oval.
ovar, v.n. to lay eggs.
ovario, sm. ovary. [(sea).
oveja, sf. ewe; -s, pl. white horses
ovejero, sm. shepherd.
ovejuno, na, a. relating to ewes.
ovillar, v.n. to reel off; to coil up; -se,
to double oneself up.
ovillo, sm. clew.
ovíparo, ra, a. oviparous, egg-bearing.
ovoso, sa, a. full of sea-weed.
óxido, sf. (chem.) oxide.
oxígeno, sm. (chem.) oxygen.
oyente, a. & sm. & f. hearing; auditor,
hearer.

P

pabellón, sm. pavilion; summer-house.
pábilo, sm. wick; snuff of a candle.
pábulo, sm. food, provender; aliment.
paca, sf. bale, bundle.
pacato, ta, a. pacific, quiet, mild, gentle,
peaceable.
pacer, v.a. to pasture, to graze.
paciencia, sf. patience.
paciente, a. & sm. patient. [mind.
pacificación, sf. pacification; peace of

pacificar, v.a. to pacify, to appease; —,
v.n. to treat for peace.
pacífico, ca, a. pacific, peaceful.
pacotilla, sf. private speculation (at sea).
pactar, v.a. to contract, to stipulate.
pacto, sm. contract, pact.
pachorra, sf. sluggishness.
padecer, v.a. to suffer; to sustain an injury; to be liable to.
padecimien'o, sm. suffering.

padrastro, sm. stepfather.
padrazo, sm. over-indulgent father.
padre, sm. father : **-s,** pl. parents ; ancestors.
padrino, sm. godfather ; second (in duel) ; protector, assistant.   [tern, model.
padrón, sm. poll ; indulgent parent ; patpat-
paella, sf. pillau, savoury rice.
paga, sf. payment, fee.
pagadero, ra, a. payable.
pagador, sm. payer ; paymaster.
paganismo, sm. paganism, heathenism.
pagano, sm. heathen, pagan ; —, **na,** a. heathenish ; pagan.
pagar, v.a. to pay ; to requite ; **-se,** to be pleased with oneself.
pagaré, sm. bond, note of hand, promissory note, I. O. U. (I owe you).
página, sf. page of a book.
pago, sm. payment ; reward.
país, sm. country, region.
paisaje, sm. landscape.
paisajista, sm. landscape-painter.
paisano, na, a. of the same country ; —, sm. countryman.   [with straws.
paja, sf. straw ; **echar -s,** to draw lots
pajar, sm. straw-loft.   [loiter about.
pajarear, v.a. to go bird-catching ; to
pajarera, sf. aviary.
pajarero, sm. bird-catcher.
pájaro, sm. bird ; sly, acute fellow.
pajarota, pajarotada, sf. false, idle report.
pajarraco, pajarruco, sm. large bird ; cunning fellow.
paje, sm. page.
pajero, sm. dealer in straw.
pajizo, za, a. made of straw ; thatched with straw ; straw-coloured.
pajuela, sf. match, torch.
pala, sf. shovel ; fire-shovel.
palabra, sf. word ; **á media —,** at the least hint ; **de —,** by word of mouth.
palabrada, sf. low language.
palabrita, sf. word full of meaning : pregnant saying, dictum.
palaciego, ga, a. pertaining or relating to the palace ; —, sm. courtier.
palacio, sm. palace.
palada, sf. a shovel-full.
paladar, sm. palate ; taste, relish.
paladín, sm. paladin.
paladino, na, a. manifest, clear, public.
palafrén, sm. palfrey.
palafrenero, sm. groom.
palanca, sf. lever.
palancada, sf. leverage.
palancana, palangana, sf. basin.
palanquera, sf. enclosure made with stakes.
palanqueta, sf. bar-shot ; small lever.
palatinado, sm. palatinate.

palatino, na, a. belonging to the palace or courtiers.
palco, sm. box in a theatre.
palenque, sm. palisade.
palestra, sf. inclosure, palisade ; palestra ; art of wrestling.
paleta, sf. shovel ; palette ; trowel.
paletada, sf. trowel-full.
paleto, sm. fallow deer ; clown, rustic.
palia, sf. altar-cloth ; square.   [cloak.
paliar, v.a. to palliate, to excuse ; to
paliativo, va, a. palliative.
palidez, sf. paleness, wanness.
pálido, da, a. pallid, pale.
palillero, sm. one who make or sells tooth-picks ; tooth-pick case.
palillo, sm. knitting-needle case ; rolling-pin ; bobbin.
palinodia, sf. palinode, recantation
palio, sm. cloak ; pall.
palique, sm. trifling conversation.
palitroque, sm. rough, ill-shaped stick.
paliza, sf. cudgelling, drubbing with a
palizada, sf. palisade.   [stick.
palma, sf. date palm-tree ; palm of the hand ; palm-leaf.
palmada, sf. slap with the hand ; clapping of hands.
palmatoria, sf. flat candle-stick.
palmear, v.a. to slap with the open hand ; to clap.
palmera, sf. palm-tree.
palmeta, sf. ferule.
palmo, sm. palm (length).   [hand.
palmotear, v.a. to slap with the open
palmoteo, sm. clapping of hands.
palo, sm. stick ; cudgel ; blow given with a stick ; execution on the gallows ; clubs (at cards) ; mast.
paloma, sf. pigeon, dove ; — **torcaz,** ring-dove.
palomar, sm. pigeon-house.
palomera, sf. bleak place, much exposed to the wind.
palomilla, sf. young pigeon ; back-bone of a horse ; chrysalis ; horse of a milk-white colour.
palomino, sm. young pigeon.
palomo, sm. cock-pigeon.
palotada, sf. stroke with a battledore.
palote, sm. drum-stick ; **-s,** pl. thick lines copied by children learning to write.
paloteo, sm. fight with sticks ; clash.
palpable, a. palpable, evident.
palpar, v.a. to feel, to touch, to grope.
palpitación, sf. palpitation, panting.
palpitar, v.n. to palpitate.
palurdo, da, a. rustic, clownish, rude.
pámpana, sf. vine-leaf.   [tendril.
pámpano, sm. young vine-branch or

pampirolada, sf. fig. & col.) impertinence.

pamplina, sf. duck-weed ; futility, trifle.

pampringada, sf. frivolous thing.

pan, sm. bread ; loaf ; food in general ; wheat ; gold-lead, silver-leaf.

pana, sf. velveteen, plush.

panacea, sf. panacea, universal medicine.

panadería, sf. trade of a baker ; bakehouse.

panadero, sm. baker.

panadizo, sm. whitlow ; sickly person.

panal, sm. honey-comb.

panarra, sm. dolt, simpleton.

pandereta, sf., pandero, sm. tambourine.

pandilla, sf. plot, league.

pando, da, a. bulging, convex.

pandorga, sf. fat, bulky woman.

panecillo, sm. roll, small loaf.

panegírico, ca, a. eulogistic ; —, sm. eulogy.

panera, sf. granary. [person.

pánfilo, sm. slow, sluggish, heavy

pánico, ca, a. panic. [bread.

paniego, ga, a. eating or yielding much

panilla, sf. small measure of oil.

panoja, sf. ear of maize.

panorama, sm. panorama.

pantalón, sm. pantaloon.

pantalla, sf. fire-guard, lamp-shade.

pantano, sm. pool of stagnant water ; morass ; obstacle, difficulty.

pantanoso, sa, a. marshy, fenny, boggy.

panteísta, sm. pantheist.

panteón, sm. Pantheon.

pantera, sf. panther.

pantomima, sf. pantomime.

pantomímico, ca, a. pantomimical.

pantorrilla, sf. calf (of the leg).

pantuflo, sm. slipper, shoe.

panza, sf. belly, paunch.

panzada, sf. belly-full of food.

panzudo, da, a. big-bellied.

pañal, sm. swaddling-cloth ; cloth in which anything is wrapped up ; tail of a shirt.

pañero, sm. woollen-draper, clothier.

paño, sm. cloth ; breadth of cloth.

pañuelo, sm. handkerchief. [toes.

papa, sm. pope ; —, sf. pap ; -s, pl. potatoes.

papá, sm. papa.

papada, sf. double-chin.

papado, sm. popedom, papacy.

papagayo, sm. parrot.

papal, a. papal, papistical.

papalina, sf. cap with ear-flaps.

papamoscas, sm. (orn.) fly-catcher.

papanatas, sm. oaf, simpleton, ninny.

paparrucha, sf. hoax.

papel, sm. paper ; writing ; part acted in a play ; — sellado, stamped paper.

papelera, sf. writing-desk, paper-case.

papelería, sf. large bundle of papers without order.

papelero, sm. paper-manufacturer.

papeleta, sf. printed form, certificate.

papera, sf. wen on the throat.

papilla, sf. pap ; guile, deceit.

papirotada, sf. fillip on the neck or face ;

papirote, sm. fillip. [rap on the nose.

papista, sm. papist.

papo, sm. double-chin.

papudo, da, a. double-chinned

paquebote, sm. packetboat.

paquete, sm. packet, bundle.

par, a. equal, alike, even ; sin—, matchless ; —, sm. pair ; Peer.

para, pr. for, to, in order to, towards, to the end that.

parabién, sm. congratulation.

parábola, sf. parable ; parabola.

parabólico, ca, a. parabolical.

paracleto, sm. Paraclete (name given to the Holy Ghost).

parachoques, sm.pl. (rail.) buffers.

parada, sf. halt ; suspension ; pause ; relay ; dam, bank ; stake, bet ; (mil.) parade.

paradero, sm. halting-place ; term, end.

parado, da, a. remiss, careless, indolent.

paradoja, sf. paradox.

parador, sm. one who stops ; inn.

parafrasear, v.a. to paraphrase.

paráfrasis, sf. paraphrase.

paraguas, sm. umbrella.

paraíso, sm. Paradise ; (theat.) gallery.

paraje, sm. place, residence ; condition disposition.

paralelo, la, a. & sm. parallel.

paralelógramo, sm. parallelogram. long.

paralítico, ca, a. paralytic, palsied.

paralogismo, sm. paralogism, false reasoning. [place extremely cold.

páramo, sm. desert, wilderness ; any

parangón, sm. model, comparison.

parangonar, v.a. to compare, to parallel.

parapeto, sm. parapet, breast-work.

parar, v.n. to stop, to halt ; —, v.a. to stop, to detain ; to treat ill ; to stake at cards ; — en mal, to have a bad end ; sin —, instantly, without delay ; -se, to stop, to halt ; —, sm. lansquenet (game at cards).

pararrayo, sm. lightning-rod, conductor.

parasismo, sm. paroxysm, fit.

parásito, sm. parasite, sponger.

parasol, sm. parasol.

parca, sf. (poet.) Fate, Fatal Sister.

parcial, a. partial.

parcialidad, sf. partiality ; sociability ; party, faction. [moderate.

parco, ca, a. sparing, scanty ; sober.

parche, sm. plaster ; drum-skin.
pardal, a. clownish, rustic ; —, sm. grey sand-piper.
pardear, v.n. to grow grey or brownish ; to become dusky.
pardillo, sm. linnet.
pardo, da, a. grey.
pardusco, ca, a. greyish, grizzly.
parear, v.a. to match, to pair, to couple.
parecer, sm. opinion, advice, counsel ; countenance, air, mien ; —, v.n. to appear ; to seem ; -se, to resemble.
parecido, da, a. resembling, like.
pared, sf. wall.　　　　　[(dancing).
pareja, sf. pair, couple, brace ; partner
parentela, sf. parentage, kindred.
parentesco, sm. kindred ; relationship.
paréntesis, sm. parenthesis.
pares y nones, sm.pl. even or odd.
paria, sm. pariah.
parias, sf.pl. tribute paid by one prince to another as an acknowledgment of superiority.
parida, sf. woman lately delivered.
paridad, sf. parity, equality.　[woman.
pariente, ta, sm. & f. kinsman ; kins-
parihuela, sf. barrow.
parir, v.a. to bring forth ; to produce ; to lie in ; to lay eggs.
parla, sf. talk, loquacity, gossip.
parlador, ra, a. & sm. & f. prater.
parlamental, a. parliamentary.　[ley.
parlamentar, v.n. to converse ; to par-
parlamentario, sm. member of parliament ; —, a. parliamentary.
parlamento, sm. harangue ; parliament.
parlanchín, na, a. & sm. & f. chatterer, jabberer.
parlar, v.a. to chatter, to talk.
parleta, sf. small talk.　　　[gossip.
parlotear, v.n. to prate, to chatter, to
Parnaso, sm. (poet.) Parnassus.
parodia, sf. parody.
parola, sf. eloquence ; chatter.
parpadear, v.n. to blink.
párpado, sm. eyelid.
parque, sm. park ; (mil.) park of artillery.
parra, sf. vine raised on stakes.
párrafo, sm. paragraph.
parral, sm. vine-arbour.
parricida, sm. & f. parricide (person).
parricidio, sm. parricide (murder).
parrillas, sf.pl. gridiron.
parro, sm. duck.
párroco, sm. parson.
parroquia, sf. parish.
parroquial, a. parochial.
parroquiano, sm. parishioner ; customer ; —, a. parochial.
parsimonia, sf. parsimony.
parte, sf. part ; side ; party.

partero, ra, sm. & f. midwife.
partible, a. divisible, partible.
partición, sf. partition, division.
participación, sf. participation.
participar, v.a. & n. to grant ; to participate, to partake.
partícipe, a. participant, sharing.
participio, sm. participle.
partícula, sf. particle.
particular, a. particular, special ; —, sm individual ; peculiar matter, particular.　　　　[ship, intimacy.
particularidad, sf. particularity ; friend-
particularizar, v.a. & r. to particularize.
partida, sf. departure ; party of soldiers ; item in an account ; game ; -s, pl. parts, talents, accomplishments ; the laws of Castile.
partidario, sm. partisan.
partido, sm. party ; district.
partidor, sm. parter, divider.
partir, v.a. to part, to divide, to separate, to cut, to cleave ; to break ; —, v.n. to depart ; -se, to differ in opinion.
parto, sm. child-birth.
parva, sf. unthrashed corn ; multitude.
parvidad, sf. littleness, minuteness.
parvo, va, a. small, little.
párvulo, la, a. very small ; innocent ; —, sm. child.
pasa, sf. raisin.
pasada, sf. passage ; pace, step ; manner, behaviour ; de —, on the way, in passing.
pasadera, sf. stepping-stone.
pasadero, ra, a. supportable, sufferable ; passable ; —, sm. stepping-stone.
pasadizo, sm. narrow passage ; alley, subway.　　　　　[cestors.
pasado, sm. (gr.) past time ; -s, pl. an-
pasador, sm. smuggler ; bolt of a lock ; woman's brooch.
pasaje, sm. passage.
pasajero, ra, a. transient, transitory, fugitive ; —, sm. & f. traveller, passenger.
pasamanería, sf. lace-making.
pasamano, sm. lace ; balustrade.
pasante, sm. assistant of a physician or lawyer.　　　　　[lough.
pasaporte, sm. passport ; (mil.) fur-
pasar, v.a. to pass ; to surpass ; to suffer ; to go through ; —, v.n. to pass ; to happen ; -se, to go over to another party ; to become corrupt or putrid, to rot.
pasatiempo, sm. pastime, amusement.
pasavolante, sm. inconsiderate speech or action, indiscretion ; seaman entered in the muster-book, but not actually existing.
Pascua, sf. Passover ; Easter.

pascual, a. paschal.
pase, sm. pass-bill; permit, license.
paseante, sm. walker; — en corte, suitor for office, hanger-on.
pasear, v.a. & n. to walk; to walk about; -se, to walk for exercise or amusement; to loiter.
paseito, sm. stroll.
paseo, sm. walk, jaunt, pleasure-trip.
pasible, a. passible, susceptible.
pasillo, sm. narrow passage.
pasión, sf. passion.
pasionaria, sf. passion-flower.
pasito, ad. gently, softly.
pasivo, va, a. passive.
pasmar, v.a. to cause a spasm; to benumb; to amaze; -se, to suffer spasms; to be astonished.
pasmo, sm. spasm, convulsion; astonishment, amazement.
pasmoso, sa, a. marvellous, wonderful.
paso, sm. pace, step; passage; manner of walking; flight of steps; accident; (rail.) — á nivel, railway-crossing; al —, on the way, in passing.
pasquín, sm. pasquinade, lampoon.
pasta, sf. paste.
pastar, v.a. to pasture, to graze.
pastel, sm. pie; crayon for drawing.
pastelería, sf. pastrycook's shop; pastry.
pastelero, sm. pastrycook.
pastilla, sf. lozenge.   [—, abundantly.
pasto, sm. pasture; pasture-ground; á
pastor, sm. shepherd; pastor.
pastoral, pastoril, a. pastoral, rural.
pastoso, sa, a. mellow, doughy.
pastura, sf. pasture; pasture-ground.
pasturaje, sm. pasturage.
pata, sf. foot and leg of an animal; duck.
patada, sf. kick; step, pace.
patagón, sm. large, clumsy foot; dollar.
patalear, v.n. to kick about violently.
pataleo, sm. stamping one's foot.
pataleta, sf. convulsion.
patán, sm. clown, churl, countryman.
patarata, sf. fiction, false story; kick-patata, sf. potato.   [shaw.
patatús, sm. swoon, fainting-fit.
patear, v.a. to kick.
patena, sf. patine.
patente, a. patent, manifest, evident; —, sf. patent; warrant; (mar.) letters of marque; bill of health.
paternal, a. paternal, fatherly.
paternidad, sf. paternity, fatherhood.
paterno, na, a. paternal, fatherly.
patético, ca, a. pathetic.
patíbulo, sm. gibbet, gallows.
paticojo, ja, a. lame, crippled.
patilla, sf. whiskers; -s, pl. (col.) devil.
patín, sm. skate, ice-spur.

patio, sm. yard, court-yard; pit (of theatre).
patitieso, sa, a. stupefied, surprised.
patituerto, ta, a. crook-legged.
patizambo, ba, a. bandy-legged.
pato, ta, sm. & f. duck.
patochada, sf. blunder, nonsense, folly.
patología, sf. pathology.
patraña, sf. fable, invention.
patria, sf. native country.
patriarca, sm. patriarch.
patriarcado, sm. patriarchate.
patriarcal, a. patriarchal.
patricio, sm. patrician.
patrimonial, a. patrimonial.
patrimonio, sm. patrimony.
patrio, tria, a. native, paternal.
patriota, sm. & f. patriot.
patriótico, ca, a. patriotic.
patriotismo, sm. patriotism.
patrocinar, v.a. to favour, to patronise, to protect.
patrocinio, sm. protection, patronage.
patrón, sm. patron, protector; skipper of a vessel; landlord of a house or inn; employer, master; patron saint of a country, town, &c.
patrona, sf. patroness, mistress.
patronato, patronazgo, sm. patronage.
patronímico, sm. patronymic.
patrono, sm. patron; lord of the manor.
patrulla, sf. (mil.) patrol.
patrullar, v.n. to patrol.
patudo, da, a. club-footed.
paulatino, na, a. slowly, by degrees.
pausa, sf. pause; repose; á -s, by intervals.   [quiet.
pausado, da, a. slow, deliberate; calm,
pausar, v.n. to pause.
pauta, sf. ruler.
pautar, v.a. to rule (paper).
pava, sf. turkey-hen; pea-hen.
pavesa, sf. embers, hot cinders; remains, relics.
pávido, da, a. timid, fearful.
pavimento, sm. pavement.
pavipollo, sm. young turkey.
pavo, sm. turkey; — real, peacock.
pavonear, v.n. to strut, to walk with affected dignity.
pavoroso, sa, a. awful, formidable.
pavura, sf. fear, dread, terror.
payo, sm. clown, churl.
paz, sf. peace; tranquillity, ease.
pe, ad. de — á pa, entirely, from beginning to end.
peaje, sm. toll.
peal, sm. sock; worthless person.
peana, sf. pedestal.
peatón, sm. rural postman.
peazgo, sm. bridge-toll.

pebete, sf. pastille for fumigation ; fusee,
pebetero, sm. censer.   [match.
peca, sf. freckle, spot.
pecado, sm. sin.
pecador, ra, sm. & f. sinner.
pecaminoso, sa, a. sinful.
pecar, v.n. to sin.
pécora, sf. sheep ; cunning fellow, knave.
pecoso, sa, a. freckled.
pectoral, a. pectoral ; —, sm. cross worn
    by bishops on the breast.
peculiar, a. peculiar, special.
peculio, sm. allowance (money).
pecunia, sf. hard cash, specie.
pecuniario, ria, a. pecuniary.
pechar, v.n. to pay taxes.
pechera, sf. stomacher ; frill.
pechero, ra, a. liable to pay tazes ; —,
    sm. commoner, plebeian ; bib.
pecho, sm. breast ; teat ; bosom ; cou-
    rage, valour ; tax, contribution ;
    tener —, to have patience ; tomar á -s,
    to take to heart.
pechuga, sf. breast of a fowl ; bosom.
pechuguera, sf. cough, hoarseness.
pedagogo, sm. pedagogue.   [courts).
pedáneo, a. petty, inferior (of law
pedante, sm. pedant.
pedantear, v.n. to play the pedant.
pedantería, sf. pedantry.
pedantesco, ca, a. pedantic.
pedantismo, sm. pedantry.
pedazo, sm. piece, bit.
pedernal, sm. flint.
pedestal, sm. pedestal, foot.
pedicular, a. lousy.
pedicuro, sm. chiropodist.
pedido, sm. voluntary contribution to
    the State ; request.
pedigüeño, ña, a. begging.
pedimento, sm. petition.
pedir, v.a. to petition, to beg, to suppli-
    cate, to solicit.
pedo, sm. wind from the bowels.
pedorrero, ra, a. flatulent.
pedrada, sf. throw of a stone.
pedrea, sf. stone-throwing.   [stones.
pedregal, sm. shingle ; place full of
pedregoso, sa, a. stony.
pedrera, sf. quarry, stone-pit.
pedrería, sf. collection of precious stones.
pedrero, sm. stone-cutter ; slinger ;
    lapidary.
pedrisco, sm. hail-stone.
pedrusco, sm. rough piece of marble.
pega, sf. pitch ; glue.   [tagious.
pegadizo, za, a. sticky, viscous ; con-
pegado, sm. sticking-plaster, cataplasm.
pegadura, sf. pitching.
pegajoso, sa, a. sticky, viscous ; con-
    tagious ; attractive.

pegar, v.a. to cement ; to join, to unite ;
    to beat ; — fuego, to set fire to ; —,
    v.n. to take root ; to stick ; -se, to
    intrude, to steal in.
Pegaso, sm. Pegasus.
pegote, sm. pitch-plaster ; impertinent
    intruder, hanger-on, sponger.
peinado, sm. combed, dressed.   [gown.
peinador, sm. hair-dresser ; dressing
peinar, v.a. to comb.
peine, sm. comb.
peinero, sm. & f. comb-maker.
peladilla, sf. sugared almond ; small
    pebble.
peladura, sf. plucking.
pelafustán, sm. ragamuffin.   [hair.
pelaje, sm. colour or tint of animals'
pelambre, sm. tufts of hair.
pelar, v.a. to pluck ; to peel, to strip.
peldaño, sm. step, stair.
pelea, sf. battle, fight ; quarrel.
pelear, v.a. to fight, to combat ; -se, to
    scuffle.   [cant fellow.
pelele, sm. man of straw ; insignifi-
peletería, sf. trade of a furrier ; fell-
    monger's shop.
peletero, sm. furrier.
peliagudo, da, a. furry ; arduous, diffi-
    cult ; ingenious, dexterous.
pelícano, sm. pelican ; —, a. grey-
    haired ; hoary.
pelicorto, ta, a. short-haired.
película, sf. pellicle.
peligrar, v.n. to be in danger ; to risk.
peligro, sm. danger, risk, peril.
peligroso, sa, a. dangerous, perilous.
pelillo, sm. short, tender hair ; trifle.
pelma, sf., pelmazo, sm. heavy paste ;
    food which lies heavy on the stomach.
pelo, sm. hair ; pile ; flaw (in precious
    stones) ; á —, to the purpose, timely.
pelón, ona, a. hairless, bald.
pelota, sf. ball ; — de viento, football.
pelotazo, sm. blow with a ball.
pelote, sm. goat's hair.
pelotear, v.n. to play at ball ; to argue,
    to dispute.
pelotera, sf. women's quarrel.
pelotero, sm. ball-maker.
pelotón, sm. large ball ; (mil.) platoon.
peltre, sm. pewter.
peltrero, sm. pewterer.
peluca, sf. wig, peruke ; reproof.
peludo, da, a. hairy.
peluquería, sf. hair-dresser's shop.
peluquero, sm. hair-dresser, barber.
pelusa, sf. fluff.
pella, sf. ball ; clew ; mass of crude
    metal ; unprepared lard ; (orn.) heron.
pellada, sf. gentle blow.
pelleja, sf. skin stripped from an animal.

pellejería, sf.- fellmonger's shop.
pellejero, sm. fellmonger, leather-dresser.
pellejo, sm. skin, hide; pelt; peel; wine-skin; oil-skin; tippler, drunkard, fuddler.
pellejudo, da, a. thick-skinned.
pellica, sf. coverlet of fine furs.
pellico, sm. fur coat.
pelliza, sf. pelisse.
pellizcar, v.a. to pinch.
pellizco, sm. pinch; nip; small bit; (fig.) remorse.
pena, sf. punishment, pain; á duras -s, with great difficulty or trouble.
penacho, sm. tuft, plume; crest; pride, haughtiness.
penal, a. penal. [ship; penalty.
penalidad, sf. suffering, trouble; hard-
penar, v.n. to suffer pain; —, v.a. to chastise; -se, to grieve, to mourn.
penates, sm.pl. Penates, household-gods, pl. [lash.
penca, sf. prickly leaf of a plant; scourge,
pendencia, sf. quarrel, dispute.
pendenciero, ra, a. quarrelsome.
pender, v.n. to hang, to impend; to depend; to be irresolute.
pendiente, sm. & f. slope, declivity; -s, pl. ear-rings.
péndola, sf. pendulum.
pendolista, sm. penman, writer.
pendón, sm. standard; banner.
péndulo, la, a. pendent, hanging; —, sm. pendulum.
penetrable, a. penetrable; comprehensible. [intelligence.
penetración, sf. penetration; complete
penetrar, v.a. to penetrate; -se, to coexist as two bodies in the same place.
península, sf. peninsula.
penique, sm. penny.
penitencia, sf. penitence; penance.
penitencial, a. penitential.
penitenciar, v.a. to impose a penance.
penitenciaría, sf. prison.
penitenciario, sm. penitentiary.
penitenta, sf. female penitent.
penitente, a. penitent, repentant; —, sm. penitent.
penoso, sa, a. painful.
pensado, de —, sm. on purpose. [pansy.
pensamiento, sm. thought, thinking;
pensar, v.n. to think.
pensativo, va, a. pensive, thoughtful.
pensión, sf. pension; toil. [pensionary.
pensionado, da, sm. & f. pensioner,
pensionar, v.a. to impose a task; to pension.
pensionista, sm. & f. pensioner, pensionary; boarder.
Pentatéuco, sm, the Pentateuch.

Pentecostés, sm. Pentecost, Whitsuntide.
penúltimo, ma, a. penultimate, last but one. [neediness, extreme want.
penuria, sf. penury, poverty, indigence,
peña, sf. rock, large stone.
peñascal, sm. rocky hill or mountain.
peñasco, sm. large rock; strong, rough cloth.
peñascoso, sa, a. rocky, mountainous.
peñón, sm. rocky mountain.
peón, sm. pedestrian; day-labourer; foot-soldier; pawn (at chess); bee-
peonía, sf. (bot.) peony. [hive.
peonza, sf. whip-top; noisy little fellow-
peor, a. & ad. worse.
peoría, sf. deterioration, detriment.
pepinar, sm. cucumber-field.
pepino, sm. cucumber.
pepita, sf. kernel; pip; pellet.
pepitoria, sf. fricassee made of giblets, livers, and jights.
pequeñez, sf. littleness; trifle.
pequeño, ña, a. little, small; young.
pera, sf. pear.
perada, sf. conserve of pears.
peral, sm. pear-tree.
percalina, sf. cloth (binding). [success.
percance, sm. perquisite; bad luck, non-
percepción, sf. perception, notion.
perceptible, a. perceptible.
percibir, v.a. to receive; to perceive, to comprehend.
percusión, sf. percussion.
percha, sf. perch; peg.
perder, v.a. to lose; -se, to go astray; to be lost; to be spoiled.
perdición, sf. losing of a thing; perdition, ruin, loss.
pérdida, sf. loss, damage; object lost.
perdidizo, za, a. lost on purpose.
perdigar, v.a. to broil partridges slightly before they are roasted; to stew larded meat in an earthen pan.
perdigón, sm. partridge trained to decoy others; -ones, pl. hail-shot.
perdiguero, ra, a. setting, pointing (of dogs).
perdiz, sf. partridge.
perdón, sm. pardon.
perdonable, a. pardonable.
perdonar, v.a. to pardon, to forgive.
perdulario, ria, a. careless of one's own interest, heedless.
perdurable, a. perpetual, everlasting.
perecedero, ra, a. perishable; —, sm. misery, extreme want.
perecer, v.n. to perish, to die; -se, to die of love or envy.
peregrinación, sf. pilgrimage.
peregrinamente, ad. rarely, curiously.
peregrinar, v.a. to go on a pilgrimage.

peregrino, na, a. foreign, travelling ; going on a pilgrimage ; strange ; —, sm. pilgrim.

perejil, sm. parsley.

perendengues, sm.pl. ear-rings, pl.

perenne, a. perennial, perpetual. [sive.

perentorio, ria, a. peremptory, decisive.

pereza, sf. laziness, idleness.

perezoso, sa, a. lazy, idle.

perfección, sf. perfection.

perfeccionar, v.a. to perfect, to complete, to finish.

perfecto, ta, a. perfect, complete.

perfidia, sf. perfidy.

pérfido, da, a. perfidious.

perfil, sm. profile.

perfilado, da, a. delicate (of features).

perfiladura, sf sketching of outlines.

perfilar, v.a. to draw profiles ; to sketch outlines ; -se, to incline. [pan.

perfumador, sm. perfumer ; perfuming-pan.

perfumar, v.a. to perfume.

perfume, sm. perfume.

perfumería, sf. perfumer's shop.

pergamino, sm. parchment. [ship.

pericia, sf. skill, knowledge, connoisseur-ship.

pericón, sm. large fan.

perifollo, sm. common chervil ; ribbon or other women's ornament.

perifrasear, v.a. to periphrase. [tion.

perífrasis, sf. periphrasis, circumlocution.

perigallo, sm. loose skin of old persons ; tall, lank person ; sling made of twine.

perihelio, sm. perihelium.

perilla, sf. small pear ; pear-shaped ornament ; pommel ; de -s, at the proper time. [grant.

perillán, ana, a. artful, knavish, vagrant.

perímetro sm. circumference, compass.

periódico, ca, a. periodical ; —, sm. newspaper.

periodista, sm. journalist.

período, sm. period.

peripatético, sm. peripatetic.

peripecia, sf. vicissitude, accident.

peripuesto, ta, a. tricked up, very spruce in dress.

periquito, sm. parroquet.

perito, ta, a. skilful, experienced, expert.

perjudicar, v.a. to prejudice, to injure, to hurt, to damage.

perjudicial, a. prejudicial, damaging.

perjuicio, sm. prejudice, injury.

perjurar, v.n. to forswear ; to swear ; -se, to perjure oneself.

perjurio, sm. perjury, false oath.

perjuro, ra, a. perjured, forsworn.

perla, sf. pearl ; de -s, much to the purpose ; splendid.

perlático, ca, a. paralytic, palsied.

perlesía, sf. paralysis, palsy.

permanecer, v.n. to persist. [ance.

permanencia, sf. permanence, perseverance.

permanente, a. permanent.

permisión, sf. permission, leave.

permiso, sm. permission, leave, licence.

permitir, v.a. to permit, to give leave.

permuta, sf. barter, exchange.

permutar, v.a. to exchange.

pernada, sf. kick.

pernear, v.n. to kick, to shake the legs ; to fret.

pernetas (en —), ad. bare-legged.

pernicioso, sa, a. pernicious, destructive.

pernil, sm. ham, gammon.

pernio, sm. hinge of door.

perniquebrar, v.a. to break the legs ; -se, to break one's leg.

pernoctar, v.n. to pass the night ; to be awake the whole night.

pero, sm. kind of apple ; —, c. but, yet.

perogrullada, sf. truism, platitude.

perol, sm. boiler, kettle.

peroración, sf. peroration, the conclusion of a speech.

perorar, v.a. to end a speech ; to make an harangue.

perorata, sf. tedious harangue.

perpendicular, a. perpendicular.

perpendículo, sm. plumb, plummet.

perpetrar, v.a. to perpetrate, to commit a crime.

perpetua, sf. everlasting flower.

perpetuar, v.a. to perpetuate.

perpetuidad, sf. perpetuity.

perpetuo, tua, a. perpetual.

perplejidad, sf. perplexity.

perplejo, ja, a. perplexed.

perra, sf. bitch ; drunkenness, intoxication ; — chica, halfpenny (5 centimos).

perrera, sf. kennel.

perrería, sf. pack of dogs ; drudgery.

perrillo, sm. little dog ; trigger ; — de falda, lap-dog.

perro, sm. dog ; obstinate person ; — de aguas, water-dog ; — grande, penny.

persecución, sf. persecution ; toil, trouble, fatigue.

perseguidor, sm. persecutor.

perseguir, v.a. to pursue ; to dun ; to persecute. u

perseverancia, sf. perseverance, constancy.

perseverar, v.n. to persevere, to persist.

persiana, sf. Venetian blind.

persignarse, v.r. to make the sign of the cross.

persistencia, sf. persistence, steadiness.

persistir, v.n. to persist.

persona, sf. person.

personaje, sm. personage.

personal, a. personal.
personalidad, sf. personality.
personero, sm. deputy, agent, attorney.
personificar, v.a. to personify.
perspectiva, sf. perspective ; false, deceitful appearance.
perspicacia, sf. perspicacity, clear-sightedness.
perspicaz, a. perspicacious, quick-sighted; sagacious. [persuaded.
persuadir, v.a. to persuade ; -se, to be
persuasión, sf. persuasion.
persuasiva, sf. persuasiveness.
persuasivo, va, a. persuasive.
pertenecer, v.n. to belong, to appertain, to concern.
pertenencia, sf. right of property ; appurtenance, dependence.
pértiga, sf. long pole or rod.
pertiguero, sm. verger.
pertinacia, sf. pertinacity, obstinacy, stubbornness.
pertinaz, a. pertinacious, obstinate.
pertrechar, v.a. to supply a place with ammunition and other warlike stores ; to dispose, to arrange, to prepare ; -se, to be provided with the necessary defensive stores and arms.
pertrechos, sm.pl. tools, instruments ; ammunition, warlike stores.
perturbación, sf. perturbation, disquiet.
perturbador, sm. perturbator, disturber.
perturbar, v.a. to perturb, to disturb.
perversidad, sf. perversity, malignity.
perversión, sf. perversion ; depravation, corruption. [wicked.
perverso, sa, a. perverse, extremely
pervertir, v.a. to pervert, to corrupt.
pesa, sf. weight (in a balance).
pesadez, sf. heaviness ; gravity, weight ; slowness ; peevishness, fretfulness ; trouble, fatigue.
pesadilla, sf. nightmare.
pesado, da, a. peevish, troublesome, cumbersome ; tedious, injurious ; heavy, weighty.
pesadumbre, sf. weightiness, gravity ; quarrel, dispute ; grief, trouble.
pésame, sm. message of condolence.
pesantez, sf. heaviness.
pesar, sm. sorrow, grief ; repentance ; á —, ad. in spite of, notwithstanding ; —, v.n. to weigh, to be of weight ; to repent ; —, v.a. to weigh.
pesaroso, sa, a. sorrowful, full of repentance ; restless, uneasy.
pesca, sf. fishing, fishery.
pescadería, sf. fish-market.
pescado, sm. fish (in general).
pescador, sm. fisher, fisherman.
pescante, sm. coach-box.

pescar, v.a. to fish, to catch fish.
pescozón, sm. slap on the neck with the open hand.
pescuezo, sm. neck.
pesebre, sm. crib, manger.
pesebrera, sf. row of mangers in a stable.
pesebrón, sm. boot of a coach.
peseta, sf. peseta (about 10d.).
pesillo, sm. small scales for weighing coin.
pesimista, sm. pessimist.
pésimo, ma, a. very bad. [scales ; dollar.
peso, sm. weight, heaviness ; balance-
pespuntar, v.a. to back-stitch.
pespunte, sm. back-stitching.
pesquera, sf. fishery.
pesquisa, sf. inquiry, examination.
pesquisar, v.a. to inquire.
pesquisidor, sm. examiner, inquirer.
pestaña, sf. eye-lash.
pestañear, v.a. to blink.
pestañeo, sm. blinking.
peste, sf. pest, plague, pestilence.
pestífero, ra, a. pestilential.
pestilencia, sf. pestilence.
pestillo, sm. bolt.
pesuña, s. hoof.
petaca, sf. pannier ; cigar-case.
petar, v.a. to please, to content.
petardear, v.a. to beat down with petards ; —, v.n. to cheat.
petardista, sm. & f. deceiver, cheat.
petardo, sm. petard ; cheat, fraud, imposition.
petate, sm. straw-bed ; sleeping-mat ; (mar.) sailors' bedding ; poor fellow.
petición, sf. petition, demand.
petimetre, sm. fop, coxcomb, beau.
petirrojo, sm. (orn.) red-breast.
petitorio, ria, a. petitionary ; —, sm. impertinent and repeated petition.
peto, sm. breast-plate ; plastron.
petrificación, sf. petrification, petrifaction.
petrificar, -se, v.r. to petrify.
petroleo, sm. petroleum, paraffin.
petulancia, sf. petulance, insolence.
petulante, a. petulant, insolent.
pez, sm. fish ; —, sf. rosin, pitch.
pezón, sm. leaf-stalk ; nipple.
pezonera, sf. linch-pin.
pezuña, sf. hoof. [chickens.
piada, sf. chirping of birds ; puling of
piadoso, sa, a. pious, mild, merciful ; moderate.
pian piano, ad. gently, softly.
piano, sm. pianoforte.
piar, v.n. to squeak, to pule, to chirp.
piara, sf. herd of swine ; flock of ewes.
pica, sf. pike.
picacho, sm. sharp point.
picada, sf. puncture.

picadero, sm. riding-school; **-s**, pl. blocks of wood put under the keel of a ship, while she is building.

picadillo, sm. minced meat, hash.

picador, sm. riding-master; pricker; horseman (in bull-ring). [clothes.

picadura, sf. prick; puncture; gusset in

picante, sm. piquancy; —, a. piquant.

picapedrero sm. stone-cutter.

picaporte, sm. door-lock, picklock.

picar, v.a. to prick; to sting; to mince; to nibble; to pursue an enemy; to itch; **-se**, to be piqued; to be moth-eaten; to begin to rot.

picardía, sm. knavery, roguery; deceit, malice; lewdness.

picaresco, ca, a. roguish, knavish.

pícaro, ra, a. knavish, roguish; mischievous, malicious; sly; merry, gay; —, sm. & f. rogue, knave.

picarote, sm. notorious villain, great impostor. [pleasure.

picazón, sf. itching, prurience; dis-

pico, sm. beak; bill, nib; spout; peak; loquacity; pick-axe.

picoso, sa, a. pitted with small-pox.

picotazo, sm. peck of a bird.

picote, sm. coarse stuff made of goat's hair; glossy silk stuff.

picotear, v.a. to peck (of birds); —, v.n. to prattle, to chatter; **-se**, to wrangle (applied to women). [prattling.

picotero, ra, a. wrangling, chattering.

picudo, da, a. beaked; sharp-pointed.

pichón, sm. young pigeon.

pie, sm. foot; leg; basis; trunk (of trees); foundation; occasion; á —, on foot; á — enjuto, without labour or pain; dry-shod.

piedad, sf. piety; mercy, pity.

piedra, sf. stone; gravel; hail.

piel, sf. skin; hide; peel.

piélago, sm. high sea; plenty, abundance.

pienso, sm. a feed for horse or mule.

pierna, sf. leg; leg of mutton; stroke (in writing); cheek of a printing-press.

pieza, sf. piece; piece of furniture.

pífano, sm. fife; fife-player, piper.

pigmeo, mea, sm. & a. dwarf; dwarfish.

pila, sf. water-trough; font; pile, heap; holy-water basin; **nombre de —**, Christian name; **sacar de —**, to stand godfather or godmother.

pilada, sf. quantity of mortar made at once; pile, heap.

pilar, sm. large water-basin of a fountain; pillar.

pilastra, sf. pilaster.

píldora, sf. pill. [trough; loaf of sugar.

pilón, sm. large water-basin, drinking-

pilongo, ga, a. lean, meagre.

pilotaje, sm. pilotage.

piloto, sm. pilot.

piltrafa, sf. skinny piece of meat.

pillada, sf. knavish trick.

pillaje, sm. pillage, plunder.

pillar, v.a. to pillage, to plunder, to foray, to seize; to chop at.

pillería, sf. gang of vagabonds or rogues; knavish trick.

pillo, lla, a. & sm. thievish, rascally; scamp.

pimentero, sm. pepper-box; pepper-tree.

pimentón, sm. ground fruit of the pepper plant.

pimienta, sf. pepper.

pimiento, sm. (bot.) pepper-tree.

pimpollo, sm. sucker; bud.

pina, sf. landmark in the form of a cone; felloe of a wheel.

pináculo, sm. pinnacle.

pinar, sm. grove of pines.

pincel, sm. paint-brush.

pincelada, sf. dash with a pencil; touch.

pinchadura, sf. puncture.

pinchar, v.a. to prick.

pincho, sm. thorn.

pindonguear, v.n. to gad about.

pingajo, sm. rag, tatter.

pingüe, a. fat, greasy; fertile.

pino, sm. (bot.) pine; á —, upright.

pinta, sf. spot, blemish, scar; mark on playing cards; pint. (to fit exactly.

pintado, da, a. painted, mottled; **venir —**,

pintamonas, sm. bad painter, dauber.

pintar, v.a. to paint, to picture; to limn, to describe; to exaggerate; —, v.n. to begin to ripen; to show, to give signs; **-se**, to paint one's face.

pintarrajar, v.a. to variegate.

pintarrajo, sm. daub. [resembling

pintiparado, da, a. exactly like, closely

pintiparar, v.a. to compare.

pintor, sm. painter.

pintoresco, ca, a. picturesque.

pintorrear, v.a. to daub.

pintura, sf. painting; picture.

pinzas, sf.pl. nippers, small pincers.

pinzón, sm. chaffinch.

piña, sf. pine-apple; fir-cone; group.

piñón, sm. pine-apple seed; pinion; cog-wheel.

piñonata, sf. conserve of almonds.

piñonate, sm. fruit paste.

pío, pía, a. pious, devout; mild, merciful; —, sm. cry of chickens.

piocha, sf. ornament for women's head-dresses.

piojería, sf. lousiness; misery.

piojo, sm. louse; troublesome hanger-on.

piojoso, sa, a. lousy; miserable, stingy.

pipa, sf. wine-cask; pipe (liquid measure); tobacco-pipe; reed of a clarion; fusee of a bomb.

pipero, sm. cooper.

pipiar, v.n. to pule, to chirp.

pipote, sm. keg.

pique, sm. pique, offence taken; echar á —, to sink a ship; á —, in danger, on the point of.

piquera, sf. bung-hole.

piquete, sm. slight prick or sting; tracing-picket; (mil.) picket.

pira, sf. funeral pile.

piramidal, a. pyramidal.

pirámide, sf. pyramid.

pirata, sm. pirate; cruel wretch.

piratería, sf. piracy. [pliment.

piropo, sm. carbuncle; (fig.) witty compliment.

pirueta, sf. pirouette.

pisada, sf. footstep; kick.

pisar, v.a. to tread, to trample; to stamp on the ground; to tamp paving-stones; to despise.

pisaverde, sm. fop, coxcomb, jackanapes.

piscina, sf. fish-pond.

Piscis, sm. Pisces, Fishes (sign of the zodiac). [ment; floor, storey.

piso, sm. tread, trampling; floor, pavement.

pisón, sm. rammer. [foot.

pisotear, v.a. to trample, to tread under

pista, sf. trace, footprint. [little.

pisto, sm. thick broth; á -s, little by little.

pistola, sf. pistol.

pistoletazo, sm. pistol-shot.

pistolete, sm. pocket-pistol.

pita, sf. (bot.) agave, aloe.

pitagórico, ca, a. Pythagorean. [price.

pitanza, sf. pittance, daily allowance;

pito, sm. pipe; whistle; cigarette.

pitón, sm. sprig, young shoot of a tree; tenderling, sprouting horn.

pitonisa, sf. sorceress, enchantress.

pitorra, sf. woodcock.

pizarra, sf. slate.

pizarral, sm. slate-quarry, slate-pit.

pizca, sf. mite; pinch. [plied to women).

pizpereta, a. sharp, brisk, lively (applied to women).

pizpirigaña, sf. play among boys, in which they pinch one another's hands.

placa, sf. clasp; badge, star, insignia of an order of knighthood. [tion.

pláceme, sm. compliment, congratulation.

placentero, ra, a. joyful, merry.

placer, sm. pleasure delight; —, v. imp. to please.

plaga, sf. plague.

plagar, v.a. to plague, to torment.

plagiario, ria, a. & sm. plagiarising, plagiarist.

plagio, sm. plagiarism.

plan. sm. plan; design, plot.

plana, sf. trowel; page (of a book); level; — mayor, (mil.) staff-office.

plancha, sf. plate; ironing-iron.

planchar, v.a. to iron linen.

planchear, v.a. to plate, to sheath.

planeta, sm. planet.

planetario, a. planetary.

plano, na, a. plain, level, flat; —, sm. plan, ground-plot; plane.

planta, sf. sole of foot; plant; plantation; -s, pl. brag, boast.

plantación, sf. plantation.

plantador, sm. planter.

plantar, v.a. to plant; to fix upright; to strike or hit a blow; to found, to establish; -se, to stand upright.

plantear, v.a. to plan, to trace.

plantel, sm. nursery-garden.

plantificar, v.a. to plant; to beat; to box, to kick.

plantilla, sf. young plant; first sole of a shoe; vamp; plate of a gun-lock.

plantillar, v.a. to vamp or sole shoes or stockings.

plantío, tía, a. planted; ready to be planted; —, sm. planting; nursery.

plantón, sm. scion, sprout; (mil.) sentry punished with extra duty.

plañidera, sf. weeping-woman.

plañir, v.n. to lament, to grieve, to bewail.

plasta, sf. paste, soft clay. [en —, briefly.

plata, sf. silver; plate (wrought silver);

plataforma, sf. platform; (rail.) — giratoria, turn-plate, turn-table.

plátano, sm. plane-tree.

plateado, da, a. silvered; plated.

plateadura, sf. silvering.

platear, v.a. to silver.

platería, sf. silversmith's shop; trade of a silversmith.

platero, sm. silversmith.

plática, sf. discourse, conversation.

platicar, v.a. to converse, to practise.

platillo, small plate.

platino, sm. platinum.

plato, sm. dish; course (at dinner).

platónico, ca, a. platonic.

plausible, a. plausible.

playa, sf. shore, strand.

plaza, sf. square, place; fortified place; office, public employment; enrolling of soldiers.

plazo, sm. term (time); appointed date.

pleamar, sf. (mar.) high water.

plebe, sf. common people, populace.

plebeyo, ya, a. plebeian; —, sm. commoner.

plectro, sm. (poet) plectrum.

plegable, plegadizo, za, a. pliable.

plegador, sm. folding instrument; plaiter

plegadura, sf. fold, plaiting.

plegar, v.a. to fold, to plait ; —, v. imp. to please ; **plegue á Dios que,** God grant that.

plegaria, sf. public prayer.

pleiteador, sm. pleader ; wrangler.

pleitear, v.a. to plead, to litigate.

pleitista, sm. litigious person.

pleito, sm. contract, bargain ; dispute, controversy, debate ; law-suit.

plenamente, ad. fully, completely.

plenario, ria, a. complete, full.   [moon.

plenilunio, sm. full-moon, full-faced

plenipotenciario, sm. plenipotentiary.

plenitud, sf. fullness, abundance.

pleonasmo, sm. pleonasm.

pliego, sm. sheet of paper.

pliegue, sm. fold, plait ; plight ; ruff.

plomar, v.a. to seal with lead, to stop teeth.

plomero, sm. plumber.

plomizo, za, a. leaden.

plomo, sm. lead ; **á —,** perpendicularly.

pluma, sf. feather, plume.

plumada, sf. dash with a pen.

plumaje, sm. plumage ; plume.   [broom.

plumero, sm. bunch of feathers ; feather-

plumista, sm. petty scrivener, notary.

plural, a. (gr.) plural.

pluralidad, sf. plurality.

pluvial, a. rainy.

pneumático, ca, a. pneumatic.

poblacho, sm. populace, rabble.

población, sf. population.   [place.

poblado, sm. town, village, inhabited

poblador, sm. populator, founder.

poblar, v.a. to populate, to people ; to colonise ; to fill, to occupy ; — v.n. to bud, to get leaves.

pobre, a. poor, indigent. [useless person.

pobrete, s.m. poor, unfortunate man ;

pobretería, sf. poor people ; avarice.

pobreza, sf. poverty, poorness.

pocero, sm. well-digger ; scavenger.

pocilga, sf. pig-sty ; any nasty, dirty place.

pócima, sf. potion ; dose.

poco, ca, a. little, scanty ; few ; —, ad. little ; **— ha que,** lately, latterly ; **á —,** gently ; little by little ; —, sm. a small part.

poda, sf. pruning of trees.

podadera, sf. pruning-knife.

podar, v.a. to prune.

podenco, sm. hound.

poder, sm. power, authority ; command ; force ; —, v.n. to be able ; to possess the power of doing or performing.

poderhabiente, sm. attorney, representative.

poderío, sm. power, authority ; wealth, riches.   [cellent.

poderoso, sa, a. powerful ; eminent, ex-

podre, sf. pus, matter.

podredumbre, sm. rot, putrid mutton ; uneasiness.

podrir, v.n. to rot, to putrefy.

poema, sm. poem.

poesía, sf. poetry ; poesy

poeta, sm. poet.

poético, ca, a. poetical.

poetisa, sf. poetess.

poetizar, v.a. to poetize.

polaina, sf. legging, gaiter.

polar, a. polar.

polea, sf. pulley ; (mar.) tackle-block.

polémica, sf. polemics.

polémico, ca, a. polemical.

policía, sf. police ; politeness ; neatness.

poligamia, sf. polygamy.

polígamo, sm. polygamist.   [gonal.

polígono, sm. polygon ; —, **na,** a. poly-

polilla, sf. moth.

pólipo, sm. polypus.

polisílabo, ba, a. polysyllabic.

politeísmo, sm. polytheism.

política, sf. politics ; policy ; politeness.

político, ca, a. political ; polite ; —, sm. politician.

póliza, sf. certificate, ticket, docket.

polo, sm. pole.

poltrón, ona, a. idle, lazy ; commodious, easy ; **silla -ona,** elbow-chair ; —, sm. poltroon.   [ence.

poltronería, sf. idleness, laziness, indol-

polución, sf. pollution.

polvareda, sf. cloud of dust.

polvo, sm. powder, dust ; **un —,** a pinch of snuff.

pólvora, sf. gun-powder.

polvorear, v.a. to powder.

polvoriento, ta, a. dusty.

polvorín, sm. priming ; powder-flask.

polvorista, sm. manufacturer of gun-powder.

polvorizar, v.a. to pulverize ; to powder.

polvoroso, sa, a. dusty ; **poner pies en -a,** to scamper away.   [pool.

polla, sf. pullet ; money staked at cards,

pollada, sf. flock of young fowls ; hatch, covey.

pollera, hen-coop.

pollero, sm. poulterer.

pollino, sm. young ass ; dull fellow.

pollo, sm. chicken.

pomada, sf. pomatum, pomade.

pómez, sf. pumice-stone. [handle ; knob.

pomo, sm. fruit from trees ; pommel ;

pompa, sf. pomp ; bubble.

pomposo, sa, a. pompous.

ponche, sm. punch.

ponchera, sf. punchbowl.
poncho, cha, a. soft, mild ; —, sm. (am.) horseman's blanket.
poncil, a. bitter orange or lemon.
ponderable, a. wonderful.
ponderación, sf. pondering, considering ; exaggeration.
ponderar, v.a. to ponder, to weigh ; to exaggerate ; to eulogise. [bolical.
ponderativo, va, a. exaggerating, hyper-
ponedero, ra, a. egg-laying ; capable of being laid or placed ; —, sm. nest ; nest-egg.
poner, v.a. to put, to place ; to impose ; to lay eggs ; -se, to set (of stars) ; to become.
poniente, sm. west ; west wind.
pontificado, sm. pontificate.
pontifical, a. & sm. pontifical.
pontífice, sm. Pope, pontiff.
pontificio, cia, a. pontifical.
pontón, sm. pontoon.
ponzoña, sf. poison.
ponzoñoso, sa, a. poisonous.
popa, sf. (mar.) poop, stern.
populacho, sm. populace, mob.
populación, sf. population.
popular, a. popular.
popularidad, sf. popularity.
populoso, sa, a. populous. [dice.
poquedad, sf. paucity, littleness ; cowar-
por, pr. for, by, about ; by means of ; through ; on account of.
porcelana, sf. porcelain, china.
porción, sf. part, portion ; lot.
porcuno, na, a. hoggish.
pordiosear, v.a. to beg alms.
pordiosero, ra, sm. & f. beggar.
porfía, sf. obstinate quarrel ; stubbornness ; importunity ; á —, emulously ; with strife and contention.
porfiado, da, a. obstinate, stubborn.
porfiador, ra, sm. & f. disputer, wrangler.
porfiar, v.a. to dispute obstinately ; to persist.
pórfido, sm. porphyry.
pormenor, sf. detail.
poro, sm. pore.
porosidad, sf. porosity.
poroso, sa, a. porous. [ad. why ?
porque, c. because.
porqué, sm. cause, reason ; — interrog.
porquería, sf. nastiness, foulness ; rudeness ; trifle ; dirty action.
porqueriza, sf. pig-sty.
porquero, sm. swine-herd.
porra, sf. cudgel.
porrazo, sm. blow with a cudgel.
porrería, sf. stupidity, folly, silliness.
porreta, sf. green leaf of leek ; en .—, stark-naked.

porrillo (á —), ad. copiously, abundantly,
porrón, sm. earthen pitcher for water.
portabandera, sf. colour-sheath.
portacartas, sm. mail ; postman.
portada, sf. portal, porch ; frontispiece.
portador, sm. carrier, porter.
portaestandarte, sm. (mil.) standard-bearer ; ensign.
portafusil, sm. (mil.) sling of a musket.
portaguión, sm. standard-bearer of cavalry.
portal, sm. porch ; portico, piazza.
portamanteo, sm. portmanteau, cloak-bag.
portapaz, sm. & f. (eccl.) image-plate.
portar, v.a. to carry ; -se, to behave, to comport oneself.
portátil, a. portable.
portazgo, sm. toll, turnpike-duty.
portazo, sm. bang of a door ; banging a door in one's face.
porte, sm. porterage, portage ; deportment, demeanour, conduct.
portento, sm. prodigy, portent.
portentoso, sa, a. prodigious, marvellous, strange.
portería, sf. porter's lodge.
portero, sm. porter, gate-keeper.
portezuela, sf. little door ; carriage door.
pórtico, sm. portico, porch, lobby.
portillo, sm. aperture in a wall ; gap, breach ; small gate.
portón, sm. inner door of a house.
porvenir, sm. future. [suit of.
pos, en —, ad. after, behind ; in pur-
posa, sf. passing-bell.
posada, sf. lodging-house, inn, hotel ; pocket-case, containing knife, spoon, and fork.
posaderas, sf.pl. buttocks.
posadero, sm. inn-keeper ; backside.
posar, v.n. to lodge ; to sit down, to repose ; —, v.a. to lay down a burden.
posdata, sf. postscript.
poseer, v.a. to hold, to possess.
poseído, da, a. possessed with the devil.
posesión, sf. possession.
posesivo, va, a. (gr.) possessive.
posesor, ra, sm. & f. possessor.
posesorio, ria, a. possessory.
posibilidad, sf. possibility ; wealth, riches.
posible, a. possible. [tion.
posición, sf. position ; posture ; situa-
positivo, va, a. positive.
pósito, sm. public granary ; — pío, granary for charity.
poso, sm. sediment, dregs, lees.
posponer, v.a. to postpone.
posta, sf. post ; post-house ; post-stage ; —, sm. person who travels post.
poste, sm. post, pillar.

postema, sm. abscess, tumour ; dull, troublesome person.

postergación, sf. postponement, passing over.   [pass over.

postergar, v.a. to leave behind ; to

posteridad, sf. posterity.

posterior, a. posterior.   [window.

postigo, sm. wicket ; postern ; sash of a

postilla, sf. pimple.

postillón, sm. postillion.

postizo, za, a. artificial (not natural) ; —, sm. false hair.   [bettor.

postor, sm. bidder at a public sale ;

postración, sf. prostration.

postrar, v.a. to humble, to humiliate ; -se, to prostrate oneself.

postre, a. last in order ; á la —, at last ; —, sm. dessert.

postrer, postrero, ra, a. last in order, hindermost.

postrimero, ra, a. hindermost.

póstumo, ma, a. posthumous.

postura, sf. posture, position ; fixed price of eatables ; price asked or offered ; bet, wager ; agreement, convention.

potable, a. potable, drinkable.

potaje, sm. pottage ; medley of various useless things.

potasa, sf. potash.

pote, sm. pot, jar ; flower-pot ; standard measure or weight.

potencia, sf. power ; mightiness.

potentado, sm. potentate, prince.

potente, a. potent, powerful, mighty.

poterna, sf. postern, sally-port.   [tion.

potestad, sf. power, dominion ; jurisdic-

potra, sf. rupture, hernia.

potro, ra, sm. & f. colt ; foal.

potroso, sa, a. afflicted with a rupture ; fortunate, lucky.

poyo, sm. bench (near the street-door).

poza, sf. puddle ; hole.

pozal, sm. bucket, pail.   [ice-cellar.

pozo, sm. well ; — de nieve, ice-house,

práctica, sf. practice.

practicable, a. practicable, feasible.

practicante, sm. practiser ; young practitioner in surgery and medicine.

practicar, v.a. to practise.   [perienced.

práctico, ca, a. practical ; skilful, ex-

pradera, pradería, sf. meadow, mead.

prado, sm. lawn, meadow.

pragmática, sf. royal edict.   [tion.

preámbulo, sm. preamble ; circumlocu-

prebenda, sf. prebend.

prebendado, sm. prebendary.

preboste, sm. provost.

precario, ria, a. precarious.

precaución, sf. precaution.   [against.

precaver, v.a. to prevent, to guard

precedencia, sf. precedence ; preference, superiority.

precedente, p. & a. precedent, foregoing

preceder, v.a. to precede, to go before.

precepto, sm. precept, order.   [ceptor.

preceptor, sm. master, teacher, pre-

preces, sf.pl. prayers ; devotions.

preciado, da, a. proud, presumptuous.

preciarse, v.r. to boast, to take pride.

precio, sm. price, value.

preciosidad, sf. excellence, preciousness.

precioso, sa, a. precious.

precipicio, sm. precipice ; sudden fall ; ruin, destruction.

precipitación, sf. precipitation, inconsiderate haste.   [long, hasty

precipitado, da, a. precipitate, head

precipitar, v.a. to precipitate ; -se, to run headlong to one's destruction.

precisar, v.a. to fix, to define ; to compel, to oblige, to necessitate.

precisión, sf. necessity, compulsion ; preciseness.   [cise, exact.

preciso, sa, a. necessary, requisite ; pre-

precocidad, sf. precocity.

preconizar, v.a. to proclaim.

precoz, a. precocious.   [runner.

precursor, ra, sm. & f. harbinger, fore-

predecesor, ra, sm. & f. predecessor, fore-runner.

predecir, v.a. to foretell.

predestinación, sf. predestination.

predestinar, v.a. to predestine.

predial, a. relating to landed property.

predicable, a. predicable.

predicación, sf. preaching, sermon.

predicado, sm. predicate.

predicador, sm. preacher.

predicamento, sm. predicament.

predicar, v.a. to publish ; to preach.

predicción, sf. prediction.

predilección, sf. predilection.

predilecto, ta, a. darling, favourite.

predio, sm. landed property ; farm ; real estate.

predominar, v.a. to predominate, to prevail ; to command.   [superiority.

predominio, sm. predominant power,

preeminencia, sf. pre-eminence, superiority of power.

preeminente, a. pre-eminent, superior.

preexistencia, sf. pre-existence.

preexistente, p. & a. pre-existent.   [fore.

preexistir, v.n. to pre-exist, to exist be-

prefacio, sm. preface.

prefecto, sm. prefect.

prefectura, sf. prefecture.

preferencia, sf. preference.

preferible, a. preferable.

preferir, v.a. to prefer.

prefijar, v.a. to prefix, to fix beforehand.

pregón, sm. proclamation made by the common crier. [public places.

pregonar, v.a. to cry, to proclaim in

pregonero, sm. common crier ; —, ra, a. publishing.

pregunta, sf. question ; inquiry.

preguntar, v.a. to question, to ask ; to inquire.

prelacía, sf. prelacy.

prelada, sf. abbess.

prelado, sm. prelate.

preliminar, a. & sm. preliminary.

preludio, sm. prelude.

prematuro, ra, a. premature, precocious.

premeditación, sf. premeditation, fore-thought. [out.

premeditar, v.a. to premeditate, to think

premiar, v.a. to reward, to remunerate.

premio, sm. reward, recompense ; pre-premisa, sf. premise. [mium.

premura, sf. narrowness, pressure, haste, hurry.

prenda, sf. pledge ; sweetheart ; treasure ; person or thing dearly loved ; -s, pl. accomplishments, talents.

prendar, v.a. to pledge ; to ingratiate oneself ; -se, to take a fancy, to be-come enamoured.

prender, v.a. to seize, to catch, to lay hold of ; to imprison ; —, v.n. to take root ; -se, to adorn oneself.

prendido, sm. attire of women.

prendimiento, sm. seizure ; capture.

prensa, sf. press.

prensado, sm. lustre, gloss (of stuff).

prensadura, sf. pressing, pressure.

prensar, v.a. to press. [office.

prensista, sm. pressman in a printing-

preñado, da, a. full, pregnant ; —, sm. pregnancy.

preñez, sf. pregnancy.

preocupación, sf. preoccupation.

preocupar, v.a. to occupy before another, to anticipate ; to preoccupy.

preparación, sf. preparation.

preparar, v.a. to prepare.

preparativo, va, a. preparatory, qualify-ing ; —, sm. prearrangement.

preparatorio, ria, a. preparatory.

preponderancia, sf. preponderance.

preponderar, v.n. to preponderate, to prevail.

preposición, sf. (gr.) preposition.

prepucio, sm. prepuce, fore-skin.

prerrogativa, sf. prerogative, privilege.

presa, sf. capture, seizure ; mouthful ; dyke, dam, mole ; -s, pl. tusks, fangs, claws.

presagiar, v.a. to presage, to forebode.

presagio, sm. presage.

presbiterado, presbiterato, sm. priesthood.

presbiteral, a. sacerdotal.

presbiterio, sm. sanctuary.

presbítero, sm. priest, clergyman.

presciencia, sf. prescience, foreknowledge.

prescindir, v.a. to prescind, to cut off ; to abstract ; to pass over.

prescribir, v.a. to prescribe.

prescripción, sf. prescription.

presea, sf. jewel.

presencia, sf. presence.

presenciar, v.a. to assist, to be present.

presentación, sf. presentation.

presentar, v.a. to present. [sent.

presente, sm. present, gift ; —, a. pre-

presentemente, ad. presently, now.

presentimiento, sm. presentiment.

presentir, v.a. to have a presentiment.

preservación, sf. preservation.

preservador, ra, a. & sm. & f. preserver.

preservar, v.a. to preserve, to defend.

preservativo, va, a. & sm. & f. preserva-tive.

presidencia, sf. presidency.

presidente, sm. president.

presidiario, sm. convict.

presidio, sm. penitentiary, prison ; garri-son of soldiers.

presidir, v.a. to preside.

presilla, sf. loop.

presión, sf. pressure, pressing.

preso, sa, a. & sm. & f. prisoner.

prestamista, sm. borrower, lender.

préstamo, sm. loan.

prestar, v.a. to lend. [mass.

preste, sm. priest who celebrates high

presteza, sf. quickness, haste, speed.

prestigiador, sm. cheat, juggler, impostor.

prestigio, sm. prestige ; imposture.

presto, ta, a. quick, prompt, ready ; —, ad. soon, quickly.

presumible, a. presumable. [gant.

presumido, da, a. presumptuous, arro-

presumir, v.a. to presume, to conjecture ; -se, to be vain. [conceit.

presunción, sf. presumption, conjecture ;

presuntivo, va, a. presumptive.

presuntuoso, sa, a. presumptuous.

presuponer, v.a. to presuppose.

presupuesto, sm. motive, pretext, pre-tence ; estimate ; budget.

presuroso, sa, a. hasty, prompt, quick ; nimble.

pretender, v.a. to pretend, to claim ; to try, to attempt. [cant.

pretendiente, a. pretender ; suitor, appli-

pretensión, sf. pretension.

pretérito, ta, a. preterite, past.

pretextar, v.a. to allege a pretext.

pretexto, sm. pretext, pretence.

pretil, sm. battlement, breast-work.

pretina, sf. girdle, waistband ; belt.

pretor, sm. pretor.

pretorio, sm. Pretorium.   [root.

prevalecer, v.n. to prevail; to take

prevaricación, sf. prevarication.

prevaricar, v.a. to prevaricate; to fail in one's duty.

prevención, sf. disposition, preparation; supply of provisions; foresight; prevention; (mil.) police-guard.

prevenido, da, a. prepared, provided; plentiful, abundant; provident, careful, cautious, foreseeing, forecasting.

prevenir, v.a. to prepare; to foresee, to foreknow; to prevent; to advise; -se, to be prepared; to be predisposed.

preventivo, va, a. preventive.

prever, v.a. to foresee, to forecast.

previo, via, a. previous.   [cast.

previsión, sf. foresight, prevision, foreseeing.

previsor, ra, a. foreseeing.

priesa, sf. haste, speed, hurry.

prieto, ta, a. blackish; narrow-minded; indigent.   [cousin.

prima, sf. prime; treble; female

primacía, sf. priority; primateship, primacy.

primado, sm. primate.

primavera, sf. spring (the season).

primeramente, ad. in the first place, mainly.

primero, ra, a. first, prior, former; —, ad. first, rather, sooner.

primicia, sf. first-fruits.

primitivo, va, a. primitive, original.

primo, ma, a. first; —, sm. cousin.

primogénito, ta, a. & sm. & sf. first-born.

primogenitura, sf. primogeniture.

primor, sm. beauty; dexterity, ability.

primoroso, sa, a. neat, elegant, fine, excellent; handsome.

princesa, sf. princess.

principado, sm. princedom; principality.

principal, a. principal, chief.

príncipe, sm. prince.

principiante, sm. beginner, learner.

principiar, v.a. to commence, to begin.

principio, sm. beginning, commencement; principle.

pringada, sf. slice of toasted bread steeped in gravy.

pringar, v.a. to baste; to grease; to take a share in; to stain one's reputation; -se, to embezzle.

pringón, ona, a. dirty, greasy; —, sm. grease-stain.

pringoso, sa, a. greasy, fat.

pringue, sm. & f. grease, lard.

prior, sm. prior; —, a. prior, preceding.

priora, sf. prioress.

priorato, sm. priorship.

prioridad, sf. priority.

prioste, sm. steward of a brotherhood.

prisa, sf. speed, haste.   [prey.

prisión, sf. seizure, capture; prison;

prisionero, sm. prisoner.

prisma, sm. prism.

privación, sf. privation, want.

privado, da, a. private; particular; —, sm. favourite.

privanza, sf. favour at court.

privar, v.a. to deprive; to prohibit.

privativo, va, a. depriving; particular, peculiar.

privilegiar, v.a. to privilege.

privilegio, sm. privilege.

pro, sm. & f. profit, benefit, advantage buena —, much good may it do you.

proa, sf. (mar.) prow.

probabilidad, sf. probability, likelihood.

probable, a. probable, likely.

probadura, sf. trial.

probanza, sf. proof, evidence.

probar, v.a. to try; to prove; to taste; —, v.n. to suit, to agree.

probidad, sf. probity.

problema, sm. problem.

problemático, ca, a. problematical.

probóscide, sm. proboscis.

procacidad, sf. impudence, petulance.

procaz, a. impudent, petulant, forward.

procedencia, sm. derivation; origin.

proceder, sm. procedure; —, v.n. to proceed, to go on; to issue.   [procedure.

procedimiento, sm. proceeding; legal

proceloso, sa, a. tempestuous, stormy.

prócer, sm. dignitary, personage.   [cute.

procesar, v.a. to inform against, to prose-

procesión, sf. procession.

proceso, sm. process, law-suit.

proclama, sf. proclamation, publication

proclamación, sf. proclamation.

proclamar, v.a. to proclaim.

procreación, sf. procreation, generation.

procrear, v.a. to procreate, to generate.

procuración, sf. power of attorney; procurement.

procurador, sm. attorney; proctor.

procuraduría, sf. attorney's office; proctorship.

procurar, v.a. to strive, to attempt; to contrive; to act as an attorney.

prodigalidad, sf. prodigality; plenty, abundance.

prodigar, v.a. to waste, to lavish.

prodigio, sm. prodigy, monster.

prodigioso, sa, a. prodigious, monstrous; exquisite, excellent.

pródigo, ga, a. prodigal.

producción, sf. production.

producir, v.a. to produce; (law) to produce as evidence.

productivo, va, a. productive.

producto, sm. product.
proemio, sm. preface, introduction.
proeza, sf. prowess, valour, bravery.
profanación, sf. profanation.
profanar, v.a. to profane.
profano, na, a. profane.
profecia, sf. prophecy.
profesar, v.a. to profess, to declare openly ; (eccl.) to take the vows ; to take the veil.
profesión, sf. profession.
profeso, sa, a. professed.
profesor, sm. professor.
profeta, sm. prophet.
profético, ca, a. prophetic.
profetisa, sf. prophetess.
profetizar, v.a. to prophesy.
prófugo, ga, a. fugitive. [deur.
profundidad, sf. profundity ; depth ; gran-
profundizar, v.a. to deepen ; to penetrate.
profundo, da, a. profound.
profusamente, ad. profusely.
profusión, sf. profusion, prodigality.
progenie, sf. progeny, race, generation, offspring, issue. [forefather.
progenitor, sm. progenitor, ancestor,
progenitura, sf. progeny ; primogeniture.
programa, sm. programme.
progresar, v.n. to progress.
progresión, sf. progression.
progresivo, va, a. progressive.
progreso, sm. progress.
prohibicion, sf. prohibition, forbiddance.
prohibir, v.n. to prohibit, to forbid, to hinder.
prohibítivo, va, a. prohibitory.
prohijamiento, sm. adoption.
prohijar, v.a. to adopt (a son).
prohombre, sm. president of a corporation or trades-union.
prójimo, sm. fellow-creature ; neighbour.
prole, sf. issue, offspring, progeny, race.
proletario, ria, a. proletarian.
prolijidad, sf. prolixity ; minute attention to trifles.
prolijo, ja, a. prolix, tedious.
prólogo, sm. prologue.
prolongación, sf. prolongation.
prolongar, v.a. to prolong.
promediar, v.a. to share equally ; —, v.n. to interpose in a friendly manner.
promesa, sf. promise ; pious offering.
prometer, v.a. to promise, to asseverate, to assure.
prometido, sm. promise ; outbidding.
prominencia, sf. protuberance.
prominente, a. prominent, jutting out.
promiscuo, cua, a. promiscuous ; ambiguous.
promoción, sf. promotion.
promontorio, sm. promontory, cape.

promotor, sm. promoter, forwarder.
promover, v.a. to promote, to advance.
promulgación, sf. promulgation.
promulgador, sm. publisher, promulgator.
promulgar, v.a. to promulgate, to pub- pronombre, sm. pronoun. [lish.
pronosticación, sf. prognostication.
pronosticador, ra, sm. & f. foreteller, prognosticator.
pronosticar, v.a. to prognosticate, to predict, to foretell, to conjecture.
pronóstico, sm. prognostic, prediction ; omen, foretoken ; astrologer's almanac.
prontitud. sf. promptitude.
pronto, ta, a. prompt, ready ; —, ad. promptly.
prontuario, sm. memorandum-book.
pronunciación, sf. pronunciation.
pronunciamiento, sm. (law) publication ; insurrection, sedition.
pronunciar, v.a. to pronounce ; -se, to rebel.
propagación, sf. propagation ; extension.
propagador, ra, sm. & f. propagator.
propaganda, sf. college at Rome, charged with propagating the Roman Catholic faith. [to increase.
propagar, v.a. to propagate ; to dilate,
propalar, v.a. to publish, to divulge.
propasar, v.a. to go beyond, to exceed.
propender, v.n. to incline.
propensión, sf. propensity, inclination.
propenso, sa, a. prone, inclined.
propiciación, sf. propitiation, atonement.
propiciar, v.a. to propitiate.
propiciatorio, ria, a. & sm. propitiatory.
propicio, cia, a. propitious.
propiedad, sf. dominion, possession ; right of property ; propriety.
propietario, ria, a. & sm. proprietor ; -s, pl. proprietary.
propina, sf. present, fee, gratuity, tip.
propinar, v.a. to invite to drink.
propincuidad, sf. propinquity.
propincuo, cua, a. near, contiguous.
propio, pia, a. proper ; belonging ; —, sm. peculiar quality ; -s, s.pl. lands estates.
proponer, v.a. to propose.
proporcion, sf. proportion ; symmetry.
proporcionado, da, a. proportionate, fit, comfortable.
proporcional, a. proportional.
proporcionar, v.a. to proportion ; to adjust, to adapt.
proposición, sf. proposition.
propósito, sm. purpose ; á —, de —, on purpose, purposely ; fuera de —, untimely, not to the purpose.
propuesta, sf. proposal, offer.

prorrata, sf. quota.   [certain shares.
prorratear, v.a. to divide a quantity into
prorrateo, sm. distribution.
prórroga, sf. prorogation.   [rogued.
prorrogable, a. capable of being pro-
prorrogar, v.a. to prorogue.   [forth.
prorrumpir, v.n. to break forth, to burst
prosa, sf. prose.
prosador, sm. sarcastic speaker.
prosaico, ca, a. prosaic.
prosapia, sf. race, generation.
proscenio, sm. proscenium.
proscribir, v.a. to proscribe, to outlaw.
proscripción, sf. proscription.
proscripto, sm. outlaw.
prosecución, sf. prosecution, pursuit.
proseguir, v.a. to pursue, to prosecute.
prosélito, sm. proselyte.
prosista, sm. prose writer.
prosodia, sf. prosody.   [dour, pageantry.
prosopopeya, sf. personification ; splen-
prospecto, sm. prospectus.
prosperar, v.a. to make happy ; to
   favour ; —, v.n. to prosper. to thrive.
prosperidad, sf. prosperity.
próspero, ra, a. prosperous.
prostitución, sf. prostitution.
prostituir, v.a. to prostitute.
prostituta, sf. prostitute.
protección, sf. protection
protector, sm. protector.
proteger, v.a. to protect.
protervia, sf. insolence.
protervo, va, a. stubborn, peevish, arrogant, insolent.
protesta, sf. (law) protest.
protestación, sf. protestation.
protestante, sm. Protestant.
protestar, v.a. to protest ; to make
   public declaration of faith.
protocolo, sm. protocol.
protomártir, sm. the first martyr.
prototipo, sm. prototype.
provecho, sm. profit.
provechoso, sa, a. profitable.   [learning.
provecto, ta, a. advanced in years *or*
proveedor, ra, sm. & f. purveyor.
proveeduría, sf. store ; office of purveyor.
proveer, v.a. to provide ; to provision ;
   to confer an employment ; to decree.
proveído, sm. judgment, sentence, decree.
proveimiento, sm. provisioning.   [issue.
provenir, v.n. to arise, to proceed ; to
proverbial, a. proverbial.
proverbio, sm. proverb
providencia, s. providence ; foresight ;
   divine providence.
providencial, a. providential.
providenciar, v.a. to ordain, to command.
próvido, da, a. provident.
provincia, sf. province.

provincial, a. & sm. provincial.
provisión, sf. provision, store of pro
   visions ; provender.
provisional, a. provisional.
provisionalmente, ad. provisionally.
provisor, ora, sm. & f. provider ; —
   s.m. vicar-general.
provocación, sf. provocation.
provocador, ora, sm. & f. provoker.
provocar, v.a. to provoke, to excite.
provocativo, va, a. provocative ; quarrel
   some.   [birth.
proximidad, sf. proximity, kindred by
próximo, ma, a. next, nearest.
proyección, sf. projection.
proyectar, v.a. to project, to scheme.
proyecto, sm. project.
prudencia, sf. prudence, wisdom.
prudente, a. prudent.
prueba, sf. proof, reason, argument ;
   token ; experiment, essay, attempt ;
   relish, taste.
prurito, sm. prurience, itching.
púa, sf. sharp point, prickle ; shoot of
   a tree engrafted in another ; weaver's
   reed ; mental pain ; sly person.
pubertad, sf. puberty.
publicación, sf. publication.
publicar, v.a. to publish, to proclaim.
publicidad, sf. publicity.
público, ca, a. & sm. public.
pucia, sf. chemist's jar, gallipot.
puchada, sf. poultice.
puchero, sm. glazed earthen pot ; meat
   boiled in an earthen pot ; grimace
   which precedes crying.
puches, sf. pl. pap, meal-pap.   [ness.
pudicicia, sf. pudicity, chastity, chaste-
púdico, ca, a. chaste, pure.
pudiente, a. rich, opulent.
pudin, sm. pudding.
pudor, sm. bashfulness, shamefacedness.
pudrición, sf. rottenness.
pudrimiento, sm. decay.
pudrir, v.a. to make putrid ; —, v.n. to
   rot, to be rotten.
pueblo, sm. town, village ; population ;
   populace.
puente, sm. & f. bridge ; (mus.) bridge.
puerca, sf. sow, female pig.
puerco, ca, a. nasty, filthy, dirty ; rude,
   coarse ; —, sm. hog ; — espin, porcupine.
puericia, sf. boyhood.
pueril, a. boyish, childish.
puerilidad, sf. puerility, boyishness.
puerro, sm. leek.
puerta, sf. door, doorway, gateway ;
   duty paid at towngates ; — trasera,
   back-door.   [row pass, defile.
puerto, sm. port, harbour, haven ; nar-

pues, ad. then, therefore; **¡ — !** well,

puesta, sf. setting (of sun). [then.

puesto, sm. place; particular spot; retail-shop; post, employment; barracks; stand; **—,** ad. **— que,** although; since. [bad smell.

¡ puf ! fy ! exclamation of disgust at a

pugilato, sm. pugilism.

pugna, sf. combat, battle.

pugnar, v.n. to fight, to combat; to solicit earnestly. [strapping.

pujante, a. powerful, strong, robust, stout,

pujanza, sf. power, strength.

pujar, v.a. to outbid.

pujo, sm. tenesmus; violent desire.

pulcritud, sf. beauty. [in dress.

pulcro, cra, a. beautiful; affectedly nice

pulga, sf. flea; **tener malas -s,** to be easily piqued; to be ill-tempered.

pulgada, sf. inch.

pulgar, sm. thumb.

pulgarada, sf. fillip; pinch (of snuff).

pulidez, sf. neatness.

pulido, da, a. neat, nice.

pulidor, sm. polisher.

pulimento, sm. polish, glossiness.

pulir, v.a. to polish, to burnish; **-se,** to adorn oneself; to become polished.

pulmón, sm. lungs.

pulmonía, sf. inflammation of the lungs.

púlpito, sm. pulpit.

pulpo, sm. cuttle-fish; polypus.

pulposo, sa, a. pulpous.

pulsación, sf. pulsation.

pulsar, v.a. to touch; to feel the pulse; to explore, to try; **—,** v.n. to pulsate.

pulsera, sf. bracelet.

pulso, sm. pulse; firmness *or* steadiness of the hand; attention, care.

pulular, v.n. to pullulate.

pulverización, sf. pulverization.

pulverizar, v.a. to pulverize.

pulla, sf. obscene expression; repartee.

pundonor, sm. point of honour.

pundonoroso, sa, a. having a nice sense of honour, punctilious.

pungir, v.a. to punch, to prick.

punición, sf. punishment, chastisement.

punta, sf. point.

puntada, sf. stitch.

puntal, sm. prop, stay, buttress.

puntapié, sm. kick.

puntear, v.a. to play the guitar; to point out; to stitch; **—,** v.n. (mar.) to tack.

puntel, sm. tube for blowing glass.

puntería, sf. aiming (of fire-arms).

puntero, ra, a. aiming well (with fire-arms)

puntiagudo, da, a. sharp-pointed.

puntilla, sf. narrow lace-edging; **de -s,** on tiptoe

puntillazo, sm. kick.

puntillo, sm. punctilio, exaggerated trifle.

punto, sm. point, end, design; point of honour; aim, sight; stitch; mesh of a net; **al —,** instantly; **en —,** punctually.

puntuación, sf. punctuation.

puntual, a. punctual, exact.

puntualidad, sf. punctuality; certainty.

puntualizar, v.a. to fix on the mind, to accomplish.

puntuar, v.a. to punctuate, to point.

punzada, sf. prick, sting; pain; compunction.

punzadura, sf. puncture, prick.

punzar, v.a. to punch, to prick, to sting.

punzón, sm. punch.

puñada, sf. cuff, blow with the fist.

puñado, sm. handful.

puñal, sm. poniard, dagger.

puñalada, sf. stab.

puñetazo, sm. blow with the closed fist.

puño, sm. fist; handful; wristband; hilt.

pupila, sf. eye-ball, pupil; orphan girl.

pupilaje, sm. pupilage; boarding-house.

pupilar, a. pupilary.

pupilo, sm. pupil; scholar.

pupitre, sm. desk.

pureza, sf. purity, chastity.

purga, sf. purging-draught.

purgación, sf. purgation.

purgante, a. & sm. purgative.

purgar, v.a. to purge, to purify; to atone, to expiate.

purgativo, va, a. purgative, purging.

purgatorio, sm. purgatory.

purificación, sf. purification.

purificador, ora, a. & s.m. & f. purifier; purificatory.

purificar, v.a. to purify.

purismo, sm. purism, pedantry.

purista, sm. purist. [Puritan.

puritano, na, a. puritanical; **—,** sm. & f.

puro, ra, a. pure, unmingled, mere; genuine; chaste, incorrupt; **—** sm. cigar.

púrpura, sf. purple-shell.

purpurado, sm. cardinal.

purpurar, v.a. to colour with purple.

purpurear, v.n. to grow purple.

purpúreo, rea, a. purpurino, na, a. purple.

purulento, ta, a. purulent.

pus, sm. pus, matter.

pusilánime, a. pusillanimous, fainthearted.

pusilanimidad, sf. pusillanimity.

pústula, sf. pustule, pimple.

putativo, va, a. putative, supposed.

putrefacción, sf. putrefaction.

pútrido, da, a. putrid, rotten.

Q

que, rel. pn. who; which; that; —, c. that.

qué, interrog. pn. what?

quebrada, sf. broken, uneven ground.

quebradizo, za, a. brittle.

quebrado, sm. (ar.) fraction.

quebradura, sf. fracture; rupture, hernia.

quebrantadura, sf. fracture, rupture, bursting.

quebrantamiento, sm. fracture, rupture; breaking out of prison; weariness, fatigue; violation of the law.

quebrantar, v.a. to break, to crack, to burst; to pound, to grind; to violate; to fatigue; to weaken.

quebranto, sm. weakness, lassitude; great loss, severe damage.

quebrar, v.a. to break, to transgress a law, to violate; —, v.n. to fail; to go brankrupt; **-se,** to break into pieces, to be ruptured.

queda, sf. resting-time; (mil.). tattoo.

quedar, v.a. to stay, to remain; to be wanting; **-se,** to falter, to stop short.

quedito, ad. softly, gently.   [gently.

quedo, da, a. quiet, still; —, ad. softly,

quehacer, sm. business.

queja, sf. complaint.

quejarse, v.r. to complain.

quejido, sm. complaint.

quejoso, sa, a. plaintful, querulous.

quejumbroso, sa, a. complaining, plaintive.

quema, sf. burning, combustion, fire.

quemador, ra, sm. & f. incendiary; burner.

quemadura, sf. burn.

quemar, v.a. to burn; to kindle; —, v.n. to be too hot; **-se,** to be parched with heat; to burn oneself.

quemazón, sf. burn.

querella, sf. complaint, lamentation.

querellarse, v.r. to lament, to complain; to lodge a complaint in a court of justice.

querelloso, sa, a. querulous.

querer, v.a. to wish, to desire; to love, to like; to will; —, sm. will, desire.

querido, da, a. dear, beloved; —, sm. & f. darling, fondling, lover.

querubín, sm. cherub.

quesera, sf. dairy.

quesero, sm. cheesemonger.

queso, sm. cheese.

quicial, sf. side-post; jamb.

quicio, sm. hook, hinge (of a door).

quídam, sm. someone, a certain person.

quiebra, sf. crack, fracture; bankruptcy.

quiebro, sm. (mus.) trill; inclination of the body.

quien, pn. who, which; one or the other.

quién, interrog. pn. who?

quienquiera, a. whosoever, whatever.

quieto, ta, a. quiet, still, peaceable.

quietud, sf. quietness, peace, tranquillity, calmness.

quijada, sf. jaw, jaw-bone.

quijotada, sf. quixotic action.

quijote, sm. quixotic person.

quijotería, sf. quixotism.

quijotesco, ca, a. quixotic.

quilatar, v.a. to assay.

quilate, sm. carat.

quilla, sf. keel.

quimera, sf. dispute, quarrel; chimera.

quimérico, ca, a. chimerical, fantastic.

quimerista, sm. wrangler, brawler, fantastic person.

química, sf. chemistry.   [cal.

químico, sm. chemist; —, **ca, a.** chemi-

quina, sf. Peruvian bark.

quincalla, sf. hard-ware.

quince, a. & sm. fifteen.

quincenal, a. fortnightly.

quinceno, na, a. fifteenth.

Quincuagésima, sf. Quinquagesima.

quindenio, sm. period of fifteen years.

quinientos, tas, a. five hundred.

quinquina, sf. quinine.

quinquenal, a. quinquennial.

quinquenio, sm. space of five years.

quinquillería, sf. hard-ware.

quinquillero, sm. hawker, pedlar, hard-ware man.

quinta, sf. country-seat, country-house; levy, drafting of soldiers; quint (mus. and piquet).

quintaesencia, sf. quintessence.

quintal, sm. quintal, hundred-weight.

quintar, v.a. to draw one out of five; to levy, to draft soldiers.

quintería, sf. farm; grange.

quintero, sm. farmer; servant who takes care of a farm.

quintilla, sf. metrical composition of five verses.

quinto, sm. fifth; share of a pasture-ground; recruit; —, **ta,** a. fifth.

quíntuplo, pla, a. quintuple, fivefold.

quiñón, sm. dividend.

quiñonero, sm. part-owner.

quiromancia, sf. chiromancy.

quirúrgico, ca, a. surgical.

qdrurgo, sm. surgeon.

quisicosa, sf. riddle ; obscure question.
quisquilla, sf. ridiculous nicety ; trifling dispute.
quisquilloso, sa, a. nice, difficult, touchy, peevish, irritable.
quisto, ta, p. & a. only used with bien and mal ; bien —, well received, generally beloved ; mal —, ill received, hated.
quitapelillos, sm. wheedler.   [lation.
quitapesares, sm. & f. comfort, conso-

quitapón, sm. ornament for the head-stall of draught-mules.
quitar, v.a. to take away, to remove ; to fetch away ; to abrogate, to annul ; to free from an obligation ; to parry (in fencing) ; -se, to abstain ; to get rid of.
quitasol, sm. parasol.
quite, sm. obstacle, impediment. [empt.
quito, ta, a. free from an obligation, ex-
quizá, quizás, ad. perhaps.

R

rabadán, sm. head-shepherd.
rabadilla, sf. rump, croup.
rabaniza, sf. radish-seed.
rábano, sm. radish.
rabia, sf. rage, fury.
rabiar, v.n. to have rabies ; to be mad ; to be furious, to rage.
rabicorto, ta, a. short-tailed.   [temper.
rabieta, sf. touchiness, petulance, bad
rabilargo, ga, a. long-tailed.
rabino, sm. rabbi, rabbin.
rabioso, sa, a. rabid ; furious.
rabisalsera, a. petulant, saucy, impudent (applied to women).
rabo, sm. tail.
rabón, ona, a. docked, short-tailed.
rabotear, v.a. to cut or crop the tail.
rabudo, da, a. long-tailed.
racimo, sm. bunch of grapes.
racimoso, sa, a. grape-bearing.
raciocinar, v.n. to reason, to argue.
raciocinio, sm. reasoning ; argument.
ración, sf. ration ; prebend so called in Spanish cathedrals.
racional, a. rational ; reasonable.
racionalidad, sf. rationality.
racionero, sm. prebendary.
rada, sf. roadstead.
radiacion, sf. radiation.
radiaute, a. radiant.
radiar, v.n. (poet.) to radiate.
radicación, sf. taking root ; becoming rooted (of a habit).
radical, a. radical.
radicarse, v.r. to take root.
radio, sm. radius ; ray.
radioso, sa, a. radiant.
raedera, sf. scraper.
raedura, sf. erasure ; scrapings.
raer, v.a. to scrape, to grate ; to erase.
ráfaga, sf. violent squall of wind. [pudent.
raído, da, a. scraped ; worn out ; im-
raiz, sf. root ; base, basis ; origin ; bienes raíces, pl. landed property.
raja, sf. splinter, chip of wood ; chink, fissure ; coarse cloth.

rajadura, sf. fissure.   [(col.) to boast.
rajar, v.a. to split, to chop, to cleave ;
ralea, sf. race, breed ; species.
ralear, v.n. to grow thin.
raleza, sf. thinness ; rarity.
ralo, la, a. thin, rare.
ralladura, sf. mark left by the grater ; small particles taken off by grating.
rallar, v.a. to grate ; to importune.
rallo, sm. grater.
rama, sf. branch (of a tree, of a family).
ramadán, sm. Mohammedan Lent.
ramaje, sm. branches.
ramal, sm. halter ; (rail.) branch-line.
rambla, sf. sandy bank.
ramera, sf. whore, prostitute.
ramificación, sf. ramification.
ramificarse, v.r. to ramify.
ramillete, sm. nosegay.
ramilletero, sm. vase with artificial flowers for ornamenting altars.
ramo, sm. small branch ; nosegay, bouquet.
ramonear, v.n. to cut off branches.
ramoso, sa, a. branchy.
rampante, a. rampant.
rampojo, sm. rape.
rampollo, sm. shoot, sprig, sucker.
rana, sf. frog.
rancio, cia, a. rank, rancid.
ranchear, v.a. to build huts.
ranchero, sm. steward of a mess.
rancho, sm. rations ; mess, mess-room ; (am.) thatched house.
ranúnculo, sm. (bot.) crowfoot.
ranura, sf. groove.
rapacidad, sf. rapacity.
rapadura, sf. shaving ; baldness.
rapar, v.a. to shave ; to plunder.
rapaz, za, a. rapacious ; —, za, sm. & f. boy or girl.
rapazada, sf. childish action or speech.
rape, sm. shaving.
rapé, sm. rappee, snuff.
rapidez, sf. rapidity.
rápido, da, a. rapid, swift.

rapiña, sf. rapine, robbery.
rapiñar, v.a. to plunder.   [person.
raposa, sf. vixen ; cunning, deceitful
raposería, sf. trick, wile, cunning.
raposo, sm. male fox, dog fox.
rapto, sm. rapine ; ecstasy, rapture ;
     ravishment.
raptor, sm. ravisher.
raqueta, sf. racket, battledoor.
raquítico, ca, a. rickety.
raquitis, sf. rickets.
rareza, sf. rarity, rareness.
raridad, sf. rarity.   [—, ad. rarely.
raro, ra, a. rare, scarce, extraordinary ;
ras, sm. level, even surface.
rasadura, sf. levelling with a strickle (in
     measuring grain).
rasar, v.a. to graze, to scrape.   [pin.
rascador, sm. scraper ; diamond-headed
rascadura, sf. scratching, scraping, rasping
rascar, v.a. to scratch, to scrape.
rasero, sm. strickle.
rasgar, v.a. to tear, to rend.
rasgo, sm. dash, stroke ; flourish ; trait,
     feature ; exploit.
rasgón, sm. rent, rag, tatter.
rasguear, v.n. to form bold strokes with
     the pen ; (mus.) to play arpeggios.
rasgueo, sm. arpeggio.
rasguñar, v.a. to scratch, to scrape.
rasguño, sm. scratch.
raso, sm. satin ; —, sa, a. plain ; flat ;
     al —, in the open air.
raspa, sf. beard of an ear of corn ; back-
     bone of fish ; stalk of grapes ; rasp.
raspador, sm. rasp.
raspadura, sf. filing, scraping ; filings.
raspar, v.a. to scrape, to rasp : to steal.
raspear, v.n. to splutter (of pens).
rastra, sf. sledge.
rastrallar, v.n. to crack with a whip.
rastrear, v.a. to trace ; to inquire into ;
     —, v.n to skim along close to the
     ground (of birds).   [cringing.
rastrero, ra, a. creeping ; low, humble,
rastrillador, ora, sm. & f. flax-dresser,
     raker.
rastrillar, v.a. to dress flax ; to rake.
rastrillo, sm. flax-comb ; portcullis ; rake,
     harrow.
rastro, sm. track ; sign, token.
rastrojera, sf. stubble-ground.
rastrojo, sm. stubble.
rasurar, v.a. to shave.
rata, sf. rat.
ratafia, sf. ratafia (liquor).
ratear, v.a. to filch, to commit petty
     thefts ; v.n. to creep.
ratería, sf. larceny, petty theft.
ratero, ra, a. creeping, mean, vile ; —,
     sm. & f. pick-pocket.

ratificación, sf. ratification.
ratificar, v.a. to ratify, to approve.
rato, sm. moment ; space of time ; á -s
     perdidos, in leisure-time.
ratón, sm. mouse.
ratonar, v.a. to gnaw (of animals).
ratonera, sf. mouse-trap ; rat-hole.
raudal, sm. torrent.   [roach (fish).
raya,s f. stroke ; line ; frontier ; ray ;
rayado, da, a. rifled (of fire-arms).
rayano, na, a. neighbouring, contiguous.
rayar, v.a. to draw lines ; to erase ; to
     emphasize ; to stripe ; —, v.n. to be
     adjacent ; to dawn, to burst forth ; to
     excel.
rayo, sm. ray, flash, lightning ; thunder-
     bolt.
rayoso, sa, a. radiating, striped.
raza, sf. race, lineage ; quality.
razón, sf. reason ; ratiocination : reason-
     ableness ; account, calculation.
razonable, a. reasonable.
razonado, da, a. rational, prudent.
razonamiento, sm. reasoning, discourse.
razonar, v.n. to reason, to discourse ; to
     talk.
reacción, sf. reaction.
real, a. real, actual ; royal ; —, sm.
     camp ; real (a Spanish coin).
realce, sm. embossment ; flash ; lustre,
     splendour.
realengo, ga, a. royal, kingly.
realidad, sf. reality ; sincerity.
realista, sm. royalist.
realizar, v.a. to realize.
realzar, v.a. to raise, to elevate ; to
     emboss ; to heighten.
reanimar, v.a. to cheer, to encourage, to
     reanimate.
reasumir, v.a. to retake; to resume.
reata, sf. strap ; string of horses ; leading
     mule ; (fig.) submission to the opinion
     of others.   [sin.
reato, sm. obligation of atonement for a
rebaja, sf. abatement, deduction.
rebajar, v.a. to abate, to lessen, to
     diminish.
rebalsa, sf. pool, puddle.
rebalsar, v.a. to dam a stream.
rebanada, sf. slice.   [cattle.
rebaño, sm. flock of sheep, herd of
rebatir, v.a. to resist ; to parry, to ward
     off ; to refute ; to repress.   [alarm.
rebato, sm. call to arms, surprise ;
rebelarse, v.r. to revolt ; to rebel ; to
     resist.
rebelde, sm. rebel ; —, a. rebellious.
rebeldía, sf. rebelliousness, contuma-
     ciousness, disobedience ; (law) contu-
     macy ; en —, by default.
rebelión, sf. rebellion. revolt.

rebenque, sm. whip.
rebollo, sm. trunk of a tree.
rebolludo, da, a. thick-set.
rebosadura, sf. overflow. [to abound.
rebosar, v.a. to run over, to overflow;
rebotar, v.a. to clinch the point of a spike
or nail; to repel; —, v.n. to rebound.
rebote, sm. rebound.
rebozo, sm. muffling of oneself up; (fig.)
pretext; cloak.
rebullir, v.n. to stir, to begin to move.
reburujar, v.a. to wrap up, to pack up
in bundles.
rebusca, sf. search; refuge, remains.
rebuscador, ora, sm. & f. gleaner; re-
searcher. [quire.
rebuscar, v.a. to glean; to search, to in-
rebuznar, v.n. to bray.
rebuzno, sm. braying of an ass.
recabar, v.a. to obtain by entreaty.
recado, sm. message; gift; compliments
recaer, v.n. to fall back. [sent.
recaída, sf. relapse.
recalcar, v.n. to squeeze; to stuff; to
repeat, to emphasize; -se, to lean
back in a chair.
recalcitrar, v.n. to kick; to wince; to
be recalcitrant.
recalentar, v.a. to heat again.
recamar, v.a. to embroider with raised
work. [gun.
recámara, sf. wardrobe; chamber of a
recapacitar, v.a. to call to recollection.
recapitulación, sf. recapitulation.
recapitular, v.a. to recapitulate.
recargar, v.a. to recharge; to charge
again; to remand.
recargo, sm. additional load; new
charge or accusation; increase of a
fever. [modest.
recatado, da, a. prudent, circumspect,
recatar, v.a. to conceal carefully; -se, to
take care.
recato, sm. prudence, circumspection;
modesty; bashfulness.
recaudación, sf. recovery of debts; collector's office.
recaudador, sm. tax-gatherer.
recaudar, v.a. to gather; to obtain.
recazo, sm. back of knife.
recelar, v.a. to fear, to suspect.
recelo, sm. dread, suspicion, mistrust.
receloso, sa, a. mistrustful, shy.
recepción, sf. reception; acceptation.
receptáculo, sm. receptacle; refuge,
asylum. [spector.
receptor, sm. receiver, treasurer; in-
receptoría, sf. receiver's or treasurer's
office. [list.
receta, sf. recipe; prescription; account,
recetar, v.a. to prescribe medicines.

recibidor, sm. receiver. [chamber.
recibimiento, sm. reception, receipt; ante-
recibir, v.a. to accept, to receive; to
admit; to welcome.
recibo, sm. receipt, acquittance.
recién, ad. recently, lately. [ern.
reciente, ad. recent, new, fresh; mod-
recinto, sm. precinct, district.
recio, cia, a. stout, strong, robust;
coarse, thick, rude; arduous, rigid;
—, ad. strongly, stoutly; hablar —,
to talk loud.
récipe, sm. prescription; (fig.) displeasure,
disgust.
recipiente, sm. (chem.) recipient.
reciprocidad, sf. reciprocity.
recíproco, ca, a. reciprocal, mutual.
recisión, sf. abrogation.
recitación, sf. recitation.
recitar, v.a. to recite.
recitativo, va, a. recitative.
reclamación, sf. reclamation; remonstrance.
reclamar, v.a. to claim; to decoy birds;
—, v.n. to protest, to raise objection.
reclamo, sm. decoy-bird; call; allurement.
reclinación, sf. reclining. [back.
reclinar, v.a. & n. to recline, to lean
reclinatorio, sm. couch.
recluir, v.a. to shut up.
reclusión, sf. reclusion; recess.
recluta, sf. recruiting; —, sm. recruit.
reclutador, sm. recruiting-officer.
reclutar, v.a. to recruit.
recobrar, v.a. to recover; -se, to recover
from sickness.
recobro, sm. recovery.
recocer, v.a. to boil again; -se, to consume oneself with rage.
recocido, da, a. skilful, clever.
recodar, v.n. to lean on the elbow.
recodo, sm. corner or angle jutting out.
recogedero, sm. meeting-place, rendez-
.vous; collecting instrument.
recogedor, sm. harbourer, shelterer;
gatherer; scraper (instrument).
recoger, v.n. to retake, to take back; to
gather; to shelter; to compile; to
collect; -se, to take shelter or refuge;
to retire to rest; to withdraw from
the world.
recogido, da, a. retired, secluded; stout.
recogimiento, sm. retreat, shelter; abstraction from worldly concerns.
recolección, sf. summary; recollection.
recoleto, ta, sm. & f. Recollect (friar).
recomendación, sf. recommendation.
recomendar, v.a. to charge; to recommend. [pense, reward.
recompensa, sf. compensation; recom-

recompensar, v.a. to recompense, to reward.

recomponer, v.a. to repair. [semble.

reconcentrar, v.a. to concentrate; to disreconciliación, sf. reconciliation.

reconciliar, v.a. to reconcile; -se, to make one's peace.

recóndito, ta, a. recondite, secret, concealed. [reviser.

reconocedor, ra, sm. & f. examiner.

reconocer, v.a. to examine closely; to acknowledge favours received; to consider; (mil.) to reconnoitre; -se, to know oneself; to repent.

reconocido, da, a. grateful.

reconocimiento, sm. recognition; acknowledgment; gratitude; inquiry.

reconquista, sf. reconquest.

reconquistar, v.a. to reconquer. [ness.

reconvalecer, v.n. to recover from sick-

reconvención, sf. recrimination. [nate.

reconvenir, v.a. to retort, to recrimi-

recopilación, sf. summary, abridgment, code.

recopilador, sm. compiler.

recopilar, v.a. to compile.

recordación, sf. remembrance, memory.

recordar, v.a. to remind; —, v.n. to awake from sleep.

recorrer, v.a. to run over, to peruse; to mend, to repair.

recortar, v.a. to cut away, to pare off.

recorte, sm. outline; shred.

recoser, v.a. to sew again.

recostar, v.a. to lean against, to recline; -se, to go to rest.

recreación, sf. recreation, amusement.

recrear, v.a. to amuse, to delight, to recreate. [ing.

recreativo, va, a. recreative, divert-

recreo, sm. recreation.

recriminación, sf. recrimination.

recriminar, v.a. to recriminate.

rectángulo, la, a. rectangular; —, sm. rectangle.

rectificación, sf. rectification.

rectificar, v.a. to rectify.

rectilíneo, nea, a. rectilinear.

rectitud, sf. straightness; rectitude; justness, honesty; exactitude.

recto, ta, a. straight, right; just, honest.

rector, ra, sm. & f. superior of a community or establishment; rector (of a university).

rectorado, sm. rectorship.

rectoral, a. rectorial.

rectoría, sf. rectory, rectorship.

recua, sf. drove of beasts of burden.

recuento, sm. inventory.

recuerdo, sm. remembrance, memory.

recuesto, sm. declivity, gradual descent.

reculada, sf. recoil.

recular, v.n. to fall back, to recoil.

reculones, á —, ad. backwards.

recuperable, a. recoverable.

recuperación, sf. recovery.

recuperar, v.a. to recover; -se, to recover from sickness.

recurrir, v.a. to recur.

recurso, sm. recourse.

recusación, sf. refusal.

recusar, v.a. to refuse; to reject.

rechazamiento, sm. repulsion.

rechazar, v.a. to repel, to repulse.

rechazo, sm. rebound.

rechifla, sf. mockery, derision.

rechiflar, v.a. to mock, to laugh.

rechinamiento, sm. creaking of a machine; gnashing of teeth.

rechinar, v.n. to gnash the teeth.

rechino, sm. creaking.

rechoncho, cha, a. chubby.

red, sf. net; grating; snare, wile, fraud

redacción, sf. editing; editor's office.

redactar, v.a. to edit.

redactor, sm. editor.

redargüir, v.a. to retort, to reply.

redecilla, sf. hair-net. [about.

rededor, sm. environs; al —, round

redención, sf. redemption; ransom; assistance, support.

redentor, ra, sm. & f. redeemer.

redil, sm. sheep-fold, sheep-cot.

redimible, a. redeemable.

redimir, v.a. to redeem, to ransom; to succour.

redingote, sm. frock-coat.

rédito, sm. revenue, rent.

redituar, v.a. to yield, to produce.

redoblado, da, a. redoubled; stout and thick.

redoblar, v.a. to redouble; to rivet.

redoble, sm. doubling, repetition; (mil.) roll of a drum.

redoma, sf. phial.

redondear, v.a. to round; -se, to extricate oneself.

redondel, sm. round cloak; circle.

redondez, sf. roundness, circular form.

redondilla, sf. roundel, roundelay.

redondo, da, a. round.

redopelo, sm. rubbing against the grain, scuffle, affray; al —, against all rule and reason; traer al —, to vex, to drag about contemptuously.

reducción, sf. reduction; exchange, change of money.

reducible, a. reducible, convertible.

reducir, v.a. to reduce; to exchange; to convert; una, to cut down one's expenses, to economise.

reducto, sm. (mil.) redoubt.

redundancia, sf. superfluity, redundance, excess.
redundante, a. overflowing.
redundar, v.n. to overflow, to be redundant; to contribute.
reedificación, sf. rebuilding.
reedificar, v.a. to rebuild.
reeleccion, sf. re-election.
reelegir, v.a. to re-elect, to elect again.
reembolsar, v.a. to recover money advanced; to reimburse.
reembolso, sm. reimbursement.
reemplazar, v.a. to replace, to restore.
reemplazo, sm. replacing; substitute in the militia.
reencuentro, sm. recounter.
reenganchar, v.a. (mil.) to re-enlist; -se, to enlist again.
reengendrar, v.a. to reproduce.
refacción, sf. refection, refreshment.
refectorio, sm. refectory.
referencia, sf. reference.
referir, v.a. to refer, to relate, to report; -se, to refer to, to relate to.
refinador, sm. refiner.
refinadura, sf. refining.
refinar, v.a. to refine.
reflectar, reflejar, v.n. to reflect light.
reflejo, sm. reflex.   [reflection.
reflexión, sf. reflexion; meditation,
reflexionar, v.a. to reflect, to meditate,
reflexivo, va, a. reflexive.
reflorecer, v.n. to blossom again.
refluir, v.n. to flow back, to reflow.
reflujo, sm. reflux, ebb-tide; flujo y —, the tides.
refocilación, sf. restoration, refection.
refocilar, v.a. to strengthen, to revive.
reforma, sf. reform; correction; dismissal from office.
reformación, sf. reformation, reform.
reformado, sm. reformed officer.
reformar, v.a. to reform, to correct, to restore; to dissolve, to dismiss; -se, to mend, to have one's manners reformed or corrected; to be prudent and moderate in speech and conduct.
reforzado, da, a. extra thick and strong.
reforzar, v.a. to strengthen, to fortify.
refracción, sf. refraction.
refractario, ria, a. refractory.
refrán, sm. proverb.   [another.
refregar, v.a. to rub one thing against
refregón, sm. friction, rubbing
refrenamiento, sm. curb; restraint.
refrenar, v.a. to curb, to bridle; to restrain, to moderate.
refrendación, sf. countersigning.
refrendar, v.a. to countersign.
refrendario, sm. officer appointed to countersign documents.

refrendata, sf. counter-signature.
refrescar, v.a. to cool, to refresh; — v.n. to cool; to take the air.
refresco, sm. refreshment.
refriega, sf. affray, skirmish, encounter, fray.   [comfort, to refrigerate.
refrigerar, v.a. to cool, to refresh, to
refrigerio, sm. refrigeration, refreshment; consolation, comfort.
refuerzo, sm. reinforcement.   [refuge.
refugiar, v.a. to shelter; -se, to take
refugio, sm. refuge, asylum.
refulgente, a. refulgent.   [anew.
refundición, sf. act of casting metals
refundir, v.a. to melt metal again; to recast.
refunfuñadura, sf. growling, grumbling.
refunfuñar, v.n. to snarl, to growl, to grumble.
refutación, sf. refutation.
refutar, v.a. to refute,
regadera, sf. watering-pot.
regadio, dia, a. irrigated, watered.
regadizo, za, a. that can be irrigated or watered.
regadura, sf. irrigation, watering.
regalado, da, a. convenient, pleasant, delicate, dainty.
regalar, v.a. to regale; to refresh; to caress; -se, to feast; to regale oneself.
regalía, sf. regalia; privilege.   [self.
regaliza, sf. licorice.
regalo, sm. present, gift, largess; regalement; delicacy, tit-bit.
regalón, ona, a. delicate; pampered.
regañar, v.n. to growl, to grumble; to quarrel.   [sternness of look.
regaño, sm. sourness of countenance;
regañón, ona, a. snarling, growling, grumbling; troublesome.
regar, v.a. to water, to irrigate.
regata, sf. irrigating-ditch; regatta.
regatear, v.n. to use evasions; —, v.a. to haggle, to higgle.   [ing.
regateo, sm. act of haggling or barter-
regatón, sm. socket, ferrule; —, ona, a. retailing.
regazo, sm. lap of a woman.
regencia, sf. regency; regentship.
regeneración, sf. regeneration.
regenerar, v.a. to regenerate.
regentar, v.a. to rule.
regente, sm. regent; manager.
regiamente, ad. royally,
regidor, sm. alderman; governor, prefect.
régimen, sm. regimen, management.
regimiento, sm. administration, government; regimen, diet; magistracy of a city; municipality; (mil.) regiment.
regio, gia, a. royal, kingly.
región, sf. region, tract of country.

regir, v.a. to rule, to govern, to direct.
registrador, sm. registrar ; controller.
registrar, v.a. to survey, to inspect ; to examine ; to record, to enter in a register. [register.
registro, sm. examining ; enrolling office ;
regla, sf. rule, ruler.
reglado, da, a. regulated, temperate.
reglamento, sm. regulation ; by-law.
reglar, a. (eccl.) regular ; —, v.a. to rule ; to regulate ; -se, to reform.
reglón, sm. level (used by masons).
regocijar, v.a. to rejoice.
regocijo, sm. joy, pleasure, merriment, rejoicing.
regodearse, v.r. to be merry, to be delighted ; to dally, to trifle, to play the fool ; to joke, to jest.
regodeo, sm. joy, merriment, diversion.
regoldar, v.n. to belch.
regolfar, v.n. to flow back.
regona, sf. irrigation-works, pl.
regordete, a. chubby, plump.
regresar, v.n. to return, to regress.
regreso, sm. return.
regüeldo, sm. eructation, belch.
reguera, sf. canal for watering lands.
reguero, sm. small rivulet ; trickling line of spilt liquid ; drain, gutter.
regulación, sf. regulation ; comparison, computation.
regulador, ra, sm. & f. regulator.
regular, v.a. to regulate, to adjust ; —, a. regular ; ordinary.
regularidad, sf. regularity.
rehabilitación, sf. rehabilitation.
rehabilitar, v.a. to rehabilitate.
rehacer, v.a. to repair, to make again ; -se, to regain strength and vigour ; (mil.) to rally. [shouldered.
rehecho, cha, a. remade ; squat, broad-
rehén, sm. hostage.
rehilete, sm. toy dart.
rehogar, v.a. to roast.
rehusar, v.a. to refuse, to decline.
reimpresión, sf. reimpression.
reimprimir, v.a. to reimprint.
reina, sf. queen.
reinado, sm. reign.
reinar, v.a. to reign, to govern.
reincidencia, sf. relapse.
reincidir, v.n. to relapse, to fall back.
reino, sm. kingdom, reign. [tion.
reintegración, sf. reintegration, restora-
reintegrar, v.a. to reintegrate, to restore ; -se, to be reinstated or restored.
reintegro, sm. reintegration.
reir, v.n. to laugh.
reiteración, sf. repetition, reiteration.
reiterar, v.a. to reiterate, to repeat.
reja, sf. plough-share ; lattice, grating.

rejilla, sf. grating.
rejo, sm. point ; spike ; sting.
rejón, sm. dagger, poniard ; spear.
rejonazo, sm. dagger-thrust.
rejonear, v.a. to spear bulls.
rejuela, sf. foot-stove, warming-pan.
rejuvenecer, v.n. to grow young again, to be rejuvenated. [account.
relación, sf. relation ; connexion ; report;
relacionar, v.a. to relate.
relajación, sf. relaxation ; remission ; laxity ; commutation of a vow ; delivery of an offender by the ecclesiastical judge to a criminal court ; hernia.
relajar, v.a. to relax, to slacken, to remit ; -se, to be relaxed ; to labour under hernia.
relamer, v.a. to lick again ; -se, to lick one's lips ; to relish ; to paint oneself to excess. [dress.
relamido, da, a. affected, over-nice in
relámpago, sm. flash of lightning.
relampaguear, v.n. to lighten, to flash.
relapso, sa, a. relapsed.
relatar, v.a. to relate.
relativo, va, a. relative.
relato, sm. recital. [reporter.
relator, sm. relater, narrator ; (law)
relatoría, sf. office of a reporter in a court of justice.
releer, v.a. to read again.
relegación, sf. relegation, exile.
relegar, v.a. to relegate, to banish ; to exile.
relente, sm. dew.
relentecer, v.n. to be damp with dew.
relevación, sf. relevation ; alleviation, relief ; remission, pardon.
relevante, a. excellent, great, eminent.
relevar, v.a. to emboss, to work in relief ; to exonerate, to disburden ; to relieve from a burden or charge ; to assist ; to succour ; to forgive, to pardon ; to exalt, to aggrandize ; pict.) to bring out in relief ; (mil.) to relieve.
relevo, sm. (mil.) relief.
relicario, sm. reliquary.
relieve, sm. (art) relievo, relief.
religión, sf. religion.
religionario, sm. & f. Protestant.
religiosidad, sf. religiousness.
religioso, sa, a. religious, pious ; belonging to a religious Order.
relinchar, v.n. to neigh.
relincho, sm. neigh, neighing. [relic.
reliquia, sf. residue, remains ; saintly
reloj, sm. clock, watch.
relojería, sf. watch-making ; watchmaker's shop.
relojero, sm. watch-maker.

relucir, v.n. to shine, to glitter ; to excel, to be brilliant.

relumbrar, v.n. to sparkle, to shine.

relumbrón, sm. lustre.

rellano, sm. landing (of stairs).

rellenar, v.a. to fill again.

relleno, sm. forced meat ; —, na, a. satiated.

remachar, v.a. to rivet.

remansarse, v.r. to become stagnant.

remanso, sm. stagnant water ; tardiness.

remar, v.n. to row.

rematadamente, ad. entirely, totally.

rematado, da, a. totally lost, utterly ruined.

rematar, v.a. to terminate, to finish ; to adjudge to the best bidder ; —, v.n. to be at an end ; -se, to be utterly ruined. [best bid.

remate, sm. end, conclusion ; last or

remedar, v.a. to copy, to imitate, to mimic.

remediable, a. remediable.

remediador, ra, sm. & f. helper ; curer.

remediar, v.a. to remedy ; to assist, to help ; to free from danger.

remedio, sm. remedy, reparation ; help ; amendment, correction ; resource ; refuge.

remedo, sm. imitation, copy. [correct.

remendar, v.a. to patch, to mend ; to

remendón, sm. botcher, cobbler.

remero, sm. rower, oarsman.

remesa, sf. sending of goods ; remittance of money.

remiendo, sm. patch, clout.

remilgarse, v.r. to be affectedly nice or grave.

remilgo, sm. affected nicety or gravity.

reminiscencia, sf. reminiscence, recollection.

remirado, da, a. prudent, cautious.

remirar, v.a. to revise, to review ; -se, to be careful ; to consider.

remisible, a. remissible.

remisión, sf. act of sending back ; remission, forgiveness.

remiso, sa, a. remiss, careless, indolent.

remitir, v.a. to remit, to transmit ; to pardon a fault ; to suspend, to put off ; —, v.n., -se, to slacken.

remo, sm. oar ; long and hard labour ; -s, pl. limbs (of a person) ; legs (of an animal).

remoción, sf. removal.

remojadero, sm. steeping-tub.

remojar, v.a. to steep ; — la palabra, to drink liquor.

remojo, sm. steeping, soaking.

remolacha, sf. beetroot.

remolcar, v.a. (mar.) to tow.

remolinar, v.n. to spin round ; -se, to collect together tumultuously (of a crowd).

remolino, sm. whirlwind ; whirlpool.

remolón, ona, a. soft, lazy.

remolonearse, v.r. to be lazy ; to tarry.

remolque, sm. towing a ship.

remonta, sf. (mil.) remount, supply of cavalry horses.

remontar, v.a. to frighten away ; to remount cavalry ; to repair ; -se, to tower, to soar.

remontista, sm. (mil.) remount officer.

remordedor, ra, a. causing regret, disquieting, discomposing.

remorder, v.a. to cause remorse ; -se, to manifest or express concern.

remordimiento, sm. remorse.

remoto, ta, a. remote, distant, far.

remover, v.a. to remove ; to excite an animal ; to dismiss. [ness.

removimiento, sm. removal ; restless-

remozar, v.a. to rejuvenate.

rempujar, v.a. to push or shove a person out of his place.

rempujón, sm. impulse, push, thrust.

remuneración, sf. remuneration, recompense.

remunerador, ra, sm. & f. remunerator.

remunerar, v.a. to reward, to remunerate.

renacer, v.a. to be born again ; to be new-born. [birth.

renacimiento, sm. regeneration ; new

renacuajo, sm. tad-pole. [a quarrel.

rencilla, sf. slight grudge remaining after

rencilloso, sa, a. peevish, quarrelsome.

rencor, sm. rancour, grudge.

rencoroso, sa, a. rancorous. [profit.

rondición, sf. surrender ; (com.) yield,

rendidamente, ad. humbly.

rendija, sf. crevice, crack, cleft.

rendimiento, sm. weariness, submission ; surrender, compliance ; rent, income.

rendir, v.a. to subject, to subdue ; to surrender ; -se, to be tired out.

renegado, sm. apostate ; wicked person.

renegar, v.a. to deny, to disown ; to detest, to abhor ; —, v.n. to apostatize ; to blaspheme, to curse.

renglón, sm. written or printed line ; item of one's income ; -ones, pl. writings.

reniego, sm. blasphemy.

renitencia, sf. resistance, opposition, stubbornness.

renitente, a. refractory, repugnant.

renombrado, da, a. renowned.

renombre, sm. renown ; surname.

renovación, sf. renovation, renewal.

renovar, v.a. to renew, to renovate, to reform.

renquear, v.n. to limp, to halt.
renta, sf. rent, income.
rentero, sm. tenant-farmer.
rentilla, sf. game at cards.
rentoy, sm. a card-game.
renuevo, sm. sprout, shoot.
renuncia, sf. renunciation, resignation.
renunciable, a. that which can be re-nounced.
renunciar, v.a. to renounce, to resign.
renunciatario, sm. he to whom anything is resigned.
renuncio, sm. renounce (at cards).
reñido, da, a. at variance, at odds.
reñir, v.a. & n. to wrangle, to quarrel; to scold, to chide.
reo, sm. offender, criminal.　[tively.
reojo, sm. mirar de —, to examine fur-
repanchigarse, repantigarse, v.r. to stretch oneself out in a chair.
reparable, a. reparable, remediable.
reparación, sf. reparation, repair.
reparada, sf. shy of a horse.
reparar, v.a. to repair; to consider, to observe; to give heed; —, v.n. to halt, to pause.
reparativo, va, a. reparative.
reparo, sm. repair, reparation; notice; consideration; difficulty.
reparón, ona, a. too cautious.
repartición, sf. distribution.
repartidor, sm. & f. distributer; assessor of taxes.　[ment of taxes.
repartimiento, sm. distribution; assess-
repartir, v.a. to distribute.
repasadora, sf. wool-comber.　[mend.
repasar, v.n. to repass; to revise; to
repaso, sm. revision.　[clivity.
repechar, v.a. & n. to ascend a de-
repecho, sm. declivity, slope.
repelar, v.a. to tear out hair.　[reject.
repeler, v.a. to repel; to refute; to
repelón, sm. tearing of hair; á -ones, by degrees, little by little; de —, by the way; in haste.
repente, de—, ad. suddenly, on a sudden; off-hand.
repentino, na, a. sudden, unforeseen.
repentista, sm. maker of impromptu verses, improvisator.　[dent.
repentón, sm. unexpected event or inci-
repercusión, sf. reverberation.
repercutir, v.n. to reverberate.
repertorio, sm. repertory, index.
repetición, sf. repetition; (mus.) repeat.
repetidor, ra, sm. & f. repeater.
repetir, v.a. to repeat.
repicar, v.a. to chime, to ring a merry peal; to count ninety before the other player counts one at piquet); -se, to pique oneself on.

repique, sm. chime; repique, counting of ninety before the other player has counted one (at piquet).
repiquetear, v.a. to ring a merry peal on festive occasions; -se, to bicker, to wrangle.
repisa, sf. pedestal or stand.
replegar, v.a. to redouble; -se, (mil.) to fall back.
repleto, ta, a. replete, very full.
réplica, sf. reply, answer; repartee.
replicar, v.n. to reply.
replicón, ona, sm. & f. constant arguer.
repollo, sm. head of lettuce; cabbage head.
repolludo, da, a. round-headed.
reponer, v.a. to replace; to restore; -se, to recover lost health or property.
reportado, da, a. moderate, temperate.
reportar, v.a. to restrain; to obtain, to reach; to attain; to carry, to bring.
reportorio, sm. repertory; almanac.
reposado, da, a. quiet, peaceful; settled (wine).
reposar, v.n. to rest, to repose.
reposo, sm. rest, repose.
repostería, sf. repository; store.
repostero, sm. steward.
reprender, v.a. to reprehend, to blame.
reprensible, a. reprehensible.
reprensión, sf. reprehension, blame blemish, reproach.
represa, sf. stoppage, retention.
represalia, sf. reprisal, reprise.　[press.
represar, v.a. to stop, to retain, to re-
representable, a. representable.
representación, sf. representation.
representante, sm. & f. representative; actor.　[on the stage.
representar, v.a. to represent; to play
representativo, va, a. representative.
represión, sf. repression.
reprimenda, sf. reprimand.　[contain.
reprimir, v.a. to repress, to refrain, to
reprobable, a. reprehensible.
reprobación, sf. reprobation, reproof.
reprobar, v.a. to reject, to condemn, to upbraid.
réprobo, ba, a. reprobate.
reprochar, v.a. to reproach.
reproche, sm. reproach.
reproducción, sf. reproduction.
reproducir, v.a. to reproduce.
reptil, sm. reptile.
república, sf. republic.　[car.
republicano, na, a. & sm. & f. republi-
repudiar, v.a. to repudiate.
repudio, sm. repudiation.
repuesto, sm. store laid up against the future.
repugnancia, sf. reluctance, repugnance.
repugnante, a. repugnant.

repugnar, v.a. to oppose, to act with
repulgar, v.a. to hem.   [reluctance.
repulgo, sm. hem.
repulsa, sf. refusal.   [refuse.
repulsar, v.a. to reject, to decline, to
repulsión, sf. repulsion.
reputación, sf. reputation, renown.
reputar, v.a. to repute, to estimate.
requebrár, v.a. to break to pieces; to
   woo, to court; to flatter.   [intimation
requerímiento, sm. request, requisition;
requerir, v.a. to intimate, to notify; to
   request, to require, to need.
requesón, sm. cheese-curds.   [wooing.
requiebro, sm. endearing expression;
requisa, sf. inspection.
requisito, sm. requisite.
res, sf. head of cattle.
resabiar, v.a. to vitiate, to pervert; -se,
   to become vicious; to grumble.
resabio, sm. unpleasant taste left on the
   palate; vicious habit, bad custom.
resaca, sf. surge, surf.
resalado, da, a. very witty.
resaltar, v.n. to rebound; to jut out;
   to be evident.   [ration.
resarcimiento, sm. compensation, repa-
resarcir, v.a. to compensate, to make
   amends.
resbaladero, sm. slippery place or road.
resbaladizo, za, sm. & f. slippery, glib.
resbaladura, sf. mark of slip, slide.
resbalar, v.n. & r. to slip, to slide.
resbalón, sm. slip, sliding.
rescatar, v.a. to ransom, to redeem.
rescate, sm. ransom.
rescindir, v.a. to rescind, to annul.
rescisión, sf. rescission, revocation.
rescoldo, sm. embers, cinders.
rescripto, sm. rescript.
resecar, v.a. to dry again.
resellar, v.a. to coin again.
resello, sm. recoinage.
resentimiento, sm. resentment.
resentirse, v.r. to begin to give way; to
   resent.   [summary.
reseña, sf. review; muster; signal;
reseñar, v.a. to review, to summarise.
reserva, sf. reserve; reservation.
reservado, da, a. reserved, cautious, circumspect.
reservar, v.a. to reserve; -se, to reserve
   oneself; to act with circumspection.
resfriado, sm. cold, rheum.
resfriar, v.n. to begin to be cold; -se,
   to catch cold.
resfrío, sm. cold, catarrh.
resguardar, v.a. to preserve, to defend;
   -se, to be on one's guard.
resguardo, sm. uard, security, safety;
   coastguard.

residencia, sf. residence; audit.
residenciar, v.a. to call a public officer to
   account for his administration.
residente, p. & a. residing; —, sm. resident.
residir, v.n. to reside, to dwell; to be
   present.
residuo, sm. residue, remainder.
resignación, sf. resignation.
resignadamente, ad. resignedly.
resignar, v.a. to resign; -se, to submit.
resina, sf. resin; rosin.
resinoso, sa, a. resinous.
resistencia, sf. resistance, opposition.
resistero, sm. heat produced by the reflexion of the sun's rays.
resistir, v.n. to resist, to oppose; to gainsay; —, v.a. to endure.
resma, sf. ream (of paper).
resollar, v.n. to respire; to take breath.
resolución, sf. resolution, boldness; decision; activity.
resolver, v.a. to resolve, to decide; to
   analyse; -se, to resolve, to determine.
resonar, v.n. to resound.
resoplar, v.n. to snore; to snort.
resoplido, sm. heavy breathing, snorting
resorte, sm. spring (elastic body).
respaldar, v.a. to endorse; -se, to recline; —, sm. back (of seats).
respaldo, sm. back; endorsement; back
   of a seat.
respectivo, va, a. respective.
respecto, sm. relation, respect.
respetable, a. respectable.
respetar, v.a. to respect; to revere.
respeto, sm. respect, regard, considera
   tion; homage.
respetoso, sa, respetuoso, sa, a. respectful; respectable.
réspice, sm. short reply; reproof.
respigar, v.a. to glean.
respingar, v.n. to wince.
respingo, sm. wincing, wince.
respiración, sf. respiration, breathing.
respiradero, sm. vent, breathing-hole;
   rest, repose.
respirar, v.n. to respire, to breathe.
resplandecer, v.n. to emit rays of light;
   to glisten.
resplandeciente, p. & a. resplendent.
resplandor, sm. splendour, brilliancy.
responder, v.a. & n. to answer; to re-
   echo; to correspond; to be responsible.
responsable, a. responsible, accountable,
   answerable.
responsabilidad, sf. responsibility.
responso, sm. response for the dead.
responsorio, sm. (eccl.) response,
respuesta, sf. answer, reply.

resquicio, sm. aperture between the jamb and leaf of a door ; crack, cleft ; subterfuge, evasion.

resta, sf. rest, residue, remainder.

restablecer, v.a. to re-establish ; -se, to recover from a disease, &c.

restablecimiento, sm. re-establishment.

restallar, v.n. to smack, to click.

restañar, v.a. to stanch, to stop blood.

restar, v.a. to subtract ; —, v.n. to be left, to remain.

restauración, sf. restoration.

restaurar, v.a. to restore.

restitución, sf. restitution. [turn.

restituir, v.a. to restore ; -se, to return.

resto, sm. remainder, rest.

restricción, sf. restriction, limitation.

restringir, v.a. to restrain, to restrict, to limit.

restriñimiento, sm. restriction. [strain.

restriñir, v.a. to make costive ; to constrain.

resucitar, v.a. to resuscitate, to revive ; to renew.

resudar, v.n. to perspire, to transpire.

resuello, sm. breath, breathing ; shortness of breath.

resuelto, ta, a. resolute, determined, prompt.

resultado, sm. result, consequence.

resultar, v.n. to result.

resumen, sm. summary, recapitulation.

resumidamente, ad. summarily.

resumir, v.a. to abridge ; to resume.

resurrección, sf. resurrection ; revival.

retablo, sm. reredos (of altar).

retaco, sm. short gun.

retador, sm. challenger.

retaguardia, sf. rear-guard.

retahila, sf. file, range, series.

retal, sm. remnant.

retar, v.a. to challenge.

retardar, v.a. to retard, to delay.

retardo, sm. delay, procrastination.

retazo, sm. remnant.

retejar, v.a. to re-tile a house.

retejo, sm. repair of a roof.

retén, sm. store, stock, reserve.

retención, sf. retention.

retener, v.a. to retain, to keep back.

retentar, v.a. to threaten a relapse (of a former disorder).

retentiva sf. memory.

reticencia, sf. reticence.

retina, sf. retina.

retintín, sm. tingling sound.

retiñir, v.n. to tingle, to resound.

retirada, sf. (mil.) retreat.

retirar, v.a. to withdraw ; -se, to retire, to retreat.

retiro, sm. retreat, retirement.

reto, sm. challenge ; threat, menace.

retocar, v.a. to retouch (a painting) ; to mend ; to finish any work completely.

retoñar, v.n. to sprout again.

retoño, sm. aftermath. [ing.

retoque, sm. finishing stroke ; retouching.

retorcer, v.a. to twist ; to retort.

retorcimiento, sm. twisting, contortion.

retórica, sf. rhetoric. [torician.

retórico, ca, a. rhetorical ; —, sm. rhetornar,** v.a. to return, to turn, to twist ; —, v.n. to return.

retorno, sm. return ; barter, exchange

retorta, sf. retort.

retortero, sm. twirl, rotation ; **andar al** —, to twirl about.

retortijón, sm. twisting.

retozar, v.n. to frisk, to skip ; to play the fool ; —, v.a. to tickle ; to amuse.

retozo, sm. lascivious gaiety.

retozón, ona, a. wanton, romping.

retracción, sf. withdrawal.

retractación, sf. retraction, recantation.

retractar, v.a. to retract, to unsay.

retracto, sm. (law) retraction.

retraer, v.a. to draw back ; to dissuade ; -se, to take refuge ; to flee.

retranca, sf. crupper, breeching.

retrasar, v.a. to defer, to put off ; —. v.n. to retrograde, to fall off.

retraso, sm. lateness ; delay ; decadence.

retratar, v.a. to portray.

retratista, sm. portrait-painter.

retrato, sm. portrait.

retreta, sf. (mil.) retreat, tattoo.

retrete, sm. closet ; water-closet.

retribución, sf. retribution.

retribuir, v.a. to repay. [back.

retroceder, v.n. to go backward, to fly

retrocesión, sf. retrocession.

retrogradar, v.n. to retrograde.

retrógrado, da, a. retrograde. [liards).

retrucar, v.n. to screw back (at billiards).

retruécano, sm. play upon words.

retruque, sm. cannoning back of a ball at billiards.

retumbar, v.n. to resound, to jingle.

retumbo, sm. resonance, echo.

reuma, sf. rheumatism.

reumático, ca, a. rheumatic.

reumatismo, sm. rheumatism.

reunión, sf. reunion, meeting.

reunir, v.a. to reunite, to unite. [tion.

revalidación, sf. confirmation, ratification.

revalidar, v.a. to ratify, to confirm ; -se, to be admitted to a post.

revelación, sf. revelation. [graphs).

revelar, v.a. to reveal ; to develop (photo-

revendedor, ra, sm. & f. retailer, huckster.

revender, v.a. to retail.

revenirse, v.r. to grow sour (of wine and preserves).

reventadero, sm. rough, uneven ground; laborious work.

reventar, v.n. to burst, to crack; to toil, to drudge; —, v.a. to molest, to harass; to burst; to work to death.

rever, v.a. to review, to revise.

reverberación, sf. reverberation.

reverberar, v.a. to reverberate.

reverdecer, v.n. to grow green again.

reverencia, sf. reverence, respect, veneration.

reverenciar, v.a. to venerate, to revere.

reverendas, sf.pl. dimissory letters; qualities worthy of reverence.

reverendo, da, a. reverend.

reverente, a. respectful, reverent.

reversión, sf. reversion, return.

reverso, sm. reverse; back; opposite.

revés, sm. back, disappointment, mis-adventure.

revesado, da, a. obstinate; difficult, entangled, perplexed, obscure.

revesino, sm. game at cards.

revestir, v.a. to put on outer robes.

revisar, v.a. to revise, to review.

revisión, sf. revision.

revisor, sm. reviser, corrector; inspector.

revista, sf. review, revision.

revistar, v.a. to revise.

revocable, a. revocable.

revocación, sf. revocation.

revocar, v.a. to revoke.   [ling.

revocatorio, ria, a. revoking, annul-

revolcarse, v.r. to wallow.

revolotear, v.n. to flutter.

revoloteo, sm. fluttering.

revoltillo, sm. confusion, disorder.

revoltoso, sa, a. turbulent, seditious.

revolución, sf. revolution; disturbance, sedition.   [turber.

revolvedor, ra, sm. & f. revolter, dis-

revolver, v.a. to turn; to turn over; to spin round; -se, to move to and fro; to change (of the weather).

revólver, sm. revolver, m.

revoque, sm. rough-cast; dashing.

revuelta, sf. second turn; revolution, revolt.

rey, sm. king; king (in cards or chess).

reyerta, sf. dispute.

rezagar, v.a. to leave behind; to defer; -se, to remain behind.

rezago, sm. remainder, residue.

rezar, v.a. to pray, to say one's prayers.

rezo, sm. prayer; divine office.

rezongar, v.n. to grumble.   [to leak.

rezumarse, v.r. to ooze, to run gently,

ría, sf. mouth of a river; estuary.

riada, sf. inundation, overflow.

ribazo, sm. hillock, ridge.

ribera, sf. shore, strand.

ribereño, ña, a. belonging to the sea-shore or bank of a river.

ribete, sm. trimming; seam, border.

ribetear, v.a. to hem, to border.

ricacho, cha, a. very rich.

rico, ca, a. noble, rich; delicious.

ricohombre, ricohome, sm. grandee.

ridiculez, sf. ridiculous action or speech; absurdity.

ridiculizar, v.a. to ridicule.

ridículo, la, a. ridiculous.

riego, sm. irrigation.

riel, sm. rail (of railway).

rienda, sf. rein of a bridle; á — suelta, loose-reined, swiftly.

riesgo, sm. danger, risk.

rifa, sf. scuffle, dispute; raffle, lottery.

rifar, v.a. to raffle.

rigidez, sf. rigidity.

rígido, da, a. rigid, rigorous, severe.

rigor, sm. rigour, rigor.

riguroso, sa, a. rigorous.   [dispute.

rija, sf. lachrymal fistula; quarrel, scuffle,

rima, sf. rhyme.

rimar, v.a. & n. to investigate; to rhyme.

rimero, sm. pile; heap.

rincón, sm. inside corner.

rinconada, sf. corner formed by two houses, streets, &c.

rinconera, sf. small triangular table placed in a corner.

ringlera, sf. row, file.

ringorango, sm. flourish with a pen; extravagant nicety in dress.

rinoceronte, sm. rhinoceros.

riña, sf. quarrel, dispute.

riñón, sm. kidney.

río, sm. river, stream.

riolada, sf. assemblage of many things.

riqueza, sf. riches, wealth.

risa, sf. laugh, laughter.

risada, sf. horse-laugh; guffaw.

risco, sm. steep rock.

riscoso, sa, a. steep and rocky.

risible, a. risible, laughable.

ristra, sf. string of onions; row, file.

ristre, sm. socket for a lance.

risueño, na, a. smiling.

rítmico, ca, a. rhythmical.

ritmo, sm. rhythm.

rito, sm. rite, ceremony.

ritual, a. & sm. ritual.

rival, sm. rival, competitor.

rivalidad, sf. rivalry.

rivalizar, v.a. to rival, to vie with.

rizar, v.a. to curl hair; to plait.

rizo, sm. curl, frizzle; crimping; cu* velvet; (mar.) reef (of sail).

robador, ra, sm. & f. robber.

robar, v.a. to rob, to plunder; to abduct a woman.

H

roble, sm. oak-tree.

robledal, sm. oak-grove.

robo, sm. robbery, theft.   [rate.

roborar, v.a. to strengthen, to corrobo-

robustez, sf. robustness.

robusto, ta, a. robust, vigorous.

roca, sf. rock, cliff ; hard substance.

rocalla, sf. fragments of rock.

roce, sm. familiarity ; friction.

rociada, sf. aspersion, sprinkling ; dew-drops ; malicious censure.

rociador, sm. instrument for sprinkling cloth.

rociar, v.a. to sprinkle ; to scatter about ; —, v.n. to fall (of dew).

rocín, sm. hack ; heavy, stupid person.

rociante, sm. miserable hack.

rocío, sm. dew.

rodaballo, sm. turbot.

rodada, sf. rut, track of a wheel.

rodadura, sf. act of rolling.

rodaja, sf. wheel ; anything circular.

rodaje, sm. wheels.   [bedstead.

rodapié, sm. fringe round the foot of a

rodar, v.n. to rotate.

rodear, v.n. to go round ; to go a round-about way ; —, v.a. to wrap up, to circle, to compass.

rodela, sf. shield; target.

rodeo, sm. act of going round ; circuitous way ; delay ; subterfuge.

rodete, sm. bolster ; splinter-bar ; ward of a key.   [one's knees.

rodilla, sf. knee ; rubber, clout ; de -s, on

rodillazo, sm. push with the knee.

rodillo, rodo, sm. roller.

rodrigar, v.a. to prop up vines.

rodrigón, sm. prop for vines.

roedor, ra, sm. & f. gnawer ; detractor.

roedura, sf. gnawing.

roer, v.n. to gnaw, to corrode.

rogación, sf. petition, supplication ; -ones, pl. Rogation days.

rogar, v.a. to entreat ; to pray.

rogativa, sf. supplication, prayer.

rojez, sf. redness.

rojizo, za, a. reddish.

rojo, ja, a. red ; ruddy.

rol, sm. list, roll, catalogue.

rollizo, za, a. plump, robust.

rollo, sm. roll ; spiral.

romadizo, sm. catarrh.

romana, sf. steelyard.

romanar, v.n. to weigh with a steelyard.

romance, sm. common Spanish language; romance.

romancero, ra, a. romancing ; sm. collection of romances or ballads ; romancer.

romancista, sm. author writing in the vernacular ; surgeon practiser.

romano, na, a. Roman.

rombo, sm. rhomb.

romboide, sm. rhomboid.

romería, sf. pilgrimage.

romero, sm. (bot.) rosemary.

romo, ma, a. blunt ; flat-nosed.

romper, v.a. & n. to break, to dash, to fracture ; to break up land ; to pierce ; to begin.

rompimiento, sm. rupture ; crack, cleft ; first ploughing of land.

ron, sm. rum.

ronca, sf. menace ; boast, brag.

roncar, v.n. to snore ; to make a harsh noise ; to roar ; to threaten, to boast, to brag.

roncear, v.n. to use evasions.

roncería, sf. laziness, tardiness ; flattery.

roncero, ra, a. snarling, growling, flattering ; slow, tardy (applied to the sailing of a ship).

ronco, ca, a. hoarse ; husky ; coarse.

roncón, sm. drone of a bag-pipe.

roncha, sf. wheal, pustule.

ronda, sf. night-patrol.

rondador, sm. watchman, night-guard.

rondar, v.a. & n. to patrol ; to roam the streets at night ; to go round.

rondel, sm. roundelay.

ronquear, v.n. to be hoarse.

ronquera, sf. hoarseness.   [sound.

ronquido, sm. snore ; rough, harsh

ronzal, sm. halter.

ronzar, v.a. to chew, to munch, to grind.

roña, sf. scab, mange ; nastiness, filth ; vice.

roñería, sf. craft, cunning ; niggardliness.

roñoso, sa, a. scabby.

ropa, sf. cloth ; stuff ; clothing, wearing-apparel ; robe.

ropaje, sm. clothing, drapery.

ropavejería, sf. old-clothes-shop.

ropavejero, sm. old-clothes-man.

ropería, sf. clothes-shop ; wardrobe.

ropero, sm. clothes-merchant.

roque, sm. rook (at chess).

ros, sm. (mil.) Spanish shako.

rosa, sf. rose ; red spot.

rosado, da, a. crimsoned, flushed ; rosy.

rosal, sm. rose-bush.

rosario, sm. rosary.

rosca, sf. screw ; anything round and spiral.

roseta, sf. rosette.

rosetón, sm. carved rose (architecture).

rosicler, sm. bright rose colour.

rosoli, sm. punch.

rosquilla, sf. spiral-shaped cake.

rostro, sm. feature, human face.

rota, sf. rout, defeat ; ecclesiastical court.

rotación, sí. rotation.

roto, ta, a. broken, destroyed ; leaky ; debauched.

rótula, sf. knee-cap.

rotular, v.a. to inscribe, to label.

rótulo, sm. inscription on papers, label ; printed bill posted up.

rotura, sf. rupture, crack, cleft.

roya, sf. rust, corn-blight ; (bot.) madder.

rozadura, sf. graze, scratch.

rozagante, a. trailing, sweeping (of gowns) ; splendid.

rozar, v.a. to weed, to stub up ; to nibble the grass ; to scrape ; to touch slightly ; to graze ; to falter, to stammer.

roznar, v.a. to chew, to nibble ; to bray.

roznido, sm. noise made by the teeth in eating, smacking of the lips ; braying of an ass.

rozo, sm. chip of wood ; stubbing, weeding.

rubí, sm. ruby.

rubia, sf. (bot.) madder.

rubicundo, da, a. reddish, rubicund.

rubio, bia, a. reddish, ruddy ; —, sm. red gurnard.

rubor, sm. blush ; bashfulness.

rúbrica, sf. red mark ; flourish at the end of a signature ; rubric.

rubricar, v.a. to sign with one's peculiar flourish ; to sign and seal a writing.

rucio, cia, a. light grey ; grey-haired ; — rodado, dappled-grey (of horses).

ruda, sf. rue.

rudeza, sf. roughness, rudeness ; stupidity

rudimento, sm. principle ; beginning ; -s, pl. rudiments.

rudo, da, a. rude, rough, coarse ; stupid.

rueca, sf. distaff.

rueda, sf. wheel ; circle ; crown ; sun-fish.

ruedo, sm. rotation ; circuit ; border, selvage ; round mat.

ruego, sm. request, prayer, petition, entreaty, supplication.

rufián, sm. pimp, pander.

rufo, fa, a. red-haired ; frizzed, curled.

rugido, sm. roaring of beasts.

rugir, v.n. to roar, to bellow ; to crack.

rugoso, sa, a. wrinkled.

ruibarbo, sm. rhubarb.

ruido, sm. noise.

ruidoso, sa, a. noisy, clamorous, loud.

ruin, a. mean, vile, despicable ; wicked ; avaricious.

ruina, sf. ruin, downfall, destruction ; —, ruins (pl.).

ruindad, sf. meanness, baseness, avarice.

ruinoso, sa, a. worthless, ruinous, destructive.

ruiseñor, sm. nightingale.

rumbo, sm. point of the compass ; road, route, way ; pomp, ostentation.

rumboso, sa, a. pompous, liberal.

rumiar, v.a. to ruminate.

rumión, ona, a. ruminating much ; (fig.) harping on a subject.

rumor, sm. rumour, report.

runrún, sm. rumour, report.

ruptura, sf. rupture.

rural, a. rural.

rusticidad, sf. rusticity ; coarseness.

rústico, ca, a. rustic ; —, sm. peasant.

ruta, sf. route, itinerary.

rutilar, v.n. (poet.) to radiate, to shine.

rutina, sf. routine, habit formed from custom.

rutinero, a. working mechanically.

S

sábado, sm. Saturday ; sabbath.

sábana, sf. sheet ; altar-cloth.

sabandija, sf. grub, beetle, insect.

sabañón, sm. chilblain.   formed.

sabedor, ora, a. & sm. & f. well-in-

saber, v.a. to know ; to experience ; —, v.n. to taste, to savour ; —, s.m learning, knowledge.

sabido, da, a. learned, well-informed.

sabiduría, sf. learning, knowledge, wisdom, notice.

sabiendas, á, —, ad. knowingly.

sabina, sf. (bot.) savin, sabine.

sabio, bia, a. sage, wise ; —, sm. & f. sage, savant.

sablazo, sm. sabre-cut.

sable, sm. sabre, cutlass.

sabor, sm. relish, taste, savour.

saborear, v.a. to give a taste or zest ; to

taste ; to engage one's affections ; -se, to swallow slowly and with great enjoyment ; to be pleased.

saboyana, sf. wide petticoat.

sabroso, sa, a. savoury ; palatable.

sabueso, sm. blood-hound ; lime-hound.

saca, sf. exportation ; transport ; taking ; sack.   [surgeons].

sacabala, sf. bullet-drawer (used by

sacabocado(s), sm. puncheon.

sacabotas, sf. boot-jack.

sacacorchos, sm. cork-screw.

sacadinero(s), sm. tinsel finery.

sacaliña, sf. trickery.

sacamanchas, sm. scourer of clothes.

sacamuelas, sm. tooth-drawer, dentist.

sacar, v.a. to take away ; to draw out ; to except ; to pull out ; to win ; to draw lots

sacatrapos, sm. worm of a ramrod.
sacerdocio, sm. priesthood.
sacerdotal, a. sacerdotal.
sacerdote, sm. priest, clergyman.
sacerdotisa, sf. priestess.
saciar, v.a. to satiate.
saciedad, sf. satiety.
saco, sm. sack.
sacramental, a. sacramental.
sacramentar, v.a. to administer the last
  sacraments.
sacramento, sm. sacrament.
sacrificadero, sm. place of sacrifice.
sacrificar, v.a. to sacrifice ; -se, to devote
  oneself to religion.
sacrificio, sm. sacrifice.
sacrilegio, sm. sacrilege.
sacrílego, ga, a. sacrilegious.
sacristán, sm. sacristan, sexton.
sacristanía, sf. office of a sexton.
sacristía, sf. sacristry, vestry.
sacro, cra, a. holy, sacred.
sacrosanto, ta, a. very holy.
sacudida, sf. shake, jerk.
sacudidura, sf. dusting, cleaning.
sacudimiento, sm. shaking.
sacudir, v.a. to shake, to jerk ; to dart ;
  to beat, to chastise with blows ; -se,
  to reject with disdain.
saeta, sf. arrow, dart.
saetar, v.a. to wound with an arrow.
saetazo, sm. arrow-wound.
sáfico, ca, a. (poet.) sapphic.
sagacidad, sf. sagacity.
sagaz, a. sagacious.
Sagitario, Sagittarius, sm. Archer (sign
  of the zodiac).
sagrado, da, a. sacred, consecrated ; —,
  sm. asylum ; sanctuary.
sagrario, sm. deposit of relics ; cibary.
sahumar, v.a. to perfume ; to smoke, to
  fume.
saín, sm. grease or fat of an animal ;
  dirt on clothes.
sainete, sm. farce ; flavour, relish ;
  delicate bit.
sajadura, sf. scarification.
sajar, v.a. to scarify.
sal, sf. salt.
sala, sf. hall, saloon ; council-room,
  session-room ; guest-chamber.
saladero, sm. salting-place ; salting-tub.
salado, da, a. salted ; witty, facetious.
saladura, sf. salting ; saltness.
salamandra, sf. salamander.
salar, v.a. to salt.
salario, sm. salary.
salazón, sf. seasoning, salting.
salchicha, sf. sausage.
salchichería, sf. sausage-shop.
salchichero, sm. sausage-maker.

saledizo, za, a. salient.
salero, sm. salt-cellar.
saleroso, a. witty.
salida, sf. outgoing ; outlet ; issue,
  result ; rising (of sun) ; (mil.) sally ;
  —, a. in heat (of a bitch).
salina, sf. salt-pit, salt-work, salt-mine.
salinero, sm. salt-dealer.
salino, a. saline.
salir, v.n. to go out ; to depart, to set
  out ; to appear ; to issue ; to rise (of
  sun) ; -se, to drop, to leak.
salitrado, da, a. impregnated with saltpetre.
salitral, sm. saltpetre-works.
salitre, sm. saltpetre.
salitrería, sf. saltpetre-work.
salitrero, sm. saltpetre-refiner.
salitroso, sa, a. nitrous.
saliva, sf. saliva.
salivar, v.n. to spit, to salivate.
salmear, salmodiar, v.a. to sing psalms.
salmista, sm. psalmist.
salmo, sm. psalm.
salmodia, sf. psalmody.
salmón, sm. salmon.
salmonado, da, a. tasting like salmon.
salmonete, sm. red-mullet.
salmuera, sf. brine.
salobre, a. brackish, saltish.
salomar, v.n. (mar.) to sing out.
salón, sm. saloon.
salpicar, v.a. to bespatter.
salpicón, sm. a spiced dish.   [pepper.
salpimienta, sf. mixture of salt and
salpresar, v.a. to salt.
salpullir, v.a. to break out in a rash.
salsa, sf. sauce.
salsera, sf. sauce-boat.
salsero, sm. (bot.) thyme.
saltabanco, sm. mountebank.
saltadero, sm. leaping-place ; artificial
  fountain, jet.
saltado, da, a. prominent, jutting.
saltador, sm. jumper, leaper.
saltar, v.n. to leap, to jump ; to be
  irritated or agitated.
saltarín, ina, sm. & f. dancer ; restless
  young rake.
saltatriz, sf. female rope-dancer.
salteador, sm. highwayman.
saltear, v.a. to rob on the highway.
salterio, sm. Psalter.
salto, sm. leap, jump.
saltón, sm. grasshopper ; —, ona, a.
  hopping, leaping.
salubre, a. healthful.
salubridad, sf. healthfulness.
salud, sf. health, sound state of the body.
saludable, a. salubrious, wholesome.
saludar, v.a. to greet, to salute.

saludo, sm. salute.
salutación, sf. salutation, greeting; exordium.
salva, sf. salute; (mil.) salvo.
salvación, sf. salvation.
salvado, sm. bran.
Salvador, sm. Saviour.
salvaguardia, sm. safeguard.
salvaje, a. savage.
salvajería, sf. rusticity, uncouth manners.
salvajismo, sm. savagery.
salvam(i)ento, sm. safety; salvation; asylum. [danger.
salvar, v.a. to save; -se, to escape from
salvavidas, sm. life-belt.
salvia, sf. (bot.) sage.
salvilla, sf. salver. [cepting.
salvo, va, a. saved; —, ad. saving, ex-
salvoconducto, sm. safe-conduct.
sallar, v.a. to weed.
sambenito, sm. garment, with a yellow cross at back and front, worn by penitents of the Inquisition; note of infamy.
san, a. saint.
sanable, a. curable, healable.
sanalotodo, sm. panacea, general remedy.
sanamente, ad. naturally; agreeably.
sanar, v.a. & n. to heal.
sanción, sf. sanction.
sancionar, v.a. to sanction.
sandalia, sf. sandal.
sándalo, sm. sandal-wood.
sandez, sf. folly, stupidity.
sandio, dia, a. foolish, nonsensical.
saneamiento, sm. surety.
sanear, v.a. to guarantee; to indemnify.
sanedrín, sm. sanhedrim.
sangradera, sf. lancet. [surgeon.
sangrador, sm. blood-letter; (col.)
sangradura, sf. bleeding. [bled.
sangrar, v.a. & n. to bleed; -se, to be
sangre, sf. blood; á — fría, in cool blood; á — y fuego, without mercy.
sangría, sf. bleeding; wound, incision.
sangriento, ta, a. bloody, stained with blood, gory; blood-thirsty.
sanguijuela, sf. leech; sharper.
sanguinaria, sf. knot-grass; sanguine (a stone). [bloody.
sanguinario, ria, a. sanguinary, cruel
sanguíneo, nea, a. sanguine; sanguineous.
sangüís, sm. blood of Christ, as sacramental element.
sanidad, sf. soundness, health.
sano, na, a. sound, sane.
Santabárbara, sf. (mar.) powder-magazine. [eye.
santiamén, sm. moment, twinkling of an
santidad, sf. sanctity.

santificación, sf. sanctification.
santificador, sf. sanctifier.
santificar, v.a. to sanctify; to justify.
santiguador, ra, sm. & f. one who cures by making the sign of the cross.
santiguar, v.a. to make the sign of the cross; to chastise, to punish.
santimonia, sf. sanctity.
santo, ta, a. & sm. saint, holy; sacred image of a saint; (mil.) watch-word.
santón, sm. hypocrite; Mohammedan saint.
santoral, sm. lives of the saints; church-choir book.
santuario, sm. sanctuary.
santurrón, ona, sm. & f. & a. hypocrite.
saña, sf. anger, passion.
sañudo, da, a. furious, enraged.
sapo, sm. toad.
saporífero, ra, a. savoury.
saque, sm. striking out the ball.
saqueador, ra, a. & sm. & f. freebooter; plunderer.
saquear, v.a. to sack, to plunder.
saqueo, sm. sack, pillage.
sarampión, sm. measles, pl.
sarao, sm. ball, dance.
sarcasmo, sm. sarcasm.
sarcástico, ca, a. sarcastic.
sarcófago, sm. sarcophagus.
sardina, sf. sardine.
sardinero, ra, sm. & f. dealer in sardines.
sardio, sardo, sm. sardine (a stone).
sardónice, sf. sardonyx (precious stone).
sarga, sf. serge.
sargento, sm. serjeant.
sarmiento, sm. vine shoot.
sarna, sf. itch; mange; scab; (fig.) envy.
sarnoso, sa, a. itchy, scabby, mangy.
sarpullido, sm. rash.
sarpullir, v.n. to break out in rash.
sarracina, sf. tumultuous contest between a number of persons.
sarro, sm. incrustation of the tongue; tartar of the teeth; sediment which adheres to vessels.
sarroso, sa, a. incrusted.
sarta, string of beads, pearls, &c.; sf string, row.
sartén, sf. frying-pan, saucepan.
sartenada, sf. saucepan-full.
sastre, sm. tailor.
sastrería, sf. tailor's shop.
Satanás, sm. Satan.
satélite, sm. bailiff, constable; satellite.
sátira, sf. satire.
satírico, ca, a. satirical.
satirizar, v.a. to satirize.
sátiro, sm. satyr.
satisfacción, sf. satisfaction; presumption; confidence.

satisfacer, v.a. to satisfy; to atone; -se, to satisfy oneself; to avenge oneself.
satisfactorio, ria, a. satisfactory.
sátrapa, sm. satrap; sly, crafty fellow.
saturación, sf. (chem.) saturation.
saturnal, a. saturnalian.
sauce, sm. (bot.) willow.
saúco, sf. (bot.) elder.
sauquillo, am. (bot.) dwarf-elder.
savia, sf. sap.
saya, sf. skirt; gown.
sayal, sm. sackcloth.
sayo, sm. large wide coat without buttons; loose coat or dress.
sayón, sm. hulking fellow.
sayuelo, sm. small jacket, little frock.
sazón, sf. maturity; season; right time; opportunity; seasoning, flavour; en —, seasonably, opportunely.
sazonadamente, ad. maturely, seasonably.
sazonado, da, a. witty.　　　[to ripen.
sazonar, v.a. to season; to mature; -se,
se, pn. (reflexive pronoun).
sebo, sm. suet; fat.
seboso, sa, a. fat, greasy.
seca, sf. drought, dry weather; inflammation and swelling in the glands.
secadera, sm. place where fruit is dried.
secamente, ad. drily, briefly.
secano, sm. dry arable land which is not irrigated.
secansa, sf. game at cards.
secante, sm. drying-oil used for painting; —, sf. (geom.) secant.
secar, v.a. to dry; -se, to grow dry; to become meagre; to decay.
seceión, sf. section.
seco, ca, a. dry; not rainy; arid, sapless; meagre; barren.
secreta, sf. privy, water-closet; -s, pl. private orisons said by the priest at the beginning of mass.
secretaria, sf. secretary's office.
secretaría, sf. secretaryship.
secretario, sm. confidant; secretary.
secreto, ta, a. secret; hidden; —, sm. secrecy.
secta, sf. sect; doctrine.　　　[sectary.
sectario, ria, a. & sm. & f. sectarian,
secuaz, a. sectary.
secuela, sf. sequel, continuation.
secuencia, sf. (eccl.) sequence (in mass).
secuestrar, v.a. to sequestrate.
secuestro, sm. sequestration.
secular, a. secular; laical.
secularización, sf. secularization.
secularizar, v.a. to secularize.
secundario, ria, a. secondary.
secura, sf. dryness.
sed, sf. thirst; eagerness.
seda, sf. silk.

sedal, sm. fishing-line; (med.) seton.
sede, sf. see.
sedear, v.a. to clean jewels, gold or silver.
sedentario, ria, a. sedentary.
sedería, sf. silk-stuff; silk-mercer's shop.
sedero, sm. silk-mercer.
sedición, sf. sedition, mutiny.
sedicioso, sa, a. seditious, mutinous.
sediento, ta, a. thirsty; eagerly desirous.
seducción, sf. seduction.
seducir, v.a. to seduce.
seductivo, va, a. seductive.
seductor, sm. seducer.
segadera, sf. reaping-hook.
segador, ra, sm. & f. reaper, harvester.
segar, v.a. to reap, to mow, to harvest.
seglar, a. worldly; secular.
segmento, sm. segment.
segregación, sf. segregation, separation.
segregar, v.a. to separate, to set apart.
seguida, sf. following; succession; en —, at once.
seguidilla, sf. merry Spanish tune and dance; -s, pl. diarrhoea.
seguido, da, a. continued, successive.
seguidor, ra, sm. & f. follower; ruled paper for teaching to write straight.
seguimiento, sm. pursuit.
seguir, v.a. to follow, to pursue; -se, to ensue; to succeed.
según, pr. according to.　　　[second.
segundar, v.a. to second; —, v.n. to be
segundario, ria, a. secondary.
segundo, da, a. second; —, sm. second (of time).
segundón, sm. second son; younger son.
segur, sf. axe.　　　[safety.
seguridad, sf. security, surety, certainty,
seguro, ra, a. secure, sure, certain; firm, constant; —, sm. leave, licence; insurance of ships; safe-conduct.
seis, a. six, sixth; —, sm. six.
seiscientos, tas, a. six hundred.
selección, sf. selection, choice.
selecto, ta, a. select, choice.
selva, sf. forest.
sellador, sm. sealer.
selladura, sf. sealing.
sellar, v.a. to seal; to finish.
sello, sm. seal; stamp-office; postage-stamp.
semana, sf. week.
semanal, a. weekly.
semanario, ria, sm. weekly (journal).
semblante, sm. face; countenance.
sembradío, día, a. fit or prepared for sowing.
sembrado, sm. corn-field.
sembrador, sm. sower.
sembradura, sf. sowing.
sembrar, v.a. to sow.

semejante, a. similar, like.

semejanza, sf. resemblance, likeness.

semejar, v.n. to resemble.

semen, sm. semen, animal seed. [seed.

sementera, sf. sowing; land sown with

semi, sm. (in comp.) half.

semibreve, sf. (mus.) semibreve.

semicírculo, sm. semicircle.

semicorchea, sf. (mus.) semi-quaver.

semidiós, sm. demigod. [quaver.

semifusa, sf. (mus.) semi-demi-semi

semilla, sf. seed.

semillero, sm. seed-plot.

seminario, sm. seminary; origin, course.

seminarista, sm. scholar in a seminary.

semínima, sf. (mus.) crotchet.

semiplena, sf. (law) imperfect proof, half-proof.

semitono, sm. (mus.) semitone.

semivocal, a. semivowel.

sémola, sf. wheat-meal.

sempiterna, sf. serge-cloth. [ternal.

sempiterno, na, a. everlasting, sempi-

senado, sm. senate.

senadoconsulto, sm. decree of a senate.

senador, sm. senator.

senatorio, ria, a. senatorial.

sencillez, sf. simplicity; lightness; silliness. [harmless.

sencillo, lla, a. simple; light; silly;

senda, sf. sendero, sm. path, footpath.

senescal, sm. seneschal.

seno, sm. breast, bosom; lap; womb; hole, cavity; sinus; asylum, refuge.

sensación, sf. sensation, feeling.

sensato, ta, a. judicious, reasonable.

sensibilidad, sf. sensibility.

sensible, a. sensible; sensitive; causing pain.

sensitiva, sf. sensitive plant.

sensitivo, va, a. sensitive; sensible.

sensual, a. sensitive; sensual, lewd.

sensualidad, sf. sensuality.

sentado, da, a. sedate, judicious.

sentar, v.a. to fit, to set up; to seat, -se, to sit down; — plaza, (mil.) to enlist.

sentencia, sf. sentence; opinion.

sentenciar, v.a. to sentence, to pass judgment; to give one's opinion.

sentencioso, sa, a. sententious.

sentido, sm. sense; reason; signification; meaning; —, da, a. sensible, feeling.

sentimental, a. sentimental.

sentimiento, sm. sentiment; grief; resentment; judgment, opinion.

sentina, sf. sink, drain; (mar.) hold.

sentir, v.a. to feel; to hear, to perceive; to suffer; to grieve, to mourn; to judge, to think; to foresee; -se, to find oneself; to be moved, to feel pain; to crack (of walls, &c.).

seña, sf. sign, mark, token; signal; (mil.) password.

señal, sf. sign, signature, token; landmark; footstep; earnest-money.

señaladamente, ad. especially; namely.

señalado, da, a. famous, celebrated, noble.

señalamiento, sm. assignation.

señalar, v.a. to stamp, to mark; to sign decrees; to signalize; -se, to distinguish oneself, to excel.

Señor, sm. Lord; Sir; sacrament of the Eucharist; master; governor.

Señora, sf. lady; mistress; gentlewoman.

señorear, v.a. to master, to domineer; to govern one's passions; -se, to affect a peculiar gravity in one's deportment.

señoría, sf. lordship; person to whom this title is given.

señoril, a. lordly. [action.

señorío, sm. seigniory; self-control in

señuelo, sm. lure, enticement.

separable, a. separable.

separación, sf. separation.

separar, v.a. to separate; -se, to separate, to be disunited; to withdraw.

septentrión, sm. septentrion, north.

septentrional, a. septentrional, northern.

septiembre, sm. September.

séptimo, ma, a. seventh.

séptuplo, pla, a. seven-fold.

sepulcral, a. sepulchral.

sepulcro, sm. sepulchre, grave, tomb; Santo —, Holy Sepulchre.

sepultar, v.a. to bury, to inter.

sepultura, sf. sepulture, interment.

sepulturero, sm. grave-digger, sexton.

sequedad, sf. aridity, dryness.

sequía, sf. dryness; thirst; drought.

séquito, sm. retinue, suite, public applause. [sm. being.

ser, v.n. to be; to exist; to fall out; —,

sera, sf. large basket.

seráfico, ca, a. seraphic.

serafín, sm. seraph.

serenar, v.a. & n. to clear up; to settle; to grow clear; to pacify; to tranquilize; to be serene.

serenata, sf. (mus.) serenade.

sereni, sm. (mar.) light boat.

serenidad, sf. serenity.

sereno, sm. dew; night-watch; —, na, a. serene, calm, quiet.

serie, sf. series.

seriedad, sf. seriousness; sternness of mien; sincerity.

serijo, serillo, sm. small basket.

serio, ria, a. serious; severe.

sermón, sm. sermon.

sermonear, v.a. to lecture, to reprimand.

serón, sm. large pannier, &c.

seroso, sa, a. serous.

serpentear, v.n. to move like a serpent; to undulate.   [ment].

serpentón, sm. serpent (musical instrument).

serpiente, sf. serpent.

sérpol, sm. (bot.) wild thyme.

serrador, sm. sawyer.

serraduras, sf.pl. saw-dust.

serrallo, sm. seraglio.   [tainous country.

serranía, sf. range of mountains, mountainous country.

serrano, na, a. & sm. & f. mountaineer.

serrar, v.a. to saw.

serrucho, sm. hand-saw.

servible, a. serviceable.

servicial, a. obsequious, attentive.

servicio, sm. service; attendance; good-turn; divine service; sum of money voluntarily offered to the king; utility.

servidero, ra, a. serviceable.

servidor, ra, sm. & f. servant, waiter.

servidumbre, sf. attendance, servitude; staff of servants; privy, common sewer.

servil, a. servile.

servilleta, sf. napkin.

servir, v.a. to serve; to pay voluntarily a sum of money to the king; to wait at table; **-se,** to deign, to please; to make use of.

sesada, sf. fried brains.

sesenta, sm. sixty; —, a. sixtieth.

sesentón, ona, sm. person over sixty years of age.

sesera, sf. brain-pan; brain.

sesgadura, sf. slope, sloping.

sesgar, v.a. to slope, to cut slantwise.

sesgo, sm. slope; —, ga, a. sloping, oblique; grave; al —, obliquely.

sesión, sf. session; conference.

seso, sm. brain.   [siesta.

sestear, v.n. to take a nap, to sleep the siesta.

sesudo, da, a. judicious, discreet, prudent.

seta, sf. mushroom, fungus.

setecientos, tas, a. seven hundred.

setenta, a. seventy.

setentón, ona, a. turned of seventy.

setiembre, sm. September.

sétimo, ma, a. seventh.

seto, sm. fence, enclosure, hedge.

seudo, a. pseudo, false.

severidad, sf. severity; punctuality, exactness.

severo, ra, a. severe, rigorous; grave, serious; punctual, exact.

sexagenario, ria, a. sixty years old.

sexagésimo, ma, a. sixtieth.

sexenio, sm. space of six years.

sexo, sm. sex.

sexta, sf. sequence of six cards at piquet; sixth (minor canonical hour after tierce).

sexto, ta, a. sixth; —, sm. book containing canonical decrees.

si, sm. (mus.) B, seventh note of the gamut; —, c. if.

sí, ad. yes, without doubt; indeed; —, pn. himself; de por —, apart; de —, spontaneously.

sibarítico, ca, a. sybaritical, luxurious.

sibila, sf. prophetess; sibyl.

sicomoro, sm. (bot.) sycamore.

sidra, sf. cider.

siega, sf. harvest, mowing.

siembra, sf. seed-time.

siempre, ad. always; — jamás, for ever and ever.

siempreviva, sf. (bot.) immortelle.

sien, sf. temple (of the head).

sierpe, sf. serpent.

sierra, sf. saw; range of mountains.

siervo, va, sm. & f. serf, slave.

siesta, sf. siesta, mid-day nap.

siete, a. & sm. seven.

sietemesino, na, a. born seven months after conception.

sigilo, sm. seal; secret.

sigiloso, sa, a. reserved; silent.

siglo, sm. century.

signar, v.a. to sign, to seal; **-se,** to make the sign of the cross.

signatura, sf. sign, mark.

significación, sf. signification.

significado, sm. signification.

significar, v.a. to signify.

significativo, va, a. significant.

signo, sm. sign, mark.   [quent.

siguiente, a. following, successive, sequent.

sílaba, sf. syllable; metrical composition.

silabario, sm. primer.

silabear, v.a. to spell.

silbar, v.a. to hiss; —, v.n. to whistle.

silbato, sm. whistle.

silbido, silbo, sm. hiss, whistling.

silencio, sm. silence.

silencioso, sa, a. silent.

sílfide, sf. sylph.

silo, sm. subterranean granary.

silogismo, sm. syllogism.

silogizar, v.a. to reason, to argue.

silvestre, a. wild, uncultivated; savage.

silla, sf. chair; see; saddle; seat; — de manos, sedan-chair; — poltrona, elbow-chair.

sillar, sm. square hewn stone.

sillería, sf. set of chairs; saddler's shop; stalls in choir of a church.

sillero, sm. saddler; chair-maker.

silleta, sf. close-stool.

silletero, sm. chairman.

sillón, sm. arm-chair.

sima, sf. deep and dark cavern.

simbólico, ca, a, symbolical.

simbolizar, v.n. to symbolize.
símbolo, sm. symbol; device.
simetría, sf. symmetry.
simétrico, ca, a. symmetrical.
simia, sf. she-ape.
simiente, sf. seed.
símil, sm. simile; —, a. similar, like.
similitud, sf. similitude.
similor, sm. pinchbeck.
simio, sm. ape, monkey.   [Madrid.
simón, sm. & f. hackney coachman in
simonía, sf. simony.
simoníaco, ca, sm. & f. guilty of simony.
simpatía, sf. sympathy.
simpático, ca, a. sympathetic.
simple, a. single, simple, silly; insipid;
  —, sm. simple (medicinal plant).
simpleza, sf. simpleness, silliness; rusticity.
simplicidad, sf. simplicity.   [simple.
simplificar, v.a. to simplify, to make
simulación, sf. simulation.
simulacro, sm. image.   [critically.
simuladamente, ad. deceptively, hypo-
simular, v.a. to simulate; to pretend.
simultáneo, nea, a. simultaneous.
sin, pr. without, besides.
sinagoga, sf. synagogue.
sincerar, v.a. to exculpate, to justify.
sinceridad, sf. sincerity.
sincero, ra, a. sincere, ingenuous, honest.
síncopa, sf. (gr., mus.) syncope.
sincopar, v.a. to syncopate.
síncope, sf. (med.) syncope, fainting fit.
sindicado, sm. syndicate.
sindicar, v.a. to accuse.
síndico, sm. syndic.
sinfonía, sf. symphony.
singular, a. singular; particular.
singularidad, sf. singularity.
singularizar, v.a. to distinguish; to
  singularize; -se, to distinguish oneself,
  to be singular.
siniestra, sf. left hand.
siniestro, tra, a. left, sinister; unhappy;
  —, sm. depravity; evil habit;
  disaster.   [only.
sino, c. if not; but; except; besides;
sinodal, a. synodic, synodal; —, sm.
  examiner of curates and confessors.
sínodo, sm. synod; conjunction of the
  heavenly bodies.
sinónimo, ma, a. synonymous.
sinópomo, ma, a. synonymous.
sinrazón, sf. injustice.
sinsabor, sm. displeasure, disgust.
sintaxis, sf. syntax.
síntesis, sf. synthesis.
sintético, ca, a. synthetical.
síntoma, sm. symptom.
sinuosidad, sf. sinuosity.

sinuoso, sa, a. sinuous.
siquiera, c. at least; although, even if.
sirena, sf. syren.
sirga, sf. tow-rope, tow-line.
sirgar, v.a. to tow a vessel.
sirte, sf. moving sand-bank.
sirvienta, sf. female servant, serving-
  maid, maid-servant.
sirviente, sm. servant.
sisa, sf. petty theft; clippings which
  tailors steal in cutting clothes;
  assize; excise.
sisón, sm. filcher, pilferer; moor-cock.
sistema, sm. system.
sistemático, ca, a. systematic.
sitiador, sm. besieger.
sitiar, v.a. to besiege.
sitio, sm. place; situation (of a town, &c.)
  (mil.) siege, blockade.
sito, ta, a. situated.
situación, sf. situation.   [property.
situado, sm. allowance; charge on a
situar, v.a. to place, to situate; to assign
  a fund; -se, to be established in place
  or business; to station oneself.
so, pr. under; below (used in composition, it occasionally diminishes the import of the verb).
soba, sf. making soft; beating.
sobaco, sm. arm-pit, arm-hole.
sobadura, sf. kneading, rubbing.
sobajar, v.a. to scrub, to rub hard.
sobar, v.a. to handle, to soften; to
  pummel, to beat, to whip; to scrub, to
  rub hard.
sobarba, sf. nose-band.
sobarbada, sf. chuck under the chin;
  jerk; (fig.) reprimand, scolding.
soberanía, sf. sovereignty; pride, haughtiness.
soberano, na, a. & sm. & f. sovereign.
soberbia, sf. pride, haughtiness; presumption.
soberbio, bia, a. proud, haughty.
sobina, sf. wooden pin or peg.
sobornador, ra, sm. & f. suborner, briber.
sobornar, v.a. to suborn, to bribe.
soborno, sm. subornation, bribe.
sobra, sf. overplus, excess; offence;
  de —, over and above.
sobradamente, ad. superabundantly.
sobradillo, sm. penthouse; shelter over
  a balcony.   [plus.
sobrante, sm. residue, superfluity, sur-
sobrar, v.a. & n. to exceed; to be more
  than enough; to remain, to be over.
sobre, pr. above, over; moreover; —,
  sm. cover of a letter; envelope.
sobreabundancia, sf. superabundance.
sobreabundar, v.a. to superabound.
sobreagudo, sm. (mus.) highest treble.

sobrealzar, v.a. to praise, to extol.
sobrecama, sf. coverlet, quilt.
sobrecaña, sf. tumour in a horse's leg.
sobrecarga, sf. additional bundle thrown over a load ; surcharge, overburden.
sobrecargar, v.a. to overload.
sobrecargo, sm. supercargo.
sobreceja, sf. part of the forehead over the eye-brows.
sobrecejo, sobreceño, sm. frown.
sobrecoger, v.a. to surprise.
sobrecubierta, sf. double cover.
sobredicho, cha, a. above-mentioned.
sobrediente, sm. projecting tooth.
sobredorar, v.a. to overgild ; to palliate, to exculpate.
sobrehueso, sm. swelling on bones ; trouble, encumbrance.
sobrehumano, na, a. superhuman.
sobrellevar, v.a. to ease, to alleviate ; to suffer, to tolerate.
sobremanera, ad. excessively.
sobremesa, sf. table-cover ; desert ; after-dinner talk ; de —, immediately after dinner.   [to float.
sobrenadar, v.a. to swim on the surface.
sobrenatural, a. supernatural.
sobrenombre, sm. nickname. [of pay.
sobrepaga, sf. increase or augmentation
sobreparto, sm. time of lying-in.
sobrepelliz, sf. surplice.
sobrepeso, sm. overweight.
sobreplan, sm. (mar.) rider.
sobreponer, v.a. to pit one thing over or on another ; -se, to put oneself out of reach of ; to show oneself superior to.
sobreprecio, sm. extra price.
sobrepujanza, sf. excessive strength.
sobrepujar, v.a. to exceed, to surpass, to excel.
sobrerropa, sf. long robe.
sobresaliente, sm. substitute. [surpass.
sobresalir, v.a. to exceed in height, to
sobresaltar, v.a. to make an unexpected attack ; to frighten.   [dread.
sobresalto, sm. sudden assault ; sudden
sobrescrito, sm. address of a letter.
sobreseer, v.n. to desist.
sobreseimiento, sm. omission, suspension.
sobresello, sm. double seal.
sobrestante, sm. overseer ; foreman.
sobresueldo, sm. addition to one's pay or allowance.
sobretodo, sm. surtout, great-coat.
sobrevenir, v.n. to happen, to come un-expectedly ; to supervene.
sobrevivir, v.n. to survive.
sobriedad, sf. sobriety.
sobrina, sf. niece.
sobrino, sm. nephew.
sobrio, ria, a. sober, frugal.

socaliña, sf. extortion, cheating.
socaliñar, v.a. to extort by cunning.
socarrar, v.a. to half-roast.
socarrón, ona, a. cunning, sly, crafty
socarronería, sf. craft, cunning, artful-
socavar, v.a. to undermine.   [ness.
sociabilidad, sf. sociableness.
sociable, a. sociable.
social, a. social.
sociedad, sf. society.
socio, sm. associate, companion ; member (of a club).
socolor, sm. pretext, pretence.
socorredor, ra, sm. & f. succourer, helper.
socorrer, v.a. to succour.
socorrido, da, a. furnished, supplied.
socorro, sm. succour, help ; provisions.
sochantre, sm. sub-chanter.
soez, a. mean, vile, lousy.
sofisma, sm. sophism.
sofista, sm. sophist.
sofistería, sf. sophistry.
sofístico, ca, a. sophistical.
sofocar, v.a. ro suffocate.
sofrenada, sf. sudden check given to a horse with the bridle ; severe repri-mand.
sofrenar, v.a. to check a horse by a violent pull of the bridle ; to repri-mand severely.   [for shame !
soga, sf. rope of esparto grass ; ¡ — ! fy !
soguería, sf. rope-walk, rope-yard.
soguero, sm. rope-maker.
sojuzgador, sm. conqueror, subduer.
sojuzgar, v.a. to conquer, to subdue.
sol, sm. sun ; (mus.) sol.
solamente, ad. only, solely.
solana, sf. sunny place ; open gallery for taking the sun.
solano, sm. easterly wind.
solapa, sf. lappet ; pretence, pretext.
solapado, da, a. cunning, crafty, artful.
solapar, v.a. to button one's coat across ; to hide under a false pretence.
solar, sm. building lot ; ancestral man-sion ; —, a. solar ; —, v.a. to floor a room ; to sole shoes or boots.
solariego, ga, a. belonging to the an-cestral mansion of a noble family.
solaz, sm. solace, consolation ; á —, pleasantly, agreeably.
solazar, v.a. to solace, to comfort.
solazo, sm. scorching sun.
soldada, sf. wages.
soldadesca, sf. soldiery.
soldadesco, ca, a. soldierly, soldier-like.
soldado, sm. soldier ; —, raso, common soldier, private.
soldador, sm. solderer ; soldering-iron.
soldadura, sf. soldering ; solder ; cor-rection.

soldar, v.a. to solder; to mend, to correct.

solecismo, sm. solecism. [place; desert.

soledad, sf. solitude; solitariness; lonely

solemne, a. solemn; celebrated; grand, high; gay, cheerful.

solemnidad, sf. solemnity.

solemnizar, v.a. to solemnize, to praise.

soler, v.n. to be accustomed.

solfa, sf. (mus.) gamut; accordance, harmony.

solfeador, sm. songster; music-master; dealer of blows.

solfeo, sm. solfeggio.

solfista, sm. & f. skilful musician.

solicitación, sf. solicitation.

solicitar, v.a. to solicit.

solícito, ta, a. solicitous.

solicitud, sf. solicitude; petition.

solidar, v.a. to consolidate.

solidez, sf. solidity.

sólido, da, a. solid.

soliloquio, sm. soliloquy, monologue.

solimán, sm. (chem.) corrosive sublimate.

solio, sm. throne.

solitario, ria, a. solitary; —, sm. hermit.

solo, sm. (mus.) solo; —, la, a. alone, single; á solas, alone, unaided; sólo, ad. only.

solomillo, solomo, sm. loin, chine.

solsticio, sm. solstice.

soltar, v.a. to untie, to loosen; to set at liberty; -se, to get loose; to lose all decency and modesty.

soltera, sf. spinster, unmarried woman.

soltería, sf. celibacy.

soltero, sm. bachelor, unmarried man; —, a. unmarried.

soltura, sf. liberation; release; agility, activity.

soluble, a. soluble; solvable.

solución, sf. solution; catastrophe of a drama.

solvente, a. dissolvent; solvent.

sollo, sm. common pike.

sollozar, v.a. to sob.

sollozo, sm. sob.

somanta, sf. beating, severe chastisement.

somatén, sm. armed corps for defence of a city; hue and cry.

sombra, sf. shade, shadow.

sombraje, sm. border, arbour.

sombrear, v.a. to shade.

sombrerazo, sm. large hat; slap with a hat. [bur.

sombrerera, sf. hat-box; (bot.) butter

sombrerería, sf. hat-factory; hat-shop.

sombrerero, sm. hatter, hat-maker.

sombrerillo, sm. (bot.) navel-wort.

sombrero, sm. hat.

sombrilla, sf. sunshade.

sombrío, bría, a. shady, darksome, gloomy.

someter, v.a. to submit; to subdue; -se, to humble oneself; to submit.

sometimiento, sm. submission.

somnolencia, sf. sleepiness, drowsiness.

somonte, sm. de —, rough, rude.

somorgujar, v.a. to submerge; — v.n. to dive. [sound of.

son, sm. sound, report; á —, at the

sonado, da, a. celebrated; famous; generally reported.

sonaja, sf. timbrel (musical instrument).

sonámbulo, a. & sm. sleep-walking; somnambulist.

sonar, v.a. to play upon a musical instrument; —, v.n. to sound; —se, to blow one's nose.

sonata, sf. (mus.) sonata.

sonda, sf. sounding; catheter.

sondable, a. that may be sounded.

sond(e)ar, v.a. (mar.) to sound.

soneto, sm. sonnet.

sonido, sm. sound.

sonoro, ra, a. sonorous.

sonreirse, v.r. to smile.

sonrisa, sf. smile.

sonroj(e)ar, v.a. to make one blush with shame; -se, to blush.

sonrojo, sm. blush; offensive word which causes a blush.

sonros(e)ar, v.a. to dye a rose colour; -se, to blush.

sonroseo, sm. blush.

sonsacador, ra, sm. & f. wheedler.

sonsacamiento, sm. wheedling, extortion.

sonsacar, v.a. wheedle, to entice away, to worm out a secret.

sonsonete, sm. tapping noise; scornf i, derisive tone.

soñador, ra, sm. & f. dreamer.

soñar, v.a. to dream.

soñoliento, ta, a. sleepy, drowsy; causing sleep; dull, lazy.

sopa, sf. sop; soup. [poor students.

sopalanda, sf. ragged clothes worn by

sopapo, sm. slap given with the hand; sucker of a pump.

sopera, sf. soup-dish.

sopero, sm. soup-plate.

sopetear, v.a. to steep bread in sauce; to abuse with foul language.

sopetón, sm. box on the ears; de —, suddenly.

soplado, da, a. over-nice and spruce.

soplamocos, sm. slap in the face.

soplar, v.n. & a. to blow; to blow bellows; to steal in an artful manner; to suggest; to inspire; to tipple, to drink much; to accuse, to denounce any one; -se, to dress in style.

soplete, sm. blow-pipe.

soplo, sm. blowing ; puff of wind ; secret advice, hint ; instant, moment.

soplón, ona, sm. & f. tale-bearer.

soponcio, tm. (col.) dismay.

sopor, sm. drowsiness, sleepiness.

soporífero, ra, a. soporific, soporiferous.

soportable, a. tolerable, supportable.

soportal, sm. portico.

soportar, v.a. to suffer, to tolerate ; to support.

sor, sister (used only to nuns).

sorbar, v.a. to sip, to suck ; to absorb, to swallow ; to imbibe.

sorbete, sm. sherbet.

sorbo, sm. sipping ; sup; a little ; small quantity.

sordera, sf. deafness.

sordidez, sf. sordidness, nastiness, covetousness.

sórdido, da, a. sordid ; nasty, dirty ; licentious.

sordina, sf. (mus.) mute.

sordo, da, a. deaf ; silent, quiet ; secret.

sorna, sf. sluggishness, laziness, slowness.

sorprender, v.a. to surprise, to attack unexpectedly.

sorpresa, sf. surprise.

sortear, v.n. to draw or cast lots ; to dodge a bull ; to avoid.

sorteo, sm. drawing lots.

sortija, sf. ring ; hoop ; buckle.

sortilegio, sm. sorcery.

sosegado, da, a. quiet, peaceful.

sosegar, v.a. to appease, to calm ; —, v.n. to rest, to repose ; to be calm or composed.

sosería, sf. insipidity.

sosiego, sm. tranquillity, calmness.

soslayar, v.a. to slope, to slant; to place a thing crooked.

soslayo, ad. obliquely ; al ó de —, askew, sideways.

soso, sa, a. insipid, tasteless.

sospecha, sf. suspicion, mistrust.

sospechar, v.a. to suspect.

sospechoso, sa, a. suspicious, mistrustful.

sostén, sm. support ; steadiness of a ship in her course.

sostener, v.a. to sustain, to maintain ; -se, to support or maintain oneself.

sostenido, a. & sm. (mus.) sharp.

sostenimiento, sm. sustenance.

sota, sf. knave (at cards).

sotana, sf. cassock ; flogging, drubbing.

sotanilla, sf. college gown.

sótano, sm. cellar.

sotavento, sm. (mar.) leeward, lee.

sotechado, sm. roofed or covered place.

soto, sm. grove, thicket ; undergrowth.

su, pn. his, her its. theirs.

suave, a. smooth, soft, delicate ; gentle, mild, meek.

suavidad, sf. softness, sweetness ; suavity.

suavizar, v.a. to soften.

subalterno, na, a. subaltern, inferior.

subarrendador, ra, sm. & f. sub-tenant.

subarrendar, v.a. to sub-let.

subarriendo, sm. sub-lease.

subasta, subastación, sf. judicial auction, open sale.

subastar, v.a. to sell by auction.

subdelegado, sm. subdelegate.

subdiaconado, subdiaconato, sm. sub-deaconship.

subdiácono, sm. subdeacon.

súbdito, ta, a. subject.

subdividir, v.a. to subdivide.

subdivisión, sf. subdivision.

subida, sf. mounting ; ascent, acclivity, rise ; enhancement, augmentation of value or price.

subido, da, a. deep-coloured ; very fine, excellent ; expensive.

subir, v.n. to mount, to ascend, to climb; to increase, to swell ; to rise in dignity, fortune, &c. ; —, v.a. to lift, to raise ; to enhance.

súbito, ta, a. sudden, hasty, unforeseen.

subjuntivo, sm. (gr.) subjunctive.

sublevación, sf. sedition, revolt.

sublevar, v.a. to excite a rebellion ; -se, to rise in rebellion.

sublimado, sm. sublimate.

sublime, a. sublime.

sublimidad, sf. sublimity.

subordinación, sf. subordination.

subordinar, v.a. to subordinate.

subrepción, sf. hidden action, underhand business.

subrepticio, cia, a. surreptitious ; done in a clandestine manner.

subrogación, sf. substitution.

subrogar, v.a. to substitute.

subsanar, v.a. to excuse ; to mend, to repair.

subsidio, sm. subsidy, aid.

subsistencia, sf. subsistence ; permanence, stability.

subsistir, v.n. to subsist.

substancia, sf. substance.

substancial, a. substantial.

substantialmente, ad. substantially.

substanciar, v.a. to abridge ; to aver, to verify.

substancioso, sa, a. substantial, nutritive, nutritious.

substracción, sf. subtraction.

substraer, v.a. to subtract ; -se, to retire, to withdraw.

subteniente, sm. sub-lieutenant.

subterfugio, sf. subterfuge, shift.

subterráneo, nea, a. subterraneous ; —, sm. cavern.
subvenir, v.a. to aid, to succour.
subversión, sf. subversion, overthrow.
subversivo, va, a. subversive. [ruin.
subvertir, v.a. to subvert, to destroy, to
subyugar, v.a. to subdue, to subjugate.
suceder, v.n. to succeed, to inherit ; to happen, to result.
sucesión, sf. succession ; issue, offspring ; hereditary succession.
sucesivo, va, a. successive.
suceso, sm. success ; result, event.
sucesor, sm. successor ; heir. [mire.
suciedad, sf. nastiness, filthiness, dirt,
sucinto, ta, a. succinct, concise.
sucio, cia, a. dirty, nasty, filthy ; obscene ; dishonest.
suculento, ta, a. succulent, juicy.
sucumbir, v.n. to succumb.
sud, sm. south. [pugnance.
sudar, v.a. to sweat ; to give with re-
sudario, sm. sweat-cloth.
sudest, sm. south-east.
sudoeste, sm. south-west.
sudor, sm. sweat.
sudoriento, ta, a. moist with sweat.
sudorífico, ca, a. sudorific.
sudoso, sa, a. sweaty.
suegra, sf. mother-in-law..
suegro, sm. father-in-law..
suela, sf. sole of the shoe ; sole-leather.
sueldo, sm. ancient Roman coin ; wages, salary.
suelo, sm. soil, surface ; sole ; district.
suelta, sf. loosening ; release ; hobbles ; dar —, to liberate for a short time.
suelto, ta, a. loose ; expeditious, swift.
sueño, sm. sleep ; vision, dream.
suero, sm. whey.
suerte, sf. chance, lot, fortune, good-luck, haphazard ; kind, sort ; species ; manner.
suficiencia, sf. sufficiency ; á —, sufficiently, enough.
suficiente, a. sufficient ; fit, capable.
sufocación, sf. suffocating.
sufocar, v.a. to suffocate, to choke ; to quench.
sufragáneo, sm. suffragan ; —, ea, a. belonging to a suffragan.
sufragar, v.a. to aid, to assist.
sufragio, sm. vote, suffrage ; aid, assistance.
sufrible, a. sufferable.
sufrido, da, a. long suffering, patient.
sufrimiento, sm. sufferance, patience.
sufrir, v.a. to suffer, to bear with patience, to permit.
sugerir, v.a. to suggest.
sugestión, sf. suggestion.

suicida, sm. suicide, self-murderer.
suicidio, sm. suicide, self-murder.
sujeción, sf. subjection ; logical connexion.
sujetar, v.a. to subdue ; to subject.
sujeto, ta, a. subject, liable, exposed ; —, sm. subject ; matter under discussion ; person, individual.
sulfúreo, rea, a. sulphureous
sulfúrico, a. sulphuric.
sultán, sm. sultan.
sultana, sf. sultana, sultaness.
suma, sf. sum ; substance.
sumar, v.a. to add, to sum up.
sumario, ria, a. summary ; —, sm. compendium, summary.
sumergir, v.a. to submerge.
sumersión, sf. submersion, immersion.
sumidero, sm. sewer, drain.
sumiller, sm chief steward in the king's household.
suministración, sf. supply, furnishing.
suministrador, ra, sm. & f. provider.
suministrar, v.a. to supply, to furnish.
sumir, v.a. to submerge ; to bury ; to take, to receive the chalice at mass ; -se, to sink under ground ; to be sunken (of one's features).
sumisión, sf. submission.
sumiso, sa, a. submissive, humble.
sumo, ma, a. highest, greatest ; á lo —, at most ; to the highest pitch.
súmulas, sf.pl. synopsis of the first elements of logic.
suntuosidad, sf. sumptuousness.
suntuoso, sa, a. sumptuous.
supeditación, sf. trampling under foot.
supeditar, v.a. to trample under foot.
superable, a. superable, conquerable.
superabundancia, sf. superabundance.
superabundar, v.n. to superabound.
superar, v.a. to surpass.
superchería, sf. deceit, fraud.
superficial, a. superficial.
superficie, sf. superficies, surface.
superfino, na, a. superfine.
superfluidad, sf. superfluity.
superfluo, ua, a. superfluous.
superintendencia, sf. superintendence.
superintendente, sm. superintendent, intendant.
superior, a. superior ; upper (in geography) ; —, sm. superior.
superioridad, sf. superiority.
superlativo, va, a. & sm. (gr.) superlative.
supernumerario, ria, a. supernumerary.
superstición, sf. superstition.
supersticioso, sa, a. superstitious.
supino, na, a. supine, on one's back ; —, sm. (gr.) supine.
suplantación, sf. supplanting.

suplantar, v.a. to falsify *or* tamper with a document ; to supplant.
suplefaltas, sm. substitute.
suplemento, sm. supplement.
súplica, sf. petition, request, supplication.
suplicante, a. & sm. supplicant.
suplicar, v.a. to supplicate ; (law) to appeal against a sentence .
suplicio, sm. capital punishment.
suplir, v.a. to supply ; to act as substitute.
suponer, v.a. to suppose, to surmise.
suposición, sf, supposition ; authority, personal distinction.
supremo, ma, a. supreme.
supresión, sf. suppression.
suprimir, v.a. to suppress.
supuesto, sm. supposition ; —, ta, a. supposed ; — que, allowing that, granting that.
supuración, sf. suppuration.
supurar, v.n. to suppurate.
supurativo, va, a. promoting suppuration.
sur, sm. south.
surcar, v.a. to furrow.
surco, sm. furrow.
surgidero, sm. anchoring-place.
surgir, v.a. to anchor ; to surge.
surtido, sm. assortment, supply.
surtidor, ra, sm. & f. purveyor, caterer ; water-spout.
surtir, v.a. to supply, to furnish, to provide.
susceptible, a. susceptible.
suscitar, v.a. to excite, to stir up.

suscribir, v.a. to subscribe.
suscripción, sf. subscription ; signature.
suscriptor, ra, sm. & f. subscriber.
susodicho, cha, a. fore-mentioned, afore-suspender, v.a. to suspend.   [said.
suspensión, sf. suspension.
suspensivo, va, a. suspensive
suspenso, sa, a. suspended, unfinished.
suspensorio, ria, a. & sm. & f, suspensory
suspicacia, sf. suspiciousness, jealousy
suspicaz, a. suspicious, jealous.
suspirar, v.n. to sigh.
suspiro, sm. sigh ; sugar sweetmeat.
sustantivo, va, a. & sm. (gr.) substantive, noun.
sustentación, sf. sustentation, support.
sustentar, v.a. to sustain ; to support, to nourish.
sustento, sm. food, sustenance.
sustitución, sf. substitution.
sustituir, v.a. to substitute.
sustituto, a. & sm. substitute.
susto, sm. fright, sudden terror.
susurrar, v.n. to whisper, to divulge a secret ; to murmur (of streams) ; -se, to be whispered about.
susurro, sm. whisper, murmur.
sútil, a. subtile ; subtle.
sutileza, sf. subtlety.
sutilizar, v.a. to subtilize ; to polish ; to discuss profoundly.
suyo, ya, a. his, hers, theirs, one's ; de —, spontaneously ; -s, sm.pl. one's people, friends, relations, acquaintance, servants.

T

taba, sf. ankle bone ; knucklebones (game).
tabaco, sm. tobacco ; — de polvo, snuff.
tábano, sm. hornet.
tabaola, sf. noise, shouting.
tabaquera, sf. snuff-box.
tabaquero, sm. tobacconist.
tabardillo, sm. burning fever.
taberna, sf. tavern.
tabernáculo, sm. tabernacle.
tabernero, sm. tavern-keeper.
tabicar, v.a. to wall up.
tabique, sm. thin wall ; partition-wall.
tabla, sf. board ; table ; butcher's block ; index of a book ; bed of earth in a garden ; -s,pl. tables containing the Decalogue ; backgammon-board.
tablado, sm. scaffold, stage ; bedstead ; (mar.) platform.
tablajero, sm. gambler.
tablazo, sm. blow with a board ; arm of the sea *or* of a river.

tablazón, sf. boarding, planking, decks and sheathing of a ship.
tablero, sm. planed board ; chess-board ; draft-board ; gambling-house ; tailor's shop-board.
tableta, sf. tablet ; cracknel.
tabletear, v.n. to move boards noisily.
tablilla, sf. placard ; tablet ; — de mesón, sign of an inn.
tablón, sm. plank.
tabuco, sm. hut, small apartment.
taburete, sm. stool.
tacañería, sf. malicious cunning ; niggardliness.   [sordid.
tacaño, ña, a. artful, knavish ; stingy, **tácito, ta**, a. tacit, silent ; implied.
taciturno, na, a. tacit, silent, melancholy.
taco, sm. stopper, stopple ; wad ; rammer ; billiard-cue.
tacón, sm. heel (of boot).
taconear, v.n. to walk on one's heels.

taconeo, sm. clatter of the heels in dancing.

táctica, sf. tactics.

tacto, sm. touch, feeling; tact.

tacha, sf. fault, defect; small nail, tack.

tachar, v.a. to blame; to reprehend; to blot, to efface.

tachón, sm. large nail. [nails.

tachonar, v.a. to stud with gilt-headed

tachuela, sf. tack, nail.

tafetán, sm. taffety.

tafilete, sm. Morocco leather.

tahalí, sm. shoulder-belt.

tahona, sf. horse-mill; crushing-mill; bakehouse.

tahur, sm. gambler, gamester.

tahurería, sf. gaming-house; fraudulent gambling.

taimado, da, a. sly, cunning, crafty.

taja, sf. cut, incision; dissection; tally.

tajada, sf. slice; (fam.) hoarseness.

tajadera, sf. chopping-knife.

tajador, ra, sm. & f. chopper, cutter; chopping-block; trencher.

tajadura, sf. cut, notch; section.

tajamar, sm. cut-water.

tajaplumas, sm. pen-knife. [cut a quill.

tajar, v.a. to cut, to chop; to hew; to

tajo, sm. cut, incision; cutting of a quill with a pen-knife; chopping-block.

tajuela, sf., **tajuelo**, sm. stool, bench.

tal, a. such; **con —**, provided that; **no hay —**, no such thing.

tala, sf. felling of trees.

talador, ra, a. destroying.

taladrar, v.a. to bore, to pierce.

taladro, sm. gimblet, auger.

tálamo, sm. bride-chamber; bridal bed.

talanquera, sf. parapet; breastwork.

talante, sm. manner of performance; appearance, aspect; disposition; will, pleasure.

talar, v.a. to fell trees; to desolate, to ruin; —, a. trailing, down to the heels (of clothes); —, sm. wing on the heel of Mercury.

talco, sm. talc.

talega, sf. bag; bagful. [fellow.

talego, sm. sack; clumsy, awkward

taleguilla, sf. small bag.

talento, sm. talent.

talión, sf. retaliation, requital.

talismán, sm. talisman.

talón, sm. heel; heel-piece of a shoe; (rail.) luggage-ticket, receipt.

talonear, v.n. to walk fast.

talla, sf. raised work; sculpture; stature, size; measure of anything; hand, draw; **media —**, half-relief.

tallado, da, a. cut, carved, engraved.

tallador, sm. engraver.

tallar, v.a. to cut, to chop; to carve in wood; to engrave; —, sm. forest of wood fit for cutting.

talle, sm. shape, size, proportion; waist.

taller, sm. workshop, laboratory.

tallista, sm. wood-carver, engraver.

tallo, sm. shoot, sprout.

talludo, da, a. thick-stalked.

tamaño, sm. size, snape, bulk; —, **ña, a** so big, so large.

tamarindo, sm. tamarind-tree.

tamarisco, tamariz, sm. tamarisk.

tambalear, -se, v.n. to stagger, to waver.

tambaleo, sm. staggering, reeling.

también, c. & ad. also, likewise; as well.

tambor, sm. drum; drummer; iron cylinder; **— mayor**, (mil.) drum-major.

tamboril, sm. tabour, tabor.

tamiz, sm. fine sieve.

tamo, sm. fluff; corn-dust; dust behind furniture.

tampoco, ad. neither.

tan, sm. sound of the tabour; —, ad. so, so much, as well, as much.

tanda, sf. turn; rotation; task; gang, shift (of workmen); number of persons employed in a work; lot, fixed quantity.

tanganillas, en —, ad. waveringly.

tanganillo, sm. small prop or stay.

tangente, sf. (geom.) tangent.

tangible, a. tangible. [blow.

tantarantán, sm. roll of a drum; sounding

tantear, v.a. to measure, to proportion; to mark the game with counters; to consider; to examine.

tanteo, sm. computation, calculation; playing-counters; valuation.

tanto, sm. certain sum or quantity; copy of a writing; —, **ta**, a. so much, as much; very great; —, ad. so, in such a manner; a long time.

tañedor, ra, sm. & f. player on a musical instrument.

tañer, v.imp. to concern.

tañido, sm. tune; sound; clink.

tapa, sf. lid, cover; **— de los sesos**, top of the skull.

tapadera, sf. lid of a pot, cover.

tapadero, sm. large stopper.

tapadura, sf. act of covering.

tapar, v.a. to stop up, to cover; to conceal, to hide.

tapete, sm. rug, table-cover.

tapia, sf. mud-wall. [stop up.

tapiar, v.a. to enclose with a mud-wall; to

tapicería, sf. tapestry.

tapicero, sm. tapestry-maker.

tapiz, sm. tapestry.

tapizar, v.a. to hang with tapestry.

tapón, sm. cork, plug, bung.
tapujarse, v.r. to muffle oneself up.
taquigrafía, sf. short-hand writing.
taquígrafo, sm. short-hand writer.
tara, sf. tare.
taracea, sf. marquetry, checker-work.
taracear, v.a. inlay.
tarambana, sm. & f. feather-head, fool.
tarantela, sf. tarantella, Neapolitan
    peasant dance ; its tune.
tarántula, sf. tarantula.
tararira, sf. noisy mirth.
tarasca, sf. dragon borne in procession of
    Corpus Christi ; termagant, virago.
tarascada, sf. bite ; pert, harsh answer.
tarazón, sm. large slice.
tardanza, sf. slowness, delay.
tardar, v.n. to delay, to tarry.   [late.
tarde, sf. afternoon ; evening ; —, ad.
tardío, día, a. late ; slow, tardy.
tardo, da, a. sluggish, tardy.
tarea, sf. task.
tarifa, sf. tariff.
tarima, sf. movable step, platform.
tarjeta, sf. visiting-card, card ; — postal,
    post-card.
tarro, sm. glazed earthern bottle.
tarta, sf. tart.   [perplexed.
tartalear, v.n. to reel, to stagger ; to be
tartamudear, v.n. to stutter, to stammer.
tartamudo, da, a. stammering.
tartana, sf. small boat ; small carriage.
Tártaro, sm. Tartar ; (poet.) hell.
tartera, sf. baking-pan (for tarts).
tarugo, sm. wooden peg or pin.
tasa, sf. rate, assize ; measure, rule ;
    valuation.
tasación, sf. valuation, appraisement.
tasador, sm. appraiser.
tasar, v.a. to apprise, to value.
tascar, v.a. to break flax or hemp ; to
    nibble grass ; to champ the bit.
tasco, sm. refuse of flax or hemp.
tasto, sm. nasty taste.
tatarabuelo, sm. great-great-grandfather.
tataranieto, sm. great-great-grandson.
taumaturgo, sm. miracle-worker.
Tauro, sm. Taurus (sign of the zodiac).
tautología, sf. tautology.
taza, sf. cup ; basin of a fountain ; (fig. &
    fam.) buttocks, breech.
tazmía, sf. share of tithes.
te, sm. (bot.) tea.
te, pn. thee.
tea, sf. candle-wood ; torch.
teatral, a. theatrical.
teatro, sm. theatre, playhouse.
tecla, sf. key of an organ or pianoforte.
teclado, sm. key-board.
técnico, ca, a. technical.
techo, sm. roof ; dwelling-house.

techumbre, sf. lofty roof, church roof.
tedio, sm. disgust, dislike, abhorrence.
teja, sf. roof-tile.
tejado, sm. roof covered with tiles.
tejar, sm. tile-works ; —, v.a. to tile.
tejedor, sm. weaver.   [stuff.
tejedura, sf. texture, weaving ; woven
tejer, v.a. to weave.
tejera, tejería, sf. tile-kiln.
tejero, sm. tile-maker.
tejido, sm. texture, web.
tejo, sm. quoit ; yew-tree.
tejón, sm. badger.
tela, sf. cloth ; woven stuff.
telar, sm. loom.
telaraña, sf. cobweb.
telefonio, sm. telephon.
telegráfico, ca, a. telegraphic.
telégrafo, sm. telegraph.
telescopio, sm. telescope.
telón, sm. curtain (of theatre).
tema, sm. theme ; —, sf. hobby.
temblar, vn. to tremble.
temblón, ona, a. tremulous.
temblor, sm. trembling.
temer, v.a. to fear, to doubt.
temerario, ria, a. rash, temerarious.
temeridad, sf. temerity, imprudence.
temeroso, sa, a. timid, timorous.
temible, a. dreadful, terrible.
temor, sm. dread, fear.
témpano, sm. drum-skin.
temperamento, sm. temperament.
temperar, v.a. to temper, to moderate.
temperatura, sf. temperature.
tempestad, sf. tempest, storm ; violent
    commotion.
tempestuoso, sa, a. tempestuous, stormy.
templadamente, ad. temperately, moder-
    ately.
templado, da, a. temperate, tempered.
templanza, sf. temperance, moderation ;
    temperature.
templar, v.a. to temper, to moderate, to
    cool ; to tune ; -se, to be moderate.
templario, sm. templar.
temple, sm. temperature ; temper,
    temperament ; harmonious accordance
    of musical instruments ; al —, painted
    in distemper.
templo, sm. temple ; church.
Témpora, sf. Ember-days.   [period.
temporada, sf. space of time, epoch,
temporal, a. temporary, temporal ; —,
    sm. weather ; tempest, storm.
temporalidad, sf. temporality.
temprano, na, a. early, anticipated ; —,
    ad. early.
tenacillas, sf.pl. small tongs.
tenacidad, sf. tenacity ; obstinacy.
tenada, sf. sheepfold.

tenaz, a. tenacious, stubborn.

tenaza, sf. tongs, pincers.

tenazada, sf. grip with pincers or tongs; act of biting strongly.

tenazmente, ad. tenaciously; obstinately.

tenca, sf. tench.

ten con ten, sm. moderation, temperance; —, ad. equally.

tendedero, sm. drying-lines.

tendedor, sm. stretcher.

tendencia, sf. tendency.

tender, v.a. to stretch out, to expand, to extend; -se, to stretch oneself out at full length.

tendero, ra, sm. & f. haberdasher.

tendido, sm. uncovered seats at a bull fight.

tendón, sm. tendon, sinew.

tenebrario, sm. (eccl.) candelabrum used in Holy Week.

tenebroso, sa, a. dark, obscure.

tenedor, sm. holder, keeper, tenant; fork.

tenencia, sf. possession; lieutenancy.

tener, v.a. to take, to hold, to possess; to have; -se, to stand firm; to stop, to halt; to resist; to adhere.

tenería, sf. tan-yard.

teniente, sm. lieutenant.

tenor, sm. tenour; (mus.) tenor.

tensión, sf. tension.

tentación, sf. temptation. [tempter.

tentador, ra, a. & sm. & f. tempting.

tentar, v.a. to touch; to try; to grope; to tempt; to attempt; to probe.

tentativa, sf. attempt, trial.

tenue, a. thin, tenuous, slender. [trifle.

tenuidad, sf. slenderness, weakness;

teñidura, sf. dyeing.

teñir, v.a. to tinge, to dye.

teologal, a. theological.

teología, sf. theology, divinity.

teológico, ca, a. theological.

teólogo, sm. theologian, divine.

teorema, sf. theorem.

teoría, teórica, sf. theory.

teórico, ca, a. theoretical.

tercena, sf. tobacco warehouse.

tercería, sf. mediation, arbitration; depositary. [mediator.

tercero, sm. third person; pimp;

tercerola, sf. short carbine. [trio.

terceto, sm. (poet.) terzarima; (mus.)

tercia, sf. third; canonical hour falling at three o'clock; sequence of three cards.

terciado, sm. cutlass.

terciana, sf. tertian-fever.

tercianario, ria, sm. & f. person suffering from tertian-fever.

terciar, v.a. to put on sideways; to divide into three parts; to plough the third time; —, v.n. to mediate.

terciero, sm. Spanish foot-soldier (16th and 17th centuries).

tercio, cia, a. third; —, sm. third part; half a load; Spanish regiment (in the 16th century); hacer bueno —, to do a good turn, to aid. [velvety.

terciopelado, sf. velveteen; —, da, a.

terciopelero, sm. velvet-weaver.

terciopelo, sm. velvet.

terco, ca, a. pertinacious, obstinate; hard as marble.

tergiversación, sf. tergiversation, evasion.

tergiversar, v.a. to tergiversate

teriaca, sf. treacle.

terliz, sm. tick, stuff for beds.

termal, a. thermal.

termas, sf.pl. thermal-waters, pl.

terminacho, sm. rude word or phrase.

terminación, sf. termination; conclusion; last syllable of a word.

terminante, a. decisive.

terminar, v.a. to terminate. [limit.

término, sm. term; end; boundary

termómetro, sm. thermometer.

terna, sf. set of three.

ternero, ra, sm. & f. calf; veal.

terneza, sf. softness, delicacy, tenderness.

ternilla, sf. gristle.

ternilloso, sa, a. gristly, cartilaginous.

terno, sf. ternary number; ornaments for celebrating high-mass.

ternura, sf. tenderness.

terquedad, terquería, terqueza, sf. stubbornness, obstinacy.

terrado, sm. terrace.

terraja, sf. screw-plate.

terraplén, sm. rampart; terrace, platform; embankment.

terraplenar, v.a. to level (uneven ground).

terraza, sf. glazed jar with two handles.

terremoto, sm. earthquake.

terrenal, a. terrestrial, earthly.

terreno, na, a. earthly, terrestrial; —, sm. land, ground, field.

terrestre, a. terrestrial.

terrible, a. terrible, dreadful; ferocious.

territorial, a. territorial.

territorio, sm. territory.

terrón, sm. clod of earth, glebe; lump; -ones, pl. landed property.

terror, sm. terror, dread.

terrorismo, sm. terrorism.

terrorista, sm. & f. terrorist

tersar, v.a. to smooth.

terso, sa, a. smooth, glossy.

tersura, sf. smoothness, purity.

tertulia, sf. club, assembly, circle.

tertuliano, sm. member of a club or social

tesauro, sm. dictionary. [group.

tesis, sf. thesis.

tesón, sm. tenacity, firmness.

tesorería, sf. treasury.
tesorero, sm. treasurer.
tesoro, sm. treasure; exchequer.
testa, sf. head; front, face.
testado, da, a. leaving a will.
testador, sm. testator.
testadora, sf. testatrix.
testadura, sf. erasure. [tion.
testamentaría, sf. testamentary execu-
testamentario, sm. executor of a will; —,
ria, a. testamentary
testamento, sm. will, testament.
testar, v.a. & n. to make one's will; to
bequeath; to scratch out.
testarudo, da, a. obstinate, wrong-headed.
testera, sf. front of anything; back seat
of a carriage. [stubbornness
testerada, sf. blow with the head;
testículo, sm. testicle.
testificación, sf. attestation.
testificar, v.a. to attest, to witness.
testigo, sm. witness, deponent.
testimonial, a. testimonial; -es, sf.pl.
testimonials.
testimoniar, v.a. to attest, to bear witness
testimonio, sm. testimony; instrument
legalized by a notary. [gravity.
tesura, sf. stiffness, firmness; affected
teta, sf. dug, teat.
tetar, v.a. to suckle, to give suck.
tetera, sf. teapot, tea-kettle.
tetrarca, sm. tetrarch.
tétrico, ca, a. gloomy, sullen, surly.
texto, sm. text.
textual, a. textual.
tez, sf. complexion.
ti, pn. oblique case of **tú.**
tía, sf. aunt; good old woman.
tiara, sf. tiara.
tibieza, sf. lukewarmness.
tibio, bia, a. lukewarm, careless.
tiburón, sm. shark.
tiempo, sm. time; term; occasion,
opportunity; season.
tienda, sf. tent; awning; tilt; shop.
tienta, sf. probe (for surgeons).
tiento, sm. touch; circumspection; á —,
gropingly.
tierno, na, a. tender. [country.
tierra, sf. earth; land, ground; native
tieso, sa, a. stiff, hard, firm; robust;
valiant; stubborn.
tiesto, sm. potsherd; large earthen pot.
tigre, sm. tiger.
tijeras, sf.pl. scissors.
tijeretada, st. cut with scissors, clip.
tijeretas, sf.pl. tendrils.
tijeretear, v.a. to cut with scissors; to
dispose of other people's affairs at one's
pleasure. [tize.
tildar, v.a. to blot; to brand, to stigma-

tilde, sf. mark over a letter; tittle; trifle.
tilo, sm. linden-tree, lime-tree.
timbal, sm. kettle-drum.
timbalero, sm. kettle-drummer.
timbre, sm. insignia of nobility; seal;
stamp (postage); electric bell.
timidez, sf. timidity.
tímido, da, a. timid, cowardly.
timón, sm. helm, rudder.
timonear, vn. to steer.
timonel, timonero, sm. steersman.
timorato, ta, a. full of the fear of God.
tímpano, sm. kettle-drum; tympanum.
tina, sf. dyer's copper.
tinaja, sf. large earthen jar.
tinajero, sm. jar maker.
tinajón, sm. small tub.
tinglado, sm. shed, cart-house.
tiniebla, sf. darkness, obscurity; -s, pl.
ignorance, obscurity.
tino, sm. skill in feeling one's way;
judgment, prudence.
tinta, sf. tint, hue; ink.
tinte, sm. tint, dye.
tintero, sm. inkhorn, inkstand.
tinto, ta, a. red (of wine).
tintorería, sf. dyer's shop.
tintorero, sm. dyer.
tintura, sf. tincture.
tinturar, v.a. to tinge, to dye, to tincture.
tiña, sf. scab; ring-worm.
tiñoso, sa, a. scabby, scurvy; niggardly.
tío, sm. uncle; good old man.
tiple, sm. (mus.) treble; small guitar.
tipo, sm. type.
tipografía, sf. typography.
tipográfico, ca, a. typographical.
tipógrafo, sm. printer.
tira, sf. strip.
tirabuzón, sm. cork-screw.
tirada, sf. cast, throw; edition; distance
from one place to another.
tirador, ra, sm. & f. thrower; drawer.
tirana, sf. female tyrant.
tiranía, sf. tyranny.
tiránico, ca, a. tyrannical.
tiranizar, v.a. to tyrannize.
tirano, na, a. tyrannical; —, sm. tyrant.
tirante, sm. joist; trace; -s, braces; —, a.
taut, extended, drawn.
tirantez, sf. span; tautness.
tirar, v.a. to throw, to cast; to pull; to
draw; to fire off; to persuade; to print
off; to tend, to aim at.
tiritar, v.n. to shiver.
tiritona, sf. shiver.
tiro, sm. cast, throw, shot; prank, imposition; team; trace (of harness);
-s, pl. sword-belts; errar el —, to miss
(at shooting).
tirón, sm. pull, haul, tug.

tirotear, v.n. to shoot at random.
tiroteo, sm. random-shooting, sharp-shooting.
tirria, sf. antipathy.
tísico, ca, a. phthisical.
tisis, sf. phthisis.
tisú, sm. tissue. [fellow.
titere, sm. puppet; ridiculous little
titiritaina, sf. noisy sport.
titiritero, sm. puppet-player.
titubear, v.n. to totter; to stammer; to vacillate, to hesitate.
titubeo, sm. vacillation.
titular, v.a. to label, to inscribe; —, v.n. to obtain a title.
título, sm. title; name; á —, on pretence, under pretext.
tiza, sf. chalk.
tiznar, v.a. to smut; to tarnish.
tizne, sm. soot, smut of coal.
tiznón, sm. spot, stain.
tizón, sm. brand, half-burnt wood.
tizonera, sf. heap of ill-burnt charcoal.
toalla, sf. towel.
tobillo, sm. ankle.
toca, sf. hood; a thin stuff.
tocado, sm. head-dress, head-gear.
tocador, sm. dressing-room, toilet-table.
tocamiento, sm. touch, contact; inspiration.
tocante (á), pr. concerning, relating to.
tocar, v.a. to touch; (mus.) to play on; to ring a bell; to test; —, v.n. to belong; to concern; to be a duty; to import; to fall to one's share.
tocayo, ya, a. name-sake.
tocinero, sm. pork-butcher.
tocino, sm. bacon, salt pork; hog's lard; hoja de —, flitch.
todavía, ad. nevertheless; yet, still.
todo, da, a. all, entire; —, sm. whole.
todopoderoso, a. almighty.
toga, sf. toga; robe; judgeship.
togado, da, a. gowned.
Toisón, sm. Order of the Golden Fleece.
toldo, sm. awning; penthouse; booth.
tolerable, a. tolerable, supportable.
tolerancia, sf. tolerance, indulgence.
tolerante, a. tolerant.
tolerar, v.n. to tolerate, to suffer.
toleto, sm. (mar.) row-lock.
tolondro, tolondrón, sm. bump, swelling; —, ona, a. giddy, hare-brained.
tolva, sf. mill-hopper.
toma, sf. dose.
tomar, v.a. to take, to seize, to grasp; to understand, to interpret, to perceive; — á cuestas, to take upon oneself; -se, to get rusty, to rust.
tomate, sm. (bot.) tomato.
tomatera, sf. tomato-plant.

tomillo, sm. (bot.) thyme.
tomo, sm. bulk; tome; volume.
ton, sm. tone; sin — ni son, without rhyme or reason.
tonada, sf. tune, melody.
tonel, sm. cask, barrel.
tonelada, sf. tun; collection of casks in a ship. [workshop.
tonelería, sf. cooper's trade; cooper's
tonelero, sm. cooper, hooper.
tónico, ca, a. tonic, strengthening.
tonina, sf. tunny; porpoise.
tono, sm. tone.
tonsura, sf. tonsure.
tonsurar, v.a. to give the tonsure to.
tontada, sf. nonsense. [foolishly.
tontear, v.n. to talk nonsense, to act
tontería, sf. foolery, nonsense.
tontillo, sm. farthingale.
tonto, ta, a. stupid, foolish.
topacio, sm. topaz.
topar, v.a. to run or strike against.
tope, sm. butt, rub; scuffle; -s, pl. (rail.) buffers.
topera, sf. mole-hole.
topetada, sf. butt (by a horned animal).
topetar, v.a. to butt.
topetón, sm. collision, encounter, blow.
tópico, ca, a. topical.
topinera, sf. mole-hill.
topo, sm. mole; stumbler.
topografía, sf. topography.
topográfico, ca, a. topographical.
toque, sm. touch; bell-ringing; crisis.
torada, sf. drove of bulls.
torbellino, sm. whirlwind; boisterous person.
torcaz, a., paloma —, ring-dove.
torcecuello, sm. wry-neck.
torcedura, sf. twisting; poor wine.
torcer, v.a. to twist, to double, to curve, to distort; to refute an argument.
torcida, sf. wick.
torcido, da, a. oblique, tortuous.
torcimiento, sm. bending, deflection; circumlocution.
tórculo, sm. rolling press.
tordo, sm. thrush, throstle; —, da, a. speckled black and white.
toreador, sm. bull-fighter.
torear, v.n. to fight bulls.
toreo, sm. bull-fighting.
torero, sm. bull-fighter.
toril, sm. enclosure for bulls.
torillo, sm. little or young bull.
tormenta, sf. storm, tempest.
tormento, sm. torment, pain, anguish; torture; tedious affliction.
tornaboda, sf. day after a wedding.
tornaguía, sf. receipt. [to repeat.
tornar, v.a. & n. to return; to restore;

tornasol, sm. (bot.) turnsole, heliotrope.

tornasolado, a. changing colours ; shot

torneador, sm. turner.   [(of silk).

tornear, v.a. & n. to turn (on a lathe) ; to tilt at tournaments.

torneo, sm. tournament.

tornero, sm. turner.

tornillo, sm. screw.

torniscón, sm. slap in the face.

torno, sm. wheel ; revolution ; turn ; en —, around.

toro, sm. bull.

toronjil, sm. (bot.) balm.

torozón, sm. gripes (among animals).

torpe, a. dull, heavy ; torpid ; stupid ; unchaste, obscene ; infamous.

torpeza, sf. heaviness, dullness ; torpor ; obscenity ; stupidity.

torre, sf. tower ; turret.

torrente, sm. torrent.

torreznada, sf. dish of rashers.

torrezno, sm. rasher.

tórrido, da, a. torrid, parched, hot.

torrija, sf. pancake.

torta, sf. tart.

tortada, sf. meat-pie.

tortera, sf. pie-dish.

torticolis, sf. stiff neck.

tortilla, sf. omelet.

tórtola, sf. turtle-dove.

tortuga, sf tortoise.

tortuoso, sa, a. tortuous, circuitous.

tortura, sf. tortuosity, flexure ; rack,

torvo, va, a. stern, grim.   [torture.

torzal, sm. cord, twist.

tos, sf. cough.

toscamente, ad. coarsely, grossly.

tosco, ca, a. coarse, ill-bred, clumsy.

toser, v.n. to cough.

tósigo, sm. poison.

tostada, sf. slice of toasted bread ; toast.

tostado, da, a. parched, sun-burnt ; brown.   [fork.

tostador, ra, sm. & f. toaster ; toasting-

tostar, v.a. to toast, to roast.   [entire.

total, sm. whole, totality ; —, à. total,

totalidad, sf. totality.   [fetter.

traba, sf. obstacle, impediment ; trammel

trabacuenta, sf. mistake in an account ; dispute, controversy.

trabajador, ra, a. & sm. & f. labourer.

trabajar, v.a. to work, to labour.

trabajo, sm. work, labour, toil ; difficulty ; -s, pl. troubles.

trabajoso, sa, a. laborious ; painful.

trabar, v.a. to join, to unite ; to join (battle, conversation, etc.) ; to take hold of ; to fetter, to shackle.

trabazón, sf. juncture, union.

trabilla, sf. stitch dropped in knitting ; strap (of trousers).

trabucación, sf. confusion, mistake.

trabucar, v.a. to derange, to confound ; -se, to mistake.   [sudden fright.

trabucazo, sm. shot with a blunderbuss ;

trabuco, sm. blunderbuss.

tradición, sf. tradition.

traducción, sf. translation.

traducir, v.a. to translate.

traductor, sm. translator.

traer, v.a. to bring, to carry, to attract ; to persuade ; -se, to be dressed in style; to bear oneself (well or ill).

tráfago, sm. traffic, trade ; careful management of affairs.

traficación, sf. traffic, trade.

traficante, sm. merchant, dealer.

traficar, v.n. to traffic, to commerce, to do business, to deal (in).

tráfico, sm. traffic, trade.

tragadero, sm. œosophagus, gullet ; gulph, abyss ; tener buenos -s ó buenas tragaderas, to be very credulous.

tragador, ra, sm. & f. glutton, gobbler.

tragaldabas, sm. glutton.

tragaleguas, sm. great walker.

tragaluz, sm. skylight.

tragantada, sf. large draught of liquor.

tragantón, ona, sm. & f. glutton ; —, a. gluttonous.

tragar, v.a. to swallow ; -se, to dissemble.

tragedia, sf. tragedy.

trágico, ca, a. tragic, tragical.

trago, sm. draught of liquor ; adversity, misfortune ; á -s, by degrees.

tragón, ona, a. gluttonous.

traición, sf. treason.

traidor, sm. traitor ; —, ra, a. treacherous

trailla, sf. leash ; levelling machine.

traillar, v.a. to level the ground.

traje, sm. complete dress ; costume ; suit of clothes.

trajinar, v.a. to convey.

trajinero, sm. waggoner.

trama, sf. plot.

tramador, ra, sm. & f. plotter ; artful contriver.   [machinate.

tramar, v.a. to weave ; to plot, to

trámite, sm. path ; (law) procedure.

tramo, sm. piece of ground ; flight of stairs ; piece of prose or verse.

tramontana, sf. north wind ; vanity, pride.

tramontano, na, a. transmontane.

tramontar, v.n. to cross the mountains ; —, v.a. to rescue ; -se, to fly, to escape.

tramoya, sf. theatrical machinery ; craft, wile, artful trick.

tramoyista, sm. theatrical mechanic, swindler, diddler, humbug.

trampa, sf. trap, snare ; trap-door ; fraud ; debt fraudulently contracted.

trampantojo, sm. trick.
trampear, v.n. & a. to swindle, to defraud.
trampista, sm. cheat, impostor, swindler, sharper.
tramposo, sa, a. deceitful, swindling.
tramvía, sm. tramway.
tranca, sf. cross-bar, cross-beam.
trancar, v.a. to barricade.
trancazo, sm. blow with a bar.
trance, sm. crisis ; last stage of life ; sale of a debtor's property.
tranco, sm. long step or stride.
tranquilidad, sf. tranquillity ; repose, heart's ease.
tranquilizar, v.a. to tranquillize, to calm.
tranquilo, la, a. tranquil, calm, quiet.
transacción, sf. accommodation, adjustment.
transatlántico, sm. (mar.) liner.
transcribir, v.a. to transcribe, to copy.
transeunte, a. transitory ; —, sm. passenger.
transferir, v.a. to transfer ; to defer.
transfiguración, sf. transformation, transfiguration.
transfigurar, v.a. to transfigure.
transfixión, sf. transfixing.
transflorear, v.a. to enamel.
transformación, sf. transformation.
transformar, v.a. to transform.
tránsfuga, tránsfugo, sm. deserter, fugitive.
transfundir, v.a. to transfuse ; to communicate.
transfusión, sf. transfusion.
transgresión, sf. transgression.
transgresor, sm. transgressor, lawbreaker.
transición, sf. transition.
transido, da, a. worn out with anguish ; avaricious.
transigir, v.a. to accommodate differences.
transitar, v.n. to travel, to pass by.
trausitivo, va, a. (gr.) transitive.
tránsito, sm. passage ; transition ; road, way ; change, removal ; passing, decease of virtuous persons.
transitorio, ria, a. transitory.
translación, sf. removal, translation.
transmarino, na, a. transmarine.
transmigración, sf. transmigration.
transmigrar, v.n. to transmigrate, to migrate.
transmitir, v.a. to transmit.
transmutable, a. transmutable, changeable.
transmutación, sf. transmutation.
transmutar, v.a. to transmute.
transparentarse, v.r. to be transparent ; to shine through.

transparente, a. transparent.
transpirar, v.a. to perspire.
transportación, sf., transportamiento, sm. transportation, transport.
transportar, v.a. to transport, to convey ; -se, to be enraged, to be beside oneself.
transporte, sm. transport, conveyance ; transport-ship.
transposición, sf. transposition, transposal.   [ation.
transubstanciación, sf. transubstantitransversal, a. transverse ; collateral.
tranvía, sm. tramway, tram-car.
tranzadera, sf. knot of plaited cords or ribbons.
trapacear, v.n. to deceive, to defraud.
trapacería, sf. fraud, deceit.
trapacero, ra, a. deceitful.
trapacista, sm. impostor, cheat.
trapajo, sm. rag, tatter.
trapajoso, sa, a. ragged, tattered.
trápala, sf. stamping ; confused noise.
trapalear, v.n. to babble.
trapalón, ona, a. loquacious.
trapería, sf. frippery, rag-fair ; cloth shop.   [cloth-dealer.
trapero, ra, sm. & f. dealer in rags,
trapisonda, sf. bustle, hurly-burly.
trapo, sm. rag, tatter.
traquear, v.n. to crack ; —, v.a. to shake, to agitate.
traqueo, sm. noise of rockets ; bumping, clatter.
tras, pr. after, behind ; —, sm. breach, bottom ; —, —, bang, bang.
trascendencia, sf. penetration ; sagacity ; result.
trascendental, a. transcendent.
trascender, v.n. to emit a strong smell ; to come to light, to transpire ; to produce results.
trascolar, v.a. (med.) to strain ; to cross a mountain.
trascordarse, v.r. to forget.
trascoro, sm. space of a church behind the choir.
trascurso, sm. course of time.
trasegar, v.a. to overset ; to decant.
trasera, sf. back-part ; croup.
trasero, ra, a. hind, hinder ; —, sm. buttock.
trasgo, sm. hobgoblin.
trashojar, v.a. to turn over the leaves, to skim a book.
trashumar, v.a. to drive sheep to or from the mountain pasture.
trasiego, sm. removal ; decanting of liquors.
trasladar, v.a. to transport ; to translate ; to transcribe, to copy.
traslado, sm. copy ; image ; resemblance.

traslucirse, v.r. to be transparent ; to be conjectured. [vanish.

traslumbrarse, v.r. to be dazzled ; to

trasluz, sm. light passing through a transparent body. [night.

trasnochar, v.n. to watch, to sit up all

traspasar, v.n. to pass over ; —, v.a. to remove, to transport ; to transfix, to transpierce ; to repass ; to exceed ; to trespass ; to transfer. [trespass.

traspaso, sm. conveyance, transfer ;

traspié, sm. trip ; slip, stumble.

trasplantar, v.a. to transplant.

trasplante, sm. transplantation.

trasponer, v.a. to remove, to transport ; -se, to hide oneself ; to be drowsy.

traspuesta, sf. transport ; hiding-place in a wood ; flight.

traspuesto, ta, a. & p. transported.

traspunte, sm. prompter.

trasquilador, sm. shearer.

trasquiladura, sf. shearing.

trasquilar, v.a. to shear sheep ; to clip.

trasquilón, sm. stripping.

traste, sm. fret of a guitar.

trasteador, ra, sm. & f. noisy fellow.

trastejador, sm. tiler.

trastejar, v.a. to cover with tiles.

trastera, sf. lumber-room.

trastería, sf. heap of lumber ; ridiculous or foolish action.

trastienda, sf. back-room behind a shop ; prudence, foresight. [person.

trasto, sm. furniture ; lumber ; useless

trastornador, sm. & f. disturber, turbulent person. [turn ; to perplex.

trastornar, v.a. to overthrow, to over-

trastorno, sm. overthrow.

trastrocar, v.a. to invert.

trasudar, v.a. to sweat, to perspire.

trasudor, sm. gentle sweat. [shed.

trasvenarse, v.r. to be spilled ; to be

tratable, a. tractable ; compliant.

tratado, sm. treaty, convention ; treatise.

tratamiento, sm. treatment ; style of address.

tratante, sm. dealer.

tratar, v.a. to treat on a subject ; to traffic, to trade ; to use, to treat ; to attempt, to try ; -se, to maintain a friendly intercourse ; to live well or ill.

trato, sm. treatment ; manner, address ; trade, traffic ; conversation.

través, sm. bias ; disaster ; traverse of a fortress ; de ó al —, across, athwart.

travesaño, sm. cross-timber ; transom.

travesero, sm. transom ; —, ra, a. transverse, across.

travesía, sf. cross-road ; passage ; distance from point to point ; passage (by sea) ; side-wind.

travestido, da, a. disguised.

travesura, sf. running about ; penetration, lively fancy ; wickedness, knavery.

traviesa, sf. crossing (by sea).

travieso, sa, a. restless, uneasy, fidgety ; turbulent ; lively ; debauched.

traza, sf. first sketch ; trace, outline ; project ; manner ; means ; appearance.

trazar, v.a. to plan, to project ; to trace.

trazo, sm. sketch, plan, design.

trébedes, sf.pl. trevet, tripod.

trébol, sm. trefoil, clover.

trece, a. thirteen.

trecho, sm. space, distance of time or place ; á -s, at intervals.

trecientos, tas, a. three hundred.

tregua, sf. truce.

treinta, a. thirty.

treinteno, na, a. thirtieth.

tremendo, da, a. terrible, formidable ; awful, grand.

trementina, sf. turpentine.

tremés, tremesino, na, a. three months old. [to wave.

tremolar, v.a. to hoist the colours ;

tremolina, sf. rustling of the wind ; bustle.

trémulo, la, a. tremulous, trembling.

tren, sm. train, retinue ; show, ostentation ; (rail.) train ; — ordinario, — ómnibus, slow train ; — correo, mail-train ; — de mercancías, goods train.

trencillo, sm. gold or silver hat-band.

treno, sm. lamentation.

trenza, sf. braid, tress.

trenzado, sm. braided hair.

trenzar, v.a. to braid the hair ; to plait.

trepar, v.n. to climb, to crawl.

tres, a. & s. three.

treta, sf. feint in fencing ; trick, wile.

triaca, sf. treacle.

triangular, a. triangular.

triángulo, sm. triangle.

tribu, sf. tribe.

tribulación, sf. tribulation, affliction.

tribuna, sf. tribune.

tribunal, sm. tribunal, court of justice.

tribuno, sm. tribune.

tributar, v.a. to pay tribute ; to contribute to ; to pay homage and respect

tributario, ria, a. tributary.

tributo, sm. tribute.

tricolor, a. tricoloured.

tricorne, a. three-horned, three-cornered.

tridente, a. three-pronged ; —, sm. trident.

trienal, a. triennial.

trienio, sm. space of three years.

trigaza, sf. short straw.

trigésimo, ma, a. thirtieth.

trigo, sm. wheat.

trigueño, ña, a. swarthy.

triguero, ra, a. growing among wheat; —, sm. winnowing-sieve, screen; corn-merchant.

trilingüe, a. trilingual.

trillado, da, a. beaten; trite, stale, hackneyed; camino —, common routine.

trillador, sm. thrasher.

trilladura, sf. act of thrashing.

trillar, v.a. to thrash.

trillo, sm. flail.

trimestre, sm. space of three months.

trinado, sm. trill, quaver.

trinar, v.n. to trill, to quaver.

trincar, v.a. to break in pieces; (mar.) to tighten the ropes.

trinchante, sm. carver; carving-knife.

trinchar, v.a. to carve, to divide meat; to decide with authority.

trinchera, sf. trench, entrenchment.

trinchero, sm. trencher.

Trinidad, sf. Trinity.

trinitaria, sf. heart's ease, pansy.

trino, na, a. containing three distinct things; —, sm. trill.

trinquete, sm. (mar.) foremast; tennis.

trío, sm. (mus.) trio.   [vessel; core.

tripa, sf. gut, tripe, intestine; belly of a tripe, sm. velveteen.

tripero, tripicallero, ra, sm. & f. tripe-man

triple, a. triple, treble.

triplicar, v.a. to treble.

triplo, la, a. treble, triplicate.

trípode, sm. tripod, trivet.

triptongo, sm. triphthong.

tripudo, da, a. big-bellied.

tripulación, sf. crew of a ship.

tripular, v.a. to man a ship.

triquitraque, sm. clatter.

tris, sm. noise made by breaking glass; trice, instant; estar en un —, to be on the point of.

trisagio, sm. (eccl.) trisagion.   [about.

triscar, v.n. to shuffle the feet; to frisk

trisílabo, ba, a. trisyllabic.

triste, a. sad, mournful, melancholy.

tristeza, sf. melancholy, sadness.

trituración, sf. pulverization.

triturar, v.a. to reduce to powder, to grind, to pound.

triunfal, a. triumphal.   [cards.

triunfar, v.n. to triumph; to trump at

triunfo, sm. triumph; trump (at cards).

triunvirato, sm. triumvirate.

triunviro, sm. triumvir.   [place.

trivial, a. frequented; trivial, common-

trivialidad, sf. familiarity, triviality.

triza, sf. little bit, fragment; cord, rope.

trocable, a. changeable.

trocar, v.a. to exchange, to barter; -se, to be changed or reformed.

trochemoche, ad. helter-skelter.

trofeo, sm. trophy.

troj, troje, sf. granary, fruit-loft.

trompa, sf. trumpet; proboscis; elephant's trunk; large top.

trompazo, sm. heavy blow; adverse accident.

trompeta, sf. trumpet; —, sm. trumpeter.

trompetear, v.n. to sound the trumpet.

trompetero, sm. trumpeter; trumpet-maker.

trompetilla, sf. speaking-trumpet.

trompicar, v.n. & a. to stumble frequently; to trip up.

trompicón, sm. stumbling.

trompo, sm. whipping-top.

tronada, sf. thunderstorm

tronar, v.n. to thunder.

troncar, v.a. to truncate, to mutilate.

tronco, sm. trunk; log of wood; stock.

tronchar, v.a. to lop off.

troncho, sm. sprig, stem or stalk.

tronera, sm. embrasure; loop-hole; small window; hare-brained person; pocket of a billiard-table.

trono, sm. throne.

tronzar, v.a. to shatter, to break into pieces; to plait, to fold.

tropa, sf. troop.

tropel, sm. confused noise; hurry, bustle, confusion, heap of things; crowd; de —, in a tumultuous and confused manner.

tropelía, sf. precipitation, hurry, confusion, vexation, oppression.

tropezadero, sm. slippery place.

tropezar, v.n. to stumble; to be detained or obstructed; to meet accidentally.

tropezón, ona, a. stumbling; á -ones, through obstructions; —, sm. tripping.

trópico, sm. tropic; —, ca, a. tropical.

tropiezo, sm. stumble, trip; obstacle; slip, fault; quarrel; dispute.

tropo, sm. trope; metaphor.

trotador, ra, sm. & f. trotter.

trotar, v.n. to trot.

trote, sm. trot; á —, in haste.

trovador, ra, sm. & f. troubadour.

trovar, v.a. to versify; to parody.

trozo, sm. piece cut off; (rail.) section of a line; plot of ground.

trucar, v.n. to lead (at cards).

truco, sm. skilful push at trucks; -s, pl. trucks (a kind of billiards).

trucha, sf. trout; crane.

trueno, sm. thunder-clap.

trueque, sm. exchange, truck, barter.

truhán, a. buffoon; cheat.   [cheat.

truhanear, v.n. to play the buffoon; to

truhanería, sf. buffoonery; humbug.

truhanesco. ca, a. belonging to a buffoon.

trujal, sm. oil-mill.
truncado, da, a. truncated.
truncamiento, sm. truncation.
truncar, v.a. to truncate, to maim.
truque, sm. a game at cards.
tu, a. thy, thine.
tú, pn. thou.   [point.
tuáutem, sm. principal person ; essential
tubo, sm. tube.
tuerca, sf. female screw.
tuétano, sm. marrow.
tuerto, ta, a. one-eyed ; squint-eyed ; —,
    sm. wrong, injury.
tufarada, sf. strong scent or smell.
tufo, sm. warm vapour ; offensive smell ;
    lock of hair over the ear.
tulipán, sm. tulip.
tullido, da, a. crippled, maimed.
tullimiento, sm. maiming.
tullir, v.n. to drop excrement (of birds) ;
    -se, to be crippled or maimed.
tumba, sf. tomb; roof of a coach; tumble.
tumbaga, sf. pinchbeck.
tumbar, v.a. to tumble (to throw down) ;
    — vn. to tumble (to fall down) ; -se,
    (col.) to lie down to sleep.
tumor, sm. tumour.
túmulo, sm. tomb, sepulchral monument.
tumulto, sm. tumult, uproar.
tumultuoso, sa, a. tumultuous.
tuna, sf. Indian fig ; idle life.
tunante, a. & p. vagabond, profligate; —
    sm. rake, rascal.   [loiter.
tunar, v.n. to lead a licentious life ; to
tunda, sf. act of shearing cloth ; severe
    chastisement, pounding.

tundidor, sm. shearer of cloth.
tundir, v.a. to shear ; to cudgel, to flog.
túnica, sf. tunic.
tuno, sm. truant, rake.
tupé, sm. toupet.
tupir, v.a. to press close ; -se, to stuff
    oneself with eating and drinking.
turba, sf. crowd ; turf, peat.
turbación, sf. perturbation, confusion,
    trouble, disorder.
turbador, ra, sm. & f. disturber.
turbante, sm. turban.
turbar, v.a. to disturb, to trouble.
turbio, bia, a. muddy, troubled.
turbión, sm. heavy shower of rain ;
    squall.
turbulencia, sf. turbulence, disturbance.
turbulento, ta, a. turbid, muddy, turbu-
turnar, v.n. to alternate.   [lent.
turno, sm. turn ; alternation.
turquesa, sf. turquoise.
turquí, a. of a deep blue colour.
turrar, v.a. to toast, to roast.
turrón, sm. nougat (almond cake).
turronero, sm. nougat-maker or seller.
turumbón, sm. bump on the head.
tutear, v.a. to address as " thou."
tutela, sf. guardianship, tutelage.
tutelar, a. tutelar, tutelary.
tuteo, sm. familiar use of " thou " and
    " thee."
tutor, sm. guardian, tutor.
tutora, sf. tutoress.
tutoría, sf. tutelage.
tuyo, ya, a. thine ; -s, pl. friends and re-
    lations of the party addressed.

U

ú, c. or (instead of ó, when the following
    word begins with an o) ; ¡ — ! ah !
    alas !
ubre, sf. dug, teat, udder.   [fully.
ufanamente, ad. ostentatiously, boast-
ufanarse, v.r. to boast.
ufanía, sf. haughtiness.   [cheerful.
ufano, na, a. haughty, arrogant ; gay,
ujier, sm. usher.
úlcera, sf. ulcer.
ulceración, sf. ulceration.
ulcerar, v.n. to ulcerate.
ulceroso, sa, a. ulcerous.
ulterior, a. ulterior, farther, further.
ultimátum, sm. ultimatum.
último, ma, a. last, hindmost.
ultrajador, ra, a. & sm. & f. insulting ;
    outrager.   [depreciate ; to abuse.
ultrajar, v.a. to outrage ; to despise, to
ultraje, sm. outrage.

ultramar, sm. oversea colonies.
ultramarino, na, a. ultramarine, oversea.
ultramontano, na, a. ultramontane.
umbilical, a. umbilical.
umbral, sm. threshold ; architrave ;
    beginning, rudiment.
un, una, art. a.
unánime, a. unanimous.
unanimidad, sf. unanimity.
unción, sf. unction ; extreme unction.
uncir, v.a. to yoke.
undécimo, ma, a. eleventh.
undísono, na, a. roaring (of waves).
undoso, sa, a. surging.
ungido, sm. Anointed ; king ; priest.
ungir, v.a. to anoint.
ungüento, sm. unguent ; ointment.
únicamente, ad. only, simply.
único, ca, a. singular, unique.
unicornio, sm. unicorn.

unidad, sf. unity; conformity, union.

unidamente, ad. jointly, unanimously.

uniformar, v.a. to make uniform.

uniforme, a. uniform; —, sm. (mil.) uniform.

uniformidad, sf. uniformity.

unigénito, a. only-begotten.

union, sf. union.

unir, v.a. to join, to unite; to mingle, to bind, to tie; -se, to associate.

unísono, na, a. in unison.

unitivo, va, a. uniting.

universal, a. universal.

universalidad sf. universality.

universidad, sf. university; corporation.

universo, sm. universe.

uno, na, a. one; sole, only; — á otro, one another; — á —, one by one; unos, nas, some.

untar, v.a. to anoint; to grease; -se, to be greased.

unto, sm. grease fat of animals.

untuoso, sa, a. unctuous, greasy.

untura, sf. unction; unguent.

uña, sf. nail; hoof; claw, talon; pointed hook.

uñada, uñarada, sf. scratch with the nail.

uñero, sm. whitlow.

urbanidad, sf. urbanity, politeness.

urbano, na, a. polite, well-bred.

urdidura, sf. warping (in weaving).

urdiembre, urdimbre, sf. warp.

urdir, v.a. to warp; to contrive.

urgencia, sf. urgency, pressure of difficulty, need, necessity.

urgentemente, ad. urgently.

urgir, v.n. to be urgent.

urinario, ria, a. urinary.

urna, sf. urn; glass-case in which small statues or images are kept.

urraca, sf. magpie.

usado, da, a. used; experienced

usanza, sf. usage, use, custom.

usar, v.a. to use, to make use of; to practise; -se, to be in use, to be wont.

Usía, (=Vuestra Señoría), sf. Your Lordship).

uso, sm. use, service; custom; mode.

Usted, sm. & f. you (contraction of Vuestra Merced).

ustorio, a., espejo —, burning mirror.

usuario, ria, a. (law) having only the use of a thing.

usufructo, sm. usufruct.

usufructuar, v.a. to enjoy the usufruct of anything; to render productive.

usufructuario, ria, a. possessing the usufruct of any thing.

usura, sf. usury.

usurario, ria, a. belonging to usury.

usurero, sm. usurer.

usurpación, sf. usurpation.

usurpador, ra, sm. & f. usurper.

usurpar, v.a. to usurp.

utensilio, sm. utensil.

uterino, na, a. uterine.

útero, sm. uterus, womb.

útil, a. useful, profitable; —, sm. utility.

utilizar, v.a. to make useful; to utilize.

uva, sf. grape; barberry.

V

vaca, sf. cow; beef.

vacaciones, sf.pl. holidays.

vacada, sf. drove of cows.

vacante, a. vacant; —, sf. vacancy.

vacar, v.n. to be vacant.

vaciadero, sm. drain, sink.

vaciador, sm. moulder; mould.

vaciar, v.a. to empty, to clear; to mould; —, v.n. to fall, to decrease (of waters); -se, to be spilt, to be emptied.

vacilación, sf. vacillation; irresolution, hesitation.

vacilar, v.n. to vacillate; to hesitate.

vacío, cia, a. a void, empty; unoccupied; concave; vain; presumptuous; unemployed; —, sm. vacuum; concavity

vacuna, sf. cow-pox, vaccine virus.

vacunar, v.a. to vaccinate.

vacuno, na, a. belonging to horned cattle.

vade, sm. satchel.

vadeable, a. fordable.

vadear, v.a. to wade, to ford.

vado, sm. ford.

vagabundo, da, a. vagabond.

vagamundear, v.a. to rove or loiter about.

vagamundo, da, a. vagabond.

vagancia, sf. vagrancy.

vagar, v.n. to rove or loiter about; to be loose and irregular; —, sm. leisure; slowness.   [sob.

vagido, sm. cry of a child; convulsive

vago, ga, a. vagrant; restless; vague; —, sm. vagabond; en —, in vain; unsteadily.

vagón, sm. (rail.) waggon; -cama, sleeping-car.

vaguear, v.n. to rove, to loiter.

vahido, sm. vertigo, giddiness.

vaho, sm. steam, vapour.   [pod, husk.

vaina, sf. scabbard of a sword; knife-case;

vainazas, sm. humdrum, dull person.

vainilla, sf. (bot.) vanilla

vaivén, sm. fluctuation, vacillation, instability; giddiness; risk, danger.

vajilla, sf. table-service.   [I.O.U.

vale, sm. farewell; promissory note,

valedero, ra, a. valid, efficacious, binding.

valentía, sf. valour, courage; brag, boast.

valentón, sm. braggadocio, hector.

valentonada, sf. brag, boast.

valer, v.n. to be worth, to be valuable, to be deserving; to be marketable; to prevail; to avail; to serve as an asylum; to be valid; to have power; to amount to; to have influence; to be equivalent to; to be current; —, v.a. to protect, to favour; -se, to employ, to make use of; to have recourse to.   [efficacious.

valeroso, sa, a. valiant, brave; valuable;

valetudinario, ria, a. valetudinarian.

valía, sf. valuation; credit, favour; party.

validación, sf. validity.

validar, v.a. to give validity.

validez, sf. validity, stability.

valido, sm. favourite, court favourite.

válido, da, a. valid; obligatory; firm.

valiente, a. robust, vigorous; valiant, brave; boasting.

valimiento, sm. use, utility, advantage; contribution; favour, protection, support.

valona, sf. tucker; cape, pelerine.

valor, sm. value, price; validity; force; power; courage, valour.

valor(e)ar, v.a. to value.

valuación, sf. valuation.

valuar, v.a. to value, to appraise.

valla, sf. intrenchment; barricade.

vallado, sm. palisaded enclosure.

valle, sm. dale, valley.

vampiro, sm. vampire.

vanagloria, sf. vainglory.   [boast.

vanagloriarse, v.r. to be vainglorious, to

vanaglorioso, sa, a. vainglorious.

vandalismo, sm. vandalism.

vandalo, la, sm. & a. vandal.

vanguardia, sf. vanguard, van.

vanidad, sf. vanity; ostentation; futility; illusion, phantom.

vanidoso, sa, a. vain, showy; haughty, self-conceited.

vano, na, a. vain; useless; frivolous; arrogant; futile; en —, in vain.

vapor, sm. vapour, steam; breath.

vaporoso, sa, a. vaporous.

vapular, v.a. to whip, to flog.

vaqueriza, sf. cow-shed.

vaquerizo, za, a. relating to cows; —, sm. cow-herd.

vaquero, sm. cow-herd; —, **ra**, a. belonging to cow-herds.

vaqueta, sf. cow-hide.

vara, st. rod; pole, staff; yard (measure); wand, rod of office; jurisdiction; -s, pl. shafts of a coach.

varal, sm. long pole; tall, slender person.

varapalo, sm. long perch; blow with a pole; trouble, vexation.

varar, v.a. to launch a new-built ship; —, v.n. to be stranded.

vardasca, sf. a twig.

vardascazo, sm. stroke with a switch.

varear, v.a. to knock fruit down with a pole; to goad a bull; to measure or sell by the yard; -se, to grow thin or lean.

vareta, sf. lime-twig for catching birds; stripe.

variable, a. variable, changeable.

variación, sf. variation.

variado, da, a. variegated.

variar, v.a. to change; —, v.n. to vary.

variedad, sf. variety; inconstancy.

varilla, sf. small rod; curtain-rod; spindle, pivot; jaw-bone; rib of a fan.

vario, ria, a. various, different; vague; variable; variegated; -s, pl. some.

varón, sm. man, male human being; man of respectability.

varonía, sf. male issue; male descendants.

varonil, a. male, masculine; manful.

vasallaje, sm. vassalage.

vasallo, sm. vassal, liegeman.

vasar, sm., **vasera**, sf. buffet on which glasses or vessels are put, side-board.

vasija, sf. vessel for liquors.

vaso, sm. vessel; vase.

vástago, sm. bud, shoot.

vasto, ta, a. vast, huge.

vaticinador, sm. prophet, diviner.

vaticinar, v.a. to divine, to foretell.

vaticinio, sm. divination, prophecy, forecast.   [neighbourhood.

vecindad, sf. inhabitants of a place;

vecindario, sm. number of inhabitants; neighbourhood.

vecino, na, a. neighbouring; near; —, sm.neighbour, inhabitant, householder.

veda, sf. prohibition.   [impede.

vedar, v.a. to prohibit, to forbid; to

vedija, sf. entangled lock of wool; flake; tuft of entangled hair, matted hair.

veedor, sm. overseer, inspector.

veeduría, sf. inspector's office.

vega, sf. fruitful plain.

vegetación, sf. vegetation.

vegetal, a. vegetable.

vegetar, v.n. to vegetate.

vehemencia, sf. vehemence, force.

vehemente, a. vehement, violent.

vehículo, sm. vehicle.

veinte, a. & sm. twenty.

veintena, sf. score.
veinteno, na, a. twentieth. [pression.
vejación, sf. vexation, molestation, op-
vejamen, sm. taunt ; satire.
vejar, v.a. to vex, to molest ; to taunt.
vejete, sm. ricidulous old man ; actor of
an old man.
vejez, sf. old age.
vejiga, sf. bladder ; blister.
vejigatorio, sm. blistering-plaster ; —,
ria, a. raising blisters.
vela, sf. watch ; watchfulness ; night-
guard ; candle ; sail ; ship ; **hacerse á la**
—, to set sail. [benedictions.
velación, sf. watching ; veiling ; nuptual
velador, sm. watchman ; careful observer ; candlestick ; small table.
velaje, sm. sails, sailwork.
velamen, sm. set of sails.
velar, v.n. to watch ; to wake ; to be
attentive ; (mar.) to appear ; —, v.a.
to guard, to watch ; to veil ; to marry.
veleidad, sf. vain desire ; feeble will ;
inconstancy.
veleidoso, sa, a. inconstant, fickle.
velero, ra, a. swift-sailing.
veleta, sf. weather-cock.
velo, sm. veil ; pretext.
velocidad, sf. velocity.
velografo, sm. type-writer.
velón, sm. oil-lamp.
velonero, sm. lamp-maker.
veloz(mente), a. (& ad.) swift(ly).
vello, sm. down ; gossamer ; short
downy hair. [metal, copper coin.
vellón, sm. fleece ; lock of wool ; base
vellorí, sm. second-rate cloth.
velloso, sa, a. downy.
velludo, da, a. shaggy, woolly.
vena, sf. vein, blood-vessel.
venablo, sm. javelin.
venado, sm. deer ; venison.
venal, a. belonging to the veins ; saleable;
mercenary.
venalidad, sf. venality.
venático, ca, a. rather mad.
venatorio, ria, a. used in hunting.
vencedor, ra, a. & sm. & f. conqueror,
victor.
vencejo, sm. martinet (bird).
vencer, v.a. to conquer, to vanquish ;
-se, to govern one's desires and passions, to control oneself.
vencible, a. conquerable.
vencido, da, a. payable, due (of bills).
vencimiento, sm. victory ; maturity (for
payment).
venda, sf. bandage ; fillet ; diadem.
vendaje, sm. brokerage ; bandage,
dressing of wounds.
vendar, v.a. to bandage ; to hoodwink.

vendaval, sm. a strong wind from sea.
vendedor, ra, sm. & f. seller.
vender, v.a. to sell.
vendible, a. saleable, vendible.
vendimia, sf. vintage.
vendimiador, ra, sm. & f. vintager.
vendimiar, v.a. to gather the vintage.
veneno, sm. poison, venom.
venenoso, sa, a. venomous, poisonous.
venera, sf. cockle-shell ; badge of
military orders.
venerable, a. venerable.
veneración, sf. veneration, worship.
venerar, v.a. to venerate, to worship.
venéreo, rea, a. venereal.
venero, sm. deposit of metal in a mine ;
source of water.
venganza, sf. revenge, vengeance.
vengar, v.a. to revenge, to avenge ; **-se,**
to revenge oneself.
vengativo, va, a. revengeful.
venia, sf. pardon ; leave, permission ;
salute, obeisance.
venial, a. venial.
venida, sf. arrival ; return ; overflow of a
river. [posterity.
venidero, ra, a. future ; **-s,** sm.pl.
venir, v.n. to come, to arrive ; to follow,
to succeed ; to spring from ; **-se,** to
ferment.
venoso, sa, a. veiny, veined.
venta, sf. sale ; inn.
ventaja, sf. advantage.
ventajoso, sa, a. advantageous. [nostril
ventana, sf. window ; window-shutter ;
ventanaje, sm. system of windows.
ventanazo, sm. banging of a window.
ventanear, v.n. to keep gazing from the
window.
ventarrón, sm. violent wind.
ventear, v.a. to smell, to scent ; to air, to
ventilate ; to investigate, to examine ;
to expose to the air ; —, v.n. to blow.
ventero, sm. & f. inn-keeper.
ventilación, sf. ventilation ; discussion.
ventilar, v.a. to ventilate ; to fan ; to
discuss.
ventisca, sf. **ventisco,** sm. snowstorm.
ventiscar, v.n. to drift (snow).
ventisquero, sm. snow-drift ; glacier.
ventolera, sf. gust ; pride.
ventor, sm. setter-dog.
ventorrillo, sm. pot-house
ventosa, sf. cupping-glass.
ventosidad, sf. flatulency.
ventoso, sa, a. windy ; flatulent.
ventrículo, sm. ventricle.
ventrílocuo, sm. ventriloquist.
ventrudo, da, a. big-bellied.
ventura, sf. luck, favourable chance,
fortune ; **por —,** by chance.

venturoso, sa, a. lucky, fortunate, happy.
Venus, sf. Venus (planet).
ver, v.a. to see, to look ; to observe ; to visit ; -se, to be seen ; to be conspicuous ; to find oneself ; to have to do with someone ; —, sm. sense of sight ; appearance.
veracidad, sf. veracity.   [season.
veran(e)ar, v.n. to pass the summer
verano, sm. summer season.
veras, sf.pl. truth, sincerity.
veraz, a. veracious, truthful.
verbal, a. verbal.
verbena, sf. (bot.) vervain.
verbigracia, ad. for example.
verbo, sm. Word ; (gr.) verb.
verbosidad, sf. verbosity.
verboso, sa, a. verbose.
verdacho, sm. green chalk.
verdad, sf. truth, veracity, reality ; certain existence of things ; — de Perogrullo, notorious truth.
verdaderamente, ad. truly, in fact.
verdadero, ra, a. true, real ; sincere.
verde, sm. & a. green.
verdear, verdecer, v.n. to grow green.
verdecillo, sm. green-finch.
verdegay, sm. bright green.
verdin, sm. verdure.
verdinegro, gra, a. dark green.
verdor, sm. verdure ; vigour ; youth ; age of vigour.
verdoso, sa, a. greenish, greeny.
verdugo, ga, sm. young shoot of a tree ; hangman ; very cruel person.
verdulero, sf. green-grocer.
verdura, sf. verdure ; vegetables, garden-stuff.   [several towns.
vereda, sf. path ; circular order sent to
veredicto, sm. verdict.
verga, sf. (mar.) yard.
vergonzante, a. bashful, shamefaced.
vergüenza, sf. shame ; bashfulness ; confusion.
vericueto, sm. rough road.
verídico, ca, a. truthful, worthy of faith.
verificación, sf. verification.
verificar, v.a. to verify ; -se, to be verified, to turn out true.
verificativo, va, a. tending to prove.
verisímil, a. probable, verisimilar.
verisimilitud, sf. probability, likelihood.
verisimilmente, ad. probably.
verja, sf. grate, lattice.
vermífugo, a. & sm. vermifuge.
verminoso, sa, a. full of grubs.
verónica, sf. (bot.) veronica.
verosímil, a. probable.
verosimilitud, sf. probability.
verraco, sm. boar.
verraquear, v.n. to grunt like a boar.

verruga, sf. wart, pimple.
verrugoso, sa, a. warty.
versado, da, a. versed, practised.
versal, a. capital (of letters).
versar, v.n. -se, to move about, to be concerned, to be versed ; to grow skilful.
versátil, a. versatile.
versículo, sm. versicle ; verse of a chapter
versificación, sf. versification.
versificador, sm. versifier.
versificar, v.a. to versify.
versión, sf. translation, version.
verso, sm. verse.
vértebra, sf. vertebra.
vertedero, sm. sewer, drain.
vertedor, ra, sm. & f. conduit, sewer ; (mar.) scoop.
verter, v.a. to spill, to shed ; to empty ; to drain ; —, v.n. to flow down.
vertical, a. vertical.   [head.
vértice, sm. vertex, zenith ; crown of the
vertiente, sm. & f. waterfall, cascade.
vertiginoso, sa, a. giddy.
vértigo, sm. giddiness, vertigo.
Véspero, sm. Vesper (evening-star).
vespertino, na, a. vespertine.
vestíbulo, sm. vestibule, lobby.
vestido, sm. dress, suit of clothes.
vestidura, sf. dress, wearing-apparel, (eccl.) vestments.
vestigio, sm. vestige, footstep.
vestiglo, sm. horrid monster.
vestir, v.a. to clothe, to dress ; to accoutre ; to adorn ; to cloak, to disguise.
vestuario, sm. clothes ; uniform ; vestry ; green-room.   [stripe.
veta, sf. vein (in mines, wood, etc.) ;
vetado, da, a. striped, veined.
veterano, na, a. experienced, long practised ; —, sm. veteran, old soldier.
vez, sf. turn, return ; cada —, each time ; una —, once ; á veces, sometimes.
vía, sf. way, road, route ; mode, manner, method ; (rail.) railway, line.
viaducto, sm. viaduct.
viajar, v.n. to travel.
viaje, sm. journey, voyage, travel.
viajero, sm. traveller.
viático, sm. viaticum.
víbora, sf. viper.
viborezno, sm. young viper.
vibración, sf. vibration.
vibrar, v.a. to vibrate, to brandish ; to throw, to dart ; —, v.n. to vibrate.
vicaría, sf. vicarship ; vicarage.
vicariato, sm. vicarage.   [vicarial.
vicario, sm. vicar, substitute ; —, ria, a.
vice, (in comp.) vice.
vicealmirante, sm. vice-admiral.
viceconsul, sm. vice-consul.

viciar, v.n. to vitiate, to corrupt; to annul; to deprave; -se, to become vitiated; to be depraved.

vicio, sm. vice.

vicioso, sa, a. vicious.

vicisitud, sf. vicissitude.

víctima, sf. victim; sacrifice.

¡victor! interj. bravo! hurrah!

victorear, v.a. to shout, to huzza.

victoria, sf. victory.

victorioso, sa, a. victorious.

vid, sf. (bot.) vine.

vida, sf. life.   [crockery.

vidriado, sm. glazed earthenware,

vidriar, v.a. to glaze.

vidriera, sf. glass case.

vidriería, sf. glazier's shop.

vidriero, sm. glazier.

vidrio, sm. glass.   [very delicate.

vidrioso, sa, a. glassy, brittle; slippery;

viejo, ja, a. old; ancient, antiquated.

viento, sm. wind; air.

vientre, sm. belly.   [Friday.

viernes, sm. Friday; — Santo, Good-

viga, sf. beam (of timber).

vigente, a. in force.

vigésimo, ma, a. twentieth.

vigía, s⟨m⟩ (mar.) look-out; —, sm. watchman.

vigilancia, sf. vigilance, watchfulness.

vigilante, a. watchful, vigilant; —, sm. watchman, policeman.

vigilar, v.n. to watch.

vigilia, sf. nocturnal study; vigil; watch.

vigor, sm. vigour, strength.

vigoroso, sa, a. vigorous.

vihuela, sf. guitar.

vihuelista, sm. guitar-player.

vil, a. mean, sordid, low; worthless; infamous; ungrateful.

vileza, sf. meanness, lowness; abjectness.

vilipendiar, v.a. to contemn, to revile.

vilipendio, sm. contempt, disdain.

vilmente, ad. vilely; abjectly.

vilordo, da, a. lazy, heavy.

vilorta, sf. ring of ozier; a game of ball.

villa, sf. villa; town enjoying peculiar privileges; its magistracy.   [away.

Villadiego, sm., tomar las de —, to run

villancico, sm. Christmas carol.

villanesco, ca, a. rustic.

villanía, sf. lowness of birth; villainy; indecorous word or act.

villano, na, a. rustic, clownish; villainous; —, sm. villain; rustic.

villorio, sm. poor hamlet.

vinagre, sm. vinegar.

vinagrera, sf. vinegar-cruet.

vinagrero, sm. vinegar-merchant.

vinajera, sf. flagon.

vinariego, sm. vine-grower.

vinatería, sf. vintry; wine-trade.

vinatero, sm. vintner.

vinculable, a. that may be entailed.

vinculación, sf. entail.   [perpetuate.

vincular, v.a. to entail an estate; to

vínculo, sm. tie, link, chain; entail.

vindicación, sf. revenge; vindication.

vindicar, v.a. to revenge; to vindicate.

vindicativo, va, a. vindictive.

vindicta, sf. vengeance.

vino, sm. wine; — tinto, red wine.

vinolento, ta, a. given to wine.

vinoso, sa, a. vinous, vinose.

viña, sf. vineyard.

viñador, sm. wine-grower.

viñedo, sm. vineyard; wine-growing district.

viñero, sm. wine-grower, vine-dresser.

viñeta, sf. vignette.

violación, sf. violation.

violado, da, a. violent-coloured.

violador, ra, sm. & f. violator; profaner.

violar, v.a. to violate; to ravish; to profane.

violencia, sf. violence.   [means.

violentar, v.a. to enforce by violent

violento, ta, a. violent, forced; absurd.

violeta, sf. (bot.) violet.

violín, sm. violin, fiddle.

violinista, sm. violinist.

violón, sm. bass-viol.

violoncelo, sm. small bass-viol.

viperino, na, a. viperine.

vira, sf. welt of a shoe.

virada, sf. (mar.) tacking.

virar, v.a. (mar.) to tack.

virgen, a. & sm. & f. virgin.

virginal, a. virginal.

virginidad, sf. virginity, maidenhood.

Virgo, sf. Virgo (sign of the zodiac).

virgulilla, sf. comma.

viril, sm. clear and transparent glass; monstrance; —, a. virile, manly.

virilidad, sf. virility, manhood; vigour.

virola, sf. ferule.

virolento, ta, a. diseased with the small-pox; pock-pitted.

virote, sm. dart, arrow; loiterer, fop.

virreinato, sm. viceroyalty.

virreina, sf. vice queen.

virrey, sm. viceroy.

virtual, a. virtual.   [vigour, courage.

virtud, sf. virtue; efficacy, force;

virtuoso, sa, a. virtuous.

viruela, sf. small-pox.

virulencia, sf. virulence.

virulento, ta, a. virulent.

viruta, sf. shavings.

visaje, sm. grimace; visage.

víscera, sf. vital organ.

viscosidad, sf. viscosity.

viscoso, sa, a. viscous, glutinous.
visera, sf. visor.
visible, a. visible ; apparent.
visión, sf. sight, vision ; ugly person,
fright, show ; phantom.
visionario, ria, a. visionary.
visir, sm. vizier.
visita, sf. visit.
visitación, sf. visitation.
visitador, ra, sm. & f. visitor ; surveyor.
visitar, v.a. to visit ; -se, to be on visiting
terms, to visit.
vislumbrar, v.a. to catch a glimpse ; to
perceive indistinctly ; to know imperfectly, to conjecture.
vislumbre, sf. glimmering light, conjecture ; imperfect knowledge ; slight
resemblance.   [appearance.
viso, sm. out-look, prospect ; lustre ;
víspera, sf. evening before ; evening
before a festival, eve ; -s, pl. vespers.
vist, sm. whist (juego de naipes de origen
ingles).
vista, sf. sight, view ; eye ; appearance ;
prospect ; intention, purpose ; (law)
— de un pleito, trial ; —, sm. employment of a custom-house officer ; -s, pl.
presents between bride and bridegroom.
vistazo, sm. glance.
vistillas, sf.pl. out-look, height.
visto, — que, c. considering that.
vistoso, sa, a. beautiful, delightful.
visual, a. visual, belonging to the sight.
vital, a. vital.   [insurance policy.
vitalicio, cia, a. during life ; —, sm. life-
vitalidad, sf. vitality.
vitela, sf. calf ; vellum, calf-skin.
¡ vítor ! long life ! bravo !
vitorear, v.a. to acclaim, to applaud.
vitríolo, sm. vitriol.
vitualla, sf. victuals.
vituallado, da, a. victualled.
vituperable, a. blameable.
vituperación, sf. blame.
vituperador, ra, sm. & f. blamer.
vituperar, v.a. to blame.
vituperio, sm. blame ; infamy.
viuda, sf. widow.
viudedad, sf. widow's jointure.
viudez, sf. widowhood.
viudo, sm. widower.
vivacidad, sf. vivacity, liveliness.
vivamente, ad. vivaciously ; to the life.
vivandero, sm. (mil.) sutler.
vivaque, vivac, sm. (mil.) bivouac.
vivaquear, v.n. (mil.) to bivouac.
vivar, sm. warren.
vivaracho, cha, a. lively, smart, sprightly.
vivera, sf. vivero, sm. warren ; fish-pond.
víveres, sm.pl. provisions.

viveza, sf. liveliness ; energy ; strong
resemblance.
vividero, ra, a. habitable.
vividor, ra, a. & sm. & f. long-lived ;
thrifty, economical.
vivienda, sf. dwelling-house.
vivificador, ra, a. & sm. & f. vivifying, animating, enlivening ; stimulus, reviver.
vivificar, v.a. to vivify, to enliven.
vivificativo, va, a. animating, comforting.
vivíparo, ra, a. viviparous.
vivir, v.n. to live ; to last.   [life.
vivo, va, a. living ; lively ; al —, to the
vizcondado, sm. viscountship.
vizconde, sm. viscount.
vizcondesa, sf. viscountess.
vocablo, sm. word, term, diction.
vocabulario, sm. vocabulary.
vocación, sf. vocation.   [vocal, oral.
vocal, sf. vowel ; —, sm. voter ; —, a.
vocativo, va, sm. (gr.) vocative.
voceador, sm. vociferator.   [to shriek.
vocear, v.n. to cry, to scream, to bawl ;
vocería, sf. vociferation.
vociferación, sf. vociferation.
vociferador, ra, sm. & f. boaster, bragger.
vociferar, v.n. to bawl, to vociferate.
vocinglería, sf. clamour, outcry ; loquacity.
vocinglero, ra, a. brawling, prattling.
volador, ra, a. flying ; running fast ; —,
sm. flying-fish.
volandas, en —, ad. in the air. [settled.
volandero, ra, a. volatile ; casual ; un-
volandillas, en —, ad. in the air.
volante, sm. screen ; shuttle-cock ;
livery-servant, footman ; light carriage.
volar, v.n. to fly ; to pass or to move
swiftly ; —, v.a. to rouse game ; to
blow up, to explode ; to irritate.
volatería, sf. fowling ; fowls.
volátil, a. volatile ; flying.
volatilizar, v.a. to volatilize, to evaporate.
volatín, sm. rope-dancer.
volcán, sm. volcano.
volcánico, a. volcanic.
volcar, v.a. to overset, to turn up ; to
make giddy ; to irritate.
volear, v.n. to throw up in the air.
voleo, sm. volley (ball) ; step in a Spanish
dance.
voltario, ria, a. fickle, variable, inconstant.
volteador, sm. tumbler.
voltear, v.a. to whirl, to overset ; —, v.n.
to tumble.
volubilidad, sf. volubility.
voluble, a. inconstant, fickle.
volumen, sm. volume ; size.
voluminoso, sa, a. voluminous.
voluntad, sf. will.   [volunteer.
voluntario. ria, a. voluntary ; —, sm.

voluptuoso, sa, a. voluptuous.

volver, v.a. & n. to return ; to restore, to repay ; to turn ; to send back a present; to change a thing from one place to another ; -se, to turn sour ; to turn towards ; to retract an opinion.

vomitar, v.a. to vomit.

vomitivo, va, a. & sm. emetic.

vómito, sm. vomiting.

vomitona, sf. violent vomiting.

voracidad, sf. voracity.

voraz(mente), a. (& ad.) voracious(ly).

vos, pn. you, ye.

vosotros, tras, pn.pl. you, ye.

votación, sf. voting.

votador, ra, sm. & f. swearer ; voter.

votar, v.n. to vow ; to vote.

votivo, va, a. a votive.

voto, sm. vow ; vote ; opinion, advice ; wish ; supplication to God ; execration.

voz, sf. voice ; outcry ; word, term.

Vuecelencia, sf. contraction of **Vuestra Excelencia,** Your Excellency.

vuelco, sm. upset, overthrow.

vuelo, sm. flight ; wing ; projection of building ; width of clothes ; ruffle, frill ; elevation in discoursing ; **á —,** **al —,** flying, expeditiously.

vuelta, sf. turn ; circuit ; return ; revolution (of wheel) ; repartee ; repetition; excursion, stroll.

Vuesamerced, sf. Your Worship, Your Honour (contraction of **Vuestra Merced**).

Vueseñoría, sf. My Lady (contraction of **Vuestra Señoría**).

vuestro, tra, a. your, yours.

vulgacho, sm. mob, populace.

vulgar, a. common, vulgar, ordinary.

vulgaridad, sf. vulgarity ; vulgarism.

vulgata, sf. (eccl.) vulgate.

vulgo, sm. populace, mob.

vulnerar, v.a. to injure.

X

xilografía, sf. wood-engraving.

xilógrafo, sm. wood-engraver.

Y

y, c. and.

ya, ad. already ; presently ; immediately; **— que,** since, seeing that.

yacer, v.n. to lie, to lie down.

yámbico, ca, a. iambic.

yambo, sm. iambic foot (‿ —).

yate, sm. yacht.

yedra, sf. ivy.

yegua, sf. mare.

yeguada, sf. stud.

yeguar, a. belonging to a mare.

yegüero, sm. keeper of brood-mares.

yelmo, sm. helmet, helm.

yema, sf. bud, gem ; yolk ; **— del dedo,** tip of the finger.

yerba, sf. herb.

yermar, v.a. to depopulate, to lay waste.

yermo, sm. desert, wilderness ; **—, ma,** a waste, desert.

yerno, sm. son-in-law.

yerro, sm. error, mistake, fault.

yerto, ta, a. stiff, inflexible ; rigid.

yesal, yesar, sm. gypsum-pit.

yesca, sf. spunk, tinder.

yesero, sm. preparer or seller of gypsum.

yesize, a. gypseous.

yeso, sm. gypsum ; **— mate,** plaster of Paris.

yesquero, sm. tinder-box.

yo, pn. I ; **— mismo,** I myself.

yugada, sf. a measure of land.

yugo, sm. yoke.

yunque, sm. anvil ; constancy.

yunta, sf. couple, pair, yoke.

Z

zabordar, v.n. (mar.) to get ashore, to be stranded.

zabullidura, sf. submersion, ducking.

zabullir, v.a. to plunge, to immerse, to dip ; -se, to plunge suddenly under water ; to lie concealed.

zacatín. sm. clothes market.

zafar, v.a. to adorn, to embellish ; to lighten a ship ; -se, to escape ; to avoid ; to free oneself from trouble.

zafarrancho, sm. (mar.) clearing for action ; hacer **—,** (mar.) to clear.

zafio, fia, a. clownish, coarse.

zafir, zafiro. sm. sapphire.

zaga, sf. rear, back; load packed at the back of a carriage; en —, behind.

zagal, sm. swain; youth; groom.

zagala, sf. shepherdess, lass, girl.

zagalejo, sm. under-petticoat.

zaguán, sm. porch, hall.

zaheridor, ra, sm. & f. censurer.

zaherimiento; sm. censure, blame.

zaherir, v.a. to reproach; to upbraid.

zahones, sm.pl. overalls.

zahorí, sm. wizard, clairvoyant; trickster, impostor.

zahurda, sf. hogsty; dirty hole.

zaino, na, a. chestnut (of horses); vicious (applied to animals); treacherous, wicked; mirar de ó á lo —, to look sideways.

zalagarda, sf. ambuscade, ambush; trap, snare; surprise; vulgar noise.

zalamería, sf. flattery.

zalamero, ra, sm. & f. wheedler.

zalea, sf. sheepskin rug.

zamacuco, sm. dunce, dolt.

zamarra, sf. dress made of sheepskins.

zamarro, sm. shepherd's coat of sheepskin; sheep or lambskin; stupid person.

zambo, ba, a. bandy-legged.

zambomba, sf. rural drum.

zambombo, sm. clown, lubber.

zambucar, v.a. to hide.

zambullida, sf. dipping, submersion.

zambullirse, v.r. to plunge into water, to dive.

zampar, v.a. to devour eagerly; -se, to thrust oneself suddenly into any place; to intrude.

zampatortas, sm. glutton; clown, rustic.

zampear, v.a. to stake, to prop.

zampuzar, v.a. to plunge.

zampuzo, sm. submersion.

zanahoria, sf. (bot.) carrot.

zanca, sf. shank of a fowl; long shank.

zancada, sf. stride.

zancadilla, sf. trip; trick.

zancajo, sm. heel-bone.

zancajoso, sa, a. bandy-legged.

zancarrón, sm. leg-bone.

zanco, sm. stilt.

zancudo, da, a. long-shanked.

zangandongo, sm. idler; dolt.

zanganear, v.n. to live in idleness.

zángano, sm. drone; idler, sponger.

zangarrear, v.n. to scrape on a guitar.

zangolotear, v.r. waddle.

zangoloteo, sm. waddling; wagging movement.

zanja, sf. ditch, trench.

zanjar, v.a. to open ditches; to dig a foundation.

zanquear, v.n. to waddle, to hurry.

zanquilargo, ga, a. long-shanked.

zapa, sf. spade; caminar á la —, (mil.) to advance by sap or mine.

zapador, sm. (mil.) sapper.

zapapico, sm. pick-axe.

zapar, v.n. to sap, to mine.

zaparrastrar, v.n. to trail, to drag along on the ground.

zaparrazo, sm. violent fall; sudden calamity.

zapatazo, sm. blow with a shoe.

zapatear, v.a. to strike with the shoe; -se, to oppose in debating.

zapatera, sf. shoemaker's wife.

zapatería, sf. shoemaker's trade; shoemaker's shop.   [cobbler.

zapatero, sm. shoemaker; — de viejo,

zapatilla, sf. pump(shoe); slipper.

zapato, sm. shoe.

zaque, sm. wine-bag; tippler.

zar, sm. czar.

zarabanda, sf. saraband (dance).   [alls.

zarag elles, sm.pl. wide breeches; over-

zaranda, sf. frame for sifting sand; screen; winnow.

zarandajas, sf.pl. trifles.

zarandar, v.a. to winnow corn.

zarcillo, sm. ear-ring; tendril.

zarpa, sf. claw.

zarpar, v.a. to weigh anchor.

zarpazo, sm. thud.

zarrapastrón, sm. tatterdemalion.

zarrapastroso, sa, a. ragged.

zarza, sf. common bramble.

zarzal, sm. bramble brake.

zarzamora, sf. blackberry-bush.

zarzaparilla, sf. (bot.) sarsaparilla.

zarzo, sm. hurdle.

zascandil, sm. busybody; upstart.

zequí, sm. zechin (Arabic gold coin).

zipizape, sm. noisy scuffle.

zizaña, sf. disagreement; anything injurious; (bot.) darnel.

zizañar, v.a. to sow discord.

zócalo, sm. socle.

zoclo, sm. wooden shoe.

zodíaco, sm. zodiac.

zona, sf. zone; girdle.

zoología, sf. zoology.

zopenco, ca, a. doltish, very stupid.

zopo, pa, a. lame, maimed; —, sm. clumsy, stupid fellow.   [blockhead.

zoquete, sm. block; morsel of bread;

zorra, sf. vixen.

zorrastron, ona, sm. & f. cunning, roguish person.

zorrera, sf. fox-hole.   [craft.

zorrería, sf. artfulness of a fox; cunning,

zorro, sm. fox; cunning fellow.

zorzal, sm. thrush.

zote, sm. stupid, lazy person.

zozobra, sf. uneasiness, anxiety.

zozobrar, v.n. to be weather-beaten ; to be in great danger ; to be afflicted ; (mar.) to founder.

zueco, sm. wooden shoe.

zullón, sm. flatulence.

zumacar, v.a. to tan with sumach.

zumaque, sm. sumach-tree.

zumba, sf. large bell, used by carriers ; facetious raillery. [jest, to joke.

zumbar, v.n. to resound, to hum ; -se, to

zumbido, sm. humming, buzzing sound.

zumbón, ona, a. waggish.

zumo, sm. sap, juice ; — de cepas ó parras, juice of the grape, wine.

zumoso, sa, a. juicy, succulent.

zupia, sf. bad wine ; refuse.

zurcidura, sf. fine-drawing ; darning.

zurcir, v.a. to darn, to fine-draw ; to join, to unite ; to hatch lies.

zurdo, da, a. left ; left-handed.

zurra, sf. tanning ; flogging, drubbing ; drudgery.

zurrador, sm. leather-dresser, currier.

zurrapa, sf. lees, dregs ; anything vile or despicable.

zurraposo, sa, a. full of lees and dregs.

zurrar, v.a. to tan ; to chastise with a whip ; -se, to have a sudden call of nature ; to dirty oneself.

zurriaga, sf. thong ; whip for tops.

zurriagar, v.a. to flog, to whip.

zurriagazo, sm. blow, lash with a whip ;

zurriago, sm. whip. [calamity.

zurriburri, sm. ragamuffin.

zurrido, sm. humming, buzzing ; confused noise.

zurrir, v.n. to hum, to buzz, to tinkle.

zurrón, sm. shepherd's pouch ; husks of grain.

zutano, na, a. such a one ; — y fulano, such and such a one, so and so.

Nombres geográficos los más importantes, que no se corresponden en ambas lenguas.

Abisinia, f. Abyssinia.
Adriático, m. Adriatic, Adriatic Sea.
africano, a, m. & f. & a. African.
albanés, a, m. & f. & a. Albanian.
alemán, a, m. & f. & a. German.
Alemania, f. Germany.
Alpes, m.pl. Alps.
alpino, a, a. alpine.
Alsacia, f. Alsace.
Amberes, m. Antwerp.
americano, a, m. & f. & a. American.
Andalucía, f. Andalusia.
andaluz, a, m. & f. & a. Andalusian.
Anseáticas, f.pl. Hanse Towns.
Apeninos, m.pl. Apennines.
Apulia, f. Apulia.
Aquisgrán, sm. Aix la Chapelle.
árabe, m. & f., arábico, a. Arab.
aragonés, a, m. & f. & a. Aragonese.
Archipiélago, m. Archipelago.
Argel, m. Algiers.
arménico, a, armenio, a, m. & f. & a. Armenian.
asiano, a, asiático, a, m. & f. & a. Asiatic.
Atenas, f.pl. Athens.
ateniense, a, m. & f. & a. Athenian.
Atlántico, m. Atlantic.
Ausburgo, m. Augsburg.
australasino, a, m. & f. & a. Australian.
austriaco, a, m. & f. & a. Austrian.

Báltico, m. Baltic Sea.
Barbadas, f.pl. Barbadoes.
Basilea, f. Basle.

bávaro, a, m. & f. & a. Bavarian.
Baviera, f. Bavaria.
Belen, m. Bethlehem.
belga, m. & f., bélgico, a, a. Belgian.
Bélgica, f. Belgium.
Bengala, f. Bengala.
Berbería, f. Barbary.
Beocia, f. Bœtia.
beociano, a, m. & f. & a. Bœotian.   [Berlinian.
berlinés, a, m. & f. & a.
Bizancio, m. Byzantium.
bohémico, a, a., bohemo, a, m. & f. Bohemian.
Borgoña, f. Burgundy.
borgoñés, a, m. & f. & a. Burgundian.
Bósforo, m. Bosphorus.
Brasil, m. Brazil.
brasileño, a, m. & f. & a. Brazilian.
Bretaña, f. Brittany ; Gran —, Great Britain.
Brunsvick, m. Brunswick.
Bruselas, f.pl. Brussels.
búlgaro, a, m. & f. & a. Bulgarian.
Burdeos, m. Bordeaux.

Cachemir, m. Cashmere.
Cádiz, f. Cadiz.
Cafrería, f. Caffraria.
calabrés, a, m. & f. & a. Calabrian.
Caldea, f. Chaldea.
Calés, m. Calais.
calmuco, m. Calmuck.
Campeche, f. Campeachy.
Canarias, f.pl. Canaries, Canary Islands.
candiote, m. & f. & a, Candian.
Cantórberi, f. Canterbury.
Capricornio, m. Capricorn.
Carintia, f. Carinthia.
Carpetanos, m.pl. Carpathians.

Caspio, m. Caspian Sea.
castellano, a, m. & f. & a. Castilian.
Castilla, f. Castile.
catalán, a, m. & f. & a. Catalonian.
Cataluña, f. Catalonia.
Cáucaso, m. Caucasus.
Ceilán, m. Ceylon.
Cerdeña, f. Sardinia.
Champaña, f. Champagne.
chino, a, m. & f. & a. Chinese.
Chipre, m. Cyprus.
Circasia, f. Circassia.
circasiano, a, m. & f. & a. Circassian.
Colonia, f. Cologne.
Constantinopla, f. Constantinople.
Copenaga, f. Copenhagen.
Córcega, f. Corsica.
Corinto, m. Corinth.
corsés, a, corso, a, m. & f. & a. Corsican.
cosaco, m. Cossack.
Cracovia, f. Cracow.
cretense, crético, a, m. & f. & a. Cretan.
Croacia, f. Croatia.
croato, a, m. & f. & a. Croatian.
Curlandia, f. Corland.

Dalmacia, f. Dalmatia.
dalmático, a, m. & f. & a. Dalmatian.
Damasco, m. Damascus.
danés, a, m. & f. & a. Dane; Danish.
Danubio, m. Danube.
Delfinado, m. Dauphinate Dauphiny.
Delfos, f. Delphi.
Dinamarca, f. Denmark.
dinamarqués, a, a. Danish.
Dovres, m. Dover.
Dresde, f. Dresden.
Dunquerque, m. Dunkirk.
Duvre, m. Dover.

226

Edimburgo, m. Edinburgh.
Efeso, m. Ephesus.
egipciaco, a, egipciano, a, egipcio, a, m. & f. & a. Egyptian.
Egipto, m. Egypt.
Epiro, m. Epirus.
Escalda, m. Scheld.
Escandinavia, f. Scandinavia.
Esclavonia, f. Slavonia.
esclavón, a, esclavonio, a, m. & f. & a. Slavonian.
escocés, a, m. & f. & a. Scotsman, Scotchwoman; Scotch, Scottish.
Escocia, f. Scotland.
Esmirna, f. Smyrna.
España, f. Spain.
español, a, m. & f. & a. Spaniard ; Spanish.
Esparta, f. Sparta.
espartano, m. & f. & a. Spartan.
esquimales, m.pl. Esquimaux.
Estiria, f. Stiria.
estiriano, a, m. & f. & a. Stirian.
Estocolmo, m. Stockholm.
Estrasburgo, m. Strasburg.
Europa, f. Europe.
europeo, a, m. & f. & a. European.

Fenicia, f. Phœnicia.
fenicio, a, m. & f. & a. Phœnician.
finlandés, a, m. & f. & a. Finlander.
Finlandia, f. Finland.
flamenco, a, m. & f. & a. Fleming ; Flemish.
Flándes, f. Flanders.
Flesinga, f. Flushing.
Florencia, f. Florence.
florentín, a, m. & f. & a. Florentine.
francés, a, m. & f. & a. Frenchman, Frenchwoman ; French ; los franceses, the French.
Friburgo, m. Freiburg.
Frisia, f. Friesland.
frisón, a, m. & f. & a. Frieslander.

Gáles, m. Wales.
galés, a, m. & f. & a. Welsh, Gaelic.
Galia, f. Gaul.

Galicia, f. Galicia.
gálico, a, m. & f. & a. Gaul.
Galilea, f. Galilee.
Gante, m. Ghent.
Gascuña, f. Gascony.
Génova, f. Genoa.
genovés, a, m. & f. & a. Genoese.
Ginebra, f. Geneva.
ginebrés, a, m. & f. & a. Genevese.
Grecia, f. Greece.
griego, a, m. & f. & a. Greek.
Grisones, m.pl. Grisons.
Groenlandia, f. Greenland.
Groninga, f. Groningen.
Gueldres, m. Guelderland.

Habana, f. Havana.
Hamburgo, m. Hamburg.
Haya, f. Hague.
hesés, a, m. & f. & a. Hessian.
Hesia, f. Hesse.
Holanda, f. Holland.
holandés, a, m. & f. & a. Hollander, Dutchman, Dutchwoman ; Dutch.
húngaro, a, m. & f. & a. Hungarian.
Hungría, f. Hungary.

Iliria, f. Illyria.
Indias, f.pl. Indies ; — orientales, East-Indies ; — occidentales, West-Indies.
indio, a, m. & f. & a. Indian.
Inglaterra, f. England.
inglés, a, m. & f. & a. Englishman, Englishwoman ; English ; los ingleses, the English.
Irlanda, f. Ireland.
irlandés, a, m. & f. & a. Irishman, Irishwoman ; Irish.
Islanda, f. Iceland.
islandés, a, m. & f. & a. Icelander.
Italia, f. Italy.
italiano, a, m. & f. & a. Italian.

Japón, m. Japan.
japonés, a, m. & f. & a. Japanese.
Jerusalén, m. Jerusalem.
Jutlandia, f. Jutland.

lapón, a, m. & f. & a. Laplander.
Laponia, f. Lapland.
León, m. Lyons.
Líbano, m. Lebanon.
Lieja, f. Liege.
Lila, f. Lisle.
Liorna, f. Leghorn.
Lipsia, f. Leipsic.
Lisboa, f. Lisbon.
Lituania, f. Lithuania.
lituánico, a, lituaniense, m. & f. & a. Lithuanian.
livoniano, a, m. & f. & a. Livonian.
Lombardía, f. Lombardy.
lombárdico, a, a., lombardo, m. & f. & a. Lombard.
Londres, m. London.
Lorena, f. Lorraine.
Lucemburgo, Lujemburgo, m. Luxemburg.
Lusacia, f. Lusatia.
lusaciano, a, m. & f. & a. Lusatian.

macedónico, a, m. & f. & a. Macedonian.
Madera, f. Madeira.
madrileño, a, m. & f. & a. inhabitant of Madrid.
Maguncia, f. Mainz.
Malina, f. Malines.
maltés, a, m. & f. & a. Maltese.
Mallorca, f. Majorca.
Marruecos, m.pl. Morocco.
Marsella, f. Marseilles.
Meca, f. Mecca.
Mediterráneo, m. Mediterranean.
mejicano, a, m. & f. & a. Mexican.
Méjico, m. Mexico.
Menorca, f. Minorca.
Mesina, f. Messina.
Milano, m. Milan.
Molucas, f.pl. Moluccas.
moravo, a, m. & f. & a. Moravian.
moro, a, m. & f. & a. Moor ; Moorish.
Mosa, m. Meuse.
Moscovia, f. Moscovy.
Mosela, m. Moselle.

Nápoles, m. Naples.
napolitano, a, m. & f. & a. Neapolitan.
Neucastel, m. Neufchâtel, Neuchâtel.

Nilo, m. Nile.
Nimega, f. Nimeguen.
Niza, f. Nice.
Normandia, f. Normandy.
normando, a, normánico, a, m. & f. & a. Norman.
Noruega, f. Norway.
noruego, a, m. & f. & a. Norwegian.
nubio, a, m. & f. & a. Nubian.
Nueva-York, f. New York.
Nuremberga, f. Nuremberg.

Olimpo, m. Olympus.
Orcades, f.pl. Órkneys.
Ostende, f. Ostend.

Pacífico, m. Pacific.
Palatinado, m. Palatinate.
Palestina, f. Palestine.
parisiense, m. & f. & a. Parisian.
Parnaso, m. Parnassus.
Peloponeso, m. the Peloponnesus.
persa, m. & f., **persiano, a,** a. Persian.
Perú, m. Peru.
Piamonte, m. Piedmont.
piamontés, a, m. & f. & á. Piedmontese.
Pirineos, m.pl. Pyrenees.
polaco, a, m. & f. & a. Pole ; Polish.
Polonia, f. Poland.
Ponto, m. Pontus.
portugués, a, m. & f. & a. Portuguese.
Praga, f. Prague.

Provenza, f. Provence.
Prusia, f. Prussia.
prusiano, a, m. & f. & a. Prussian.

Ratisbona, f. Ratisbon.
Ravena, f. Ravenna.
Rin, Rhin, m. Rhine.
Ródano, m. Rhone.
Rodas, f.pl. Rhodes.
Roma, f. Rome.
Romania, f. Roumania.
romano, a, m. & f. & a. Roman.
Rusia, f. Russia.

Saboya, f. Savoy.
saboyano, a, m. & f. & a. Savoyard.
sajón, a, sajono, a, m. & f. & a. Saxon.
Sajonia, f. Saxony.
sardo, a, m. & f. & a. Sardinian.
Sena, m. Seine.
Sicilia, f. Sicily.
siciliano, a, m. & f. & a. Sicilian.
silesio, a, m. & ₁. & a. Silesian.
Suecia, f. Sweden.
sueco, a, m. & f. & a. Swede ; Swedish.
Suiza, f. Switzerland.
suizo, a, m. & f. & a. Swiss.
Sund, m. the Sound.

Tajo, m. Tagus.
Támesis, m. Thames.
Tartaria, f. Tartary.

**Termópilas,   f.pl. Thermopylæ.
Tesalónica, f. Thessalonica.
tésalo, a, m. & f. & a. Thessalian.   [lese.
tirolés, a, m. & f. & a. Tirolón,** m. Toulon.
Tolón, m. Toulon.
Tolosa, f. Toulouse.
Toscana, f.pl. Tuscany.
Tracia, f. Thracia.
Trento, m. Trent.
Tréveris, m. Triers.
Troya, f. Troy.   [Trojan.
troyano, a, m. & f. & a.
Túnez, f. Tunis.
turco, a, m. & f. & a. Turk ; Turkish.
Turingia, f. Thuringia.
turingio, a, m. & f. & a. Thuringian.
Turquía, f. Turkey.

Utreque, f. Utrecht.

valaco, a, m. & f. & a. Wallachian.
Valaquia, f. Wallachia.
Varsovia, f. Warsaw.
Venecia, f. Venice.
veneciano, a, m. & f. & a. Venetian.
Versalles, m. Versailles.
Vesuvio, m. Vesuvius.
Viena, f. Vienna.
vienés, a, m. & f. & a. Viennese.
Vincenas, f.pl. Vincennes.

Zelandia, f. Zealand.
Zurico, m. Zurich.

Nombres de Bautismo los más comunes, que no se corresponden en ambas lenguas.

Abrahán, Abraham.
Adán, Adam.
Adelaida, Adelaide.
Adolfo, Adolphus.
Agustín, Austin.
Alejandro, Alexander.
Alfonso, Alphonso.
Ambrosio, Ambrose.
Amalia, Amelia.
Amata, Amy.
Ana, Aun.
Andréo, Andrés, Andrew.
Anita, Nan, Nancy.
Antonio, Anthony.
Augusto, Augustus.

Bártolo, Bartolomé, Bartolomeo, Bartholomew.
Beatriz, Beatrice.
Beltrán, Bertram.
Benito, Benedict.
Bianca, Blanche.
Brígida, Bridget.
Carlos, Charles.
Carlota, Charlotte.
Carolina, Caroline.
Catalina, Catharine, Kate.
Cecilia, Cecily.
Constancia, Constance.
Cristóbal, Christopher.

Jerónimo, Jerome.

Diego, James.
Dorotea, Dorothy, Dorothea.

Eduardo, Edward.
Elena, Ellen, Eleanor.
Emilia, Emily.
Enrique, Henry.
Enriqueta, Harriet, Henrietta.

Enriquito, Harry, Hal.
Estéban, Stephan.
Ester, Esther.
Eugenio, Eugene.

Faquita, Fanny.
Federico, Frederick.
Felipe, Philip.
Fernando, Ferdinand.
Francisca, Frances.
Francisco, Francis, Frank.

Gaspar, Jasper.
Geofredo, Geoffrey, Jeffrey.
Gertrudis, Tula, Gertrude.
Ginebra, Guinevere, Genivra.
Gofredo, Godofredo, Godfrey.
Gregorio, Gregory.
Gualterio, Walter.
Guido, Guy.
Guillermo, William, Will, Willy, Bill, Billy.
Gustavo, Gustavus.

Helena, Helen.
Hilario, Hilary.
Hugo, Hugh.

Ignacio, Ignatius.
Inés, Agnes.
Isabel, Elizabeth, Eliza, Lizzie.

Jaime, James, Jem, Jemmy.
Jorge, George.
José, Joseph.
Juan, John.
Juana, Jane.
Juanita, Jenny.
Juanito, Johnny, Jack.
Juliana, Julia.
Julio, Julius.

Leonor, Eleanor.
Lucas, Luke.
Lucía, Lucy.
Luis, Lewis.
Luisa, Loiusa.

Manuel, Emanuel.
Marcos, Mark.
Margarita, Margaret, Madge, Margery, Peggy.
María, Mary.
Mariquita, Maruja, Moll, Molly.
Mateo, Matthew, Mat.
Miguel, Michael.

Pablo, Paul.
Pancho, Paquito, Frank.
Pancha, Paquita, Fanny.
Patricio, Patrick, Paddy.
Pedro, Peter.
Pepe, Pepillo, Joe.

Ramón, Raymund.
Ricardo, Richard.
Roberto, Robert, Bob, Robin.
Rogerio, Roger.
Rodolfo, Rodulfo, Ralph.

Salomón, Solomon.
Sara, Sarah, Sally.
Sofía, Sophia, Sophy.
Susana, Susan.

Teresa, Theresa.
Timóteo, Timothy.
Tomás, Thomas, Tom.

Valentino, Valentine.

Zacarias, Zachary.

Abreviaturas
que más comunmente se usan en castellano.
(Customary Abbreviations.)

A. C., Año de Cristo.
B. L. M., besa la mano.
B. L. P., besa los pies.
Cᵃ, compañia.
D., Don.
Da., Doña.
Excmo, Excma, Excelentísimo, Excelentísima.
M. S., manuscrito.
m.s a.s., muchos años.
M. SS., manuscritos.
N. S., Nuestro Señor.
Q. B. S. M. ó q. b. s. m., que besa su mano.
Q. B. S. P. ó q. b. s. p., que besa sus pies.
Q. D. G. ó q. D. g., que Dios guarde.
q. e. g. e., que en gloria esté.
R. I. P., *Requiescat in pace* (en paz descanse).
R. P., Reverendo Padre.

S. M., Su Majestad.
S. M. A., Su Majestad Apostólica.
S. M. B., Su Majestad Británica.
S. M. C., Su Majestad Católica.
S. M. F., Su Majestad Fidelísima.
S. M. I., Su Majestad Imperial.
S.r ó Sr., Señor.
Sra, Sras, Señora, Señoras.
Sres ó S.res, Señores.
S. S. S., su seguro servidor.
Sto, Sta, Santo, Santa.
U. ó Ud., Usted.
Uds., Ustedes.
V., Usted ; Véase.
V. A., Vuestra Alteza.
V. A. R., Vuestra Alteza Real.
V. E., Vuestra Excelencia ó Vuecencia.,
vg., verbigracia.
v. g. ó v. gr., verbigracia.

Monedas, Pesos y Medidas españolas.
(Spanish Currency, Weights and Measures.)

The official system of weights and measures in Spain is the metric system, thus :—

1 metro = 39.37 inches.
1 kilómetro = about ⅝ of a mile.

1 gramo = 15·43 grains.
1 kilogramo = 2·2 lbs.

1 hectarea = 2·47 acres.

1 litro = 1·76 pints.

But the old system is still often in popular use, thus :—

1 pulgada = 1 1/12 of an inch.

1 palmo = 9 pulgadas (8¼ inches).
1 pie = 12 pulgadas (11 inches).
1 vara = 3 pies (33 inches).
Long distances are commonly measured in leguas (leagues), the legua being about 3½ miles.

The Castilian libra was slightly heavier than the English lb.
1 arroba = 25 libras.
1 quintal = 100 libras.

The fanega (dry measure) = 1·6 bushels ; i.e. 8 bushels = 5 fanegas.

There are also many local weights and measures, which vary in different parts of Spain and of America.

Monedas.
(Currency.)

The monetary unit is the **peseta**, corresponding to the French franc, and worth about 9½d. at par. The **peseta** is divided into 100 **céntimos.** But sums of money are often reckoned in **duros** (dollars) of 5 pesetas. Small sums are often reckoned in **reales,** the real being not a coin, but a sum of money, viz. ¼ of a **peseta.**

The penny or piece of 10 **céntimos** is popularly called **perro gordo.**

The halfpenny or piece of 5 **céntimos** is called **perra chica.**

Irregular Verbs.[1]

Infinitivo.	Presente del Indicativo.	Pretérito perfecto.	Futuro.	Imperativo.	Participio.
abastecer	*conjugated*	*as*	nacer		
aborrecer	*conjugated*	*as*	nacer		
abrir					abierto.
absolver	yo absuelvo, tú absuelves, él absuelve, ellos absuelven			absuelve tú, absuelva él, absuelvan ellos	absuelto
acertar	yo acierto, tú aciertas, él acierta, ellos aciertan			acièrta tú, acierte él, acierten ellos	
acordar	*conjugated*	*as*	acostar		
acostar	yo acuesto, tú acuestas, él acuesta, ellos acuestan			acuesta tú, acueste él, acuesten ellos	
acrecentar	*conjugated*	*as*	acertar		
adestrar	*conjugated*	*as*	acertar		
adherir	*conjugated*	*as*	sentir		
adquirir	*conjugated*	*as*	sentir		
advertir	*conjugated*	*as*	sentir		
alentar	*conjugated*	*as*	acertar		
almorzar	*conjugated*	*as*	acostar		
amolar	*conjugated*	*as*	acostar		
andar		yo anduve, tú anduviste &c.	yo iré &c. (v. Ir.)		
apacentar	*conjugated*	*as*	acertar		
aportar	*conjugated*	*as*	acostar		
apostar	*conjugated*	*as*	acostar		
apretar	*conjugated*	*as*	acertar		
aprobar	*conjugated*	*as*	acostar		
argüir	yo arguyo, tú arguyes, él arguye, ellos arguyen			arguye tú &c.	
arrendar	*conjugated*	*as*	acertar		
arrepentirse	*conjugated*	*as*	sentir		
ascender	yo asciendo, tú asciendes, él asciende, ellos ascienden			asciende tú, ascienda él, asciendan ellos	
asentar	*conjugated*	*as*	acertar		
asir	yo asgo			asga él, asgan ellos	
asolar	*conjugated*	*as*	acostar		
atender	*conjugated*	*as*	ascender		
aterrar	*conjugated*	*as*	acertar		

[1] The persons *not* given in the tables, as well as the tenses in the columns of which a blank is left, are conjugated *regularly*.

Infinitivo.	Presente del Indicativo.	Pretérito perfecto.	Futuro.	Imperativo.	Participio.
atestar	*conjugated*	*as*	acertar		
atravesar	*conjugated*	*as*	acertar		
atribuir	*conjugated*	*as*	argüir		
bendecir [1]	yo bendigo, tú bendices, él bendice, ellos bendicen	yo bendije, tú bendijiste &c.	yo bendeciré, tú bendecirás &c.	bendice tú, bendiga él, bendigan ellos	bendido (bende-[cido)
caber	yo quepo	yo cupe, tú cupiste &c.	yo cabré, tú cabrás &c.	quepa él, quepan ellos	
caer	yo caigo	él cayó, ellos cayeron		caiga él, caigamos nosotros, caigan ellos	
calentar	*conjugated*	*as*	acertar		
cegar	*conjugated*	*as*	acertar		
ceñir	*conjugated*	*as*	pedir		
cerner	*conjugated*	*as*	ascender		
cerrar	*conjugated*	*as*	acertar		
cocer	*conjugated*	*as*	absolver		
colegir	*conjugated*	*as*	pedir		
colgar	*conjugated*	*as*	acostar		
comenzar	*conjugated*	*as*	acertar		
compeler					
competir	*conjugated*	*as*	pedir		
concebir	*conjugated*	*as*	pedir		
concertar	*conjugated*	*as*	acertar		
concluir	*conjugated*	*as*	argüir		concluso (concluido)
condoler	*conjugated*	*as*	absolver		
conducir	yo conduzco	yo conduje, tú condujiste &c.		conduzca él, conduzcamos nosotros, conduzcan ellos	
conferir	*conjugated*	*as*	sentir		
confesar	*conjugated*	*as*	acertar		
confundir					confuso (confun-[dido)
conmover	*conjugated*	*as*	absolver		
conocer	*conjugated*	*as*	nacer		
consolar	*conjugated*	*as*	acostar		
constituir	*conjugated*	*as*	argüir		
constreñir	*conjugated*	*as*	pedir		
contar	*conjugated*	*as*	acostar		
contribuir	*conjugated*	*as*	argüir		
controvertir	*conjugated*	*as*	sentir		
convencer					
convertir	*conjugated*	*as*	sentir		
costar	*conjugated*	*as*	acostar		
crecer	*conjugated*	*as*	nacer		
cubrir					cubierto
dar	yo doy	yo dí, tú díste, él dió &c.			
decir [2]	yo digo, tú dices, él dice, ellos dicen	yo dije, tú dijiste &c.	yo diré, tú dirás &c.	di tú, diga él, digamos nosotros, digan ellos	dicho
deducir	*conjugated*	*as*	conducir		
defender	*conjugated*	*as*	ascender		

[1] Gerundio: bendiciendo.   [2] Gerundio: diciendo.

Infinitivo.	Presente del Indicativo.	Pretérito perfecto.	Futuro.	Imperativo.	Participio.
deferir	*conjugated*	*as*	sentir		
degollar	*conjugated*	*as*	acostar		
demoler	*conjugated*	*as*	absolver		
derrengar	*conjugated*	*as*	acertar		
derretir	*conjugated*	*as*	pedir		
derrocar	*conjugated*	*as*	acostar		
desasir	*conjugated*	*as*	asir		
descollar	*conjugated*	*as*	acostar		
descontar	*conjugated*	*as*	acostar		
desdecir	*conjugated*	*as*	bendecir		
desleir	*conjugated*	*as*	pedir		
desmembrar	*conjugated*	*as*	acertar		
desmentir	*conjugated*	*as*	sentir		
desolar	*conjugated*	*as*	acostar		
despedir	*conjugated*	*as*	pedir		
despernar	*conjugated*	*as*	acertar		
despertar					despierto (despertado)
desterrar	*conjugated*	*as*	acertar		
destruir	*conjugated*	*as*	argüir		
detener	*conjugated*	*as*	tener		
dezmar	*conjugated*	*as*	acertar		
diferir	*conjugated*	*as*	sentir		
digerir	*conjugated*	*as*	sentir		
discernir	*conjugated*	*as*	sentir		
disolver	*conjugated*	*as*	absolver		
distribuir	*conjugated*	*as*	argüir		
divertir	*conjugated*	*as*	sentir		
doler	*conjugated*	*as*	absolver		
dormir [1]	yo duermo, tú duermes, él duerme, ellos duermen	él durmió, ellos durmieron		duerme tú, duerma él, durmamos nosotros, duerman ellos	
elegir	*conjugated*	*as*	pedir		
empedrar	*conjugated*	*as*	acertar		
empezar	*conjugated*	*as*	acertar		
emporcar	*conjugated*	*as*	acostar		
encarecer	*conjugated*	*as*	nacer		
encender	*conjugated*	*as*	ascender		
encerrar	*conjugated*	*as*	acertar		
encomendar	*conjugated*	*as*	acertar		
encontrar	*conjugated*	*as*	acostar		
encordar	*conjugated*	*as*	acostar		
engreirse	*conjugated*	*as*	pedir		
engrosar	*conjugated*	*as*	acostar		
enmendar	*conjugated*	*as*	acertar		
entender	*conjugated*	*as*	ascender		
enterrar	*conjugared*	*as*	acertar		
envestir	*conjugated*	*as*	pedir		
errar	*conjugated*	*as*	acertar		
escarmentar	*conjugated*	*as*	acertar		
escribir					escrito
esforzar	*conjugated*	*as*	acostar		
estar	yo estoy	yo estuve, tú estuviste &c.			

Gerundio: durmiendo.

Infinitivo.	Presente del Indicativo.	Pretérito perfecto.	Futuro.	Imperativo.	Participio.
estregar	*conjugated*	as	acertar		
excluir	*conjugated*	us	argüir		excluso (ex-[cluído)
expedir	*conjugated*	as	pedir		
expeler					expulso (ex [pelido]
exponer	*conjugated*	as	poner		
extender	*conjugated*	as	ascender		
extinguir					extinto (ex-.[tinguido)
extraer	*conjugated*	as	traer		
fijar					fijo (fijado)
florecer	*conjugated*	as	nacer		
fluir	*conjugated*	as	argüir		
forzar	*conjugated*	as	acostar		
fregar	*conjugated*	as	acertar		
freir	*conjugated*	as	pedir		
gemir	*conjugated*	as	pedir		
gobernar	*conjugated*	as	acertar		
guarnecer	*conjugated*	as	nacer		
haber [1]	yo he, tú has, él ha, nosotros hemos, nosotros habéis,	yo hube, tú hubiste, él hubo &c.	yo habré, tú habrás &c.	haya él, hayamos nosotros, hayan ellos	habido
hacer	yo hago [ellos han	yo hice, tú hiciste, él hizo &c.	yo haré, tú harás &c.	haz tú, haga él, hagamos nosotros, hagan ellos	hecho
heder	*conjugated*	as	ascender		
helar	*conjugated*	as	acertar		
henchir	*conjugated*	as	pedir		
hender	*conjugated*	as	ascender		
herir	*conjugated*	as	sentir		
herrar	*conjugated*	as	acertar		
hervir	*conjugated*	as	sentir		
holgar	*conjugated*	as	acostar		
hollar	*conjugated*	as	acostar		
huir	*conjugated*	as	argüir		
imbuir	*conjugated*	as	argüir		
imprimir					impreso (imprimi-do)
incluir	*conjugated*	as	argüir		incluso (in-[cluido)
inducir	*conjugated*	as	conducir		
inferir	*conjugated*	as	sentir		
ingerir	*conjugated*	as	sentir		ingerto (in-[gerido)
inquirir	*conjugated*	as	sentir		
insertar					inserto (in-[sertado)
instituir	*conjugated*	as	argüir		
instruir	*conjugated*	as	argüir		
introducir	*conjugated*	as	conducir		
invernar	*conjugated*	as	acertar		
invertir	*conjugated*	as	sentir		inverso (in-vertido)

[1] Pres. del Subj.: yo haya, &c. Imperf. del Ind.: yo había, &c. Imperf. del Subj.: yo hubiese, &c. Condic. del Ind.: yo habría, &c.; Cond. del Subj.: yo hubiera, &c. Fut. del Subj.: yo hubiere, &c. Gerundio: habiendo.

Infinitivo.	Presente del Indicativo.	Pretérito perfecto.	Futuro.	Imperativo.	Participio.
ir 1	yo voy, tú vas, él va, nosotros vamos, vosotros vais, ellos van	yo fui, tú fuiste, él fué &c.	yo iré, tú irás &c.	ve tú, vaya él, vayamos (vamos) nosotros, id vosotros, vayan ellos	
jugar	*conjugated*	*as*	acostar		
lucir	*conjugated*	*as*	nacer		
llover	*conjugated*	*as*	absolver		
maldecir	*conjugated*	*as*	bendecir		maldito (maldecido)
manifestar	*conjugated*	*as*	acertar		
mantener	*conjugated*	*as*	tener		
medir	*conjugated*	*as*	pedir		
mentar	*conjugated*	*as*	acertar		
mentir	*conjugated*	*as*	sentir		
merendar	*conjugated*	*as*	acertar		
moler	*conjugated*	*as*	absolver		
morder	*conjugated*	*as*	absolver		
morir	*conjugated*	*as*	dormir		muerto
mostrar	*conjugated*	*as*	acostar		
mover	*conjugated*	*as*	absolver		
nacer	yo nazco			nazca él, nazcan ellos	
negar	*conjugated*	*as*	acertar		
nevar	*conjugated*	*as*	acertar		
obscurecer	*conjugated*	*as*	nacer		
obstruir	*conjugated*	*as*	argüir		
ofrecer	*conjugated*	*as*	nacer		
oir 2	yo oigo, tú oyes &c.	yo oí, tú oiste, él oyó, ellos oyéron		oiga él, oigamos nosotros, oigan ellos	
oler	*conjugated*	*as*	absolver		omiso (omitido)
omitir					
oprimir					opreso (oprimido)
pacer	*conjugated*	*as*	nacer		
parecer	*conjugated*	*as*	nacer		
pensar	*conjugated*	*as*	acertar		
pedir 3	yo pido, tú pides, él pide, ellos piden	él pidió, ellos pidieron		pide tú, pida él, pidamos nosotros, pidan ellos	
perder	*conjugated*	*as*	ascender		
placer, v. def.4	me (te, le) place	me &c. plugo			
plegar	*conjugated*	*as*	ascertar		
poblar	*conjugated*	*as*	acostar		
poder 5	yo puedo, tú puedes, él puede, ellos pueden	yo pude, tú pudiste &c.	yo podré, tú podrás &c.		

1 Pres. del Subj.: yo vaya, &c. Imperf. del Ind.: yo iba, &c.: Imperf. del Subj.: yo fuese, &c. Condic. del Indic.: yo iria, &c.; Condic. del Subj.: yo fuera, &c. Fut. del Subj.: yo fuere, &c. Gerundio: yendo.

2 Gerundio: oyendo.   3 Gerundio: pidiendo.

4 Pres. del Subj.: plegue ó plazga (á Dios). Imperf. del Subj.: pluguiese (á Dios) Fut. del Subj.: si me plugiere, &c. Condic. del Subj.: pluguiera (á Dios).

5 Gerundio: pudiendo.

Infinitivo.	Presente. del Indicativo.	Pretérito perfecto.	Futuro.	Imperativo.	Participio.
podrir ⎱ pudrir ⎰	yo pudro, tú pu- dres, él pudre, ellos pudren	yo pudrí, tú pudriste &c	yo pudriré, tú pudri- rás &c.	pudre tú, pu- dra él, pudra- mos nosotros, pudran ellos	pudrido
poner	yo pongo	yo puse, tú pu- siste &c.	yo pondré, tú pon- drás &c.	pon tú, ponga él, pongamos nosotros, pon- gan ellos	
preferir	*conjugated*	*as*	sentir		[(dido]
prender					preso (pren-
prescribir					prescrito
probar	*conjugated*	*as*	acostar		[(prescribi- [do
producir	*conjugated*	*as*	conducir		
prostituir	*conjugated*	*as*	argüir		
proveer					provisto
quebrar	*conjugated*	*as* .	acertar		(proveído)
querer	yo quiero, tú qui- eres, él quiere, ellos quieren	yo quise, tú quisiste &c.	yo querré, tú querras &c.	quiere tú, qui- era él, qui- eran ellos	
recluir	*conjugated*	*as*	argüir		recluso (re-
recomendar	*conjugated*	*as*	acertar		[cluido)
reconocer	*conjugated*	*as*	nacer		
recordar	*conjugated*	*as*	acostar		
reducir	*conjugated*	*as*	conducir		
referir	*conjugated*	*as*	sentir		
regir	*conjugated*	*as*	pedir		
reir	*conjugated*	*as*	pedir		
renacer	*conjugated*	*as*.	nacer		
rendir	*conjugated*	*as*	pedir		
renovar	*conjugated*	*as*	acostar		
reñir	*conjugated*	*as*	pedir		
reprobar	*conjugated*	*as*	acostar		
resentirse	*conjugated* ·	*as*	sentir		
retentar	*conjugated*	*as*	acertar		
retorcer	*conjugated*	*as*	absolver		
retribuir	*conjugated*	*as*	argüir		
reventar	*conjugated*	*as*	acertar		
revolcarse	*conjugated*	*as*	acostar		
rodar	*conjugated*	*as*	acostar		
romper					roto (rom-
saber	yo sé(Pres.delSubj. yo sepa &c.)	yo supe, tú su- piste &c.	yo sabré, tú sabrás &c.	sepa él, sepan ellos	[pido)
salir	yo salgo		yo saldré, tú saldrás &c.	sal tú, salga él, salgamos nosotros, sal- gan ellos	
segar	*conjugated*	*as*	acertar		
seguir	*conjugated*	*as*	pedir		
sembrar	*conjugated*	*as*	acertar		
sentar	*conjugated*	*as*	acertar		
sentir	yo siento, tú sien- tes, él siente, ellos sienten	él sintió, ellos sintieron		siente tú, sien- ta él, sientan ellos	

Infinitivo.	Presente del Indicativo.	Pretérito perfecto.	Futuro.	Imperativo.	Participio.
ser [1]	yo soy, tú eres, él es, nosotros somos, vosotros sois, ellos son	yo fui, tú fuiste, él fué &c.	yo sere, tú serás &c.	se tú, sea él, seamos nosotros, sean ellos	sido
serrar	*conjugated*	*as*	acertar		
servir	*conjugated*	*as*	pedir		
soldar	*conjugated*	*as*	acostar		
soler	*conjugated*	*as*	absolver		
soltar	*conjugated*	*as*	acostar		suelto (sol- [tado)
sonar	*conjugated*	*as*	acostar		
soñar	*conjugated*	*as*	acostar		
sostener	*conjugated*	*as*	tener		
substituir	*conjugated*	*as*	argüir		
sugerir	*conjugated*	*as*	sentir		
suprimir					supreso [(suprimido)
temblar	*conjugated*	*as*	acertar		
tender	*conjugated*	*as*	ascender		
tener	yo tengo, tú tienes, él tiene, ellos tienen	yo tuve, tu tuviste &c.	yo tendre, tú tendrás &c.	ten tú, tenga él, tengamos nosotros, tengan ellos	
tentar	*conjugated*	*as*	acertar		
teñir	*conjugated*	*as*	pedir		
torcer	*conjugated*	*as*	absolver		
tostar	*conjugated*	*as*	acostar		
traducir	*conjugated*	*as*	conducir		
traer	yo traigo	yo traje, tu trajiste &c.			
tronar	*conjugated*	*as*	acostar		
trasferir	*conjugated*	*as*	sentir		
tropezar	*conjugated*	*as*	acertar		
valer	yo valgo		yo valdré, tú valdrás &c.	valga el, valgamos nosotros, valgan ellos	
venir [2]	yo vengo, tú vienes, él viene, ellos vienen	yo vine, tú viniste &c.	yo vendré, tú vendrás &c.	ven tú, venga él, vengan ellos	
ver					visto
verter	*conjugated*	*as*	ascender		
vestir	*conjugated*	*as*	pedir		
volar	*conjugated*	*as*	acostar		
volcar	*conjugated*	*as*	acostar		
volver	*conjugated*	*as*	absolver		vuelto
yacer, v. def. [3]	(yago) él yace, ellos yacen				

1 Pres. del Subj.: yo sea, &c. Imperf. del Ind.: yo era, &c., nosotros éramos; Imperf. del Subj.: yo fuese, &c. Condic. del Ind.: yo sería, &c.; Condic. del Subj.: yo fuera, &c. Futuro del Subj.: yo fuere, &c. Gerundio: siendo.
  2 Gerundio: viniendo.   3 Imperf.: él yacia, ellos yacian.

ENGLISH AND SPANISH

A

a, an, art. indef. un, una.

aback, ad. detrás, atrás; (mar.) en facha; to be taken —, ser consternado.

abacus, s. tabla aritmética; ábaco, tablero de un capitel.

abaft, ad. (mar.) á ó en popa.

abandon, v.a. abandonar, dejar.

abandonment, s. abandonamiento, abandono; desamparo.

abase, v.a. abatir, humillar, envilecer.

abasement, s. abatimiento; humillación.

abash, v.a. avergonzar, causar confusión, sonrojar.

abashment, s. confusión, vergüenza; rubor, consternación.

abate, v.a. minorar, disminuir, rebajar; —, v.n. disminuirse.

abatement, s. rebaja, diminución.

abbacy, s. abadía.

abbess, s. abadesa.

abbey, s. abadía.

abbot, s. abad.   [pendiar,

abbreviate, v.a. abreviar, acortar, com-

abbreviation, s. abreviación.

abdicate, v.a. abdicar, renunciar.

abdication, s. abdicación, renuncia.

abdomen, s. abdomen, bajo vientre.

abdominal, a. abdominal.

abduct, v.a. arrebatar, llevar por fuerza (á una mujer ó un menor).

abductor, s.m. raptor; (anat.) músculo abductor.

abed, ad. en (la) cama.

aberration, s. error, desvío; aberración.

abet, v.a. favorecer, patrocinar, sostener; excitar, animar.

abetter, abettor, s. fautor, instigador.

abeyance, s. (law) expectativa.

abhor, v.a. aborrecer, detestar.

abhorrence, -cy, s. aborrecimiento, odio.

abhorrent, a. antipático, repugnante.

abide, v.n. habitar, morar; continuar; —, v.a. soportar, sufrir, sostener, aguantar.

ability, s. potencia, habilidad, capacidad, aptitud; abilities, pl., talento.

abiding, adj. continuo; inmutable; — place, s. morada, residencia.

---

abject, a. vil, despreciable, bajo.

abjection, s. abatimiento, desesperación.

abjectness, s. bajeza, vileza, humillación.

abjectly, ad. vilmente, bajamente.

abjuration, s. abjuración.

abjure, v.a. abjurar; renunciar.

ablative, s. (gr.) ablativo.

ablaze, a. en llamas.

able, a. fuerte, capaz, hábil; to be —,   [poder.

able-bodied, a. robusto, vigoroso.

ablution, s. ablución.

ably, ad. con habilidad, hábilmente.

abnegate, v.a. negar, renunciar.

abnegation, s. abnegación, resignación.

abnormal, a. irregular, deforme; inusitado.

aboard, ad. abordo.

abode, s. morada, residencia, domicilio.

abolish, v.a. abolir, anular, revocar.

abolition, s. abolición, anulación.

abolitionist, s. abolicionista.

abominable, a. abominable, detestable, -bly, ad. abominablemente.

abominate, v.a. abominar, detestar, aborrecer.

abomination, s. abominación, detestación.

aboriginal, a. aborigen, indígena, primitivo.

aborigines, s.pl. aborígenes, indígenas.

abort, v.n. abortar, malparir.

abortion, s. aborto, malparto.

abortive, a. abortivo; intempestivo, malogrado; -ly, intempestivamte, inútilmente.   [abundar de.

abound, v.n. abundar; to — with,

about, pr. cerca de, alrededor de, hacia; acerca, tocante á. I carry no money — me, no traigo dinero; to go — a thing, emprender alguna cosa; — ad. en contorno, aquí y allá; to be — to, estar para.

above, pr. encima, sobre; —, ad. arriba; — all, sobre todo, principalmente; — mentioned, ya mencionado.

abrade, v.a. raer.

abrasion, s. raspadura; lo que se quita de la superficie raspando.

abreast, ad. de frente; de costado.

abridge, v.a. abreviar, compendiar; acortar.

abridgment, s. compendio.   [barrenar.

abroach, ad. para derramarse; to set —,

abroad, ad. fuera de casa ó del país; en todas partes; to go —, salir; to set —, divulgar, publicar.

abrogate, v.a. abrogar, anular.

abrogation, s. abrogación, anulación.

abrupt, a. quebrado, desigual; precipitado, repentino; rudo; -ly, precipitadamente; bruscamente.

abruptness, s. precipitación, inconsideración; descortesía.

abscess, s. absceso, apostema.

abscind, v.a. cortar, tajar, trinchar.

abscission, s. cortadura.

abscond, v.n. esconderse; huirse.

absconder, s. fugitivo; desertor.

absence, s. ausencia; distracción; negligencia.

absent, a. ausente; distraído; — oneself, v.r. ausentarse.   [empleo, &c.

absentee, s. el que está ausente de su

absinth, s. ajenjo.

absolute, a. absoluto; categórico; positivo; arbitrario; -ly, absolutamente.

absoluteness, s. amplitud, carácter positivo de una cosa.

absolution, s. absolución.

absolutism, s. absolutismo.

absolutist, s. absolutista.

absolve, v.a. absolver, dispensar, exentar.

absorb, v.a. absorber.

absorbed, adj. preocupado.

absorbent, s. & a. absorbente (medicina).

absorption, s. absorción; preocupación.

abstain, v.n. abstenerse, privarse.

abstemious, a. abstemio, sobrio, moderado; -ly, ad. moderadamente.

abstemiousness, s. sobriedad, templanza, abstinencia.

abstention, s. abstensión.   [abstergente.

abstergent, a. lo que sirve para purificar.

abstinence, s. abstinencia; templanza.

abstinent, a. abstinente, sobrio; -ly, abstinentemente.

abstract, v.a. abstraer; —, robar; —, a. abstracto; —, s. extracto; sumario; in the —, de un modo abstracto.

abstracted, a. separado; abstraído; -ly, abstractivamente.

abstraction, s. abstracción; distracción.

abstractly, ad. en abstracto.

abstruse, a. abstruso, recondito, obscuro; -ly, obscuramente.

abstruseness, s. obscuridad, dificultad; misterio.

absurd, a. absurdo; -ly, ad. absurdamente

absurdity, s. absurdidad.

abundance, s. abundancia, copia.

abundant, a. abundante; -ly, ad. abundantemente, en copia.

abuse, v.a. abusar; engañar; ultrajar, violar; —, s. abuso, engaño; corruptela, seducción; injuria, afrenta.

abusive, a. abusivo, injurioso; -ly, ad. abusivamente.

abusiveness, s. palabras injuriosas.

abut, v.n. terminar, confinar.

abutment, s. confín, límite.

abysmal, a. abismal; insondable.

abyss, s. abismo; golfo; infierno.

acacia, s. acacia.

academic(al), a. académico.

academician, s. académico.

academy, s. academia, universidad.

acanthus, s. (bot.) acanto.

accede, v.n. acceder, convenir en alguna cosa, asentir.

accelerate, v.a. acelerar.

acceleration, s. aceleración.

accelerative, a. acelerativo.

accent, s. acento, modulación, tono; (poet.) lenguaje; —, v.a. acentuar, colocar los acentos.

accentuate, v.a. acentuar.

accentuation, s. acentuación.

accept, v.a. aceptar; admitir; recibir cariñosamente.

acceptable, a. aceptable, grato, digno de aceptación.

acceptability, s. aceptabilidad.

acceptably, ad. gustosamente, gratamente.

acceptance, acceptation, s. aceptación, recepción; recibimiento; acepcion.

acception, s. acepción, aceptacion, sentido ó significado en que se toma alguna cosa.

access, s. acceso; entrada; aumento, acceso periódico (de alguna enfermedad).

accessarily, ad. accesoriamente.

accessary, s. cómplice; —, a. accesorio; eventual, casual.

accessible, a. accesible.

accession, s. aumento, acrecentamiento; advenimiento; acceso.   [cómplice.

accessory, a. accesorio; confederado; -s,

accidence, s. rudimentos de la gramática.

accident, s. accidente; casualidad; suceso imprevisto, lance (funesto).

accidental, a. casual, contingente; -ly, ad. accidentalmente.

acclaim, v.a. aclamar, aplaudir.

acclamation, s. aclamación; aplauso.

acclimatise, v.a. aclimatar.

acclivity, s. cuesta, rampa, subida, ladera.

accolade, s. acolada, abrazo.

accommodate, v.a. acomodar. ajustar; — oneself, conformarse.

accommodating, a. servicial, obsequioso.
accommodation, s. comodidad, conveniencia, adaptación ; ajuste ; conciliación.
accommodation-bill, s. letra pro forma.
accompaniment, s. (mus.) acompañamiento. [acompañante.
accompanist, s. (mus.) acompañador,
accompany, v.a. acompañar.
accomplice, s. cómplice.
accomplish, v.a. efectuar, completar.
accomplished, a. perfecto, completó, elegante, consumado.
accomplishment, s. cumplimiento entero de alguna cosa ; perfección ; -s, pl. talentos, conocimientos.
accord, s. acuerdo, convenio ; armonía ; simetría ; with one —, unánimemente ; of one's own —, espontáneamente ; —, v.a. otorgar, conceder.
accordance, s. conformidad ; acuerdo.
accordant, a. acorde, conforme, conveniente.
according, pr. según, conforme ; — as, según que, como ; -ly, en conformidad, de consiguiente, en efecto, pues.
accordion, s. (mus.) acordeón.
accost, v.a. saludar á uno yendo hacia él; trabar conversación.
accoucheur, s. comadrón, partero.
account, s. cuenta, cálculo ; caso, estimación, aprecio ; narrativa de alguna cosa ; on no —, de ninguna manera ; por ningún título ; on — of, por motivo de ; to turn to —, hacer provechoso ; —, v.a. tener, reputar ; contar, computar.
accountability, s. responsabilidad.
accountable, a. responsable.
accountant, s. contador.
account-book, s. libro de cuentas.
accoutre, v.a. equipar, vestir.
accoutrement, s. atavío, apresto ; vestidura ; ornamento.
accredit, v.a. acreditar, patrocinar.
accretion, s. aumento, acrecentación.
accrue, v.n. resultar, provenir.
accumulate, v.a. acumular ; amontonar ; —, v.n. crecer. [namiento.
accumulation, s. acumulación ; amontonamiento.
accumulative, a. acumulativo.
accumulator, s. acumulador.
accuracy, s. exactitud, esmero. [mente.
accurate, a. exacto, puntual ; -ly, exactamente.
accursed, a. maldito, maldecido ; execrable ; excomulgado ; fatal ; — be ! ¡ mal haya !
accusation, s. acusación.
accusative, s. (gr.) acusativo.
accusatory, a. acusatorio.
accuse, v.a. acusar ; culpar

accuser, s. acusador ; denunciador.
accustom, v.a. acostumbrar, habituar.
accustomed, a. acostumbrado, habitual.
ace, s. as ; atomo ; migaja, partícula, f. ; within an — of, casi, casi ; por poco . . .
acephalous, a. acéfalo.
acerbity, s. acerbidad, amargura, severidad, aspereza, dureza.
acetic, a. (chem.) acético. [doler.
ache, s. dolor continuo, mal ; —, v.n.
achievable, a., hacedero, ejecutable.
achieve, v.a. ejecutar, perfeccionar ; ganar, obtener, acabar. [hazaña.
achievement, s. ejecución ; acción heroica.
achromatic, a. (opt.) acromático.
acid, a. ácido, agrio, acedo.
acidify, v.a. (chem.) acidificar.
acidity, s. agrura, acedía, acidez, acritud.
acknowledge, v.a. reconocer, confesar.
acknowledgment, s. reconocimiento ; gratitud ; concesión.
acme, s. crisis ; cima ; cenit, apogeo.
acolyte, s. acólito.
aconite, s. (bot.) acónito.
acorn, s. bellota.
acoustic, a. acústico.
acoustics, s. acústica.
acquaint, v.a. informar, advertir, avisar.
acquaintance, s. conocimiento ; familiaridad ; conocido. [terse.
acquiesce, v.n. consentir, asentir, someterse.
acquiescence, s. asenso, consentimiento.
acquiescent, a. deferente.
acquirable, a. adquirible.
acquire, v.a. adquirir, ganar, aprender.
acquirement, s. adquisición ; conocimientos, talento.
acquisition, adquisición ; cosa obtenida.
acquisitiveness, s. disposición á adquirir.
acquit, v.a. libertar, descargar, absolver.
acquitment, s. absolución ; descargo.
acquittal, s. absolución.
acquittance, s. descargo; recibo, finiquito.
acre, s. acre (medida de tierra que tiene cerca de 5800 varas cuadradas).
acrid, a. acre, mordaz.
acridity, s. acidez. [rosivo.
acrimonious, a. acre, aspero, duro, corrosivo.
acrimony, acrimonia, acritud.
acrobat, s. acróbata, funámbulo.
across, ad. de través, de una parte á otra; pr. á través de.
acrostic, s. poema acróstico.
act, a. representar ; obrar ; —, v.n. conducirse, obrar ; —, s. acto, hecho ; acción ; efecto ; jornada (de una comedia).
acting, s. acción ; representación, f
action, s. acción, operación : batalla ; gesticulación ; proceso.

actionable, a. punible ; procesable.
active, a. active ; eficaz ; ocupado ; ágil ;
  -ly, activamente, ágilmente, eficazmente.
activeness, activity, s. agilidad, actividad;
  prontitud ; vivacidad. [teatros).
actor, s. agente ; cómico, actor (en los
actress, s. comedianta, actriz.
actual, a. actual ; cierto, real ; efectivo ;
  -ly, en efecto, realmente.
actuality, s. actualidad.
actuary, s. secretario ; registrador.
actuate, v.a. excitar ; poner en acción.
acumen, s. agudeza, perspicacia, penetración.
acute, a. agudo ; ingenioso ; -ly, con
  agudeza. [sagacidad.
acuteness, s. agudeza ; perspicacia,
adage, s. refrán.
adamant, s. adamante.
adamantine, a. adamantino.
adapt, v.a. adaptar, acomodar una cosa á
  otra ; ajustar.
adaptability, s. facilidad de adaptarse.
adaptable, a. adaptable.
adaptation, adaptación.
adapted, a. proprio, útil. [up, sumar.
add, v.a. añadir, aumentar ; juntar ; to —
addendum, s. suplemento.
adder, s. víbora.
addict, v.a. dedicar ; to — one's self, en-
  tregarse á . . .
addictedness, addiction, s. inclinación,
  propensión, dedicación, afición.
addition, s. adición.
additional, a. adicional ; -ly, por adición ; además.
addle, v.a. hacer estéril.
addled, a. estéril, podrido.
addle-headed, -pated, a. bobo, aturdido.
address, v.a. hablar ; dirigir ; —, s.
  petición ; memorial ; dedicatoria ; destreza.
adduce, v.a. alegar, aducir
adept, s. adepto, sabio ; —, a. adepto.
adequacy, s. suficiencia ; proporcionali-
  dad.
adequate, a. adecuado, proporcionado ;
  suficiente ; -ly, adecuadamente.
adequateness, s. suficiencia, proporción
  exacta.
adhere, v.n. adherir, pegarse ; aficionarse.
adherence, s. adherencia, anexión, unión.
adherent, a. pegajoso ; tenaz ; adherente;
  —, s. adherente, partidario.
adhesion, s. adhesión.
adhesive, a. pegajoso, tenaz.
adhesiveness, s. adhesividad, tenacidad.
adieu, interj. á Dios, adiós ; —, s. despedida.
adipose, a. adiposo.

adit, s. conducto subterráneo ; entrada
  de una mina.
adjacency, contigüidad, vecindad.
adjacent, a. adyacente, contiguo.
adjectival, a. adjetival ; -ly, adjetiva-
  mente. [jetivo.
adjective, s. adjetivo ; -ly, como ad-
adjoin, v.a. juntar ; unir ; —, v.n. estar
  contiguo.
adjoining, a. contiguo, inmediato, junto.
adjourn, v.a. diferir, remitir.
adjournment, s. prórroga, emplazo, suspensión. [condenar ; decretar.
adjudge, adjudicate, v.a. adjudicar ;
adjunct, s. adjunto.
adjuration, s. conjuro, juramento.
adjure, v.a. juramentar ; conjurar.
adjust, v.a. ajustar, acomodar.
adjustment, s. ajustamiento, arreglo.
adjutancy, s. (mil.) ayudantía.
adjutant, s. (mil.) ayudante.
admeasurement, s. medida.
administer, v.a. administrar ; gobernar ;
  contribuir ; to — an oath, tomar juramento. [erno.
administration, s. administración ; gobi-
administrative, a. administrativo.
administrator, s. administrador.
administratrix, s. administradora.
admirable, a. admirable ; -bly, admirable
  mente, á maravilla.
admiral, s. almirante.
admiralship, dignidad de almirante.
admiralty, s. almirantazgo.
admiration, s. admiración ; maravilla
admire, v.a. admirar ; amar.
admirer, s. admirador ; amante.
admiringly, ad. con admiración.
admissible, a. admisible.
admissibility, s. admisibilidad.
admission, a. admisión, recepción, entrada. [permitir.
admit, v.a. admitir ; recibir, conceder,
admittance, s. entrada, admisión.
admittedly, ad. sin duda, sin denegación.
admixture, s. mistura, mezcla.
admonish, v.a. amonestar, reprender.
admonition, s. amonestación ; consejo,
  aviso.
admonitory, a. lo que amonesta, ex-
  hortatorio. [fatiga.
ado, s. dificultad ; bullicio, tumulto ;
adolescence (-cy), s. adolescencia.
adopt, v.a. adoptar, prohijar.
adoption, s. adopción.
adoptive, a. adoptivo.
adorable, a. adorable.
adorableness, s. excelencia.
adorably, ad. de un modo adorable.
adoration, s. adoración.
adore, v.a. adorar.

adorer, s. adorador, amante. [adornar.
adorn, v.a. hermosear con adornos,
adornment, s. adorno, atavío.
adrift, ad. flotando á merced de las olas ;
á la ventura.
adroit, a. diestro, hábil, mañoso.
adroitness, s. destreza.
adulation, s. adulación, lisonja, zalamería.
adulatory, a. lisonjero.
adult, a. adulto ; —, s. adulto ; adulta.
adulterate, v.a. adulterar, corromper,
falsificar ; —, a. adulterado, falsificado.
adulteration, s. adulteración, corrupción.
adulterator, s. falsificador.
adulterer, s. adúltero.
adulteress, s. adúltera. [espurio.
adulterous, a. adúltero ; adulterino ;
adultery, s. adulterio.
adumbrate, v.a. bosquejar.
advance, v.a. avanzar ; promover ; pagar
adelantado ; —, v.n. adelantar, hacer
progresos ; s. avance, paga adelantada.
advancement, s. adelantamiento ; progreso ; promoción.
advantage, s. ventaja, superioridad ;
provecho ; lucro ; ocasión favorable ;
to take — of, aprovecharse de ; —, v.a.
ayudar, favorecer.
advantage-ground, s. puesto ventajoso.
advantageous, a. ventajoso, útil ; -ly,
ventajosamente.
advantageousness, s. ventaja, utilidad.
advent, s. venida ; Advent, s. Adviento.
adventitious, a. adventicio, accidental.
adventure, s. aventura ; riesgo ; lance ; v.n.
osar, emprender ; —, va. aventurar.
adventurer, s. aventurero.
adventuress, s. aventurera.
adventurous, a. intrépido, atrevido,
valeroso ; -ly, arriesgadamente.
adverb, s. adverbio. [mente.
adverbial, a. adverbial ; -ly, adverbial-
adversary, s. adversario, enemigo.
adversative, a. (gram.) adversativo.
adverse, a. adverso, contrario ; -ly, contrariamente.
adversity, s. adversidad, calamidad ; infortunio. [mente.
advert, v.n. advertir, considerar atenta-
advertence, s. atención.
advertise, v.a. avisar, advertir.
advertisement, s. aviso ; reclamo.
advertiser, s. avisador.
advertising, s. anuncio.
advice, s. consejo ; aviso. [aviso.
advice-boat, s. (mar.) embarcación de
advisability, s. conveniencia.
advisable, a. conveniente.
advise, v.a. aconsejar ; avisar ; —, v.n.
considerar, deliberar. [mente.
advisedly, ad. avisadamente, deliberada-

advisedness, s. prudencia.
adviser, s. consejero, aconsejador.
advisory, a. consultor, autorizado para
aconsejar. [logía.
advocacy, s. vindicación, defensa, apo-
advocate, s. abogado ; protector ; —, v.a.
sostener.
advocateship, s. abogacía. [eclesiástico.
advowee, s. patrón de un beneficio
advowson, s. patronato de un beneficio.
adze, s. azuela.
ægis, s. egida, escudo.
æon, s. eón, eternidad.
aerate, v.a. ventilar.
aerated, a. gaseoso.
aerial, a. aéreo, etéreo.
aerodrome, s. aeródromo.
aerolite, s. aerolito.
aerometer, s. aerómetro.
aeronaut, s. aeronauta.
aeronautic, s. aeronautica, aerostación.
aeroplane, s. aeroplano.
aerostat, s. globo aerostático.
aerostatics, aerostation, s. aerostática.
aesthetic, a. estetico.
aesthetics, s. estetíca.
afar, ad. lejos,; from —, desde lejos.
affability, s. afabilidad, urbanidad, dulzura. [afablemente.
affable, a. afable, complaciente ; -bly,
affair, s. asunto ; negocio ; (mil.) acción.
affect, v.a. conmover, emocionar, in-
presionar ; afectar.
affectation, s. afectación.
affected, p. & a. afectado, lleno de afectación ; inclinado ;-ly, con afectación.
affecting, a. sensible, lastimoso ; -ly
tiernamente, patéticamente.
affection, s. afección ; amor ; afición.
affectionate, a. afectuoso, benévolo ; -ly,
cariñosamente.
affiance, s. desposorio, esponsales, confianza ; —, v.a. desposar, prometer en
esponsales.
affianced, a. desposado, novio, novia.
affidavit, s. declaración jurada.
affiliate, v.a. ahijar ; afiliar.
affiliation, s. adopción, afiliacion.
affinity, s. afinidad, parentesco por matrimonio ; atracción.
affirm, v.a. afirmar, declarar, confirmar.
affirmation, s. afirmación. [mente.
affirmative, a. afirmativo ; -ly, afirmativa-
affix, v.a. anexar, añadir, fijar ; —, s.
(gr.) afijo.
afflatus, s. soplo ; inspiración poética.
afflict, v.a. afligir ; atormentar.
afflicted, a. afligido, desgraciado.
afflicting, a. penoso, lastimoso.
affliction, s. aflicción, dolor, pena.
afflictive, a. aflictivo, penoso.

affluence, s. afluencia, concurrencia, concurso ; copia, abundancia, opulencia.
affluent, a. afluente, opulento ; s. afluente,
rio que se echa en otro.
afflux, s. confluencia, afluencia.
afford, v.a. dar ; proveer ; producir.
afforest, v.a. plantar con arboles.
afforestation, s. plantío, plantación.
affray, s. asalto; tumulto.
affreight, v.a. fletar, alquilar (un barco).
affright, v.a. espantar ; —, s. espanto.
affront, s. afrenta, injuria ; —, v.a.
afrentar, insultar, ultrajar.
affusion, s. afusión.
afield, ad. en campo abierto, fuera.
afire, ad. en llamas.
aflame, ad. en llamas.
afloat, ad. flotante, á flote.
afoot, ad. á pie.
afore, ad. antes.
aforesaid, a. ya mencionado, susodicho.
aforethought, a. premeditado.
aforetime, ad. antiguamente.
afraid, a. medroso, tímido ; I am —,
temo.
afresh, ad. de nuevo, otra vez.
aft, ad. (mar.) á popa.
after, pr. después de ; detrás ; según ;
all, en fin, en suma. [venideros.
after-ages, s.pl. tiempos venideros, siglos
after-birth, s. secundinas.
after-crop, s. segunda cosecha.
afterglow, s. crepúsculo.
aftermath, s. retoño, segunda cosecha.
aftermost, a. último.
afternoon, s. tarde.
after-part, s. parte posterior.
after-piece, s. sainete representado después de una comedia.
after-taste, s. resabio.
after-thought, s. reflexión tardía ; reparo.
afterward, afterwards, ad. después, más
tarde.
again, ad. otra vez, de nuevo ; — and —,
muchas veces ; as much —, el doble.
against, pr. contra ; — the grain, á contrapelo ; de mala gana.
agape, a. boca abierta.
agapé, s. ágapas.
agate, s. ágata (piedra preciosa).
agave, s. pita.
age, s. edad ; siglo ; vejez ; under —,
menor ; —, v.a. envejecer.
aged, a. viejo, anciano.
agency, s. agencia.
agent, s. agente, factor, delegado.
agglomerate, v.a. aglomerar ; —, v.n.
aglomerarse.
agglomeration, s. aglomeración.
agglutinate, v.a. conglutinar, unir.

agglutination, s. conglutinación.
aggrandize, v.a. engrandecer ; elevar.
aggrandizement, s. engrandecimiento.
aggravate, v.a. agravar ; exagerar.
aggravation, s. agravación. [conjunto.
aggregate, a. agregado ; — s. coleccion,
aggregation, s. agregación.
aggress, v.n. acometer.
aggression, s. agresión, cfensa ; asalto.
aggressive, a. ofensivo.
aggressor, s. agresor.
aggrieve, v.a. injuriar, gravar, dañar :
apesadumbrar ; —, v.n. lamentar.
aggroup, v.a. agrupar.
aghast, a. horrorizado.
agile, a. ágil, vivo ; diestro.
agility, s. agilidad ; destreza.
agio, s. agio.
agitate, v.a. agitar ; discutir.
agitation, s. agitación ; perturbación.
agitator, s. agitador, incitador.
aglet, aiglet, s. herrete de cordón.
agnate, a. & s. agnado ; agnada.
agnostic, s. & a. agnostico, -ca.
agnosticism, s. agnosticismo.
ago, ad. two years —, hace dos anos ;
how long —, ¿ cuanto ha ? or ¿ cuanto
hace ?
agog, a. deseoso, presuroso.
agoing, ad. en acción, en movimiento.
agonise, v.n. agonizar ; —, v.a. atormentar.
agonising, a. doloroso, atroz.
agony, s. agonía ; angustia extrema.
agrarian, a. agrario.
agree, v.n. concordar, convenir.
agreeable, a. conveniente, agradable ;
amable ; -bly, agradablemente ; -bly
with, según, conforme á.
agreeableness, s. conformidad, amabilidad, gracia.
agreed, a. convenido. [unión.
agreement, s. concordia ; conformidad,
agricultural, a. agricola.
agriculture, s. agricultura.
agriculturist, s. agricultor.
aground, ad. (mar.) varado, encallado.
ague, s. fiebre, calentura intermitente.
aguish, a. febril.
ah ! ¡ ah ! ¡ ay ! [por la proa.
ahead, ad. más allá, adelante (mar.)
ahoy ! (mar.) ¡ ohé ! ¡ ahupa !
aid, v.a. ayudar, socorrer ; —, s. ayuda ;
auxilio, socorro.
aide-de-camp, s. (mil.) ayudante de
campo. [cómplice.
aider, s. auxiliador ; — and abetter, (law)
aigret, s. cresta, penacho.
ail, v.a. afligir, molestar ; what -s you ?
¿ qué le duele á U.?
ailing, a. doliente, enfermizo.

ailment, s. dolencia, indisposición.

aim, v.a. apuntar, asestar el tiro con el ojo; aspirar; intentar; —, s. de signio; mira; puntería.

aimless, a. sin designio, sin objeto.

air, s. aire; aire de música; semblante; —, v.a. airear; secar; ventilar.

air-balloon, s. globo aerostático.

air-cushion, s. cojinete rellenado de aire.

air-gun, s. escopeta de viento.

air-hole, s. respiradero.

airily, ad. ligeramente, airosamente.

airiness, s. ventilación.

airing, s. paseo; ventilación.

airless, a. falto de ventilación, sofocado.

airman, s. aviador.

air-pump, s. máquina neumática.

air-shaft, s. respiradero de mina.

airship, s. dirigible.

air-tight, a. herméticamente cerrado.

airy, a. aéreo.

aisle, s. nave de una iglesia.

ajar, a. entreabierto.

akimbo, a. with arms —, de jarras, en [jarras.

akin, a. consanguíneo, emparentado.

alabaster, s. alabastro; —, a. alabastrino.

alack(-a-day) ! ¡ay ! (exclamación de dolor ó lástima).

alacrity, s. ardor, viveza. [quietar.

alarm, s. alarma; —, v.a. alarmar; in-

alarm-bell, s. campana de rebato.

alarm-clock, s. reloj despertador.

alarming, a. formidable.

alarmist, s. alarmista.

alarm-post, s. puesto de aviso.

alarum, s. alarma.

alas, ¡ay !

alb, s. alba.

albatross, s. alcatraz.

albeit, c. aunque.

albino, s. albino.

album, s. album.

albumen, s. albumen.

albuminous, a. albuminoso.

alchemist, s. alquimista.

alchemy, s. alquimia. [vino.

alcohol, s. alcohol, espíritu rectificado de

alcoholic, a. alcohólico.

alcoran, s. el corán.

alcove, s. alcoba.

alder, s. aliso (árbol).

alderman, s. regidor (oficial municipal).

ale, s. cerveza.

alehouse, s. cervecería, taberna.

alehouse-keeper, s. cervecero.

alert, a. alerta, vigilante; vivo.

alertness, s. cuidado; vigilancia, viveza, actividad.

alga, s. alga (planta que se cría en el mar.).

algebra, s. álgebra.

algebraic(al), a. algebraico.

algebraist, s. algebrista.

alias, ad. alias; —, s. nombre falso.

alibi, s. (law) coartada.

alien, a. & s. extraño; forastero.

alienable, a. enajenable.

alienate, v.a. enajenar. [extravío

alienation, s. enajenación; — of mind.

alight, v.n. bajar (de un coche ó de caballo apearse; —, a. encendido; ardiente.

alignment, s. alineamiento. [mente.

alike, a. semejante, igual; —, ad. igual-

aliment, s. alimento. [nutritivo.

alimental, alimentary, a. alimentoso,

alimentation, s. alimentación.

alimony, s. alimentos.

aliquot part, s. parte alícuota.

alive, a. vivo, viviente; activo.

alkali, s. álcali.

alkaline, a. alcalino.

alkaloid, s. & a. alcaloide.

all, a. todo; —, ad. enteramente; — at once, — of a sudden, de repente; — the same, sin embargo; — the better, tanto mejor; not at —, no por cierto; once for —, una vez por todas; —, s. todo.

allay, v.a. aliviar, apaciguar.

allayment, s. alivio, desahogo.

allegation, s. alegación.

allege, v.a. alegar; declarar.

allegiance, s. lealtad, fidelidad.

allegorical, a. alegórico; -ly, alegóri-camente.

allegorise, v.a. alegorizar.

allegory, s. alegoría.

allegro, s. (mus.) alegro.

alleluia, int. alleluya.

alleviate, v.a. aliviar, aligerar.

alleviation, s. alivio; mitigación.

alley, s. paseo de árboles; callejuela.

all-hallowmas, all-hallow-tide, fiesta de todos los Santos.

alliance, s. alianza.

allied, a. aliado, confederado.

alligation, s. aligación.

alligator, s. caimán; cocodrilo Americano

alliteration, s. aliteración.

allocate, v.a. asignar.

allocation, s. colocación; distribución.

allocution, s. alocución.

allodial, a. alodial.

allodium, s. alodio.

allopathy, s. alopatía.

allot, v.a. distribuir por suerte; asignar.

allotment, s. asignación; repartimiento.

allow, v.a. conceder, aprobar; permitir; dar, pagar.

allowable, a. admisible, permitido, justo.

allowance, s. concesión; lic   a; (mar.) ración, alimentos.

alloy, v.a. ligar, mezclar un metal con otro ; quilatar oro ; —, s. liga, mezcla ; quilate.
allspice, s. pimiento.
allude, v.n. aludir.
allure, v.a. alucinar, cebar.
alluringly, ad. seductoramente.
allurement, s. halago, cebo, aliciente, atractivo.
allusion, s. alusión. [alusivo.
allusive, a. alusivo ; -ly, de un modo
alluvial, a. aluvial.
alluvion, alluvium, s. aluvión. [alianza.
ally, s. aliado ; pariente ; —, v.a. hacer
allwise, a. omniscio.
almanac, s. almanaque.
almighty, s. omnipotente, todopoderoso.
almond, s. almendra.
almond-tree, s. almendro.
almoner, s. limosnero.
almonry, s. hospicio para pobres.
almost, ad. casi, cerca.
alms, s. limosna.
alms-house, s. hospicio para pobres.
aloe, s. áloe, liniáloe.
aloft, ad. arriba.
alone, a. solo ; —, ad. solamente, sólo ; to let —, dejar en paz.
along, ad. á lo largo ; adelante ; — with, junto con : -side (mar.), al costado.
aloof, ad. lejos, aparte, á lo largo.
aloud, ad. alto, en alta voz.
alphabet, s. alfabeto. [camente.
alphabetical, a. alfabético ; -ly, alfabéti-
alpine, a. alpino.
already, ad. ya.
also, ad. también, igualmente, además.
altar, s. altar.
altar-piece, s. retablo.
alter, v.a. alterar, mudar.
alterable, a. alterable, mudable.
alteration, s. cambio, alteración.
alterative, a. alterativo.
altercation, s. altercación, disputa.
altercate, v.n. trabarse de palabras, disputar, altercar.
alternate, a. alternativo, recíproco ; —, v.a. alternar ; -ly, alternativamente.
alternation, s. alternación.
alternative, s. alternativa, —, a. alternativo ; -ly, alternativamente.
although, altho', c. aunque, bien que.
altitude, s. altitud, altura.
altogether, ad. del todo, completamente.
alum, s. alumbre.
aluminium, s. (chem.) aluminio.
aluminous, a. aluminoso.
always, ad. siempre, constantemente, sin cesar. [samente.
amain, ad. con vehemencia, vigoro-
amalgam, s. amalgama.

amalgamate, v.a. & n. amalgamar.
amalgamation, s. amalgamación.
amanuensis, s. amanuense, secretario.
amaranth, s. (bot.) amaranto.
amaryllis, s. (bot.) amarilis.
amass, v.a. acumular, amontonar.
amateur, s. aficionado.
amativeness, s. amatividad.
amatory, a. amatorio ; erótico.
amaze, v.a. espantar ; sorprender.
amazedly, ad. fuera de sí.
amazement, s. asombro, pasmo.
amazing, a. extraño, pasmoso, asombroso -ly, pasmosamente.
amazon, s. amazona.
ambassador, s. embajador.
ambassadress, s. embajadora.
amber, s. ámbar ; —, a. ambarino.
ambidextrous, a. ambidextro.
ambient, a. ambiente.
ambiguity, s. ambigüedad, duda ; equi- voco. [mente.
ambiguous, a. ambiguo ; -ly, ambigua-
ambit, s. circúito ; circumferencia.
ambition, s. ambición.
ambitious, a. ambicioso ; -ly, ambiciosa- mente.
amble, s. ambladura ; —, v.n. amblar.
ambler, s. amblador.
ambrosia, s. ambrosia.
ambrosial, a. delicioso.
ambulance, s. (mil.) hospital de campaña.
ambulant, a. ambulante.
ambulatory, s. galería, pasadizo.
ambuscade, ambush, s. emboscada, celada, acecho ; to lie in —, estar em- boscado, acechar.
ambush, v.a. emboscar.
ameliorate, v.a. mejorar.
amelioration, s. mejoramiento.
amenable, a. responsable ; tratable.
amend, v.a. enmendar ; —, v.n. enmen- darse, reformarse, restablecerse.
amendable, a. reparable, corregible.
amendment, s. enmienda, reforma.
amends, s. recompensa, compensación.
amenity, s. amenidad.
amerce, v.a. multar.
amercement, s. multa.
Americanism, s. Americanismo ; idiot- ismo Americano.
amethyst, s. amatista.
amiability, s. amabilidad.
amiable, a. amable, amigable.
amiableness, s. amabilidad, gracia.
amiably, ad. amablemente.
amianthus, s. amianto.
amicable, a. amigable, amistoso ; -bly, amigablemente.
amice, s. amito, ornamento sagrado.
amid(st), pr. entre, en medio de.

amidships, ad. en medio del barco. [mal.
amiss, ad. culpablemente, erradamente,
amity, s. amistad.
ammonia, s. amoníaco.
ammonite, s. amonita.
ammunition, s. munición.
amnesty, s. amnistía ; olvido general.
among(st), pr. entre, en medio de.
amorous, a. amoroso ; -ly, amorosa-
mente. [rosa.
amorousness, s. amor, inclinación amo-
amorphous, a. informe.
amortise, v.a. amortizar.
amortisement, s. amortización.
amount, s. importe ; —, v.n. montar,
importar, subir, ascender.
amour, s. intriga de amor.
amphibian, s. anfibio.
amphibious, a. anfibio.
amphitheatre, s. anfiteatro.
ample, a. amplio, extenso, copioso.
ampleness, s. amplitud, abundancia.
amplification, s. amplificación ; extensión.
amplify, v.a. ampliar, extender.
amplitude, s. amplitud, extensión ;
abundancia.
amply, ad. ampliamente, copiosamente.
amputate, v.a. amputar. [miento.
amputation, s. amputación ; corta-
amuck, ad. furiosamente.
amulet, s. amuleto.
amuse, v.a. entretener, divertir.
amusement, s. diversión, pasatiempo,
entretenimiento. [mente.
amusing, divertido ; -ly, entretenida-
an, art. un, una.
anabaptism, s. herejía de los anabaptistas.
anabaptist, s. anabaptista.
anachronism, s. anacronismo.
anæmia, s. anemia.
anæmic, a. anémico.
anagram, s. anagrama. [camente.
analogical, a. analógico ; -ly, analógi-
analogous, a. análogo.
analogy, s. analogía, conformidad.
analysis, s. análisis.
analyse, v.a. analizar.
analyst, s. analizador. [mente.
analytical, a. analítico ; -ly, analítica-
anarchic(al), a. anárquico, confuso.
anarchy, s. anarquía.
anathema, s. anatema, excomunión.
anathematize, v.a. anatematizar.
anatomical, a. anatómico ; -ly, anatómi-
camente.
anatomist, s. anatomista.
anatomize, v.a. anatomizar.
anatomy, s. anatomía.
ancestor, s. abuelo ; -s, pl. antepasados.
ancestral, a. hereditario.

ancestry, s. linaje de antepasados ; raza,
alcurnia. [las anclas
anchor, s. ancla, áncora ; —, v.n. echar
anchorage, s. anclaje.
anchorite, s. anacoreta.
anchovy, s. anchova, anchoa.
ancient, a. antiguo ; -ly, antiguamente.
and, c. y, é.
andiron, s. morillo, caballete de hierro.
anecdotal, a. anecdótico.
anecdote, s. anécdota.
anemone, s. (bot.) anémona, anémone.
anent, pr. contra ; sobre.
aneurism, s. aneurisma.
anew, ad de nuevo, nuevamente.
angel, s. ángel.
angelic(al), a. angélico.
anger, s. ira, cólera ; —, v.a. enojar,
irritar, encolerizar.
angle, s. ángulo ; caña de pescar ; —, v.n.
pescar con caña ; halagar.
angled, a. anguloso.
angler, s. pescador de caña.
Anglican, a. anglicano.
anglicism, s. anglicismo.
angling, s. pesca con caña.
angling-line, s. sedal.
angling-rod, s. caña de pescar.
angrily, ad. coléricamente, con ira.
angry, a. colérico, irritado.
anguish, s. ansia, pena, angustia.
angular, s. angular.
angularity, s. forma angular.
anil, s. añil.
aniline, s. anilina. [vertencia ; represión.
animadversion, s. animadversión ; ad-
animadvert, v.n. considerar, observar ;
censurar ; reprochar.
animal, s. & a. animal.
animalcule, s. animalejo.
animalism, s. animalismo.
animality, s. vida animal. [animado,
animate, v.a. animar ; —, a. viviente,
animated, a. animado, vivo.
animation, s. animación.
animosity, s. animosidad.
animus, s. voluntad ; intención ; animosidad.
anise, s. anís.
aniseed, anise'te, s. anís.
anker, s. medida de líquidos, baril.
ankle, s. tobillo, maléolo ; -bone, hueso
del tobillo.
annalist, s. analista, cronista.
annals, s. anales.
anneal, v.a. templar (metal ó vidrio).
annex, v.a. anexar, unir ; —, s. anexo,
dependencia.
annexation, s. anexión.
annihilate, v.a. aniquilar.
annihilation, s. aniquilación.

anniversary, s. aniversario ; —, s. anual.
annotate, v.n. anotar.
annotation, s. anotación.
announce, v.a. anunciar, publicar.
announcement, s. advertencia, aviso, anuncio.
annoy, v.a. molestar.
annoyance, s. molestia.
annoying, s. enfadoso, molesto, fastidioso, importuno.
annual, a. anual ; -ly, anualmente, todos los años. . .   [vitalicia.
annuitant, s. proprietario de renta
annuity, s. renta vitalicia.
annul, v.a. anular, aniquilar.
annular, a. anular.
annulment, s. anulación.
annunciate, v.a. anunciar.
annunciation, s. anunciación.
anodyne, a. (med.) anodino.
anoint, v.a. untar, ungir.
anomalous, a. anómalo, irregular ; -ly, irregularmente.
anomaly, s. anomalía, irregularidad.
anon, ad. luego.
anonymous, a. anónimo ; -ly, anónimamente.   [otro.
another, a. otro, diferente ; one —, uno á
answer, v.n. contestar ; responder, corresponder ; surtir efecto ; —, s. contestación, respuesta.
answerable, a. responsable ; conforme.
ant, s. hormiga.
antagonism, s. antagonismo, rivalidad.
antagonist, s. antagonista, adversario.
antarctic, a. antártico.
ant-bear, ant-eater, s. oso hormiguero.
antecedence, s. precedencia.
antecedent, a. antecedente.
antechamber, s. antecamara.
antedate, v.a. antedatar.
antediluvian, a. antediluviano.
antelope, s. antílope, gacela.
antemeridian, a. antes de mediodía.
antennae, s.pl. antenas.
antepenultimate, s. antepenúltima.
anterior, a. anterior, precedente.
anteriority, s. anterioridad, precedencia.
ante-room, s. anticamera.
anthem, s. antífona.
anther, s. (bot.) antera.
ant-hill, s. hormiguero.
anthology, s. antología.   [Antón.
Anthony's fire, s. (med.) fuego de San
anthracite, s. antracita.
anthrax, s. (med.) antrax, avispero.
anthropology, s. antropología.
antic, a. grotesco ; —, s. bufón
Antichrist, s. Antecristo, m.
anticipate, v.a. anticipar, prevenir.
anticipation, s. anticipación.

anticipatory, anticipant, a. antici-ante.
anti-climax, s. anticlimax.
antics, s. bufonadas.
antidote, s. antídoto, contraveneno.
antimony, s. antimonio.
antipathetic, a. antipático.
antipathy, s. antipatía.
antipodes, s.pl. antipodas.
antipope, s. antipapa.
antiquarian, antiquary, s. anticuario.
antiquated, a. anticuado.
antique, a. antíguo ; —, s. antigualla, antigüedad.
antiquity, s. antigüedad ; ancianidad.
antiseptic, a. antiséptico.
antithesis, s. antítesis, contrariedad.
antitype, s. antitipo.
antler, s. cercetas, mogotes del ciervo.
anus, s. ano.
anvil, s. yunque, bigornia.
anxiety, s. ansiedad, ansia, afán.
anxious, a. ansioso ; -ly, ansiosamente.
any, a. & pn. cualquier, cualquiera, alguno, alguna, todo ; -body, -one, alguno, cualquiera ; -how, de cualquier modo ; -thing, algo ; -where, en cualquier lugar.
aorta, s. aorta.   [tud.
apace, ad. apriesa, con presteza ó prontiapart, ad. aparte, separadamente.
apart, ad. aparte, separadamente.
apartment, s. cuarto.
apathetic, a. apático.
apathy, s. apatía.
ape, s. mono ; —, v.a remedar, contrahacer, imitar.
aperient, aperitive, a. (med.) aperitivo.
aperture, s. abertura.
apex, s. ápice, colmo ; cima.
aphorism, s. aforismo ; máxima.
aphoristical, a. aforístico.
apiary, s. colmena.
apiece, ad. por cabeza, por persona.
apish, a. remedador, gestero, mímico, monero.
Apocalypse, s. Apocalípsis.
apocrypha, s.pl. libros apócrifos, pl.
apocryphal, a. apócrifo, no canónico.
apologetic, a. apologético.
apologise, v.n. disculparse, excusarse.
apologist, s. apologista.
apology, s. apología, defensa.
apophthegm, s. apotegma.
apoplectic, a. apopletico.
apoplexy, s. apoplejía.
apostasy, s. apostasía.
apostate, s. apóstata.
apostatise, v.n. apostatar.
aposteme, apostume, s. apostema, absceso.
apostle, s. apóstol.
apostleship, s. apostolado.
apostolic(al), a. apostólico

apostrophe, s. apóstrofe, (gr.) apóstrofo.
apostrophise, v.a. apostrofar. [botica.
apothecary, s. boticario ; -'s _hop, s.
apotheosis, s. apoteosis, deificación.
appal, v.a. espantar, asustar.
appalling, a. espantoso.
appanage, s. alimentos ; heredamiento, infantazgo.
apparatus, s. aparato, aparejo.
apparel, s. traje, vestido ; —, v.a. vestir ; adornar. [apariencia.
apparent, a. evidente, aparente ; -ly, en
apparition, s. aparición, visión.
apparitor, s. ujier ; alguacil.
appeal, v.n. apelar, recurrir á un tribunal superior ; —, s. (law) apelación.
appear, v.n. aparecer, ser evidente.
appearance, s. apariencia, probabilidad.
appeasable, a. aplacable, reconciliable.
appease, v.a. aplacar, reconciliar.
appellant, s. (law) apelante.
appellation, s. título, nombre.
appellee, s. (law) apelado, intimado.
append, v.a. añadir, agregar. [miento.
appendage, s. dependencia ; hereda-
appendix, s. apéndice.
appertain, v.n. pertenecer, tocar á.
appetence, s. concupiscencia.
appetising, a. apetitivo, gustoso.
appetite, s. apetito. [aclamar.
applaud, v.a. aplaudir ; alabar ; palmear ;
applauder, s. aclamador.
applause, s. aplauso.
apple, s. manzana : pupila del ojo.
apple-pie, s. pastelillo de manzanas ; in — order, en sumo orden.
apple-tree, s. manzano.
appliance, s. recurso ; aparato.
applicability, s. aptitud.
applicable, a. aplicable, apto ; conforme ; -bly, de un modo aplicable.
applicant, s. aspirante, pretendiente.
application, s. aplicación.
apply, v.a. aplicar, acomodar ; —, v.n. dirigirse, recurrir.
appoint, v.a. señalar, determimar ; nombrar, eligir.
appointment, s. decreto, mandato ; nombramiento ; puesto ; convenio para una entrevista.
apportion, v.a. proporcionar, repartir.
apportionment, s. repartición.
appose, v.a. cuestionar, examinar.
apposite, a. adaptado ; propio ; -ly, convenientemente, á propósito.
apposition, s. aposición.
appraise, v.a. apreciar ; tasar ; estimar.
appraisement, s. aprecio, valuación, estimación. [dor.
appraiser, s. apreciador, tasador valua-
appreciable, a. apreciable.

appreciate, v.a. apreciar, estimar, valuar.
appreciation, s. aprecio ; tasa.
appreciative, a. apreciativo.
apprehend, v.a. aprehender, prender ; concebir, comprender ; temer.
apprehension, s. aprehensión ; recelo ; presa, captura. [perspicaz.
apprehensive, a. aprehensivo, tímido ;
apprentice, s. aprendiz ; —, v.a. poner á alguno de aprendiz.
apprenticeship, s. aprendizaje.
apprise, v.a. informar, instruir.
approach, v.a. (& n.) aproximar(se) ; —, s. acceso.
approachable, a. accesible.
approbation, s. aprobación.
appropriate, v.a. apropiar, adaptar ; tomar para sí ; —, a. apropiado, apto, conveniente.
approvable, a. digno de aprobación.
approval, s. aprobación.
approve, v.a. aprobar.
approver, s. aprobador ; (leg.) revelador.
approximate, v.a. (& n.) acercar(se) ; —, a. aproximativo.
approximation, s. aproximación.
approximative, a. aproximativo.
appurtenance, s. (law) dependencia, pertenencia.
apricot, s. albaricoque.
April, s. abril.
apron, s. delantal.
apsis, s. ábside.
apt, a. apto, idóneo ; -ly, aptamente.
aptitude, aptness, s. aptitud ; disposición natural.
aqua fortis, s. agua fuerte.
aquarium, s. aquarium.
Aquarius, s. Acuario (signo del zodiaco).
aquatic, a. acuático, acuátil.
aqueduct, s. acueducto.
aqueous, a. acuoso.
aquiline, a. aguileño.
arabesque, s. arabesco.
arable, a. labrantío.
arbiter, s. arbitrador, árbitro.
arbitrament, s. arbitrio.
arbitrarily, ad. arbitrariamente.
arbitrariness, s. carácter caprichoso ó absoluto.
arbitrary, a. arbitrario, despótico, caprichoso. [árbitro.
arbitrate, v.a. arbitrar, juzgar como
arbitration, s. arbitramento, arbitrio.
arbitrator, s. arbitrador, árbitro.
arborescent, a. arborescente.
arbour, s. emparrado ; enramada.
arbute, arbutus, s. madroño.
arc, s. arco.
arcade, s. arcada, galería de arcos.
arcanum, s. arcano.

arch, s. arco ; —, v.a. cubrir con arcos ; arquear, corvar ; —, a. travieso, stuto ; principal, insigne ; grande ; se usa en composición como aumentativo).

archæological, a. arqueológico.

archæology, s. arqueología.

archaic, a. arcaico.

archaism, s. arcaísmo.

archangel, s. arcángel.

archbishop, s. arzobispo.

archbishopric, s. arzobispado.

archdeacon, s. arcediano.

archduchess, s. archiduquesa.

archduke, s. archiduque.

archdukedom, s. archiducado.

arched, a. arqueado, encorvado.

archer, s. arquero.

archery, s. arte de tirar con arco y flecha.

archiepiscopal, a. arzobispal.

archipelago, s. archipiélago.

architect, s. arquitecto.

architectural, a. arquitectonico.

architecture, s. arquitectura.

archives, s.pl. archivos.

archivist, s. archivero.

archly, ad. jocosamente ; sútilmente.

archness, s. astucia, travesura.

archpriest, s. arcipreste.

archway, s. arcada, bóveda ; portal.

arctic, a. ártico, septentrional.

ardency, ardour, s. ardor ; vehemencia ; pasión.

ardent, a. ardiente ; apasionado ; -ly, con pasión.

arduous, a. arduo ; laborioso ; difícil.

area, s. área, superficie, espacio.

arenaceous, a. arenoso.

aerometer, s. areómetro.

argentiferous, a. argentífero.

argil, s. arcilla.

argillaceous, a. arcilloso.

argosy, s. barco grande mercante.

argue, v.n. disputar, discurrir.

argument, s. argumento, controversia.

argumentation, s. argumentación.

argumentative, a. argumentador.

Arian, s. & a. Arriano.

arid, a. árido, seco, estéril.

aridity, s. sequedad.

Aries, s. Aries (signo del zodíaco).

aright, ad. rectamente, justamente, bien; to set —, rectificar.

arise, v.n. levantarse ; provenir.

aristocracy, s. aristocracia.

aristocrat, s. aristócrata.

aristocratic, a. aristocrático ; -ally, aristocráticamente.

arithmetic, s. aritmética.

arithmetical, a. aritmético ; -ly, aritméticamente.

arithmetician, s. aritmético.

ark, s. arca.

arm, s. brazo ; rama del árbol ; arma ; — v.a. (& n.) armar(se).

armadillo, s. armadillo, molito.(am.)

armament, s. (mar.) armamento de navíos ; (mil.) armamento.

arm-chair, s. sillón.

armful, s. brazada.

arm-hole, s. sobaco.

armistice, s. armisticio.

armlet, s. brazuelo ; brazalete ; guardabrazo de la armadura.

armorial, a. heráldico.

armour, s. armadura.

armour-bearer, s. escudero.

armoured, a. acorazado.

armourer, s. armero, armador.   [cas.

armoury, s. armería ; insignias genealógi-

arm-pit, s. sobaco.

arms (herald.) s. armas, escudo.

army, s. ejército ; tropas, pl.

aroma, s. aroma.

aromatic(nl), a. aromático.

around, pr. cerca ; —, ad. al rededor.

arouse, v.a. despertar ; excitar ; sublevar.

arquebuse, s. arcabuz.

arrack, s. aguardiente de arroz.

arraign, v.a. citar, delatar en justicia ; acusar.   [criminal.

arraignment, s. acusación, proceso

arrange, v.a. colocar, poner en orden.

arrangement, s. colocación ; orden, arreglo.

arrant, a. malo, perverso ; infame.

arras, s. tapiz, tapicería.

array, s. adorno, vestido ; orden de batalla ; —, v.a. colocar ; vestir, adornar.

arrears, s. resto de una deuda ; atraso.

arrest, s. prisión ; arresto ; —, v.a. prender, arrestar, embargar.

arrival, s. arribo ; llegada, venida.

arrive, v.n. llegar, arribar.

arrogance, s. arrogancia, presunción.

arrogant, a. arrogante, presuntuoso ; -ly, arrogantemente.

arrogate, v.a. arrogarse, reclamar.

arrow, s. flecha, saeta.

arsenal, s. (mil.) arsenal.

arsenic, s. arsénico.   [incendiar.

arson, s. fuego incendiario, delito de

art, s. arte ; industria ; ciencia.

arterial, a. arterial, arterioso.

artery, s. arteria.

artesian well, s. pozo artesiano.

artful, a. artificioso ; diestro ; -ly, artificiosamente, diestramente.

artfulness, s. astucia, habilidad.

artichoke, s. alcachofa.   [aprendizage.

article, s. artículo ; —, v.a. poner en

articulate, a. articulado, claro, distinto ;
-ly, distintamente ; —, v.a. articular,
pronunciar distintamente.
articulation, s. articulación ; (bot.) nudo
en las plantas.
artifice, s. artificio ; fraude.
artificer, s. artesano, artífice.
artificial, a. artificial ; artificioso, postizo ;
-ly, artificialmente ; artificiosomente.
artillery, s. artillería.
artillery-man, s. artillero.
artillery-practice, s. cañoneo.
artisan, s. artesano, artífice.
artist, s. artista.
artistic, a. artístico.
artless, a. sencillo, simple ; -ly, sencilla-
mente, naturalmente.
artlessness, s. sencillez.
as, c. como ; mientras ; visto que, pues
que ; — for, — to, en cuanto á.
asbestos, s. asbesto, amianto.
ascend, v.n. ascender, subir.
ascendant, s. ascendiente ; —, a. superior,
predominante.
ascendency, s. influjo, poder.
ascension, s. ascensión.
ascent, s. subida ; eminencia ; altura.
ascertain, v a. cerciorarse de, aprender,
asegurar.
ascertainable, a. conocible.
ascetic, a. ascético ; —, s. asceto.
asceticism, s. asceticismo.   [judicar.
ascribe, v.a. adscribir ; atribuir ; ad-
ascription, s. atribución.
aseptic, a. aséptico.
ash, s. (bot.) fresno : ceniza.
ashamed, a. avergonzado, vergonzoso.
ash-coloured, a. ceniciento.
ashen, a. hecho de fresno.
ash-hole, -pan, -pit, s. cenicero, ceñizal.
ashore, ad. en tierra, á tierra ; to go —,
desembarcar.
Ash-Wednesday, s. miércoles de ceniza.
ashy, a. cenizoso, ceniciento.
aside, ad. al lado, á parte.
asinine, a. asnal, bobo.
ask, v.a. pedir, rogar, interrogar ; convidar.   [oblicuamente.
askance, askant, ad. al sesgo, al soslayo,
askew, ad. al lado ; de lado ; de través.
aslant, a. & ad. oblícuo, oblícuamente.
asleep, a. dormido ; to fall —, dormirse.
asp, s. áspid.
asparagus, s. espárrago.
aspect, s. aspecto ; vista ; aire ; semblante.
aspen(-tree), s. álamo temblón ; —, a. de
álamo temblón, trémulo.
asperity, s. aspereza, rudeza.
asperse, v.a. calumniar, infamar.
aspersion, s. aspersión, defamación,
calumnía.

asphalt, s. asfalto.
asphyxia, s. (med.) asfixia.
asphyxiate, v.a. asfixiar, ahogar.
aspirant, s. aspirante. pretendiente.
aspirate, v.a. aspirar, pronunciar con
aspiración ; —, s. sonido aspirado.
aspiration, s. aspiración.
aspire, v.n. aspirar, anhelar, desear.
ass, s. burro, borrico, asno ; she —, borrica.
assail, v.a. asaltar, atacar.
assailable, a. vulnerable.
assailant, assailer, s. asaltador, agresor.
assassin, s. asesino, matador.
assassinate, v.a. asesinar, matar.
assassination, s. asesinato.   [asaltar.
assault, s. asalto ; —, v.a. acometer,
assay, s. ensayo ; prueba ; experimento ;
—, v.a. tentar ; probar, ensayar.
assayer, s. ensayador.
assemblage, s. agregado ; multitud.
assemble, v.a. congregar, convocar ; —,
v.n. juntarse.
assembly, s. asamblea, junta ; congreso.
assent, s. asenso ; aprobación ; —, v.n.
asentir, convenir.   [asegurar.
assert, v.a. sostener, mantener ; afirmar ;
assertion, s. aserción.
assertive, a. perentorio. categórico.
assess, v.a. amillarar, fijar.
assessable, a. contributario.
assessment, s. amillaramiento, fijación.
assets, s.pl. capital, caudal ; activo.
assever, asseverate, v.a. aseverar, afirmar.
asseveration, s. aseveración, afirmación.
assiduity, s. asiduidad, aplicación ; constancia.
assiduous, a. asiduo, aplicado ; -ly, constantemente ; diligentemente.
assign, v.a. asignar ; transferir algún
derecho á otro.
assignable, a. asignable.
assignation, s. asignación ; cesión ; cita.
assignee, s. síndico, apoderado ; ceșion-
ario.   [señalamiento.
assignment, s. asignación ; cesión ;
assimilate, v.a. asimilar, asemejar.
assimilation, s. asimilación.
assist, v.a. asistir, ayudar, socorrer.
assistance, s. asistencia ; socorro.
assistant, s. asistente, ayudante.
assize, s. sesión semestral de los tribunales
en los condados ingleses.
associate, v.a. asociar ; acompañar ; —
with, acompañar, frecuentar ; —, s.
asociado ; socio, compañero.
association, s. asociación, unión, sociedad.
assonance, s. asonancia.
assort, v.a. clasificar, distribuir ; —
with, v.n. concordar, acordar.
assortment, s. surtido.

assuage, v.a. mitigar, suavizar ; —, v.n.
disminuir ; apaciguarse.
assuagement, s. mitigación, calma.
assume, v.a. arrogar, apropiar, presumir ; —, v.n. arrogarse.
assuming, a. presuntuoso, altivo.
assumption, s. presunción ; postulado ;
Assumption, s. Asunción.
assurance, s. seguridad, certeza ; fianza.
assure, v.a. asegurar, afirmar.
assuredly, ad. ciertamente, sin duda.
asterisk, s. asterisco.
astern, ad. (mar.) por la popa.
asthma, s. asma.
asthmatic, a. asmático.
astir, ad. en turbación, en movimiento.
astonish, v.a. sorprender, asombrar.
astonishing, a. asombroso ; -ly, asom-
brosamente.
astonishment, s. asombro ; sorpresa,
pasmo.   [turbar.
astound, v.a. consternar, pasmar, con-
astounding, a. asombroso, pasmoso.
astraddle, ad. á horcajadas.
astral, a. astral, de los astros.
astray, a. & ad. extraviado, descaminado;
to lead —, desviar, seducir.
astriction, s. astricción.
astride, ad. á horcajadas.
astringent, a. astringente.
astrolabe, s. astrolabio.
astrologer, s. astrólogo.
astrological, s. astrológico.
astrology, astrología.
astronomer, s. astrónomo.
astronomical, a. astronómico.
astronomy, s. astronomía.
astute, a. astuto ; aleve.
asunder, ad. separadamente, à parte.
asylum, s. asilo, refugio.
at, pr. en ; — once, en seguida ; — all
events, de todos modos ; — first, al
principio ; — last, en fin.
atheism, s. ateísmo.
atheist, s. ateísta, ateo.
atheistic(al), a. ateo.
athirst, a. sediento, con gana de beber.
athlete, s. atleta.
athletic, a. atlético, vigoroso.
athwart, pr. & ad. al través.
atlas, s. atlas.
atmosphere, s. atmósfera.
atmospherical, a. atmosférico.
atom, s. átomo.
atomic(al), a. atómico.
atone, v.a. expiar.
atonement, s. expiación, propiciación.
atop, ad. encima.
atrabilious, a. atrabiliario, melancólico.
atrocious, a. atroz ; enorme ; odioso ; -ly,
atrozmente.

atrocity, s. atrocidad, enormidad.
atrophy, s. (med.) atrofia.
attach, v.a. enganchar, atar ; prender,
asir, coger.
attaché, s. agregado á alguna legación.
attached, a. aficionado, afecto.
attachment, s. adherencia ; afecto;
secuestro.   [ataque.
attack, v.a. atacar ; acometer ; —, s.
attain, v.a. ganar, conseguir, obtener.
attainable, a. asequible.
attainder, s. proscripción.
attainment, s. logro ; consecución de lo
que se pretende ; -s, pl. conocimientos.
attaint, v.a. proscribir, condenar ; corromper, viciar, manchar ; —, s. mácula.
attar, s. aceite rosado ó de rosas.
attempt, v.a. tentar ; probar, experimentar ; —, s. empresa ; experimento;
tentativa.
attend, v.a. servir, asistir, acompañar ;
—, v.n. prestar atención ; considerar.
attendance, s. tren, séquito ; servicio.
attendant, s. sirviente, acompañante,
dependiente.
attention, s. atención ; cuidado.
attentive, a. atento ; cuidadoso ; -ly, con
atención.
attenuate, v.a. atenuar, disminuir.
attenuation, s. atenuación.
attest, v.a. atestiguar.
attestation, s. atestación ; testimonio.
attic, s. desván ; guardilla ; —, a. ático,
juicioso, picante (aplícase al estilo).
attire, s. atavío, m. ; —, v.a. adornar,
ataviar.
attitude, s. actitud, postura.
attitudinise, v.n. tomar posturas estrañas.
attorney, s. procurador, poderhabiente ;
-general, fiscal.
attract, v.a. atraer, persuadir.
attraction, s. atracción ; atractivo.
attractive, a. atractivo, halagüeño ; -ly,
por atracción.
attributable, a. imputable.   [atributo.
attribute, v.a. atribuir, imputar ; —, s.
attribution, s. atributo ; reputación.
attrition, s. trituración ; atrición.
attune, v.a. acordar ; armonizar.
auburn, a. castaño.
auction, s. venta pública, almoneda,
subasta, remate (am).
auctioneer, s. corredor de almoneda.
audacious, a. audaz, temerario ; -ly, atrevidamente.
audacity, s. audacia, osadía.
audible, a. oible ; -bly, ad. alto.
audience, s. audencia ; auditorio.
audit, s. revisión, examen de una cuenta;
—, v.a. examinar una cuenta
auditor, s. oidor.

auditory, s. auditorio ; —, a. auditívo.
auger, s. barrena.
aught, pn. algo, alguna cosa.
augment, v.a. aumentar, acrecentar ; —, v.n. crecer.
augmentation, s. aumentación ; aumento.
augmentative, a. aumentativo. [jeturas.
augur, v.n. augurar, adivinar por con-
augury, s. agüero, presagio.
August, s. agosto.
august, a. augusto ; majestuoso.
augustness, s. grandeza.
auk, s. penguino.
aulic, a. aulico.
aunt, s. tía.
aureola, s. auréola.
auricle, s. aurícula.
auricular, a. auricular, dicho al oído ; -ly, al oído ; secretamente.
auriferous, a. aurífero.
aurist, s. aurista, médico para el oido.
aurora, s. aurora ; — borealis, aurora boreal.
auscultation, s. auscultación. [boreal.
auspices, s.pl. auspicio ; protección.
auspicious, a. próspero, favorable ; propicio ; -ly, prósperamente.
austere, a. austero, severo, rígido ; -ly, austeramente.
austerity, s. austeridad ; mortificación.
austral, a. austral, austrino. [amente.
authentic, a. auténtico ; -ly, auténtic-
authenticate, v.a. autenticar.
authenticity, s. autenticidad.
author, s. autor ; escritor.
authoress, s. autora, escritora.
authorisation, s. autorización.
authorise, v.a. autorizar.
authoritative, a. autoritativo ; -ly, au-toritativamente, con autoridad.
authoritativeness, s. presunción ; apari-encia autoritativa.
authority, s. autoridad.
authorship, s. calidad de autor, pro-veniencia (de un libro).
autobiography, s. autobiografía.
autocracy, s. autocracia.
autocrat, s. autócrata.
autocratic(al), a. autocrático.
autograph, s. autógrafo.
automatic, a. automático.
automaton, s. automata.
autonomy, s. autonomía.
automobile, s. automóvil.
autopsy, s. autopsia.
autumn, s. otoño.
autumnal, a. otoñal.
auxiliary, a. auxiliar, asistente.
auxiliaries, s.pl. tropas auxiliares.
avail, v.n. servir, ser ventajoso ; — one-self of, aprovecharse de ; —, s. pro-vecho ; ventaja.

available, a. disponible ; útil, ventajoso.
avalanche, s. alud, lurte.
avarice, s. avaricia.
avaricious, a. avaro ; -ly, avaramente.
avaunt, interj. ¡ fuera ! ¡ quita !
avast, int. (mar.) ¡ alto ! ¡ basta !
avenge, v.a. vengar.
avenger, s. vengador. [alameda.
avenue, s. calle de árboles ; avenida,
aver, a.v. afirmar, verificar, declarar.
average, v.a. tomar un término medio ; —, s. término medio ; (mar.) avería.
averse, a. contrario, repugnante.
aversion, s. aversión, disgusto.
avert, v.a. desviar, apartar.
aviary, s. pajarera.
aviator, s. aviador.
aviation, s. aviación.
avidity, s. codicia, avidez.
avocation, s. ocupación. [anular.
avoid, v.a. evitar, escapar, huir ; (law)
avoidable, a. evitable.
avoidance, s. evitación, fuga.
avoirdupois, s. sistema de pesos ingleses.
avouch, v.a. afirmar, justificar, sostener.
avow, v.a. confesar, declarar.
avowal, s. declaración, confesión.
avowedly, declaradamente, abiertamente.
avuncular, a. perteneciente á un tío.
await, v.a. aguardar. [despierto.
awake, v.a. & n. despertar ; —, a.
awaken, v.a. & n. despertar.
awaking, s. despertamiento.
award, v.a. juzgar, sentenciar ; —, s, sentencia, decisión.
aware, a. cauto, vigilante.
away, ad. ausente, fuera ; —! ¡ fuera, quita de ahí, marcha ! far and —, de mucho, con mucho.
awe, s. miedo, temor reverencial ; —, v.a. infundir miedo ó temor reverencial.
aweary, a. cansado.
awful, a. tremendo ; funesto ; -ly, con respeto y veneración.
awfulness, s. veneración ; horror.
awhile, ad. un rato, algún tiempo.
awkward, a. tosco, inculto, rudo, poco diestro ; -ly, groseramente, tosca-mente. [poca habilidad.
awkwardness, s. tosquedad, grosería,
awl, s. lesna. [del sol).
awning, s. (mar.) toldo (para guardarse
awry, ad. oblicuamente, torcidamente,
axe, s. segur, hacha. [al través.
axiom, s. axioma.
axis, s. eje.
axle(-tree), s. eje de una rueda. [siempre.
ay, aye, ad. sí ; seguramente ; para
azalea, s. (bot.) azalea.
azimuth, s. azimut.
azure, a. azulado ; —, s. color cerúleo.

B

baa, s. balido ; ·—, v.n. balar.
babble, v.n. charlar, parlotear ; —, babbling, s. charla, cháchara.
babbler, s. charlador, charlatán.
babe, baby, s. niño pequeño, nene ; infante.   [de voces.
Babel, babel, s. Babel ; babel, confusión
baboon, s. cinocéfalo, mono grande.
babyhood, s. niñez.
babyish, a. niñero ; pueril.
baby-linen, s. envoltura de una criatura recién nacida.   [disoluto.
bacchanalian, a. disipado, licencioso,
bacchic, a. báquico.
bachelor, s. soltero ; bachiller.
bachelorship, s. celibato ; bachillerato.
back, s. dorso ; revés ; recazo ; —, ad. atrás, detrás ; **a few years** —, algunos años ha ; —, v.a. montar (á caballo) ; sostener, apoyar, favorecer.
backbite, v.a. hablar mal del que está ausente ; difamar.
backbiter, s. detractor.
back-board, s. (mar.) respaldo de bote.
backbone, s. hueso dorsal, espinazo.
backdoor, s. puerta trasera.
backer, s. partidario.   [tablas.
backgammon, s. juego de chaquete ó
background, s. fondo.   [mano.
back-handed, ad. con el revés de la
back-number, s. número atrasado de algún periódico.
back-payment, s. paga atrasada.
backside, s. trasero.
backslide, v.n. apostatar ; tergiversar.
backstairs, s.pl. escalera secreta.
backward, a. tardo, lento ; —, -s, atrás, hacia atrás.
backwardness, s. torpeza, tardanza.
backwoods, s.pl. bosques remotos, monte, selvas.
bacon, s. toci.   [indispuesto ; -ly, mal.
bad, a. mal, malo ; perverso ; dañoso ;
badge, s. señal ; símbolo ; divisa.
badger, s. tejón ; —, v.a. atormentar, embromar.
badness, s. maldad, mala calidad.
baffle, v.a. eludir ; confundir ; acosar.
bag, s. saco ; talega ; bolsa ; —, v.a. entalegar.
baggage, s. equipaje, bagaje.   [traje.
baggy, a. (col.) ancho (hablando de ropa ó
bagman, (col.) s. viajante.
bagnio, s. estufa ; burdel.
bagpipe, s. gaita.
bail, s. fianza, caución (juratoria) ; fiador ; —, v.a. caucionar, fiar.

bailable, a. caucionable.
bailiff, s. alguacil ; mayordomo.
bairn, s. niño, nene.
bait, v.a. cebar ; atraer ; tormentar ; azuzar ; —, s. cebo ; anzuelo.
baize, s. bayeta.
bake, v.a. cocer en horno.
bakehouse, bakery, s. panadería.
baker, s. hornero, panadero ; -'s **dozen** trece piezas.
balance, s. balanza ; equilibrio ; volante de reloj ; saldo de una cuenta ; —, v.a pesar en balanza ; contrapesar, saldar ; considerar, examinar.
balance-sheet, s. balance.
balcony, s. balcón.
bald, a. calvo ; rudo ; sin disfraz.
baldachin, s. dosel, baldaquin.
balderdash, s. (col.) disparate.
baldness, s. calvez ; desnudez.
baldric, s. correa de espada.
bale, s. fardo de mercaderías ; —, v.a. (mar.) tirar el agua del bote.
baleful, a. triste, funesto ; -ly, tristemente ; miserablemente.
balk, s. viga ; contratiempo ; agravio, perjuicio ; —, v.a. frustrar ; — v.n. pararse con sobresalto.
ball, s. pelota, bola ; bala ; baile.
ballad, s. balada ó balata.
ballad-singer, s. jacarero.
ballast, s. lastre ; —, v.a. lastrar.
ballet, s. bailete.
balloon, s. globo.
balloonist, s. aeronauta.
ballot, s. balota ó bolilla para votar ; escrutinio ; —, v.n. votar con balotas.
ballot-box, s. urna de escrutinio.
balm, balsam, s. bálsamo ; —, v.a. untar con bálsamo ; suavizar.
balmy, balsamic, a. balsámico ; fragante ; lo que mitiga y suaviza.
baluster, s. balaustre.
balustrade, s. balaustrada.
bamboo, s. bamboa.
bamboozle, v.a. (col.) engañar ; burlar.
ban, s. bando, anuncio ; proscripción ; entredicho ; —, v.a. proscribir, entredecir.
banana, s. banana.
band, s. venda, faja, unión ; cuadrilla, banda (de soldados) ; orquesta, capilla ; —, v.a. unir, juntar.
bandage, s. venda, faja ; vendaje ; —, v.a. vendar, fajar.
bandana, s. bandanas.
bandbox, s. caja de cartón.

bandit, s. bandido.
band-master, s. (mus.) maestro de capilla.
bandoleer, s. bandolera, correa de escopeta.
bandsman, s. músico de banda.
bandy, v.a. trocar (palabras ó dimes y diretes) ; pelotear ; discutir.
bandy-legged, a. patizambo.
bane, s. veneno ; ruina ; rat's —, arsénico.
baneful, a. venenoso, destructivo, funesto.
bang, s. puñada ; golpe ; —, v.a. golpear, sacudir ; cerrar con violencia.
bangle, s. brazalete delgado.
banish, v.a. desterrar, echar fuera, proscribir, expatriar.
banishment, s. destierro.
banjo, s. guitarra de los negros.
bank, s. orilla (de río) ; montón de tierra ; banco ; dique ; escollo ; —, v.a. poner dinero en un banco ; detener el agua con diques.
banker, s. banquero, cambista.
bank-holiday, s. día de vacación oficial y general.
bank-note, s. billete de banco.
bankrupt, a. insolvente ; —, s. fallido, quebrado.
bankruptcy, s. bancarrota, quiebra.
banner, s. bandera ; estandarte, pabellón.
banneret, s. caballero de pendón.
banns, s.pl. anuncio solemne ó bando de desposorio.
bannister, s. balaustre.
banquet, s. banquete ; —, v.a. banquetear.
bantam, s. especie de gallina pequeña.
banter, v.a. zumbar ; embromar ; —, s. zumba, burla, broma.
bantling, s. chicuelo ; chicuela ; nene.
baptise, v.a. bautizar.
baptism, s. bautismo.
baptismal, a. bautismal.
baptistery, s. bautisterio.
bar, s. barra ; tranca ; obstáculo ; mostrador para venta de bebidas ; (law) cuerpo ó gremio de abogados ; —, v.a. cerrar con barras ; impedir ; prohibir ; excluir.
barb, s. lengüeta de flecha ó anzuelo ; caballo de Berbería ; —, v.a. armar flechas con lengüetas.
barbarian, s. & a. bárbaro.
barbaric, a. bárbaro.
barbarism, s. (gr.) barbarismo ; crueldad.
barbarity, s. barbaridad, inhumanidad.
barbarous, a. bárbaro, cruel ; -ly, bárbaramente, cruelmente.
barbecue, s. asado campestre.
barber, s. barbero, peluquero.
barbican, s. barbacana.
bard, s. bardo ; poeta.

bare, a. desnudo, descubierto ; simple ; público ; pobre ; puro ; —, v.a. desnudar, descubrir, privar.
barefaced, a. desvergonzado, impudente.
barefoot(ed), a. descalzo.
bareheaded, a. descubierto, sin sombrero.
barelegged, a. con las piernas desnudas.
barely, ad. apenas, solamente ; pobremente.
bareness, s. desnudez ; pobreza.
bargain, s. contrato, pacto ; compra ó venta ; una buena compra ; —, v.n. pactar ; negociar.
barge, s. falúa, chalupa, chata.
bargeman, bargee, s. barquero, botero
bar-iron, s. hierro en barras.
baritone, s. (mus.) baritono.
bark, s. corteza ; ladra (del perro) ; —, v.a. descortezar ; —, v.n. ladrar.
barley, s. cebada.
barm, s. levadura.
barmaid, s. moza de taberna.
barn, s. granero, henil, pajar.
barnacle, s. barnacle, especie de molusco.
barometer, s. barómetro
baron, s. barón.
baronage, s. baronía.
baroness, s. baronesa.
baronet, s. título de honor inferior al de barón y superior al de caballero.
baronetcy, s. dignidad de baronet.
baronial, a. de barón, noble.
barony, s. baronía.
barque, s. (mar.) barco.
barrack, s. cuartel.
barratry, s. baratería ; fraude ; engaño.
barrel, s. barril ; cañon de escopeta ; cilindro.
barrel-organ, s. organillo de cilindro.
barren, a. estéril, infructuoso ; -ly, infructuosamente, sin fruto.
barrenness, s. esterilidad, infecundidad ; falta de ingenio.
barricade, s. barricada; estacada; barrera ; —, v.a. cerrar con barreras, empalizar
barrier, s. barrera ; obstáculo.
barring, ad. excepto, fuera de.
barrister, s. abogado.
barrow, s. angarillas ; túmulo.
barter, v.n. baratar, traficar ; —, v.a. cambiar, trocar.
basalt, s. basalto.
base, s. fondo ; basa ; pedestal ; —, v.a. apoyar ; —, a. bajo, vil ; -ly, bajamente.
baseless, a. sin fondo ó base, falso.
basement, s. sótanos.
baseness, s. bajeza, vileza ; ilegitimidad de nacimiento ; mezquinería.
bashaw, s. bajá.
bashful, a. vergonzoso, modesto, tímido.

basilisk, s. basilisco.
basin, s. jofaina, bacía.
basis, s. base ; fundamento.
bask, v.n. tomar el sol, asolearse.
basket, s. cesta, canasta, canasto.
bass, s. estera ; —, (mus.) contrabajo.
bassoon, s. bajón.
bass-viol, s. viola.
bastard, s. & a. bastardo.
bastardy, s. bastardía.
baste, v.a. dar golpes con un bastón ;
    pringar la carne en el asador.
bastinado, s. bastonada ; —, v.a. golpear
    con un bastón.
bassinet, s. cuna.
bastion, s. (mil.) bastión.
bat, s. pala ; raqueta ; murciélago.
batch, s. hornada, cantidad que se
    despacha de una vez.
bate, v.a. minorar ; bajar.   [baja.
bated, a. bajo ; with — breath, con voz
bath, s. baño.
bathe, v.a. (& n.) bañar(se).
bathing-gown, s. peinador.
bath-keeper, s. bañero.
bathos, s. estilo bajo en la poesía.
bath-tub, s. baño (la cuba).
baton, s. bastón.
battalion, s. (mil.) batallón.   [engordar.
batten, s. astilla ; —, v.a. cebar ; —, v.n.
batter, v.a. apalear ; batir, cañonear ;
    demoler ; —, s. batido.
battering-ram, s. (mil.) ariete.
battery, s. batería.
battle, s. combate ; batalla ; pelea ; —,
    v.n. batallar, combatir.
battle-array, s. orden de batalla.
battledore, s. raqueta.
battlement, s. muralla almenada.
bauble, s. chuchería, cosa de poca im-
    portancia.
baulk, s. & v.a. V. balk.
bawdy, a. obsceno.
bawl, v.n. gritar, vocear.
bay, s. bahía ; laurel, lauro ; —, v.n.
    ladrar ; balar ; —, a. colorado.
bayonet, s. bayoneta ; —, v.a. traspasar
    con la bayoneta.
bay-window, s. ventana salediza.
bazaar, s. bazar.
be. v.n. ser ; estar.
beach, s. playa ; —, v.a. (mar.) encallar.
beacon, s. almenara, baliza.
bead, s. cuenta ; -s, s.pl. rosario.
beadle, s. macero ; bedel (en las universi-
    dades) ; alguacil (en los tribunales).
beagle, s. perro lebrel.
beak, s. pico.
beaker, s. taza ó vaso grande.
beam, s. viga ; rayo de luz ; brazos de
    balanza ; —, v.n. emitir rayos, brillar.

beaming, a. radiante.   [frijoles.
bean, s. haba ; French —, habichuelas ;
bear, v.a. llevar como carga ; sostener,
    soportar ; producir ; parir ; —, v.n.
    dirigirse, tender.
bear, s. oso ; she —, osa.
bearable, a. soportable.
beard, s. barba ; arista de espiga ; —,
    v.a. afrontar, encararse.
bearded, a. barbado, barbudo.
beardless, a. imberbe, joven.
bearer, s. portador ; árbol fructífero.
bearing, s. porte, ademán.
bearish, a. grosero.
beast, s. bestia ; hombre brutal ; — of
    burden, acémila.
beastliness, s. bestialidad, brutalidad.
beastly, a. bestial, brutal.
beat, v.a. golpear ; batir ; tocar (un
    tambor) ; pisar ; abatir ; —, v.n.
    pulsar, palpitar ; —, s. golpe ; pul-
    sación.
beatific, a. beatífico.
beatify, v.a. beatificar, sanctificar.
beating, s. paliza, pulsación.
beatitude, s. beatitud, felicidad.
beau, s. petimetre, currutaco, pisaverde.
beauteous, a. bello, hermoso.
beautiful, a. hermoso, bello ; -ly, con
    belleza ó perfección.   [adornar.
beautify, v.a. hermosear ; embellecer ;
beauty, s. hermosura, belleza ; — spot,
    s. lunar.   [castor.
beaver, s. castor ; sombrero de pelo de
becalmed, a. (mar.) inmóvil por falta de
    viento.
because, c. porque ; — of, á causa de.
beck, s. seña, indicación muda.
beckon, v.n. llamar con seña de cabeza,
    ó de mano.   [v.n. ponerse, hacerse.
become, v.a. convenir ; estar bien ; —,
becoming, a. decente, conveniente ; -ly,
    decentemente.   [acostar.
bed, s. cama ; —, v.a. meter en la cama
bedaub, v.a. jalbegar.
bed-chamber, s. dormitorio.
bed-clothes, bedding, s. ropa de cama.
bedeck, v.a. ataviar.
bedecked, a. adornado.
bedew, v.a. rociar ; regar.
bedim, v.a. obscurecer.   [travagancia.
bedizen, v.a. ataviar, adornar con ex-
bedlam, s. manicomio.
bedlamite, s. loco, orate.
bed-post, s. pilar de cama.
bedraggled, a. enlodado.
bedridden, a. postrado en cama.
bedside, s. lado de cama ; cabecera.
bedstead, s. armazón de cama.
bed-time, s. hora de dormir.
bee, s. abeja.

beech, s. haya.
beechen, a. de haya.
beech-mast, beech-nut, s. hayuco.
beef, carne de vaca ; vaca ó buey ; beeves, pl. ganado vacuno.
beef-eater, s. alabardero real.
beef-steak, s. biftec, bife (am.).
beef-tea, s. caldo.
bee-hive, s. colmena.
bee-line, s. línea recta.   [floja.
beer, s. cerveza ; small —, cerveza
beery, a. borracho.
beeswax, s. cera.
beet, s. acelga, remolacha.
beetle, s. escarabajo ; pisón.
beetling, a. precipitoso, colgante.
beet-root, s. betarraga.   [venir.
befall, v.n. suceder, acontecer, sobre-
befit, v.a. convenir.
befool, v.a. infatuar, engañar, chasquear.
before, ad. & pr. delante, enfrente ; ante, antes de.   [padamente.
beforehand, ad. de antemano, antici-
befoul, v.a. ensuciar, emporcar.
befriend, v.a. favorecer, proteger, amparar.   [v.n. mendigar.
beg, v.a. mendigar, rogar ; suplicar ; —,
beget, v.a. engendrar.
begetter, s. engendrador ; padre ; autor.
beggar, s. mendigo ; —, v.a. empobrecer.
beggarliness, s. mezquindad, pobreza, miseria.
beggarly, a. pobre, miserable.
beggary, s. mendicidad, mendiguez.
begin, v.a. & n. empezar, comenzar, principiar.   [tirón.
beginner, s. principiante ; novicio ;
beginning, s. principio, origen ; -s, pl. rudimentos, pl.
begone, ¡ fuera ! ¡ mandese mudar !
begrime, v.a. encenagar, ennegrecer, embarrar, manchar.
begrudge, v.a. envidiar.
beguile, v.a. engañar.   [ción.
behalf, s. favor, patrocinio ; considera-
behave, v.n. comportarse, portarse.
behaviour, s. conducta ; modo de portarse.
behead, v.a. decapitar, cortar la cabeza.
behest, s. mandato, precepto.
behind, pr. & ad. detrás ; atrás.
behindhand, ad. con atraso.
behold, v.a. ver, contemplar, observar ; — ! ¡ he aquí !
beholden, a. obligado (por gratitud).
behoof, s. provecho ; utilidad, ventaja.
behove, v.a. convenir, importar, ser útil ó necesario.
being, s. existencia ; estado ; ente ; persona (que existe).
belabour, v.n. apalear, dar puñadas.

belated, a. trasnochado.   [eructación.
belch, v.n. eructar ; —, s. eructo ;
beldam, s. vejezuela ; bruja.
beleaguer, v.a. sitiar, bloquear.
belfry, s. campanario.   [calumniar.
belie, v.a. contrahacer ; desmentir.
belief, s. fe, creencia ; opinión ; credo.
believable, a. creible.   [imaginar.
believe, v.a. creer ; —, v.n. pensar,
believer, s. creyente, fiel.
bell, s. campana ; to bear the —, ser el primero ; —, v.n. gritar (como los ciervos).
belle, s. señorita bella y elegante.
bellicose, a. belicoso.
belligerent, a. beligerante.
bellman, s. pregonero.
bellow, v.n. bramar ; rugir ; vociferar ; —, s. bramido.
bellows, s. fuelle.   [panilla.
bell-pull, bell-rope, s. cuerda de campanilla.
bell-ringer, s. campanero.   [cencerro.
bell-wether, s. carnero que lleva el
belly, s. vientre ; panza.
belly-band, s. cincha.
bellyful, s. panzada ; hartura.
belong, v.n. pertenecer, tocar.
belongings, s.pl. bienes.
beloved, a. querido, amado.
below, ad. & pr. debajo, abajo.
belt, s. cinturón, cinto, faja.
bemoan, v.a. deplorar, lamentar.
bench, s. banco ; King's —, tribunal principal de justicia.   [abogados.
bencher, s. decano de un colegio de
bend, v.a. encorvar, inclinar, plegar ; —, v.n. encorvarse, inclinarse ; —, s. comba, encorvadura.
beneath, ad. & pr. debajo, abajo.
benedict, s. el recien casado.
benediction, s. bendición.
benefact on, s. beneficio.
benefactor, s. bienhechor.
benefactress, s. bienhechora.   [ástico.
benefice, s. beneficio ; beneficio eclesi-
beneficence, s. beneficencia, liberalidad.
beneficent, a. benéfico ; -ly, ad. benéficamente.
beneficial, a. beneficioso, provechoso, útil ; -ly, ad. provechosamente, ventajosamente.
beneficiary, s. beneficiario ; beneficiado.
benefit, s. beneficio ; utilidad ; provecho ; —, v.a. beneficiar ; —, v.n. sacar provecho.
benefit-night, s. representación dramática al beneficio de un actor ó de una actriz, beneficio.   [gratuito.
benevolence, s. benevolencia ; donativo
benevolent, a. benévolo.
benighted, (p. &) a, anochecido,

benign, a. benigno ; afable ; liberal ; -ly, benignamente.

benignant, a. bondadoso.

benignity, s. benignidad, bondad, dulzura.

benison, s. bendición.   [cia.

bent, s. inclinación, propensión, tenden-

benumb, v.a. entorpecer.

benzine, s. (chem.) benzina.

benzoin, s. benjuí.

bepraise, v.a. lisonjear.

bequeath, v.a. legar en testamento.

bequeather, s. testador.

bequest, s. legado.

bereave, v.a. despojar, privar.

bereavement, s. despojo.

berlin, s. berlina (coche).

berry, s. baya, grano.

berth, s. (mar.) hamaca ; cama abordo ; anclaje, amarradero de un barco.

beseech, v.a. suplicar, implorar, conjurar, rogar.

beseem, v.n. convenir.

beset, v.a. sitiar ; cercar ; perseguir.

besetting, a. habitual.

beside, pr. al lado de ; junto á ; fuera de.

beside(s), ad. además, aun.

besiege, v.a. sitiar, bloquear.

besieger, s. sitiador.

besmear, v.a. salpicar, ensuciar.

besom, s. escoba.

besotted, a. borracho, embrutecido.

bespatter, v.a. salpicar, manchar ; disfamar.

bespeak, v.a. ordenar, encargar de antemano, apalabrar.

besprinkle, v.a. rociar, esparcir.

best, a. & ad. mejor.   [mente.

bestial, a. bestial, brutal ; -ly, bestial-

bestiality, s. bestialidad, brutalidad.

bestir oneself, v.r. removerse.

bestow, v.a. dar, conferir ; otorgar ; regalar.   [acción de dar.

bestowal, s. donación, otorgamiento.

bestrew, v.a. esparcir ó derramar sobre ; polvorear, salpicar.   [jadas.

bestride, v.a. atrancar ; montar á horca-

bet, s. apuesta ; —, v.a. apostar.

betake oneself, v.a. recurrir, acudir.

bethink oneself, v.a. acordarse ; —, v.n. considerar, pensar.

betide, v.n. acaecer, suceder.

betoken, v.a. anunciar ; denotar.   [pronto.

betime(s), ad. con tiempo, en sazón.

betray, v.a. traicionar ; divulgar.

betrayal, s. traición.

betroth, v.a. desposar.

betrothal, s. esponsales, pl.

better, a. & ad. mejor ; so much the —, tanto mejor ; -s, s.pl. superiores, pl. ; —, v.a. mejorar, reformar.

between, betwixt, pr. entre, en medio de.

bevel, s. bisel.

beverage, s. brebaje, bebida, refresco.

bevy, s. bandada.

bewail, v.a. lamentar, deplorar.

beware, v.n. guardarse.

bewilder, v.a. embarazar ; turbar.

bewilderment, s. extravío ; embarazo.

bewitch, v.a. encantar, hechizar.

bewitcher, s. encantador ; hechizero.

bewitching, a. encantador ; -ly, halagüenamente.   [fuera de.

beyond, pr. más allá, más adelante,

bezoar, s. bezar.

bias, s. propensión, inclinación ; sesgo ; —, v.a. inclinar ; preocupar.

bib, s. babador.

bibber, s. bebedor, borrachón.

Bible, s. Biblia (la sagrada escritura).

biblical, a. bíblico.

bibliography, s. bibliografía.

bibliophile, s. bibliófilo.

biceps, s. (anat.) biceps.

bicker, v.n. escaramucear, reñir, disputar.

bicycle, s. bicicleta.

bid, v.a. convidar ; mandar, ordenar ; ofrecer en comprando.

bidding, s. orden, mandato ; ofrecimiento de un comprador.   [residir.

bide, v.a. sufrir, aguantar ; —, v.n.

biennial, a. bienal.

bier, s. féretro, ataúd.

bifurcated, a. bifurcado, ahorquillado.

big, a. grande, grueso.

bigamist, s. bígamo.

bigamy, s. bigamia.

bight, s. bahía.

bigness, s. grandeza ; tamaño, bulto.

bigot, s. beatón ; fanático.

bigoted, a. santurrón, beatón ; fanático.

big-wig, (col.) s. personaje.

bilberry, s. arándano, una fruta silvestre.

bilbo, s. cepo con grillos, carcel.

bile, bilis ; cólera.

bilge, s. (mar.) pantoque ; —, v.a. (mar.) hacer agua ; — water, s. agua de pantoque.

bilingual, a. bilingüe.

bilious, a. bilioso.

bilk, v.a. (col.) chasquear, engañar.

bill, s. pico de ave ; papel, billete ; cédula ; cuenta ; — of exchange, letra de cambio ; — of lading, (mar.) conocimiento ; -s-receivable, s. letras aceptables ; —, v.n. arrullar, acariciar.

bill-broker, corredor.

billet, s. billete ; leño ; alojamiento ; (met.) empleo ; —, v.a. alojar (soldados).

billiard-ball, s. billa.

billiards, s. billar.

billiard-table, s. billar.

Billingsgate, s. pescadería en Londres ; lenguaje bajo.

billion, s. millón de millones.

billow, s. ola grande, onda.

billowy, a. ondeado, undoso.   [despensa.

bin, s. artesón, cofre ; armario ; estante ;

bind, v.a. atar ; unir ; encuadernar ; obligar, poner á uno á servir.

binder, s. encuadernador.   [obligatorio.

binding, s. venda, faja ; — a. formal ;

bindweed, s. correhuela, enredadera.

binnacle, s. (mar.) bitácora.

binocular, a. (opt.) binocular.

binomial, s. binomio.

biographer, s. biógrafo.

biographical, a. biográfico.

biography, s. biografía.

biology, s. biología.

biped, s. bípede.

biplane, s. biplano.

birch, s. abedul ; —, v.a. (col.) varear.

birchen, a. de abedul.

bird, s. ave ; pájaro.

bird-cage, s. jaula.

bird-lime, s. liga.

bird's-eye view, s. vista de pájaro.

birth, s. nacimiento ; origen ; parto.

birth-day, s. cumpleaños.

birth-place, s. suelo nativo, patria.

birth-right, s. derechos de nacimiento ; primogenitura.

biscuit, s. galleta.

bisection, s. bisección.

bisect, v.a. dividir en dos partes,

bishop, s. obispo.

bishopric, s. obispado.

bismuth, s. bismuto.

bison, s. bisonte.

bit, s. pedacito ; — of a bridle, bocado del freno ; —, v.a. enfrenar.

bitch, s. perra.

bite, v.a. morder ; picar ; — the dust, mascar tierra, morir ; —, s. morde- dura ; bocado.

biter, s. mordedor.

biting, a. mordaz ; picante.

bitter, a. amargo, áspero ; mordaz, satírico ; penoso ; -ly, amargamente ; con pena ; severamente.

bittern, s. alcaraván, bitor.   [dolor.

bitterness, s. amargura ; rencor ; pena ;

bitters, s.pl. brebaje amargo, aperitivo.

bitumen, s. betún.

bituminous, a. bituminoso.

bivalve, s. bivalvo.

bivouac, s. (mil.) vivac, vivaque ; —, v.n. vivaquear.

bizarre, a. raro, extravagante.

blab, v.a. parlar, charlar, divulgar.

black, a. negro, obscuro ; tétrico, malvado ; funesto ; —, s. color negro ;

—, v.a. teñir de negro, negrecer ; limpiar (botas).

blackamoor, s. negro.

black-art, s. nigromancia.

black-ball, v.a. excluir á un candidato en votando con una bolita negra.

blackberry, s. zarzamora.

blackbird, s. merla.

black-board, s. tabla, plancha para cálculos en las clases escolares.

black-draught, s. infusión de sene.

blacken, v.a. teñir de negro ; ennegrecer.

blacking, s. lustre para botas.

blackfriar, s. dominicano.

blackguard, s. galopín, bribón ; —, v.a. insultar.

black-lead, s. lápiz-plomo.

blackleg, s. bribón.

black-letter, s. letra gótica.

blackmail, s. rescate que los viajeros pagan á los salteadores.

blackness, s. negrura, oscuridad.

black-pudding, s. morcilla.

blacksmith, s. herrero.

black-thorn, s. endrino.

bladder, s. vejiga.

blade, s. brizna ú hoja (de yerba) ; hoja (de cuchillo) ; pala (de remo) ; espada (poet.), jaquetón ; guapo.

blamable, a. culpable ; vituperable ; -bly, culpablemente.

blame, v.a. culpar, vituperar ; —, s. culpa, vituperación, imputación.

blameless, a. inocente, irreprensible, puro ; -ly, inocentemente.

blameworthy, a. culpable.

blanch, v.a. blanquear ; —, v.n. palidecer.

bland, a. blando, suave, dulce, apacible.

blandishment, s. halago ; zalamería ; caricia.

blank, a. blanco ; aturdido ; (poet.) sin rima ; —, s. blanco.   [cama.

blanket, s. frazada, manta, cubierta de

blare, s. son (de trompetas).

blaspheme, v.a. blasfemar ; vituperar.

blasphemous, a. blasfemo ; -ly, blas- femamente.

blasphemy, s. blasfemia.

blast, s. soplo de aire ; influjo maligno ; —, v.a. marchitar, secar ; arruinar ; infamar ; volar por medio de pólvora.

blast-furnace, s. fundería, horno de   [fundición.

blatant, a. vocinglero.

blaze, s. llama ; brillo ; —, v.n. encen- derse en llama ; brillar, resplandecer ; —, v.a. divulgar.

blazon, v.a. blasonar ; decorar ; publicar.

blazon, blasonry, s. blasón.   [blanquear.

bleach, v.a. blanquear al sol ; —, v.n.

bleak, a. pálido, descolorido ; desierto, esteril, triste (paisaje).

bleakness, s. palidez ; esterilidad, tristeza.
blear(-eyed), a. lagañoso.
bleat, s. balido ; —, v.n. balar.
bleed, v.n. perder sangre ; —, v.a. sangrar.
bleeding, s. sangría.
blemish, v.a. manchar, suciar ; infamar ; — s. mancha, tacha ; deshonra, infamia.
blench, estremecerse ; ejar, recular.
blend, v.a. mezclar, templar ; —, s. mezcla.
bless, v.a. bendecir. [beatitud.
blessed, a. feliz, beato ; **-ness,** s. felicidad;
blessing, s. bendición ; favores del cielo.
blight, s. pulgón ; alheña ; peste ; —, v.a. apestar, enfermar ; arruinar.
blind, a. ciego ; oculto ; obscuro ; — **alley,** s. callejón sin salida ; —, v.a. cegar ; deslumbrar ; —, s. velo ; (Venetian —) persiana.
blindfold, v.a. vendar los ojos ; —, a. con los ojos vendados.
blindly, ad. ciegamente, á ciegas.
blindman's-buff, s. gallina ciega (un juego).
blindness, s. ceguedad ; alucinación.
blind-side, s. el lado flaco.
blind-worm, s. cecilia. [lumbre.
blink, v.n. pestañear ; —, s. ojeada, vis-
blinkers, s. anteojeras.
bliss, s. felicidad.
blissful, a. feliz ; beato, bienaventu-rado ; **-ly,** felizmente.
blissfulness, s. suprema felicidad.
blister, s. vejiga, ampolla ; vejigatorio ; —, v.a. & n. ampollar(se).
blithe, a. alegre, contento, gozoso.
blizzard, s. (am.) huracán nevoso.
bloat, v.a. hinchar ; **-ed,** a. hinchado, turgente, grueso.
bloater, s. arenque ahumado.
block, s. pedazo, trozo (de piedra ó de ma-dera); obstáculo ; —, v.a. cerrar ; obstar.
blockade, s. bloqueo ; —, v.a. bloquear.
blockhead, s. necio, zopenco.
blonde, a. & s. rubio.
blood, s. sangre ; linaje, parentesco ; —, v.a. sangrar, ensangrentar.
blood-guiltiness, s. homicidio, asesinato.
blood-hound, s. sabueso. [mente.
bloodily, ad. cruelmente, inhumana-
bloodiness, s. (fig.) crueldad.
bloodless, a. exangüe ; anémico ; pálido ; débil, sin efusión de sangre.
blood-letting, s. sangría. [matanza.
bloodshed, s. efusión de sangre.
bloodshot, a. ensangrentado (de los ojos).
blood-sucker, s. sanguijuela ; (fig.) desollador.
blood-vessel, s. vena.
bloody, a. sangriento, ensangrentado ; cruel.

bloom, s. flor ; (also fig.) ; —, v.n. florecer.
blossom, s. flor, (fig.) flor, nata ; — v.n florecer, echar flor.
blot, v.a. manchar (lo escrito) ; cancelar, borrar, denigrar ; —, s. mancha, borrón.
blotch, s. mancha ; pústula.
blotting-case, -pad, s. papelería.
blotting-paper, s. papel secante ; teleta.
blouse, s. blusa.
blow, v.n. soplar ; sonar ; florecer ; —, v.a. soplar ; inflar ; **to — up,** volar(se) por medio de pólvora ; —, s. golpe.
blow-pipe, s. soplete.
blowzy, a. rubicunda, inelegante (mujer).
blubber, s. grasa de ballena ; —, v.n. & a. llorar hasta hincharse los carrillos.
bluchers, s.pl. botas gruesas.
bludgeon, s. cachiporra ; garrote macana.
blue, a. & s. azul ; —, v.a. azular.
blue-bell, s. jacinto selvaje.
blue-bottle, f. corónida (mosca).
blue-devils, blues, s.pl. melancolío, jaqueca.
blue-eyed, a. ojizarco.
blueness, s. color azul.
blue-peter, s. (mar.) pabellón de partida.
blue-stocking, s. (col.) mujer docta.
bluff, a. rústico, franco ; —, s. cabo, pro-montorio.
bluffness, s. franqueza ó desenvoltura rústica.
bluish, a. azulado.
blunder, s. desatino ; error ; —, v.a. & n. confundir ; desatinar, desacertar.
blunderbuss, s. trabuco.
blunt, a. obtuso embotado, brusco ; bronco ; —, v.a. embotar ; enervar ; calmar (un dolor).
bluntly, sin artificio ; francamente.
bluntness, s. embotadura, franqueza in-formal.
blur, s. mancha ; —, v.a. manchar ; defamar.
blurt (out), v.a. soltar (noticias) impensa damente.
blush, s. rubor ; sonrojo ; —, v.n. ponerse colorado, sonrojarse.
bluster, s. ruido, tumulto ; jactancia ; —, v.n. vocear, vociferar, fanfarronear.
boa, s. boa (serpiente).
boar, s. verraco ; **wild —,** jabalí.
board, s. tabla ; mesa ; tribunal, consejo ; **on —,** (mar.) abordo ; —, v.a. abordar ; —, v.n. estar en hospedaje ; — v.a tomar huespedes.
boarder, s. pensionista, pupilo, huesped.
boarding-house, s. casa de pupilos ; casa de huéspedes. [internos.
boarding-school, s. escuela ó colegio de
board-wages, s. ración en dinero que se da á los criados para mantenerse.

boast, v.n. jactarse ; —, s. jactancia ; ostentación ; -er, s. fanfarrón.
boastful, a. jactancioso.
boat, s. bote ; barca, chalupa, bote.
boathook, s. (mar.) bichero.
boating, s. paseo en barquilla.
boatman, s. barquero.
boatswain, s. contramaestre.
bob, s. cosa oscilante, colcajo ; oscilación. —, v.a. & n. balancear, mover(se), [oscilar.
bobbin, s. canilla, broca.
bobtail, s. rabón ; cola cortada.
bob-wig, s. peluca pequeña.
bode, v.a. presagiar, pronosticar. [femenil.
bodice, s. parte superior del vestido
bodiless, a. incorpóreo.
bodily, a. corpóreo ; —, ad. por completo.
bodkin, s. punzón de sastre ; aguja grande.
body, s. cuerpo ; individuo ; gremio ; any—, cualquier ; every —, cada uno.
body-guard, s. (mil.) guardia de corps.
bog, s. pantano.
bogey, s. duende.
boggle, v.n. titubear, vacilar, balancear.
boggy, a. pantanoso.
bogus, (col.) a. postizo.
bohea, s. te negro de la China.
boil, v.n. hervir; bullir; hervir (la sangre) ; —, v.a. cocer ; —, s. furúnculo, tumorcillo.
boiler, s. caldero, caldera.
boisterous, a. borrascoso, tempestuoso ; violento ; -ly, tumultuosamente, furiosamente.
bold, a. ardiente, valiente ; audaz ; temerario ; impudente ; -ly, audazmente, descaradamente.
boldness, s. intrepidez ; valentía ; osadía.
bole, s. tronco.
bolster, s. cabezal ; —, v.a. apoyar.
bolt, s. dardo ; flecha ; cerrojo ; —, v.a. cerrar con cerrojo ; engullir ; — v.n. (col.) huirse.
bolus, s. (med.) bola, píldora.
bomb, s. (mil.) bomba, obus.
bombard, v.a. bombardear.
bombardier, s. bombardero.
bombardment, s. bombardeo.
bombast, s. fanfarronería.
bombastic, a. hinchado, fanfarrón.
bond, s. ligadura ; vínculo ; vale ; obligación ; —, v.a. poner en depósito.
bondage, s. esclavitud, servidumbre.
bond-holder, s. accionista.
bond(s)man, s. esclavo, siervo.
bone, s. hueso ; —, v.a. desosar.
boneless, a. sin huesos ; desosado.
bonesetter, s. cirujano.
bonfire, s. fuego de regocijo.
bonnet, s. gorra ; bonete.

bonny, a. bonito, galán, gentil.
bonus, s. regalo, adehala.
bony, a. osudo.
booby, s. hombre bobo.
book, s. libro ; v.a. asentar en un libro ; (rail) tomar el billete.
book-binder, s. encuadernador de libros.
book-case, s. armario ó estante para libros. [billetes.
booking-office, s. (rail) despacho de
book-keeper, s. tenedor de libros.
book-keeping, s. teneduría de libros, contabilidad.
book-maker, s. apostador (de oficio).
book-seller, s. librero.
book-worm, s. polilla que roe los libros ; estudiante muy aplicado á los libros.
boom, s. (mar.) botalón ; cadena para cerrar un puerto ; —, v.n. zumbar.
boon, s. presente, regalo ; favor.
boor, s. patán, villano.
boorish, a. rústico, agreste.
boorishness, s. rusticidad, grosería.
boot, s. bota ; — v.n. valer, servir ; to —, ad. además.
booted, a. calzado con botas.
booth, s. barraca, cabaña.
boot-jack, s. sacabotas.
bootless, a. inútil, sin provecho, vano.
bootmaker, s. zapatero.
boot-tree, s. horma de bota.
booty, s. botín ; presa.
booze, v.n. emborracharse.
borax, s. borraj.
border, s. orilla ; borde ; margen ; frontera ; —, v.n. confinar ; —, v.a. ribetear ; limitar.
borderer, s. hombre fronterizo.
bore, v.a. taladrar ; barrenar ; fastidiar ; —, s. taladro ; calibre ; hombre enfadoso.
boreal, a. septentrional, boreal.
boredom, s. fastidio.
born, a. nacido.
borough, s. villa ; burgo.
borrow, v.a. tomar fiado ; pedir prestado.
borrower, s. deudor de un empréstito.
boscage, s. boscaje ; arboleda.
bosh, s. (col.) galimatías.
bosom, s. seno, pecho.
bosom-friend, s. amigo íntimo.
boss, s. clavo ; giba, joroba ; —, (am.) patrón, maestro.
botanic(al), a. botánico.
botanise, v.a. herborizar.
botanist, s. botánico ; **botany**, s. botánica.
botch, s. remiendo ; roncha ; úlcera ; —, v.a. remendar ; chapuzar.
botcher, s. chapucero.
both, a. ambos, entrambos ; c. —...and, tanto ... como.

bother, v.a. molestar, enfadar; — s molestia, fastidio.　　　　[botellar.

bottle, s. botella; frasco; —, v.a. em-

bottom, s. fondo; fundamento; valle; buque; —, a. inferior; — upwards, ad. lo de arriba abajo, al revés.

bottomless, a. insondable;

bottomry, s. (mar.) hipoteca de un barco.

boudoir, s. saloncito privado de señora.

bough, s. brazo del árbol; rama.

boulder, s. guijarro.

bounce, v.n. brincar; saltar, jactarse; —, s. salto, brinco; bravata.

bound, s. límite; salto; —, v.a. confinar, limitar; reprimir; —, v.n. resaltar; — for, a. destinado á.

boundary, límite; frontera.

bounden, a. obligado; obligatorio.

boundless, a. ilimitado, infinito.

bounteous, bountiful, a. liberal, generoso; -ly, generosamente, liberalmente.

bounty, s. liberalidad, bondad.

bouquet, s. ramillete de flores, ramo.

bourn, s. confín; destino; fin.

bout, s. vez; experimento; rato.

bovine, a. bovino.

bow, v.a. encorvar, doblar, oprimir; —, v.n. encorvarse; hacer reverencia; —, s. reverencia, inclinación.　　[nudo.

bow, s. arco; arco de violín; corbata;

bowels, s.pl. intestinos, pl.; entrañas, pl.; ternura, compasión.

bower, s. enramada; aposento retirado.

bowie-knife, s. puñal largo y ancho.

bowl, s. taza; bola; —, v.n. jugar á las bochas.

bow-legged, a. estevado, patiestevado.

bowline, s. (mar.) bolina.

bowling-green, s. boleo.

bowsprit, s. (mar.) bauprés.

bowstring, s. cuerda del arco.

bow-window, s. ventana arqueada.

bowler, s. tirador de la pelota en los juegos.

box, s. boj (árbol); caja, cajita; palco de teatro; — on the ear, bofetada; —, v.a. encajar; apuñetear; —, v.n. combatir á puñadas.

boxen, a. hecho de boj.

boxer, s. púgil.

boxing-day, s. día de San Estéban.

box-seat, s. pescante.

boy, s. muchacho; niño;

boycot, v.a. excluir á una persona de todo trato, social y comercial.

boyhood, s. muchachez.　　　　[mente.

boyish, a. pueril; frívolo; -ly, pueril-

boyishness, s. puerilidad, muchachería.

brace, s. lazo, atadura; abrazadera; sopanda de coche; par de aves ó de animales de caza; -s, pl. tirantes de pantalones, pl.; —, v.a. ligar, amarrar; (mar.) bracear.

bracelet, s. brazalete.

bracken, s. (bot.) helecho.

bracket, s. puntal; corchete, razgo que circunda una ó más palabras; to — with, v.a. unir, ligar.

brackish, a. salobre.　　　　[cante (clima).

bracing, a. vivo, invigorizante, fortifi-

brad, s. tachuela, punta.

brad-awl, s. lesna.　　　　[fanfarronear.

brag, s. jactancia; —, v.n. jactarse,

braggadocio, s. fanfarrón.

braggart, a. & s. jactancioso; fanfarrón.

braid, s. trenza; —, v.a. trenzar.

brain, s. cerebro; seso; juicio; —, v.a. descerebrar.

brain-fever, s. cerebritis.

brainless, a. tonto, insensato.

brain-pan, s. cráneo.

brain-sick, a. frenético.

brake, s. maleza, matorral; (rail.) freno.

brakesman, s. (rail.) guardafrenos.

bramble, s. zarza, espina.

bran, s. salvado.　　　　[carse.

branch, s. ramo; rama; —, v.n. ramifi-

branch-line, s. (rail.) ramal.

brand, s. tizón; mancha; señal; —, v.a. herrar, marcar con hierro encendido; infamar.

brandish, v.a. blandir, ondear.

bran(d) new, a. flamante.

brandy, s. aguardiente.

brass, s. bronce; desvergüenza.

brass-founder, s. fundidor de bronce.

brat, s. rapáz.

bravado, s. baladronada.

brave, a. valiente, atrevido; —, v.a. atacar, atreyirse; -ly, con valor.

bravery, s. valor; magnificencia. [¡bravo!

bravo, s. espadachín, jácaro; —, interj.

brawl, s. riña, disputa, camorra; —, v.n. alborotar; vocinglear.

brawn, s. pulpa; carne de verraco.

brawny, a. carnoso, musculoso.

bray, v.a. triturar; —, v.n. rebuznar; —, s. rebuzno (del asno).

braze, v.a. soldar con latón; broncear.

brazen, a. de bronce; desvergonzado, impudente; —, v.a. hacerse descarado.

brazier, s. latonero; brasero,

breach, s. rotura; brecha; violación.

bread, s. pan.

breadstuffs, s.pl. granos, pl.

breadth, s. anchura.

break, v.a. romper; quebrantar; violar; domar; arruinar; interrumpir; —, v.n. romperse; reventarse; separarse; (com.) quebrar; to — out, abrirse salida; derramarse, desaguar; —,

s. rotura, abertura ; interrupción;
— of day, alba, amanecer.

breakage, s. rompimiento.

breakdown, s. vuelca, caída, fracaso.

breakfast, s. desayuno, almuerzo ; v.n.
—, desayunar, almorzar. [rio.

breakneck, a. (col.) precipitoso ; temera-

breakwater, s. rompeolas, dique.

breast, s. pecho, seno ; tetas ; corazón ;
—, v.a. resistir.

breast-bone, s. esternón.

breast-high, a. alto hasta el pecho.

breast-plate, s. peto ; pectoral ; coraza.

breast-work, s. parapeto.　　　[aire.

breath, s. aliento, respiración ; soplo de

breathe, v.a. & n. respirar ; exhalar.

breathing, s. aspiración ; respiración ;
aliento.

breathing-time, s. descanso, reposo.

breathless, a. falto de aliento ; desalentado.　　　　　　　　　　[ó fusil].

breech, s. trasero ; culata de cañón

breeches, s.pl. calzones, pantalones, pl.

breed, s. casta, raza ; —, v.a. procrear,
engendrar ; producir ; educar ; —,
v.n. parir ; multiplicarse.

breeder, s. criador ;

breeding, s. crianza ; buena educación.

breeze, s. brisa.

breezy, a. ventoso.　　[(en estilo grave).

brethren, s.pl. (de brother) hermanos, pl.

brevet, s. despacho, título.

breviary, s. breviario.

brevity, s. brevedad.

brew, v.a. hacer (cerveza ú otros licores),
tramar, maquinar ; —, s. calderada
de cerveza.

brewer, s. cervecero.

brewery, s. cervecería.

briar, brier, s. zarza, espino.

bribe, s. cohecho, soborno ; —, v.a.
cohechar, corromper, sobornar.

bribery, s. cohecho, soborno.

brick, s. ladrillo ; hombre alegre, compadre ; —, v.a. enladrillar.

brick-bat, s. pedazo de ladrillo.

brick-layer, s. albañil.

bridal, a. nupcial : —, s. boda.

bride, s. novia, esposa.

bridegroom, s. novio.

bridesmaid, s. madrina de boda.

Bridewell, s. carcel, prisión.

bridge, s. puente ; caballete de la nariz ;
puente de violín ; to — (over), v.a.
construir un puente, atravesar.

bridle, s. brida, freno ; —, v.a. embridar ;
reprimir, refrenar.

brief, a. breve, conciso, sucinto ; —, s.
compendio ; breve ; cédula ; -less, a.
(abogado) sin causas.

briefly, ad. brevemente en pocas palabras.

brier, s. zarza.

brig, brigantine, s. (mar.) bergantín.

brigade, s. (mil.) brigada.

brigadier, s. (mil.) brigadier.

brigand, s. bandido. [espléndidamente.

bright, a. claro, luciente, brillante ; -ly

brighten, v.a. pulir, lustrar, ilustrar : —,
v.n. aclarar.　　　　[agudeza ; claridad.

brightness, s. esplendor, brillantez ;

brill, s. barbosa (pez).

brilliancy, s. brillantez.

brilliant, a. brilliante ; -ly, espléndidamente ; —, s. brillante (diamante).

brim, s. borde, boca extremo, orilla ; —
(of hat), alas ; —, v.a. llenar hasta el
borde ; —, v.n. estar lleno.

brimful, a. lleno hasta el borde.

brimstone, s. azufre.

brindled, a. abigarrado.

brine, s. salmuera.

bring, v.a. llevar, traer ; conducir ; inducir, persuadir ; to — about, efectuar ;
to — forth, producir ; parir ; to — up,
educar.

brink, s. orilla ; margen, borde.

briny, s. salado.

brisk, a. vivo, alegre, jovial ; fresco.

brisket, s. pecho (de vaca).

briskly, ad. vigorosamente ; alegremente ;
vivamente.

briskness, s. vivacidad, alegría.

bristle, s. cerda, seta ; —, v.n. erizarse.

bristly, a. cerdoso, lleno de cerdas.

brittle, a. quebradizo, frágil.

brittleness, s. fragilidad.

broach, s. asador ; —, v.a. espetar ; proferir, abrir (un asunto) ; barrenar.

broad, a. ancho ; abierto ; grosero ; at —
noon, al medio día.

broadcast, ad. (sembrando) al vuelo con
la mano ; (fig.) públicamente (esparcido.)

broadcloth, s. paño fino.

broaden, v.a. & n. ensanchar(se).

broadly, ad. anchamente.

broadness, s. ancho ; anchura ; grosería.

broadside, s. costado de navío ; andanada.

broadsword, s. espada ancha ; alfanje.

broadwise, ad. de costado.

brocade, s. brocado.

broccoli, s. bróculi, especie de col.

brogue, s. abarca ; idioma corrompido.

broider, v.a. bordar.

broil, s. tumulto ; riña ; —, v.a. asar
(carne) ; —, v.n. padecer calor.

broiling, a. (calor) sofocante.

broken, p. roto, interrumpido ; —
english, inglés mal articulado.

broker, s. corredor ; factor.

brokerage, s. corretaje.

bronchial, a. bronquial.

bronchitis, s. bronquitis.
bronze, s. bronce ; —, v.a. broncear.
brooch, s. broche de metal fino ó de piedras preciosas.
brood, v.n. empollar ; meditar, abstraerse, ensimismarse ; madurar ; —, s. raza ; nidada.
brood-hen, s. gallina clueca.
brook, s. arroyo ; —, v.n. sufrir, tolerar.
broom, s. hiniesta ; escoba.
broom-stick, s. palo de escoba.
broth, s. caldo.
brothel, s. burdel.
brother, s. hermano.
brotherhood, s. hermandad ; fraternidad.
brother-in-law, s. cuñado.
brotherly, a. fraternal.
brougham, s. coche cerrado.
brow, s. ceja ; frente ; cima. [acallar.
browbeat, v.a. arrumbar, desconcertar,
brown, a. moreno ; obscuro ; **to be in a — study,** estar ensimismado ; **— paper,** s. papel de estraza ; **— sugar,** s. azúcar terciado ; —, s. color moreno.
brownie, s. duende.
browse, v.n. pacer, ramonear.
bruin, (col.) s. oso.
bruise, v.a. magullar, machacar, abollar, majar ; pulverizar ; —, s. magulladura, contusión.
bruit, v.a. publicar, esparcir.
brummagem, a. (col. de Birmingham), mal hecho ; ordinario ; cachivaches.
brunette, s. mujer morena.
brunt, s. choque ; golpe.
brush, s. cepillo ; escobilla ; bruza ; pincel ; asalto ; combate ; —, v.a. acepillar, cepillar ; —, v.n. moverse apresuradamente ; pasar ligeramente.
brushwood, s. breñal, zarzal.
brushy, a. cerdoso ; velludo.
brutal, a. brutal ; **-ly,** ad. brutalmente.
brutality, s. brutalidad.
brutalize, v.a. embrutecer. [irracional.
brute, s. bruto ; —, a. feroz, bestial ;
brutish, a. bruto, brutal, bestial ; feroz ; **-ly,** brutalmente.
bubble, s. burbuja ; friolera, una nada ; engañifa ; —, v.n. burbujear, bullir ; —, v.a. engañar.
buccanier, s. corsario, filibustero.
buck, s. gamo ; macho (de algunos animales) ; (fig.) mozo guapetón, majo.
bucket, s. cubo, pozal, balde.
buckle, s. hebilla ; —, v.a. hebillar ; ajustar ; —, v.n. encorvarse.
buckler, s. escudo ; adarga.
buckram, s. bocací. [tido.
buckskin, s. ante, cuero de gamo curbuckwheat,** s. trigo negro.
bucolic, a. bucólico. agreste,

bud, s. pimpollo, botón ; —, v.a., ingertar, ingerir ; — v.n. brotar, abotonar.
budge, v.n. moverse, mudarse.
budget, s. atado de papeles, presupuesto de los gastos del Estado.
buff, s. ante ; color de amarillo ligero ; —, a. de ante.
buffalo, s. búfalo.
buffer, s. (rail.) tope.
buffet, s. puñada ; bofetada ; aparador ; —, v.n. abofetear.
buffoon, s. bufón, chocarrero.
buffoonery, s. bufonada, bufonería.
bug, s. chinche. [objeto de odio.
bugbear, s. espantajo, coco, pesadilla,
buggy, s. volanta, cochecito americano.
bugle (horn), s. trompa de caza.
buhl, s. obra francesa de metal y madera fina (muebles).
build, v.a. edificar ; construir ; —, v.n. fiarse. [tro de obras.
builder, s. arquitecto ; edificador ; maesbuilding,** s. edificio ; construcción.
bulb, s. bulbo ; cebolla.
bulbous, a. bulboso.
bulge, v.n. combarse ; encorvarse.
bulk, s. masa ; volumen ; grosura ; tamaño ; mayor parte ; capacidad de un buque ; **in —,** en grueso.
bulkhead, s. mamparo.
bulkiness, s. bulto ; masa, magnitud.
bulky, a. macizo, grueso, grande.
bull, s. toro ; bula, breve pontificio ; dicho absurdo.
bull-baiting, s. combate de toros y perros.
bull-dog, s. especie de perro bajo, corpulento y fuerte.
bullet, s. bala.
bulletin, s. boletín.
bull-finch, s. (orn.) pinzón real.
bullion, s. oro ó plata en barras.
bull's-eye, claraboya redonda ; (mil.) centro del blanco ; linterna de policía.
bullock, s. novillo capado, buey.
bully, s. espadachín, gallo, fanfarron ; —, v.a. & n. intimidar, atormentar gallear, bravear.
bulrush, s. junco.
bulwark, s. baluarte.
bumble-bee, s. abejarrón, abejón, zángaro
bumboat, s. bote vivandero.
bump, s. golpe, choque ; hinchazón ; bollo —, v.a. & n. golpear(se) ; chocar.
bumper, s. copa ; vaso lleno.
bumpkin, s. patán ; villano.
bumptious, a. presumido, hinchado.
bun, s. bizcocho, panecillo dulce.
bunch, s. manojo, atado, fardo ; racimo ; ramo de flores ; hinchazón ; nudo ; —, v.a. & n. atar, reunir : formar corcova, acurrucarse.

bunchy, a. corcovado, espeso, corpulento.

bundle, s. atado, fardo, haz (de leña, &c.); paquete ; rollo ; —, v.a. atar, liar.

bung, s. tapón ; —, v.a. tapar, atarugar.

bungalow, s. quinta de piso bajo en las Indias.

bung-hole, s. boca (para envasar licores).

bungle, v.a. chapucear, chafallar ; —, v.n. desacertar, desatinar ; —, s. yerro ; obra mal hecha.

bunk, s. cama de marinero.

bunkum, s. (col.) embuste.

bun(n)ion, s. juanete, callosidad que se forma en los pies.

bunting, s. lanilla para banderas.

buoy, s. (mar.) boya ; —, v.a. boyar.

buoyancy, s. capacidad de flotar ; animación, viveza

buoyant, a. flotador.

bur, s. (bot.) bardana, cardencha ; acento gutural.

burden, s. carga ; estrambote ; —, v.a. cargar ; embarazar.   [cómodo.

burdensome, a. gravoso, molesto, in-

burdock, s. bardana (planta).

bureau, s. armario ; escritorio.

bureaucrat, s. burócrata.

burg, s. *V.* borough.

burgess, s. ciudadano.

burgher, s. ciudadano, vecino.   [noche.

burglar, s. ladrón que roba una casa de

burglary, s. robo nocturno de una casa.

burgomaster, s. burgomaestre, alcalde.

burial, s. enterramiento ; exequias, pl.

burial-place, s. cimenterio.

burlesque, s. & a. burlesco ; — v.a. parodiar, remedar por risa.

burly, a. corpulento, grueso.

burn, v.a. quemar, abrasar, incendiar ; —, v.n. arder ; —, s. quemadura.

burner, s. mechero, piquera de gas ó de lámpara.

burning, a. (fig.) ardiente, fragante.

burning-glass, s. lente ; espejo ustorio.

burnish, v.a. bruñir, lustrar.

burnisher, s. bruñidor.

burr, s. *V.* bur.

burrow, s. conejera ; —, v.n. minar, cavar como los conejos.

bursar, s. tesorero.

burst, v.n. reventar ; abrirse ; —, v.a. romper, quebrar ; to — into tears, prorrumpir en lágrimas ; to — with laughing, descoyuntarse de risa ; —, s. reventón, estallido.

burthen, s. *V.* burden.

bury, v.a. enterrar, sepultar ; esconder.

burying-ground, s. cimenterio.

bus, s. (col.) ómnibus.

busby, s. gorra de húsar.

bush, s. arbusto ; bosque.

bushel, s. fanega.

bushranger, s. salteador (de selva).

bushy, a. espeso, lleno de arbustos ; lanudo.

busily, ad. solícitamente, diligentemente, apresuradamente.

business, s. empleo ; ocupación ; negocio.

buskin, s. borceguí ; coturno.

buss, s. beso.

bust, s. busto.

bustard, s. abutarda.

bustle, v.n. agitarse, moverse, apresurarse ; —, s. baraúnda ; ruido.

busy, a. ocupado ; entremetido ; —, v.a. ocupar.

busybody, s. entremetido, oficioso, bullebulle.

but, c. pero, sino ; —, ad. excepto menos ; solamente.

butcher, s. carnicero ; —, v.a. matar.

butcher's shop, s. carnicería.

butchery, s. carnicería ; matanza.

butler, s. despensero, mayordomo.

butt, s. blanco, hito; terrero ; hazmereir ; — v.a. topar con cabezadas (como cabras).

butt-end, s. culata.

butter, s. manteca ; —, v.a. untar con manteca.   [de león.

butter-cup, s. (bot.) amargón, diente

butterfly, s. mariposa.

butter-milk, s. suero de manteca.

buttery, s. despensa ; —, a. mantecoso.

buttock, s. nalga, anca ; (mar.) cucharros, pl.

button, s. botón ; —, v.a. abotonar.

button-hole, s. ojal.

button-hook, s. abotonador.

buttress, s. (arch.) contrafuerte, estribo ; apoyo ; —, v.a. estribar.

buxom, a. gordo y jovial.

buy, v.a. comprar.

buyer, s. comprador.   [cuchuchear.

buzz, s. susurro, soplo ; —, v.n. zumbar ;

buzzard, s. buaro, especie de milano.

by, pr. por ; á ; cerca, al lado de ; — the —, de paso ; — much, con mucho

bygone, a. pasado.

by-lane, s. sendero, callejuela.

by-law, s. ley local.

by-path, s. atajo, trocha.

by-road, s. camino vecinal.

bystander, s. mirador ; circunstante.

by-street, s. calle extraviada.

by-word, s. refrán ; tipo de mal ejemplo.

C

cab, s. coche de plaza ; -driver,'s. cochero.
cabal, s. cábala, camarilla ; maquinación, trama.
cabalistic, a. cabalístico.   [retazos.
cabbage, s. berza, col ; —, v.a. hurtar
cabin, s. cabaña ; cámara de navío, camarote ; —, v.a. & n. encerrar en cabaña ; vivir en cabaña.
cabin-boy, s. (mar.) grumete.
cabinet, s. gabinete ; escritorio : consejo le ministros.   [ministros.
cabinet-council, s. sesión del consejo de
cabinet-maker, s. ebanista.
cable, s. (mar.) cable ; —'s length, medida de 120 brazas.
cabman, s. cochero de plaza, simón.
caboose, s. (mar.) cocina.
cabstand, s. punto de los coches de plaza.
cacao, s. cacao.
cache, s. (am.) escondite, silo.
cackle, v.a. cacarear ó graznar ; —, s. carcareo ; charla.
cackler, s. cacareador ; parlanchín.
cactus, s. cactus, pita.
cad, s. (col.) hombre grosero y inculto.
cadaverous, a. cadavérico, palido.
caddy, s. caja para el te.
cadence, s. ritmo, cadencia.
cadet, s. cadete ; hermano menor.
cage, s. jaula ; —, v.a. enjaular.
cairn, s. túmulo ; montón de piedras.
caitiff, s. bribón, picaro, miserable.
cajole, v.a. lisonjear ; engañar.
cajolery, a. adulación, lisonja ; zalamería, engaño.
cake, s. bollo, torta, biscocho ; masa espesa (de cera, argilla, &c.) ; —, v.n. endurecerse (como el pan en el horno).
calabash, s. calabaza.
calamitous, a. calamitoso.
calamity, s. calamidad, miseria.
calcareous, a. calcáreo.
calcine, v.a. calcinar.
calculable, a. calculable.
calculate, v.a. calcular, contar.
calculation, s. calculación ; cálculo.
calculus, s. cálculo.
caldron, s. caldera.
calendar, s. calendario, almanaque.
calf, s. ternero ; ternera.
calibre, s. calibre.
calico, s. tela de algodón, algodón.
caligraphy, s. caligrafía.
caliph, s. califa ; -ate, s. califato.   [pl.
calisthenics, s.pl. ejercicios gimnásticos,
calk, v.a. (mar.) calafatear un navío.
call, v.a. llamar, nombrar ; convocar,

citar ; apelar ; **to — for,** preguntar por alguno, ir á buscarle ; **to — names,** injuriar ; **to — upon,** visitar ; —, s. llamada ; instancia ; invitación ; vocación ; (mar.) pito.
caller, s. visitador.
calligraphy, s. caligrafía.
calling, s. profesión, vocación.
callosity, s. callosidad.
callous, a. calloso, endurecido : insensible, sin compasión.
callow, a. implume (pajarito) ; (fig.) imberbe, simple, sin experiencia.
calm, s. calma, tranquilidad ; —, a. quieto, tranquilo ; —, v.a. calmar ; aplacar, aquietar : -ly, tranquilamente, quieta y sosegadamente.
calmness, s. tranquilidad, calma.
calomel, s. calomel.
caloric, s. calórico.
calumet, s. cañutillo de una pipa de fumar.
calumniation, calumny, s. calumnia.
calumniate, v.a. calumniar.
calumnious, a. calumnioso.
Calvary, s. calvario.
calve, v.n. parir (la vaca).
Calvinist, s. calvinista.
calyx, s. (bot.) cáliz.
cambric, s. batista.
camel, s. camello.
camellia, s. (bot.) camelia.
camelopard, s. camellopardal, girafa.
cameo, s. camafeo.
camera, s. máquina fotográfica ; **in —** (law), en sesión secreta.
camlet, s. camelote.
camomile, s. manzanilla.
camp, s. (mil.) campamento ; —, v.n. acampar.
campaign, s. campaña ; —, v.n. servir en campaña.
campaigner, s. experto en la vida de campaña.
camphor, s. alcanfor.
camp-stool, s. silla de tijera.   [metal.
can, v.n. poder ; —, s. copa ó balde de
canal, s. canal.
canary(-bird), s. canario.   [invalidar.
cancel, v.a. cancelar, borrar ; anular,
cancer, s. cáncer.
cancerous, a. canceroso.
candid, a. cándido, sencillo, ingenuo, sincero ; -ly, cándidamente, francamente.
candidate, s. candidato ; pretendiente.
candied, a. bañado de azúcar.
candle, s. vela.

Candlemas, s. Candelaria.
candle-snuffers, s. despabiladeras, pl.
candlestick, s. candelero ; branched —, araña. [genuidad.
candour, s. candor ; sinceridad, in-
candy, v.a. confitar ; —, s. confites.
cane, s. caña ; bastón ; —, v.n. apalear con un bastón ó caña aporrear.
cane-bottom(ed) chair, s. silla de caña.
canicular, a. canicular.
canine, a. canino, perruno.
caning, s. aporreo. [&c.).
canister, s. vasija (para tener te, tabaco,
canister-shot, s. metralla.
canker, s. gangrena ; corrupción ; —, v.a. roer, corromper ; —, v.n. corromperse, roerse.
cannibal, s. caníbal ; antropófago.
cannibalism, s. canibalismo.
cannon, s. cañón.
cannonade, s. cañoneo ; —, v.a. cañonear.
cannon-ball, s. bala de artillería.
cannonier, s. cañonero, artillero.
cannon-shot, s. cañonazo.
canny, a. prudente, cuerdo.
canoe, s. canoa. [canónico.
canon, s. canon ; regla ; -law, derecho
canoness, s. canonesa. [clericales, pl.
canonical, a. canónico ; -s, s.pl. vestidos
canonization, s. canonización.
canonize, v.a. canonizar.
canonry, s. canonicato.
canopy, s. dosel.
cant, s. jerigonza ; salmodia ; hipocresía ; lenguaje afectado é insincero ; —, v.n. hablar en jerigonza, salmear, decir hipocresías.
cantankerous, a. áspero, fastidioso.
canteen, s. cantina.
canter, s. hipócrita ; galope corto.
cantharides, s.pl. cantáridas, pl.
canticle, s. cántico, salmo.
canton, s. cantón ; —, v.a. acantonar, acuartelar.
cantonment, s. acantonamiento de tropas. [cuadro.
canvas, s. cañamazo ; tela de pintor ;
canvass, v.a. & n. solicitar (votos) ; examinar, escudriñar ; —er, s. solici-tador.
caoutchouc, cautchuc, goma elástica.
cap, s. gorra ; birreta ; —, v.a. vencer en el juego de citar versos ó cuentos.
capability, s. capacidad, aptitud, in-teligencia.
capable, a. capaz, idóneo.
capacious, a. capaz ; espacioso, vasto.
capacitate, v.a. hacer capaz.
capacity, s. capacidad ; intelligencia, habilidad ; calidad. [en blanca.
cap-à-pie, ad. de pies a cabeza, de punta

caparison, s. caparazón ; —, v.a. en-jaezar un caballo.
cape, s. cabo, promontorio ; capa.
caper, s. cabriola ; (bot.) alcaparra ; to cut a —, cabriolar ; —, v.n. hacer cabriolas.
capillary, a. capilar.
capital, a. capital, excelente ; principal ; punible con la muerte ; —, s. (arch.) capitel ; capital (la ciudad principal) ; capital, fondo ; mayúscula ; — punish-ment, s. pena de muerte ; -ly, superior-mente ; admirablemente, capitalmente.
capitalise, v.a. capitalizar.
capitalist, s. capitalista.
capitation, s. capitación.
capitulary, s. capitular (individuo de algún capítulo).
capitulate, v.n. (mil.) capitular.
capitulation, s. capitulación.
capon, s. capón.
capote, s. capote, levitón.
caprice, s. capricho ; extravagancia.
capricious, a. caprichoso ; -ly, ad. caprichosamente.
capricorn, s. capricornio.
capsize, v.a. & n. (mar.) volcar, zozobrar.
capstan, s. (mar.) cabrestante.
capsule, s. cápsula.
captain, s. capitán.
captaincy, captainship, s. capitanía.
captious, a. sofístico, caviloso ; quis-quilloso ; -ly, cavilosamente.
captiousness, s. cavilación.
captivate, v.a. cautivar.
captivation, s. atractivo, encanto.
captive, s. cautivo, esclavo.
captivity, s. cautividad, esclavitud, cautiverio.
captor, s. apresador.
capture, s. captura ; presa ; —, v.a. apresar, capturar.
capuchin, s. capuchino ; capucha.
car, s. carreta ; carro.
carabine, s. carabina.
carabinier, s. carabinero. [jinete.
caracole, s. caracol, vuelta que hace el
caramel, s. caramelo.
caravan, s. caravana.
caravansary, s. caravanera.
caraway, s. (bot.) alcaravea.
carbolic acid, s. ácido carbólico.
carbon, s. (chem.) carbón.
carboniferous, a. carbonífero.
carbonize, v.a. carbonizar.
carbuncle, s. carbúnculo ; carbunco, tumor maligno.
carcass, s. (mil.) cadáver.
card, s. naipe ; carta ; cardencha ; pack of —s, baraja de naipes ; —, v.a. cardar lana.
card-board, s. cartón.

cardiac, a. cardíaco.   [cardenal.
cardinal, a. cardinal, principal ; —, s.
card-sharper, s. trampista truhán.
card-table, s. mesa para jugar.
care, s. cuidado ; solicitud ; —, v.n.
cuidar, tener cuidado ó pena, inquietarse.
careen, v.a. carenar.
career, s. carrera ; curso ; —, v.n. correr
á carrera tendida.
careful, a. cuidadoso, ansioso, diligente ;
prudente ; —, ad. cuidadosamente.
carefulness, s. cuidado, cautela, atención,
diligencia.
careless, a. descuidado, negligente ;
indolente ; **-ly,** descuidadamente.
carelessness, s. negligencia, indiferencia.
caress, s. caricia ; —, v.a. acariciar,
alhagar.
caressing, a. cariñoso ; **-ly,** con cariño.
careworn, a. fatigado, ansioso.
cargo, s. cargamento de navío.
caricature, s. caricatura ; —, v.a. hacer
caricaturas, ridiculizar.
caricaturist, s. caricaturista.
caries, s. (med.) caries.
carman, s. carretero.
Carmelite, s. carmelita.
carmine, s. carmín.
carnage, s. carnicería, matanza. [mente.
carnal, a. carnal ; sensual ; **-ly,** carnal-
carnation, s. clavel (flor.).
carnival, s. carnaval.
carnivorous, a. carnívoro.
carol, s. villancico, canción de alegría ó
piedad ; —, v.n. cantar villancicos.
carotid (artery), s. carótida.
carousal, s. festín vinoso ; jarana.
carouse, v.a. festejarse bebiendo ; jaranear.   [criticar, reprobar.
carp, s. carpa (pez) ; —, v.n. censurar,
carpenter, s. carpintero.
carpentry, s. carpintería.
carper, s. critición, censurador
carpet, s. alfombra ; —, v.a. alfombrar.
carpet-bag, s. maleta de tela, saco de
noche.
carpet-knight, s. caballerete.
carping, a. capcioso, caviloso ; **-ly,** malignamente.
carriage, s. porte, talante ; coche,
carruaje ; vehículo ; carga ; cureña de
cañón.
carriage-free (-paid), a. franco de porte.
carrier, s. portador, carretero.
carrier-pigeon, s. paloma correo, paloma
mensajera.
carrion, s. carroña.
carronade, s. carronada.
carrot, s. chirivía.
carroty, a. (col.) pelirrojo.

carry, v.a. llevar, traer, conducir, portar,
lograr ; **to — the day,** quedar victorioso ; **to — on,** conducir.
cart, s. carro ; carreta ; —, v.a. & n.
carretear ; usar carretas ó carros.
cartage, carting, s. carretaje.
cartel, s. cartel.
carter, s. carretero.
cart-horse, s. caballo de tiro.
Carthusian, s. cartujo (monje).
cartilage, s. cartílago ; ternilla
cart-load, s. carretada.
cartoon, s. cartón, dibujo.
cartouch, cartridge, s. cartucho ; **ball —,**
cartucho con bala ; **blank —,** cartucho
sin bala.
cartridge-box, s. cartuchera.
carve, v.a. cincelar ; trinchear ; grabar ;
—, v.n. esculpir.
carver, s. escultor, trinchante.
carving, s. escultura.
carving-knife, s. cuchillo grande de mesa.
cascade, s. cascada, catarata.
case, s. estado ; situación ; caso ;
estuche ; vaina ; **in —,** si acaso.
case-hardened, a. acerado, endurecido.
casemate, s. (mil.) casamata.
casement, s. puerta ventana.
case-shot, s. metralla.   [(un cheque).
cash, s. dinero contante ; —, v.a. pagar
cashier, s. cajero, ; —, v.a. privar á uno
de su empleo.
cashmire, s. cachemira.
casing, s. forro, cubierta.
cask, s. barril, tonel ; —, v.a. entonelar.
casket, s. cajita para joyas, cajita.
casque, s. yelmo.
cassation, s. (law) casación ; **court of —,**
tribunal que anula ó confirma las
sentencias de los tribunales inferiores.
cassock, s. sotana.
cassowary, s. (ornit.) casoar.
cast, v.a. tirar, lanzar ; modelar ; fundir
(metal) ; condenar ; **to — an account,**
ajustar una cuenta ; **to — lots,** echar
suertes ; —, s. tiro, golpe ; forma ;
echamiento ; **(of the eyes)** mirada
bisoja.
castanets, s. pl. castañuelas, pl.
castaway, s. réprobo, perdido.
cast-down, a. humillado, desesperado.
caste, s. casta, corporación.
castigate, v.a. castigar.
castigation, s. castigo ; pena.
casting-voice (-vote), s. voto decisivo.
castings, s. pl. obras de fundición, pl.
cast-iron, s. hierro fundido.
castle, s. castillo ; fortaleza.   [de castor.
castor, s. castor ; sombrero de pelo
castor-oil, s. aceite de ricino ó de palmacristi.

castrate, v.a., capar, castrar.
castration, s. capadura, castración.
casual, a. casual, fortuito ; **-ly,** casualmente, fortuitamente.
casualty, s. casualidad ; acaso, accidente.
casuist, s. casuísta.
casuistical, a. casuístico.
cat, s. gato ; gata ; — **o' nine tails,** s.
azote con nueve cordeles ; —**'s
paw** (mar.), soplo ; (fig.) agente
obsequioso, persona explotada ó
abusada.
cataclysm, s. cataclismo.
catacombs, s. pl. catacumbas, pl.
catalepsy, s. catalepsis.
catalogue, s. catálogo.
catamount, s. gato montaraz.
cataplasm, s. cataplasma.
catapult, s. catapulta.
cataract, s. cascada ; catarata.
catarrh, s. catarro ; reuma.
catastrophe, s. catástrofe.
cat-call, s. silbido.
catch, v.a. coger, agarrar, asir ; atrapar ;
sorprender ; tomar (infección) ; **to —
cold,** resfriarse ; **to — fire,** encenderse ;
—, s. presa ; captura ; idea (mus.)
cosa repetida ; provecho ; trampa.
catching, s. contagioso.
catchword, s. refrán.
catechise, v.a. catequizar, examinar.
catechism, s. catecismo.
catechist, s. catequista.   [camente.
categorical, a. categórico ; **-ly,** categóri-
category, s. categoría.
cater, v.n. abastecer, proveer.
caterer, s. proveedor, abastecedor.
caterpillar, s. oruga.
caterwaul, v.n. maullar ; —, s. maullido.
cat-gut, s. cuerda de violón.
cathartic, a. purgante.
cathedral, s. catedral.
catholic, a. & s. católico (m.).
catholicism, s. catolicismo.
catkin, s. flor del sauce.
cattle, s. ganado.
cattle-show, s. exposición de ganados.
cattle-van, cattle-box, s. (rail.) vagón
cuadra.
caucus, s. (am.) junta electoral.
caudle, s. especie de caldo.
cauliflower, s. coliflor.
caulk, s. & v.a. V. calk.
cause, s. causa ; razón ; motivo ;
proceso : —, v.a. causar, hacer.
causeless, a. infundado, sin razón.
causeway, s. arrecife.
caustic, a. & s. cáustico (m.) ; **lunar —,**
s. piedra infernal, nitrato de plata.
cauterise, v.a. cauterizar.
cautery, s. cauterio.

caution, s. prudencia, precaución ; aviso ,
—, v.a. avisar ; amonestar ; advertir.
cautionary, a. dado á fianzas.
cautious, a. prudente, circunspecto, cauto.
cavalcade, s. cabalgata, cabalgada.
cavalier, s. jinete ; caballero.
cavalry, s. caballería.
cave, cavern, s. caverna ; bodega,
caveat, s. (law) notificación.
cavernous, a. cavernoso.
caviar(e), s. cavial, caviar.
cavil, s. cavilación, sofistería ; —, v.n.
cavilar ; criticar.
caviller, s. sofista, enredador.
cavity, s. hueco.
caw, v.n. graznar, crascitar.
cease, v.a. parar, suspender, dejar ; —,
v.n. desistir, pararse, acabar, terminar.
ceaseless, a. incesante, continuo ; **-ly,**
perpetuamente.
cedar, s. cedro.
cede, v.a. ceder, transferir.
ceil, v.a. techar.   [ción.
ceiling, s. techo o cielo raso de una habita-
celebrate, v.a. celebrar ; elogiar.
celebration, s. celebración ; alabanza.
celebrity, s. celebridad, fama.
celerity, s. celeridad, velocidad.
celery, s. apio.
celestial, a. celeste, divino ; —, s. celícola
celibacy, s. celibato.
celibate, a. soltero ; soltera.
cell, s. celda, celdilla ; alvéolo ; cueva,
cellar, s. sótano ; bodega.
cellaret, s. cantina, frasquera.
cellular, a. celular.
cellule, s. celdita.
cellulose, a celuloso ; —, s. celulosa.
cement, s. argamasa ; cimento ; (fig.)
vínculo ; —, v.a. pegar con cimento.
cemetery, s. cimenterio.
cenotaph, s. cenotafio.
censer, s. incensario.
censor, s. censor ; crítico.   [severamente.
censorious, a. severo, crítico ; **-ly,**
censorship, s. censura, (oficio).
censurable, a. digno de censura, culpable.
censure, s. censura, reprensión ; —, v.a.
censurar, reprender ; criticar.
census, s. censo, encabezamiento.
cent, s. ciento ; centésimo de un duro (am.)
centenarian, s. centenario ; centenaria.
centenary, s. centena ; —, a. centenario.
centennial, a. centenario.
centipede, s. escolopendra   [el centro.
central, a. central ; **-ly,** centralmente, en
centralize, v.a. centralizar.
centre, s. centro ; —, v.a. colocar en un
centro ; reconcentrar.
centrifugal, a. centrífugo.
centripetal, a. centrípeto.

centuple, a. céntuplo ; —, v.a. centuplicar.
century, s. centuria ; siglo.
cereals, s. pl. cereales, pl. [ceremonial.
ceremonial, s. ceremonia, rito ; —, a,
ceremonious, a. ceremonioso ; -ly, ceremoniosamente.
ceremony, s. ceremonia.
certain, a. cierto, evidente ; seguro ;
-ly, ciertamente, sin duda. [dad.
certainty, certitude, s. certeza ; seguridad.
certificate, s. certificado, testimonio.
certify, v. a. certificar, afirmar.
cerulean, a. cerúleo, azulado.
cessation, s. cesación ; — of arms, suspensión de armas.
cession, s. cesión.
cesspool, s. cloaca ; sumidero.
chafe, v.a. frotar, enojar, irritar ; —, v.n.
acalorarse, irritarse.
chaff, s. zurrón, hollejo ; paja menuda ;
(col.) burla, broma ; —, v.a. (col.) embromar.
chaffer, v.n. regatear, baratear.
chaffinch, s. pinzón. [mesa.
chafing-dish, s. estafeta, braserito de
chagrin, s. enfado, mortificación.
chain, s. cadena ; serie, sucesión ; -s,
pl. esclavitud ; —, v.a. encadenar,
atar con cadena.
chain-shot, s. balas encadenadas, pl.
chair, s. silla ; asiento portátil ; —, v.a.
llevar en triunfo.
chair-man, s. presidente ;
chaise, s. volante ; coche.
chaldron, s. V. caldron.
chalice, s. cáliz.
chalk, s. tiza, creta.
chalk-pit, s. gredera.
chalky, a. gredoso.
challenge, s. desafío, cartel ; —, v.a.
desafiar ; provocar ; reclamar ; (mil.)
llamar ¿ quién vive ?
challenger, s. desafiador.
chalybeate, a. ferruginoso.
chamber, s. cámara ; aposento.
chamberlain, s. camarero.
chamberlainship, s. camarería.
chamber-maid, s. moza de cámara.
chamber-pot, s. orinal. [camarera.
chameleon, s. camaleón.
chamois-leather, s. gamuza.
champ, v.a. morder, mascar.
champagne, s. vino de Champaña.
champaign, s. campiña, llanura.
champion, s. campeón ; —, v.a. proteger,
apoyar. [atletas).
championship, s. triunfo, premio (entre
chance, s. ventura, suerte ; acaso ;
riesgo ; by —, por acaso ; —, v.n.
acaecer, acontecer.

chancel, s. presbiterio (en la iglesia).
chancellor, s. canciller.
chancery, s. chancillería.
chandelier, s. araña de luces ; candelero.
chandler, s. cerero ; ship's —, s. proveedor de barcos.
change, v.a. cambiar ; trasmutar ; —,
v.n. variar, alterarse ; —, s. mudanza,
variedad ; vicisitud ; cambio.
changeable, changeful, a. variable,
inconstante ; mudable. [constancia.
changeableness, s. mutabilidad, inchangeless, a. constante, inmutable.
changeling, s. niño cambiado (por otro),
hijo supuesto. [lar, estriar.
channel, s. canal, álveo ; —, v.a. acanachant, s. canto (llano) ; —, v.a. cantar.
chanticleer, s. gallo ;
chantry, s. chantría.
chaos, s. caos ; confusión.
chaotic, a. confuso, caótico.
chap, v.n. rajarse, henderse el cutis ;
—, s. hendrija, rendija ; mandíbula.
chap, s. (col.) mozo, joven.
chapel, s. capilla.
chap-fallen, a. cabizbajo.
chaplain, s. capellán.
chaplet, s. guirnalda ; rosario.
chapman, s. vendedor ; traficante.
chapter, s. capítulo ; cabildo.
char, v.a. hacer carbón de leña ; —
v.n. trabajar á jornal (las mujeres).
character, s. carácter ; señal ; forma de
la letra ; calidad.
characteristic, a. característico ; -ally,
característicamente.
characterize, v.a. caracterizar, imprimir.
characterless, a. sin carácter.
charade, s. charada.
charcoal, s. carbón de leña. [quejar.
charcoal-pencil, s. carboncillo para boscharge, v.a. encargar, comisionar ; cargar ; acusar, imputar ; —, s. cargo,
cuidado ; mandato ; acusación ; (mil.)
ataque, carga, embestida.
chargeable, a. imputable. [de guerra.
charger, s. fuente, plato grande ; caballo
chariness, s. circunspección, parsimonia.
chariot, s. carro.
charioteer, s. cochero, auriga (poet.).
charitable, a. caritativo ; benigno, clemente ; -bly, caritativamente.
charitableness, s. caridad. [limosna.
charity, s. caridad, benevolencia ;
charity-school, s. escuela gratuita.
charlatan, s. charlatán.
Charles's-Wain, s. Osa Mayor.
charm, s. encanto ; talismán ; atractivo ; —, v.a. encantar, embelesar,
atraer.
charmingly, ad. agradablemente.

charnel-house, s. carnero.

chart, s. carta de navegar.

charter, s. letra patente ; privilegio ; —, v.a. fletar un buque.

char-woman, s. jornalera.

chary, a. circunspecto ; frugal.

chase, v.a. cazar ; perseguir ; cincelar ; —, s. caza.

chasing, s. cinceladura.

chasm, s. hendidura ; vacío, abismo.

chaste, a. casto ; puro ; púdico.

chasten, v.a. corregir, castigar.

chastise, v.a. castigar, reformar, corregir.

chastisement, s. castigo. [gir.

chastity, s. castidad, pureza.

chasuble, s. casulla.

chat, v.n. charlar ; —, s. charla, cháchara ; garrulidad.

chattel, s. bienes muebles, pl.

chatter, v.n. cotorrear ; charlar ; —, s. chirrido ; charla. [dor, gárrulo.

chatter-box, chatterer, s. parlero, habla-

chatty, a. locuaz, parlanchín.

chaw, v.a. *V.* chew

cheap, a. barato ; -ly á poco precio.

cheapen, v.a. regatear ; abaratar.

cheapness, s. baratura ; bajo precio.

cheat, v.a. engañar, defraudar ; trampear ; —, s. trampa, f. ; fraude, engaño ; trampista, fraudulento.

check, v.a. reprimir, refrenar ; registrar ; —, s. restricción ; freno ; represión ; cheque ; pagaré.

checker, v.a. taracear.

checker-work, s. taracea.

check-mate, s. jaque-mate (en ajedrez).

checkers, s. pl. juego de damas.

cheek, s. carrillo ; mejilla ; (col.) desvergüenza ; atrevimiento ; — by jowl, cara á cara.

cheek-bone, s. hueso del carrillo.

cheeky, a. (col.) impudente, audaz.

cheer, s. alegría ; aplauso ; buen humor ; vigor ; manjares, pl. ; —, v.a. animar, alentar, aclamar, aplaudir ; —, v.n. alegrarse. [alegremente.

cheerful, a. alegre, vivo, jovial ; -ly,

cheerfulness, cheeriness, cheerily, s. alegría ; buen humor.

cheerless, a. triste, melancólico.

cheese, s. queso.

cheese-dairy, s. quesera. [queso.

cheese-monger, s. quesero, el que vende

cheese-paring, s. raedura de queso ; (fig.) parsimonia.

chemical, a. químico.

chemist, s. químico ; boticario.

chemistry, s. química.

cheque, s. cheque.

chequered, a. taraceado ; variado. [teger.

cherish, v.a. mantener, fomentar, pro-

cheroot, especie de cigarro de India ó de Manila.

cherry, s. cereza.

cherry-stone, s. cuesco de cereza.

cherry-tree, s. cerezo.

cherub, s. querubín.

chess, s. juego del ajedrez.

chess-board, s. ajedrez (el tablero).

chess-man, s. pieza de ajedrez, peón.

chest, s. pecho ; arca ; — of drawers, cómoda.

chestnut, s. castaña ; color de castaña.

chestnut-tree, s. castaño.

chew, v.a. mascar, masticar ; rumiar meditar, reflexionar.

chicane, s. cavilación, trampa ; —, v.n. cavilar, sofisticar.

chicanery, s. sofistería, enredo.

chick(en), s. pollo, polluelo ; (fig.) joven.

chicken-hearted, a. cobarde, tímido, gallina.

chicken-pox, s. viruelas locas, pl.

chick-pea, s. garbanzo.

chicory, s. achicoria. [reñir, alborotar.

chide, v.a. reprobar, regañar ; —, v.n.

chider, s. regañón.

chief, a. principal, capital ; -ly, principalmente ; —, s. jefe, principal.

chieftain, s. jefe, caudillo, cacique.

chilblain, s. sabañon.

child, s. infante, niño, hijo ; hija ; from a —, desde niño ; with —, preñada, embarazada ; -bed, -birth, s. sobreparto.

childhood, s. infancia, niñez.

childish, a. pueril ; -ly, puerilmente.

childishness, s. puerilidad.

childless, a. sin hijos.

childlike, a. pueril.

children, s. pl. niños.

chill, a. frío, fresco ; —, s. frío, resfrío ; —, v. a. enfriar.

chilliness, s. calofrío ; tiritona

chilly, a. friolero, friolento.

chime, s. armonía ; el conjunto de campanas ; —, v.n. sonar con armonía ; concordar.

chimera, s. quimera. [mente.

chimerical, a. quimérico ; -ly, quimérica-

chimney, s. chimenea. [chimenea.

chimney-piece, s. dintel que adorna la

chimney-sweeper, s. limpia-chimeneas, deshollinador.

chin, s. barba.

china(-ware), s. porcelana, loza de China.

chine, s. espinazo ; solomo.

chink, s. grieta, hendedura, sonido de dinero ; —, v.n. resonar.

chintz, s. zaraza.

chip, v.a. desmenuzar, picar ; —, v.n. desprenderse pedacitos ; —, s. brizna, astilla ; raspadura fragmento

chiromancy, s. quiromancia.
chiropodist, s. pedicuro.   [chirrido.
chirp, v.n. chirriar, gorjear ; —, s. gorjeo,
chirping, s. canto de las aves.
chirrup, v.n. & s.   *V.* chirp.
chisel, s. escoplo, cincel ; —, v.a. escoplear, cincelar, grabar.
chit, s. niño ; tallo (del grano).
chit-chat, s. charla, parlería.
chitterlings, s. embuchado de tripas.
chivalrous, chivalric, a. caballeresco.
chivalry, s. caballería.
chives, s. pl. cebolleta.
chloral, s. (chem.) cloral.
chloroform, s. cloroformo.
chlorosis, s. (med.) clorosis.
chock-full, choke-full, a. de bote en bote,
completamente lleno.
chocolate, s. chocolate.
chocolate-pot, s. chocolatera.
choice, s. elección, preferencia ; —, a.
selecto, exquisito, excelente ; -ly,
escogidamente, primorosamente.
choiceness, s. delicadeza.
choir, s. coro.
choke, v.a. sofocar ; oprimir ; tapar ;
— v.n. sofocarse, ahogarse.
choker, s. (col.) cravata.
choler, s. cólera, f. ; bilis, ira.
cholera, s. cólera-morbo.
choleric, a. colérico.
choose, v.a. escoger, elegir.
chop, v.a. tajar, cortar ; picar ; —, v.n.
girar, mudar ; —, s. tajada de carne ;
costilla de ternera ó de carnero ; raja ;
-s, pl. quijadas, pl.
chopper, s. cuchillo de carnicero.
chopfallen, a.   *V.* chap-fallen.
chopping-block, s. tajo de cocina.
choppy, a. (mar) agitado.
choral, a. coral.
chord, s. cuerda ; —, v.a. encordar.
chorister, s. corista.
chorus, s. coro.
chough, s. (orn.), chova.
chrism, s. crisma.
christen, v.a. bautizar, cristianar.   [dad.
christendom, s. cristianismo ; cristian-
christening, s. bautismo.
Christian, a. & s. cristiano ; — name,
nombre de bautismo.
christianise, y.a. cristianizar.
Christianity, s. cristianismo,; cristiandad.
Christmas, s. Navidad, Natividad.
Christmas-box, s. aguinaldo.
chromatic, a. cromático.
chromolithography, s. cromolitografía.
chronic, a. crónico.
chronicle, s. crónica ; —, v.a. historiar,
relatar.
chronicler, s. cronista,

chronological, a. cronológico ; -ly,
cronológicamente.
chronology, s. cronología.
chronometer, s. cronómetro.
chrysalis, s. crisálida.
chub, s. bobio (pez).
chubby, a. gordo, cariancho.
chuck, v.a. dar una sobarbada ; (col.
tirar, arrojar, dejar ; —, s. sobarbada.
chuckle, v.a. cloquear ; —, v.n. reirse,
divertirse.   (antes).
chum, s. (col.) compañero (entre estudi-
chump, chunk, s. tajo, tronco.
church, s. iglesia.
churching, s. ceremonia de la purificación.
church-law, s. derecho canónico.
churchman, s. feligrés ; sacerdote,
eclesiástico.   [parroquia.
church-warden, s. prohombre de una
churchyard, s. cimenterio.
churl, s. patán, rústico.
churlish, a. rústico, grosero ; tacaño ;
-ly, rudamente, brutalmente.
churn, s. mantequera ; —, v.a. mazar,
batir la leche para hacer manteca.
cicatrice, s. cicatriz.
cider, s. sidra.
cigar, s. cigarro, tabaco.
cigarette, s. cigarro de papel, cigarillo.
cigar-holder, s. boquilla, portacigar-
ros.
cimeter, s. cimitarra.
cincture, s. cinto, ceñidor.
cinder, s. ceniza.
cinematograph, s. cinematógrafo.
cinnabar, s. cinabrio, bermellón.
cinnamon, s. canela.
cipher, s. cifra; cero; (fig.) cero, persona
insignificante ; —, v.n. numerar,
calcular.
circle, s. círculo ; corrillo ; asamblea ;
—, v.a. circundar ; cercar, ceñir ; —,
v.n. circular.
circlet, s. círculo pequeño, collar.
circuit, s. circuito ; recinto.
circuitous, a. tortuoso, indirecto.
circular, a. circular, redondo ; —, s. carta
circular.   [dor
circulate, v.n. circular ; moverse al rede-
circulation, s. circulación.
circumcise, v.a. circuncidar.
circumcision, s. circuncisión.
circumference, s. circunferencia ; circuito.
circumflex, s. acento circunflejo.
circumlocution, s. circunlocución, perífrasis.
circumnavigate, v.a. circumnavegar.
circumnavigation, s. circumnavegación.
circumscribe, v.a. circunscribir, confinar,
limitar.   [tación.
circumscription, s. circunscripción, limi-

circumspect, a. circunspecto, prudente, reservado.

circumspection, s. circunspección, prudencia.

circumstance, s. circunstancia, condición ; incidente.

circumstantial, a. accidental ; accesorio ; -ly, detalladamente.

circumvent, v.a. frustrar, enredar.

circus, s. circo.

cistern, s. cisterna.

citadel, s. ciudadela, fortaleza.

citation, s. citación, cita.

cite, v.a. citar ; alegar ; referirse.

cithern, s. cítara.

citizen, s. ciudadano.

citizenship, s. ciudadanía.

citron, cidra.

citron-tree, s. cidro.

city, s. ciudad.

civet, s. gato de algalia ; algalia.

civic, a. cívico. [cortésmente.

civil, a. civil ; cortés ; -ly, civilmente ;

civilian, s. juris consulto ; —, s. & a. civil (opuesto á *militar*).

civilisation, s. civilización.

civilise, v.a. civilizar.

civility, s. civilidad, urbanidad, cortesía.

clack, s. ruido continuo, estrépito ; —, v.n. cencerrear.

clad, a. vestido, cubierto.

claim, v.a. reclamar, pretender ; —, s. pretensión, reclamación ; derecho.

claimant, s. pretendiente ; demandador.

clam, v.a. empastar, pegar.

clamber, v.n. gatear, trepar.

clamminess, s. viscosidad.

clammy, a. viscoso, pegadizo.

clamorous, a. clamoroso, tumultuoso, estrepitoso ; -ly, clamorosamente.

clamour, s. clamor, grito ; —, v.n. vociferar, gritar. [empalmar, lañar.

clamp, s. empalmadura ; laña ; —, v.a.

clan, s. família, tribu, raza.

clandestine, a. clandestino, oculto ; -ly, clandestinamente. [v.n. rechinar.

clang, clank, s. rechino, retintín ; —,

clangorous, a. ruidoso, resonante.

clangour, s. rechinamiento.

clap, v.a. batir ; aplicar ; palmear ; —, s. estrépito ; golpe ; trueno ; palmoteo.

clapper, s. palmoteador ; badajo de campana ; cítola de molino.

clapping, s. palmada ; aplauso, palmoteo.

clap-trap, s. embeleco, embuste.

claret, s. clarete (vino).

clarification, s. clarificación.

clarify, v.a. clarificar, aclarar ; —, v.n. ponerse claro.

clarinet, s. clarinete.

clarion, s. clarín.

clash, v.n. rechinar ; encontrarse ; contradecir ; —, s. rechino, crujido ; estrépito ; disputa ; choque.

clasp, s. broche ; hebilla ; abrazo ; —, v.a. abrochar ; abrazar.

clasp-knife, s. navaja. [coordinar.

class, s. clase ; orden ; —, v.a. clasificar,

classic(al), a. clásico ; —, s. autor clásico.

classification, s. clasificación.

classify, v.a. clasificar. [ruido.

clatter, v.n. resonar ; hacer ruido ; —, s.

clause, s. cláusula ; artículo.

claustral, a. claustral.

clavicle, s. clavícula. [arañar.

claw, s. garra ; garfa ; —, v.a. desgarrar,

clay, s. arcilla.

clayey, clayish, a. arcilloso.

clay-pit, s. barrizal.

clean, a. limpio ; casto ; —, ad. enteramente ; —, v.a. limpiar.

cleanliness, s. limpieza.

cleanly, a. limpio ; puro, delicado.

cleanness, s. limpieza ; pureza.

cleanse, v.a. limpiar, purificar ; purgar.

clear, a. claro ; neto ; diáfano ; sereno ; evidente ; inocente ; -ly, claramente ; —, v.a. clarificar, aclarar ; justificar, absolver ; —, v.n. aclararse.

clearance, s. despejo, removimiento ; (mar.) patente ó certificado de pago de derechos de aduana.

clear-headed, a. perspicaz.

clearly, ad. claramente, evidentemente.

clearness, s. claridad, transparencia ; esplendor ; perspicacia ; sinceridad.

clear-sighted, a. perspicaz, juicioso.

clearstarch, v.a. almidonar.

cleave, v.a. hender ; partir ; dividir ; — v.n. pegarse.

cleaver, s. cuchillo de carnicero.

cleft, s. hendedura, abertura.

clematis, s. clemátide.

clemency, s. clemencia.

clement, a. clemente, benigno.

clenched, a. cerrado (dícese de la mano ó del puño).

clergy, s. clero. [ástico.

clergyman, s. clerigo, sacerdote, eclesiclerical, a. clerical, eclesiástico.

clerk, s. eclesiástico, clérigo ; estudiante ; escribiente.

clerkship, s. empleo de escribiente.

clever, a. diestro, hábil, mañoso ; propio ; -ly, diestramente, hábilmente.

cleverness, s. destreza, habilidad.

clew, s. ovillo de hilo ; (fig.) seña, guía, indicio para indagar un misterio ; (mar.) niño ó extremo de la vela.

click, v.n. retiñir ; —, s. retintín.

client, s. cliente.

cliff, s. peñasco ; roca escarpada.

climacteric, a. climaterico.

climate, s. clima ; temperatura.

climatic, a. relativo al clima.

climax, s. clímax.

climb, v.a. & n. escalar, trepar.

clinch, v.a. empuñar, cerrar el puño ; remachar un clavo ; fijar, asegurar.

cling, v.n. colgar, adherirse, pegarse.

clinic(al), a. clínico.

clink, v.a. hacer resonar ; —, v.n. retiñir, resonar ; —, s. retintín.

clinker, s. cagafierro ; escoria de horno.

clip, v.a. cortar ; escatimar.

clipper, s. cortador, cercenador de monedas ; (mar.) barco á vela ligero.

clippings, s. pl. tundizno.

clique, s. camarilla, pandilla, trinca.

cloak, s. capa ; pretexto ; —, v.n. encapotar ; —, v.a. paliar.

cloak-room, s. vestuario ; (rail.) depósito de equipajes.

clock, s. reloj ; what o'clock is it ? ¿ qué hora es ?

clock-maker, s. relojero.

clock-work, s. máquina de reloj ; mecanismo de resorte ó muelle.

clod, s. terrón ; zoquete ; —, v.n. coagularse.

clog, s. obstáculo ; galocha ; —, v.a. cargar, embarazar ; —, v.n. coagularse ; unirse.

cloister, s. claustro, monasterio.

close, v.a. cerrar ; concluir, terminar ; —, v.n. cerrarse, unirse ; —, s. cercado ; fin ; conclusión ; —, a. cerrado ; estrecho, angosto ; ajustado ; secreto ; avaro ; retirado ; cercano ; denso ; reservado ; —, ad. de cerca ; — by, junto, cerca.

close-fisted, a. apretado, avaro.

closely, ad. estrechamente ; secretamente, atentamente.

closeness, s. estrechez, espesura ; reclusión.

closet, s. retrete ; gabinete ; —, v.a. encerrar en un gabinete.

closure, s. cerradura ; conclusión.

clot, s. grumo, cuajarón, coágulo ; —, v.n. engrumecerse, coagularse.

cloth, s. paño ; mantel ; vestido ; lienzo.

clothe, v.a. vestir, cubrir.

clothes, s. pl. vestidura ; ropaje ; suit of —, s. traje ; bed—, cobertores, ropa de cama.

clothes-peg, s. percha.

clothier, s. pañero.

clothing, s. vestido.

cloud, s. nube ; nublado ; manchita ; (fig.) adversidad ; —, v.a. anublar, obscurecer ; —, v.n. anublarse, obscurecerse.

cloudily, ad. obscuramente.

cloudiness, s. nublosidad ; obscuridad.

cloudless, a. sin nubes, claro, sereno.

cloudy, a. nublado, nubloso ; obscuro ; sombrío, melancólico.

clout, s. rodilla ; remiendo ; —, v.a. remendar ; chapucear.

clove, s. clavo (especia).

clover, s. trébol ; to live in —, vivir lujosamente.

clown, s. patán, rústico ; payaso.

clownish, a. rústico ; grosero ; -ly, toscamente, groseramente.

cloy, v.a. saciar, hartar.

club, s. clava, cachiporra ; club ; —, v.n. contribuir ; unirse.

clue, s. V. clew.

clump, s. trozo sin forma ; bosquecillo.

clumsily, ad. zafiamente, groseramente.

clumsiness, s. zafiedad, rustiquez, grosería.

clumsy, a. tosco, pesado ; sin arte.

cluster, s. racimo ; manada ; pelotón ; —, v.a. agrupar ; —, v.n. arracimarse.

clutch, s. apresamiento, garras ; —, v.a. empuñar.

coach, s. coche ; carroza ; —, (col.) v.a. enseñar.

coach-box, s. pescante de coche.

coach-hire, s. alquiler de coche.

coach-house, s. cochera.

coachman, s. cochero.

coadjutor, s. coadjutor, compañero.

coagulate, s.a. coagular, cuajar ; —, v.n. coagularse, cuajarse, espesarse.

coagulation, s. coagulación.

coal, s. carbón de piedra.

coalesce, v.n. juntarse, incorporarse.

coalescence, s. unión, incorporación.

coal-heaver, s. mozo de carbonero.

coal-hole, s. carbonera.

coalition, s. coalición, confederación.

coal-mine, coal-pit, s. mina de carbón, carbonería.

coal-scuttle, s. caja de carbon.

coarse, a. basto, rústico, grosero ; -ly, groseramente.

coarseness, s. tosquedad, grosería.

coast, s. costa ; —, v.n. costear.

coaster, s. buque costanero, costero.

coastguard, s. guardacosta.

coat, s. casaca ; frac ; hábito ; saya ; saco ; — of mail, cota de malla ; — of arms, escudo.

coating, s. capa, mano (de pintura).

coax, v.a. lisonjear, acariciar.

coaxer, s. adulador, mimador.

cob, s. mazorca de maíz ; caballo bajo y fuerte.

cobble, v.a. chapucear ; remendar (zapatos) ; —, s. piedra redonda de empedrado.

cobbler, s. remendón.

cobweb, s. telaraña.

cochineal, s. cochinilla, grana.
cock, s. gallo; pájaro macho; pie de gato de escopeta; weather—, veleta; hay—, montoncillo de heno; at half —, desamartillado (fusil); at full — amartillado, montado (fusil): —, v.a. amartillar, montar una escopeta.
cockade, s cucarda.
cock-a-doodle-doo, s. canto del gallo.
cockatoo, s. cacatoy.
cockatrice, s. basilisco.
cock-chafer, s. especie de escarabajo.
cock-crow, s. canto del gallo; alba.
cocker, v.a. (col.) acariciar, mimar.
cockerel, s. gallipollo.
cock-fight(ing), s. riña de gallos.
cockle, s. caracol de mar; (bot.) zizaña; —, v.a. arrugar; doblar; —, v.n. plegarse, doblarse.
cock-loft, s. desván, zaquizamí.
cockney, s. (col.) Londinense, habitante de la capital.
cock-pit, s. reñidero de gallos; (mar.) entarimado del sollado.   [currutaco.
cock's comb, s. cresta de gallo; (fig.)
cockswain, coxwain, s. patrón de bote.
cockroach, s. escarabajo negro.
cocoa, s. cacao.
cocoa-nut, s. coco.
cocoon, s. capullo de insecto.
cod, s. bacalao; merluza; (bot.) vaina.
coddle, v.a. acariciar; afeminar.
code, s. código.
codicil, s. (law) codicilo.
codify, v.a. codificar.
cod-liver oil, s. aceite de merluza.
coefficient, s. coeficiente.
coequal, a. igual.
coerce, v.a. refrenar; restringir, obligar.
coercion, s. coerción, opresión.
coercive, a. coercitivo.
coeval, a. & s coevo; contemporáneo.
coexistence, s. coexistencia.
coffee, s. café.
coffee-berry, s. fruto del café.
coffee-house, s. café.
coffee-pot, s. cafetera.
coffer, s. cofre; caja.   [en un ataúd.
coffin, s. féretro, ataúd; —, v.a. meter
cog, s. diente (de rueda).
cogency, s. urgencia.
cogent, a. convincente, urgente; -ly, de un modo convincente.
cogitate, v.n. pensar, meditar.
cogitation, s. meditación.
cognate, a. cognado.
cognition, s. conocimiento; convicción.
cognizance, s. conocimiento; divisa.
cognizant, a. informado; (law) competente.
cog-wheel, s, rueda dentada.

cohabit, v.n. cohabitar.
cohabitation, s. cohabitación.
coheir, s. coheredero.
coheiress, s. coheredera.   [conformarse.
cohere, v.n. pegarse; unirse; convenir,
coherence, s. coherencia, conexión.
coherent, a. coherente; consiguiente.
cohesion, s. coherencia.
cohesive, a. coherente.
coif, s. cofia, redecilla.
coil, v.a. recoger; to — a cable, (mar.) adujar un cable; —, s. baraúnda; fracaso; (mar.) adujada.
coin, s. rincón; moneda acuñada; dinero; —, v.a. acuñar moneda, falsificar; inventar.
coinage, s. acuñación, braceaje; falsificación; invención.
coincide, v.n. coincidar, concurrir.
coincidence, s. coincidencia.
coincident, a. coincidente.
coiner, s. acuñador de moneda, monedero falso; inventor.
coke, s. cok.
colander, s. coladera; colador.
cold, a. frío; indiferente, insensible; reservado; -ly, fríamente; indiferentemente; —, s. frío: frialdad.
cold-blooded, a. impasible.
coldness, s. frialdad; indiferencia, insensibilidad, apatía.
cole-wort, s. (bot.) berza verde.
colic, s. cólico.
collaborate, v.a. cooperar, colaborar.
collaboration, s. cooperación, colaboración.
collapse, v.n. descaecer; —, s. hundimiento; (med.) colapso.
collar, s. cuello (de camisa), collar; collera; —, (col.) v.a. agarrar á uno de los cabezones; arrollar.
collar-bone, s. clavícula.
collate, v.a. comparar.
collateral, a. colateral; indirecto; -ly, colateralmente; indirectamente.
collation, s. colación; comparación.
colleague, s. colega, compañero.
collect, v.a. recoger, colegir; —, s. colecta.
collection, s. colección; compilación.
collective, a. colectivo, congregado; -ly, colectivamente.
college, s. colegio.   [colegio.
collegian, s. colegial, miembro de un
collegiate, a. colegial.
collide, v.n. ludir, chocar.
collie (dog), s. perro de pastor.
collier, s. carbonero; barco carbonero.
colliery, s. mina de carbón.
collision, s. colisión; ludimiento.
collocation, s, colocación.

collonade, s. columnata, galeria de columnas.

collop, s. tajada (pequeña) de carne.

colloquial, a. íntimo, familiar; **-ly,** familiarmente.

col'oquialism, s. idiotismo familiar.

colloquy, s. coloquio; conversación, plática.

collusion, s. colusión.   [mente.

collusive, a. colusorio; **-ly,** colusoria-

colon, s. (gr.) colon (:).

colonel, s. (mil.) coronel.

colonelcy, s. coronelía.

colonial, a. colonial.

colonise, v.a. colonizar.

colonist, s. colono.

colony, s. colonia.

colossal, a. colosal.

colossus, s. coloso.

colour, s. color; pretexto; **-s,** pl. bandera; —, **v.a.** colorar; paliar; —, **v.n.** ponerse colorado.

colourable, a. especioso, plausible.

colourably, ad. plausiblemente.

colour-blind, a. daltoniano.]

colouring, s. colorido.

colourist, s. colorista.

colourless, a. descolorido, sin color.

colt, s. potro; (fig.) mozuelo sin juicio.

colter, s. reja de arado.

columbine, s. (bot.) aguileña.

column, s. columna.

columnar, a. columnario.

coma, s. coma; letargo.

comatose, a. comatoso.   [(lana).

comb, s. peine; —, **v.a.** peinar; cardar

combat, s. combate; batalla; single —, duelo; —, **v.n.** combatir; —, **v.a.** resistir.

combatant, s. combatiente.

combative, a. quisquilloso.   [nación.

combination, s. combinación, coordi-

combine, v.a. combinar; —, **v.n.** unirse.

combustible, a. & s. combustible.

combustion, s. combustión; incendio.

come, v.n. venir; acontecer; proceder.

comedian, s. comediante, cómico.

comedy, s. comedia.

comeliness, s. gracia; garbo, hermosura.

comely, a. garboso, decente.

comestible, a. comestible.

comet, s. cometa.

comfit, s. confite.

comfort, s. ayuda; consuelo; comodidad, agrado; —, **v.a.** confortar; alentar, consolar.

comfortable, a. cómodo, consolatorio.

comfortably, ad. agradablemente, cómodamente.

comforter, consolador; bufanda.   [able.

comfortless, a. desconsolado; desagrad-

comic(al), a. original, divertido, risible; **-ly,** risiblemente.

comicalness, s. gracejo, chiste.

coming, s. venida, llegada; —, **a.** venidero.

comma, s. (gr.) coma.

command, v.a. mandar, ordenar; —, **v.n.** gobernar; —, **s.** orden, mando, mandamiento.

commander, s. comandante.

commandment, s. mandato, precepto.

commemorate, v.a. conmemorar; celebrar.

commemoration, s. conmemoración.

commence, v.a. & n. comenzar, empezar

commencement, s. principio.

commend, v.a. encomendar; alabar.

commendable, a. recomendable.

commendably, ad. loablemente.

commendation, s. recomendación.

commendatory, a. recomendatorio

commensurate, v.a. conmensurar; —, **a.** commensurativo, proporcionado.

comment, s. comento; glosa; —, **v.a.** comentar, glosar.   [tación.

commentary, s. comentario; interpre-

commentator, s. comentador.   [negocio.

commerce, s. comercio, tráfico, trato.

commercial, a. comercial.

commination, s. conminación, amenaza

comminatory, a. conminatorio.

commingle, v.a. (& n.) mezclar(se).

commiserate, v.a. compadecer.

commiseration, s. conmiseración, compasión.

commissariat, s. (mil.) abastecimiento, provisión de víveres

commissary, s. comisario.

commission, s. comisión; patente; —, **v.a.** comisionar; encargar, apoderar

commissioner, s. comisionado, delegado.

commit, v.a. cometer; depositar; en cargar.

commitment, committal, s. auto de prisión.

committee, s. junta, comité.

commodious, a. cómodo, conveniente; **-ly,** cómodamente.

commodity, s. ventaja, utilidad; provecho; comodidad; mercaderías, pl.

commodore, s. (mar.) jefe de escuadra.

common, a. común; ordinario; in —, comúnmente; —, **s.** pasto comunal.

commonage, s. derecho de pastar ganados en algún común.

commonalty, s. comunidad, pueblo.

common-council, s. concejo municipal.

commoner, s. miembro de la cámara baja (en Inglaterra); ciudadano pechero

common-law, s. derecho fundamental[y] acostumbrado.

commonly, ad. comúnmente ; frecuente-
mente.
commonness, s. frecuencia ; vulgaridad.
common-place, s. lugares comunes, pl.;
—, a. trivial.
commons, s.pl. generalidad del pueblo ;
cámara baja (en Inglaterra).
commonweal(th), s. república, estado.
commotion, s. tumulto ; perturbación del
ánimo.
commune, v.a. conversar, conferir.
communicable, a. comunicable, **im-
partible.**
communicant, s. (eccl.) comulgante.
communicate, v.a. comunicar, participar;
participar ; — v.n. comulgar.
communication, s. comunicación ; participación.
communicative, a. comunicativo.
communicativeness, s. carácter comunicativo.
communion, s. comunidad ; comunión.
communism, s. comunismo.
communist, s. comunista.
community, s. comunidad ; república.
commutable, a. conmutable, cambiable.
commutation, s. conmutación, trueco.
commute, v.a. conmutar, trocar.
compact, a. compacto, sólido, denso ; —,
s. pacto, convenio ; **-ly,** estrechamente,
con brevedad.
compactness, s. solidez, densidad.
companion, s. compañero, socio.
companionable, a. sociable.
companionship, s. sociedad, compañía.
company, s. compañía, sociedad ; compañía de comercio.
comparable, a. comparable.
comparative, a. comparativo ; **-ly,** com-
parativamente.
compare, v.a. comparar, cotejar ; —,
s. comparación ; semejanza.   [símil.
comparison, s. comparación, cotejo ;
compartment, s. compartimiento.
compass, s. circuito, alcance ; circunferencia ; compás de la voz ; compás ;
brújula ; —, v.a. circundar ; conseguir;
acabar.   [para trazar círculos).
compasses, s.pl. compás (instrumento
compassion, s. compasión, sinpatía.
compassionate, v.a. compadecer ; —, a.
compasivo.
compatibility, s. compatibilidad.
compatible, a. compatible.
compatriot, s. compatriota, paisano.
compeer, s. colega, el que es par ó igual
en razón.
compel, v.a. obligar, constreñir, forzar.
compendium, s. compendio, epítome.
compendious, a. compendioso, sucinto,
breve ; **-ly,** compendiosamente.

compensate, v.a. compensar.   [miento.
compensation, s. compensación ; resarci-
compete, v.n. concurrir, competir.
competence, s. suficiencia.
competent, a. competente, bastante ;
-ly, competentemente, hábilmente.
competition, s. competencia ; concurrencia.   [(exámen).
competitive, a. de concurso ó oposición
competitor, s. competidor, rival.
compilation, s. compilación.
compile, v.a. compilar.
complacence, complaisance, s. complacencia, deferencia, cortésia.
complacent, complaisant, a. complaciente,
afable, cortés.
complain, v.n. quejar(se), lamentar(se).
complaint, s. queja ; lamento, llanto,
▸ quejido ; (col.) enfermedad.
complement, s. complemento.
complete, a. completo, perfecto ; **-ly**
completamente ; —, v.a. completar
acabar.
completion, s. complemento, colmo.
complex, a. complexo, compuesto ; complicado.
complexion, s. tez, aspecto.
complexioned, complexionado.
complexity, s. complexo.
compliance, s. complacencia, sumisión,
condescendencia.
compliant, a. complaciente, oficioso.
complicate, v.a. complicar.
complication, s. complicación.
complicity, s. complicidad.
compliment, s. cumplimiento ; —, v.a.
cumplimentar ; hacer ceremonias.
complimentary, a. cumplimentero, ceremonioso ; laudatorio.
compline, s. completas, pl. (vísperas).
comply, v.n. cumplir ; conformarse,
ceder, asentir.
component, a. componente.
comport, v.n. convenir, concordar ; — v.r.
portarse, comportarse.
compose, v.a. componer ; sosegar ;
concertar, reglar, ordenar.
composed, a. compuesto, moderato ; **-ly,**
tranquilamente, serenamente.
composer, s. compositor (de música).
composition, s. composición ; compuesto ;
accomodamiento.
compositor, s. cajista.
compost, s. abono, estiércol.
composure, s. tranquilidad, sangre fría.
compound, v.a. componer, combinar ; —,
v.n. concertarse ; ajustar ; —, a. & s.
compuesto.   [entender.
comprehend, v.a. comprender, contener ;
comprehensible, a. comprensible ; **-ly,**
comprensiblemente.

comprehension, s. comprensión; inteligencia. [comprensivamente.
comprehensive,' a. comprensivo; -ly,
comprehensiveness, s. alcance, cabida.
compress, v.a. comprimir, estrechar; —, s. (med.) cabezal.
compression, s. compresión.
comprise, v.a. comprender, incluir.
compromise, s. compromiso, acomodamiento; —, v.a. comprometer.
(**compulsion, s.** compulsión; apremio.
compulsive, compulsory, a. compulsivo; -ly, por fuerza.
compunction, s. compunción, contrición.
computable, a. computable, calculable.
computation, s. computación, cuenta hecha.
compute, v.a. computar, calcular.
comrade, s. camarada, compañero.
con, ad. pro and —, en favor y en contra; —, v.a. meditar, estudiar, reflexionar.
concatenation, s. encadenamiento; serie.
concave, a. cóncavo.
concavity, s. concavidad.
conceal, v.a. ocultar, esconder.
concealment, s. ocultación; encubrimiento.
concede, v.a. conceder, asentir.
conceit, s. concepción; capricho; pensamiento; presunción; —, v.n. imaginar, creer.
conceited, a. afectado, vano, presumido; -ly, fantásticamente, con vanidad.
conceivable, a. concebible, inteligible.
conceive, v.a. concebir, comprender; imaginar.
concentrate, v.a. concentrar.
concentration, s. concentración.
concentric(al), a. concéntrico.
conception, s. concepción; sentimiento.
concern, v.a. concernir, importar, pertenecer; interesar; afligir; —, s. negocio; interés; importancia, consecuencia; afecto.
concerning, pr. tocante á; sobre.
concert, s. concierto; convenio; —, v.a. (& n.) concertar(se).
concession, s. concesión, privilegio.
conch, s. concha.
conciliate, v.a. conciliar; atraer.
conciliation, s. conciliación.
conciliator, s. conciliador.
conciliatory, a. conciliativo, complaciente.
concise, a. conciso, sucinto; -ly, concisamente.
conciseness, s. concisión; laconismo.
conclave, s. conclave.
conclude, v.a. concluir; decidir; determinar. [fin.
conclusion, s. conclusión, determinación;

conclusive, a. decisivo, conclusivo; -ly, concluyentemente. [madurar.
concoct, v.a. cocer, componer, preparar;
concoction, s. maduración, preparación; (col.), brebaje ó manjar estraño.
concomitant, a. concomitante.
concord, s. concordia, armonía; buena inteligencia.
concordance, s. concordancia.
concordant, a. concordante, conforme.
concordat, s. concordato; convenio.
concourse, s. concurso; multitud, gentío.
concrete, a. concreto; s. cimiento, argamasa.
concretion, s. concreción; agregado.
concubinage, s. concubinato, amancebamiento.
concubine, s. concubina, manceba.
concupiscence, s. concupiscencia, codicia.
concur, v.n. concurrir; juntarse.
concurrence, s. concurrencia; unión; concordia, asenso.
concussion, s. concusión, golpe.
condemn, v.a. condenar; desaprobar; vituperar.
condemnation, s. condenación.
condemnatory, a. condenatorio.
condensation, s. condensación.
condense, v.a. & n. condensar(se).
condescend, v.n. condescender; consentir.
condescension, s. condescendencia.
condign, a. condigno, merecido.
condiment, s. condimento; salsa.
condition, s. situación, condición, calidad; estado.
conditional, a. condicional, hipotético; -ly, condicionalmente.
conditioned, a. acondicionado.
condole, v.n. condoler(se), compadecer.
condolence, s. compasión, lástima.
condonation, s. perdón, condonación.
condone, v.a. perdonar, condonar.
conduce, v.a. conducir, concurrir.
conducive, a. conducente, oportuno.
conduct, s. conducta; manejo, proceder; conducción (de tropas); —, v.a. conducir, guiar.
conductor, s. conductor; guía, director; conductor de electricidad.
conduit, s. conducto; caño.
cone, cono.
confabulate, v.n. (col.) platicar.
confection, s. confitura; confección.
confectioner, s. confitero.
confectionery, s. dulces, confites.
confederacy, s. confederación.
confederate, v.n. confederarse; —, a. & s. confederado. [gar, dar.
confer, v.n. conferenciar; —, v.a. otorconference, s.** conferencia.

confess, v.a. (& n.) confesar(se).
confessedly, ad. conocidamente, sin contradicción.
confession, s. confesión.
confessional, s. confesionario.
confessor, s. confesor.
confidant, s. confidente, amigo íntimo.
confide, v.a. & n. confiar ; fiarse.
confidence, s. confianza, seguridad.
confident, a. cierto, seguro ; confiado ; atrevido. [fianza.
confidential, a. confidencial ; de confiding, a. sin sospechas.
configuration, s. configuración.
confine, s. confín, límite ;' —, v.a. limitar ; aprisionar ; —, v.n. confinar.
confinement, s. prisión, encierro ; sobreparto.
confirm, v.a. confirmar ; ratificar.
confirmation, s. confirmación ; ratificación : prueba. [firmativo.
confirmative, confirmatory, a. confiscate, v.a. confiscar.
confiscation, s. confiscación. [general.
conflagration, s. conflagración, incendio
conflict, s. conflicto ; combate ; pelea ; —, v.a. contender ; combatir, discordar.
confluence, s. confluencia ; concurso.
confluent, a. confluente.
conform, v.a. (& n.) conformar(se).
conformable, a. conforme, conveniente ; -bly, conformemente, segun.
conformation, s. conformación.
conformity, s. conformidad, conveniencia.
confound, v.a. turbar, confundir ; destruir. [comparar.
confront, v.a. afrontar ; confrontar ;
confraternity, s. cofradía, hermandad.
confuse, v.a. confundir ; desordenar.
confusedly, ad. confusamente.
confusion, s. confusión ; peturbación ; desorden.
confute, v.a. confutar, refutar.
congeal, v.a. (& n.) helar, congelar(se).
congelation, s. congelación.
congenial, a. congenial.
congeniality, s. semejanza de genio, simpatía de carácter.
congenital, a. congénito.
conger, s. congrio.
congestion, s. congestión ; formación de una masa, acumulación.
conglomerate, v.a. conglomerar, aglomerar ; —, a. aglomerado.
conglomeration, s. aglomeración.
congratulate, v.a. congratular, felicitar.
congratulation, s. congratulación.
congratulatory, a. congratulatorio.
congregate, v.a. & n. congregar(se), reunir(se) con.
congregation, s. congregación, reunión.

congress, s. congreso ; conferencia.
congruity, s. congruencia.
congruous, a. idóneo, congruo, apto.
conic(al), a. cónico ; -ally, en forma cónica.
coniferous, a. (bot.) conífero.
conjectural, a. conjetural ; -ly, conjeturalmente.
conjecture, s. conjetura, opinión ; —, v.a. conjeturar ; pronosticar.
conjoin, v.a. juntar ; asociar ; — v.n. unirse, ligarse.
conjoint, a. asociado, confederado.
conjugal, a. conyugal, matrimonial ; -ly, conyugalmente.
conjugate, v.a. (gr.) conjugar.
conjugation, s. (gr.) conjugación.
conjunction, s. conjunción ; unión.
conjunctive, a. conjunto ; conjuntivo.
conjuncture, s. coyuntura ; ocasión ; tiempo crítico. [spiración.
conjuration, s. súplica ardiente ; conjure, v.a. rogar, pedir con instancia ; — v.n. conjurar, exorcizar ; encantar ; hechizar.
conjurer, s. conjurador, encantador.
connect, v.a. juntar, unir, enlazar.
connectedly, ad. coordinadamente, lógicamente.
connexion, s. conexión, relación.
connivance, s. connivencia.
connive, v.n. guiñar el ojo ; tolerar.
connoisseur, s. conocedor.
connubial, a. conyugal, matrimonial.
conquer, v.a. conquistar ; vencer.
conqueror, s. vencedor, conquistador.
conquest, s. conquista.
consanguineous, a. consanguíneo.
consanguinity, s. consanguinidad.
conscience, s conciencia, escrúpulo.
conscientious, a. concienzudo, escrupuloso ; -ly, según conciencia, honradamente. [das.
conscious, a. sabedor ; -ly, á sabiendas.
conscript, a. conscripto.
conscription, s. asiento en algún registro ; (mil.) reclutamiento.
consecrate, v.a. consagrar ; dedicar.
consecration, s. consagración.
consecutive, a. consecutivo ; -ly, consecutivamente.
consent, s consentimiento, asenso ; aprobación ; —, v.n. consentir ; aprobar. [[ancia.
consequence, s. consecuencia ; import-
consequent, a. consecutivo, resultante ; -ly, consiguientemente.
consequential, a. presumido.
conservation, s. conservación.
conservative, a. conservativo, conservador
conservator, s. conservador ; defensor.

conservatory, s. invernáculo.

conserve, v.a. conservar.

consider, v.a. considerar, examinar ; —, v.n. pensar, deliberar.

considerable, a. considerable ; importante ; -bly, considerablemente.

considerate, a. discreto ; atento, razonable ; -ly, juiciosamente ; atentamente.

consideration, s. consideración ; deliberación ; importancia ; valor, mérito.

considering, ad. en atención á ; — that, á causa de ; visto que, en razón á.

consign, v.a. consignar.

consignee, s. agente.

consignment, s. consignación.

consist, v.n. consistir ; corresponder, acordarse.   [pondencia.

consistence(cy), s. consistencia, corres-

consistent, a. consistente ; conveniente, conforme ; -ly, conformemente.

consistory, s. consistorio.

consolable, a. consolable.

consolation, s. consolación ; consuelo.

consolatory, a. consolatorio.

console, v.a. consolar.

consolidate, v.a. (& n.) consolidar(se).

consolidation, s. consolidación.   [pl.

consols, s. pl. consolidados (fondos),

consonance, s. consonancia ; armonía.

consonant, a. consonante, conforme ; —, s. (gr.) consonante.

consort, s. consorte, socio ; esposo ; esposa ; —, v.n. asociarse.

conspicuous, a. conspicuo, aparente ; notable ; -ly, claramente, insignemente.

conspiracy, s. conspiración.

conspirator, s. conspirador.

conspire, v.n. conspirar, maquinar.

constable, s. condestable; alguacil,guardia.

constabulary, s. policía, guardia civil.

constancy, s. constancia, perseverancia, persistencia.

constant, a. constante ; perseverante ; -ly, constantemente.

constellation, s. constelación.   [terror.

consternation, s. consternación ; pasmo,

constipate, v.a. obstruir ; (med) constipar.

constituency, s. distrito electoral.

constituent, s. constitutivo ; —, a. constituyente, votador.   [formar.

constitute, v.a. constituir ; establecer ;

constitution, s. constitución ; estado ; temperamento.

constitutional, a. constitucional, legal.

constrain, v.a. constreñir, forzar ; restringir.

constrainedly, ad. por fuerza.

constraint, s. constreñimiento ; fuerza, violencia.

constrict, v.a. constreñir, estrechar.

constringent, a. constrictivo.

construct, v.a. construir, edificar.

construction, s. construcción ; interpretación.

constructive, a. inductivo.

construe, v.a. construir ; interpretar.

consul, s. cónsul.

consular, a. consular.

consulate, consulship, s. consulado.

consult, v.a. & n. consultar, deliberar.

consultation, s. consulta, deliberación.

consumable, a. consumible, destruible.

consume, v.a. consumir ; disipar ; v.n. consumirse.

consumer, s. consumidor, comprador.

consummate, v.a. consumar, acabar, perfeccionar ; —, a. cumplido, consumado

consummation, s. consumación, perfección.   [tisis.

consumption, s. consunción ; consumo ;

consumptive, a. tísico, ético.

contact, s. contacto.

contagion, s. contagio.

contagious, a. contagioso.

contain, v.a. contener, comprender ; reprimir, refrenar.

contaminate, v.a. contaminar ; corromper ; —, a. contaminado, corrompido.

contamination, s. contaminación.

contemn, v.a. despreciar, menospreciar, desestimar ; desdeñar.

contemplate, v.a. contemplar.

contemplation, s. contemplación.

contemplative, a. contemplativo ; -ly, con atención y estudio.

contemporaneous, contemporary, a. contemporáneo.

contempt, s. desprecio, desdén.

contemptible, a. despreciable, vil ; -bly, vilmente.

contemptuous, a. desdeñoso, insolente ; -ly, con desdén.   [alegar.

contend, v.n. contender, disputar, argüir,

content, a. contento, satisfecho ; —, v.a. contentar, satisfacer ; —, s. contento satisfacción ; -s, pl. contenido.

contentedly, ad. de un modo satisfecho ; con paciencia.

contention, s. contención, altercación ; argumento, alegación.

contentious, a. contencioso, litigioso ; -ly, contenciosamente.

contentment, s. contentamiento, placer, contento.

contest, v.a. contestar, disputar, litigar, —, s. disputa, contestación, altercación.

context, s. contexto ; contextura.

contiguity, s. contigüidad,

contiguous, a. contiguo, vecino.
continence(cy), s. continencia ; castidad.
continent, a. continente, casto ; -ly, casta-
mente ; —, s. continente.
continental, a. continental.
contingency, s. contingencia ; acontecimiento ; eventualidad.
contingent, a. contingente ; cuota ; —,
a. contingente, casual ; -ly, casualmente.   [mente.
continual, a. continuo ; -ly, continua-
continuance, s. permanencia ; duración.
continuation, s. continuación, serie.
continue, v.a. continuar ; —, v.n. durar,
perseverar, persistir.   [miento.
continuity, s. continuidad, encadena-
continuous, a. continuo, unido.
contort, v.a. torcer.
contortion, s. contorsión.
contour, s. contorno.   [hibido, ilegal.
contraband, s. contrabando ; —, a. pro-
contrabandist, s. contrabandista.
contract, v.a. contraer ; abreviar ; contratar ; —, v.n. contraerse ; —, s. contrato, pacto.   [tura.
contraction, s. contracción ; abrevia-
contractor, s. contratante.
contradict, v.a. contradecir.
contradiction, s. contradicción, oposición.
contradictoriness, s. oposición.
contradictory, a. contradictorio.
contrariety, contrariness, s. contrariedad,
oposición.
contrary, a. contrario, opuesto ; —, s.
contrario ; on the —, al contrario.
contrariwise, ad. al contrario.
contrast, s. contraste ; oposición ; —, v.a.
contrastar, oponer.
contravene, v.a. contravenir. infringir.
contravention, s. contravención.
contributary, a. contributario.
contribute, v.a. contribuir, ayudar.
contribution, s. contribución ; tributo.
contributor, s. contribuidor.
contributory, contributive, a. contribuyente ; tributario.
contrite, a. contrito, arrepentido.
contrition, s. penitencia, contrición.
contrivance, s. designio ; invención ; concepto.   [manejar ; combinar.
contrive, v.a. inventar, trazar, maquinar;
control, s. autoridad, mando ; inspección;
—, v.a. restringir ; gobernar ; registrar.
controller, s. veedor, registrador, inspector
controversial, a. polémico.
controversy, s. controversia.
controvert, v.a. controvertir, disputar.
contumacious, a. contumaz ; -ly, con-
tumazmente.
contumacy, s. contumacia, resistencia.

contumelious, a. contumelioso, injurioso
-ly, contumeliosamente.
contumely, s. contumelia, injuria.
contusion, s. contusión.
conundrum, acertijo, enigma.
convalescence, convalencia.
convalescent, a. convaleciente.
convene, v.a. convocar ; juntar, unir ; —,
v.n. convenir, juntarse.
convenience, s. conveniencia, comodidad,
conformidad.
convenient, a. conveniente, apto, cómodo,
propio ; -ly, cómodamente, oportunamente.   [terio.
convent, s. convento, claustro, monas-
conventicle, s. conventículo.
convention, s. convención ; contrato,
tratado.   [ordinario.
conventional, a. convencional, estipulado;
conventual, a. conventual.
converge, v.n. convergir.
convergence, s. convergencia.
convergent, a. convergente.
conversable, a. conversable, sociable.
conversant, a. versado.   [dad.
converation, s. conversación, familiari-
converse, v.n. conversar ; platicar ; —, s.
conversación, plática ; familiaridad ;
comercio.   [mente.
conversely, ad. mutuamente, recíproca-
conversion, s. conversión, transmutación.
convert, v.a. (& n.) convertir(se) ; —, s.
converso, convertido.
convertible, a. convertible, transmutable.
convex, a. convexo.
convexity, s. convexidad.
convey, v.a. transportar ; transmitir,
trasferir, transferir.
conveyance, s. transporte ; conducción ;
(law) traspaso, escritura de traspaso.
conveyancer, s. notario que hace la
escritura de traspaso.
convict, v.a. convencer, probar un delito,
condenar ; —, s. convicto, condenado,
conviction, s. convicción ; refutación.
convince, v.a. convencer, persuadir.
convincingly, ad. de un modo convincente.
convivial, a. sociable ; hospitalario.
conviviality, s. sociabilidad.
convocation, s. convocación ; sínodo.
convoke, v.a. convocar, reunir.
convulvulus, s. convólvulo.
convoy, v.a. convoyar, escoltar ; —, s.
convoy ; escolta.
convulse, v.a. conmover, trastornar.
convulsion, s. convulsión ; conmoción ;
tumulto.   [sivamente.
convulsive, a. convulsivo ; -ly, convul-
cony, s. conejo.
coo, v.n. arrullar,

cooing, s. arrullo de palomas ; halago.
cook, s. cocinero ; cocinera ; —, v.a. aderezar las viandas ; —, v.n. cocinar ; guisar.
cookery, s. arte culinaria, cocina.
cool, a. fresco ; indiferente ; —, s. frescura ; —, v.a. enfriar, refrescar, atemperar.
cooler, s. enfriadera ; (med.) refrigerante.
coolly, ad. frescamente ; indiferentemente.
coolness, s. fresco ; frialdad, frescura.
coop, s. caponera ; redil ; —, v.a. enjaular, encarcelar.
cooper, s. cubero, tonelero.
cooperate, v.n. cooperar.
cooperation, s. cooperación.
cooperative, a. cooperativo ; cooperante.
coordination, s. coordinación.
coot, s. (orn.) negreta.
copartner, s. compañero, socio.
cope, s. capa ; cobertura ; —, v.n. competir, lidiar con otro.
copier, s. copista.
coping, albardilla, caballete de un muro.
copious, a. copioso, abundante ; -ly, en abundancia.
copiousness, s. abundancia, copia.
copper, s. cobre,; calderón ; moneda de cobre, calderilla.
copperas, s. caparrosa.   [estampa.
copper-plate, s. lámina de cobre ;
coppersmith, s. calderero.
coppice, **copse**, s. bosquecillo, soto, tallar.
copy, s. copia ; ejemplar de algún libro ; —, v.a. copiar ; imitar.
copying-clerk, s. expedicionero.
copying-machine, **-press**, s. copiador.
copyist, s. copista.
copyright, s. propiedad de una · obra literaria ; derechos de autor, pl.
coquet, v.n. coquetear, cortejar.
coquetry, s. coquetería.
coquettish, a. pisaverde, coqueta.
coral, s. coral.
cord, s. cuerda ; cordel ; montón de leña ; —, v.a. encordelar.
cordage, s. cordaje.
cordial, a. cordial, de corazón, amistoso ; -ly, cordialmente ; —, s. remedio confortativo.
cordiality, s. cordialidad.   [espeso.
corduroy, s. especie de paño duro y
core, s. cuesco ; interior, centro, corazón.
cork, s. alcornoque ; corcho ; —, v.a. tapar botellas con corchos.
cork-screw, s. tirabuzón.
cormorant, s. corvejón ; glotón.
corn, s. grano ; callo ; —, v.a. salar (carne)
corn-cob, s. (am.) mazorca.
cornelian, cornerina.

corner, s. ángulo ; rincón, esquina.
corner-stone, s. mocheta.
cornet, s. corneta ; alférez.
cornetcy, s. alferecía.
corn-exchange, s. lonja de granos.
corn-field, s. sembrado.
corn-flower, s. azulejo, aciano.
cornice, s. cornisa.
corollary, s. corolario.
coronation, s. coronación.
coroner, s. oficial que hace la inspección jurídica de los cadáveres.
coronet, s. corona pequeña.
corporal, s. cabo, caporal ; —, a. corpóreo; material ; -ly, corporalmente.
corporate, a. formado en cuerpo ó en comunidad.
corporation, s. corporación ; gremio.
corporeal, a. corpóreo.
corps, s. cuerpo de ejército ; regimiento.
corpse, s. cadáver.
corpulence(cy), s. corpulencia.
corpulent, a. corpulento, gordo.
corpuscle, corpúsculo.
correct, v.a. corregir, reprender, castigar; enmendar, amonestar ; —, a. correcto, revisto ; -ly, correctamente.
correction, s. corrección ; castigo ; enmienda ; censura.   [restricción.
corrective, a. correctivo ; —, s. correctivo;
correctness, s. exactitud.
correlative, a. correlativo.
correspond, v.n. corresponder ; corresponderse.   [teligencia
correspondence, s. correspondencia ; incorrespondent**, a. correspondiente, conforme ; —, s. corresponsal.
corridor, s. pasadizo, galería.
corrigible, a. corregible.
corroborate, v.a. corroborar.
corroboration, s. corroboración
corroborative, a. corroborativo
corrode, v.a. corroer.
corrosion, s. corrosión.
corrugate, v.a. arrugar.
corrupt, v.a. corromper ; sobornar ; infectar ; —, v.n. corromperse, pudrirse ; —, a. corrompido ; depravado.
corruptible, a. corruptible.
corruption, s. corrupción ; depravación ; alteración ; pus.
corruptive, a. corruptivo.   [vicio.
corruptness, s. corruptela, **corrupción**,
corsair, s. corsario, pirata.
corset, s. corsé.
coruscation, s. resplandor.
corvette, s. (mar.) corbeta.
cosily, ad. (col.) cómodamente.
cosmetic, a. & s. cosmético.
cosmographer, s. cosmógrafo.   [mopolita.
cosmopolitan, **cosmopolite**, a. & s. cos-

cosset, v.a. mimar.

cost, s. coste, precio ; expensas, gastos, pl. ; —, v.n. costar.

coster, coster-monger, s. frutero.

costive, a. restriñente.

costiveness, s. constipación.

costliness, s. suntuosidad.

costly, a. costoso, suntuoso, caro ; espléndido, suntuoso.

costume, s. traje, vestido.

cosy, (col.) a. cómodo.

cot, s. cabaña ; catre ; cuna.

cotillion, s. cotillón.

cottage, s. cabaña, casucha.

cottager, s. aldeano, lugareño.

cotton, s. algodón.

cotton-plant, s. algodonero.

cotton-wool, s. algodón basto.

couch, v.n. agobiarse ; —, v.a. acostar ; esconder ; bajar (los ojos) ; (in writing) componer ; —, s. cama, lecho ; canapé.

cough, s. tos ; —, v.n. toser.

council, s. concilio, concejo ; sínodo.

councillor, s. concejal, jurisconsulto.

counsel, s. consejo, aviso ; abogado.

counsellor, s. consejero ; abogado.

count, v.a. contar, numerar ; calcular ; reputar ; —, s. cuenta ; cálculo ; conde.

countenance, s. rostro ; aspecto ; (buena ó mala) cara ; protección ; favor ; aire ; —, v.a. proteger, favorecer.

counter, s. contador ; mostrador ; —, ad. contra, al contrario, al revés.

counteract, v.a. contrariar, impedir, estorbar ; frustrar.

counteraction, s. oposición.

counterbalance, v.a. contrapesar ; igualar, compensar ; —, s. contrapeso.

counterfeit, v.a. contrahacer, imitar, falsear ; —, s. impostor ; falsificación ; —, a. falsificado ; fingido.

counterfeiter, s. falsario ; — of coin, monedero falso.

counter-foil, s. contramarca.   [vocar.

countermand, v.a. contramandar ; re-

counterpane, s. colcha de cama ; cobertor.

counterpart, s. contraparte, cópia, equivalente.

counterplot, s. contratreta.

counterpoise, v.a. contrapesar ; —, s. contrapeso.

counterscarp, s. contraescarpa.

countersign, v.a. refrendar.   [trarrestar.

countervail, v.a. contrapesar, con-

countess, s. condesa.

counting-house, s. despacho, escritorio.

countless, a. innumerable.

countrified, a. rústico ; tosco, rudo.

country, s. país ; campo ; región ; patria ; —, a. rústico ; campestre, rural.

country-dance, s. contradanza.

country-house, s. casa de campo, granja, quinta.

countryman, s. paisano ; compatriota.

county, s. condado.   [casar.

couple, s. par ; lazo ; —, v.a. unir, parear;

couplet, s. copla ; par.

courage, s. coraje, valor.

courageous, a. animoso, valiente, valeroso ; -ly, valerosamente.

courier, s. correo, mensajero, expreso.

course, s. curso ; carrera ; camino ; ruta ; rumbo ; curso ; método ; regularidad, orden, serie ; —, v.a. & n. cazar ; corretear ; of—, por supuesto, sin duda,

courser, s. corcel.

court, s. corte ; palacio ; tribunal de justicia ; cortejo ; patio ; —, v.a. cortejar ; solicitar, adular.

courteous, a. cortés ; -ly, cortésmente.

courtesan, s. cortesana.

courtesy, s. cortesía ; benignidad ; —, v.n. hacer la reverencia.

court-house, s. foro, tribunal.

courtier, s. cortesano, palaciego.

courtliness, s. cortesía, urbanidad, política ; elegancia.

courtly, a. cortesano, elegante.

court-martial, s. (mil.) tribunal militar.

court-plaster, s. tafetán inglés.

courtship, s. cortejo ; galantería.

court-yard, s. patio.

cousin, s. primo ; prima ; first —, primo hermano.

cove, s. (mar.) ensenada, caleat.

covenant, s. contrato ; convención ; —, v.n. pactar, estipular.

cover, s. cubierta ; abrigo ; pretexto ; —, v.a. cubrir ; tapar ; ocultar ; proteger ; paliar, honestar.

covering, s. ropa ; vestido.

coverlet, coverlid, s. colcha.

covert, s. cubierto ; refugio ; matorral, bosquecillo ; —, a. cubierto ; oculto, secreto ; -ly, secretamente.

coverture, s. abrigo, refugio.

covet, v.a. codiciar, desear con ansia.

covetous, a. avariento, codicioso ; -ly, codiciosamente.

covetousness, s. codicia, avaricia.

covey, s. nidada, pollada de perdices.

cow, s. vaca ; —, v.a. acobardar, intimidar.

coward, s. cobarde, medroso.

cowardice, s. cobardía, timidez.

cowardly, a. cobarde ; pusilánime.

cower, v.n. agacharse, acurrucarse.

cow-herd, s. vaquero.

cow-hide, s. cuero.

cowl, s. capuz, cogulla, capucha.

cowslip, s. (bot.) vellorita-

coxcomb, s. petimetre.   [con esquivez
coy, a. recatado, modesto ; esquivo ; -ly,
coyness, s. esquivez, modestia.
coz. s. (col.) primo ; prima.
cozen, v.a. engañar, defraudar.
cozenage, s. engaño ; trampa.
crab, s. cangrejo.
crab-apple, s. manzana silvestre.
crabbed, a. áspero, austero, bronco,
   tosco ; -ly, de mal humor ; ásperamente.
crack, s. crujido ; hendedura, quebraja ;
   —, v.a. hender, rajar ; romper ; —,
   v.n. reventar ; jactarse ; —, s. (col.)
   raro, fino.
crack-brained, a. alocado.
cracker, s. triquitraque ; galleta.
crackle, v.n. crujir, chillar.
crackling, s. estallido, crujido.
cradle, s. cuna ; —. v.a. meter en cuna.
craft, s. arte ; artificio : astucia.
craftily, ad. astutamente.
craftiness, s. astucia, estratagema.
craftsman, s. artífice, artesano.
crafty, a. astuto, artificioso.
crag, s. despeñadero.
cragged, a. escabroso, áspero.
cragginess, s. escabrosidad, aspereza.
craggy, a. escabroso, áspero.
cram, v.a. rellenar, embutir ; engordar ;
   —, v.n. atracarse de comida.
cramp, s. calambre ; laña ; —, v.a. lañar ;
cramp-iron, s. laña.   [constreñir.
cranberry, s. arándano.
crane, s. grulla ; grúa.
crank, s. eje articulado, manubrio.
crannied, a. hendido.
cranny, s. grieta, hendedura.
crape, s. crespón.
crash, v.n. estallar ; —, s. estallido,
   fracaso.   [grosero.
crass, a. craso, grueso, basto, tosco,
crate, s. cesta grande.
crater, s. cráter, boca de volcán.
cravat, s. corbata.
crave, v.a. rogar, suplicar.
craven, s. cobarde, pusilánime.
craving, a. insaciable, pedigüeño ; —, s.
   deseo ardiente.
craw, s. buche de ave.
crawfish, s. cangrejo de agua dulce.
crawl, v.n. arrastrarse, gatear ; to —
   with, hormiguear.
crayfish, s. cangrejo de río.
crayon, s. lápiz.   [manía, locura.
craze, v.a. embobar, entontecer ; —, s.
craziness, s. locura.   [simple.
crazy, a. decrépito ; caduco ; fatuo,
creak, v.n. crujir, estallar.
cream, s. nata, crema ; —, v.a. desnatar ;
   —, v.n. criar nata.

creamy, a. lleno de crema.
crease, s. pliegue ; —, v.a. plegar,
create, v.a. crear ; causar.
creation, s. creación ; nombramiento.
creative, a. creativo.
creator, s. Criador, Hacedor ; autor.
creature, s. criatura.
credence, s. creencia, fe.
credentials, s.pl. cartas credenciales, pl.
credibility, s. credibilidad.
credible, a. creíble ; -bly, creíblemente.
credit, s. crédito ; creencia ; reputación ;
   autoridad ; —, v.a. creer, fiarse.
creditable, a. estimable, honorífico ; -bly,
   honorablemente, con crédito.
creditor, s. acreedor.
credulity, s. credulidad.
credulous, a. crédulo ; -ly, con credulidad.
creed, s. credo.
creek, s. bahía pequeña ; (am.) arroyo.
creep, v.n. arrastrar, serpear.
creel, s. cesta de pescador.
creeper, s. planta enredadera ; reptil.
cremate, v.a. incinerar (cadáveres).
cremation, s. cremación.
crenellated, a. dentado.
creole, a. & s. criollo.
crescent, a. & s. creciente.
cress, s. lepidio, mastuerzo, berro.
crest, s. cresta ; copete ; penacho.
crested, a. crestado.
crest-fallen, a. cabizbajo, abatido.
cretaceous, a. cretáceo.
crevice, s. raja, hendedura,
crew, s. banda, tropa ; (mar.) tripulación.
crewel, s. estambre fino.
crib, s. pesebre ; casucha.
crick, s. calambre ; tortícolis.
cricket, s. grillo ; juego de pelota inglés.
crier, s. pregonero.
crime, s. crimen ; culpa.
criminal, a. & s. criminal, reo convicto ;
   -ly, criminalmente ; —, s. reo convicto.
criminality, s. criminalidad.
criminate, v.a. acriminar,
crimination, s. criminación.
crimp, v.a. rizar, encrespar ; arrugar ;
   —, s. (col.) enganchador.
crimson, a. & s. carmesí.
cringe, s. bajeza ; —, v.n. incensar,
   adular con bajeza.
crinkle, s. sinuosidad, arrugación ; —,
   v.a. & n. encrespar(se), arrugar(se).
crinoline, s. crinolina.
cripple, s. & a. estropeado, cojo ; —,
   v.a. estropear, inutilizar.
crisis, s. crisis.   [v.a. crespar, rizar,
crisp, a. crespo ; duro y quebradizo ; —,
crispness, s. friabilidad, fragilidad,
criterion, s. criterio.
critic, s. crítico ; crítica,

critic(al), a. crítico ; exacto ; delicado ; -ally, exactamente, rigurosamente.

criticise, v.a. criticar, censurar.

criticism, s. crítica.

croak, v.n. graznar, crocitar, crascitar.

crochet, s. especie de bordadura.

crockery, s. loza ; vasijas de barro, pl.; vidriado.

crocodile, s. cocodrilo.

crocus, s. (bot.), azafrán.

croft, s. campecito, huerta.

crone, s. anciana, vieja. [padre.

crony s., amigo, antiguo ; (col.) com-

crook, s. gancho ; artificio ; —, v.a. encorvar, torcer. •

crooked, a. torcido, corvo ; perverso ; -ly, torcidamente, perversamente, con doblez.

croon, v.n. zumbir ; arrullar.

crop, s. buche de ave ; cosecha ; —, v.a. cultivar, sembrar y segar ; cortar (el pelo, las orejas, &c.).

croquet, s. juego de pelota.

crosier, s. cayado pastoral de obispo.

cross, s. cruz ; (fig.) carga ; trabajo ; pena, aflicción ; tormento ; —, a. contrario, opuesto, atravesado ; mal humorado, ceñudo ; —, v.a. atravesar, cruzar.

cross-bar, -beam, s. travesaño.

cross-examine, v.a. (law) repreguntar, examinar á un testigo.

cross-eyed, a. bisojo.

cross-grained, a. perverso, intratable.

crossing, s. paso, travesía, pasaje.

crossly, ad. contrariamente, de mal humor.

crossness, s. espíritu de contradicción ; mal humor ; malicia, travesía.

cross-purpose, s. equivocación mutua en conversación.

cross-road, s. encrucijada.

crotchet, s. capricho ; corchete ; (mus.) corchea.

crouch, v.n. agacharse, bajarse.

croup, s. grupa (de caballo) ; coqueluche.

crow, s. cuervo ; canto del gallo ; —, bar, barra de hierro ; —, v.n. cantar (el gallo).

crowd, s. tropel ; turba, muchedumbre ; —, v.a. & n. amontonarse ; agrupar(se), estrecharse.

crown, s. corona ; guirnalda de flores ; moneda de cinco chelines (plata) ; complemento, colmo ; —, v.a. coronar ; recompensar ; dar cima.

crown-prince, s. príncipe real.

crozier, s. See crosier.

crucial, a. crucial ; crítico, sumamente importante.

crucible, s. crisol.

crucifix, s. crucifijo.

crucify, v.a. crucificar.

crude, a. crudo, indigesto, imperfecto ; -ly, crudamente.

crudity, s. crudeza.

cruel, a. cruel, inhumano ; -ly, cruelmente

cruelty, s. crueldad.

cruet, s. vinagrera.

cruet-stand, s. angarillas, pl.

cruise, s. jícara ; (mar.) crucero, viaje ; —, v.n. (mar.) navegar.

cruiser, s. crucero.

crumb, s. miga. [—, v.n. desmigajarse.

crumble, v.a. desmigajar, desmenuzar ;

crumple, v.a. arrugar.

crunch, v.a. mascar, magullar.

crupper, grupera.

crusade, s. cruzada. [—, s. turba.

crush, v.a. apretar, oprimir ; amilanar

crust, s. costra ; corteza ; —, v.a. (& n.) encostrar(se).

crustaceous, a. crustáceo ; conchado.

crustily, ad. enojadamente, broncamente.

crustiness, s. dureza de la costra ; mal genio, dureza.

crusty, a. costroso ; bronco, áspero.

crutch, s. muleta.

crux, s. crisis, punta decisiva.

cry, v.a. & n. gritar ; pregonar ; exclamar ; llorar ; —, s. grito ; lloro ; clamor.

crypt, s. cripta (bóveda subterránea).

cryptic, a. enigmático, misterioso, oscuro.

crystal, s. cristal.

crystalline, a. cristalino ; transparente.

crystallisation, s. cristalización.

crystallise, v.a. (& n.) cristalizar(se).

cub, s. cachorro ; —, v.n. parir (la osa ó zorra).

cube, s. cubo.

cubic(al), a. cúbico.

cubiform, a. cúbico.

cubit, s. codo (medida).

cuckoo, s. cuclillo, cuco .

cucumber, s. cohombro, pepino.

cud, s. panza, primer estómago de los rumiantes ; pasto contenido en la panza ; to chew the —, rumiar ; (fig.) reflexionar. [v.n. agacharse.

cuddle, v.a. (col.) abrazar, acariciar ; —,

cuddy, s. camarote de proa (mar.).

cudgel, s. garrote, palo ; —, v.a. apalear.

cudgelling, s. bastonada.

cue; s. coleta ; apunte de comedia ; humor ; taco (de billar). [vestido.

cuff, s. puñada ; vuelta de manga de cuirass, s. coraza.

cuirassier, s. coracero.

culinary, a. culinario, de la cocina.

cull, v.a. escoger, elegir, coger (flores).

culminate v.n. culminar.

culpability, s. culpabilidad.

culpable, a. culpable, criminal; -bly, culpablemente, criminalmente, por la vía criminal.

culprit, s. culpable, reo convicto.

cultivate, v.n. cultivar, mejorar; perfeccionar.

cultivation, s. cultivación; cultivo.

culture, s. cultura.

culverin, s. (mil.) culebrina.

culvert, s. (rail.) desagüe.

cumber, v.a. embarazar, embrollar. [ado.

cumbersome, cumbrous, a. engorroso, pescumbrance, s. carga, estorbo, peso.

cumulative, a. cumulativo.

cunning, a. experto; artificioso, astuto; intrigante; -ly, astutamente; expertamente; —, s. astucia, sutileza.

cup, s. copa, taza, jícara; (bot.) cáliz; — and ball, boliche; —, v.a. sangrar.

cupboard, s. armario.

cupidity, s. concupiscencia, codicia.

cupola, s. cúpola.

cupping-glass, s. ventosa.

cur, perro de mala ralea.

curable, a. curable.

curacy, s. tenencia; vicariato.

curate, s. teniente de cura.

curative, a. curativo.

urator, s. curador; guardián.

curb, s. barbada; freno; restricción; —, v.a. refrenar, contener, moderar.

curb-stone, s. margen de acera.

curd, s. cuajada; —, curdle, v.a. & n. cuajar(se), coagular(se). [sanar.

cure, s. cura; remedio; —, v.a. curar,

curfew, s. campanada del anochecer.

curing, s. curación.

curiosity, s. curiosidad.

curious, a. curioso, exacto, delicado; raro; -ly, curiosamente.

curl, s. rizo de pelo; tortuosidad; —, v.a. encrespar el pelo; ondear; —, curly, a. rizado.   [v.n. rizarse.

curmudgeon, s. hombre tacaño.

currant, s. uva de Corinto.

currency, s. circulación; moneda corriente; duración.

current, a. corriente, común; —, s. curso, progreso, marcha; corriente, fluido (eléctrico).

currently, ad. corrientemente; á la moda.

curriculum, s. curso de estudio.

currier, s. curtidor.   [brutalmente.

currish, æ. perruno, brutal, regañón; -ly,

curry, v.a. zurrar; almohazar; —, s. mezcla picante de especias.

currycomb, s. almohaza.

curse, v.a. maldecir; —, v.n. imprecar; blasfemar; —, s. maldición; imprecación.

cursedly, ad. miserablemente, abominablemente.

cursive, a. cursivo.

cursorily, ad. de paso, brevemente

cursory, a. breve, inconsiderado.

curt, a. sucinto; brusco.

curtail, v.a. cortar; mutilar.

curtain, s. cortina; telón en los teatros —, v.a. cubrir con cortinas.

curtain-rod, s. varilla de cortinaje.

curtsy, s. saludo ó reverencia.

curvated, a. corvo, encorvado.

curvature, s. curvatura.

curve, v.a. encorvar; —, s. corva, combadura.

curvet, s. corveta; —, v.n. corcovear saltar de alegría.

cushion, s. cojín, almohada.

custard, s. natillas, pl., crema.

custodian, s. custodio, guardián.

custody, s. custodia; prisión.

custom, s. costumbre, uso; -s, derechos de aduana, pl.

customarily, de costumbre, comúnmente, ordinariamente.   [ordinario.

customary, a. usual, acostumbrado,

customer, s. comprador, marchante.

custom-house, s. aduana.

cut, v.a. cortar; separar; herir; dividir; alzar los naipes; (col.) evitar, desconocer; to — short, interrumpir, cortar la palabra; to — capers, cabriolar; to — teeth, nacerle los dientes (á un niño); —, v.n. traspasar; cruzarse; —, s. cortadura; estampa; grabado; hechura, figura; herida; — and dry, a. pronto, arreglado.

cuticle, s. epidermis.

cutlass, s. machete; alfanje.

cutler, s. cuchillero.

cutlery, s. cuchillería.

cutlet, s. costilla de carnero ó de ternera.

cut-purse, s. ladrón.

cutter, s. cortador; (mar.) cúter.

cut-throat, s. asesino.

cutting, s. cortadura; incisión; alce de naipes; —, a. picante, mordaz.

cuttle-fish, s. jibia, sepia.

cutwater, s. (mar.) tajamar.

cycle, s. ciclo.

cyclopædia, s. enciclopedia.

cyclopean, a. ciclópeo.

cygnet, s. pollo del cisne.

cylinder, s. cilindro; rollo.

cylindric(al), a. cilíndrico.

cymbal, s. címbalo.

cynic(al), a. cínico; —, s. cínico (filósofo).

Cynosure, s. Cinosura.

cypress, s. ciprés.

czar, s. Zar.

czarina, s. Zarina

D

dab, v.a. rociar ; empapar ; —, pedazo pequeño ; salpicadura ; golpe blando ; barbada (pez).

dabble, v.a. rociar, salpicar ; —, v.n. chapotear.

dabbler, s. chapucero, chisgaravís.

dace, s. albur (pez).

dad(dy), s. papá.

dado, s. dado.

daffodil, s. narciso.

daft, a. imbécil, bobo.

dagger, s. puñal.

dahlia, s. (bot.) dalia.

daily, a. diario, cotidiano ; —, ad. diariamente, cada día.

daintily, ad. delicadamente.

daintiness, s. elegancia ; delicadeza.

dainty, a. delicado ; elegante ; —, s. bocado exquisito, golosina.

dairy, s. lechería.

dairy-maid, s. lechera, mantequera.

daisy, s. margarita, maya.

dale, s. cañada ; valle.

dalliance, s. regodeo, retozo ; dilación.

dally, v.n. regodear, retozar ; tardar.

dam, s. madre (en los animales) ; dique ; azud, presa, barraje ; —, v.a. represar estamar (agua).

damage, s. daño, detrimento ; resarcimiento de daño ; —, v.a. dañar.

damask, s. damasco ; —, a. de damasco ; —, v.a. adamascar.

dame, s. dama, señora.

damn, v.a. condenar.

damnable, a. condenable ; -bly, de un modo condenable ; horriblemente, detestablemente.

damnation, s. condenación.

damp, a. húmedo ; humedad ; (fig.) tristeza ; —, v.a. humedecer ; desanimar, abatir.

dampen, v.a. humedecer.

damper, s. apagador ;

dampness, s. humedad.

damsel, s. damisela, señorita.

damson, s. damascena.

dance, s. danza ; baile ; —, v.n. bailar ; **to — attendance**, servir con prontitud y atención, cortejar.

dancer, s. danzarín, -na ; bailarín, -na.

dancing-master, s. maestro de baile ó danza.

dandelion, s. (bot.) diente de león.

dandle, v.a. mecer ; halagar, acariciar.

dandruff, s. caspa.

dandy, s. petimetre, currutaco.

danger, s. peligro, riesgo.

dangerous, a. peligroso ; -ly, peligrosamente.

dangle, v.a. & n. menear, vibrar ; oscilar, temblar, fluctuar ;.

dangler, s. Juan de las damas.

dank, a. húmedo, oscuro.

dapper, a. activo, vivaz, despierto.

dapple, v.a. abigarrar ; —, a. vareteado ; rayado ; **—-grey horse**, s. caballo tordo.

dare, v.n. osar, atreverse, arriesgarse ; —, v.a. desafiar, provocar. [chín.

daredevil, s. hombre temerario, espada-

daring, s. osadía ; —, a. osado, temerario; emprendedor ; **-ly**, atrevidamente, osadamente.

dark, a. oscuro ; opaco ; secreto ; **-ly**, oscuramente, secretamente ; —, s. oscuridad ; ignorancia.

darken, v.a. (& n.) obscurecer(se).

dark-lantern, s. linterna sorda.

darkness, s. oscuridad ; tinieblas, pl.

darksome, a. oscuro, opaco, sombrío.

darling, a. & s. favorito, querido, amado.

darn, v.a. zurcir, remendar.

darnel, s. zizaña.

dart, s. dardo ; —, v.a. lanzar, tirar ; — v.n. volar como dardo.

dash, v.a. arrojar, chocar, romper ; salpicar ; borrar ; confundir ; —, v.n. saltar, lanzarse, arrojarse ; —, s. colisión ; choque ; colpe ; **— of a pen**, rasgo de pluma ; **at one —**, de un golpe.

dash-board, s. paralodo.

dashing, a. vistoso, brillante ; valiente.

dastard, s. collón, cobarde.

dastardly, a. cobarde, miserable.

date, s. data, fecha ; plazo ; (bot.) dátil ; —, v.a. datar.

dative, a. & s. dativo ; [ensuciar.

daub, v.a. pintorrear ; untar ; manchar,

dauber, s. pintor tosco.

daughter, s. hija ; **-in-law**, nuera.

daunt, v.a. intimidar, espantar.

dauntless, a. intrépido.

Dauphin, s. delfín (de Francia).

daw, s. corneja.

dawdle, v.n. gastar tiempo, tardar.

dawdler, s. haragán.

dawn, s. alba ; albor ; —, v.n. amanecer.

day, s. día ; **by —**, de día ; **— by —**, de día en día.

day-book, s. diario.

day-break, s. alba.

day-labourer, s. jornalero.

day-light, s. luz del día, luz natural.

day-scholar, s. externo.

day-spring, s. alba.

day-star, s. lucero del alba.

daze, dazzle, v.a. deslumbrar, ofuscar.

dazed, a. confuso, aturdido.

deacon, s. diácono.

dead, a. muerto ; flojo, entorpecido ; vacío, inútil, triste ; apagado, sin espíritu ; despoblado ; marchito ; devuelto (hablando de cartas) ; the —, pl. los finados.

dead-drunk, a. hecho un cuero.

deaden, v.a. amortecer.

dead-heat, s. corrida indecisa.

deadlock, s. complicación ineludible, controversia sin salida.

deadly, a. mortal ; terrible, implacable.

deadness, s. flojedad, inercia ; amortiguamiento.

deaf, a. sordo.

deafen, v.a. ensordar, ensordecer.

deafness, s. sordera ; desinclinación á oir.

deal, s. parte ; cantidad ; madera de pino; contrato, compra ; **a great** —, mucho ; **a good** —, bastante ; —, v.a. distribuir; dar ; —, v.n. traficar, comerciar ; **to** — **with,** tratar con ; ser marchante.

dealer, s. mercader, traficante ; el que da las cartas en el juego de naipes.

dealing, s. conducta ; trato ; tráfico, comercio.

dean, s. deán.

deanery, s. deanato.

dear, a. querido, amado ; caro, costoso ; -ly, tiernamente, con cariño ; caro.

dearness, s. cariño, amor ; carestía.

dearth, s. carestía ; esterilidad.

death, s. muerte. [agonía.

death-bed, s. cama del moribundo ;

death-blow, s. golpe mortal.

death-dealing, a. mortífero.

deathlike, a. quedo ; letárgico.

death-throe, s. agonía.

death-warrant, s. sentencia de muerte.

debar, v.a. excluir, prohibir.

debarkation, s. desembarco.

debase, v.a. humillar, envilecer ; alterar (moneda). [cimiento.

debasement, s. abatimiento ; envile-

debatable, a. disputable.

debate, s. debate ; riña, disputa ; —, v.a. discutir ; examinar ; —, v.n. deliberar; disputar.

debater, s. controversista.

debauch, s. vida disoluta ; exceso ; —, v.a. & n. corromper ; hacer excesos.

debauchee, s. calavera.

debauchery, s. desarreglo ; disolución.

debenture, s. cédula de hipoteca.

debilitate, v.a. debilitar, enervar.

debility, s. debilidad, languidez.

debit, s. (com.) debe ; —, v.a. adeudar, cargar en una cuenta.

debouch, v.n. (mil.) desfilar ; desembocar un río.

debt, s. deuda ; débito ; obligación ; **to run into** —, adeudar(se).

debtor, s. deudor.

decade, s. década.

decadence, s. decadencia.

Decalogue, s. Decálogo.

decamp, v.n. (mil.) decampar ; (col.) escapar, mudarse.

decampment, s. (mil.) levantamiento de un campamento. [discurrir.

decant, v.a. decantar ; (col.) razonar,

decanter, s. garrafa.

decapitate, v.a. decapitar, degollar.

decapitation, s. decapitación.

decay, v.n. decaer, descaecer, declinar ; degenerar ; —, s. descaecimiento ; decadencia, declinación, diminución.

decease, s. muerte.

deceit, s. engaño, fraude, impostura.

deceitful, a. fraudulento, engañoso ; falaz ; -ly, falsamente.

deceive, v.a. engañar, defraudar.

deceiver, s. engañador, trapacista.

December, s. diciembre.

decency, s. decencia ; modestia.

decennial, a. decenal.

decent, a. decente, razonable ; propio, conveniente ; -ly, decentemente.

decentralise, v.a. repartir. [engaño.

deception, s. decepción, impostura

deceptive, a. falso, engañoso.

decide, v.a. & n. decidir, determinar, resolver, juzgar.

decidedly, ad. determinadamente.

deciduous, a. (bot.) decedente.

decimal, a. decimal.

decimate, v.a. diezmar.

decimation, s. diezmo.

decipher, v.a. descifrar.

decision, s. decisión, determinación, resolución. [mente.

decisive, a. decisivo ; -ly, decisiva-

deck, s. (mar.) puente ; cubierta ; —, v.a. adornar.

declaim, v.n. declamar, perorar.

declamation, s. declamación, arenga.

declamatory, a. declamatorio.

declaration, s. declaración, publicación ; explicación.

declare, v.a. declarar, manifestar.

declension, s. declinación ; declivio.

declination, s. declinación ; decremento.

decline, v.a. evitar ; rehusar ; (gr.) declinar ; —, v.n. decaer, desmejorar; inclinarse ; —, s. declinación, decadencia ; tisis. [cuesta.

declivity, s. declividad ; pendiente ;

decoct, v.a. cocer, componer.

decoction, s. cocción ; (med.) cocimiento.

decompose, v.a. & n. descomponer(se).
decomposition, s. descomposición.
decorate, v.a. decorar, adornar.
decoration, s. decoración.
decorative, a. decorativo.
decorator, s. decorador, adornista; guarnecedor. [decorosamente.
decorous, a. decente, decoroso; -ly, ad.
decorum, s. decoro, garbo; decencia; conveniencia.
decoy, v.a. atraer (algún pájaro); embaucar, engañar; —, s. seducción; cazadero con señuelo.
decoy-bird, s. pájaro de reclamo.
decrease, v.a. & n. disminuir(se), minorar(se); —, s. decremento; descaecimiento, diminución.
decree, s. decreto, edicto; —, v.a decretar; ordenar.
decrepit, a. decrépito.
decrier, s. difamador.
decry, v.a. desacreditar, censurar públicamente, difamar.
dedicate, v.a. dedicar; consagrar.
dedication, s. dedicación; dedicatoria.
dedicatory, a. dedicatorio.
deduce, v.a. deducir; concluir, inferir.
deduct, v.a. deducir, sustraer.
deduction, s. deducción, consecuencia; descuento. [cia.
deductively, ad. por ilación ó consecuen-
deed, s. acción; hecho; hazaña; (law) cédula, instrumento auténtico.
deem, v.n. juzgar, pensar, estimar.
deep, a. profundo; sagaz; artificioso; grave; oscuro; —, s. (poet) mar.
deepen, v.a. profundizar.
deeply, ad. profundamente; astutamente.
deepness, s. profundidad.
deer, s. ciervo, venado.
deface, v.a. borrar; desfigurar, afear.
defacement, s. desfiguración.
defalcate, v.a. desfalcar.
defamation, s. difamación, calumnia.
defamatory, a. calumnioso, difamatorio.
defame, v.a. disfamar; calumniar.
default, s. culpa; delito; defecto; falta; —, v.n. faltar.
defaulter, s. (law) contumaz; desfalcador.
defeat, s. derrota; vencimiento; —, v.a. derrotar; frustrar.
defect, s. defecto; falta.
defection, s. defección.
defective, a. defectivo, imperfecto.
defence, s. defensa; protección, amparo.
defenceless, a. indefenso; desamparado.
defend, v.a. defender; proteger.
defendant, s. defensor; reo demandado.
defender, s. defensor, protector.
defensive, a. defensivo; -ly, de un modo defensivo; —, s. defensiva.

defer, v.a. diferir, retardar.
deference, s. deferencia; respeto; consideración.
deferential, a. respetoso.
defiance, s. desafío. [rebelde.
defiant, a. provocante, amenazante.
deficiency, s. defecto, imperfección, falta; déficit. [falto; imbécil.
deficient, a. deficiente; incompleto,
deficit, s. déficit, descubierto.
defile, s. desfiladero; —, v.a. ensuciar.
definable, a. definible; determinable.
define, v.a. definir; limitar; determinar; —, v.n. decidir, juzgar.
definite, a. definido, exacto, preciso, limitado, cierto.
definition, s. definición. [mente.
definitive, a. definitivo; -ly, definitiva-
deflect, v.a. & n. desviar(se); ladear(se).
deflection, s. desvío, rodeo.
deflour, deflower, v.a. desflorar, estuprar.
defoliation, s. caída de las hojas, defoliación.
deform, v.a. desformar, desfigurar.
deformity, s. deformidad.
defraud, v.a. defraudar.
defray, v.a. costear, pagar.
deft, a. hábil, despejado, diestro; -ly, con destreza.
defunct, a. difunto, muerto.
defy, v.a. desafiar; provocar, despreciar.
degeneracy, s. degeneración, depravación.
degenerate, v.n. degenerar; —, a. degenerado.
degeneration, s. degeneración.
degradation, s. degradación; degeneración. [vilecer.
degrade, d.v.a. degradar; deshonrar, envilecer.
degree, s. grado; rango; condición; by -s, gradualmente.
deification, s. apoteosis.
deify, v.a. deificar; divinizar.
deign, v.n. dignarse.
deism, s' deísmo.
deist, s. deísta.
deity, s. deidad, divinidad.
deject, v.a. abatir, desanimar.
dejection, s. tristeza, aflicción.
delay, v.a. diferir; retardar; —, v.n. tardar; —, s. dilación; retardo.
delectable, a. deleitoso; -bly, deleitosamente; con gusto.
delegate, v.a. delegar, diputar; —, s. delegado, diputado. [comisión.
delegation, s. delegación, diputación,
delf(t), s. loza vidriada.
deliberate, v.a. deliberar, considerar; —, a. cauto; avisado; -ly, deliberadamente.
deliberateness, deliberation, s. deliberación, circunspección, miramiento.

deliberative, a. deliberativo.
delicacy, s. delicadeza ; tenuidad ; golosina, manjar exquisito.
delicate, a. delicado ; exquisito ; afeminado ; **-ly,** delicadamente ; afeminadamente.   [liciosamente.
delicious, a. delicioso ; exquisito ; **-ly,** deliciousness, s. delicia ; gusto.
deliciousness, s. delicia ; gusto.
delight, s. delicia ; placer, gozo, encanto ; —, v.a. (& n.) deleitar(se).
delightful, a. delicioso ; deleitable ; **-ly** deliciosamente.
delimitation, s. amojonamiento.
delineate, v.a. delinear, diseñar.
delineation, s. delineación ; delineamento.
delinquency, s. delito ; culpa.
delinquent, s. delincuente, culpable.
delirious, a. delirante, desvariado.
delirium, s. delirio.   [relatar ; partear.
deliver, v.a. dar; rendir ; libertar ; recitar,
deliverance, s. libramiento.
delivery, s. entrega ; libramiento ; parto.
dell, s. valle hondo ; hondonada.
delta, s. delta.
delude, v.a. engañar.   [empapar.
deluge, s. inundación ; diluvio ; v.a. —,
delusion, s. engaño ; ilusión.
delusive, a. engañoso, falaz.
delve, v.a. cavar.
demagogue, s. demagogo.
demand, s. demanda ; petición ; —, v.a. demandar, reclamar.
demarcate, v.a. amojonar.
demarcation, s. demarcación.
demean, v.n. portarse.
demeanour, s. porte, ademán, modales.
demented, a. demente, loco.
demerit, s. demérito, culpa.
demesne, s. tierra solariega.
demise, v.a. legar, dejar en testamento ; —, s. muerte.
demigod, s. semidiós.
democracy, s. democracia.
democrat, s. demócrata.
democratic(al), a. democrático.
demolish, v.a. demoler, arruinar ; arrasar.
demolition, s. demolición.
demon, s. demonio, diablo.
demoniac, a. demoniaco ; endemoniado ; —, s. energúmeno.
demonstrable, a. demostrable ; **-bly,** demonstrablemente.
demonstrate, v.a. demostrar, probar.
demonstration, s. demostración.
demonstrative, a. demostrativo ; **-ly,** ad. demostrativamente.
demoralization, s. desmoralización.
demoralize, v.a. desmoralizar.
demur, v.n. objetar ; vacilar, escrupulizar ; —, s. duda, vacilación, escrupulos.

demure, a. reservado ; decente ; grave, serio ; **-ly,** modestamente.   [aspecto.
demureness, s. seriedad, gravedad de
demurrer, s. (law) demora, prorroga.
den, s. caverna ; antro.
deniable, a. negable.
denial, s. denegación.
denizen, s. habitante ; (law) extranjero naturalizado ; —, v.a. naturalizar.
denominate, v.a. denominar, nombrar.
denomination, s. denominación ; título, nombre, apelativo.
denote, v.a. denotar, indicar.
denounce, v.a. denunciar.
dense, a. denso, espeso.
density, s. densidad, solidez.
dent, s. mella, raja, señal de un golpe ; — v.a. rajar, mellar.
dental, a. dental ; —, s. letra dental.
dentifrice, s. dentrífico.
dentist, s. dentista.
dentistry, s. arte del dentista.
denudation, s. denudación.
denude, v.a. desnudar, despojar.
denunciate, v.a. denunciar, delatar.
denunciation, s. denunciación.
deny, v.a. negar, rehusar ; renunciar ; abjurar.
deodorize, v.a. desinficionar.
depart, v.n. partir(se) ; marcharse, salir.
department, s. departamento, distrito.
departure, s. partida ; salida.
depend, v.n. depender, estar dependiente ; — on ó upon, confiar ; it **-s,** según |
dependent, a. & s. dependiente .
dependence, dependency, s. dependencia ; confianza ; **foreign** —, colonia.
depict, v.a. pintar, retratar ; describir.
depletion, s. diminución.
deplorable, a. deplorable, lamentable ; **-bly,** deplorablemente.
deplore, v.a. deplorar, lamentar.
deploy, v.a. (mil.) desplegar.
deponent, s. (law) deponente, declarante.
depopulate, v.a. despoblar, devastar.
depopulation, s. despoblación ; devastación.
deport, v.a. desterrar.
deportation, s. deportación ; destierro.
deportment, s. conducta ; porte, manejo.
depose, v.a. deponer ; destronar ; testificar.
deposit, v.a. depositar ; —, s. depósito.
deposition, s. deposición, testimonio ; destitución.
depository, s. almacén.
deprave, v.a. depravar, corromper.
depraved, a. depravado.
depravity, s. depravación.
deprecate, v.a. deprecar.   [males.
deprecation, s. súplica para conjurar los

depreciate, v.a. rebajar el precio;
  despreciar, deprimir.
depreciation, s. descrédito; desestimación.
depredation, s. depredación; pillaje.
depress, v.a. deprimir, humillar.
depressed, a. abatido, desanimado.
depression, s. depresión; abatimiento;
  hueco.
deprivation, s. privación, pérdida.
deprive, v.a. privar, despojar.
depth, s. hondura, profundidad; abismo;
  oscuridad.
deputation, s. diputación.
depute, v.a. diputar, delegar.
deputy, s. diputado, delegado.
derange, v.a. desarreglar, desordenar.
deranged, a. imbécil.
derangement, s. desarreglo, desorden.
derelict, a. (mar.) abandonado en alta
  mar.
dereliction, s. desamparo, abandono.
deride, v.a. burlar, mofar.   [burla.
derision, s. irrisión, mofa; escarnio;
derisive, a. irrisorio.
derivable, a. derivable, deducible.
derivation, s. derivación.   [proceder.
derive, v.a. (& n.) derivar(se); descender,
derogate, v.n. derogar.
derogation, s. derogación.
derogatory, a. derogatorio.   [grúa.
derrick, s. máquina para levantar pesos,
dervish, s. derviche.
descant, v.n. discantar; discurrir; —,
  s. (mus.) discante.
descend, v.n. descender, bajar.
descendent, a. descendiente.
descent, s. bajada, descenso; pendiente;
  invasión; descendencia, posteridad.
describe, v.a. describir, delinear.
description, s. descripción.
descriptive, a. descriptivo.
descry, v.a. entrever, espiar; observar.
desecrate, v.a. profanar.
desecration, s. profanación.
desert, s. desierto; soledad; —, a.
  desierto, solitario.   [mérito.
desert, v.a. abandonar; desertar; —, s.
deserter, s. desertor, trásfuga.
desertion, s. deserción.
deserve, v.a. merecer; ser digno.
deservedly, ad. merecidamente, dignamente.
deserving, a. meritorio.
desideratum, s. desiderátum; lo que falta.
design, v.a. designar, proyectar; tramar;
  diseñar; —, s. designio, intento;
  empresa; diseño.   [tinguir.
designate, v.a. apuntar, señalar; dis-
designation, s. designación.
designatory, a. designativo.
designedly, ad. de propósito, de intento.

designing, a. insidioso, astuto.
desirable, a. deseable.   [desear, apetecer.
desire, s. deseo; apetencia; —, v.a.
desirous, a. deseoso, ansioso; -ly, ansiosamente.
desist, v.n. desistir.   [atril (de coro).
desk, s. escritorio, papelera; bufete;
desolate, v.a. desolar; devastar; —, a.
  desolado; solitario.
desolation, s. desolación, ruina, destrucción.   [desesperar.
despair, s. desesperación; —, v.n.
despairingly, ad. desesperadamente.
despatch, v.a. despachar; —, s. despacho;
  expreso.
despatch-boat, s. (mar.) aviso.
despatch-box, s. escritorio portátil.
desperado, s. hombre furioso ó criminal.
desperate, a. desesperado; furioso; -ly,
  ad. desesperadamente, furiosamente.
desperation, s. desesperación.
despicable, a. despreciable, bajo; -bly,
  despreciablemente.
despise, v.a. despreciar; desdeñar.
despite, s. despecho; malicia; in — of,
  á despecho de.
despoil, v.a. despojar; privar.
despond, v.n. desconfiar, abatirse;
  desesperar.   [miento.
despondency, s. desesperación; abati-
despot, s. déspota.
despotic(al), a. despótico, absoluto;
  -ally, ad. despóticamente.
despotism, s. despotismo.
dessert, s. postres, pl.
dessicated, a. seco, secado.
destination, s. destinación.
destine, v.a. destinar, señalar.
destiny, s. destino, hado; suerte.
destitute, a. destituído, abandonado,
  privado, indigente.
destitution, s. destitución, privación
  abandono, indigencia.
destroy, v.a. destruir, arruinar.
destruction, s. destrucción, ruina.
destructive, a. destructivo, ruinoso; -ly,
  destructivamente.
desuetude, s. desuso.
desultoriness, s. instabilidad, falta de
  método.   [método.
desultory, a. irregular, inconstante, sin
detach, v.a. separar; (mil.) destacar.
detachment, separación, apartimiento;
  (mil.) destacamento.
detail, s. detalle, menudencia; (mil.) destacamento; in —, al por menor; —,
  v.a. detallar; referir por menor;
  menudear.
detain, v.a. retener, detener; impedir.
detect, v.a. descubrir.
detection, s. descubrimiento; revelación.

detective, s. oficial de policía secreta.
detention, 's. detención, retención ; cautividad ; cantiverio.
deter, v.a. disuadir ; impedir.
detergent, a. (med.) detergente.
deteriorate, v.a. deteriorar.
deterioration, s. deterioración.
determinable, a. determinable.
determinate, a. determinado, decidido.
determination, s. determinación ; decisión.
determine, v.a. determinar, decidir ; —, v.n. terminar, concluir.
deterrent, a. & s. obstructivo ; obstáculo.
detest, v.a. detestar, aborrecer.
detestable, a. detestable, abominable ; -bly, detestablemente. [miento.
detestation, s. detestación ; aborreci-
dethrone, v.a. destronar.
dethronement, s. destronamiento.
detonate, v.n. (chem.) detonar.
detonation, s. detonación. [minuir.
detract, v.a. detractar, infamar ; dis-
detraction, s. detracción.
detriment, s. detrimento, daño, perjuicio.
detrimental, a. perjudicial.
deuce, s. dos (en los juegos) ; diantre.
devastate, v.a. devastar ; robar.
devastation, s. devastación, ruina.
develop, v.a. & n. desenvolver(se) ; desarrollar(se) ; revelar (fotografías).
development, s. desarrollo.
deviate, v.n. desviarse.
deviation, s. desvío ; deviación.
device, s. proyecto, expediente ; invención ; divisa.
devil, s. diablo, demonio. [camente.
devilish, a. diabólico ; -ly, diabóli-
devilment, s. pillada, bribonada ; broma.
devilry, s. diablura ; maleficio.
devious, a. desviado ; errante. [legar.
devise, v.a. trazar ; inventar ; idear ;
deviser, s. inventor.
devisor, s. testador.
devoid, a. vacío ; privado.
devolve, v.n. recaer, traspasar.
devote, v.a. dedicar ; consagrar.
devotedness, s. devoción.
devotee, s. santurrón ; beato. [afición.
devotion, s. devoción ; oración, rezo ;
devotional, a. devoto, religioso.
devour, v.a. devorar ; engullir.
devout, a. devoto, piadoso ; -ly, devotamente.
dew, s. rocío ; —, v.a. rociar.
dewlap, s. papada del buey.
dewy, a. rociado.
dexterity, s. destreza. [mente.
dexterous, a. diestro, hábil ; -ly, diestra-
diabetes, s. diabetes. [camente.
diabolic(al), a. diabólico ; -ally, diaboli-

diadem, s. diadema.
diagnose, v.a. (med.) diagnosticar.
diagnosis, (med.) s. diagnosis.
diagnostic, s. diagnóstico. [mente.
diagonal, s. diagonal ; -ly, diagonal-
diagram, s. diagrama.
dial, s. reloj solar ; cuadrante.
dialect, s. dialecto.
dialogue, s. diálogo.
diameter, s. diámetro.
diametrical, a. diametral ; -ly, diametralmente. [oros, pl.
diamond, s. diamante ; (at cards)
diamond-cutter, s. diamantista.
diaper, s. lienzo adamascado ; —, v.a matizar ; adamascar.
diapason, s. (mus.) diapasón.
diaphanous, a. diáfano, trasparente.
diaphragm, s. diafragma.
diarrhœa, s. diarrea.
diary, s. diario.
dibble, s. plantador, almocafré ; — v.a. plantar con plantador.
dice, s.pl. dados, pl.
dice-box, s. cubilete de dados.
dickens, s. (col.) diablo
dictate, v.a. dictar.
dictation, s. dictado.
dictator, s. dictador.
dictatorial, a. autoritativo ; magistral.
dictatorship, s. dictadura ; dictatura.
diction, s. dicción ; estilo.
dictionary, s. diccionario.
didactic(al), a. didáctico. [marchitarse.
die, v.n. morir, expirar ; desvanecerse
die, s. dado ; cuño.
diet, s. dieta ; régimen ; asamblea ; —, v.a. poner á dieta. [cinal.
dietary, a. dietético ; —, s. dieta medi-
differ, v.n. diferenciarse ; contradecir.
difference, s. diferencia, disparidad.
different, a. diferente ; desemejante ; -ly, diferentemente.
differentiate, v.a. diferenciar.
difficult, a. difícil, áspero.
difficulty, s. dificultad ; obstáculo ; duda.
diffidence, s. diffidencia.
diffident, a. desconfiado ; tímido ; -ly, desconfiadamente.
diffraction, s. difracción.
diffuse, v.a. difundir, esparcir ; —, a. difundido, esparcido ; prolijo ; -ly, copiosamente. [parcimiento.
diffusion, s. difusión, prolijidad ; es-
diffusive, a. difusivo ; prolijo.
dig, v.a. cavar, ahondar, azadonar ; —, s. (col.) codazo.
digest, v.a. digerir, ordenar ; rumiar ; —, s. (law) digesto ; — of the case, resumen del pleito.
digestible, a. digerible.

digestion, s. digestión.
digestive, a. & s. digestivo.
digger, s. cavador.
dignified, a. altivo, grave.
dignify, v.a. exaltar, elevar.
dignitary, s. personaje, dignidad.
dignity, s. dignidad ; rango ; aire noble.
digress, v.n. hacer digresión.
digression, s. digresión ; desvío.
digressive, a. digresivo, prolijo.
dike, s. dique.
dilapidate, v.a. dilapidar, echar á perder.
dilapidated, a. arruinado, gastado.
dilapidation, s. dilapidación ; ruina.
dilate, v.a. & n. hinchar(se), dilatar(se),
extender(se) ; discurrir, descantar.
dilatory, a. tardo, dilatorio.
dilemma, s. dilema.
diligence, s. diligencia ; exactitud.
diligent, a. diligente, asiduo ; -ly, diligentemente.
dilly-dally, v.n. (col.) tardar, vacilar.
dilute, v.a. diluir, templar.
dilution, s. diluición.
diluvial, a. diluviano.
dim, a. turbio de vista, lerdo ; obscuro ;
—, v.a. ofuscar, obscurecer ; eclipsar.
dimension, s. dimensión, medida, extensión.   [crecer.
diminish, v.a. & n. disminuir(se), de-
diminution, s. diminución.
diminutive, s. & a. diminutivo.
dimity, s. fustán, algodón fuerte.
dimly, ad. obscuramente.
dimness, s. ofuscamiento ; estupidez.
dimple, s. hoyuelo de la mejilla.
din, s. ruido violento, alboroto ; —, v.a.
insistir.
dine, v.n. comer, cenar.   [insistir.
dinghy, s. botecito.
dingy, a. deslucido, sucio, moreno.
dining-hall, dining-room, s. comedor ;
refectorio.
dinner, s. comida.
dinner-time, s. hora de comer.
dint, s. golpe ; mella ; by — of, á fuerza de.
diocese, s. diócesis, diócesi.
diorama, s. diorama.
dip, v.a. remojar, sumergir ; repasar
ligeramente ; —, v.n. sumergirse ;
penetrar ; inclinación ; plumada de
tinta ; inmersión.
diphtheria, s. difteritis.
dipthong, s. diptongo.
diploma, s. diploma ; letra patente.
diplomacy, s. diplomática.
diplomatic, a. diplomático.
diplomat(ist), s. diplomático.
dipsomania, s. dipsomanía.
dire, a. horrendo ; terrible.
direct, a. directo, derecho ; claro ; —,
v.a. dirigir, enderezar ; reglar, ordenar.

direction, s. dirección ; instrucción ;
mandado ; rumbo.
directly, ad. directamente, inmediatamente ; en seguida.
director, s. director.
directory, s. directorio.
dirge, s. canción lúgubre, lamento.
dirt, s. lodo ; basura, suciedad.
dirtily, ad. puercamente ; vilmente.
dirtiness, s. suciedad ; bajeza.
dirty, a. sucio ; vil, bajo ; —, v.a. ensuciar.   [incapacidad.
disability, s. impotencia ; inhabilidad,
disability, s. incapacidad.
disable, v.a. incapacitar ; desmontar,
estropear.
disabled, a. estrepeado.
disablement, s. incapacidad, impedimento, estropeamiento.
disabuse, v.a. desengañar.
disadvantage, s. desventaja ; daño ; —,
v.a. dañar, perjudicar.
disadvantageous, a. desventajoso ; -ly,
desventajosamente.
disaffect, v.a. descontentar ; indisponer.
disaffection, s. desafecto, deslealtad ;
desamor.
disagree, v.n. desconvenir, discordar.
disagreeable, a. desagradable, contrario
-bly, desagradablemente.
disagreeableness, s. desavenencia ; contradicción.
disagreement, s. diferencia ; discordia.
disallow, v.a. desaprobar ; —, v.n. negar,
prohibir.
disappear, v.n. desaparecer ; ausentarse.
disappearance, s. desaparecimiento.
disappoint, v.a. frustrar, faltar á la
palabra ; engañar.
disappointment, s. chasco ; contratiempo;
desengaño.   [ción, censura.
disapprobation, disapproval, s. desaproba
disapprove, v.a. desaprobar.
disarm, v.a. desarmar, privar de armas.
disarmament, s. desarmamiento.   [lar.
disarray, s. desarreglo ; —, v.a. desarreg-
disaster, s. desastre ; infortunio.
disastrous, a. desastroso, infeliz ; calamitoso ; -ly, desastradamente.
disavow, v.a. negar ; desconocer.
disavowal, s. denegación.
disband, v.a. (mil.) descartar, despedir.
disbelief, s. incredulidad, desconfianza.
disbelieve, v.a. descreer, desconfiar.
disbeliever, s. descreído, incrédulo.
disburden, v.a. descargar.
disburse, v.a. desembolsar, pagar.
disbursement, s. desembolso, gasto.
disc, disk, s. disco, tejo.
discard, v.a. despedir, apartar, arrojar,
descartar.

discern, v.a. discernir, percibir, distinguir.
discernible, a. perceptible ; sensible.
discerning, a. juicioso, perspicaz.
discharge, v.a. descargar, pagar (una deuda) ; dispensar ; ejecutar, cumplir ; descartar ; despedir ; —, s. descarga ; descargo ; finiquito ; dimisión ; absolución.
disciple, discípulo.
disciplinarian, s. disciplinario ; dómine.
discipline, s. disciplina ; enseñanza ; rigor ; —, v.a. disciplinar, instruir.
disclaim, v.a. negar, renunciar, desconocer.
disclaimer, s. denegación.
disclose, v.n. descubrir ; revelar.
disclosure, s. descubrimiento ; revelación.
discoloration, s. descoloramiento.
discolour, v.a. descolorar.
discomfit, v.a. derrotar, vencer ; turbar, desconcertar.
discomfiture, s. derrota ; vencimiento ; abatimiento, turbación.
discomfort, s. incomodidad, molestia.
discommode, v.a. incomodar, molestar.
discompose, v.a. descomponer ; desordenar ; turbar. [fusión.
discomposure, s. descomposición ; confusión.
disconcert, v.a. desconcertar, confundir, turbar.
disconnect, v.a. desunir.
disconnected, a. inconsiguiente.
disconnection, s. desunión.
disconsolate, a. inconsolable ; -ly, ad. desconsoladamente.
discontent, s. descontento ; —, a. malcontento ; —, v.a. descontentar.
discontinuation, s. descontinuación, cesación, interrupción.
discontinue, v.a. & n. descontinuar, interrumpir ; cesar.
discord, discordance, s. discordia ; discordancia, disensión.
discordant, a. discorde ; incongruo ; -ly, con discordancia. [descontar.
discount, s. descuento ; rebaja ; —, v.a.
discountenance, v.a. desaprobar.
discourage, v.a. desalentar, desanimar.
discouragement, s. desaliento.
discourse, s. discurso ; tratado ; —, v.n. conversar, discurrir, tratar.
discoursive, a. discursivo.
discourteous, a. descortés, grosero ; -ly, descortesmente.
discourtesy, s. descortesía, grosería.
discover, v.a. descubrir ; revelar ; manifestar.
discoverable, a. descubrible. [lación.
discovery, s. descubrimiento ; reve-
discredit, s. descrédito, oprobio ; —, v.a. desacreditar, deshonrar.

discreditable, a. ignominioso.
discreet, a. discreto ; circumspecto ; -ly, discretamente.
discrepancy, s. discrepancia, diferencia.
discretion, s. discreción.
discretionary, a. discrecional, á discreción.
discriminate, v.a. distinguir ; señalar.
discrimination, s. discernimiento, distinción. [mente.
discursive, a. discursivo ; -ly, prolija-
discuss, v.a. discutir.
discussion, s. discusión.
disdain, v.a. desdeñar, despreciar ; —, s. desdén, desprecio. [deñosamente.
disdainful, a. desdeñoso ; -ly, des-
disease, s. mal ; enfermedad.
diseased, a. enfermo.
disembarcation, s. desembarco.
disembark, v.a. & n. desembarcar.
disembarrass, v.a. desembarazar.
disembodied, a. incorpóreo, inmaterial, espiritual.
disembogue, v.n. desembocar.
disenchant, v.a. desencantar.
disenchantment, s. desencanto.
disencumber, v.a. desembarazar.
disencumbrance, s. desembarazo.
disengage, v.a. desenredar, librar.
disentangle, v.a. desenredar, separar ; desembarazar.
disentanglement, s. desenredo.
disentomb, v.a. exhumar.
disestablish, v.a. desalojar, desentablar.
disfavour, v.a. desfavorecer ; —, s. disfavor, disgusto.
disfigurement, s. deformidad.
disfigure, v.a. desfigurar, afear.
disfranchise, v.a. quitar franquicias, inhabilitar.
disgorge, v.a. vomitar ; devolver.
disgrace, s. deshonra ; disfavor ; oprobio ; —, v.a. deshonrar.
disgraceful, a. deshonroso, ignominioso ; -ly, vergonzosamente.
disguise, v.a. disfrazar, enmascarar ; disimular ; —, s. disfraz. [disgustar.
disgust, s. disgusto ; aversión ; —, v.a.
dish, s. fuente, plato ; taza ; —, v.a. servir la vianda.
dish-clout, s. rodilla, pañuelo.
dishearten, v.a. desalentar, desanimar.
dishevel, v.a. desgreñar.
dishonest, a. deshonesto ; fraudulento ; -ly, deshonestamente.
dishonesty, deshonestidad, engaño, fraude.
dishonour, s. deshonra, ignominia ; —, v.a. deshonrar, infamar.
dishonourable, a. deshonroso, afrentoso, indecoroso ; -bly, ignominiosamente.
disillusionment, s. desengaño.
disinclination, s. desafecto, aversión.

disincline, v.a. desinclinar.
disinfect, v.a. desinficionar.
disinfectant, a. & s. desinfectante.
disingenuous, a. falso, disimulado.
disinherit, v.a. desheredar.
disinter, v.a. desenterrar.
disintegrate, v.a. despedazar, desmenuzar.
disintegration, s. desagregación.
disinterested, a. desinteresado; **-ly,** desinteresadamente.
disinterestedness, s. desinterés.
disinterment, s. desenterramiento.
disjoint, v.a. dislocar, desmembrar.
dislike, s. aversión; disgusto; —, v.a. odiar, desaprobar.
dislocate, v.a. dislocar, descoyuntar.
dislocation, s. dislocación; descoyuntamiento.
dislodge, v.a. & n. desalojar. [mente.
disloyal, a. desleal; infiel; **-ly,** deslealmente.
disloyalty, s. deslealtad, infidelidad, perfidia.
dismal, a. triste, funesto; horrendo.
dismantle, v.a. (mil.) desmantelar (una plaza); (mar.) desaparejar.
dismast, v.a. desarbolar (un navío).
dismay, s. desmayo; pasmo; turbación; —, v.a. & n. desmayar(se).
dismember, v.a. desmembrar, despedazar.
dismiss, v.a. despedir; echar; descartar.
dismissal, dismission, despedida; dimisión.
dismount, v.a. desmontar; —, v.n. bajar, descender; apearse (del caballo).
disobedience, s. desobediencia.
disobedient, a. desobediente.
disobey, v.a. desobedecer.
disobliging, a. descortés, egoista, tieso.
disorder, s. desorden; confusión; indisposición; —, v.a. desordenar, confundir, perturbar. [sedicioso.
disorderly, a. desarreglado, confuso;
disorganization, s. desorganización, desarreglo.
disorganize, v.a. desorganizar.
disown, v.a. negar, desconocer, renunciar.
disparage, v.a. envilecer; desdorar.
disparagement, s. censura; desprecio.
disparity, s. disparidad, desigualdad.
dispassionate, a. sereno, desapasionado; templado.
dispatch, s. & v. *V.* **despatch.**
dispel, v.a. expeler, disipar.
dispensary, s. despensa, botica.
dispensation, s. distribución; dispensa.
dispense, v.a. dispensar; distribuir.
dispeople, v.a. *V.* **depopulate.**
disperse, v.a. esparcir, disipar; distribuir.
dispersion, s. dispersión; separación.
dispirit, v.a. desalentar, desanimar.
displace, v.a. dislocar, desordenar.

display, v.a. desplegar; explicar; exponer; ostentar; —, s. ostentación.
displease, v.a. desplacer, disgustar; ofender. [indignación.
displeasure, s. desplacer, disgusto;
disport, (oneself), v.n. & r. juguetear; divertirse.
disposal, s. disposición.
dispose, v.a. disponer, dar; arreglar; — of, v.a. vender; transferir.
disposed, a. dispuesto, inclinado.
disposition, s. disposición; orden; índole; inclinación.
dispossess, v.a. desposeer, privar.
dispraise, v.a. desaprobar, censurar; —, s. censura, reprobación. [dad.
disproportion, s. desproporción, desigualdad.
disproportionate, a. desproporcionado.
disprove, v.a. confutar.
disputable, a. disputable, contestable.
disputant, s. disputador.
disputation, s. disputa, controversia.
disputatious, a. disputador, quisquilloso.
dispute, s. disputa, controversia; —, v.a. & n. disputar, controvertir, argüir.
disqualification, s. inhabilidad.
disqualify, v.a. inhabilitar.
disquiet, s. inquietud, perturbación; —, v.a. inquietar, turbar, desasosegar.
disquietude, s. inquietud, desasosiego.
disquisition, s. disquisición; discurso.
disregard, v.a. desatender, desdeñar; —, s. desatención; desdén.
disregardful, a. desatento, negligente.
disrelish, s. disgusto, tedio, hastío; —, v.a. desaprobar; tener fastidio.
disrepair, s. mal estado, dilapidación.
disreputable, a. deshonroso; desaliñado; **-bly,** deshonrosamente.
disrespect, s. irreverencia.
disrespectful, a. irrespetuoso, irreverente, descortés; **-ly,** irreverentemente, sin respeto.
disrobe, v.a. & n. desnudar(se), despojar.
disruption, s. rompimiento, disolución.
dissatisfaction, s. descontento, disgusto.
dissatisfy, v.a. descontentar, desagradar.
dissect, v.a. disecar.
dissection, s. disección, anatomía; examen minucioso.
dissemble, v.a. & n. disimular. [esparcir.
disseminate, v.a. diseminar, sembrar,
dissension, s. disensión, discordia.
dissent, v.n. disentir, diferenciarse; —, s. disensión, contrariedad de opinión.
dissenter, s. disidente; hereje, no conformista.
dissentient, a. discrepante.
dissertation, s. disertación.
dissever, v.a. partir, dividir, separar.
dissimilar, a. desemejante, heterogéneo.

dissimilarity, s. desemejanza, diversidad, diferencia.
dissimulate, v.a. disimular.
dissimulation, s. disimulación.
dissipate, v.a. disipar.
dissipation, s. disipación ; dispersión.
dissociate, v.a. disociar.
dissoluble, a. disoluble.
dissolute, a. disoluto, libertino.
dissolution, s. disolución ; muerte.
dissolve, v.a. disolver ; —, v.n. disolverse, derretirse.
dissolvent, s. disolvente.
dissonance, s. disonancia ; desconcierto.
dissonant, a. disonante ; discordante ; [diferente.
dissuade, v.a. disuadir.
dissuasion, s. disuasión.
dissuasive, a. disuasivo.
dissylable, a. disílabo.
distaff, s. rueca.
distance, s. distancia ; esquivez ; **at a —,** de lejos ; —, v.a. sobrepasar.
distant, a. distante ; lejano ; esquivo.
distaste, s. hastío, disgusto, tedio.
distasteful, a. desabrido, desagradable ; fastidioso.
distemper, s. indisposición, enfermedad ; desasosiego ; desorden ; —, v.a. perturbar. [hincharse.
distend, v.a. extender, ensanchar; —, v.n.
distension, s. dilatación, hinchazón.
distich, s. dístico ; copla.
distil, v.a. & n. destilar ; gotear.
distillation, s. destilación. [iente.
distillery, s.destilatorio,fábrica de aguard-
distinct, a. distinto, diferente, diverso ; claro, sonoro ; -**ly,** distintamente.
distinction, s. distinción, diferencia.
distinctive, a. distintivo ; -**ly,** distintamente, claramente.
distinctness, s. distinción, claridad.
distinguish, v.a. distinguir ; discernir.
distinguishable, a. distinguible, notable.
distort, v.a. torcer ; desviar.
distortion, s. torcimiento.
distract, v.a. distraer ; separar ; perturbar
distracted, a. perturbado, enloquecido ; -**ly,** locamente. [frenesí.
distraction, s. distracción ; confusión ;
distrain, v.a. embargar, secuestrar.
distraint, s. (law) secuestro.
distress, s. calamidad, miseria ; (law) se-cuestro ; —, v.a. angustiar, congojar.
distressing, a. penoso. [partir.
distribute, v.a. distribuir, dividir, re-
distribution, s. distribución.
district, s. distrito ; región.
distrust, v.a. desconfiar, dudar ; —, s. desconfianza, sospecha.
distrustful, a. desconfiado ; sospechoso ; -**ly,** desconfiadamente.

disturb, v.a. perturbar, estorbar.
disturbance, s. disturbio ; confusión ; tumulto.
disunion, s. desunión, discordia.
disunite, v.a. (& n.) desunir(se), separar (se). [desacostumbrar, dejar.
disuse, s. desuso ; —, v.a. desusar.
ditch, s. zanja ; foso.
ditto, s. lo dicho, idem.
ditty, s. canción, jácara.
diuretic, a. (med.) diurético.
diurnal, a. diurno, cotidiano.
dive, v.n. sumergirse ; bucear.
diver, s. buzo : (orn) colimbo.
diverge, v.n. divergir, desviarse.
divergence, s. divergencia.
divergent, a. divergente.
divers, a. varios, diversos, muchos, pl.
diverse, a. diverso, diferente ; variado ; -**ly,** diversamente.
diversify, v.a. variar, diversificar.
diversion, s. diversión ; pasatiempo.
diversity, s. diversidad ; variegación.
divert, v.a. desviar ; divertir ; recrear.
divest, v.a. desnudar ; privar, despojar.
divide, v.a. dividir, distribuir ; desunir ; —, v.n. desunirse, dividirse.
dividend, s. dividendo.
divider, s. (ar.) divisor ; distribuidor.
divination, s. divinación.
divine, a. divino, sublime, excelente ; —, s. teólogo ; —, v.a. adivinar ; conje-
divinely, ad. divinamente. [turar.
diving-bell, s. campana de buzo.
divinity, s. divinidad ; deidad ; teología.
divisibility, s. divisibilidad.
divisible, a. divisible.
division, s. división ; desunión.
divisor, s. (ar.) divisor.
divorce, s. divorcio ; —, v.a. divorciar.
divulge, v.a. divulgar, publicar.
dizziness, s. vahido, vértigo ; ligereza.
dizzy, a. vertiginoso ; ligero.
do, v.a. & auxil. hacer, ejecutar, obrar ; finalizar ; despachar ; cocer ; —, v.n. comportarse ; estar. [amar.
doat, v.n. chochear ; — **on,** v.a. mimar,
docile, a. dócil, apacible.
docility, s. docilidad.
dock, s. bardana ; lampazo ; trozo ; (rail.) dock ; (mar.) dique ; atarazana ; —, v.a. descolar ; cortar. [rotular.
docket, s. rótulo ; extracto ; —, v.a.
dockyard, s. (mar.) astillero. [cinar.
doctor, s. doctor ; médico ; —, v.a. medi-
doctrinal, a. doctrinal, dogmático.
doctrine, s. doctrina, erudición.
document, s. documento.
documentary, a. documental.
dodge, v.a. & n. (coi.) trampear; esquivar; — s. trampa, artificio.

dodger, s. trampista.

doe, s. gama ; — -rabbit, coneja.

doer, s. autor, ejecutor.

doff, v.a. quitar (sombrero, vestido).

dog, s. perro ; —, v.a. espiar, seguir.

dog-cheap, a. muy barato.

dog-days, s.pl. dias caniculares, pl.

doge, s. dux (de Venecia y Génova).

dogged, a. ceñudo, intratable, áspero, brutal ; -ly, con ceño.

doggedness, s. ceño ; mohina, bronquedad

doggerel, a. & s. malos versos; burlesco.

dog-kennel, s. perrera.

dog-latin, s. latín bárbaro.

dogmatic(al), a. dogmatico ; -ly, dogmáticamente.

dog-rose, s. rosa silvestre.

dog's-ear, s. pliegue en los ángulos de la hoja de un libro.

Dog-star, s. Sirio ; canícula.

doings, s.pl. hechos, pl.; acciones, pl.; conducta, procedimiento.

doldrums, s.pl. (mar.) calma y vientos variables del Ecuador ; (col.) mal humor.

dole, s. distribución ; porción ; limosna : —, v.a. repartir, distribuir.

doleful, a. doloroso, lúgubre, triste.

doll, s. muñeca.

dollar, s. peso, duro.

dolomite, s. dolomia.

dolour, s. dolor, pesar, dolencia.

dolphin, s. delfín.

dolt, s. hombre bobo.

domain, s. dominio.

dome, s. cúpula.

domestic, a. doméstico, intestino.

domesticate, v.a. domesticar.

domestication, s. domesticación.

domesticity, s. domesticidad.

domicile, s. domicilio.

domiciliary, a. domiciliario.

dominate, v.n. dominar, predominar.

domination, s. dominación ; imperio.

domineer, v.n. dominar, señorear.

dominie, s. (col.) dómine, maestro.

dominion, s. dominio, territorio ; soberanía.

domino, s. dominó, traje de máscara ; -es, pl. dominó (juego). [profesor.

don, v.a. meter (el vestido) ; —, s. (col.)

donate, v.a. (am.) donar.

donation, s. donación.

done, p. & a. hecho ; cocido, asado.

donkey, s. asno, borrico ; — -engine, s. secunda máquina de los vapores.

donor, s. donador.

doom, s. sentencia, condena ; suerte ; —, v.a. juzgar, condenar.

doomsday, s. día del juicio universal.

door, s. puerta : within -s, en casa.

door-keeper, s. portero.

door-plate, s. planchuela, letrero.

doric, a dórico ; — s. dialecto.

dormant, a. durmiente ; secreto.

dormer-window, s. lumbrera.

dormitory, s. dormitorio.

dormouse, s. lirón.

dorsal, a. dorsal.

dose, s. dosis, porción ; —, v.a. medicinar.

dot, s. tilde ; —, v.a. tildar.

dotage, s. chochera, chochez.

dotard, s. viejo que chochea.

dotation, s. dotación.

dote, v.n. chochear.

dotingly, ad. con cariño excesivo.

double, a. doble, duplicado ; falso ; —, v.a. doblar ; plegar ; —, s. doble, duplo ; engaño ; artificio.

double-chin, s. papada.

double-dealing, s. duplicidad.

double-edged, a. con dos filas.

double-entry, s. (com.) partida doble.

double-lock, v.a. echar segunda vuelta á la llave.

doublet, s. justillo.

double-tongued, a. falso.

doubloon, s. doblón.

doubly, ad. doblemente.

doubt, s. duda, sospecha ; —, v.a. & n. dudar ; sospechar.

doubtful, a. dudoso, dudable ; incierto ; -ly, dudosamente.

doubtless, a. indubitable.

dough, s. masa (de pan).

doughty, a. bravo, valeroso.

douse, v.a. zabullir.

dove, s. paloma.

dove-cot, dove-house, s. palomar.

dovelike, a. columbino, inocente.

dove-tail, s. (carp.) cola de milano ; — v.a. ensamblar.

dowager, s. viuda de calidad que goza viudedad de su marido.

dowdy, a. (col.) desaliñado.

dower, s. dote, viudedad ; dotación.

dowered, a. dotado. [to sit —, sentarse.

down, s. plumón ; flojel ; —, ad. abajo ;

downcast, a. apesadumbrado, cabizbajo.

downfall, s. ruina, decadencia.

down-hill, a. pendiente, declive ; —, ad. cuesta abajo.

downright, a. patente, manifiesto ; franco, sincero ; —, ad. á plomo.

down-train, s. (rail.) tren descendente, el que viene de la capital.

downward, a. inclinado ; cabizbajo, triste ; -(s), ad. hacia abajo.

downy, a. velloso ; suave.

doxology, s. el *Gloria Patri*. [cabecear.

doze, s. medio sueño ; —, v.n. dormitar,

dozen, s. docena.

drab. s. especie de paño pardo ; (col.) mujerzuela ; —, a. de color entre gris y moreno.

drachm, s. dracma.

draft, s. dibujo ; letra de cambio ; —, v.a. dibujar ; (mil.) destacar.

drag, v.a. arrastrar ; tirar con fuerza ; —, v.n. arrastrar por el suelo ; —, s. carretilla ; freno de coche.

draggle, v.a. & n. ensuciar(se) alguna cosa arrastrandola por el suelo.

drag-net, s. red barredera.

dragoman, s. dragomán.

dragon, s. dragón.

dragon-fly, s. (entom.) libélula.

dragoon, s. (mil.) dragón.

drain, v.a. desaguar ; secar ; —, s. desaguadero.

drainage, s. desagüe ; derramamiento ; desecamiento, sistema de zanjas ó caños.

drake, s. ánade macho.

dram, s. copita ; trago.

drama, s. drama.

dramatic(al), a. dramático ; -ally, dramáticamente.

dramatist, s. dramático.

dramatize, v.a. dramatizar.

drape, v.a. vestir, cubrir, velar.

draper, s. pañero.

drapery, s. ropería ; ropaje.

drastic, a. eficaz, activo.

draught, s. trago ; poción ; bebida medicinal ; dibujo ; letra de cambio ; corriente de aire.

draught-board, s. tablero.

draught-horse, s. caballo de tiro.

draughts, s.pl. juego de las damas.

draughty, a. airoso, ventoso.

draw, v.a. tirar, traer ; atraer ; arrastrar ; dibujar ; to — nigh, acercarse.

drawback, s. desventaja ; (com.) rebaja, descuento.

draw-bridge, s. puente levadizo.

drawer, s. aguador ; mozo de taberna ; gaveta ; -s, pl. calzoncillos, pl.

drawing, s. dibujo.

drawing-room, s. sala, salón.

drawing-board, s. tabla para dibujar.

drawl, v.n. hablar con pesadez.

draw-well, s. pozo hondo.

dray, s. carro.

dray-man, s. carretero.

dread, s. miedo, terror, espanto ; —, a. terrible ; —, v.a. temer.

dreadful, a. terrible, espantoso ; -ly, terriblemente.

dreadnought, s. (mar.) navío acorazado grande y poderoso.

dream, s. sueño ; fantasía ; v.n. soñar ; imaginar.

dreaminess, s. sopor, letargo.

dreamy, a. quimérico, fabuloso.

drearily, ad. tristemente.

dreary, a. triste, tedioso.

dredge, v.a. (mar.) rastrear, cavar.

dredger, s. pescador de ostras ; barco rastreador ó excavador.

dregs, s.pl. hez ; morralla.

drench, v.a. empapar, humedecer ; abrevar ; purgar ; —, s. bebida purgante (para ciertos animales).

dress, v.a. vestir, ataviar ; curar las heridas ; ajustar ; cocinar ; aderezar ; —, v.n. vestirse ; —, s. vestido ; atavio, tocado.

dress-circle, s. balcón (de teatro).

dress-coat, s. frac.

dresser, s. estante de cocina ; aparador.

dressing, s. curación ; adorno, aderezo.

dressing-gown, s. peinador ; bata.

dressing-room, s. gabinete-tocador.

dressing-table, s. tocador.

dribble, v.n. gotear, babear ; —, v.a. hacer gotear.

dribblet, s. gota ; pedacito.

drift, s. impulso ; dirección, tendencia ; fuerza de un movimiento ; montón (de nieve ó de arena ; objeto de discurso ; designio ; — of sand, arena movediza ; —, v.n. vagar ó arrastrarse con el viento ; amontonarse (nieve).

drift-wood, s. leña acarreada por el agua.

drill, s. taladro ; terraja ; (mil.) instrucción de reclutas ; —, v.a. taladrar ; (mil.) disciplinar.

drink, v.a. & n. beber, embeber, absorber ; embriagarse ; —, s. bebida.

drinkable, a. potable.

drinking-bout, s. borrachera.

drip, v.a. despedir algún líquido á gotas ; —, v.n. gotear, destilar ; —, s. gotilla.

dripping, s. pringue.

dripping-pan, s. grasera.

drive, v.a. & n. impeler ; guiar, conducir (algún carruaje) ; llevar, forzar ; andar en coche ; to — at, designar ; —, s. paseo en coche.

drivel, s. baba ; cháchara, galimatías ; —, v.n. babear ; balbucir.

driver, s. empujador ; cochero ; carretero ; boyero;

drizzle, v.n. gotear ; lloviznar ; —, s. llovizna.

droll, a. jocoso, gracioso ; original ; -ly, jocosamente.

drollery, s. bufonería, bufonada, farsa.

dromedary, s. dromedario.

drone, s. zángano de colmena ; haragán ; —, v.n. zanganear ; dar un sonido sordo.

droop, v.n. descaecer ; penar, consumirse ; desfallecer.

drooping, a. lánguido.

drop, s. gota ; joya pendiente ; —, v.a. destilar ; soltar ; cesar ; dejar ; —, v.n. gotear ; desvanecerse ; caerse.

drop-scene, s. telón de entreacto.

dropsical, a. hidrópico.

dropsy, s. hidropesía.

dross, s. escoria de metales ; hez.

drought, s. seca ; sequedad ; sed.

drove, s. manada : hato ;

drover, s. ganadero.

drown, v.a. & n. ahogar(se) ; anegar(se).

drowsily, ad. soñolientamente ; lentamente.

drowsiness, s. somnolencia, pereza, indolencia.

drowsy, a. soñoliento ; estúpido.

drub, v.a. apalear, sacudir.

drubbing, s. paliza.

drudge, v.n. afanarse ; —, s. ganapán ; yunque, esclavo.

drudgery, s. trabajo vil.

drudgingly, ad. trabajosamente.

drug, s. droga ; —, v.a. adulterar ó envenenar (víveres) ; adormecer con narcóticos.

drugget, s. droguete.

druggist, s. droguero.

druid, s. druida.

drum, s. tambor ; tímpano (del oído) , —, v.n. tocar el tambor.

drum-major, s. tambor mayor.

drummer, s. tambor ; (am.) viajante con mercaderías.

drum-stick, s. palillo de tambor ; hueso de la pierna de un pollo.

drunk, a. borracho, ebrio, embriagado.

drunkard, s. borrachón, cuero ; bebedor.

drunken, a. ebrio.

drunkenness, s. embriaguez ; borrachera.

dry, a. árido, seco ; sediento ; frío ; insípido , —, v.a. secar ; enjugar ; —, v.n. secarse, enjugarse.

dryly, ad. secamente, fríamente ; estérilmente.

dryness, s. sequedad ; aridez de estilo.

drynurse, s. ama que cuida á un niño sin darle de mamar ; —, v.a. criar á un niño sin darle de mamar.

dry-rot, s. podre, podredumbre.

dry-shod, a. á pie enjuto, con los pies secos.

dual, a. binario.

dub, v.a. nombrar, titular.

dubiety, s. duda.

dubious, a. dudoso ; **-ly,** dudosamente

ducal, a. ducal.

ducat, s. ducado.

duchess, s. duquesa.

duchy, s. ducado.

duck, s. ánade ; tela para velas ; mona, querida (voz de cariño) ; —, v.a. (& n.) zabullir(se).

duckling, s. anadeja.

duckweed, s. lenteja acuática.

duct, s. (anat.) canal.

ductile, a. dúctil, flexible ; tratable

ductility, s. ductilidad ; docilidad

dudgeon, s. ojeriza, malicia.

duds, s.pl. (col.) atavío.

due, a. propio, debido, apto ; —, s. derecho ; tributo, impuesto.

duel, s. duelo.

duellist, s. duelista.

duet, s. (mus.) dúo.

duffer, s. (col.) estúpido.

dug, s. teta.

dug-out, s. (am.) piragua.

duke, s. duque.

dukedom, s. ducado.

dulcimer, s. (mus.) tímpano.

dull, a. lerdo, estúpido ; insípido ; obtuso ; tosco ; triste, murrio ; opaco ; — **of hearing,** algo sordo ; —, v.a. entontecer ; obstruir ; contristar ; ofuscar ; **-y,** estúpidamente ; lentamente.

dullard, s. estólido.

dulness, s. estupidez, torpeza ; somnolencia ; pereza ; pesadez.

duly, ad. debidamente ; puntualmente.

dumb, a. mudo.

dumbfounder, v.a. confundir ; enmudecer.

dumbness, mudez ; silencio.

dumb-show, s. pantomima. [de servicio.

dumb-waiter, s. mesita giratoria, mesa

dummy, s. espantajo ; maniquí.

dump, s. golpe de una caída ; —, v.a. tirar al suelo (un peso ó fardo).

dumpling, s. bola de pasta.

dumps, s.pl. murria, tristeza.

dumpy, a. gordo, rollizo.

dun, a. bruno ; sombrío ; —, —, s. acreedor importuno ; —, v.a. importunar un acreedor á su deudor.

dunce, s. zote, zopenco.

dune, s. médano, duna.

dung, s. estiércol ; —, v.a. estercolar.

dungeon, s. calabozo.

dung-hill, s. estercolero.

duodecimo, s. libro en dozavo.

dupe, s. bobo ; —, v.a. engañar, embaucar.

duplicate, a. & s. duplicado ; copia.

duplicity, s. doblez, duplicidad.

durability, s. estabilidad ; dura, duración.

durable, a. durable, duradero.

durance, s. cautividad.

duration, s. duración.

during, pr. mientras.
dusk, a. obscurecido, fusco; —, s. color fusco; crepúsculo.
duskily, ad. oscuramente.
dusky, a. obscuro.
dust, s. polvo; —, v.a. desempolvar.
dust-cart, s. carro de basura.
duster, s. rodilla.
dustman, s. basurero.
dusty, a. polvoriento.
duteous, a. fiel, leal.
dutiful, a. bueno, meritorio, obediente, sumiso; respetoso; -ly, debidamente, respetosamente.
dutifulness, s. exactitud, mérito, obediencia; respeto.
duly, s. deber; obligación; respeto, homenaje; derechos de aduanas, pl.

dwarf, s. enano; enana; —, v.a. achicar.
dwarfish, a. enano, pequeño.
dwell, v.n. habitar, morar; dilatarse.
dwelling, s. habitación; domicilio.
dwindle, v.n. mermar, disminuirse; degenerar; consumirse.
dye, v.a. teñir; —, s. tinte.
dyer, s. tintorero.
dyeing, s. tintorería, tintura.
dying, p. & a. agonizante, moribundo.
dynamics, s. dinamica. [—, s. muerte.
dynamite, s. dinámita.
dynamiter, s. dinamitista.
dynamo, s. dínamo.
dynasty, s. dinastía.
dysentery, s. disentería.
dyspepsia, s. (med.) dispepsia.
dyspeptic, a. dispéptico.

E

each, pn. cada uno; — other, unos á otros, mutuamente.
eager, a. deseoso; fogoso; ardiente, vehemente; -ly, vehementemente, ardientemente.
eagerness, s. ansia; anhelo; vehemencia; ardor.   [americana.
eagle, s. águila; moneda de oro norteeagle-eyed, a. de vista lince.
eaglet, s. aguilucho.
ear, s. oreja; oído; asa; espiga; by —, de oreja; —, v.n. espigar.
ear-ache, s. dolor de oídos.
earl, s. conde.
earldom, s. condado.
earliness, s. precocidad; presteza, prontitud.   [prano.
early, a. temprano, presto; —, ad. temear-mark, v.a. marcar, señalar; destinar.
earn, v.a. ganar, obtener, conseguir.
earnest, a. ardiente, fervoroso, serio, importante; —, s. señal; esperanza; prueba; in —, de buena fe; con sinceridad; -ly, seriamente; ansiosaearnest-money, s. caparra.   [mente.
earnestness, s. ansia; ardor, celo; seriedad, vehemencia.
earnings, s.pl. sueldo, salario.
ear-ring, s. zarcillo, pendiente.
earth, s. tierra; el globo; —, v.a. cubrir con tierra.
earth-born, a. terrestre, mortal.
earthen, a. terreno; hecho de tierra.
earthenware, s. loza de barro.
earthiness, s. terrenidad; grosería.
earthliness, s. vanidad mundana.
earthly, a. terrestre, mundano; sensual.
earthquake, s. terremoto, temblor de tierra.

earth-worm, s. lombriz.
ear-wig, s. tijereta.
ease, s. quietud; reposo, ocio; comodidad; facilidad; at —, con desahogo; —, v.a. aliviar; mitigar.
easel, s. caballete (de los pintores).
easement, s. alivio, apoyo; ventaja.
easily, ad. fácilmente; quietamente.
easiness, s. facilidad; quietud; comeast, s. oriente; este.   [placencia.
Easter, s. Pascua de resurrección; —-Eve, Sábado santo.
easterly, eastern, a. oriental.
eastward, ad. hacia el oriente.
easy, a. fácil; cortés, sociable; cómodo, pronto; libre; tranquilo, aliviado;
easy-going, inalterable, sereno.   [tarse.
eat, v.a. comer; roer; —, v.n. alimeneatable, a. comestible; -s, s.pl. viveres,pl.
eating-house, s. bodegón, fonda; ristorante, hostería.
eaves, s.pl. socarrén.
eaves-drop, v.a. escuchar á la ventana lo que se habla dentro de la casa.
ebb, s. baja ó caída del mareo; menguante; decremento; —, v.n. bajar, menguar; decaer, disminuir, bajar.
ebon, a. de ébano; negro.
ebony, s. ébano.
ebullition, s. ebullición, fermentación.
eccentric, a. excéntrico, raro.
eccentricity, s. excentricidad.
ecclesiastic, a. & s. eclesiástico.
echo, s. eco; —, v.n. resonar; —, v.a. repercutir.
eclectic, a. ecléctico.
eclipse, s. eclipse; —, v.a. eclipsar.
ecliptic, s. eclíptica.   [moderado.
economic(al), a. económico, frugal, parco,

economics, s.pl. ciencia económica.
economise, v.a. & n. economizar, ahorrar.
economist, s. economista.
economy, s. economía ; frugalidad.
ecstasy, s. éxtasi, éxtaxis. [tasis.
ecstatic(al), a. extático ; **-ally,** en ex-
ecumenical, a. ecuménico.
eczema, s. (med.) eczema.
eddy, s. remolino ; —, v.n. remolinar.
edge, s. filo ; punta ; esquina ; margen ;
  acrimonia ; —, v.a. ribetear ; introducir.
edge-tool, s. herramienta cortante.
edge-ways, ad. de filo, de lado.
edging, s. orla, orilla.
edible, a. comestible.
edict, s. edicto, mandato.
edification, s. edificación.
edifice, s. edificio.
edify, v.a. edificar ; instruir.
edit, v.a. comentar ó preparar una obra
  para la prensa. [presión.
edition, s. edición ; publicación ; im-
editor, s. editor.
editorial, a. editorial.
educate, v.a. educar ; enseñar.
education, s. educación, crianza.
educe, v.a. educir.
eel, s. anguila.
eerie, a. aduendado.
efface, v.a. borrar, destruir.
effacement, s. anulación, canceladura.
effect, s. efecto ; realidad ; **-s,** s.pl. efectos,
  bienes, pl. ; —, v.a. efectuar, ejecutar.
effective, a. eficaz ; efectivo ; real ; **-ly,**
  efectivamente, en efecto. [mente.
effectual, a. eficaz ; efectivo ; **-ly,** eficaz-
effeminacy, s. afeminación.
effeminate, v.a. afeminar, debilitar ; —,
  v.n. afeminarse, enervarse ; —, a.
  afeminado ; **-ly,** con afeminación.
effervesce, v.n. hervir, bullir.
effervescence, s. efervescencia ; hervor.
effete, a. degenerado ; inútil ; estéril.
efficacious, a. eficaz ; **-ly,** eficazmente
efficacy, s. eficacia.
efficiency, s. eficiencia, actividad, virtud.
efficient, a. eficaz.
effigy, s. efigie, imagen, retrato.
efflorescence, s. eflorescencia ; excre-
  cencia.
effluvium, s. efluvio ; emanación.
effort, s. esfuerzo, empeño.
effrontery, s. descaro ; impudencia, desvergüenza.
effulgence, s. esplendor, fulgor.
effulgent, a. resplandeciente.
effusion, s. efusión ; flujo de palabras.
eft, s. lagartija. [pujar.
egg. s. huevo ; **to — on,** v.a. incitar, em-
egg-cup, s. huevera.

egg-shell, s. cáscara de huevo.
eglantine, s. (bot.) escaramujo, rosí
  silvestre.
egoism, s. egoísmo (teórico ó filosófico)
egoist, s. egoísta.
egotism, s. egoísmo.
egotist, s. egoísta.
egotistic(al), a. egoísta.
egregious, a. egregio, famoso, excelente ;
  -ly, egregiamente.
egress, egression, s. salida.
eiderdown, s. edredón, plumón de ave.
eight, a. ocho.
eighteen, a. diez y ocho.
eighteenth, a. décimoctavo.
eighth, a. octavo ; **-ly,** en el octavo lugar.
eightieth, a. octogésimo.
eighty, a. ochenta. [c. ó.
either, pn. cualquiera, uno de dos ; —,
ejaculate, v.a. exclamar, gritar.
ejaculation, s. exclamación, grito.
eject, v.a. expeler, desechar.
ejection, s. expulsión.
eke, v.a. suplir, alargar ; prolongar.
elaborate, v.a. elaborar ; —, a. elaborado,
  primoroso ; **-ly,** cuidadosamente.
elapse, v.n. pasar, correr (el tiempo).
elastic, a. elástico ; repercusivo.
elasticity, s. elasticidad.
elate, a. altivo, orgulloso ; —, v.a.
  ensoberbecer ; exaltar, elevar.
elation, s. altivez, soberbia.
elbow, s. codo ; —, v.a. codear.
elbow-chair, s. sillón.
elbow-room, s. anchura ; espacio suficiente ; (fig.) libertad, latitud.
elder, s. (bot.) saúco ; —, a. mayor.
elderly, a. de edad ya madura. [pl.
elders, s.pl. ancianos, parientes mayores,
eldest, a. el más anciano, el mayor.
eldritch, (Scot.) a. aduendado, satánico.
elect, v.a. elegir ; —, a. elegido, escogido
election, s. elección.
electioneering, s. maniobras electorales,
  solicitación de votos.
elective, a. electivo.
elector, s. elector.
electoral, a. electoral.
electorate, s. electorado.
electric(al), a. eléctrico.
electrician, s. electricista.
electricity, v.a. electricidad. [pasmar.
electrify, v.a. electrizar ; asombrar,
electro-magnetism, s. electro-magnet-
  ismo.
electro-plating, s. plateadura eléctrica.
electrize, v.a. electrizar.
electuary, s. electuario. [limosna.
eleemosinary, a. pobre que vive de
elegance, s. elegancia. [elegantemente.
elegant, a. elegante, delicado ; **-ly,**

elegiac, a. elegíaco.
elegy, s. elegía.
element, s. elemento ; fundamento.
elemental, elementary, a. elemental, simple, inicial.
elephant, s. elefante.
elephantine, a. inmenso.
elevate, v.a. elevar, alzar, exaltar.
elevation, s. elevación ; altura ; alteza (de pensamientos).
eleven, a. once.
eleventh, a. onceno, undécimo.
elf, s. duende, trasgo.
elfin, a. aduendado.
elicit, v.a. sacar á luz, descubrir, revelar.
eligibility, s. elegibilidad.
eligible, a. elegible ; deseable.
eliminate, v.a. eliminar, descartar.
elk, s. ana (medida).
ell, s. ana (medida).
ellipse, s. (gr.) elipsis ; (geom.).
elliptic(al), a. elíptico.
elm, s. olmo.
elocution, s. elocución ; habla.
elocutionist, s. profesor de declamación.
elongate, v.a. alargar, prolongar.
elope, v.n. escapar, huir, evadirse.
elopement, s. fuga, huída, evasión (de amantes ó de novios).
eloquence, s. elocuencia.
eloquent, a. elocuente ; -ly, elocuentemente. [manera ; sino.
else, pn. otro ; —, c. de otro módo ó
elsewhere, ad. en otra parte.
elucidate, v.a. dilucidar, explicar.
elucidation, s. elucidación, explicación.
elude, v.a. eludir, evitar.
elusion, s. escapatoria ; fraude, artificio.
elusive, elusory, a. vago, artificioso, falaz.
elvish, a. aduendado.
elysian, a. elíseo, delicioso, celestial.
elysium, s. Elíseo.
emaciate, v.a. & n. enflaquecer.
emaciation, s. emaciación ; enflaquecimiento.
emanate, v.n. emanar.
emanation, s. emanación ; origen.
emancipate, v.a. emancipar ; libertar.
emancipation, s. emancipación.
emasculate, v.a. castrar ; enervar, debilitar ; —, a. enervado, débil.
embalm, v.a. embalsamar.
embank, v.a. terraplenar.
embankment, s. terraplén; dique, barraje.
embargo, s. embargo (detención de buques).
embark, v.a. & n. embarcar(se).
embarkation, s. embarcación.
embarrass, v.a. embarazar, enredar.
embarrassment, s. embarazo, enredo.
embassy, s. embajada.

embattle, v.a. formar en orden de batalla.
embellish, v.a. hermosear, adornar.
embellishment, s. adorno.
ember-days, s.pl. Témpora.
embers, s.pl. rescoldo.
embezzle, v.a. apropiarse bienes encargados, hurtar lo confiado.
embezzlement, s. hurto.
embitter, v.a. amargar, empeorar.
emblazon, v.a. blasonar.
emblem, s. emblema.
emblematic(al), a. emblemático, simbólico. [ficación.
embodiment, s. incorporación, personi-
embody, v.a. incorporar.
embolden, v.a. animar, [en relieve.
emboss, v.a. relevar, formar alguna cosa
embrace, v.a. abrazar ; contener ; —, s. abrazo.
embrasure, s. tronera.
embrocation, s. (med.) embrocación.
embroider, v.a. bordar.
embroidery, s. bordado ; bordadura.
embroil, v.a. embrollar ; confundir.
embryo(n), s. embrión. [imperfecto.
embryonic, a. embrionario, rudimental,
emendation, s. enmienda, corrección.
emerald, s. esmeralda.
emerge, v.n. salir, proceder.
emergency, s. emergencia ; necesidad urgente, crisis.
emery, s. esmeril.
emetic, s. emético, vomitivo.
emigrant, a. & s. emigrante, emigrado.
emigrate, v.n. emigrar.
emigration, s. emigración.
eminence, s. altura, sumidad ; eminencia, excelencia.
eminent, a. eminente, elevado ; distinguido ; -ly, eminentemente.
emissary, s. emisario ; agente.
emission, s. emisión.
emit, v.a. emitir ; arrojar, despedir.
emmet, s. hormiga.
emollient, a. emoliente.
emolument, s. emolumento, pago, saldo.
emotion, s. agitación del ánimo, conmoción, emoción. [nervioso.
emotional, a. concitativo, agitante ;
empale, v.a. empalar.
emperor, s. emperador.
emphasis, s. énfasis.
emphasise, v.a. acentuar, señalar.
emphatic(al), a. enfático ; -ally, enfáticamente.
empire, s. imperio.
empiric, s. empírico, medicastro ; -al, a. empírico ; -ally, empíricamente.
employ, v.a. emplear, ocupar ; —, s. empleo ; ocupación.
employer, s. amo, patrón.

employment, s. empleo ; ocupación.
emporium, s. emporio, almacén.
empower, v.a. autorizar, habilitar.
empress, s. emperatriz.
emptiness, s. vaciedad ; vacuo ; futilidad.
empty, a. vacío ; vano ; —, v.a. vaciar, evacuar.
empyrean, a. empíreo.
emu, s. casoar.
emulate, v.a. emular, competir ; imitar.
emulation, s. emulación ; rivalidad.
emulgent, a. emulgente.
emulous, a. émulo ; -ly, á competencia.
emulsion, s. emulsión.
enable, v.n. habilitar.
enact, v.a. decretar, ordenar.
enactment, s. (leg.) decreto, dictamen.
enamel, s. esmalte ; —, v.a. esmaltar.
enamour, v.a. enamorar.
encage, v.a. enjaular, encerrar.
encamp, v.a. acamparse.
encampment, s. campamento.
encase, v.a. encajar, encajonar.
encaustic, a. encáustico.
enchain, v.a. encadenar.
enchant, v.a. encantar ; -er, s. encantador -ress, encantadora.
enchantingly, ad. de un modo deleitoso.
enchantment, s. encanto, encantamiento.
encircle, v.a. cercar, circundar.
enclose, v.a. cercar, circumvalar, circundar ; incluir.
enclosure, s. cercamiento ; cercado.
encomium, s. encomio, elogio. [circuir.
encompass, v.a. circundar ; cercar ;
encore, ad. ¡ bis !, otra vez ; —, v.a. pedir que un actor repita lo cantado.
encounter, s. encuentro ; duelo ; pelea ; —, v.a. encontrar ; —, v.n. encontrarse ; combatir.
encourage, v.a. animar, alentar.
encouragement, s. estímulo, patrocinio.
encroach, v.a. usurpar, avanzar gradualmente.
encroachment, s. usurpación, intrusión.
encrust, incrustar.
encumber, v.a. embarazar, cargar.
encumbrance, s. embarazo, impedimento.
encyclical, encíclica.
end, s. fin ; extremidad ; término ; resolución ; intento ; on —, en pie, parado ; —, v.a. acabar ; concluir, fenecer ; —, v.n. acabarse, terminarse.
endanger, v.a. peligrar, arriesgar.
endear, v.a. encarecer.
endearment, s. requiebro, mimo, cariño.
endeavour, v.n. esforzarse ; intentar ; —, v.a. tentar ; —, s. esfuerzo.
endemic, a. endémico.
ending, s. conclusión, cesación, fin.

endive, s. (bot.) endibia.
endless, a. infinito, perpetuo ; -ly, sin fin, perpetuamente. [rizar.
endorse, v.a. endosar ; confirmar, auto-
endorsement, s. endoso, confirmación
endorser, s. endosador, endosante.
endow, v.a. dotar.
endowment, s. dote, dotación.
endurable, a. sufrible, tolerable.
endurance, s. paciencia ; tolerancia, sufrimiento. [durar.
endure, v.a. sufrir, soportar ; — v.n.
endways, endwise, ad. de punta, derecho.
enemy, s. enemigo, antagonista.
energetic, a. enérgico, vigoroso.
energy, s. energía, fuerza.
enervate, v.a. enervar, debilitar.
enfeeble, v.a. debilitar, enervar.
enfilade, s. fila, hilera ; —, v.a. (mil.) enfilar.
enfold, v.a. envolver, arrollar ; rodear.
enforce, v.a. esforzar ; violentar ; compeler.
enforcement, s. compulsión, coacción, fuerza ; sanción ; aprieto.
enfranchise, v.a. franquear ; naturalizar.
engage, v.a. empeñar, obligar, comprometer, halagar ; ocupar ; —, v.n. empeñarse ; (mil.) pelear.
engagement, s. empeño ; combate ; pelea ; obligación, compromiso ; desposorio.
engagingly, ad. de un modo halagüeño.
engender, v.a. engendrar ; producir ; —, v.n. producirse. [instrumento.
engine, s. ingenio ; máquina ; locomotora;
engine-driver, s. maquinista.
engineer, s. ingeniero ; maquinista.
engineering, sl. ingenería.
engrave, v.a. grabar ; esculpir ; tallar.
engraving, s. grabado ; estampa.
engross, v.a. copiar en limpio ; monopolizar.
engulf, v.a. engolfar ; engullir.
enhance, v.a. encarecer, levantar en alto; agravar.
enigma, s. enigma.
enigmatical, a. enigmático ; -ly, enigmáticamente .
enjoin, v.a. ordenar, prescribir ; advertir.
enjoy, v.a. gozar ; poseer. [fruición.
enjoyment, s. goce, disfrute ; placer, fruición.
enlarge, v.a. engrandecer, dilatar, extender ; desaprisionar ; —, v.n. extenderse, dilatarse.
enlargement, s. aumento ; ampliación, soltura.
enlighten, v.a. alumbrar ; iluminar ; instruir.
enlightenment, s. luces, pl., ilustración.
enlist, v.a. alistar.

enlistment, s. alistamiento.
enliven, v.a. animar ; avivar ; alegrar.
enmesh, v.a. enredar.
enmity, s. enemistad ; odio.
ennoble, v.a. ennoblecer.
enormity, s. enormidad ; atrocidad.
enormous, a. enorme ; **-ly,** enormemente
enough, ad. bastantemente ; suficiente
   —, s. bastante ; suficiencia.
enounce, v.a. declarar.
enquire, v.a. & n. informarse, tomar in-
    formes, averiguar, inquirir.
enquiry, s. indagación.
enrage, v.a. enfurecer, irritar. [encantar.
enrapture, v.a. arrebatar, entusiasmar
enrich, v.a. enriquecer ; adornar.
enrichment, s. enriquecimiento.
enrol, v.a. registrar ; arrollar.
ensconce, v.a. esconder.
enshrine, v.a. guardar para reliquia ;
    entronizar, exaltar.   [alférez.
ensign, s. (mil.) bandera ; abanderado,
ensign-bearer, s. abanderado, alférez.
enslave, v.a. esclavizar, cautivar.
ensnare, v.a. entrampar ; engañar.
ensue, v.n. seguirse ; suceder.
ensure, v.a. asegurar.
entablature, s. entablamento.
entail, s. (law) vínculo, mayorazgo ; —,
    v.a. vincular.   [embarazar.
entangle, v.a. enmarañar, embrollar,
entanglement, s. enredo, embarazo.
enter, v.a. entrar ; registrar ; empezar ;
   —, v.n. entrar ; empeñarse en algo ;
    emprender.
enterprise, s. empresa.
entertain, v.a. tratar ; hospedar ; man-
    tener ; entretener.
entertainer, s. huésped.
entertainment, s. conversación ; festejo ,
    mantenimiento ; entretenimiento, pa-
    satiempo.
enthral, v.a. oprimir, esclavizar ; (fig.)
    cautivar, encantar.
enthralling, a. interesante, absorbante.
enthrone, v.a. entronizar.
enthusiasm, s. entusiasmo.
enthusiast, s. entusiasta.
enthusiastic(al), a. entusiasmado.
entice, v.a. halagar, acariciar, excitar,
    inducir.
entire, s. entero, cumplido, completo,
    perfecto ; **-ly,** enteramente.
entirety, s. entereza, integridad.
entitle, v.a. intitular ; nombrar ; autorizar.
entity, s. entidad, existencia.
entomb, v.a. sepultar.
entomologist, s. entomólogo.
entomology, s. entomología.
entrails, s.pl. entrañas, pl.   [cipio.
entrance, s. entrada ; admisión ; prin-

entrance-hall, s. pórtico, vestíbulo.
entrance-money, s. entrada.   [ganar.
entrap, v.a. entrampar ; enredar ; en-
entreat, v.a. rogar, suplicar.
entreaty, s. petición, suplica, instancia.
entrust, v.a. confiar, encomendar.
entry, s. entrada.
entwine, v.a. entrelazar, enroscar.
enumerate, v.a. enumerar, numerar,
    contar.
enumeration, s. enumeración.
enunciate, v.a. enunciar, declarar.
enunciation, s. enunciación.
envelop, v.a. envolver.
envelope, s. sobre, cubierta.
envenom, v.a. envenenar, atosigar.
enviable, a. envidiable.
envious, a. envidioso ; **-ly,** envidiosa-
    mente.
environs, s.pl. vecindad , contornos, pl.
envoy, s. enviado ; mensajero.   [vidiar.
envy, s. envidia, malicia ; —, v.a. en-
enwray, v.a. envolver.
eolian, a. eolio.
epaulet, s. (mil.) charretera.
ephemeral, a. efímero.
epic, s. épico.
epicure, s. epicúreo.
epicurean, a. epicúreo ; epicúreo.
epidemic, a. epidémico ; —, s. epidemia
epigram, s. epígrama.
epigrammatic, a. epigramático.
epilepsy, s. epilepsia.
epileptic, a. epiléptico.
epilogue, s. ep logo.
Epiphany, s. Epifanía.
episcopacy, s. episcopado.
episcopal, -ian, a. episcopa .
episcopate, s. episcopado.
episode, s. episodio.
epistle, s. epístola.
epistolary, a. epistolar.
epitaph, s. epitafio.
epithet, s. epíteto.
epitome, s. epítome, compendio.
epitomize, v.a. epitomar, abreviar
epoch, s. época.
equable, a. uniforme, constante , **-bly,**
    uniformemente.
equal, a. igual ; justo ; semejante ;
    imparcial ; —, s. compañero, par , —,
    v.a. igualar ; compensar.
equalisation, s. igualamiento.
equalise, v.a. igualar.
equality, s. igualdad, uniformidad.
equally, ad. igualmente.
equanimity, s. ecuanimidad.
equation, s. ecuación.
equator, s. ecuador.
equatorial, a. ecuatorial, ecuatorio.
equerry, s. caballerizo del rey.

equestrian, a. ecuestre.
equidistant, a. equidistante.
equilateral, a. equilátero.
equilibrium, a. equilibrio.
equine, a. caballar.
equinoctial, a. equinoccial.
equinox, s. equinoccio. [armar.
equip, v.a. equipar, pertrechar ; aprestar,
equipage, s. equipaje, tren ; coche.
equipment, s. equipaje ; apresto.
equipoise, s. equilibrio.
equitable, a. equitativo, imparcial ; -bly,
equitativamente. [dad.
equity, s. equidad, justicia, imparciali-
equivalence, s. equivalencia.
equivalent, a. & s. equivalente.
equivocal, a. equívoco, ambiguo ; -ly,
equivocadamente, ambiguamente.
equivocate, v.a. usar equívocos.
equivocation, s. equívoco ; anfibología.
era, s. era, período.
eradicate, v.a. desarraigar, extirpar.
eradication, s. extirpación.
erase, v.a. cancelar, rayar, borrar.
eraser, s. raspador.
erasure, s. rascadura, borradura.
ere, pr. & c. antes, antes que.
erect, v.a. erigir ; establecer ; —, a.
derecho, en pie, parado.
erection, s. establecimiento, estructura.
ermine, s. armiño.
erotic, a. erótico.
err, v.n. vagar, errar ; desviarse.
errand, s. recado, mensaje.
errant, a. errante ; vagabundo, andante.
errantry, s. vida errante ; caballería
andante.
erratum, errata.
erratic, a. errático, errante ; irregular.
erring, a. errado, errante.
erroneous, a. erróneo ; falso ; equivocado;
-ly, erróneamente.
error, s. error, yerro.
eructation, s. eructación ; eructo.
erudite, a. erudito.
erudition, s. erudición ; doctrina.
eruption, s. erupción ; excursión hostil.
erysipelas, s. erisipela.
escalade, s. escalada. ·
escape, v.a. evitar ; escapar ; —, v.n.
evadirse, salvarse ; huirse ; —, s.
escapada, huída, fuga.
escarpment, s. (mil.) escarpe.
eschalot, s. (bot.) chalote.
escheat, s. bienes mostrencos ; —, v.a.
confiscar ; v.n. caducar al fisco.
eschew, v.a. huir, evitar, evadir.
escort, s. escolta ; —, v.a. escoltar,
· convoyar.
esculant, a. comestible, comedero.
escutcheon, s. escudo.

esoteric, a. esotérico.
especial, a. especial ; -ly, especialmente.
espial, espionage, s. espionaje.
esplanade, s. (mil.) esplanada.
espousals, s.pl. esponsales, desposorio.
espouse, v.a. desposar.
espy, v.a. espiar ; percibir ; descubrir.
Esquire, s. Señor (título).
essay, v.a. ensayar, tentar, probar ; —,
s. conato, ensayo : tentativa ; prueba,
experiencia ; tratado, folleto.
essayist, s. tratadista, escritor de folletos
ó artículos.
essence, s. esencia ; perfume.
essential, s. esencia ; —, a. esencial,
substancial, principal ; -ly, esencial-
mente. [confirmar.
establish, v.a. establecer, fundar, fijar ;
establishment, s. establecimiento ; fundación ; institución. [bienes.
estate, s. estado ; rango ; hacienda ;
esteem, v.a. estimar, apreciar ; pensar ;
—, s. estima ; consideración.
esthetic(al), a. estético.
estimable, a. estimable.
estimate, v.a. estimar, apreciar, tasar.
estimation, s. estimación, valuación ;
opinión.
estrange, v.a. extrañar, apartar, enajenar.
estrangement, s. enajenamiento ; extrañeza, distancia.
estuary, s. estuario, ría.
etch, v.a. grabar al agua fuerte.
etching, s. grabado al agua fuerte.
eternal, a. eterno, perpetuo, inmortal ;
-ly, eternamente.
eternity, s. eternidad.
ether, s. éter.
ethereal, a. etéreo, celeste.
ethic(al), a. ético ; -ally, moralmente ;
-s, s.pl. ética.
etymological, a. etimológico.
etymologist, s. etimologista.
etymology, s. etimología.
Eucharist, s. Eucaristía.
eulogise, v.a. elogiar.
eulogy, s. elogio, encomio ; alabanza.
eunuch, s. eunuco.
euphemism, s. eufemismo.
euphony, s. eufonía.
euphuism, s. gongorismo, estilo delicado
y afectado.
evacuate, v.a. evacuar.
evacuation, s. evacuación.
evade, v.a. evadir, escapar, evitar.
evanescent, a. fugitivo ; imperceptible.
evangelic(al), a. evangélico ; -ally, evan-
gélicamente.
evangelist, s. evangelista.
evaporate, v.a. & n. evaporar(se),
vaporizar(se), volatizar(se).

evaporation, s. evaporación.

evasion, s. evasión ; escape, efugio.

evasive, a. evasivo ; sofístico ; -ly, sofísticamente.

eve(n), s. tardecita ; vigilia, víspera.

even, a. llano, igual ; par, semejante ; —, ad. aun ; — as, como ; — so, lo mismo, de veras ; —, v.a. igualar, allanar.

even-handed, a. imparcial, equitativo.

evening, s. tarde.

evenly, ad. igualmente, llanamente.

evenness, s. igualdad ; uniformidad ; llanura ; imparcialidad.

evensong, s. (eccl.) vísperas.

event, s. evento, acontecimiento ; éxito.

eventful, a. lleno de acontecimientos, crítico, importante.

eventual, a. eventual; contingente, consecuente, final ; -ly, por consecuencia, en fin.

eventuality, s. eventualidad, suceso.

ever, ad. siempre ; for — and —, siempre jamás, eternamente ; — since, desde, desde que ; —, — and anon, de cuando en cuando.

evergreen, a. siempre verde.

everlasting, a. eterno.   [jamás.

evermore, ad. eternamente, para siempre

every, a. cada uno ó cada una ; — where, en ó por todas partes ; -thing, todo ; -one, -body, cada uno, cada una.

evict, v.a. despojar jurídicamente.

eviction, s. evicción, despojo jurídico.

evidence, s. evidencia ; testimonio, prueba ; —, v.a. evidenciar.

evident, a. evidente ; patente, manifiesto ; -ly, evidentemente.

evil, a. malo, depravado, pernicioso ; dañoso ; —, s. maldad ; daño ; calamidad.

evil-doer, s. malhechor.

evilly, ad. malamente, mal.

evil-minded, a. malo, malicioso, mal intencionado.   [muración, calumnia.

evil-speaking, s. maledicencia, mur-

evince, v.a. probar, justificar, demostrar.

eviscerate, s.a. destripar.

evocation, s. evocación.

evoke, v.a. evocar.

evolution, s. desplegadura ; evolución ; desarrollo.   [arse ; extraer.

evolve, v.a. & n. desenvolver ; desplég-

ewe, s. oveja (hembra del carnero).

ewer, s. palancana ó palangana, aljofaina.

exacerbate, v.a. exasperar, amargar.

exact, a. exacto, puntual ; cuidadoso ; —, v.a. exigir.

exaction, s. exacción, extorsión.

exactly, a. exactamente, puntualmente.

exactness, exactitude, s. exactitud.

exaggerate, v.a. exagerar.

exaggeration, s. exageración.

exalt, v.a. exaltar, elevar ; alabar ; realzar.

exaltation, s. exaltación, elevación.

examination, s. examen.

examine, v.a. examinar ; escudriñar.

example, s. ejemplar ; ejemplo.

exasperate, v.a. exasperar, irritar, enojar, provocar ; agravar, amargar.

exasperation, s. exasperación, irritación

excavate, v.a. excavar, ahondar.

excavation, s. excavación ; cavidad ; excava.

exceed, v.a. & n. exceder ; sobrepujar.

exceeding, a. excesivo ; -ly, extremamente, en sumo grado.

excel, v.a. sobresalir, exceder.

excellence, s. excelencia ; preeminencia.

Excellency, s. Excelencia (título).

excellent, s. excelente ; -ly, excelentemente.

except, v.a. exceptuar, excluir ; —, v.n. recusar ; -(ing), pr. excepto, á excepción de.

exception, s. excepción, exclusión.

exceptionable, a. recusable, expuesto á reparos y contradicciones.

exceptional, a. excepcional.   [extraer.

excerpt, s. extracto, selección ; — v.a.

excess, s. exceso ; intemperancia.

excessive, a. excesivo ; -ly, excesivamente.

exchange, v.a. cambiar; trocar, permutar; —, s. cambio ; bolsa, lonja.

exchangeable, a. cambiable.

exchequer, s. fisco ; tesorería.   [real.

exchequer-bill, exchequer-bond, s. vale

excise, s. sisa ; — v.a. sisar.

exciseman, s. sisero.

excision, s. excisión, extirpación.

excitability, s. excitabilidad.

excitable, a. excitable, nervioso, inquieto.

excite, v.a. excitar ; estimular.

excitement, s. estímulo, incitamento.

exclaim, v.n. exclamar, gritar.   [grito.

exclamation, s. exclamación ; clamor,

exclamatory, a. exclamatorio.

exclude, v.a. excluir ; exceptuar.

exclusion, s. exclusión, exclusiva, excepción.   [clusivamente.

exclusive, a. exclusivo ; -ly, ex-

excommunicate, v.a. excomulgar.

excommunication, s. excomunión.

excoriate, v.a. escoriar.

excoriation, s. excoriación.   [ales, pl.

excrement, s. excremento, materias fec-

excrescence, s. excrescencia.

excruciating, a. doloroso, penoso, atroz.

exculpate, v.a. disculpar ; justificar.

exculpation, s. disculpa.

exculpatory, a. justificativo.

excursion, s. excursión ; digresión.
excursionist, s. turista.
excusable, a. excusable.   [excusa.
excuse, v.a. excusar ; perdonar ; —, s.
execrable, a. execrable, detestable.
execrably, ad. execrablemente.
execrate, v.a. execrar, maldecir.
execration, s. execración, maldición.
execute, v.a. ejecutar ; ajusticiar.
execution, s. ejecución.
executioner, s. ejecutor ; verdugo.
executive, a. ejecutivo ; s. gobierno, administración, poder ejecutivo.
executor, s. albacea, testamentario.
exegesis, s. exegesis, interpretación.
exemplar, s. ejemplar, original, modelo.
exemplary, a. ejemplar.
exemplify, v.a. ejemplificar.
exempt, a. exento, inmune.
exemption, s. exención, franquicia.
exercise, s. ejercicio ; ensayo ; tarea ;
  práctica ; —, v.a. ejercitar ; atarear.
exert, v.a. emplear, aplicar ; to — one's
  self, esforzarse.
exertion, s. esfuerzo.
exfoliate, v.n. exfoliarse.
exfoliation, s. exfoliación.
exhalation, s. exhalación ; vapor.
exhale, v.a. exhalar.
exhaust, v.a. apurar, agotar, acabar,
  consumir.   [fatiga.
exhaustion, s. agotamiento, acabamiento.
exhaustive, a. profundo, escudriñador.
exhibit, v.a. exhibir ; mostrar ; —, s.
  (law) memorial, libelo.
exhibition, s. exhibición, presentación ;
  espectáculo ; exposición ; (acad.) beca.
exhibitioner, s. (acad.) beca, colegial
  prebendado.
exhibitor, s. expositor.
exhilarate, v.a. alegrar, animar.
exhilaration, s. alegría ; buen humor,
  regocijo.
exhort, v.a. exhortar, excitar.
exhortation, s. exhortación.
exhume, v.a. exhumar, desenterrar.
exigency, s. exigencia, necesidad, urgencia.   [deportar.
exile, s. destierro ; —, v.a. desterrar,
exist, v.n. existir.
existence, s. existencia.   [presente.
existent, existing, a. existente ; actual,
exit, s. partida, salida ; éxito.
exodus, s. éxodo ; emigración.
exonerate, v.a. exonerar, descargar.
exoneration, s. exoneración.
exorbitance, s. exorbitancia, enormidad.
exorbitant, s. exorbitante, excesivo.
exorcise, v.a. exorcisar, conjurar.
exorcism, s. exorcismo.
exordium, s. exordio.

exotic, a. exótico, extranjero ; —, s.
  planta exótica.
expand, v.a. extender, dilatar.
expanse, s. extensión de lugar, espacio.
expansive, a. expansivo.
expatiate, v.n. espaciarse.
expatriate, v.a. expatriar, desterrar.
expect, v.a. esperar, aguardar.
expectance, expectancy, s. expectación,
  esperanza.
expectant, a. & s. esperador.
expectation, s. expectación, expectativa.
expectorate, v.a. expectorar, escupir.
expectoration, s. expectoración.
expediency, s. propriedad ; conveniencia,
  oportunidad.
expedient, a. oportuno, conveniente ; —,
  s. expediente, medio ; -ly, conveniente-
  mente, prudentemente.
expedite, v.a. acelerar ; expedir.
expedition, s. expedición, priesa.
expeditious, a. pronto, expedito ; -ly,
  prontamente.
expel, v.a. expeler, desterrar.
expend, v.a. expender ; desembolsar.
expenditure, s. gasto, desembolso.
expense, s. gasto, costa, expensas, pl.
expensive, a. pródigo ; costoso ; -ly,
  costosamente.
experience, s. experiencia ; práctica ; —
  v.a. experimentar, probar.
experiment, s. experimento, ensayo ; —
  v.a. experimentar.
experimental, a. experimental ; -ly,
  experimentalmente.   [diestro.
expert, a. & s. perito, experto, práctico,
expertness, s. maña, destreza, habilidad.
expiate, v.a. expiar ; reparar.
expiation, s. expiación.
expiatory, a. expiatorio.   [mino, plazo.
expiration, s. expiración ; remate, tér-
expire, v.n. expirar.
expiry, s.   V. expiration.
explain, v.a. explicar.
explanation, s. explicación.
explanatory, a. explicativo.
expletive, a. expletivo.
explicable, a. explicable.
explicit, a. explícito ; -ly, explícitamente,
  categóricamente.
explode, v.a. & n. estallar(se) ; hacer
  explosión ; disipar (un error).
exploit, s. hazaña ; hecho heroico.
exploration, s. exploración ; examen.
explore, v.a. explorar, examinar; sondear.
explorer, s. explorador.
explosion, s. explosión.
explosive, a. explosivo.
exponent, s. expositor, representante ;
  (ar.) exponente.
export, v.a. exportar.

export, exportation, s. exportación.
expose, v.a. exponer ; mostrar ; descubrir; desenmascarar, sacar á luz.
exposition, exposición, interpretación.
expostulate, v.n. reconvenir, debatir, contender.   [debate ; disputa.
expostulation, s. queja, reconvención,
exposure, s. exposición, desnudez, desámparo.
expound, v.a. exponer ; interpretar.
express, v.a exprimir ; representar ; —, a. expreso, claro; —, s. expreso, correo ; (rail.) tren expreso.
expression, s. expresión ; locución, animación del rostro.
expressionless, a. sin expresión (cara).
expressive, a. expresivo, -ly, expresivamente.
expressly, ad. expresamente, de propósito.
expropriate, v.a. expropriar (por causa de utilidad pública).
expropriation, s. (law) expropiación.
expulsion, s. expulsión.
expunge, v.a. borrar, cancelar.
expurgate, v.a. expurgar.
expurgation, s. purificación, expurgo.
exquisite, a. exquisito, perfecto, excelente; -ly, exquisitamente.
exquisiteness, s. primor, excelencia.
extant, s. estante, existente.
extemporaneous, extemporary, a. extemporáneo, improviso.
extempore, ad. de improviso, in promptu.
extemporize, v.n. improvisar.
extend, v.a. extender ; amplificar ; —, v.n. extenderse.
extension, s. extensión. [extensivamente.
extensive, a. extenso, dilatado ; -ly,
extent, s. extensión.   [atenuar.
extenuate, v.a. extenuar, disminuir,
extenuation, s. extenuación ; mitigación.
exterior, a. & s. exterior.
exterminate, v.a. exterminar ; extirpar.
extermination, s. exterminación, extirpación.
external, a. externo ; -ly, exteriormente ; -s, s.pl. exterior, formas, pl., apariencia.
extinct, a. extinto ; abolido.
extinction, s. extinción ; abolición.
extinguish, v.a. extinguir ; suprimir.
extinguisher, s. matacandelas.

extirpate, v.a. extirpar.
extirpation, s. extirpación ; exterminio.
extol, v.a. alabar, magnificaı, alzar, exaltar, ponderar.
extort, v.a. sacar por fuerza ; adquirir por violencia.
extortion, s. extorsión.
extortionate, a. avaro, opresivo, violento.
extortioner, s. exactor opresivo ó violento.   [extraordinario.
extra, ad. extra ; —, a. adicional,
extract, v.a. extraer, extractar ; —, s. extracto ; compendio.
extraction, s. extracción, descendencia.
extradite, v.a. (law) devolver un reo refugiado al gobierno de su país.
extradition, s. (law) extradición.
extraneous, a. extraño, exótico, ajeno.
extraordinarily, ad. extraordinariamente.
extraordinary, a. extraordinario.
extravagance, s. extravagancia ; gastos excesivos, pl., predigálidad.
extravagant, a. extravagante, singular, exorbitante ; pródigo ; -ly, extravagantemente.
extreme, a. extremo, supremo ; último ; —, s. extremo ; -ly, extremamente.
extremity, s. extremidad.
extricate, v.a. desembarazar, desenredar.
extrication, s. desembarazo.
extrinsic(al), a. extrínseco.   [dancia.
exuberance, s. exuberancia, suma abun-
exuberant, a. exuberant, abundantísmo ; -ly, abundantemente.
exude, v.n. transpirar, exudar.
exult, v.a. exultar, regocijarse, triunfar.
exultation, s. exultación ; regocijo
eye, s. ojo ; corcheta ; (bot.) botón ; —, —, v.a. ojear, contemplar, observar.
eye-ball, s. globo del ojo.
eye-brow, s. ceja.
eye-glass, s. anteojo ; lente.
eye-lash, s. pestaña.
eyelet, s. ojete.
eye-lid, s. párpado.
eye-sight, s. vista.
eye-sore, s. objeto odioso, pesadilla.
eye-tooth, s. colmillo.
eye-wash, s. colirio.
eye-witness, s. testigo ocular.
eyry, eyrie, s. nido de ave de rapiña.

F

fable. s. fábula ; ficción.   [tejido.
fabric, s. fábrica ; edificio ; manufactura ;
fabricate, v.a. fabricar, edificar, fingir.
fabrication, s. fabricación, ficción.
fabulous, a. fabuloso : -ly, fabulosamente.

face, s. cara, faz, rostro, haz ; superficie ; fachada ; frente ; aspecto ; aparencia ; atrevimiento ; in my —, á mi presencia. —, v.a. encararse ; hacer frente.
face-ache, s. nevralgia facial.

facet, s. faceta.
facetious, a. chistoso, alegre, gracioso ; -ly, chistosamente.
facial, a. facial.
facile, a. fácil, afable.
facilitate, v.a. facilitar.
facility, s. facilidad, ligereza ; afabilidad.
facing, s. paramento ; —, a. en frente.
fac-simile, s. facsímile, copia exacta.
fact, s. hecho ; realidad ; in the —, en el acto.
faction, s. facción ; disensión.
factionary, factionist, s. faccioso, inquieto.
factious, a. faccioso; -ly, sediciosamente.
factiousness, s. espíritu de facción.
factitious, a. facticio.
factor, s. factor (agente) ; (ar.) factor.
factory, s. factoría, fábrica.
factotum, s. factótum.
faculty, s. facultad ; poder, privilegio.
fad, s. (col.) manía.
fade, v.n. decaer, marchitarse, fallecer.
fag, s. (col.) trabajador ; esclavo ; —, v.n. desmayarse ; (col.) afanarse, esforzarse.
fag-end, s. cadillos, pl., desechos, pl.
fagot, s. haz, gavilla de leña.
fail, v.a. & n. omitir, abandonar ; descuidar ; faltar ; perecer ; perderse.
failing, s. falta ; defecto, vicio.
failure, s. falta ; culpa ; descuido ; quiebra, bancarrota.
fain, a. inclinado, gustoso ; —, ad. de buena gana.
faint, v.n. desmayarse, desfallecer, debilitarse ; —, s. desmayo, deliquio ; —, a. débil, lánguido ; cobarde ; -ly, débilmente.
faint-hearted, a. cobarde, medroso, pusilánime ; -ly, medrosamente.
faintness, s. languidez, flaqueza ; timidez.
fair, a. hermoso, bello ; blanco ; rubio ; claro, sereno ; recto, justo ; franco ; —, s. feria.
fairly, ad. decentemente, justamente.
fairness, s. hermosura ; honradez ; candor.
fair-play, s. lealtad, candidez.
fair-spoken, a. bien hablado, cortés.
fairy, s. duende ; bruja, encantadora ; —, a duendado, mágico, encantador.
faith, s. fe ; dogma de fe ; fidelidad, sinceridad.
faithful, a. fiel, leal ; -ly, fielmente.
faithfulness, s. fidelidad, lealtad.
faithless, a. infiel, pérfido, desleal.
fakir, s. faquir.
falchion, s. cimitarra, (poet.) espada.
falcon, s. halcón.
falconer, s. halconero.

falconry, s. halconería.
fall, v.n. caer(se) ; disminuir, decrecer, bajar ; to — asleep, dormirse ; to — short, faltar ; to — sick, enfermar ; to — in love, enamorarse ; to — off, separarse ; disminuir ; apostatar ; to — out, reñir, disputar ; acaecer, acontecer ; to — upon, atacar, asaltar ; —, s. caída ; declive ; catarata.
fallacious, a. falaz, fraudulento ; -ly, falazmente.
fallacy, s. falacia, sofistería ; engaño.
fallibility, s. falibilidad.
fallible, a. falible.
falling-sickness, s. epilepsia.
falling-star, s estrella fugaz.
fallow, a. flavo ; (agr.) no sembrado ; — deer, s. corzo ; corza.
false, a. falso, pérfido ; -ly, falsamente ; pérfidamente.
falsehood, falseness, s. falsedad ; perfidia.
falsetto, a. & s. falsete.
falsify, v.a. falsificar.
falsity, s. falsedad, mentira.
falter, v.n. tartamudear ; vacilar.
faltering, s. debilidad ; defecto ; —, a. balbuciente, tartamudo.
fame, s. fama ; renombre.
famed, a. famoso, renombrado.
familiar, a. familiar ; casero ; -ly, familiarmente ; —, s. amigo íntimo.
familiarity, s. familiaridad.
familiarize, v.a. familiarizar.
family, s. familia ; linaje ; clase, especie.
famine, s. hambre ; carestía.
famish, v.a. hambrear ; —, v.n. morirse de hambre.
famous, a. famoso, renombrado ; -ly, famosamente.
fan, s. abanico ; —, v.a. abanicar ; aventar.
fanatic, a. & s. fanático.
fanaticism, s. fanatismo.
fanciful, a. imaginativo, caprichoso ; -ly, caprichosamente.
fancifulness, s. antojo, capricho.
fancy, s. fantasía, imaginación ; capricho ; —, v.n. imaginar ; amar ; apasionarse, figurarse ; fantasear.
fancy-articles, fancy-goods, s.pl. novedades, modas, pl.
fancy-ball, s. baile de máscaras.
fancy-fair, s. bazar.
fancy-free, a. libre de amores
fane, s. (poet.) templo.
fanfare, s. (mus.) charanga.
fang, s. colmillo ; garra, uña.
fanged, a. colmilludo.
fantastic(al), a. fantástico ; caprichoso ; -ally, fantásticamente.
fantasy, s. fantasía.

far, ad. lejos ; —, a. lejano, distante, remoto ; — and away, con mucho, de mucho ; — off, lejano.

farce, s. farsa.

farcical, a. ridículo, absurdo.

fare, s. comida ; pasaje ; —, v.n. viajar ; ir, andar (mal ó bien).

farewell, s. despedida ; —! ad. ¡ á Dios ! ¡ siga U. bueno !

far-fetched, a. exagerado, forzado.

farinaceous, a. harinoso, farináceo.

farm, s. tierra arrendada ; alquería ; —, v.a. arrendar ; tomar en arriendo ; cultivar.   [brantia ; labrador.

farmer, s. arrendatario de tierra la-

farm-house, s. granja.

farming, s. agricultura.

farm-yard, s. corral.

farrago, s. fárrago ; broza.

farrier, s. herrador.

farriery, s. albeitería.

far-seeing, a. perspicaz.

farther, farthest, comp. y superl. de far, a. & ad. más lejos, lo más lejos.

farthing, s. cuarto de penique ; ardite.

fascinate, v.a. fascinar, encantar.

fascination, s. fascinación ; encanto.

fascine, s. fajina, haz.

fashion, s. forma, figura ; moda ; uso ; —, v.a. formar, amoldar.

fashionable, a. hecho á la moda ; elegante ; -bly, á ó según la moda.

fast, v.n. ayunar ; —, s. ayuno ; —, a. firme, estable ; veloz, pronto ; —, ad. firmemente ; estrechamente ; de prisa.

fast-day, s. día de ayuno.

fasten, v.a. afirmar, asegurar, atar ; fijar ; —, v.n. pegarse.   [fastidiosamente.

fastidious, a. fastidioso, desdeñoso ; -ly,

fastness, s. prontitud ; firmeza ; fortaleza.

fat, a. gordo, pingüe ; —, s. gordo ; grasa.

fatal, a. fatal ; funesto ; -ly, fatalmente.

fatalist, s. fatalista.

fatality, s. fatalidad, predestinación.

fate, s. hado, destino ; -s, pl. (poet.) Parcas, pl.

fated, a. destinado ; inevitable.

fateful, a. fatídico, portentoso.

father, s. padre.

fatherhood, s. paternidad.

father-in-law, s. suegro.

fatherland, s. patria.

fatherless, a. huérfano de padre.

fatherly, a. paternal.

fathom, s. braza (medida) ; —, v.a. sondar ; penetrar.

fathomless, a. insondable.   [fatigar.

fatigue, s. fatiga, cansancio ; —, v.a.

fatness, s. gordura, pinguosidad.

fatten, v.a. cebar, engordar ; —, v.n. engrosarse.

fattening, s. cebadura.

fatty, a. untoso, craso, píngüe.

fatuity, s. fatuidad, simpleza.

fatuous, a. fatuo, tonto, imbécil.

fault, s. falta, culpa ; delito ; defecto.

fault-finder, s. censurador.

faultily, ad. defectuosamente.

faultiness, s. culpa ; defecto.

faultless, a. perfecto, intachable.

faulty, a. culpable, defectuoso.

faun, s. fauno.

favour, s. favor, beneficio ; patrocinio ; blandura ; —, v.a. favorecer, proteger.

favourable, a. favorable, propicio ; -bly, favorablemente.

favoured, a. favorecido.

favourite, s. favorito ; —, a. favorecido.

fawn, s. cervato ; —, v.n. adular servilmente.

fawningly, lisonjeramente.

fay, s. duende.

fealty, s. homenaje ; fidelidad, lealtad.

fear, v.n. temer ; —, s. miedo.

fearful, a. medroso, temeroso ; tímido ; -ly, medrosamente, temerosamente ; terriblemente.   [sin miedo.

fearless, a. intrépido, atrevido ; -ly,

fearlessness, s. intrepidez.

feasibility, s. posibilidad.

feasible, a. factible, hacedero.

feast, s. banquete, festín ; fiesta ; —, v.a. v.a. festejar, regalar ; —, v.n. comer opíparamente.

feaster, s. goloso ; anfitrión.

feat, hecho ; acción, hazaña.

feather, s. pluma ; (fig.) bagatela ; —, v.a. emplumar.

feather-bed, s. plumón.

feathery, a. plumado ; ligero.

feature, s. rostro ; facción del rostro ; forma.

febrile, a. febril.

February, s. febrero.

fecund, a. fecundo, fértil.   [abundancia.

fecundity, s. fecundidad, fertilidad ;

federal, a. federal.

federalist, s. federalista.

federate, a. conferado.

federation, s. confederación.

fee, s. feudo ; paga, gratificación ; salario ; —, v.a. pagar ; premiar.

feeble, a. flaco, débil.

feebleness, s. debilidad.

feebly, ad. débilmente.

feed, v.a. pacer ; nutrir ; alimentar ; —, v.n. nutrirse ; engordar ; —, s. pasto.

feeder, s. el que da de comer ; glotón ; babadero.

feeding-bottle, s. bebedero.

feel, v.a. sentir ; palpar ; —, v.n. tener sensibilidad ; —, s. tacto, sentido.

feeler, s. antenas, pl. ; (fig.) tentativa.
feeling, s. tacto ; sensibilidad.
feelingly, ad. sensiblemente.
feet, s. plur. de **foot**.
feign, a. inventar, fingir ; disimular.
feignedly, ad. fingidamente.
feint, s. ficción ; finta.
felicitate, v.a. felicitar ; congratular.
felicitation, s. felicitación, congratu-
felicitous, a. feliz, dichoso.   [lación.
felicity, s. felicidad, dicha.
feline, a. gatuno.
fell, a. cruel, bárbaro ; —, s. cuero ;
piel ; pellejo ; —, v.a. cortar (arboles).
felloe, **felly**, s. pina de una rueda..
fellow, s. compañero, camarada ; socio
de algún colegio.
fellow-citizen, s. conciudadano.
fellow-creature, s. prójimo.
fellow-feeling, s. simpatía.
fellow-prisoner, s. compañero de prisión.
fellowship, s. compañía, sociedad ; beca
(en un colegio).
fellow-soldier, s. conmilitón.
fellow-student, s. condiscípulo.
fellow-sufferer, s. compañero de infortunio.
fellow-traveller, s. compañero de viaje.
felon, s. reo de un delito serio ; —, a.
cruel, traidor.   [oramente.
felonious, a. traidor, pérfido ; **-ly**, traid-
felony, s. felonía.
felt, s. fieltro.
felucca, s. feluca.
female, s. hembra ; —, a. femenino.
feminine, a. feminino ; femenil, tierno ;
afeminado, amujerado.
fen, s. almarjal, pantano.
fence, s. cerca, palizada ; defensa ; —,
v.a. cercar ; defender, preservar ; —,
v.n. esgrimir.   [cercado.
fenceless, a. abierto, lo que no está
fencing, s. esgrima.
fencing-master, s. maestro de armas.
fend, v.a. parar ; rechazar ; —, v.n.
defenderse.   [lante del hogar.
fender, s. barandilla que se pone de-
fennel, s. (bot.) hinojo.
ferment, s. fermento ; —, v.a. & n. hacer
fermentar ; fermentar.
fermentation, s. fermentación.
fern, s. (bot.) helecho.
fernery, s. helechar.
ferocious, a. feroz ; fiero ; **-ly**, ferozmente.
ferocity, s. ferocidad, fiereza.
ferret, s. hurón ; —, v.a. huronear ; **to —
out**, descubrir, escudriñar.
ferruginous, a. ferruginoso.
ferrule, s. virola, regatón.
ferry, s. barca de transporte ; v.a. —,
llevar en barca.

ferry-man, s. barquero.
fertile, a. fértil, fecundo.
fertilise, v.a. fertilizar.
fertility, s. fertilidad, fecundidad.
ferule, s. férula, palmeta.
fervency, s. fervor, celo.   [fervor.
fervent, a. ferviente ; fervoroso ; **-ly**, con
fervid, a. ardiente, vehemente.
fervour, s. fervor, ardor.
festal, **festive**, a. festivo.
fester, v.n. enconarse, inflamarse.
festival, a. festivo ; —, s. día festivo.
festivity, s. festividad.
festoon, s. festón ; —, v.a. festonear.
fetch, v.a. traer ; producir ; llevar
fetid, a. fétido, hediondo.
fetlock, s. cerneja.
fetter, v.a. atar con cadenas.
fetters, s.pl. grillos, pl.
feud, s. riña, contienda ; feudo
feudal, a. feudal.
feudalism, s. feudalismo.
feudatory, s. feudatario.
fever, s. fiebre ; **yellow —**, vómito negro.
feverish, a. febril.
few, a. poco ; **a —**, algunos ; **— and far
between**, pocos y raros.
fewness, s. poquedad ; corto número.
fiat, s. mandato absoluto, fiat.
fib, mentira ; —, v.n. mentir.
fibre, s. fibra, hebra.
fibrous, a. fibroso.   [ligero.
fickle, a. voluble, inconstante, mudable,
fickleness, s. volubilidad, inconstancia.
fiction, s. ficción ; invención.
fictitious, a. ficticio ; fingido ; **-ly**, fingidamente.
fiddle, s. violín ; —, v.n. tocar el violín ;
juguetear, travesear.
fiddler, s. violinista.   [naná !
fiddlesticks, s.pl. (col.) disparates ; ¡ nini
fiddle-string, s. cuerda de violín.
fidelity, s. fidelidad, lealtad.
fidget, v.n. inquietarse, atrafagarse, cazcalear ; —, s. agitación inquieta ;
hombre azogado, azogue.
fidgety, a. (col.) inquieto, impaciente.
fiduciary, a. & s. fiduciario.
fie, ¡ vaya !
fief, s. feudo.
field, s. campo ; campaña ; espacio.
field-day, s. (mil.) día de maniobras.
fieldfare, s. zorzal (pájaro).
field-marshal, s. (mil.) general en jefe.
field-mouse, s. turón.
field-piece, s. artillería de campaña.
field-sports, s.pl. caza.
fiend, s. demonio.
fiendish, a. demoniaco.   [furiosamente.
fierce, a. fiero, feroz ; cruel, furioso ; **-ly**,
fierceness, s. fiereza, ferocidad.

fieriness. s. ardor ; fogosidad.
fiery, a. ígneo ; fogoso, colérico.
fife, s. pífano.
fifteen, a. quince.
fifteenth, a. décimoquinto.
fifth, s. quinto ; -ly, en quinto lugar.
fiftieth, a. quincuagésimo.
fifty, a. cincuenta.
fig, s. higo ; (fig.) ardite.
fig-pecker, s. becafigo.
fig-tree, s. higuera.
fight, v.a. & n. reñir ; batallar ; combatir ;
    —, s. batalla ; combate ; pelea.
figment, s. ficción.   [damente.
figurative, a. figurativo ; -ly, figura-
figure, s. figura, forma, hechura ; imagen;
    cifra ; —, v.a. figurar.
figure-head, s. (mar.) figura de proa.
filament, s. filamento ; fibra.
filbert, s. avellana de cáscara delgada.
filch, v.n. ratear.
filcher, s. ratero, ladroncillo.
file, hilo ; lista ; (mil.) fila, hilera ; lima ;
    —, v.a. enhilar ; limar ; pulir ; to — off,
    (mil.) desfilar.
file-cutter, s. picador de limas.
filial, a. filial.
filibuster, s. pirata, filibustero.
filigree, s. filigrana.
filings, s.pl. limaduras, pl.
fill, v.a. llenar, henchir ; hartar ; —, v.n.
    hartarse ; —, s. hartura, abundancia.
fillet, s. venda, faja ; lonja de carne.
fillip, s. capirotazo.
filly, s. potranca.
film, s. película, membrana.
filter, s. filtro ; —, v.a. filtrar.
filth(iness), s. inmundicia, porquería ;
    fango, lodo.
filthily, ad. suciamente.
filthy, a. sucio.
filtration, s. filtración.
fin, s. aleta (de pez).
final, a. final, último ; -ly, finalmente.
finance, s. hacienda pública, adminis-
    tración del fisco.
financial, a. rentístico.   [financiero.
financier, s. estadista de hacienda ;
finch, s. pinzón.   [s. hallazgo.
find, v.a. hallar, descubrir ; proveer ; —,
fine, a. fino ; agudo, cortante ; claro,
    trasparènte ; delicado ; astuto ; diestro;
    galán, lindo ; elegante ; bello ; bien
    criado ; —, s. multa ; in —, finalmente,
    por fin ; —, v.a. afinar, refinar ; multar.
finely, ad. con elegancia.
fineness, s. fineza, delicadeza, hermosura.
finery, s. adorno, atavío.
fine-spun, a. (fig.) sútil.   [manejar.
finger, s. dedo ; —, v.a. tocar, manosear ;
finger-board, s. teclado ; teclas, pl.

finger-glass, s. enjuague.
finger-post, s. poste de señal ; indicador.
finger-stall, s. dedal.
finical, a. afectado.
finish, v.a. acabar, terminar, concluir.
finite, a. finito.
finny, a. armado de aletas.
fir(-tree), s. abeto.
fire, s. fuego ; incendio ; —, v.a. quemar,
    inflamar ; —, v.n. encenderse ; (mil.)
    tirar, hacer fuego.
fire-arms, s.pl. armas de fuego, pl.
fire-ball, s. granada real ó de mano ;
    metéoro, meteoro.   [dor.
fire-brand, s. tizón ; incendiario ; agita-
fire-brigade, s. bomberos.
fire-damp, s. aire inflamable en las
    minas.
fire-eater, s. fanfarrón, espadachín.
fire-engine, s. bomba de apagar los in-
    cendios.   [para incendios.
fire-escape, s. aparato de salvamento
fire-fly, s. luciérnaga.
fire-man, s. bombero ; (rail.) fogonero.
fire-place, s. hogar, fogón.   [bustible.
fire-proof, a. á prueba de fuego ; incom-
fire-shovel, s. paleta ; badil.
fire-side, s. hogar.
fire-wood, s. leña.
fireworks, s.pl. fuegos artificiales.
firing, s. leña ; (mil.) descarga. [barrel]
firkin, s. cuarterola (medida inglesa=¼
firm, a. firme, estable, constante ; —, s.
    (com.) firma ; -ly, ad. firmemente.
firmament, s. firmamento.
firmness, s. firmeza ; constancia.
first, a. primero ; —, ad. primeramente ;
    at —, al principio ; -ly, en primer lugar.
first-born, firstling, s. primogénito.
first-fruits, s.pl. primicias.
first-rate, a. de primera clase, excelente.
firth, s. ría.
fisc, s. fisco, Hacienda pública.
fiscal, a. fiscal.
fish, s. pez, pescado ; —, v.n. pescar.
fisher, fisherman, s. pescador.
fishery, s. pesca ; pesquera.
fish-hook, s. anzuelo.
fishing, s. pesca.
fishing-line, s. sedal.
fishing-rod, s. caña de pescar.
fish-market, s. pescadería.
fish-monger, s. pescadero.
fish-pond, s. estanque de peces.
fish-wife, s. pescadera.
fishy, a. abundante de pescado ; (col.)
    sospechoso, equívoco.
fissure, s. grieta, hendedura.
fist, s. puño.
fisticuffs, s.pl. (col.) combate á puñadas.
fistula, s. fístula, fístola.

fit, s. paroxismo ; convulsión ; capricho ; ímpetu, arranque ; —, a. apto, idóneo, capaz ; cómodo ; justo ; —, v.a. ajustar, acomodar, adaptar ; to — out, proveer, equipar ; —, v.n. convenir.

fitful, a. variable, caprichoso.

fitly, ad. aptamente, justamente.

fitness, s. aptitud, conveniencia ; proporción ; oportunidad.

fitting, a. conveniente, idóneo, justo ; -s, pl. guarnición, mueblaje.

five, s. cinco.

fives, s.pl. juego de pelota.

fix, v.a. fijar, establecer ; —, v.n. fijarse, determinarse ; s. (col.) dilema.

fixedly, ad. fijamente, ciertamente.

fixedness, fixity, s. firmeza ; constancia.

fixture, s. mueble fijo de una casa.

fizz(le), v.n. silbar.

flabby, a. blando, flojo, lacio.

flaccid, a. flojo, flaco ; flácido.

flag, s. bandera ; pabellón ; losa ; (bot.) espadaña ; —, v.a. (with stones) enlosar ; —, v.n. pender ; debilitarse.

flagellate, v.a. azotar.

flageolet, s. caramillo ; flauta.

flagitious, a. facineroso, malvado.

flag-officer, s. (mar.) jefe de una escuadra.

flagon, s. frasco.

flagrancy, s. escándalo ; enormidad.

flagrant, a. flagrante ; notorio.

flag-ship, s. nave capitana ó almiranta.

flag-staff, s. asta del pabellón.

flag-stone, s. losa.

flail, s. mayal.

flake, s. copo (de nieve ó de lana) ; lámina ; —, v.n. romperse en láminas.

flaky, a. vedijoso ; roto en pequeñas laminillas.

flamboyant, a. flamígero ; jactancioso.

flame, s. llama ; fuego (del amor) ; —, v.n. arder ; brillar.

flaming, a. ardiente, inflamado, compuesto de llamas.

flange, s. realce, ribete, borde.

flank, s. ijada ; (mil.) flanco ; —, v.a. atacar el flanco ; flanquear.

flannel, s. franela, flanela.

flap, s. falda, faldilla ; válvula ; oreja (de los zapatos) ; golpe ligero ; —, v.a. mosquear ; —, v.n. agitarse, menearse.

flare, v.n. lucir, brillar ; —, s. llama.

flash, s. relámpago ; llamarada ; brillo ; — of wit, agudeza ; —, v.n. relampaguear, brillar ; —, a. falso, contrahecho.

flashy, a. superficial, ostentador, insulso, desabrido.

flask, s. frasco ; botella.

flat, a. llano, plano ; insípido ; —, s. llanura ; plano ; (mar.) bajío ; (mus.)

bemol ; (col.) bobo, simple ; -ly, horizontalmente ; llanamente ; enteramente ; de plano ; francamente.

flatness, s. llanura ; insipidez.

flatten, v.a. allanar ; abatir ; —, v.n. aplanarse.

flatter, v.a. adular, lisonjear.

flatterer, s. adulador.

flattery, s. adulación, lisonja.

flatulence, s. (med.) flatulencia.

flatulent, a. flatulento ; hinchado, vano, fútil, frívolo, caduco. [earse.

flaunt, v.a. & n. ostentar, lucir ; pavonflavour, s. sabor, gusto ; —, v.a. sazonar (manjares).

flavourless, a. desabrido, soso. [tacha.

flaw, s. resquebradura, hendedura ; falta, flawless, a. sin defecto, perfecto.

flax, s. lino.

flaxen, flaxy, a. de lino ; blondo.

flay, v.a. descortezar.

flea, s. pulga.

fleck, s. tacha, mancha.

fledge, v.a. & n. pelechar, emplumecer.

fledgling, s. pajarito.

flee, v.a. & n. escapar ; huir.

fleece, s. vellón ; —, v.a. esquilar, desnudar, despojar.

fleecy, a. lanudo. [ligero.

fleet, s. flota ; —, a. veloz, acelerado, fleeting, a. pasajero, fugitivo.

fleetness, s. velocidad, ligereza.

flesh, s. carne ; —, v.a. hartar ; cebar.

fleshiness, s. gordura extremada.

fleshless, a. flaco ; descarnado.

fleshy, a. carnoso, pulposo.

flexibility, s. flexibilidad.

flexible, a. flexible.

flexion, s. flexión, corvadura.

flick, v.a. latigazo ó abanicazo leve ; v.a. rozar levemente con látigo ó guante ó servieta.

flicker, v.n. aletear ; fluctuar.

flight, s. huída, fuga ; vuelo ; bandada (de pájaros) ; (fig.) elevación.

flighty, a. veloz, inconstante.

flimsiness, s. textura débil, delgadez, mezquindad.

flimsy, a. débil, delgado ; fútil.

flinch, v.n. vacilar ; faltar ; retirarse.

fling, v.a. lanzar, echar ; —, v.n. brincar, resentirse ; —, s. tiro ; burla.

flint, s. pedernal.

flinty, a. roqueño ; pedregoso ; inexorable.

flip, v.a. rozar ; — s, golpecito, capirotazo.

flippancy, s. ligereza ; petulancia ; impertinencia.

flippant, a. ligero ; petulante, locuaz.

flirt, v.a. arrojar, lanzar ; —, v.n. mofar ; coquetear ; —, s. coqueta.

flirtation, s. coquetería.

flit, v.n. volar, aletear; huir; (col.) mudarse.

flitch, s. hoja de tocino.

float, v.n. flotar; fluctuar; —, v.a. sostener (lo que flota); —, s. corcho de caña de pescar; barco chato.

floating-bridge, s. pontón.

flock, s. manada; rebaño; gentío; vedija de lana; —, v.n. congregarse.

floe, s. masa de hielo flotante.

flog, v.a. azotar.

flogging, s. tunda, zurra.

flood, s. diluvio; inundación; flujo; —, v.a. inundar.

floor, s. pavimento, suelo, piso; piso de una casa; —, v.a. solar.

flooring, s. estrado; ensamblaje de madera para suelos.

flop, v.n. (col.) caer con pesadez.

floral, a. floral.

florescence, s. florescencia.

florid, a. florido.

florin, s. florín.

florist, s. florista.

floss-silk, s. seda floja.

flossy, a. blando como la seda.

flotilla, s. (mar.) flotilla. [frágio.

flotsam, s. restos flotantes de un nau-

flounce, s. farfalá; —, v.a. guarnecer con fáralas.

flounder, s. acedía, platija (pez de mar); —, v.n. patear, brincar, revolcarse.

flour, s. harina.

flourish, v.a. exornar, adornar; vibrar (una espada); —, v.n. florecer; gozar de prosperidad; jactarse; escribir haciendo lazos con la pluma; amplificar; (mus.) preludiar, florear; —, s. floreo de palabras; (mus.) floreo, preludio. [burla.

flout, v.a. mofar, burlarse; —, s. mofa.

flow, v.n. fluir, manar; crecer la marea; ondear; —, s. creciente de la marea; abundancia; flujo. [florecer.

flower, s. flor; —, v.a. & n. florear

flower-bed, s. cuadro (en un jardín).

flower-girl, s. florera.

floweret, s. florecilla, florecita.

flower-pot, s. tiesto de flores, maceta.

flowery, a. florido.

flower-show, s. exposición de flores.

fluctuate, v.n. fluctuar; estar suspenso.

fluctuation, s. fluctuación.

flue, s. humero; pelusa.

fluency, s. fluidez; volubilidad.

fluent, a. fluido; fluente; fácil; -ly, con facundia.

fluff, s. pelusa.

fluid, a. & s. fluido.

fluidity, s. fluidez.

fluke, s. lengüeta de áncora; acedía (pez).

flummery, s. gachas de harina de avena, pl.; lisonja grosera.

flunkey, s. lacayo; estafero.

flurry, s. ráfaga; priesa, agitación; —, v.a. confundir; alarmar.

flush, v.a. sonrojar; excitar; —, v.n. fluir con violencia; ponerse colorado; —, s. flujo rápido; (at cards) flux; rubor suelto; —, a. fresco, robusto, opulento.

fluster, v.a. confundir, atropellar.

flute, s. flauta; estría; —, v.a. estriar.

flutist, s. flautista.

flutter, v.a. turbar, desordenar; —, v.n. aletear, revolotear; estar en agitación; —, s. confusión; agitación; undulación.

fluvial, a. fluvial.

flux, s. flujo; concurso; disentería.

fly, v.a. & n. volar; pasar ligeramente; saltar, reventar; huir, escapar; —, s. mosca; volante (coche); Spanish cantárida.

fly-blow, s. cresa.

fly-leaf, s. página blanca.

flying-fish, s. volador, pez volante.

foal, s. potro, potra; —, v.a. parir una yegua.

foam, s. espuma; —, v.n. espumar.

foamy, a. espumoso.

fob, s. faltriquera pequeña.

focus, s. foco, el punto céntrico.

fodder, s. forraje.

foe(man), s. adversario, enemigo.

fog, s. niebla.

fogey, s. (col.) tipo antjcuado, vejete.

foggy, a. nebuloso, brumoso.

foible, s. debilidad, parte flaca, manía.

foil, v.a. vencer; frustrar; —, hoja (de estaño); florete; fondo ó engaste de piedra preciosa.

foist, v.a. insertar (subrepticiamente).

fold, s. redil, aprisco; plegadura; —, v.a. apriscar el ganado; plegar.

folder, s. plegador, plegadera.

folding, s. plegadura.

folding-bed, s. catre de tijera ó de campaña.

folding-chair, s. silla de tijera.

folding-door, s. media puerta.

folding-screen, s. biombo.

foliage, s. follaje.

foliation, s. (bot.) foliación.

folio, s. libro en folio.

folk, s. gente, mundo.

folk-lore, s. cuentos y creencias de pago.

follow, v.a. seguir; acompañar; imitar; —, v.n. seguirse, resultar, provenir.

follower, s. seguidor; imitador; secuaz, partidario; adherente; compañero.

folly, s. tontería, locura ; indiscreción.

foment, v.a. fomentar.

fomentation, s. fomentación ; fomento.

fond, a. loco, enamorado, apasionado, cariñoso ;₂ -ly, locamente, cariñosamente.

fondle, v.a. mimar, hacer caricias.

fondling, s. favorito, niño mimado.

fondness, s. terneza, cariño, pasión loca ; indulgencia.

font, s. pila bautismal.

food, s. alimento ; comida.

fool, s. loco, tonto ; bufón ; —, v.a. engañar ; infatuar ; —, v.n. tontear.

foolery, s. tontería, bobería.

foolhardiness, s. temeridad, locura.

foolhardy, a. temerario.

foolish, a. bobo, tonto ; -ly, bobamente; sin juicio.

foolscap, s. papel de cierto tamaño.

foot, s. pie ; base ; infantería ; — by —, paso entre paso ; on ó by —, á pie ; —, v.n. bailar ; ir á pie.

foot-ball, s. balón para jugar con los pies.

foot-bridge, s. puentecilla.

foot-guards, s.pl. guardias de infantería.

foot-hold, s. espacio en que cabe el pie.

footing, s. base ; piso ; estado ; condición; fundamento. [pl.

foot-lights, s.pl. lámparas del proscenio.

footman, s. lacayo.

foot-note, s. anotación al pie de la página.

foot-pace, s. paso lento ó corto.

foot-pad, s. salteador á pie.

foot-path, s. senda, acera.

foot-pavement, s. acera.

foot-print, s. huella, pisada.

foot-step, s. paso, vestigio ; huella.

foot-stool, s. escabelo.

foot-warmer, s. estufilla.

fop, s. petimetre, pisaverde. [vestirse].

foppery, s. tontería ; afectación (en el foppish, vanidoso ; afectado.

for, pr. por, á causa de ; para ; —, c. porque, pues ; as — me, tocante á mi ; what — ? á que ? ? á qué fin ? ¿ para qué ? [saquear.

forage, s. forraje ; —, v.a. forrajear ;

forager, s. forrajero.

forasmuch as, c. visto que, porque.

foray, s. incursión, pillage.

forbear, v.n. cesar, detenerse, abstenerse.

forbearance, s. paciencia, indulgencia.

forbears, s.pl. antepasados.

forbid, v.a. prohibir, vedar ; impedir.

force, s. fuerza ; poder, vigor ; violencia ; necesidad ; -s, pl. tropas ; —, v.a. forzar, violentar ; esforzar ; constreñir.

forcedly, ad. forzosamente, por fuerza.

forceps, s. fórceps, tenaza.

forcible, a. fuerte, eficaz, poderoso, prevaleciente ; -bly, fuertemente, forzadamente.

ford, s. vádo ; —, v.a. vadear.

fordable, a. vadeable.

fore, a. anterior ; —, ad. delante, antes.

forearm, s. antibrazo.

forebode, v.n. pronosticar, presagiar.

forecast, v.n. prever ; conjeturar de antemano ; —, s. previsión, profecía.

forecastle, s. (mar.) castillo de proa.

foreclose, v.a. ejecutar (una hipoteca) : impedir ; excluir.

foreclosure, s. ejecución (de hipoteca).

foredoom, v.a. predestinar.

forefather, s. abuelo, antecesor.

forefend, v.a. prohibir, vedar.

forefinger, s. índice.

forego, v.a. ceder, abandonar.

foregone, a. pasado ó ido.

foreground, s. primer plano (en pintura).

forehead, s. frente.

foreign, a. extranjero ; extraño.

foreigner, s extranjero, forastero.

foreknowledge, s. presciencia.

foreland, s. cabo, promontorio.

forelock, s. melena, copete. [capataz.

foreman, s. presidente (del jurado) ;

foremast, s. (mar.) palo de trinquete.

forementioned, a. ya citado, arriba citado.

foremost, a. delantero, primero.

forenoon, s. mañana.

forensic, a. forense.

forepart, s. delantera.

forerunner, s. precursor ; predecesor.

forerun, v.a. preceder.

foresail, s. (mar.) vela de trinquete.

foresee, v.a. prever.

foreshadow, v.a. pronosticar ; simbolizar.

foreshore, s. playa.

foreshorten, v.a. recortar.

foresight, s. previsión ; presciencia.

forest, s. bosque ; selva.

forestall, v.a. anticipar ; preocupar, prevenir ; monopolizar.

forester, s. guardabosque.

forestry, s. arboricultura. [pación.

foretaste, v.a. goce anticipado, antici-

foretell, v.a. predecir, profetizar.

foreteller, s. profeta.

forethought, s. providencia ; premeditación.

forever, ad. para siempre. [antemano.

forewarn, v.a. prevenir ; amonestar de

forfeit, s. multa ; confiscación ; confiscado ; —, v.a. confiscar ; perder ; pagar una multa.

forfeiture, s. confiscación ; multa.

forge, s. fragua ; fábrica de metales ; —, v.a. forjar ; contrahacer ; inventar.

forger, s. falsario.

forgery, s. falsificación.
forget, v.a. olvidar ; descuidar.
forgetful, a. olvidadizo ; descuidado.
forgetfulness, s. olvido ; negligencia.
forget-me-not, s. (bot.) miosotis, no-me-olvides.
forgive, v.a. perdonar, remitir.
forgiveness, s. perdón ; remisión.
fork, s. tenedor ; horca ; —, v.n. bifurcarse.
forked, forky, a. horcado.
forlorn, a. abandonado, perdido.
forlornness, s. miseria ; soledad ; abandono, desamparo.
form, s. forma ; modelo ; modo ; formalidad ; método ; banco ; molde ; —, v.a. formar.
formal, a. formal, metódico ; ceremonioso ; -ly, formalmente.
formalism, s. formalismo.
formalist, s. formalista.
formality, s. formalidad ; ceremonia.
formation, s. formación.
former, a. precedente ; anterior, pasado ; -ly, antiguamente, en tiempos pasados, antes.
formidable, a. formidable, terrible.
formula, s. fórmula.
formulary, s. formulario.
formulate, v.a. formular, articular.
forsake, v.a. dejar, abandonar.
forsooth, ad. en verdad, ciertamente.
forswear, v.a. renunciar con juramento ; perjurar.
fort, s. castillo ; fortaleza.
forth, ad. en adelante ; fuera ; hasta lo último ; and so —, et cetera. [ente.
forthcoming, a. venidero, pronto, inminforthwith, a. inmediatamente, sin tardanza, en seguida.
fortieth, s. cuadragésimo.
fortification, s. fortificación.
fortify, v.a. fortificar ; corroborar.
fortitude, s. fortaleza ; valor.
fortnight, s. quince días, pl ; dos semanas, pl.; -ly, a. & ad. cada quince días.
fortress, s. (mil.) fortaleza.
fortuitous, a. impensado ; casual ; -ly, fortuitamente.
fortunate, a. afortunado ; felizmente.
fortune, s. fortuna, suerte ; estado ; condición ; bienes de fortuna, pl.; hacienda, dote.
fortune-hunter, s. aventurero ; el que busca esposa rica.
fortune-teller, s. sortílego, adivino.
forty, a. cuarenta.
forward, a. apresurado ; presumido ; anterior ; pronto, activo, dispuesto ; —, ad. adelante, más allá ; -ly, apresuradamente ; atrevidamente ; —, v.a.
acelerar ; promover, patrocinar ; despachar, transmitir (equipaje, cartas, precocidad ; audacia. [etc.).
forwarder, s. promotor.
forwardness, s. prontitud ; progreso, precocidad ; audacia.
forwards, ad. adelante.
foss, s. foso, zanca.
fossil, a. & s. fósil.
foster, v.a. criar, nutrir.
foster-brother, s. hermano de leche.
foster-child, s. alumno.
foster-mother, s. ama de leche.
foster-son, s. hijo de leche.
foul, a. sucio ; impuro, detestable ; -ly, ad. suciamente ; ilegítimamente ; —, v.a. ensuciar.
foulmouthed, a. deslenguado, obsceno.
foulness, s. suciedad, porquería ; deformidad. [fundir.
found, v.a. fundar, establecer ; edificar ;
foundation, s. fundación ; fundamento.
foundation-stone, s. piedra fundamental.
founder, s. fundador ; fundidor ; —, v.n. (mar.) irse á pique.
foundling, s. niño expósito.
fount, fountain, s. fuente.
fountain-head, s. origen.
four, a. cuatro.
fourfold, a. cuádruplo.
four-footed, a. cuadrúpedo.
fourscore, a. ochenta.
fourteen, a. catorce.
fourteenth, a. décimocuarto.
fourth, a. cuarto ; -ly, en cuarto lugar.
fowl, s. ave ; volatería.
fowler, pajarero, cazador.
fowling, s. caza de aves.
fowling-piece, s. escopeta.
fox, s. zorra ; (fig.) zorro.
fox-glove, s. (bot.) dedalera.
foxy, a. (col.) astuto, taimado.
fraction, s. fracción.
fractional, a. fraccionario.
fractious, a. regañón, enojadizo.
fracture, s. fractura ; —, v.a. fracturar, romper.
fragile, a. frágil ; debil. [flaqueza.
fragility, s. fragilidad ; debilidad. fla-fragment, s. fragmento.
fragmentary, a. fragmentario.
fragrance, s. fragrancia. [fragrancia.
fragrant, a. fragrante, oloroso ; -ly, con
frail, a. frágil, débil.
frailty, s. fragilidad ; debilidad.
frame, s. fábrica ; marco, cerco ; bastidor ; telar ; cuadro de vidriera ; estructura ; sistema ; organización, orden, disposición ; figura, forma, cuerpo ; forjadura ; —, v.a. fabricar, componer, construir, formar ; ajustar ; idear ; poner en bastidor ; forjar.

frame-work, s. armazón, estructura.

franchise, s. franquicia ; privilegio.

frank, a. franco, liberal ; —, s. carta franca ; —, v.a. franquear una carta.

frankincense, s. incienso.

frankly, ad. francamente.

frankness, s. franqueza.

frantic, a. frenético, furioso.

fraternal, a., -ly, fraternal(mente).

fraternity, s. fraternidad.

fraternize, v.n. fraternizar, amistarse.

fratricide, s. fratricidio ; fratricida.

fraud, s. fraude, engaño.

fraudulence, s. fraudulencia. [lentamente.

fraudulent, a. fraudulento ; -ly, fraudulentamente.

fraught, a. cargado, lleno.

fray, s. riña, disputa, querella ; —, v.a estregar.

freak, s. fantasía ; capricho.

freckle, s. peca.

freckled, a. pecoso.

free, a. libre ; liberal ; franco, ingenuo ; exento, dispensado, privilegiado ; —, v.a. libertar ; librar ; eximir.

freebooter, s. filibustero.

freedman, s. esclavo manumiso.

freedom, s. libertad ; inmunidad.

free-hearted, a. liberal, generoso.

freehold, a. & s. feudo franco, propiedad absoluta.

freely, ad. libremente ; espontáneamente ; liberalmente.

freeman, s. hombre libre ; ciudadano.

freemason, s. francmasón.

freemasonry, s. francmasonería. [dad.

freeness, s. libertad ; sinceridad ; liberalifree-spoken, a. franco, de habla abierta.

free-thinker, s. libre pensador ; escéptico.

free-trade, s. libre cambio.

free-will, s. libre albedrío; espontaneidad.

freeze, v.n. helar(se) ; —, v.a. congelar.

freight, s. carga ; flete ; —, v.a. (mar.) fletar ; a. agua dulce.

freighter s. fletador.

frenchify, v.a. afrancesar.

frenzied, a. loco, delirante.

frenzy, s. frenesí ; locura.

frequency, s. frecuencia ; multitud.

frequent, a. -ly, frecuente(mente) ; — v.a. frecuentar.

frequenter, s. frecuentador.

fresco, s. pintura al fresco.

fresh, a. fresco ; nuevo, reciente ; — water, s. agua dulce.

freshen, v.a. (& n.) refrescar(se).

freshet, s. avenida, creciente de un río.

freshly, ad. frescamente ; recientemente.

freshness, s. frescura ; fresco.

fret, s. enojo ; —, v.a. frotar ; corroer ; irritar ; agitar enojar ; —, v.n. agitarse, enojarse.

fretful, a. enojadizo, colérico ; -ly, de mala gana.

fretfulness, s. enojo, mal humor.

fret-saw, s. sierra pequeña y flexible.

fretting, s. agitación.

friability, s. friabilidad.

friable, a. friable, desmenuzable.

friar, s. fraile.

friary, s. convento de frailes.

fricassee, s. guisado. [Santo.

Friday, s. viernes ; Good —, Viernes

friend, s. amigo ; amiga.

friendless, a. sin amigos. [bondad.

friendliness, s. amistad, benevolencia,

friendly, a. amigable, amistoso.

friendship, s. amistad.

frieze, s. friso.

frigate, s. (mar.) fragata.

fright, s. espanto, terror.

frighten, v.a. espantar.

frightful, a. espantoso, horrible ; -ly, espantosamente, terriblemente.

frigid, a. frío, frígido ; -ly, fríamente.

frigidity, s. frialdad ; indiferencia.

frill, s. escote, vuelo. [franjas.

fringe, s. franja ; —, v.a. guarnecer con

frippery, s. ropa vieja ; atavío descompuesto. [gambeta ; brinco.

frisk, v.n. saltar, cabriolar ; —, s.

frisky, a. alegre, placentero.

frith, s. ría. [v.a. disipar.

fritter, s. fruta de sarten, buñuelo ; —,

frivolity, s. frivolidad.

frivolous, a. frívolo, vano ; -ly, frívolamente, sin substancia.

frizz(le), v.a. frisar ; rizar.

fro, ad. to go to and —, ir y venir.

frock, s. blusa ; bata de niño ; sayo ; túnica.

frog, s. rana.

frolic(k), a. alegre, vivo ; —, s. fantasía ; capricho ; —, v.n. loquear, juguetear, triscar.

frolicsome, a. juguetón, travieso.

from, pr. de ; desde.

frond, s. rama verde.

front, s. frente ; —, v.a. hacer frente.

frontage, s. fachada. [frente.

frontal, s. venda ; —, a. frontero, de frontier, s. frontera.

frontispiece, s. frontispicio ; frontis grabado de un libro.

frontlet, s. frontal ; venda para la frente.

frost, s. helada ; hielo. [hielo.

frost-bitten, a. helado, quemado del

frosty, a. helado, frío como el hielo.

froth, s. espuma (de algún líquido) ; —, v.n. espumar.

frothy, s. espumoso ; frívolo, vano.

froward, a. incorregible ; inpertinente ; -ly, insolentemente.

frowardness, s. mal genio ; petulancia.

frown, v.n. fruncir las cejas ; —, s. ceño ; enojo.

frowzy, a. desaliñado.

frozen, a. helado.

frugal, a. frugal ; económico ; sobrio ; -ly, frugalmente.

frugality, s. frugalidad, moderación.

fruit, s. fruta, fruto ; producto.

fruiterer, s. frutero.

fruitful, a. fructífero, fértil ; provechoso, útil : -ly, con fertilidad.

fruitfulness, s. fertilidad.

fruition, s. goce.

fruitless, a. estéril ; inútil ; -ly, vanamente, inútilimente, de balde.

fruit-tree, s. frutal.

frump, s. (col.) vieja desaliñada.

frustrate, v.a. frustrar ; anular.

frustration, s. contratiempo, chasco.

fry, s. fritura ; enjambre ; —, v.a. freír

frying-pan, s. sartén.

fuchsia, s. (bot.) fuchsia.

fuddle, v.a. emborrachar.

fudge, s. disparate ; ¡ caracoles !

fuel, s. combustible.

fugitive, a. & s. fugitivo.

fugue, s. (mus.) fuga.

fugleman, s. guía.

fulcrum, s. apoyo de palanca ó alzaprima.

fulfil, v.a. colmar ; cumplir.   [ción.

fulfilment, s. cumplimiento ; consuma-

full, a. lleno, repleto, completo ; perfecto; —, s. total ; complemento ; —, ad. enteramente, del todo ; —, v.a. batanar el paño.

full-blown, a. desplegado completamente (hablando de las flores).

full-cock, a. montado, amartillado (dícese de una escopeta).

full-dress, s. vestido de gala.

fuller, s. batanero.

full-length, s. grandeza natural.

fulling-mill, s. batán.

full-moon, s. plenilunio ; luna llena.

fully, ad. llenamente, enteramente, ampliamente.

fulminant, a. fulminante.

fulminate, v.a. & n. fulminar.

fulmination, s. fulminación.

fulness, s. plenitud, llenura, abundancia.

fulsome, a. servil en adulación.

fumble, v.a. & n. chapucear, muchachear; andar á tientas.

fume, s. humo, vapor ; cólera ; vanidad ; —, v.a. ahumar ; —, v.n. humear, exhalar ; encolerizarse.

fumigate, v.a. fumigar, sahumar.

fumigation, s. sahumerio : fumigación.

fumigator, s. máquina fumigatoria.

fun, s. chanza, burla.

function, s. función ; empleo.

functionary, s. empleado.

fund, s. caudal, fondo ; fondos públicos, pl.; —, v.a. consolidar (deudas) ; invertir fondos.

fundament, s. fundamento.

fundamental, a. fundamental ; -ly, fundamentalmente.

funeral, s. entierro, exequias

funereal, a. funeral, fúnebre.

fungous, a. fungoso ; esponjoso.

fungus, —, s. hongo ; seta.

funk, s. (col.) miedo ; cobarde.

funnel, s. embudo ; cañón (de chimenea).

funny, a. risible, entretenido, bufón.

fur, s. forro de pieles ; pelo.

furbelow, s. falbalá.

furbish, v.a. acicalar, pulir.   [furia.

furious, a. furioso, frenético ; -ly, con

furl, v.a. doblar ; (mar.) aferrar las velas.

furlong, s. estadio (octava parte de una milla).

furlough, s. (mil.) licencia.

furnace, s. horno.

furnish, v.a. suplir, proveer ; equipar ; (a house) amueblar una casa.

furnisher, s. proveedor.   [aparejo.

furniture, s. muebles, mueblaje, ajuar ;

furrier, s. peletero.

furrow, s. surco ; —, v.a. surcar ; estriar.

furry, a. hecho ó guarnecido de pieles.

further, a. ulterior, más distante ; —, ad. más lejos, más adelante ; aun ; además de eso ; —, v.a. adelantar, promover, ayudar.

furtherance, s. adelantamiento ; progreso; ayuda, asistencia.

furthermore, s. además.

furthest, a. & ad. superl. de further, lo más lejos.

furtive, a. furtivo ; secreto ; -ly, furtivamente.

fury, s. furor ; furia ; ira.

furze, s. (bot.) tojo.

fuse, v.a. & n. fundir ; derretir(se) ; —, s. mecha.

fusible, a. fusible, fundible.

fusilier, s. fusilero.

fusion, s. fusión, licuación.

fuss, s. alboroto, tumulto.

fussy, a. inquieto, nervioso.

fustian, s. fustán ; estilo altisonante.

fusty, a. mohoso.

futile, a. fútil, frívolo.

futility, s. futilidad, vanidad.

future, a. venidero, futuro ; —, s. lo futuro, el tiempo venidero.

futurity, s. futuro ; tiempos venideros, pl.

fy, ¡ vaya !

G

gab, s. (col.) locuacidad. [algarabía.

gabble, v.n. charlar, parlotear ; —, s.

gable, gable-end, s. remate triangular de un tejado.

gaby, s. papanatas.

gad, v.n. tunar, corretear, andorrear.

gad-fly, s. tábano.

gaff, s. (mar.) cangreja. [con mordaza.

gag, s. mordaza ; —, v.a. tapar la boca

gage, s. prenda.

gaiety, s. alegría.

gaily, ad. alegremente.

gain, s. ganancia ; interés, provecho ; —, v.a. ganar ; conseguir ; —, v.n. enriquecerse ; prevalecer, obtener influjo.

gainer, s. ganador.

gainings, s. pl.ganancia ; provecho.

gainsay, v.a. contradecir ; negar ; contrariar.

gait, s. marcha ; porte.

gaiter, s. polaina. [bellezas.

galaxy, s galaxia ; (fig.) reunión de

gale, s. (mar.) viento fresco.

gall, s. hiel ; rencor, odio ; —, v.a. frotar, desollar.

gallant, a. galante, elegante ; valeroso ; -ly. galantemente ; bravamente ; —, s. galán, cortejo.

gallantry, s. galantería ; bravura.

galleon, s. (mar.) galeón.

gallery, s. galería ; corredor.

galley, s. (mar.) galera.

galley-slave, s. galeote.

gallinaceous, a. galináceo.

gallipot, s. orza.

gallon, s. galón (medida).

gallop, s. galope ; —, v.n. galopear.

gallows, s. horca.

galosh, galoche, s. V. golosn.

galvanic, a. galvánico.

galvanise, v.a. galvanizar.

galvanism, s. galvanismo.

gambit, s. gambito.

gamble, v.n. apostar al juego.

gambler, s. jugador, garitero, fullero.

gambling-house, s. garito ; casa de juego.

gamboge, s. gutagamba.

gambol, s. cabriola ; —, v.n. brincar, saltar.

game, s. juego ; pasatiempo ; burla ; animales ó aves de caza ; —, v.n. jugar.

game-bag, s. mochila de un cazador.

game-cock, s. gallo de riña.

game-keeper, s. guarda de coto.

gamesome, a. juguetón, retozón ; -ly. alegremente.

gamester, tahur, jugador.

gaming, s. juego.

gammon, s. jamón ; (col.) embustes, disparates ; —, v.a. engañar.

gamut, s. (mus.) gama.

gander, s. ganso.

gang, s. cuadrilla, banda.

gangrene, s. gangrena. [mano, escalera.

gangway, s. paso, pasadizo ; (mar) pasa-

gaol, s. cárcel, prisión.

gaol-bird, s. bribón, criminal.

gaoler, s. carcelero.

gap, s. boquete ; brecha. [hendirse.

gape, v.n. bostezar, boquear ; ansiar,

gaping, s. bostezo.

garb, s. vestidura ; traje.

garbage, s. tripas, desecho.

garble, v.a. entresacar ; torcer, falsificar.

garden, s. huerto ; jardín ; —, v.n. cultivar un jardín ó un huerto.

garden-hose, s. regadera.

gardener, s. jardinero ; jardinera.

gardening, s. jardinería. [gargarismo.

gargle, v.a. & n. gargarizar ; —, s. gargoyle, s. gárgola.

garish, a. pomposo, ostentoso.

garland, s. guirnalda.

garlic, s. (bot.) ajo.

garment, s. vestidura.

garner, s. granero ; —, v.a. almacenar.

garnet, s. granate.

garnish, v.a. guarnecer, adornar ; —, s. guarnición ; adorno.

garret, s. guardilla ; desván.

garrison, s. (mil.) guarnición ; —, v.a. (mil.) guarnecer.

garrote, v.a. estrangular y robar.

garrulity, s. garrulidad, locuacidad, charla.

garrulous, a. gárrulo, locuaz, charlador.

garter, s. liga ; jarretera.

gas, s. gas.

gasalier, s. candil de gas.

gas-burner, s. mechero de gas.

gaseous, a. gaseoso.

gash, s. cuchillada ; cicatriz ; —, v.a. dar una cuchillada, tajar.

gas-holder, gasometer, s. gasómetro.

gasp, v.n. boquear ; anhelar ; —, s. respiración difícil, suspiro.

gastric, a. gástrico.

gastronomic, a. gastronómico.

gate, s. puerta.

gate-way, s. puerta cochera.

gather, v.a. recoger, amontonar ; inferir ; plegar ; —, v.n. condensarse, aumentarse, juntarse; supurar.

gathering, s. acumulación ; colecta.
gaudily, ad. ostentosamente, fastosamente.
gaudiness, s. pompa ; ostentación.
gaudy, a. fastoso ; pomposo ; —, s. fiesta; festín.
gauge, v.a. aforar ; -s, vara de aforador.
gauger, s. aforador.
gaunt, a. & s. flaco, delgado.
gauntlet, s. guantelete ; manopla.
gauze, s. gasa.
gawky, a. desmañado, bobo.
gay, a. alegre [mirada.
gaze, v.n. contemplar, considerar ; —, s.
gazelle, s. gacela.
gazer, s. mirón.
gazette, s. gaceta.
gazetteer, s. diccionario geográfico.
gear, s. atavío ; vestido ; aparejo, equi-
gelatine, s. gelatina. [paje.
gelatinous, a. gelatinoso.
geld, v.a. castrar, capar.
gelding, s. caballo capón.
gem, s. joya ; —, v.a. adornar con piedras preciosas.
Gemini, s. Géminis (signo del zodíaco).
gender, s. género.
genealogical, a. genealógico.
genealogy, s. genealogía.
general, a. general, común, usual ; in —, por lo común ; -ly, generalmente ; —, s. general.
generalisation, s. generalización.
generalise, v.a. generalizar.
generality, s. generalidad, mayor parte.
generalship, s. generalato. [causar.
generate, v.a. engendrar ; producir ;
generation, s. generación.
generator, s. engendrador.
generic, a. genérico.
generosity, s. generosidad, liberalidad.
generous, a. generoso ; -ly, magnánimamente.
genial, a. genial, cordial, alegre ; -ly, genialmente. [queza.
geniality, s. alegría, cordialidad, fran-
genitive, s. genitivo.
genius, s. genio. [-ly, gentilmente.
genteel, a. gentil, lindo, galán, elegante ;
gentian, s. (bot.) genciana.
gentile, s. gentil, pagano.
gentility, s. gentileza ; gentilidad ; nobleza de sangre. [benigno.
gentle, a. suave, dócil, manso, moderado ;
gentlefolks, s.pl. gente bien nacida.
gentleman, s. gentilhombre, caballero ; hidalgo.
gentlemanlike, a. caballeroso, urbano.
gentleness, s. dulzura, suavidad de carácter ; nobleza.
gentlowoman, a. señora, dama.

gently, ad. gentilmente, despacio.
gentry, s. gente noble (sin título) ; aristocracia.
genuflexion, s. genuflexión.
genuine, a. genuino, puro, auténtico, real ; -ly, puramente, realmente.
genuineness, s. pureza ; autenticidad.
genus, s. género.
geographer, s. geógrafo.
geographical, a. geográfico.
geography, s. geografía.
geological, a. geológico.
geologist, s. geólogo.
geology, s. geología.
geometric(al), a. geométrico.
geometrician, s. geómetra.
geometry, s. geometría.
geranium, s. (bot.) geranio.
germ, s. (bot.) germen.
German, a. alemán.
germane, a. anejo.
germinal, a. germinativo.
germinate, v.n. brotar.
gerund, s. gerundio.
gesticulate, v.n. gesticular.
gesticulation, s. gesticulación.
gesture, s. gesto, movimiento expresivo.
get, v.a. granjear, ganar ; conseguir, obtener, alcanzar ; coger ; agarrar, persuadir ; —, v.n. alcanzar ; llegar, venir ; hacerse, ponerse ; to — by heart, aprender de memoria ; to — the better, salir vencedor, sobrepujar
gewgaw, s. chuchería ; mirifiaque.
Geyser, s. Géiser ; fuente caliente.
ghastliness, s. palidez, cara cadavérica.
ghastly, a. pálido ; espantoso.
gherkin, s. pepini'llo. cohombrillo.
ghost, s. alma, espíritu ; espectro, fantasma.
ghostly, a. espiritual.
giant, s. gigante.
gibberish, s. jerigonza.
gibbet, s. horca ; —, v.a. ahorcar.
gibe, v.n. escarnecer, burlarse, mofar ; —, s. mofa, burla.
giblets, s.pl. menudillos (de aves), pl.
giddily, ad. con vértigos ; descuidadamente.
giddiness, s. vértigo ; inconstancia.
giddy, a. vertiginoso ; inconstante.
gift, s. don ; dádiva ; talento.
gifted, a. talentoso, hábil.
gig, s. calesín ; esquife.
gigantic, a. gigante, gigantesco.
giggle, v.n. fisgar sonriéndose.
gild, v.a. dorar.
gilding, gilt, s. doradura.
gill, s. medida de licores ; -s, pl. barbas del gallo, pl.; agallas de los peces, pl.

gillyflower, s. (bot.) alelí.

gimcrack, s. juguete, chuchería.

gimlet, s. barrena pequeña.

gimp, s. encaje de hilo ó seda.

gin, s. trampa ; ginebra.

ginger, s. jengibre.

gingerbread, s. pan de jengibre.

ginger-beer, s. cerveza de jengibre.

gin-palace, s. tienda de aguardiente, pulpería (am.).

gipsy, s. gitano.

giraffe, s. jirafa.

gird, v a ceñir ; cercar ; —, v.n. mofarse.

girder, s. viga.

girdle, s. cinturón ; —, v.a. ceñir.

girl, s. muchacha ; niña, moza.

girlhood, s. doncellez, niñez.

girlish, s. juvenil.

girth, s. cincha ; circunferencia.

gist, s. lo esencial, medula.

give, v.a. dar, donar ; conceder ; pronunciar ; — up, renunciar, abandonar ; — in, v.n. ceder.

gizzard, s. molleja.

glacial, a. glacial.

glacier, s. ventisquero.   [mente.

glad, a. alegre, contento ; -ly, alegre-

gladden, v.a. alegrar, recrear.

glade, s. pradecito entre bosques ; alameda.

gladiator, s. gladiator.

gladness, s. alegría.

gladsome, a. alegre, contento.

glamour, s. encanto, atractivo, lumbre.

glance, s. vislumbre ; relámpago ; ojeada ; —, v.a. lanzar miradas ; rasar, pasar ligeramente ; —, v.n. centellar ; hojear.

gland s. glándula

glanders, s. muermo.

glare, s. deslumbramiento ; mirada feroz y penetrante ; —, v.n. relumbrar, brillar ; echar miradas de indignación.

glaring, a. deslumbrante ; manifiesto ; flagrante.

glass, s. vidrio ; telescopio ; vaso para beber ; espejo ; barómetro ; -es, pl. anteojos, lentes.

glassy, a. vítreo, cristalino, vidrioso.

glaze, v.a. vidriar ; embarnizar.

glazier, s. vidriero.

gleam, s. relámpago, rayo, brillo ; —, v.n. relampaguear, brillar.

glean, v.a. espigar ; recoger.

glebe, s. gleba ; terrón.   [canción.

glee, s. alegría ; gozo ; jovialidad ;

gleeful, a. alegre, gozoso.

glen, s. valle.   [mente.

glib, a. voluble, plausible ; -ly, voluble-

glide, v.n. resbalar ; pasar ligeramente.

glim, s. (col.) lumbre.   [lumbrarse.

glimmer, s. vislumbre ; —, v.n. vis-

glimpse, s. vislumbre ; ojeada ; —, v.a. (am.) descubrir, percibir.

glisten, glitter, v.n. relucir, brillar.

gloaming, s. crepúsculo.

gloat, v.n. ojear.

globe, s. globo ; esfera.

globular, a. globoso.

globule, s. glóbulo.

gloom, gloominess, s. obscuridad ; melancolía, tristeza ; -ily, obscuramente ; tristemente.

gloomy, a. sombrío, obscuro ; nublado ; triste, melancólico.

glorification, s. glorificación, alabanza.

glorify, v.a. glorificar, celebrar.

glorious, a. glorioso, ilustre ; -ly, gloriosamente.

glory, s. gloria, fama, celebridad ; aureola ; —, v.n. gloriarse, jactarse.

gloss, s. glosa ; escolio ; lustre ; —, v.a. glosar, comentar.

glossary, s. glosario.

glossy, a. lustroso, brillante.

glove, s. guante.

glover, s. guantero.

glow, v.n. arder ; inflamarse ; relucir ; —, s. color vivo ; viveza de color ; vehemencia de una pasión.

glower, v.n. mirar con ceño.

glow-worm, s. luciérnaga.

gloze, v.n. adular, lisonjear ; falsificar, mentir.

glue, s. cola ; visco ; —, v.a. encolar, pegar.

gluey, a. viscoso, pegajoso.

glum, a. (col.) tétrico, triste.

glut, v a engullir, tragar, devorar ; saciar ; —, s. hartura, abundancia.

gluten, s. gluten.

glutinous, a. glutinoso, viscoso.

glutton, s. glotón, tragón.

gluttony, s. glotonería.

glycerine, s. glicerina.

gnarled, a. nudoso.

gnash, v.a. crujir (los dientes).

gnat, s. mosquito.

gnaw, v.a. roer ; mordicar.

gnome, s. gnomo.

go, v.n. ir, irse, andar, caminar ; partir(se), marchar ; huir ; pasar.

goad, s. aguijada, aijada ; — v.a. aguijar, estimular, incitar.

goal, s. meta ; fin.

goat, s. cabra, chiva ; he——, cabrón.

goat-herd, s. cabrero.

gobble, v.a. engullir, tragar ; —, v.n. gorgorear como los gallipavos.

go-between, s. mediador ; entremetido.

goblet, s. copa.

goblin, s. espíritu ambulante, duende,

go-cart, carretilla de niño,

M

God, s. Dios.
god-child, s. ahijado, hijo de pila.
god-daughter, s. ahijada, hija de pila.
goddess, s. diosa.
god-father, s. padrino.
godhead, s. deidad, divinidad.
godless, a. infiel, impío, sin Dios, ateo.
godlike, a. divino.
godliness, s. piedad, devoción, santidad.
godly, a. piadoso, devoto, religioso ; recto, justificado.
god-mother, s. madrina.
god-send, s. don de Dios, suceso dichoso.
god-son, s. ahijado.
goer, s. andador.
goggle, v.n. volver los ojos.
goggles, s.pl. (dol.) anteojos grandes ; quevedos. [progreso.
going, s. paso ; andadura ; partida ;
goitre, s. papera.
gold, s. oro.
gold-beater, s. batidor de oro, batihoja.
golden a. áureo, de oro ; excelente.
goldfinch, s. pinzón.
gold-fish, s. dorado.
gold-leaf, s. hoja de oro batido.
goldsmith, s. orífice.
golf, s. juego de pelota escocés.
golosh, galocha, zapato de goma elástica.
gondola, s. góndola.
gondolier, s. gondolero. [muerto.
gone, a. ido ; perdido ; pasado ; gastado ;
gong, s. atabal chino.
good, a. bueno, benévolo, cariñoso ; conveniente, apto ; —, s. bien, prosperidad, ventaja ; **-s,** pl. bienes ; mercaderías, pl.
good-bye, ¡ á Dios ! ¡ adiós !
goodies, s.pl. (col.) golosinas, pl.
goodliness, s. hermosura, elegancia, gracia.
goodly, a. hermoso, espléndido.
good-nature, s. bondad.
good-natured, a. bondadoso.
goodness, s. bondad.
goodwill, s. benevolencia, bondad.
goose, s. ganso ; oca ; plancha de sastre.
gooseberry, s. grosella.
gopher, s. turón.
gore, s. sangre cuajada ; —, v.a. punzar ; herir con puñal , herir con cuernos (un animal).
goose-flesh, s. (col.) estremecimiento.
gorge, s. gorja, garganta ; —, v.a. & n. engullir, tragar.
gorgeous, a. primoroso, brillante, vistoso, **-ly,** con esplendor y magnificencia.
gorget, s. gola.
Gorgon, s. Gorgona.
gormandize, v.n. glotonear.
gormandizer, s. glotón.

gory, a. cubierto de sangre grumosa.
goshawk, s halcón.
gosling, s. gansarón.
gospel, s. evangelio.
gossamer, s. telaraña.
gossip, s. compadre ; comadre ; charla ; —, v.n. charlar.
gothic, a. gótico.
gouge, s. gubia ; escoplo.
gourd, s. (bot.) calabaza.
gout, s. gota (enfermedad).
gouty, a. gotoso.
govern, v.a. gobernar, dirigir, regir.
governable, a. dócil, manejable.
governess, s. gobernadora.
government, governance, s. gobierno ; administración pública.
governor, s. gobernador. [mujer ; bata.
gown, s. toga ; ropa talar, vestido de
gownsman, s. estudiante de universidad.
grab, v.a. (col.) agarrar, robar.
grace, s. gracia ; favor ; merced ; perdón ; **to say —,** bendecir la mesa ; —, v.a. adornar ; agraciar.
Grace, s. Alteza (título).
graceful, a. elegante, primoroso ; **-ly,** elegantemente, con gracia. [malvado.
graceless, a. desagraciado ; réprobo,
gracious, a. condescendiente, bondadoso ; favorable ; **-ly,** bondadosamente.
graciousness, s. bondad, condescendencia.
gradation, s. graduación.
grade, s. grado. [pendiente.
gradient, s. (rail.) pendiente y contra-
gradual, a. gradual ; **-ly,** gradualmente.
graduate, v.a. & n. graduar(se) ; adelantar.
graduation, s. graduación.
graft, s. injerto ; —, v.a. injertar, ingerir.
grafting-knife, s. ingeridor.
grain, s. grano ; semilla ; grana ; disposición, índole ; **against the —,** contra pelo ; con repugnancia.
grained, a. áspero , rayado.
gram, s. gramo (peso).
grammar, s. gramática.
grammarian, s. gramático. [(mente)
grammatic(al), a. **-ally,** gramatical-
grampus, s. delfín.
granary, s. granero.
grand, a. grande, ilustre.
grandchild, s. nieto ; nieta. [nieta.
granddaughter, s. nieta ; **great—,** biz-
grandee, s. grande (de España).
grandeur, s. grandeza ; pompa. [buelo.
grandfather, s. abuelo ; **great—,** bisa-
grandiloquent, a. grandílocuo.
grandiose, a. grandioso. [mente.
grandly, ad. grandemente, sublime-
grandmother, s. abuela ; **great—,** bisabuela.

grand-sire, s. abuelo.
grandson, s. nieto ; **great——,** bisnieto.
grange, s. granja.
granite, s. granito.
grant, v.a. conceder ; **to take for granted,** presuponer ; **—,** s. concesión, don.
granulate, v.a. & n. granular(se). íuvas.
grape, s. uva ; **bunch of -s,** racimo de
grape-shot, s. (mil.) metralla.
grape-stone, s. granuja.
graphic, a. gráfico ; pintoresco ; **-ally,** gráficamente.
grapple, v.a. (& n.) agarrar(se).
grasp, v.a. empuñar, asir, agarrar ; **—,** v.n. esforzarse á agarrar ; **—,** s. puño, puñado ; poder, alcance, comprensión.
grass, s. hierba ; herbaje.
grass-hopper, s. langosta, saltamontes.
grass-plot. s. césped. [marido está ausente.
grass-widow, s. (col.) mujer cuyo
grassy, a. herboso.
grate, s. reja, verja, rejilla ; **—,** v.a. rallar ; rechinar (los dientes) ; ofender.
grateful, a. grato, agradecido ; **-ly,** agradecidamente.
gratefulness, s. gratitud.
grater, s. rallo.
gratification, s. gratificación.
gratify, v.a. contentar ; gratificar.
grating, s. reja, verja ; **—,** a. áspero ; ofensivo.
gratis, ad. gratis, de balde.
gratitude, s. gratitud. [gratuitamente.
gratuitous, a. gratuito, voluntario ; **-ly,**
gratuity, s. gratificación, recompensa.
gratulate, v.a. congratular.
gratulation, s. congratulación.
grave, s. sepultura ; **—,** v.a. grabar, esculpir ; **—,** a. grave, serio ; **-ly,** con gravedad, seriamente.
grave-clothes, s.pl. mortaja.
grave-digger, s. sepulturero.
gravel, s. casquijo, guijo ; (med.) cálculo ; **—,** v.a. cubrir con guijo ; embarazar.
gravelly, a. arenisco, cascajoso.
gravel-pit, s. arenaria.
graven, a. grabado.
graver, s. grabador ; buril.
grave-stone, s. piedra sepulcral, losa.
gravitate, v.n. gravitar.
gravitation, s. gravitación.
gravity, s. gravedad.
gravy, s. jugo de la carne ; salsa.
gray, a. g⁻is ⁻ cano ; **—,** s. gris.
gray-beard, s. barbicano.
grayish, a. pardusco ; entrecano.
grayling, s. umbra (pez).
grayness, s. color gris.
graze, v.a. pastorear ; rozar, tocar ligeramente : **—,** v.n. pacer.

grazier, s. ganadero.
grease, s. grasa ; **—,** v.a. untar.
greasiness, s. grasa, pringue.
greasy, a. grasiento, craso, gordo.
great, a. gran, grande ; principal ; ilustre ; noble, magnánimo ; **-ly,** muy, mucho ; grandemente.
great-coat, s. sobretodo.
greatness, s. grandeza ; dignidad ; poder ; magnanimidad.
greedily, ad. vorazmente, ansiosamente.
greediness, greed, s. voracidad ; gula ; codicia. [deseoso ; insaciable.
greedy, a. voraz, hambriento ; ansioso,
Greek, a. s. griego.
green, a. verde, fresco, reciente ; inmaturo ; **—,** s. verde ; pradera ; **-s,** pl.
green-gage, s. ciruela verdal. [verdura.
green-grocer, s. verdulero.
green-horn, s. (col.) joven sin experiencia.
green-house, s. invernáculo.
greenish, a. verdoso.
greenness, s. verdín, verdor, vigor ; frescura, falta de experiencia; novedad.
green-room, s. vestuario (de teatro).
green-sward, s. césped.
green-wood, s. bosque verde.
greet, v.a. saludar.
greeting, s. salutación.
gregarious, a. gregal.
grenade, s. (mil.) granada.
grenadier, s. granadero.
grey, a. gris, pardo.
greyhound, s. galgo.
gridiron, s. parrillas, pl.
grief, s. dolor ; aflicción, pena.
grievance, s. pesar ; molestia ; agravio ; injusticia ; perjuicio. [afligirse ; llorar.
grieve, v.a. agraviar, afligir ; **—,** v.n.
grievous, a. doloroso ; enorme, atroz ; **-ly,** penosamente, cruelmente.
griffin, s. grifo.
grig. s. grillo.
grill, v.a. asar en parrillas.
grim, a. feo ; horrendo ; ceñudo
grimace, s. visaje ; mueca.
grimalkin, s. gatazo. [suciar.
grime, s. negrura, suciedad ; **—,** v.a. en-
grimness, s. grima ; horror.
grimy, a. ensuciado.
grin, s. mueca ; risa irónica ; **—,** v.n. hacer muecas ; reír sardónicamente.
grind, v.a. moler ; pulverizar ; afilar ; estregar ; mascar ; rechinar los dientes.
grinder, s. molinero ; molinillo ; amolador ; muela.
grindstone, s. piedra amoladera.
grip, s. caz, desagüe.
grip, gripe, v.a. asir, agarrar, empuñar ; dar cólico ; **—,** s. toma . presa ; opresión ; **-s,** pl. (col.) dolor cólico.

griskin, s. costilla de tocino.
grisly, grisled, a. áspero, horroroso.
grist, s. molienda ; provisión.
gristle, s. cartílago.
grit, s. moyuelo ; avena medio molida ;
arena ; (am.) fortaleza, coraje.
gritty. a. arenoso. [pardusco.
grizzled, grizzly, a. mezclado con gris,
groan, v.n. gemir, suspirar ; —, s.
gemido, suspiro.
groat, s. moneda de cuatro peniques.
grocer, s. especiero, abacero.
grocery, s. especería, abacería.
grog, s. grog, ponche.
groggy, a. medio borracho.
groin, s. ingle. [v.a. cuidar los caballos
groom, s. establero ; criado ; novio ; —,
groomsman, s. padrino de boda.
groove, s. estría, muesca ; —, v.a. estriar,
acanalar. [obscuras ; andar á tientas.
grope, v.a. & n. tentar, buscar á ob-
gross, a. grueso, corpulento, espeso ;
grosero ; estúpido ; -ly, groseramente ;
—, s. grueso ; íntegro ; doce do-
cenas, pl.
grossness, s. rudeza, grosería.
grot(to), s. gruta.
grotesque, s. grotesco.
ground, s. tierra, país ; terreno, suelo,
pavimento ; fundamento ; razón fundamental ; campo (de batalla) ; fondo ;
-s, pl. hez ; poso ; —, v.a. establecer ;
(mar.) varar.
ground-floor, s. piso bajo.
ground-ivy, s. hiedra terrestre.
groundless, a. infundado ; -ly, sin fund
amento, sin razón ó motivo.
groundlessness, s. falta de razón ó fundamento.
ground-plot, s. solar, terreno.
groundsel, s. yerba caña.
ground-work, s. plan, fundamento.
group, s. grupo ; —, v.a. agrupar.
grouse, s. especie de ave de caza.
grove, s. arboleda ; boscaje.
grovel, v.n. serpear ; bajarse.
grow, v.a. cultivar ; —, v.n. crecer,
aumentarse ; nacer ; vegetar ; adelantar ; hacerse, ponerse, volverse ;
— up, crecer.
grower, s. cultivador. [—, s. gruñido.
growl, v.n. regañar, gruñir, rezongar ;
growth, s. vegetación ; crecimiento ;
producto ; aumento ; progreso, ade-
lanto. [gar ; cavar.
grub, s. gorgojo, larva ; —, v.a. desarrai-
grudge, s. rencor, odio ; envidia ; —, v.a.
& n. envidiar ; repugnar. [gana.
grudgingly, con repugnancia, de mala
gruel, s. caldo de harina. [mente.
gruff, a. ceñudo, grosero ; -ly, áspera-

gruffness, s. aspereza, severidad.
grumble, v.n. gruñir ; murmurar.
grumpy, a. regañón, ceñudo.
grunt, v.n. gruñir ; gemir.
guarantee, guaranty, s. garante, fiador
garantía ; —, v.a. garantir.
guard, s. guarda, guardia ; (rail.) conductor ; —, v.a. guardar ; defender.
guarded, a. mesurado, circunspecto.
guard-house, guard-room, s. (mil.)
cuerpo de guardia.
guardian, s. tutor ; curador ; guardián.
guardianship, s. tutela.
guard-ship, s. navío de guardia ó de ronda.
guava, s. guayaba.
gudgeon, s. gobio (pez).
guerdon, s. galardón. [—, s. conjetura.
guess, v.a. & n. conjeturar ; adivinar ;
guest, s. huésped, convidado.
guffaw, s. carcajada.
guidance, s. gobierno ; dirección.
guide, v.a. guiar, dirigir ; —, s. guía.
guide-book, s. itinerario.
guild, s. gremio ; corporación.
guild-hall, s. casa municipal.
guile, s. engaño, fraude.
guileful, a. engañoso, impostor.
guileless, a. cándido, sincero. [tinar.
guillotine, s. guillotina ; —, v.a. guillo-
guilt, s. delito ; culpa.
guiltless, a. inocente, libre de culpa.
guilty, a. reo, culpable.
guinea, s. guinea (moneda).
guinea-hen, s. gallinaza de Indias.
guise, s. modo ; manera.
guitar, s. guitarra.
gulch, s. cañada, cañón.
gulf, s. golfo ; abismo.
gull, s. gaviota ; bobo ; —, v.a. engañar
gullet, s. gaznate ; gola.
gullibility, s. credulidad.
gullible, a. crédulo.
gully, v.n. cañada.
gulp, s. trago ; —, v n. engullir, tragar.
gum, s. goma ; encía ; —, v.a. engomar.
gummy, a. gomoso.
gumption, s. (col.) intelligencia ; juicio,
vigor.
gum-tree, s. eucalipto.
gun, s. arma de fuego ; cañón, escopeta.
gun-boat, s. lancha cañonera.
gun-carriage, s. cureña.
gun-metal, s. bronce de cañones.
gunnel, s. (mar.) borda.
gunner, s. artillero.
gunnery, s. artillería.
gunpowder, s. pólvora.
gun-room, s. (mar.) Santabárbara.
gun-shot, s. tiro de escopeta.
gunsmith, s. arcabucero, armero.
gun-stock, s. caja de escopeta.

gunwale, s. (mar.) borda.
gurgle, s. chorro, ruido de agua ; —, v.n. murmurar (agua).
gush, v.n. brotar ; chorrear ; —, s. chorro.
gusset, s. cuadrado (de camisa).
gust, s. gusto ; soplo de aire.
gusty, a. tempestuoso. [destripar.
gut, s. intestino ; —, v.a. desventrar,

gutter, s. gotera.
guttural, a. gutural.
guy, s. (mar.) retenida; Juan de las Viñas.
guzzle, v.a. & n. engullir.
gymnasium, s. gimnasio.
gymnast, s. gimnasta. [gimnástica.
gymnastic(al), a. gimnástico ; **-s,** s.
gyrate, v.n. girar.

H

haberdasher, s. tendero.
haberdashery, s. mercería.
habiliment, s. vestido.
habit, s. hábito, vestido ; uso, costumbre ; complexión.
habitable, a. habitable.
habitation, s. habitación ; domicilio.
habitual, a. habitual ; **-ly,** habitualmente.
habituate, v.a. habituar, acostumbrar.
habitude, s. costumbre.
hack, s. caballo de alquiler, rocín ; muesca ; —, v.a. tajar, cortar.
hackle, rastrillo ; seda cruda ; —, v.a. rastrillar.
hackney, caballo de alquiler ; —, a. alquilado.
hackneyed, a. trillado, vulgarizado.
haddock, s. especie de merluza.
haft, s. mango ; asa.
hag, s. bruja, hechicera. [henil.
haggard, a. flaco, macilento ; —, s. pajar.
haggle, v.n. regatear.
haggler, s. regatón.
ha-ha, s. zanja.
hail, s. granizo ; llamamiento, saludo ; —, v.a. llamar ; —, v. imp. granizar ; —, ¡ salve !
hail-fellow, s. compañero, compadre.
hail-stone, s. piedra de granizo.
hair, s. pelo ; cabello. [nada.
hair-breadth, s. ancho de un pelo ; casi
hair-cloth, s. cilicio.
hair-dresser, s. peluquero, peinador.
hairless, a. calvo.
hair-pin, s. alfiler para cabellos.
hair-splitting, s. quisquilla.
hairy, a. peludo, velludo, cabelludo.
halberd, s. alabarda.
halberdier, s. alabardero.
halcyon, a. quieto, tranquilo ; —, s. alción (ave).
hale, a. sano, vigoroso.
half, s. mitad ; —, a. & ad. medio.
half-bred, half-caste, a. mestizo.
half-cock, a. desmontado (escopeta).
half-moon, s. semilunio.
half-penny, s. medio penique.
half-seas over, a. medio borracho.

halfway, ad. á medio camino.
half-witted, a. medio imbécil.
halibut, s. especie de pez.
hall, s. vestíbulo ; salón, colegio.
hall-mark, s. marca oficial de plata ; v.a. marcar, señalar.
halloo, ¡ hola !, ¡ ea ! —, v.n. azuzar (á los perros en la caza).
hallow, v.a. consagrar, santificar.
hallucination, s. alucinación.
halo, s. aureola.
halt, v.n. cojear ; parar ; dudar ; —, s. cojera ; parada ; alto.
halter, s. soga ; cuerda.
halve, v.a. partir en dos
halyard, s. (mar.) driza.
ham, s. corva ; jamón.
hamlet, s. villorrio.
hammer, s. martillo ; serpentín de fusil ; subasta ; —, v.a. martillar ; forjar.
hammer-cloth, s. paño del pescante de un coche.
hammock, s. hamaca.
hamper, s. cuévano ; —, v.a. embarazar.
hamstring, s. tendón de la corva ; —, v.a. desjarretar.
hand, s. mano (medida) ; carácter de escritura ; talento ; (mar.) marinero; obrero ; mano de un reloj ; at —, á la mano, al lado ; —, v.a. guiar por la mano ; entregar, transmitir.
hand-barrow, s. angarillas, pl.
hand-bell, s. campanilla.
hand-bill, s. cartel.
hand-book, s. manual.
hand-cuff, s. manilla. [á otro.
handed, a. transmitido, pasado de uno
handful, s. manojo, puñado.
hand-gallop, s. galope corto.
handicap, s. carrera de competidores igualizados por diferencia de distancia ó de peso ; —, v.a. igualizar (competidores).
handicraft, s. arte mecánica.
handicraftsman, s. artesano.
handily, ad. mañosamente.
handiness, s. maña, habilidad.
handiwork, s. obra.

handkerchief, s. pañuelo.

handle, s. mango, puño ; asa, manija ; —, v.a. manejar ; tratar.

handling, s. manejo ; toque.

handmaid, s. servidora.

hand-mill, s. molinillo.

hand-rail, s. guardalado.

handsel, s. estreno ; —, v.a. estrenar.

handsome, a. hermoso, bello, gentil ; -ly, hermosamente, generosamente.

hand-spike, s. palanca.   [letra.

hand-writing, s. carácter de escritura.

handy, a. diestro, mañoso.

hang, v.a. colgar, suspender ; ahorcar ; entapizar ; —, v.n. colgar ; pegarse ; quedarse s penso ; depender.

hanger, s. al nje.

hanger-on, s. dependiente ; mogollón.

hangings, s.pl. tapicería.

hangman, s. verdugo.

hank, s. madeja de hilo.

hanker, v.n. ansiar, apetecer.

hanky-panky, s. (col.) juglería, truhan-ería, embuste.

hansom, s. cabriolé.

hap, s. suerte, casualidad.

hap-hazard, s. accidente, lance.

hapless, a. desgraciado, desventurado.

haply, ad. por casualidad.

happen, v.n. acontecer, acaecer, suceder.

happily, ad. felizmente.

happiness, s. felicidad, dicha.

happy, a. feliz, dichoso.

harangue, s. arenga ; —, v.n. arengar.

harass, v.a. fatigar, molestar, atormentar

harbinger, s. precursor.

harbour, s. albergue ; puerto ; asilo ; —, v.a. albergar ; hospedar ; —, v.n. tomar albergue.

hard, a. duro, firme ; difícil ; penoso ; cruel, severo, rígido ; — of hearing, medio sordo ; —, ad. con fuerza ; — by, muy cerca.

harden, v.a. (& n.) endurecer(se).

hard-hearted, a. duro de corazón, in-sensible.

hardihood, s. atrevimiento, valor.

hardiness, s. intrepidez ; fuerza, robustez.

hardly, ad. apenas ; severamente.

hardness, s. dureza ; dificultad ; in-humanidad ; severidad.

hardship, s. injuria, opresión ; injusticia ; penalidad ; trabajo ; molestia, fatiga.

hardware, s. quinquillería.

hardy, a. atrevido, bravo, intrépido ; fuerte, robusto.

hare, s. liebre.

harebell, s. (bot.) campanilla.

hare-brained, a. aturdido, atolondrado.

hare-lipped, a. labihendido.

hark, ¡ oye !

harlequin, s. arlequín, bufón.

harlot, s. ramera, puta, meretriz.

harm, s. mal, daño ; desgracia ; perjuicio; —, v.a. dañar, injuriar, ofender.

harmful, a. dañoso ; perjudicial ; -ly, dañosamente.

harmless, a. sencillo, mocente : -ly, ino-centemente ; sin daño.

harmonic, a. armónico. [moniosamente.

harmonious, a. armonioso ; -ly, ar-harmonise, v.a. ajustar, concertar ; —, v.n. convenir, corresponder.

harmony, s. armonía. [—, v.a. enjaezar.

harness, s. arreos de un caballo, pl.

harp, s. arpa ; —, v.a. & n. tocar el arpa ; descantar.

harpist, s. arpista.

harpoon, s. arpón.

harpsichord, s. clavicordio.

harpy, s. arpía.

harridan, s. viejezuela.

harrier, s. perro lebrero.

harrow, s. grada ; rastro ; —, v.a. gradar.

harry, v.a. tormentar ; devastar.

harsh, a. áspero, agrio, rígido, duro, austero ; -ly, ásperamente, severa-mente. [austeridad, severidad.

harshness, s. aspereza, dureza, rudeza,

hart, s. ciervo.

hartshorn, s. cuerno de ciervo.

harum-scarum, a. precipitado, atolon-drado. [recoger las mieses, segar.

harvest, s. cosecha ; agosto ; —, v.a.

harvester, s. agostero, segador.

harvest-home, s. fiesta al acabar la siega.

hash, s. jigote ; —, v.a. picar.

hasp, s. aldaba de candado ; broche ; —, v.a. abrochar ; cerrar con aldaba.

hassock, s. cojín de paja.

haste, s. prisa ; presteza.

hasten, v.a. acelerar, apresurar ; —, v.n. correr, apresurarse. [mente.

hastily, ad. precipitadamente ; airada-

hastiness, s. precipitación.

hasty, a. apresurado ; colérico.

hasty-pudding, s. papilla de leche y harina.

hat, s. sombrero.

hat-band, s. cinta del sombrero.

hat-box, hat-case, s. sombrerera.

hatch, v.a. criar (pollos) ; empollar ; tramar ; —, s. pollada, nidada ; media puerta ; (mar.) cuarteles.

hatchet, s. destral ; hacha pequeña.

hatchment, s. escudo fúnebre.

hatchway, s. (mar.) escotilla.

hate, s. odio, aborrecimiento ; —, v.a. odiar, detestar.

hateful, a. odioso, detestable ; -ly, de-testablemente, con tirria.

hatred, s. odio, aborrecimiento.

hatter, s. sombrerero. [mente.
haughtily, ad. fieramente, orgullosa-
haughtiness, s. orgullo; altivez.
haughty, a. altanero, altivo, orgulloso.
haul, v.a. tirar, halar; —, s. estirón.
haulage, s. acción de halar.
haunch, s. anca. [guarida; querencia.
haunt, v.a. frecuentar, rondar; —, s.
haunted, a. misterioso, legendario.
hautboy, s. (mus.) oboe.
have, v.a. haber; tener; poseer.
haven, s. puerto; abrigo, asilo.
haversack, s. mochila.
havoc, s. estrago; ruina.
haw, s. cerca; baya de espino; —, v.n.
tartamudear.
hawk, s. halcón; —, v.n. cazar con
halcón; vender mercaderías por las
calles.
hawker, s. mercachifle, buhonero.
hawser, s. (mar.) guindaleza.
haw-thorn, s. espino blanco.
hay, s. heno.
hay-cock, s. pila de heno.
hay-loft, s. henil.
hay-rick, hay-stack, s. niara.
hazard, s. azar, accidente; riesgo;
juego de azar á los dados; —, v.a.
arriesgar; aventurar.
hazardous, a. arriesgado, peligroso; -ly,
peligrosamente.
haze, s. niebla.
hazel, s. avellano.
hazel-nut, s. avellana. [ambiguo.
hazy, a. aneblado; obscuro; dudoso,
he, pn. el.
head, s. cabeza; jefe; juicio; talento;
puño (de bastón); fuente; nacimiento de un río; —, v.a. gobernar,
dirigir.
head-ache, s. dolor de cabeza.
head-dress, s. cofia; tocado.
headiness, s. precipitación, obstinación.
head-land, s. promontorio.
headless, a. inconsiderado.
headlong, a. & ad. temerario, inconsiderado; temerariamente; precipitadamente.
head-master, s. rector de un colegio.
headmost, a. primero.
head-piece, s. casco, yelmo; (col.) seso,
entendimiento.
head-quarters, s. (mil.) cuartel general.
headship, s. primado; autoridad.
headsman, s. degollador, verdugo.
headstall, s. cabestral. [obstinado.
headstrong, a. testarudo, cabezudo,
head-way, s. adelantamiento de un barco.
healy, a. temerario; obstinado; violento.
heal, v.a. & n. curar; sanar.
health, s. salud, sanidad; brindis.

healthiness, s. sanidad, salud.
healthy, a. sano; salubre.
heap, s. montón; turba; —, v.a.
amontonar, acumular.
hear, v.a. oir,; entender; obedecer; —,
v.n. oir; escuchar.
hearer, s. oyente, oidor.
hearing, s. oído; audiencia.
hearken, v.n. escuchar, atender.
hearsay, s. rumor; fama.
hearse, s. ataúd, féretro.
heart, s. corazón; interior, centro;
ánimo,valor; amor; by —, de memoria.
heart-breaking, a. congojoso.
heart-burning, s. cardialgía; afflicción.
hearth, s. hogar, fogón.
heartily, ad. sinceramente, cordialmente.
heartiness, s. cordialidad, sinceridad.
heartless, insensible, cruel; -ly, insensiblemente.
heartrending, a. penoso.
heart-sick, a. dolorido, afligido.
heart-whole, a. libre de amores.
hearty, a. sincero; sano; vigoroso.
heat, s. ardor, calor, vehemencia; animosidad; —, v.a. calentar, encender
heater, s. escalfador.
heath, heather, s. (bot.) brezo; brezal.
heathen, s. gentil, pagano; -ish, a.
gentílico; salvaje; -ishly, á la manera de los paganos.
heathenism, s. paganismo.
heave, v.a. alzar; elevar; hincharse; —,
v.n. palpitar; respirar trabajosamente;
—, s. esfuerzo para levantarse.
heaven, s. cielo; firmamento.
heavenly, a. celeste, divino.
heavily, ad. pesadamente.
heaviness, s. pesadez; aflicción; opresión.
heavy, a. grave, pesado; opresivo,
penoso, molesto; triste; tardo, soñoliento.
hebrew, s. hebreo, judío.
hecatomb, s. hecatombe.
hectic, a. hético.
hector, v.n. baladronear, bravear.
hedge, s. seto, cerco; —, v.a. cercar con
un seto.
hedge-hog, s. erizo.
hedger, s. cercador.
hedge-row, s. seto vivo.
heed, v.a. atender, observar; —, s.
cuidado; atención, precaución.
heedful, a. vigilante, atento; circunspecto; -ly, cautelosamente.
heedless, a. descuidado, negligente; -ly,
negligentemente.
heel, s. talón; to take to one's -s, apretar
los talones, huir.
heeltaps s. restos de bebida en la copa.
Hegira, s. égira, era de los mahometanos.

heifer, s. novilla, vaquilla.   [sublimidad.
height, s. altura, elevación, sumidad ;
heighten, v.a. realzar. adelantar, mejorar ; exaltar.   [mente, horriblemente.
heinous, a. atroz, odioso ; **-ly,** atroz-
heir, s. heredero ; **— apparent,** heredero
forzoso.
heirdom, heirship, s. herencia, heredad.
heiress, s. heredera.
heirloom, s. vínculo de bienes muebles.
heliograph, s. heliógrafo.
hell, s. infierno.
hellenism, s. helenismo.
hellenist, s. helenista.
hellish, a. infernal, malvado.
helm, s. (mar.) timón, gobernalle.
helm, helmet, s. yelmo.
helmsman, s. timonero.
help, v.a. (& n.) ayudar, asistir, socorrer;
aliviar, remediar, reparar ; **I cannot —
it** ; no puedo dejarlo de hacer ; **—,**
s. ayuda ; socorro, remedio.
helper, s. ayudador, auxiliador, socorredor.
help-mate, help-meet, esposa.
helpful, a. útil ; saludable.
helpless, a. abandonado ; irremediable ;
-ly, irremediablemente, sin recurso.
helter-skelter, ad. á trochemoche, en
desorden.
helve, s. mango ; astil de hacha.
hem, s. ribete ; **—,** v.a. ribetear ; repulgar ; **—,** v.n. toser de fingido ;
— ¡ interj. ¡ ho ! ¡ he !
hemisphere, s. hemisferio.
hemlock, s. cicuta.
hemorrhage, s. hemorragía.
hemorrhoids, s.pl. hemorroides, pl.
hemp, s. cáñamo.
hempen, a. cañameño.
hen, s. gallina.
hence, ad. de aquí ; por esto.
henceforth, henceforward, ad. en adelante, desde ahora ; en lo venidero.
henchman, s. paje, mozo de confianza.
hen-coop, hen-house, s. gallinero.
hen-pecked, a. consentido.
hen-roost, s. gallinero.
her, pn. su, ella, de ella, á ella.
herald, s. heraldo.
heraldic, a. heráldico.
heraldry, s. heráldica.
herb, s. yerba ; -s, pl. legumbre, hortaliza.
herbaceous, a. herbáceo.
herbage, s. herbaje.
herbalist, s. herbolario.
herbivorous, a. herbívoro.
herculean, a. herculeo.
herd, s. hato, rebaño ; manada ; grey ;
—, v.n. ir en hatos ; asociarse.
herdsman, s. pastor, vaquero.

here, ad. aquí, acá.
hereabout(s), ad. aquí alrededor.
hereafter, ad. en adelante, en lo futuro ;
—, s. vida futura.
hereby, ad. por esto.
hereditary, a. hereditario.
heredity, s. derecho de sucesión.
herefrom, ad. de aquí.
herein, ad. en esto.
hereof, ad. de esto.
heresy, s. herejía.
heretic, s. hereje ; **—,** a. herético.
hereto, ad. á esto, para esto.
heretofore, ad. antes, en tiempos pasados.
hereupon, ad. sobre esto.
herewith, ad. con esto.
heritance, s. herencia.   [méticamente.
hermetic(al), a. hermético ; **-ly,** her-
hermit, s. ermitaño, eremita.
hermitage, s. ermita.
hernia, s. hernia.
hero, s. héroe.
heroic(al), a. heroico; **-ally,** heroicamente.
heroine, s. heroína.
heroism, s. heroísmo.
heron, s. garza.
heronry, s. lugar para criar las garzas.
herring, s. arenque.
hers, pn. suyo, de ella.
herself, pn. ella misma.
hesitate, v.a. dudar, vacilar, tardar.
hesitancy, hesitation, s. vacilación, duda,
irresolución.
heterodox, a. heterodoxo.
heterogeneous, a. heterogeneo.
hew, v.a. leñar ; tajar ; cortar, picar.
hewer, s. leñador.
hey, ¡ he !
heyday, s. alegría ; gozo ; **—** ! ¡ he !
hiatus, s. abertura, hendedura ;   (gr.)
hibernate, v.n. invernar.   [hiato.
hiccough, s. hipo ; **—,** v.n. tener hipo.
hickory, s. noguera americana.
hide, v.a. & n. esconder(se) ; (vulg.)
apalear ; **—,** s. cuero, piel.
hideous,ra. feo, repugnante ; **-ly,** horriblemente.
hiding-place, s. escondite, escondrijo.
hie, v.n. irse.
hierarchy, s. jerarquía.
hieroglyphic, a. & s. jeroglífico.
higgle, v.n. regatear.   [mente.
higgledy-piggledy, ad. (col.) confusa-
higgler, s. revendedor, regatón.
high, a. alto, elevado ; arduo ; altivo ;
noble, ilustre ; sublime ; solemne ;
caro.
high-altar, s. altar mayor.   [miento.
high-born, a. noble, ilustre por naci-
high-coloured, a. subido de color, de
colores vivos ; exagerado.

high-flown, a. hinchado, presuntuoso.
highland, s. serranía.
highlander, s. montañés.
highly, ad. altamente; em sumo grado; arrogantemente; ambiciosamente.
high-mettled, a. ardiente, bravo.
high-minded, a. magnánimo, generoso.
highness, s. altura; alteza.
high-water, s. marea alta.
high-road, highway, s. camino real.
highwayman, s. salteador.
hilarious, a. alegre.
hilarity, s. hilaridad, alegría; regocijo.
hill, s. cerro, collado.
hillock, s. cerrito, colina; otero.
hilly, a. montañoso.
hilt, s. puño de espada.
him, pn. le, á él.
himself, pn. á él mismo.
hind, a. trasero, posterior; —, s. cierva (hembra del ciervo); criado; patán.
hinder, v.a. impedir, embarazar.
hinder, a. trasero.
hind(e)rance, s. impedimento, obstáculo.
hind(er)most, a. postrero, último.
Hindu, Hindoo, a. & s. Indio.
hinge, s. gozne, charnela, bisagra; razón principal; —, v.a. engoznar.
hint, s. seña; sugestión, insinuación; luz; aviso; —, v.a. apuntar, insinuar; sugerir; hacer señas.
hip, cadera.
hippodrome, s. hipódromo.
hippopotamus, s. hipopótamo.
hire, v.a. alquilar; arrendar; —, s. alquiler; salario.
hireling, s. jornalero; hombre mercenario; —, a. mercenario, venal.
hirsute, a. hirsuto, velludo, áspero.
his, pn. su, suyo, de él.
hiss, v.a. & n. silbar.
hist, ¡ chito! ¡ chitón!
historian, s. historiador. [camente.
historic(al), a. histórico; -ally, histó-
history, s. historia, narración.
histrionic, a. histriónico.
hit, v.a. golpear; atinar; —, s. golpe; suerte feliz; alcance.
hitch, v.n. menearse; engancharse; —, s. nudo, impedimento; (mar.) vuelta de cabo.
hither, ad. acá; á este fin; —, a. citerior; -to, hasta ahora, hasta aquí.
hive, s. colmena; —, v.a. enjambrar; —, v.n. vivir muchos juntos, hormiguear.
hoar, a. blanco, cano.
hoard, s. montón; tesoro escondido; —, v.a. atesorar, acumular.
hoar-frost, s. escarcha.
hoariness, s. blancura; canas de viejo, pl.

hoarse, a. ronco; -ly, roncamente.
hoarseness, s. ronquera, carraspera.
hoary, a. blanquecino, cano.
hoax, s. burla; petardo; —, v.a. engañar, burlar.
hob, s. patán; calentador en la chimenea.
hobble, v.n. cojear; —, v.a. manear; —, s. maneas, maniotas; dificultad.
hobby, hobby-horse, s. caballico de niños; estudio ó pasatiempo predilecto; manía.
hobgoblin, s. duende, gnomo.
hobnail, s. clavo de herradura.
hob-nob, v.n. hermanarse con otro.
Hobson's choice, s. alternativa entre eso ó nada.
hock, s. vino del Rin; jarrete, corvejón.
hockey, s. juego de pelota inglés.
hocus, s. truhán; truhanería; —, v.a. engañar; narcotizar.
hocus-pocus, s. embuste, truhanería.
hodge-podge, s. olla almodrote.
hodman, s. peon de albañil.
hoe, s. azada; —, v.a. cavar con azada.
hog, s. cerdo, puerco.
hoggish, a. porcuno.
hogshead, s. pipa (de vino ó cerveza).
hoiden, hoyden, s. muchacha retozona.
hoist, v.a. alzar; izar. [pizpereta.
hoity-toity, interj. ¡ caracoles !
hold, v.a. tener, asir; detener; sostener; mantener; juzgar, reputar; poseer; continuar, proseguir; contener; —, v.n. valer; mantenerse; durar; abstenerse; adherirse, depender; — ¡ tente! ¡ para! éstate quieto; —, s. presa; mango; asa; prisión; custodia; (mar.) bodega.
holdfast, s. grapa, laña.
holding, s. tenencia, arrendamiento.
hole, s. agujero; cueva; hoyo. [ciones, pl.
holiday, s. día de fiesta; -s, pl. vaca-
holiness, s. santidad.
holland, s. tela holandesa.
hollow, a. hueco; vacío; inútil; s. cavidad, caverna; —, v.a. excavar, ahuecar. [insinceridad.
hollowness, s. cavidad; simulación;
holly, s. (bot.) acebo.
holly-hock, s. malva hortense.
holocaust, s. holocausto.
holster, s. funda de pistola.
holy, a. santo, pío; consagrado.
holy-water, s. agua bendita.
holy-week, s. semana santa.
homage, s. homenaje. [patria; domicilio.
home, s. casa propia, morada; hogar;
home-bred, a. nativo; casero.
homeless, a. sin casa ni hogar.
homeliness, s. simpleza; grosería.
homely, a. casero, modesto, simple.

home-made, a. hecho en casa.
home-rule, s. autonomía regional.
home-ruler, s. partidario de autonomía irlandesa; separatista.
home-sick, a. nostálgico.
home-sickness, s. mal del país, nostalgia.
homestead, s. granja.
homeward, a. hacia casa, hacia su país.
homicidal, a. homicida.
homicide, s. homicidio; homicida.
homily, s. homilia.
homœopathist, s. homeopatista.
homœopathy, s. homeopatía.
homogenous, a. homogéneo.
hone, s. piedra amoladera.
honest, a. honesto; justo; honrado; -ly, honestamente.
honesty, s. honestidad, justicia.
honey, s. miel; dulzura.
honey-comb, s. panal.
honeymoon, s. luna de miel.
honey-suckle, s. (bot.) madreselva.
honied, a. dulce, meloso, enmelado.
honorarium, s. pago, saldo.
honorary, a. honorario.
honour, s. honra; honor; —, v.a. honrar; hacer honor á una letra de cambio.
honourable, a. honorable; ilustre.
honourably, ad. honorablemente.
hood, s. caperuza; capirote (de graduados); capucha (de religioso); —, v.a. vendar los ojos, cegar.
hoodwink, v.a. engañar, capotear.
hoof, s. casco de las bestias caballares.
hook, s. gancho; anzuelo; by — or crook, de un modo ú otro; —, v.a. enganchar.
hooked, a. enganchado, encorvado.
hook-nosed, a. cariaguileño.
hoop, s. cerco de barril; tontillo; —, v.a. cercar.
hooping-cough, s. tos convulsiva.
hoopoo, s. abubilla (ave).
hoot, v.n. gritar; —, s. grito.
hop, s. (bot.) lúpulo, hombrecillo; salto; —, v.n. saltar, brincar.
hope, s. esperanza; —, v.n. esperar.
hopeful, a. esperador, confidente; precoz, industrioso (de los jóvenes); -ly, con esperanza.
hopefulness, s. buena esperanza.
hopeless, a. desesperado; -ly, sin esperanza.
hop-garden, s. plantío de lúpulos.
hopper, s. saltador; tolva (en los molinos).
hop-pole, s. estaca de lúpulo.
hopscotch, s. un juego de niños.
horde, s. horda.
horizon, s. horizonte.   [zontalmente.
horizontal, a. horizontal; -ly, hori-

horn, s. cuerno; corneta.
horn-blower, s. trompetero.
horned, a. cornudo.
hornet, s. avispón.
horn-owl, s. buho cornudo.
horn-pipe, s. fandango de marineros.
horny, a. hecho de cuerno; calloso.
horologe, s. reloj.
horoscope, s. horóscopo.
horrible, a. horrible, terrible.   [mente.
horribly, ad. horriblemente; enorme-
horrid, a. hórrido, horrible.
horrific, a. horrífico; horroroso.
horror, s. horror, terror.
horse, s. caballo; caballería; caballete.
horseback, ad. on —, á caballo.
horse-block, s. montadero.
horse-breaker, s. domador de caballos.
horse-chesnut, s. castaño de Indias.
horse-cloth, s. jerga de caballo.
horse-dealer, s. chalán, traficante en caballos.
horse-fly, s. moscarda, moscardón. [pl.
horse-guards, s.pl. guardias de á caballo.
horse-hair, s. crin de caballo.
horse-laugh, s. carcajada.
horse-leech, s. sanguijuela.
horseman, s. jinete.
horsemanship, s. equitación.
horseplay, s. chanza pesada.
horsepond, s. abrevadero.   [caballos.
horse-race, s. carrera ó corrida de
horse-radish, s. rábano picante.
horse-shoe, s. herradura de caballo.
horsewhip, s. látigo; —, v.a. azotar.
horsewoman, s. caballera.
horticulture, s. horticultura, jardinería.
horticulturist, s. hortelano, jardinero.
hose, s. bragas, pl.; calzones, mangueras, tubo elástico.
hosier, s. tendero.
hosiery, s. tienda.
hospitable, a. hospitable, generoso.
hospitably, ad. con hospitalidad.
hospital, s. hospital.
hospitality, s. hospitalidad.   [hostia.
host, s. huésped; mesonero; ejército;
hostage, s. rehén.
hostess, s. huespeda; posadera, mesonera.
hostile, a. hostil.
hostility, s. hostilidad.
hostler, s. mozo de paja.   [lento.
hot, a. cálido, ardiente; fervoroso; vio-
hot-bed, s. era.
hotch-potch, s. olla podrida.
hotel, s. fonda, posada.
hot-house, s. invernáculo.
hotly, ad. con calor; violentamente. [ear.
hough, s. jarrete, corvejón; —, v.a. jarret-
hound, s. sabueso.
hour, s. hora.

hour-glass, s. reloj de arena. [las horas.
hour-hand, s. mano del reloj que señala
houri, s. hurí.
hourly, ad. á cada hora.
house, s. casa; linaje; cámara (del
parlamento); —, v.a. & n. albergar;
residir.
house-breaker, s. ladrón.
household, s. familia; manejo doméstico;
-bread, pan casero.
householder, s. amo de casa, vecino.
housekeeper, s. ama de llaves.
housekeeping, s. gobierno doméstico.
houseless, a. sin habitación ó sin casa.
house-maid, s. criada, camarera.
house-warming, s. festín al estrenar una
casa nueva.
housewife, s. ama de casa; ama de
gobierno, mujer económica; —, cos-
turero.
housing, s. almacenaje; -s, pl. gualdrapa.
hovel, s. choza, cabaña. [rondar.
hover, v.n. revolotear, aletear; dudar;
how, ad. como; — much? cuanto; —
do you do? ¿cómo le va á U.?
how(so)ever, ad. como quiera que sea;
de cualquier modo; no obstante.
howitzer, s. (mil.) obús; mortero.
howl, v.n. aullar; —, s. aullo.
hub, s. centro de una rueda.
hubbub, s. ruido; alboroto, tumulto.
huckaback, s. lienzo, grueso para toallas.
huckster, s. revendedor, chalán.
huddle, v.a. & n. amontonar(se), acur-
rucar(se); —, confusión, baraunda.
hue, s. color; tez del rostro; matiz; —
and cry, alarma que se da contra un
criminal. [bravear.
huff, s. arrebato; cólera; —, v.a. bufar,
hug, v.a. abrazar, acariciar; —, s.
abrazo apretado. [mente.
huge, a. vasto, enorme; -ly, inmensa-
hugeness, s. grandeza enorme ó des-
mesurada.
hulk, s. (mar.) casco, cuerpo de barco.
hull, s. (mar.) casco de un buque.
hum, v.n. zumbar, susurrar; murmurar;
—, s. zumbido; —! ¡ya!
human, a. humano. [humanamente.
humane, a. humano; benigno; -ly,
humanise, v.a. humanizar.
humanist, s. humanista.
humanity, s. humanidad. [humano.
humankind, s. el género ó linaje
humanly, ad. humanamente.
humble, a. humilde, modesto; —, v.a.
humillar, postrar.
humble-bee, s. zángano.
humbleness, s. humildad.
humbly, ad. con humildad.

humbug, s. trampa, embuste, disparate;
embustero; —, v.a. engañar, chasquear.
humdrum, a. lerdo, estúpido; monótono.
humid, a. húmedo.
humidity, s. humedad.
humiliate, v.a. humillar. [cación.
humiliation, s. humillación, mortifi-
humility, s. humildad. [jarito).
humming-bird, s. picaflor, colibrí (pa-
humming-top, s. trompo, peonza. [oso.
humorist, s. hombre entretenido, graci-
humorous, a. chistoso, placentero; -ly,
de buen humor; agudamente.
humorsome, a. petulante, caprichoso.
humour, s. humor; humorada, fantasía;
capricho; agudeza; —, v.a. complacer, dar gusto.
hump, s. jiba, joroba.
humpbacked, a. jorobado, jiboso.
hunch, s. puñada; pedazo (de pan);
jiba; -backed, a. jorobado, jiboso.
hundred, a. ciento; —, s. centenar; un
ciento.
hundredfold, a. céntuplo.
hundredth, a. centésimo.
hundred-weight, s. quintal.
hunger, s. hambre; —, v.n. hambrear.
hungrily, ad. hambrientamente.
hungry, a. hambriento; voraz.
hunk, s. pedazo grande.
hunt, v.a. cazar; perseguir; buscar; —,
v.n. cazar; —, s. caza.
hunter, s. cazador; caballo de caza.
hunting, s. montería, caza.
hunting-box, s. casa de campo.
hunting-crop, s. rebenque.
hunting-horn, s. corneta de caza.
huntress, s. cazadora.
huntsman, s. cazador, montero.
hurdle, s. zarzo.
hurdy-gurdy, s. orgán mecánico.
hurl, v.a. tirar con violencia; arrojar.
hurly-burly, s. babalonia, trapisonda,
baraunda.
hurricane, s. huracán.
hurry, v.a. & n. acelerar, precipitar;
apresurar(se); —, s. prisa, precipitación.
hurt, v.a. dañar; herir; ofender; —, s
mal, daño, perjuicio; herida.
hurtful, a. dañoso, nocivo; injurioso;
-ly, dañosamente.
hurtfulness, s. mal, daño.
husband, s. marido; labrador; —, v.a
gobernar con economía; ahorrar.
husbandman, s. labrador, viñador.
husbandry, s. agricultura; economía.
hush! ¡chitón! ¡silencio! —, v.a
aquietar; acallar; —, v.n. estar quieto.

hush-money, s. cohecho que se da á alguno para que calle.
husk, s. cáscara; pellejo; —, v.a. descascarar, mondar.
huskiness, s. ronquedad.
husky, a. ronco.
hussar, s. húsar.
hussy, s. mujercilla.
hustings, s. tribuna para las elecciones.
hustle, v.a. correr, acosar, empujar.
hut, s. cabaña, barraca.
hutch, s. arca; cofre; jaula.
hyacinth, s. jacinto.   [dráulica.
hydraulic(al), a. hidráulico; -s, s.pl. hi-
hydrographer, s. hidrógrafo.
hydrophobia, s. hidrofobia.
hydrostatics, s.pl. hidrostática.
hyena, s. hiena.

hygiene, s. higiena.
hymen, s. himeneo.
hymeneal, a. nupcial.
hymn, s. himno.
hyperbole, s. hipérbole; exageración.
hyperbolic(al), a. hiperbólico; -ally hiperbólicamente.
hypercritical, a. criticón, riguroso.
hypochondria, s. hipocondría.
hypochondriac, a. & s. hipocondriaco.
hypocrisy, s. hipocresía.
hypocrite, s. hipócrita.
hypocritic(al), a. hipocrita, disimulado.
hypothesis, s. hipótesis.   [dicionalmente.
hypothetic(al), a. hipotético; -ly, con-
hyssop, s. hisopo.
hysteric(al), a. histérico.
hysterics, s.pl. paroxismo histérico.

I

I, pn. yo.
iambic, a. iámbico; —, s. iambo.
ice, hielo; —, v.a. helar (licores).
ice-bound, a. rodeado de hielos.
ice-box, ice-cellar, -icehouse, ice-safe, s. nevería.
icicle, s. cerrión.
iconoclast, s. iconoclasta.
icy, a. helado; frío.
idea, s. idea, imagen mental.
ideal, a. ideal; -ly, idealmente.
identic(al), a. idéntico.
identify, v.a. identificar.
identity, s. identidad.
idiocy, s. idiotez.
idiom, s. idioma; idiotismo.
idiomatic(al), a. idiomático, castizo.
idiosyncrasy, s. idiosincrasia.
idiot, s. idiota, necio.
idiotic(al), a. tonto, bobo.
idle, a. ocioso, perezoso, desocupado, holgazán; inútil, vano, frívolo; —, v.n. holgazanear; estar ocioso.
idleness, s. ociosidad, pereza; negligencia; frivolidad.
idler, s. holgazán.
idly, ad. ociosamente; vanamente.
idol, s. ídolo; imagen.
idolater, s. idólatra.
idolatrous, a. idolátrico.
idolatry, s. idolatría.
idolise, v.a. idolatrar.
idyl, s. idilio.
idyllic, a. idílico.
if, c. si; aunque, supuesto que;   [sino.
igneous, a. ígneo.   [San Telmo.
ignis-fatuus, s. fuego fatuo; fuego de
ignite, v.a. & n. encender(se), abrasar(se).

ignition, s. ignición.
ignoble, a. innoble; bajo.
ignobly, ad. vilmente, bajamente.
ignominious, a. ignominioso; -ly, igno- miniosamente.
ignominy, s. ignominia, infamia.
ignoramus, s. ignorante, tonto.
ignorance, s. ignorancia.   [mente.
ignorant, a. ignorante; -ly, ignorante-
ignore, v.a. ignorar.
ill, a. malo, enfermo, doliente; —, s. mal, infortunio; —, ad. mal, malamente.
illegal, a. -ly, ad. ilegal(mente).
illegality, s. ilegalidad.
illegible, a. ilegible.
illegibly, ad. de un modo ilegible.
illegitimacy, s. ilegitimidad.
illegitimate, a. ilegítimo; bastardo; -ly, ilegitimamente.
ill-favoured, a. feo.   [quinamente.
illiberal, a. innoble; mezquino; -ly, mes-
illiberality, s. cortedad de ánimo; mezquindad, roñería.
illicit, a. ilcito.
illimitable, a. ilimitado.
illiterate, a. indocto, iliterato.
illness, s. enfermedad; maldad.
illogical, a. ilógico.
ill-shaped, a. disforme; mal hecho.
ill-starred, a. desdichado.
ill-tempered, a. colérico.
ill-timed, a. intempestivo, á deshora.
ill-treat, ill-use, v.a. maltratar.
illuminate, v.a. iluminar.
illumination, s. iluminación.
illumine, v.a. iluminar.
illusion, s. ilusión.
illusive, illusory, a. ilusivo, ilusorio.

illustrate, v.a. ilustrar; explicar.
illustration, s. ilustración; elucidación.
illustrative, a. explicativo.
illustrious, a. ilustre, insigne, célebre; -ly, ilustremente.
ill-will, s. malquerencia, malevolencia.
image, s. imagen, estatua; —, v.a. imaginar, representar.
imagery, s. imagen; metáfora; vuelos de la fantasía, pl.
imaginable, a. imaginable, concebible.
imaginary, a. imaginario.
imagination, s. imaginación; idea fantástica.
imaginative, a. imaginativo.
imagine, v.a. imaginar, figurarse; idear, inventar.
imbecile, a. imbécil, necio. [idiotez.
imbecility, s. imbecilidad, mentecatez.
imbedded, a. enterrado, engastado.
imbibe, v.a. embeber; chupar.
imbroglio, s. embrollo; maraña.
imbrue, v.a. remojar, teñir.
imbue, v.a. imbuir, infundir.
imitable, a. imitable.
imitate, v.a. imitar, remedar, copiar.
imitation, s. imitación, copia.
imitative, a. imitativo.
immaculate, a. inmaculado, puro.
immaterial, a. inmaterial; poco importante.
immature, a. inmaturo.
immeasurable, a. inmensurable, inmenso.
immeasurably, ad. inmensamente, inmensurablemente.
immediate, a. inmediato; -ly, inmediatamente, incontinente.
immemorial, a. inmemorial.
immense, a. inmenso; vasto; -ly, inmensamente. [dumbre.
immensity, s. inmensidad, muchedumbre.
immerge, immerse, v.a. sumergir, zambullir.
immersion, s. inmersión.
immigrant, s. inmigrante.
imminent, a. inminente.
immobile, a. inmovil.
immobility, s. inmovilidad.
immoderate, a. inmoderado, excésivo; -ly, inmoderadamente.
immodest, a. inmodesto; desvergonzado; -ly, inmodestamente.
immodesty, s. inmodestia, desvergüenza.
immolate, v.a. inmolar, sacrificar.
immolation, s. inmolación.
immoral, a. inmoral, depravado.
immorality, s. inmoralidad, pravedad, corrupción.
immortal, a. inmortal.
immortalise, v.a. inmortalizar, eternizar.
immortality, s. inmortalidad.

immovable, a. inmoble; inmovible; -s, s.pl. muebles fijos, pl.
immovably, a. inmóblemente.
immunity, s. inmunidad, franquicia, privilegio.
immure, v.a. emparedar.
immutability, s. inmutabilidad.
immutable, a. inmutable.
immutably, ad. inmutablemente.
imp, s. diablillo, duende.
impact, s. choque, impacción. [minuir,
impair, v.a. empeorar, deteriorar; disimpale, v.a. empalar.
impalpable, a. impalpable.
impannel, v.a. (law) citar á los jurados.
impart, v.a. communicar, dar parte.
impartial, a. -ly, imparcial(mente).
impartiality, s. imparcialidad.
impassable, a. intransitable.
impassibility, s. impasibilidad.
impassive, a. impasible.
impatience, s. impaciencia.
impatient, a. -ly, impaciente(mente).
impeach, v.a. acusar, denunciar.
impeachable, a. delatable.
impeachment, s. acusación pública.
impeccable, a. impecable.
impecunious, a. indigente.
impede, v.a. impedir, embarazar.
impediment, s. impedimento, obstáculo.
impel, v.a. impeler, empujar.
impend, v.n. acercarse, estar inminente.
impenetrability, s. impenetrabilidad.
impenetrable, a. impenetrable.
impenetrably, ad. impenetrablemente.
impenitence, s. impenitencia.
impenitent, a. impenitente; -ly, sin penitencia.
imperative, a. imperativo; -ly, imperativamente.
imperceptible, a. imperceptible.
imperceptibly, ad. imperceptiblemente.
imperfect, a. imperfecto, defectuoso; -ly, imperfectamente; —, s. (gr.) pretérito imperfecto.
imperfection, s. imperfección, defecto.
imperial, a. imperial.
imperil, v.a. arriesgar. [periosamente.
imperious, a. imperioso; altivo; -ly, imperishable, a. indestructible; eterno.
impermeable, a. impermeable.
impersonal, a. -ly, impersonal(mente).
impersonate, v.a. representar. [actor).
impersonation, s. representación (de un impertinence, s. impertinencia; descaro.
impertinent, a. impertinente; -ly, impertinentemente; fuera de propósito.
imperturbable, a. imperturbable; -bly, sin perturbación.
impervious, a. impermeable.
impetuosity, s. impetuosidad, impetu.

impetuous, a. impetuoso ; **-ly**, impetuosa-mente.
impetus, s. ímpetu.
impiety, s. impiedad, irreligión.
impinge (on), v.a. tocar, rasar.
impious, a. impío, irreligioso ; **-ly**, im-píamente.
implacable, a. implacable, irreconciliable.
implacably, ad. implacablemente.
implant, v.a. plantar ; injertar ; im-primir.
implement, s. herramienta.
implicate, v.a. implicar, envolver.
implication, s. implicación. [mente.
implicit, a. implícito ; **-ly**, impl cita-
implore, v.a. implorar, suplicar.
imply, v.a. implicar.
impolite, a. descortés, mal criado.
impoliteness, s. desco tesía.
impolitic, a. imprudente ; impolítico.
import, v.a. importar ; significar ; —, s. importancia ; importe ; sentido ; sig-nificación ; **-duty**, derechos de entrada.
importance, s. importancia. [pl.
important, a. importante.
importation, s. importación. [tranjeros.
importer, s. introductor de géneros ex-
importunate, a. importuno ; **-ly**, im-portunamente.
importune, v.a. importunar.
importunity, s. importunidad.
impose, v.a. imponer ; — **upon**, engañar.
imposing, a. imponente, impresion-ante. [postura.
imposition, s. imposición, carga ; im-
impossibility, s. imposibilidad.
impossible, a. imposible.
impost, s. impuesto, tributo.
impostor, s. impostor.
imposture, s. impostura ; engaño.
impotence, s. impotencia ; incapacidad.
impotent, a. impotente ; incapaz ; **-ly**; sin poder, inútilmente.
impound, v.a. encerrar, acorralar.
impoverish, v.a. empobrecer.
impoverishment, s. empobrecimiento.
impracticability, s. imposibilidad.
impracticable, a.impracticable, imposible.
imprecate. v.a. maldecir.
imprecation, s. imprecación, maldición.
impregnable, a. inexpugnable.
impregnate, v.a. empreñar ; impregnar.
impregnation, s. fecundación ; impreg-nación.
impress, v.a. imprimir, estampar ; en-ganchar por fuerza, levar ; —, s. im-presión ; estampa. [presionable.
impressible, **impressionable**, a. im-
impression, s. impresión ; edición.
impressive, a. penetrante ; imponente ; **-ly**, eficazmente.

imprint, v.a. imprimir ; estampar.
imprison, v.a. aprisionar.
imprisonment, s. prisión ; encierro.
improbability, s. improbabilidad, in-verisimilitud.
improbable, a. improbable, inverisímil.
improbably, ad. improbablemente.
improbity, s. deshonestidad.
impromptu, a. extemporáneamente.
improper, a. inconveniente, impropio, in-decente ; **-ly**, impropiamente.
impropriety, s. inconveniencia, impro-piedad, incongruencia.
improve, v.a. & n. mejorar, perfeccionar mejorar ; hacer progresos.
improvement, s. progreso, mejoramiento.
improvidence, s. imprudencia, impre-visión. [próvidamente.
improvident, a. impróvido ; **-ly**, im-
improvise, v.a. improvisar.
imprudence, s. imprudencia.
imprudent, a. imprudente , **-ly**, impru dentemente.
impudence, s. descaro, desvergüenza.
impudent, a. descarado ; **-ly**, desvergon-zadamente.
impugn, v.a. impugnar.
impulse, impulsion, s. impulsión; impulso.
impulsive, a. impulsivo, precipitado.
impunity, s. impunidad.
impure, a. impuro ; impúdico, sucio , **-ly**, impuramente.
impurity, s. impuridad, impureza.
imputation, s. imputación.
impute, v.a. imputar.
in, pr. en.
inability, s. inhabilidad, incapacidad.
inaccessible, a. inaccessible.
inaccuracy, s. incorrección, inexactitud.
inaccurate, a. inexacto.
inaction, s. inacción.
inactive, a. inactivo, inerte , flojo, perezoso, negligente.
inactivity, s. ociosidad, desidia.
inadequate, a. inadecuado, defectuoso ; imperfecto, insuficiente.
inadmissible, a. inadmisible.
inadvertence, s. inadvertencia.
inadvertently, ad. inadvertidamente
inalienable, a. inajenable, inalienable.
inanimate, a. inanimado.
inanition, s. inanición.
inanity, s. vacuidad ; nulidad.
inapplicable, a. inaplicable.
inapposite, a. impropio, mal puesto.
inappreciable, a. inapreciable.
inappropriate, a. impropio.
inaptitude, s. ineptitud, inconveniencia.
inarticulate, a. inarticulado ; **-ly**, in-distintamente.
inasmuch, ad. visto ó puesto que.

inattention, s. desatención; descuido.
inattentive, a. desatento, descuidado.
inaudible, a. inaudible.
inaugural, a. inaugural.
inaugurate, v.a. inaugurar.
inauguration, s. inauguración.
inauspicious, a. malaventurado; -ly,
 desgraciadamente.
inborn, inbred, a. innato, ínsito.
incalculable, a. incalculable.
incandescent, a. incandescente.
incantation, s. encantamiento.
incapability, s. incapacidad.
incapable, a. incapaz, inhábil.
incapacitate, v.a. inhabilitar.
incapacity, s. incapacidad.
incarcerate, v.a. encarcelar, aprisionar.
incarnate, a. encarnado.
incarnation, s. encarnación.
incase, v.a. encajar, incluir. [mente.
incautious, a. incauto; -ly, incauta-
incendiary, s. incendiario.
incense, s. incienso; —, v.a. exasperar,
 irritar, provocar.
incentive, s. estímulo.
inception, s. principio.
incertitude, s. incertidumbre.
incessant, a. incesante, constante; -ly,
 continuamente.
incest, s. incesto.
incestuous, a. incestuoso.
inch, s. pulgada (duodécima parte de un
 pie); — by —, palmo á palmo.
inchoate, a. ya empezado, imperfecto.
incidence, s. incidencia.
incident, a. incidente; dependiente; —,
 s. casualidad, episodio.
incidental, a. accidental, casual; —, in-
 cidentemente.
incipient, a. incipiente.
incise, v.a. tajar, cortar, grabar.
incision, s. incisión.
incisive, a. incisivo, incisorio.
incisor, a. & s. incisivo.
incite, v.a. incitar, estimular.
incivility, s. incivilidad, descortesía.
inclemency, s. inclemencia, severidad.
inclement, a. inclemente. [declive.
inclination, s. inclinación, propensión;
incline, v.a. & n. inclinar(se).
include, v.a. incluir, comprender.
inclusive, a. inclusivo; -ly, inclusiva-
incognito, ad. de incógnito. [mente.
incoherence, s. incoherencia.
incoherent, a. incoherente, inconsecuente;
 -ly, incongruamente.
incombustible, a. incombustible.
income, s. renta.
incommensurable, inconmensurable.
incommode, v.a. incomodar.
incommodious, a. incómodo; molesto.

incomparable, a. incomparable, excelente.
incomparably, ad. incomparablemente.
incompatibility, s. incompatibilidad.
incompatible, a. incompatible, opuesto.
incompetence, incompetency, s. incapacidad, ineptitud.
incompetent, a. -ly, incompetente-
 (mente).
incomplete, a. incompleto, falto, imperfecto.
incomprehensibility, s. incomprensi-
 bilidad.
incomprehensible, a. incomprensible.
inconceivable, a. inconcebible.
inconclusive, a. no concluyente, no
 decisivo; -ly, ad. sin conclusión.
incongruity, s. incongruencia, incon-
 gruidad.
incongruous, s. incongruo; -ly, incongruamente.
inconsequent, a. inconsecuente.
inconsiderable, a. de poca importancia.
inconsiderate, a. inconsiderado; desatento; -ly, inconsideradamente.
inconsistency, s. contradicción, incon-
 sistencia, incongruencia.
inconsistent, a. inconsistente; -ly, incongruamente.
inconsolable, a. inconsolable.
inconstancy, s. inconstancia.
inconstant, a. inconstante, mudable.
incontestable, a. incontestable.
incontestably, ad. incontestablemente.
incontinence, s. incontinencia.
incontinent, a. incontinente; -ly, in-
 continentemente.
incontrovertible, a. incontrovertible.
inconvenience, s. inconveniencia, incomodidad; —, v.a. incomodar.
inconvenient, a. incómodo, inconveniente; -ly, incómodamente.
inconvertible, a. inconvertible.
incorporate, v.a. incorporar(se); —, a.
 incorporado.
incorporation, s. incorporación.
incorporeal, a. incorpóreo, incorporal.
incorrect, a. incorrecto; -ly, inexacta-
incorrigible, a. incorregible. [mente.
incorrupt, a. incorrupto.
incorruptibility, s. incorruptibilidad.
incorruptible, a. incorruptible.
increase, v.a. acrecentar, aumentar; —,
 v.n. crecer, tomar aumento; —, s.
 aumento, acrecentamiento.
incredibility, s. incredibilidad.
incredible, a. increíble.
incredibly, ad. increíblemente.
incredulity, s. incredulidad.
incredulous, a. incrédulo.
increment, s. incremento.
incriminate, v.a. acriminar, acusar.

incrust, v.a. incrustar.
incubate, v.n. empollar.
incubator, s. aparato para empollar.
incubus, s. íncubo.
inculcate, v.a. inculcar.
inculpate, v.a. inculpar.
incumbency, s. posesión de un beneficio
　eslesiástico.　　　　　　　[ficiado.
incumbent, a. obligatorio ; —, s. bene-
incur, v.a. incurrir.
incurable, a. incurable.
incurably, ad. de un modo incurable.
incursion, s. incursión, invasión.
indebted, a. endeudado, empeñado.
indebtedness, s. deudo.
indecency, s. indecencia.　　　　[mente.
indecent, a. indecente ; -ly, indecente-
indecision, s. irresolución.
indecisive, a. indeciso.
indecorous, a. indecoroso, indecente.
indeed, ad. verdaderamente, de veras.
indefatigable, a. infatigable.
indefinite, a. indefinido, indeterminado ;
　-ly, indefinidamente.
indelible, a. indeleble.
indelicacy, s. falta de delicadeza,
　grosería, indecencia.
indelicate, a. poco delicado, grosero.
indemnification, s. indemnización ; re-
　sarcimiento de daño.
indemnify, v.a. indemnizar.
indemnity, s. indemnidad.
indent, v.a. dentar, mellar.　　　[mella.
indentation, s. recortadura, dentada,
indenture, s. contrato de un aprendiz.
independence, s. independencia.
independent, a. independiente ; -ly, in-
　dependientemente.
indescribable, a. indescriptible.
indestructible, a. indestructible.
indeterminate, a. indeterminado ; -ly,
　indeterminadamente.
index, s. indicio ; índice, tabla de un libro.
india-rubber, s. goma elástica.
indicate, v.a. indicar.
indication, s. indicación ; indicio ; señal
indicative, a. & s. (gr.) indicativo.
indicator, s. indicador, apuntador.
indictment, s. acusación.　　　　[alidad.
indifference, s. indiferencia, imparci
indifferent, a. indiferente ; -ly, indifer-
　entemente.
indigence, s. indigencia, pobreza.
indigenous, a. indígena.
indigent, a. indigente, pobre.
indigestible, a. indigestible.
indigestion, s. indigestión.
indignant, a. indignado, airado.
indignation, s. indignación ; despecho.
indignity, s¹ indignidad.
indigo, s. añil.

indirect, a. indirecto ; -ly, indirectamente.
indiscreet, a. indiscreto, inconsiderado ;
　-ly, indiscretamente.
indiscretion, s. indiscreción, imprudencia,
　inconsideración.　　　　　　　[tinción.
indiscriminate, a. indistinto ; -ly, sin dis-
indispensable, a. indispensable.
indispensably, ad. indispensablemente.
indispose, v.a. indisponer.
indisposed, a. indispuesto, achacoso.
indisposition, s. indisposición ; mala gana.
indisputable, a. indisputable.
indisputably, ad. indisputablemente.
indissoluble, a. indisoluble.
indistinct, a. indistinto, confuso ; -ly, in-
　distintamente.
indistinguishable, a. indistinguible.
indite, v.a. escribir, redactar.
individual, a. individual, individuo ; -ly
　individualmente ; —, s. individuo.
individuality, s. individualidad.
indivisible, a. indivisible ; -bly, indi-
　visiblemente.
indocil, a. indócil.
indocility, s. indocilidad.
indolence, s. indolencia, pereza.　[gencia.
indolent, a. indolente ; -ly, con negli-
indomitable, a. indomable.
indoor, a. casero ; -s, adv. en casa.
indorse, v.a. endosar.
indubitable, a. indubitable.
indubitably, ad. indubitablemente.
induce, v.a. inducir, persuadir ; causar.
inducement, s. inducimiento, motivo,
　atractivo.
induction, s. inducción ; ilación.
inductive, a. inductivo ; ilativo.
indue, v.a. vestir ; dotar ; proveer.
indulge, v.a. & n. favorecer ; conceder ;
　ser indulgente.
indulgence, s. indulgencia.
indulgent, a. indulgente ; -ly, de un modo
　indulgente.
induration, s. endurecimiento.
industrial, a. industrial.
industrious, a. industrioso ; trabajador ;
　laborioso ; -ly, industriosamente.
industry, s. industria.
inebriate, v.a. embriagar.
inebriation, inebriety, s. embriaguez.
ineffable, a. inefable.
ineffaceable, a. indeleble.
ineffective, ineffectual, a. ineficaz ; -ly,
　sin efecto.
inefficacious, a. ineficaz.
inefficiency, s. ineficacia.
inefficient, a. incapaz, inepto.
inelegant, a. inelegante.　　　　[elección.
ineligibility, s. calidad que excluye
ineptitude, s. ineptitud.　　　　[diferencia.
inequality, s. desigualdad, disparidad.

inequitable, a. injusto. [mente.
inert, a. inerte, perezoso ; -ly, indolente-
inertness, inercia.
inestimable, a. inestimable, inapreciable.
inevitable, a. inevitable.
inexcusable, a. inexcusable.
inexcusably, ad. inexcusablemente.
inexhaustible, a. inexhausto, inagotable.
inexorable, a. inexorable, inflexible, duro.
inexpediency, s. inconveniencia, falta de
oportunidad.
inexpedient, s. impropio, inconveniente.
inexpensive, a. barato, económico.
inexperience, s. inexperiencia, impericia.
inexpert, a. inexperto.
inexpiable, a. inexpiable.
inexplicable, a. inexplicable.
inexpressible, a. indecible.
inexpressibly, ad. indeciblemente.
inextricable, a. inextricable.
infallibility, s. infalibilidad.
infallible, a. infalible.
infallibly, ad. infaliblemente. [mente.
infamous, a. vil, infame ; -ly, infame
infamy, s. infamia.
infancy, s. infancia.
infant, s. infante ; niño.
infanta, s. infanta.
infanticide, s. infanticidio ; infanticida.
infantile, infantine, a. pueril, infantil.
infantry, s. infantería.
infatuate, v.a. infatuar, embobar.
infatuation, s. infatuación.
infect, v.a. infectar.
infection, s. infección. [por infección.
infectious, a. infecto, inficionado ; -ly,
infer, v.a. inferir.
inference, s. inferencia, ilación.
inferior, a. inferior ; —, s. oficial subordinado.
inferiority, s. inferioridad.
infernal, a. infernal.
infest, v.a. infestar, incomodar.
infidel, s. infiel ; pagano.
infidelity, s. infidelidad ; perfidia.
infiltrate, v.n. infiltrar.
infinite, a. infinito, innumerable ; -ly,
infinitamente.
infinitesimal, a. infinitesimal.
infinitive, a. infinitivo.
infirm, a. enfermo, débil.
infirmary, s. enfermería.
infirmity, s. fragilidad, enfermedad.
inflame, v.a. (& n.) inflamar(se).
inflammable, a. inflamable.
inflammation, s. inflamación.
inflammatory, s. inflamatorio.
inflate, v.a. inflar, hinchar.
inflation, s. inflación ; hinchazón. [voz.
inflection, s. inflexión ; modulación de la
inflexibility, s. inflexibilidad.

inflexible, a. inmoble, inflexible.
inflexibly, ad. inflexiblemente.
inflict, v.a. imponer, infligir.
infliction, s. imposición, pena, molestia.
influence, s. influencia ; —, v.a. influir.
influential, a. influente.
influenza, s. catarro febril, gripe.
influx, s. influjo ; infusión.
inform, v.a. cerciorar, informar, enseñar.
informal, a. informal ; irregular.
informality, s. informalidad. [mante.
informant, s. el que da informes, infor-
information, s. información, instrucción.
infraction, s. infracción.
infrequent, a. raro, insólito ; -ly, raramente. [contravenir.
infringe, v.a. violar (una ley ó pacto) ;
infringer, s. violador, contraventor.
infuriate, v.a. irritar, provocar, enfurecer.
infuse, v.a. infundir.
infusion, s. infusión.
ingathering, s. cosecha. [mente.
ingenious, a. ingenioso ; -ly, ingeniosa-
ingenuity, s. ingeniosidad ; destreza.
ingenuous, n. ingenuo, sincero ; -ly, in
ingenuamente.
ingle, s. chimenea.
inglorious, a. ignominioso, vergonzoso ;
-ly, ignominiosamente.
ingot, s. barra de metal (sin labrar).
ingraft, v.a. injertar.
ingrained, a. inveterado.
ingrate, a. ingrato. [graciarse.
ingratiate (oneself), v.r. insinuarse ; con-
ingratitude, s. ingratitud.
ingredient, s. ingrediente.
ingress, s. entrada.
ingulf, v.a. engolfar, tragar, sumir.
inhabit, v.a. & n. habitar ; vivir, residir.
inhabitant, s. habitador, habitante.
inhale, v.a. inspirar, inhalar.
inharmonious, a. disonante, discordante.
inherent, a. inherente.
inherit, v.a. heredar.
inheritance, s. herencia.
inheritor, s. heredero. [able.
inhospitable, a. inhospitable, inhosped-
inhospitality, a. inhospitalidad.
inhuman, a. inhumano, cruel ; -ly, in-
humanamente.
inhumanity, s. inhumanidad, crueldad.
inhume, v.a. enterrar, sepultar.
inimical, a. enemigo, hostil.
inimitable, a. inimitable.
iniquitous, a. inicuo, injusto.
iniquity, s. iniquidad, injusticia.
initial, a. inicial ; —, s. letra inicial.
initiate, v.a. principiar, iniciar.
initiation, s. principio ; iniciación.
inject, v.a. inyectar.
injection, s. inyección.

injudicious, a. indiscreto, imprudente ;
-ly, sin juicio.
injunction, s. mandato, precepto, orden.
injure, v.a. injuriar, ofender.
injurious, a. injurioso, dañoso, perjuicial;
-ly, injuriosamente.
injury, s. injuria, afrenta ; daño.
injustice, s. injusticia ; agravio.
ink, s. tinta ; —, v.a. marcar con tinta.
ink-horn, s. tintero (de faltriquera).
inkling, s. insinuación, conjetura.
ink-stand, s. tintero.
inky, a. manchado con tinta ; negro.
inlaid, a. ataraceado.   [país.
inland, a. interior ; —, ad. dentro de un
inlay, v.a. ataracear ; —, s. ataracea.
inlet, s. bahía.
inmate, s. persona alojada ; interno.
inmost, a. íntimo.
inn, s. posada ; mesón, fonda.
innate, a. innato, natural, ínsito
inner, a. interior.
inmost, innermost, a. íntimo.
inn-keeper, s. posadero, mesonero.
innocence, s. inocencia.   [mente.
innocent, a. inocente ; -ly, inocente-
innocuous, a. innocuo, inocente ; -ly,
inocentemente.
innovate, v.a. innovar.
innovation, s. innovación.
innoxious, a. inocente ; no nocivo ; -ly,
sin hacer daño.
innuendo, s. indirecta, insinuación.
innumerable, a. innumerable.
inoculate, v.a. inocular ; injertar.
inoculation, s. inoculación.
inoffensive, a. inofensivo, pacífico.
inoperative, a. ineficaz.   [tuno.
inopportune, a. inconveniente, inopor-
inordinate, a. irregular, exagerado ; -ly,
fuera de orden.
inorganic, a. inorgánico.
inquest, s. pesquisa.
inquietude, s. inquietud.
inquire, v.a. preguntar ; —, v.n. inquirir,
examinar.
inquiry, s. interrogación ; pesquisa.
inquisition, s. inquisición ; escudriñamiento.   [-ly, inquisitivamente.
inquisitive, a. inquisitivo, curioso ;
inquisitor, s. juez pesquisidor ; inquisidor.
inroad, s. incursión, invasión.
insane, a. insano, loco, demente.
insanity, s. insania ; locura.
insatiable, a. insaciable.
inscribe, v.a. inscribir ; dedicar.
inscription, s. inscripción ; dedicación.
inscrutable, a. inescrutable.
insect, s. insecto.
insecure, a. desconfiado ; inseguro.
insecurity, s. peligro, riesgo.

insensate, a. insensato.
insensibility, s. insensibilidad ; estupidez.
insensible, a. insensible ; imperceptible.
insensibly, ad. insensiblemente.
inseparable, a. inseparable.
inseparably, ad. inseparablemente.
insert, v.a. insertar, ingerir, encajar.
insertion, s. inserción.
inside, s. interior ; ad. adentro, dentro.
insidious, a. insidioso ; -ly, insidiosa-
mente.
insight, s. perspicacia.
insignia, s.pl. insignia, divisa.
insignificance, s. insignificancia, nulidad.
insignificant, a. insignificante, frívolo.
insincere, a. poco sincero, doble.
insincerity, s. disimulación, doblez.
insinuate, v.a. insinuar.
insinuation, s. insinuación.   [mente.
insipid, a. insípido ; insulso ; -ly, insulsa-
insipidity, s. insipidez, insulsez.
insist, v.n. insistir, persistir.
insistance, s. insistencia.
insolence, s. insolencia.   [mente.
insolent, a. insolente ; —ly, insolente-
insoluble, a. insoluble ; indisoluble.
insolvency, s. insolvencia.
insolvent, a. insolvente.
insomuch, ad. de manera, así.
inspect, v.a. reconocer, examinar, inspeccionar.
inspection, s. inspección.
inspector, s. inspector, superintendente.
inspiration, s. inspiración.   [sugerir.
inspire, v.a. inspirar (el aire) ; inspirar,
inspirit, v.a. alentar, animar.
instability, s. instabilidad, inconstancia.
instal, v.a. instalar.
installation, s. instalación.
instalment, s. instalación ; pago parcial.
instance, s. instancia ; solicitación ;
ejemplo, documento ; for —, por
ejemplo ; —, v.a. alegar (ejemplos).
instant, a. instante, urgente ; -ly, instantáneamente ; —, s. instante, momento.
instantaneous, a. instantáneo ; -ly,
instantáneamente.
instead (of), pr. en lugar de, en vez de.
instep, s. empeine del pie.
instigate, v.a. instigar, mover.
instigation, s. instigación, sugestión.
instil, v.a. insinuar, instilar.
instinct, s. instinto ; —, a. vivo. [stinto.
instinctive, a. instintivo ; -ly, por in-
institute, v.a. instituir, establecer ; —,
s. instituto.
institution, s. institución.
instruct, v.a. instruir, enseñar.
instruction, s. instrucción, enseñanza.
instructive, a. instructivo.

instructor, s. instructor.
instrument, s. instrumento ; contrato.
instrumental, a. instrumental.
insubordinate, a. insubordinado.
insubordination, s. insubordinación.
insufferable, a. insufrible, insoportable
insufferably, ad. inaguantablemente, de
  un modo insoportable.
insufficiency, s. insuficiencia.
insufficient, a. insuficiente ; **-ly**, in-
  suficientemente.
insular, a. insular, isleño. [eléctricas).
insulate, v.a. aislar (las corrientes
insult, v.a. insultar ; —, s. insulto.
insulter, s. insultador.
insultingly, ad. con insolencia.
insuperable, a. insuperable.
insuperably, ad. invenciblemente.
insupportable, a. insoportable, inaguantable. [soportablemente.
insupportably, ad. intolerablemente, in-
insurance, s. (com.) seguro ; seguridad.
insure, v.a. asegurar.
insurgent, s. ingursente, rebelde.
insurmountable, a. insuperable.
insurrection, s. insurrección, sedición.
insurrectionary, a. rebelde.
intact, a. intacto, entero.
intaker, s. recaudador. [—, s. todo.
integral, a. íntegro.
integrity, s. integridad ; pureza.
intellect, s. entendimiento.
intellectual, a. intelectual, mental.
intelligence, s. intelligencia ; conocimiento ; nueva, noticia ; concierto.
intelligent, a. inteligente.
intelligible, a. inteligible.
intelligibly, ad. inteligiblemente.
intemperance, s. intemperancia.
intemperate, a. destemplado ; inmoderado ; **-ly**, destempladamente, inmoderadamente.
intend, v.a. intentar, proyectar.
intendant, s. intendente.
intense, a. intenso ; vehemente ; **-ly**,
  intensamente.
intensify, v.a. aumentar, agravar.
intensity, s. intensidad.
intent, a. atento, cuidadoso ; **-ly**, con
  aplicación ; —, s. intento, designio.
intention, s. intención ; designio.
intentional, a. intencional; **-ly**, de intento.
inter, v.a. enterrar, soterrar.
intercalate, v.a. intercalar.
intercede, v.n. interceder, mediar.
intercept, v.a. interceptar.
intercession, s. intercesión, mediación.
intercessor, s. intercesor, mediador.
interchange, v.a. alternar, trocar ; —, s.
  trueco ; permuta de géneros..
intercourse, s. comercio ; comunicación.

interdict, **-ion**, s. entredicho ; —, v.a.
  interdecir ; entredecir.
interest, v.a. interesar ; empeñar ; —, s.
  interés, provecho ; influjo, empeño ;
  compound —, interés de interés.
interfere, v.n. entremeterse, mezclarse.
interference, s. interposición, mediación.
interim, s. intermedio, interín ; ad —,
  entre tanto ; en el ínterin.
interior, a. interior, interno.
interjection, s. (gr.) interjección.
interlace, v.a. entretejer.
interlard, v.a. mechar ; entreponer.
interleave, v.a. interpolar hojas blancas
  entre las impresas de un libro.
interline, v.a. interlinear.
interlocution, s. interlocución.
interlocutor, s. interlocutor. [licencia.
interlope, v.n. entremeterse ; traficar sin
interloper, s. entremetido ; intruso.
intermarriage, s. doble ó repetido casamiento entre dos familias. [miento
intermarry, v.n. unirse por un doble casa-
intermediate, a. intermedio.
interment, s. entierro ; sepultura.
interminable, a. interminable, ilimitado.
intermingle, v.a. & n. entremezclar ;
  mezclarse.
intermission, s. intermisión, interrupción.
intermit, v.a. intermitir.
intermittent, a. intermitente.
internal, a. interno ; **-ly**, internamente.
international, a. internacional.
interpellation, s. interpelación.
interpolate, v.a. interpolar.
interpolation, s. interpolación.
interpose, v.a. interponer, entreponer ;
  —, v.n. interponerse.
interposition, s. interposición.
interpret, v.a. interpretar.
interpretation, s. interpretación.
interpreter, s. intérprete.
interregnum, s. interregno.
interrogate, v.a. interrogar, examinar.
interrogation, s. interrogación, pregunta.
interrogative, **interrogatory**, a. interro-
  gativo.
interrupt, v.a. interrumpir.
interruptedly, ad. con interrupción.
interruption, s. interrupción. [carse
intersect, v.a. cruzar ; —, v.n. interse
intersection, s. intersección.
intersperse, v.a. entremezclar.
interstice, s. intersticio, intervalo.
intertwine, v.a. entretejer.
interval, s. intervalo.
intervene, v.n. intervenir ; ocurrir.
intervention, s. intervención, inte
  posición.
interview, s. entrevista ; —, v.a. pes
  cudar (á los políticos).

interviewer, s. periodista que va pescu-
dando á los hombres de Estado.
interweave, v.a. entretejer, enlazar.
intestate, a. intestado.
intestinal, a. intestinal.
intestine, a. intestino, doméstico; **-s,**
s.pl. intestinos, pl.
inthral, v.a. *V.* enthrall.
intimacy, s. intimidad, confianza.
intimate, a. & s. íntimo, familiar; **-ly,**
íntimamente; —, v.a. insinuar, dar
á entender.
intimation, s. insinuación, informe.
intimidate, v.a. intimidar.
into, pr. en, dentro, adentro.
intolerable, a. intolerable.
intolerably, ad. intolerablemente.
intolerance, s. intolerancia.
intolerant, a. intolerante.
intonation, s. entonación.
intoxicate, v.a. embriagar.
intoxication, s. embriaguez.
intractable, a. intratable.
intransitive, a. (gr.) intransitivo.
intrench, v.a. atrincherar; —, v.n.
usurpar, invadir.   [trépidamente.
intrepid, a. arrojado; intrépido; **-ly,** in-
intrepidity, s. intrepidez.   [cultad.
intricacy, s. embrollo, embarazo; difi-
intricate, a. intricado, complicado.
intrigue, s. intriga; —, v.n. intrigar.
intrinsic(al), a. intrínseco, interno; **-ally,**
intrínsecamente.
introduce, v.a. introducir.
introduction, s. introducción.
introductory, a. previo, preliminar.
introspection, s. examen de sí mismo;
contemplación.
introspective, a. introspectivo.
intrude, v.n. entremeterse, introducirse.
intruder, s. intruso, entremetido.
intrusion, s. intrusión entremetimiento.
intrusive, a. intruso.
intrust, v.a. confiar.
intuition, s. intuición.
intuitive, a. intuitivo.
inundate, v.a. inundar.
inundation, s. inundación.
inure, v.a. acostumbrar, habituar.
inutility, s. inutilidad.
invade, v.a. invadir, asaltar.
invader, s. invasor.
invalid, a. inválido, nulo; —, s. enfermo.
invalidate, v.a. invalidar, anular.
invalidity, s. invalidación, nulidad.
invaluable, a. inapreciable.   [mente.
invariable, a. invariable; **-bly,** invariable-
invasion, s. invasión.
invective, s. invectiva.
inveigh, v.n. escribir ó decir invectivas,
inveigle, v.a. seducir, persuadir.

invent, v.a. inventar.
invention, s. invención.
inventive, a. inventivo.
inventor, s. inventor.
inventory, s. inventario.
inverse, a. inverso, trastornado.
inversion, a. inversión.
invert, v.a. invertir, trastrocar.
invertebrate, a. invertebrado.
invest, v.a. investir.
investigate, v.a. investigar, indagar.
investigation, s. investigación, pesquisa
investiture, s. investidura.
investment, s. acción de investir; inversión (de dinero).
inveterate, a. inveterado.   [mente
invidious, a. envidioso; **-ly,** envidiosa
invigorate, v.a. vigorar, vigorizar.
invincible, a. invencible.
invincibly, ad. invenciblemente.
inviolable, a. inviolable.
inviolate, a. ileso.
invisibility, s. invisibilidad.
invisible, a. invisible.
invisibly, ad. invisiblemente.
invitation, s. convite, invitación.
invite, v.a. convidar
invocation, s. invocación.
invoice, s. (com.) factura.
invoke, v.a. invocar.
involuntarily, ad. involuntariamente.
involuntary, a. involuntario.
involve, v.a. envolver, implicar.
invulnerable, a. invulnerable.
inward, a. interior; interno; —, **-s,** ad.
hacia dentro, adentro; **-ly,** interiormente, dentro.
iodine, s. (chem.) iodo.
irascible, a. irascible.
irate, ireful, a. irato, iracundo.
ire, s. ira, iracundia.
iridescent, a. iridescente.
iris, s. arco iris; (anat.) iris.
irksome, a. tedioso, fastidioso.
iron, s. hierro, fierro; —, a. férreo; —,
v.a. aplanchar; poner en grillos.
iron-dust, s. limadura de hierro.
ironclad, a. & s. acorazado.
ironic(al), a. irónico; **-ly,** a. con ironía.
ironing, s. planchado.
iron-monger, s. quinquillero, ferretero.
iron(-)mould, s. robín.
iron-ware, s. ferretería; quincallería.
iron-work, s. herraje; **-s,** pl. herrería.
irony, s. ironía.
irradiate, v.a. & n. irradiar; brillar.
irrational, a. irracional.
irreclaimable, a. incorregible.
irreconcilable, s. irreconciliable, implacable.   [remediable.
irrecoverable, a. irrecuperable; ir-

irredeemable, a. irredimible, no amor-
irrefragable, a. irrefragable.   [tizable.
irregular, a. -ly, irregular(mente).
irregularity, s. irregularidad.
irrelevant, a. inaplicable ; improprio.
irreligion, s. irreligión, impiedad. [mente.
irreligious, s. irreligioso ; -ly, irreligiosa-
irremediable, a. irremediable ; -bly, irremediablemente.
irreparable, a. irreparable.   [tachable.
irreproachable, a. irreprensible, in-
irresistible, a. irresistible.   [lutamente.
irresolute, a. irresoluto ; -ly, irreso-
irresolution, s. irresolución.   [siderar.
irrespective, a. excluyendo, sin con-
irresponsible, a. no responsable, frívolo.
irretrievable, a. irrecuperable, irreparable.
irretrievably, a. irreparablemente.
irreverence, s. irreverencia.   [entemente.
irreverent, a. irreverente ; -ly, irrever-
irrevocable, a. irrevocable.
irrigate, v.a. regar.
irrigation, s. riego.
irritability, s. irritabilidad.
irritable, a. irritable.
irritant, a. & s. (med.) irritante.

irruption, s. irrupción, entrada forzada.
isinglass, s. colapez.
Islamism, s. islamismo.
island, s. isla.
islander, s. isleño.
isle, islet, s. islote, isleta.
isolate, v.a. aislar.
issue, s. salida ; evento ; resulta ; fin,
término ; prole, progenie ; —, v.n.
salir ; prorrumpir ; brotar ; venir ; proceder ; provenir ; —, v.a. echar ; expedir, despachar ; publicar ; emitir.
isthmus, s. istmo.
it, pn. él, ella, ello, lo, la, le.
italic, s. letra cursiva.
italicize, v.a. (fig.) tildar.
itch, s. sarna ; picazón ; prurito ; —, v.n.
picar.   [artículo.
item, ad. ítem, otrosí, aun más ; —, s.
iteration, s. reiteración.
itinerant, a. ambulante, errante.
itinerary, s. itinerario.
its, pn. su, suyo.
itself, pn. mismo.
ivory, s. marfil.
ivy, s. hiedra.

J

jabber, v.n. charlar, farfullar.
jabberer, s. farfullador, parlanchín.
jack, s. sacabotas ; torno de asador ; cota
de malla ; boliche ; macho ; burro ;
lucio (pez) ; —o'-lantern, fuego fatuo ;
— of all trades, factótum, chapucero.
jackal, s. adiva, adive, chacal.   [eso.
jackanapes, s. mequetrefe ; rapaz travi-
jack-ass, s. garañón, burro.   [pl.
jack-boots, s.pl. botas grandes y fuertes,
jack-daw, s. grajo.
jacket, s. chaqueta, jaqueta.
jade, s. rocín ; —, v.a. cansar.
jag, s. mella ; —, v.a. dentar.
jagged, s. desigual, dentado.
jaguar, s. jaguar, tigre (am.).
jail, s. cárcel.
jail-bird, s. preso, bribón.
jailer, s. carcelero.   [apretar, estrechar.
jam, s. conserva ; mermelada ; —, v.a.
jamb, s. quicial.
jangle, v.n. resonar ; reñir, altercar.
janiter, s. ujier, portero.
Janizary, s. genízaro.
January, s. enero.
japan, s. charol ; —, v.a. charolar.
Japanese, a. & s. japonés.
japanner, s. charolista.
jar, v.n. chocar ; (mus.) discordar ; reñir ;
—, s. jarro ; tinaja ; riña ; sonido
desapacible.

jargon, s. jerga, jerigonza.
jasper, s. jaspe.
jaundice, s. ictericia.
jaundiced, a. ictérico.
jaunt, s. excursión.
jaunty, a. alegre, festivo.
jaw, s. quijada ; boca.
jay, s. (orn.) picaza, urraca, marica
javelin, s. jabalina.
jealous, a. celoso ; envidioso.
jealousy, s. celos, pl.
jean, s. lienzo.
jeer, v.n. befar, mofar, escarnecer ; —,
s. befa, mofa, burla.
Jehu, s. cochero.
jelly, s. jalea.
jelly-fish, s. medusa.
jennet, s. jaca ; mula.
jeopard(ise), v.a. arriesgar.
jerk, s. sacudida, sobarbada ; —, v.a.
sacudir.
jerkin, s. coleto.
jessamine, s. jazmín.
jest, s. chanza, burla.
jester, s. mofador, bufón.
jestingly, ad. de burlas.   [cascarilla.
Jesuit, s. jesuita ; —'s bark, quina,
jesuitic(al), a. jesuítico.
jet, s. azabache.
jetsam, jettison, s. (mar.) bienes arro
jados al mar.

jetty, a. azabachado, negro ; —, s. muelle.
Jew, s. judío.
jewel, s. joyal, dije.
jeweller, s. joyero.
jewelry, s. joyería.
Jewess, s. judía.
jewish, a. judaico, judío.
jewry, s. judería.
Jews' harp, s. birimbao.
jib, s. (mar.) maraguto, foque ; —, v.n. pararse ; vacilar.
jig, s. baile alegre   [novio).
jilt, s. coqueta ; —, v.n. despedir (áun
jingle, v.n. retiñir, resonar; —, s. retintín, resonido.
jingo, a. & s. (col.) partidario de una [política agresiva.
job, s. destajo, obrita ; engañifa ; —, v.a. & n. traficar.
jobber, s. destajero, traficante ; agiotista.
job-master, s. alquilador de caballos.
jockey, s. jinete (en las carreras) ; engañabobos ; —, v.a. trampear, engañar.
jocose, a. jocoso, burlesco ; **-ly,** jocosamente.
jocosity, s. jocosidad, chanza.
jocular, jocund, a. jocoso, alegre.
jog, v.a. empujar ; dar un golpe suave ; —, v.n. andar al trotecito ; —, s. empellón ; traqueo.
jog-trot, s. trotecito ; rutina.
John Bull, s. apodo de los ingleses.
John-dory, s. dorado (pez).
join, v.a. juntar, unir ; —, v.n. unirse, juntarse, asociarse.
joiner, s. carpintero.
joinery, s. carpintería.
joint, s. coyuntura, articulación ; tajo (de carne) ; nudo (de una planta) ; —, a. unido ; participante ; — **heir,** s. coheredero ; —, v.a. juntar ; descuartizar.
jointly, ad. juntamente.
joint-stock-company, s. (com.) sociedad por acciones.
jointure, s. viudedad.
joist, s. viga de bovedilla ó de suelo.
joke, s. chanza, burla ; —, v.n. chancear.
jollification, s. gaudeamus.
jollity, s. alegría ; regocijo.
jolly, a. alegre, gallardo.
jolly-boat, s. botequín.   [queo.
jolt, v.a. traquear, sacudir ; —, s. tra-
Jonathan, Brother —, s. apodo de los americanos del norte.
jorum, s. vaso : trago.
jostle, v. rempujar, codear.
jot, s. jota, punto
journal, s. diario.
journalism, s. periodismo.
journalist, s. periodista.
journey, s. viaje ; —, v.a. viajar.
journeyman, s. jornalero.

joust, s. torneo ; justa ; —, v.n. justar.
jovial, a. jovial, alegre ; **-ly,** con jovialidad.
joviality, s. jovialidad.
joy, s. alegría ; júbilo ; **to give** or **wish** —, congratular.   [alegremente.
joyful, joyous, s. alegre, gozoso ; **-ly,**
joyless, a. triste, sin alegría.
jubilant, a. lleno de júbilo.
jubilation, s. júbilo, regocijo.
jubilee, s. jubileo.
Judaism, s. judaísmo.
judge, s. juez ; —, v.n. juzgar ; inferir.
judgment, s. juicio ; sentir ; opinión, decisión.
judicature, s. judicatura.
judicial, a. **-ly,** judicial(mente).
judicious, a. juicioso, prudente ; **-ly,** juiciosamente.
jug, s. jarro ; —, v.a. guisar.
juggle, s. juego de manos ; —, v.n. hacer juegos de manos, trampear. [truhán.
juggler, s. jugador de manos, juglar,
jugular, a. yugular.
juice, s. zumo, jugo ; suco.
juicy, a. jugoso.
July, s. julio (mes).
jumble, v.a. mezclar confusamente ; —, s. mezcla, confusión.
jump, v.n. saltar, brincar ; convenir, concordar ; —, s. salto.   [palme.
junction, s. junta, unión ; (rail.) em-
juncture, s. juntura, coyuntura ; crisis.
June, s. junio (mes).
jungle, s. selva tropical, matorral.
junior, a. más joven.
juniper, s. (bot.) enebro.
junk, s. barco chino.
junket, s. cuajada ; dulce ; festín, convite. —, v.n. festejarse.
juridic(al), a. jurídico, judicial ; **-ly,** jurídicamente.
jurisdiction, s. jurisdicción.
jurisprudence, s. jurisprudencia.
jurist, s. jurista.
juror, juryman, s. jurado.
jury, s. jurado.   [provisado.
jury-mast, s. (mar.) bandola, mastil im-
just, a. justo, honrado ; —, ad. justamente, exactamente ; **-ly,** con honradez ; — **now,** ahora mismo.
justice, s. justicia ; juez.
justifiable, a. justo, razonable.
justifiably, ad. con justicia y rectitud
justification, s. justificación ; defensa.
justify, v.a. justificar.
justness, s. justicia, equidad, exactitud
jut, v.n. sobresalir, volar.
jute, s. lienzo grueso de India.
juvenile, a. juvenil.
juxtaposition, s. yuxtaposición.

K

Kaffir, s. cafre.
kale, s. col.
kaleidoscope, s. kaleidóscopo.
kangaroo, s. canguro.
keel, s. (mar.) quilla.
keen, a. afilado, agudo; penetrante, sútil, vivo; vehemente; satírico, picante; -ly, agudamente; con viveza.
keenness, s. agudeza, perspicacia; viveza.
keen-sighted, a. perspicaz.
keep, v.a. tener, mantener, retener; preservar, guardar; proteger; detener; conservar; reservar; observar; solemnizar; —, v.n. perseverar; soler; mantenerse; quedar; vivir, residir; —, s. torre; guardia; sustentación.
keeper, s. guardián.
keepsake, s. recuerdo; regalo.
keeping, s. custodia; guarda.
keg, s. barrica.
ken, s. vista, conocimiento.
kennel, s. perrera; jauría; zorrera.
kerb-stone, s. brocal de pozo, margen de acera.
kerchief, s. pañuelo.
kernel, s. almendra, pepita; meollo.
ketch, s. (mar.) queche.
kettle, s. caldera.
kettle-drum, s. timbal, atabal.
key, s. llave; (mus.) clave; tecla.
key-board, s. (mus.) teclado.
key-hole, s. agujero de la llave.
key-note, s. (mus.) tónica.
key-ring, s. colgajo de llaves.
key-stone, s. llave de un arce ó bóveda.
kick, v.a. acocear; —, v.n. patear; —, s. puntapié; patada.
kickshaw, s. (col.) golosina; bocado'
kid, s. cabrito.
kidnap, v.a. arrebatar niños ú hombres.
kidney, s. riñón; (fig.) especie, jaez.
kill, v.a. matar, asesinar.
kiln, s. horno.
kiln-dry, v.a. secar ó quemar en horno.
kilt, s. saya de los escoceses serranos.
kimbo, s.; to set one's arms a-, ponerse en asas, ponerse en jarras.
kin, s. parentesco; afinidad; next of —, pariente proximo.
kind, a. benévolo, benigno, afable, cariñoso; —, s. género; especie, naturaleza, manera; calidad.
kindle, v.a. & n. encender; arder.
kindliness, s. benevolencia.
kindly, a. blando, suave, tratable; —, ad. benignamente; [ficio.
kindness, s. benevolencia; favor, bene-

kindred, s. parentesco; parentela, casta; —, a. emparentado.
king, s. rey.
kingdom, s. reíno.
king-fisher, s. (orn.) martín pescador.
kinglike, kingly, a, real; regio.
king's evil, s. escrófula.
kinsfolk, s. parientes, pl.
kinship, s. parentela.
kinsman, s pariente.
kinswoman, parienta.
kirtle, s. manta.
kipper, s. arenque fumado.
kiss, s. beso, ósculo; —, v.a. besar.
kissing, s. beso; — of hand, besamano.
kit, s. equipaje.
kitchen, s. cocina.
kitchen-dresser, s. estante de cocina.
kitchen-garden, s. huerta.
kitchen-range, s. fogón inglés de cocina.
kite, s. milano; cometa, birlocha.
kith, s. amigos, conocidos.
kitten, s. gatillo; —, v.n. parir (la gata).
kleptomania, s. kleptomanía.
knack, s. chuchería; maña, destreza.
knacker, s. carnicero de caballos.
knapsack, s. mochila. [sota.
knave, s. bribón, pícaro; (at cards)
knavery, s. picardía, bribonada.
knavish, a. fraudulento; pícaro; -ly,
knead, v.a. amasar. [pícaramente.
kneading-trough, s. amasadera.
knee, s. rodilla; (mar.) curva; ángulo.
knee-deep, a. metido hasta las rodillas.
kneel, v.n. arrodillarse.
knee-pan, s. rótula.
knell, s. toque de campana á muerto.
knickerbockers, s.pl. calzones cortos.
knick-knacks, s.pl. bujería; juguetes.
knife, s. cuchillo. [caballero.
knight, s. caballero; —, v.a. crear á unq
knight-errant, s. caballero andante.
knighthood, s. caballería (dignidad de caballero).
knightly, a. caballeresco.
knit, v.a. & n. enlazar; atar, unir; trabajar á punto de aguja; to — the brows, fruncir las cejas.
knitter, s. calcetero, mediero. [media.
knitting-needle, s. aguja de hacer
knob, s. bulto; nudo, prominencia; botón de las flores.
knobby, a. nudoso.
knock, v.a. & n. chocar; golpear, tocar; to — down, derribar; —, s. golpe; llamada.
knocker, s. aldaba.

knock-kneed, a. cojuelo.
knoll, s. colina.
knot, s. nudo ; lazo ; maraña ; dificultad ;
agrupación ; —, v.a. enredar, juntar.
knotty, a. nudoso ; dificultoso.
knout, s. bastonada rusa.
know, v.a. & n. conocer, saber.

knowing, a. agudo, entendido ; **-ly,**
hábilmente ; á sabiendas ; á propósito.
knowledge, s. conocimiento ; ciencia ;
inteligencia, habilidad.
knuckle, s. nudillo ; jarrete de ternero.
koran, s. alcorán.
kraal, s. (afr.) corral.

L

label, s. marbete ; rótulo, marca ; —,
v.a. rotular ó señalar alguna cosa con
un rótulo.
labial, a. labial.
laboratory, s. laboratorio.
laborious, a. trabajador, laborioso ;
difícil ; **-ly,** laboriosamente.
labour, s. trabajo ; labor ; fatiga ; **to be in**
—, estar de parto ; —, v.a. trabajar ;
afanarse ; estar con dolores de parto.
labourer, s. labrador ; trabajador.
laburnum, s. (bot.) codeso.
labyrinth, s. laberinto.
lac, s. laca, goma laca.
lace, s. lazo, cordón ; encaje ; randa ;
galón ; —, v.a. abrochar, encordonar ;
galonear.
lacerate, v.a. lacerar, rasgar
lachrymose, a. lloroso, lacrimoso.
lack, v.a. & n. carecer, necesitar ; faltar
algo ; —, s. falta.
lackey, s. lacayo.
laconic(al), a. lacónico.   [distraído.
lackadaisical, a. (col.) sentimental,
lacquer, s. laca.
lad, s. mozo, muchacho.
ladder, s. escala ó escalera portátil.
lade, v.a. cargar.
lading, s. carga ; cargamento.
ladle, s. cucharón.
ladleful, s. cucharada.
lady, s. señora, señorita, dama.
lady-bird, s. vaquita de Dios (insecto).
Lady-day, s. día de la Anunciación.
lady-like, a. elegante ; muy señora, bien
educada.
lady-love, s. dama, querida.
ladyship, s. señoría.
lag, v.n. quedarse atrás, tardar.
laggard, lagger, s. haragán, holgazán.
lagoon, s. laguna.
laic, a. lego.
lair, s. cubil.
laird, s. (Scot.) hacendado.
laity, s. estado seglar ó lego.
lake, s. lago ; laguna.
lamb, s. cordero ; —, v.n. parir corderos.
lambent, a. centelleante.
lambkin, s. corderito.

lame, a. cojo ; imperfecto ; **-ly,** con
cojera ; imperfectamente ; —, v.a.
lisiar, estropear
lameness, s. cojera ; imperfección.
lament, v.a. (& n.) lamentar(se) ; —, s.
lamento.
lamentable, s. lamentable, deplorable.
lamentation, s. lamentación.
lamp, s. lámpara.
lamp-black, s. negro de humo.
lampoon, s. sátira ; libelo ; —, v.a.
satirizar.
lamp-post, s. candelabro.
lamprey, s. lamprea (pez).
lance, s. lanza ; —, v.a. dar un lancetazo ;
(med.) abrir con lanceta.
lancer, s. (mil.) lancero.
lancet, s. lanceta.
land, s. país ; región ; territorio, tierra ;
—, v.a. & n. desembarcar ; saltar en
tierra.
landau, s. landó (coche).
landed, a. hacendado.
land-forces, s.pl. tropas de tierra, pl.
land-holder, s. hacendado.
landing, s. desembarco.
landing(-place), s. desembarcadero.
landlady, s. patrona, dueña ; mesonera,
posadera.
land-locked, a. cercado de tierra, bien
abrigado (puerto ó golfo).   [posadero.
landlord, s. patrón, dueño ; huésped,
land-lubber, s. (col.) marinero de río.
land-mark, s. mojón ; (fig.) marca, señal,
punto importante.
landscape, s. paisaje.
land-slip, s. hundimiento, desploma-
miento de un terreno.
land-tax, s. tributo sobre tierras.
landward, ad. hacia la tierra.
lane, s. callejuela.
language, s. idioma, lengua ; lenguaje.
languid, a. lánguido, débil ; **-ly,** lánguida-
mente, débilmente.
languish, v.n. entristecerse, afligirse.
languor, s. languidez.
lank(y), a. alto y delgado.
lantern, s. linterna ; farol, **dark** —, lín-
terna sorda.

lanyard, s. (mar.) cuerda.
lap, s. faldas, pl.; regazo; —, v.a. arrollar, envolver; lamer.
lap-dog, s. perro de faldas.
lapidary, s. lapidario.
lappet, s. falda.
lapse, s. caída; falta ligera; translación de derecho ó dominio; lapso; —, v.n. escurrir, manar; deslizarse.
lapwing, s. (orn.) avefría.
larboard, s. (mar.) babor (lado izquierdo del navío).
larceny, s. robo.
larch, s. alerce, lárice, (árbol). mechar.
lard, s. lardo, tocino gordo; —, v.a.
larder, s. despensa.
large, a. amplio, vasto; largo, liberal; at —, á lo largo; -ly, largamente, copio-samente, liberalmente.
largeness, s. grandor; anchura, amplitud.
largess, s. dádiva, largueza.
lark, s. alondra.
larva, s. larva, oruga.
lascivious, a. lascivo; -ly, lascivamente.
lash, s. latigazo; punta del látigo; pihuela; (fig.) sarcasmo; —, v.a. azotear; atar; satirizar.
lass, s. doncella, moza.
lassitude, s. lasitud, fatiga.
last, a. último, postrero, pasado; at —, últimamente; al fin; -ly, al fin; final-mente; —, s. horma de zapatero; —, v.n. durar. [perpetuamente.
lasting, a. duradero, permanente; -ly,
latch, s. cerradura; —, v.a. cerrar.
latchet, s. correa (de zapatos).
latch-key, s. llave.
late, a. tardío; tardo, lento; atrasado; difunto; —, ad. tarde; of —, de poco tiempo acá; -ly, ad. poco ha, re-cientemente.
lateness, s. tardanza, hora avanzada.
latent, a. escondido, oculto.
lateral, a. -ly, lateral(mente).
lath, s. lata; listón.
lathe, s. torno.
lather, s. jabonaduras, pl.; —, v.a. & n. bañar con espuma de jabón; espumar.
latten, s. latón.
latter, a. posterior, último; -ly, últi-mamente, recientemente.
lattice, s. celosía; —, v.a. enrejar.
laudable, a. laudable, loable.   [mente.
laudably, ad. laudablemente, loable-
laudanum, s. opio.
laudatory, a. laudatorio.
laugh, v.n. reir; —, s. risa, risada.
laughable, a. risible.
laughingly, ad. alegremente, con risa.
laughing-stock, s. hazmerreir.
laughter, s. risa, risada.

launch, v.a. (& n.) lanzar(se); (mar.) botar (un barco); —, s. lancha.
laundress, s. lavandera.
laundry, s. lavadero.
laureate, laurelled, a. laureado.
laurel, s. laurel.
lava, s. lava.
lavender, s. (bot.) espliego, lavándula.
lavish, a. pródigo; -ly, pródigamente; —, v.a. prodigar.
law, s. ley; derecho; litigio judicial; jurisprudencia.   [mente
lawful, a. legal; legítimo; -ly, legal-
law-giver, s. legislador.
lawless, a. ilegal; anárquico.
lawlessness, s. ilegalidad, desorden, anarquía.
law-maker, s. legislador.
lawn, s. prado; linón.
law-suit, s. proceso, lite.
lawyer, s. abogado, jurisperito.
lax, a. laxo, flojo.
laxative, a. & s. laxativo.
laxity, s. laxitud, flojedad.
lay, v.a. poner, colocar, extender; cal-mar, sosegar; imputar; apostar; exhibir; to — claim, reclamar; pre-tender; —, v.n. aovar, poner huevos las aves; tramar
layer, s. lecho; plancha; mano (de pintura); pimpollo; gallina que pone.
lay-figure, s. maniquí.
layman, s. lego, seglar.
lazaretto, lazar-house, s. lazareto.
lazily, ad. perezosamente; lentamente.
laziness, s. pereza.
lazy, a. perezoso, tardo, pesado.
lea, s. prado, pradera.
lead, s. plomo; -s, pl. techo emplomado.
lead, v.a. conducir, guiar; gobernar; —, v.n. mandar en jefe; ser mano (en el juego de naipes); —, s. conducta; (at cards) mano.   [estúpido.
leaden, a. hecho de plomo; pesado;
leader, s. guía, conductor; jefe, general.
leading, a. principal; capital; — article, s. artículo de fondo de una gaceta.
lending-strings, s.pl. andadores, pl.; trailla.   [de puerta.
leaf, s. hoja; hoja de un libro; hoja
leaflet, s. hojita, folleto.
leafy, a. frondoso, hojudo.   [confederarse.
league, s. liga, alianza; legua; —, v.n.
leak, s. gotera, grieta donde pasa el agua; —, v.n. (mar.) hacer agua.
leakage, s. derrame, merma.
leaky, a. roto, agujereado.
leal, a. leal.
lean, v.a. & n. ladear, inclinar; apoyarse; —, a. magro.
leaning(s), s. ladeo; inclinación.

leanness, s. magrura.
leap, v.n. saltar, brincar; salir con ímpetu; palpitar; —, s. salto.
leap-frog, salta la burra (juego).
leap-year, s. año bisiesto.
learn, v.a. & n. aprender.
learned, a. docto, erudito; -ly, docta- mente.
learner, s. tirón; escolar; aprendiz.
learning, s. literatura, ciencia, erudición.
lease, s. arriendo, contrato de arriendo con plazo; —, v.a. arrendar por tiempo fijo.
leasehold, s. arriendo. [con correa.
leash, s. pihuela, correa; —, v.a. atar
least, a. mínimo; at —, á lo menos.
leather, s. cuero, pellejo.
leathern, a. (hecho) de cuero.
leathery, a. correoso.
leave, s. licencia; permiso; despedida; to take —, despedirse; —, v.a. dejar, abandonar; ceder.
leaven, s. levadura; fermento; —, v.a. templar el pan con levadura.
leavings, s.pl. sobras, pl.
lecherous, a. lascivo.
lecture, s. lección, discurso, conferencia; represión; —, v.a. & n. disertar; dar conferencias ó discursos; censurar.
lecturer, s. lector, instructor.
ledge, s. borde.
ledger, s. (com.) libro mayor.
led-horse, s. caballo de mano. [ventado.
lee, s. (mar.) sotavento; —, a. sota-
leech, s. sanguijuela; médico.
leek, s. (bot.) puerro.
leer, s. ojeada; — v.n ojear al través.
lees, s.pl. heces, pl.; sedimento, poso.
lee-shore, s. costa de sotavento.
lee-side, s. (mar.) banda de sotavento.
leeward, a. & ad. (mar.) á sotavento.
lee-way, s. (mar.) deriva. [quierda.
left, a. izquierdo; on the —, á la iz-
left-handed, a. zurdo, morganático.
leg, s. pierna; pie.
legacy, s. legado.
legal, a. legal, legítimo; -ly, legalmente.
legality, s. legalidad, legitimidad.
legalize, v.a. legalizar, autorizar.
legate, s. legado, diputado.
legatee, s. legatario.
legation, s. legación, embajada.
legend, s. leyenda, legenda.
legendary, a. fabuloso.
legerdemain, s. juego de manos.
legible, a. legible.
legibly, ad. legiblemente.
legion, s. legión.
legislate, v.a. legislar.
legislation, s. legislación.
legislative, a. legislativo.

legislator, s. legislador.
legislature, s. legislatura.
legitimacy, s. legitimidad.
legitimate, a. legítimo; -ly, legítima- mente; —, v.a. legitimar.
leguminous, a. (bot.) leguminoso.
leisure, s. desocupación; ocio; at —, leisurely, ad. á sus anchas, con sosiego.
lemon, s. limón.
lemonade, s. limonada.
lemon-tree, s. limonero.
lend, v.a. prestar.
length, s. longitud; duración; distancia; at —, finalmente. [garse, dilatarse.
lengthen, v.a. alargar; —, v.n. alar-
lengthy, a. largo; fastidioso.
leniency, s. clemencia, benignidad.
lenient, a. clemente.
lenitive, a. & s. lenitivo.
lenity, s. benignidad, blandura.
lens, s. lente (vidrio convexo).
lent, s. cuaresma.
lentil, s. lenteja.
leonine, a. leonino.
leopard, s. leopardo.
leper, s. leproso.
leprosy, s. lepra.
leprous, a. leproso.
lesion, s. lesión, daño.
less, a. menor; —, ad. menos.
lessee, s. arrendatario. [ir(se).
lessen, v.a. & n. minorar(se), disminu-
lesser, a. menor, más pequeño.
lesson, s. lección; represión.
lessor, s. arrendador.
lest, c. para que no, de miedo que.
let, v.a. dejar, permitir; arrendar, im- pedir.
lethal, a. letal.
lethargic(al), a. letárgico.
lethargy, s. letargo.
letter, s. letra; carta.
letter-box, s. buzón.
letter-case, s. cartera.
lettered, a. letrado, docto.
letter-press, s. impresión.
lettuce, s. lechuga.
levant, s. levante, oriente.
levee, s. corte; besamanos
level, a. llano, igual; nivelado; alla- nado; —, s. llanura; plano; nivel; —, v.a. allanar; nivelar.
lever, s. palanca.
leverage, s. fuerza de una palanca.
leveret, s. lebrato.
levite, s. levita.
levity, s. levedad, ligereza; inconstancia, veleidad. [leva.
levy, s. leva (de tropas); —, v.a. hacer
lewd, a. lascivo, disoluto.
lewdness, s. lascivia, disolución.

lexicographer, s. lexicógrafo.
lexicon, s. diccionario.
liability, s. responsibilidad.
liable, a. sujeto, expuesto ; responsable.
liar, s. mentiroso.
libation, s. libación.
libel, s. libelo ; —, v.a. difamar.
libeller, s. libelista.
libellous, a. difamatorio.   [mente.
liberal, a. liberal, generoso ; -ly, liberal-
liberality, s. liberalidad, generosidad.
liberate, v.a. librar, libertar.
liberation, s. liberación.
liberator, s. libertador.
libertine, s. libertino ; —, a. disoluto.
liberty, s. libertad ; privilegio.
Libra, s. Libra (signo del zodiaco).
librarian, s. bibliotecario.
library, s. librería ; biblioteca.
lice, s. piojos.
licence, s. licencia ; permiso.   [mente.
licentious, a. licencioso ; -ly, licenciosa-
lichen, s. (bot.) liquen.
lick, v.a. lamer, chupar ; (col.) golpear.
licking, s. paliza.
lid, s. tapa ; párpado.
lie, s. mentira ; —, v.n. mentir ; echarse ;
    reposar, acostarse ; yacer.
lief, ad. de buena gana.
liege, a. (law) ligio ; súbdito.
lien, s. (law) derecho de retención.
lieu, s. lugar ; in — of, en vez de.
lieutenancy, s. lugartenencia.   [ente.
lieutenant, s. lugarteniente ; (mil.) teni-
life, s. vida ; conducta ; vivacidad ;
    mundo ; to the —, al natural.
life-boat, a. lancha de salvación.
life-belt, s. cinturón para nadar.
life-guard, s. guardia de corps.
lifeless, a. muerto, inanimado ; sin
    vivacidad.
life-long, a. por la vida.
life-size, a. de grandeza natural.
life-time, s. duración de la vida.
lift, v.a. alzar, elevar, levantar ; hurtar,
    robar ; —, s. esfuerzo para levantar
    alguna cosa pesada ; alzamiento ;
    alza ; ayuda ; ascensor (hidráulico).
ligament, ligature, s. ligamento ; ligadura.
light, s. luz ; claridad ; conocimiento ;
    día ; —, a. ligero, leve, fácil ; frívolo ;
    superficial ; ágil ; inconstante ; claro ;
    blondo ; —, v.a. encender ; alumbrar ;
    —, v.n. hallar, encontrar ; desmon-
    tarse ; apearse.   [iluminar, aligerar.
lighten, v.n. relampaguear ; —, v.a.
lighter, s. (mar.) alijador.
lighterman, s. (mar.) lanchonero.
light-headed, a. delirante, aturdido ;
    casquivano, ligero de cascos.
light-hearted, a. ligero, alegre.

light-house, s. (mar.) faro, fanal.
lighting, s. iluminación.
lightly, ad. ligeramente ; fácilmente.
lightness, s. ligereza ; agilidad, velocidad
lightning, s. relámpago.   [pararrayos
lightning-conductor, lightning-rod, s.
lights, s.pl. bofes, pl.
lightsome, a. alegre.
ligneous, a. leñoso.
like, a. semejante ; igual ; verosímil ; —,
    s. semejante ; semejanza ; —, ad. del
    mismo modo que ; —, v.a. querer,
    amar.
likelihood, s. probabilidad, verisimilitud
likely, a. probable, verisímil.
liken, v.a. asemejar ; comparar.
likeness, s. semejanza ; igualdad ; retrato
likewise, ad. también ; igualmente.
liking, s. robustez ; gusto, agrado.
lilac, s. lila ; lilas.
lilt, s. canción.
lily, s. lirio.
limb, s. miembro.
limbo, s. limbo.
limber, a. manejable, flexible ; —, s.
    (mil.) avantrén.
lime, s. cal ; lima (especie de limón) ;
    (-tree), tilo ; —, v.a. untar con liga.
lime-kiln, s. horno de cal.
lime-stone, s. piedra de cal, caliza.
limit, s. límite, término ; —, v.a. limitar
    restringir.
limitation, s. limitación ; restricción
limitless, a. inmenso.
limn, v.a. pintar.
limner, s. pintor.
limp, v.n. cojear ; —, s. cojera ; —, a.
    débil, flaco.
limpet, s. lepada (molusco).
limpid, a. claro, transparente.
linch-pin, s. pezonera.
linden(-tree), s. tilo.
line, s. línea ; (mil.) línea de batalla ;
    raya ; esquicio, contorno ; ecuador ;
    renglón ; verso ; linaje ; cordón (muy
    delgado) ; —, v.a. forrar ; revestir.
lineage, s. linaje ; descendencia.
lineal, s. lineal ; -ly, en línea recta.
lineament, s. lineamentos, pl.
linear, a. lineal.   [lienzo.
linen, s. lienzo, lino ; —, a. hecho de
linen-draper, s. lencero.
liner, s. (mar.) barco grande de pasajeros,
    transatlántico.
ling, s. brezo ; merluza.
linger, v.n. tardar.
lingering, a. tardo, prolongado, duro ; -ly,
    lentamente ; lánguidamente.
linguist, s. lingüista.
liniment, s. linimento.
lining, s. forro.

link, s. eslabón; cadena; hacha, antorcha;
— , v.a. juntar ; encadenar.
link-boy, s. paje de hacha.
linnet, s. pardillo.
linseed, s. linaza.
linsey-woolsey, s. tejido de lana grosero
y con mezcla de hilo.
linstock, s. (mil.) mechero.
lint, s. lino ; hilas.
lintel, s. dintel, tranquero.
lion, -ess, s. león, leona.
lip, s. labio, borde. [liquidarse.
liquefy, v.a. licuar, liquidar ; — , v.n.
liqueur, s. licor delicado.
liquid, a. líquido ; — , licor.
liquidate, v.a. liquidar.
liquidation, s. liquidación.
liquor, s. licor.
liquorice, s. orozuz, regaliz.
lisp, v.n. cecear ; — , s. ceceo.
lissom, a. V. lithe.
list, s. lista ; gana ; voluntad ; — , v.n.
querer, desear ; — , v.a. registrar ;
(mil.) alistar.
listen, v.n. escuchar. [negligentemente.
listless, a. indiferente, descuidado ; -ly,
listlessness, s. descuido.
litany, s. letanía.
literal, a. -ly, literal(mente).
literary, a. literario.
literature, s. literatura.
lithe, a. flexible, ágil. [litografiar.
lithograph, s. litografía ; — , v.a.
lithographer, s. litógrafo.
lithography, s. litografía.
litigant, s. litigante.
litigate, v.a. litigar, pleitear.
litigation, s. litigio.
litigious, a. litigioso.
litter, s. litera, cama portátil ; lechigada,
ventregada ; — , v.a. parir los animales ; desordenar.
little, a. pequeño, poco ; — , s. poco ;
porción pequena.
littleness, s. pequeñez.
liturgical, a. litúrgico.
liturgy, s. liturgia. [a. vivo.
live, v.n. vivir ; mantenerse ; habitar ; —,
livelihood, s. vida ; subsistencia.
liveliness, s. vivacidad.
lively, a. vivo, brioso ; gallardo.
liver, s. vividor ; hígado.
livery, s. librea ; — stables, pl. caballeriza pública.
live-stock, s. (agr.) ganado.
livid, a. lívido, cárdeno. [—, a. vivo.
living, s. modo de vivir ; subsistencia ;
lizard, s. lagarto.
lo, ¡ bé aquí !, ¡ ved aquí !
load, v.a. cargar ; —, s. carga.
loadstar, lodestar, s. estrella polar.

loadstone, s. imán.
loaf, s. pan ; (of sugar), pilón de azúcar.
loafer, s. holgazán, gandul, azotacalles.
loam, s. marga.
loan, s. préstamo, empréstito.
loathe, v.a. aborrecer ; tener hastío ; —,
v.n. fastidiar ; — , a. V. loth.
loathing, s. disgusto, aversión.
loathly, loathsome, a. detestable, fastidioso.
lobby, s. vestíbulo.
lobe, s. lóbulo.
lobster, s. langosta.
local, a. local.
locality, s. localidad.
localize, v.a. localizar.
loch, s. lago (en Escocia).
lock, s. cerradura, cerraja ; llave de
fusil ; vedija de lana ; guedeja ; represa (de canal) ; —, v.a. cerrar ; to
— out, excluir cerrando la puerta.
locker, s. armario.
locket, s. broche, corchete ; medallón.
lock-jaw, s. trismo.
lock-out, s. cesación del trabajo.
locksmith, s. cerrajero.
locomotion, s. locomoción.
locomotive, s. locomotora.
locust, s. langosta.
lodge, s. casita ; —, v.a. alojar ; fijar en
la memoria ; —, v.n. residir, habitar.
lodger, s. huésped.
lodging, s. posada ; -s, pl. cuarto alquilado.
lodging-house, s. posada.
loft, s. piso ; desván.
loftiness, s. altura; sublimidad; soberbia.
lofty, a. alto ; sublime; altivo. [quilla.
log, s. leño, trozo de árbol ; (mar.) bar-
logarithm, s. logaritmo. [gación.
log(-book), s. (mar.) diario de nave-
loggerhead, s. zote.
logic, s. lógica.
logical, a. lógico.
logician, s. lógico.
log-line, s. (mar.) corredera.
logwood, s. palo de Campeche.
loin, lomo ; -s, pl. lomos, pl.
loiter, v.n. tardar, haraganear.
loiterer, s. haragán, holgazán.
loll, v.n. apoyarse, recostarse.
lollipop, s. (col.) golosina, dulce.
lone(ly), lonesome, a. solitario ; solo.
loneliness, s. soledad.
long, a. largo ; —, ad. á una gran distancia ; mucho ; —, v.n. desear con
vehemencia, anhelar.
long-bow, s. arco ; to draw the —, v.n.
exagerar. [de la vida.
longevity, s. longevidad, duración larga
longing, s. deseo vehemente, anhelo.

longitude, s. longitud.

longitudinal, a. longitudinal.

long-sighted, a. présbite.

loo, s. especie de juego de naipes.

look, v. n.mirar, considerar, pensar, contemplar; parecer; — for, v.a. buscar, esperar; —, s. aspecto; mirada.

looker-on, s. espectador, presente.

looking-glass, s. espejo. [vigía.

look-out, s. (mil.) centinela; (mar.)

loom, s. telar; —, v.n. asomar; destacarse, encimarse.

loop, s. ojal; presilla.

loop-hole, s. tronera; escapatoria.

loose, a. suelto, desatado; flojo; vago, relajado; disoluto; desenredado; descuidado; -ly, sueltamente; —, loosen, v.a. aflojar, laxar, desliar.

looseness, s. flojedad; relajación.

loot, v.a. saquear; s. botín.

lop, v.a. desmochar.

lop-eared, a. con las orejas caídas.

lop-sided, a. ladeado, sesgado.

loquacious, a. locuaz, charlador. [dad.

loquacity, s. locuacidad, charla, garruli-

Lord, s. señor; Dios; amo, dueño; Lord; — Mayor, alcalde; —, v.n. señorear, dominar.

lordliness, s. señorío; altivez; orgullo.

lordling, s. lord pequeño.

lordly, a. señoril; orgulloso, imperioso.

Lordship, s. Excelencia, Señoría.

lore, s. erudición, ciencia, doctrina.

lose, v.a. perder; disipar.

lorn, a. abandonado, desamparado

loser, s. perdedor. [desatinar.

loss, s. pérdida; daño; to be at a —,

lot, s. suerte; lote; cuota; porción.

loth, a. repugnante, disgustado.

lotion, s. loción.

lottery, s. lotería, rifa. [altamente.

loud, a. ruidoso, alto; clamoroso; -ly,

loudness, s. tono elevado; ruido.

lounge, v.n. haraganear.

louse, (pl. lice), s. piojo.

lousy, a. piojoso; miserable, vil.

lout, s. patán, rústico, zafio.

loutish, a. rústico, tosco.

lovable, a. amable.

love, s. amor, cariño; galanteo, to fall in —, enamorarse; —, v.a. amar; querer.

love-letter, s. esquela, carta amorosa.

loveliness, s. amabilidad, agrado; belleza.

lovely, a. amable, hermoso.

lover, s. amante, galán, cortejo.

love-sick, a. enamorado; herido de amor.

loving, a. cariñoso, afectuoso; -ly, afectuosamente. [bilidad.

loving-kindness, s. benignidad, ama-

low, a. bajo, pequeño; hondo; abatido; vil; —, ad. á precio bajo; vilmente.

low, v.n. mugir.

low-bred, a. mal criado.

lower, a. más bajo; —, v.a. abajar, humillar; disminuir; —, v.n. disminuirse; encapotarse.

lowering, a. sombrío.

lowermost, lowest, a. más bajo, ínfimo.

lowing, s. mugido.

lowland, s. tierra baja, planicie.

lowliness, s. bajeza; humildad.

lowly, a. humilde.

lowness, s. bajeza.

low-water, s. bajamar.

loyal, a. leal, fiel; -ly, lealmente.

loyalty, s. lealtad; fidelidad.

lozenge, s. rombo; pastilla de boca.

lubber, s. bobo; bigardo.

lubberly, a. perezoso, bigardo.

lubricate, v.a. lubricar.

lucid, a. luminoso; lúcido, claro.

lucidity, s. lucidez. [fósforo.

Lucifer, s. Lucero; —(-match), cerilla,

luck, s. fortuna, suerte. [mente.

luckily, ad. por fortuna, afortunada.

luckless, a. infeliz, desventurado.

lucky, a. afortunado, feliz, venturoso.

lucrative, a. lucrativo.

lucre, s. lucro; ganancia.

lucubration, s. lucubración.

ludicrous, a. ridículo.

luff, v.a. (mar.) orzar.

lug, v.a. tirar; (mar.) halar.

luggage, s. equipaje, bulto. [cías.

luggage-train, s. (rail.) tren de mercan-

luggage-van, s. (rail.) vagón de equipajes.

lugger, s. (mar.) lugre.

lugubrious, a. lúgubre, triste.

lukewarm, a. tibio; -ly, tibiamente.

lull, v.a. arrullar; adormecer; v.n. calmar(se) (el viento); —, s. intervalo de calma.

lullaby, s. arrullo.

lumbago, s. lumbago. [trastera.

lumber, s. armatoste, trastos; -room, s.

luminary, s. luminar.

luminous, a. luminoso, resplandeciente.

lump, s. masa informe; by the —, por grueso ó por junto; — sugar, s. azúcar blanco; —, v.a. tomar alguna cosa por junto ó por mayor.

lunacy, s. locura, frenesí. [de plata.

lunar, a. lunar; — caustic, s. nitrato

lunatic, a. & s. lunático, frenético; fantástico.

lunch, luncheon, s. merienda.

lunette, s. (mil.) media luna.

lung, pulmón.

lunge, s. estocada; — v.n. hacer una estocada (de esgrima).

lurch, s. abandono, ladeo, traqueo ; —, v.n. ladear, traquear. [atraer, inducir.
lure, s. señuelo, añagaza ; cebo ; —, v.a.
lurid, a. pálido, sombrío.
lurk, v.n. esconderse, ponerse en acecho.
lurking-place, s. escondrijo ; guarida.
luscious, a. dulce ; delicioso.
lust, s. lujuria, sensualidad ; concupiscencia ; —, v.n. lujuriar.
lustful, a. lujurioso, voluptuoso ; -ly, lujuriosamente.
lustily, ad. vigorosamente.
lustiness, s. vigor ; robustez.
lustre, s. lustre ; brillantez.
lustring, s. lustrina (tela).
lusty, a. fuerte, vigoroso.
lute, s. laúd ; luten.
lute-string, s. V. lustring.

Lutheran, s. luterano.
luxuriance, s. exuberancia, superabundancia.
luxuriant, a. exuberante, superabundante.
luxuriate, v.n. crecer con exuberancia.
luxurious, a. lujoso ; exuberante ; -ly lujosamente.
luxury, s. lujo ; exuberancia.
lyceum, s. liceo.
lying, s. acto de mentir ; mentira.
lying-in, s. parto.
lymph, s. linfa.
lymphatic, a. linfático.   [(am.).
lynch, v.a. ajusticiar al reo el populacho
lynx, s. lince.
lyre, s. lira.
lyric(al), a. lírico.

M

macadamize, v.a. empedrar un camino al estilo de MacAdam.
macaroni, s. macarrones, pl.
macaroon, s. almendrado.
mace, s. maza ; macis.   [cuerpo.
macerate, v.a. macerar ; mortificar el
machinate, v.n. maquinar.
machination, s. maquinación, trama.
machine, s. máquina.
machinery, s. maquinaria, mecanismo.
machinist, s. maquinista.
mackerel, s. escombro (pez).
mackintosh, s. sobretodo impermeable.
mad, a. loco, furioso, rabioso, insensato.
madam, s. madama, señora.
mad-cap, s. locarias, orate.
madden, v.a. enloquecer.
madder, s. (bot.) rubia.
mad-house, s. manicomio.
madly, ad. furiosamente ; como un loco.
madman, s. loco.
madness, s. locura, manía ; furor.
madrigal, s. madrigal.
magazine, s. almacén ; periódico, revista ; (mar.) Santabárbara.
maggot, s. gusano ; (col.) capricho.
magic, s. magia negra ; —, a. mágico ; -ally, mágicamente.
magician, s. mago, nigromante.
magisterial, a. magistral ; imperioso ; -ly, magistralmente.
magistracy, s. magistratura.
magistrate, s. magistrado.
magnanimity, s. magnanimidad.
magnanimous, a. magnánimo ; -ly, magnánimamente.
magnet, s. imán, piedra imán.
magnetic(al), a. magnético.

magnetism, s. magnetismo.
magnificence, s. magnificencia.
magnificent, a. magnífico ; -ly, pomposamente.   [exagerar.
magnify, v.a. magnificar, exaltar,
magnitude, s. magnitud, grandeza.
magpie, s. urraca, picaza.
mahogany, s. caoba, caobana.
mahometan, a. & s. mahometano.
maid(en), s. doncella, joven ; moza, criada.   [intacto.
maiden, a. virgíneo, virginal ; nuevo,
maidenhood, s. doncellez, virginidad.
maidenly, a. virginal, púdico.
maiden-speech, s. primer discurso de un diputado en el parlamento.
mail, s. cota de malla ; mala, correo.
mail-coach, s. diligencia.
mail-train, s. (rail.) tren correo.
maim, v.a. mutilar ; estropear.
main, a. principal ; esencial ; —, s. grueso ; océano, alta mar ; fuerza ; in the —, en general.
mainland, s. tierra firme, continente.
main-line, s. (rail.) línea principal, tronco.
mainly, ad. principalmente, sobre todo.
main-mast, s. (mar.) palo mayor.
maintain, v.a. & n. mantener, sostener.
maintenance, s. mantenimiento ; protección ; sustento.
maize, s. maíz.
majestic(al), a. majestuoso ; grande ; -ally, majestuosamente.
majesty, s. majestad.
major, a. mayor ; —, s. (mil.) mayor, comandante ; primera proposición de un silogismo.
majority, s. mayoría ; pluralidad.

make, v.a. hacer, crear, producir;
formar, fabricar; ejecutar; obligar,
forzar; —, v.n. hacerse; ir, encamin-
arse; —, s. hechura, forma, figura.
make-believe, s. disimulo; pretexto.
makeshift, s. expediente, arreglo provisional, chapucería.
make-weight, s. contrapeso. [hechura.
making, s. composición; estructura,
malachite, s. malaquita.
malady, s. enfermedad.
malapert, a. descarado, impertinente.
malaria, s. fiebre local, fiebre palúdica.
malcontent, a. & s. malcontento.
male, a. masculino; —, s. macho.
malediction, s. maldición.
malefactor, s. malhechor.
maleficent, a. maléfico, maligno.
malevolence, s. malevolencia. [namente.
malevolent, a. malévolo; -ly, malig-
malice, s. malicia. [mente.
malicious, a. malicioso; -ly, maliciosa-
malign, a. maligno; dañoso; —, v.a.
calumniar. [namente.
malignant, a. maligno; -ly, ad. malig-
malignity, s. malignidad.
malinger, v.n. fingir enfermedad.
malingerer, s. enfermo fingido.
malleable, a. maleable.
mallet, s. mazo.
mallow, s. (bot.) malva.
malmsey, s. malvasía.
malpractice, s. malversación; maltrato.
malt, s. cebada preparada para hacer la
cerveza; — liquor, s. cerveza.
maltreat, v.a. maltratar.
maltster, s. obrero que prepara la cebada
para hacer cerveza.
malversation, s. malversación.
mamma, s. mamá.
mammal, s. mamífero.
mammon, s. lucro.
man, s. hombre; marido; criado; peón;
— of war, navío de guerra; —, v.a.
(mar.) tripular, armar.
manacle, s. manilla; -s, pl. esposas; —,
v.a. maniatar. [ministrar.
manage, v.a. manejar, gobernar, ad-
manageable, a. manejable; dócil, tratable.
management, s. manejo; administración;
conducta. [hombre económico.
manager, s. administrador, director;
mandate, s. mandato; comisión.
mandatory, s. mandatario.
mandible, s. quijada, mandíbula.
mandrake, s. (bot.) mandrágora.
mane, s. crines del caballo, pl.
man-eater, s. antropófago.
manful, a. valiente; -ly, valerosamente.
mange, s. roña, sarna perruna.
manger, s. pesebre.

mangle, s. calandria; —, v.a. pasar por
la calandria; mutilar.
mangold, s. especie de nabo.
mango, s. mango.
mangrove, s. (bot.) mangle.
mangy, a. sarnoso.
manhood, s. edad viril; valor.
mania, s. manía.
maniac(al), a. maniático, maniaco.
manichean, a. maniqueo.
manifest, a. manifiesto, patente; —, s
manifiesto; —, v.a. manifestar.
manifestation, s. manifestación.
manifold, a. muchos, varios.
manikin, s. hombrecillo, títere, maniquí.
manipulate, v.a. manejar.
manipulation, s. manipulación.
mankind, s. género ó linaje humano.
manlike, a. varonil.
manliness, s. valentía; valor.
manly, a. varonil, valeroso.
man-midwife, s. comadrón, partero.
manner, s. manera; modo; forma;
método; maña; hábito; moda;
especie; -s, pl. modales; urbanidad,
crianza. [dad.
mannerism, s. idiosincrasia, particulari-
mannerly, a. cortés. [brar.
manoeuvre, s. maniobra; —, v.n. manio-
manor, s. señorío; feudo.
manorial, a. señorial.
manse, s. (Scot.) casa del párroco.
mansion, s. mansión, morada, residencia,
manslaughter, s. homicidio.
mantel-piece, s. repisa de chimenea.
mantle, s. manto.
manual, a. & s. manual.
manufactory, s. fábrica, manufactura.
manufacture, s. manufactura; artefacto;
—, v.a. fabricar, manufacturar.
manufacturer, s. fabricante.
manumission, s. manumisión.
manure, s. abono; estiércol; fimo; —,
v.a. abonar, estercolar.
manuscript, s. manuscrito.
many, a. muchos; — a time, muchas
veces; how —? ¿cuántos? as — as,
tantos como.
map, s. mapa; —, v.a. delinear en mapas.
maple, s. arce (plátano falso).
mar, v.a. dañar, corromper.
marauder, s. merodeador.
marble, s. mármol; bolilla de mármol;
—, a. marmóreo; —, v.a. jaspear.
March, s. marzo (mes). [caminar.
march, —, s. marcha; —, v.n. marchar,
marchioness, s. marquesa.
mare, s. yegua.
margarine, s. margarina.
margin, s. margen, borde; orilla; —
v.a. marginar.

marginal, a. marginal.

marigold, s. (bot.) caléndula.

marine, a. marino ; —, s. marina ; soldado de marina.

mariner, s. marinero.

marital, a. marital.

maritime, a. marítimo, naval.

marjoram, s. (bot.) mejorana.

mark, s. marca ; señal, nota ; blanco ; —, v.a. marcar ; —, v.n. advertir.

market, s. mercado.

marketable, a. vendible.

marksman, s. tirador.

marl, s. marga ; —, v.a. margar.

marl-pit, s. marguera.

marly, a. margoso.

marmalade, s. mermelada.

marmoset, s. mico pequeño.

marmot, s. marmota.

maroon, s. cólor castaño.

maroon, s. cimarrón ; —, v.a. (mar.) abandonar á alguien en tierra selvaje.

marquee, s. marquesina.

marquetry, s. marquetería, ataracea.

marquess, marquis, s. marqués.

marquisate, s. marquesado.

marriage, s. matrimonio ; casamiento.

marriageable, a. casadero, núbil.

marriage settlement, s. contrato matrimonial.

married, a. casado, conyugal.

marrow, s. meollo ; medula.

marry, v.a. & n. casar(se).

marsh, s. pantano.

marshal, s. mariscal.

marshy, a. pantanoso.

marsupial, a. marsupial.

mart, s. mercado, emporio ; feria.

marten, s. marta.

martial, a. marcial, guerrero ; — law, s. derecho militar.   [disciplina.

martinet, s. instructor muy tieso en la

Martinmas, s. día de S. Martín.

martyr, s. mártir.

martyrdom, s. martirio.

martyrology, s. martirologio.

marvel, s. maravilla ; —, v.n. maravillar(se).   [villosamente.

marvellous, a. maravilloso ; -ly, mara-

masculine, a. masculino, varonil.

mash, s. mezcla ; fárrago ; —, v.a. amasar ; mezclar.

mask, s. máscara ; pretexto, color ; —, v.a. enmascarar ; disimular, ocultar ; —, v.n. andar enmascarado.

masker, s. máscara (persona enmascarada).

mason, s. albañil.

masonry, s. albañilería.

masquerade, s. mascarada.

masquerader, s. máscara.

mass, s. masa ; montón ; (eccl.) misa.

massacre, s. carnicería, matanza ; —, v.a. matar atrozmente, hacer una carnicería.

massive, a. macizo, sólido.   [fabuco

mast, s. árbol de navío, palo ; (bot.)

master, s. amo, dueño ; maestro ; señor, señorito ; (mar.) capitán, patrón, —, v.a. domar, domeñar ; gobernar, dominar.

masterly, a. imperioso, despótico ; diestro, hábil ; —, ad. con maestría.

master-piece, s. obra maestra.

master-stroke, master-touch, s. golpe de maestro.

mastery, s. superioridad, maestría.

masticate, v.a. mascar, masticar.

mastiff, s. mastín.

mat, s. estera, esterilla ; —, v.a. esterar

mat, a. sin lustre.

match, s. mecha, pajuela ; fósforo, cerilla ; partido, competencia en juego ; contrincante ; pareja ; casamiento ; —, v.a. igualar ; aparear ; casar ; —, v.n. hermanarse.

match-box, s. cajita de fósforos.

matchless, s. incomparable, sin par.

match-maker, s. casamentero.

mate, s. consorte ; compañero ; compañera ; (mar.) piloto ; —, v.a. desposar(se), igualar.

material, s. -ly, material(mente).

materialism, s. materialismo.

maternal, a. maternal, materno.

maternity, s. maternidad.

mathematic(al), a. matemático ; -ly, matemáticamente.

mathematician, s. matemático.

mathematics, s.pl. matemáticas, pl.

matins, s.pl. maitines, pl.

matricide, s. matricidio ; matricida.

matriculate, v.a. matricular.

matriculation, s. matriculación.

matrimonial, a. matrimonial, marital

matrimony, s. matrimonio, casamiento.

matron, s. matrona.

matronly, a. matronal, seria, grave.

matted, a. entretejido.

matter, s. materia, substancia material ; asunto, objeto ; cuestión, importancia. it is no —, no importa ; what is the —? de qué se trata ? —, v.n. importar.

matter-of-fact, a. práctico, sensato.

mattings, s.pl. esteras, pl.

mattock, s. azadón.

mattress, s. colchón.

mature, a. maduro ; —, v.a. madurar.

maturity, s. madurez.

maudlin, a. medio borracho, absurda mente sentimental.

maul, v.a. apalear, maltratar á golpes,

maul-stick, s. tiento.
Maundy-Thursday, s. Jueves Santo.
mausoleum, s. mausoleo.
maw, s. estómago ; molleja de las aves.
mawkish, a. fastidioso, nauseabundo.
maxim, s. máxima, refrán.
may, v.n. poder ; -be, ad. acaso, quizá.
May, s. mayo (mes.).
May-day, s. primer de mayo.
May-pole, s. mayo (arbol).
mayor, s. alcalde.
mayoralty, s. alcaldía.
mayoress, s. alcadesa.
maze, s. laberinto ; perplejidad.
mazy, a. confuso, embrollado.
me, pn. me.
mead, s. aguamiel.
mead(ow), s. pradería ; prado.
meagre, a. magro ; flaco ; -ly, pobremente, estérilmente.
meagreness, s. flaqueza ; escasez.
meal, s. comida ; harina.
mealy, a. harinoso.
mean, a. bajo, vil, despreciable ; abatido;
mediocre ; -time, -while, ínterin,
mientras tanto ; —, s. medio ; expediente ; -s, pl. medios, pl.; caudal ;
—, v.a. & n. significar ; hacer intención, pensar.
meander, s. laberinto, camino tortuoso ;
— v.n. vagar, fluir con corriente tortuoso.   [sentido, significado.
meaning, s. intención ; inteligencia ;
meanly, ad. mediocremente ; pobremente ; vilmente.
meanness, s. bajeza ; pobreza ; mezquindad ; mediocridad.
measles, s.pl. sarampión.
measurable, a. mensurable.
measure, s. medida ; (mus.) compás ; —,
v.a. medir ; ajustar.
measurement, s. medida.
measurer, s. medidor.
meat, s. carne ; vianda.
mechanic, s. mecánico.
mechanical, a. mecánico ; servil, bajo ;
-ly, mecánicamente.
mechanician, mechanist, s. mecánico,
maquinista.
mechanics, s.pl. mecánica.
mechanism, s. mecanismo.
medal, s. medalla.
medallion, s. medallón.
meddle, v.n. entremeterse.
meddler, s. entremetido.
mediæval, medieval, a. de la edad media.
mediate, v.n. mediar.
mediation, s. mediación, interposición.
medical, a. médico.
medicament, s. medicamento.
medicate, v.a. impregnar con medicina.

medicinal, a. medicinal.
medicine, s. medicina, medicamento.
mediocrity, s. mediocridad.
meditate, v.a. meditar, idear.
meditation, s. meditación.
meditative, a. meditativo, contemplativo.
mediterranean, a. mediterráneo.   [ción.
medium, s. medio ; expediente ; modera-
medlar, s. níspero ; níspola.
medley, s. miscelánea, mezcla.
meek, a. mego, apacible ; dulce ; -ly,
suavemente.   [dulzura.
meekness, s. suavidad ; modestia ;
meerschaum, s. espuma de mar.
meet, v.a. encontrar ; —, v.n. encontrarse ; juntarse ; —, a. idóneo, propio.
meeting, s. asamblea ; congreso ; entrevista ; conventículo.   [cólico.
melancholy, s. melancolía ; —, a. melan-
mellifluous, a. melifluo.
mellow, a. maduro, meloso ; tierno ; —,
v.a. (& n.) madurar(se).
mellowness, s. madurez.   [mente.
melodious, a. melodioso ; -ly, melodiosa
melodrama, s. melodrama.
melody, s. melodía.
melon, s. melón.
melt, v.a. derretir, fundir ; liquidar ; enternecer ; —, v.n. derretirse, liquidarse.
member, s. miembro ; parte ; individuo,
socio.
membrane, s. membrana.
memento, s. memento.
memoir, s. memoria, relación, narrativa.
memorable, a. memorable.
memorably, ad. memorablemente.
memorandum, memorándum.
memorial, s. memoria ; memorial.
memory, s. memoria ; recuerdo.
menace, s. amenaza ; —, v.a. amenazar.
menagerie, menagery, s. colección de
fieras ó animales raros.
mend, v.a. reparar, remendar, retocar ;
mejorar ; corregir.
mendacious, a. mendoso, mentiroso.
mendacity, s. falsedad, mentira.
mendicancy, mendicity, s. mendiguez,
mendicidad.
mendicant, a. & s. mendicante, mendigo.
menial, a. servil, doméstico.   [struc-
menstruation, s. menstruación, men-
mensuration, s. medición.
mental, a. mental, intelectual ; -ly,
mentalmente, intelectualmente.
mention, s. mención ; —, v.a. mencionar.
Mentor, s. mentor ayo, guía.
mephitic(al), a. mefítico.
mercantile, a. mercantil.
mercenary, a. & s. mercenario.
mercer, s. mercero, sedero.
mercery, s. mercería, sedería.

merchandise, s. mercancía.
merchant, s. comerciante.
merchantman, s. navío mercantil.
merchant-service, s. marina mercantil.
merciful, a. misericordioso ; -ly, misericordiosamente.
merciless, a. duro de corazón, inhumano; -ly, cruelmente.
mercurial, a. vivo, activo ; mercurial.
mercury, s. mercurio, azogue.
mercy, s. misericordia, piedad ; perdón.
mere, a. mero, puro ; -ly, simplemente ; puramente.
meretricious, a. meretricio.
merge, v.a. sumergir ; — v.n. hundirse, confundirse.
meridian, s. mediodía ; meridiano.
meridional, a. meridional.
merit, s. mérito ; —, v.a. merecer.
meritorious, a. meritorio ; -ly, meritoriamente.
mermaid, s. sirena.
merrily, ad. alegremente.
merriment, s. diversión ; regocijo, alegría.
merry, a. alegre, jovial, festivo.
Merry-Andrew, s. bufón, chulo.
mesh, s. malla (de red).
Mesmerism, s. mesmerismo.
mess, s. plato ; rancho ; porción ; (col.) olla podrida, masa sucia, confusión.
message, s. mensaje, recado.
messenger, s. mensajero.
mess-mate, s. comensal. [habitación.
messuage, s. menaje, ajuar de casa ;
metal, s. metal ; (fig.) coraje, espíritu.
metallic, a. metálico.
metallurgy, s. metalurgia.
metamorphose, v.a. transformar.
metamorphosis, s. metamorfosis.
metaphor, s. metáfora.
metaphoric(al), a. metafórico.
metaphysic(al), a. metafísico ; -ly, metafísicamente.
metaphysics, s.pl. metafísica.
mete, v.a. medir, distribuir.
meteor, s. metéoro, meteoro.
meteorite, s. meteorito.
meteorological, a. meteorológico.
meteorology, s. meteorología.
meter, s. medidor. [pienso.
methinks, v. imp. me parece, creo,
method, s. método. [dicamente.
methodic(al), a. metódico ; -ly, metó-
methodist, metodista.
metre, s. metro.
metrical, a. métrico.
metropolis, s. metrópoli ; la capital corte.
metropolitan, s. metropolitano.
mettle, s. brío, valor, coraje, ardor.
mettled, mettlesome, a. brioso, vivo, ardiente.

mew, s. gaviota ; jaula ; caballeriza ; —, v.a. enjaular ; —, v.n. maullar (como el gato).
microscope, s. microscopio.
microscopic(al), microscópico.
mid, a. medio. [camino.
mid-course, s. media carrera ; medio
mid-day, s. mediodía.
middle, a. medio, intermedio ; mediocre ; —, s. medio, centro.
middle-aged, a. de edad madura.
middleman, s. intermedio.
middling, a. mediano, mediocre.
midland, a. mediterráneo.
midnight, s. media noche.
midriff, s. diafragma.
midshipman, middy, s. guardia marina.
midst, s. medio, centro [del estío.
midsummer, s. solsticio estival ; rigor
midway, s. medio camino ; —, ad. á medio camino.
midwife, s. comadre, partera.
midwifery, s. obstetricia.
mien, s. semblante.
might, s. poder ; fuerza ; — and main, suma fuerza.
mightily, ad. poderosamente, sumamente.
mightiness, s. poder ; potencia.
mighty, a. fuerte, potente.
mignonette, s. (bot.) reseda. [cilio.
migrate, v.n. mudarse, cambiar de domi-
migration, s. mudanza, migración.
migratory, a. migratorio.
milch, a. lactífero.
mild, a. indulgente, blando, dulce, apacible, suave, moderado ; -ly, suavemente, con blandura.
mildew, s. tizón, tizoncillo.
mildness, s. clemencia, dulzura.
mile, s. milla.
mileage, s. pago por milla.
mile-stone, s. mijero.
militant, a. militante.
military, a. & s. militar.
militate, v.n. oponerse.
militia, s. milicia.
milk, s. leche ; —, v.a. ordeñar.
milk-maid, s. lechera.
milk-sop, s. marica.
milky, a. lácteo, lactífero ; lechal ; —, way, s. galaxia, via láctea.
mill, s. molino ; —, v.a. moler ; batir con el molinillo ; estampar.
mill-dam, s. esclusa de molino.
millennium, s. milenario.
miller, s. molinero.
millet, s. (bot.) mijo.
milliner, s. modista.
millinery, s. modas.
million, s. millón, cuento.
millionth, a. millonésimo.

mill-race, s. canal de molino.

mill-stone, s. muela.

mime, mimic, s. mimo, bufón.

mimic, v.a. imitar, remedar, contrahacer.

mimicry, s. mímica.

mince, v.a. picar la carne; v.n. melindrear. [drosamente.

mincingly, ad. con afectación, melindmind, s. mente; entendimiento; gusto, afecto; voluntad, intención; pensamiento; opinión; ánimo; —, v.a. notar, observar, considerar; pensar.

minded, a. inclinado, dispuesto.

mindful, a. atento, diligente; -ly, atentamente.

mindless, a. descuidado, negligente.

mine, pn. mío, mi; —, s. mina; —, v.n. minar, cavar.

miner, s. minero.

mineral, a. & s. mineral.

mineralogy, s. mineralogía.

minaret, s. minarete.

mingle, v.a. & n. mezclar(se).

miniature, s. miniatura.

minim, s. (mus.) mínima.

minimise, v.a. apocar.

minimum, s. mínimum.

minion, s. favorito.

minister, s. ministro; —, v.a. ministrar; servir; suministrar; proveer; socorrer.

ministerial, a. ministerial.

ministration, s. agencia; ministerio.

ministry, s. ministerio.

minnow, s. vario (pez).

minor, a. menor, pequeño; inferior; —, s. menor (de edad). [menor.

minority, s. minoridad; minoría; edad menor.

minster, s. iglesia catedral.

minstrel, s. ministril.

mint, s. (bot.) menta; ceca, casa de moneda; —, v.a. acuñar.

minuet, s. minuete, minué.

minus, ad. menos. [exactamente.

minute, a. menudo, pequeño; -ly, minute, s. minuto; memento, instante; minuta.

minute-book, s. libro de minutas.

minuteness, s. minucia, pequeñez.

minutiae, s.pl. menudencias.

minx, s. muchacha despejada, pícara.

miracle, s. milagro; maravilla.

miraculous, a. milagroso; -ly, maravillosamente.

mirage, s. espejismo.

mire, s. fango, limo.

mirror, s. espejo.

mirth, s. alegría; regocijo.

mirthful, a. alegre, jovial.

miry, a. cenagoso, lodoso.

misadventure, s. desventura; infortunio.

misalliance, s. matrimonio desigual.

misanthrope, s. misántropo.

misanthropy, s. misantropía.

misapplication, s. mala aplicación.

misapply, v.a. usar impropiamente.

misapprehend, v.a. entender mal.

misapprehension, s. error, yerro.

misbehave, v.n. portarse mal.

misbehaviour, s. mala conducta.

misbelief, s. opinión falsa; heterodoxia.

misbeliever, s. hereje.

miscalculate, v.a. desatinar.

miscarriage, s. éxito infeliz de alguna empresa; aborto. [abortar.

miscarry, v.n. frustrarse, malograrse;

miscellaneous, a. misceláneo.

miscellany, s. miscelánea.

mischance, s. desventura; infortunio.

mischief, s. mal, daño, infortunio.

mischief-maker, s. derramasolaces, destripamariendas.

mischievous, a. dañoso, malicioso, malévolo; -ly, malignamente.

misconceive, v.a. entender mal, errar.

misconception, s. equivocación.

misconduct, s. mala conducta; —, v.r. portarse mal.

misconstruction, s. mala construcción, interpretación siniestra.

misconstrue, v.a. interpretar mal.

miscreant, s. infiel, incrédulo; malvado, malhechor.

misdeed, s. mal hecho, delito.

misdemeanour, s. mala conducta.

misdirect, v.a. dirigir erradamente, desviar.

misdoubt, v.a. recelar, sospechar.

miser, s. avaro. [mezquino.

miserable, a. miserable, infeliz; pobre;

miserably, ad. miserablemente.

miserly, a. avaro, mezquino, tacaño.

misery, s. miseria; infortunio.

misfit, s. vestido mal hecho.

misfortune, s. infortunio; calamidad.

misgive, v.a. llenar de dudas; hacer temer. [miento.

misgiving, s. recelo; duda; presenti-misgovern, v.a. gobernar mal.

misguide, v.a. guiar mal.

mishap, s. desventura; desastre.

misinform, v.a. informar mal.

misinterpret, v.a. interpretar mal

misjudge, v.n. juzgar mal.

mislay, v.a. extraviar, perder. [seducir.

mislead, v.a. extraviar, descaminar;

mismanage, v.a. manejar mal.

mismanagement, s. mala administración; desarreglo.

misname, v.a. dar un nombre falso.

misnomer, s. nombre ó título falso.

misogynist, s. aborrecedor de mujeres.

misplace, v.a. colocar mal.

misprint, v.a. imprimir mal ; —, s. errata de un libro.
misrepresent, v.a. representar mal.
misrepresentation, s. representación falsa.
misrule, s. tumulto ; confusión.
miss, s. señorita ; pérdida, falta ; —, v.a. errar, perder ; omitir ; —, v.n. frustrarse ; faltar.
missal, s. misal.
misshape, v.a. deformar, desfigurar.
missile, s. proyectil.
missing, s. lo que falta ; perdido.
mission, s. misión, comisión.
missionary, s. misionero.
missive, s. carta misiva ; —, a. misivo.
mist, s. niebla.
mistake, v.a. entender mal ; —, v.n. equivocarse, engañarse ; **to be mistaken,** haberse equivocado ; —, s. equivocación ; yerro, engaño.
Mister, s. Señor (título).
mistiness, s. nebulosidad.
mistletoe, s. (bot.) muérdago ; liga.
mistress, s. ama ; concubina ; —, señora, doña ; dueña.
mistrust, v.a. desconfiar ; sospechar ; —, s. desconfianza, sospecha.
mistrustful, a. desconfiado, sospechoso.
misty, a. nebuloso.
misunderstand, v.a. entender mal.
misuse, v.a. maltratar ; abusar ; — s, abuso.
mite, s. cresa ; pizca.
mitigate, v.a. mitigar, calmar.
mitigation, s. mitigación ; alivio.
mitre, s. mitra.
mittens, s.pl. mitones, pl.
mix, v.a. mezclar.
mixture, s. mistura, mixtura, mezcla.
mizzen s. (mar.) mesana.
mizzle, v.n. molliznar, lloviznar.
moan, s. lamento, gemido ; —, v.a. lamentar, gemir ; —, v.n. afligirse.
moat, s. foso de defensa.   [correr, acosar.
mob, s. populacho, canalla ; —, v.a
mobilise, v.a. (mil.) movilizar.
mobility, s. movilidad ; (col.) populacho.
moccasin, s. alpargata de los Indios.
mock, v.a. mofar, burlar ; —, s. mofa ; burla ; —, a. ficticio, falso.
mockery, s. mofa, burla, zumba.
mocking-bird, s. estornino (ave).
mock-turtle, s. tortuga fingida (especie de sopa).   [costumbre.
mode, s. modo ; forma ; manera ;
model, s. modelo ; —, v.a. modelar.
modeller, s. trazador, dibujador.
moderate, a. moderado ; mediocre ; -ly, moderadamente ; —, v.a. moderar.
moderation, s. moderación.
modern, a. moderno, reciente.

modernize, v.a. modernizar.
modest, a. modesto ; -ly, modestamente.
modesty, s. modestia, decencia.
modicum, s. porción moderada.
modification, s. modificación.
modify, v.a. modificar.
modish, a. á la moda.
modulate, v.a. modular.
modulation, s. (mus.) modulación.
mohair, s. tela hecha de pelo de cabra.
moiety, s. mitad.
moist, a. húmedo, mojado.
moisten, v.a. humedecer.
moisture, s. humedad ; jugo.
molar, a. molar ; —, s. muela.
molasses, s.pl. melaza.
mole, s. lunar ; muelle, dique ; topo.
mole-hill, s. topinera.
molest, v.a. molestar, atormentar.
molestation, s. molestia.
mollify, v.a. ablandar.
mollusc, mollusk, s. molusco.
molten, a. derretido.
moment, s. momento ; importancia.
momentarily, ad. á cada momento.
momentary, a. momentáneo.
momentous, a. importante.
momentum, s. (mec.) momento.
monarch, s. monarca.
monarchic(al), a. monárquico.
monarchy, s. monarquía.
monastery, s. monasterio, convento.
monastic(al), a. monástico.
Monday, s. lunes.
monetary, a. monetario.
money, s. moneda ; dinero , **ready** dinero contante.
moneyed, monied, a. adinerado, rico.
money-lender, s. prestamista.
money-market, s. la Bolsa.
monger, s. tratante, traficante.
mongrel, a. & s. mestizo.
monition, s. amonestación.
monitor, s. admonitor ; monitor.
monitory, a. monitorio.
monk, s. monje.
monkey, s. mono.
monkish, a. monástico.
monograph, s. monografía.
monomaniac, a. monomaniaco.
monoplane, s. monoplano.
monopolist, s. monopolista.
monopolize, v.a. monopolizar.
monopoly, s. monopolio.   [silábica
monosyllabic, a. monosílabo, mono-
monosyllable, s. monosílabo.
monotonous, a. monótono.
monotony, s. monotonía.
monsoon, s. (mar.) monzón.
monster, s. monstruo.
monstrosity, s. monstruosidad.

monstrous, a. monstruoso ; -ly, monstruosamente.

month, s. mes.

monthly, s. (& ad.) mensual(mente).

monument, s. monumento.

monumental, a. monumental.

mood, s. (gr.) modo ; humor, capricho.

moodiness, s. mal humor.

moody, a. sombrío, mal humorado.

moon, s. luna.

moon-beam, s. rayos lunares, pl.

moon-shine, s. claridad de la luna ; (fig.) ilusión.

moon-struck, a. lunático, loco.

moor, s. pantano, marjal ; moro, negro ; —, v.a. (mar.) amarrar.

moot, v.a. sugerir, introducir.

mop, s. estropajo ; —, v.a. aljofifar.

mope, v.n. dormitar, entontecerse, estar triste.

moral, a.-ly, ad. moral(mente) ; ejemplo (de un cuento) ; -s, s. pl. costumbres, moralidad.

moralise, v.a. & n. moralizar.

moralist, s. moralista.

morality, s. ética, moralidad.

morass, s. lavajo, pantano.

morbid, a. enfermo, morboso.

more, a. & ad. más ; never —, nunca más, jamás ; once —, otra vez ; so much the —, cuanto más.

moreover, ad. además, también.

morning, (poet.) morn, s. mañana ; good —, buenos días, pl.

morning-gown, s. bata.

morning-star, s. lucero del alba.

morocco(-leather), s. marroquí.

morose, a. moroso ; cabezudo ; -ly, morosamente.

morrow, s. mañana. [morosamente.

morse, s. (zool.) morsa.

morsel, s. bocado.

mortal, a. mortal , humano ; -ly mortalmente ; —, s. mortal.

mortality, s. mortalidad.

mortar, s. mortero.

mortgage, s. hipoteca ; —, v.a. hipotecar.

mortgagee, s. acreedor hipotecario.

mortgager, s. deudor hipotecario.

mortification, s. mortificación ; gangrena.

mortify, v.a. (& n.) mortificar(se).

mortise, s. cotana , v.a. encajar un madero en la cotana.

mortmain, s. mano muerta.

mortuary, a. funeral ; s. casa mortuoria.

mosaic, s. obra mosaica ; —, a. mosaico.

mosque, s. mezquita.

mosquito, s. mosquito.

moss, (bot.) musgo ; moho.

mossy, a. mohoso.

most, a. lo más ; —, ad. sumamente, en sumo grado ; —, s. los más ; mayor

número ; at —, á lo más ; -ly, por lo común.

mote, s. mota ; átomo.

moth, s. polilla.

moth-eaten, apolillado. [perla.

mother, s. madre ; -of-pearl, madre-

motherhood, s. maternidad.

mother-in-law, s. suegra.

motherless, a. sin madre.

motherly, a. maternal, materno.

motion, s. movimiento, moción ; proposición.

motionless, a. inmoble, inmóvil.

motive, a. & s. razón ; motivo.

motley, mottled, a. abigarrado, gayado.

motor-car, s. automóvil.

motto, s. mote ; divisa.

mould, s. moho ; tierra ; suelo ; molde ; matriz ; —, v.a. moldar ; formar ; —, v.n. enmohecerse.

moulder, s. moldeador ; —, v.a. (& n.) convertir(se) en polvo.

mouldiness, s. moho. [miento.

moulding, s. molduras, pl., cornisa-

mouldy, a. mohoso, lleno de moho.

moult, v.n. mudar la pluma (las aves).

mound, s. terraplén, baluarte, dique.

mount, s. monte ; cerro ; —, v.a. subir, levantar ; montar ; —, v.n. subir.

mountain, s. montaña, sierra, monte.

mountain-ash, s. (bot.) mostajo.

mountaineer, s. montañés.

mountainous, a. montañoso.

mountebank, s. saltimbanco, charlatán.

mourn, v.a. deplorar ; —, v.n. lamentar ; llevar luto.

mourner, s. lamentador ; llorón.

mournful, a. triste ; -ly, tristemente.

mourning, s. lamento ; luto.

mourningly, ad. tristemente.

mouse, s. (mice, pl.) ratón.

mouser, s. gato cazador de ratones.

moustache, s. bigotes, pl.

mouth, s. boca ; entrada ; embocadura ; —, v.a. & n. mascar ; vociferar, vocear.

mouthful, s. bocado.

mouth-piece, s. boquilla de un instrumento de música. [muebles.

movable, a. movible, movedizo ; -s,

move, v.a. mover ; proponer ; excitar ; persuadir ; mover á piedad ; —, v.n. moverse, menearse ; andar ; marchar un ejército ; —, s. movimiento ; movimiento (en el juego de ajedrez).

movement, s. movimiento ; moción.

mover, s. motor, movedor ; proponedor, autor.

moving, s movimiento , —, a. patético, persuasivo ; -ly, patéticamente.

mow, v.a. segar, guadañar.

mower, s. segador, guadañero.

much, a. & ad. mucho ; con mucho.
mucilage, s. mucílago.
mucous, a. mocoso, viscoso.
mucus, s. moco.
mud, s. fango, limo.
muddle, v.a. enturbiar ; embriagar.
muddy, a. cenagoso ; turbio.
mudlark, s. muchacho vagabundo.
mud-wall, s. tapia.
muff, s. manguito ; (col.) bobo.
muffle, v.a. embozar ; envolver.
mug, s. cubilete.
muggy, a. húmedo y tibio   [morera.
mulberry, s. mora ; — -tree, moral,
mulct, v.a. multar ; —, s. multa.
mule, s. mulo ; mula.
mule-driver, muleteer, s. arriero, mulatero, mozo de mulas.
mull, v.a. templar y calentar (licor).
mullet, s. mujol, sargo (pez).
mullion, s. (arch.) columna de ventana.
multifarious, a. vario, diferente.
multiple, a. multíplice ; —, s. múltiplo
multiplication, s. multiplicación ; —
   -table, tabla de multiplicar.
multiplicity, s. multiplicidad.
multiply, v.a. multiplicar.
multitude, s. multitud ; vulgo.
multitudinous, a. numeroso.
mum, ¡ chito !, ¡ silencio !
mumble, v.a. barbotar.
mummer, s. máscara, momero.
mummery, s. momería.
mummy, s. momia.
mumps, s.pl. (med.) paperas ; (col.) mal
   humor.
munch, v.a. masticar.
mundane, a. mundano.
municipal, a. municipal.
municipality, s. municipalidad.
munificence, s. munificencia, liberalidad.
munificent, a. munífico, liberal.
muniment, s. fortificación, defensa ;
   (law) título, documento.
munition, s. municion.
mural, a. mural.   [asesinar
murder, s. asesinato, homicidio ; —, v.a.
murderer, s. asesino.
murderess, s. matadora.
murderous, a. sanguinario, cruel.
murky, a. obscuro, lóbrego.
murmur, s. murmullo, murmurio ; —,
   v.n. murmurar.
murrain, s. morriña.
muscatel, s. moscatel.
muscle, s. músculo.

muscular, a. muscular.
muse, s. musa ; meditación profunda ;
   —, v.r. meditar ; pensar profundamente.
museum, s. museo.
mushroom, s. (bot.) seta.
music, s. música.   [con armonía.
musical, a. musical ; melodioso ; -ly,
music-hall, s. sala de concierto.
musician, s. músico.
musing, s. meditación.
musk, s. musco, almizcle.
musket, s. mosquete.
musketeer, s. mosquetero.
musketry, s. mosquetería.
muslin, s. muselina.
mussel, s. marisco.
mussulman, a. & s. mahometano.
must, v. imp. & def. estar obligado ;
   ser menester, ser necesario.
mustard, s. mostaza.
muster, v.a. revistar ; agregar ; —, s.
   (mil.) revista.
muster-roll, s. lista de tropas
musty, a. mohoso, añejo.
mutability, s. mutabilidad, inconstancia.
mutation, s. mudanza ; mutación.
mute, a. mudo, silencioso ; -ly, muda-
   mente, sin chistar.
mutilate, v.a. mutilar.
mutilation, s. mutilación.
mutineer, s. amotinador, sedicioso.
mutinous, a. sedicioso ; -ly, amotinada
   mente.
mutiny, s. motín, tumulto ; —, v.n.
   amotinarse, rebelarse.
mutter, v.a. & n. murmurar, musitar ;
   —, s. murmuración.
mutton, s. carnero.
mutual, a. mutuo, mutual, recíproco ;
   -ly, mutuamente, recíprocamente.
muzzle, s. bozal, frenillo ; hocico ; —,
   v.a. embozar.
my, a. mi ; mío.
myriad, s. miriada ; gran número.
myrrh, s. mirra.
myrtle, s. mirto, arrayán.
myself, pn. yo mismo.   [teriosamente.
mysterious, a. misterioso ; -ly, mis-
mystery, s. misterio.   [mente.
mystic(al), a. místico ; -ally, mística-
mystification, s. equivocación, chasco ;
mystify, v.a. chasquear, burlar. [burla.
myth, s. fábula.
mythologic(al), a. mitológico.
mythology, s. mitología.

N

nab, v.a. (col.) atrapar, apiolar, prender.
nabob, s. nabab ; (col.) ricacho.
nacre, s. madre perla.
nadir, s. nadir.
nag, s. haca, jaca.
nail, s. uña; garra; clavo; —, v.a. clavar.
naive, a. ingenuo, simple.
naked, a. desnudo ; evidente ; puro,
simple ; **-ly,** desnudamente ; claramente, patentemente.
nakedness, s. desnudez ; claridad.
namby-pamby, a. sentimental, afectado.
name, s. nombre ; fama, reputación ; —,
v.n. nombrar ; mencionar.
nameless, a. anónimo.
namely, ad. á saber.
namesake, s. tocayo, colombroño.
nankeen,. s mahón.
nap, s. sueño ligero ; lanilla. ·
nape, s. nuca.
naphtha, s. nafta.
napkin, s. servilleta.
narcissus, s. (bot.) narciso.
narcotic, a. & s. narcótico.
narrate, v.a. narrar, relatar.
narration, s. narración, relación.
narrative, a. narrativo.
narrow, a. angosto, estrecho ; avariento ;
tieso ; **-ly,** estrechamente ; —, v.a.
estrechar ; limitar.   [pobreza.
narrowness, s. angostura, estrechez ;
nasal, a. nasal.
nascent, a. naciente.
nastily, ad. suciamente.
nastiness, s. porquería, disgusto.
nasty, a. repugnante, displicente, sucio,
puerco ; obsceno ; sórdido.
natal, a. nativo ; natal.
natation, s. natación.
nation, s. nación.
national, a. **-ly,** nacional(mente).
nationalise, v.a. nacionalizar.
nationality, s. nacionalidad.
native, a. nativo ; —, s. natural. [scopo.
nativity, s. nacimiento ; origen ; horó-
natty, a. neto, pulido, bonito.
natural, a. natural ; sencillo ; ilégítimo ;
-ly, naturalmente ; —, s. (mus.) becuadro.
naturalist, s. naturalista.
naturalise, v.a. naturalizar.
nature, s. naturaleza ; índole.
naught, s. nada.
naughtily, ad. malvadamente.
naughtiness, s. maldad, extravio, desobediencia, malignidad.
naughty, a. malo, malvado.

nausea, s. náusea, asco. [tener disgusto.
nauseate, v.a. dar disgusto ; nausear,
nauseous, a. disgustante ; **-ly,** con náusea.
nautical, naval, a. náutico, naval.
nautilus, s. nautilo.
nave, s. cubo (de rueda); nave (de iglesia).
navel, s. ombligo.
navigable, a. navegable.
navigate, v.n. navegar.
navigation, s. navegación.
navvy, s. cavador, labrador de ferrocarril
navy, s. marina ; armada.
nay, ad. no ; y aun, aun más.
near, pr. cerca de, junto á ; —, ad. casi ;
cerca ; —, a. cereano; próximo, inmediato.
nearly, ad. casi, por poco.
nearness, s. proximidad ; mezquindad.
near-sighted, a. miope.
neat, a. hermoso, pulido ; puro ; neto;
vacuno. **-ly,** elegantemente ; —, s.
vaca.
neatness, s. pulidez, elegancia.
nebulous, a. nebuloso.
necessaries, s.pl. lo necesario.
necessarily, ad. necesariamente.
necessary, a. necesario, preciso.
necessitate, v.a. necesitar.
necessitous, a. indigente, pobre.
necessity, s. necesidad.
neck, s. cuello, nuca ; — **of land,** lengua
de tierra entre dos mares.
neckcloth, neckerchief, s. corbata ; pañuelo de cuello.
necklace, s. collar.
necktie, s. corbata.
necromancy, s. nigromancia.
nectar, s. néctar.
nectarine, s. melocoton.
need, s. necesidad ; pobreza ; —, v.a.
pedir ; necesitar.   [necesariamente.
needful, a. necesario, indispensable; **-ly,**
neediness, s. indigencia, pobrezá.
needle, s. aguja.
needle-case, s. alfiletero, palillero.
needless, a. superfluo, inútil.
needle-woman, s. costurera.
needle-work, s. costura ; bordado de
aguja ; obra de punto.
needs, ad. necesariamente.
needy, a. indigente, necesitado, pobre.
nefarious, a. nefario.
negation, s. negación.
negative, a. negativo ; **-ly,** negativa-
mente ; —, s. negativa.
neglect, v.a. descuidar, desatender ; —,
s. negligencia.

negligence, s. negligencia ; descuido.
negligent, s. negligente, descuidado ; -ly, negligentemente.
negotiable, a. negociable.
negotiate, v.n. negociar, comerciar.
negotiation, s. negociación.
negress, s. negra.
negro, s. negro.
negus, s. carraspada.
neigh, v.n. relinchar ; —, s. relincho.
neighbour, s. vecino ; —, v.a. confinar.
neighbourhood, s. vecindad ; vecindario.
neighbourly, a. sociable.   [ni otro.
neither, c. ni ; —, pn. ninguno, ni uno
neophyte, s. neófito, novicio.
nephew, s. sobrino.
nepotism, s. nepotismo.
nerve, s. nervio ; vigor.
nerveless, a. enervado, débil.
nervous, a. nervoso, nervioso ; nervudo.
nest, s. nido ; nidada.
nestle, v.a. anidarse.
nestling, s. pollo.
net, s. red ; —, -t, a. neto.
nether, a. inferior, más bajo.
nethermost, a. lo más bajo, ínfimo.
netting, s. mallado.
nettle, s. ortiga ; —, v.a. picar ; irritar.
neuter, a. neutral, indiferente ; (gr.) neutro.
neutral, a. neutral ; -ly, neutralmente.
neutrality, s. neutralidad.
neutralize, v.a. neutralizar.
never, ad. nunca, jamás.
nevertheless, ad. sin embargo.
new, a. nuevo, fresco, reciente ; —, -ly, nuevamente.
new-comer, s. recién llegado.
new-fangled, a. moderno, poco probado.
newness, s. novedad.
news, s.pl. novedad, nuevas, noticias.
news-monger, s. noticiero.
newspaper, s. gaceta, periódico.
newt, s. lagartija.
next, a. próximo ; the — day, el día siguiente ; —, ad. luego, inmediatamente después.
nib, s. pico ; punta.
nibble, v.a. & n. roer, mascullar ; criticar
nice, a. delicado, exacto, solícito ; circunspecto ; tierno ; fino ; elegante ; escrupuloso ; -ly, primorosamente.
niceness, nicety, s. exactitud ; esmero ; delicadeza.
niche, s. nicho.
nick, s. punto crítico ; ocasión oportuna.
nickel, s. níquel.
nick-nack, s.   *V.* knick-knack.
nickname, s. mote, apodo ; —, v.a. poner apodos.
niece, s. sobrina.

niggard, s. hombre avaro y mezquino.
niggardliness, s. tacañería.
niggardly, a. avaro, sórdido.
nigger, s. negro.
nigh, pr. cerca ; —, ad. cerca ; —, a. cercano.   [good —, buenas noches.
night, s. noche ; by —, de noche ;
night-cap, s. gorro de dormir ; (col.) copa al acostarse.
night-fall, s. anochecer.
nightingale, s. ruiseñor.
night-light, s. vela de noche.
nightly, ad. todas las noches ; —, a. nocturno.
night-mare, s. pesadilla.
night-shade, s. (bot.) hierbamora.
nihilist, s. nihilista.
nimble, a. ligero, activo, listo, ágil.
nimbly, ad. ágilmente.
nimbus, s. auréola.
nincompoop, s. (col.),   *V* ninny.
nine, a. nueve.
nine-pins, s. juego de bolos.
nineteen, a. diez y nueve.
nineteenth, a. décimonono.
ninetieth, a. nonagésimo.
ninety, a. noventa.
ninny, s. badulaque, bobo.   [lugar.
ninth, a. nono, noveno ; -ly, en nono
nip, v.a. arañar, rasguñar ; morder ; (col.) chupar (licores).
nippers, s.pl. alicates, pl.
nipping, a. sensible (frío), picante.
nipple, s. pezón, chimenea (de escopeta).
nit, s. liendre.
nitre, s. nitro.
no, ad. no ; —, a. ningún, ninguno.
nobility, s. nobleza.   [noble.
noble, a. noble ; insigne , generoso ; —, s.
nobleman, s. noble.
nobleness, s. nobleza.
nobly, ad. noblemente.
nobody, s. nadie.
nocturnal, a. nocturnal, nocturno.
nod, s. cabeceo ; señal , —, v.n. cabecear ; amodorrarse.
node, s. nudo ; nodo, tumor.
nodule, s. nódulo.
noise, s. ruido, estruendo ; rumor ; —, v.a. divulgar.
noiseless, a. silencioso.
noisily, ad. con ruido.   [alboroto.
noisiness, s. estrépito, ruido, tumulto,
noisome, a. nocivo, malsano ; asqueroso.
noisy, a. ruidoso, turbulento.
nomad, nomadic, s. & a. nómada.
nomenclature, s. nomenclatura.
nominal, a. -ly, ad. nominal(mente).
nominate, v.a. nombrar.
nomination, s. nominación.
nominative, s. (gr.) nominativo.

nominee, s. el nombrado.
non-age, s. menor edad.
nonagenarian, a. nonagenario.
non-attendance, s. ausencia.
nonce, s. ocasión presente.
nonconformist, a. & s. no conformista, separatista.
nonconformity, s. sectas de separatistas.
non-descript, a. indescriptible, extraño.
none, a. ninguno.
nonentity, s. nada; persona insignificante.
non-performance, s. falta de ejecución.
nonplus, s. embarazo; perplejidad; —, v.a. confundir, embarazar.
non-resistance, s. sumisión pasiva.
nonsense, s. disparate, absurdo.
nonsensical, a. absurdo.
nonsuit, s. desistimiento de un proceso; —, v.a. absolver de la instancia.
noodle, s. simplón, mentecato.
nook, s. rincón.
noon, noontide, s. mediodía.
noose, s. lazo corredizo; —, v.a. enlazar.
nor, c. ni.
normal, a. normal.
north, s. norte; —, a. septentrional.
northerly, northern, a. septentrional.
north-pole, s. polo ártico.
northward(s), ad. hacia el norte.
nose, s. nariz; olfato; sagacidad.
nose-bag, s. morral.
nosegay, s. ramillete.
nostril, s. ventana de la nariz.
nostrum, s. panacea, remedio de charlatán.
not, ad. no.
notable, a. notable; memorable.
notably, ad. notablemente.
notary, s. notario.
notch, s. muesca; —, v.a. hacer muescas.
note, s. nota, marca; señal; billete; noticia; —, v.a. notar, marcar; observar.
note-book, s. librito de apuntes.
noted, a. afamado, célebre.
nothing, s. nada; good for —, a. lo que sirve para nada, inútil.
notice, s. noticia; aviso; —, v.a. observar.
noticeable, a. notable, reparable.
notification, s. notificación.
notify, v.a. notificar.
notion, s. noción; opinión; idea.
notoriety, s. notoriedad.
notorious, a. notorio; -ly, notoriamente.
notwithstanding, c. no obstante.
nought, s. nada.
noun, s. (gr.) nombre, sustantivo.

nourish, v.a. nutrir, alimentar.
nourishment, s. nutrimiento, alimento.
nous, s. (col.) seso, entendimiento.
novel, s. novela; — a. recente, moderno.
novelist, s. novelador.
novelty, s. novedad.
November, s. noviembre.
novice, s. novicio.
noviciate, s. noviciado.
now, ad. ahora, en el tiempo presente; — and then, de cuando en cuando.
nowadays, ad. hoy día.
nowhere, ad. en ninguna parte.
nowise, ad. de ningún modo.
noxious, a. nocivo, dañoso; -ly, perniciosamente.
nozzle, s. pico, boquilla.
nucleus, s. núcleo.
nude, a. desnudo, en carnes, en cueros, sin vestido.
nudge, v.a. codear.
nudity, s. desnudez.
nugatory, a. nugatorio, frívolo.
nugget, s. pepita.
nuisance, s. daño, perjuicio; incomodidad.
null, a. nulo, inválido.
nullify, v.a. anular, invalidar.
nullity, s. nulidad.
numb, a. entorpecido; —, v.a. entorpecer.
number, s. número; cantidad; —, v.a. numerar.
numberless, a. innumerable, sin número.
numbness, s. torpor.
numeral, a. numeral.
numeration, s. numeración.
numerical, a. numérico.
numerous, a. numeroso.
numismatics, s.pl. numismática.
numskull, s. zote.
nun, monja, religiosa.
nunnery, s. convento de monjas.
nuptial, a. nupcial; -s, pl. nupcias, boda.
nurse, s. ama de cría; enfermera; —, v.a. criar; alimentar.
nursery, s. crianza; plantel.
nursling, s. niño de teta.
nurture, v.a. criar, educar.
nut, s. nuez.
nut-crackers, s.pl. cascanueces.
nutmeg, s. nuez moscada.
nutriment, s. nutrimento, alimento.
nutrition, s. nutrición; nutrimento.
nutritious, nutritive, a. nutritivo, alimentoso.
nut-shell, s. cáscara de nuez.
nut-tree, s. avellano.
nymph, s. ninfa.

O

oaf, s. idiota, zoquete.
oak, s. roble.
oak-apple, s. agalla.
oaken, a. (hecho) de roble.
oakum, s. (mar.) estopa.
oar, s. remo.
oarsman, s. remero.
oasis, s. oasis.
oat, s. avena.
oatmeal, s. harina de avena.
oath, s. juramento.
obduracy, s. endurecimiento ; dureza de
    corazón.   [camente, ásperamente.
obdurate, a. endurecido, duro ; -ly, ter-
obedience, s. obediencia.
obedient, a. -ly, ad. obediente(mente).
obeisance, s. cortesía, reverencia.
obelisk, s. obelisco.
obese, a. obeso, gordo.
obesity, s. obesidad, crasitud.
obey, v.a. obedecer.
obituary, s. necrología.
object, s. objeto ; —, v.a. objetar
objection, s. oposición, objeción, réplica.
objectionable, a. displicente.
objective, a. objetivo.
oblation, s. oblación, ofrenda.
obligation, s. obligación.
obligatory, a. obligatorio.
oblige, v.a. obligar ; complacer favorecer.
obliging, a. servicial ; -ly, cortésmente.
oblique, a. oblicuo ; indirecto ; -ly, ob-
    licuamente.
obliquity, s. oblicuidad.
obliterate, v.a. borrar.
oblivion, s. olvido.
oblivious, a. olvidadizo.
oblong, a. oblongo.
obloquy, s. maledicencia ; deshonra.
obnoxious, a. sujeto , culpable , ofensivo.
obscene, a. obsceno, impúdico.
obscenity, s. obscenidad.
obscure, a. obscuro ; -ly, obscuramente ;
    —, v.a. obscurecer.
obscurity, s. obscuridad.
obsequies, s.pl. exequias.
obsequious, a. obsequioso ; servil ; -ly,
    servilmente.
observable, a. notable, conspicuo.
observance, s. observancia ; reverencia.
observant, a. observante, respetuoso.
observation, s. observación.
observatory, s. observatorio.
observe, -v.a. observar, mirar ; —, v.n.
    ser circunspecto.
observer, s. observador.   [mente.
observingly, ad. cuidadosamente, atenta-

obsolete, a. obsoleto.
obstacle, s. obstáculo.
obstinacy, s. obstinación.   [damente.
obstinate, a. obstinado ; -ly, obstina-
obstreperous, a. estrepitoso, turbulento.
obstruct, v.a. obstruir ; impedir.
obstruction, s. obstrucción ; impedi-
    mento.
obtain, v.a. obtener ; —, conseguir, ad-
    quirir ; —, v.n. estar establecido.
obtainable, a. asequible.   [forzar.
obtrude, v.a. introducir con violencia,
obtrusive, a. intruso, importuno.
obtuse, a. obtuso, sin punta ; lerdo, torpe.
obverse, s. anverso, haz principal de una
    moneda.
obviate, v.a. obviar, evitar   [mente.
obvious, a. obvio, evidente ; -ly, patente-
occasion, s. ocasión, ocurrencia ; tiempo
    oportuno ; —, v.a. ocasionar, causar.
occasional, a. casual ; -ly, de vez en
    cuando.
occidental, a. occidental.
occult, a. oculto, escondido.
occupancy, s. posesión.
occupant, occupier, s. ocupador ; posee-
    dor , inquilino.
occupation, s. ocupación , empleo.
occupy, v.a. ocupar, emplear.
occur, v.n. ocurrir ; acontecer.
occurrence, s. ocurrencia ; incidente.
ocean, s. océano ; alta mar.
oceanic, a. oceánico.
ochre, s. ocra.
octave, s. octava.
October, s. octubre.
ocular, a. ocular
oculist, s. oculista.
odd, a. impar ; particular ; extravagante ;
    extraño ; -ly, extrañamente.   [rareza.
oddity, s. singularidad, particularidad,
oddness, s. disparidad ; desigualdad ;
    singularidad.   [superioridad.
odds, s. diferencia, disparidad ; ventaja,
ode, s. oda.
odious, a. odioso ; -ly, odiosamente.
odium, s. odio.
odorous, a. odorífero.
odour, s. olor ; fragrancia.
o'er, pr. & ad.   V over.
of, pr. de ; tocante.
off, ad. fuera, lejos ; —hand, de re-
    pente ; —! ¡ fuera !.
offal, s. sobras, pl.; desecho.
offence, s. ofensa ; injuria.
offend, v.a. ofender, irritar ; injuriar ; —,
    v.n. pecar.

offender, s. delincuente, ofensor.
offensive, a. ofensivo; injurioso; -ly,
   ofensivamente.
offer, v.a. ofrecer; inmolar; atentar; —,
   v.n. ofrecerse; —, s. oferta.
offering, s. sacrificio; oferta.
offertory, s. ofertorio.
office, s. oficio, empleo; servicio.
officer, s. oficial, empleado. [empleado.
official, a. oficial; -ly, de oficio; —, s.
officiate, v.n. oficiar.
officious, a. oficioso; -ly, oficiosamente.
offing, s. pleamar.
offscouring, s. basura; lavaduras.
offset, s. pimpollo; equivalente.
offspring, s. prole; linaje; descendencia.
oft, often, oftentimes, ad. muchas veces;
   á menudo, con frecuencia.
ogle, v.a. mirar al soslayo; guiñar.
ogre, s. ogro.
oil, s. aceite; óleo; —, v.a. aceitar.
oil-cloth, s. encerado, hule.
oil-colour, s. color preparado con aceite.
oilman, s. aceitero.
oil-painting, s. pintura al óleo.
oil-silk, oil-skin, s. encerado, hule.
oily, a. aceitoso, oleaginoso.
ointment, a. ungüento.   [antiguamente.
old, olden, a. viejo; antiguo; of —,
old-fashioned, a. pasado de moda.
oleaginous, a. oleaginoso.
oleander, s. (bot.) adelfa; baladre.
olfactory, a. olfatorio.
olive(-fruit), s. aceituna.
olive(-tree), s. olivo.
olive-grove, s. olivar.
olive-oil, s. aceite de olivas.
oligarchy, s. oligarquía.
omelet, s. tortilla de huevos.
omen, s. agüero, presagio.
omened, a. fatídico, augural.   [mente.
ominous, a. ominoso; -ly, ominosa-
omission, s. omisión; descuido.
omit, v.a. omitir.
omnibus, s. ómnibus.
omnipotence, s. omnipotencia.   [deroso.
omnipotent, a. omnipotente, todopo-
omniscience, s. omnisciencia.
on, pr. sobre, encima, en; á; —, ad.
   adelante; — ! ¡ vamos !, ¡ adelante !
once, ad. una vez; — for all, una vez por
   todas; at —, de un golpe; all at —, de
   una vez.
one, a. un, uno; — by —, uno á uno.
one-armed, a. manco.
one-eyed, a. tuerto.
onerous, a. oneroso, molesto.
oneself, pn. sí mismo.
one-sided, a. desigual, parcial.
onion, s. cebolla.   [sólo.
only, a. único, solo; —, ad. solamente,

onset, onslaught, s. primer ímpetu;
   ataque.
onward(s), ad. adelante.
onyx, s. ónice.
ooze, s. fango; —, v.n. manar un
   líquido lentamente.
opacity, s. opacidad.
opal, s. ópalo.
opaque, a. opaco.
open, a. abierto; patente, evidente;
   sincero, franco; -ly, ad. con franqueza;
   —, v.a. (& n.) abrir(se); descubrir(se).
open-handed, a. dadivoso, liberal.
open-hearted, a. franco, sincero, sencillo.
opening, s. abertura; principio, oportunidad.   [ceridad.
openness, s. claridad; franqueza, sin-
open-work, s. obra á claros.
opera, s. ópera.
opera-glass, s. anteojo de ópera.
opera-hat, s. clac.
operate, v.n. obrar, operar.
operatic(al), a. de ópera.
operation, s. operación; efecto.
operative, a. operativo.
operator, s. operario; (med) operador.
ophthalmia, ophthalmy, s. oftalmía.
opiate, s. opiata.
opine, v.n. opinar, juzgar.
opinion, s. opinión; juicio.
opinionative, a. obstinado, pertinaz.
opossum, s. zorra mochilera.
opponent, s. antagonista.   [mente.
opportune, a. oportuno; -ly, oportuna-
opportunity, s. oportunidad, sazón.
oppose, v.a. & n. oponer(se).
opposite, a. fronterizo, opuesto; contrario; —, s. antagonista, adversario.
opposition, s. oposición; resistencia;
   impedimento.
oppress, v.a. oprimir.
oppression, s. opresión, vejación.
oppressive, a. opresivo, cruel.
oppressor, s. opresor.
opprobrious, a. oprobioso, ignominioso.
opprobrium, s. ignominia; oprobio.
optic(al), a. óptico, -s, s.pl. óptica.
optician, s. optico.
optimist, s. optimista.
option, s. opción.
optional, a. facultativo.
opulence, s. opulencia, riqueza.
opulent, a. opulento; -ly, opulentemente.
or, ó; ú.
oracle, s. oráculo.
oracular, a. obscuro, ambiguo.
oral, a. oral, vocal; -ly, verbalmente; de
   palabra.
orange, s. naranja.
orange-tree, s. naranjo.
oration, s. oración, arenga.

orator, s. orador.

oratorio(al), a. retórico, oratorio.

oratory, s. oratoria ; oratorio ; elocuencia.

orb, s. orbe ; esfera ; globo.

orbit, s. órbita.

orchard, s. pomar.

orchestra, s. orquesta.

orchid, s. orquídeo.

ordain, v.a. ordenar ; establecer.

ordeal, s. ordalías.

order, s. orden, regla ; mandato ; serie, clase ; —, v.a. ordenar, arreglar ; mandar.   [sición.

ordering, s. manejo ; dirección, dispo-

orderly, a. ordenado, regular ; (mil.) soldado de oficio.

ordinance, s. ordenanza.

ordinarily, ad. ordinariamente.

ordinary, a. ordinario.

ordination, s. ordenación.

ordnance, s. artillería.

ore, s. mineral.

organ, s. órgano.

organic, a. orgánico.

organisation, s. organización.

organise, v.a. organizar.

organism, s. organismo.

organist, s. organista.

organ-pipe, s. fístula de órgano.

orgy, s. orgía.

oriental, a. oriental.

orifice, s. orificio.

origin, s. origen, principio.

original, a. original, primitivo ; -ly, originalmente.

originality, s. originalidad.

originate, v.a. (& n.) originar(se).

orison, s. oración ; rezo.

ormolu, s. oro molido.

ornament, s. ornamento ; —, v.a. orna-mentar, adornar.

ornamental, a. lo que sirve de adorno.

ornate, a. adornado, ataviado.

orphan, a. & s. huérfano.

orphanage, s. orfandad.   [huérfanos.

orphanage, orphan-asylum, s. casa de

orthodox, a. ortodoxo.

orthodoxy, s. ortodoxia.

othography, s. ortografía.

oscillate, v.n. oscilar, vibrar.

oscillation, s. oscilación, vibración.

osier, s. (bot.) mimbrera.

osprey, s. águila marina.

ossification, s. osificación.

ossify, v.a. & n. osificar(se).

ostensible, a. ostensible.

ostensibly, ad. ostensiblemente.

ostentation, s. ostentación.

ostentatious, a. ostentoso, fastuoso ; -ly, pomposamente.

ostler, s. mozo de caballos.

ostracise, v.a. desterrar por medio del ostracismo.

ostrich, s. avestruz.

other, pn. otro.   [parte.

otherwise, ad. de otra manera, por otra

otter, s. nutra, nutria.   [sofá.

ottoman, a. & s. otomano, turco ; —, s.

ought, v.imp. & def. deber.

ounce, s. onza.

our, ours, a. nuestro.

ourselves, pn. pl. nosotros mismos.

oust, v.a. quitar ; desposeer.

out, ad. fuera, afuera.

outbid, v.a. pujar.

outbreak, s. erupción.

outburst, s. explosión.   [pulso.

outcast, a. desechado ; desterrado, ex-

outcry, s. clamor ; gritería.

outdo, v.a. exceder, sobrepujar.

outdoor, a. externo, campesino.

outer, a. exterior.

outermost, a. extremo ; lo más exterior.

outfit, s. vestidos, ropa, equipaje.

outfitter, s. confeccionador.

outgoing, s. salida ; -s, pl. gasto.

outflank, v.a. (mil.) ; hacer flanqueo.

outgrow, v.a. sobrecrecer, exceder en vegetación.   [galpón (am.).

outhouse, s. dependencia de una casa,

outing, s. excursión.

outlandish, a. extraño, exótico, raro.

outlast, v.a. exceder en duración.

outlaw, s. proscripto ; bandido ; —, v.a. proscribir.

outlawry, s. proscripción.

outlay, s. gastos, pl.

outlet, s. salida.

outline, s. contorno ; bosquejo.

outlive, v.a. sobrevivir.

outlying, a. distante.

outnumber, v.a. exceder en número.

out of doors, ad. fuera de casa.

outpost, s. puesto avanzado.

outrage, s. ultraje ; —, v.a. ultrajar.

outrageous, a. ultrajoso ; atroz ; -ly, injuriosamente ; enormemente.

outrider, s. palafrenero.

outright, ad. completamente.

outrun, v.a. correr más que otro.

outset, s. principio.   [eclipsar.

outshine, v.a. exceder en brillantez,

outside, s. superficie; exterior; apariencia.

outsiders, s.pl. los no admitidos.

outskirt, s. parte exterior ; suburbio.

outstretch, v.a. extenderse, alargar.

outstrip, v.a. dejar atrás ; sobrepujar.

outward, a. exterior, externo ; —, -s, hácia fuera, para el exterior ; -ly, ad. fuera ; exteriormente.

outweigh, v.a. preponderar

outwit, v.a. engañar.

outworks. s.pl. (mil.) obras avanzadas.
oval, s. óvalo ; —, a. oval.
ovary, s. ovario.
ovation, s. ovación.
oven, s. horno.
over, pr. sobre, encima ; —, ad. más, demás ; — again, otra vez ; — against, enfrente ; — and —, repetidas veces.
overall, s. sobretodo.   [respeto.
overawe, v.a. tener á freno ; imponer
overbalance, v.a. & n. volcar, perder el equilibrio.
overbear, v.a. sujetar, oprimir.
overbearing, a. imperioso, despótico.
overboard, ad. (mar.) al mar.
overburden, v.a. sobrecargar.
overcast, v.a. anublar, obscurecer ; repulgar ; —, a. nublado.
overcharge, v.a. sobrecargar ; cobrar demasiado.
overcloud, v.a. cubrir de nubes.
overcome, v.a. vencer ; superar.
over-confident, a. demasiado atrevido.
overdo, v.a. hacer con exceso.
overdraft, s. (com.) adelantos, pl.
overdraw, v.a. & n. exceder la suma del crédito ; exagerar.
overdress, v.a. engalanar con exceso.
over-eat, v.a. oir por casualidad. tupirse.
overflow, v.a. & n. inundar ; salir de madre ; rebosar ; —, s. inundación ; superabundancia.
overgrow, v.n. crecer demasiado.
overhang, v.a. estar colgando sobre alguna cosa ; salir algo fuera del nivel de un edificio.
overhead, ad. sobre la cabeza, en lo alto.
overhear, v.a. oir por casualidad.
overheat, v.a. acalorar.
overjoyed, a. muy gozoso.
overlay, v.a. abrumar.
overlook, v.a. mirar desde lo alto ; examinar ; rever ; repasar ; pasar por alto, tolerar ; descuidar ; desdeñar.
overmuch, a. demasiado.
overpass, v.a. pasar por alto ; omitir.
overplus, s. sobrante.

overpower, v.a. predominar, oprimir.
overrate, v.a. apreciar ó valuar demasiado.
overreach, v.a. engañar.
overrule, v.a. dominar, acallar.
overrun, v.a. hacer correrías ; cubrir enteramente ; inundar ; infestar ; repasar ; —, v.n. rebosar.
oversee, v.a. inspeccionar.
overseer, s. superintendente.
overset, v.a. volcar ; trastornar ; —, v.n. volcarse, caerse.
overshadow, v.a. asombrar, obscurecer.
overshoe, s. galocha.
overshoot, v.a. tirar más allá del blanco, sobresalir ; —, v.n. pasar de raya.
oversight, s. yerro ; equivocación.
oversleep, v.a. dormir demasiado.
overspread, v.a. desparramar, cubrir.
overstate, v.n. exagerar.
overstep, v.a. pasar más allá.   [mente.
overt, a. abierto ; público ; -ly, abierta-
overtake, v.a. alcanzar.
overtax, v.a. oprimir con tributos.
overthrow, v.a. trastornar ; demoler ; destruir ; —, s. trastorno ; ruina, derrota.   [obertura.
overture, s. abertura, sugestión ; (mus.)
overturn, v.a. subvertir, trastornar.
overweening, a. presuntuoso.
overweight, s. preponderancia ; exceso en el peso.   [sumergir.
overwhelm, v.a. abrumar ; oprimir ;
overwork, v.a. & n. fatigar(se), agotar(se) con trabajo.
oviparous, a. ovíparo.   [obligado.
owe, v.a. deber, tener deudas ; estar
owing, a. debido ; — to, por causa de.
owl, owlet, s. lechuza.
own, a. propio ; my —, mío ; —, v.a. reconocer ; poseer ; confesar.
owner, s. dueño, propietario.
ownership, s. dominio ; propiedad.
ox, s. buey.
oxidize, v.a. oxidar.
oxygen, s. oxígeno.
oyster, s. ostra.
ozone, s. ozono.

P

pace, s. paso ; —, v.a. medir á pasos ; —, v.n. pasear.
pacer, s. caballo de paso de andadura.
pacha, s. bajá.
pacific(al), a. pacífico.
pacification, s. pacificación.
pacify, v.a. pacificar.
pack, s. lío, fardo ; baraja de naipes; muta, perrada ; cuadrilla ; —, v.a. enfardelar, embalar, embaular ; empaquetar.

package, s. fardo ; embalaje.
packet, s. paquete.
packet-boat, s. paquebote.
pack-horse, s. caballo de carga.
packing, s. embalaje.
pack-thread, s. bramante, guita.
pact, s. pacto.
pad, s. haca ; salteador de caminos á pie, cojín, cojinillo, forro ; —, v.a. acolchar con forro.

paddle, v.n. remar ; chapotear ; —, s. canalete (especie de remo), rueda (de un vapor).
paddock, s. pradito, cercado, potrero.
padlock, s. candado.
pagan, a. & s. pagano.
paganism, s. paganismo.
page, s. página ; paje ; —, v.a. foliar.
pageant, s. espectáculo público.
pageantry, s. fasto ; pompa.
pail, s. colodra ; cubo, pozal, balde.
pain, s. pena ; castigo ; dolor ; —, v.a. afligir. [dolorosamente, con pena.
painful, a. dolorido ; penoso ; -ly,
painless, a. sin pena ; sin dolor.
painstaking, a. laborioso.
paint, v.a. & v.n. pintar ; afeitarse.
painter, s. pintor.
painting, s. pintura.
pair, s. par ; —, v.a. (& n.) parear(se).
palace, s. palacio.
palatable, a. sabroso.
palate, s. paladar ; gusto.
palatial, a. magnífico, suntuoso.
palatinate, s. palatinado.
palatine, a. palatino.
palaver, s. charla ; fruslería ; zalamería ; —, v.n. & n. congraciarse con zalamerías ; charlar.
pale, a. pálido ; claro ; —, s. palidez ; palizada, cerco.
paleness, s. palidez.
palette, s. paleta.
palfrey, s. palfrén.
paling, palisade, s. estacada, palizada.
pall, s. paño de tumba ; palio de arzobispo ; — v.a. fastidiar.
pallet, s. camilla, cama pequeña y pobre.
palliate, v.a. paliar.
palliation, s. paliación.
palliative, a. & s. paliativo.
pallid, a. pálido.
pallor, s. palidez.
palm, s. (bot.) palma ; victoria ; palma (de la mano) ; —, v.a. escamotar ; encajar, manosear.
palmated, s. palmeado.
palmer, s. pelerino.
palmistry, s. quiromancia.
Palm-Sunday, s. domingo de ramos.
palmy, a. floreciente.
palpable, a. palpable ; evidente.
palpably, ad. palpablemente ; claramente.
palpitate, v.n. palpitar.
palpitation, s. palpitación.
palsied, a. paralítico.
palsy, s. parálisis, perlesía.
paltry, a. vil ; mezquino.
pamper, v.a. mimar, engordar.
pamphlet, s. folleto, librejo.
pamphleteer, s. folletista.

pan, s. cazuela.
panacea, s. panacea.
pancake, s. buñuelo.
pandemonium, s. pandemonio.
pander, s. alcahuete ; —, v.n. obsequiar, ser indulgente.
pane, s. cuadro de vidrio.
panegyric, s. panegírico.
panel, s. entrepaño; (law) lista de jurados
pang, s. angustia, congoja.
panic, a. & s. pánico ; terror pánico.
pannier, s. cuévano, angarillas.
panoply, s. panoplia.
panorama, s. panorama.
pansy, s. (bot.) trinitaria, pensamiento.
pant, v.n. palpitar ; jadear ; to — for, or after, suspirar por. [pantalones, pl.
pantaloon, s. Pantalón, bufón ; -s, pl.
panther, s. pantera.
pantomime, s. pantomimo ; pantomima.
pantry, s. despensa de casa. [la fruta.
pap, s. pezón ; papa, papilla ; carne (de
papacy, s. papado.
papal, s. papal.
paper, s. papel ; jornal ; -s, pl. escrituras, pl. ;—, a. de papel ; —, v.a. entapizar con papel.
paper-weight, s. sujetapapeles.
papist, s. papista.
papyrus, s. papiro. [(com.) á la par.
par, s. equivalencia ; igualdad ; at —,
parable, s. parábola.
parade, s. ostentación, pompa ; (mil.) parada ; —, v.a. & n. formar parada ; pasear ; hacer gala.
paradise, s. paraíso.
paradoxical, a. paradójico, paradojo.
paragon, s. modelo perfecto.
paragraph, s. párrafo.
parallel, a. paralelo ; —, s. línea paralela ; —, v.a. parangonar.
paralyse, v.a. paralizar.
paralysis, s. parálisis.
paralytic(al), a. paralític
paramount, a. supremo, superior.
paramour, s. cortejo, manceba.
parasite, s. parásito, gorrista. [jero.
parasitic, a. parasítico, adulatorio, lison-
parasol, s. quitasol.
parboil, v.a. medio cocer.
parcel, s. paquete ; porción, cantidad ; equipaje, bulto ; —, v.a. partir, dividir.
parch, v.a. tostar.
parchment, s. pergamino.
pardon, s. perdón ; —, v.a. perdonar.
pardonable, a. perdonable.
pare, v.a. recortar.
parent, s. padre ; madre.
parentage, s. parentela ; extracción.
parental, a. paternal.
parenthesis, s. paréntesis.

parish, s. parroquia ; —, a. parroquial.
parishioner, s. parroquiano, feligrés.
park, s. parque.
parlance, s. lenguaje. [platicar.
parley, s. conferencia, plática , —, v.n.
parliament, s. parlamento.
parliamentary, a. parlamentario.
parlour, s. parlatorio ; sala de recibi-
parochial, a. parroquial. [miento.
parody, s. parodia ; —, v.a. parodiar.
paroquet, s. lorito.
paroxysm, s. paroxismo.
parricide, s. parricidio ; parricida.
parrot, s. papagayo, loro.
parry, v.n. parar (en esgrima) ; frustrar
parse, v.a. (gr.) construir.
parsimonious, a. económico, moderado en
  sus gastos ; -ly, con parsimonia.
parsimony, s. parsimonia.
parsley, s. (bot.) perejil.
parsnip, s. (bot.) chirivía.
parson, s. párroco.
parsonage, s. casa del cura.
part, s. parte ; partido , oficio ; papel (de
  un actor) ; -s, pl. partes, paraje,
  distrito ; —, v.a. partir, separar ;
  desunir ; —, v.n. partirse, separarse ;
  -ly, en parte. [parte en.
partake, v.a. & n. participar ; tomar
partaker, s. participante.
partial, a. -ly, ad. parcial(mente).
partiality, s. parcialidad.
participant, a. participante, partícipe.
participate, v.a. participar.
participation, s. participación.
participle, s. (gr.) participio.
particle, s. partícula.
particular, a. particular, singular ; -ly,
  particularmente ; —, s. particular ;
  particularidad.
particularise, s. particularizar. [stancia.
particularity, s. patricularidad, circun-
parting, s. separación, partida ; raya (en
  los cabellos).
partisan, s. partidario.
partition, s. partición, separación ; —,
  v.a. partir, dividir en varias partes.
partner, s. socio, compañero. [comercio.
partnership, s. compañía, sociedad de
partridge, s. perdiz.
party, s. partido ; parte ; tertulia ; (mil)
  partida.
party-coloured, a. abigarrado.
party-man, s. partidario, faccionario.
party-wall, s. pared medianera.
paschal, a. pascual.
pasha, s. bajá.
pass, v.a. pasar ; traspasar ; transferir ;
  —, v.n. pasar, ocurrir ; —, s. pasillo ;
  paso, camino ; pase ; estado ; condición : estocada.

passable, a. pasadero, transitable ;
  mediano, regular.
passage, s. pasaje ; travesía ; pasadizo ;
  acontecimiento.
passenger, s. pasajero.
passer-by, s. el que pasa.
passing, a. transitorio, sobresaliente ; —,
  ad. eminentemente. [muerto.
passing-bell, s. campana que toca á
passion, s. pasión ; amor ; celo, ardor.
passionate, a. apasionado ; colérico ; -ly
  apasionadamente ; ardientemente.
passion-flower, s. (bot.) pasionaria.
Passion-week, s. semana de Pasión.
passive, a. pasivo ; -ly, pasivamente.
pass-key, s. llave maestra.
Passover, s. Pascua.
passport, s. pasaporte.
pass-word, s. (mil.) santo, seña.
past, a. pasado ; gastado ; —, s. (gr.)
  pretérito ; —, pr. más allá, fuera de.
paste, s. pasta ; engrudo ; —, v.a. engrudar.
pasteboard, s. cartón fuerte.
pastel, s. pintura al pastel.
pastern, s. cuartilla del caballo.
pastime, s. pasatiempo ; diversión.
pastor, s. pastor, sacerdote.
pastoral, a. pastoril ; pastoral.
pastry, s. pastelería.
pasturage, s. pasturaje.
pasture, s. pastura ; —, v.a. pastar,
  apacentar ; —, v.n. pastar, pacer.
pasty, s. pastel.
pat, a. apto, conveniente, propio ; —, s.
  golpecillo ; —, v.a. dar golpecillos.
patch, s. remiendo ; lunar ; —, v.a.
  remendar.
patch-work, s. obra de retacitos ;
  chapucería.
pate, s. (col.) cabeza.
paten, s. patena de cáliz.
patent, a. patente ; evidente ; —, s.
  patente ; —, v.a. asegurar con patente
  (una invención).
patentee, s. privilegiado ; concesionario.
patent-leather, s. cuero de charol.
paternal, a. paternal.
paternity, s. paternidad.
path(way), s. senda. [patetícamente.
pathetic(al), a. patético ; -ally, ad
pathless, a. sin senda, intransitable.
pathological, a. patológico.
pathology, s. patología.
pathos, s. lo patético.
patience, s. paciencia.
patient, a. paciente, sufrido ; -ly, con
  paciencia ; —, s. enfermo.
patriarch, a. patriarca.
patrimony, s. patrimonio.
patriot, s. patriota,

patriotic, a. patriótico.
patriotism, s. patriotismo.
patrol, s. patrulla ; —, v.n. patrullar.
patron, s. patrón, protector.
patronage, s. patrocinio ; patronato, patronazgo.
patroness, s. patrona.
patronise, v.a. patrocinar, proteger.
patronymic, s. apellido.
patten, s. galocha ; base de columna.
patter, v.n. menudear golpecitos, como graniza ó el trotecito de niños ; recitar, charlar.
pattern, s. modelo ; ejemplar.
patty, s. pastelillo.
paucity, s. poquedad, pequeña cantidad.
paunch, s. panza ; vientre.
pauper, s. pobre.
pauperism, s. pauperismo.
pause, s. pausa ; —, v.a. pausar ; deliberar.
pave, v.a. empedrar ; enlosar, embaldosar.
pavement, s. pavimento, empedrado de calle.
pavilion, s. pabellón (tienda). .
paving-stone, s. losa.
paw, s. garra ; —, v.a. herir con el pie delantero ; manosear.
pawn, s. prenda ; peón ; —, v.a. empeñar.
pawn-broker, s. prendero.
pay, v.a. pagar ; —, s. paga ; salario.
payable, a. pagadero.
pay-day, s. día de paga.
payee, s. creditor, recibidor.
pay-master, s. pagador.
payment, s. paga ; pagamento, pago.
pea, s. (peas ó pease, pl.) guisante.
peace, s. paz ; — ! ¡ paz !, ¡ silencio !
peaceable, peaceful, a. tranquilo, pacífico.
peach, s. melocotón, durazno.
peach-tree, s. melocotonero.
peacock, s. pavón, pavo real.
peahen, s. pava real.
peak, s. cima.
peaked, a. formado en punta.
peal, s. campaneo ; —, v.a. & n. hacer resonar.
pear, s. pera.
pearl, s. perla.
pearly, a. lo que tiene perlas ó es semejante á ellas, traslúcido.
pear-tree, s. peral.
peasant, s. campesino, labriego, patán.
pea-shooter, s. cerbatana.
peat, s. turba (tierra).
pebble, s. guija ; guijarro.
pebbly, a. guijarroso.
peccadillo, s. pecadillo.
peck, picotazo ; celemín (medida de granos) ; —, v.a. picotear ; picar.
pectoral, a. pectoral ; —, s. medicamento pectoral.
peculate, v.n. robar al público. [pectoral.

peculation, s. peculado.
peculiar, a. peculiar, particular, singular . -ly, peculiarmente.   [laridad.
peculiarity, s. particularidad, singu-
pecuniary, a. .pecuniario.
pedagogue, s. pedagogo.
pedal, s. pedal.
pedant, s. pedante.
pedantic(al), s. pedantesco.
pedantry, s. pedantería.
peddle, v.a. & n. vender buhonerías, ocuparse en frioleras.
peddling, a. fútil, frívolo.
pedestal, s. pedestal.   [pedestre.
pedestrian, s. andador, peón ; —, a,
pedigree, s. genealogía.
pediment, s. frontis.
pedlar, pedler, s. buhonero.
peel, v.a. descortezar ; —, s. corteza ; pellejo (de frutas).
peep, v.n. asomar ; atisbar ; piar los pollos ; —, s. asomo ; alba ; ojeada.
peep-hole, s. atisbadero.
peer, s. compañero ; Par (grande de Inglaterra) ; —, v.n. atisbar.
peerage, s. dignidad de Par.
peeress, s. mujer de un Par.
peerless, a. incomparable, sin par.
peevish, a. regañón, bronco ; enojadizo -ly, con impertinencia.
peevishness, s. mal humor.
peg, s. clavija, espita ; —, v.a. clavar.
peg-top, s. trombo.
pelf, s. riquezas, pl.
pelican, s. pelicano.
pelisse, s. ropón, capote.
pell, s. pellejo, cuero.
pellet, s. pelotilla.
pellicle, s. película.
pell-mell, ad. á trochemoche.
pellucid, a. claro, transparente.
pelt, s. pellejo, cuero ; —, v.a. apedrear.
peltry, s. pieles.
pen, s. pluma ; caponera ; —, v.a en-jaular, encerrar ; escribir.
penal, a. penal.
penalty, s. pena ; castigo ; multa.
penance, s. penitencia.
pence, s.pl. de penny.
pencil, s. pincel ; lápiz ; —, v.a. pintar escribir con lápiz.
pencil-case, s. lapicero.
pendant, s. pendiente ; (mar.) gallardete.
pendent, a. pendiente.
pending, a. pendiente, indeciso.
pendulum, s. péndulo.
penetrate, v.a. & n. penetrar.
penetration, s. penetración, sagacidad.
penguin, s. (orn.) penguin.
pen-holder, s. portapluma,
peninsula, s. península.

penitence, s. penitencia.
penitent, a. & s. penitente ; -ly, con arrepentimiento.
penitential, a. penitencial.
penitentiary, s. penitenciario.
pen-knife, s. cortaplumas.
penman, s. pendolista ; autor, escritor.
penmanship, s. caligrafía ; profesión de escritor. [banderola.
pennant, pennon, s. (mar.) flámula,
penniless, a. falto de dinero.
penny, s. penique.
penny-a-liner, s. gacetista que recibe un penique por cada línea.
penny-post, s. correo interior.
pennyweight, s. peso de 20 granos.
penny-wise, a. económico de manera falsa ; — and pound-foolish, ganador en los gastos menores, gastador en los mayores.
penny-worth s. valor de un penique.
pension, s. pensión ; —, v.a. pensionar.
pensionary, pensioner, s. pensionista, pensionado. [camente.
pensive, a. pensativo ; -ly, melancóli-
pent, a. incluso, preso.
pentagon, s. pentágono.
Pentecost, s. Pentecostés.
penthouse, s. cobertizo, tejadillo.
penultimate, a. penúltimo.
penumbra, s. penumbra.
penurious, a. tacaño, avaro.
penury, s. penuria, carestía.
peony, s. peonía.
people, s. pueblo ; nación ; vulgo ; gente ; —, v.a. poblar.
pepper, s. pimienta ; —, v.a. sazonar con pimienta ; herir con munición menuda.
pepper-box, s. pimentero.
pepper-corn, s. semilla de pimienta.
per, pr. por.
peradventure, ad. quizá, tal vez ; acaso.
perambulate, v.a. recorrer.
perambulator, s. cochecito para niños.
perceivable, a. perceptible.
perceive, v.a. percibir, comprender.
percentage, s. tasa del por ciento.
perceptibility, s. perceptibilidad.
perceptible, a. perceptible.
perceptibly, ad. perceptiblemente.
perception, s. percepción, idea, noción.
perch, s. percha ; —, v.n. posarse.
perchance, ad. acaso, quizá.
percolate, v.a. colar ; filtrar.
percussion, s. percusión ; golpe.
percussion-cap, s. cápsula de fusil.
perdition, s. pérdida, ruina.
peregrination, s. peregrinación.
peremptorily, ad. perentoriamente ; definitivamente.
peremptoriness, s. decisión absoluta.

peremptory, a. perentorio. decisivo.
perennial, a. perenne ; perpetuo.
perfect, a. perfecto, acabado ; puro ; -ly, perfectamente ; —, v.a. perfeccionar.
perfection, s. perfección. [fidamente.
perfidious, a. pérfido, desleal ; -ly, pérfidy, s. perfidia.
perforate, v.a. horadar.
perforation, s. perforación.
perforce, ad. forzosamente.
perform, v.a. ejecutar ; efectuar ; —, v.n. representar, hacer papel.
performance, s. ejecución ; cumplimiento; obra ; representación teatral, función.
performer, s. ejecutor ; actor.
perfume, s. perfume ; fragancia ; —, v.a. perfumar.
perfumer, s. perfumero, perfumista.
perfunctory, a. superficial.
perhaps, ad. quizá, quizás, tal vez.
peril, s. peligro, riesgo. [mente.
perilous, a. peligroso ; -ly, peligrosa-
period, s. período.
periodic(al), a. periódico ; -ly, periódicamente ; —, s. jornal, periódico.
peripatetic(al), a. peripatético.
periphrase, s. perífrasis, circunlocución.
perish, v.n. perecer.
perishable, a. perecedero.
peristyle, s. peristilo.
periwig, s. peluca.
periwinkle, s. caracol marino.
perjure, v.a. perjurar.
perjury, s. perjurio.
perk, v.n. (col.) alzar la cabeza, animarse.
permanence, s. permanencia. [(mente).
permanent, a. -ly, ad. permanente-
permeate, v.a. penetrar.
permissible, a. lícito, permiso.
permission, s. permisión, licencia.
permissive, a. admisible.
permit, v.a. permitir ; —, s. guía ; permiso.
permutation, s. permutación.
pernicious, a. pernicioso ; perjudicial ; -ly, perniciosamente.
peroration, s. peroración.
perpendicular, a. -ly, perpendicular-(mente) ; —, s. línea perpendicular.
perpetrate, v.a. perpetrar, cometer.
perpetration, s. perpetración. [mente.
perpetual, a. perpetuo ; -ly, perpetua-
perpetuate, v.a. perpetuar, eternizar.
perpetuation, s. perpetuación.
perpetuity, s. perpetuidad.
perplex, v.a. confundir, embrollar.
perplexity, s. perplejidad.
perquisite, s. percance.
perry, s. cidra de peras.
persecute, v.a. perseguir, importunar.
persecution, s. persecución.
perseverance, s. perseverancia.

persevere, v.n. perseverar.
perseveringly, ad. con perseverancia.
persist, v.n. persistir.
persistency, s. persistencia.
persistent, a. persistente.
person, s. persona.
personage, s. personaje.
personal, a. -ly, ad. personal(mente) ; — estate, — goods, bienes muebles, pl.
personality, s. personalidad.
personally, s. (law) bienes muebles, pl.
personate, v.a. contrahacer otra personalidad.
personation, s. simulación de otro sujeto.
personification, s. prosopopeya, personificación.
personify, v.a. personificar. [spectivo.
perspective, s. perspectiva ; —, a. perperspicacious, a. perspicaz, penetrante.
perspicacity, s. perspicacia.
perspicuity, s. perspicuidad.
perspiration, s. transpiración.
perspire, v.n. transpirar, sudar.
persuade, v.a. persuadir.
persuasion, s. persuasión.
persuasive, a. persuasivo ; -ly, de un modo persuasivo.
pert, a. listo, vivo ; petulante.
pertain, v.n. pertenecer.
pertinacious, a. pertinaz, obstinado ; -ly, pertinazmente.
pertinacity, s. pertinacia. [cosa con otra.
pertinence, s. conexión, relación de una
pertinent, a. pertinente ; perteneciente ; -ly, oportunamente.
pertness, s. impertinencia ; vivacidad.
perturb, v.a. perturbar. [de ánimo.
perturbation, s. perturbación, agitación
peruke, s. peluca.
perusal, s. lectura, lección.
peruse, v.a. leer ; examinar atentamente.
Peruvian-bark, s. quina.
pervade, v.a. penetrar, llenar.
perverse, a. perverso, depravado ; -ly, perversamente.
perversion, s. perversión.
perversity, s. perversidad.
pervert, v.a. pervertir, corromper.
pervious, a. permeable.
pessimist, s. pesimista.
pest, s. peste, pestilencia.
pester, v.a. molestar, importunar.
pest-house, s. lazareto.
pestilence, s. pestilencia.
pestilent, pestilential, a. pestilente, pestilencial. [de mortero.
pestle, s. mano de almirez, majadero
pet, s. enojo, enfado ; favorito ; —, v.a. mimar.
petal, s. (bot.) pétalo.
petard, s. petardo.

petition, s. memorial ; petición, súplica ; —, v.a. suplicar ; requerir en justicia.
petitioner, s. suplicante.
petrel, s. (orn.) petrel.
petrification, s. petrificación.
petrify, v.a. & n. petrificar.
petroleum, s. petróleo [quiña.
petticoat, s. guardapiés, zagalejo, baspettifogger, s. abogado de guardilla.
pettifogging, a. picapleito, intrigante.
pettiness, s. pequeñez.
pettish, a. caprichudo, regañón.
petty, a. pequeño, corto.
petulance, s. petulancia.
petulant, a. petulante; -ly, con petulancia.
pew, s. banco de iglesia.
pewter, s. peltre.
phaeton, s. faetón.
phalanx, s. falange.
phantasm, phantom, s. fantasma.
pharisaic(al), a. farisaico.
pharisee, fariseo.
pharmaceutic(al), a. farmacéutico.
pharmacopœia, s. farmacopea.
pharmacy, s. farmacia.
phase, phasis, s. fase.
pheasant, s. faisán.
phenomenal, a. fenomenal.
phenomenon, s. fenómeno.
phial, s. redomilla.
philander, v.n. coquetear.
philanthropic(al), a. filantrópico.
philanthropist, s. filántropo.
philanthropy, s. filantropía.
philological, a. filológico.
philologist, s. filólogo.
philology, s. filología.
philosopher, s. filósofo. [sóficamente.
philosophic(al), a. filosófico; -ally filophilosophise, v.n. filosofar.
philosophy, s. filosofía ; natural —, física.
philter, s. filtro.
phiz, s. (col.) facha, cara.
phlegm, s. flema.
phlegmatic(al), a. flemático.
phœnix, s. fénix.
phonetic, a. fonético.
phonograph, s. fonógrafo.
phosphoric, a. fosfórico.
phosphorus, s. fósforo. [fotografiar
photograph, s. fotografía ; —, v.a.
photographer, s. fotógrafo.
photographic(al), a. fotográfico.
photograph, s. fotografía.
phrase, s. frase ; —, v.a. expresar.
phraseology, s. lenguaje, estilo.
phrenology, s. frenología.
phthisical, a. tísico, ético.
phthisis, s. tisis.
physic, s. medicina, medicamento ; -s, pl física ; —, v.a. medicinar, purgar-

physical, a. físico; **-ly,** físicamente.
physician, s. médico.
physiognomist, s. fisonomista, fisónomo.
physiognomy, s. fisonomía.
physiological, a. fisiológico.
physiologist, s. fisiologista, fisiólogo.
physiology, s. fisiología.
physique, s. físico, constitución.
pianist, s. pianista.
piano, s. pianoforte.
piaster, s. escudo (moneda).
picaroon, s. picarón.
pick, v.a. escoger, elegir; recoger; picar; —, v.n. masticar, roer; —, s. pico; lo escogido.
pickaback, ad. en espaldas.
pick-axe, s. pico.
pickerel, s. sollito (pez).
picket, s. (mil.) piquete. [escabechar.
pickle, s. escabeche, salmuera; —, v.a.
picklock, s. ganzúa.
pickpocket, pickpurse, s. cortabolsas.
picnic, s. merienda campestre, comida al fresco.
pictorial, a. pictórico.
picture, s. pintura, cuadro; —, v.a. pintar; figurar.
picturesque, a. pintoresco.
pie, s. pastel; marica.
piebald, a. pío, overo.
piece, s. pedazo; pieza, obra; cañón, fusil; —, v.a. remendar. [dividido.
piecemeal, ad. en pedazos, á trozos; —, a.
pied, a. variado.
pier, s. estribo de puente; muelle.
pierce, v.a. penetrar, agujerear, taladrar.
piercingly, ad. agudamente.
pier-glass, s. espejo grande.
piety, s. piedad, devoción.
pig, s. puerco, cerdo; lingote.
pigeon, s. palomo; paloma.
pigeon-hole, cajita para guardar cartas.
pigeon-house, s. palomar.
pig-headed, a. obstinado, estúpido.
pigment, s. afeite, pigmento, pintura.
pigmy, s. pigmeo.
pig-sty, s. zahurda.
pike, s. lucio; pica.
pilaster, s. pilastra.
pile, s. estaca; pila; montón; pira; edificio grande y macizo; pelillo (en las telas de lana); **-s,** pl. almorranas, pl.; —, v.a. amontonar, apilar.
pilfer, v.a. ratear.
pilgrim, s. peregrino, romero.
pilgrimage, s. peregrinación.
pill, s. píldora.
pillage, s. pillaje, botín, saqueo; —, v.a. pillar, hurtar.
pillar, s. pilar.
pillion, s. albarda, sillón.

pillory, s. argolla; cepo; —, v.a. empicotar, poner á un malhechor en la picota.
pillow, s. almohada.
pillow-case, s. funda.
pilot, s. piloto; —, v.a. guiar un navío en su navegación.
pilotage, s. pilotaje.
pimp, s. alcahuete.
pimpernel, s. pimpinela.
pimple, s. postilla, pupa, buba.
pimpled, a. engranujado.
pin, s. alfiler; —, v.a. prender con alfileres; fijar con clavija.
pinafore, s. delantal.
pin-case, s. alfiletero.
pincers, s. pinzas, tenazuelas, pl.
pinch, v.a. pellizcar, apretar con pinzas; v.n. ser frugal, excusar gastos; —, s. pellizco; pulgarada; aprieto.
pinch-beck, s. similor, similoro.
pin-cushion, s. acerico.
pine, s. (bot.) pino; —, v.n. estar lánguido; ansiar alguna cosa.
pine-apple, s. anana, piña.
pinion, s. piñón; ala; —, v.a. atar las alas; maniatar. [—, a. rojizo.
pink, s. (bot.) clavel; (mar.) pingüe;
pin-money, s. alfileres, pl.
pinnace, s. (mar.) pinaza.
pinnacle, s. pináculo, chapitel.
pint, s. pinta (medida de líquidos).
pioneer, s. explorador; (mil.) zapador.
pious, a. pío, devoto; **-ly,** piadosamente.
pip, s. pepita; —, v.n. piar ciertas aves.
pipe, s. tubo, cañón, conducto, caño; pipa para fumar; churumbela; —, v.n. tocar la flauta; graznar.
pipe-clay, s. arcilla refractaria.
piper, s. flautero, flautista.
piping, s. enfermizo; hirviente.
pipkin, s. pucherito.
pippin, s. (bot.) esperiega.
piquancy, s. picante.
piquant, a. punzante, picante.
pique, s. pique; desazón; ojeriza; pundonor; —, v.a. picar; irritar.
piquet, s. juego de los cientos.
piracy, s. piratería.
pirate, s. pirata, forbante.
piratical, a. pirático.
Pisces, s. Piscis (signo del zódíaco).
pish! ¡ quite allá !
pismire, s. hormiga.
pistachio, s. (bot.) alfónsigo, pistacho.
pistol, s. pistolete.
pistol-shot, s. pistoletazo.
piston, s. émbolo, pistón.
pit, s. hoyo; sepultura; patio; —, v.a. azuzar á uno para que riña.
pit-a-pat, ad. con palpitación.

pitch, s. pez ; cima ; grado de elevación ; —, **v.a.** fijar, plantar ; colocar, ordenar ; tirar, arrojar ; embrear ; —, **v.n.** caerse hacia abajo ; caer de cabeza.

pitch-dark, a. negro como la pez.

pitcher, s. cántaro.

pitchfork, s. horca ; (mus.) diapasón.

piteous, a. lastimoso ; compasivo, tierno ; miserable ; **-ly,** lastimosamente.

pitfall, s. trampa.

pith, s. meollo ; médula ; **energía.**

pithily, ad. vigorosamente.

pithy, a. enérgico ; meduloso.

pitiable, a. lastimoso.   [mosamente.

pitiful, a. lastimoso, compasivo ; **-ly,** lasti-

pitifulness, s. compasión, piedad, misericordia.   [cruelmente.

pitiless; a. desapiadado, cruel ; **-ly,**

pittance, s. pitanza, ración ; porcioncilla.

pitted, a. cavado, picado   [compadecer.

pity, s. piedad, compasión ; — **v.a.**

pivot, s. espigón, quicio.

pix, s. píxide.

pixie, pixy, s. duende.

placable, a. aplacable.

placard, s. placarte.

place, s. lugar, sitio ; (mil.) plaza, fortaleza ; rango, empleo ; —, **v.a.** colocar ; poner dinero á ganancias.   [mente.

placid, a. plácido, quieto ; **-ly,** apacible-

placidity, s. quietud, tranquilidad.

plagiarism, s. plagio.

plague, s. peste, plaga ; —, **v.a.** atormentar ; infestar, apestar.

plaguily, ad. molestamente.

plaice, s. platija (pez).

plaid, s. capa suelta de sarga listada que usan los montañeses de Escocia.

plain, a. liso, llano, abierto ; sincero ; puro, simple, común ; claro, evidente, distinto ; **-ly,** llanamente ; claramente ; —, **s.** llano, llanura, planicie.

plain-dealing, s. buena fe.   [claridad.

plainness, s. igualdad ; sinceridad ;

plaint, s. queja ; lamento.

plaintiff, s. (law) demandador.

plaintive, a. lamentoso, lastimoso ; **-ly,** de un modo lastimoso.

plait, s. pliegue ; trenza ; —, **v.a.** plegar, trenzar ; rizar ; tejer.

plan, s. plano ; delineación (de un edificio) ; —, **v.a.** proyectar.

plane, s. plano ; cepillo de carpintero ; —, **v.a.** allanar ; acepillar.

planet, s. planeta.

planetary, a. planetario.

plane-tree, s. plátano.   [entablar.

plank, s. tablón ; (mar.) tablaje ; —, **v.a.**

plant, s. planta ; —, **v.a.** plantar.

plantain, s. (bot.) llantén, plátano.

plantation, s. plantación ; colonia.

planter, s. plantador ; colono.

plash, s. charquillo, lagunajo ; —, **v.a.** salpicar.   [enyesar ; emplastar.

plaster, s. yeso ; emplasto ; —, **v.a.**

plastic, a. plástico.

plat, s. pedazo de tierra ; cintilla de paja ; estera ; —, **v.a.** entretejer.

plate, s. plancha ó lámina de metal ; plata labrada ; vajilla ; plato ; —, **v.a.** planchear ; batir hoja.

plate-layer, s. (rail.) asentador de vía.

platform, s. plataforma ; (rail.) andén.

platinum, s. platino.

platitude, s. sentencia superficial.

platoon, s. (mil.) pelotón.

platter, s. fuente, plato grande.

plaudit, s. aplauso.

plausibility, s. plausibilidad.

plausible, a. plausible.

plausibly, ad. plausiblemente.

play, s. juego ; representación dramática ; —, **v.a. & n.** jugar ; juguetear ; burlarse ; representar ; (mus.) tocar.

play-bill, s. programa de espectáculo.

player, s. jugador ; comediante, actor ; tocador.

play-fellow, play-mate, s. camarada.

playful, a. juguetón, travieso ; **-ly,** juguetonamente, retozando.

playfulness, s. jovialidad.

play-house, s. teatro.

plaything, s. juguete.

play-wright, s. poeta dramático.

plea, s. defensa ; excusa ; pretexto, socolor, efugio.

plead, v.n. & a. abogar ; alegar.

pleader, s. abogado ; defensor.

pleading, s. acto de abogar.

pleasant, a. agradable ; placentero, alegre ; **-ly,** alegremente, placenteramente.

pleasantness, s. alegría ; placer, recreo.

pleasantry, s. chocarrería, chanza.

please, v.a. agradar, complacer.

pleasing, a. agradable, placentero.

pleasurable, a. deleitable, divertido, alegre.

pleasure, s. gusto, placer ; arbitrio.

pleasure-ground, s. parque de recreo, jardín.

plebeian, a. & s. vulgar, bajo ; plebeyo.

pledge, s. prenda ; fianza ; —, **v.a.** empeñar, dar fianzas.

pleiades, s.pl. pléyadas, pléyades.

plenary, a. plenario, entero.

plenipotentiary, s. & a. plenipotenciario.

plenitude, s. plenitud, abundancia.

plenteous, plentiful, a. copioso, abundante ; **-ly,** con abundancia.

plenty, s. copia, abundancia.

pleonasm, s. pleonasmo.

plethora, s. plétora, replecion.
plethoric, a. pletórico, repleto.
pleurisy, s. pleuresía.
pliable, pliant, a. flexible, dócil.
pliancy, s. flexibilidad.   [condición.
plight, v.a. empeñar ; —, s. estado ;
plinth, s. (arch.) plinto.
plod, v.n. afanarse mucho, ajetrearse.
plot, s. pedazo pequeño de terreno ;
    plano ; conspiración, trama ; estrata-
    gema ; —, v.a. & n. trazar ; conspirar ;
    tramar.
plotter, s. conspirador.   [(la tierra).
plough, s. arado ; —, v.a. arar, labrar
plough-boy, s. arador.
plough-share, s. reja de arado.
plover, s. frailecillo (ave).
pluck, v.a. tirar con fuerza ; coger
    (flores) ; arrancar ; desplumar ; —, s.
    asadura ; arranque, tirón ; (col.) coraje.
plucky, a. guapo, gallardo.
plug, s. tapón, tarugo ; —, v.a. atarugar.
plum, s. ciruela.
plumage, s. plumaje.   [—, v.a. aplomar.
plumb, s. plomada ; —, ad. á plomo.
plumbago, s. lápiz plomo.
plumber, s. plomero.
plumb-line, s. cuerda de plomada ; nivel.
plume, -s. pluma ; plumaje, penacho ; —,
    v.a. adornar con plumas ; — oneself,
    lucirse, jactarse.
plummet, s. plomada.
plump, a. gordo, rollizo ; —, ad. de
    repente ; —, v.a. & n. hinchar ; caer á
    plomo.   [obesidad.
plumpness, s. gordura, corpulencia,
plum-pudding, s. pudín.
plum-tree, s. ciruelo.
plunder, v.a. saquear, pillar, robar ; —,
    s. pillaje, botín.   [tarse.
plunge, v.a. & n. sumergir(se), precipi-
plunger, s. buzo.
plural, a. & s. plural.
plurality, s. pluralidad.
plush, s. tripe (tela felpada).
ply, v.a. aplicar con ahinco ; importunar,
    solicitar ; —, v.n. afanarse ; aplicarse ;
    (mar.) barloventear.
pneumatic, a. neumático.
pneumonia, s. neumonía.
poach, v.a. estrellar (huevos) ; **poached
    eggs,** s.pl. huevos estrellados ; —, v.n.
    cazar en vedado.
poacher, s. cazador furtivo.
pock, s. viruela, pústula.
pocket, s. bolsillo ; faltriquera ; —, v.a.
    embolsar ; aguantar.   [cartera.
pocket-book, s. librito de memoria ;
pocket-money, s. dinero para los gastos
pod, s. vaina.   [menudos.
poem, s. poema.

poesy, s. poesía.
poet, s. poeta.
poetaster, s. poetastro.
poetess, s. poetisa.
poetic(al), a. poético ; -ly, poéticamente.
poetry, s. poesía.
poignancy, s. picante ; acrimonia.
poignant, a. picante ; punzante ; satírico;
    -ly, con satirización.
point, s. punta ; punto ; promontorio ;
    puntillo ; —, v.a. apuntar ; aguzar.
point-blank, ad. directamente, á boca de
    fusil.   [-ly, sútilmente.
pointed, a. puntiagudo, epigramático ;
pointer, s. apuntador ; perro de punta.
pointless, a. obtuso, sin punta.
poise, s. peso ; equilibrio , —, v.a. pesar,
    equilibrar.   [atosigar
poison, s. veneno ; —, v.a. envenenar,
poisoner, s. envenenador ; corruptor.
poisonous, a. venenoso.
poke, s. barjuleta, bolsa ; —, v.a. picar ;
    —, v.n. andar á tientas ; hurgar (la
    lumbre).
poker, s. hurgón.
polar, a. polar.   [coche ; percha.
pole, s. polo ; palo ; pértiga ; lanza de
pole-axe, s. hachuela de mano.
pole-cat, s. gato montés.
polemic, a. polémico ; -s, s.pl. polémica.
pole-star, s. estrella polar, estrella del
    norte.
police, s. policía.
police-court, s. tribunal de policía.
policeman, s. oficial de policía, celador,
    guardia, vigilante.
policy, s. política, astucia.
polish, v.a. pulir, alisar ; limar ; —, v.n.
    recibir pulimento ; —, s. pulimento.
polished, a. elegante, pulido.
polite, a. pulido, cortés; -ly, urbanamente.
politeness, s. cortesía.
politic, a. político ; astuto.
political, a. político ; -ly, políticamente
politician, s. político.
politics, s.pl. política.
polity, s. gobierno, policía, república.
polka, s. polca.
poll, s. cabeza ; lista de los que votan en
    alguna elección ; —, v.a. descabezar ;
    desmochar ; —, v.n. dar voto en las
    elecciones.
pollard, s. árbol desmochado.
pollen, s. (bot.) polen.
poll-tax, s. capitación.
pollute, v.a. ensuciar ; corromper.
polluter, s. corruptor.
pollution, s. polución, contaminación.
poltroon, s. cobarde, collón (col.).
polygamist, s. polígamo.
polygamy, s. poligamia.

polyglot, a. & s. poligloto.
polygon, s. polígono.
polypus, s. pólipo.
polysyllable, s. polisílabo.
polytheism, s. politeísmo.
pomade, pomatum, s. pomada.
pomegranate, s. (bot.) granado ; granada.
pommel, s. pomo de espada ; —, v.a.
pomp, s. pomp ; esplendor.   [cascar.
pomposity, s. ostentación ; boato.
pompous, a. pomposo ; -ly, pomposo.
pond, s. estanque de agua.   [mente.
ponder, v.a. & n. ponderar, considerar.
ponderous, a. ponderoso, pesado ; -ly,
   pesadamente.
poniard, s. puñal.
pontiff, s. pontífice, papa.
pontifical, a. & s. pontifical (libro).
pontificate, s. pontificado, papado.
pontoon, s. pontón.
pony, s. haca, jaca.
poodle, s. perro de aguas.
pooh, interj. ¡ caracoles !
pooh-pooh, v.a. (col.) desdeñar.
pool, s. charco ; lago.
poop, s. (mar.) popa.
poor, a. pobre ; humilde ; de poco valor ;
   estéril ; -ly, pobremente , the —, s. los
   pobres.
poor-box, s. cepo para limosnas.
poor-house, s. asilo de indigentes.
poor-law, s. ley de asistencia pública.
poorness, s. pobreza.   [de los pobres.
poor-rate, s. contribución al provecho
pop, s. chasquido ; —, v.a. & n. entrar ó
   salir de sopetón ; meter alguna cosa
Pope, s. papa.   [repentinamente.
Popedom, s. papado.
popery, s. papismo.
pop-gun, s. escopetilla con que juegan
   los muchachos.
popinjay, s. papagayo ; pisaverde.
popish, a. papal, romano ; -ly, á la
   manera de los papistas.
poplar, s. álamo.
poplin, s. moselina de lana y seda.
poppy, s. (bot.) adormidera, amapola.
populace, s. populacho.
popular, a. -ly, popular(mente).
popularity, s. popularidad.
popularize, v.a. popularizar.
populate, v.n. poblar.
population, s. población.
populous, a. populoso, poblado.
porcelain, s. porcelana, china, loza fina.
porch, s. pórtico, vestíbulo.
porcupine, s. puerco espín.
pore, s. poro.
pork, s. carne de cerdo.
porker, s. porcino, cochino.
porosity, s. porosidad.

porous, a. poroso.
porphyry, s. pórfido.
porpoise, s. puerco marino, delfín.
porridge, s. sopa de avena.
porringer, s. escudilla.
port, s. puerto ; (mar.) babor ; vino de
   Oporto.
portable, a. portátil.
portal, s. portal, portada.
portcullis, s. (arch.) rastrillo.
portend, v.a. pronosticar.
portent, s. portento, prodigio.
portentous, a. portentoso.
porter, s. portero ; mozo ; cerveza negra.
porterage, s. porte.
portfolio, s. cartera, carpeta.
porthole, s. (mar.) ventanilla.
portico, s. pórtico.
portion, s. porción, parte ; dote ; —, v.a.
   partir, dividir ; dotar.
portliness, s. porte corpulento
portly, a. majestuoso ; rollizo.
portmanteau, s. portamanteo, maleta.
portrait, s. retrato.
portraiture, s. arte de retratar.
portray, v.a. retratar.
portrayer, s. retratista.
pose, v.a. parar ; confundir ; preguntar ;
   posarse, tomar aires afectados ; —, s.
   posición, porte, ademán.   [confunde.
poser, s. examinador ; pregunta que
position, s. posición, situación ; proposición.
positive, a. positivo, real, verdadero ;
   -ly, positivamente ; ciertamente ; perentoriamente.
positiveness, s. carácter positivo ; realidad ; determinación ; obstinación.
positivist, s. positivista.
posse, s. fuerza armada.
possess, v.a. poseer ; gozar.
possession, s. posesión.
possessive, a. posesivo.
posset, s. suero, agua de leche.
possibility, s. posibilidad.   [tal vez.
possible, a. posible ; -ly, quizá, quizás,
post, s. posta, estafeta ; correo ; puesto ;
   empleo ; poste ; —, v.a. poner, apostar ;
   despachar por correo ; —, v.n. ir en
   posta, correr la posta.
postage, s. porte de carta.
postage-stamp, s. sello, sello de correo.
post-boy, s. postillón.
post-captain, s. capitán de navío.
post-card, s. tarjeta postal.
post-chaise, s. carruaje de posta.
posterior, a. posterior, trasero.
posterity, s. posteridad.
poster, s. cartel, placarte.
postern, s. postigo ; poterna.
post-haste, ad. á rienda suelta.

posthumous, a. póstumo.
postilion, s. postillón.
posting, s. viaje en posta.
postman, s. cartero ; correo.
post-mark, s. timbre de correo.
post-master, s. administrador de correos.
post-mortem,s.(med.)exámen del cadáver.
post-office, s. casa de correos.
post-paid, a. franco.   [poner:
postpone, v.a. diferir, suspender ; pos-
postscript, s. posdata.
post-prandial, a. después de comer.
postulant, s. postulante.
posture, s. postura ; positura.
posy, s. mote ; ramillete de flores.
pot, s. marmita ; olla ; —, v.a. preservar
    en marmitas.
potable, a. potable.
potash, s. potasa.
potation, s. trago.
potato, s. patata.
pot-bellied, a. panzudo.
pot-boiler, s. (col.) obra mediana, para
    ganar el pan.
pot-boy, s. mozo de cervecero.
potency, s. fuerza.
potent, a. potente, poderoso, eficaz.
potentate, s. potentado.
potential, a. potencial.
pother, s. baraúnda ; alboroto, bullicio.
pot-herb, s. hortaliza.
pot-hook, s. garabato para colgar ollas ;
    (col.) letra informe, garabato.
pot-house, s. ventorrillo.
potion, s. poción, bebida medicinal.
pot-luck, s. comida ordinaria, convite
    familiar.
potsherd, s. tiesto.
potter, s. alfarero.
pottery, s. alfar.
pouch, s. bolsillo ; faltriquera.
poulterer, s. pollero, gallinero.
poultice, s. cataplasma.
poultry, s. aves caseras.
poultry-yard, s. corral de aves caseras.
pounce, s. grasilla ; cisquero ; —, v.a.
    apomazar ; —, v.n. lanzarse, caer
    encima.
pound, s. libra ; libra esterlina ; corral
    de concejo ; —, v.a. machacar.
pound-foolish, a. pródigo.
pour, v.a. echar ó vaciar líquidos de una
    parte en otra ; arrojar alguna cosa
    continuadamente ; —, v.n. fluir con
    rapidez ; llover á cántaros.
pout, v.n. hacer muecas ; —, s. mueca.
poverty, s. pobreza ; —stricken,
    -struck, a. pobre.
powder, s. polvo ; pólvora ; —, v.a.
    pulverizar ; salar.
powder-chest, s.pl. (mar.) caja de fuego.

powder-horn, s. frasco para pólvora.
powdery, a. polvoriento.
power, s. poder ; potestad ; imperio ;
    potencia ; autoridad ;
powerful, a. poderoso ; -ly, poderosa-
    mente, con mucha fuerza.
powerless, a. impotente.
pox, s. viruelas, pl.; chicken—, viruelas
    locas, pl.; cow—, vacuna.   [cosa.
practicability, s. posibilidad de hacer una
practicable, a. practicable ; hacedero.
practical, a. práctico ; -ly, prácticamente.
practice, s. práctica ; uso, costumbre ; -s,
    pl. intrigas.
practise, v.a. & n. practicar, ejercer.
practitioner, s. práctico (médico).
pragmatic(al), a. pragmático.
prairie, s. pradería, sabana, llano.
praise, s. fama ; renombre ; alabanza ;
    —, v.a. celebrar, alabar.
praiseworthy, a. laudable.
prance, v.n. cabriolar.
prank, s. travesura, extravagancia.
prate, v.a. charlar ; —, s. charla.
prattle,v.n. charlar; —, s. parlería, charla.
prawn, s. langostín.
pray, v.a. & n. suplicar, rogar ; orar.
prayer, s. oración, súplica ; Lord's —,
    Padre nuestro.
prayer-book, s. libro de devociones.
preach, v.a. & n. predicar.
preacher, s. predicador.
preaching, s. predicación.
preamble, s. preámbulo.
prebend, s. prebenda.
prebendary, s. prebendado.
precarious, a. precario, incierto ; -ly,
    precariamente.
precariousness, s. incertidumbre.
precaution, s. precaución.
precautionary, a. preventivo.
precede, v.a. anteceder, preceder.
precedence, s. precedencia.
precedent, a. & s. precedente, ejemplo.
precentor, s. chantre.
precept, s. precepto.
preceptor, s. preceptor, maestro.
precinct, s. límite, lindero.
precious, a. precioso.
preciousness, s. preciosidad.
precipice, s. precipicio.
precipitance, precipitancy, precipitation,
    s. precipitación, prisa, inconsideración.
precipitate, v.a. & n. precipitar(se) ;
    a. precipitado ; -ly, precipitadamente ;
    —, s. precipitado.
precipitous, a. precipitoso.
precise, s. preciso, exacto ; -ly, precisa-
    mente, exactamente.
precisian, s. rigorista.
precision, s. precisión, limitación exacta.

preclude, v.a. prescindir, prevenir, impedir [maturo.

precocious, a. precoz, temprano, pre-

precocity, s. precocidad.

preconceive, v.a. opinar ó imaginar con antelación.

preconception, s. preocupación.

preconcert, v.a. concertar, convenir ó estipular de antemano.

preeursor, s. precursor.

predatory, a. rapaz, voraz.

predecease, v.a. preceder en muerte.

predecessor, s. predecesor, antecesor.

predestination, s. predestinación.

predestine, v.a. predestinar.

predicament, s. predicamento ; categoría ; embarazo.

predicate, v.a. afirmar ; —, s. predicado

predication, s. afirmación.

predict, v.a. predecir.

prediction, s. predicción.

predilection, s. predilección.

predispose, v.a. predisponer.

predisposition, s. predisposición.

predominance, s. predominio.

predominant, a. predominante.

predominate, v.a. predominar.

pre-eminence, s. preeminencia.

pre-eminent, a. preeminente.

pre-emption, s. compra de antemano.

preen, v.a. aderezar el plumaje (las aves).

pre-engagement, s. empeño anterior.

pre-existence, s. preexistencia.

preface, s. prólogo ; —, v.a. introducir con prólogo.

prefatory, a. preliminar.

prefect, s. prefecto.

prefecture, s. prefectura.

prefer, v.a. preferir, proponer en público ; exhibir.

preferable, a. preferible.

preference, s. preferencia.

preferential, a. con privilegio.

preferment, s. promoción ; preferencia.

prefix, v.a. prefijar ; —, s. (gr.) prefijo.

pregnancy, s. preñez.

pregnant, a. preñada ; fértil.

prehensile, a. (zool.) prehensil.

prehistoric, a. prehistórico.

prejudge, v.a. prejuzgar.

prejudice, s. perjuicio ; —, v.a. perjudicar.

prejudicial, a. perjudicial, dañoso.

prelacy, s. prelacía.

prelate, s. prelado.

preliminary, a. preliminar.

prelude, s. preludio ; —, v.a. (mus.) florear. [padamente.

premature, a. prematuro ; -ly, antici-

premeditation, s. premeditación.

premier, s. primer ministro ; —, a. principal.

premise, v.a. alegar al principio.

premise, s. premisa ; -s, pl. estancia, establecimiento. [prima.

premium, s. premio ; remuneración ;

premonitory, a. preventivo.

preoccupation, s. anticipación de la adquisición ; preocupación (del ánimo).

preordain, v.a. preordinar. [parada.

preparation, s. preparación ; cosa pre-

preparatory, a. preparatorio.

prepare, v.a. &(n.) preparar(se).

prepay, v.a. pagar con anticipación franquear (una carta)..

prepense, a. (law) premeditado.

preponderance, s. preponderancia.

preponderate, v.a. & n. preponderar.

preposition, s. preposición.

prepossessing, s. atractivo.

prepossession, s. preocupación ; opinion anticipada.

preposterous, a. prepóstero ; absurdo, -ly, al revés, sin razón.

prerogative, s. prerrogativa. [presagiar.

presage, s. presagio, pronóstico ; —, v.a.

presbyterian, a. & s. presbiteriano.

prescience, s. presciencia.

prescient, a. profético. [recetar

prescribe, v.a. & n. prescribir, ordenar ;

prescription, s. prescripción ; receta medicinal.

presence, s. presencia ; talle, porte.

presence-chamber, s. sala de recibimiento.

present, s. presente, regalo ; —, a. presente ; -ly, al presente ; —, v.a ofrecer, presentar ; regalar.

presentable, a. decente, decoroso.

presentation, s. presentación ; regalo.

presentation-copy, s. ejemplar regalado.

presentiment, s. presentimiento.

presentment, s. presentación.

preservation, s. preservación.

preservative, a. & s. preservativo.

preserve, v.a. preservar, conservar ; —, s. conserva, confitura.

preside, v.n. presidir ; dirigir.

presidency, s. presidencia.

president, s. presidente.

press, v.a. aprensar, apretar ; oprimir, angustiar ; compeler ; importunar ; estrechar ; reclutar por fuerza ; —, v.n. apresurarse ; agolparse la gente al rededor de una persona ó cosa ; —, s. prensa ; turba ; armario.

press-gang, s. (mar.) ronda de matrícula.

pressing, p. & a. -ly, urgente(mente).

pressure, s. prensadura; presión; opresión.

presumable, a. presumible.

presume, v.n. presumir, suponer.

presumption, s. presunción.

presumptuous, a. presuntuoso ; -ly, presuntuosamente

presuppose, v.a. presuponer.
presupposition, s. presuposición.
pretence, s. pretexto ; pretensión.
pretend, v.a. & n. pretender ; presumir.
pretender, s. pretendiente.
pretendingly, ad. presuntuosamente.
pretension, s. pretensión.
preterite, s. pretérito.
preternatural, s. preternatural.
pretext, s. pretexto, socolor.   [mente.
prettily, ad. bonitamente ; agradable-
prettiness, s. lindeza ; belleza.
pretty, a. lindo, bien parecido ; hermoso ;
—, ad. algo, un poco.
prevail, v.n. prevalecer, predominar.
prevailing, a. dominante (uso, costumbre)
prevalence, s. predominio ; superioridad.
prevalent, a. predominante, eficaz.
prevaricate, v.n. prevaricar.
prevarication, s. prevaricación.
prevent, v.a. prevenir ; impedir.
prevention, s. prevención ; obstrucción.
preventive, a. & s. preventivo, preservativo.   [antemano.
previous, a. previo ; antecedente ; -ly, de
prey, s. botín ; rapiña ; —, v.a. rapiñar,
pillar, robar.
price, s. precio ; premio.
priceless, a. inapreciable.
prick, v.a. punzar, picar ; apuntar ;
excitar, espolear ; —, s. puntura ;
picadura ; punzada.
pricking, s. picadura ; punzada.
prickle, s. pincho ; espina.
prickly, a. espinoso.
pride, s. orgullo ; soberbia ; — oneself,
v.r. jactarse.
priest, s. sacerdote, presbítero.
priestess, s. sacerdotisa.
priesthood, s. clerecía ; sacerdocio.
priestly, a. sacerdotal.
priest-ridden, a. beato, supersticioso.
prig, v.a. (col.) hurtar, ratear ; —, s.
pedante.
priggish, a. afectado.
prim. a. melindroso.
primacy, s. primacía.
primarily, ad. primariamente, sobre todo.
primary, a. primario, principal, primero.
primate, s. primado.
prime, a. primero , primoroso, excelente ;
— s. principio, madrugada, alba , (fig.)
flor, nata , primavera , —, v.a. cebar
(una arma de fuego).
primer, a. cartilla para los niños.
primeval, a. primitivo.
priming, s. cebo.   [mente.
primitive, a. primitivo ; -ly, primitiva-
primness, s. melindres.
primogeniture, s. primogenitura.
primordial, a. primordial

primrose, s. (bot.) prímula.
prince, s. príncipe, soberano.
princedom, s. principado.
princely, a. correspondiente á un prín
cipe ; real, magnífico.
princess, s. princesa.
principal, a. -ly, principal(mente) ; —, s-
principal, jefe.
principality, s. principado.
principle, s. principio ; causa primitiva ,
fundamento, motivo.
print, v.a. estampar, imprimir ; —, s
impresión, estampa, edición ; impreso ;
out of —, vendido, agotado (libros).
printer, s. impresor ; -'s reader, corrector
printing-house, printing-office, s. imprenta.   [(prelado).
prior, a. anterior, precedente ; —, s. prior
prioress, s. priora.
priority, s. prioridad.
priory, s. priorato.
prism, s. prisma.
prison, s. prisión, cárcel.
prisoner, s. prisionero.
pristine, a. prístino, antiguo.
prithee, ¡ por favor !
privacy, s. secreto ; retiro.
private, a. secreto, privado ; particular ;
— soldier, s. soldado raso ; -ly, en
secreto, en particular.
privateer, s. corsario.
privation, s. privación.   [legiar.
privilege, s. privilegio ; —, v.a. privi-
privily, a. secretamente.
privity, s. confianza ; consentimiento.
privy, a. privado, secreto, secreto ; confidente ; —, s. excusado.
prize, s. premio ; precio ; presa ; —, v.a.
apreciar, valuar ; — fight, combate de
atletas ; — money, (mar.) presa re-
partida.
pro, ad. en favor : -s and cons, argu-
mentos favorables y opuestos.
probability, s. probabilidad, verisimilitud.
probable, a. probable, verisímil ; -bly,
probablemente.
probate, s. verificación de los testa-
mentos.
probation, s. prueba, examen; noviciado.
probationary, a. probatorio.
probationer, s. novicio.   [(una herida).
probe, s. (med.) tienta ; —, v.a. tentar
probity, s. probidad, sinceridad.
problem, s. problema.
problematical, a. problemático ; -ly,
problemáticamente.
proboscis, s. probóscide.   [proceso.
procedure, s. procedimiento ; progreso,
proceed, v.n. proceder ; provenir ; portarse ; originarse ; -s, s.pl. producto ;
rédito.

proceeding, s. procedimiento ; proceso ; conducta.
process, s. proceso ; progreso.
procession, s. procesión. [publicar.
proclaim, v.a. proclamar, promulgar ;
proclamation, s. proclamación ; decreto, bando.
proclivity, s. propensión, inclinación.
proconsul, s. procónsul.
procrastinate, v.a. diferir, retardar.
procrastination, s. dilación, tardanza.
procrastinator, s. pelmazo.
procreate, v.a. procrear.
proctor, s. procurador ; juez escolástico.
proctorship, s. procuraduría.
procurable, a. asequible.
procuration, s. procuración.
procurator, s. procurador.
procure, v.a. procurar.
procurement, s. procuración.
procurer, s. alcahuete.
procuress, s. alcahueta.
prodigal, a. pródigo ; **-ly,** pródigamente ; —, s. disipador.
prodigality, s. prodigalidad. [mente.
prodigious, a. prodigioso ; **-ly,** prodigiosa-
prodigy, s. prodigio. [s. producto.
produce, v.a. producir, criar ; causar ; —,
product, s. producto ; obra ; efecto.
production, s. producción ; producto.
productive, a. productivo.
productiveness, s. fertilidad.
profanation, s. profanación.
profane, a. profano ; **-ly,** profanamente ; —, v.a. profanar.
profess, v.a. profesar ; declarar.
professedly, ad. declaradamente ; públicamente.
profession, s. profesión.
professional, a. profesional ; oficial (opuesto al aficionado).
professor, s. profesor, catedrático.
professorship, s. profesorado ; cátedra.
proffer, v.a. proponer, ofrecer ; —, s. oferta.
proficiency, s. talento, destreza.
proficient, a. proficiente, adelantado.
profile, s. perfil.
profit, s. ganancia ; provecho ; ventaja ; —, v.a. & n. aprovechar, servir, ser útil ; adelantar ; aprovecharse.
profitable, a. provechoso, ventajoso ; **-bly,** provechosamente.
profitableness, s. ganancia ; provecho.
profitless, a. inútil, sin provecho.
profligacy, s. disolución ; desarreglo.
profligate, a. licencioso, perdido ; **-ly,** disolutamente. [mente.
profound, a. profundo ; **-ly,** profunda-
profundity, s. profundidad. [fusamente.
profuse, a. profuso, pródigo ; **-ly,** pro-

profusion, s. prodigalidad ; abundancia.
progenitor, s. progenitor.
progeny, s. progenie, casta.
prognostic, s. pronóstico.
prognosticate, v.a. pronosticar. [nóstico.
prognostication, s. pronosticación ; pro-
programme, s. programa.
progress, s. progreso ; viaje, curso ; —, v.n. hacer progresos. [miento.
progression, s. progresión ; adelanta-
progressive, a. progresivo; **-ly,** progresivamente.
prohibit, v.a. prohibir, vedar ; impedir.
prohibition, s. prohibición ; auto pro hibitorio.
prohibitive, prohibitory, a. prohibitivo.
project, v.a. proyectar, trazar ; —, s. proyecto.
projectile, s. proyectil.
projection, s. proyección ; proyectura.
projector, s. proyectista.
proletarian, a. proletario, vulgar.
proletariat, s. populacho.
prolific, a. prolífico, fecundo.
prolix, a. prolijo, difuso.
prolixity, s. prolijidad.
prologue, s. prólogo.
prolong, v.a. prolongar.
prolongation, s. prolongación.
promenade, v.n. pasearse ; —, s. paseo.
prominence, s. prominencia.
prominent, a. prominente, saledizo.
promiscuous, a. promiscuo ; **-ly,** pro miscuamente.
promise, s. promesa ; —, v.a. prometer.
promissory, a. [promisorio ; — **note,** s. pagaré.
promontory, s. promontorio.
promote, v.a. promover.
promoter, s. promotor, promovedor.
promotion, s. promoción.
prompt, a. pronto ; constante ; **-ly,** prontamente ; —, v.a. sugerir, insinuar ; apuntar (en el teatro).
prompter, s. apuntador de teatro.
promptitude, promptness, s. prontitud, presteza.
promulgate, v.a. promulgar, publicar.
promulgation, s. promulgación.
prone, a. prono, inclinado.
proneness, s. inclinación, propensión.
prong, s. diente de una horca.
pronominal, a. pronominal.
pronoun, s. pronombre.
pronounce, v.a. pronunciar ; recitar.
pronunciation, s. pronunciación.
proof, s. prueba ; —, a. impenetrable ; de prueba.
proof-sheets, s.pl. pruebas.
prop, v.a. sostener ; apuntalar ; —, s. apoyo, puntal ; sostén.

propaganda, s. propaganda.
propagate, v.a. propagar.
propagation, s. propagación.
propel, v.a. impeler.
propeller, s. (mar.) hélice.
propensity, s. propensión, tendencia.
proper, a. propio ; conveniente ; exacto ;
bien parecido ; **-ly,** propiamente, justa-
property, s. propiedad ; calidad. [mente.
prophecy, s. profecía.
prophesy, v.a. profetizar ; predicar.
prophet, s. profeta.
prophetess, s. profetisa. [camente.
prophetic(al), a. profético ; **-ally,** proféti-
prophylactic, a. & s. (med.) profiláctico,
preservativo. [dad ; parentesco.
propinquity, s. propincuidad, proximi-
propitiate, v.n. propiciar.
propitiation, s. propiciación.
propitiatory, a. propiciatorio.
propitious, a. propicio, favorable ; **-ly,**
propiciamente. [v.a. proporcionar.
proportion, s. proporción; simetría ; —,
proportional, a. proporcional, pro-
porcionable. [oferta.
proposal, s. propuesta, proposición ;
propose, v.a. proponer.
proposition, s. proposición, propuesta.
propound, v.a. proponer ; sentar una
proposición.
proprietary, a. propio, proprietario.
proprietor, s. propietario, dueño.
proprietress, s. propietaria, dueña.
propriety, s. conveniencia.
prorogation, s. prorrogación.
prorogue, v.a. prorrogar.
prosaic, a. prosaico, en prosa.
proscenium, s. proscenio.
proscribe, v.a. proscribir.
proscription, s. proscripción.
prose, s. prosa.
prosecute, v.a. proseguir.
prosecution, s. prosecución ; seguimiento de una causa criminal.
prosecutor, s. acusador.
proselyte, s. prosélito.
prosody, s. prosodia.
prospect, s. perspectiva ; esperanza.
prospective, a. venidero ; próvido.
prospectus, s. prospecto.
prosper, v.a. & n. prosperar.
prosperity, s. prosperidad.
prosperous, a. próspero, feliz ; **-ly,** ad.
prósperamente. [tuta, ramera.
prostitute, v.a. prostituir ; —, s. prosti-
prostitution, s. prostitución.
prostrate, a. prosternado ; —, v.a. postrar.
prostration, s. postración.
protect, v.a. proteger ; amparar.
protection, s. protección.
protective, a. protectorio.

protector, s. protector, patrono.
protest, v.n. protestar ; —, s. protesta,
protestant, s. protestante. [protesto.
protestantism, s. protestantismo.
protestation, s. protestación ; protesta.
protocol, s. protocolo.
prototype, s. prototipo.
protract, v.a. prolongar, dilatar.
protraction, s. prolongación, dilatación.
protrude, v.a. empujar ; impeler ; —, v.n.
empujarse, sobresalir.
protuberance, s. protuberancia.
protuberant, a. prominente, saliente.
proud, a. soberbio, orgulloso ; **-ly,** sober
biamente.
prove, v.a. probar, justificar ; experimentar ; —, v.n. resultar ; salir (bien ó
mal).
provender, s. forraje.
proverb, s. refrán, proverbio.
proverbial, a. **-ly,** proverbial(mente).
provide, v.a. proveer.
provided, (— that), c. con tal que.
providence, s. providencia ; economía.
provident, a. próvido ; providente ; **-ly,**
próvidamente.
providential, a. **-ly,** providencial(mente).
province, s. provincia ; obligación par
ticular.
provincial, a. & s. provincial.
provincialism, s. provincialismo.
provision, s. provisión ; precaución.
provisional, a. **-ly,** provisional(mente).
proviso, s. estipulación.
provisory. a. provisorio.
provocation, s. provocación ; apelación.
provoke, v.a. provocar ; apelar.
provokingly, ad. de un modo provocativo.
provost, s. preboste.
prow, s. (mar.) proa.
prowess, s. proeza, valentía.
prowl, v.n. andar en busca de pillaje ;
rondar, vagar.
prowler, s. vago, ladrón, estafador.
proximate, a. próximo ; **-ly,** próxima-
mente.
proximity, s. proximidad.
proximo, a. (mes) que viene.
proxy, s. procuración ; procurador.
prude, s. mojigato, rigorista en escrúpulos.
prudence, s. prudencia. [con juicio.
prudent, a. prudente, circunspecto ; **-ly,**
prudential, a. juicioso.
prudentials, s.pl. máximas de prudencia.
prudery, s. gazmoñería, mojigatez.
prudish, a. gazmoño, melindroso.
prune, v.a. podar ; escamondar los
árboles ; —, s. ciruela pasa.
prunella, s. tela de lana.
pruning-hook, pruning-knife, s. podade a.

pruriency, s. comezón ; prurito.
prurient, a. concupiscente, lascivo.
prussic acid, s. ácido azul.
pry, v.n. espiar, acechar, atisbar.
psalm, s. salmo.
psalter, s. salterio, libro de salmos.
pseudonym, s. seudónimo.
pshaw ! | vaya !, | quita !.
psychologic(al), a. sicológico.
psychology, s. sicología.
puberty, s. pubertad.
public, a. público ; común ; notorio ; -ly, públicamente ; —, s. público. .
publican, s. publicano ; tabernero.
publication, s. publicación ; edición.
public-house, taberna.
publicist, s. publicista.
publicity, s. publicidad.
publish, v.a. publicar.
publisher, s. publicador, editor.
puce, a. & s. purpúreo.
puck, s. duende.
pucker, v.a. arrugar, hacer pliegues.
pudding, s. pudín, morcilla.
puddle, s. lodazal, cenagal ; —, v.a. enlodar ; enturbiar el agua con lodo.
pudenda, s. partes vergonzosas, pl.
pudicity, s. pudor, recato.
puerile, a. pueril.
puff, s. bufido, soplo ; borla para empolvar ; rizado ; reclamo ; —, v.a. hinchar ; soplar ; ensoberbecer ; —, v.n. inflarse ; bufar ; resoplar.
puffiness, s. hinchazón.
puffing, s. reclamo.
puffy, a. hinchado, entumecido.
pug, s. perrillo fino.
pugilism, s. pugilato.
pugilist, s. pugil.
pugnacious, a. pugnaz.
pug-nose, s. nariz chata.
puisne, a. (law) inferior ; segundón (juez).
puke, v.n. vomitar.
puling, s. gemido ; piamiento.
pull, v.a. tirar ; coger ; rasgar, desgarrar ; to — off, arrancar ; —, s. pullet, s. polla. [tirón ; sacudida.
pulley, s. polea, garrucha.
pulmonary, pulmonic(al), a. pulmoníaco.
pulp, s. pulpa.
pulpit, s. púlpito.
pulpy, a. pulposo.
pulsate, v.n. pulsar, latir.
pulsation, s. pulsación.
pulse, s. pulso ; legumbres, pl.
pulverization, s. pulverización.
pulverize, v.a. pulverizar.
pumice, s. piedra pómez.
pummel, v.a. golpear, pegar.
pump, s. bomba ; escarpín ; —, v.a. dar á la bomba ; sondear ; sonsacar.

pumpkin, s. calabaza. [mas.
pump-room, s. pabellón para beber termun, s. equívoco, chiste ; —, v.n. jugar del vocablo, decir equívocos.
punch, s. punzón ; ponche (bebida) ; arlequín. [veinte arrobas.
puncheon, s. punzón ; cuño ; medida de
punchinello, s. títere, bufón.
punctilio, s. puntillo.
punctilious, a. puntoso, escrupuloso.
punctual, a. puntual, exacto ; -ly, puntualmente.
punctuality, s. exactitud, puntualidad.
punctuate, v.n. puntuar.
punctuation, s. pintuación.
puncture, s. puntura.
pundit, s. erudito.
pungency, s. acrimonia ; picante.
pungent, a. picante, acre, mordaz.
punic, a. púnico.
punish, v.a. castigar, penar.
punishable, a. punible.
punishment, s. castigo ; pena.
punster, s. dichero.
punt, v.a. apuntar, parar (poner el dinero á las cartas) ; —, s. barco llano
punter, s. apuntador (en el juego de faraón).
puny, a. pequeño, débil, inferior.
pup, s. cachorrillo ; —, v.n. parir la perra.
pupil, s. pupilo ; pupila ; discípulo.
pupilage, s. pupilaje.
puppet, s. títere, muñeco.
puppet-show, s. representación de títeres
puppy, s. perrillo ; (col.) trasto, pisaverde
purblind, a. miope, cegató.
purchase, v.a. comprar ; mercar ; —, s. compra ; adquisición.
purchaser, s. comprador.
pure, a. puro ; -ly, puramente.
purgation, s. purgación.
purgative, a. purgativo.
purgatory, s. purgatorio.
purge, v.a. purgar.
purification, s. purificación.
purify, v.a. purificar.
purist, s. purista.
puritan, s. puritano.
purity, s. pureza.
purl, s. cerveza calentada ; murmullo ; —, v.n. murmurar.
purlieu, s. comarca.
purloin, v.a. hurtar, robar.
purple, a. purpúreo ; —, s. púrpura.
purport, s. designio ; contenido ; —, v.a. significar, designar.
purpose, s. intención ; designio, proyecto ; to the —, al propósito ; to no —, inútilmente ; on —, de propósito ; —, v.n. proponer.
purposeless, a. inútil.

purr, v.n. susurrar (los gatos).
purse, s. bolsa ; —, v.a. embolsar.
purse-proud, a. plutocrático.
purslain, s. (bot.) verdolaga.
pursuance, s. prosecución.
pursuant, a. consiguiente.
pursue, v.a. & n. perseguir ; seguir, acosar ; continuar.
pursuit, s. perseguimiento ; ocupación.
pursy, a. gordito, asmático.
purulence, s. purulencia.
purulent, a. purulento.
purvey, v.a. & n. proveer ; procurar.
purveyance, s. abasto ; provisión.
purveyor, s. abastecedor, proveedor.
purview, s. objeto, límites.
pus, s. (med.) pus.
push, v.a. empujar ; estrechar, apretar ; —, v.n. hacer esfuerzos ; —, s. impulso; empujón ; esfuerzo ; asalto.
pushing, a. emprendedor.
pusillanimity, s. pusilanimidad.

pusillanimous, a. pusilánime.
puss(y), s. miz (vos de cariño para el gato).
pustule, s. pústula.
put, v.a. poner, meter, colocar ; propoa er ; imponer, obligar ; — off, dilatar.
putative, a. putativo, reputado.
putrefaction, s. putrefacción.
putrefy, v.a. pudrirse.
putrescence, s. pudrición.
putrescent, putrid, a. podrido, pútrido.
putridness, s. podredumbre, pudrición.
putty, s. cimento.
puzzle, s. embarazo ; perplejidad ; —, v.a. embrollar ; —, v.n. confundirse.
pygmy, s. V. pigmy.
pyramid, s. pirámide.
pyramidal, a. piramidal.
pyre, s. pira, hoguera.
pyrotechnics, s.pl. pirotecnia.
python, s. (zool.) boa.
pythoness, s. pitonisa.
pyx, s. pixide, copón.

Q

quack, v.n. graznar (como un pato) ; —, s. charlatán.
quackery, s. charlatanería.
quadragesima, s. cuadragésima.
quadrangle, s. cuadrángulo.
quadrant, s. cuadrante.
quadrennial, a. cuadrienal.
quadrilateral, a. cuadrilátero.
quadrille, s. contradanza.
quadroon, s. cuarterón.
quadruped, s. cuadrúpedo.
quadruple, a. cuádruplo.
quaff, v.a. beber á grandes tragos.
quagmire, s. tremedal.
quail, s. codorniz.
quaint, a. curioso, original.
quaintness, s. curiosidad.
quake, v.n. temblar ; tiritar.
quaker, s. cuácaro (sectario).
qualification, s. calificación ; prendas.
qualify, v.a. calificar ; modificar ; templar ; — v.n. prepararse, cumplir lo debido (un pretendiente).
qualitative, a. cualitativo.
quality, s. calidad.
qualm, s. nausea, escrúpulo.
qualmish, a. desfallecido, lánguido.
quandary, s. incertidumbre, embarazo.
quantitative, a. cuantitativo.
quantity, s. cantidad.
quantum, s. tanto, porción.
quarantine, s. cuarentena.
quarrel, s. quimera, riña, contienda ; —, v.n. reñir, disputar.
quarreller, s. quimerista.

quarrelsome, a. pendenciero, quimerista.
quarry, s. cantera ; (sport) presa, animal de caza.
quarryman, s. cavador de cantera.
quart, s. cuarta (en el juego de los cientos) ; media azumbre.
quartan, s. cuartana.
quarter, s. cuarto ; cuarta parte ; cuartel ; barrio ; — of an hour, un cuarto de hora ; —, v.a. cuartear ; acuartelar.
quarter-day, s. día trimestral de paga.
quarter-deck, s. (mar.) alcázar.
quarterly, a. trimestral.
quartern, s. cuarta parte de una medida
quarter-sessions, s.pl. (law) sesión trimestral de los tribunales.
quartet, s. (mus.) cuarteto.
quarto, s. libro en cuarto.
quartz, s. (min.) cuarzo.
quash, v.a. fracasar ; cascar ; anular, abrogar. [goritear, trinar.
quaver, s. (mus.) corchea ; —, v.n. gorquay, s. muelle.
quean, s. mujercilla.
queasiness, s. hastío.
queasy, a. nauseabundo ; fastidioso.
queen, s. reina ; dama (en el juego de damas y en el ajedrez). [mente.
queer, a. estraño ; ridículo ; -ly, ridiculaqueerness, s. rareza, ridiculez.
quell, v.a. subyugar, postrar, avasallar.
quench, v.a. apagar ; extinguir
quenchless, a. inextinguible
querist, s. inquisidor, preguntador.
querulous, a. quejoso ; -ly, quejosamente.

querulousness, s. la disposición ó costumbre de quejarse.   [guntar.
query, s. cuestión, pregunta ; —, v.a. pre-
quest, s. pesquisa, inquisición, busca.
question, s. cuestión ; disquisición ; duda; cuestión de tormento ; —, v.a. cuestionar, preguntar ; —, v.n. dudar, desconfiar.
questionable, a. cuestionable, dudoso.
questioner, s. inquiridor, preguntador.
quibble, s. argumento engañoso ; —, v.n. cavilar, decir equívocos.
quick, a. vivo, viviente ; veloz ; ligero; pronto ; ágil, ardiente, penetrante ; **-ly,** con presteza ; —, s. carne viva.
quicken, v.a. vivificar ; acelerar ; animar.
quick-lime, s. cal viva.   [penetración.
quickness, s. [presteza ; actividad ; viveza.
quick-sand, s. arena movediza.
quickset, s. plantón ; —hedge, seto vivo.
quicksilver, s. azogue, mercurio.
quick-witted, a. agudo, perspicaz.
quid, s. pedazo de tabaco que mascan los marineros.
quiddity, s. esencia, cuestión sutil, cavilación, trampa legal.
quidnunc, s. fanfarrón.
quiescence, s. quietud.
quiescent, a. quieto, descansado.
quiet, a. quedo, quieto, tranquilo ; **-ly,** quietamente.
quietism, s. tranquilidad de ánimo.
quietness, quietude, s. quietud, tranquilidad ; finiquito ; muerte.   [dad.
quietus, s. finiquito ; muerte.
quill, s. pluma (para escribir).

quill-driver, s. cagatinta.
quilt, s. colcha.
quince, s. (bot.) membrillero, membrillo.
quincunx, s. quincunce.
quinine, s. quinina.
quinquennial, a. quinquenal.
quinsy, s. esquinancia, angina.   [naipes).
quint, s. quinta (en algunos juegos de
quintescence, s. quinta esencia.
quintet, s. (mus.) quinteto.
quintuple, a. quíntuplo.
quip, s. indirecta ; —, v.a. echar pullas.
quire, s. mano de papel.
quirk, s. pulla ; sutileza.
quit, v.a. descargar ; desempeñar ; absolver ; dejar, abandonar ; —, a. libre, descargado.
quite, ad. totalmente, enteramente, absolutamente.
quits, ¡ en paz !
quittance, s. finiquito, desempeño.
quiver, s. aljaba ; —, v.n. temblar ; **-ed,** a. armado con aljaba.
quixotic, a. quijotesco.
quiz, v.a. burlar, chulear.
quizzing-glass, s. anteojo de puño.
quoit, s. tejo.
quondam, a. antiguo.
quorum, s. número competente de jueces
quota, s. cuota.
quotation, s. citación, cita.
quote, v.a. citar.
quoth, v.imp. — **I,** dije yo ; — **he,** él dijo.
quotidian, a. cotidiano.
quotient, s. cuociente.

R

rabbet, s. ranura.
rabbi, s. rabí, rabino.
rabbit, s. conejo.
rabble, s. gentuza, canalla.
rabid, a. rabioso, furioso.
race, s. raza, casta ; carrera ; —, v.n. correr con ligereza.
racer, s. caballo de carrera.
racial, a. de raza.
raciness, s. calidad rancia del vino ; gracia en conversación.   [ciega.
racing, s. corrida de caballos, carrera
rack, s. tormento ; rueca ; morillos de asador, pl.; —, v.n. atormentar.
racket, s. baraúnda, confusión; raqueta.
rack-rent, s. arriendo suficiente.
racy, a. rancio ; entretenido, gracioso.
radiance, s. brillo, esplendor.
radiant, a. radiante, brillante.
radiate, v.n. echar rayos, centellear.
radiation, s. radiación.
radical, a. -ly, radical(mente).

radicalism, s. radicalismo.
radish, s. rábano.
radius, s. radio, semidiámetro.
raffle, s. rifa (juego) ; —, v.n. rifar.
raft, s. balsa ; jangada.
rafter, s. cabrio, viga.
rag, s. trapo, andrajo, girón.
ragamuffin, s. andrajo, mendigo, pordiosero ; bribón.   [encolerizarse.
rage, s. rabia ; furor ; —, v.n. rabiar ;
rag-gatherer, (—man, —picker), s. trapero.
ragged, a. andrajoso.   [mente.
raging, s. furia, rabia ; **-ly,** rabiosa-
raid, s. invasión.
raider, s. merodeador.
rail, s. baranda, barrera ; balaustrada ; (rail.) rail, riel, carril de los caminos de hierro ; —, v.a. cercar con balaustradas ; —, v.n. injuriar de palabra.
railer, s. maldiciente, murmurador.
raillery, s. chocarrería, burla.

railroad, railway, s. ferrocarril.
raiment, s. ropa ; vestido.
rain, s. lluvia ; —, v.n. llover.
rainbow, s. arco íris, arco celeste.
rain-water, s. agua llovediza.
rainy, a. lluvioso.
raise, v.a. levantar, alzar ; fabricar, edificar ; engrandecer, elevar ; excitar, causar.
raisin, s. pasa (uva seca).   [sar.
rake, s. rastro, rastrillo ; tunante, calavera ; —, v.a. rastrillar ; raer ; rebuscar.
rakish, a. libertino, disoluto.
rally, v.a. (mil.) reunir ; ridiculizar ; —, v.n. reunirse.   [peler con violencia.
ram, s. morueco ; ariete ; —, v.a. impeler con violencia.
ramble, v.n. vagar ; callejear ; —, s. correría, paseo.
rambler, s. vagabundo, callejero.
ramification, s. ramificación.
ramify, v.n. ramificarse.
rammer, s. maza ; baqueta de escopeta.
rampant, a. exuberante.
rampage, v.n. (col.) excitarse, meter barullo.   [muralla.
rampart, s. plataforma ; terraplén ; (mil.)
ramrod, s. baqueta ; atacador.
ramshackle, a. ruinoso.
rancid, a. rancio.
rancidity, s. rancidez.
rancour, s. rencor.   [trochemoche.
random, s. ventura, casualidad ; at —, á
range, v.a. colocar, ordenar ; cerner ; —, v.n. vagar ; —, s. clase ; orden ; hilera ; correría ; alcance de un tiro, aparato de cocina inglés.
ranger, s. andador ; guardabosque.
rank, a. exuberante ; rancio ; fétido ; —, s. fila, hilera, clase ; grado de dignidad.
rankle, v.n. enconarse, inflamarse.
rankness, s. exuberancia ; olor ó gusto rancio ; fuerza, vigor.
ransack, v.a. registrar ; saquear, pillar.
ransom, v.a. rescatar ; —, s. rescate.
rant, v.n. decir disparates ; descantar.
ranter, s. declamador.
rap, v.a. & n. dar un golpe vivo y repentino ; arrebatar ; —, s. golpe ligero y vivo.
rapacious, a. rapaz ; -ly, con rapacidad.
rapacity, s. rapacidad.   [silvestre.
rape, s. fuerza ; estupro ; (bot.) nabo
rapid, a. rápido ; -ly, rápidamente.
rapidity, s. rapidez.
rapids, s.pl. catarata.
rapier, s. espadín.
rapine, s. rapiña.
rappee, s. rapé.
rapper, s. llamador ∠ aldabón de puerta.
rapscallion, s. bribón.
rapt. a. encantado, enajenado.

rapture, s. éxtasis.
rapturous, a. delicioso.   [mente.
rare, a. raro, extraordinario ; -ly, rararareeshow, s. mundinovi, mundinuevo.
rarefaction, s. rarefacción.
rarefy, v.a. rarificar.
rarity, s. raridad, rareza.
rascal, s. pícaro, bribón.
rascality, s. pillada.
rascallion, s. villano.
rase, v.a. arrasar, destruir.
rash, a. precipitado, temerario ; -ly, temerariamente ; —, s. roncha.
rasher, s. torrezno.
rashness, s. temeridad, arrojo.
rasp, s. raspador ; —, v.a. raspar ; escofinar.   [bueso.
raspberry, s. frambuesa ; —bush, framrat, s. rata ; —, v.n. (col.) desertar.
rate, s. tasa, precio, valor ; grado manera ; —, v.a. tasar, apreciar ; reñir.
rather, ad. más bien ; antes.
ratification, s. ratificación.
ratify, v.a. ratificar.
ratio, s. razón.
ration, s. (mil.) ración ; proporción.
rational, a. racional ; razonable ; -ly, racionalmente.
rationality, s. razón, luz natural.
rat's-bane, s. arsénico.   [Malaya).
rattan, s. (bot.) rotén, rota (caña de
ratteen, s. ratina (tela de lana).
rattle, v.a. & n. hacer ruido, regañar ; zumbar, zurrir ; —, s. sonido rechino, sonajero.
rattle-snake, s. culebra de cascabel.
raucus, a. ronco.   [s. saqueo.
ravage, v.a. saquear, pillar ; asolar ; —.
rave, v.n. delirar ; enfurecerse.
ravel, v.a. embrollar ; —, v.n. enredarse.
raven, s. cuervo.
ravenous, a. -ly, voraz(mente).
ravine, s. barranca.
raving, a. furioso, frenético.
ravish, v.a. estuprar ; arrebatar.
ravisher, s. estuprador, forzador.
ravishingly, ad. de un modo encantador.
ravishment, s. rapto ; éxtasis.
raw, a. crudo ; puro ; nuevo ; novato.
raw-boned, a. huesudo ; magro.
rawness, s. crudeza ; inexperiencia.
ray, s. rayo de luz ; raya (pez).
rayless, a. sin brillo, apagado.
raze, v.a. arrasar, extirpar ; borrar.
razor, s. navaja de barbero.
reach, v.a. alcanzar ; llegar hasta ; —, v.n. extenderse, llegar ; alcanzar, penetrar ; esforzarse ; —, s. alcance, poder ; capacidad ; astucia.   [accionar.
react, v.a. obrar reciprocamente ; rereaction, s. reacción.

read, v.a. leer ; enseñar en público ; —,
    v.n. estudiar.
readable, a. legible.
reader, s. lector.
readily, ad. prontamente ; de buena gana.
readiness, s. facilidad ; vivacidad del
    ingenio ; voluntad, gana ; prontitud.
reading, s. lectura.
reading-room, s. gabinete de lectura.
re-adjust, v.a. recomponer.
ready, a. listo, pronto ; inclinado ; fácil ;
    ligero ; —, ad. prontamente, presto.
ready-made, a.hecho sin medida (vestido).
ready-money, s. moneda contante.
real, a. real, verdadero, efectivo ; -ly,
    realmente.
realism, s. realismo.
reality, s. realidad, entidad.
realization, s. realización.
realize, v.a. realizar.
realm, s. reino.
realty, real estate, s. bienes inmobles.
ream, s. resma.
re-animate, v.a. reanimar.
reap, v.a. segar.
reaper, s. segador.
reaping-hook, s. hoz.
reappear, v.n. reaparecer.
rear, s. retaguardia ; última clase ; —,
    v.a. & n. levantar(se) alzar(se).
rear-admiral, s. contraalmirante.
rear-guard, s. retaguardia.
re-ascend, v.n. volver á subir.
reason, s. razón ; causa, motivo ; —, v.a.
    & n. razonar, raciocinar.
reasonable, a. razonable.
reasonableness, s. razón ; racionalidad.
reasonably, ad. razonablemente.
reasoner, s. razonador.
reasoning, s. raciocinio.
re-assure, v.a. reanimar ; (com.) dar un
    nuevo seguro.
rebate, v.a. rebajar.
rebel, s. rebelde ; —, v.n. rebelarse.
rebellion, s. rebelión.
rebellious, a. rebelde.   [saltar.
rebound, v.n. repercutir, rebotar, re-
rebuff, s. resistencia, denegación, derrota;
    —, v.a. rechazar.
rebuild, v.a. reedificar.   [reprensión.
rebuke, v.a. reprender, regañar ; —, s.
rebus, s. acertijo.
rebut, v.a. rechazar, repeler.
recalcitrant, s. recalcitrante.
recall, v.a. revocar ; —, s. revocación.
recant, v.a.& n. retractar(se), desdecir(se).
recantation, s. retractación.
recapitulate, v.a. recapitular.
recapitulation, s. recapitulación.
recapture, s. represa ; —, v.a. recobrar.
recede, v.n. retroceder ; desistir.

receipt, s. recibo ; receta ; -s, s.pl. (com.)
receivable, a. recibidero.   [ingresos.
receive, v.a. recibir ; aceptar, admitir.
recent, a. reciente, nuevo ; fresco ; -ly,
    recientemente.
receptacle, s. receptáculo.
reception, s. acogida.
recess, s. rincón, retiro ; fondo.
recession, s. retirada.
recipe, s. receta.
recipient, s. recipiente.   [mente
reciprocal, a. recíproco ; -ly, recíproca-
reciprocate, v.a. reciprocar, corresponder.
reciprocity, s. reciprocidad.
recital, recitation, s. recitación.
recitative, s. (mus.) recitativo.
recite, v.a. recitar ; referir, relatar.
reck, v.n. & n. cuidar.   [con descuido.
reckless, a. descuidado, omiso ; -ly,
reckon, v.a. contar, numerar ; —, v.n.
    computar, calcular.
reckoning, s. cuenta ; calculación.
reclaim, v.a. reformar, corregir ; re-
reclaimable, a. redimible.   [clamar.
recline, v.a. & n. reclinar ; reposar.
recluse, a. recluso, retirado ; —, s. per-
    sona retirado del mundo.
reclusion, s. reclusión.   [gación.
recognisance, s. reconocimiento ; obli-
recognise, v.a. reconocer.
recognition, s. reconocimiento ; recuerdo.
recoil, v.n. recular.
recollect, v.a. acordarse ; recobrarse.
recollection, s. recuerdo ; reminiscencia.
recommence, v.a. empezar de nuevo.
recommend, v.a. recomendar.
recommendation, s. recomendación.
recommendatory, a. recomendatorio.
recompense, s. recompensa, premio ; —,
    v.a. recompensar.
recompose, v.a. recomponer.
reconcilable, a. reconciliable.
reconcile, v.a. reconciliar.
reconciliation, s. reconciliación.
recondite, a. recondito, reservado.
reconnaisance, s. (mil.) reconocimiento.
reconnoitre, v.a. (mil.) reconocer.
reconsider, v.a. considerar de nuevo.
reconstruct, v.a. reedificar, reconstruir.
record, v.a. registrar ; protocolar ; —, s.
    registro, archivo ; -s, pl. anales.
recorder, s. registrador, archivero ; juez
    municipal.
recount, v.a. referir ; contar de nuevo.
recourse, s. recurso.
recover, v.a. recobrar ; reparar ; restab-
    lecer ; —, v.n. convalecer, restable-
    cerse , to — one's self, volver en sí.
recoverable, a. recuperable.
recovery, s. convalecencia ; recobro.
recreant, a. & s. cobarde ; apóstata.

recreate, v.a. recrear, deleitar, divertir.
recreation, s. recreación.
recreative, s. recreativo.
recriminate, v.a. & n. recriminar.
recrimination, s. recriminación.
recrudescence, s. recrudescencia.
recruit, v.a. reclutar ; to — one's self, restablecerse ; —, s. (mil.) recluta.
recruiting, s. recluta, reclutamiento.
rectangle, s. rectángulo.
rectangular, a. rectangular.
rectification, s. rectificación.
rectify, v.a. rectificar.
rectilinear, a. rectilíneo.
rectitude, s. rectitud, derechura.
rector, s. rector ; párroco ; jefe.
rectorship, s. rectorado.
rectorial, a. rectoral.
rectory, s. rectoría ; casa del rector (cura).
recumbent, a. recostado, reclinado.
recuperative, a. recuperativo.
recur, v.n. recurrir.
recurrence, s. retorno ; vuelta.
recurrent, a. repetido, periódico.
recusant, s. nonconformista.
red, a. rojo, colorado, rubio ; —, s. rojez.
redan, s. (mil.) estrella.
red-breast, s. pitirrojo.
redcoat, s. soldado inglés.
redden, v.a. teñir de color rojo ; —, v.n. ponerse colorado.
reddish, a. rojizo.
redeem, v.a. redimir, rescatar.
redeemable, a. redimible.
redeemer, s. redentor.
redemption, s. redención.
red-handed, a. fragante, en el acto.
red-hot, a. candente, ardiente.
red-lead, s. minio.
red-letter day, s. día colendo, día festivo.
redness, s. rojez, bermejura.
redolence, s. fragancia.
redolent, a. fragante, fragrante, oloroso.
redouble, v.a. (& n.) redoblar(se).
redoubt, s. (mil.) reducto.
redoubtable, a. formidable, terrible.
redound, v.n. redundar.
redress, v.a. corregir ; reformar ; rectificar —, s. reforma, corrección.
red-tape, s. (col.) enredos oficiales.
reduce, v.a. reducir ; disminuir ; sujetar.
reducible, a. reducible.
reduction, s. reducción.
redundancy, s. redundancia.
redundant, a. redundante, superfluo.
reduplicate, v.a. reduplicar.
reduplication, s. reduplicación.
re-echo, v.n. resonar.
reed, s. caña ; flecha.
reef, v.a. (mar.) tomar rizos á las velas ; —, s. arrecife.

reek, s. humo, vapor ; —, v.n. humear ; vahear ; oler.
reel, s. aspa, devanadera ; un baile ; —, v.a. aspar ; —, v.n. vacilar al andar.
re-election, s. reelección.
re-engage, v.a. empeñar de nuevo.
re-enter, v.a. volver á entrar.
re-establish, v.a. restablecer. [restauración
re-establishment, s. restablecimiento ;
refection, s. refección.
refectory, s. refectorio.
refer, v.a. & n. referir, remitir ; referirse.
referee, s. arbitrador, árbitro.
reference, s. referencia, relación.
refine, v.a. refinar, purificar.
refined, a. elegante, bien educado.
refinement, s. refinación ; refinadura ;
refinery, s. refinería.   [elegancia.
refit, v.a reparar ; (mar.) embonar, re parar.
reflect, v.a. & n. reflejar, repercutir ; reflectar ; reflexionar ; recaer, refluir.
reflection, s. reflexión, meditación.
reflective, reflexive, a. reflexivo.
reflector, a. reflector.
reflex, a. reflejo.
reform, v.a. (& n.) v.a. reformar(se).
reform, reformation, s. reformación, re forma.
reformer, s. reformador.
refract, v.a. refractar, refringir.
refraction, s. refracción.
refractoriness, s. obstinación, terqueza.
refractory, a. refractario, obstinado.
refrain, v.a. & n. refrenar(se), reprimir(se); desistir.
refresh, v.a. refrescar, renovar.
refreshment, s. refresco, recreación.
refreshment-bar, s. despacho de bebidas.
refrigerator, s. enfriadera.
refuge, s. refugio, asilo.
refugee, s. refugiado.   [brillo.
refulgence, refulgency, s. resplandor,
refund, v.a. restituir ; pagar.
refusal, s. repulsa, denegación.
refuse, v.a. rehusar, repulsar ; —, s. desecho, zupia, sobra.
refutation, s. refutación.
refute, v.a. refutar.
regain, v.a. recobrar.
regal, a. real.
regale, v.a. regalar.
regalia, s. insignias, pl.
regard, v.a. estimar ; considerar ; —, s. consideración ; respeto.
regardful, a. atento ; -ly, atentamente.
regarding, pr. respeto á, sobre.
regardless, a. descuidado, negligente.
regatta, s. regata.
regency, s. regencia.   [generado.
regenerate, v.a. regenerar ; —, a. re

o

regeneration, s. regeneración.
regent, s. regente.
regicide, s. regicida ; regicidio.
regimen, s. régimen ; dieta.
regiment, s. regimiento, batallón.
regimentals, s.pl. uniforme.
region, s. región ; distrito.
register, s. registro ; —, v.a. registrar, encabezar, empadronar ; -ed letter, s. carta certificada.
registrar, s. registrador.   [miento.
registration, s. registro ; empadrona-
registry, s. asiento, registro.
regret, s. arrepentimiento, sentimiento ; —, v.a. sentir.
regretful, a. pesaroso.
regular, a. regular ; ordinario ; -ly, regularmente ; —, s. regular, reglar.
regularity, s. regularidad.
regulate, v.a. regular, ordenar.
regulation, s. regulación ; arreglo.
regulator, s. regulador ; registro de reloj.
rehabilitate, v.a. rehabilitar.
rehabilitation, s. rehabilitación.
rehearsal, s. repetición ; relación ; prueba (de una pieza de teatro).
rehearse, v.a. repetir, recitar.
reign, s. reinado, reino ; —, v.n. reinar, prevalecer.
reimburse, v.a. reembolsar, recompensar.
reimbursement, s. reembolso.
rein, s. rienda ; —, v.a. refrenar.
reins, s.pl. riñones.
reindeer, s. reno, rangífero.
re-insert, v.a. insertar de nuevo, reponer.
re-instate, v.a. reinstalar ; restablecer.
re-issue, s. nueva edición.
reiterate, v.a. reiterar.
reiteration, s. reiteración. repetición.
reject, v.a. rechazar, rebatir.
rejection, s. desecho, repulsa.
rejoice, v.a. (& n.) regocijar(se).
rejoicing, s. regocijo.
rejoin, v.a. volver á juntar(se) ; —, v.n. replicar, contestar.
rejoinder, s. contrarréplica.
relapse, v.n. recaer ; —, s. reincidencia.
relate, v.a. & n. relatar, referirse.
related, a. emparentado.
relation, s. relación ; parentesco ; pariente.
relationship, s. parentesco.
relative, a. relativo ; -ly, relativamente ; —, s. pariente.
relax, v.a. & n. relajar, aflojar.
relaxation, s. relajación, recreación.
relay, s. parada ó posta, muda de caballos.
release, v.a. soltar, libertar ; — s. soltura ; descargo.
relegate, v.a. desterrar, relegar.

relegation, s. relegación ; destierro.
relent, v.n. relentecer, ablandarse.
relentless, a. empedernido, inflexible.
relevance, relevancy, s. aplicabilidad, pertinencia.
relevant, a. aplicable, proprio, anejo.
reliance, s. confianza, fe.
relic, s. reliquia.
relict, s. viuda.
relief, s. relieve ; alivio, consuelo.
relieve, v.a. aliviar, consolar ; socorrer.
relieving-officer, s. limosnero.
religion, s. religión.   [mente.
religious, a. religioso ; -ly, religiosa-
religiousness, s. religiosidad.
relinquish, v.a. abandonar, dejar.
relinquishment, s. abandono.
reliquary, s. relicario.
relish, s. sainete, sabor ; gusto, deleite ; — v.a. tener buen gusto ; gustar, agradar.
reluctance, s. repugnancia.   [gana.
reluctant, a. repugnante ; -ly, de mala
rely, v.n. confiar en ; contar con.
remain, v.n. quedar, restar, permanecer.
remainder, s. resto, residuo.   [durar.
remains, s.pl. restos, residuos, sobras.
remand, v.a. aplazar (al reo).
remark, s. observación, nota ; —, v.a. notar, observar.
remarkable, a. notable, interesante.
remarkably, ad. notablemente.
remediable, a. remediable.
remedial, a. curativo.
remedy, s. remedio, medicamento ; —, v.a. remediar.   [cordar.
remember, v.a. acordarse, mentar ; re-
remembrance, s. memoria ; recuerdo.
remind, v.a. acordar, recordar.
reminiscence, s. reminiscencia.
remiss, a. remiso, flojo, perezoso, negligente ; -ly, negligentemente.
remission, s. remisión ; perdón.
remissness, s. incuria, indolencia.
remit, v.a. & n. remitir, perdonar ; disminuir ; debilitarse
remittance, s. remesa.
remnant, s. resto, residuo.
remodel, v.a. reformar.
remonstrance, s. súplica, advertencia, censura.
remonstrate, v.n. representar, suplicar, arguir.
remorse, s. remordimiento ; compunción.
remorseless, a. insensible á los remordimientos.   [mente, lejos.
remote, a. remoto, lejano ; -ly, remota-
remoteness, s. alejamiento ; distancia.
remount, v.a. & n. remontar ; volver á subir.
removable, a. amovible.
removal, s. remoción, deposición.

remove, v.a. remover, alejar ; deponer del empleo ; —, v.n. mudarse ; —, s. cambio de puesto ; partida.
remunerate, v.a. remunerar.
remuneration, s. remuneración. [tivo.
remunerative, a. remuneratorio ; lucra-
renaissance, s. renacimiento.
rencounter, s. encuentro ; (mil.) refriega.
rend, v.a. lacerar, hacer pedazos, rasgar.
render, v.a. volver, restituir ; traducir ; rendir.
rendezvous, s. cita ; lugar señalado para encontrarse.
renegade, s. renegado, apóstata.
renew, v.a. renovar, restablecer.
renewal, s. renovación.
rennet, s. cuajo.
renounce, v.a. renunciar.
renovate, v.a. renovar.
renovation, s. renovación.
renown, s. renombre ; fama, celebridad.
renowned, a. célebre, renombrado.
rent, s. renta ; arrendamiento ; alquiler ; rasgón ; cisma ; —, v.a. arrendar, alquilar.
rental, s. lista de arriendos.
renunciation, s. renuncia, renunciación.
reopen, v.a. abrir de nuevo.
reorganization, s. reorganización.
reorganize, v.a. reorganizar.
repair, v.a. reparar ; resarcir ; —, v.n. irse, acudir ; —, s. reparo.
reparable, a. reparable.
reparation, s. reparación.
repartee, s. réplica picante, agudeza.
repast, s. comida, colación.
repay, v.a. pagar, restituir.
repayment, s. pago.
repeal, v.a. abrogar, revocar ; —, s. revocación, anulación.
repeat, v.a. repetir.
repeatedly, ad. repetidamente.
repeater, s. reloj de repetición.
repel, v.a. repeler, rechazar.
repent, v.n. arrepentirse.
repentance, s. arrepentimiento.
repentant, a. arrepentido.
repeople, v.a. repoblar.
repertory, s. repertorio.
repercussion, s. repercusión.
repetition, s. repetición, reiteración.
repine, v.n. afligirse, arrepentirse.
replace, v.a. reemplazar ; reponer.
replenish, v.a. llenar, surtir.
replete, a. repleto, lleno.
repletion, s. repleción, plenitud.
reply, s. contestación, réplica, respuesta ; —, v.a. & n. replicar, contestar.
report, v.a. referir, contar ; dar cuenta ; —, s. voz ; rumor ; fama ; relación.
reporter, s. relator ; estenógrafo.

repose, v.a. componer, depositar, confiar; —, v.n. reposar ; descansar ; —, s. reposo, descanso.
reposite, v.a. depositar.
repository, s. depósito.
repossess, v.a. recuperar.
reprehend, v.a. reprender
reprehensible, a. reprensible.
reprehension, s. reprensión, fraterna.
represent, v.a. representar.
representation, s. representación.
representative, a. representativo ; —, s. representante.
repress, v.a. reprimir, domar.
repression, s. represión.
repressive, a. represivo.
reprieve, v.a. suspender (una ejecución) ; —, s. dilación (de algún castigo).
reprimand, v.a. reprender, corregir ; —, s. reprensión ; reprimenda.
reprint, v.a. reimprimir.
reprisal, s. represalia.
reproach, s. reprensión, censura ; impro-perio, oprobio ; —, v.a. improperar ; reprender.
reproachful, a. reprobador, oprobioso, ignominioso ; -ly, ignominiosamente.
reprobate, v.a. reprobar ; —, s. réprobo, malvado.]
reprobation, s. reprobación.
reproduce, v.a. reproducir.
reproduction, s. reproducción.
reproof, s. reprensión.
reprove, v.a. censurar ; reprender.
reptile, s. reptil.
republic, s. república.
republican, a. & s. republicano.
republicanism, s. republicanismo.
repudiate, v.a. repudiar.
repugnance, s. repugnancia, desgana.
repugnant, a. repugnante.
repulse, v.a. repulsar, desechar ; —, s. repulsa ; rechazo.
repulsion, s. repulsión, repulsa.
repulsive, a. repulsivo.
repurchase, v.a. recomprar.
reputable, a. honroso.
reputably, ad. honrosamente.
reputation, s. reputación.
repute, v.a. reputar. [rogar, suplicar.
request, s. petición, súplica ; —, v.a.
require, v.a. requerir, demandar.
requirement, s. requisito ; exigencia.
requisite, a. necesario, indispensable ; —, s. requisito. [requisición.
requisition, s. petición, demanda ; (mil.)
requital, s. retorno ; recompensa.
requite, v.a. recompensar.
reredos, s. retablo.
rescind, v.a. rescindir, abrogar.
rescript, s. rescripto, edicto.

rescue, v.a. librar, rescatar ; —, s. libramiento, recobro.

research, s. escudriñamiento, estudio.

resemblance, s. semejanza.

resemble, v.a. asemejarse, parecerse á.

resent, v.a. resentirse.

resentful, a. resentido ; vengativo ; -ly, con resentimiento.

resentment, s. resentimiento.

reservation, s. reservación, reserva ; restricción mental.

reserve, v.a. reservar ; —, s. reserva.

reservedly, ad. con reserva.

reside, v.n. residir, morar.

residence, s. residencia, morada.

resident, a. residente.

residuary, a. sobrado ; — **legatee,** s. (law) legatario universal.

residue, s. residuo, resto.

residuum, s. (chem.) residuo.

resign, v.a. & n. resignar, renunciar, ceder ; resignarse, rendirse.

resignation, s. resignación.

resin, s. resina.

resinous, a. resinoso.

resist, v.a. resistir, oponerse.

resistance, s. resistencia.

resistless, a. irresistible.

resolute, a. resuelto ; -ly, resueltamente.

resolution, s. resolución.

resolve, v.a. & n. resolver(se).

resonance, s. resonancia.

resonant, a. resonante.　　　　[concurso.

resort, v.n. recurrir, frecuentar ; —, s.

resound, v.n. resonar.

resource, s. recurso ; expediente.

respect, s. respecto ; respeto ; motivo ; —, v.a. apreciar ; respetar ; venerar.

respectability, s. consideración, carácter respetable.

respectable, a. respetable ; considerable ; -bly, notablemente.　　　[mente.

respectful, a. respetuoso ; -ly, respetuosa-

respecting, pr. con respecto á.

respective, a. respectivo, relativo ; -ly, respectivamente.

respirador, s. respirador.

respiratory, a. respiratorio.

respire, v.n. respirar.

respite, s. suspensión ; respiro ; —, v.a. suspender, diferir.

resplendence, s. resplandor, brillo.

resplendent, a. resplandeciente.

respond, v.a. responder ; corresponder.

respondent, s. (law) defensor.　　　[réplica.

response, s. contestación, respuesta.

responsibility, s. responsabilidad.

responsible, a. responsable.

responsive, a. conforme, correspondiente.

rest, s. reposo ; sueño ; quietud ; (mus.) pausa ; resto, residuo ; —, v.a. des-

cansar ; apoyar ; —, v.n. dormir, reposar.

resting-place, s. descansadero.

restitution, s. restitución.

restive, a. repropio, inquieto ; obstinado.

restless, a. inquieto, agitado.

restoration, s. restauración.

restorative, a. & s. restaurativo.

restore, v.a. restaurar, restituir.

restrain, v.a. restringir, restriñir.

restraint, s. refrenamiento, constreñi-

restrict, v.a. restringir, limitar. [miento.

restriction, s. restricción.

restrictive, a. restrictivo.

result, v.n. resultar ; —, s. resulta.

resume, v.a. resumir ; empezar de nuevo

resumption, s. reasunción.

resurrection, s. resurrección.

resuscitate, v.a. resucitar.

retail, v.a. revender, regatonear ; —, s. venta por menor.

retain, v.a. retener, guardar.　　　[iente.

retainer, s. adherente, partidario; depend-

retake, v.a. recoger, recobrar.

retaliate, v.a. talionar.

retaliation, s. talión.

retard, v.a. retardar.

retardation, s. retardación.

retch, v.n. tener bascas.

retention, s. retención.

retentive, a. retentivo.

reticence, s. reticencia.

reticent, a. reservado, taciturno.

reticle, reticule, s. redecilla, saquita (entre las mujeres).

retina, s. retina (del ojo).

retire, v.a. (& n.) retirar(se).

retired, a. apartado, retirado.

retirement, s. retiro, retiramiento.

retort, v.a. redargüir, retorcer (un argumento) ; —, s. redargución ; (chem.)

retouch, v.a. retocar.　　　[retorta.

retrace, v.a. volver á trazar ; desandar.

retract, v.a. retraer ; retractar.

retreat, s. retirada ; —, v.a. retirarse.

retrench, v.a. cercenar ; —, v.n. cercenar sus gastos.

retrenchment, s. rebaja, cercenamiento.

retribution, s. retribución, recompensa.

retrievable, a. recuperable ; reparable.

retrieve, v.a. recuperar, recobrar.

retriever, s. sabueso.　　　[gradar.

retrograde, a. retrógrado ; —, v.n. retro-

retrogression, s. retrogradación, retroceso.

retrospect, retrospection, s. reflexión de las cosas pasadas.

retrospective, a. retrospectivo.

return, v.a. retribuir ; restituir ; volver ; —, s. retorno ; vuelta ; recompensa, retribución ; vicisitud ; recaída.

returnable, a. que se puede volver.

reunion, s. reunión.
reunite, v.a. (& n.) reunir(se).
reveal, v.a. revelar. [jarana, fiesta.
revel, v.n. jaranear, festejarse ; —, s.
revelation, s. revelación.
reveller, s. camarada de fiesta, vividor.
revelry, s. borrachera.
revenge, v.a. vengar ; —, s. venganza.
revengeful, a. vengativo.
revenue, s. renta ; rédito.
reverberate, v.a. & n. reverberar ;
resonar, retumbar.
reverberation, s. reverberación.
revere, v.a. reverenciar, venerar.
reverie, s. ensueño, reflexión profunda.
reverence, s. reverencia ; —, v.a. reverenciar.
reverend, a. reverendo ; venerable.
reverent, reverential, a. reverencial,
respetuoso ; -ly, reverencialmente.
reversal, s. revocación de una sentencia.
reverse, v.a. trastrocar ; abolir ; —, s.
vicisitud ; contrario ; derrota ; reverso
(de una moneda).
reversible, a. reversible, revocable.
reversion, s. futura ; reversión.
reversionary, a. reversible. [revertir.
revert, v.a. & n. trastrocar ; volverse,
revertible, a. reversible.
revictual, v.a. volver á proveer de víveres.
review, v.n. rever ; (mil.) revistar ; —, s.
revista ; reseña. [revista.
reviewer, s. revisor ; escritor en una
revile, v.a. ultrajar ; disfamar.
revise, v.a. rever ; —, s. revista ; segunda
prueba de un pliego.
reviser, s. revisor.
revision, s. revisión.
revisit, v.a. volver á visitar.
revival, s. restauración. [revivir.
revive, v.a. avivar ; restablecer ; —, v.n.
revocable, a. revocable.
revocation, s. revocación.
revoke, v.a. revocar, anular.
revolt, v.n. rebelarse ; —, v.a. disgustar ;
—, s. rebelión.
revolting, a. escandaloso.
revolution, s. revolución.
revolutionary, a. revolucionario.
revolutionist, s. revolucionario. [girar.
revolve, v.a. revolver ; meditar ; —, v.n.
revolver, s. revólver (pistola).
revolving, a. periódico, giratorio.
revulsion, s. revulsión. [pensar.
reward, s. recompensa ; —, v.a. recompensar.
rewarder, s. remunerador.
rhapsody, s. rapsodia.
rhetoric, s. retórica.
rhetorical, a. retórico.
rhetorician, s. retórico.
rheum, s. reuma.

rheumatic, a. reumático.
rheumatism, s. reumatismo.
rhinoceros, s. rinoceronte.
rhomb, s. rombo.
rhomboid, s. romboide.
rhubarb, s. ruibarbo.
rhyme, s. rima ; poema ; —, v.n. rimar.
rhym(st)er, s. versista.
rhythm, s. ritmo.
rhythmical, a. rítmico.
rib, s. costilla.
ribald, s. hombre lascivo ó grosero. l
ribaldry, s. lenguaje obsceno ó rudo.
riband, ribbon, s. listón, cinta.
rice, s. arroz. [ricamente.
rich, a. rico ; opulento ; abundante ; -ly,
riches, s.pl. riqueza.
richness, s. riqueza ; abundancia.
rick, s. niara, pila de cereal.
rickets, s. raquitis.
rickety, a. raquítico ; instable.
rid, v.a. librar, desembarazar ; —, a
franco.
riddance, s. libramiento ; zafada.
riddle, s. acertijo, enigma ; criba ; —,
v.a. cribar.
ride, v.n. cabalgar ; —, s. paseo á caballo.
rider, s. caballero, cabalgador, jinete.
ridge, s. espinazo, lomo ; cumbre.
ridicule, s. ridiculez ; ridículo ; —, v.a.
ridiculizar. [mente.
ridiculous, a. ridiculoso ; -ly, ridículamente.
riding, s. acción de andar á caballo.
riding-habit, s. traje de amazona.
riding-school, s. picadero.
riding-whip, s. látigo, rebenque.
rife, a. común, frecuente.
riff-raff, s. desecho, desperdicio, canalla.
rifle, v.a. robar, pillar ; estriar, rayar ;
—, s. fusil rayado, rifle.
rifle-man, s. fusilero. [s. (col.) burla.
rig, v.a. ataviar ; (mar.) aparejar ;
rigging, s. (mar.) aparejo.
right, a. derecho, recto ; justo ; honesto ;
— ! ¡ bien !, ¡ bueno ! -ly, rectamente,
justamente ; —, s. justicia ; razón ;
derecho ; mano derecha ; —, v.a.
hacer justicia. [justamente.
righteous, a. justo, honrado ; -ly,
righteousness, s. equidad ; honradez.
rigid, a. rígido ; austero, severo ; -ly, con
rigidez.
rigidity, s. rigidez, austeridad.
rigmarole, s. galimatías.
rigorous, a. rigoroso ; -ly, rigorosamente.
rigour, s. rigor ; severidad.
rill, s. riachuelo.
rim, s. margen ; orilla.
rime s. escarcha.
rimy, a. escarchado.
rind. s. corteza ; cáscara.

ring, s. círculo, cerco ; anillo ; campaneo ; —, v.a. sonar ; —, v.n. retiñir, retumbar ; to — the bell, tirar de la campanilla.

ringer, s. campanero.

ring-finger, s. dedo anular.

ring-leader, s. cabeza ó caudillo de partido.

ringlet, s. rizo.

ring-worm, s. (med.) tiña favosa, bando.

rink, s. lugar para patinar.

rinse, v.a. lavar, limpiar.

riot, s. tumulto, bullicio ; borrachera ; —, v.n. causar alborotos.

rioter, hombre sedicioso.

riotous, a. bullicioso, sedicioso ; disoluto ; -ly, disolutamente.

rip, v.a. rasgar, lacerar ; descoser.

ripe, a. maduro, sazonado ; -ly, madura- [mente.

ripen, v.a. & n. madurar.

ripeness, s. madurez. [borbotones.

ripple, v.n. manar ó hervir el agua á

rippling, s. movimiento del agua á borbollones.

rise, v.n. levantarse ; nacer, salir (hablando de los astros) ; rebelarse ; ascender ; hincharse ; elevarse ; —, s. levantamiento ; elevación ; subida ; salida (del sol) ; causa.

risible, a. risible. [ó sesión.

rising, s. salida del sol ; fin de una junta

risk, s. riesgo, peligro ; —, v.a. arriesgar.

risky, a. peligroso.

rite, s. rito.

ritual, a. & s. ritual. [petir, emular.

rival, a. émulo ; —, s. rival ; —, v.a. com-

rivalry, s. rivalidad.

rive, v.a. (& n.) hender(se).

river, s. rio. [roblar.

rivet, s. remache ; —, v.a. remachar,

rivulet, s. riachuelo.

roach, s. raya (pez).

road, s. camino, carretera ; -side, apar-

roadstead, s. (mar.) rada.

roadster, s. caballo de viaje.

roam, v.a. (& n.) corretear ; vagar.

roan, a. roano, ruano.

roar, v.n. rugir ; aullar ; bramar ; —, s. rugido ; bramido, mugido.

roast, v.a. asar ; tostar.

roastbeef, s. asado de vaca.

rob, v.a. robar, hurtar.

robber, s. robador, ladrón.

robbery, s. robo. [gala.

robe, s. manto ; toga ; —, v.a. vestir de

robin-(redbreast), s. petirrojo.

robust, a. robusto.

robustness, s. robustez.

rock, s. roca ; piedra ; escollo ; —, v.a. mecer ; arrullar ; —, v.n. bambolear.

rocker, s. cunera.

rocket, s. cohete.

rocking-horse, s. caballito de madera.

rock-oil, s. petróleo.

rock-salt, s. sal gema, sal piedra.

rock-work, s. grutesco.

rocky, a. peñascoso, pedroso.

rod, s. varilla, verga, caña.

rodents, s.pl. roedores, pl.

rodomontade, s. fanfarria.

roe, s. corzo ; hueva.

roebuck, s. corzo.

rogation, s. rogaciones, pl.

rogue, s. bribón, pícaro, villano.

roguery, s. picardía.

roguish, a. pícaro.

roister, v.n. bravear, tanfarronear.

roll, v.a. rodar ; volver ; arrollar ; —, v.n. rodar ; girar ; (mar.) balancear ; —, s. rodadura ; rollo ; lista ; catálogo ; roleo ; voluta ; bollo ; panecillo.

roller, s. rodillo, cilindro.

rollicking, a. vivaracho, juguetón.

rolling-pin, s. rodillo de pastelero.

romance, s. romance ; ficción ; cuento, fábula.

romancist, s. romancero.

romantic(al), a. romántico.

romish, a. romano.

romp, s. muchacha retozona ; —, v.n. retozar.

rood, s. medida inglesa (décima parte de una hectárea) ; cruz.

roof, s. techo, tejado ; —, v.a. techar.

roofing, s. tejado.

rook, s. corneja de pico blanco ; roque (en el juego de ajedrez) ; trampista ; —, v.a. (col.) robar, pelar.

rookery, s. arboles donde hacen sus nidos muchas cornejas, pl.; colonia de méndigos.

room, s. lugar, espacio ; aposento ; cámara, cuarto, pieza.

roominess, s. espaciosidad, capacidad.

roomy, espacioso.

roost, s. pértiga del gallinero ; —, v.n. dormir las aves en una pértiga.

root, s. raíz ; origen ; —, v.a. & n. (— out) desarraigar ; arraigar.

rooted, a. inveterado. [cuerda.

rope, s. cuerda ; cordel ; —, v.a. atar con

rope-dancer, s. funámbulo.

rope-maker, s. cordelero.

rope-walk, rope-yard, s. cordelería.

rosary, s. rosario.

rose, s. rosa.

roseate, a. róseo.

rose-bed, s. campo de rosales.

rose-bud, s. capullo de rosa.

rosemary, s. (bot.) romero.

rose-tree, s. rosal.

rosette, s. roseta.

rosin, s. trementina, resina.

rosiness, s. color róseo.

rosy, a. róseo.   [facción.

rot. v.n. pudrirse ; —, s. morriña ; putre-

rotate, v.a. & n. girar.

rotation, s. rotación.

rotatory, a. rotatorio.

rote, s. repetición mecánica de lecciones.

rotten, a. podrido, corrompido.

rottenness, s. podredumbre, putrefacción.

rotund, a. rotundo, redondo, circular, esférico.

rotundity, s. rotundidad, redondez.

rouge, s. arrebol, colorete.

rough, a. áspero, tosco ; bronco, bruto, brusco ; tempestuoso ; -ly, rudamente.

rough-cast, v.a. bosquejar una figura ó cuadro ; —, s. modelo en bruto.

rough-copy, s. borrador.

roughen, v.a. poner áspero.

rough-hew, v.a. formar el modelo tosco de alguna cosa.   [dad ; tempestad.

roughness, s. aspereza ; rudeza, tosque-

round, a. redondo ; cabal ; franco, sincero ; —, s. círculo ; redondez ; vuelta ; giro ; escalón ; (mil.) ronda ; descarga ; —, ad. alrededor ; -ly, ad. redondamente ; francamente ; —, v.a. cercar, rodear ; redondear.

roundabout, a. indirecto, vago.

roundelay, s. coplas que se cantan en rueda, pl.

roundness, s. redondez.

rouse, v.a. despertar ; excitar.

rout, s. rota, derrota ; —, v.a. derrotar.

route, s. ruta ; camino.

rove, v.n. vagar, vaguear.

rover, s. vagamundo ; pirata.

row, s. camorra ; zipizape. [remar, bogar.

row, s. hilera, fila ; —, v.a. & n. (mar.)

rowan(-tree), s. (bot.) serbal.

rowdy, a. & s. (col.) alborotador, tararira, bullanguero.

rowel, s. estrella de espuela.

rower, s. remero.

row-lock, s. (mar.) escálamo, tolete.

royal, a. real ; regio ; -ly, regiamente.

royalist, s. realista.

royalty, s. realeza, dignidad real ; pago por cantidad minada al dueño de la mina ; pago á un escritor por cada ejemplar vendido.

rub, v.a. estregar, fregar, frotar ; raspar ; —, s. frotamiento ; (fig.) embarazo ; dificultad.

rubber, s. estropajo ; escofina ; partido de naipes. V. india-rubber.   [jos. pl.

rubbish, s. escombro ; ruinas, pl.; andra-

rubicund, a. rubicundo.

rubric, s. rúbrica.

ruby, s. rubí.

rudder, s. timón.

ruddiness, s. tez rubia y sana.

ruddy, a. colorado, rubio.

rude, a. rudo, brutal, rústico, grosero ; tosco ; -ly, rudamente, groseramente.

rudeness, s. descortesía ; rudeza, in-

rudiment, s. rudimentos, pl. [solencia.

rudimentary, a. elemental.

rue, v.n. compadecerse ; —, s. (bot.) ruda.

rueful, a. lamentable, triste.

ruff, s. lechuguilla.

ruffian, s. malhechor, bandolero.

ruffianly, a. brutal, criminal.

ruffle, v.a. desordenar, desazonar ; rizar ; —, s. pliego ; tumulto.

rug, s. paño burdo ; frazada.

rugged, a. áspero, tosco; brutal; peludo.

ruin, s. ruina ; perdición ; escombros, pl.; — v.a. arruinar ; destruir.

ruinous, a. ruinoso ; -ly, ruinosamente.

rule, s. mando ; regla ; regularidad ; —, v.a. & n. gobernar ; reglar, arreglar.

ruler, s. gobernador ; regla.   [dirigir.

rum, s. ron ; —, a. (col.) extraño, singular.

rumble, v.n. crujir, rugir.

ruminate, v.a. rumiar.

rumination, s. meditación.

rummage, v.a. trastornar ; —, s. tumulto.

rumour, s. rumor ; —, v.a. divulgar alguna noticia.

rump, s. anca, nalga.

rumple, v.a. arrugar, desordenar.

rumpus, (col.) riña, alboroto.

run, v.n. correr ; fluir, manar ; pasar rápidamente ; proceder ; —, s. corrida, carrera ; curso ; serie ; ataque.

runagate, runaway, s. fugitivo, escapado, desertor.

run(d)let, s. barrilejo.   [de mano).

rung, s. escalón, peldaño (de escalera

runner, s. corredor ; correo, mensajero.

running, s. carrera, corrida ; curso.

rupture, s. rotura ; hernia, quebradura ; —, v.a. reventar, romper.

rural, a. rural, campestre, rústico.

ruse, s. astucia, maña, artería.

rush, s. junco ; (fig.) bledo, ardite ; ímpetu ; —, v.n. lanzarse, tirarse.

rush-light, s. vela ó lamparilla de noche.

rusk, s. galleta.

russet, a. bermejizo.

Russia-leather, s. cuero de Moscovia.

rust, s. orín, herrumbre ; robín ; — v.n. enmohecerse.

rustic(al), a. rústico ; —, s. patán, rústico.

rusticate, v.n. vivir en el campo ; —, v.a. desterrar de la universidad.

rustication, s. vida campestre, destierro universitario.

rusticity, s. rusticidad.

rustiness, s. herrumbre.

rustle, v.n. crujir, rechinar.
rustling, s. estruendo ; crujido, susurro.
rusty, a. oriniento, mohoso ; rancio.
rut, v.n. bramar los venados y ciervos cuando están en celo ; —, s. carril, huella de rueda.   [humanamente.
ruthless, a. cruel, insensible ; -ly, in-
rye, s. (bot.) centeno.

S

sabbatarian, s. puritano riguroso.
sabbath, s. sábado.
sable, s. cebellina.
sabre, s. sable ; —, v.a. matar con sable.
sacerdotal, a. sacerdotal.   [v.a. saquear.
sack, s. saco ; vino seco ; saqueo ; —,
sackcloth, s. brea.
sacrament, s. sacramento ; Eucaristía.
sacramental, a. -ly, sacramental(mente).
sacred, s. sagrado, sacro ; inviolable ; -ly,
    sagradamente, inviolablemente.
sacredness, s. santidad.   [ficar.
sacrifice, s. sacrificio ; —, v.a. & n, sacri-
sacrificial, a. sacrificador.
sacrilege, s. sacrilegio.
sacrilegious, a. sacrílego.
sad, a. triste, melancólico ; infausto ;
    obscuro ; -ly, tristemente.
sadden, v.a. entristecer.
saddle, s. silla ; —, v.a. ensillar.
saddle-bag, s. alforja, maleta (am.)
saddle-cloth, s. jerga de silla.
saddle-horse, s. caballo de montar.
saddler, s. sillero.   [pl.
saddlery, s. guarnicionería ; guarniciones,
sadness, s. tristeza ; aspecto tétrico.
safe, a. seguro ; -ly, á salvo ; — and
    sound, sano y salvo ; —, s. cofre fuerte.
safe-conduct, s. salvoconducto.
safe-guard, s. salvaguardia.
safety, s. seguridad.
safety-valve, s. llave de seguridad.
saffron, s. azafrán.   [mente.
sagacious, a. sagaz, sutil ; -ly, sagaz-
sagacity, s. sagacidad, astucia.
sage, s. sabio (bot.) salvia ; —, a. sabio ;
    -ly, sabiamente.
sago, s. (bot.) sagú.
sail, s. vela ; —, v.n. dar á la vela, navegar
sailing, s. navegación.
sailor, s. marinero.
saint, s. santo ; santa.
saint, sainted, saintly, a. santo, beato.
sake, s. causa, razón ; **for God's —,**
    por amor de Dios.
salad s. ensalada.
salad-bowl, s. ensaladera.
salad-oil, s' aceite de olivas.
salamander, s. salamandra.
salary, s. salario.
sale, s. venta.
saleable, a. vendible.

salesman, s. vendedor, tendero.
salient, a. saliente, saledizo.
saline, a. salino.
saliva, s. saliva.
sallow, a. cetrino, pálido.   [salir.
sally, s. (mil.) salida, surtida ; —, v.n
salmon, s. salmón.
salmon-trout, s. trucha salmonada.
saloon, s. salón.
salt, s. sal ; (fig.) sabor ; agudeza ; —,
    a. salado ; —, v.a. salar.
salt-cellar, s. salero (en la mesa).
saltpetre, s. nitro, salitre.
salubrious, a. salubre, saludable.
salubrity, s. salubridad.
salutary, a. salubre, salutífero.
salutation, s. salutación.
salute, v.a. saludar ; —, s. salutación.
salvage, s. (mar.) percance de salvamento.
salvation, s. salvación.
salve, s. emplasto, ungüento.
salver, s. salvilla, bandeja.
salvo, s. reservación, excusa.
same, a. mismo, idéntico.
sameness, s. identidad.
samphire, s. hinojo marino.   [probar.
sample, s. muestra ; ejemplo ; —, v.a.
sampler, s. dechado, modelo.   [gración.
sanctification, s. santificación ; consa-
sanctify, v.a. santificar.   [crita.
sanctimonious, a. devoto, beato ; hipó-
sanction, s. sanción ; —, v.a. sancionar,
sanctity, s. santidad.
sanctuary, s. santuario ; asilo.
sanctum, s. despacho retirado.
sand, s. arena ; —, v.a. enarenar.
sandal, s. sandalia.
sand-bags, s. pl. (mil.) sacos de tierra
sanded, a. arenoso.
sand-pit, s. arenal.
sandstone, s. piedra arenisca.
sandy, a. arenoso, arenisco.
sane, a. sano.
sanguinary, a. sanguinario.
sanguine, a. sanguíneo, animoso.
sanguineness, s. coraje, ánimo, anhelo.
sanguineous, a. sanguino ; sanguíneo.
sanitation, s. higiene.
sanity, s.sanidad, juicio sano.
sap, s. savia ; (mil.) zapa ; —, v.a. zapar.
sapient, a. sabio, cuerdo.
sapling, s. renuevo.

sapper, s. (mil.) zapador.
sapphire, s. zafir, zafiro.
sarcasm, s. sarcasmo. [mordazmente.
sarcastic(al), a. mordaz, cáustico; -ally,
sarcenet, s. tafetán de Florencia.
sarcophagus, s. sarcófago, sepulcro.
sardine, s. sardina.
sash, s. cíngulo, cinta, faja.
sash-window, s. ventana corrediza.
Satan, s. Sátanas.
satanic(al), a. diabólico.
satchel, s. mochila, vademecum.
satellite, s. satélite.
satiate, sate, v.a. saciar, hartar.
satiety, s. saciedad, hartura.
satin, s. raso.
satinet, s. rasete.
satire, s. sátira.
satiric(al), a. satírico; -ly, satíricamente.
satirist, s. autor satírico.
satirize, v.a. satirizar.
satisfaction, s. satisfacción.
satisfactorily, ad. satisfactoriamente.
satisfactory, a. satisfactorio.
satisfy, v.a. satisfacer.
satrap, s. sátrapa.
saturate, v.a. saturar.
saturday, s. sábado.
saturnine, a. saturnino, melancólico.
satyr, s. sátiro.
sauce, s. salsa; —, v.a. condimentar.
saucepan, s. cacerola.
saucer, s. platillo.
saucily, ad. desvergonzadamente.
sauciness, s. insolencia, impudencia.
saucy, a. insolente.
saunter, v.n. callejear, corretear.
sausage, s. salchicha.
savage, a. salvaje, bárbaro; -ly, bárbaramente; —, s. salvaje.
savageness, s. salvajería; crueldad.
savagery, s. yermo; crueldad.
savannah, s. sabana.
save, v.a. salvar; economizar; conservar; —, ad. salvo, excepto.
saveloy, s. chorizo.
saver, s. libertador; ahorrador.
saving, a. frugal, económico; —, pr.
fuera de, excepto; -ly, ad. económi-
camente, parcamente; —, s. salva-
miento; -s, pl. aborros.
Saviour, s. Redentor. [saborear.
savour, s. olor; sabor; —, v.a. gustar.
savouriness, s. paladar; fragrancia.
savoury, a. sabroso.
saw, s. sierra; —, v.a. serrar.
sawbones, s. (col.) médico, sangrador.
saw-dust, s. aserraduras, pl.
saw-fish, s. priste.
saw-mill, s. molino de aserrar.
saw-pit, s. aserradero.

sawyer, s. aserrador.
say, v.a. decir, hablar; —, s. habla.
saying, s. dicho, proverbio.
scab, s. roña; sarna.
scabbard, s. vaina de espada; cobertura
scabbiness, s. estado roñoso.
scabby, a. sarnoso.
scaffold, s. andamio; cadalso.
scaffolding, s. armazón de andamio.
scald, v.a. escaldar.
scalding, a. hirviente.
scale, s. balanza; escama; laminita,
escala; (mus.) gama; **pair of -s,** peso,
balanza; —, v.a. & n. escalar; descostrarse.
Scales, s.pl. Libra (signo del zodíaco).
scaling-ladder, s. escala de sitio.
scallop, s. concha; punta dentada.
scalp, s. cráneo; —, v.a. descortezar
el cráneo.
scamp, s. pícaro; —, v.a. frangollar.
scamper, v.n. correr, apresurarse.
scan, v.a. escudriñar; medir las sílabas
de un verso.
scandal, s. escándalo, infamia.
scandalize, v.a. escandalizar.
scandalous, a. escandaloso; -ly, escanda-
scansion, s. prosodia. [losamente.
scant, scanty, a. escaso, parco; sórdido.
scantily, ad. escasamente, estrechamente.
scantiness, s. estrechez, escasez.
scantling, s. pedacito.
scape-goat, s. víctima; sujeto expiatorio.
scape-grace, s. pícaro.
scar, s. cicatriz; —, v.a. mellar.
scarce, a. raro; -ly, apenas.
scarcity, s. escasez; raridad.
scare, v.a. espantar.
scarecrow, s. espantajo.
scarf, s. trena, corbata.
scarify, v.a. sajar.
scarlatina, s. escarlatina.
scarlet, s. escarlata; —, a. de color de
scarp, s. escarpa. [escarlata ó grana.
scatter, v.a. & n. esparcir(se); disipar(se).
scavenger, s. basurero.
scene, s. escena.
scenery, s. paisaje; decoración (de teatro).
scenic(al), a. escénico. [oler.
scent, s. olfato; olor; rastro; —, v.a.
scent-bottle, s. frasquito con agua de olor.
scentless, a. sin olfato, inodoro.
sceptic, s. escéptico.
sceptic(al), a. escéptico.
scepticism, s. escepticismo.
sceptre, s. cetro.
schedule, s. esquela; cédula.
scheme, s. proyecto, designio; plan,
modelo; —, v.a. proyectar. [trampista.
schemer, s. proyectista, invencionero;
schism, s. cisma.

schismatic(al), s. cismático.
scholar, s. escolar, estudiante ; literato.
scholarship, s. ciencia; educación literaria; prebenda colegial.
scholastic, a. escolástico.
school, s. escuela ; —, v.a. enseñar.
school-boy, s. niño de escuela, colegial.
schooling, s. instrucción.
schoolfellow, s. camarada de escuela.
school-master, s. maestro de escuela.
school-mistress, s. maestra de niños ó niñas.
schooner, s. (mar.) goleta.
sciatica, s. ciática.
science, s. ciencia.
scientific(al), a. científico; -ally, científicamente.
scimitar, s. cimitarra.
scintillate, v.n. chispear, centellar.
scintillation, s. chispazo.
sciolist, s. sabio somero, chárlatán.
scion, s. verduguillo ; vástago.
scissors, s.pl. tijeras, pl.
scoff, v.n. mofarse, burlarse; —, s. mofa, burla.
scoffer, s. mofador.
scoffingly, ad. con mofa y escarnio.
scold, v.a. & n. regañar, reñir, refunfuñar.
sconce, s. candelabro.
scoop, s. cucharón; —, v.a. cavar, socavar
scope, s. objeto alcance, designio, espacio.
scorbutic, a. escorbútico.
scorch, v.a. quemar por encima ; tostar ; —, v.n. quemarse, secarse.
score, s. muesca, consideración ; cuenta ; escote ; razón ; motivo ; veintena ; —, v.a. sentar alguna deuda ; señalar con una línea.
scoria, s. escoria, hez,.   [menosprecio.
scorn, v.a. & n. despreciar ; —, s. desdén,
scorner, s. desdeñador.
scornful, a. desdeñoso ; -ly, con desdén.
scorpion, s. escorpión.
scot, s. escote.   [escoplear, herir.
scotch, s. cortadura, incisión ; —, v.a.
scot-free, a. sin pagar.
scoundrel, s. belitre, bribón.
scoundrelly, a. ruin, pícaro.
scour, v.a. fregar, estregar ; limpiar ; —, v.a. & n. recorrer, correr.
scourge, s. azote ; castigo ; —, v.a. azotar, castigar.
scout, s. (mil.) batidor de la campaña ; centinela avanzada ; espía ; —, v.a. & n. (mil.) reconocer ; —, v. a. desdeñar, rechazar.   [semblante ceñudo.
scowl, v.n. mirar con ceño ; —, s. ceño,
scowlingly, ad. con ceño.
scrag, s. pedazo de carne huesudo.
scragginess, s. flaqueza ; aspereza.
scraggy, a. áspero ; macilento.
scramble, v.n. arrapar ; trepar ; disputar ; —, s. disputa ; juego de muchachos.
scrap, s. migaja ; sobras, pl ; pedacito.

scrap-book, s. album.
scrape, v.a. & n. raer, raspar ; arañar ; tocar mal un instrumento ; —, s. embarazo ; dificultad.
scraper, s. rascador.
scratch, v.a. rascar, raspar ; raer, garrapatear ; —, s. rascadura.
scratch-wig, s. peluca chica.
scrawl, v.a. & n. garrapatear ; —, s. garabatos, pl.
scream, screech, v.n. chillar, dar alaridos; —, s. chillido, grito, alarido.
screech-owl, s. zumaya.
screen, s. biombo, mámpara ; harnero ; criba ; —, v.a. abrigar, esconder ; cribar, cerner.
screw, s. tornillo ; (mar.) hélice ; (col.) tacaño, avaro ; —, v.a. torcer con tornillo ; forzar, apretar, estrechar.
screw-driver, s. destornillador.
screw-nut, s. tuerca.
screw-steamer, s. navío á hélice.
scribble, v.a. escarabajear ; —, s. escrito de poco mérito.
scribe, s. escritor ; escriba.
scrimmage, s. turbamulta.
scrip, s. bolsa, taleguilla ; cédula.
scriptural, a. bíblico.
Scripture, s. Escritura sagrada.
scrivener, s. escribano, notario público.
scrofula, s. escrófula.
scrofulous, a. escrofuloso.
scroll, s. rollo (de papel ó pergamino).
scrub, v.a. estregar, fregar ; maleza ; —, (col.) belitre.
scruple, s. escrúpulo ; —, v.n. escrupulizar, tener duda.
scrupulosity, s. escrupulosidad.
scrupulous, a. escrupuloso ; -ly, escrupulosamente.
scrutinize, v.a. escudriñar, examinar.
scrutiny, s. escrutinio, examen.
scud, s. nube ventosa ; —, v.n. huirse, escaparse.   [pelear.
souffle, s. quimera, riña ; —, v.n. reñir,
scull, s. cráneo ; remo pequeño ; —, v.n. remar con dos remos.
sculler, s. remero.
scullery, s. fregadero.
scullion, s. marmitón ; fregona.
sculptor, s. escultor.
sculpture, s. escultura ; —, v.a. esculpir.
scum, s. nata ; espuma ; escoria.
scurf, s. tiña ; costra de una herida.
scurrility, s. bufonería, bufonada.
scurrilous, a. vil, bajo ; injurioso ; -ly, injuriosamente
scurvily, ad. vilmente.
scurviness, s. ruindad ; malignidad.
scurvy, s. escorbuto ; —, a. escorbútico ; vil, despreciable.
scutcheon, s. escudo de armas.

scuttle, s. banasta; —, v.n. correr,
scythe, s. guadaña. [escaparse.
sea, s. mar.
sea-faring, a. marino, marinero.
sea-green, a. verdemar.
sea-gull, s. gaviota. [v.a. sellar.
seal, s. sello; foca, lobo marino; —,
sealing-wax, s. lacre.
sealskin, s. piel de foca.
seam, s. costura; —, v.a. coser.
seaman, s. marinero.
seamanship, s. pericia en la navegación.
seamstress, s. costurera.
seamy, a. lo que tiene costuras; (fig.) vil,
miserable.
sea-piece, sea-scape, s. pintura marítima.
sear, v.a. cauterizar.
search, v.a. examinar; escudriñar; inquirir, tentar; investigar, buscar; —,
s. pesquisa; busca; buscada.
search-light, s. reflector eléctrico.
sea-shore, s. ribera, litoral, costa.
sea-sick, a. mareado.
sea-sickness, s. mareamiento, mareo.
sea-side, s. orilla ó ribera del mar, costa.
season, s. estación; tiempo oportuno;
sazón; —, v.a. sazonar.
seasonable, a. oportuno, á propósito.
seasonably, ad. en sazón.
seasoning, s. condimento.
season-ticket, s. (rail.) abono de pasaje.
seat, s. silla; morada; domicilio; situación; —, v.a. situar; colocar; asentar.
sea-urchin, s. equino, erizo marino.
seaward(s), ad. hacia el mar.
sea-weed, s. alga marina.
sea-worthy, a. (mar.) proprio para navegar (barco).
secede, v.n. apartarse, separarse.
secession, s. apartamiento; separación.
seclude, v.a. apartar, excluir.
seclusion, s. separación; retiro.
second, a. segundo; -ly, en segundo
lugar; —, s. padrino; (mus.) segunda;
—, v.a. ayudar; segundar.
secondary, a. secundario.
secondhand, a. usado (artículo reven-
dido). [oculto.
second-sight, s. vista misteriosa de lo
secrecy, s. secreto, silencio cuidadoso.
secret, a. & s. secreto; -ly, secretamente.
secretary, s. secretario.
secretaryship, s. secretaría.
secrete, v.a. esconder; (med.) secretar.
secretion, s. secreción.
secretive, a. taciturno.
sect, s. secta.
sectarian, sectary, s. sectario.
section, s. sección.
sector, s. sector.
secular, a. secular, seglar.

secularity, s. apego á las cosas mundanas.
secularize, v.a. secularizar.
secure, a. seguro; salvo; -ly, seguramente; —, v.a. asegurar; salvar.
security, s. seguridad; defensa; confianza; fianza.
sedan(-chair), s. silla de manos.
sedate, a. sosegado, tranquilo; -ly,
tranquilamente.
sedateness, s. tranquilidad.
sedative, a. sedativo.
sedentary, a. sedentario.
sederunt, s. (law Scot.) estrados.
sedge, s. (bot.) espadaña.
sediment, s. sedimento, hez, poso.
sedition, s. sedición; tumulto, alboroto,
motín; revuelta. [mente
seditious, a. sedicioso; -ly, sediciosa-
seditiousness, s. turbulencia.
seduce, v.a. seducir; engañar.
seducer, s. seductor.
seduction, s. seducción.
seductive, a. seductivo. [mente.
sedulous, a. asiduo; -ly, diligente-
see, v.a. & n. ver, observar, descubrir;
advertir; conocer, juzgar; comprender; —, ¡ mira ! —, s. diocesis, séo.
seed, s. semilla, simiente; —, v.n. granar.
seedling, s. planta de semilla.
seed-plot, s. semillero, plantel.
seedsman, s. tratante en semillas.
seed-time, s. sementera, siembra.
seedy, a. granado, lleno de granos; (fig.)
miserable; gastado.
seeing, s. vista; acto de ver; — that,
visto que.
seek, v.a. buscar; pretender.
seem, v.a. parecer.
seeming, s. apariencia; -ly, al parecer.
seemliness, s. decencia.
seemly, a. decente, propio.
seer, s. profeta.
seesaw, s. vaivén; —, v.n. balancear.
seethe, v.n. hervir, bullir.
segment, s. segmento de un círculo.
segregate, v.a. segregar.
segregation, s. segregación.
seine(net), s. almadraba.
seize, v.a. asir, agarrar; secuestrar.
seizure, s. captura; secuestro.
seldom, ad. raramente, rara vez.
select, v.a. elegir, escoger; —, a. selecto,
escogido.
selection, s. selección.
self, pr. mismo.
self-command, s. serenidad, aplomo.
self-conceit, s. presunción.
self-confident, a. audaz.
self-defence, s. defensa propria.
self-denial, s. abnegación.
self-evident, a. evidente, claro.

self-interest, s. propio interés.
selfish, a. egoista ; -ly, interesadamente.
selfishness, s. egoismo.
self-possession, s. sangre fría, tranquilidad
　　de ánimo. [dad.
self-respect, s. estima de sí mismo, digni-
self-same, a. idéntico, mismo.
self-seeking, a. egoista.
self-willed, a. obstinado.
sell, v.a. & n. vender ; traficar ; —, s.
　　(col.) engaño, chasco.
seller, s. vendedor.
selling-off, s. (com.) liquidación.
selvage, s. orilla del paño.
semblance, s. semejanza, apariencia.
semaphore, s. semáforo.
semicircle, s. semicírculo.
semicircular, a. semicircular.
semicolon, s. punto y coma.
seminary, s. seminario.
semiquaver, s. (mus.) semicorchea.
semitone, s. (mus.) semitono.
sempstress, s. costurera.
sempiternal, a. sempiterno.
senate, s. senado.
senator, s. senador.
senatorial, a. senatorio.
send, v.a. enviar, despachar, mandar ;
　　enviar ; producir.
seneschal, s. senescal.
senile, a. senil.
senility, s. senectud ; vejez.
senior, s. mayor de edad.
seniority, s. precedencia de edad, an-
　　tigüedad, ancianidad.
senna, s. (bot.) sen, sena.
sennight, s. ocho días, pl.; semana.
sensation, s. sensación.
sense, s. sentido ; entendimiento ; razón ;
　　juicio ; sentimiento. [insensatamente.
senseless, a. insensible ; insensato ; -ly,
senselessness, s. tontería, insensatez.
sensibility, s. sensibilidad.
sensible, a. sensible, sensitivo ; juicioso.
sensibly, ad. sensiblemente.
sensitive, a. sensitivo.
sensual, a. -ly, ad. sensual(mente).
sensuous, a. estético, afectivo, patético.
sensualist, s. persona sensual.
sensuality, s. sensualidad. [condenar.
sentence, s. sentencia ; —, v.a. sentenciar,
sententious, a. sentencioso ; -ly, sen-
　　tenciosamente.
sentient, a. sensitivo, sentidor.
sentiment, s. sentimiento ; opinión.
sentimental, a. sentimental.
sentinel, sentry, s. centinela.
sentry-box, s. garita de centinela.
separable, a. separable.
separate, v.a. (& n.) separar(se) ; —, a.
　　separado ; -ly, ad. separadamente

separation, s. separación. [orientales.
sepoy, s. soldado natural de las Indias
September, s. setiembre.
septennial, a. sieteñal.
septic, a. (med.) séptico.
septuagenarian, s. septuagenario.
sepulchral, a. sepulcral, fúnebre.
sepulchre, s. sepulcro.
sepulture, s. sepultura.
sequel, s. secuela, consecuencia.
sequence, s. serie, continuación.
sequester, sequestrate, v.a. secuestrar,
sequestration, s. secuestro.
seraglio, s. serallo.
seraph, s. serafín.
sere, a. marchito, seco. [serenatas.
serenade, s. serenata ; —, v.a. dar
serene, a. sereno ; -ly, serenamente.
serenity, s. serenidad.
serf, s. siervo, esclavo.
serge, s. sarga (tela de lana fina).
sergeant, serjeant, s. sargento ; alguacil ;
　　abogado de primera clase.
serial, a. & s. periódico ; folleto peri-
　　ódico.
series, s. serie.
serious, a. serio, grave ; -ly, seriamente.
sermon, s. sermón ; predicación.
sermonise, v.a. sermonear.
serous, a. seroso, acuoso.
serpent, s. serpiente, sierpe. [serpentina.
serpentine, a. serpentino ; —, s. (chem.)
serrated, a. serrado.
serum, s. suero.
servant, s. criado ; criada.
servant-girl, servant-maid, s. criada.
serve, v.a. & n. servir ; asistir (á la mesa);
　　ser á propósito, bastar.
service, s. servicio; servidumbre, utilidad ;
　　culto divino ; acomodo.
serviceable, a. servicial ; oficioso.
servile, a. -ly, ad. servil(mente).
servility, s. servilismo, bajeza, vileza de
　　ánimo.
servitude, s. servidumbre, esclavitud.
session, s. junta ; sesión.
set, v.a. poner, colocar, fijar ; establecer,
　　determinar ; parar (en el juego) ; —,
　　v.n. ponerse (el sol ó los astros) ; cua-
　　jarse ; aplicarse ; —, s. juego, conjunto
　　de buenas cartas ; servicio (de plata) ;
　　conjunto ó agregado de muchas cosas ;
　　cuadrilla, bandada ; —, a. puesto, fijo.
settee, s. canapé pequeño.
setter, s. perro de muestra.
setter-on, s. instigador.
setting, s. establecimiento, fijación ; en-
　　gaste ; — of the sun, puesta del sol.
settle, v.a. colocar, fijar, afirmar ; ar-
　　reglar ; calmar ; —, v.n. reposarse ;
　　establecerse : sosegarse ; —, s. banco.

settlement, s. establecimiento ; domicilio ; contrato ; empleo ; poso ; colonia.
settler, s. colono.
set-to, s. riña ; combate.
seven, a. siete.
sevenfold, a. séptuplo.
seventeen, a. diez y siete.
seventeenth, a. décimoséptimo. [lugar.
seventh, a. [séptimo ; -ly, en séptimo
seventieth, a. septuagésimo.
seventy, a. setenta.
sever, v.a. & n. separar, cortar.
several, a. diversos, muchos, pl. ; particular ; -ly, separadamente.
severance, s. separación.
severe, a. severo, riguroso, áspero, duro ; -ly, severamente.
severity, s. severidad.
sew, v.a. & n. coser.
sewage, s. basura.
sewer, s. albañal, caño maestro ; —, cos turera. [agua de sumidero.
sewerage, s. construcción de albañales ;
sex, s. sexo.
sexennial, a. lo que dura ó acontece en
sextant, s. sextante. [seis años.
sexton, s. sepulturero ; sacristán.
sextuple, a. séxtuplo.
sexual, a. sexual.
shabbily, ad. vilmente, mezquinamente.
shabbiness, s. vileza, bajeza, miseria.
shabby, a. vil, bajo ; desharrapado ; tacaño. [pl.
shackle, v.a. encadenar ; -s, s.pl. grillos,
shad, s. alosa, (pez.)
shade, s. sombra, obscuridad ; matiz ; sombrilla ; —, v.a. asombrar ; abrigar ; proteger.
shadiness, s. sombraje ; umbría.
shadow, s. sombra ; protección. [mérico.
shadowy, a. umbroso ; obscuro ; quimérico.
shady, a. opaco, obscuro, sombrío ; (fig.) sospechoso, equívoco, deshonesto.
shaft, s. flecha, saeta ; fuste de columna ; lanza de los coches.
shag, s. pelo áspero y lanudo ; felpa.
shaggy, a. afelpado.
shagreen, s. piel de zapa, lija.
shake, v.a. sacudir ; agitar ; —, v.n. vacilar ; temblar ; to — hands, darse las manos ; —, s. concusión, sacudida.
shaking, s. sacudimiento ; temblor.
shaky, a. titubeante.
shale, s. arcilla laminosa.
shall, v.n. def. deber.
shallop, s. (mar.) chalupa.
shallow, a. somero, superficial, poco profundo ; trivial ; —, s. bajío (banco de arena.)
shallowness, s. poca profundidad ; necedad.

sham, v.a. & n. simular, trampear, fingir ; —, s. socolor ; fingimiento ; impostura ; —, a. fingido, disimulado.
shambles, s.pl. carnicería.
shambling, a. lo que se mueve toscamente ; medio cojo.
shame, s. vergüenza ; deshonra ; —, v.a. avergonzar, deshonrar.
shamefaced, a. vergonzoso, pudoroso.
shameful, a. vergonzoso ; deshonroso ; -ly, ignominiosamente.
shameless, a. desvergonzado ; -ly, desvergonzadamente. [dencia.
shamelessness, s. desvergüenza, impu-
shampoo, v.a. dar las friegas ; — s. friega.
shamrock, s. trébol.
shank, s. pierna ; asta ; cañón de pipa.
shanty, s. (col.) cabaña, choza.
shape, v.a. & n. formar ; proporcionar ; concebir ; —, s. forma, figura ; modelo.
shapeless, a. informe.
shapely, a. bien hecho, hermoso.
share, s. parte, porción ; (com.) acción ; reja del arado ; —, v.a. & n. repartir ; participar.
shareholder, s. (com.) accionista.
sharer, s. partícipe.
shark, s. tiburón ; petardista.
sharp, a. agudo, aguzado ; astuto ; perspicaz ; penetrante ; acre, mordaz, severo, rígido ; vivo, violento ; —, s. (mus.) becuadro.
sharpen, v.a. afilar, aguzar.
sharper, s. petardista, estafador.
sharply, ad. con filo ; severamente, agudamente ; ingeniosamente.
sharpness, s. agudeza ; sutileza, perspicacia ; acrimonia.
sharpshooter, s. tirador, guerillero.
shatter, v.a. destrozar, estrellar ; —, v.n. hacerse pedazos.
shave, v.a. rasurar ; afeitar ; raspar ; rozar ; (fig.) escatimar. [rapaz.
shaver, s. barbero ; (fig.) muchacho,
shaving, s. raedura ; rasura.
shawl, s. chal.
she, pn. ella.
sheaf, s. gavilla ; —, v.a. agavillar.
shear, v.a. atusar ; tundir, esquilar ; —, s.pl. tijeras grandes.
sheath, s. vaina ; —, v.a. envainar ; (mar.) aforrar el fondo de un navío.
shed, v.a. verter, derramar ; esparcir ; —, s. sotechado, tejadillo ; cabaña ; [galpón (am.).
sheen, s. resplandor.
sheep, s. oveja ; carnero ; (fig.) papanatas.
sheep-cot, sheep-fold, s. redil.
sheepish, a. vergonzoso ; tímido.
sheepishness, s. timidez, cortedad de genio.

sheep's-eye, s. mirada al soslayo; ojeada codiciosa.

sheepskin, s. piel de carnero.

sheep-walk, s. dehesa carneril, pasto de ovejas.

sheer, a. puro, claro; precipitoso; —, ad. de un golpe; —, v.n. alargarse, escaparse.

sheet, s. sábana; pliego de papel; (mar.) escota.

sheet-anchor, s. áncora mayor.

sheeting, s. tela para sábanas.

shelf, s. anaquel; (mar.) arrecife; escollera; on the —, desecho.

shell, s. cáscara; concha; corteza; —, v.a. descascarar, descortezar; —, v.n. descascararse.

shelter, s. guarida; amparo, abrigo; asilo, refugio; —, v.a. guarecer, abrigar; acoger.

shelterless, a. sin asilo.

shelve, v.a. echar á un lado, arrinconar.

shelving, shelvy, a. inclinado, en declive.

shepherd, s. pastor; zagal.

shepherdess, s. pastora; zagala.

sherbet, s. sorbete.

sheriff, s. jerif.

sherry, s. vino de Jerez. [defender.

shield, s. escudo; patrocinio; —, v.a.

shift, v.n. cambiarse; mudarse el vestido; ingeniarse; maquinar; —, v.a. mudar, cambiar; transportar; —, s. último recurso; artificio; astucia; efugio; camisa de mujer.

shifter, s. tramoyista.

shillelagh, s. macana.

shilling, s. chelín.

shilly-shally, v.n. (col.) vacilar.

shin(-bone), s. espinilla.

shine, v.n. lucir, brillar, resplandecer.

shingle, s. ripia; guijarros de la playa; -s, pl. (med.) herpes, pl. [plendor.

shining, a. resplandeciente; —, s. es-

shiny, a. brillante, luciente.

ship, s. nave; barco, navío, buque; —, v.a. embarcar.

ship-board, s. on —, abordo.

ship-boy, s. grumete.

shipbroker, s. corredor marítimo.

ship-building, s. arquitectura naval.

shipmate, s. (mar.) camarada de abordo.

shipment, s. cargazón.

ship-owner, s. naviero.

shipper, s. fletador.

ship-shape, a. bien arreglado.

shipwreck, s. naufragio.

shipwright, ship-builder, s. constructor de barcos.

shire, s. condado (de Inglaterra).

shirk, v.a. evitar, eludir.

shirt, s. camisa.

shirting, s. Indiana para camisas.

shiver, s. cacho, pedazo, fragmento; —, v.n. tiritar de frío; —, v.a. estrellar, shivering, s. horripilación; temblor.

shoal, s. multitud, muchedumbre; bajío; —, a. lleno de bajíos; —, v.n. estar lleno de bajíos, encallarse.

shock, s. choque, encuentro; combate; ofensa; hacina; —, v.a. sacudir; ofender.

shock-headed, a. peludo, despeinado.

shoddy, s. cadura, paño barato.

shoe, s. zapato; herradura de caballo; —, v.a. calzar; herrar un caballo.

shoe-black, shoe-boy, s. limpiabotas.

shoeing, s. acto de herrar.

shoeing-horn, s. calzador.

shoelace, shoe-string, s. cordón de zapato.

shoemaker, s. zapatero.

shoot, v.a. tirar, arrojar, lanzar, disparar; —, v.n. brotar, germinar; sobresalir; lanzarse; —, s. tiro; vástago.

shooter, s. tirador.

shooting, s. caza con escopeta; tiro.

shop, s. tienda; taller.

shop-front, s. escaparate.

shop-keeper, s. tendero, mercader.

shop-lifter, s. ladrón de tiendas.

shop-man, s. mancebo de tienda; hortera (col.).

shop-walker, s. celador de tienda.

shop-woman, s. tendera.

shore, s. costa, ribera, playa; puntal, sostén; —, v.a. apuntalar, apoyar.

short, a. corto, breve, sucinto, conciso; -ly, brevemente; presto; en pocas palabras.

shortcoming, s. insuficiencia; déficit.

shorten, v.a. acortar; abreviar.

shorthand, s. taquigrafía, estenografía.

shorthand-writer, s. taquígrafo, estenógrafo.

shortness, s. cortedad; brevedad.

short-sighted, a. corto de vista.

short-sightedness, s. cortedad de vista.

shot, s. tiro; alcance; perdigones, pl.; escote.

shoulder, s. hombro; brazuelo; —, v.a. cargar al hombro.

shoulder-blade, s. omoplato.

shout, v.n. gritar, vocear; —, s. grito, gritería y exclamación.

shove, v.a. & n. empujar; impeler; —, s. empujón.

shovel, s. pala; —, v.a. traspalar.

show, v.a. mostrar; descubrir; manifestar; probar; enseñar, explicar; —, v.n. parecer; —, s. espectáculo; muestra; exposición, parada.

shower, s. llovizna; (fig.) abundancia; —, v.n. llover.

showery, a. lluvioso.

showman, a. tiritero, dueño de teatro ambulante.
showy, a. ostentoso.
shrapnel, s. (mil.) metralla.
shred, s. cacho, pedacito ; —, v.a. picar.
shrew, s. mujer de mal genio ; musgaño.
shrewd, a. astuto ; maligno ; -ly, astuta- **shrewdness**, s. astucia. [mente.
shrewish, a. regañón ; -ly, con mal humor.
shrewmouse, s. musgaño, musaraña.
shriek, v.n. chillar ; —, s. chillido.
shrike, s. (orn.) picaza.
shrill, a. agudo, penetrante.
shrillness, s. agudeza del sonido ó de la voz.
shrimp, s. camarón ; (fig.) enano, hombrecillo.
shrine, s. relicario ; altar, santuario.
shrink, v.n. encogerse, retroceder, vacilar; angostarse, acortarse, disminuir.
shrivel, v.a. & n. arrugar(se), encoger(se); tostar(se), hacer(se) cenizas.
shroud, s. cubierta ; mortaja ; -s, s.pl.; (mar.) obenques, pl.; —, v.a. cubrir, defender ; amortajar ; proteger ; —, v.n. guarecerse, refugiarse.
shrovetide, s. martes de carnaval.
shrub, s. arbusto.
shrubbery, a. plantío de arbustos, bosque.
shrug, v.a. encomerse, coscarse ; —, s. encogimiento de hombros.
shudder, v.n. estremecerse, despeluzarse ; —, s. despeluzamiento, temblor.
shuffle, v.a. & n. poner en confusión, desordenar ; barajar (los naipes) ; trampear ; tergiversar ; —, s. barajadura ; treta.
shuffling, s. tramoya.
shun, v.a. huir, evitar.
shunt, v.a. desvair, quitar ; (rail.) mover vagones á otra vía.
shut, v.a. cerrar, encerrar.
shutter, s. puertaventana, celosía.
shuttle, s. lanzadera.
shuttle-cock, s. volante, rehilete.
shy, a. tímido ; reservado ; vergonzoso, contenido ; -ly, tímidamente.
shyness, s. timidez.
sibilant, a. & s. silbidor, sibilante.
sibyl, s. sibila, profetisa.
sick, a. malo, enfermo ; disgustado.
sicken, v.a. & n. enfermar(se).
sickle, s. hoz.
sickliness, s. indisposición habitual.
sickly, a. enfermizo.
sickness, s. enfermedad.
side, s. lado ; costado ; facción ; partido ; (col.) jactancia, ostentación ; —, a. lateral ; oblicuo ; —, v.a. unirse con alguno.
sideboard, s. aparador ; alacena.
sideface, ad. en perfil.

sidelong, a. lateral ; -ly, de lado.
side-saddle, s. silla de dama.
side-scene, s. bastidores de teatro.
sideways, ad. de lado, al través.
siding, s. (rail.) aguja.
sidle, v.n. ir de lado, insinuarse.
siege, s. (mil.) sitio.
sieve, s. tamiz ; criba ; cribo. [vestigar.
sift, v.a. cerner ; cribar ; examinar ; in- **siftings**, s.pl. granzas, pl.
sigh, v.n. suspirar, gemir ; —, s. suspiro.
sight, s. vista ; mira.
sightless, a. ciego.
sightly, a. vistoso, hermoso.
sight-seeing, s. visita de curiosidades.
sign, s. señal, indicio ; tablilla ; signo ; firma ; seña ; —, v.a. señalar ; hacer señas, firmar. [señalado.
signal, s. señal, aviso ; —, a. insigne, **signalize**, v.a. señalar.
signal-light, s. (rail.) farol.
signal-man, s. (rail.) guardavía.
signature, s. firma, rúbrica.
signet, s. sello.
significance, a. importancia.
significant, a. significante.
signification, s. significación ; sentido.
signify, v.a. significar ; —, v.n. importar
sign-painter, s. pintor de letreros.
sign-post, s. pilar de anuncio.
silence, s. silencio ; —, v.a. enmudecer, acallar.
silent, a. silencioso ; -ly, silenciosamente.
silhouette, s. silueta, retrato trazado del perfil.
silk, s. seda.
silken, a. hecho de seda ; sedeño.
silkiness, s. blandura, molicie.
silk-pod, s. capullo del gusano de seda.
silk-worm, s. gusano de seda.
silky, a. hecho de seda ; sedeño.
sill, s. umbral de puerta.
sillily, ad. tontamente. [necedad.
silliness, s. simpleza, bobería, tontería.
silly, a. tonto, mentecato, imbécil.
silver, s. plata ; —, a. de plata ; —, v.a. platear.
silverer, **silversmith**, s. platero.
silvery, a. plateado. [mente.
similar, a. similar ; semejante ; -ly, igual
similarity, **similitude**, s. semejanza.
simile, s. semejanza, similitud.
simmer, v.n. hervir á fuego lento.
simony, s. simonía.
simper, v.n. sonreirse, melindrear ; —, s. sonrisa, melindres, pl.
simple, a. simple, puro, sencillo.
simpleton, s. bobo, necio. [simpleza.
simplicity, s. sencillez, simplicidad.
simplification, s. simplificación.
simplify, v.a. simplificar.

simply, ad. simplemente.
simulate, v.a. simular, fingir.
simulation, s. simulación.
simultaneous, a. simultáneo.
sin, s. pecado ; —, v.n. pecar, faltar.
since, ad. ya que ; desde que ; pues que ; —, pr. desde. [mente.
sincere, a. sincero ; franco ; -ly, sincera-
sincerity, s. sinceridad.
sinecure, s. sinecura.
sinew, s. tendón ; nervio.
sinewy, a. nervoso, robusto.
sinful, a. pecaminoso, malvado ; -ly, malvadamente. [pecador.
sinfulness, s. corrupción, estado de
sing, v.n. & a. cantar ; gorjear los pájaros ;
(poet.) celebrar.
singe, v.a. chamuscar.
singer, s. cantor ; cantora.
singing, s. canto.
single, a. sencillo, simple, solo ; soltero ;
—, v.a. singularizar ; separar.
singleness, s. sencillez, sinceridad ;
singly, ad. separadamente. [celibato.
singular, a. singular, peculiar ; -ly, singu-
larmente.
sing-song, s. canto monótono.
singularity, s. singularidad. [funesto.
sinister, a. siniestro ; viciado ; infeliz,
sink, v.n. hundirse ; sumergirse ; bajarse ;
penetrar ; arruinarse, decaer ; —, v.a.
hundir, echar á lo hondo ; deprimir,
destruir ; —, s. sentina, sumidero.
sinking-fund, s. caja de amortización.
sinner, s. pecador ; pecadora.
sin-offering, s. sacrificio propiciatorio.
sinuosity, s. sinuosidad.
sinuous, a. sinuoso.
sip, v.a. beborrotear, sorber ; —, s. sorbo.
siphon, s. sifón.
sippet, s. rebanada de pan, tostada.
Sir, s. Señor.
sire, s. engendrador, padre.
siren, s. sirena.
sirloin, s. lomo de buey ó vaca.
sirup, s. sorbete.
sister, a. hermana ; religiosa.
sisterhood, s. hermandad.
sister-in-law, s. cuñada.
sisterly, a. cariñosa.
sit, v.n. sentarse ; estar situado.
site, s. sitio ; situación.
sitting, s. sesión, junta ; sentada.
situate, a. situado.
situation, s. situación.
six, a. seis. [pl.
sixpence, s. seis peniques (medio chelin),
sixteen, a. diez y seis.
sixteenth, a. décimosexto.
sixth, a. sexto ; -ly, en sexto lugar.
sixtieth, a. sexagésimo.

sixty, a. sesenta. [universidad.
sizar, s. estudiante premiado en la
size, s. tamaño, talle ; calibre ; dimensión ;
l. estatura ; cola de retazo ; —, v.a.
l. encolar. [grandor de las cosas.
sized, a. lo que pertenece al tamaño ó
skate, s. lija (pez) ; patín ; —, v.n. patinar.
skating-rink, s. lugar para patinar.
skein, s. madeja.
skeleton, s. esqueleto.
skeleton-key, s. llave maestra.
sketch, s. esbozo ; esquicio ; —, v.a.
esquiciar, bosquejar.
skew, a. oblicuo. [—, v.a. espetar.
skewer, s. aguja de lardear ; espetón ;
skid, s. arrastradera de un carruaje ; —,
v.n. resbalar, deslizarse.
skiff, s. esquife. [mente.
skilful, a. práctico, diestro ; -ly, diestra-
skilfulness, s. destreza.
skill, s. destreza, arte, pericia.
skilled, a. práctico, diestro.
skillet, s. marmita pequeña.
skim, v.a. espumar ; tratar superficial-
mente ; —, s. espuma.
skimmer, s. espumadera.
skin, cutis ; —, v.a. desollar.
skinned, s. desollado.
skinner, s. pellejero ; peletero.
skinflint, s. tacaño, avariento.
skinny, a. flaco, macilento.
skip, v.n. saltar, brincar ; —, v.a. pasar,
omitir ; atrancar ; —, s. salto, brinco.
skipper, s. patrón, capitán de barco.
skirmish, s. escaramuza ; —, v.n. escaramuzar.
skirmisher, s. escaramuzador. [costear.
skirt, s. falda, orla ; —, v.a. orillar ;
skit, s. burla, zumba ; sátira.
skittish, a. retozón ; inconstante ; -ly,
caprichosamente.
skittle, s. bola ; -s, (col.) ¡ disparates !
skulk, v.n. acechar.
skull, s. cráneo.
skull-cap, s. gorro.
skunk, s. (zool.) mofeta ; (fig.) hombre
vil y despreciable.
sky, s. cielo, firmamento.
sky-light, s. claraboya.
sky-rocket, s. cohete.
slab, s. losa.
slack, a. flojo ; perezoso, negligente, lento.
slack(en), v.a. & n. aflojar ; ablandar ;
entibiarse ; decaer ; relajar ; aliviar.
slackness, s. flojedad, remisión ; descuido.
slag, s. escoria.
slake, v.a. extinguir.
slam, s. golpe violento, capote (en los
juegos de naipes) ; —, v.a. cerrar ó
empujar con violencia. [calumnia.
slander, v.a. calumniar, infamar ; —, s.

slanderer, s. calumniador, maldiciente.
slanderous, a. calumnioso ; -ly, calumni-
slang, s. jerigonza.   [osamente.
slant, v.n. pender oblicuamente.
slanting, a. sesgado, oblicuo.
slap, s. manotada ; bofetada ; —, ad. de
  un golpe ; —, v.a. golpear, dar una
  bofetada.   [mente.
slap-dash, ad. de sopetón, precipitada-
slash, v.a. acuchillar ; golpear ; —, s.
  cuchillada, golpe.
slashing, a. mordaz ; impetuoso.
slate, s. pizarra.
slate-pencil, s. lápiz de pizarra.
slater, s. pizarrero.
slating, s. techo de pizarras.
slattern, s. mujer desaliñada.
slatternly, a. desaliñada.
slaughter, s. carnicería, matanza ; —, v.a.
  matar atrozmente ; matar (reses).
slaughter-house, s. matadero, rastro.
slaughterer, s. matador, asesino.
slave, s. esclavo ; esclava ; —, v.n. trabajar como esclavo, afanarse.
slaver, slave-ship, s. negrero (navío).
slaver, s. baba ; —, v.n. babosear.
slavery, s. esclavitud.   [mente.
slavish, a. servil, humilde ; -ly, servil-
slavishness, s. bajeza, servilismo.
slay, v.a. matar, quitar la vida.
slayer, s. matador.   [trineo.
sled, sledge, sleigh, s. rastra, narria ;
sledge-hammer, s. macho.   [pulir.
sleek, a. liso, bruñido ; —, v.a. alisar,
sleep, v.n. dormir ; —, s. sueño.
sleeper, s. dormilón ; (rail.) durmiente.
sleepily, ad. con somnolencia ó torpeza.
sleepiness, s. adormecimiento, somnolencia.
sleeping-room, s. dormitorio.
sleepless, a. desvelado.
sleep-walking, s. sonambulismo.   [sueño.
sleepy, a. soñoliento ; to be, —, tener
sleet, s. aguanieve ; —, v.n. caer aguan-
sleeve, s. manga.   [ieve.
sleight, s. astucia, maña.
sleight-of-hand, s. prestidigitación.
slender, a. delgado, sutil, débil, pequeño-
  escaso ; -ly, delgadamente.
slenderness, s. delgadez ; tenuidad.
slice, s. rebanada, lonja ; tajada, espátula
  —, v.a. rebanar.
slide, v.n. resbalar, deslizarse ; correr por
  encima del hielo ; —, s. resbalón ;
  resbaladero ; corredera.
sliding, s. deslizamiento.
sliding-scale, s. (com.) escala movible.
slight, a. ligero, leve, pequeño ; —, s.
  descuido ; desaire ; —, v.a. despreciar.
slightingly, ad. con desprecio.
slightly, ligeramente.

slightness, s. debilidad ; negligencia.
slim, a. delgado, sutil.
slime, s. lodo ; substancia viscosa.
sliminess, s. viscosidad.
slimy, a. viscoso, pegajoso. [con honda.
sling, s. honda ; hondazo ; —, v.a. tirar
slink, v.n. escaparse ; deslizarse.
slip, v.n. resbalar ; escapar, huirse ; —,
  v.a. meter ó introducir secretamente ;
  dejar ; —, s. resbalón ; tropiezo
  escapada.
slipper, s. chinela.
slipperiness, s. calidad resbaladiza.
slippery, a. resbaladizo.
slipshod, a. en chancleta ;] (fig.) desaliñado, negligente.   [dedura.
slit, v.a. rajar, hender ; —, s. raja, hen-
slobber, s. baba ; —, v.n. babear.
sloe, s. endrina.
sloop, s. (mar.) balandra.
slop, s. aguachirle ; lodazal ; -s, pl.
  gregüescos, pl.   [v.a. sesgar.
slope, s. sesgo ; declivio ; escarpa ; —,
sloping, a. oblicuo ; declive.
slop-pail, s. cubeta.
sloppy, a. lodoso.   [América.
sloth, s. pereza ; perezoso (animal de
slothful, a. perezoso.
slouch, v.a. & n. estar cabizbajo (como
  un patán) ; bambolearse pesadamente.
slough, s. lodazal ; —, pellejo de serpiente;
  escara (de una herida).
sloughy, a. lodoso.
sloven, s. hombre desaliñado.
slovenliness, s. desaliño.
slovenly, a. desaliñado, sucio.
slow, a. tardío, lento, torpe, perezoso ;
  -ly, lentamente.
slowness, s. lentitud, tardanza, pesadez.
slow-worm, s. cecilia. [pedazo de metal.
slug, s. babosa, holgazán, zángano ;
sluggard, s. haragán, holgazán.
sluggish, a. perezoso ; lento ; -ly, perezosamente.
sluggishness, s. pereza.
sluice, s. compuerta, esclusa ; —, v.a.
  cubrir con agua, empapar.
slum, s. garito ; callejuela.   [ligero.
slumber, v.n. dormitar ; —, s. sueño
slump, s. (com.) baja repentina.
slur, v.a. ensuciar ; manchar ; pasar
  ligeramente ; —, s. (mus.) ligado.
slush, s. lodo, barro, cieno.
slut, mujer sucia, mujerzuela.
sly, a. astuto ; -ly, astutamente.
sly-boots, s. (col.) pícaro, astuto.
slyness, s. astucia, maña.
smack, s. sabor, gusto ; manotada ; beso
  fuerte (que se oye) ; chasquido de
  latigo ; —, v.n. saber ; manotear.
small, a. pequeño, menudo.

smallish, a. algo pequeño.
smallness, s. pequeñez.
small-pox, s. viruelas, pl.
small-talk, s. charla.
smalt, s. esmalte.
smart, s. escozor ; —, a. punzante, agudo, agrio ; ingenioso ; mordaz ; doloroso ; —, v.n. escocer.
smartly, ad. agudamente, vivamente.
smartness, s. agudeza, viveza, sutileza.
smash, v.a. romper, quebrantar ; —, s. fracaso.
smatterer, s. erudito somero.
smattering, s. conocimiento superficial.
smear, v.a. untar ; emporcar.
smell, v.a. & n. oler ; percibir ; —, s. olfato ; olor ; hediondez.
smelling-bottle, s. pomito de olor.
smelt, s. espirenque (pez) ; —, v.a.
smelter, s. fundidor.   [fundir (el metal).
smile, v.n. sonreirse ; —, s. sonrisa.
smirk, v.n. sonreirse con afectación.
smite, v.a. herir, golpear.
smith, s. herrero, forjador de metales.
smithery, smithy, s. herrería, fragua.
smock, s. camisa de mujer.
smock-frock, s. blusa.
smoke, s. humo ; vapor ; —, v.a. & n. ahumar ; humear ; fumar (tobacco).
smoke-dry, v.a. ahumar, secar al humo.
smokeless, a. sin humo.
smoker, s. fumador.
smoky, a. humeante ; humoso.
smooth, a. liso, pulido, llano ; suave ; afable ; —, v.a. allanar ; alisar ; lisonjear.
smoothly, ad. llanamente ; con blandura.
smoothness, s. lisura ; llanura ; suavidad.
smother, v.a. sofocar ; ahogar ; suprimir ; —, s. humareda.
smoulder, v.n. arder debajo la ceniza.
smudge, v.a. mancha, mugre ; —, v.a. manchar, ennegrecer.   [esto.
smug, a. atildado, nimiamente compu-
smuggle, v.a. hacer el contrabando, matutear.
smuggler, s. contrabandista.
smuggling, s. contrabando.
smut, s. tiznón, mancha ; tizón ; suciedad —, v.a. tiznar ; ensuciar.
smuttiness, s. tizne ; obscenidad.
smutty, a. tiznado ; anieblado ; obsceno.
snack, s. parte, porción.
snaffle, s. brida sencilla.   [sumergido.
snag, s. dentadura ; corcova ; arbol
snail, s. caracol.
snake, s. culebra, serpiente.
snaky, a. serpentino.
snap, v.a. & n. romper ; agarrar ; morder ; insultar ; (one's fingers) castañetear ; —, s. estallido.

snapdragon, s. (bot.) antirrino.
snappish, a. mordaz ; regañón ; -ly, agria-mente.
snappishness, s. irritabilidad.
snare, s. lazo ; trampa.
snarl, v.n. regañar, gruñir.
snarler, s. regañón.
snatch, v.a. arrebatar ; agarrar ; —, s. arrebatamiento ; bocado.   [servil.
sneak, v.n. arrastrarse ; —, s. hombre
sneer, v.n. hablar con desprecio ; fisgarse ; —, s. fisga.
sneeringly, ad. con desprecio.
sneeze, v.n. estornudar.
sniff, v.n. resollar, hacer muecas.
snigger, v.n. reir con intención sarcástica.
snip, v.a. tijeretear ; —, s. tijeretada, pedazo pequeño ; porción.
snipe, s. chocha.
snivel, s. moquita ; —, v.n. moquear.
sniveller, s. lloraduelos.
snob, s. medrado ; galopín.
snobbish, a. cursi.
snood, s. cinta de cabello.
snooze, s. sueño ligero.
snore, v.n. roncar ; —, s. ronquido.
snort, v.n. resoplar (bufar como un caballo fogoso).
snout, s. hocico.
snow, s. nieve ; —, v.n. nevar.
snow-ball, s. pelota de nieve.
snow-drop, s. (bot.) campanilla blanca.
snowy, a. nevoso ; nevado.
snub, v.a. reprender, regañar.
snub-nosed, a. romo.
snuff, s. moco de candela ; pábilo ; tabaco de polvo ; [rapé] ; —, v.a. atraer en la nariz con el aliento ; despabilar ;
snuff-box, s. tabaquera.   [oler.
snuffers, s.pl. despabiladeras, pl.
snuffle, v.n. ganguear, hablar gangoso.
snug, a. abrigado ; conveniente, cómodo, agradable, grato.
snuggery, s. despacho retirado.
so, ad. así ; tan ; de modo que ; and — forth, y así de lo demás.
soak, v.n. & a. remojarse ; calarse ; empapar, remojar.
soaker, s. beberrón.
soap, s. jabón ; —, v.a. jabonar.
soap-boiler, s. jabonero.
soap-bubble, s. ampolla de jabón.
soap-suds, s. jabonaduras, pl.
soapy, a. jabonoso.
soar, v.n. volar, remontarse, sublimarse.
soaring, s. vuelo muy alto.
sob, s. sollozo ; —, v.n. sollozar.
sober, a. sobrio ; serio ; -ly, sobriamente ; juiciosamente.   [fría.
sobriety, s. sobriedad; seriedad, sangre
sociability, s. sociabilidad.

sociable, a. sociable, communicativo.
sociably, ad. sociablemente. [mente.
social, a. social, sociable ; -ly, sociable-
socialism, s. socialismo.
socialist, s. socialista.
society, s. sociedad ; compañía.
sock, s. escarpín ; media.
socket, s. cañón del candelero ; cuenca del ojo ; alvéolo de un diente.
socle, s. zócalo, plinto.
sod, s. césped ; turba.
soda, s. sosa, soda.
soever, s. que sea.
sofa, s. sofá.
soft, a. blando, mole, suavecito ; benigno, tierno ; jugoso ; afeminado ; -ly, suavemente ; despacio.
soften, v.a. ablandar, mitigar ; enternecer
soft-hearted, a. compasivo.
softness, s. blandura, dulzura.
soft-spoken, a. afable.
soil, v.a. ensuciar, emporcar ; —, s. mancha, porquería ; terreno ; tierra.
sojourn, v.n. residir, morar ; —, s. morada ; residencia. [consuelo.
solace, v.a. solazar, consolar ; —, s.
solar, a. solar.
sold, s. sueldo, estipendio.
solder, v.a. soldar ; —, s. soldadura.
soldier, s. soldado.
soldierlike, soldierly, a. soldadesco.
soldiery, s. soldadesca.
sole, s. planta del pie ; suela del zapato ; —, a. único, solo ; —, v.a. solar.
solecism, s. (gr.) solecismo.
solemn, a. -ly, ad. solemne(mente).
solemnity, s. solemnidad.
solemnization, s. solemnización.
solemnize, v.a. solemnizar.
solicit, v.a. solicitar ; implorar.
solicitation, s. solicitación.
solicitor, s. procurador, solicitador.
solicitous, a. solícito, diligente ; -ly, solícitamente.
solicitude, s. solicitud. [mente.
solid, a. sólido, compacto ; -ly, sólida-
solidify, v.a. solidificar.
solidity, s. solidez.
soliloquize, v.n. hablar á solas.
soliloquy, s. soliloquio.
solitaire, s. solitario.
solitarily, ad. solitariamente.
solitariness, s. soledad ; retiro.
solitary, a. solitario, retirado ; —, s. ermitaño.
solitude, s. soledad ; vida solitaria.
solo, s. (mus.) solo.
solstice, s. solsticio.
soluble, a. soluble.
solution, s. solución.
solve, v.a. solver, disolver.

solvency, s. solvencia.
solvent, a. solvente.
some, a. algo de, un poco, algún, alguno, alguna, unos, pocos, ciertos.
somebody, s. alguien.
somehow, ad. de algún modo.
somerset, somersault, s. salto de volteo.
something, s. alguna cosa, algo ; —, ad algún tanto. [guamente.
sometime, ad. en algún tiempo, anti-
sometimes, ad. algunas veces.
somewhat, s. alguna cosa, algo ; —, ad. algún tanto, un poco.
somewhere, ad. en alguna parte.
somnambulism, s. somnambulismo.
somnambulist, s. sonámbulo.
somnolence, s. somnolencia.
somnolent, a. somnolente, soñoliento.
son, s. hijo.
sonata, s. (mus.) sonata.
song, s. canción.
songster, s. cantor.
songstress, s. cantatriz.
son-in-law, s. yerno.
sonnet, s. soneto.
sonorous, a. sonoro ; -ly, sonoramente.
soon, ad. presto, pronto ; as — as, luego
sooner, ad. antes, más pronto.] [que.
soot, s. hollín. [mente.
sooth, s. verdad ; in good —, verdadera·
soothe, v.a. adular ; calmar.
soothsayer, s. adivino.
sooty, a. holliniento, fuliginoso.
sop, s. sopa.
sophism s. sofisma.
sophist, s. sofista.
sophistic(al), a. sofístico.
sophisticate, v.a. sofisticar ; falsificar.
sophistry, s. sofistería.
soporific, a. soporífero.
sorcerer, s. hechicero.
sorceress, s. hechicera.
sorcery, s. hechizo, encanto.
sordid, a. sórdido, sucio ; avariento ; -ly, codiciosamente.
sordidness, s. sordidez, mezquindad.
sore, s. llaga, úlcera ; —, a. doloroso penoso ; -ly, penosamente.
soreness, s. dolencia ; mal.
sorrel, s. (bot.) acedera ; —, a. alazán rojo.
sorrily, ad. malamente, pobremente.
sorrow, s. pesar ; tristeza ; —, v.n. entristecerse. [con aflicción.
sorrowful, a. pesaroso, afligido ; -ly,
sorry, a. triste, afligido ; I am — for it, lo siento.
sort, s. suerte ; género ; especie ; calidad ; manera ; —, v.a. separar en distintas clases ; escoger, elegir.
so-so, a. (col.) ordinario.
sot, s. zote.

sottish, a. torpe, rudo ; -ly, torpemente.
soul, s. alma ; esencia ; persona.
sound, a. sano ; entero ; puro ; firme ;
-ly, sanamente, vigorosamente ; —, s.
tienta, sonda ; sonido, ruido ; —, v.a.
sondar ; sonar, tocar ; celebrar ; —,
v.n. sonar, resonar.
sound(ing)-board, s. sombrero de púlpito.
sounding-lead, s. escandallo.
sounding-line, s. sondalesa.
soundings, s.pl. (mar.) sondeo.
soundness, s. sanidad ; fuerza, solidez.
soup, s. sopa.
sour, a. agrio, ácido ; áspero ; -ly, agria-
mente ; —, v.a. & n. agriar, acedar ;
agriarse.
source, s. manantial ; principio.
sourness, s. acedía, agrura ; acrimonia.
souse, s. salmuera ; —, ad. (col.) zas, con
violencia ; —, v.a. escabechar ; chapu-
south, s. mediodía, sud, sur. [zar.
southerly, southern, a. meridional.
southward, ad. hacia el mediodía.
southwester, s. (mar.) viento de sudoeste;
sombrero grande de los marineros.
sovereign, a. & s. soberano.
sovereignty, s. soberanía.
sow, s. cerda, puerca, marrana.
sow, v.a. sembrar, esparcir.
sowing-time, s. sementera, siembra.
space, s. espacio ; intersticio.
spacious, a. espacioso, amplio ; -ly, con
bastante espacio.
spaciousness, s. espaciosidad. [naipes.
spade, s. laya, azada ; espadas, (en los
span, s. palmo ; —, v.a. medir á palmos ;
cruzar, atravesar.
spangle, s. lentejuela ; —, v.a. adornar
con lentejuelas.
spaniel, s. sabueso.
Spanish fly, s. cantárida.
Spanish leather, s. cordobán.
spar, s. espato ; (mar.) palo ; —, v.n. fingir
un combate á puñadas.
spare, v.a. & n. ahorrar, economizar ;
perdonar ; vivir con economía ; —, a.
escaso, económico ; -ly, escasamente.
sparing, a. escaso, raro, económico ; -ly,
parcamente, frugalmente.
spark, s. chispa ; centella ; pisaverde.
sparkle, s. centella, chispa ; —, v.n.
chispear ; espumar.
sparrow, s. gorrión, pardal.
sparrow-hawk, s. gavilán.
sparse, a. delgado ; tenue ; -ly, tenue-
mente.
spasm, s. espasmo.
spasmodic, a. espasmódico.
spatter, v.a. salpicar, manchar.
spatterdashes, spats, s.pl. polainas, pl.
spatula, s. espátula.

spavin, s. esparaván. [engendrar.
spawn, s. freza ; —, v.a. & n. desovar ;
spawning, s. freza.
speak, v.a. & n. hablar ; decir ; arengar ;
conversar ; pronunciar.
speaker, s. el que habla ; orador.
speaking-trumpet, s. bocina.
spear, s. lanza ; arpón ; —, v.a. herir con
lanza. [cialmente.
special, a. especial, particular ; -ly, espe-
specialty, speciality, s. especialidad.
specie, s. dinero contante.
species, s. especie.
specific(al), a. específico ; —, s. específico.
specifically, ad. específicamente.
specification, s. especificación.
specify, v.a. especificar.
specimen, s. muestra ; prueba.
specious, a. especioso, plausible ; -ly,
especiosamente. [abigarrar, manchar.
speck(le), s. mácula, tacha ; —, v.a.
spectacle, s. espectáculo ; -s, pl. anteojos.
spectator, s. espectador. [pl.
spectral, a. aduendado ; — analysis,
s. análisis del espectro solar.
spectre, s. espectro ; fantasma.
spectrum, s. espectro.
speculate, v.n. especular ; reflexionar.
speculation, s. especulación; especulativa;
meditación.
speculative, a. especulativo, teórico.
speech, s. habla ; arenga ; conversación.
speechify, v.n. arengar.
speechless, a. mudo.
speed, s. prisa ; celeridad ; —, v.a. apresurar ; despachar ; ayudar ; —, v.n.
darse priesa ; salir bien.
speedily, ad. aceleradamente, de priesa.
speediness, s. celeridad, prontitud, pre
cipitación.
speedy, a. veloz, pronto, diligente.
spell, s. hechizo, encanto ; —, v.a. & n.
escribir correctamente ; deletrear.
spelling-book, s. silabario.
spell-bound, a. encantado, mudo.
spelter, s. zinc.
spend, v.a. gastar ; disipar ; consumir ;
—, v.n. hacer gastos ; consumirse.
spendthrift, s. pródigo.
spent, a. agotado ; agobiado.
sperm, s. esperma.
spermaceti, s. espermaceti.
spew, v.n. vomitar.
sphere, s. esfera.
spheric(al), a. esférico ; -ly, en forma
esférica. [especiar.
spice, s. especia ; migaja ; —, v.a.
spicily, ad. de un modo picante.
spick-and-span, a. flamante.
spicy, a. aromático.
spider, s. araña ; —'s web, telaraña.

spigot, s. espita ó llave de un baril.

spike, s. espiga de grano ; espigón ; —, v.n. clavar con espigones.

spikenard, s. nardo. [espiga.

spill, v.a. derramar, verter ; —, s. clavija,

spin, v.a. hilar ; alargar, prolongar ; —, v.n. hilar ; correr hilo á hilo.

spinach, spinage, s. espinaca.

spinal, a. espinal.

spindle, s. huso ; quicio.

spindle-legged, -shanked, a. zanquivano.

spine, s. espinazo, espina.

spinet, s. (mus.) espineta.

spinner, s. hilador ; hilandera.

spinney, s. matorral, bosquecito.

spinning-jenny, s. máquina de hilar.

spinning-wheel, s. torno de hilar.

spinster, s. hilandera ; doncella, soltera.

spiral, a. & s. espiral ; -ly, en figura de espiral. [torre).

spire, s. espira ; pirámide ; aguja (de una

spirit, s. aliento ; espíritu ; ánimo, valor ; brío ; humor ; fantasma ; —, v.a. incitar, animar ; to — away, quitar secretamente.

spirited, a. vivo, brioso ; -ly, con espíritu.

spirit-lamp, s. calentador alimentado con alcohol.

spiritless, a. abatido, sin espíritu.

spiritual, a. -ly, espiritual(mente).

spiritualist, s. espiritualista.

spirituality, s. espiritualidad.

spirituous, s. espirit(u)oso.

spirt, v.a. & n. arrojar un líquido en un chorro ; jeringar. [escupir.

spit, s. asador ; —, v.a. & n. espetar ;

spite, s. rencor, malevolencia ; in — of, á pesar de, á despecho ; —, v.a. dar pesar. [malignamente, con tirria.

spiteful, a. rencoroso, malicioso ; -ly,

spitefulness, s. malicia, rencor.

spitfire, s. locarias, matasiete.

spittle, s. saliva ; esputo.

spittoon, s. escupidera.

splash, v.a. salpicar, enlodar.

splash-board, s. mantelete.

splay, v.a. desplegar, extender.

splay-footed, a. con los pies chatos.

spleen, s. bazo ; mal humor.

splendid, a. espléndido, magnífico ; -ly, ad. espléndidamente.

splendour, s. esplendor ; pompa.

splenetic(al), a. atrabiliario.

splice, v.a. (mar.) empalmar, empleitar.

splint, s. astilla ; -s, pl. brazales, pl.

splinter, s. cacho ; astilla ; brisna ; —, v.a. (& n.) hender(se).

split, v.a. hender, rajar ; —, v.n. henderse

spoil, v.a. pillar, robar ; despojar ; arruinar ; —, v.n. corromperse, dañarse ; —, s. despojo, botín ; ruina.

spoiler, s. corruptor, robador.

spoke, s. rayo de la rueda.

spokesman, s. orador, intérprete.

spoliate, v.a. robar, pillar. [bienes.

spoliation, s. despojo ; espoliación de

sponge, s. esponja ; —, v.a. limpiar con esponja ; —, v.n. meterse de mogollón.

sponge-bath, s. baño movible.

sponger, s. pegote, mogollón.

sponginess, s. calidad esponjosa.

sponging-house, s. posada para deudores presos.

spongy, a. esponjoso.

sponsor, s. fiador ; padrino ; madrina.

spontaneity, s. espontaneidad, voluntariedad.

spontaneous, a. espontáneo ; -ly, espontáneamente.

spool, s. canilla, broca.

spoon, s. cuchara.

spoonful, s. cucharada.

sporadic(al), a. esporádico.

sport, s. juego, retozo ; juguete, divertimiento, recreo, pasatiempo ; —, v.a. divertirse ; —, v.n. chancear, juguetear.

sportive, a. festivo, juguetón.

sportiveness, s. festividad, holganza.

sportsman, s. Cazador.

spot, s. mancha ; borrón ; sitio, lugar ; —, v.a. abigarrar ; manchar.

spotless, a. limpio, inmaculado.

spotted, spotty, a. lleno de manchas, sucio.

spousal, s. nupcias, pl. ; —, a. matrimonial, nupcial.

spouse, s. esposo ; esposa.

spout, v.a. & n. arrojar agua ; borbotar ; chorrear ; (fig.) arengar ; —, s. llave de fuente ; gárgola.

sprain, a. descoyuntar ; —, s. dislocación.

sprat, s. especie de arenque (pez).

sprawl, v.n. revolcarse.

spray, s. ramito ; vástago ; espuma de la mar ; —, v.a. salpicar, rociar.

spread, v.a. extender, desplegar ; esparcir, divulgar ; —, v.n. extenderse, desplegarse ; —, s. extensión, dilatación.

spree, s. (col.) excursión, fiesta, festín.

sprig, s. ramito.

sprightliness, s. alegría, vivacidad.

sprightly, a. alegre, despierto, vivaracho.

spring, v.n. brotar, arrojarse ; nacer, provenir ; dimanar, originarse ; saltar, brincar ; —, v.a. excitar ; hacer volar ; —, s. primavera ; elasticidad ; muelle, resorte ; salto ; manantial.

springe, s. lazo de cazador.

springiness, s. elasticidad.

spring-tide, s. marea fuerte.

spring-water, s. agua de fuente.

springy, a. elástico. [mentar.
sprinkle, v.a. rociar; hisopear; salpi-
sprint, v.n. (col.) esfuerzo en corriendo;
　—, v.n. esforzerse á correr.
sprite, s. espíritu; fantasma.
sprout, s. vástago, renuevo; -s, s.pl.
　bretones; —, v.n. brotar.
spruce, a. pulido, gentil; -ly, bellamente,
　lindamente; — oneself, v.r. vestirse
　con afectación; —, s. especie de pino,
　abeto.
spruceness, s. lindeza, hermosura.
spume, s. espuma; —, v.n. espumar,
spunk, s. (col.) coraje.
spur, s. espuela; espolón (del gallo);
　estímulo; —, v.a. espolear; estimular.
spurious, a. espurio, falso; contrahecho;
　supuesto; bastardo.
spurn, v.a. acocear; despreciar.
spurt, v.a. & n. manar, brotar; V.
　sprint.
sputter, v.n. babosear; barbotar.
sputterer, s. farámallero. [columbrar.
spy, s. espía; —, v.a. & n. espiar;
spy-glass, s. anteojo de larga vista.
squab, a. implume; cachigordo, re-
　gordete; —, s. pichón. [riña, disputa.
squabble, v.n. reñir, disputar; —, s.
squabbler, s. pendenciero.
squad, s. escuadra de soldados.
squadron, s. (mil. & mar.) escuadra.
squalid, a. mezquino, sucio.
squall, s. chubasco; —, v.n. chillar.
squally, a. borrascoso.
squalor, s. miseria, suciedad.
squander, v.a. malgastar, disipar.
square, a. cuadrado, cuadrángulo;
　exacto; cabal; —, s. cuadro; plaza;
　—, v.n. cuadrar; ajustar, arreglar;
　—, v.n. ajustarse.
squash, v.a. aplastar.
squat, v.n. agacharse; —, a. agachado;
　rechoncho.
squatter, s. colono usurpador.
squaw, s. mujer india.
squeak, v.n. plañir, chillar; —, s. grito.
squeal, v.n. plañir, gritar. [plañido.
squeamish, a. fastidioso; demasiado
　delicado. [char; —, s. compresión.
squeeze, v.a. apretar, comprimir; estre-
squib, s. cohete; (col.) sátira. [quear.
squint, s. ojizaino; bizco; —, v.n. biz-
Squire, s. Caballero (tratamiento de
squirrel, s. ardilla. [cortesía).
squirt, v.a. jeringar; —, s. jeringa;
　chorro. [lada.
stab, v.a. herir con puñal; —, s. puña-
stability, s. estabilidad, solidez.
stable, s. establo; caballeriza; —, v.a.
　poner en el establo; —, a. estable.
stabling, s. caballerizas.

stack, s. niara; —, v.a. hacinar.
staff, s. báculo, palo, bastón; apoyo
　(mil.) estado mayor.
stag, s. ciervo.
stage, s. tablado; teatro; escalón.
stager, s. veterano.
stagger, v.n. vacilar, titubear; estar inci-
　erto; —, v.a. asustar; hacer vacilar.
stagnancy, **stagnation**, s. estagnación.
stagnant, a. estancado.
stagnate, v.n. estancarse.
staid, a. grave, serio.
staidness, s. gravedad.
stain, v.a. manchar; —, s. mancha; des-
　honra.
stainer, s. tinterero.
stainless, a. limpio; inmaculado.
stair, s. escalón; -s, pl. escalera.
staircase, s. escalera.
stake, s. estaca; posta (en el juego); —,
　v.a. estacar; poner en el juego.
stalactite, s. estalactita.
stalagmite, s. estalagmita.
stale, a. añejo, viejo, rancio; —, s. orina;
　—, v.n. orinar (los animales).
staleness, s. vejez; rancidez.
stalk, v.n. andar con paso majestuoso;
　—, v.a. circunvenir (la caza); —, s.
　paso orgulloso; tallo, pie, tronco,
　troncho (de hortalizas).
stalking-horse, s. caballo verdadero ó
　figurado que sirve á los cazadores para
　ocultarse y cazar, máscara; disfraz.
stall, s. pesebre; tienda portátil;
　tabanco; silla (de coro); butaca en el
　teatro; —, v.a. metre en el establo.
stallion, s. caballo, entero.
stalwart, a. robusto, vigoroso.
stamen, s. estambre; fundamento.
stamina, s. fuerza física.
stammer, v.n. tartamudear.
stammerer, s. tartamudo.
stamp, v.a. patear; moler, majar;
　estampar, imprimir; acuñar; andar
　con mucha pesadez; —, s. cuño; sello;
　impresión; estampa.
stampede, s. susto, terror pánico; —, v.n.
　huir en terror.
stanch, v.a. (& n.) estancar(se); —, a.
　sano; firme, seguro, zeloso.
stand, v.n. estar en pie ó derecho;
　sostenerse; resistir; permanecer; par-
　arse, hacer alto, estar situado; ha-
　llarse; —, v.a. sostener, aguantar; —,
　s. puesto, sitio; posición, situación;
　parada; estado; estante, vasar.
standard, s. estandarte; modelo; precio
　ordinario; norma.
standing, a. permanente, fijado, es-
　tablecido; estancado; —, s. duración;
　posición; puesto.

stand-still, s. pausa ; alto.
stanza, s. estrofa.
staple, s. emporio de comercio ; escala de depósito ; cerradero ; —, a. establecido, principal.
star, s. estrella ; asterisco.
starboard, s. estribor.
starch, s. almidón ; —, v.a. almidonar.
stare, v.n. clavar la vista ; —, s. mirada fija.
staringly, ad. brillantemente. [fija.
stark, a. fuerte, áspero ; puro ; —, ad. del todo.
starless, a. sin estrellas. [todo.
starling, s. estornino.
starred, starry, a. estrellado.
start, v.n. sobrecogerse, sobresaltarse, estremecerse ; levantarse de repente ; salir, partir, marcharse ; —, v.a. sobrecoger ; suscitar ; descubrir ; —, s. sobresalto ; ímpetu ; paso primero, salida. [en las carreras.
starter, s. el oficial que da la salida
starting-point, s. poste de salida (en las carreras), raya.
startle, v.a. sobresaltar, estremecer ; —, s. espanto, susto repentino. [ción.
starvation, s. muerte de hambre, inanistarve, v.n. perecer de hambre.
starveling, s. hombre hambriento.
state, s. estado ; condición ; Estado (político) ; pompa, grandeza ; —, v.a. alegar, afirmar.
stateliness, s. grandeza, pompa.
stately, a. augusto, majestuoso.
statement, s. relación, cuenta.
statesman, s. estadista, político.
statesmanlike, a. hábil en la política.
statesmanship, s. política.
statics, s. estática.
station, s. estación ; empleo, puesto ; situación, postura ; grado ; condición ; (rail.) estación ; —, v.a. apostar, colocar.
stationary, a. estacionario, fijo.
stationer, s. librero-papelero.
stationery, s. toda especie de papel y demás cosas necesarias para escribir.
statist, statistician, s. estadista.
statistic(al), a. estadístico.
statistics, s.pl. estadística.
statuary, s. estatuario, escultor ; estatuaria ; colección de estatuas.
statue, s. estatua.
stature, s. estatura, talle.
status, s. estado, rango.
statute, s. estatuto ; reglamento.
stave, v.a. descabezar algún barril ; —, s. canción ; -s, s.pl. duelas de barril, pl.
stay, s. estancia, mansión ; -s, s.pl. corsé, justillo ; —, v.n. quedarse, estarse ; tardar, detenerse ; aguardarse, esperarse ; —, v.a. detener ; contener ; apoyar.

stead, s. lugar.
steadfast, a. firme, estable, sólido ; **-ly,** firmamente, con constancia.
steadfastness, s. firmeza, constancia.
steadily, ad. firmemente ; invariablemente.
steadiness, s. firmeza, estabilidad.
steady, a. firme, fijo ; —, v.a. hacer firme.
steak, s. tajada de carne.
steal, v.a. & n. hurtar, robar ; introducirse clandestinamente ; deslizarse.
stealth, s. hurto ; by —, á hurtadillas.
stealthily, ad. furtivamente.
stealthy, a. furtivo.
steam, s. vapor ; —, v.n. vahear.
steam-boiler, s. caldera de una máquina de vapor.
steam-engine, s. máquina de vapor.
steamer, steam-boat, steam-vessel, s. vapor, buque á vapor.
steed, s. caballo.
steel, s. acero ; eslabón ; —, v.a. acerar ; fortalecer, endurecer.
steelyard, s. romana.
steep, a. escarpado ; —, s. precipicio ; —, v.a. empapar.
steeple, s. torre ; campanario.
steeple-chase, s. carrera por los campos.
steepness, s. precipicio ; escarpa.
steer, s. novillo ; —, v.a. (mar.) gobernar, timonear.
steerage, s. parte posterior de un barco ; pasaje de tercera clase.
stellar, a. estrellado.
stem, s. tallo ; estirpe ; (mar.) proa, tajamar ; —, v.a. cortar la corriente.
stench, s. hedor.
stencil, s. (art) patrón, modelo.
stenographer, s. estenógrafo.
stenographic(al), a. estenográfico.
stenography, s. estenografía.
stentorian, a. estentoreo.
step, s. paso, escalón ; huella ; —, v.n. dar un paso ; andar.
step-brother, s. medio hermano.
step-daughter, s. hijastra.
step-father, s. padrastro.
step-mother, s. madrastra.
stepping-stone, s. pasadera.
step-sister, s. media hermana.
step-son, s. hijastro.
stereotype, s. estereotipía —, v.a. esterotipar.
sterile, a. estéril.
sterility, s. esterilidad.
sterling, a. esterlín, genuino, verdadero ; —, s. moneda esterlina.
stern, a. austero, rígido, severo ; —, s. (mar.) popa ; **-ly,** austeramente.
stertorous, a. roncador, estertoroso.
stethoscope, s. (med.) estetoscopio.

stevedore, s. (mar.) estivador.
stew, v.a. guisar ; —, s. guisado ; (fig.) agitación.		[pensero.
steward, s. mayordomo ; (mar.) des-
stewardship, s. mayordomía.
stew-pan, s. cazuela.
stick, s. palo, palillo, bastón ; vara ; —, v.a. pegar, hincar ; —, v.n. pegarse ; detenerse ; perseverar ; dudar.
stickiness, s. viscosidad.
stickle, v.n. tomar partido ; disputar.
stickleback, s. espinola (pez).		[dario.
stickler, s. padrino en un duelo ; parti-
sticky, a. viscoso, tenaz.
stiff, a. tieso ; duro, torpe ; rígido ; obstinado ; -ly, obstinadamente.
stiffen, v.a. atiesar, endurecer ; —, v.n. endurecerse.
stiff-neck, s. torticoli.
stiff-necked, a. obstinado.
stiffness, s. tesura, rigidez ; obstinación.
stifle, v.a. sofocar.
stigma, s. nota de infamia.
stigmatize, v.a. infamar, manchar.
stile, s. portillo con escalones (para pasar de un cercado á otro) ; gnomon ; estilo.
stiletto, s. puñal.
still, v.a. aquietar, aplacar ; —, a. silencioso, tranquilo ; —, s. alam- bique ; —, ad. todavía ; siempre, hasta ahora ; no obstante.
still-born, a. nacido muerto.
still-life, s. (art) naturaleza muerta.
stillness, s. calma, quietud.
stilts, s.pl. zancos, pl.
stimulant, s. estimulante.
stimulate, v.a. estimular, aguijonear.
stimulation, s. estímulo ; estimulación.
stimulative, a. estimulante.
stimulus, s. estímulo.
sting, v.a. picar ó morder (un insecto) ; —, s. aguijón ; punzada, picadura, picada ; remordimiento de conciencia.
stingily, ad. avaramente.
stinginess, s. tacañería, avaricia.
stinging-nettle, s. ortiga.
stingy, a. mezquino, tacaño, avaro.
stink, v.n. heder ; —, s. hedor.
stint, v.a. limitar ; —, límite ; restricción.
stipend, s. estipendio ; sueldo, salario.
stipendiary, a. estipendiario.
stipulate, v.n. estipular.
stipulation, s. estipulación ; contrato.
stir, v.a. remover ; agitar ; incitar ; —, v.n. moverse ; —, s. tumulto ; turbu- lencia.
stirrer, s. instigador.
stirrup, s. estribo.
stirrup-cup, s. copa de despedida.
stirrup-leather, s. ación.
stitch, v.a. coser ; —, s. puntada ; punto.

stiver, s. moneda holandesa ; (fig.) ardite.
stoat, s. comadreja.
stock, s. tronco ; injerto ; zoquete, estólido ; mango ; estirpe, linaje ; capital, principal ; fondo ; -s, pl. acciones en los fondos públicos, pl.; —, v.a. proveer, abastecer.
stockade, s. palizada ; estocada.
stock-exchange, s. (com.) Bolsa.
stock-fish, s. bacalao seco.
stock-holder, s. accionista.
stocking, s. media.
stock-jobber, s. corredor de bolsa.
stock-still, a. inmoble, inmóvil.
stoic, s. estoico.
stoical, a. estoico ; -ly, estoicamente.
stoicism, s. estoicismo.
stoker, s. fogonero.
stole, s. estola.
stolid, a. estólido.
stolidity, s. estolidez.		[aguantar.
stomach, s. estómago ; apetito ; —, v.a.
stomacher, s. peto.
stomachic(al), a. estomático ; —, s. medicamento estomacal.
stone, s. piedra ; cálculo ; pepita ; cuesco, hueso de fruta ; peso de catorce libras; —, a. de piedra ; —, v.a. apedrear ; quitar los huesos de las frutas.
stone-blind, a. enteramente ciego.
stone-cutter, s. picapedrero.
stone-dead, a. muerto.
stone-fruit, s. fruta de hueso.
stone-pit, s. cantera.
stone-ware, s. loza de piedra.
stoning, s. apedreamiento.
stony, a. pedregoso, pétreo ; duro.
stool, s. banquillo, taburete ; letrina, evacuación.
stoop, v.n. encorvarse, inclinarse ; ba- jarse ; —, s. inclinación hacia abajo ; abatimiento.
stop, v.a. detener, parar, diferir ; tapar ; —, v.n. pararse, hacer alto ; —, s. pausa ; obstáculo.
stop-gap, s. expediente provisorio.
stoppage, stopping, s. obstrucción ; im- pedimento ; (rail.) alto.
stopper, stopple, s. tapón.
stop-watch, s. reloj para marcar carreras.
storage, s. almacenamiento ; almacenaje.
store, s. abundancia ; provisión ; al- macén ; —, v.a. surtir, proveer, abastecer.
store-keeper, s. guardaalmacén.
storey, s. piso de una casa.
storied, a. historiado.
stork, s. cigüeña.
storm, tempestad, borrasca ; asalto ; —, v.a. tomar por asalto ; —, v.n. tem- pestar, enfurecerse.

stormily, a. violentamente.
stormy, a. tempestuoso ; violento.
story, s. historia ; fábula. *V.* storey.
stoup, s. cántaro, vaso.
stout, a. robusto, corpulento, vigoroso ;
terco ; -ly, valientemente ; obstinadamente ; —, s. cerveza negra.
stoutness, s. valor ; fuerza ; corpulencia.
stove, s. estufa.
stow, v.a. ordenar, colocar; (mar.) estivar.
stowage, s. almacenaje ; (mar.) arrumaje.
stowaway, s. (mar.) refugiado abordo.
straggle, v.n. vagar.   [bundo.
straggler, s. soldado rezagado ; vaga-
straight, a. derecho ; estrecho ; —, ad.
luego ; directamente.
straighten, v.a. enderezar.   [leal.
straightforward, a. derecho ; franco ;
straightforwardness, s. derechura, franqueza.
straightway, ad. inmediatamente, luego.
strain, v.a. colar, filtrar ; apretar lá uno
contra sí ; forzar, violentar ; —, v.n.
esforzarse ; —, s. retorcimiento ; raza ;
linaje ; estilo ; sonido ; armonía.
strainer, s. colador ; coladera.
strait, a. estrecho, angosto ; íntimo ;
rígido, exacto ; escaso ; -ly, estrechamente ; —, s. estrecho ; aprieto,
peligro ; penuria.
straiten, v.a. acortar, estrechar.   [dad.
straitness, s. estrechez ; penuria ; severi-
strait-waistcoat, s. casaca para asujetar
frenéticos.   [(mar.) encallar.
strand, s. costa, playa ; —, v.a. & n.
strange, a. extranjero ; extraño ; -ly,
extrañamente, extraordinariamente.
strangeness, s. extrañeza, rareza.
stranger, s. extranjero.
strangle, v.a. ahogar.
strangulation, s. ahogamiento.
strap, s. correa, tira de cuero ; —, v.a.
atar con correa.
strapping, a. abultado, corpulento.
stratagem, s. estratagema ; astucia.
strategic, a. estratégico.
strategy, s. estrategia.
stratum, s. estrato, lecho ; bancal.
straw, s. paja ; (fig.) ardite.
strawberry, s. fresa.
straw-cutter, s. tajador (máquina).
stray, v.n. extraviarse ; perder el camino ;
—, a. extraviado, casual.
streak, s. raya, lista ; —, v.a. rayar.
streaky, a. rayado.
stream, s. arroyo, rio, torrente ; —, v.n.
correr ; echar rayos
streamer, s. (mar.) flámula.
streamlet, s. arroyo, arroyuelo.
street, s. calle.   [fortaleza.
strength, s. fuerza, robustez ; vigor ;

strengthen, v.a. fortificar ; corroborar.
strenuous, a. estrenuo, valeroso ; asiduo ;
-ly, acérrimamente ; valerosamente.
strenuousness, s. valor, esfuerzo ; vigor.
stress, s. fuerza ; peso ; importancia ;
acento.
stretch, v.a. & n. extender, alargar ;
estirar ; extenderse ; esforzarse ; —, s.
extensión ; esfuerzo ; estirón.
stretcher, s. horma para estirar ; (mar.)
travesaño de bote á remo.
strew, v.a. esparcir ; sembrar.
striated, a. estriado.
strict, a. estricto, estrecho ; exacto,
riguroso, severo ; -ly, exactamente,
con severidad.
strictness, s. exactitud ; severidad.
stricture, s. contracción ; censura.
stride, s. tranco ; —, v.n. atrancar.
strident, a. estridente.
strife, s. contienda, disputa.
strike, v.a. & n. golpear ; herir ; castigar ;
tocar ; chocar ; sonar ; cesar de trabajar ; —, s. cesación de trabajadores,
huelga.
striking, a. imponente, notable.
string, s. cordón ; hilo ; cuerda ; hilera,
fibra ; —, v.a. encordar ; enhilar ;
estirar.
stringent, a. astringente.
stringy, a. fibroso.
strip, v.a. desnudar, despojar ; —, s. tira.
stripe, s. raya, lista ; azote ; —, v.a. rayar.
stripling, s. mozuelo, mozalbete.
strive, v.n. esforzarse ; empeñarse ; disputar, contender.
stroke, s. golpe ; toque (en la pintura) ;
sonido (del reloj) ; plumada ; —, v.a.
acariciar.
stroll, v.n. pasear, vagar.
strolling, a. ambulante.
strong, a. fuerte, vigoroso, robusto ;
poderoso ; violento ; -ly, fuertemente,
con violencia.
strong-box, s. cofre fuerte.
stronghold, s. plaza fuerte.
strop, s. cuero para navajas, suavizador.
strophe, s. estrofa.
structure, s. estructura ; edificio.
struggle, v.n. esforzarse ; luchar ; agitarse.
struggling, s. esfuerzo ; contienda,
lucha.
strum, v.a. (mus.) tocar casualmente.
strumpet, s. ramera, puta.
strut, v.n. pavonearse ; —, s. contoneo ;
(arch.) puntal.
stub, s. tocón ; —, v.a. desarraigar.
stubble, s. rastrojo.
stubborn, a. obstinado, testarudo ; -ly,
obstinadamente.
stubbornness, s. obstinación, pertinacia.

stubby, a. cachigordete ; gordo.
stucco, s. estuco.
stud, s. estaca ; tachón ; botón ; caballeriza para criar ; —, v.a. tachonar.
student, s. estudiante.
studied, a. docto ; premeditado.
studio, s. estudio de un artista.
studious, a. estudioso ; **-ly,** estudiosamente.
study, s. estudio ; aplicación ; meditación profunda ; —, v.a. estudiar ; observar ; —, v.n. estudiar ; aplicarse.
stuff, s. materia ; material ; estofa ; — ! ¡ bagatela !, ¡ niñería ! ; —, v.a. henchir, llenar ; forrar ; —, v.n. (col.)
stuffing, s. relleno [atracarse.
stuffy, a. (col.) mal ventilado.
stultify, v.a. atontar ; anular, confutar.
stumble, v.n. tropezar ; —, s. traspié, tropiezo. [de escándalo.
stumbling-block, s. tropezadero ; piedra
stump, s. tronco ; tocón ; —, v.a. andar con pesadez.
stump-orator, s. orador de populacho.
stumpy, a. (col.) cachigordo.
stun, v.a. aturdir, ensordecer.
stunt, v.a. no dejar crecer ; achicar.
stunted, a. bajo de talle.
stupefaction, s. aturdimiento, estupor.
stupefy, v.a. atontar, atolondrar.
stupendous, a. estupendo, maravilloso.
stupid, a. estúpido ; **-ly,** estúpidamente.
stupidity, s. estupidez.
stupor, s. estupor.
sturdily, ad. vigorosamente. [ción.
sturdiness, s. fuerza, fortaleza ; obstina-
sturdy, a. fuerte, tieso, robusto.
sturgeon, s. esturión.
stutter, v.n. tartamudear.
sty, s. zahurda ; pocilga.
sty(e), s. (med.) orzuelo.
style, s. estilo ; título ; gnomon ; modo ; —, v.a. intitular, nombrar. [cete.
stylish, a. elegante, en buen estilo ; galansuasion, s. persuasión.
suave, a. suave ; **-ly,** suavemente.
suavity, s. suavidad, dulzura.
subaltern, a. (mil.) subalterno.
subdivide, v.a. subdividir.
subdivision, s. subdivisión.
subdual, s. sujeción. [mortificar.
subdue, v.a. sojuzgar, sujetar ; conquistar,
subject, a. sujeto ; sometido á ; —, s. sujeto ; —, v.a. sujetar ; exponer.
subjection, s. sujeción.
subjoin, v.a. sobreañadir.
subjugate, v.a. sojuzgar, sujetar.
subjugation, s. sujeción.
subjunctive, s. subjuntivo.
sublet, v.a. subarrendar. [limar.
sublimate, s. sublimado ; —, v.a. sub-

sublime, a. sublime, excelso ; **-ly,** de un modo sublime ; —, s. **sublime.**
sublimity, s. sublimidad.
sublunar(y), a. sublunar ; terrestre.
submarine, a. submarino.
submerge, v.a. sumergir.
submersion, s. sumersión.
submission, s. sumisión.
submissive, a. sumiso, obsequioso ; **-ly,** con sumisión.
submissiveness, s. sumisión.
submit, v.a. (& n.) someter(se).
subordinate, a. subordinado, inferior ; —, v.a. subordinar.
subordination, s. subordinación.
suborn, s. soborar, cohechar.
subornation, s. soborno. [citar.
subpoena, s. (law) comparendo ; — v.a
subscribe, v.a. & n. suscribir, firmar, consentir.
subscriber, suscriptor.
subscription, s. suscripción.
subsequent, a. **-ly,** subsiguiente(mente), posterior(mente).
subserve, v.a. servir, estar subordinado.
subserviency, s. servicio ; utilidad ; concurso ; ayuda.
subservient, a. subordinado ; útil.
subside, v.n. bajar, someterse, tranquilizarse.
subsidence, s. baja, derrumbamiento.
subsidiary, a. subsidiario.
subsidize, v.a. dar subsidios, proveer.
subsidy, s. subsidio, socorro.
subsist, v.n. subsistir ; existir.
subsistence, s. existencia ; subsistencia.
subsoil, s. subsuelo. [esencia.
substance, s. substancia ; entidad ;
substantial, a. substancial ; real, material ; substancioso ; fuerte ; **-ly,** substancialmente.
substantiate, v.a. confirmar, probar.
substantive, s. sustantivo.
substitute, v.a. sustituir.
substitution, s. sustitución.
substratum, s. lecho, subsuelo.
subterfuge, s. subterfugio ; evasión.
subterranean, a. subterráneo.
subtile, a. sútil, delicado, tenue ; penetrante, agudo ; **-ly,** sútilmente.
subtility, s. sutilidad.
subtle, a. sútil, astuto.
subtlety, s. sutileza, astucia.
subtly, ad. sútilmente.
subtract, v.a. (ar.) sustraer.
suburb, s. suburbio.
suburban, a. suburbano.
subversion, s. subversión.
subversive, a. subversivo.
subvert, v.a. subvertir, destruir.
subway, s. túnel.

succeed, v.n. & a. suceder, seguir; conseguir, lograr, tener suceso, salir con, prosperar.

success, s. suceso, éxito.

successful, a. próspero, dichoso; -ly, prósperamente. [herencia.

succession, s. sucesión; descendencia;

successive, a. sucesivo; -ly, sucesivamente.

successor, s. sucesor. [con brevedad.

succinct, a. sucinto, compendioso; -ly,

succour, v.a. socorrer, ayudar; —, s. socorro; ayuda, asistencia.

succulence, s. jugosidad.

succulent, a. suculento, jugoso.

succumb, v.n. sucumbir. [los que.

such, pn. tal, semejante; — as, el que,

suck, v.a. & n. chupar; mamar; amamantar.

sucking-pig, s. lechoncillo.

suckle, v.a. amamantar.

suckling, s. mamantón.

suction, s. succión. [súbitamente.

sudden, a. repentino; -ly, de repente,

suddenness, s. precipitación.

sudorific, a. & s. sudorífico.

suds, s. jabonadura, agua de jabón.

sue, v.a.& n. poner por justicia, perseguir, procesar; suplicar.

suet, s. sebo. [permitir.

suffer, v.a. & n. sufrir, padecer; tolerar,

sufferable, a. sufrible, soportable.

sufferance, s. sufrimiento; tolerancia.

suffering, s. pena; dolor.

suffice, v.n bastar, ser suficiente.

sufficiency, s. suficiencia; capacidad.

sufficient, a. suficiente; -ly, bastante.

suffix, s. (gr.) sufijo.

suffocate, v.a. sofocar, ahogar.

suffocation, s. sofocación.

suffragan, s. sufragáneo.

suffrage, s sufragio, voto.

suffuse, v.a. imbuir, difundir, derramar.

suffusion, s. (med.) sufusión.

sugar, s. azúcar; —, v.a. azucarar.

sugar-basin, s. azucarero.

sugar-beet, s. (bot.) remolacha.

sugar-cane, s. caña de azúcar.

sugar-loaf, s. pan de azúcar.

sugar-plum, s. confite.

sugary, a. azucarado.

suggest, v.a. sugerir.

suggestion, s. sugestión.

suicidal, a. de suicida, fatal.

suicide, s. suicidio; suicida.

suit, s. galanteo; petición; pleito; traje, vestido entero; —, v.a. & n. adaptar; surtir; ajustarse, acomodarse, convenir.

suitable, a. conforme, conveniente. [encia.

suitableness, s. conformidad, conveni-

suitably, ad. según, conforme.

suite, s. serie; tren, comitiva.

suitor, s. suplicante; amante, cortejo;

sulkiness, s. mal humor. [pleiteante.

sulky, a. regañón; terco.

sullen, a. malcontento; intratable; -ly, de mal humor; tercamente.

sullenness, s. mal humor; obstinación, pertinacia, terquedad.

sully, v.a. manchar, ensuciar.

sulphur, s. azufre.

sulphurous, a. sulfúreo, azufroso.

sultan, s. sultán.

sultana, s. sultana.

sultriness, s. bochorno.

sultry, a. caluroso; sufocante.

sum, s. suma; —, v.a. sumar.

summarily, ad. sumariamente.

summary, a. & s. sumario.

summer, s. verano, estío.

summer-house, s. glorieta.

summit, s. ápice; cima.

summon, v.a. llamar, convocar, convidar; (leg.) citar; (mil.) intimar la rendición.

summons, s. citación; requerimiento.

sumptuary, a. suntuario. [mente.

sumptuous, a. suntuoso; -ly, suntuosa-

sumptuousness, s. suntuosidad.

sun, s. sol.

sun-beam, s. rayo del sol. [asoleado.

sun-burnt, a. tostado por el sol,

Sunday, s. domingo.

sunder, v.a. separar, apartar.

sun-dial, s. reloj de sol, cuadrante.

sun-down, s. V. sunset.

sundry, a. varios, muchos, diversos.

sunflower, s. girasol.

sunless, a. sin sol; sin luz.

sun-light, s. luz del sol. [gre.

sunny, a. asoleado; brillante; (fig.) ale-

sun-rise, sun-rising, s. salida del sol.

sunset, s. puesta del sol.

sun-shade, s. quitasol.

sun-shine, s. luz, claridad del sol.

sun-stroke, s. insolación.

sup, v.a. sorber, beber á sorbos; —, v.n. cenar; —, s. sorbo.

super, s. V. supernumerary.

superabound, v.n. superabundar.

superabundance, s. superabundancia; lo superfluo. [(mente.

superabundant, a. -ly, superabundante-

superadd, v.a. sobreañadir.

superannuated, a. pensionado, retirado.

superannuation, s. jubilación; retiro.

superb, a. soberbio; -ly, soberbiamente.

supercargo, s. (mar.) sobrecargo.

supercilious, a. altanero; -ly, con altivez.

supererogation, s. supererogación.

superficial, a. somero, superficial; -ly, superficial(mente).
superficies, s. superficie, sobrefaz.
superfine, a. superfino.
superfluity, s. superfluidad.
superfluous, a. superfluo.
superhuman, a. sobrehumano.
superintend, v.a. inspeccionar, vigilar.
superintendence, s. superintendencia.
superintendent, s. superintendente.
superior, a. & s. superior.
superiority, s. superioridad.
superlative, a. & s. superlativo; -ly, superlativamente, en sumo grado.
supernatural, s. sobrenatural. [parsa.
supernumerary, a. supernumerario, com-
superscribe, v.a. sobrescribir.
superscription, s. sobrescrito.
supersede, v.a. sobreseer; suspender; reemplazar.
superstition, s. superstición.
superstitious, a. supersticioso; -ly, supersticiosamente. [sobre otro.
superstructure, s. edificio levantado
supervene, v.n. sobrevenir, suceder.
supervise, v.a. inspeccionar, revistar.
supervision, supervisal, s. superintenden-
supervisor, s. superintendente. [cia.
supine, a. supino; negligente; -ly, descuidadamente.
supineness, s. negligencia.
supper, s. cena; Lord's —, Eucaristía.
supperless, a. sin cena.
supplant, v.a. suplantar.
supple, a. flexible, manejable; blando.
supplement, s. suplemento. [cional.
supplemental, supplementary, a. adi-
suppleness, s. flexibilidad.
suppli(c)ant, a. & s. suplicante.
supplicate, v.a. suplicar.
supplication, s. súplica, suplicación.
supplicatory, a. suplicante.
supply, v.a. suplir, completar; surtir; —, s. surtido, subsidios, víveres, pl. socorro.
support, v.a. sostener; soportar, asistir.
supportable, a. soportable. [tector.
supporter, s. sustentáculo; apoyo; pro-
suppose, v.a. suponer, creer.
supposition, s. suposición.
supposititious, a. supuesto, falso, fingido.
suppress, v.a. suprimir.
suppression, s. supresión.
suppurate, v.n. supurar.
suppuration, s. supuración.
supremacy, s. supremacía. [mente.
supreme, a. supremo; -ly, suprema-
surcease, s. cesación, parada; —, v.a. & n. parar, cesar.
surcharge, v.a. sobrecargar.
surcingle, s. sobrecincha.
sure, a seguro, cierto; firme; estable;

to be —, de veras; -ly, ciertamente, seguramente, sin duda.
sureness, s. certeza, seguridad.
surety, s. seguridad; fiador.
surf, s. (mar.) resaca.
surface, s. superficie, sobrefaz.
surfeit, v.a. & n. hartar, saciar; ahitarse, saciarse; —, s. ahito, empacho; indigestión. [cerse el mar.
surge, s. ola, onda; —, v.n. embrave-
surgeon, s. cirujano.
surgery, s. cirujía.
surgical, a. quirúrgico.
surlily, ad. con mal humor.
surliness, s. mal humor, ceño.
surly, a. ceñudo, tétrico.
surmise, v.a. sospechar; —, s. sospecha.
surmount, v.a. sobrepujar; superar, domar.
surmountable, a. superable.
surname, s. apellido. [ceder, aventajar.
surpass, v.a. sobresalir, sobrepujar, ex-
surpassing, a. sobresaliente.
surplice, s. sobrepelliz.
surplus(age), s. sobrante.
surprise, v.a. sorprender; —, s. sorpresa.
surprising, a. maravilloso.
surrender, v.a. & n. rendir; ceder; rendirse; —, s. rendición.
surreptitious, a. subrepticio; -ly, subrepticiamente.
surrogate, s. subrogado, vicario.
surround, v.a. circundar, cercar, rodear.
surroundings, s.pl. contornos; circunstancias.
survey, v.a. inspeccionar, examinar; apear, medir; s. inspección; apeo (de tierras).
surveyor, s. sobrestante; agrimensor.
surveyorship, s. superintendencia.
survive, v.n. sobrevivir.
survivor, s. sobreviviente.
susceptibility, s. susceptibilidad.
susceptible, a. susceptible.
suspect, v.a. & n. sospechar.
suspend, v.a. suspender.
suspense, s. suspensión; detención; incertidumbre. [tregua.
suspension, s. suspensión; — of arms,
suspension-bridge, s. puente colgante ó colgado. [braguero.
suspensor(y), a. dudoso; —, s. (med.)
suspicion, s. sospecha.
suspicious, a. suspicaz, sospechoso; -ly, sospechosamente. [anza.
suspiciousness, s. suspicacia, desconfi-
sustain, v.a. sostener, sustentar, mantener; apoyar; sufrir.
sustainable, a. sustentable.
sustainer, s. apoyo, sostén.
sustenance, s. sostenimiento, sustento.

sutler, s. vivandero.

suture, s. sutura, costura.

swab, s. lampazo ; (fig.) zopenco.

swaddle, v.a. fajar.

swaddling-clothes, s.pl. pañales, pl.

swag, s. (col.) botín.

swagger, v.n. baladronear.

swaggerer, s. fanfarrón, baladrón.

swain, s. zagal, joven aldeano, pastorcillo.

swallow, s. golondrina ; gula ; —, v.a. tragar, engullir.

swamp, s. pantano.

swampy, a. pantanoso.

swan, s. cisne.

swap, v.a. cambalachear, trocar.

sward, s. césped.

swarm, s. enjambre ; gentío ; hormiguero ; —, v.n. enjambrar ; hormiguear ; abundar.

swart, swarthy, a. atezado, moreno.

swarthiness, s. tez morena.

swash-buckler, s. fanfarrón.

swath, s. tajo de hierba segada.

swathe, v.a. fajar ; —, s. faja.

sway, v.a. empuñar ; dominar, gobernar ; —, v.n. ladearse, inclinarse ; tener influjo ; —, s. bamboneo ; poder, imperio, influjo. [juramentar.

swear, v.a. & n. jurar ; hacer jurar ;

sweat, s. sudor ; —, v.n. [sudar ; afanarse.

sweep, v.a. & n. barrer ; arrebatar ; deshollinar ; rozar ; —, s. barredura ; giro.

sweeping, a. rápido, completo ; -s, pl. barreduras, pl.

sweep-stake, s. conjunto de apuestas entre varios.

sweet, a. dulce, grato, gustoso ; suave ; oloroso ; melodioso ; hermoso ; amable; —, -ly, dulcemente, suavemente.

sweet-bread, s. lechecillas, molleja de ternera, pl.

sweeten, v.a. endulzar ; suavizar ; aplacar ; limpiar, ventilar.

sweetheart, s. galanteador ; novia.

sweetmeats, s.pl. dulces.

sweetness, s. dulzura, suavidad.

sweet-scented, a. perfumado.

sweet-william, s. (bot.) dianto.

swell, v.n. hincharse ; ensoberbecerse ; embravecerse ; —, v.a. hinchar, inflar, agravar ; —, s. hinchazón ; bulto ; mar de leva ; (col.) elegante ; —, a. á la moda, cursí, elegante.

swelling, s. hinchazón, tumor.

swelter, v.a. & n. ahogar(se) de calor.

swerve, v.n. vagar ; desviarse.

swift, a. veloz, ligero, rápido ; —, s. (orn.) vencejo.

swiftly, ad. velozmente.

swiftness, s. velocidad, rapidez.

swill, v.a. beber con exceso ; —, s. trago profundo, bazofia. [vertiginoso,

swim, v.n. nadar ; abundar en ; ser

swimming, s. natación ; vértigo ; -ly, lisamente, sin dificultad.

swindle, v.a. petardear, estafar.

swindler, s. petardista, trampista.

swine, s. sing. & pl. cerdo, puerco, cochino,

swine-herd, s. porquero.

swing, v.n. balancear, columpiarse ; vibrar ; agitarse ; —, v.a. vibrar ; —, vibración ; balanceo ; columpio.

swing-bridge, s. puente movedizo.

swing-door, s. puerta que se cierra automáticamente.

swinish, a. porcuno, cochino ; grosero.

swirl, s. remolino ; —, v.n. remolinar.

switch, s. varilla ; (rail.) aguja ; —, v.a. varear ; desviar.

switchback railway, s. montaña rusa.

switchman, s. (rail.) guardaagujas.

swipes, s. (col.) cerveza barata.

swivel, s. eje, charnela.

swoon, v.n. desmayarse ; —, s. desmayo, deliquio, pasmo.

swoop, v.a. & n. agarrar al vuelo ; arrojarse (las aves) ; —, s. ímpetu de una ave de rapiña ; **at one** —, de un golpe.

sword, s. espada.

sword-arm, s. brazo derecho.

sword-fish, s. pez espada.

swordsman, s. espada, soldado.

sybarite, s. sibarita.

sybaritic, a. sibarítico. [falso.

sycamore, s. sicomoro (árbol), plátano

sycophant, s. sicofante.

syllabic(al), a. silábico.

syllable, s. sílaba.

syllabus, s. extracto, resumen,

syllogism, s. silogismo.

sylph, s. sílfide, ninfa.

sylvan, a. silvestre.

symbol, s. símbolo.

symbolic(al), a. simbólico.

symbolise, v.a. simbolizar. [simetría.

symmetrical, a. simétrico ; -ly, con

symmetry, s. simetría.

sympathetic(al), a. simpático, compasivo; -ally, compasivamente.

sympathize, v.n. compadecerse.

sympathy, s. simpatia, compasión.

symphony, s. sinfonía.

symptom, s. síntoma.

synagogue, s. sinagoga.

synchronism, s. sincronismo,

syndic, s. síndico.

syndicate, s. sindicato.

synod, s. sínodo.

synonyme, s. sinónimo,

synonymous, s. sinónimo ; -ly, con sinonimia.

synopsis, s. sinopsis, sumario.
synoptical, a. sinóptico.
syntax, s. sintaxis.
synthesis, s. síntesis.

syringe, s. jeringa, lavativa ; —, v.a.
system, s. sistema.   [jeringar.
systematic(al), a. sistemático ; -ally,
     sistemáticamente.

T

tabby, s. tabí ; gata.
tabernacle, s. tabernáculo.
table, s. mesa ; tabla ; —, v.a. apuntar en
     forma sinóptica ; — d'hôte, mesa re-
table-cloth, s. mantel.   [donda.
table-land, s. meseta.
table-spoon, s. cuchara grande.
tablet, s. tabla, tableta ; plancha (gra-
     bada ó pintada).
taboo, v.a. interdecir ; —, s. interdicción.
tabular, a. reducido á índices.
tacit, a. tácito ; -ly, tácitamente.
taciturn, a. taciturno, callado.
taciturnity, s. taciturnidad.
tack, s. tachuela ; —, (mar.) bordada,
     virada ; —, v.a. atar ; pegar ; —, v.n.
     (mar.) virar.
tackle, s. aparejo, armazón ; (mar.) cor-
     daje, jarcia.
tact, s. tacto.
tactician, s. táctico.
tactics, s.pl. táctica.
tactless, a. sin tacto, grosero.
tadpole, s. ranilla ; sapillo.
taffeta, s. tafetán.
tag, s. herrete.
tagrag, s. canalla.
tail, s. cola, rabo.
tailor, s. sastre.
taint, v.a. manchar ; inficionar ; alterar,
     viciar ; —, s. mancha ; corrupción, in-
     fección.   [sin tacha.
taintless, a. incorrupto, incontaminado.
take, v.a. tomar, coger, asir ; recibir,
     aceptar ; prender ; admitir ; entender ;
     —, v.n. salir bien, efectuarse una cosa ;
     arraigarse ; —, s. toma ; presa.
take-in, s. engaño.
take-off, s. caricatura.
taking, a. agradable, atrayente.
tale, s. cuento ; fábula.
tale-bearer, s. soplón.
talent, s. talento ; capacidad.
talented, a. talentoso.
talisman, s. talismán.
talk, v.n. hablar, conversar ; charlar ;
     —, s. plática, habla ; charla ; fama.
talkative, a. gárrulo, locuaz.
talkativeness, s. locuacidad.
tall, a. alto, elevado.
tallness, s. talle, estatura.
tallow, s. sebo ; —, v.a. ensebar.
tallowy, a. seboso.

tally, v.a. ajustar ; tarjar ; —, s. tarja,
     palito para tarjar.
talon, s. garra del ave de rapiña.
tamable, a. domable.
tamarind, s. tamarindo.
tamarisk, s. tamarisco.
tambourine, s. tamboril.
tame, a. manso, amansado, domado, do-
     mesticado ; abatido ; sumiso ; -ly,
     mansamente ; bajamente ; —, v.a.
     domar, domesticar.
tameness, s. domesticidad ; sumisión ;
     carácter apocado.
tamper, v.n. experimentar, maquinar,
     entremeterse.   [de roble.
tan, v.a. curtir, zurrar ; —, s. corteza
tandem, ad. con dos caballos en fila.
tangent, s. tangente.
tangible, a. tangible.
tangle, v.a. enredar, embrollar ; —, s.
     enredo, embrollo.
tank, s. cisterna ; aljibe.
tankard, s. cántaro con tapadera.
tanner, s. curtidor.
tannin, s. tanino.
tantalize, v.a. atormentar á alguno
     mostrándole placeres que no puede
tantamount, a. equivalente.   [alcanzar.
tantivy, ad. á rienda suelta, á escape.
tan-yard, s. tenería.
tap, v.a. tocar ligeramente ; barrenar ;
     extraer el jugo de un árbol por in-
     cisión ; sacar agua del cuerpo humano ;
     —, s. palmada suave ; toque ligero ;
     espita ; despacho de bebidas.
tape, s. cinta ; galón.
taper, s. cirio ; —, a. cónico ; —, v.n.
     rematar en punta.
tapestry, s. tapiz ; tapicería.
tape-worm, s. tenia.
tap-room, s. taberna.   [embrear.
tar, s. brea ; (col.) marinero ; —, v.a.
tardily, ad. lentamente.
tardiness, s. lentitud, tardanza.
tardy, a. tardo, lento.
tare, s. (bot.) zizaña.
target, s. rodela ; blanco (para tirar).
tariff, s. tarifa.
tarlatan, s. tarlatana.
tarn, s. laguna entre montañas.
tarnish, v.a. (& n.) deslustrar(se).
tarpaulin, s. tela embreada.
tarragon, s. (bot.) estragón.

tarry, v.n. tardar, pararse ; —, a. embreado.
tart, a. acedo, acre ; -ly, agriamente.
tart, tartlet, s. tarta, torta.
tartar, s. tártaro.
tartness, s. agrura, acedía.
task, s: tarea ; —, v.a. atarear.
tassel, s. borlita.
taste, s. gustadura ; gusto ; sabor ; saboreo ; ensayo ; —, v.a. & n. gustar ; probar ; experimentar ; agradar ; tener sabor.
tasteful, a. sabroso ; de buen gusto, artístico ; -ly, sabrosamente.
tasteless, a. insípido, sin sabor ; inculto, inartístico.
taster, s. catador.
tastily, ad. con gusto.
tasty, a. gustoso.
tatter, s. andrajo, arrapiezo.
tatterdemalion, s. pobre andrajoso.
tattle, v.n. charlar, parlotear; —, s. charla
tattler, s. faramallero.
tattoo, s. (mil.) retreta, queda ; picadura y pintura del cuerpo ; —, v.a. pintarse el cuerpo los salvajes.
taunt, v.a. mofar ; ridiculizar ; dar chanza ; —, s. mofa, burla, chanza.
tauntingly, ad. con mofa.
Taurus, s. Tauro (signo del zodíaco).
taut, a. tieso, apretado ; bien arreglado.
tautological, a. tautológico.
tautology, s. tautología.
tavern, s. taberna.
tavern-keeper, s. tabernero. [de mármol.
taw, v.a. ablandar pieles ; —, s. bolita
tawdriness, s. oropel.
tawdry, a. vistoso, chabacano.
tawny, a. curtido, moreno.
tax, s. impuesto ; contribución ; —, v.a. imponer tributos ; tasar, acusar.
taxable, a. sujeto á impuestos, pechero.
taxation, s. imposición de impuestos.
tax-gatherer, s. colector de impuestos.
taxing-master, s. tasador.
tea, s. te.
tea-caddy, s. caja para te.
teach, v.a. enseñar, instruir.
teachable, a. dócil.
teacher, s. preceptor, enseñador.
teak, s. teca (árbol).
tea-kettle, s. caldera para te.
teal, s. (orn.) cerceta, especie de pato.
team, s. tiro de caballos.
teamster, s. galerero, cochero.
tea-pot, s. tetera.
tear, v.a. despedazar, lacerar ; rasgar.
tearful, a. lloroso ; -ly, con lloro.
tearless, a. sin lágrimas.
tease, v.a. cardar (lana ó lino) ; importunar, molestar.
teasel, teazel, teazle, s. capota, cardo.

tea-service, tea-set, tea-things, s.pl.
teat, s. ubre, teta. [servicio para te.
technical, a. técnico.
technicalities, s.pl. términos técnicos, pl.
technology, s. tecnología.
techy, a. V. tetchy. [tidiosamente.
tedious, a. tedioso, fastidioso ; -ly, fastediousness, tedium, s. tedio, fastidio.
teem, v.n. parir ; abundar ; v.a. (mar.) sacar agua del bote, vaciar.
teens, s.pl. años desde 13 hasta 20 años.
teeth, s.pl. de tooth ; —, v.n. endentecer.
teetotal, a. abstemio. [stemio.
teetotaller, s.; el que no bebe vino, abteetotum, s. perinola.
telegram, s. telegrama, despacho.
telegraph, s. telégrafo.
telegraphic, a. telegráfico.
telegraphy, s. telegrafía.
telephone, s. teléfono.
telescope, s. telescopio.
telescopic(al), a. telescópico. [numerar.
tell, v.a. & n. decir ; informar, contar,
teller, s. relator ; computista.
telling a. impresionante, decisivo.
tell-tale, s. soplón.
temerity, s. temeridad.
temper, v.a. templar, moderar ; atemperar ; —, s. temperamento ; ira.
temperament, s. temperamento.
temperance, s. templanza, moderación.
temperate, a. templado, moderado, sobrio : -ly, templadamente.
temperature, s. temperatura, temperie.
tempered, a. templado, acondicionado.
tempest, s. tempestad, tormenta.
tempestuous, a. tempestuoso, proceloso.
templar, s. estudiante de leyes.
temple, s. templo ; sien.
temporal, a. -ly, temporal(mente).
temporarily, ad. temporalmente.
temporary, a. temporario, temporal.
temporise, v.n. temporizar.
tempt, v.a. tentar ; provocar.
temptation, s. tentación.
ten, a. & s. diez.
tenable, a. defendible.
tenacious, a. -ly, tenaz(mente).
tenacity, s. tenacidad ; porfía.
tenancy, s. tenencia, arrendamiento.
tenant, s. arrendatario, inquilino.
tenantless, a. sin inquilinos.
tenantry, s. conjunto de los arrenda
tench, s. tenca (pez). [tarios.
tend, v.a. guardar, velar ; —, v.n. tirar, tendency, s. tendencia. [dirigirse.
tender, a. tierno, delicado ; sensible ; -ly, tiernamente ; —, s. oferta ; (mar.) patache ; (rail.) ténder ; —, v.a. ofrecer.
tenderness, s. terneza, delicadeza.

tendon, s. tendón.

tendril, s. zarcillo.

tenement, s. arriendo ; habitación ar-
tenet, s. dogma ; aserción.   [rendada.

tenfold, a. décuplo.

tennis, s. raqueta (juego).

tennis-court, s. sitio en que se juega la
raqueta.   [stancia.

tenor, s. (mus.) tenor ; contenido ; sub-

tense, a. tieso, tenso ; —, s. (gr.) tiempo.

tension, s. tensión, tirantez.

tent, s. (mil.) tienda de campaña.

tentacle, s. tentáculo.

tentative, a. tentativo ; -ly, por prueba.

tenter, s. varilla, colgador.

tenter-hook, s. garabato, clavo ; **to be on**
-s, estar suspenso.

tenth, a. décimo ; -ly, en décimo lugar.

tenuity, s. tenuidad.

tenure, s. tenencia.

tepid, a. tibio.

tergiversation, s. tergiversación.

term, s. término, confín ; dicción ;
vocablo ; condición, estipulación ; —,
v.a. nombrar, llamar.

termagant, s. diabla, marimacho.

terminate, v.a. & n. terminar, limitar.

termination, s. terminación, conclusión.

terminus, s. (rail.) estación terminal.

terrace, s. terrado ; terraplén ; —, v.a.
terraplenar.

terrestrial, a. terrestre, terreno.

terrible, a. terrible.

terribly, ad. terriblemente.

terrier, s. perro raposero.

terrific, a. terrífico.

terrify, v.a. aterrar, espantar.

territorial, a. territorial.

territory, s. territorio, distrito.

terror, s. terror, pavor.

terrorist, s. terrorista.

terse, a. terso, pulido ; -ly, con pulidez.

terseness, s. tersura, brevedad expresiva.

tertian, a. terciana.

tertiary, a. terciario (en geología).

tesselate, v.a. taracear.

test, s. prueba ; criterio.

testaceous, a. testáceo.

testament, s. testamento.

testamentary, a. testamentario.

testator, s. testador.

testatrix, s. testadora.

tester, s. cielo de cama.

testicles, s.pl. testículos, pl.

testifier, s. testificante.

testify, v.a. testificar, atestiguar.

testily, ad. con morosidad.

testimonial, s. atestación, carta de
recomendación.

testimony, s. testimonio.

testiness, s. petulancia, irritación.

testy, tetchy, a. petulante, irritable.

tether, s. maniota.

text, s. texto.

textile, a. textile.

textual, a. textual.

texture, s. textura ; tejido.

than, ad. que, de.

thank, v.a. agradecer, dar gracias.

thankful, a. grato, agradecido ; -ly, con

thankfulness, s. gratitud.   [gratitud.

thankless, a. ingrato.   [de gracias.

thank-offering, s. ofrecimiento en acción

thanks, s.pl. gracias, pl.

thanks-giving, s. acción de gracias ; fiesta
nacional americana.

that, pn. aquel, aquello ; este ; —, c. que,
porque ; para que ; so —, de modo que.

thatch, s. techo de paja ; —, v.a. techar
con paja.   [lar(se).

thaw, s. deshielo ; —, v.a. & n. deshe-
the, art. el.

theatre, s. teatro.

theatrical, a. teatral ; histriónico ; -ly,
histriónicamente ; -s, s.pl. representación de aficionados.

thee, pn. te, á ti.

theft, s. hurto.

their, pn. su, suyo ; de ellos, de ellas ; -s,
el suyo ; de ellos, de ellas.

theism, s. teísmo, deísmo.

theist, s. teísta, deísta.

them, pn. los ; ellos.

theme, s. tema.

themselves, pn. pl. ellos mismos, ellas
mismas ; sí mismos.

then, ad. entonces, después ; en tal caso ;
now and —, de cuando en cuando.

thence, ad. desde allí, de ahí, por eso.

thenceforth, ad. desde entonces.

theocracy, s. teocracia.

theocratic(al), a. teocrático.

theologic(al), a. teológico.

theologian, s. teólogo.

theology, s. teología.

theorem, s. teorema.   [mente.

theoretic(al), a. teórico ; -ly, teórica-

theorise, v.a. teorizar.

theorist, s. teórico.

theory, s. teoría.

theosophy, s. teosofía.

therapeutics, s. terapéutica.

there, ad. allí, allá.

thereabout(s), ad. por ahí, acerca.

thereafter, ad. después.

thereat, ad. por eso, á causa de eso.

thereby, ad. por eso ; per medio de eso.

therefore, ad. por eso ; por esta razón.

therefrom, ad. de allí, de allá ; de eso, de
aquello.

therein, ad. en aquello, en eso.

thereof, ad. de esto, de aquello, de ello.

thereon, ad. en eso, sobre eso.
thereunder, ad. debajo de eso.
there(un)to, a. á eso, á ello.
thereupon, ad. entonces.
therewith, ad. con eso ; luego.
thermal waters, s.pl. termas, pl.
thermometer, s. termómetro.
these, pn. pl. estos.
thesis, s. tesis.
thew, s. tendón, músculo.
they, pn. pl. ellos.
thick, a. espeso, denso, turbio ; grueso ;
frecuente ; grosero ; **to speak —,** hablar
con media lengua ; **-ly,** ad. frecuente-
mente, continuadamente.
thicken, v.a. & n. espesar, condensar ;
condensar(se).
thicket, s. matorral ; bosque.
thick-head(ed), a. estúpido.
thickness, s. espesura, densidad ; grosería.
thick-set, a. plantado muy espeso ; re-
thief, s. ladrón. [choncho.
thief-catcher, s. alguacil.
thieve, v.n. hurtar, robar. [ladrón.
thievish, a. ladrón, ladronesco ; **-ly,** como
thievishness, s. ladronicio.
thigh, s. muslo.
thill, s. vara de un carro.
thimble, s. dedal.
thimble-rigger, s. petardista, truhán.
thin, a. delgado, delicado, sútil, flaco ;
claro ; ralo ;—, v.a. enrarecer, atenuar;
adelgazar ; aclarar.
thine, pn. tuyo.
thing, s. cosa ; asunto.
think, v.a. & n. pensar, imaginar, meditar,
considerar ; creer, juzgar.
thinker, s. pensador.
thinking, s. pensamiento ; juicio ;
opinión. [número.
thinly, ad. delgadamente ; en corto
thinness, s. tenuidad, delgadez, raleza.
third, a. tercero ; —, s. tercio ; **-ly,** en
tercer lugar.
thirst, s. sed ; —, v.n. tener ó padecer sed.
thirstily, ad. con anhelo.
thirsty, a. sediento.
thirteen, a. trece.
thirteenth, a. décimotercio.
thirtieth, a. trigésimo.
thirty, a. treinta.
this, pn. este, esto.
thistle, s. cardo.
thither, ad. allá, á aquel lugar.
thole(-pin), s. (mar.) tolete, escálamo.
thong, s. correa, correhuela.
thorn, s. espino ; espina.
thorny, a. espinoso ; arduo.
thorough, pr. por, por medio ; —, a.
entero, cabal, perfecto ; **-ly,** enteramente, cabalmente.

thoroughbred, a. castizo, de sangre, de
casta.
thoroughfare, s. paso, tránsito.
thorough-paced, a. cabal, perfecto.
those, pn. pl. aquellos.
thou, pn. tú.
though, c. aunque, bien que ; **as —,** como
que, como sí. [cuidado.
thought, s. pensamiento, juicio ; opinión;
thoughtful, a. pensativo, meditabundo ;
-ly, atentamente ; de pensado.
thoughtfulness, s. meditación, atención.
thoughtless, a. descuidado ; insensato ;
-ly, descuidadamente, sin reflexión.
thoughtlessness, s. descuido ; inadverten-
thousand, a. mil. [cia.
thousandfold, a. mil veces tanto.
thousandth, a. milésimo.
thraldom, s. esclavitud. [cautivar.
thrall, s. esclavo ; esclava ; —, v.a.
thrash, v.a. trillar (grano) ; golpear.
thrasher, s. trillador.
thrashing-floor, s. era. [vesar.
thread, s. hilo ; —, v.a. enhebrar ; atra-
threadbare, a. raído, muy usado.
threat, s. amenaza.
threaten, v.a. amenazar. [amenazas.
threatening, a. amenazador ; **-ly** con,
three, a. tres.
three-cornered, a. triangular.
threefold, a. tríplice, triplo. [palos.
three-master, s. (mar.) buque de tres
threescore, a. & s. sesenta.
threshold, s. umbral.
thrice, ad. tres veces.
thrift, s. ganancia, economía, frugalidad.
thriftily, ad. frugalmente.
thriftiness, s. frugalidad, parsimonia.
thriftless, a. maniroto, pródigo.
thrifty, a. frugal, económico.
thrill, v.a. taladrar, horadar ; —, v.a.
& n. estremecer(se) ; —, s. estremecimiento.
thrive, v.n. prosperar, adelantar.
thrivingly, ad. prósperamente.
throat, s. garganta.
throb, v.n. palpitar ; —, s. palpitación.
throe, s. dolor, agonía.
throne, s. trono.
throng, s. tropel de gente ; —, v.a. & n.
agruparse ; venir de tropel ; cubrir ó
estrechar con gente.
throttle, s. gaznate, garguero ; —, v.a.
ahogar.
through, pr. por ; por medio de ; a
través de ; —, **and —** de un lado á otro.
throughout, pr. por todo ; —, ad. en
todas partes.
throw, v.a. echar ; arrojar, tirar, lanzar ;
—, s. tiro ; golpe. [strumento.
thrum, v.a. rascar las cuerdas de un in-

P

thrush, s. tordo (ave).

thrust, v.a. & n. empujar, impeler; estrechar; entremeterse, introducirse; —, s. estocada; puñalada; lanzada.

thud, s. estrépito de un golpe.

thumb, s. pulgar; —, v.a. manosear; ensuciar con los dedos.

thump, s. porrazo, golpe; —, v.a. aporrear, apuñetear.

thumping, a. grueso, pesado.

thunder, s. trueno; —, v.n. tronar; atronar; fulminar.

thunder-bolt, s. rayo.

thunder-clap, s. tronada.

thunder-storm, s. temporal.

thunder-struck, a. atónito, pasmado, consternado.

Thursday, s. jueves.

thus, ad. así, de este modo.

thwack, v.a. aporrear, apuñear.

thwart, v.a. cruzar, atravesar; contradecir, frustrar; —, s. banco de remero.

thy, a. tu.

thyme, s. (bot.) tomillo.

thyself, pn. ti mismo.

tiara, s. tiara.

tick, s. garrapata (insecto); funda de almohada; (col.) crédito.

ticket, s. boleta; cédula; (rail.) billete

ticket-collector, s. (rail.) revisor de billetes.

ticket-office, s. (rail.) despacho.

ticking, s. terliz; tic-tac.

tickle, v.a. hacer cosquillas á alguno, —, v.n. tener cosquillas.

tickling, s. cosquillas. pl.

ticklish, a. cosquilloso.

tidal, a. (mar.) de la marea.

tide, s. tiempo; estación; marea.

tide-waiter, s. aduanero en el litoral.

tidily, ad. mañosamente.

tidiness, s. maña, prontitud; aseo.

tidings, s.pl. nuevas, noticias.

tidy, a. neto, bonito; aseado; diestro.

tie, v.a. anudar, atar; —, s. nudo; atadura; lazo.

tiff, s. bebida; (col.) pique, disgusto.

tiffany, s. tafetán sencillo.

tiger, s. tigre; lacayo.

tight, a. tirante, tieso, apretado, estrechado, tenso; (col.) borracho.

tighten, v.a. tirar, estirar; apretar, estrechar.

tightly, ad. estrechamente.

tightness, s. tensión, tirantez, estrechez.

tights, s.pl. pantalón ajustado de tigress, s. tigra.   [bailarines.

tile, s. teja; —, v.a. tejar.

tiling, s. tejado.

till, pr. & c. hasta que, hasta; —, s. cajón; gaveta; —, v.a. cultivar, labrar.

tillage, s. labranza.   [timón.

tiller, s. agricultor; (mar.) caña del

tilling, s. labranza.

tilt, s. toldo de un vagón; justa; torneo; —, v.a. inclinar, sesgar; apuntar la lanza; —, v.n. justar.

tilth, s. labranza.

timber, s. madera de construcción; vigas maestras, pl.; —, v.a. enmaderar.

timber-work, s. maderaje.

timbrel, s. pandero.

time, s. tiempo; (mus.) compás; in — tiempo; from — to —, de cuando en cuando; —, v.a. adaptar al tiempo,

time-keeper, s. reloj.

timeliness, s. oportunidad.

timely, ad. con tiempo; á propósito; —, a. oportuno.

time-piece, s. reloj.

time-server, s. (fig.) veleta.

time-serving, s. servilismo.

time-worn, a. usado, deslustrado.

timid, a. tímido, temeroso; -ly, con

timidity, s. timidez.   [timidez.

timorous, a. temeroso; -ly, temerosamente.

tin, s. estaño; —, v.a estañar. [tinturar.

tincture, s. tintura; tinte; —, v.a. teñir,

tinder, s. yesca.

tinge, v.a. tinturar, teñir.   [punzar.

tingle, v.n. zumbar los oídos; latir,

tingling, s. zumbido de oídos; latido.

tinker, s. latonero; calderero remendón.

tinkle, v.a. & n. cencerrear.

tinman, tinsmith, s. hojalatero.

tin-plate, s. hoja de lata.

tinsel, s. oropel.

tint, s. tinte; —, v.a. teñir.

tin-tack, s. tachuela de estaño.

tiny, a. (col.) pequeño, chico.

tip, s. punta, extremidad; (col.) propina; —, v.a. herretear; golpear ligeramente.   [mente.

tippet, s. palatina.

tipple, v.n. beber con exceso; —, s.

tipsiness, s. embriaguez.   [bebida.

tipstaff, s. alguacil.

tipsy, a. borrachuelo, entre dos vinos.

tiptoe, s. punta del pie; on —, empinando.

tiptop, a. (col.) excelente; —, s. cumbre.

tirade, s. invectiva.

tire, s. atavío, toca; —, v.a. cansar, fatigar; —, v.n. cansarse, fastidiarse.

tiresome, a. tedioso, molesto.

tiresomeness, s. tedio, fastidio.

tiring-room, s. vestuario.

tissue, s. tisú; —, v.a. entretejer.

tit, s. pajarito; — for tat, ad. taz á taz.

titbit, s. bocado.

tithe, s. diezmo.

titillate, v.n. titilar.

title, s. título.
titled, a. titulado.
title-deed, s. título, documento de propiedad.
title-page, s. frontispicio de un libro.
titmouse, s. paro. [femenil.
titter, v.n. reirse fátuamente; —, s. risa
tittle, s. tilde; jota.
tittle-tattle, s. charla; —, v.n. charlar.
titular, a. titular.
to, pr. á, para; por; hasta; delante de un verbo, indica sólo el infinitivo y no se traduce.
toad, s. sapo, escuerzo.
toad-stool, s. (bot.) hongo.
toady, v.n. andar de gorra; —, s. pegote, hombre servil.
toadyism, s. servilismo. [brindis.
toast, v.a. tostar; brindar; —, s. tostada;
toaster, s. parrillas, pl.
tobacco, s. tabaco.
tobacco-box, s. tabaquera.
tobacconist, s. tabaquero.
tobacco-pouch, s. petaca.
tocsin, s. campana á rebato.
to-day, ad. hoy.
toddle, v'n. (col.) trotar (niño).
toddy, s. grog.
to-do, s. (col.) agitación, tumulto.
toe, s. dedo del pie.
together, ad. junto, juntamente; al mismo tiempo. [ropa.
toggery, s. (col.) fruslería; ropavejería,
toil, v.n. fatigarse, trabajar mucho; afanarse; —, s. trabajo; fatiga; afán.
toilet, s. acción de vestirse; vestido.
toilsome, a. trabajoso; fatigoso.
token, s. señal; recuerdo.
tolerable, a. tolerable; mediocre.
tolerably, ad. tolerablemente; así así.
tolerance, toleration, s. tolerancia.
tolerant, a. tolerante.
tolerate, v.a. tolerar.
toll, s. peaje; —, v.a. tocar una campana.
toll-gatherer, s. portazguero.
tomahawk, s. hacha de los indios
tomato, s. tomate. [americanos.
tomb, s. tumba; sepulcro.
tomboy, s. doncella pizpireta y retozona.
tomb-stone, s. piedra sepulcral.
tom-cat, s. gato macho.
tome, s. tomo.
tomfoolery, s. pataratas, frioleras. pl.
to-morrow, ad. mañana.
tomtit, s. (orn.) paro (pájaro).
ton, s. tonelada.
tone, s. tono de la voz; acento; estilo.
tongs, s.pl. tenazas.
tongue, s. lengua; habla; promontorio; (of a balance) lengua en el peso; to hold the —, callar.

tongue-tied, a. mudo.
tonic, a. (med.) tónico.
to-night, ad. esta noche.
tonnage, s. porte de un buque.
tonsil, s. agallas, pl.
tonsure, s. tonsura.
tontine, s. tontina.
too, ad. demasiado; también, aun.
tool, s. herramienta; utensilio.
tooth, s. diente; gusto; —, v.a. dentar.
tooth-ache, s. dolor de muelas.
tooth-brush, s. cepillo de dientes.
toothless, a. desdentado.
toothpick, s. mondadientes, palito.
toothpowder, s. dentífrico.
toothsome, a. sabroso; comedero.
top, s. cima, cumbre; peonza; trompo; (mar.) cofa; —, v.a. & n. encimarse; sobrepujar, exceder; descabezar los árboles.
topaz, s. topacio.
top-coat, s. sobretodo.
toper, s. borrachón, bebedor.
top-heavy, a. pesado por arriba.
topic, s. asunto, lugar, materia.
topmost, a. lo más alto.
topographic(al), s. topográfico.
topography, s. topografía.
topple, v.n. volcarse, derribarse.
topsy-turvy, ad. al revés.
torch, s. antorcha, hacha.
torch-bearer, s. hachero.
torch-light, s. luz de antorcha.
torment, v.a. atormentar; —, s. tormento.
tornado, s. turbonada; huracán.
torpedo, s. torpedo.
torpid, a. entorpecido.
torpor, s. entorpecimiento, estupor.
torrent, s. torrente.
torrid, a. tórrido, tostado.
tortoise, s. tortuga.
tortoise-shell, s. concha de tortuga.
tortuous, a. tortuoso, sinuoso.
torture, s. tortura; —, v.a. atormentar.
Tory, s. tory (partido conservativo de Inglaterra).
toss, v.a. & n. tirar, lanzar, arrojar; agitar(se), sacudir(se); (in a blanket) mantear; —, s. sacudida; cabezada.
total, a. total, entero; -ly, totalmente.
totality, s. totalidad.
totter, v.n. bambolear; vacilar.
touch, v.a. & n. tocar, palpar; —, s. tocamiento; contacto; tacto; toque; prueba.
touch-hole, s. luz (de cañon).
touchiness, s. susceptibilidad.
touching, a. patético, conmovedor; —, pr. respeto á, sobre.
touch-me-not, s. (bot.) mercurial.

touch-stone, s. piedra de toque.
touch-wood, s. yesca.
touchy, a. cosquilloso, vidrioso.
tough, a. correoso ; tieso ; viscoso, duro.
toughen, v.a. & n. endurecer(se). [tesura.
toughness, s. tenacidad ; viscosidad ;
tour, s. viaje ; peregrinación.
tourist, s. viajero.
tournament, s. torneo ; justa.
tout, s. revendedor, truhán, agente servil.
tow, s. estopa ; remolque ; —, v.a. (mar.)
    remolcar, atoar.
towage, s. (mar.) remolque, atoaje.
toward(s), pr. & ad. hacia, con dirección á.
towel, s. toalla.
towel-horse, s. enjugador.
tower, s. torre ; ciudadela ; —, v.n. en-
    cimarse ; elevarse.
town, s. ciudad, pueblo, villa.
town-councillor, s. concejal, concejil.
town-crier, s. pregonero.
town-hall, town-house, s. casa consis-
    torial, casa municipal.
townsfolk, s.pl. gente de la ciudad.
township, s. territorio municipal, muni-
    cipalidad.
townsman, s. conciudadano.
toy, s. chuchería ; miriñaque, juguete ;
    —, v.n. jugar, divertirse. [delinear.
trace, s. huella, pisada ; —, v.a. trazar,
track, s. vestigio ; huella ; senda, rodada ;
    —, v.a. rastrear. [desierto.
trackless, a. sin huella, sin senda ;
tract, s. trecho ; región, comarca ;
    tratado.
tractable, a. tratable, afable.
tractableness, s. afabilidad, docilidad.
tractably, ad. dócilmente.
traction, s. tracción.
trade, s. comercio, tráfico ; negocio,
    trato ; ocupación ; —, v.n. comerciar,
    traficar. [mercante.
trader, s. comerciante, traficante ; navío
tradesman, s. tendero, mercader.
trades-union, s. asociación de artesanos,
    gremio.
trade-winds, s.pl. (mar.) vientos alisios.
trading, s. comercio ; —, a. comercial.
tradition, s. tradición.
traditional, a. tradicional ; **-ly,** por
    tradición. [acusar
traduce, v.a. vituperar ; calumniar ;
traffic, s. tráfico ; mercaderías ; —, v.n.
    traficar, comerciar.
trafficker, s. traficante, comerciante,
    negociante, mercader.
tragedian, s. actor trágico.
tragedy, s. tragedia. [mente.
tragedic(al), a. trágico ; **-ally,** trágica-
tragicomedy, s. tragicomedia.
tragi-comical, a. tragi-cómico.

trail, v.a. & n. rastrear ; arrastrar ; —,
    s. rastro ; pisada ; cola.
train, v.a. arrastrar ; amaestrar, enseñar,
    criar, adiestrar ; disciplicar ; —, s.
    estratagema, engaño ; serie ; séquito,
    tren ; (rail.) tren.
train-bands, s.pl. milicias, pl.
trainer, s. maestro, enseñador.
training, s. educación, disciplina.
train-oil, s. aceite de ballena.
trait, s. rasgo de carácter.
traitor, s. traidor. [traidoramente.
traitorous, a. perfido, traidor ; **-ly,**
traitress, s. traidora.
trammel, s. trasmallo ; impedimento ; —,
    v.a. embarazar, impedir.
tramp, s. v.a. & n. pisar, viajar á pie ;
    —, s. viajero ó pie, vagabundo, mén-
    digo.
trample, v.n. pisar ; insultar. [digo.
trampling, s. pataleo.
tram-way, s. tranvía.
trance, s. rapto ; éxtasi. [mente.
tranquil, a. tranquilo ; **-ly,** tranquila-
tranquillity, s. tranquilidad.
tranquillize, v.a. tranquilizar.
transact, v.a. negociar ; transigir.
transaction, s. transacción ; negociación ;
    -s, pl. memorias, pl.
transatlantic, s. transatlántico. [ceder.
transcend, v.a. transcender, pasar ; ex-
transcendency, s. excelencia.
transcendent, a. sobresaliente ; **-ly,** ex-
    celentemente.
transcribe, v.a. trascribir, copiar.
transcriber, s. copiante.
transcript, s. trasunto.
transcription, s. traslado ; copia.
transept, s. nave transversal de una
    iglesia. [s. cesión.
transfer, v.a. transferir, transportar ; —,
transferable, a. transferible.
transfiguration, s. transfiguración.
transfigure, v.a. transformar.
transfix, v.a. traspasar.
transform, v.a. transformar.
transformation, s. transformación.
transgress, v.a. & n. transgredir, violar.
transgression, s. transgresión.
transgressor, s. transgresor.
transient, a. pasajero, transitorio.
transit, s. tránsito.
transition, s. tránsito ; transición.
transitional, a. provisional.
transitive, a. transitivo.
transitoriness, s. brevedad.
transitory, a. transitorio.
translate, v.a. trasladar, traducir.
translation, s. translación ; traducción.
translator, s. traductor.
translucent, a. trasluciente, diáfano.
transmarine, s. trasmarino.

transmigration, a. transmigración.
transmission, s. transmisión.
transmit, v.a. transmitir.
transmutation, s. transmutación.
transom, s. travesaño.   [parencia.
transparence, transparency, s. trans-
transparent, a. transparente, diáfano.
transpire, v.n. transpirar; revelarse;
    suceder.
transplantation, s. trasplante.
transport, v.a. transportar; deportar;
    —, s. transportación; (mar.) trans-
    porte; criminal condenado á la de-
    portación.   [portamiento.
transportation, s. transportación, trans-
transporting, a. embelesador.
transpose, v.a. transponer.
transposition, s. transposición.
transubstantiation, s. transubstancia-
    ción.   [versalmente.
transverse, a. transverso; -ly, trans-
trap, s. trampa; —, v.a. coger en trampa.
trap-door, s. puerta disimulada; escotil-
trapeze, s. trapecio.   [lón.
trapper, s. cazador de animales pelíferos.
trappings, s.pl. jaeces, pl.
trappist, s. cartujo.
trash, s. heces, pl., desecho; zupia.
trashy, a. vil, despreciable, sin valor.
travail, s. afan; dolores de parto.
travel, v.n. viajar; —, s. viaje.
traveller, s. viajante, viajero.
travelling, s. viajes, pl.
traverse, v.a. atravesar, cruzar.
travesty, s. disfraz; caricatura; —, a.
    disfrazado; —, v.a. disfrazar; satirizar.
trawl, v.n. rastrear (pescando).
tray, s. salvilla, batea; artesa.
treacherous, a. traidor, pérfido; -ly, trai-
    doramente.
treachery, s. perfidia, deslealtad, traición.
treacle, s. triaca, melaza.
tread, v.a. n. pisar, hollar, apretar con
    el pie; pisotear; patalear; caminar con
    majestad; —, s. pisa; pisada.
treadle, s. pedal, cárcola.
treason, s. traición; 'high —, delito de
    lesa majestad.
treasonable, a. traidor; -bly, á traición.
treasure, s. tesoro; —, v.a. atesorar.
treasurer, s. tesorero.
treasury, s. tesorería.
treat, v.a. & n. tratar; regalar; —, s.
    trato, banquete, festín.
treatise, s. tratado.
treatment, s. trato.
treaty, s. tratado.
treble, a. triplice; —, v.a. & n. tripli-
    car(se); —, s. (mus.) tiple.
trebly, ad. triplicadamente.
tree, s. árbol; cepo, asta.

trefoil, s. trébol.
trellis, s. enrejado.
tremble, v.n. temblar.
trembling, s. temblor; trino.
tremblingly, ad. trémulamente. [mente.
tremendous, a. tremendo; -ly, terrible-
tremor, s. tremor, temblor.
tremulous, a. trémulo.
tremulousness, s. temblor.
trench, v.a. cortar; atrincherar; —, s.
    foso; (mil.) trinchera.
trenchant, a. afilado, cortante; decisivo.
trencher, s. plato de madera.
trencher-man, s. comedor.
trepan, s. trépano; —, v.a. trepanar.
trespass, v.a. quebrantar, transpasar,
    violar; —, s. transgresión, violación.
trespasser, s. transgresor.
tress, s. trenza; rizo de pelo.
trestle, s. bastidor, caballete, trébedes.
trial, s. prueba; ensayo; (law) examen
    (judicial), proceso.
triangle, s. triángulo.
triangular, a. triangular.
tribal, a. perteneciente á una tribu.
tribe, s. tribu; raza, casta.
tribulation, s. tribulación.
tribunal, s. tribunal.
tribune, s. tribuno, púlpito; tribuna.
tributary, a. & s. tributario.
tribute, s. tributo.
trice, s. momento, tris.
tricycle, s. tricicleta.
trick, s. engaño, fraude; superchería,
    astucia; burla; maña; baza ,(en el
    juego de naipes); —, v.a. engañar,
    trampear, ataviar.
trickery, s. engaño, dolo.
trickster, s. engañador, petardista.
trickle, v.n. gotear.
tricky, a. astuto, artificioso.
trident, s. tridente (cetro).
triennial, a. trienal.
trifle, s. bagatela, niñería; —, v.n.
    bobear; chancear, juguetear.
trifler, s. necio; persona frívola; haragán.
trifling, a. frívolo, trivial; -ly, frívol-
    mente, sin consecuencia.
trigger, s. gatillo de escopeta (ó pistola).
trigonometry, s. trigonometría.
trill, s. trino; —, v.a. trinar.
trim, a. compuesto, ataviado; —, v.a.
    aparejar, preparar; acomodar; ador-
    nar; podar; (mar.) enderezar; orien-
    tar (las velas); —, v.n. balancear,
    vacilar; —, s. atavío, adorno, aderezo.
trimly, ad. lindamente, con primor.
trimming, s. guarnición de vestido.
Trinity, s. Trinidad.   [juguetes.
trinket, s. joya, alhaja; adorno; bujería;
trio, s. (mus.) trio.

trip, v.a. hacer tropezar ; —, v.n. tropezar ; resbalar ; hacer un viaje corto ; —, s. zancadilla ; resbalón ; viaje corto.

tripartite, a. tripartito.

tripe, s. tripa ; intestino.

triple, a. tríplice, triplo ; —, v.a. triplicar.

triplet, s. (poet.) tercerilla ; -s, pl. tres gemelos, pl.

tripod, v.a. trípode.   [melos, pl.

tripos, s. examen universitario.

tripping, a. veloz, ligero, ágil ; —, s. baile ligero ; tropiezo ; -ly, velozmente.

trireme, s. trirreme.   [mente.

trisect, v.a. tripartir.

trisyllable, s. palabra trisilábica.

trite, a. usado ; trivial ; superficial, común.

triteness, s. falta de originalidad.

triturate, v.a. triturar.

triumph, s. triunfo ; —, v.n. triunfar.

triumphal, a. triunfal.   [-ly, en triunfo.

triumphant, a. triunfante ; victorioso ;

triumvirate, s. triumvirato.

trivet, s. trébedes, pl.   [mente.

trivial, a. trivial, vulgar ; -ly, trivial-

triviality, s. trivialidad.   [trawl.

troll, v.a. voltear ; —, v.n. girar. V.

trolley, s. (rail.) lorri.

trollop, s. mujerzuela, gorrona.

troop, s. tropa ; cuadrilla, turba ; —, v.n. atroparse.

trooper, s. soldado á caballo.

trope, s. tropo, frase figurativa.

trophy, s. trofeo.

tropical, a. trópico.

tropics, s.pl. trópico.

trot, s. trote ; —, v.n. trotar.

troth, s. fe, fidelidad, verdad.

trotter, s. caballo trotón.

trouble, v.a. disturbar ; afligir ; —, s. turbación ; disturbio ; inquietud ; aflicción, pena ; congoja.   [tuno, molesto.

troublesome, a. penoso, fatigoso ; impor-

troublesomeness, s. incomodidad, molestia.

troublous, a. turbulento, confuso.

trough, s. artesa, gamella ; dornajo.

trousers, s.pl. pantalones.

trout, s. trucha (pez).

trow, v.a. creer, suponer.

trowel, s. trulla, llana.

truant, a. & s. vago, vagabundo, holgazán, haragán.

truce, s. tregua, suspensión de armas.

truck, v.n. trocar, cambiar ; —, s. cambio, trueque; rueda de cureña; (rail.) vagón,

truckle, v.n. someterse ; —, s. ruedecita.

truckle-bed, s. carriola.   [especie.

truck-system, s. paga de los obreros en

truculence, s. fiereza, crueldad.

truculent, a. truculento, cruel.

trudge, v.n. andar á pie con afán.

true, a. verdadero, cierto; sincero; exacto.

true-born, a. legítimo.

true-bred, a. de casta legítima, castizo.

true-hearted, a. leal, sincero, franco, fiel.

truffle, s. criadilla de tierra.

truism, s. verdad indubitable, lugares comunes, axioma.

truly, ad. en verdad ; sinceramente.

trump, s. trompeta ; triunfo (en el juego de naipes) ; —, v.a. ganar con el triunfo ; to — up, forjar ; inventar.

trumpery, s. hojarasca ; bujería, baratija.

trumpet, s. trompeta ; —, v.a. trompetear ; divulgar.

trumpeter, s. trompetero.

truncate, v.a. truncar ; troncar.

truncheon, s. cachiporra, macana.

trundle, s. rueda baja ; carreta de ruedas bajas ; rodillo ; —, v.a. rodar.

trunk, s. tronco, baúl, cofre ; trompa de elefante.   [línea principal.

trunk-line, trunk-road, (rail.) tronco,

trunk-maker, s. cofrero.

trunnion, s. (mil.) eje de cañón.

truss, s. braguero ; haz ; atado ; —, v.a. empaquetar ; apretar.

trust, s. confianza ; cargo, depósito ; crédito ; asociación comercial para monopolizar la venta de algún género ; —, v.a. & n. confiar ; confiarse, fiarse dar crédito ; esperar.

trustee, s. fideicomisario, curador.

trustful, a. fiel ; confiado.

trustily, a. fielmente.

trustiness, s. fidelidad, probidad.

trustworthy, a. digno de confianza, honrado.   [in —, en verdad.

trusty, a. fiel, leal ; seguro.

truth, s. verdad ; fidelidad ; realidad ;

truthful, a. verídico.

truthfulness, s. veracidad.

try, v.a. & n. examinar, ensayar, probar; experimentar ; tentar ; intentar ; juzgar ; purificar, refinar.

trying, a. crítico ; penoso ; fastidioso.

tryst, s. cita, lugar de cita.

tub, s. cubo ; tina de madera.

tube, s. tubo, cañón, cañuto.

tubercle, s. (med.) tubérculo.

tuberose, s. (bot.) tuberosa.

tubular, a. tubular.   [mangar, recoger.

tuck, s. alforza ; pliegue ; —, v.a. arre-

tucker, s. babador.

Tuesday, s. martes.

tuft, s. borla ; penacho ; melena ; grupo ; moño ; espesura de hierba ó de verdura.

tufted, a. frondoso, velludo.

tuft-hunter, s. parasito, pegote.

tug, v.a. tirar con fuerza ; arrancar ; —, v.n. esforzarse ; —, s. tirada ; esfuerzo; (mar.) remolcador.

tuition, s. tutoría, tutela.

tulip, s. tulipa ; tulipán.

tumble, v.n. caer, hundirse, voltear ; revolcarse ; —, v.a. revolver ; rodar ; volcar ; —, s. caída ; vuelco.

tumble-down, a. arruinado.

tumbler, s. volteador ; saltimbanque ; vaso (sin pie) para beber.

tumbrel, s. (mil.) carro de municiones ; chirrión.

tumefy, v.a. & n. hinchar(se).

tumor, s. tumor, hinchazón.

tumult, s. tumulto.   [tuariamente.

tumultuous, a. tumultuoso ; -ly, tumul-

tun, s. tonel.

tune, s. tono ; armonía ; aria ; humor ; —, v.a. templar un instrumento músico.

tuneful, a. armonioso, acorde, melodioso.

tuneless, a. disonante.

tunic, s. túnica.

tuning-fork, s. (mus.) horquilla tónica.

tunnel, s. cañón de chimenea ; túnel, mina ; —, v.a. & n. minar, socavar.

tunnelling, s. abertura de un túnel.

tunny, s. atún (pez).

turban, s. turbante.

turbid, a. turbio, cenagoso.

turbot, s. rodaballo, rombo (pez).

turbulence, s. turbulencia, confusión.

turbulent, a. turbulento, tumultuoso ; -ly, tumultuariamente.

tureen, s. sopera.

turf, s. césped ; turba ; el pasatiempo de corrida de caballos ; —, v.a. cubrir con céspedes.

turgid, a. túmido, inflado.

turkey, s. pavo ; pava.

turmoil, s. disturbio ; baraúnda.

turn, v.a. volver, trocar ; verter, traducir ; cambiar ; tornear ; —, v.n. volver, girar, rodar ; voltear ; dar vueltas ; volverse á, mudarse, transformarse ; volver casaca ; —, s. vuelta ; giro ; rodeo ; turno ; vez ; procedimiento, modo de portarse ; inclinación ; forma.

turncoat, s. desertor, renegado.

turncock, s. fontanero.

turner, s. torneador, tornero.

turning, s. vuelta ; rodeo.

turning-in, s. pliegue.

turning-lathe, s. torno.

turnip, s. (bot.) nabo.

turnkey, s. carcelero, alguacil de cárcel.

turn-out, s. aparejo de coche ; producto.

turnpike, s. barrera de portazgo.

turn-plate, turn-rail, turn-table, s. (rail.) plataforma giratoria, tornavía.

turnscrew, s. destornillador.

turnspit, s. galopín de cocina que da vueltas al asador ; especie de perro.

turnstile, s. molinete.

turpentine, s. trementina.

turpitude, s. torpeza, infamia.

turquoise, s. turquesa.

turret, s. torrecilla.

turreted, a. armado con torrecillas.

turtle, s. tórtola ; tortuga de mar.

turtle-dove, s. tórtola.

tush ! tut ! ¡ calla !, ¡ disparates !

tusk, s. colmillo.

tusked, a. colmilludo.

tussle, s. alboroto ; riña.

tutelage, s. tutela, tutoría.

tutelar, a. tutelar.

tutor, s. tutor ; preceptor ; — v.a. enseñar, instruir ; señorear.

tutoress, s. tutriz, aya.

twaddle, v.n. charlar ; —, charla, disparates.

twain, a. dos.

twang, v.a. & n. resonar ; restallar ; —, s. gangueo ; sonido agudo.

tweak, v.a. pinzar.

tweed, s. paño.

tweezers, s.pl. tenacillas, pl.

twelfth, a. duodécimo.

Twelfth-day, Twelfth-night, s. día de reyes ; Epifanía.

twelve, a. doce.

twelvemonth, s. año (doce meses).

twentieth, a. vigésimo.

twenty, a. veinte.

twice, ad. dos veces ; al doble.

twig, s. vareta, varilla ; vástago.

twilight, s. crepúsculo.

twill, s. tela cruzada.

twin, s. gemelo.

twine, v.a. torcer ; enroscar ; —, v.n. en trelazarse ; caracolear ; —, s. guita.

twinge, v.a. punzar, pellizcar ; —, s. dolor agudo ó punzante.

twinkle, v.n. centellear ; parpadear.

twinkling, s. vislumbre ; guiñada ; pestañeo.   [tación.

twirl, v.a. & n. voltear, girar ; —, s. rotwist, v.a. & n. torcer, retorcer ; entretejer ; retortijarse ; —, s. trenza ; cordón ; torcedura.

twit, v.a. regañar, reprender.

twitch, v.a. pellizcar ; —, v.n. encogerse, sacudirse ; —, s. pellizco ; sacudida.

twitter, v.n. gorjear ; —, s. gorjeo.

two, a. dos.

twofold, a. doble, duplicado ; —, ad. al doble.

tympan(um), s. tímpano.

type, s. tipo ; letra.

typewriter, s. máquina de escribir.

typhoid, a. tifoideo.

typhus, s. tifo.

typical, a. típico ; -ly, simbólicamente.

typify, v.a. figurar.
typographer, s. tipógrafo.
typographic(al), a. tipográfico.
typography, s. tipografía.   [camente.
tyrannic(al), a. tiránico; -ly, tiráni-

tyrannize, v.a. tiranizar.
tyranny, s. tiranía; crueldad.
tyrant, s. tirano.
tyre, s. llanta.
tyro, s. tirón, bisoño.

U

ubiquitous, a. ubicuo.
ubiquity, s. ubicuidad.
udder, s. ubre.
ugliness, s. fealdad, deformidad.
ugly, a. feo, disforme.
ulcer, s. úlcera.
ulcerate, v.a. ulcerar.
ulceration, s. ulceración.
ulterior, a. ulterior.
ultimate, a. último; -ly, últimamente.
ultimatum, x. ultimátum.
ultramarine, a. ultramarino.
ultramontane, a. ultramontano.
umber, s. (art) tierra de sombras.
umbrage, s. sombra; sospecha; enojo;
   take —, tener sospecha, enojarse.
umbrageous, a. sombrío, umbrío, som-
umbrella, s. paraguas.   [broso.
umpire, s. árbitro.
unabashed, v.a. descocado.
unabated, a. no disminuido; cabal.
unable, a. incapaz.
unaccommodating, a. inconveniente, poco
   complaciente.
unaccompanied, a. solo, sin acompañamiento.   [bado.
unaccomplished, a. incompleto, no aca-
unaccountable, a. inexplicable, extraño.
unaccountably, ad. extrañamente.
unaccustomed, a. desacostumbrado, desusado.
unacknowledged, a. desconocido; negado.
unacquainted, a. ignorante.
unadorned, a. sin adorno, simple.
unadulterated, a. genuino, puro; sin
   mezcla.   [-ly, naturalmente.
unaffected, a. sincero, sin afectación;
unaided, a. sin ayuda.
unaltered, a. invariado.
unambitious, a. no ambicioso.
unanimity, s. unanimidad.   [mente.
unanimous, a. unánime; -ly, unánime-
unanswerable, a. incontrovertible, incontestable.
unanswered, a. no respondido.
unapproachable, a. inaccesible.
unarmed, a. inerme, desarmado.
unasked, a. no llamado, no convidado.
unassailable, a. libre de ataque, seguro.
unassisted, a. sin socorro, sin auxilio, sin
unassuming, a. modesto.   [ayuda.
unattached, a. independiente; disponible.

unattainable, a. inasequible. [intentado.
unattempted, a. no experimentado; no
unattended, a. sin comitiva.
unavailing, a. inútil, vano, infructuoso.
unavoidable, a. inevitable.
unavoidably, ad. inevitablemente.
unaware, s. descuidado, ignorante.
unawares, ad. de improviso.
unbar, v.a. desatrancar.
unbearable, a. intolerable.
unbecoming, a. indecente, indecoroso;
   -ly, indecentemente.
unbelief, s. incredulidad.
unbeliever, s. incrédulo, infiel.
unbend, v.a. & n. aflojar(se).
unbending, a. inflexible.
unbiassed, a. imparcial.
unbidden, a. no convidado; espontáneo.
unbind, v.a. desatar.
unbleached, a. no blanqueado.
unblemished, a. sin mancha, sin tacha,
   irreprensible.
unblest, a. maldito; desgraciado.
unblushing, a. impudente.
unbolt, v.a. desatrancar.
unborn, a. que no ha nacido aun; embrión; venidero.
unbosom, v.a. abrir el pecho, revelar.
unbound, a. no encuadernado; desatado.
unbounded, a. infinito; ilimitado; -ly,
   ilimitadamente.
unbridle, v.a. desenfrenar; -d, a. desenfrenado, licencioso.
unbroken, a. indómito.
unbuckle, v.a. deshebillar.   [aliviar.
unburden, unburthen, v.a. descargar
unburied, a. insepulto.
unbutton, v.a. desabotonar.
uncalled for, a. gratuito, superfluo.
unceasing, a. continuo.
uncertain, a. incierto, dudoso.
uncertainty, s. incertidumbre.
unchain, v.a. desencadenar.
unchangeable, a. inmutable.
unchangeably, ad. inmutablemente.
unchanged, a. constante.
unchanging, a. inalterable, inmutable.
uncharitable, a. incompasivo, duro.
uncharitableness, s. falta de caridad,
unchecked, a. desenfrenado.   [dureza.
unchaste, a. incasto.
unchecked, a. desenfrenado

unchristian, a. indigno de un cristiano.
uncivil, a. grosero, descortés. [lizado.
uncivilized, a. tosco, salvaje, no civi-
unclad, a. desnudo.
unclaimed, a. no reclamado ; mostrenco.
unele, s. tío ; (col.) prendero.
unclean, a. inmundo, sucio.
uncleanness, uncleanliness, s. suciedad ;
impureza.
unclose, v.a. abrir ; descubrir, revelar.
unclouded, a. sereno.
uncock, v.a. desmontar una escopeta.
uncoil, v.a. desarrollar.
uncombed, a. despeinado.
uncomely, a. indecente ; feo.
uncomfortable, a. desconsolado ; desagradable, incómodo.
uncomfortableness, s. descomodidad.
uncomfortably, ad. desconsoladamente ;
incómodamente ; tristemente.
uncommon, a. raro, extraordinario ; **-ly,**
extraordinariamente ; raramente.
uncommonness, s. raridad.
uncompromising, a. irreconciliable.
unconcern, s. indiferencia ; descuido.
unconcerned, a. indiferente ; **-ly,** con indiferencia. [soluto.
unconditional, a. sin condiciones, ab-
unconfined, a. libre, ilimitado.
unconquerable, a. invencible, insuperable.
unconscionable, a. desrazonable ; **-bly,**
sin razón.
unconscious, a. inconsciente ; desmayado;
-ly, sin conocimiento ó conciencia de
las cosas.
unconstrained, a. libre, voluntario.
uncontrolled, a. desenfrenado, libre.
unconvincing, a. no convincente.
uncork, v.a. destapar.
uncorrected, a. incorrecto, no corregido.
uncorrupted, a. incorrupto, íntegro.
uncouple, v.a. soltar, desatraillar.
uncouth, a. extraño ; grosero ; **-ly,**
groseramente.
uncouthness, s. extrañeza, rareza.
uncover, v.a. descubrir.
uncrown, v.a. destronar.
unction, s. unción.
unctuous, a. untuoso ; (fig.) pomposo.
uncultivated, a. inculto.
uncured, a. no salado ; fresco.
uncurl, v.a. desenrizar el pelo.
uncut, a. no cortado, entero.
undamaged, a. ileso, libre de daño.
undaunted, a. intrépido.
undeceive, v.a. desengañar.
undecided, a. indeciso.
undefiled, a. impoluto, puro.
undeniable, a. innegable, incontestable ;
-bly, indubitablemente.
under, pr. & ad. debajo ; **menos de.**

underclothing, s. paños menores.
undercurrent, corriente submarino ; tendencia secreta.
undercut, s. solomo.
underdone, a. poco cocido.
undergo, v.a. sufrir ; sostener.
undergraduate, s. estudiante no graduado.
underground, a. soterráneo.
undergrowth, s. soto, monte tallar.
underhand, ad. clandestinamente ; **—,** a.
secreto, clandestino.
underlie, v.n. estar debajo, esconderse.
underline, v.a. rayar (las palabras).
underling, s. dependiente.
undermine, v.a. minar.
undermost, a. ínfimo.
underneath, ad. debajo.
under-part, s. parte inferior.
underpin, v.a. (arch.) apuntalar.
underrate, v.a. desapreciar.
under-secretary, s. subsecretario. [otro.
undersell, v.a. vender por menos que
undersized, a. muy pequeño.
understand, v.a. entender, comprender.
understanding, s. entendimiento ; inteligencia ; conocimiento ; correspondencia ; **—,** a. inteligente, perito.
undertake, v.a. emprender ; empeñarse.
undertaker, s. empresario ; asentista.
undertaking, s. empresa ; empeño.
undertone, s. voz baja.
undervalue, v.a. desapreciar ; desestimar.
underwood, s. monte bajo, mata.
underwrite, v.a. suscribir ; asegurar
contra los riesgos del mar.
under-writer, s. asegurador. [mente.
undeserved, a. inmérito ; **-ly,** inmérita-
undeserving, a. indigno. [intención.
undesigned, a. involuntario, hecho sin
undesigning, a. sincero, sencillo.
undesirable, a. no deseable, malo.
undetermined, a. indeterminado, indeciso.
undeviating, a. firme, estable, constante.
undigested, a. indigesto.
undiminished, a. entero, no disminuido.
undiscerning, a. inobservante, insensible.
undisciplined, a. indisciplinado. [sincero.
undisguised, a. sin disfraz, cándido,
undismayed, a. intrépido.
undisputed, a. incontestable.
undisturbed, a. quieto, tranquilo.
undivided, a. indiviso, entero.
undo, v.a. deshacer, desatar.
undoubted, a. indubitado, evidente ; **-ly,**
indubitablemente. [ropa de casa.
undress, v.a. & n. desnudar(se) ; **—,** s.
undue, a. indebido ; injusto.
undulate, v.n. ondear.
undulation, s. undulación.
unduly, ad. **indebidamente ; ilícitamente.**

undutiful, a. desobediente ; -ly, inobedientemente. [de respeto.

undutifulness, s. desobediencia ; falta

undying, a. inmortal.

unearth, v.a. desenterrar ; descubrir.

unearthly, a. sobrenatural, aduendado ; celeste. [mente.

uneasily, ad. inquietamente, incómoda-

uneasy, a. inquieto, desasosegado ; incómodo. [ejemplo.

unedifying, a. poco edificante ; de mal

unemployed, a. desocupado ; ocioso.

unenlightened, a. no iluminado ; indocto.

unentertaining, a. monótono, insípido.

unenviable, a. no envidiable.

unequal, a. -ly, ad. desigual(mente).

unequalled, a. incomparable.

unerring, a. -ly, ad. infalible(mente).

uneven, a. desigual ; impar ; -ly, desigualmente.

unevenness, s. desigualdad.

unexampled, a. sin ejemplo, único.

unexceptionable, a. irreprensible.

unexpected, a. inesperado ; inopinado ; -ly, de repente ; inopinadamente.

unexplored, a. ignorado, no descubierto.

unfading, a. inmarcesible.

unfailing, a. infalible, seguro.

unfair, a. doble, falso ; injusto ; -ly, injustamente.

unfaithful, a. infiel, pérfido.

unfaithfulness, s. infidelidad, perfidia.

unfaltering, a. firme, asegurado.

unfamiliar, a. desacostumbrado, poco común. [contra la moda.

unfashionable, a. opuesto á la moda ; -bly,

unfasten, v.a. desatar, soltar, aflojar.

unfathomable, a. insondable, impenetrable.

unfavourable, a. desfavorable.

unfavourably, ad. contrariamente.

unfed, a. falto de alimento.

unfeeling, a. insensible, duro de corazón.

unfeigned, a. verdadero, genuino ; -ly, sinceramente.

unfelt, a. no sentido, imperceptible.

unfilial, a. indigno de un hijo.

unfinished, a. imperfecto, no acabado.

unfit, a. desconveniente, inepto, incapaz ; -ly, impropiamente ; —, v.a. inhabilitar.

unfitness, s. ineptitud ; impropiedad.

unfitting, a. desconvenible ; impropio

unfix, v.a. soltar, aflojar.

unfixed, a. errante, vacilante.

unfledged, a. implume. [cerrar.

unfold, v.a. desplegar ; revelar ; desen-

unforeseen, a. imprevisto.

unforgiving, a. implacable.

unfortunate, a. desafortunado, infeliz ; -ly, por desgracia, infelizmente.

unfounded, a. sin fundamento.

unfrequent, a. *V.* infrequent.

unfrequented, a. solitario.

unfriendliness, s. falta de benevolencia.

unfriendly, a. nada afable.

unfruitful, a. estéril ; infructuoso.

unfruitfulness, s. esterilidad, infecundidad, infructuosidad.

unfurl, v.a. desplegar, extender.

unfurnished, a. sin muebles ; desprovisto.

ungainly, a. zafio, desmañado.

ungenerous, a. ignoble, bajo, tacaño.

ungentlemanly, a. mal criado, grosero.

unglazed, a. sin vidrieras ; sin vidriar.

ungodliness, s. impiedad.

ungodly, a. impío. [able.

ungovernable, a. indomable, ingobern-

ungoverned, a. desgobernado, desenfrenado. [reglas de la gramática.

ungrammatical, a. contrario á las

ungrateful, a. ingrato ; desagradable ; -ly, ingratamente.

ungratefulness, s. ingratitud.

ungrounded, a. infundado.

ungrudgingly, ad. de buena gana.

unguarded, a. negligente, descuidado.

unhallowed, a. profano.

unhand, v.a. soltar.

unhandsome, a. feo, falto de gracia ; mezquino ; -ly, sin gracia ; feamente.

unhandy, a. desmañado.

unhappily, ad. infelizmente.

unhappiness, s. infelicidad.

unhappy, a. infeliz.

unharmed, a. ileso, sano y salvo. [salud.

unhealthiness, s. insalubridad ; falta de

unhealthy, a. enfermizo. [ejemplo.

unheard (of), a. inaudito, extraño, sin

unheeded, a. no atendido, despreciado.

unheedful, unheeding, a. negligente ; distraído.

unhinge, v.a. desquiciar ; desordenar.

unholy, a. profano, impío.

unhonoured, a. despreciado, no venerado.

unhook, v.a. desganchar.

unhoped (for), a. inesperado.

unhorse, v.a. botar de la silla al jinete.

unhurt, a. ileso.

unicorn, s. unicornio. [s. uniforme.

uniform, a. -ly, uniforme(mente) ; —,

unify, v.a. unir, unificar.

unimaginable, a. inimaginable.

unimpaired, a. no disminuido, no alterado

unimpeachable, a. incontestable.

unimportant, a. nada importante, trivial.

uninformed, a. ignorante.

uninhabitable, a. inhabitable. [poblado.

uninhabited, a. inhabitado, desierto, des-

uninjured, a. ileso, no dañado.

uninstructed, a. ignorante, indocto.

unintelligible, a. ininteligible. [teligible.

unintelligibly, a. de un modo inin-

unintentional, a. involuntario.
uninteresting, a. poco interesante.
uninterrupted, a. sin interrupción, continuo ; -ly, continuamente.
uninvited, a. no convidado.
union, s. unión.
unionist, s. unitario.
unique, a. único, uno, singular.
unison, s. unisonancia ; unisón.
unit, s. uno, individuo, unidad.
unitarian, s. unitario.
unite, v.a. & n. unir(se), juntarse.
unitedly, ad. unidamente, de acuerdo.
unity, s. unidad, concordia, conformidad.
universal, a. -ly, ad. universal(mente).
universality, a. universalidad.
universe, s. universo.
university, s. universidad.
unjust, a. injusto ; -ly, injustamente.
unjustifiable, a. indisculpable ; -bly, inexcusablemente.
unkempt, a. (fig.) despeinado, tosco, impolítico.
unkind(ly), a. descortés, cruel.
unkindness, s. desafecto ; malignidad.
unknowingly, ad. sin saberlo.
unknown, a. incógnito.
unlace, v.a. desabrochar ; desenlazar.
unlawful, a. ilegítimo, ilícito ; -ly, ilegítimamente.
unlawfulness, s. ilegalidad.
unlearn, v.a. desaprender.
unlearned, a. indocto.
unleavened, a. ázimo.
unless, c. á menos que, si no.
unlettered, a. iliterato, indocto.
unlicensed, a. sin licencia.
unlike, a. diferente, disímil ; improbable; inverisímil.
unlikelihood, s. inverisimilitud.
unlikely, a. improbable, inverisímil.
unlimited, a. ilimitado ; -ly, ilimitadamente.
unload, v.a. descargar.
unlock, v.a. abrir alguna cerradura.
unlooked (for), a. inopinado.
unloose, v.a. desatar.
unluckily, ad. desafortunadamente.
unlucky, a. desafortunado ; siniestro.
unmake, v.a. deshacer.
unman, v.a. afeminar ; castrar ; acobardar.   [tratable.
unmanageable, a. inmanejable, in-
unmanly, a. afeminado.
unmannered, a. rudo, brutal, grosero.
unmanneriness, s. mala crianza, descortesía.
unmannerly, a. malcriado, descortés.
unmarried, a. soltero.
unmask, v.a. desenmascarar.
unmeaning, a. insignificativo.

unmentionable, a. indecible ; impropio, nefando.
unmerciful, a. severo, cruel.
unmerited, a. inmérito, inmerecido.
unmindful, a. olvidadizo, negligente.
unmistakable, a. evidente ; -bly, con evidencia.
unmoor, v.a. (mar.) desamarrar.
unmoved, a. inmoto, firme.
unnatural, a. no natural ; -ly, contra la naturaleza.   [útilmente.
unnecessarily, ad. sin necesidad ; in-
unnecessary, a. inútil, no necesario.
unneighbourly, a. poco atento con sus vecinos,, inhospitalario ; descortés.
unnerve, v.a. enervar ; acobardar.
unnoticed, unobserved, a. inadvertido.
unnumbered, a. innumerable.
unobtainable, a. inasequible.
unobtrusuve, a. modesto.
unoccupied, a. desocupado.
unoffending, a. inocente, inofensivo.
unorthodox, a. heterodoxo.
unpack, v.a. desempaquetar, desembaular ; desenvolver.
unpaid, a. no pagado ; gratúito.
unpalatable, a. desabrido.
unparalleled, a. sin paralelo ; sin par.
unpardonable, a. irremisible.
unpardonably, ad. sin perdón.
unparliamentary, a. contrario á las reglas del parlamento.
unpeople, v.a. despoblar.
unperceived, a. desapercibido.
unpitying, a. incompasivo.   [(mente).
unpleasant, a. -ly, ad. desagradable.
unpleasantness, s. desagrado.
unpolished, a. que no está pulido ; inculto, rudo, grosero.
unpolluted, a. impoluto, inmaculado.
unpopular, a. impopular.
unpractised, a. inexperto, no versado.
unprecedented, a. sin ejemplo.
unprejudiced, a. no preocupado.
unpremeditated, a. no premeditado ; in promptu.   [cibido.
unprepared, a. no preparado, desaper-
unpretending, a. sin pretensiones, mo-
unprincipled, a. sin escrúpulos.   [desto.
unproductive, a. estéril.
unprofitable, a. inútil, vano.
unprofitableness, s. inutilidad.   [vecho.
unprofitably, ad. inútilmente, sin pro-
unpropitious, a. infausto, no favorable.
unprotected, a. desvalido, desamparado.
unprovided, a. desprovisto.
unpublished, a. secreto, oculto, no publicado ; inédito.
unpunctual, a. inexacto.
unpunished, a. impune.
unquenchable, a. inextinguible.

unquestionable, a. indubitable, indisputable; -bly, sin duda, sin disputa. [guntado.
unquestioned, a. incontestable; no pre-
unquiet, a. inquieto, agitado.
unravel, v.a. desenredar.
unread, a. no leído; ignorante.
unready, a. desprevenido, no preparado.
unreal, a. sin realidad; vano, fantástico.
unreasonable, a. desrazonable.
unreasonableness, s. sinrazón.
unreasonably, ad. irracionalmente.
unregarded, a. despreciado.
unrelenting, a. incompasivo, inflexible.
unremitting, a. constante, incansable.
unrepentant, unrepenting, a. impenitente.
unreserved, a. sin restricción; franco; -ly, abjertamente.
unresisting, a. que no resiste; sumiso.
unrest, s. agitación, inquietud.
unrestrained, a. desenfrenado; ilimitado.
unriddle, v.a. explicar.
unrighteous, a. injusto; -ly, inicuamente. [justicia.
unrighteousness, s. inicuidad, in-
unripe(ned), a. inmaturo.
unripeness, s. falta de madurez.
unrivalled, a. incomparable, sin par.
unroll, v.a. desarrollar.
unroof, v.a. destechar.
unruffle, v.n. calmar.
unruliness, s. turbulencia; desenfreno.
unruly, a. desenfrenado, desarreglado.
unsaddle, v.a. desensillar. [sedicioso.
unsafe, a. inseguro, peligroso; -ly, peli-
unsaleable, a. invendible. [grosamente.
unsatisfactory, a. insuficiente, improprio.
unsatisfied, a. descontento; no harto.
unsavouriness, s. insipidez.
unsavoury, a. desabrido, insípido.
unschooled, a. indocto.
unscrew, v.a. desentornillar.
unseasonable, a. intempestivo, fuera de propósito.
unseasonably, ad. fuera de sazón.
unseat, v.a. destituir, reemplazar.
unseemliness, s. indecencia.
unseemly, a. indecente.
unseen, a. invisible; no visto; oculto.
unselfish, a. desinteresado.
unsettle, v.a. perturbar. [resuelto.
unsettled, a. voluble, inconstante, ir-
unshaken, a. firme, estable, inmoble.
unshaven, a. no afeitado, barbudo.
unsheath, v.a. desenvainar.
unsheltered, a. desvalido; expuesto; desabrigado.
unship, v.a. desembarcar.
unshod, a. descalzo; desherrado.
unshorn, a. que no ha sido esquilado.
unshrinking, a. intrépido.

unsightliness, s. fealdad, deformidad.
unsightly, a. desagradable á la vista, feo.
unskilful, a. inhábil, poco mañoso; -ly, sin destreza.
unskilfulness, s. impericia.
unskilled, a. inhábil. [huraño.
unsociable, a. insociable, intratable,
unsold, a. no vendido. [un soldado.
unsoldierlike, unsoldierly, a. indigno de
unsought, a. no buscado; inopinado.
unsound, a. falta de salud; erróneo; podrido. [solidez.
unsoundness, s. heterodoxia; falta de
unsparing, a. liberal, generoso; abundante; inexorable.
unspeakable, a. inefable, indecible.
unspeakably, ad. indeciblemente.
unstable, a. instable, inconstante.
unsteadily, ad. ligeramente, inconstantemente.
unsteadiness, s. ligereza, inconstancia.
unsteady, a. voluble, inconstante.
unstudied, a. no estudiado; no premeditado; improvisado, espontáneo.
unsubdued, a. indomado.
unsubstantial, a. impalpable.
unsuccessful, a. infeliz, desafortunado; -ly, infelizmente, sin éxito.
unsuitable, a. desproporcionado, incongruente, impropio.
unsullied, a. inmaculado, puro.
untamable, a. indomable.
untamed, a. indómito, indomado.
untaught, a. ignorante; indocto, novato.
unteachable, a. incapaz de instrucción, refractorio.
untenable, a. insostenible.
untenanted, a. desarrendado, vacío.
unthankful, a. ingrato; -ly, ingratamente
unthankfulness, s. ingratitud.
unthinking, a. desatento, indiscreto.
unthought of, a. impensado.
untidiness, s. desaliño.
untidy, a. desaliñado, negligente.
untie, v.a. desatar, deshacer, soltar.
until, ad. hasta; hasta que. [tivamente.
untimely, a. intempestivo; -ly, intempes-
untiring, a. incansable.
unto, pr. á, hasta.
untold, a. que no se ha referido, callado.
untouched, a. intacto.
untoward, a. testarudo, desmañado; siniestro, adverso; -ly, indócilmente; fatalmente. [pasajeros; casero.
untravelled, a. no frecuentado de
untried, a. no ensayado ó probado.
untrod(den), a. no pisado, desierto.
untroubled, a. no perturbado, tranquilo.
untrue, a. falso; pérfido.
untruly, ad. falsamente.
untrustworthy, a. indigno de la confianza.

untruth, s. falsedad, mentira.
untutored, a. indocto, tirón.
unused, a. inusitado, no usado ; insólito.
unusual, a. inusitado, raro ; **-ly,** inusitadamente, raramente.
unutterable, a. inefable.
unvaried, a. invariado.
unvarying, a. invariable.
unveil, v.n. revelar, descubrir.
unversed, a. inexperto, no versado.
unwarrantable, a. indisculpable.
unwarranted, a no autorizado.
unwary, a. incauto, imprudente.
unwed(ded), a. soltero.
unwelcome, a. desagradable, mal visto,
unwell, a. enfermizo, malo. [mal venido.
unwholesome, a. malsano, insalubre.
unwieldy, a. pesado.
unwilling, a. desinclinado ; **-ly,** de mala gana. [nancia.
unwillingness, s. mala gana, repug-
unwind, v.a. desenredar, desenmarañar.
unwise, a. imprudente.
unwittingly, ad. sin saber.
unwonted, a. insólito.
unworthily, ad. indignamente.
unworthiness, s. indignidad, bajeza.
unworthy, a. indigno ; vil.
unyielding, a. inflexible, recio.
unyoke, v.a. desuncir.
up, ad. arriba, en lo alto ; levantado ; — !
¡ arriba ! ; **— to,** pr. hacia ; hasta ; —
and down, acá y allá, arriba y abajo.
upbraid, v.a. echar en cara, vituperar.
upbraidingly, ad. por vía de reconvención.
upheaval, s. alzamiento ; sedición, catástrofe.
uphill, a. difícil, penoso ; —, s. subida.
uphold, v.n. levantar en alto ; sostener, apoyar, proteger.
upholder, s. fautor ; sustentáculo, apoyo.
upholsterer, s. tapicero. [elevado.
upland, s. país montañoso ; —, a. alto,
uplift, v.a. levantar.
upon, pr. sobre, encima.
upper, a. superior ; más elevado.
upper-hand, s. superioridad.
uppermost, a. lo más alto, supremo.
uppish, a. (col.) engreído, altivo.
upright, a. derecho, perpendicular, recto ;
puesto en pie ; equitativo ; **-ly,** derechamente, rectamente ; sinceramente.
uprightness, s. elevación perpendicular ;
rectitud, probidad.
uproar, s. tumulto, alboroto.

uproot, v.a. desarraigar.
upset, v.a. trastornar, volcar.
upshot, s. remate ; fin ; conclusión.
upside-down, ad. al revés.
upstairs, ad. arriba, en los pisos altos.
upstart, s. medrado.
uptrain, s. (rail.) tren ascendente, tren para la capital.
upward(s), ad. hacia arriba.
urban, a. urbano.
urbanity, s. urbanidad. [erizo.
urchin, s. (col.) muchacho, rapaz ; (zool.)
urethra, s. uretra. [urgir.
urge, v.a. & n. incitar ; activar ; irritar ;
urgency, s. urgencia.
urgent, a. urgente; **-ly,** instantemente.
urinal, s. orinal.
urinary, a. urinario.
urine, s. orina.
urn, s. urna.
us, pn. nos ; nosotros.
usable, a. apto.
usage, s. costumbre.
usance, s. usanza.
use, s. uso ; servicio ; utilidad práctica ;
—, v.a. usar, emplear, servirse ; acostumbrar ; tratar ; practicar ; soler.
useful, a. **-ly,** útil(mente).
usefulness, s. utilidad.
useless, a. inútil ; **-ly,** inútilmente.
uselessness, s. inutilidad.
usher, s. ujier, maestro (de escuela) ; —,
v.a. introducir ; anunciar.
usual, a. usual, común, usado ; **-ly,** usualmente, ordinariamente.
usufruct, s. (law) usufructo.
usurer, s. usurero.
usurious, a. usurario.
usurp, v.a. usurpar.
usurpation, s. usurpación.
usury, s. usura.
utensil, s. utensilio.
uterine, a. uterino.
utilise, v.a. utilizar.
utilitarian, a. & s. utilitario.
utility, s. utilidad.
utmost, a. extremo, sumo ; último.
utter, a. exterior ; todo ; extremo ;
entero ; —, v.a. proferir ; expresar ;
publicar. [venta.
utterance, s. prolación, habla, expresión ;
utterly, ad. enteramente, del todo.
uvula, s. gallillo.
uxorious, a. gurrumino ; **-ly,** con gurrumina.

V

vacancy, s. vacío ; vacante.

vacant, a. vacío ; desocupado ; vacante.

vacate, v.a. dejar, renunciar.

vacation, s. vacación.

vaccinate, v.a. vacunar.

vaccination, s. vacunación.

vacillate, v.n. vacilar.

vacillation, s. vacilación, vaivén.

vacuity, s. vacuidad.

vacuous, a. vacío, vano, necio.

vacuum, s. vacuo. [mundo

vagabond, a. & s. vagabundo ; vaga-

vagary, s. capricho ; extravagancia.

vagrancy, s. holgazanería, mendiguez, tuna.

vagrant, a. & s. vagabundo, mendigo.

vague, a. vago ; -ly, vagamente.

vails, s.pl. propina.

vain, a. vano, inútil ; vanidoso.

vainglorious, a. vanaglorioso.

vainglory, s. vanagloria.

vainly, ad. vanamente.

valance, s. cenefa, franja de cama.

vale, s. (poet.) valle.

valediction, s. despedida, vale.

valedictory, a. por despedida.

valentine, s. billete amoroso del 14 del febrero ; novio elegido aquel día.

valerian, s. (bot.) valeriana.

valet, s. criado. [fermizo.

valetudinarian, a. valetudinario, en-

valiant, a. valiente, valeroso ; -ly, valien-

valid, a. válido, fuerte. [temente.

validity, s. validación, fuerza.

valise, s. valija, maleta.

valley, s. valle.

valorous, a. valeroso ; -ly, con valor.

valour, s. valor, aliento, brío, esfuerzo ; fortaleza. [preciosas.

valuable, a. precioso ; -s, s. pl. cosas

valuation, s. tasa, valuación.

value, s. valor, precio ; —, v.a. valuar ; estimar, apreciar.

valueless, a. sin valor, inútil.

valve, s. válvula.

vamose, v.n. (am.) escaparse.

vamp, v.a. empeine de calzado ; —, v.a. remendar ; improvisar, inventar.

vampire, s. vampiro.

van, s. vanguardia ; bieldo ; carro.

vandalism, s. vandalismo.

vane, s. veleta ; (mar.) grímpola.

vanguard, s. vanguardia.

vanilla, s. vainilla.

vanish, v.n. desvanecerse, desapareser.

vanity, s. vanidad.

vanquish, v.a. vencer, conquistar.

vanquisher, s. vencedor.

vantage(-ground), s. ventaja ; provecho ; oportunidad ; superioridad.

vapid, a. exhalado, evaporado ; insípido.

vapidness, s. insipidez.

vaporous, a. vaporoso.

vapour, s. vapor ; exhalación.

variable, a. variable. [stancia.

variableness, s. instabilidad, incon-

variably, ad. variablemente.

variance, s. discordia, desavenencia.

variation, s. variación, mudanza.

varicose vein, s. várice.

variegated, a. abigarrado, variado.

variety, s. variedad.

various, a. vario, diverso, diferente ; -ly, variamente.

varlet, s. criado ; pícaro.

varnish, s. barniz ; —, v.a. barnizar.

varnisher, s. embarnizador.

vary, v.a. & n. variar, diferenciar ; cambiar, mudarse, discrepar.

vase, s. vaso.

vassal, s. vasallo.

vassalage, s. vasallaje. [mente.

vast, a. vasto ; inmenso ; -ly, excesiva-

vastness, s. vastedad, inmensidad.

vat, s. tina.

vault, s. bóveda ; cueva ; caverna ; —, v.a. abovedar ; —, v.n. voltear.

vaunt, v.n. jactarse, vanagloriarse.

vaunter, s. baladrón, fanfarrón.

veal, s. ternera ; ternero.

veer, v.n. cambiar de dirección ; (mar.) virar. [-s, pl. legumbre.

vegetable, a. vegetable ; —, s. vegetal ;

vegetarian, s. vegetariano.

vegetate, v.n. vegetar.

vegetation, s. vegetación.

vegetative, a. vegetativo.

vehemence(cy), s. vehemencia, violencia.

vehement, a. vehemente, violento ; -ly, vehementemente, patéticamente.

vehicle, s. vehículo ; carruaje.

veil, s. velo ; disfraz ; —, v.a. encubrir, ocultar. [humor.

vein, s. vena ; inclinación del ingenio ;

veined, veiny, a. venoso ; vetado.

vellum, s. vitela.

velocipede, s. velocípedo.

velocity, s. velocidad.

velvet, s. terciopelo ; —, a. hecho de terciopelo ; terciopelado.

velveteen, s. felpa, velludo.

venal, a. venal, mercenario.

venality, s. venalidad.

vend, v.a. vendér.

vendor, s. vendedor.
veneer, v.a. taracear ; —, s. embutido.
venerable, a. venerable.
venerably, ad. venerablemente.
venerate, v.a. venerar, honrar.
veneration, s. veneración.
venereal, a. venéreo.
venery, s. caza.
venetian blind, s. persiana.
vengeance, s. venganza.
vengeful, a. vengativo.
venial, a. venial.
venison, s. (carne de) venado.
venom, s. veneno. [mente.
venomous, a. venenoso ; -ly, venenosa-
venomousness, s. venenosidad.
vent, s. respiradero ; salida ; venta ; —,
v.a. dar salida; echar fuera; divulgar (un proyecto, &c.) ; ventear.
vent-hole, s. respiradero.
ventilate, v.a. ventilar ; aventar ; discutir.
ventilation, s. ventilación.
ventral, a. ventral.
ventricle, s. ventrículo.
ventriloquist, s. ventrílocuo.
venture, s. riesgo ; ventura ; **at a —,** á
ventura ; —, v.n. osar, aventurarse ;
atreverse ; —, v.a. aventurar, arriesgar.
venturesome, venturous, a. osado, atrevido ; -ly, osadamente. [causa.
venue, s. (law) lugar destinado para una
veracious, a. veraz.
veracity, s. veracidad.
veranda, s. galería exterior.
verb, s. (gr.) verbo.
verbal, a. verbal, literal; -ly, verbalmente.
verbatim, ad. palabra por palabra.
verbiage, s. habladuría, lenguaje hinchado.
verbose, a. verboso.
verbosity, s. verbosidad.
verdant, a. verde.
verdict, s. (law) veredicto ; dictamen.
verdigris, s. cardenillo, verdín.
verdure, s. verdura.
verge, s. vara ; maza ; borde ; margen ;
—, v.n. inclinarse, doblarse; acercarse, tocar, tirar.
verger, s. pertiguero, sacristán.
verification, s. verificación.
verify, v.a. verificar.
verily, v.a. ad. en verdad.
verjuice, s. agraz.
vermicelli, s.pl. fideos.
vermicular, a. vermicular.
vermifuge, s. vermífugo.
vermilion, s. bermellón.
vermin, s. bichos, pl. ; sabandijas, pl.
vernacular, a. vernaculo.
vernal, a. vernal.
versatile, a. versátil, voluble.

versatility, s. versatilidad.
verse, s. verso ; versículo.
versed, a. versado.
version, s. versión, traducción.
versus, pr. contra.
vertebra, s. vértebra.
vertebral, vertebrate, a. vertebral.
vertibrate, a. vertebrado.
vertex, s. vórtice, remolino.
vertical, a. -ly, vertical(mente).
vertigo, s. vértigo.
vervain, s. (bot.) verbena.
very, a. verdadero, real ; idéntico, mismo ;
—, ad. muy, mucho, sumamente.
vesicle, s. vejigüela.
vespers, s.pl. vísperas, pl.
vessel, s. vasija ; vaso ; buque, bejel.
vest, s. chaleco ; —, v.a. vestir ; investir.
vestal, a. vestal (virgen).
vested, a. vestido, envestido.
vestibule, s. vestíbulo, zaguán.
vestige, s. vestigio, huella.
vestment, s. vestido ; vestidura.
vestry, s. sacristía ; concejo parroquial.
vesture, s. vestido ; vestidura.
vetch, s. (bot.) alverjana.
veteran, a. & s. veterano.
veterinary surgeon, s. veterinario.
veto, s. veto.
vex, v.a. vejar, molestar.
vexation, s. vejación, molestia.
vexatious, a. penoso, molesto, enfadoso ;
-ly, penosamente.
viaduct, s. viaducto.
vial, s. redoma, ampolleta.
viand, s. vianda.
viaticum, a. viático.
vibrate, v.a. vibrar.
vibration, s. vibración.
vicar, s. vicario.
vicarage, s. vicaría ; curato, casa del
párroco.
vicarious, a. sustituto, vicario.
vice, s. vicio ; culpa ; prensa de tornillo ;
tornillo de banco ; garra ; —, ad. (in
comp.) vice.
viceroy, s. virrey.
vicinity, s. vecindad, proximidad.
vicious, a. vicioso ; -ly, viciosamente,
malamente.
vicissitude, s. vicisitud.
victim, s. víctima.
victimize, v.a. sacrificar.
victor, s. vencedor. [mente.
victorious, a. victorioso ; -ly, victoriosa-
victory, s. victoria.
victual, v.a. abastecer.
victualler, s. abastecedor, proveedor.
victuals, s.pl. vituallas, pl.
videlicet, ad. á saber.
vie, v.n. competir, rivalizar.

view, a. vista; perspectiva; aspecto; examen; apariencia; —, v.a. mirar, ver; examinar.
viewless, a. invisible.
vigil, s. vela; vigilia.
vigilance, s. vigilancia.   [vigilancia.
vigilant. a. vigilante, atento; -ly, con
vignette, s. viñeta.   [mente.
vigorous, a. vigoroso; -ly, vigorosa-
vigour, s. vigor; robustez; energía.
vile, a. vil, bajo; -ly, vilmente.
vileness, s. vileza, bajeza.
vilify, v.a. envilecer.
villa, s. quinta, casa de campo.
village, s. aldea
villager, s. aldeano.
villainy, s. villanía, vileza.
villanous, a. bellaco, vil, ruin; villano; -ly, vilmente.
vindicate, v.a. vindicar, defender.
vindication, s. vindicación; justificación.
vindictive, a. vengativo; -ly, con rencor.
vine, s. vid.
vine-branch, s. sarmiento.
vine-dresser, s. viñador.
vinegar, s. vinagre.
vine-grower, s. viticultor.
vine-growing, s. viticultura.
vine-stock, s. cepa.
vineyard, s. viña.
vinous, a. vinoso.
vintage, s. vendimia.
vintager, s. vendimiador.
vintner, s. vinatero.
viol, s. (mus.) viola.
violate, v.a. violar.
violation, s. violación.
violator, s. violador.
violence, s. violencia.
violent, a. violento; -ly, violentamente.
violet, s. (bot.) violeta.
violin, s. (mus.) violín.
violinist, s. violinista.
violoncello, s. (mus.) violón, violoncello.
viper, s. víbora.
viperine, viperous, s. viperino.
virago, s. marimacho.
virgin, s. virgen; —, a. virginal.
virginal, a. virginal.
virginity, s. virginidad.
Virgo, s. Virgo (signo del zodíaco).
virile, a. viril.
virility, s. virilidad.
virtu, s. gusto (en las bellas artes).
virtual, a. -ly, virtual(mente).
virtue, s. virtud.
virtuous, a. virtuoso; -ly, virtuosamente.
virulence, s. virulencia.
virulent, a. virulento; -ly, malignamente.
virus, s. virus.
visage, s. rostro; cara.

viscera, s.pl. intestinos, pl.
viscosity, s. viscosidad.
viscount, s. vizconde.
viscountess, s. vizcondesa.
viscous, a. viscoso, glutinoso
visibility, s. visibilidad.
visible, a. visible.
visibly, ad. visiblemente.
vision, s. visión; fantasma.
visionary, a. & s. visionario.
visit, v.a. visitar; —, s. visita.
visitant, s. visitador.
visitation, s. visitación.
visitor, s. visitador, huesped.
visor, s. visera; máscara.
visored, a. enmascarado, disfrazado.
vista, s. vista, perspectiva.
vital, a. vital; -ly, vitalmente; -s, s.pl. partes vitales.
vitality, s. vitalidad.
vitiate, v.a. viciar, corromper.
vitiation, s. depravación.
vitreous, a. vítreo, de vidrio.
vitrify, v.a. (& n.) vitrificar(se).
vitriol, s. vitriolo.
vituperate, v.a. vituperar, .
vivacious, a. vivaz, despejado.
vivacity, s. vivacidad.
vivid, a. vivo; -ly, vivamente.
vividness, s. claridad.
vivify, v.a. vivificar.
viviparous, a. vivíparo.
vivisection, s. vivisección.   [sección,
vivisectionist, s. partidario de la vivi-
vivisector, s. vivisector.
vixen, s. zorra, raposa; mujer vocinglera.
viz, ad. V. videlicet.
vizier, s. visir.
vocabulary, s. vocabulario.
vocal, a. vocal.
vocalist, s. cantador; cantatriz.
vocation, s. vocación; oficio; carrera,
vocative, s. vocativo.   [profesión.
vociferate, v.n. vociferar.
vociferation, s. vocería, grita.
vociferous, a. vocinglero, clamoroso; -ly, con clamor.
vogue, s. moda; boga.
voice, s. voz; sufragio.
voiceless, a. mudo.
void, a. vacío, desocupado, nulo; falto, privado; —, s. vacuo; —, v.a. vaciar,
volatile, a. volátil; voluble. [desocupar.
volatility, a. volatilidad.
volcanic, a. volcánico.
volcano, s. volcán.
vole, s. campañol.
volition, s. voluntad.
volley, s. descarga de armas de fuego; salva; rociada de insultos, &c.
volubility, s. volubilidad.

voluble, a. voluble.
volume, s. volumen ; libro ; tomo.
voluminous, a. voluminoso.
voluntarily, ad. voluntariamente.
voluntary, a. voluntario ; —, s. (mus.) capricho.
volunteer, s. (mil.) voluntario ; —, v.n. [ofrecerse.
voluptuary, voluptuoso, calavera.
voluptuous, a. voluptuoso ; -ly, voluptuosamente.
voluptuousness, s. sensualidad.
volute, s. voluta (roleo de columna).
vomica, s. (med.) vómica.
vomit, v.a. vomitar ; —, s. vómito ; vomitivo.
voracious, a. -ly, voraz(mente).
voracity, s. voracidad.
vortex, s. remolino, torbellino.
votary, s. apasionado, aficionado.

vote, s. voto, sufragio ; —, v.a. votar.
voter, s. votante.
votive, a. votivo.
vouch, v.a. atestiguar, certificar, afirmar.
voucher, s. testigo ; documento justificativo. [dignarse.
vouchsafe, v.a. conceder ; —, v.n.
vow, s. voto ; —, v.a. dedicar, consagrar ;
vowel, s. vocal. [votar.
voyage, s. viaje por mar ; —, v.n. hacer un viaje por mar.
voyager, s. viajero. [vulgo, populacho.
vulgar, a. -ly, ad. vulgar(mente) ; —, s.
vulgarism, a. palabrota.
vulgarity, s. vulgaridad ; bajeza.
vulgarize, v.a. vulgarizar.
vulnerable, a. vulnerable.
vulpine, a. zorruno, vulpino.
vulture, s. buitre.
vying, s. emulación.

W

wad, s. atado de paja ; borra ; taco ; —, —, v.a. acolchar.
wadding, s. entretela ; taco.
waddle, v.n. anadear.
wade, v.n. vadear.
wafer, s. hostia ; oblea.
waft, v.a. llevar por el aire ó por el agua ; —, v.n. flotar ; —, s. soplo, banderín. [sona chocarrera ; juguetón.
wag, v.a. mover ligeramente ; —, s. perwage, v.a. hacer (guerra).
wager, s. apuesta ; —, v.a. apostar.
wages, s.pl. salario.
waggery, s. chocarrería, bufonada.
waggish, a. chocarrero.
waggishness, s. juguete ; chocarrería.
waggle, v.a. & n. menear(se), anadear.
waggon, s. carro ; (rail.) vagón.
waggoner, s. carretero.
wagtail, s. (orn.) motolita, nevatilla.
waif, s. bienes mostrencos, pl.; vagabundo. [mentar, gemir.
wail, s. lamento, gemido ; —; v.n. lawain, s. carro.
wainscot, s. enmaderamiento de ensambladura ; —, v.a. entablar.
waist, s. cintura.
waistcoat, s. chaleco.
wait, v.a. & n. esperar, aguardar, acechar; quedarse ; —, s. espera, demora ; acecho ; to lay —, acechar.
waiter, s. mozo de café, sirviente.
waiting, s. espera ; servicio.
waiting-maid, (-woman), waitress, s. doncella, criada.
waits, s.pl. murga, músicos que tocan en tiempo de Navidad.

waive, v.a. abandonar, ceder.
wake, v.n. velar ; despertarse ; —, v.a. despertar ; —, s. vela ; vigilia ; (mar.) estela.
wakeful, a. vigilante ; despierto.
wakefulness, s. vigilancia ; insomnia.
waken, v.a. (& n.) despertar(se).
waking, s. vela.
wale, s. raya (de látigo) ; (mar.) cinta.
walk, v.a. & n. pasear, ir ; andar, caminar —, s. paseo ; sitio para pasearse, senda.
walker, s. paseador, andador.
walking, s. paseo.
walking-stick, s. bastón.
walk-over, s. victoria fácil.
wall, s. pared ; muralla ; muro ; —, v.a. cercar con muros.
wallet, s. mochila ; morral de viandante.
wall-flower, s. (bot.) alelí doble.
wall-fruit, s. fruta de espalera.
wallow, v.n. encenagarse.
walnut, s. nogal ; nuez.
walrus, s. caballo marino ; vaca marina.
waltz, s. vals (baile).
wan, a. pálido.
wand, s. vara.
wander, v.n. errar ; vagar ; rodar.
wanderer, s. vagamundo.
wandering, s. paseos, pl.; extravío.
wane, v.n. disminuir ; decaer ; —, s. decadencia ; (of the moon) menguante de la luna.
wanness, s. palidez.
want, v.a. & n. necesitar ; faltar ; —, s. necesidad ; indigencia ; falta.
wanting, a. falto, defectuoso.

wanton, a. lascivo, licencioso ; juguetón ; —, s. hombre ó mujer lasciva ; —, v.n. retozar, juguetear.

wantonly, ad. lascivamente; alegremente.

wantonness, s. lascivia, impudicia ; juguete ; chanza.

war, s. guerra ; —, v.n. guerrear.

warble, v.n. trinar ; gorjear.

warbler. s. pájaro cantador.

war-cry, s. grito de guerra.

ward, v.a. guardar, defender ; (off), evitar ; —, s. guarda, defensa ; cárcel ; barrio ; cuartel ; tutela ; pupilo.

warden, s. custodio, guardián ; bedel ; gobernador.

warder, s. guarda, guardia.   [vestido.

wardrobe, s. guardarropa; conjunto de

wardship, s. tutela.

ware, s. mercadería.

warehouse, s. almacén.

warehouse-keeper, warehouse-man, s. guarda-almacén, almacenero.

warfare, s. guerra ; vida soldadesca.

warily, ad. prudentemente.

wariness, s. cautela, prudencia.

warlike, a. guerrero, belicoso.

warlock, s. brujo, hechicero.

warm, a. cálido ; caliente ; irritado ; —, v.a. calentar.

warming-pan, s. calentador.

warmly, ad. con calor, ardientemente.

warmth, s. calor (moderado).

warn, v.a. avisar ; advertir, precaver.

warp, s. urdimbre ; (mar.) espía ; —, v.n. torcerse, alabearse ; —, v.a. torcer ; urdir ; remolcar.

war-path, s. to be on the —, trabar guerra, armar lucha.

warrant, v.a. autorizar ; privilegiar ; garantir, asegurar ; —, s. testimonio ; justificación, autorización ; decreto de prisión.

warrantable, a. abonable, justificable.

warranty, s. garantía, seguridad.

warren, s. conejero.

warrior, s. guerrero, soldado.

wart, s. verruga.

warty, a. verrugoso.

wary, a. cauto, prudente.

wash, v.a. lavar ; bañar ; —, v.n. lavarse, —, s. lavadura ; loción, ablución ; bazofia.

washer-woman, s. lavandera.

washhand-basin, s. jofaina.

wash-house, s. lavadero.

washing, s. lavadura.

washy, a. húmedo, mojado ; débil.

wasp, s. avispa.

waspish, a. enojadizo, caprichudo.

wassail, s. brindis, festejo, orgía.

waste, v.a. disminuir, disipar ; destruir,

arruinar, asolar ; —, v.n. gastarse ; —, desperdicio ; destrucción ; despilfarro ; desierto ; —, a. baldío.

wasteful, a. destructivo ; pródigo ; **-ly,** pródigamente.

wastefulness, s. prodigalidad.

waste-paper, s. papel de desecho.

waster, s. disipador, gastador.

watch, s. desvelo ; vigilia ; vela ; centinela, reloj ; —, v.a. & n. velar, guardar, custodiar ; espiar, observar.

watch-dog, s. perro de guardia.

watcher, s. observador, espía.

watch-fire, s. fuego de vivaque.   [mente.

watchful, a. vigilante ; **-ly,** cuidadosa-

watchfulness, s. vigilancia.

watch-light, s. farol.

watch-maker, s. relojero.

watch-man, s. sereno.

watch-tower, s. atalaya.

watch-word, s. (mil.) santo y seña.

water, s. agua ; —, v.a. regar, humedecer, mojar, bañar ; —, v.n. chorrear agua.

water-closet, s. retrete.   [pl.

water-colour, s. acuarela ; **-s,** s.pl. aguadas,

water-course, s. corriente de agua, acequia, canal.

water-cresses, s. (bot.) berros, pl.

water-cure, s. hidropatía.

water-fall, s. cascada.

watering, s. riego ; abrevadura.

watering-place, s. abrevadero.

watering-pot, s. regadera.

water-lily, s. (bot.) ninfea, nenúfar.

water-line, s. (mar.) línea de flotación.

water-logged, a. (mar.) anegado.

water-man, s. barquero, botero.

water-melon, s. zandía.

water-power, s. fuerza del agua.

water-shed, s. cumbre de las vertientes de las aguas.

water-spout, s. manga, bomba marina.

water-tight, a. impermeable.   [aguas.

water-works, s.pl. establecimiento de

watery, a. acuoso, acueo.

wattle, s. zarzo, tejido de varas ; barbas de gallo, pl. ; —, v.a. enzarzar.

wave, s. ola, onda ; —, v.n. ondear ; fluctuar.   [suspenso.

waver, v.n. vacilar, balancear, estar

wavering, a. inconstante ; —, s. irresolución.

wavy, a. ondeado, undoso.

wax, s. cera ; —, v.a. encerar ; —, v.n. crecer ; hacerse.

waxen, a. de cera.

wax-work, s. figura de cera.

waxy, a. semejante á cera.

way, s. camino ; vía ; ruta ; modo ; expediente ; **to give —,** ceder, **-s and means, s.pl.** medios, términos, pl.

wayfarer, s. pasajero, viandante.
waylay, v.a. acechar.
wayside, s. orilla del camino, apartadero.
wayward, a. caprichoso, cabezudo.
we, pn. nosotros, nosotras.
weak, a. -ly, débil(mente).
weaken, v.a. debilitar. [delicada.
weakling, s. alfeñique ; persona muy
weakness, s. debilidad ; parte flaca de
una persona.
weal, s. prosperidad ; bien.
wealth, s. riqueza ; bienes, pl.
wealthily, ad. ricamente, opulentamente.
wealthiness, s. opulencia.
wealthy, a. rico, opulento.
wean, v.a. destetar.
weapon, s. arma.
wear, v.a. gastar, consumir ; usar,
llevar ; —, v.n. consumirse ; —, s. uso.
weariness, s. cansancio ; fatiga ; enfado.
wearisome, a. tedioso ; -ly, enfadosa-
mente.
weary, v.a. cansar, fatigar ; molestar ;
—, a. cansado, fatigado ; tedioso.
weasel, s. comadreja.
weather, s. tiempo, temperatura ; tempestad ; —, v.a. (mar.) doblar (un
cabo) ; sufrir, superar. [intemperie.
weather-beaten, a. endurecido á la
weather-cock, s. giraldilla, veleta.
weather-glass, s. barómetro. [del tiempo.
weatherwise, s. perito en las mudanzas
weave, v.a. tejer ; trenzar.
weaver, s. tejedor.
weaving, s. tejido.
web, s. tela ; tejido.
webbed, web-footed, a. (orn.) palmeado.
wed, v.a. (& n.) casar(se).
wedding, s. nupcias, pl. ; casamiento.
wedge, s. cuña ; —, v.a. acuñar.
wedlock, s. matrimonio.
Wednesday, s. miércoles.
wee, a. pequeñito. [cigarro.
weed, s. mala hierba ; (col.) tabaco,
vestido de luto ; —, v.a. escardar.
weedy, a. lleno de malas hierbas, flaco.
week, s. semana.
week-day, s. día de trabajo.
weekly, a. semanal ; —, ad. semanal-
mente, por semana.
ween, v.a. pensar, creer.
weep, v.a. & n. llorar ; lamentar.
weevil, s. gorgojo (insecto).
weft, s. trama ; tejido. [siderar.
weigh, v.a. & n. pesar ; examinar, con-
weight, s. peso ; pesadez.
weightily, ad. pesadamente.
weightiness, s. importancia, gravedad.
weighty, a. ponderoso ; importante.
weir, s. azud.
weird, a. mágico, portentoso, extraño.

welcome, a. bienquisto, grato, bien
venido ; —, s. bienvenida, acogida ;
—, v.a. dar la bienvenida á alguno,
recibir, acoger.
weld, v.a. soldar (hierro).
welfare, s. prosperidad ; bienestar.
welkin, s. cielo.
well, s. fuente ; manantial pozo ; —,
a. bueno, sano ; —, ad. bien, felizmente ; favorablemente ; conveniente-
mente ; as — as, así como, lo mismo
que.
well-being, s. felicidad, prosperidad.
well-bred, a. bien criado, bien educado.
well-doing, s. virtud, conducta digna de
beneficio.
well-favoured, a. bonito, bello.
well-met, ¡ bien hallado ! .
well-nigh, ad. casi.
well-read, a. docto, ilustrado.
well-to-do, well-off, a. rico.
well-wisher, s. amigo, partidario.
welt, s. ribete ; (col.) raya (de latigo) ; —
v.a. ribetear.
welter, v.n. revolcarse en lodo.
wen, s. lobanillo, lupia.
wench, s. mozuela.
wend, v.a. ir. [occidental.
west, s. poniente, occidente ; —, a.
westerly, western, a. occidental. [dente.
westward, ad. á poniente, hacia occi-
wet, a. húmedo, mojado ; —, s. humedad;
—, v.a. mojar, humedecer.
wether, s. carnero castrado.
wetness, s. humedad.
wetnurse, s. ama de leche.
whack, v.a. aporrear ; —, s. golpe.
whale, s. ballena.
whale-bone, s. ballena.
whaler, s. pescador de ballena.
wharf, s. muelle.
wharfage, s. muellaje.
wharfinger, s. fiel ó dueño de muelle.
what, pn. que, lo que. [cosa, que sea
what(so)ever, pn. cualquier ó cualquiera
wheat, s. trigo.
wheaten, a. de trigo. [lisonjas.
wheedle, v.a. halagar, engañar con
wheedler, s. caroquero.
wheel, s. rueda ; —, v.a. (hacer) rodar ;
volver, girar ; —, v.n. rodar.
wheel-barrow, s. carretilla.
wheel-wright, s. carpintero que hace
ruedas, carretero.
wheeze, v.n. jadear.
whelm, v.a. cubrir ; oprimir.
whelk, s. concha. [perra.
whelp, s. cachorro ; —, v.n. parir (la
when, ad. cuando.
whence, ad. de donde ; de quien.
whencesoever, ad. de donde quiera.

when(so)ever, ad. cuando quiera que, siempre que.

where, ad. donde; any-, en cualquier parte; every-, en todas partes.

whereabout(s), ad. hacia donde; —, s. paradero.   [pues que, ya que.

whereas, ad. por cuanto, mientras que;

whereat, ad. á lo cual.

whereby, ad. por lo cual, con lo cual, por donde, de que.   [motivo.

wherefore, ad. por lo que, por cuyo

wherefrom, ad. de donde.

wherein, ad. en donde, en lo cual, en que.

whereof, ad. de lo cual, de que.

whereon, ad. sobre lo cual, sobre que.

wheresoever, ad. donde quiera, doquiera.

where(un)to, ad. á lo que, á que.

whereupon, ad. sobre lo cual, entonces.

wherever, ad. donde quiera que, doquiera que.

wherewith(al), ad. con que, con lo cual.

wherry, s. esquife; barca.

whet, v.a. afilar, amolar; excitar.

whether, ad. si; sea, sea que; —, pn. cual, cual de los dos.

whetstone, s. aguzadera.

whey, s. suero.   [las cuales.

which, pn. que, el cual, la cual, los cuales,

which(so)ever, pn. cualquiera.   [fumada.

whiff, s. vaharada; bocanada de humo,

Whig, s. antiguo partido de liberales moderados en Inglaterra.

while, s. rato; vez; a — ago, rato ha.

while, whilst, ad. mientras.

whim, s. antojo, capricho.

whimper,, v.n. sollozar, gemir; —, s. sollozo.

whimsical, a. caprichoso, fantástico.

whine, v.n. llorar, lamentar; —, s. quejido, lamento.

whinny, v.n. relinchar (los caballos).

whip, s. azote; látigo; —, v.a. & n.

whip-hand, s. ventaja.   [azotar.

whipper-in, s. guía de perros de caza; director de votantes en el Parlamento

whir, v.n. girar con ruido; —, s. ruido de máquinas.

whirl, v.a. & n. girar; hacer girar; mover(se) rápidamente; —, s. giro muy rápido.

whirligig, s. perinola.

whirlpool, s. vórtice de agua.

whirlwind, s. torbellino.

whisk, s. escobilla; cepillo.

whisker, s. patilla.

whisky, s. aguardiente de cebada.

whisper, v.n. cuchichear; susurrar.

whispering, s. cuchicheo; susurro.

whist, s. juego de naipes.

whistle, v.a. & n. silbar; chiflar; —, s. silbo, silbido.

whit, s. algo; not a —, nada.

white, a. blanco, pálido; cano; —, s. color blanco; clara del huevo.

whitebait, s. pescado menudo.

white-lead, s. albayalde (cal de plomo).

white-heat, s. incandescencia.

white-hot, a. incandescente.

whiten, v.a. & n. blanquear.

whiteness, s. blancura; palidez.

white-wash, s. blanqueo; enlucimiento; —, v.a. encalar; jalbegar.

whither, ad. adonde, donde.

whithersoever, ad. adonde quiera.

whiting, s. especie de pez de mar.

whitish, a. blanquizco, blanquecino.

whitlow, s. panadizo, panarizo.

Whitsuntide, s. Pentecostés.

whittle, v.a. cortar con navaja.

whiz, v.n. zumbar, silbar.

who, pn. quien, que.   [quiera que.

who(so)ever, pn. quienquiera que, cualwhole, a. todo, total; sano, entero; —, s.

wholesale, s. venta por mayor.   [total.

wholesome, a. sano, saludable; -ly, saludablemente.

wholesomeness, s. salubridad.

wholly, ad. enteramente.   [gritar.

whoop, s. gritería; —, v.n. huchear,

whooping-cough, s. tos convulsiva.

whore, s. puta.

why, ad. porque.

wick, s. torcida, pábilo.   [malamente.

wicked, a. malo, malvado, perverso; -ly,

wickedness, s. perversidad, malignidad.

wicker, s. mimbre; —, a. tejido de mimbres.

wicket, s. postigo; portezuela.

wide, a. ancho, vasto, remoto; -ly, anchamente; far and —, por todos lados.

wide-awake, a. despierto.

widen, v.a. ensanchar, extender.

wideness, s. anchura, extensión.

widgeon, s. especie de pato de caza.

widow, s. viuda; —, v.a. privar á una mujer de su marido.

widower, s. viudo.

widowhood, s. viudez.

width, s. anchura.

wield, v.a. manejar, empuñar.

wife, s. esposa, consorte; mujer.

wifely, a. propio de una esposa.

wig, s. peluca.

wig-block, s. cabeza de madera.

wight, s. persona, criatura racional.

wig-maker, s. peluquero, cabana.

wigwam, s. toldo de los indios, cabaña.

wild, a. silvestre, feroz; desierto; salvaje; —, s. yermo, desierto.

wilderness, s. desierto.

wildfire, s. fuego incendiario.

wildly, ad. sin cultivo; desatinadamente.

wildness, s. selvatiquez; brutalidad, furor.
wile- s. dolo, engaño; astucia.
wilful, a. voluntarioso, temoso; -ly, obstinadamente.
wilfulness, s. obstinación.
wiliness, s. fraude, engaño.
will, s. voluntad; testamento; —, v.a. querer, desear. [buena gana.
willing, a. inclinado, pronto; -ly, de
willingness, s. buena voluntad, buena
willow, s. sauce (árbol.). [gana.
wily, a. astuto, insidioso.
wimple, s. toca, velo. [lograr.
win, v.a. ganar, conquistar; alcanzar;
wince, v.n. recular, estremecerse.
winch, s. cigüeña de torno.
wind, s. viento; aliento; pedo.
wind, v.a. & n. dar vuelta; torcer; ventear; serpentear; envolver.
wind-bag, s. (col.) charlatán.
winded, a. desalentado, jadeante.
windiness, s. ventosidad, flatulencia.
winding, s. vuelta, revuelta; —, a. tor-
winding-sheet, s. mortaja. [tuoso.
windlass, s. árgana, grúa.
wind-mill, s. molino de viento.
window, s. ventana.
wind-pipe, s. traquea.
wind-up, v.a. terminar; acabar; liquidar.
windward, ad. (mar.) á barlovento.
windy, a. ventoso.
wine, s. vino.
wine-bibber, s. borracho.
wine-press, s. prensa; lagar. [teatro.
wing, s. ala; aventador; bastidor de
winged, a. alado.
wink, v.n. guiñar; —, s. pestañeo; guiño.
winner, s. ganador, vencedor.
winning, s. ganancia; lucro; —, a. atractivo, encantador.
winnow, v.a. aventar.
winsome, a. alegre, jovial.
winter, s. invierno; —, v.n. invernar.
wintry, a. brumal, invernal.
wipe, v.a. limpiar; borrar.
wire, s. alambre.
wiredraw, v.a. tirar á hilo algunos metales; prolongar.
wireless, a. sin hilos, inalámbrico.
wire-puller, s. tiritero; intrigante.
wire-pulling, s. maquinaciones secretas.
wiry, a. fuerte, musculoso.
wisdom, s. sabiduría, prudencia.
wise, a. sabio, docto, juicioso, prudente; —, s. modo, manera.
wiseacre, s. necio pedante.
wisely, ad. sabiamente, con prudencia.
wish, v.a. desear, anhelar, ansiar; —, s. anhelo, deseo.
wishful, a. descoso; -ly, con anhelo.

wisp, s. manojo de heno, &c. [mente.
wistful, a. pensativo, ansioso; -ly, atenta-
wit, entendimiento, ingenio; to —, ad. á
witch, s. bruja, hechicera. [saber.
witchcraft, s. brujería; sortilegio.
witchery, s. hechicería.
with, pr. con.
withal, ad. además, también.
withdraw, v.a. quitar; retirar; —, v.n. retirarse, apartarse.
withdrawal, s. retiro, retirada.
withe, s. mimbre. [v.a. marchitar.
wither, v.n. marchitarse, secarse; —,
withhold, v.a. detener, impedir, retener.
within, pr. dentro, adentro; —, ad. interiormente; en casa.
without, pr. sin, con falta de; —, ad. fuera, afuera; exteriormente; —, c. si no, sin que, á ménos que.
withstand, v.a. resistir.
withy, s. mimbre.
witless, a. necio, tonto, falto de ingenio.
witling, s. truhán, chocarrero.
witness, s. testimonio; testigo; —, v.a. & n. atestiguar, testificar; presenciar.
wittily, ad. ingeniosamente.
wittiness, s. agudeza; chiste ingenioso; viveza de ingenio.
wittingly, ad. adrede, de propósito.
witty, a. ingenioso, agudo, chistoso,
wizard, s. brujo, hechicero. [gracioso.
woad, s. (bot.) gualda.
woe, s. dolor; miseria. [mente.
woeful, a. triste, funesto; -ly, triste-
wolf, s. lobo; she—, loba.
wolfish, a. lobero.
woman, s. mujer.
womanhood, s. estado de mujer.
womanish, a. mujeril.
womankind, s. mujeriego.
womanly, a. mujeril, mujeriego.
womb, s. útero.
wonder, s. milagro; maravilla; —, v.n. maravillarse. [villosamente.
wonderful, maravilloso; -ly, mara-
wondrous, a. maravilloso.
won't, abrev. de will not.
wont, s. uso, costumbre.
wonted, a. acostumbrado, usual.
woo, v.a. cortejar, requerir de amores.
wood, s. bosque; selva; madera; leña-
wood-bine, s. (bot.) madreselva.
wood-cock, s. chocha, becada.
wood-cut, s. estampa de madera.
wood-cutter, s. grabador en madera, xilógrafo.
wooded, a. arbolado.
wooden, a. hecho de madera.
wood-land, s. arbolado.
wood-louse, s. cucaracha.
woodman, s. guardabosque.

wood-pecker, s. picamaderos.
wooer, s. galanteador, pretendiente.
woof, s. trama.
wool, s. lana.
wool-gathering, a. his wits have gone —, está distraído.
woolly, a. lanudo, lanoso.
word, s. palabra, voz ; —, v.a. expresar ; componer en escritura.
wordiness, s. verbosidad.
wordy, a. verboso.
work, v.n. trabajar ; obrar ; estar en movimiento ó en acción ; —, v.a. trabajar, labrar ; ' fabricar, manu-facturar ; —, s. trabajo ; fábrica ; obra (de manos) ; fatiga.
worker, s. trabajador, obrero.
work-house, s. asilo de pobres.
working-day, s. día de trabajo.
workman, s. artífice, labrador.
workmanship, s. manufactura ; destreza del artífice.
workshop, s. taller.
work-woman, s. costurera ; obrera.
world, s. mundo ; universo ; vida ; gente, gentío.
worldliness, s. mundanalidad.
worldling, s. hombre mundano.
worldly, a. mundano, terreno.
worm, s. lombriz, gusano, gorgojo ; —, v.a. & n. insinuar, minar.
worm-eaten, a. carcomido, apolillado.
wormwood, s. (bot.) ajenjo.
worry, v.a. molestar, atormentar.
worse, a. & ad. peor.
worship, s. culto ; adoración ; your —, Usía ; —, v.a. adorar, venerar.
worshipful, a. venerable.
worshipping, s. adoración.
worst, a. pésimo, lo peor ; —, v.a. vencer, sujetar.
worsted, s. estambre. [digno, que vale.
worth, s. valor, precio ; mérito ; —, a.
worthily, ad. dignamente, conveniente-mente.
worthiness, s. dignidad ; mérito.
worthless, a. indigno ; vil, inútil.
worthlessness, s. indignidad, vileza.
worthy, a. digno, benemérito ; —, s. varón ilustre.
would-be, a. pretendido.
wound, s. herida, llaga ; —, v.a. herir, llagar.
wove(n), a. participio de weave.

wraith, s. fantasma.
wrangle, v.n. reñir ; —, s. pelotera, riña
wrangler, s. pendenciero, disputador.
wrap, v.a. arrollar ; envolver.
wrapper, s. envolvedero ; chal.
wrath, s. ira, rabia, cólera.
wrathful, a. furioso, irritado.
wreak, v.a. vengar ; to — one's anger, descargar la cólera.
wreath, s. corona, guirnalda ; —, v.a. coronar ; enroscar, torcer.
wreck, s. naufragio ; destrucción ; navío naufragado ; —, v.a. arruinar.
wreckage, s. despojos de naufragio.
wren, s. reyezuelo (avecilla).
wrench, v.a. arrancar ; dislocar ; torcer ; —, s. torcedura ; destornillador.
wrest, v.a. arrancar, quitar á fuerza, ar-rebatar.
wrestle, v.a. luchar ; disputar ; —, s. lucha.
wrestling, s. lucha.
wretch, s. picarón, bribón ; pobre infeliz, hombre muy miserable.
wretched, a. infeliz, miserable ; mezquino ; -ly, miserablemente.
wretchedness, s. miseria ; vileza, bajeza.
wriggle, v.n. menearse, agitarse.
wright, s. artesano, obrero.
wring, v.a. torcer ; arrancar ; estrujar.
wrinkle, s. arruga (de la cara, del paño) ; —, v.a. arrugar.
wrist, s. muñeca.
wrist-band, s. puño de camisa.
writ, s. escrito ; escritura ; orden.
write, v.a. escribir ; componer.
writer, s. escritor, autor.
writhe, v.a. & n. torcer(se).
writing, s. escritura ; escrito ; manuscrito.
writing-book, s. cuaderno.
writing-desk, s. escritorio.
writing-master, s. maestro de escribir.
writing-paper, s. papel para escribir.
wrong, s. injuria ; injusticia ; perjuicio ; error ; —, a. malo, injusto, errado, falso ; —, ad. mal, injustamente ; al revés ; —, v.a. agraviar, injuriar.
wrongful, a. injusto, inicuo ; -ly, injusta-mente.
wroth, a. encoleradizo.
wrought, a. trabajado, forjado ; her-moseado.
wry, a. torcido, tuerto, no derecho.
wry-neck, s. torcecuello (ave).

X

xebec, s. (mar.) jabeque.
Xmas, s. V. Christmas.

xylography, s. arte de grabar en madera, xilografía.

Y

yacht, s. (mar.) yate, embarcación de
yam, s. (bot.) batata. [recreo.
Yankee, s. (col.) cuidadano de los Estados Únidos. [verga.
yard, s. corral ; yarda (medida) ; (mar.)
yarn, s. estambre ; hilo de lino.
yarrow, s. (bot.) milhojas.
yawl, s. (mar.) serení, canoa.
yawn, v.n. bostezar.
yclept, a. nombrado, llamado.
ye, pn. vos.
yea, ad. sí, verdaderamente.
yean, v.n. parir la oveja.
year, s. año.
yearling, s. animal que tiene un año.
yearly, a. anual ; —, ad. anualmente,
todos los años.
yearn, v.n. compadecerse ; afligirse interiormente ; — for, v.a. ansiar.
yearning, s. compasión.
yeast, s. levadura, jiste.
yell, v.n. aullar ; —, s. aullido.
yellow, a. amarillo ; —, s. color amarillo.
yellow fever, s. (med.) vómito negro.
yellowish, a. amarillento.
yellowness, s. amarillez.
yelp, v.n. latir, gañir.
yelping, s. gañido.

yeoman, s. dueño de un terreno modesto ;
guardia palaciego.
yeomanry, s. conjunto de hacendados
modestos ; milicia rural á caballo.
yerk, v.a. arrojar, lanzar.
yes, (vulg.) ad, sí.
yesterday, ad. ayer. [más; aun,
yet, s. sin embargo ; pero ; —, ad. ade-
yew, s. tejo (árbol).
yield, v.a. dar, producir ; ceder, admitir ;
conceder ; —, v.n. rendirse, someterse ;
yielding, a. condescendiente. [asentir.
yoke, s. yugo ; yunta ; —, v.a. uncir ;
yokel, s. campesino. [sojuzgar.
yolk, yelk, s. yema de huevo.
yon(der), ad. allí, allá.
yore, s, tiempo antiguo.
you, pn. vosotros, Vd., Vds.
young, a. joven, mozo.
youngish, a. mozuelo, jovencillo.
youngster, s. jovéncito, joven.
your(s), pn. vuestro, de U(ds).
yourself, Vd. mismo.
youth, s. juventud, adolescencia ; joven.
youthful, a. juvenil ; -ly, de un modo
juvenil.
youthfulness, s. juventud.
yule, s. Návidad.

Z

zany, s. gracioso (de las comedias
italianas) ; bufón.
zeal, s. celo ; ardor.
zealot, s. faniátco. [celo.
zealous, a. asiduo, ardiente ; -ly, con
zenith, s. cenit.
zephyr, s. céfiro.
zero, s. zero, cero.
zest, s. gusto, sabor.

zigzag, s. ese ; zigzag ; —, a. en zigzag.
zinc, s. zinc (metal).
zodiac, s. zodíaco.
zone, s. banda, faja ; zona.
zoological, a. zoológico.
zoologist, s. zoólogo.
zoology, s. zoología.
zoophyte, s. zoofito.
zounds, ¡ cáscaras !

List of some names, differing in the two languages.

Abruzzi, Abruzos, pl.
Abyssinia, Abisinia.
African, s. & a. africano.
Albanian, s. & a. albanés.
Algiers, s. Argel.
Alpine, a. alpino, pl.
Alps, s.pl. Alpes, pl.
Alsace, Alsacia.
Alsatian, s. & a. alsaciano.
American, s. & a. americano.
Andalusia, Andalucía.
Andalusian, s. & a. andaluz.
Antwerp, Amberes.   [luz.
Apennines, Apeninos, pl.
Arab, Arabian, s. & a. árabe, arábigo. [gonés.
Aragonese, s. & a. aragonese.
Archipelago, Archipiélago.
Armenian, s. & a. armenio, arménico.   [asiano.
Asiatic, s. & a. asiático.
Athenian, s. & a. ateniense.
Athens, Atenas, pl.
Atlantic, (Mar) Atlántico.
Augsburg, Ausburgo.
Australian, s. & a. australiano.
Austrian, s. & a. austriaco.

Baltic, Mar Báltico.
Barbadoes, Barbadas, pl.
Barbary, Berbería.
Basle, Basilea.
Batavian, s. & a. bátavo.
Bavaria, Baviera.
Bavarian, s. & a. bávaro.
Belgian, s. & a. belga ; bélBelgium, Bélgica.   [gico.
Bengal, Bengala.
Bengalese, s. & a. bengalí.
Bethlehem, Belén.
Biscay, Vizcaya.
Bœotia, Beocia.
Bœotian, s. & a. beocio.
Bohemian, s. & a. bohemio ; bohémico.
Bordeaux, Burdeos.
Bosphorous, Bósforo.
Brazil, Brasil.
Brazilian, s. & a. brasileño.

Breton, s. bretón.   taña.
Britain (Great-), Gran Bre-
Brittany, Bretaña.
British, británico ; a. — Channel, la Mancha.
Brunswic(k), Brunsvick.
Brussels, Bruselas, pl.
Bulgarian, s. & a. búlgaro.
Burgundian, s. & a. borgoñón.
Burgundy, Borgoña.
Byzantium, Bizancio.

Calabrian, s. & a. calabrés.
Campeachy, Campeche.
Canaries, Canary Islands, Canarias, pl.
Canterbury, Cantórberi.
Carinthia, Carintia.
Caspian Sea, (Mar) Caspio.
Castile, Castilla.
Castilian, s. & a. castellano.
Catalonia, Cataluña.
Catalonian, s. & a. catalán.
Caucasus, Cáucaso.
Ceylon, Ceilan.
Chaldea, Caldea.
Champagne, Champaña.
Chinese, s. & a. chino, chinesco.
Circassia, Circasia.
Circassian, s. & a. Circasiano.
Cologne, Colonia.   [nopla.
Constantinople, Constantinopla.
Corinth, Corinto.
Corsica, Córcega.
Corsican, s. & a. corso.
Cossack, cosaco.
Courland, Curlandia.
Cracow, Cracovia.
Cretan, s. & a. cretense ; crético.
Croatia, Croacia.
Croatian, s. & a. croato.
Cyprus, Chipre.

Dalmatia, Dalmacia.
Dalmatian, s. & a. dálmata, dalmático.
Damascus, Damasco.

Dane, s. dinamarqués.
Danish, a. dánico, dinamarqués.
Danube, Danubio.
Dauphinate, Dauphiny, Delfinado.
Denmark, Dinamarca.
Dover, Dovres.
Dresden, Dresde.
Dunkirk, Dunquerque.
Dutch, s. & a. holandés, holandesa.

East Indies, Indias orientales, pl.
Edinburgh, Edimburgo.
Egypt, Egipto.
Egyptian, s. & a. egipciaco, egipciano, egipcio.
England, Inglaterra.
English, Englishman, a. inglés ; — Channel, la Mancha.
Ephesus, Éfeso.
Eskimo, Esquimau, s. & a. esquimal.
Europe, Europa.
European, s. & a. europeo.
Euxine, Mar Negro.
Finland, Finlandia.
Finlander, s. & a. finlandés
Flanders, Flandes.
Fleming, s. & a. flamenco.
Flemish, a. flamenco.
Florence, Florencia.
Florentine, s. & a. florentín, florentino.
Flushing, Flesinga.
France, Francia.
Freiburg, Friburgo.
French, a. francés.
Frenchman, Frenchwoman, francés, francesa.
Friesland, Frisia.
Frieslander, s. & a. frisón.

Gaelic, s. & a. céltico, Galilee, Galilea.   [gaélico.
Gascony, Gascuña.
Gaul, s. & a. Galia ; gálico.
Geneva, Ginebra.

441

Genevese, s. & a. ginebrés, ginebrino.
Genoa, Génova.
Genoese, s. & a. genovés.
German, s. & a. alemán.
Germany, Alemania.
Ghent, Gante.
Grecian, s. & a. griego.
Greece, Grecia.
Greek, s. & a. griego.
Greenland, Groenlandia.
Greenlander, s. & a. groenlandés.
Grisons, Grisones, pl.
Groningen, Groninga.
Guelderland, Gueldres.

Hague, a. Haya.
Hamburg, Hamburgo.
Hanse, s. ansa.
Hanse Towns, Ciudades Anseáticas, pl.
Havannah, a. La Habana.
Helvetia, Helvecia.
Hesse, Hesia.
Hessian, s. & a. hesés.
Holland, Holanda.
Hollander, holandés.
Hungarian, s. & a. húngaro.
Hungary, Hungría.

Iceland, Islanda.
Icelander, s. & a. islandés ; islándico.
Illyria, Iliria.
Indian, s. & a. indiano ; indio.
Indies, las Indias.
Ireland, Irlanda.
Irish, Irishman, s. & a. irlandés.
Italian, s. & a. italiano.
Italy, Italia.

Japan, Japón.
Japanese, s. & a. japonés.
Jerusalem, Jerusalén.
Jutland, Jutlandia.

Lapland, Laponia.
Laplander, s. & a. lapón.
Lebanon, Líbano.
Leghorn, Liorna.
Liege, Lieja.
Lisbon, Lisboa.
Lisle, Lila.
Lithuania, Lituania.
Lombard, s. & a. lombardo, lombárdico.
Lombardy, Lombardía.
London, Londres.

Lorraine, Lorena.　[jos.
Low Countries, Países Bajos.
Lyons, León de Francia.

Macedonian, s. & a. macedón, macedónio ; macedónico.
Madeira, Madera.
Majorca, Mallorca.
Malines, Malinas.
Maltese, s. & a. maltés.
Marseilles, Marsella.
Mecca, Meca.
Mediterranean, Mediterráneo.
Mentz, Maguncia.
Messina, Mesina.
Mexican, s. & a. mejicano.
Mexico, Méjico.
Milan, Milano.
Minorca, Menorca.
Moluccas, Molucas, pl.
Moor, Moorish, a. moro.
Moravian, s. & a. moravo.
Morocco, Marruecos, pl.
Moscow, Moscú.
Moselle, Mosela.
Mulatto, mulato.

Naples, Nápoles.
Neapolitan, s. & a. napolitano.
Netherlands, Países Bajos, pl.
Newfoundland, Terranova.
New York, Nueva York.
Nice, Niza.
Nile, Nilo.
Nimeguen, Nimega.
Norman, s. & a. normano, normando.
Normandy, Normandía.
North America, América del Norte.
Norway, Noruega.
Norwegian, s.& a. noruego.
Nubian, s. & a. nubio.

Olympus, Olimpo.
Orkneys, Orcadas, pl.
Ostend, Ostende.

Pacific, (Mar) Pacífico.
Palatinate, Palatinado.
Palestine, Palestina.
Parisian, s. & a. parisiense.
Parnassus, Parnaso.
Peloponnesus, Peloponeso.
Persian, s. & a. persa ; persiano.
Phenicia, Fenicia.

Phenician, s. & a. fenicio.
Piedmont, Piamonte.
Piedmontese, s. & a. piamontés.
Poland, Polonia.　[montés.
Pole, Polish, a. polaco.
Portuguese, s. & a. portugués.
Prague, Praga.　[gués.
Provence, Provenza.
Prussia, Prusia.
Prussian, s. & a. prusiano.
Pyrenees, Pirineos, pl.

Ratisbon, Ratisbona.
Ravenna, Ravena.
Rhine, Rin.
Rhodes, Rodas, pl.
Rhone, Ródano.
Roman, s. & a. romano.
Rome, Roma.
Russia, Rusia.
Russian, s. & a. ruso.

Sardinia, Cerdeña.
Sardinian, s. & a. sardo.
Savoy, Saboya.
Savoyard, s. & a. saboyano.
Saxon, s. & a. sajón.
Saxony, Sajonia.
Scandinavia, Escandinavia
Schaffhausen, Escafusa.
Scheldt, Escalda.
Sclavonia, Esclavonia.
Sclavonian, s. & a. esclavón ; esclavonio.
Scotch, -man, escocés.
Scotland, Escocia.
Scottish, a. escocés.
Seine, Sena.
Servian, s. & a. servio.
Siberia, Siberia.
Siberian, s. & a. siberiano.
Sicilian, s. & a. siciliano.
Sicily, Sicilia.
Silesian, s. & a. silesiano ; silesio.
Smyrna, Esmirna.
South Sea, Mar del Sur, Pacífico.
Spain, España.
Spaniard, s. español.
Spanish, a. español.
Sparta, Esparta.
Spartan, s. & a. espartano
Stiria, Estiria.
Stirian, s. & a. estiriano.
Stockholm, Estocolmo.
Strasburg, Estrasburgo.
Swede, s. sueco.
Sweden, Suecia.
Swedish, a. sueco.
Swiss, s. & a. suizo.

Switzerland, Suiza.
Syracuse, Siracusa.

Tagus, Tajo.
Tartar, s. & a. tártaro.
Tartary, Tartaria.
Thames, Támesis.
Thermopylæ, Termópilas.
Thessalian, s. & a. tesaliense, tésalo.
Thessalonica, Tesalónica.
Thessaly, Tesalia.
Thracia, Tracia.
Thuringia, Turingia.
Thuringian, s. & a. turingiano, turingio.
Toulon, Tolón.

Toulouse, Tolosa.
Transylvania, Transilvania.
Trent, Trento.
Treves, Tréveris.
Trojan, s. & a. troyano.
Troy, Troya.
Tunis, Túnez.
Turk, s. turco, a.
Turkey, Turquia.
Turkish, a. turco.
Tuscany, Toscana.
Tyrol, el Tirol.
Tyrolese, s. & a. tirolés.

the United States (of North America), Estados Unidos, pl.

Venetian, s. & a. veneciano.
Venice, Venecia.
Versailles, Versalles.
Vesuvius, Vesuvio.
Vienna, Viena.
Viennese, s. & a. vienés.
Vincennes, Vincenas, pl.

Wales, Gales.
Wallachia, Valaquia.
Wallachian, s. & a. valaWarsaw, Varsovia. [quo.
Welsh, s. natural de Gales.
West Indies, Indias occidentales, pl.

Zealand, Zelanda

List of the most usual Christian Names, that differ in the two languages.

Abraham, Abrahán.
Adam, Adán.
Adelaide, Adelaida.
Adolphus, Adolfo.
Alexander, Alejandro.
Alphonso, Alfonso.
Ambrose, Ambrosio.
Amelia, Amalia.
Andrew, Andrés.
Ann, Ana.
Anthony, Antonio.
Augustus, Augusto.
Austin, Agustín.

Bartholomew, Bartolomé, Bartolomeo, Bártolo.
Beatrice, Beatriz.
Ben, Benjaminito.
Benedict, Benito.
Bernard, Bernardo.
Bertha, Berta.
Bertram, Bertie, Beltrán.
Bess, Bessy, Betsey, Isabelita.
Biddy, Brigidita.
Bill, Billy, abreviatura de William.
Blanche, Blanca.
Bob, Bobby, abreviatura de Robert.
Bridget, Brígida.

Carry, abreviatura de Caroline. Carolina.

Catherine, Catalina.
Cecily, Cecilia.
Charles, Carlos.
Charlotte, Carlota.
Christ, Cristo.
Christopher, Cristóbal.
Constance, Constanza.
Constantine, Constantino.

Dan, abreviatura de Daniel.
Dick, Ricardito.
Doll(y), Doroteita.
Dorothy, Dorotea.

Edward, Eduardo.
Eleanor, Leonor.
Elizabeth, Isabel.
Ellen, Elena.
Emily, Emilia.
Esther, Ester.
Eugene, Eugenio.
Eva, Eve, Eva.

Fanny, Pancha, Panchita.
Ferdinand, Fernando.
Frances, Francisca.
Francis, Frank, Francisco, Pancho.
Frederica, Federica.
Frederic(k), Federico.

Geoffr(e)y, Geofredo.
George, Jorge.

Godfrey, Gofredo, Godofredo.
Gregory, Gregorio.
Gustavus, Gustavo.
Guy, Guido.

Hal, Euriquito.
Hannah, Ana.
Harriet, Enriqueta.
Helen, Helena.
Henry, Harry, Enrique
Hilary, Hilario.
Hugh, Hugo.
Humphrey, Hunfredo.

Ignatius, Ignacio.

Jack, por John, Juanillo, Juanito. [tiago.
James, Diego, Jaime, SanJane, Juana.
Jasper, Gaspar.
Jemmy, abreviatura de James.
Jenny, Juanita.
Jeremy, Jeremías.
Jerry, abreviatura de Jeremy. [James.
Jim, abreviatura de Joan, Juana.
Joe, Pepe.
John, Juan.
Johnny, Juanito.
Joseph, José, Pepe.

Kate, Kit, Kitty, abreviatura de Catherine.
Kit, abreviatura de Christopher.

Laurence, Lorenzo.
Lewis, Luis.
Lucretia, Lucrecia.
Lucy, Lucía.

Madeline, Magdalen, Magdalena.
Madge, Margery, abreviatura de Margaret.
Margaret, Meg, Margarita.
Mark, Marcos.
Martha, Marta.
Mary, María.
Matthew, Mat, Mateo.
Matilda, Matilde.
Maud, abreviatura de Magdalen.
Michael, Miguel.
Moll, Molly, (por Mary), Mariquita, Maruja.
Morris, Mauricio.

Nancy, Anita.   [ward.
Ned, abreviatura de Edward.
Nell, Nelly, abreviatura de Eleanor.
Nicholas, Nick, Nicolas.

Oliver, Oliverio.

Paul, Pablo.
Peg, Peggy, por Margaret.
Peter, Pedro.
Phil, abreviatura de Philip, Felipe.
Poll, Polly, Maruja.

Ralph, Rodolfo.   [món.
Raymond, Raimundo, Ramón.
Richard, Ricardo.
Robin, por Robert, Roberto.
Rose, Rosie, Rosa.
Rowland, Roldán, Rolando

Sal, Sally, por Sarah, Sara.
Samuel, Sam, Samuel.
Sandy, abreviatura de Alexander.

Solomon, Salomón.
Sophia, Sophy, Sofía.
Stephen, Esteban.
Susan, Susannah, Susana.

Ted, Teddy, por Edward.
Theresa, Teresa.
Tim, abreviatura de Timothy.
Timothy, Timoteo.
Tobias, Toby, Tobías.
Tom, Tommy, por Thomas, Tomás.
Tony, abreviatura de Anthony.

Valentine, Valentín.
Violet, Violeta.

Walter, Gualterio.
Will, abreviatura de William, Guilielmo, Guillermo.

Zachary, Zacarías.

A List of the most usual Abbreviations in Writing and Printing.

A.B., able-bodied seaman.
Abp., Archbishop.
a/c, account.
A.D., *anno Domini,* in the year of our Lord.
A.D.C., aide-de-camp.
ad lib., ad libit., *ad libitum,* at pleasure.
a.m., *ante meridiem,* before noon.
Anon., anonymous.
A.R.A., Associate of the Royal Academy.
avdp., avoirdupois.

b., born.
B.A., Bachelor of Arts.
Bart., Bt., Baronet.
B.C., b.c., before Christ.
B.C.L., Bachelor of Civil Law.
B.D., Bachelor of Divinity.
B.L., Bachelor of Law.
Bp., Bishop.
Bros., Brothers.
B.Sc., Bachelor of Science.

Cam., Camb., Cambridge.   [dent.
Cantab., *Cantabrigiensis,* Cambridge stu-
Capt., captain.
C.B., Companion of the Bath.
cf., *confer,* compare.
chap., chapter.
Co., Company ; county.
Col., Colonel.
Coll., College.
con., *contra,* against.
C.S.I., Companion of the Star of India.
cwt., hundredweight.

d., died ; *denarius,* penny.
D.C.L., Doctor of Civil Law.
D.D., Doctor of Divinity.
D.G., *Dei gratia,* by the grace of God.
D.L., Deputy-Lieutenant.
do., Do., ditto, the same.
doz., dozen.
Dr., Doctor.
D.V., *Deo volente,* God willing.
lwt., pennyweight.

Ed., editor.
e.g., *exempli gratia,* for instance.

E. long., eastern longitude.
E.N.E., east-north-east.
E.S.E., east-south-east.
Esq., Esqr., Esquire.
etc., &c., *et cetera,* and so on.

Fahr, Fahrenheit (thermometer).
F.M., Field-marshal.
F.O.B., fob., free on board.
F.P., fire plug.   [Physicians.
F.R.C.P., Fellow of the Royal College of
F.R.C.S., Fellow of the Royal College of Surgeons.   [phical Society.
F.R.G.S., Fellow of the Royal Geogra-
F.R.Hist.S., Fellow of the Royal His-
torical Society.
F.R.S., Fellow of the Royal Society.
F.S.A., Fellow of the Society of Anti-
ft., foot, feet.   [quaries.
F.Z.S., Fellow of the Zoological Society.

G.C.B., Grand Cross of the Bath.
G.C.S.I., Grand Commander of the Star
Geo., George.   [of India.
G.M.S.I., Grand Master of the Star of
Gov.-Gen., Governor-General.   [India.
G.P.O., General Post Office.

H.B.M., Her *or* His Britannic Majesty.
H.H., His *or* Her Highness.
hhd., hogshead.
H.I.H., His *or* Her Imperial Highness.
H.M., His *or* Her Majesty.
Hon., Honourable.
H.P., horse-power.
H.R.H., His *or* Her Royal Highness.
H.S.H., His *or* Her Serene Highness.

I., Is., island, islands.
ib., ibid., *ibidem.*
id., *idem.*
i.e., *id est,* that is.
Ill., Illinois.
in., inch, inches.
incog., incognito.
inst., instant.
I.O.U., I owe you.

Jas., James.

445

Jno., John.
Jos., Joseph.
J.P., Justice of the Peace.
jr., junr., junior.

K.B., Knight of the Bath.
K.C., King's Counsel.
K.C.B., Knight Commander of the Bath.
K.C.S.I., Knight Commander of the Star
K.G., Knight of the Garter.   [of India
Knt., Knight.
Ky., Kentucky.

L., l., £, pound sterling.
La., Louisiana.
lat., latitude.
lb., *libra,* pound in weight.
Lieut., Lt., Lieutenant.
Litt.D., Doctor of Literature.
LL.D., *legum doctor,* Doctor of Laws.
loc. cit., l.c., *loco citato,* in the place
long., longitude.   [quoted.
loq., *loquitar,* he *or* she speaks.
L.S.D., £.s.d., pounds, shillings, pence.

M.A., *magister artium,* Master of Arts.
Mass., Massachusetts.   [of Medicine.
M.B., *medicinæ baccalaureus,* Bachelor
M.C., Member of Congress.   [cine.
M.D., *medicinæ doctor,* Doctor of Medi-
Md., Maryland.
Me., Maine.
mem., memorandum.
Messrs., Messieurs.
M.F.H., Master of Fox Hounds.
Mgr., Monsignor.
Mi., Mississippi.
Mich., Michigan.
Miss., Mississippi.
Minn., Minnesota.
Mn., Michigan.
Mo., Missouri.
M.P., Member of Parliament.
Mr., Mister (title).   [of Surgeons.
M.R.C.S., Member of the Royal College
Mrs., mistress (title).
Ms., manuscript ; **Mss.,** manuscripts.
Mus. Doc., *musicæ doctor,* Doctor of
    Music.

N., north.
N.B., *nota bene,* note well, take notice ;
    North Britain (Scotland) ; New Bruns-
    wick.
N.E., north-east.   [opposing.
nem. con., *nemine contradicente,* no one
N.H., New Hampshire.
N.J., New Jersey.
N. lat., north latitude.
N.N.E., north-north-east.
N.N.W., north-north-west.

No., *numero,* number ; **Nos.,** numbers.
N.S., Nova Scotia ; New Style (of the
N.T., New Testament.   [calendar)
N.W., north-west.
N.Y., New York.

O., Ohio.
ob., *obiit,* died.
O.H.M.S., on Her or His Majesty's
    Service.
O.S., Old Style (of the calendar).
O.T., Old Testament.
Oxon., Oxford.
oz., ounce, ounces.

p., page.
Pa., Pennsylvania.
par., paragraph.
p.c., per cent., *per centum.*
P.C., Privy Council ; Privy Councillor ;
pd., paid.   [Police Constable.
Penn., Pennsylvania.
Ph.D., *philosophiæ doctor,* Doctor of
    Philosophy.
p.m., *post meridiem,* after noon.
P.O., Post Office ; Postal Order.
P.O.O., Post Office Order.
P.P., parish priest.
P.P.C., *pour prendre congé,* to take leave.
P.R.A., President of the Royal Academy.
Prof., Professor.
prox., *proximo,* of the next month.
P.R.S., President of the Royal Society.
Ps., Psalm.
P.S., postscript.
P.T.O., please turn over.

Q.C., Queen's Council.
q.e., *quod est,* which is.
Q.E.D., *quod erat demonstrandum.*
qr., quarter ; **qrs.,** quarters.
qt., quart ; **qts.,** quarts.
q.v., *quod vide,* which see.

R., Rex ; Regina.
R.A., Royal Academy.
R.C., Roman Catholic.
R.E., Royal Engineers.
recd., received.
Rev., Revd., Reverend.
R.N., Royal Navy.
Rs., rupees.
R.S.V.P., *répondez s'il vous plait,* please
    to answer.
Rt. Hon., Right Honourable ; **Rt. Rev.,**
    Right Reverend.
Ry., railway.

s., shilling.
sc., *sculpsit,* sculpted by   ..
sc., scil., *scilicet,* that's to say.

S.C., South Carolina.
S.E., south-east.
sec., secretary.
serv., servt., servant.
S.J., Society of Jesus; Jesuit.
S. lat., south latitude.
S.P.C.K., Society for Promoting Christian Knowledge.
sq., square.
s.s., steamship.
S.S.E., south-south-east.
S.S.W., south-south-west.
St. Saint.
S.W., south-west.

Thos., Thomas.
Tim., Timothy.

U.C. Upper Canada.
ult., ultimo.
U.S.A., United States of (North) America.

v., *versus*, against ; *vide*, see.
Va., Virginia.
V.C., Victoria Cross.
Ven., Venerable (title).
viz., *videlicet*, that is to say.
vol., volume ; **vols.,** volumes.
V.P., Vice-President.
V.S., Veterinary Surgeon.
Vt., Vermont.

W., west.
W. long., western longitude.
W.N.W., west-north-west.
Wpful., Worshipful (title).
W.S.W., west-south-west.
wt., weight.

Xmas, Christmas.
Xtian, Christian.

yd., yard ; **yds.,** yards.
yr., your ; year ; **yrs.,** yours.

British Currency, Weights and Measures.
(Monedas, Pesos y Medidas inglesas.)

Currency (Monedas).

Sovereign (de oro), Pound Sterling (£) = 20 shillings = 240 pence = 25 pesetas.
Shilling (s.) (de plata) = 12 pence = 1·25 pesetas.
Penny (d.) (de cobre) = 4 farthings = 10·04 céntimos.
Guinea = 21 shillings = 26·25 pesetas.
Crown (de plata) = 5 shillings = 6·25 pesetas.
Florin (de plata) = 2 shillings = 2·50 pesetas.
Papel-moneda : Billetes del Banco de Inglaterra, en series de 5, 10, 20, 50, y 100 pounds sterling.

Weights (Pesos).

Troy pound (lb.) = 12 ounces = 373·25 gramos.
Avoirdupois pound (avdp.) = 16 ounces = 454 gramos.
Ounce (oz.) = 16 drams = 28 38 gramos.
Dram = 1·7 gramos.
Hundredweight (cwt.) = 50·803 kilogramos.
Ton = 20 hundredweight = 1015 kilogramos.

Linear Measure (Medidas longitudinales).

Yard = 3 feet = 9·15 decímetros.
Foot (Pie) = 12 inches = 3·05 decímetros.
Inch (Pulgada) = 2·54 centímetros.
Fathom (brazo) = 2 yards = 1·83 metro.
Cable-length = 120 fathoms = 219·60 metros.
Furlong = 220 yards = 201·3 metros.
Mile = 1760 yards = 1·609 kilómetros.
Sea-Mile *or* **Knot** = 1·855 kilómetros.

Dry Measure (Medidas para áridos).

Imperial Quarter = 8 bushels = 2·908
Bushel = 36·35 litros.   [hectolitros.

Liquid Measure (Medidas para líquidos).

Gallon = 4·543 litros.
Quart = ¼ gallon = 1·136 litros.
Pint = ½ Quart = 0·568 litro.

Square Measure (Medidas agrarias).

Square Yard = 8·36 decímetros cuadrados.
Square Pole = 30¼ square yards = 25·29 metros cuadrados.
Acre of land = 160 square poles = 4840 square yards = 40·46 áreas.
30 acres = 12 hectáreas.
640 acres = 1 square mile = 259 hectáreas.

Table of the Irregular Verbs.*

Present.	Past.	Participle.	Present.	Past.	Participle.
abide	abode	abode	deal	dealt	dealt
am	was	been	dig	dug*	dug*
arise	arose	arisen	dip	dipt*	dipt*
awake	awoke*	awoke	distract	distracted	distraught*
bear	bore, bare	borne, born	do	did	done
beat	beat	beaten	draw	drew	drawn
become	became	become	dream	dreamt*	dreamt*
it befalls	it befell	befallen	drink	drank	drunk
beget	begot	begot, be-gotten	drive	drove	driven
			dwell	dwelt*	dwelt*
begin	began	begun	eat	ate, eat	eaten
behold	beheld	beheld	engrave	engraved	engraven*
bend	bent	bent	fall	fell	fallen
bereave	bereft*	bereft*	feed	fed	fed
beseech	besought	besought	feel	felt	felt
beset	beset	beset	fight	fought	fought
bestride	bestrode	bestrid, be-stridden	find	found	found
			flee	fled	fled
betake	betook	betaken	fling	flung	flung
bid	bid, bade	bid, bidden	fly	flew	flown
bind	bound	bound	forbear	forbore	forborne
bite	bit	bit, bitten	forbid	forbade	forbidden
bleed	bled	bled	forego	forewent	foregone
blow	blew	blown	foresee	foresaw	foreseen
break	broke	broken	foretell	foretold	foretold
breed	bred	bred	forget	forgot	forgot, for-gotten
bring	brought	brought			
build	built	built	forgive	forgave	forgiven
burn	burnt*	burnt*	forsake	forsook	forsaken
burst	burst	burst	forswear	forswore	forsworn
buy	bought	bought	freeze	froze	frozen
can	could	—	freight	fraught*	fraught*
cast	cast	cast	geld	gelt*	gelt*
catch	caught	caught	get	got	got, gotten
chide	chid	chid, chidden	gild	gilt*	gilt*
choose	chose	chosen	gird	girt*	girt*
cleave,	cleft, clove*	cleft, cloven	give	gave	given
cling	clung	clung	go	went	gone
clothe	clad*	clad*	grave	graved	graven*
come	came	come	grind	ground	ground
cost	cost	cost	grow	grew	grown
creep	crept	crept	hang	hung*	hung*
crow	crew*	crowed	have	had	had
cut	cut	cut	hear	heard	heard
dare	durst*	durst*	heave	hove*	hove*

* Significa que este verbe se conjuga también regularmente.

448

Present.	Past.	Participle.	Present.	Past.	Participle.
hew	hewed	hewn*	overshoot	overshot	overshot
hide	hid	hid, hidden	overtake	overtook	overtaken
hit	hit	hit	overthrow	overthrew	overthrown
hold	held	held, holden	partake	partook	partaken
hurt	hurt	hurt	pay	paid	paid
inlay	inlaid	inlaid	pen	pent	pent
interweave	interwove	interwoven	put	put	put
keep	kept	kept	quit	quitted	quit, quitted
kneel	knelt*	knel:*	read	read	read
knit	knit*	knit*	rebuild	rebuilt*	rebuilt*
know	knew	known	rend	rent	rent
lade	laded	laden*	repay	repaid	repaid
lay	laid	laid	retake	retook	retaken
lead	led	led	retell	retold	retold
lean	leant*	leant*	rid	rid	rid
leap	leapt*	leapt	ride	rode	ridden
learn	learnt*	learnt*	ring	rang	rung
leave	left	left	rise	rose	risen
lend	lent	lent	rot	rotted	rotten
let	let	let	run	ran	run
lie	lay	lain	saw	sawed	sawn*
load	loaded	laden*	say	said	said
lose	lost	lost	see	saw	seen
make	made	made	seek	sought	sought
may	might	—	seethe	seethed	sodden
mean	meant	meant	sell	sold	sold
meet	met	met	send	sent	sent
melt	melted	molten*	set	set	set
methinks	methought	—	shake	shook	shaken
misgive	misgave	misgiven	shape	shaped	shapen*
mislay	mislaid	mislaid	shave	shaved	shaven*
mislead	misled	misled	shear	shore*	shorn*
misspell	misspelt*	misspelt*	shed	shed	shed
mistake	mistook	mistaken	shew	shewed	shewn*
mow	mowed	mown	shine	shone	shone
outbid	outbid	outbid, out-bidden	shoe	shod	shod
			shoot	shot	shot
outdo	outdid	outdone	show	showed	shown*
outgo	outwent	outgone	shrink	shrunk, shrank	shrunk, shrunken
outgrow	outgrew	outgrown			
outride	outrode, outrid	outrid, outridden	shrive	shrove	shriven
			shut	shut	shut
outrun	outran	outrun	sing	sang	sung
outsell	outsold	outsold	sink	sank	sunk
outshine	outshone	outshone	sit	sat	sat
outshoot	outshot	outshot	slay	slew	slain
overcome	overcame	overcome	sleep	slept	slept
overdo	overdid	overdone	slide	slid	slid, slidden
overdrive	overdrove	overdriven	sling	slung	slung
overhang	overhung*	overhung*	slink	slunk	slunk
overhear	overheard	overheard	slit	slit	slit
overlade	overladed	overladen*	smell	smelt*	smelt*
overlay	overlaid	overlaid	smite	smote	smitten
override	overrode	overridden	sow	sowed	sown*
overrun	overran	overrun	speak	spoke	spoken
oversee	oversaw	overseen	speed	sped	sped
overset	overset	overset	spell	spelt*	spelt*

Present.	Past.	Participle.	Present.	Past.	Participle.
spend	spent	spent	unbend	unbent*	unbent*
spill	spilt*	spilt*	unbind	unbound	unbound
spin	spun, span	spun	underbid	underbid	underbidden
spit	spit, spat	spit	undergird	undergirt*	undergirt*
split	split	split	undergo	underwent	undergone
spread	spread	spread	underlay	underlaid	underlaid
spring	sprang	sprung	undersell	undersold	undersold
stand	stood	stood	understand	understood	understood
steal	stole	stolen	undertake	undertook	undertaken
stick	stuck	stuck	underwrite	underwrote	underwritten
sting	stung	stung	undo	undid	undone
stink	stank, stunk	stunk	ungird	ungirt*	ungirt
strew	strewed	strewn*	unlade	unladed	unladen
stride	strode	strid, stridden	unsay	unsaid	unsaid
strike	struck	struck, stricken	unstring	unstrung	unstrung
string	strung	strung	unwind	unwound	unwound
strive	strove	striven	uphold	upheld	upheld, upholden
strow	strowed	strown*	uprise	uprose	uprisen
swear	swore	sworn	upset	upset	upset
sweep	swept	swept	wake	woke*	waked
swell	swelled	swollen, swoln*	wash	washed	washen*
			waylay	waylaid	waylaid
swim	swam	swum	wear	wore	worn
swing	swung	swung	weave	wove	woven
take	took	taken	weep	wept	wept
teach	taught	taught	win	won	won
tear	tore	torn	wind	wound	wound
tell	told	told	wis	wist	wist
think	thought	thought	withdraw	withdrew	withdrawn
thrive	throve*	thriven*	withhold	withheld	withheld, withholden
throw	threw	thrown			
thrust	thrust	thrust	withstand	withstood	withstood
toss	tost*	tost*	wring	wrung	wrung
tread	trod	trod, trodden	write	wrote	written